PROMISES TO KEEP

A 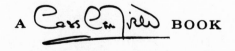 BOOK

BOOKS BY CHESTER BOWLES

Promises to Keep

A View from New Delhi

The Makings of a Just Society

The Conscience of a Liberal

The Coming Political Breakthrough

Ideas, People and Peace

American Politics in a Revolutionary World

Africa's Challenge to America

The New Dimensions of Peace

Ambassador's Report

Tomorrow Without Fear

PROMISES TO KEEP

MY YEARS IN PUBLIC LIFE

1941-1969

CHESTER BOWLES

1817

HARPER & ROW, PUBLISHERS

NEW YORK, EVANSTON, SAN FRANCISCO, LONDON

PROMISES TO KEEP. *Copyright © 1971 by Chester Bowles. All rights reserved. Printed in the United States of America. No part of this book may be used or reproduced in any manner whatsoever without written permission except in the case of brief quotations embodied in critical articles and reviews. For information address Harper & Row, Publishers, Inc., 49 East 33rd Street, New York, N.Y. 10016. Published simultaneously in Canada by Fitzhenry & Whiteside Limited, Toronto.*

FIRST EDITION

LIBRARY OF CONGRESS CATALOG CARD NUMBER: 76-123917

TO STEB

CONTENTS

Acknowledgment   xi

PROLOGUE: THE EARLIER YEARS   I

PART I
Wartime Administrator

1. MADISON AVENUE TO OAK STREET   13
2. INTRODUCTION TO WASHINGTON   29
3. THE BUSINESSMEN VS. THE PROFESSORS   43
4. SETTING THE RULES   51
5. INVOLVING A NATION   61
6. WHO GETS WHAT — AND HOW MUCH?   75
7. DOING BATTLE WITH THE LOBBYISTS   86
8. JOURNEYS TO CAPITOL HILL   102
9. MY RELATIONS WITH FDR   116
10. THE LINE BEGINS TO BEND   126
11. THE LINE FINALLY BREAKS   143

PART II
Connecticut Politics

12. INTRODUCTION TO POLITICS   161
13. THE CAMPAIGN OF 1948   176

14. THE LEGISLATIVE CONFRONTATION   189

15. THE SPECIAL SESSIONS   207

16. POLITICIANS AND POLITICS   218

17. THE CAMPAIGN OF 1950   232

18. INTERLUDE   244

19. THE SENATE CAMPAIGN OF 1958   258

20. CONGRESSMAN FROM CONNECTICUT   269

PART III
Working with Kennedy

21. A NEW ADMINISTRATION   285

22. THE TEAM OF RUSK AND BOWLES   299

23. EMBASSIES AND AMBASSADORS   315

24. THE BAY OF PIGS   326

25. THE LAOS CRISIS   334

26. SPELLING OUT OUR DIFFERENCES   342

27. THE CONFLICT COMES TO THE SURFACE   352

28. THE CONFLICT BOILS OVER   360

29. LAUNCHED IN A NEW ROLE   368

30. FOREIGN ECONOMIC ASSISTANCE   379

31. A FRESH LOOK AT CHINA   391

32. VIETNAM: THE MAKINGS OF A DEBACLE   404

33. CHALLENGE IN AFRICA: THE CONGO CRISIS   418

34. FROM WASHINGTON TO NEW DELHI   430

35. JOHN F. KENNEDY   443

PART IV
Ambassador to India:
A Search for Alternatives in Asia

36. THE AMERICAN MISSION IN INDIA   457

37. A LOST OPPORTUNITY   472

38. IMPRESSIONS OF JAWAHARLAL NEHRU   487

39. LAL BAHADUR SHASTRI   497

40. NEHRU'S DAUGHTER TAKES THE HELM   508

41. LBJ AND AMERICAN WHEAT   523

42. CHINA, RUSSIA AND INDIA   537

43. PROSPECTS FOR INDIA   547

44. FAREWELL TO INDIA AND ASIA   574

    EPILOGUE   585

APPENDICES:

  I. *Inaugural Address as Governor of Connecticut, January 5, 1949*   593
 II. *Considerations Regarding the Selection of Top Policy-makers,*
     December 18, 1960   603
III. *Some Requirements of American Foreign Policy, July 1, 1961*   608
 IV. *Letter to Adlai Stevenson in Paris, July 23, 1961*   619
  V. *Random Musings about Chester Bowles and the Department of*
     State by Samuel W. Lewis, May 26, 1963   626
 VI. *Letter to Prime Minister Shastri, October 17, 1964*   631
VII. *"Train to Allahabad," by Steb Bowles, in* News Circle, *March, 1966*   638

Index   645

A section of illustrations will be found following page 178.

ACKNOWLEDGMENT

During my twenty-nine years in public life I have been the beneficiary of the imagination, wisdom and insights of a series of remarkable assistants, all of whom came to me while in their twenties and many of whom have gone on to impressive careers of their own.

These include Edward J. Logue, now President of the New York State Urban Development Corporation; Abram Chayes, now Professor of Law at Harvard; Harris Wofford, now President of Bryn Mawr; Thomas L. Hughes, now President of the Carnegie Endowment for Peace; James C. Thomson, Jr., now Associate Professor of Chinese History at Harvard; Richard F. Celeste, now launched on a promising political career in Cleveland, Ohio; Douglas J. Bennet, Jr., now Administrative Assistant to Senator Thomas F. Eagleton of Missouri; Daniel L. Miller, now Executive Assistant to Edward Logue; Thomas A. Dine, now on the staff of Senator Frank Church of Idaho; several young members of the Foreign Service, including John Shirley, Brandon Grove and Samuel W. Lewis; and my present personal assistant, Bryant Robey, formerly of the Peace Corps, who has been working closely with me on this book for the last twelve months.

Each of these men contributed to my efforts in his own special way and for their assistance I am eternally grateful. I particularly appreciate the thoroughness with which they searched their memories and their files for material for this volume.

In addition, I have benefited from the criticisms and suggestions of former colleagues such as Philip Coombs, Robert R. R. Brooks, William Weathersby, David Ginsburg, James G. Rogers, Douglas J. Bennet, Sr.,

Bice Clemow, Richard Field, David Cavers, Jean Joyce, Leonard Weiss and many others. For any omissions, mistakes or misconceptions I, of course, assume full responsibility.

I am also indebted to John A. Herfort, Gregory B. Craig, Drucilla Ramey and Steven D. Bartelstone, students at Harvard, Yale and the University of Connecticut Law Schools, for digging out facts, quotations and other material from libraries, newspaper morgues and other sources, and for their criticisms and suggestions.

I would particularly like to thank my secretary, Mrs. Lorre Parsons, who tirelessly typed and retyped the manuscript in its many drafts, and Mrs. Frances O'Dell, who assisted her.

PROMISES TO KEEP

PROLOGUE: THE EARLIER YEARS

THIS BOOK IS NOT A BIOGRAPHY. It is a record of my public life, which began twenty-nine years ago when I was in my fortieth year. Inevitably it will evoke a wide variety of reactions. My contemporaries will consider it against the background of their own memories and experiences. But to many younger readers for whom Roosevelt is old history and Kennedy is already fading into myth, it may appear simply as the record of one man's futile effort to buck the so-called "Establishment."

Written words, after the events, cannot fully convey the anticipation of great accomplishments or the anguish of disappointment. But to the extent that this story tells how my generation failed to realize past possibilities or recognize new challenges, it may contain some lessons.

In the 1930's and 1940's I and many of my contemporaries were motivated by a sense of commitment and idealism similar in many respects to the feelings that characterize so many men and women now under thirty. During the Great Depression we broke loose from traditional economic and political concepts to broaden the federal government's responsibility for the functioning of our economy and for the assurance of a greater measure of dignity and economic, political and social justice. Following Pearl Harbor we mustered our national and human resources on an unprecedented scale to win a world war; we conceived and organized the United Nations; some of us even dreamed of world government.

Following the war, we were genuinely convinced that we were entering a new era, and that if we invested enough vision, energy and money, we could not only eliminate poverty and privation in the United States but ultimately extend the ideas and ideals of the American Revolution to the entire world. A permanent American Revolution, we called it; a World New Deal, a War on Want, the Century of the Common Man.

As this is written, the pendulum has swung from our earlier euphoria to a sense of impending catastrophe.

The deepening of our difficulties and their convergence into one supreme test of human reason and politics present us with awesome dangers. They are compounded by the fact that most of those who largely control our economic, political and social system—the Establishment—oppose meaningful changes in our traditional ways of doing things. As a consequence, on most critical issues such as Southeast Asia, racial discrimination, national priorities, maldistribution of wealth and resources, and the militarization of our society, our national policies have been dangerously out of touch with the realities.

Throughout my public life I have challenged the positions taken by the Establishment on these and other issues and expended most of my time and energies in an effort to shape public policy to the realities of our revolutionary new world. Significantly, I have chosen to pursue this course *within* our system of government. Many members of the younger generation assert that such efforts as mine are doomed to fail. As they see it, the more just, free and creative society which we seek requires not only the elimination of the Establishment but the destruction of the system itself.

On this I believe they are mistaken. It is not our democratic system which is at fault; it is those who control the levers of power within the system and who use that power to serve their own narrow interests, concepts and privileges. The challenge facing the younger generation, as I see it, is how to provide our democratic society with a fresh sense of priorities, values and relevance. This they can do only by involving themselves deeply in the process by which our system works.

In this perspective, the cycle of success and failure which I shall describe should be considered not as nostalgia for old battles won or lost, but as the first skirmishes of the struggle which lies ahead. If the members of the emerging new generation are not to pass on to their children a world of even graver problems, they must do far better than we did.

A brief review of my earlier years may help throw light on what I did and attempted to do in the varied and sometimes turbulent years with which this book is concerned.

An early Bowles, I am told, came from England to the Massachusetts Bay Colony in 1632, but I don't know what kind of pioneer he was—

a Puritan with religious motives, an adventurer, an entrepreneur in search of fortune or simply a man fleeing the Old World. Over a span of three hundred years anyone can claim direct descent from more than six thousand individuals—quite a pot to choose from.

My grandfather, Samuel Bowles, editor of the Springfield *Republican,* died in 1882, nineteen years before I was born. At an early age I read his liberal editorials in support of Abraham Lincoln during the Civil War and his prophetic writings about the development of the American West, and was deeply influenced by them. The period following the Civil War which encompassed my father's boyhood was one of intense political conflict, and my grandfather was a man with strong views which he never hesitated to express.

My father was in the paper business in Springfield, Massachusetts, not the newspaper business, but as a sales agent for wood pulp used in the manufacturing of paper. Although we did not have a great deal of money, we had a car probably as early as 1914, and lived comfortably in a middle-class neighborhood.

Like most Yankee businessmen of his day, my father grew up hating and fearing government. He believed that government had no useful purpose other than putting out fires, delivering the mails and maintaining law and order.

My mother came from Rutland, Vermont, where her father, Joel B. Harris, was a manufacturer. She had a vivid imagination and I remember her as a wise, sensitive person who was always great fun. Like my father she was a deeply committed Republican. During the election campaign of 1936 she said to me: "If 'that man' is re-elected President, I shall pull down every shade in this house and not raise them again until he leaves the White House." But she cheerfully forgave me for my own political sins.

My brother, Allen, who died in 1946, and my sister, Dorothy, who died in 1968, were much older than I. I felt close to both of them. Dorothy was a true New Englander and the custodian of our family traditions. Only on Thanksgiving Day and Christmas were we allowed to use my Grandmother Harris' red and gold china. In regard to politics, she not only forgave me for being a Democrat, she became one herself. However, I admit that there is little evidence that her party loyalties extended beyond the activities of her younger brother. Just before the Massachusetts State election of 1948, she asked me plaintively, "As a Democrat do I really *have* to vote for the re-election of Governor Dever?"

My early views on history, economics and politics were profoundly influenced not only by my grandfather's career but by the deep convictions of my father's older sister, Ruth Standish Baldwin, who lived first in the town of Washington in western Connecticut and later with her children in New Hope, Pennsylvania. She was a mild Socialist, a pacifist and an admirer and friend of Norman Thomas, with keen insights in regard to politics, international affairs and, particularly, civil rights.

She was a founder of the NAACP, the Urban League and the Highlander Folk School in Monteagle, Tennessee, which trained Southern labor leaders and which was consequently charged with being "radical." She was also a trustee of Smith College. I eagerly looked forward to her visits to our home in Springfield.

My father subscribed to an ultraconservative magazine known as *Harvey's Weekly*, which was committed to the early political demise of my Aunt Ruth's hero, Woodrow Wilson. During World War I and immediately thereafter a line in bold type would appear at the bottom of each page; one week it would say: "Only 133 days more of Woodrow Wilson." The next week it would be: "Only 126 days left"; and so on.

At the age of fourteen at my aunt's suggestion, I read Professor Charles Seymour's *Diplomatic Background of the War—1870–1914* and as a result was soon able to win most of our dinner table debates on the origins of World War I. Although my father was opposed to my gradually evolving liberal views, and smilingly blamed them on his sister, I think he enjoyed our arguments.

My education included ten years in the Springfield public schools, followed by two years at the Choate School in Wallingford, Connecticut, where I first met Adlai Stevenson. My father and older brother had both graduated from Yale and it never occurred to me to do otherwise. They had both taken a special three-year liberal arts course which did not require Latin and which for some obscure reason was attached to Yale's Sheffield Scientific School. At that time a large number of "Sheff" students took this general all-purpose course; only a little more than half actually majored in science.

I decided to break this particular family tradition by taking the full four-year liberal arts course at Yale College. However, at that time Yale was about to go through a long overdue reorganization, and the college was short of dormitory space. Consequently, some university authorities persuaded several of us to go to the Sheffield Scientific School, where we were assured more comfortable accommodations and the choice of whatever courses appealed to us. I accepted their advice and became a student in the Scientific School.

Unhappily for us, Yale had just recruited as Dean of the Sheffield Scientific School a scientist from M.I.T., and not unreasonably he insisted that the school should become what it always should have been—a genuine scientific school designed to turn out genuine scientists. As a result several classmates and I, who had no intention of becoming scientists, were faced with a choice: we could shift over to Yale College and lose a year, or we could take the absolute minimum of scientific courses at "Sheff" and then try to carry some liberal arts courses as well.

Like almost everyone else at that age I was in a rush and so I decided on the latter course of action. As a result I averaged nearly thirty hours of classes each week during my last two years, about double the normal schedule. The only extracurricular activity I had time for was golf. As a member of the Yale golf team I lost only one match in three years; in my senior year I was elected captain.

I think back now on my four years at Yale as a period of overwork, confusion and missed opportunities; I vaguely sensed that something was wrong, something that I could not clearly define. In the roaring twenties the national mood was apathetic and shallow; it was unfashionable in or out of college to think much about anything.

With the exception of Norman Thomas and the elder Robert La Follette, I can remember no political leader who articulately expressed a liberal or humanistic view of our society. In my class of some seven hundred students, I doubt that there were thirty who would admit to being Democrats, and they were largely from the South. Following graduation in 1924 most of my classmates rushed off to highly paid jobs on Wall Street. As far as I know, I was the only one who even considered public service.

My first choice, however, was journalism. Since my childhood I had assumed that after graduation I would go to work on our family newspaper, the Springfield *Republican*, and I actually worked there for nearly a year. However, I found myself in a dilemma. The Springfield *Republican* and its companion evening paper, the Springfield *Daily News*, were tightly controlled by my cousin, Sherman Bowles, who at that time was in his early forties.

It was soon evident that Sherman and I did not see eye to eye. My objective was to restore our family paper to the prestige, integrity and liberal orientation which it had during my grandfather's and uncle's lifetime. But as my cousin saw it, a newspaper was no more nor less than a commercial enterprise designed to make money. He begrudged even the meager salaries paid to the editorial writers.

In the course of several long talks, Sherman made it clear that he had no desire to see me stay on the newspaper. "We already have too many cousins," he said, and I was inclined to agree with him.

Twenty years later when I attempted to buy the Springfield *Republican* in the hope that I might restore it to its former position of influence, he refused even to discuss the possibility.

My second choice as a career was the Foreign Service, which, I assume, grew out of my admiration for Woodrow Wilson and my Aunt Ruth's influence. After several interviews arranged by my father's close friend, Frederick B. Gillette from Westfield, Massachusetts, who was at that time Speaker of the House of Representatives, I was offered an opportunity to serve in the Consulate in Shanghai. But at that point my father suddenly became ill and I did not feel free to leave the country.

Had I gone to China at that time, it is intriguing to speculate that I would have almost certainly emerged as a charter member of the Old China Hands Club, who were charged by Senator Joseph McCarthy in the early 1950's with a long list of crimes ranging from gross stupidity to acting as undercover agents for Mao Tse-tung.

My next attempt was in the Department of Commerce, of which Herbert Hoover was then Secretary. However, when a job failed to materialize, I wrote to Speaker Gillette that since I could not find a promising opportunity in government, I had decided to go into business, with a solemn pledge to myself that I would leave when I was thirty-five. If I made a go of it, fine; if I were unsuccessful, I would leave anyway. I was to miss my goal by only four years.

In 1925 after turning down a $12-a-week job at the *New York Times*, I landed one at $25 a week in a New York advertising company then known as the George Batten Company, now Batten, Barton, Durstine & Osborn. In July of that year I married Julia Fisk of Springfield.

The three years I worked at B.B.D. & O. were largely spent as a copywriter. But increasingly I dreamed of establishing a company of my own, which might enable me more quickly to achieve a degree of financial independence.

William Benton, who had been two years ahead of me at Yale and whom I had come to know at the George Batten Company, had a similar objective, and soon we began to talk of a partnership. In early 1929 we called on several top officials of the General Foods Corporation, including Ralph Starr Butler and Charles Mortimer, for each of whom I came to have great respect and affection. We described the improved service which they might expect from a small advertising agency with a fresh point of view and its future at stake, and for a time seemed to be making progress.

When they learned that I was barely twenty-eight years old and Benton was only one year older, their early enthusiasm began to diminish. However, they finally decided to take a chance, and on July 10, 1929, with a total capital of $12,000 the wobbly new firm of Benton & Bowles moved into a two-room office in the old Chanin Building on Forty-second Street in Manhattan. Our total business consisted of two small General Foods accounts, our staff of one secretary, an office boy and a young man just out of college.

On the same day our office opened the stock market boom reached its peak. Then four months later came the Wall Street crash leading to the Great Depression. Paradoxically, I believe that the Depression itself gave added impetus to our growth. We were a fresh new organization in a period of economic upheaval. The managements of most corporations, under the pressure of sagging sales and disappearing profits, were in a mood for change, *any* change, and firing their advertising agency was an effective way to prove to their directors and stockholders that they were on the job. In any event, when the economy hit rock bottom in 1933, Benton & Bowles, Inc. was busily hiring more and more people and moving into larger offices.

During the early Depression years I began to realize that my formal education had been dreadfully inadequate, and I decided to embark on a methodical reading schedule. For the next eight or ten years everything I read, outside of business reading and the daily newspapers, conformed to a plan. The first year I concentrated on world history, economics and philosophy. From then on I devoted one full year of reading to each major country—for instance, a year of French history, economics, literature, music, art and culture, followed by a similar one-year concentration on Germany, China, Russia and the United Kingdom.

Whatever knowledge I may now have of history, philosophy, economics and government has its roots in this self-imposed routine. Although it was no substitute for a well-rounded education at a good university, with the daily give-and-take with professors and fellow students, I was able to make up considerable ground by my early thirties.

During these years my ideas were also shaped by experience. For instance, I saw at first hand the plight of the millions of jobless Americans. In January, 1931, I made several hundred house-to-house calls in upper New York State and Ohio to see why housewives bought certain products and rejected others. Most of the homes on which I called were in low- or middle-income neighborhoods, and it was there that I saw the shattering effects of the Depression on American society. I can still see vividly the weary husbands returning home from another fruitless day of job hunting with a look of stark fear and hopelessness in their eyes.

On several occasions college friends who had gone directly from

Yale into brokerage or banking and had promptly begun to earn large incomes, called on me in desperation to say they did not have enough money in the house to buy food and to ask for a loan. The contrast between our own good fortune and the ordeal endured by most American families made me conscious of the injustices in our society and the need for fundamental changes.

I also became increasingly aware of the limitations of advertising and sales promotion. It was clear that skillful advertising could persuade millions of people to try a new product. But advertising could not sell a bad product twice. Sustained high volume and profits depended primarily on the quality and public acceptance of the product itself. Out of this experience came some new research techniques for the pretesting of products to determine how well they suited the public taste.

Even a modest reduction in the retail price of a good product, we discovered, would often result in an extraordinary growth in sales. Over a period of years we succeeded in persuading our clients to lower the price of fourteen different products and simultaneously to improve their quality, even though in several instances this required a sizable reduction in advertising expenditures. On each occasion, sales expanded rapidly and soon the product was earning a substantially higher profit at the lower consumer price. In later years as Administrator of OPA I remembered these lessons.

In 1932 my first marriage ended in a divorce, and eighteen months later I married Dorothy Stebbins of Newton, Massachusetts. This was by far the most important event in shaping my later life. For more than thirty-five years "Steb" has cheerfully shared both my victories and defeats. In everything I have done or attempted to do, she has been a wise and dedicated participant, while also serving in several difficult situations as my conscience.

The five Bowles children—Barbara and Chester, Jr., who were born in 1927 and 1928 of my first marriage, and Cynthia, Sarah and Samuel, born in 1936, 1938 and 1939—have, each in his own way, been full-fledged partners in our various undertakings, while retaining his or her own personal identity and viewpoint. With their cooperation, we now have eleven grandchildren.

Steb and I have long been keenly interested in sailing, and in 1935 we built a seventy-two-foot schooner, *Nordlys*. In the next six years we sailed her for many thousands of miles, including six passages to Bermuda, three to Nova Scotia, one to Newfoundland and innumerable cruises to Maine. In 1936 we began to spend our weekends in Old Saybrook, Connecticut, and in 1939 we built a house on the beautiful

Connecticut River at Essex, which we have considered home ever since.

By 1935 the annual volume of Benton & Bowles business had reached some $15 million, and we had more than four hundred employees. This was the year in which I had planned to leave business and to begin a new career in either government or education. But one day Bill Benton told me that for years he had contemplated doing precisely what I had planned to do: leave the business, sell his stock to me and other partners and move into educational work.

The time for him to leave, he said, had come. He had been offered a challenging job at the University of Chicago, then headed by his close friend, Robert Hutchins. Since Benton was a year older and had spoken first, I had no alternative but to wish him well and do the best I could to keep the company going.

The business continued to grow, and by 1938 I began to feel that the time had come for me to sell my share of the business to my partners and take up other work as I had always intended. Unhappily, when I announced my plans, two of our largest clients reacted negatively, and one of my associates seized upon the opportunity to start his own agency with some of our most important accounts. Again I had no alternative but to stay in the business full time to regain the lost ground.

In those years my outside activities were limited. It was not until 1940, for example, that I made my first speech. The subject was "product research," and my audience was a business group of some forty people in New York. My first article appeared the next year in a magazine on sailing. Entitled "Man Overboard," it described the most effective procedures for rescuing a shipmate who falls off the deck of a sailing vessel at sea, an experience that happened to me in 1937 midway between New London, Connecticut, and Bermuda.

When World War II broke out in 1939, I was sorely torn about whether or not we should become involved. The tragic repudiation of Woodrow Wilson's League of Nations by the United States Senate in 1919 had convinced me and millions of others that the American people were not yet ready to participate effectively in world affairs; nor was it in our American anticolonial tradition to subsidize and protect the British, French, Belgian and Dutch empires in Asia and Africa. Our first national responsibility, I thought, was to fulfill the promises of the Rooseveltian New Deal.

While opposing United States participation in World War II unless we were attacked, I rejected the isolationist argument that we could cut ourselves off from the rest of mankind. My strong feelings led me to write an article in 1941, for an excellent but long since defunct magazine, *Common Sense*. It was entitled "What's Wrong with the Isolationists by a Non Interventionist."

This article has a familiar ring in these days of public protest over Vietnam. For instance, I wrote: "We have already spent enough on the Second World War (in assistance to Britain, France and the U.S.S.R.) to clear away all our slums, build millions of homes, new schoolhouses, new parks and new buildings, dramatically to raise our health standards and to send hundreds of thousands of our young people to college."

Posing the question of whether, when the war was over, American military power could be expected to keep peace in all the far-flung corners of the world, I concluded: "We cannot guarantee the future of our civilization behind a barricade of armaments, nor can we establish world democracy with the sword."

In 1941 I once again began to explore possibilities of leaving business. A venture that particularly interested me was a new newspaper to be published in Hartford, Connecticut. I also thought of buying an existing paper such as the New London *Day* or the Middletown *Press,* and about educational administration and teaching.

In early December, 1941, I received a call from Charles Seymour, president of Yale, who asked me to stop at his New Haven office on Friday, December 5, on my way to Essex for the weekend. In the course of a two-hour talk, President Seymour said he was anxious to strengthen the administration of Yale and felt that my practical business experience would be helpful. The possibility was intriguing, and I promised to consider it seriously. Two days later Pearl Harbor was attacked, and the question of precisely how to leave my business behind and to embark on a public career was suddenly settled for me by events.

My friends and family often comment on my reluctance to discuss my early years in business. I suppose the honest answer is that I look on them with mixed feelings. Although I had a high personal regard for many of my associates (and still have), I honestly believe that I would have been happier and more effective if I had gone into public service immediately following my graduation from college.

On the other hand, I realize that the grinding effort that I put into these early years enabled my family and me to build a capital reserve which has assured us far greater independence and made it possible for me to travel, to write, to speak my mind, and to move from one career to the next as various challenges presented themselves.

PART I

Wartime Administrator

◆

"The highest and best form of efficiency is
the spontaneous cooperation of a free people."

WOODROW WILSON

CHAPTER 1

MADISON AVENUE TO OAK STREET

LATE SUNDAY AFTERNOON, December 7, 1941, Steb and I drove my oldest son, Chester, Jr., back to Pomfret School in northeastern Connecticut after a weekend at home in Essex.

It was clear and cold, and on the long drive home I remember that we stopped briefly on two or three occasions to look at the northern lights, which were putting on a spectacular show. As we pulled up in front of our house a little before 7:00 P.M., the telephone was ringing in the front hall, and I rushed in to answer it. It was my sister, Dorothy, calling from Springfield, Massachusetts.

"What do you think of the terrible news?" she asked. I had no idea what she meant. "The Japanese have just attacked Pear Harbor." This was an event which would drastically change our lives and those of tens of millions of others. But, of course, we had no idea how great the change was to be.

The next morning I drove to Hartford to keep an appointment that I had made the previous week with Connecticut's Governor Robert A. Hurley. A mutual friend had told me some weeks before that the Governor had mentioned the possibility of my becoming Director of the State Defense Council, which had been created in 1940 by the National Defense Advisory Commission as one of a network of such councils throughout the country to deal with state emergencies.

Steb was already a board member, with responsibility for health, welfare and education problems growing out of the influx of workers from New Hampshire, Vermont and Maine attracted by the high-paying jobs in Connecticut's burgeoning defense industries.

However, instead of discussing the Defense Council, Governor

Hurley handed me an urgent telegram he had just received from President Roosevelt requesting him immediately to appoint someone to take responsibility for rationing automobile tires in Connecticut. With all of Southeast Asia now cut off from the United States by the Japanese Navy, he said, we were faced with a critical rubber shortage.

Frankly, I found the idea of becoming the Connecticut State Tire Ration Administrator unappealing—even if it was essential for the war effort. I thanked the Governor but said that I was not the man for the job. When he pressed further, I told him that I had a bad cold (which was an understatement) and needed time to talk to Steb and to consider the alternatives. I would call him the next day and give him my answer. It would be easier, I thought, to refuse the job over the telephone.

Shortly after I arrived home a reporter from the Hartford *Courant* telephoned. "Congratulations on your new job," he told me. "We would like a statement for tomorrow morning's edition on your immediate plans for setting up the new tire-rationing organization."

My first instinct was to say that there must have been some misunderstanding. While I was annoyed at having been boxed in, I felt I could not embarrass the Governor, who was obviously desperate for a tire rationer; the best I could do under the circumstances was to limit the length of my commitment. So I told the reporter that I planned to serve only three months; by that time the program should be set up and running, and someone else could take over.

The next morning I called my partners in New York City to tell them what had happened. Although they expressed concern about my taking a leave of absence from the business, they were understanding and cooperative.

My departure from Madison Avenue was almost as inconspicuous as my arrival. The *New York Times* reported it in a remote corner of the financial section under the heading "Personnel." I had, said the *Times,* "received a leave of absence of from six weeks to three months from Benton & Bowles to set up a statewide rationing system in Connecticut. His first duty will be the allotment of tires."

I knew even then that I would never return to the business world. It had treated me well, but my personal interests were elsewhere, and, however undramatically, I had finally cut the Gordian knot; or, more accurately, it had been cut for me.

As a believer in man's ability (within certain obvious limits) to shape his own future, I find it disconcerting to look back and discover the role that external events and accidents have played in shaping my career. My decision to leave the business world for government was hardly a decision at all. Even though I had been preparing to leave business for ten years, I was finally propelled out of it.

At that point the only appeal that I could see in my new job as State Tire Rationer was the fact that no one had ever done it before. Although the idea of telling the people of Connecticut who could and who could not have a rubber tire was not interesting in itself, the prospect of doing something altogether new in government carried a certain challenge.

With the shock of Pearl Harbor still fresh, the early moves to mobilize the domestic war effort were speedy and surprisingly efficient. On

"The most marvellous thing about it—the tires came through without a scratch."

Tires were the first item to be rationed in the program launched a few days after Pearl Harbor. Though the public found it hard to believe we could run short of anything, the program was accepted in good humor and surprising cooperation. *Drawing by Garrett Price; Copyright © 1942, 1970 The New Yorker Magazine, Inc.*

December 12, at the request of President Roosevelt, Governor Hurley issued an executive order banning the sale of all tires, and "to stop a consumers' buying wave," he imposed a strict state enforcement of the ban.

The production and sale of new passenger tires came to an abrupt halt, and the production of new truck tires was drastically curtailed. During the following weeks rumors spread that the federal government even planned to seize all private cars for use by the armed forces or in essential civilian services.

The public response was at first skeptical. During the long years of the Depression, the American people had been conditioned to think only in terms of surpluses. Suddenly to find our economy faced with shortages was difficult for many people to accept.

It was understandable that Germany, France and Britain with their limited resources had to regulate prices and impose rationing, but why, they asked, should a country as wealthy as the United States have to disrupt the lives of its citizens with restrictive government regulations? Someone must have blundered; some bureaucrats somewhere in the vast machinery of government must be at fault.

Shortly after my appointment the Governor assigned me a small staff and an even smaller office on Oak Street in Hartford near the State Capitol. My new associates included an extraordinarily efficient secretary, Marcella Eastman, who was to remain with me until her death in 1950; Stanley Crute, a senior civil servant in the Highway Department who acted as my general assistant; Asa Scranton, a State Senator who, I was told, knew what buttons to push to break down bureaucratic barriers; Francis Quinlan, a newspaperman from Bridgeport in charge of press relations; and one or two others.

One of our first responsibilities was to convince the public that the problem we faced was genuine. The Connecticut radio stations volunteered to make available whatever time I needed, and I began a regular series of statewide broadcasts, every Monday night for a half-hour.

It seems strange now to think that these were the first public statements that I ever made. Because I was dealing with an enormously complex and unfamiliar situation, I went out of my way to keep my presentations simple and earthy. *Broadcast Magazine,* at least, felt that I succeeded; it reported that "Bowles spoke without oratorical flourish and in idiom, mixing metaphors, split infinitives and common sense into a verbal porridge which the people found palatable. He is earthy and sincere and fluffs words like a neophyte. He skips high-sounding phrases."

Whatever my technical defects as a broadcaster, I was soon deluged with mail, almost all of it favorable. One lady even went so far as to write:

> I want you to know that I think you are the tops in broadcasting. Even Lowell Thomas, whom I admire greatly, does not quite compare with you! I never miss one of your broadcasts, and for clarity and hitting the nail on the head no one can best you. You put the rationing question so clearly that no one could possibly misunderstand it.

The facts of the "rationing question" were dramatic. Before Pearl Harbor 95 percent of the raw rubber used by the United States had come from the Southeast Asia area. Although it was several months before the rubber-producing countries such as Indonesia, Malaya and Singapore were actually occupied by the Japanese, shipping from Southeast Asia to our West Coast ports was stopped within two or three weeks.

Before the war, the United States imported about 800,000 tons of crude rubber annually, 75 percent of which was used for tires. On December 7, 1941, we had on hand a *total* of only 650,000 tons of rubber —510,000 tons already in inventories in this country and another 140,000 en route. With the present limited stock and the skyrocketing rate of demand, the rubber supply in the country would have been exhausted in sixty days.

Although the process of artificial rubber production had been developed, the costs were still so high that it had not been extensively used. A crash manufacturing program was launched immediately, but it would be many months before the output would begin to meet even our minimum needs.

The rubber industry itself was keenly aware of this situation and supported the drastic actions of the government. John L. Collyer, the president of B. F. Goodrich, proclaimed rationing as "both necessary and fair." He said, "From now on, one of the big jobs facing the tire industry is to make every motorist a tire expert who knows how to keep his tires from premature old age."

Under the new rationing system, each state was allotted a quota of tires every month (usually about one-fourth of the normal sales) for distribution to those whose needs were essential for the war effort. Vehicles performing vital services, such as fire engines, police cars, ambulances, school buses and doctors' automobiles, received top priority. Public transportation systems and essential trucking services followed. Then came workers who used their cars to drive to their jobs at defense plants.

Very wisely, it was decided that local volunteer boards would be responsible for the distribution of automobile tires and whatever other products might be rationed in the future under regulations and criteria worked out in Washington. Our immediate task was to set up these ration boards in the 169 cities and towns of Connecticut. Since they had to be functioning by January 5, we had less than a month for a task that might normally take a year.

From fifteen years in business, I had come to believe that a successful operation depended not only on the judgment, energy and imagination of the policy-makers, but even more on the sense of involvement and personal commitment generated among the rank and file. In setting up our new Connecticut ration boards, therefore, three points seemed to me essential. First, the ration board chairmen must be able administrators, respected and trusted by their fellow citizens; second, each board must represent a genuine cross section of the city or town; and, third, political influence must, at any cost, be avoided; the objectivity and integrity of the boards must be beyond question.

My conviction that a politically based rationing system would be a disaster put me on a collision course with Democratic political leaders throughout the state. At that time the Democrats controlled the Connecticut State Administration. During the Depression years of mass unemployment political considerations had come to play a key role in staffing the lower levels of federal and state agencies. For millions of people a government job often meant the difference between hunger and enough food for the family. It was assumed—even by the opposition —that the party in power would distribute whatever government jobs might be available and that loyal party workers would receive a high priority.

Inevitably, most state Democratic leaders looked upon my rapidly expanding new agency as a political bonanza. This view was reinforced when it became known that in addition to the volunteer board members a large number of paid clerical employees would be necessary.

The day following the opening of our small office on Oak Street I received an invitation to lunch from the genial Commissioner of Motor Vehicles, John T. McCarthy, the Governor's right-hand man on political affairs. McCarthy was no exception to the conditioning of the Depression. He began by saying he assumed that before selecting ration board members I would consult with local Democratic leaders and ask for their nominees. I replied that I would welcome suggestions, but would make the appointments totally on the basis of merit. The rationing system would never work, I argued, unless it was respected by everyone regardless of how he voted.

After a lengthy exchange I convinced McCarthy that I could not be moved on this issue. However, he suggested that surely the several hundred paid clerical employees who would serve the ration boards throughout the state were a different matter. I repeated that every aspect of rationing in Connecticut—and I hoped everywhere else—had to be above politics, even in the absence of Civil Service requirements. The board members would be solely responsible for the hiring and firing of their own paid employees.

Admitting my lack of political experience, I then asked why the Democrats in Connecticut or anywhere else should want to assume public responsibility for withholding tires and eventually sugar, gasoline, coffee, shoes, canned goods, meats and butter? It was inevitable, I pointed out, that no matter how well handled, rationing would be subject to heavy criticism. Wouldn't it be wiser for the Democrats to share with the Republicans both the credit, which was likely to be meager, and the blame, which was likely to be extensive?

Although McCarthy seemed only mildly impressed with this political logic, we were both aware that as a practical matter I knew very few people throughout the state and would be forced to compromise somewhat in the rush to form our 169 boards by January 5. Although on a number of occasions I did consult with local political leaders in choosing ration board chairmen and in some cases acted on their recommendations, I took the precaution of making each of these early appointments temporary. As I came to know the chairmen better, and as I met more and more people around the state, I planned to replace any incompetents who might have slipped through with men and women in whom I had personal confidence.

Between January 5 and March 1, 1942, I visited each of the 169 cities and towns in the sate to meet personally with every ration board and to make my own judgments. In the course of these visits I met several Democratic leaders who, interestingly enough, had taken my advice to Commissioner McCarthy so much to heart that they had recommended their political enemies for positions on the ration boards.

By early December of 1942, whether because of our effort to be unbiased or the Democratic leaders' desire to "share the blame," there were 897 Republicans, 476 Democrats and 356 Independents appointed to the Connecticut ration boards.[1] In all fairness I should add that once the depth of my convictions was recognized by Governor Hurley and his political associates, most of them genuinely cooperated.

Equal to the need to keep the ration boards free of party politics was the importance, in my opinion, of seeing that each of the boards

1. The Republican majority is explained by the fact that there were more small-town ration boards than large-city ration boards and most small towns in Connecticut tended (and still do) to be Republican.

represented all segments of the local community which it served. In Connecticut as elsewhere civic activities are more often than not organized and run by well-to-do business leaders, many of them retired, who not only have the administrative experience but also more free time. Naturally, they tend to recruit men and women to work with them whom they know personally, with the result that a large percentage are from the upper-income groups.

To avoid this imbalance in our ration boards, I established firm rules for the composition of their membership. Of the five members, who in the early stages of the program constituted the average board, one should be a businessman, one a schoolteacher, one a member of organized labor, one a shopkeeper, or in rural areas a farmer, and one a respected individual who need not be from any particular category, for instance a clergyman.

Later, when larger boards were required, we simply increased the numbers in each category equally. Because the Connecticut boards were both representative and nonpolitical, they quickly achieved, and with very few exceptions maintained, a degree of prestige and respect which would have been impossible for a politically based board or a board confined to members from the economic upper crust.

In the early weeks of 1942, even as the volunteer tire-rationing boards were being set up, it was becoming clear that rapid war mobilization would require a broader administrative structure to deal with new rationing problems and also with the administration of price and rent controls.

In the first few months of 1942 the Office of Price Administration (OPA), which had been set up by Congress as an executive agency of the President, created nine regional offices covering the entire country, with ninety-four districts operating under their jurisdiction. New England was designated a region with headquarters in Boston, and each of its six states became a district. In March I was asked to become Connecticut District Director, a Civil Service post with a salary of $7,500 annually—3 percent of my earned income in New York the previous year.

Since Pearl Harbor I had been considering the possibility of enlisting in the Navy. Although I had many years' experience in deep-sea sailing, my request for sea duty was turned down because I had only one good ear as a result of a mastoid condition in my childhood. While this did not interfere with my ability to hear a fog horn or a bell buoy, I could not determine the direction of the sound. I was, however, offered a commission as Lieutenant Commander, with an assignment to teach nautical astronomy, navigation and piloting to "ninety-day wonders"— the young ensigns who were being given crash courses before their seagoing assignments.

Since this prospect seemed tedious, unappealing and of less importance than OPA, I decided, with Steb's strong support, to accept the OPA appointment. Because of the remote possibility of a conflict of interest in some future situation, I decided to sever my financial connections with Benton & Bowles. In view of the unpredictable impact of the war and of my withdrawal, my partners were uncertain about the future prosperity of the business; but eventually a price for my stock was agreed upon which seemed fair to everyone, and I became a full-blown civil servant. I might add that the forebodings of my former partners turned out to be unjustified. After my departure the business grew even more rapidly and has continued to grow ever since.

The knowledge that my move from New York to Hartford was now no longer temporary called for a major personal adjustment. I had left behind a spacious, well-equipped office on Madison Avenue with a well-paid, competent staff of four hundred people for a tiny cubbyhole jammed with harried volunteers in a dingy building on Oak Street. The only other tenant in the building was a little man upstairs whose job it was to take care of the gravestones of Spanish-American War veterans. After twenty years on the job, he had begun to look like one himself.

At Benton & Bowles we had known more or less what we were doing and what worked and what did not. We had been able to hire the people we needed at whatever salaries were necessary without red tape or delay.

In Hartford I faced a totally new kind of administrative challenge with no experience to guide me. Our small staff was literally overwhelmed with clerical tasks—addressing envelopes, writing instructions to all the ration boards, sending out literature explaining the emergency, and compiling questionnaires to determine public reaction. When truck drivers came in to deliver supplies, we often talked them into a half-hour of emergency envelope-stuffing before going on to their next delivery.

When we were finally authorized by the federal government to hire a more adequate office staff, I found myself sinking into the unfamiliar and seemingly bottomless pit of Civil Service procedures. We could not do anything, from hiring stenographers to buying typewriters, without "clearance," and clearance involved filling out endless papers and enduring long delays while the regional office in Boston "processed" our requests. I remember coming into the office one morning particularly frustrated and proclaiming that we would that very day hire fifteen secretaries, no matter what, and we would buy fifteen typewriters for them to work with, no matter what.

But I soon learned that bureaucracy is a formidable force; the girls we hired did not get paid, and the bill for the typewriters ended up on my desk. Only after a pilgrimage to the regional Civil Service office in Boston during which I threw myself on their mercy and humbly promised henceforth to work within the "system" did they agree to bail me out.

New employees began to arrive without warning from Washington. One day, for example, I walked into my office after lunch and found a stranger sitting in my chair with his feet on my desk discussing with someone over the telephone how to handle his difficult new boss. My initial reaction was chilly. And it did not improve when I found that he was one of several new employees who had been selected by the central office to help staff the new professional organization that was gradually replacing the emergency (and in Washington's view amateur) organization set up by the states. But by that time I was becoming resigned to the "system" invariably winning, and after some discussion I told my new employee that he was welcome if I could have the one assurance that he would help me to build a down-to-earth, community-based organization, even though our administrative setup might not precisely fit the Washington pattern.

I soon learned that this new employee, Douglas J. Bennet, had great ability. Within a few weeks he was on his way to becoming my top associate in the Connecticut OPA, and he later joined me for three years in Washington in a key role. When I ran for Governor in 1946, 1948 and 1950, Doug was my campaign manager; and all during my Administration in Hartford he worked as my executive secretary at a major sacrifice in income. In 1958, when I ran for the Senate nomination against Thomas J. Dodd, he was once again in the thick of it. After the war Doug and his wife, Phoebe, bought a home on Hamburg Cove just across the Connecticut River from us and are among our very closest friends.

With a satisfactory staff finally assembled, we established a good working relationship with the OPA regional office in Boston and also began to develop some contacts with Washington. The Connecticut program was off to a good start, and many of our techniques were being borrowed for use in other parts of the country.

By early spring, 1942, in addition to rationing we were being given increasing responsibilities for retail and wholesale price control. I was also asked to recruit a state rent control director and three area directors to work under my jurisdiction in freezing all rents throughout the state.

One welcome aspect of my new job was that it allowed my family and me to continue to live in Essex, forty-one miles from Hartford. With an OPA-imposed forty-mile-an-hour speed limit, this meant a three-hour round trip daily, which I made with three other Essex residents in a car pool.

Shortly after I had become the State Rationing Director, Steb resigned her position as a member of the State Defense Council and was elected a member of the Essex school board, later becoming its chairman.

Steb was determined to raise all the food we could on our own land. For several months, with the help of an old Yankee friend, Archie Looby, and his ox, Brindle (the only surviving ox in Essex), we worked every Sunday to clear out four or five acres of woodland near our house as a pasture and hay lot. Steb's day began at 6 A.M., first milking the cow and then getting the children off to school. Each morning the children walked a mile through the woods to the main road, where they were picked up by the school bus, with another mile hike back each night. They have never been healthier.

Steb's "farm" turned out to be a two-way asset. First, it enabled us to grow nearly half of all our food. At the peak of her farming efforts we had two cows, three pigs, a half-dozen sheep and 150 chickens. Second, it provided me with a never-ending supply of anecdotes with which to convince our rural citizenry that I had a down-to-earth understanding of their problems.

The public reaction to rationing was mixed and seemed to change from week to week. As more and more commodities came under the rationing system, public resistance began to increase, and as price and rent controls were enforced more strictly, landlords, retailers, wholesalers and farmers began to react.

We gave high priority to a program to inform and educate the public about the purposes of rationing, price and rent control programs and their relation to the war effort. In addition to my weekly broadcasts, we distributed posters throughout the state explaining why rationing was necessary and prepared a series of one-minute radio spots directed toward specific groups, which appeared during sports broadcasts, news programs, soap operas and music shows.

A typical radio spot aimed primarily at housewives might ask: "Do you drive your husband to the station every morning? Well, you women can save your automobile tires by taking turns and driving your men to the station in just one car. The state rationing administration asks that you cut your driving 25 percent. Walk more, take the train or bus wherever possible."

The newspapers also were helpful in explaining why government controls were essential to the war effort. Even those which opposed the Administration on other issues supported it on this one. For example, an editorial in the strongly anti-Administration Hartford *Courant,* during the Congressional debate over the Emergency Price Control Act, stated, "If the public wants to be protected against inflation, it can let Congress know that it need have no fear to enact a price control bill that will work."

It quickly became evident to those who set national policy in Washington that if we were effectively to control one commodity we would need to control related commodities, which led to an ever-increasing number of regulations. For example, motorists were required to get their old tires retreaded instead of perfunctorily submitting applications for new tires. This meant two additional elements in our rationing operation: a standard, fixed cost for retreading old tires to which local garages must adhere and an uncorruptible system of inspection to determine whether or not an old tire should be reworked or discarded. This required a system of control over all garages.

The number of rationed products grew steadily. On April 20, 1942, the rationing of sugar was ordered. This meant the first distribution of the famous ration books. In Connecticut we had to rush to make the deadline, May 4, since the ration books did not arrive from the printer in Washington until the morning they were supposed to be distributed. Somehow we managed to get them to our 169 local ration boards by noon of that day, where thousands of schoolteachers, working as volunteers, registered each individual citizen and distributed the books. Three-quarters of a pound of sugar were allotted to each person every week.

By May, 1942, in addition to automobile tires and sugar, we were also administering the rationing of fuel oil and gasoline, with shoes, meat, coffee and canned fruits and vegetables yet to come, in addition to a wide range of price and rent controls. (During the summer it was announced from Washington that an additional group of rubber products were being classified as national necessities. These included hot-water bottles, fire hoses, nipples for babies' bottles and raincoats for police and firemen. Within twenty-four hours after the list had been published, a well-organized lobby of militant women succeeded in pressing the OPA in Washington to add girdles to the list of national necessities vital to the war effort.)

Today there are few who remember the near-disaster we faced in the winter of 1943 because of the shortage of fuel oil and gasoline. It was the coldest winter in memory. Temperatures were consistently sub-zero and many fuel oil dealers were receiving as many as two hundred calls a day from customers pleading for emergency delivery.

On January 5, 1943, I issued a public statement to underscore the magnitude of the crisis and the need for care. "Right now," I said, "there is only one day's supply of fuel oil in dealers' supply tanks in the State of Connecticut. Since mid-December there has never been more than three days' supply of fuel oil on hand at any one time."

The fuel oil and gasoline shortage was largely caused by transportation difficulties. The pipe lines to carry petroleum products from Texas and Oklahoma to the East Coast had not yet been completed and the only means of transportation was by tankers, which were an easy target for German submarines. I was told one night fourteen blazing tankers were visible from the lighthouse at Cape Hatteras.

Our office, which had now moved to Ann Street in Hartford, was not exempt from these privations. In mid-December a headline appeared in the Hartford *Times,* "Penetrating Cold Penetrates OPA Office." The article reported that some of our OPA employees had to be sent home because we lacked oil to heat the office.

Our house in Essex was built in 1939 for a large family and a heavy flow of guests, and it normally consumed a lot of fuel. However, when fuel rationing began, we shut off all the heat in two-thirds of the house and lived in the rest. Our dining room became our living room, the nearby front hall was piled high with firewood, and with an open coal fire going day and night we, like millions of other families, nursed our sharply reduced oil supply through the winter.

We also faced a shortage of gasoline, which by the winter of 1943 was far more serious than the rubber shortage and almost as serious as the fuel crisis. Although the rationing system had cut the amount of gasoline used in half, it was almost impossible to go below that amount without a total breakdown of transportation.

To deal with this emergency, the OPA headquarters in Washington announced on January 7, 1943, a ban on all "pleasure driving" which was to be effective in all the East Coast states regardless of the ration tickets a motorist might have received from his ration board. From the beginning it was clear to us that this edict was totally unenforceable, and the public soon came to realize it.

From this experience I learned a valuable lesson in government: a very small percentage of the public—perhaps 2 or 3 percent—are inherently dishonest; while something like 20 percent can be trusted to obey the law regardless of what others do. The remaining 75 percent or so genuinely *want* to be honest, but they are also determined not to confirm P. T. Barnum's assertion that "a sucker is born every minute"; breaking a law or two is a small price to pay to escape the unpleasant sense of being had. The solution clearly is to avoid unenforceable laws and rigidly to enforce those which the majority are prepared to support.

Although the strain was unrelenting, I found the experience of work-

ing closely with people in local communities deeply rewarding. We had
set out in Connecticut to build a system that involved the people as
much as it served them. We had also made a massive effort to explain
why certain actions were necessary, to admit our mistakes and to seek
advice on how we could improve our operation. Out of this combination
evolved a crusading spirit of cooperation that gave the statewide program
life and purpose.

As OPA came under increasingly heavy fire in late 1942 and early
1943, beleaguered OPA officials caught in the Washington cross-fire
often remarked wistfully how much they envied our relationship with
the people of Connecticut. While I sought to explain our relative freedom
from public and press abuse on the ground that Connecticut was a small
state, I began to receive suggestions that I accept a post in the national
OPA organization.

In late 1942, Leon Henderson, the first Administrator of OPA, asked
me to become head of the national rationing operation. In the spring of
1943, Prentiss M. Brown, Henderson's successor, invited me on several
occasions to work in Washington, though in a rather vague general
capacity. Each time I refused.

Although I had been attracted to government for many years, the
idea of working in Washington D.C., had never appealed to me under
the best of circumstances. I had returned from a number of conferences
there appalled at the bureaucratic confusion in the OPA national organization. Only by a total reorganization and the introduction of
scores of able new people, I thought, could anyone straighten out the
administrative mess, and this did not appear likely.

I was also concerned by the fact that in some parts of the country
OPA was gradually becoming a haven for defeated politicians. The
Congressional election of 1942 had gone against the Democrats and
many of the losers had turned up on the OPA payroll. I could also observe
a growing readiness to bend to political pressures in an effort to win
more support from Congress.

In May, 1943, concerned about the resignation of the New York
District Director, Russell Potter, who had left because of political pressures, I wrote to Prentiss Brown:

> Because I am worried about some recent developments, I am taking
> the liberty of writing to you about a subject which is officially none of
> my affair.
>
> Both Ken Backman and Prescott Vose[2] are registered Republicans, and

2. Kenneth B. Backman, Regional Director for the Northeast, and Prescott Vose,
District Director for Maine.

there are persistent rumors that they, too, will soon be dismissed and replaced by organization Democrats. . . .

Rationing and price control will never be really popular. Although the public will accept rationing and price control as necessary, there will always be irritations in the administration of the essential rules and regulations.

If well-substantiated charges of political influence and patronage are added to the burden which the field organization already carries in attempting to administer unpopular regulations, I am fearful that the public reaction in our part of the country will be devastating. . . .

If it is once established that the OPA has "gone political," we will quickly lose many of our best people, both on our paid staff and on our local boards, and public confidence in the OPA will be dealt a blow from which I do not believe we could hope to recover. . . . If respected employees of the OPA who have done outstanding work over a period of months are replaced for no other reason than the fact that they are Republicans, I feel there is grave danger that your OPA organization, in New England at least, may collapse.

In the letter I also responded to Brown's recent request for me to share the management of OPA with Lou R. Maxon, head of OPA's information department. "In my opinion, the reorganization and rejuvenation of OPA which are immediately essential," I said, "can only be achieved by setting up a General Manager who would act as your Deputy with full authority over *all* operations and responsible *only* to you on matters of policy. It would be a tough and thankless job. No sensible person would seek it."

I specifically said that if I were placed in charge, one of my first acts would be to get rid of any newly acquired political appointees who were not clearly qualified. Because of an uneasy conscience, I assume, I ended up by conceding somewhat more than I had on any previous occasion: "If you should ever decide to reorganize the OPA on that basis now or sometime in the future and if you are willing to place the complete management responsibility in my hands, I shall accept it." Since the chance of such sweeping preconditions' being accepted seemed remote, I reassured Steb that she need not worry about our moving to Washington, D.C.

In early July, 1943, after a year and a half of intensive work without a breathing spell, I left with Steb and our daughter Cynthia, then seven years old, for a two-week sail from South Dartmouth on Buzzards Bay to Nantucket and Martha's Vineyard. In view of the gasoline shortage we would rely completely on sail; if the wind died, we would sit there until it came up again.

At about the halfway mark on our cruise we anchored one noon just off the lovely beach in Quick's Hole which faces the channel between Naushon and Nashawena islands and went ashore for a swim and picnic lunch. An hour or so later a Coast Guard cutter anchored near us and some of the crew came ashore. Steb and I offered them part of our lunch, and we chatted with them until they returned to their boat and proceeded toward Cuttyhunk, their home port.

During the next week we saw no one, and since our radio had broken down, we heard nothing. On a late Sunday afternoon we put in at Woods Hole and went ashore for some supplies. When I picked up a copy of the *New York Times*, I was startled to see a front-page headline, "Search for Bowles Continues."

At first I thought this must be some other Bowles. But as I read the story I realized that what I had solemnly assured Steb would never happen had in fact happened: President Roosevelt and Prentiss Brown had accepted my terms. For better or for worse, I was to become General Manager of the most complex and most controversial of all the agencies of the federal government.

According to the news story, the Administration had been searching for me for more than a week and I was nowhere to be found. Since we had talked to the skipper and crew of a Coast Guard cutter only a week before, this puzzled us.

From a pay telephone on the Woods Hole dock I called Prentiss Brown, who told me that he fully accepted my conditions. When he asked how soon I could get to Washington, I replied that I would be there in forty-eight hours.

CHAPTER 2

INTRODUCTION TO WASHINGTON

As I WALKED DOWN THE LONG PLATFORM to the Washington station on Tuesday morning, July 27, 1943, I was convinced that I had agreed to undertake an impossible job. I had been in Washington no more than a dozen times in my life and knew very few people there—two of them being our Connecticut Senators, Francis Maloney and John A. Danaher. Although I had talked to Mrs. Roosevelt on several occasions, I had never met the President.

Later that morning in his office, Prentiss Brown compounded my concern by announcing that he was leaving in two days for his home in Michigan, that he was uncertain when he would return and that as of that moment he was turning the whole operation over to me. Thus I suddenly found myself General Manager and Acting Administrator of a federal agency second in size only to the Post Office, which had been hurriedly put together against strong opposition to handle a task never before attempted.

At least one incident brightened my first day in office—a letter from a Chief Boatswain's Mate in the United States Coast Guard who identified himself as skipper of the Coast Guard cutter we had seen at Quick's Hole. "I was sent to find you," he wrote, "but your wife told me how badly you needed a rest and I just couldn't believe it was all that important for you to come to Washington right then. So I returned to my base and reported that I could not find you." A year later after exacting a promise that he would not take the Boatswain's Mate to task I showed this letter to Secretary of the Navy James V. Forrestal, who agreed that in this particular case the Coast Guard had acted with laudable independence.

29

Less than four months before I arrived in Washington President
Roosevelt had issued one of the most important administrative actions
of his Presidency, the so-called "hold the line" order of April 8.

"The only way to hold the line," the President said, "is to stop trying
to find justifications for not holding it here or not holding it there. No
one straw can break a camel's back, but there is always the last straw.
We can't afford to take further chances or relax the line. We already
have taken too many."

The order provided for the actual rollback of food prices by direct
income payments to the farmers which would enable them to cover
any increase in costs and to maintain their incomes. The "hold the line"
program included "dollars and cents ceilings" to be posted in every
grocery store (that is, ceiling prices with specific amounts for each item).

At the same time the President vetoed the so-called "Bankhead
Bill," which would have made further increases in farm prices man-
datory. The veto message was a strong reiteration of the President's determination to maintain a stable economy. Farm incomes during the war,
he stressed, had risen by almost 50 percent more than the average income of the nonfarm population.

The order also directed that all items affecting the cost of living
should be brought under control. No further price increases would be
allowed except under exceptional circumstances. Price increases would
no longer be used to stimulate increases in production. In those cases
where production incentives were necessary they must be provided
through subsidies.

Bidding for labor by offering higher wages was likewise banned.
The War Manpower Commission was directed to prevent any workers
already employed in a defense industry from moving to higher-paid jobs.

The "hold the line" order was the climax of a long struggle to develop
workable, integrated stabilization programs that would enable us to
avoid the costly inflation which had occurred during and after World
War I. By 1919 the war effort had added $30 billion to the public debt
and created over 22,000 new millionaires. Public money was flowing
into private pockets at an unprecedented rate, and, worse still, it was
justified on the specious grounds that, like it or not, the only way to
increase production in a capitalist economy was to open the door wide
to unlimited profits. Since maximum production was vital, it was argued,
manufacturers should be given what amounted to a blank check.

The regulations designed to hold down prices during the war had been
largely ineffective, and on Armistice Day, 1918, even those were abandoned. As a consequence, prices rose even more rapidly, and the next

eighteen months saw an economic collapse which left tens of thousands of returning veterans jobless, homeless and bitter.

Profiteering had been so scandalous that both the Democratic and Republican parties included planks in their 1924 platforms recommending that in the event of any future war special powers be granted to the President. Said the Republicans, "The President [should] be empowered to draft such material resources and such services as may be required to stabilize the prices of services and essential commodities, whether used in warfare or private activities."

The Democrats expressed similar sentiments. "In the event of war in which the manpower of the Nation is drafted," the Democratic platform said, "all other resources should also be drafted. This will tend to discourage war by depriving it of its profits."

In 1930 Congress passed a joint resolution creating the War Policies Commission to consider ways of removing the profits from war, of authorizing the public seizure of private property during wartime, and of equalizing the burdens of war. When the Attorney General ruled that it was unconstitutional to fix prices merely to prevent profiteering, the Commission recommended that a constitutional amendment be passed granting Congress the power to prevent profiteering in time of war; but predictably nothing came of it.

In 1936, when the rumble of approaching conflict once again began to be heard in Europe, the Senate created a special Senate committee, headed by Gerald P. Nye of North Dakota, to consider seven bills that had been introduced regulating domestic economic activity during wartime. After investigating the munitions industry, the Nye Committee issued a pessimistic report, declaring that the goods needed for a modern war could never be produced "without the evils of profiteering, mountainous debts, and inflation. Whenever attempts are made to eliminate these evils, they will be in direct conflict with the efforts to stimulate production; it is the former rather than the latter which must be sacrificed."

Nevertheless, several political leaders continued their search for a rational answer. In the summer of 1938, Senator Joseph C. O'Mahoney of Wyoming, chairman of the Temporary National Economic Committee, appointed a government economist, Leon Henderson, as executive secretary of the committee, with instructions to explore, among other questions, means of assuring a reasonable measure of economic stabilization in wartime.

On May, 28, 1940, during the Battle of Dunkirk, President Roosevelt revived the National Defense Advisory Commission, a body originally created by an old World War I statute passed in 1916. Leon Henderson was placed in charge of Price Stabilization, with Sidney Hillman responsible for Labor, Harriet Elliott for Consumer Protection, and William S. Knudsen for Industrial Production.

Leon Henderson regarded his role as more than that of a mere adviser. The time had come, he thought, to consider the need for stand-by price controls, and he proceeded to explore the requirements. On February 17, 1941, David Ginsburg and John E. Hamm, Henderson's two top associates, issued the first of the now famous "price schedules." The initial order was aimed at stabilizing the prices of secondhand machine tools.

Although the schedule had no legal authority behind it, there were dark hints of legal action against those who did not obey the price recommendations. A period of "jawbone control," which was to last through 1941, had begun. Congressman Wright Patman of Texas called the price schedules "fixing prices by the banging-on-the-table method"; Congressman Henry Steagall of Alabama wryly suggested that "The legality of these price schedules is unquestionable; they rest firmly on the constitutional right of free speech."

The standing of the price schedules had been enhanced two months later by an Executive Order issued by President Roosevelt on April 11, 1941, setting up the Office of Price Administration and Civilian Supply, intended to serve as a stopgap measure until Congress could pass the necessary legislation. On August 28, again by Executive Order, Roosevelt essentially split OPACS into two parts, the Office of Price Administration and the Supply Priorities and Allocations Board.

The obstacles to effective long-range planning in economic stabilization were formidable and were reflected in the difficulties encountered in enacting meaningful legislation for price control. Businessmen knew that price controls would tend to limit profits, labor leaders feared (correctly) that they would lead to wage controls, and orthodox economists rejected them on the basis that the only way to increase production and to bring out scarce supplies was to boost the profits to whatever level might be necessary. This strange alliance of interests—plus pure inertia— made the passage of a Price Control Bill slow going.

In the fall of 1941 Congressional committees listened for a leisurely five weeks to testimony about price controls. But there was little indication that they were prepared to move beyond the attitude of the 1936 Nye Committee and give the executive branch the necessary authority to control the economy during wartime.

To understand this reluctance, it is important to consider the public state of mind. Since 1929 almost everyone had been living through an extremely lean period, and here at last, many thought, was a well-deserved opportunity to make up for lost time.

Hundreds of thousands of farmers had been forced off their land by catastrophically low prices. Most businessmen had opposed the New Deal and Roosevelt and his "creeping socialists" out of a fear, which was for the most part genuine and deep-rooted, that "too much government" was dangerous. Now they feared that if under the "cover" of the wartime emergency rigid controls were established throughout our economy, they would become a permanent fixture.

Labor was equally skittish. Although the unions trusted the Roosevelt Administration more than did private enterprise, they feared that the President under wartime pressures might reverse his favorable labor policies.

The public in general had not forgotten Roosevelt's efforts to restore our national confidence in the dark days of the Depression, and to take steps, however inadequate, to ease the problems of the "forgotten third." But it was weary, impatient and confused.

Supporters of price control were divided into two groups—the "selectivists," those who advocated price control only on a few basic commodities such as steel, wheat and cotton, and those who advocated a price freeze, an across-the-board price control, backed by effective wage controls.

One of those who most effectively opposed selective price control was Representative Albert Gore of Tennessee, who eloquently summed up the case against this method in the following terms: "To try to halt general price levels by placing a ceiling on selective commodities is like trying to impound the water of a stream by building a dam only halfway across it."

The case against both the selectivists and those who opposed price control altogether became increasingly stronger in late 1941. Inflationary pressures were growing steadily. In order to fight a two-front war, the military planners agreed that something close to $100 billion annually would be required for the military alone. This was reflected later in Roosevelt's State of the Union message on January 3, 1942, in which he called for the production of five million tons of shipping annually and fifty thousand airplanes.

But the entire Gross National Product in 1940, the last prewar year, was slightly less than $100 billion. Since some ten or twelve million of our ablest young men would be moved out of the domestic economy into the armed services, many economists were convinced that even with a longer work week and many women and normally unemployable men at work no more than $30 or $40 billion in additional production would be available to meet the entire needs of our domestic economy. The goals set by the President in his January 3 speech, they said, were unrealistic, and could only be justified as propaganda designed to alarm our enemies.

Among the handful of individuals who challenged this pessimistic view was Walter P. Reuther, president of the United Automobile Workers. Reuther was convinced that our economy could generate $100 billion of wartime production and at the same time provide an additional $100 billion for the domestic economy even with several million of our men in the armed services. This view, which was dismissed at the time as hopelessly visionary, turned out to be prophetic.

As an increasing number of witnesses testified before Congress on the necessity for price controls, it was Leon Henderson who emerged as the man who most clearly understood the situation. He had been in the government since 1931, and as the head of research and planning for the National Recovery Administration he had become closely associated with the New Deal. The *New York Times* described Henderson as "the first government economist to predict the 1937 recession."

Henderson was well known on Capitol Hill for his ability to marshal complex information and organize it into a persuasive argument. Wright Patman, who became one of OPA's strongest supporters in Congress, told Henderson, "I have never seen a witness in a committee or in a courthouse—and I have had some experience in both—who knew more about any subject. And I say that conscientiously."

With a boost from Pearl Harbor, the bill was finally passed and signed into law by President Roosevelt on January 30, 1942; Henderson became the logical choice for the post of Administrator.

When President Roosevelt invited Henderson to his office to inform him of his appointment, he said, "For this job I need the toughest damned bastard in town, and, Leon, you are it." Only a few disagreed. Joseph Martin of Massachusetts, a powerful Republican in the House, recommended that Herbert Hoover be asked to take on this responsibility. Almost everybody else, however, was pleased with Leon Henderson.

Henderson further strengthened his position by recruiting some of the most able associates who have ever served our government. David Ginsburg, who was less than thirty years old when he joined Henderson's staff, soon to become OPA General Counsel, was a creative, forceful and eloquent graduate of the Harvard Law School. As one political observer described him in 1940, he seemed to be "three to six months ahead of anyone else in Washington."

As Deputy Administrator for Price, Henderson chose John Kenneth Galbraith, who was then a brilliant young economist at Princeton and who had done some imaginative work in agricultural economics. Paul A. Porter, a Washington lawyer, became Deputy Administrator for Rent, and Paul M. O'Leary, Deputy Administrator for Rationing.

Although the Emergency Price Control Act was not everything that the President or his Price Administrator wanted, it was much the furthest an American Congress had ever gone in delegating economic power to the executive branch.

Soon after the bill passed Congress, Leon Henderson said, stressing its strengths, "This is the only price control bill in the world that has standards in it which are binding on those who administer it. It is the only price control bill . . . which has embodied in it the rights of appeal to the courts for those who feel that they are aggrieved. . . . The bill is the only one that has a standard of profits in it. . . . It was not by accident that that bill contained standards. It was not by accident that there was a clear channel to the aggrieved that he might have his case reviewed by other than the administrative authority, and it was not by any fortuitous circumstances that it had a standard in there which undertook to say to a price administrator, be he Leon Henderson or those who came after, 'You must give due regard to costs and profits.' "

The legislation opened with a declaration of purposes, broad enough to justify almost any action taken by the Price Administrator to control prices. The purpose of the law, it said, was "to stabilize prices, and rents, and to prevent profiteering, hoarding and speculation; to assure that defense appropriations are not dissipated by excessive prices; to protect those with fixed incomes from undue impairment of their living standards; to assist in securing adequate production; and to prevent postemergency collapse of values."

A second section involved the formal delegation of power. To fix maximum prices by regulations, the law said, the ceilings had to be "generally fair and equitable" and such as would "effectuate the purpose of this act."

The third section, however, contained a serious weakness which had caused Henderson to urge the President to veto the bill in spite of its many good features; it strictly limited the controls that could be exercised over agricultural prices. Since food prices were at the heart of any economic stabilization program, Henderson asserted quite correctly that the cost of living could never be controlled unless there was direct control over the price of food and wages.

In regard to administration and enforcement, the Office of Price Administration was established as an independent agency run by a single Administrator. Senator Robert A. Taft of Ohio unsuccessfully argued that the ultimate decision-making power should be vested in a board. The Administrator was granted subpoena power so that he might make studies and reports and investigate records of private enterprise.

Rent control was recognized as a task of monumental proportions. As war industries sprang into being, hundreds of thousands of workers

left the communities where they had lived for higher-paying jobs elsewhere. The competition for housing resulted in a rapid increase in rents.
Since rents for the average working family amounted to an average of
20 percent in the cost of living, this generated still greater pressures
for higher wages.

Under the Emergency Price Control Act, the OPA Administrator
was authorized to designate defense-rental areas and recommend that
local action for stabilization and reduction in rents should take place
in these areas. If after sixty days the rents had not been stabilized in
accordance with these recommendations, he was empowered to roll
back rents to the levels of April 1, 1941. If rents had already been
significantly increased prior to April 1, 1941, due to defense activity, the
Administrator had the authority to select an earlier date, but not earlier
than April 1, 1940.

By the fall of 1942 OPA had designated 443 rent control areas with a
total population of 133 million people, which in effect extended rent
control to the entire nation. During the entire war period rents increased
less than one percent. Without this program the stabilization of our wartime economy would have been impossible.

Whatever its weaknesses, the Emergency Price Control Act of January,
1942, was brilliantly conceived and drafted. It gave OPA a mandate to
do what needed to be done and enabled those who administered OPA,
when under pressure, simply to point out that the legislation compelled
them to act as they did.

Effective implementation of the Act was another matter. By early
March, 1942, price controls had been applied to little more than half the
economy and then only at the wholesale level. Retail prices of food,
clothing, housing, furnishings and rents were still rising rapidly.

While the general public was gradually beginning to understand
the danger of inflation and to support measures to contain it, lobbyists
representing manufacturers, retailers, workers and farmers were crowding into Washington to plead "special rights" for exemption of one kind
or another from the impending price regulations. All major economic
groups were in competition not only with each other but with the government. Each advocated firm control over other segments of the
economy but resisted control over its own.

Yet, as the weeks passed, the vastness and complexity of the inflation
danger became increasingly obvious. As a result a consensus began to
take shape among almost all economic factions, and within the federal
government itself, that an integrated and comprehensive program of
inflationary controls was essential. In general but imprecise terms this

was understood to include wage controls, price and rent controls, rationing of scarce products, production controls and measures to siphon off much more of the rapidly rising purchasing power through higher taxes or enforced savings.

This gradual public acceptance of the need to close legislative gaps was due in large measure to Henderson's constant reiteration of the fact that price controls without wage controls were bound to fail, and that without firm control over food prices wage controls were impossible. Among Henderson's strongest supporters was Harold D. Smith, Director of the Budget. Indeed, Smith's efforts in the first few months of 1942 were largely responsible for the first major steps toward a truly integrated stabilization effort.

The Anti-Inflation Committee, which had been established by the President to prepare an integrated program, reached agreement in mid-March, 1942. Its report called for a Seven Point Program, the first item of which was a general freeze of all prices as of April 1, 1942, with a recommendation that the special protection given to agricultural commodities in the Price Control Act should be at once repealed and these prices frozen at their current levels.

If further incentives were needed to encourage the production of particular commodities, whether agricultural or otherwise, the committee recommended that cash subsidies should be paid by the government directly to the producers, which would enable them to maintain their income and allow prices to the consumer to remain unchanged. All rents should be frozen promptly. All wage and salary rates should be frozen at the current level and a forty-eight-hour normal work week established in the war industries, with overtime payment in the form of war bonds which would not be redeemed until after the war.

The committee also recommended a heavy increase in income taxes, plus an increase in Social Security payments and a higher national retail sales tax. Rationing should be extended broadly, with controls over inventories, residential and industrial construction, and installment buying should be tightened or eliminated.

This report was submitted to the President on March 26 by Judge Samuel I. Rosenman, the President's General Counsel and long-time assistant, who played a key role in working out the differences among the various government departments involved. The program was approved by the President with the statement, "Only a program as drastic and broad as here outlined can stop inflation. Every element is essential; any lesser approach must fail."

On April 27, 1942, the President submitted to Congress a cost-of-living message outlining in general terms this Seven Point Program. The next evening he went on the radio for a "fireside chat," in which he pointed out the inflationary dangers and told of his determination to meet them.

Immediately following the President's announcement OPA moved to establish the general price freeze as of April 1, 1942, under the so-called General Maximum Price Regulation. But the President's message was still unclear on the crucial questions of food prices and wages. In spite of his brave words about a general price freeze, the goal he set could not be attained as long as food prices were largely exempted from controls and wages were allowed to creep upward.

When Leon Henderson in a public statement stressed that by wage stabilization he meant direct control over wages, he was subjected to bitter attacks by leaders of organized labor, who had previously looked upon him as a liberal New Dealer who had been strongly pro-labor. Now, as they saw it, their champion had let them down. The fact that Henderson was committed to serving no special interest group and was concerned only with maintaining a stable economy seemed to have escaped their attention as it had escaped that of so many others.

During the late spring and summer of 1942, the controversy continued over the desirability of wage and food price controls. After the establishment of the price control freeze as of April 1, many manufacturers and distributors found themselves caught between fixed prices established by the government and rising costs which included increasing wages. Those manufacturers whose profits were high could absorb these increases, but there were many who could not.

The Little Steel Formula of July, 1942, was designed to place some ceiling on across-the-board wage increases in the steel industry by limiting wage increases to 15 percent over January, 1941, wage levels. Although this narrowed the differences in wages between workers in the large steel plants and those in the smaller ones, its net effect was inflationary.

Wage pressures were further increased by the massive shift of manpower from one industry to another and particularly from the farms to the cities in response to higher wages. To ease this pressure, it was proposed that a manpower control program similar to that in the United Kingdom should be adopted. Under this program almost everyone would have been assigned to a specific job until the war was over. Its advocates pointed out that if a man could be drafted into the armed services, why could his neighbor not be drafted to work in a shipyard?

By midsummer, 1942, it was clear that the President's Seven Point Program, which was in effect only two-thirds of a program, was inadequate. Under the pressure of rising wages and farm prices the price control regulations put into effect in April were beginning to falter. Public confidence, never very great, was diminishing. The farm bloc, organized labor and business spokesmen were each effectively protecting their own narrow interests, and Congress was in an increasingly contentious mood.

As the bureaucratic struggle continued between those who believed in a firm price and wage freeze and those who felt that the problem could best be handled on a more flexible basis, an incident occurred which brought the situation to a head. In early July pressure developed for a substantial increase in the wages of aircraft workers on the Pacific Coast. Although the Office of Price Administration had the legal authority to set direct price ceilings on airplanes and other military equipment, this power had not been used; each contract was, however, subject to renegotiation if profits were later found to be out of line.

Faced with the threat of a new surge of wage increases running through the entire economy set off by the aircraft workers' demands, the Office of Price Administration let it be known that any increase in wages would have to be absorbed by the corporation involved. Under no circumstances would OPA allow this increase to be used to justify a price increase.

The OPA statement included the following language:

> While the Office of Price Administration does not have the responsibility directly to determine wages, it does have the responsibility for determining prices, and we will recognize as grounds for price adjustments only such wage increases as are required to meet a hardship situation. The country is at war; the country expects economic stabilization; wage stabilization means no wage increases except those required to eliminate inequalities or sub-standards of living. This is an essential step toward stabilization.[1]

I believe that it was this statement that led to the final breakthrough. In mid-August, Samuel Rosenman, drawing from proposals by Henderson, Smith and others, prepared an Executive Order which established an integrated stabilization program under the direct authority of an Economic Stabilization Director. Justice James F. Byrnes agreed to step down from the Supreme Court to assume the new post of Director and to become the chief coordinator of the economic stabilization program. Later Byrnes moved into the White House to become in effect deputy to the President, responsible for all nonmilitary aspects of the war effort.

1. Richard Gilbert, OPA Director of Research, who represented Leon Henderson at the July, 1942, Air Frame Wage Conference in Los Angeles, was largely responsible for the language and substance of this statement.

In late August, 1942, President Roosevelt announced his intention to deliver a major speech early in September on the subject of stabilizing prices and wages. However, on the afternoon of September 5, he made a key decision. If Congress failed to provide the necessary legislation, he would go ahead with the new stabilization program by administrative action under his own wartime powers as President. He would first place the problem squarely in the lap of Congress and force it to face up to the mounting public pressure which he was confident would now support an effective price and wage control effort. And then if Congress failed to act, he would do so.

The President's Labor Day message on September 7 was a demand for immediate, comprehensive action by Congress to stabilize our economy. The message pointed out that Congress had failed to act on the program the President had proposed in April in regard to taxes and farm prices. Since then the Administration had been doing its best to carry out the program by executive action, and a good start had been made on price controls, rent controls, rationing and the tightening of consumer credit. But events of the last few months had demonstrated that the control of wages and the control of farm prices were interdependent; one could not be achieved without the other. Consequently, he said, Congressional action to establish effective control of farm prices was the key to effective wage control, which in turn was essential to the program as a whole.

The President recalled the bleak days of 1933 when the Congress, "alive to the needs of that period, had formulated and enacted whatever was required. It did so without long debate, without party politics, and without the heat and pressure of any special group working in advantage for itself. . . . Unless Congress passes the required legislation, we cannot hold the price of food and clothing down to the present levels beyond October 1."

The President then laid the issue squarely on the line. "Action on your part by that date," he said to the Congress, "is your inescapable responsibility to the people of this country to assure that the war effort is no longer imperiled by the threat of economic chaos. In the event that the Congress should fail to act and act adequately, I shall accept responsibility and I shall act."

Although the President's "ultimatum" was resented by many and the debate was bitter, public opinion was now turning strongly toward the President's position. The legislation was passed, and on October 2 the President signed the new stabilization act, which immediately became law.

Another major legislative battle had been won. But there was still one missing element: as long as food prices continued to rise, however gradually, wage controls would remain under an unbearable strain. As Henderson had consistently argued, there was only one answer: government subsidies paid directly to the farmers. Such subsidies would enable farm prices to be held to the present level while providing the farmer with a reasonable return for his work.

In early December, OPA Administrator Henderson resigned, a sick, weary and harried man who had courageously and successfully led the fight for a stable economy. He had thrown all his energies and abilities into the task and in the process had brought down upon his head the wrath of every economic group in the country.

The choice of Prentiss Brown, a Democratic Senator from Michigan who had fought hard for the price control legislation in Congress and who in November, 1942, had been defeated at the polls, was calculated to ease the deteriorating relationship between the Office of Price Administration and the Congress and at the same time to provide an Administrator whose commitment to the program was unquestioned.

Meanwhile, labor, which had gone along with the President on wage controls on the understanding that the cost of living, including food, would henceforth be held firmly in check, began, for the first time, to emerge as the militant representative of the American consumer. Labor's strategy was to bring such strong pressure to bear on the Administration and on Congress that the government would be forced to take the necessary action in regard to prices.

By early spring the President saw that he must go the whole way. On April 8, 1943, he issued the "hold the line" order to which I have already referred. This action may be credited not only to the courage of the President and of those leaders in Congress who understood the dangers, but also to the efforts of such men as Leon Henderson, David Ginsburg, one of the most brilliant architects of the program, and John Kenneth Galbraith, who served as Deputy Administrator for Price during these crucial negotiations.

The President also included in his message a plea that Congress should act further to increase taxes. He pointed out that inflation could not be stopped solely by price, rent and wage ceilings. If the OPA price control dam was to be maintained, the accumulating pressure of increased purchasing power behind the dam must be eased. But the Treasury Department was opposed, and Congress could not be budged. As we shall see later, this omission was costly.

Between the issuance of the "hold the line" order and my arrival in July, the retail price of food actually dropped 3 percent as a consequence of the rollback made possible by the subsidy payments to farmers. The

long struggle for the necessary legislation and policy decisions was behind us. Labor had been given a major stake in the success of the
program and most businessmen were beginning to realize that a stable
economy was essential to their long-range interests.

Although the farmers were restless, they, too, were beginning to
understand that under the present price ceilings, with increased production and with direct subsidies available where needed, they were
assured substantial incomes. The leaders of the farm lobbies and their
Congressional spokesmen were still opposed to subsidies, and this
was a battle that I would have to fight and to win. But we had come a
long way.

CHAPTER 3

THE BUSINESSMEN VS.
THE PROFESSORS

ALTHOUGH THE LEGAL FOUNDATION for economic stabilization was largely completed and had some degree of public support before I reached Washington, OPA itself was misunderstood, distrusted and disorganized. If it was to carry out its responsibilities, a major reorganization would be required. Unless OPA could soon emerge in the minds of Congress, press and public as an effective, realistic government operation, no amount of commitment, sincerity and good intentions could save it or its program from disaster.

By the summer of 1943 the Office of Price Administration had more than 70,000 salaried employees, nearly half a million volunteers, 5,000 volunteer ration boards, 443 area rent control offices, 103 district offices and 9 regional offices. This vast organization necessarily had been put together on a crash basis, and it was not surprising that it was the target for considerable criticism.

The steady barrage of complicated new rationing programs had baffled and irritated almost everyone, and the price and rent regulations, many of which were necessarily intricate, had engulfed many businessmen in a maze of red tape. Members of Congress, besieged with letters and calls from influential constituents charging OPA with destroying their businesses, were uneasy, and morale throughout the OPA organization itself was at a low ebb.

Two weeks before my appointment, Lou Maxon, the chief information officer for the Office of Price Administration, had held a press conference and announced his resignation. OPA, said Maxon, was full of "confusion, indecision and compromise." Citing a famous OPA price order on fruitcake which occupied six pages of fine print, Maxon said, "Miles of legalistic red tape clutter up the place. There is so much of it that Houdini himself couldn't untangle it."

Like many of the critics before him, Maxon aimed the brunt of his attack at "the professors and theorists whose unworkable ideas have been conceived in the rarefied atmosphere of the classroom. . . . Their thinking takes wings and soars through the clouds unimpeded by facts and unhindered by actuality." He called for a "liberal transfusion of horse sense and a drastic reorganization." Maxon concluded by recommending that OPA rid itself of those "who wish to control just for control's sake."

The shrill eloquence of Maxon's rhetoric gave OPA critics some additional ammunition, and the cries to "Get the theorists out of price control" redoubled in number and in vigor. A rash of editorials appeared denouncing the pinko professors, ex-Communists, or near-Communists, New Dealers and reformers who, it was alleged, were arbitrarily determining price control policies and making a mess of rationing.

In a fit of frustration, Congress had even passed a statute requiring anyone working in a policy-making position in the Office of Price Administration to have had a year of business experience. The law was senseless—a year working in the local grocery store would have met the requirements—but it indicated the antipathy to the "theorists." Unhappily, these were often the lawyers and the economists who had best understood the need for the program and who were by and large most deeply committed to its success. A number of them, such as Ken Galbraith, were experienced departmental and bureau chiefs who would be particularly difficult to replace.

Because I was a businessman who had passed the acid test of having met a payroll, the announcement of my appointment was favorably received in conservative circles; I was generally looked upon as a naïve but honest businessman who was about to be thrown to the jackals of Washington, D.C. Editorials entitled "Mr. Bowles Goes to Washington" and "Poor Mr. Bowles" indicated sympathy for my predicament, but little hope.

Even the strongly anti-Administration Hartford *Courant* had a kindly word to say. On July 16, a few days before my appointment, the following editorial appeared:

What a Mess for Mr. Bowles!

Making due allowance for the state of Mr. Maxon's feelings and conceding that he has not yet mastered the art of effective understatement, the picture he has drawn of OPA is one that impresses the public as being essentially correct in its broad outlines. Into this picture steps Mr. Chester Bowles. . . .

The general opinion seems to be that Mr. Bowles has performed his difficult and thankless task in Connecticut extremely well. He has done all that anyone could do to explain to the public the thousand and one OPA regulations and try to make them palatable. . . . Should he go to Washington, as it is expected, he will find there ample opportunity for the exercise of his talents as an organizer.

The New Haven *Register* added the cheerful reminder: "Mr. Bowles, those Washington wolves are mean. They will be after your heels, your neck, and your scalp seven days a week." *Time* magazine predicted that "Bowles won't last six weeks."

Under these forbidding circumstances, Steb and I decided that the wisest course was for her and the three youngest children (Barbara was at school in New York and Chester, Jr. was still at Pomfret) to remain in Essex until the situation became somewhat clearer. I rented a small apartment in the Wardham Park Hotel and tried to get to Essex for a weekend once a month, while Steb made occasional visits to Washington.

When I took office, the final decision on each price regulation was almost completely in the hands of the lawyers, who felt with justification that they had a crucial role to play. They had carried the torch of price control and rationing within the agency for two long years, and they were deeply committed to keeping the flame burning. Before any policy decision on prices was made, they were expected under existing procedures to provide a legal opinion as to whether it met the requirements of the Price Control Act, and that opinion was decisive.

However, many of the lawyers and the economists had little understanding of the practical problems business faced under price controls. They were also inclined to be skeptical of business motives (often with justification) and impatient with business procedures. Inevitably, these attitudes produced a counterreaction among members of the business community, many of whom were still confirmed Roosevelt haters who regarded all government officials as rude, arrogant, power-hungry ideologues.

Another cause of business criticism was the complexity of many OPA regulations. While much of this was unavoidable because of the complexity of the program itself, some OPA lawyers found it difficult to strike a balance between the legal tightness required to carry out our mission and the clarity necessary to assure compliance.

In the summer of 1942 an effort at simplification had begun under the leadership of David F. Cavers. During the next year under Cavers' direction substantial progress was made in simplifying the form and style of the regulations, especially those applying to small businesses.

There was indeed a kernel of truth in the charges that OPA econo-mists were using price controls to transform American capitalism. Many economists in OPA were interested in making the free enterprise system both economically more efficient and more sensitive to the broader inter-ests of the consumer. When they ran across what appeared to be an unnecessary or unjust business procedure, there was often a compulsion to change it by using the power of price control.

For example, one OPA economist discovered that, instead of a single set of wholesalers selling fruits and vegetables to the retailers in New York City, there was for no clear reason an additional layer of whole-salers. Since these extra middlemen seemed to serve only to raise the price of vegetables, OPA proceeded to squeeze them out and thereby pre-sumably effect a savings for vegetable customers. Unhappily, unknown to OPA, the second layer of wholesalers had been performing an essential marketing function, and the fruit and vegetable market was thrown into chaos until the old system was reinstated.

In view of the often irrational abuse to which they had been subjected in the last few years, it was not surprising that even many of the ablest OPA lawyers and economists had become insensitive and in-different to public or Congressional opinion. Shortly after my arrival in Washington, this led to a near-disaster. At that time OPA was just completing its plans for a massive canned fruit and vegetable rationing program. Everything was set for a public announcement, the ration books had been printed, and I assumed that everything was in good order.

However, since I knew from my Connecticut experience the practical problems ration boards faced on a new program of this kind, I decided even at this late hour briefly to review the plans. To my horror, I discovered that under the new program the amount of fruits and vege-tables householders had raised in their "victory gardens" and preserved in their own kitchens would be subtracted from the ration coupons assigned to each family for the purchase of commercially canned vegetables and fruits in the stores. This would deprive the millions of householders who, at the government's request, had grown victory gardens, of the benefits of their efforts. If this particular program had not been stopped in its tracks, I believe that public confidence in the rationing system would have been destroyed.

My experience in Connecticut had made me aware of the genuine frustrations of many businessmen in dealing with OPA. But I was convinced that the technical skills of the lawyers and economists and their deep personal commitment to the inflation control program were es-sential if we were effectively to carry out the April, 1943, "hold the line" order. If I restricted the price-setting role of the lawyers, I would be charged with selling out to business interests, but unless I could at least blunt the criticisms of the business community and their Congressional spokesmen, OPA could be destroyed.

In this delicate situation I took a carefully calculated risk. An administrative order to end the veto power of the Legal Division and to assign all lawyers to the role of "legal advisers" in the Price, Rent and Rationing bureaus, had been on the books since April 2, 1943. The General Counsel alone would be responsible directly to the Administrator. However, owing to the chaotic conditions in OPA, the order had never been carried out. I decided to carry it out immediately.

In a memorandum which I found extremely difficult to write I stated that "It is my personal responsibility as acting price administrator to see that bureau heads and section chiefs faithfully carry out our policies in accordance with the law. This requires an ironclad chain of command." Under my reorganization plan lawyers were to advise the department, bureau or section chiefs as to the legality of a proposed price action, but they would no longer make the ultimate decision.

I also began to bring in a significant number of able new people experienced in business procedures to give OPA the "new look" required to gain public and Congressional support. My first and most important business appointee was an old associate, James F. Brownlee, a former excutive vice president of the General Foods Corporation, which had been a client of Benton & Bowles. Brownlee, who had recently left General Foods to become president of Frankfort Distilleries, agreed to become Deputy Administrator for Price (Galbraith's old job).

Brownlee was an extraordinarily incisive and clear-thinking executive, one of the few businessmen I have known who could hold his own intellectually in a group of top-flight economists. Much of the credit for whatever we were able to accomplish in the next three years belongs to him.

Since Jim was slight in stature and meek in appearance, hostile Congressmen in the first months following his appointment assumed that he would be an ideal target for their attacks. One day during a committee hearing, John Taber of New York, the ranking Republican on the House Appropriations Committee, launched into one of his familiar diatribes about freeloading within the bureaucracy. Turning to Brownlee, he demanded, "How much money did you make before you went into government?"

Jim was embarrassed and hesitated. His hesitancy confirmed Taber in his judgment that he had caught a featherbedder in the act and he pressed confidently on. "Out with it!" he demanded. "How much did you make before you worked for OPA?" After some further hesitation, Jim admitted that his income in the previous year in business had been $250,000.

For the post of Deputy Administrator I recruited James G. Rogers, Jr., who had been one of my most capable associates at Benton & Bowles and had a genius for orderly procedures and for getting things done. To head a talent hunt for other businessmen, I hired Robert Smallwood, president of Lipton Tea. Within a few weeks we had filled forty-six key positions.

Most of these newcomers had been in the selling end of their businesses, from which in the sellers' market stimulated by the war they could be most easily spared. Although they had a genuine desire to contribute to the war effort, most of them had very little economic or legal experience, almost no understanding of the dynamics of inflation, and the conviction—not unlike that of the lawyers—that they alone could do the job. I was conscious that many of our new recruits had come to Washington to correct what they felt to be unfairly low price levels, rather than to "hold the price line" as the President had called on us to do. Just give us a month or so, some of them were reported to have said as they left for the national capital, and we will straighten out this price control mess.

I knew that the integration of these businessmen, however well intentioned, into OPA would be difficult, and, indeed, the tension turned out to be as great as I had feared. But with the firm support of Jim Brownlee, Jim Rogers and sophisticated economists and lawyers such as Donald H. Wallace, Richard V. Gilbert, Henry Hart, Richard H. Field and David Cavers, who understood my decision, we welcomed them aboard and hoped for the best.

In early October, 1943, came the inevitable explosion. Some four or five weeks after the influx of businessmen, I was invited to a dinner given by them at the Sheraton Park Hotel in Washington. When Jim Brownlee dropped by my office to drive out with me, I asked what he thought was the purpose of the dinner. Jim replied, "They have been here for a while and begun to feel involved, and they probably just want to give you a dinner."

The minute we entered the dining room I sensed tension. The usual easy flow of conversation and laughter were missing, and the atmosphere seemed strained. After we had finished an uncomfortable dinner, a new recruit from the furniture industry arose, tapped his water glass for silence and—somewhat nervously—began to speak.

The businessmen, he said, had come to Washington with the understanding that their views on prices would be decisive, subject only to my approval as Price Administrator. However, in spite of the impressive-sounding jobs to which I had assigned them, the lawyers and economists were still setting the policies. This, they said, was an intolerable situation. Unless they were given more authority, they would resign en masse. This bombshell was followed by a general nodding of heads and an ominous silence.

The economic stabilization program had arrived at a testing point. The resignation of some forty newly hired businessmen would presumably be followed by a public charge that they had been prevented from carrying out their responsibilities. With Congressional opinion, under pressure from various lobbies and individual businessmen, already hostile to OPA over the alleged power of the "theorists," there was an excellent chance that the entire stabilization program would collapse. But as I rose to reply, I had no question about the right course.

I told the group that I had asked them to come to Washington because I knew from my own experience in business that OPA needed men in responsible positions who understood the problems, procedures and language of industry and management. However, they had been brought to Washington not to raise prices in response to industry pressures but to help make our price actions under the Price Control Act more practical, more enforceable and easier for businessmen and farmers to live with.

Their withdrawal would be a severe setback and, coming in the midst of the war effort, could only be described as reckless and irresponsible. Although I sincerely hoped that they would change their minds, they should be under no illusions about my position. If they forced me to choose between businessmen who wanted to raise prices and lawyers and economists who wanted to hold them down, I would without hesitation pick the lawyers and economists and we would carry on as best we could.

Jim Brownlee promptly supported my position and added that he was embarrassed and shocked by their demands, which he described as "only a little short of blackmail."

For a few minutes there was general confusion. Then individual businessmen rose to say that their case had been overstated, that they recognized my difficulties and that I could count on their assistance. The revolution collapsed, and with three or four exceptions the businessmen stuck to their posts. Within a few months the great majority had become as deeply committed to "holding the price line" as any of us.

One of the most rewarding aspects of the next few years was the teamwork which gradually evolved between the businessmen and the lawyers and economists. At first the issues brought to me for settlement reflected in large measure their differences in ideology and priorities. Gradually the ideological dividing lines became blurred; lawyers would argue against lawyers and businessmen against businessmen.

Yet the problem of juggling the various constituencies within OPA as well as outside of the agency, the problem of keeping one foot in everyone's camp and of maintaining credibility with people who were at each other's throats, stayed with me in one way or another from my first day in Washington to my departure three years later.

CHAPTER 4

SETTING THE RULES

WITHIN A WEEK AFTER ARRIVING in Washington I became convinced that unless we adopted consistent pricing standards and formulated and publicized an interpretation of the law acceptable to both Congress and the courts, the price line could not be firmly held, and we would soon find ourselves administering price inflation instead of price control. One journalist had credited me with perseverance which, he said, "depending on one's individual viewpoint, may be traced to his New England heritage or likened to the stubbornness of a Missouri mule." But perseverance alone would not enable us to carry out our responsibilities. What we needed now was a solid base on which to persevere.

Previously the OPA had operated on the basis of what the lawyers characterized as the "flexible approach." All price regulations were issued under the price freeze of March, 1942; exceptions were made on a case-by-case basis whenever there was proof of undue hardship.

The key phrase in the Price Control Act was the directive that the prices established by OPA must be "generally fair and equitable." As long as we failed to define this phrase precisely and to apply that interpretation to all pricing decisions, any ingenious lawyer with the price of a ticket to Washington could argue that the OPA should accept his client's version of what "fair and equitable" meant. With the help of his Senator or Congressman there was an excellent chance that he could get what he wanted. This meant that under the current "flexible" system it was inevitable that OPA would be pressured into inconsistent and often inflationary decisions.

As we discussed the problem, one point emerged clearly: no price could be fair for everybody; some inequities are inevitable in wartime as in peace. Everything depended on the meaning of the word "generally." With strong dissents from several members of our staff, it was decided that "generally fair and equitable" would henceforth be interpreted according to the following formula: "Only if the profits before taxes of a sizable percentage of the *entire industry* in question, say 30 to 40 percent, had fallen below the 1936–1939 level, could a price increase be granted."

The opposition within OPA argued that such a statement would "tie our hands." But my objective was precisely that: to see that our hands were, in fact, so tied that we could resist the pressures. If businessmen and their lawyers knew in advance how each request for a price increase would be judged, and if the courts and Congress upheld our interpretation, we would be literally forced to hold the price line.

I presented the problem and our solution to the Banking and Currency Committees of the House and Senate in public hearings, and to my relief I found many strong supporters.

"The Price Control Act," I said, "was passed by Congress. It is now our task to interpret what it means and yours to change the language if you disagree with our interpretation. . . . Let me say at the outset that I can see no reason why the government should guarantee a profit to every firm no matter how inefficient it might be in either wartime or peacetime. Our economic system is based on competition, and those who cannot make a profit fall by the wayside. During wartime, with sharply increased sales and decreased advertising costs, the number of failures should be, and indeed is, substantially less.

"As long as 60 or 70 percent of an industry," I continued, "is able to maintain the industry level of prewar profit, I think the objectives of the price control legislation have been met. The relatively few high-cost producers who run into difficulties can usually find some defense work to do where prices are set by negotiations and not by direct controls. If the new pricing standards which I hereby propose do not reflect the intent of Congress, I shall change them, but only if you specifically direct me to do so."

This interpretation was generally accepted in both houses of Congress, with some dissenters such as Senator Taft. Once the Congressional hurdle had been cleared, the focus switched to the courts. Thanks to David Ginsburg, OPA's first General Counsel, the Emergency Price Control Act included an ingeniously effective procedure for judicial review. A special nationwide Emergency Court of Appeals was established under the Act staffed by judges drawn from the federal bench, with the exclusive jurisdiction to determine the legality of OPA regulations.

This meant that the Federal District Courts were bypassed. Any OPA regulation would remain in effect unless it were thrown out by an adverse ruling of the nationwide Emergency Court. Without this system, each challenge would have been brought separately into a Federal District Court, with each decision binding only on that one district unless the question was settled by an appeal to the Supreme Court. The result would have been the collapse of the price and rent control system.

In practical terms it was a long road to the Emergency Court of Appeals. Upon the announcement of a new regulation, a hearing would be held by an administrative board within OPA. Any businessman affected by the regulation could then challenge the board's finding and appeal to the Emergency Court, where only the appeal record was considered.

The final recourse was direct appeal from the Emergency Court to the Supreme Court. In May, 1943, the Supreme Court upheld the Emergency Court's exclusive jurisdiction, and later, in March, 1944, upheld price control. In August, 1944, our new "industry earnings" standard was also upheld unanimously by the Supreme Court in *Gillespie Rogers–Pyatt Co.* v. *Bowles.*

With a court-enforced standard, we could meet any request by a single company with an objective rule rather than a subjective ruling. Every lawyer in the country knew precisely the standard by which his request for a price increase would be judged in Washington, and as a result fewer and fewer made the trip.

The creation of this solid legal base was the work of some of the finest young legal minds in the country. Although at first many of our legal staff had their doubts about the political wisdom of this self-imposed, court-enforced "strait jacket," it proved invaluable in meeting the challenges of Congressional groups, often stimulated by special interests. I recall, for example, one hearing before the Senate Small Business Committee at which Senator Kenneth S. Wherry of Nebraska (whom one journalist described as "a perennial and bloodthirsty critic of all that is OPA") repeatedly badgered me with the question, "Is there any legislative authority for you to regulate profits?" I answered, "We do not regulate profits; we regulate prices. The courts have established that this is clearly within our authority."

Wherry then asked, "Has the price Act on which you rely been amended to give you that authority?" I answered, "*You* members of Congress set up the price Act and wrote the language; *you* then set up a court to determine and interpret the intent of that language. The court which was your creation decided that we were acting in line with what was intended . . . therefore, I would say the intent of Congress was abundantly clear and that intent is now being carried out. . . . If Congress does not approve what the courts have done, Congress can change the Act."

Where a manufacturer was entitled to a price increase, we attempted to distribute the burden fairly. On the assumption that the consumer was least able to absorb the increased cost, we introduced what someone called the "collapsible telescope" approach. If a manufacturer was authorized to increase the price of his product by, let us say, $1.00, the percentage markup taken by the wholesaler and the retailer might result in the consumer paying not simply the additional $1.00, but $1.25.

Under our new standards the wholesalers were required to absorb the increase granted to the manufacturer unless this drove the wholesaler's profit below the "generally fair and equitable" industry level of 1936–39; in that case we shifted the burden to the retailer.

Only if first the manufacturer, then the wholesaler and finally the retailer could demonstrate hardship under our standards, did the cost reach the consumer in the form of a price increase.

This three-level approach was upheld by the Emergency Court of Appeals, which on December 15, 1943, stated:

> When such price increases are permitted it is the duty of the Administrator so far as possible to require them to be absorbed at some appropriate intermediate step in the process of production and distribution at which there may be an existing margin of profit reasonably sufficient to absorb them.

This decision was crucial to holding the price line; not the least of its advantages was the fact that it made involuntary allies of the wholesalers and retailers in the struggle against higher manufacturers' prices.

As this legal and administrative structure gradually took shape, we began to feel more confident that through well-administered price controls and the limited use of subsidies we could hold the price line for the duration of the war emergency.

Moreover, it was my impression that most members of Congress, privately at least, welcomed our new legally buttressed position. If some prices were rising while others were being held down, the pressures from their constituents would have become almost as heavy on them as on us. Now when a Congressman asked me to raise the price of a product produced by one of his constituents, I could say, "Mr. Congressman, I would like to go along but I can't. This price like all others is set by a law passed by Congress and confirmed by the courts. In asking me to raise this one price you are in effect asking me to raise thousands of other prices, which I cannot legally do." When the Congressman had passed this answer on to his constituent, he had done all that he could do and his constituent knew it.

As I mentioned in an earlier chapter, national labor policy in the early stages of the economic stabilization program was neither clear nor firm. Wages had been frozen by President Roosevelt's "hold the line" order of April, 1943, and once our price standards were firmly established and the subsidies required to hold down food prices were available, the problem of wage stabilization was greatly eased.

But the government still lacked legal authority to channel new-comers to the labor market into war-critical industries, and, because the authority was not available, the responsibility had been in large measure placed on OPA. By establishing a relatively low-ceiling price on non-essential items we could make it difficult and even impossible for the manufacturers of these items to divert newcomers into the labor market away from the essential defense industries by offering them higher wages. It was not our job, but we had no alternative except to do the best we could to fill the legislative gap.

Although responsible labor leaders agreed that we had carried out our promises "to hold the line," thus relieving the pressure on wages, they were with good reason skeptical of our ability to persuade Congress to continue the food subsidies which were essential to the price-wage structure.

Following the President's "hold the line" order, the Congress had reluctantly and tentatively authorized the limited use of subsidies to farmers. What Lou Maxon had decried as the fruit of "left-wingers or new thinkers" was simply a program of cash grants paid directly to the producer to cover increased costs and thereby avoid a retail price increase.

Any unbiased observer who took the trouble to explore the question could see that subsidies on critically important products were a bargain for its producers, its consumers and the taxpayers in general. The alternative was continuing price hikes, which labor would quite understandably use to force further increases in wages.

But the opposition to food subsidies formed by the farm lobbies remained strong, and it was evident that until Congress accepted the need for the subsidy payments, labor's pressure on wages would never be entirely relieved. Therefore, three months after my arrival in Washington I presented to the Banking and Currency Committees of the House and the Senate the case for continuing these subsidies as an essential element in the stabilization program. In my presentation I estimated that the $800 million the government had paid out in subsidies thus far had saved the country close to $15 billion by eliminating the need for price increases, and I asked for additional funds to carry on the program.

Although a clear majority in both committees supported our recommendations, the opposition from the farm bloc spokesmen was unbending. Subsidies were described as a "form of bribery and blackmail perpetrated by enemies of the American way of life." Among the most vocal opponents were the cattle raisers and the meat packers.

The president of the Pork Producers Association testified that "Hog raisers are disgusted and discouraged by the way they are being regulated. Every American has the right and obligation to pay his own grub bill."

The argument against subsidies was largely based on the gnawing fear of government control which had developed during the 1930's. While the farm bloc leaders admitted that subsidies enabled the farmers to get a fair return on their labor, they were concerned that they might in some way lead to "socialism."

But our case was convincing and eventually the battle was won. Congress was impressed by what we had achieved. Subsidy payments on agricultural products were being held well within the $4.5 billion annually which we had anticipated, and by assuring stable food prices this investment had allowed us to avoid the expenditure of tens of billions of dollars for wage increases. These increases not only would have greatly added to inflationary pressures, but would also have caused a sharp rise in defense expenditures and, consequently, in our national debt.

We used a similar subsidy program to hold down the prices of copper and petroleum. Under the pressure of war it was essential to get every last ounce of production, which meant that all available sources had to be used regardless of production costs. The only alternative to subsidies in this case was to set price ceilings at a level which would cover the costs of production in the least efficient copper mines and oil wells. But the owners of the more efficient mines and wells would then make a killing at the public expense. By paying direct subsidies to cover the extra cost of these inefficient mines and wells, we avoided an across-the-board price increase.

My job was made more bearable by the knowledge that I could count fully on President Roosevelt's support under any circumstances. Although powerful political leaders continually pressed him to direct me to do this or that, on no occasion did he ever ask—or even suggest—that we change a decision on prices.

Indeed, only once did he even raise a question with me about any price regulation: this involved peaches. With his skill in simplifying complex situations, FDR had explained to his peach-raising neighbors of Warm Springs, Georgia, that price controls were required only on essential products. Peaches, he said, were a good example. Since they were not essential to the war effort, there would be no point in setting price ceilings, and the peach growers could rest easy. Unhappily, our subsequent decision to control the price of peaches in order to keep labor from moving into the peach orchards instead of into defense industries occurred when the President was enjoying a weekend rest in Georgia.

His telephone call the following morning came just as I entered my office. You have ruined me, he said. My peach-growing neighbors will hardly speak to me. Tell me, how can the price of peaches in Georgia be related to our efforts to win the war?

I explained the problem, describing the spectacle of several thousand would-be newcomers to the labor market bypassing the defense factories for the peach orchards, where, because of the absence of price ceilings, higher wages could be paid. Finally, with a sigh, he said he would do his best to explain it to his neighbors.

Donald M. Nelson, who headed the War Production Board, once told me that the only time the President had indicated the slightest concern about a WPB decision was when the WPB had been forced to postpone the completion of the St. Lawrence waterway because of the shortage of steel. On this occasion FDR had simply said, "Donald, the St. Lawrence waterway has been my favorite development project ever since my years as Governor of New York. Do you really have to suspend it now?"

When Nelson explained the priority need for steel elsewhere in our war economy, FDR said, "The decision is yours to make, and you have my full support."

The one instance during Roosevelt's lifetime in which I was overruled on a price decision occurred almost by accident. In 1943 we had established a ceiling price on synthetic rubber that the industry felt was unfair. Since synthetic rubber was a new product on which there were no established cost records and because OPA wanted to provide a genuine incentive to encourage maximum production, we reached an understanding with the industry. We agreed to set a higher price than we felt was justified, with the understanding that if experience demonstrated their costs were in fact less than they had expected, the price would later be reduced.

When the test period was completed, the figures showed the industry generally was making substantially larger profits than they or we had anticipated. Therefore we adjusted the price downward in line with our agreement. The industry, which by that time had become accustomed to bonanza profits, protested to the Office of War Mobilization and asked that I be overruled. Since James Byrnes was out of town, the issue arrived on the desk of his new deputy, Lucius Clay. The pressure was intense; one irate producer even threatened to abandon production of rubber and "sit out the war in Florida" unless he had his way. Clay, bending to the pressure, sent me a directive ordering me to put the price back to its original level.

When Byrnes returned to Washington, I sent him a vigorous protest. The Office of Price Administration, I said, was operating under clearly established legal standards and there was no way under these standards to justify this price increase. I could carry out Clay's directive only if our present pricing standards were amended.

With tongue in cheek I suggested several possibilities. We could in such cases relate our price ceilings to the blood pressure of the industry representatives, or perhaps to some medically approved pulse rate. However, it was his responsibility to decide how high the blood pressure or pulse rate must go before a price increase was indicated.

Byrnes called the next day and said, in effect, that, while fun was fun, this decision had unfortunately slipped by when he was away and please would I help him out of a delicate situation by going along. It would never, he assured me, happen again. And it never did.

Although I had direct access to Roosevelt and saw him every two or three weeks, Byrnes was my immediate boss. The heads of all war agencies such as OPA reported directly to Byrnes. These included Donald Nelson of WPB, responsible for over-all defense production; Paul V. McNutt, responsible for manpower mobilization; Marvin Jones, in charge of the War Food Administration; Harold L. Ickes, responsible for petroleum development; Frederick M. Vinson, Director of the Office of Economic Stabilization, which Byrnes had originally headed before moving into the White House; William H. Davis, Chairman of the Wage Control Board; and Elmer H. Davis of the War Information Agency.

Byrnes' War Mobilization Office in the White House operated with a small staff of no more than thirty or forty people. The Economic Stabilization staff was also small, no more than forty or fifty. It was the task of Byrnes and his staff to see that realistic goals were set and met, that the various agencies responsible for administering the various programs were working effectively, and to settle any conflicts that might develop. Byrnes had over-all responsibility for all policy on price, rent and wage controls, agriculture and industrial production, and, indirectly, for tax policy.

I had met Byrnes on my second day in Washington to discuss my new responsibilities, and in the following months I grew to know him well. As majority leader of the Senate in the 1930's he had played a key role in putting the New Deal through Congress. When Roosevelt appointed him to the Supreme Court, Byrnes had attained his highest ambition. But when Roosevelt had asked him in October, 1942, to resign from the Court to become Director of the new Office of Economic Stabilization, Byrnes without hesitation agreed to do so.

When Prentiss Brown resigned in early October, 1943, and I took over as Price Administrator, I suggested to Byrnes that I meet with him once a week for a review of the domestic economy in general and economic stabilization in particular. I was carrying vast responsibilities and I felt the need to keep him fully informed about our operation and to get his judgment on the highly complex questions with which we were dealing.

Byrnes said that he could see no need for it, but he agreed and a weekly meeting was scheduled each Wednesday afternoon at four o'clock. However, his heart was never in it; after a few minutes' discussion of current problems he would reach in his desk for a bottle of bourbon, pour a couple of drinks, add some "branch water" and launch into a story of his early political career in South Carolina.

When I attempted to switch the conversation back to the more worrisome problems on my agenda, he was usually content to express his confidence that I would reach the right decision, and then return to his favorite subject of politics. As far as my operation was concerned, the decisions I made, he said, would be unequivocally backed by him and by the President.

His letters would often follow the same tack. In his reply to my request for advice on hiring a certain individual whom I knew he could influence, he wrote in March, 1944:

DEAR CHET:

I have taken the position from the beginning that this should be solely a policymaking office. The last thing on earth that I want here would be the questions of personnel. The fact is that I have consistently avoided anything approaching it.

When you were appointed, I felt differently. . . . You were asked to take what I contend is the most difficult post in Washington. Whenever you made a request of me to help with personnel, I gladly complied. . . . You have done such a wonderful job that I confess I do not now have the same sympathy for you.

With the letter came a photograph inscribed, "To Chester Bowles who has made life much easier for James F. Byrnes."

Byrnes' only failing as an administrator was his occasional slowness in foreseeing difficulties and planning how to handle them before they hit the headlines. However, when they did come to a head, he almost always managed with awesome skill to work out a last-minute solution.

The new generation who knew him only in his later years as a segregationist and archconservative will no doubt view these comments with skepticism. But I sincerely hope that historians will take note of the integrity and competence with which he served our country in his earlier years.

CHAPTER 5

INVOLVING A NATION

ANOTHER NECESSARY PART of the reorganization of OPA was to bring our operation closer to the people it was set up to serve. Most bureaucratic organizations accumulate too many people in their central office, and ours was no exception. As a result the practical problems of price, rent and rationing controls were often lost sight of.

I can still remember the sinking sensation I felt on many occasions when as OPA Director in Connecticut I learned for the first time in my morning newspaper of new programs for which I would presumably be responsible—programs which had been conceived in Washington with little regard for or understanding of the difficulties involved in putting them into effect.

Within ninety days after my arrival in Washington we had worked out a reorganization that reduced our Washington staff from twelve thousand to slightly more than four thousand. Only relatively few of the people subject to this reduction lost their jobs; most of them were transferred directly to the regional offices, which were asked to reassign the maximum possible number to the district offices under their jurisdiction where they would be dealing directly with the people. However, we soon found that the regional offices suffered from the same zeal for building up their own staffs as had the Washington office, and a second effort was required to persuade the regional offices that we were serious in our intentions.

We underscored our determination to decentralize by announcing that from then on only nine appointments outside of Washington would be made directly by me and the national office; these were the nine regional directors themselves. The regional directors in turn would pick only their own staff members and the district directors who served in their regions. Similarly, the district directors would be responsible for recruitment of their own staffs and the appointment of ration board chairmen in their districts. Only in regard to a few particularly key posts where special circumstances were involved was it necessary for the regional offices to discuss a personnel problem with my office. We relied heavily on regular monthly visits by the regional directors to Washington and frequent trips my staff and I made around the country to keep in touch with the district as well as regional directors.

We knew that the heart of the Office of Price Administration consisted of 5,600 local war price and ration boards, and the primary objective of the decentralization program was to give them more effective support. These boards were manned by more than a quarter of a million volunteers who worked an average of thirty-two hours a week without compensation. This was by all odds the greatest grass-roots administrative effort in our history; the success or failure of the stabilization program depended in large measure on these volunteers. The area rent offices were separate from the local boards, but also operated under the jurisdiction of the national and regional offices.

A volunteer member of a local ration board was subject not only to heavy pressures but often to considerable abuse. He had to be part public servant, part diplomat and part publicist. It was his task not only to administer the OPA policies in his own hometown and neighborhood, but to explain the reason for these policies and, above all, the importance of everyone's abiding by them as part of the war effort. He had to learn how to disappoint people without making them feel they were being unfairly treated and to bring in line, by persuasion if possible, or by legal action if necessary, those who were dishonest about their rationing allotments.

Inevitably, ration board members often faced situations for which there was no answer in the rule books. For instance, on a visit to a ration board in a small town in rural Iowa, I once overheard a revealing conversation between an earnest OPA volunteer and a young farm woman who insisted that her kerosene ration was inadequate.

In the winter months, she explained, far more kerosene was needed for lighting than during the summer. To this the ration board member, of course, agreed. Moreover, during the winter months she often had to lower a kerosene lantern into the well to keep the surface of the water from freezing, and on particularly cold nights she put another kerosene lantern in the potato cellar to keep the potatoes from freezing.

When the ration board member tried to determine how often she had to lower the lamp into the well or provide the lamp for the potato cellar, the woman explained, "Some winters I have to warm the well every night. Other winters I only have to warm it twice a week. You see, it all depends on the winter."

All our offices were also deluged with letters, and we insisted that each one should be promptly and sympathetically answered. My files include one such letter in which a Connecticut lady described her problem of feeding her cats. She wrote:

> I have fourteen cats and kittens at present, one of them being a large stud. I have been feeding the stud pork kidneys, which require two ration points a pound, and now I am unable to get the points for them.
>
> I have been raising cats for three years, helping to put my son through the seminary, and I cannot kill them or do away with them. They simply do not like dry food unless it is mixed with meat. If the stud does not get some meat pretty soon, I am afraid he will become very vicious. He weighs almost 16 pounds now and if he ever leaped at me it would be terrible as I am a woman 55 years of age. Now if you could please allow me ration stamps which I could buy the kidneys with, I would appreciate it and it would certainly save me a lot of worrying.

The rationing officer rose to the occasion:

> We have carefully gone through the meat rationing regulations, but unhappily we can find no provisions for cats. However, last night I discussed your problem with my wife, who has had considerable experience with cats, and she suggests that you feed him fresh fish, which many cats prefer to meat. Some friends of mine who own many cats also tell me that their cats eagerly respond to broth made of bouillon cubes and non-meat fats. In some cases, they say, they even seem to like it better.

In order to increase public confidence in our ration board organization, we required that the membership of each board should be diversified so that all economic groups in the community were represented. This was the plan we had orginally worked out in Connecticut, and it proved equally effective elsewhere.

In addition, the ration boards were, like the regional and district offices, given increased control over personnel. Each ration board employed at least one and in larger communities a dozen or more full-time clerks who were paid by the federal government. The local ration board chairman was responsible for the recruitment, guided by standards laid down by us. The district offices were responsible only for seeing that these standards were met.

To improve the morale and effectiveness of the Washington office, we insisted on high standards of performance and strict adherence to principles of equality in recruiting personnel. For example, 14 percent of our Washington staff were blacks at a time when the average throughout the rest of the government was no more than one percent. Several blacks filled key positions, which at that time was practically unheard of. In large measure this record was due to the efforts of Miss Frances Williams, a remarkable black woman from St. Louis, whom I asked to assume responsibility for interpreting our organization to minority groups and who served as my special assistant.

Our personnel standards required all our offices totally to disregard racial or religious questions in hiring new people. On several occasions when district directors persistently ignored the regulation, I decided that they should be replaced. But before any action could be taken Frances would ask me for authorization first to visit the district and attempt to persuade the director to consider the situation from a fresh perspective; and on each occasion she succeeded. Later after the OPA organization had been disbanded I received letters from several former directors saying that through Frances Williams' patient efforts their minds had been opened to new dimensions of democracy and that this would always be a memorable part of their OPA experience.

In order to keep our staff informed of our problems, the steps that we were taking to meet them, and to encourage their participation, I held monthly meetings with the entire Washington staff. Because this involved some four thousand people, these meetings were held in the cafeteria of the old Census Building, and I had to stand on a table to be seen and heard. Over the months, OPA morale improved to a point where it was generally agreed to be the highest of any wartime agency.

Our administrative office under Jim Rogers kept close watch over our operations so that we could not be charged with waste while asking sacrifice of others. I remember one incident involving typewriters, which were in short supply during the war. At night, at Jim Rogers' direction, teams from the administrative department visited every office, loaded every seventh typewriter on a cart and rolled it away. They then waited to see who would complain the following morning. In nearly half of the cases the typewriters apparently were never missed.

The same technique was then applied to filing cabinets, also in short supply. Here the procedure was to remove a filing cabinet unless at least one individual working within two hundred feet of it knew what was in it. If no one knew, it would be rolled away until somebody complained, and frequently no one did.

To build an administrative structure which would improve our relations with business and to bring our regulations closer to existing business procedures, we also set out to strengthen the system of industry advisory committees. OPA was required by law to set up such committees for every industry which requested one. However, by executive order we went much further. This order, which I signed a few months after arriving in Washington, directed that no significant change could be made in any price, rent or rationing regulation until it had been discussed with an advisory committee representing that industry.

We soon had more than one thousand advisory committees, each of which reflected as nearly as possible a cross section of the industry or business it represented. These industry advisory committees were by no means window dressing. Although they could not change a price ceiling which was established according to our legal standards, they helped save us from administrative blunders, assure more realistic procedures and provide more easily enforced regulations.

At first most members of these advisory committees came to Washington focused on their own problems and determined to raise the roof if they did not have their own way. But we turned most of these critics into cooperative partners by placing the question the committee had been invited to discuss in the general framework of the war effort as a whole.

Before starting to discuss the regulation in question, a military expert would review the progress of the war in North Africa or the Pacific. He would be followed by a representative of the Treasury Department who would describe the awesome inflationary pressures we were striving to control. He in turn would be followed by a representative of the War Labor Board who would describe the pressures for higher wages and why the price line must be held if wages were to be kept in check.

It was only after such a briefing on the relation of economic stabilization to the war effort that discussion about the specific regulation on the agenda was begun. As a result pricing procedures which had seemed frustrating back home became more acceptable. These meetings, three or four thousand of which were held every year, with few exceptions went smoothly and helped greatly to improve our relations with industry.

To underline the importance of this effort, I created the Office of Advisory Committees, directly attached to my own office. The director, Mrs. Ethel Gilbert, had an incredible capacity to soothe the most irate entrepreneurs, often turning them into ardent supporters of the stabilization program.

It would be a mistake to look back on the relationship between OPA and business as a battle between the "good guys" and the "bad guys." Although many businessmen strongly opposed price controls and fought them by all means, fair and foul, the fact remains that most businessmen, who might be termed the "vast silent majority," realized their importance and did all they could to make them work.

The Committee for Economic Development, headed by Paul G. Hoffman, president of Studebaker, and entirely financed and organized by businessmen, was one of the most constructive and powerful forces during the war period. So was the National Chamber of Commerce under the leadership of Eric Johnston.

The CED put out a series of carefully developed memoranda which objectively and thoughtfully presented the economic problems we were facing. Although the CED studies did not always agree with those of OPA, they were without exception responsible documents which had a wide and healthy effect.

Our relations with labor were also of critical importance. Because it was known that I had insisted industrial or other workers should be assigned to every ration board in Connecticut, most labor leaders looked on my appointment favorably. I also had several personal friends in the labor movement, such as Donald E. Montgomery of the United Automobile Workers, who helped me get off to a good start.

At that time, Robert R. R. Brooks, a distinguished young labor economist, who had taught first at Yale University and later at Williams College, was in charge of OPA's labor relationships. Thanks to Bob's efforts, a national labor advisory committee had already been set up and, now with my support, he proceeded to strengthen it. Normally one meeting took place each week (or at the very least once every other week), and usually I was present.

On several occasions, my patience wore thin. Several militant members of the committee seemed to assume that the best way to strengthen the price and rent control program was to hit me and my OPA associates on one side of the head to compensate for business' hitting us on the other side. Since the U.S.S.R. was our wartime ally, several Communist union leaders were accepted as members of the committee, and they were particularly aggressive.

Under Bob Brooks' leadership we patiently explained our problems and worked to win their confidence. One of our first steps was to set up labor advisory committees in all district and regional offices to meet regularly with the regional and district directors.

In September, 1943, after I had been in Washington only two months, I was able to say to the national convention of the American Federation of Labor that "more than 700 representatives of organized labor are now serving as members of our 94 district OPA advisory committees in every state of the Union and there are more than 4,000 members serving as members of local war price and rationing boards."

Several thousand more were working on plant transportation committees, as part of the tire-rationing program, while many wives of workers were employed by the price and ration boards.

Although we managed generally to hold the support of labor during the most difficult war years, I felt that we deserved more backing than we received, particularly in the difficult transitional period following the war.

To win the confidence of farmers was a more difficult task. From the time I arrived in Washington until March of 1944, the farm bloc strongly opposed the use of subsidies as a device to hold down food prices. I met this challenge head on and succeeded in winning Congressional approval. Once this issue was settled, the farm bloc support for the inflation control program began to grow surprisingly, and I was able to maintain close ties with the farm leaders for the next three years. Much of the credit belongs to a small but highly competent staff responsible directly to me which I established to maintain constant contact between OPA and the farm organizations throughout the country.

We also set up a national farmer's advisory committee along the lines of the labor advisory committee with whom I met at least once a month. Although I tried to persuade the Department of Agriculture to participate in this undertaking, many of their key people were concerned about their own postwar relationship with farmers and unwilling to become involved in any operation that might become controversial.

A total of some seventy-two OPA farmer advisory committees were set up in the district offices, where they met regularly with the directors. These farmer committees, like the labor and business committees, provided a setting in which the more militant members could blow off steam, and at the same time enabled those present to learn something about our complex problems. Attached to each district office, in addition, were special committees with which we consulted in setting prices on all fruits and vegetables, which we required to be posted in each retail store. Since these products were perishables that came into the market on an uneven schedule, the price changes often had to be made every week, with the committees meeting each Friday afternoon with price officials in the district offices to set the prices for the following week.

Although most of the farm lobby spokesmen in Congress persisted in their knee-jerk reaction to the Office of Price Administration, the farm organizations themselves gradually grew not only to accept OPA but to support it. Dramatic proof of this transformation came in May, 1945, when Senator Kenneth S. Wherry introduced an amendment which was designed to win the approval of the farmers by upsetting the whole wage-price balance.

In preparing the case against this amendment I called on the president of each of the major farm organizations and asked him to provide me with a statement that I could read over a national radio hookup voicing his personal opposition to the Wherry amendment—and to my amazement they all agreed to do so. These strongly worded statements from the farm bloc leaders themselves left their self-styled representatives in Congress, particularly Senator Wherry, badly shaken.

The relatively favorable relationship we were able to create with the farm organizations can, I think, be rather simply explained: gradually the farmers came to understand that the prices of the things they bought were being held down while they were assured generous prices and a guaranteed market for all they could produce.

With the memory of first the boom and then the collapse of farm prices of the World War I period in their minds, as the end of the war came closer, this relationship became even stronger. In 1945 I was even given a special gold medal by the Farmer's Union for my "contribution to American agriculture during the war," and a few months later, to my dismay, the Ohio State Grange went so far as to pass a resolution urging that price controls be continued for five years after the hostilities had ended. As a guest speaker at their convention I decided that the discreet thing to do was first to thank them warmly for their support but then to oppose the resolution itself to avoid being once again charged by Ohio's own Senator Taft with seeking to remain OPA Administrator for life.

Even the conservative Edward A. O'Neal, the so-called "Grand Field Marshall of the farm bloc," became one of my warm friends, and, to the surprise of our opponents in Congress, he supported us on many key questions.

While the support of business, labor and farm organizations was important, we knew that the final word lay with the consumers, and we set out vigorously to secure and maintain their understanding and support. Our objective was to involve the American people in this domestic war program to the limit of our capacity, to make them feel part of the effort, and to share with us responsibility for the results. Barring some occasional conflicts, I think it is fair to say we succeeded.

Consumer advisory committees were established in all OPA district offices, and since many members of organized labor had begun to develop a "consumer viewpoint," most of these committees had strong support from local labor leaders. Their major function was to develop close relationships with local, state and national organizations and to provide them with a flow of information about price and rationing control.

Within a year or less we managed to put together literally a maze of well-informed grass-roots committees in which close to fifty thousand individuals representing agriculture, labor, consumers and businessmen participated—in addition to the volunteer ration boards—and they played a key role in gaining and maintaining public acceptance.

Our Consumer Information Service received massive support from radio stations, advertising concerns, insurance companies and the like. As in Connecticut, I also used radio regularly as a means of talking directly to the people. Once a week I spoke over a nationwide network of nearly four hundred stations, explaining to housewives and their husbands the dangers of inflation and how we were trying to meet these dangers. I explained and then explained again why OPA's programs were needed and how they could best be made to work. Following is an excerpt from one broadcast:

> Difficulties of production, shortages of labor and transportation, the huge food demands of our armed forces and the increased wartime demands of civilians—all these factors will make it necessary for us to watch rationing carefully, to keep food prices under control.
>
> I want to assure all of you that we at OPA to the best of our ability will carry out our two difficult wartime responsibilities. First, our job of rationing scarce supplies so that everyone gets an equal share of the food actually available. And, second, our job of continuing to keep food prices down. You people have entrusted those jobs to us—to protect you and your families from scarcities and from a skyrocketing cost of living. I know you will continue to give us now, as you have in the past, your full understanding and support.

These broadcasts were part of a frank effort to strengthen our position with Congress by gaining the support of the public. In them I pulled no punches, as indicated by the following excerpts from a broadcast shortly before the Congress was to act on the renewal of the Price Control Act:

> The big argument that is shaping up here in Washington these days is one that concerns you—and every member of your family—an argument which concerns your special G.I. Joe or WAVE or WAC and every other man or woman in our Army, Air Force, Navy, Coast Guard and Marines.
>
> The outcome of this debate may have a decisive effect on your chances of a postwar job, the size of your paycheck, whether your business will prosper or go bankrupt, whether your farm will flourish or go on the auction block. This argument will be settled in the next thirty days.
>
> On one side is a group that says that some prices and rents should

go up now. No great harm will be done, they say, if some rents go higher, if some prices go up on food and clothing; it won't make too much difference if that new auto or your new radio or the house you have been dreaming of in these difficult wartime years costs you a little more.

That's the way one group is talking. Now let's hear from the other side. This group says, "Prices and rents must be held where they are now. We must keep on holding the price line firmly on food, rent, clothing and other necessities. It's our only hope now and in the period of peace that lies ahead; it's the only way we can avoid the inflationary boom and the crash which brought disaster to millions upon millions of people everywhere following the last war."

You will know the decision very shortly. The law under which wartime prices and rents are controlled by OPA runs out next month on June 30.

Before that time, after hearing all the pros and cons, Congress will vote on the Price Control Bill. They will either continue our power to keep prices and rents from rising (as one side is urging them to do) or they will modify our power to control inflation (as the other side is demanding so loudly). . . . In large measure the vote will be decided by what you do or say.

I will keep you posted on how this battle is going and on its outcome; after all it is your battle—you win or lose. Next week I shall describe some particularly damaging amendments which are being proposed. Until then good-bye to you all.

Although it may be reasonably charged that some of these weekly broadcasts oversimplified a complex subject (one reporter called them my "entre nous or off-the-record revelations of common knowledge"), they developed a large audience and consequently they were resented by our opposition.

I was accused—quite accurately—of lobbying in behalf of a program which was then being debated in Congress and of which I was administrator. When questions were raised before Congressional committees, I frankly admitted the charge. Many lobbies, I said, were spending millions of dollars in an attempt to destroy price and rent controls and to make a fortune out of the war. Someone had to speak up for the consumer, and as long as I was Administrator of the OPA I would continue to do so.

For example, during one of my regular appearances before the Senate Banking and Currency Committee, Senator Taft attacked my "OPA propaganda," charging, "You are propagandizing for the continuation of your agency at government expense."

I agreed with Taft as I had with others that our mailings, advertisements, and radio programs were designed to win public support, but, I said, "If this, as you say, is propaganda, it is propaganda against inflation, and I know of no one who is in favor of inflation, including you, Senator." I added that "If you are accusing me of trying to make this essential wartime program more democratic and more responsive to people, then I plead guilty."

At one point Congress threatened to cut our information budget. I testified that if they deprived us of the means of explaining our program to the people, our requirements for investigators and inspectors to enforce our regulations would be greatly increased. With a $5 million annual budget for information, I said I could keep the American people reasonably informed about our regulations and their own obligations and rights as citizens. But if Congress cut this $5 million, I would have no alternative but to make a public request for $15 million to hire law enforcement inspectors to prosecute the many people who, often through their own ignorance and lack of information, had acted illegally. If Congress preferred this, it was their prerogative. I myself preferred persuasion to police-state tactics.

In August, 1943, we launched the "Home Front Pledge" campaign. All over the country, citizens were urged to sign the pledge:

I will pay no more than legal prices.
I accept no rationed goods without giving up ration stamps.

The twenty million consumers who signed were given a sticker portraying the American housewife with her right hand raised in oath. After a year or so of our intensive cultivation of public understanding and support, a cartoon appeared of me attempting to hypnotize Joe Citizen by saying, "THERE IS NO CIGARETTE SHORTAGE! You just think there is because there are no cigarettes."

The success of our public information policy was reflected in the surprisingly strong public support for the Office of Price Administration, which lasted until the spring of 1946. For about three years public opinion polls showed 60 percent or so strongly in favor of our program, another 30 percent who felt we were doing a "fairly good job," and well under 10 percent who were opposed.

This public support had an interesting effect on my career. When I agreed to become General Manager and then Administrator of the Office of Price Administration in the summer of 1943, I had told President Roosevelt that I was anxious to run for the United States Senate from Connecticut in 1944, and that this was one reason I had hesitated to accept this appointment. He replied that if, as he anticipated, I could put OPA into reasonably good shape by June, 1944, he would not only allow me to withdraw but would speak strongly in my behalf for the Senate.

But when June, 1944, rolled around and I reminded the President of my plan to run for the Senate, he told me that he now had no alternative except to ask me to stick to what I was doing, adding with a smile that as he was my "Commander in Chief" in wartime he knew I would agree.

He doubted whether the Republican nominee for President would attack the war effort itself, since this would be bound to react against him. Therefore the major attacks would be launched against the domestic programs, which would be considered fair political game.

The Office of Price Administration, the President said, was much the most important agency dealing with domestic affairs, and, since its work touched every family in the country, he assumed that a major political attack would be made on the administration of price control, rationing and rent control. Consequently, the most important contribution I could make to the war effort and to him personally was to stay precisely where I was, to keep the OPA out of politics and to make it as invulnerable as possible to attack from his political opponents.

Although I was disappointed, I accepted the President's judgment. A few days later I sent a memorandum to every member of the OPA organization saying that anyone who wanted to go actively into politics on either side should do so, but that those who did should first resign from the Office of Price Administration. If we were to maintain public support, we must keep the OPA not only nonpolitical in fact but also free of any basis for suspicion in this regard.

Within a week, two violations of this rule came to my attention. One was a labor leader on a Boston ration board who made a stirring speech in behalf of Roosevelt; the other was a businessman, chairman of the ration board in Holyoke, Massachusetts, and an old friend of my father, who attacked Roosevelt and the New Deal. I seized upon the occasion to ask for the resignations of both individuals, thereby dramatizing my determination both to carry out the rule and to avoid favoring one side or the other.

One example of an attempt to play politics with OPA's relationship with the public, which occurred shortly after I came to Washington, involved that professional political warrior, Fiorello La Guardia, Mayor of New York. Although I had met La Guardia casually only once or twice, I had great admiration for him as a man of integrity and liberal convictions. When my secretary told me that he was calling me on the telephone, I was delighted to talk with him.

I was somewhat less pleased as he began to establish his point. He pointed out that as Mayor of New York it was essential that he maintain the support of the people. Right now many New Yorkers were concerned about the shortage of meat, and therefore he was planning to deliver a blast at the rationing and price control system. It would appear in the papers the following day, and he hoped I would not take it personally.

The next morning the New York newspapers carried a front-page story of a press conference by La Guardia in which he accused me of depriving New York of its proper share of food and gasoline and other scarce commodities, and demanded that I adopt regulations to see that New Yorkers got their proper share.

I telephoned La Guardia to say that I had just read the news story and, although I had very little experience in politics, could clearly understand the need for a statement of that kind. But he also must understand how important it was for me to reject such pressures and to denounce those who brought them against me. I hoped he would not be distressed over the stories that would appear in tomorrow's papers of my own reactions.

I then prepared a statement charging La Guardia with playing politics with price control and rationing and trying to improve his political position in New York at the expense of the rest of the country.

Shortly after that I met La Guardia in New York and discovered that instead of making an enemy I had made a fast friend. For the next three years La Guardia was generally one of our strongest supporters, and I saw him frequently in New York and Washington.

However, shortly after V-J Day, in the fall of 1945 when many businessmen were attacking OPA on the specious ground that we were holding up production, we went through a somewhat similar exchange. On this occasion, La Guardia attacked OPA before a Congressional committee. Although he was careful not to suggest that prices should go up, he charged us with standing in the way of expanding output. At the end of his testimony La Guardia announced that he planned to call upon me and demand a change in our policies.

A few days later La Guardia requested an appointment. When I went out to greet him, he was walking down the corridor followed by at least fifty press people with paper and pens at the ready. I asked Fiorello to come into my office, closed the door, sat down on the sofa and launched into an attack.

"With your lifelong concern for the consumer and the little man," I said, "I am startled to see that you advocate that we allow the National Association of Manufacturers and other such groups to blackmail OPA into raising prices which do not need to be raised and which are ample to provide substantial profits."

I went on to say that I assumed by the large number of press people outside that he intended to make a statement after he left my office. I told him that I would like to turn it into a joint press conference in which I would express my amazement that such a popular liberal as he would support the most conservative elements in the business community in a demand that they be allowed to make a killing at the expense of the people.

As an alternative I suggested that since neither one of us could win such an argument we let the matter drop; the decision was up to him.

Upon leaving my office he shook my hand warmly and made only a brief statement to the effect that he was convinced I was doing my best to hold down prices and at the same time encourage full production. The OPA, he said, had done an admirable job during the war and that no one had supported it more consistently than he.

Thomas E. Dewey, in his vigorous campaign for the Presidency in 1944, never, as far as I know, mentioned the Office of Price Administration. I was told later that Dewey, who had planned to make OPA a major target for his attack, as Roosevelt had anticipated, had become convinced by a series of public opinion polls that such an attack would boomerang.

CHAPTER 6

WHO GETS WHAT—AND HOW MUCH?

As I IMPLIED IN THE PREVIOUS CHAPTER, there were two essentially opposite ways to secure compliance with price, rent and rationing regulations. The first was to convict wrongdoers by a major increase in the OPA enforcement program, with stiffer legal penalties for violations. The second was to prevent violations by a greater emphasis on public education and cooperation and thereby allow the enforcement program largely to concentrate on prosecuting the willful violators.

Our efforts to convince the people that price and rent controls and rationing regulations were essential to the war effort, and that each individual had a major personal stake in making them work, gave me confidence that we could get by with a relatively modest enforcement program.

Since OPA's creation in early 1942 it had had its own investigation staff as part of the Legal Division. The Emergency Price Control Act of 1942 gave the President the power to bring criminal and civil proceedings against violators. The Justice Department was charged with instituting criminal proceedings, based on facts provided by OPA's investigators, while OPA itself handled civil sanctions, armed with such weapons as the injunction, "treble damage" action, and suspension of licenses.

As part of my organizational changes involving the function of the lawyers in September, 1943, I set up the OPA enforcement program as a separate department under the direction of Thomas I. Emerson, who later became a professor at Yale Law School. Nationwide, his staff consisted of some 3,000 investigators and 850 attorneys. This may sound like an excessive number of investigators, but it was spread extremely thin since literally millions of manufacturers, wholesalers, retailers and landlords were subject to OPA regulations.

The criminal sanction was never a consistent or effective deterrent. The power to institute criminal proceedings was vested in the United States Attorneys in each state. Although the Criminal Division of the Justice Department in Washington could act directly, it rarely did, and the Attorney General was reluctant to force the United States Attorneys in each state to act. Many of them failed to prosecute OPA cases, in part because of the enormous workload which they were already carrying. But, in addition, there was a certain reluctance to become involved in the complex problems of OPA enforcement.

Consequently, we came largely to depend on civil enforcement powers granted us by the Price Control Act, over which OPA had direct control. OPA had the power to license anyone who produced or sold a product under price control. Since the threat of license revocation was a constant unspoken deterrent to petty violators, who knew that OPA had the legal power to put them out of business, we rarely used this sanction or even threatened to use it.

Another OPA enforcement procedure was the treble damage suit. In the event of an overcharge, any aggrieved consumer, upon substantial proof, could bring suit against a retailer for either $50 or a sum equal to three times the amount of the overcharge, whichever was higher. Although this ingenious device was effective, we were fearful that treble damage suits, if used on any large scale, might set the purchasers against the merchants and create a divisive force in the community. Most retail violations were careless, not willful, and by and large the public had the good sense not to sue merchants for $50 damages over such grievances as a five-cent inadvertent overcharge on a can of peas.

The treble damages section of the Act also enabled OPA to initiate such a suit in the name of the OPA Administrator against alleged violators at the wholesale and manufacturing levels, where the most important overcharges occurred. This we used much more freely. On one occasion, for example, we filed a treble damage suit for $9 million against forty lumber operators. On another, we settled a treble damage claim for overcharges on sales of woolen cloth for more than $2 million.

Existing criminal statutes proved effective in the enforcement of our rationing program. False claims of inventory, for example, were punishable by up to $10,000 in fines and/or ten years' imprisonment. In addition, the Emergency Act gave OPA the power to punish anyone who falsified his records. Another criminal statute prohibiting the theft of government property put many black marketeers out of business permanently, as did heavy penalties imposed for counterfeiting or conspiracy.

In August, 1944, the OPA Administrator was given the right to sue if an aggrieved consumer or tenant did not do so within thirty days. This was especially useful in rent cases where the tenant preferred to pay excess rent without a fuss rather than risk eviction or other reprisal.

We learned that the most effective approach to enforcement was through nationwide enforcement drives in special areas where we knew compliance was particularly lax. This required close coordination between those responsible for setting price and rationing regulations on the one hand and the enforcement staffs of our regional and district offices on the other.

For example, an enforcement drive on sugar rationing was broken down into two main areas: first, control of the prices charged by the producers, and second, control of the prices charged by wholesalers and retailers. In order to insure the effective rationing of the limited supply, we had to know exactly the size of the sugar stocks held by each of the three groups.

In this particular case we discovered that 83 percent of the institutional sugar users (soft drink manufacturers, bakeries, candy manufacturers and the like) had either deliberately or through carelessness misstated their sugar inventories, despite the fact that most fraudulent misrepresentation was a criminal offense. However, our workload was so heavy that in this instance we decided to let a majority of the violators off with warnings; only the worst offenders were prosecuted in the courts. As a result of this drive, however, most of the leakage of sugar into the black markets was eliminated.

The magnitude of our enforcement operation, even with an effective public information program, is indicated by the fact that in 1944 various sanctions were applied to 338,000 violators. The great majority of these were handled without actual prosecution since they involved only minor infractions. However, approximately fifty thousand were subject to license warnings or revocations, monetary settlement, or other administrative action; and another fifty thousand were settled by suits for treble damages, court injunctions or criminal prosecution. In all, some $21 million were collected in fines that one year.

Of all our enforcement programs the rationing of gasoline, beginning in December, 1942, presented by far the greatest challenge. The gasoline shortage was a major problem throughout the country, and particularly in the East, which suffered from a number of geographic disadvantages.

Most of the coastal vessels normally used for shipping gasoline and petroleum products to the East Coast from the Southwest were now being used by the armed services, and many oil tankers that continued in this service were sunk by submarines. Since the pipe lines were still under construction, gasoline and fuel oil had to be shipped east by rail. To add to the difficulties, most of the oil for the petroleum products for the military in Europe and Africa had to be shipped from the East Coast.

We repeatedly reminded the public by radio that the war was run on petroleum. "As the number of our soldiers and sailors increases," we announced, "and we step up the tempo of our air raids and our land fighting, the demands on our oil and gasoline supply become constantly greater."

Our problems with gasoline and oil rationing were compounded by the division of responsibility among the government agencies. Most of them were willing and even eager to let OPA absorb the inevitable complaints. For instance, Harold Ickes, Secretary of the Interior and the Petroleum Administrator for War, often created difficulties for OPA by announcing unduly optimistic estimates of the amounts available for civilian consumption. On August 13, 1943, three weeks after I arrived in Washington, Ickes announced, "The transportation [of gasoline supplies] difficulty, after months of struggle, has now been overcome." This gross misstatement of fact led millions of people to apply for gasoline which did not exist. On such occasions it was my unpleasant task to force the public to face up to the realities.

To clarify OPA's actual role, I pointed out in a speech in December, 1943:

> The Office of Price Administration is not responsible for our gasoline supply. That responsibility rests with the Petroleum Administrator for War. . . . After meeting the military requirements in full, he divides the remaining supply on the basis of requests made by the claimant agencies.
>
> The War Food Administration claims a certain percentage of the gasoline supply for use in farm vehicles. The Office of Defense Transportation estimates the total amount of gasoline required to maintain all forms of domestic transportation . . . what portion of this total amount shall go for the operation of railroads, waterways, buses, trucks and passenger cars. This month the amount which they allocated for passenger cars is only 33 percent of the total supply. This is all that OPA has to ration to you car owners.

In addition to the administrative problems, gasoline rationing presented a dangerously ripe field for black market operations. Individual motorists were supplied with "A," "B" or "C" ration tickets. An "A" card was given to those car owners who had no special war-related reason for a larger ration. The "A" card allotment allowed only very limited driving, to the store, to visit a nearby friend or a relative and the like.

The "B" card was given to those persons who had to travel to and from regular jobs in which regular use of public transportation or car pool arrangements were impractical. The "C" card was given to car owners whose activities involved essential travel, such as doctors and defense workers.

The system worked as follows: A motorist would go to a gas station and request, let us say, ten gallons of gasoline. In addition to paying the dealer the controlled price for the gas, he would also give him ration coupons for the ten gallons. The station owner would then paste these coupons on a card which he was given for the purpose. When he wished to replenish his own gasoline supply, he would pass the card with the coupons on to his wholesaler, who then authorized the replacement of the appropriate number of gallons in the dealer's tanks.

The wholesaler in turn could replenish his own supply only by presenting the requisite number of ration coupons, which he had collected from his customers, to his wholesale supplier. Thus the ration ticket stream flowed from the motorist to the dealer to the distributor to the supplier.

A black market in gasoline was created by the injection of counterfeit or stolen ration tickets into the normal flow. The procedure was as follows: A black market operator would offer his illegally acquired ration tickets to various gasoline dealers. The gasoline dealers who purchased these black market coupons were then in a position to offer their customers a choice: gasoline at an inflated price without ration tickets or gasoline at the regular ceiling price with the payment of ration tickets. As a result many motorists were able to buy gasoline far in excess of their ration. When the time came to refill his tanks, the black market dealer would simply paste his illegally acquired tickets (either counterfeit or stolen) on his card in place of the regular tickets which he had failed to collect.

Some of the black market ration coupons were procured by professional criminals breaking into storage vaults. One enterprising black market gang managed to bore through eighteen inches of solid concrete to reach a large store of ration coupons in a vault in Grand Rapids, Michigan. But it was the counterfeiters, most important among them the so-called "Purple Gang" in Detroit, who, in the spring and summer of 1944, very nearly broke the entire system.

The penalties were stiff for counterfeiting ration coupons or for illegally transferring them—a $1,000 fine and up to ten years' imprisonment. As he sentenced a gasoline black marketeer to six years in prison, one West Coast judge denounced ration ticket counterfeiting as "akin to treason." Nevertheless, the rewards were so great that for some months the black market increased alarmingly.

Finally, with the help of counterfeiting experts in the Treasury Department we found a way to break the system. The first step was to require all gasoline ration coupons which gasoline stations turned over to the wholesalers to be processed through a central office. There each card with its coupons was passed under an infrared light which immediately distinguished any counterfeits.

An OPA investigator would then call on the gasoline dealer whose cards contained the counterfeits and show him the result of the test. If it was a matter of only two or three counterfeits, they would usually be disregarded on the assumption that the dealer might have accepted them in good faith from a customer who had himself bought them from a counterfeiter. But if the number was significant, the dealer's next gas allotment would be reduced by the amount of the counterfeits he had turned in. Eventually, of course, this could put him out of business.

The final step was to trace the counterfeit coupons back to their source. We could generally count on a number of retailers to reveal where they had purchased the counterfeit coupons. The chain of sales was then traced back to the black market salesman and finally to the actual counterfeiters, many of whom received long prison terms.

With the exception of the "pleasure driving ban" fiasco in early 1943, the gasoline rationing program worked phenomenally well. In 1942, 1943 and 1944 the use of gasoline and fuel oil was cut by about 50 percent in the face of the vastly increased need for motor transport. Hundreds of thousands of defense workers, for instance, who had given up their prewar jobs in towns and rural areas, were driving forty, fifty and even sixty miles, six days a week, to urban defense plants.

The program worked for two reasons. First, we went to great lengths to explain it constantly to the public, and second, everyone recognized that the decision in regard to his ration was made not by some bureaucrat in Washington but by members of his own community who served on the local volunteer ration board.

Although rationing programs were by and large highly successful, it was inevitable that in an operation of this magnitude there would be mistakes and blunders. The most memorable of these occurred in December, 1944, when we tried to solve the problem created by an excess accumulation of outstanding food ration coupons.

This excess was created by householders who did not need all the coupons they had been allotted and passed them on to people they knew who wanted more. A country cousin or a friend with a large "victory garden" who raised and canned her own fruits and vegetables would send her unused coupons to relatives or friends in the cities. Moreover, on the assumption that many ration book holders, particularly those living in rural areas, would not use all their food ration stamps, it was our practice to issue somewhat more food ration stamps than could actually be matched by the available commodities.

On several occasions, to prevent a rush to cash in food ration stamps in the retail stores at either the beginning or end of a ration period, we had assured the public that ration coupons could be held indefinitely and used whenever the holder wished to do so.

However, in the fall of 1944 it gradually became apparent that a much larger number of unused ration stamps had accumulated than we anticipated, and many of these "excess" stamps were understandably —but quite illegally—finding their way into the market, thereby threatening to upset the always fragile balance between outstanding ration stamps and the available supplies.

As the unexpected redemption of excess coupons began to cause increasing scarcities of rationed products such as sugar and canned goods, the problem became acute. If consumers once began to realize that the number of food ration stamps available was significantly greater than the supplies, a run which we could not cope with would almost certainly start in the retail stores.

As a consequence, I had an extraordinarily difficult set of choices. Should I go back on the government's assurance that it would not repudiate outstanding ration coupons? Or should I stand by the government's word and run the risk of a collapse of the food rationing system?

My top associates and I considered and reconsidered these questions. I also privately consulted with Fred Vinson and James Byrnes. Since either action would put the food rationing program in jeopardy, it was a choice between which was worse.

Finally, we decided reluctantly to invalidate the stamps. But how best to inform the public? Clearly, the new program had to go into effect simultaneously in every part of the nation; a public announcement from Washington without a well-worked-out administrative plan could have created the very run we were trying to avoid. There was also a legal problem. By law, the local boards must receive written orders from Washington if the change was to be valid in their areas.

This meant that we could not rely on a radio announcement or general press announcement to implement the policy nationally. Rather, the new regulation had to be drafted, typed, approved, carried to the

Federal Register and published before it would have any legal status. And somehow, throughout this entire operation, absolute secrecy would have to be maintained.

With impressive, if inexperienced, cloak-and-dagger techniques, we proceeded with a great bureaucratic type-in. Clustered in a sealed-off corridor, the top dozen OPA officials groped for the least objectionable euphemism for what was being done. It was a rare thing, at least in those days, for the government to repudiate a promise to the American public, and we were not eager to set a precedent.

Hunched before typewriters and mimeograph machines, this small group of officials cautiously stabbed out and duplicated the final drafts of the messages. Meanwhile, hair-splitting timetables were being devised to govern the mailings. Based upon thousands of airline, train and trucking schedules, these tables were designed to assure us of the simultaneous arrival of the materials at every locality in the country.

As we completed stuffing, addressing and stamping the sea of envelopes all around us, the tension steadily grew and did not subside until the exit of the last bundle, headed, I assume, for the office building next door.

The press release was of particular importance. As on previous occasions, we decided that the best explanation was the truth. In familiar, homely terms we described the situation that had developed and our difficult choices. In conclusion I asked for public support in a painful situation.

We then sat back to wait the reaction. It turned out to be as powerful as we had feared. One distressed OPA rationing official under heavy attack from an angry public told me, "When my grandchildren ever ask me what I did during the Great War, I'm going to tell them it was too horrible to talk about."

In those areas where the material was delivered on schedule our attempt to cushion the impact proved remarkably successful. For instance, everybody *east* of the Mississippi—every OPA office and every newspaper editor—received the order and press release together, at almost exactly the same time. But, by some perverse happenstance, the order reached all points *west* of the Mississippi before the explanation was made available to editors and radio commentators.

Almost without exception, the informed editors east of the Mississippi recognized our dilemma and supported our decision. The Washington *Post,* for example, ran an editorial in which it said: "The tightening and expansion of the rationing program, together with the invalidation of a large number of unused pre-December ration stamps, will, we believe, be welcomed by people who take the trouble to find out the reasons of the announced changes."

Western editors, who failed to receive the explanation in time, generally denounced the government for breaking faith with the public. A San Francisco *Chronicle* editorial entitled "Confounding Housewives" said: "OPA gives the housewife a handful of points supposed to be good indefinitely. This encourages hoarding of points, perfectly legitimate hoarding. With some special occasion in mind . . . the housewife skimps to save up her red points for a roast. At that moment OPA cancels her points and the guests at the 'special occasion' feast on creamed codfish."

Although it took weeks in the Western states for the explanation to catch up with the event, gradually the situation eased. Nevertheless, this incident will always be remembered by those of us who participated in it as our most painful hour.

As I thought back on the subject, what particularly distressed me was the fact that there had been actually a third alternative which for some reason never occurred to us. Instead of canceling the stamps altogether, we could have frankly explained the problem and then suspended the validity of these unused stamps for a specific period, after which they would have again become valid. In this way, we could have worked them gradually back into the ration currency stream without risking the "run" we so greatly feared.

As the war went on, I became increasingly concerned with the possibilities of shady dealings within OPA itself. Our staff had been hastily recruited, and because of the demands of the armed services our personnel turnover, except at the very top levels, was rapid. Moreover, our staff was badly overworked and subject to constant pressures for quick decisions. Finally, the opportunities for malpractice were readily available. By deliberately misplacing a digit in a single price control order, for example, a member of our OPA staff could put several million dollars into someone's pocket.

I finally decided to outline my fears to President Roosevelt. I pointed out that decisions from our various bureaus involving tens of millions of dollars came across my desk daily, figures which I had to accept on faith as honestly arrived at. With all the pressures of wartime decision-making, corruption was a danger in every government agency; but OPA, I thought, was by far the most vulnerable.

Sooner or later, I said, the political opposition would take over, and we must assume that they would search every nook and cranny of the war effort for evidence of malpractices and corruption which could be used to castigate the present Administration. This, I said, could have a devastating impact on the record of his Presidency. Roosevelt agreed and asked me to bring him a plan that might lessen this danger.

My first thought was of the Federal Bureau of Investigation. Even if it did not like to investigate price violations by presumably respectable business firms, it would, I thought, agree to help police the internal operations of the largest and most vulnerable of the wartime agencies. To my surprise and chagrin, the Attorney General said that all they could do was to investigate specific cases which I might bring to their attention.

The solution to the problem was finally provided by Mayor Fiorello La Guardia. He had a passion for honesty in public affairs, and when I described my worries and asked for his advice, he was immediately responsive.

La Guardia told me that his success in keeping the administration of New York City clean was largely due to an independent investigatory group he had set up under a Commissioner of Investigations who reported directly to the Mayor himself. When any hint of corruption occurred, this team of investigators would be called upon to dig out the facts. Since everyone in the city government knew that this group was on the lookout for corruption and that it was responsible only to the city executive, the operation was remarkably effective.

To adapt this plan to OPA I asked the President for twenty-five operatives from the Secret Service branch of the Treasury Department, which was probably as well equipped as the FBI to handle such an assignment. The President agreed, and the Secretary of the Treasury, Henry Morgenthau, assigned to my office a picked detachment of experienced investigators.

I then wrote a letter to every ration board member and to each OPA employee, announcing the existence and purpose of this new investigatory group. I pointed out that, as an employee of OPA, each of us was a participant in the war effort. Ten, twenty or thirty years from now we would all want to look back on the OPA organization as one we could be proud of. I asked each employee to write me personally about any knowledge he might have of wrongdoing anywhere in the organization; I would see that the situation was immediately, tactfully and discreetly investigated.

In this way we extended to our employees both an invitation to help us police OPA themselves and at the same time warned the few individuals who might be tempted into wrongdoing that Secret Service investigators were now on the job. From that moment on, every rumor from whatever source in every part of the country was carefully traced.

In the Washington office, where most prices were determined, I know of only one effort to bribe an OPA official, and this failed. A textile manufacturer had been pressing the price department to raise the price ceiling of one of his products. The appropriate bureau, acting in accordance with our price standards, repeatedly told him that this was impossible. As he left his office after the last meeting, he handed the OPA price executive who was responsible for this area an envelope, saying, "Please read this memorandum carefully; perhaps it will change your mind."

After this individual had left the office the OPA price executive opened the envelope and out fell the halves of five one-thousand dollar bills. A note explained that the other halves would be in a certain hotel safe in the OPA man's name after the price increase went through. The guilty man was arrested at his hotel two hours later.

Several similar incidents occurred in our regional and district offices, but I doubt that the total was more than ten, which, in view of the magnitude of our operation, was an impressive testimony to the integrity and sense of commitment of our volunteers and paid employees.

On one occasion during a Congressional hearing an influential Senator charged that there had been an advance disclosure by OPA employees of information concerning a new price regulation for rye, and then refused to give me the evidence. I protested vigorously before the committee and then wrote him a letter in which I said:

> You and I, as responsible government officials, cannot condone such a position. Your informant has suggested that members of our staff are guilty of what I consider to be the worst possible breach of faith by a pricing official. I do not think that such implied charges should be allowed to stand on the record unless they can be substantiated.

I continued by informing the Senator:

> I have, in my office, a confidential staff of investigators who will quietly and efficiently undertake an intensive investigaton of any specific charges against our own employees of improper conduct. . . . I assure you that it is a matter of grave concern to me.

He never answered my letter. Later, when the Republicans gained control of both houses, they hired an investigating staff, which I was told totaled one hundred people, to probe into the OPA operation in search of evidence of wrongdoing that might provide political ammunition for attacking the preceding Administration.

Among all the hundreds of thousands of price decisions involving billions of dollars they were unable to come up with a single charge.

CHAPTER 7

DOING BATTLE WITH THE LOBBYISTS

EVEN IN "NORMAL" TIMES Washington is full of lobbyists. Many of them have been set up to protect the public interest and do so with varying degrees of effectiveness. But a larger number are concerned solely with promoting their own special interests at the expense of our society as a whole.

During World War II, when the government inevitably played a much greater role in our economy, the determination and resources of the lobbies, responsible and irresponsible alike, were significantly increased. Since OPA's decisions affected in some degree the daily life of every American consumer, worker, farmer or business, we were a primary target for profiteers, corner-cutters and honest citizens who were just plain frustrated. Much of their shooting was directed at me personally as Administrator of OPA.

In dealing with these pressures I followed a formula: (1) promptly investigate every responsible criticism and where indicated admit and correct our mistake or misjudgment; (2) when the attack had no basis in fact, meet the critics head on.

My counterattacks made me "controversial." As one journalist noted: "Threatened by pressure groups and plagued by lobbies, [Bowles] has astonished Washington by publicly labeling some of his vociferous tormentors 'pressure groups' and 'lobbyists.'"

Much of the public seemed gratified to be privy to these governmental shenanigans. The *New Republic* highlighted this public interest in an editorial of early 1945:

> The Price Stabilization Act, which expires in June, is coming before Congress this week for consideration. It will be under attack from nearly

every special interest, every pressure group in the country. They will display the bloody carcasses of their gored oxen before the Banking and Currency Committees, in the corridors of the Capitol and in the magazines and newspapers of the land. Hamstringing amendments of all kinds will be urged from all sides. This is the fight to watch—the whole people, the public, all of us (and a lot of us asleep) against the special interests.

An example of a confrontation with a professionally organized lobbying campaign in 1944 concerned the stove industry. OPA had set price ceilings on stoves at a level which, as was often the case, many members of the industry felt was inadequate, and the result was a highly publicized uproar. One day I received an anonymous letter, presumably from a stove manufacturer in Chicago. The writer began by saying that one of his two sons had been killed in the Pacific and that he was a strong supporter of our efforts on the home front. He felt it was his duty as a citizen to inform me about a conspiracy among certain members of the stove industry designed to force me to raise their ceiling price.

He enclosed a copy of a meticulous plan prepared by a New York City public relations firm. It involved carefully scheduled use of canned editorials, from letters to Congressmen, bogus cost analyses by economists and, finally, well-publicized investigations of OPA and of me personally by certain "cooperative members" of key Congressional committees.

At first we were skeptical and waited to see if anything would happen. When the editorials and the attacks by presumably subsidized economists began to appear in the newspapers on the precise schedule outlined in the plan, we decided to use this incident publicly to dramatize the forces with which we were contending. In my next radio broadcast I described the plan in full.

"Recently," I said, "you may have seen a headline in your local newspaper, 'Economists Assail OPA Price Policies.' . . . This is the opening gun of a professionally designed effort to force us to raise the prices which you pay for stoves." I said that I had in my hand the detailed day-by-day lobby plans, bought and paid for by a number of manufacturers, of which the news story was only a first step. The assumption, I told the public, was that, through fake news releases, planted editorials and pressures generated by inaccurate testimony in Congressional hearings, OPA would be forced to raise the present ceilings.

According to the plan schedule, I was supposed to receive a subpoena two days later to appear before a Congressional investigatory committee the following week. That no subpoena was ever served[1] can be credited

1. As a matter of fact, on no occasion during my three years as OPA Administrator was I ever served with a subpoena.

to the fact that many editors across the country, all of whom received copies of my broadcast, strongly supported my action in giving the public the facts. The following editorial in the San Francisco *Chronicle* was one of many:

> The public's most effective protection against such tactics [the stove lobby's plan] is to be forewarned about their nature. . . . If we are to maintain economic order in wartime, we must remain vigilantly on guard against the few who chisel exorbitant profits at the expense of all.

It was no surprise that some Congressmen and Senators would become lobbyists for these groups on Capitol Hill, but it certainly created problems for us. Even Senators and Congressmen who normally acted responsibly did not hesitate to promote the narrow interest groups in their states or districts, often bolstering their arguments with distorted literature provided by the lobbies with which they cooperated.

One could actually chart the yearly sweep of the sun by the sequence of proposed amendments to the Price Control Act. When Congressman James H. Morrison got up to speak, we knew it was strawberry season in Louisiana; when Congressman Richard M. Kleberg, owner of the largest cattle ranch in Texas, rose to demand higher prices for meat, we knew it was springtime on the range; and there were dozens more.

The primary argument of these members of Congress, which was expressed in different ways for different occasions, was that production could be increased only if price controls were either eliminated or placed at much higher levels. In rebuttal I pointed out that under wartime conditions increases in prices could not possibly produce increases in production since our workers were all fully employed and our factories going full blast. What higher prices would do was produce economic chaos as businessmen faced rapidly rising costs and a never-ending speculative scramble for raw materials. The result would very likely be not more production but less.

Many key officials on the War Production Board, including Chairman Donald Nelson, under heavy industry pressures, disagreed with OPA's position. Senator Robert Taft and many other influential and presumably informed political leaders supported Nelson. In the face of massive evidence to the contrary, Nelson and Taft remained genuinely convinced that only by raising prices could production meet our wartime targets. They ignored the overwhelming evidence that, since the earliest months of the war, production had risen far beyond the expectations of most economists and that, with few exceptions, industrialists, distributors and farmers were earning significantly higher profits than before the war.

Farm income, labor earnings and profits of corporations and small businesses all increased phenomenally throughout the war period. In 1944, with two or three million young farmers serving in our armed forces, farm production was 25 percent greater than in 1939, and 14 percent above the 1938–42 average. Industrial production increased 116 percent between 1939 and 1944.

When presented with these facts, the opponents of price controls would often shift their arguments to the "psychological problems" allegedly created by OPA. As long as industries had the *impression* that they were being shackled by price ceilings, they would, it was said, drag their feet. Convinced as I was that when and if such foot-dragging occurred it would be the result of hard dollars-and-cents calculations rather than of psychological depressions brought on by price ceilings, we stuck to our pricing standards.

Even among those who sincerely supported price controls in general there were many who sought higher price ceilings on specific items; and consequently the battle raged often within the government itself. On some issues it was difficult to distinguish between certain key lobbies and their governmental spokesmen.

Curiously enough, our principal adversary within the government was Harold Ickes, Secretary of the Interior and Petroleum Administrator for War, and long respected as a liberal force in the Roosevelt Administration. For reasons which I have never understood, he became the most vigorous spokesman for the big oil companies during the war.

In 1943 Ickes proposed an across-the-board increase in crude oil prices of 35 cents per barrel. I opposed the proposed price hike because the large oil producers were already reaping a handsome profit and needed no price raise "to stimulate production," while the smaller producers were receiving direct subsidies to assure their maximum production.

Economic Stabilization Director Fred Vinson supported OPA's position, and we were also able to convince Congress that OPA's subsidy plan to the oil industry, which cost the government only $50 million, was to be preferred to Ickes' price increases, which would cost $525 million.

Because of what he believed to be his responsibility to his industrial "clients" and my commitment to "hold the line," Ickes and I collided head on. Curiously enough, the treaty of peace to which we ultimately subscribed grew out of another difference, this time involving fur prices. The situation was similar to the one involving peach prices that so concerned FDR.

Since furs were considered luxuries, they were not at first subject to price ceilings. However, as purchasing power rose, demand for fur coats rose correspondingly, and soon the fur industry began to offer higher wages. Unless we used our pricing powers to hold down wages in the fur industry, as in other nonessential industries, thousands of workers entering the labor force for the first time, who were not yet under wage control, would be making mink coats instead of uniforms and parachutes.

However, we discovered that the pattern for all fur prices was established traditionally by the price of sealskins sold in the annual St. Louis auction, and consequently it was the prices of sealskins that must first be placed under control. Unhappily, high prices for sealskins were a special interest of the Secretary of the Interior, who by law was responsible for the Alaskan seal "harvest" and for the marketing of hides. To make matters worse, we discovered this fact only three days before the fur auction was due to start.

But there was no out. I nervously sent Ickes a letter informing him that we planned to freeze all sealskin prices at $54 a pelt on the following day. Ickes had been counting on getting at least $80 a pelt, and his response was predictably violent.

Ickes wrote letters in vast numbers and at great length, and as I read and reread his torrid comments about our sealskin prices, I was somewhat shaken, since, in spite of our occasional disagreements on the pricing of petroleum products in which he had an interest, I had always regarded Ickes as a great and awesome figure in American public life. He had been a crusader for clean government in Chicago and, although he was a lifelong Republican, Roosevelt had asked him to become a member of his New Deal Cabinet, in which he served with distinction. Nevertheless, I decided my only hope of holding my own was to go on the offensive.

After offering our apologies for giving him almost no warning of our decision on seal prices I went on to express my long admiration for him as a liberal and then described my personal distress at receiving such abusive letters from a man whom I had looked forward to knowing.

But, I said, my distress was now giving way to awe. How could a man with such overwhelming governmental responsibilities—and I listed them all—find the time to turn out such a prodigious number of personally written letters? It was not so much the quantity that impressed me as the quality. Much as I often disagreed with their contents, I marveled at the brilliance with which he expressed himself. Clearly, he must devote a major part of his time to this hobby.

In closing I said that in recent weeks I had learned, with relief, that I was not, in fact, the sole recipient of harsh words from the Secretary of the Interior. Indeed, I was told that almost every old hand with a responsible job in Washington could practically paper his office wall with similar missives. With considerable misgivings, I mailed the letter. Two days later, Ickes asked me to lunch. Our many differences were not even discussed, and we emerged and remained close personal friends.

By 1944, apparel, which was one of the few areas in which prices were still rising, had become perhaps the greatest remaining threat to the "hold the line" program. Even if we had had the full cooperation of the manufacturers and merchants (which we didn't), it would have been a difficult job. This problem was aggravated by the general wartime economic situation, in which shortages in textiles and greatly increased consumer spending power had combined to produce a sellers' market in apparel. Worse still, the various lobbies representing the industry were well financed, powerful and had great influence on Capitol Hill.

With no cars, refrigerators or washing machines available for purchase, the rush of millions of families, where breadwinners at long last had regular full-time jobs, to buy more clothes was intensified. Under these circumstances and with inadequate controls over production, most manufacturers shifted all the production they could to the higher-priced items and lowered the quality of the rest.

The structure of the industry itself was complex. Cotton textiles, rayons and woolens were produced by 3,500 mills, processed by 18,000 apparel manufactures, and distributed to the public through 3,400 wholesalers and 900,000 retailers.

The products themselves ranged infinitely in characteristics—color, styling and materials—to the point where it was nearly impossible to set any price that would be of general applicability. If we priced a dress with a rose on the left shoulder, the manufacturer would simply shift it to the right shoulder—and it would have to be priced as a different dress.

On three different occasions Congress was persuaded by industry pressure to enact amendments that further weakened our ability to keep down textile and apparel prices. These amendments were due in large part to the tenacious and astute lobbying efforts of the textile industry and National Retail Dry Goods Association.

I remember one occasion in September of 1945 when the NRDGA issued a grossly inaccurate alarmist report forecasting the demise of the retail dry goods industry if it were forced to absorb any of the increased costs of manufactured dry goods. The NRDGA itself had been one of the prime movers for the very price hike which had increased these costs.

During this period many textile manufacturers and merchants were reaping profits 1000 percent higher than prewar levels. Before taxes, the profits of the textile industry as a whole actually rose from $94 million in 1936–39 to $675 million in 1944, and those of apparel manufacturers rose tenfold. Although I made sure that every member of Congress knew these facts, the lobbies could usually garner enough votes to shoot down our attempts to impose some kind of regulation on what the industry produced and in what quantities.

Our conflicts with Congress in regard to textiles were very nearly matched by the battles we were once again forced to fight within the government, notably with the War Production Board. Although the WPB had full authority over all consumer production, it consistently took the position that its only function was to assure that the needs of the military were met. Despite our constant prodding, the WPB refused to set production standards for apparel or to divert consumer production to the areas where the needs were greatest.

I was eager to adopt the highly effective British system, which limited production in any one line of apparel to about one hundred basic garments with only relatively minor differences in style. The legal retail selling price on each garment was actually sewn into the label, and consumers could see for themselves exactly what price the retailer was authorized to charge.

By July of 1944 the WPB, even under constant OPA pressure, had refused to go beyond allocating somewhat more fabrics for the production of low-cost ladies' house dresses. OPA promptly established price ceilings on each of these items, spelled out in specific dollars and cents, and these particular prices at least were thereby stabilized. But beyond that the WPB refused to go, and as a consequence by one device or another garment prices continued their gradual but steady rise.

It was understandable that the manufacturers with whom the WPB was in close contact would be able to gain WPB support for higher prices on the grounds they were necessary as "further incentives." But the position of the Office of Economic Stabilization and its Director, Fred Vinson, was more difficult to understand, particularly since on most questions Vinson gave us his support. I urged him on innumerable occasions to use his legal power to direct WPB to give us the necessary help through production controls, but he refused to do so.

Then one Saturday afternoon an extraordinary incident occurred. Elmer Davis, head of the Office of War Information and a strong supporter of the anti-inflation programs, called to say he had just read the annual report to the President from the Office of Economic Stabilization. In this report Vinson stated that the Office of Price Administration had failed to hold down clothing prices adequately and that he hoped the Price Administrator would improve OPA's performance in the coming year. Davis, who knew of my efforts to deal with this question, wanted to be sure I knew about the report before it appeared in the newspapers.

I could hardly believe my ears. I had been fighting and bleeding for months to establish the necessary controls, while Vinson had consistently looked the other way. When Davis told me that the report was scheduled for release for the Monday morning papers, I asked him to hold it up until I called him back. I then telephoned Vinson.

Up to that point I had assumed, somewhat charitably, that the report must have been written by a staff member, that the comment on textiles must have escaped Vinson's attention, and that he would quickly agree to change the report to coincide with the facts. But to my amazement Vinson stood his ground.

I told Vinson that since it was his repeated failure to establish controls over production despite my persistent requests that he direct the WPB to do so, his criticism could not have been made in good faith, and I hung up the telephone. I then called my immediate boss, James Byrnes, head of the War Mobilization Board and only one step short of the President.

I briefly described the comments in Vinson's report and added that, while I had no desire to create a difficult situation, I would have no alternative if it appeared in the press as scheduled on Monday but to call a press conference to challenge its accuracy. I would document the number of times and the dates when we had pressed the WPB and Vinson for the tighter controls on the production of clothing that were essential for effective price controls. I would then document the number of times my efforts had been shot down. Under no circumstances, I said, could I accept the report without public comment.

Byrnes as usual was sympathetic and told me not to worry; he would take care of it. Within five minutes Vinson called to say that after talking to me earlier it occurred to him that I might not realize that he was joking and so he was calling me to put his own mind at ease. The report came out with the reference to OPA and to apparel prices omitted.

Vinson, who later became Secretary of the Treasury and then Chief Justice of the Supreme Court, had a reputation for toughness under pressure which in general he had earned. However, on this and two or three other occasions, he took actions which were difficult to justify.

These occasional lapses may be explained by the fact that, unlike most of the wartime administrators, Vinson had political ambitions.

Although the textile lobby continued to oppose each new regulation as a threat to the American way of life, we managed to make some progress after Donald Nelson left WPB. In cooperation with Nelson's successor, Julius A. Krug, we established a maximum average price regulation at the apparel manufacturing level, requiring manufacturers to maintain the same average prices for each category of goods as prevailed in 1943. The WPB was to channel fabrics to low-priced manufacturers of apparel, while the OPA put dollars-and-cents ceilings on each item of their clothing as it was produced. The *New Republic* noted our efforts:

> Bowles and WPB's Captain Krug, in a commendable and almost unique spirit of agency cooperation, are now undertaking, by a system of priority and price control, to divert a large percentage of cotton and other fibers from the limited civilian supply available, back into moderate priced merchandise.

In late 1944, under renewed industry pressure, Congress applied a time restriction on this effort, knowing that in the short period this left us we could not muster and train the people necessary to handle such a complex program. So the price and enforcement divisions continued their brave efforts at keeping track of restless style changes, while prices in this one field continued to creep gradually upward. Interagency disharmony, Congressional hostility and, above all, amazingly successful lobbying combined to keep the textile and apparel industry a hornet's nest for OPA and a needless problem for the consumer.

Meat pricing generated only slightly less pressure than clothing. Here again we encountered a deadly combination of economic imperative and political interference, aggravated by interagency strife.

As early as November 15, 1943, the Washington *Post* ran the headline, "Worst Meat Dearth Predicted by Livestock Men—OPA Hit." The article read in part:

> Five hundred livestock and poultry men descended on Washington to oppose subsidies as a means of holding down meat prices. . . . Representatives of all the livestock groups said that should the OPA regulations continue, next year will see the beginning of reduction of herds to the point that it will take many years to build them up again to normalcy.
>
> "We're getting damn sick of being governed by regulations written by some economist in Washington instead of by law," said counsel for the Texas and Southwestern Cattle Raisers Association.

I found this onslaught particularly difficult to understand. In July, 1942, price ceilings had been imposed on packers and wholesalers of beef and veal, but it wasn't until some time later that livestock itself was controlled.

It had been our hope that with time the ceiling on processed meat would be reflected downward and result in lower livestock prices. Instead, the big meat packers teamed up with the cattlemen to prevent this development.

The War Department, for reasons they never could make clear, scheduled most of their meat purchases for the armed services (which amounted to about 30 percent of the total meat supply) in the spring, which it so happened was the time that the Price Control Act came up for renewal in Congress. The cattlemen would then deliberately keep their remaining cattle on the range, thereby creating artificial meat shortages in the consumer market while they lobbied in Washington for higher prices.

Although the smaller meat packers were often caught in a squeeze between high livestock prices and low ceilings, the cattlemen and big packers would reap unconscionable profits. I finally persuaded President Roosevelt to order the War Department to spread its purchase of meat over a longer period, *not* in the spring. But to the bitter end by one device or another the big packers and many large cattlemen still managed to arrange meat shortages in the retail stores at the time best calculated to create difficulties for us in Congress.

In 1945 we devised a special subsidy arrangement for meat processors. Maximum prices were established for products resulting from the processing of cattle, calves, lambs, sheep and hogs. I found it ironic that Joseph C. Montague, the chief lobbyist for the cattlemen, referred to all such subsidies as a "form of bribery and blackmail," since the cattlemen had consistently informed OPA that only a higher meat ceiling could bring the cattle in from the range.

Caught in the midst of all this hurly-burly were the consumers. Very few people believed it, but the amount of meat available for consumers in the war period was more per capita than before the war. The explanation is that during the depressed 1930's, with millions unemployed, most families were unable to afford meat more than once or twice a week. With the war came full employment, and, as with clothing, the American consumer's demand for meat rose sharply.

While the system was steadily improved and the rise in meat prices generally curtailed, meat pricing remained more or less a political football. On one occasion I was told by a Congressional critic that the

Mitchell County Fair at Osage, Iowa, had been forced to cancel its greased-pig contest because of price uncertainty in the hog market.

Some pressure groups required greater tactical ability on our part than others. I remember one day receiving an urgent call from Senator Allen J. Ellender of Louisiana. "Chet," he said, "I am in a real jam. There's an army of muskrat hunters from Louisiana outside my office, as mad as they can be about your price ceilings on muskrat hides. They're ready to tar and feather any available government employee. Can I send them up to see you?"

By that time I had accumulated considerable experience in dealing with irate entrepreneurs from all walks of life, but I was admittedly leery of taking on a group of enraged muskrat hunters fresh from the Louisiana swamplands. As they marched militantly into my office wearing hunting shirts and heavy boots, they were a formidable-looking delegation.

I offered them chairs, sat down myself and remarked, "Before we talk about the price of muskrat skins, I'd like to know something for my own information. As a boy I used to trap muskrats in the woods of western Massachusetts, and I wondered what kind of traps you now use in Louisiana? Where do you set them and how do you bait them?" For the next forty minutes the ins and outs of trapping were thoroughly explored, with my visitors obviously delighted to find someone in Washington, D.C., who was interested in their day-to-day problems.

The meeting abruptly ended when one of my aides, according to a prearranged plan, opened the door, excused his interruption and said, "The President wants to see you at the White House immediately!" I apologized to the muskrat hunters for my sudden departure, assured them of my continued interest in their problems and then beat a hasty retreat to a dependable sanctuary. I never heard from the muskrat hunters again.

The professionally staffed lobby of the National Association of Manufacturers was a major headache, pressing in the most irresponsible manner for the elimination of controls over prices regardless of the effect on the war effort or on our postwar economy. When we met them head on, as I was ultimately forced to do, they simply dug in deeper.

On one occasion, I was asked to speak at the NAM annual dinner at the Waldorf-Astoria in New York. I had prepared a written speech and according to the usual practice had released it to the newspapers for publication following delivery.

After dinner the speaker immediately preceding me launched into a harsh attack on our program and on me personally, questioning OPA's competence and my own motives. As I was wondering how to handle

The National Association of Manufacturers, one of the most bitter opponents of price control, argued that removing controls would bring prices down. Obviously, Little Red Riding Hood was unconvinced in this cartoon by Herblock. © *1961 by Herblock in The Washington Post.*

this situation, I was tipped off by an anonymous note from an unknown friend at the head table that the speaker scheduled to follow me could be expected to launch a similar onslaught.

I decided to scrap my prepared speech and speak extemporaneously. I said that I had been invited to the dinner as a guest to discuss our common problems and I had not anticipated a personal attack of this kind. I knew the problems of business first hand, and as OPA Administrator I had done my best to ease the impact of the wartime regulations on businessmen as on others. However, the government in time of war had a right to expect the cooperation of business, as well as of labor and the farmers, and this the membership of the NAM had consistently refused to give.

I suggested that the NAM take a moment to examine its own record. If the programs which its official representatives had proposed in 1941 and 1942 before Congressional committees had actually been accepted by Congress, the war, because of the higher prices which the government would have been forced to pay, would have already cost some $80 billion more that it had cost thus far and added this vast amount to the national debt. In other words, the American people had already saved $80 billion by *not* taking the advice of the National Association of Manufacturers.

I emphasized that I did not place the blame for this massive misjudgment on the individual members, who I doubted had ever been consulted, but primarily on the NAM staff.

When I sat down, I expected to be greeted at best by silence and more likely by boos. But to my surprise I received a generous round of applause. I was further encouraged by more than one hundred letters from businessmen who had been present, expressing their personal regrets over the rigged proceedings and disassociating themselves from them.

Perhaps the most dramatic instance of the manipulation of Congressmen by a pressure group in which I was involved took place in the fall of 1945 when the National Automobile Dealers Association launched an all-out attack on the prices we had just set on the first postwar automobiles. It was a case, as one newsman put it, of "open lobbying, wholesale and by remote control."

Following V-J Day we were anxious to emphasize our determination and obligation to control inflation by keeping new cars on the market at the same price as in October, 1941, just before Pearl Harbor. When studies indicated that a 2.5 percent increase in the manufacturer's price was called for under our standards, we required the dealers, as our pricing standards specified, to absorb this 2.5 percent from their own profit margins.

Although the net margins which resulted were in fact still far in excess of the actual prewar margins, the dealers organized an all-out campaign to break our new ceilings. As the well-publicized avalanche of outraged dealers descended on Washington, I said in the course of a radio speech: "Automobile dealers today are doing a very profitable business, thanks to repairs on old cars, the sale of used cars, and the sale of the sprinkling of newly produced cars, which will soon grow to an increasing flood."

Just prior to the scheduled hearings of the House Small Business Committee, the NADA people swamped the OPA central office with over five thousand telegrams and telephone calls, which provided us with ample warning of the uproar we could except at the hearing.

Came the big day, and there assembled were not only four hundred embittered, well-rehearsed dealers, but more than three hundred members of Congress (nearly three-fourths of the whole membership) to demonstrate their personal support for their well-heeled constituents. Indeed, so many Congressmen showed up that the hearings had to be shifted to the huge Caucus Room of the Old House Office Building.

At the outset I was impressed with the irony of the situation. Wright Patman of Texas, who as chairman of the House Small Business Committee had been asked to call the meeting, had on many occasions been helpful to OPA. As he called the meeting to order, I suspected that he must be feeling uncomfortable.

The first witness was NADA's president, W. L. Mallon, who launched into an impassioned twenty-page plea for what amounted to the right of the dealers to charge whatever the public was prepared to pay.

The dealers, he said, would go broke if they had to absorb the 2.5 percent increase which we planned to give the manufacturers. He added that there were 35,000 dealers in the country and that all 35,000 wanted to come to Washington to speak for themselves. He said he had forestalled this by "wiring them they'd have to sleep in the park." When he finished, there was applause as enthusiastic as on the opening night of *Oklahoma!*

Representative Leonard W. Hall of New York promptly rose to answer that he, for one, was convinced. That very day he would introduce a resolution calling on OPA to hold everything until the committee had finished its investigation. More applause.

Representative G. Evan Howell of Illinois suggested that the resolution in question be forwarded to the OPA at once by special messenger. Still more applause.

Underlining my own opening statement in rebuttal was my concern over the kind of tactics which had been employed and their apparent success. As Marquis Childs noted in his column of November 25, 1945:

> The idea of government by pressure, as Bowles pointed out, assumes that officials should base their decisions not on the merits of an issue, but on the degree of pressure which can be focused on a given point. It's the principle of a steam boiler. If a lobby can generate enough heat to force the needle in the gauge up to the proper notch, then action must automatically follow.
>
> What is more, Congress seems to accept this technique. . . .

On the way back to the office for a brief lunch, one of my staff suddenly remembered an incident in the debates on the renewal of the Price Control Act the previous spring. In an effort firmly to establish our legal right to require first the wholesaler and then the retailer to absorb any price increase which the manufacturers could not absorb, as long as their own profits remained "generally" above the 1936–40 average, we had asked Patman in the course of the debate to speak in support of this identical pricing procedure; and he had done so, reading into the record a memorandum prepared by our Legal Division.

In this speech, a copy of which was soon on my desk, Patman had clearly outlined our legal right and responsibility to carry out the precise procedure which the automobile dealers were now so belligerently demanding that we abandon. Since there had been no challenge to Patman's interpretation of Congressional intent at the time, this had served to anchor the principle into the law.

When I returned to the hearing room after lunch, I showed Wright a copy of his speech. A few minutes later he called the meeting to order and abruptly announced that he was confident I would do everything I properly could to be helpful under the law. To the accompaniment of considerable muttering from the amazed auto dealers, who had assumed that the performance was just getting under way, the meeting was then adjourned.

In defense of the auto dealers' position, it should be said that for many years before the war they had been forced by the manufacturers to operate on a tight profit margin; it was only after a long struggle that they had been able to raise the level to around 25 percent. What worried them now was that once their margin had been lowered from 25 to 22.5 percent and the sellers' market period had passed, it would be difficult for them to persuade the manufacturers to restore the pre-war margin.

But any automobile dealer who was honest with himself would agree that as the new cars became available at the end of the war it would be in a sellers' market, with an opportunity to make a very generous profit.

Moreover, with customers standing in line for new cars the dealers would be in a position either to refuse trade-ins entirely or else to price a trade-in car at a level well below its normal value. In addition, advertising costs for at least two or three years would be minimal. Under these conditions our regulation could not reasonably be questioned.

AGAIN, BOWLES' BOYS HOLD THAT LINE !

As the war drew to a close, American industry, eager to reconvert to the production of peacetime items, brought heavy pressure on OPA to allow price increases. In November, 1945, automobile dealers descended on Washington, but without success, as depicted in this cartoon by R. A. Lewis which appeared with the caption, "Again Bowles' boys hold that line!"

CHAPTER 8

JOURNEYS TO CAPITOL HILL

OUR PRIMARY POLITICAL PROBLEM each year was obtaining the authorization from Congress to stay alive. The Price Control Act was authorized for only one year at a time, and each spring for three consecutive years, 1944–46, I was called upon to make formal presentations to the Banking and Currency Committees of both houses, to which OPA was directly responsible, and also to the Appropriations Committees.

For three or four months each year I spent two-thirds of my time before these Congressional committees, and several top members of my staff were equally occupied.

The chairman of the Senate Banking and Currency Committee was an old friend, Robert Wagner, Senator from New York and author of much of the New Deal legislation. He and a majority of his committee, including several Republicans, notably Charles W. Tobey of New Hampshire, were strong supporters of OPA. Bob Taft, of course, was the most articulate spokesman for the opposition, which included Kenneth Wherry of Nebraska.

The chairman of the House Banking and Currency Committee was Brent Spence of Kentucky, who was also a staunch advocate of the economic stabilization program. He was joined by Congressman A. S. Mike Monroney of Oklahoma and many others who understood what we were trying to do and did everything in their power to help us do it.

Mike Monroney in particular could always be counted upon in difficult situations during House committee hearings and also in debates on the House floor. On one occasion when a bill directing us to raise oil prices by 10 percent slipped unexpectedly through the Senate, I asked

Monroney whom we should call upon to mobilize opposition to the bill when it reached the floor of the House.

Mike insisted on organizing the opposition himself in spite of my warning that this would assure the bitter opposition of powerful oil interests in Oklahoma to his re-election the following November. The oil companies did make him a primary target, but he was re-elected, thereby demonstrating that men with integrity and courage can survive in the political arena.

The annual authorization ordeals gave scores of lobbyists an opportunity not only to attack us on specific issues but periodically to bring pressure to bear directly on the members of Congress. When they failed to persuade Congress to order us to do what they wanted us to do, they blamed those members who had failed to succumb to their arguments.

On several occasions with this point in mind, I privately asked Congressional leaders if it would not be easier for Congress as well as for the Administration if OPA legislation were authorized for the duration of the war, plus a readjustment period of six months or a year. Although most members of the committees agreed, on each occasion when I proposed this change someone managed to block it.

And while it was true that on no occasion did the White House suggest that OPA succumb to pressure to raise a price, it offered very little direct support in our dealings with Congress. The heads of the wartime agencies were regarded as politically expendable, and we were left to fight our own battles, with each other, with the lobbies and with Congress, with whatever support we could muster from the general public.

Although the Secretaries of the Treasury, Labor, Commerce and Agriculture each had a major stake in the ability of OPA to maintain a stable price level, on no occasion during my three years as OPA Administrator, if my memory is correct, did any member of the Cabinet testify in our behalf before Congress.

Everyone had his own problems. The Secretary of Agriculture did not want to tangle with the farmers; the Secretary of Labor had no desire to upset labor; the Secretary of Commerce traditionally represented business within the Administration; the Secretary of the Treasury was reluctant to take on the battle for higher taxes; and other members of the government, such as Paul V. McNutt, Director of the War Manpower Commission, were still dreaming of someday becoming President. All we could expect were private good wishes and public indifference.

Obviously, this meant that our relations with Congress must be given the very highest priority. Soon after my arrival in Washington I set out to develop a more effective system of communications with members of the Senate and House. The first step was the establishment of a special Congressional liaison section attached to my office under the direction of an able businessman and long-time Republican, Zenas L. Potter, whom I had known in New York. We directed that every letter from a member of Congress should be answered within three days.

When it was apparent that an important issue involving a price, rent or rationing regulation was beginning to shape up, every member of Congress was promptly provided with an easy-to-understand explanation of our responsibilities under the law, the procedures available to us in meeting this particular responsibility and precisely why we had taken the action. Our explanation usually arrived before the protests from home began to reach their desks.

Under Potter's general direction, an OPA information office was established on Capitol Hill, the staff of which could quickly respond to all Congressional inquiries on OPA policy and regulations. Through this office or directly through the appropriate OPA bureaus, we answered over 750,000 letters and 30,000 telephone calls from Congressmen every year. When I described this vast flow of correspondence to Alben Barkley of Kentucky, who was then Senate majority leader and later became Vice President, he said, "In the interest of the consumer I hope that only a limited number of these calls are successful."

I was concerned that, despite our efforts to inform and cooperate with Congress, the only occasions when my top associates and I had personal contact with members of the House or Senate, with the exception of social contacts with a few personal friends, were when they were under public pressure to force us into inflationary actions.

I proposed to the two Banking and Currency Committee chairmen, Bob Wagner and Brent Spence, that we experiment with new ways of keeping the committees better informed and of resolving whatever differences might develop over our regulations before they erupted in public hearings, which often took on some of the aspects of a three-ring circus. The American people, I said, might be regarded as the stockholders, Congress as the board of directors and the Administration as the management. As the administrators of policies laid down by Congress, we were eager for a closer working relationship.

I proposed that once a month I and two or three of my senior staff members should meet with each of the two Banking and Currency Committees for general discussions of broad questions of policy and administration.

"It would be enormously helpful," I wrote,

if I were in a position to spell out regularly to the appropriate Congressional committee, in an unemotional setting, the problems that we foresee in the future and the ways in which we can cope with them. I suggest this not only because it would give us an opportunity to give you and your committee members a better understanding of our difficulties, but also because we would gain a great deal from your advice and counsel.

This proposal was promptly approved by both chairmen, and the meetings were duly scheduled. Unhappily, they were not a success. Those who attended were largely our supporters, while those who were usually critical and with whom I was then most eager to communicate stayed away. After a few months the meetings petered out.

In early February, 1944, I was scheduled for my major Congressional debut before the Senate and House Banking and Currency Committees in support of the extension of the Emergency Price Control Act. Because we knew that this presentation would be crucial to the future of price control, rent control and rationing, we took great care in working out an effective presentation. Potter, who was absorbed eighteen hours a day in answering criticisms of OPA, wrote me on February 3, advising:

> We have got to prove to Congress and the public that we have done a remarkable job in spite of some delays and mistakes. The primary point is that the price line has been held under great difficulties as we promised to do and here we are on firm ground. . . . But once a critic in an open hearing with a real or imagined cause for complaint gets us involved in arguing the details of his special problem we are licked.
>
> We have the guns and the ammunition, and the hour is late. We should follow the policy of Marshal Joffre who said, "My left flank is turned; my right is falling back. The situation is excellent. I shall attack." Just proving we're reasonable men won't suffice. We've got to resell the need for wartime inflation controls, which is one of the biggest selling jobs of all time.

I agreed that the most effective strategy would be to let the exceptions—our more glaring instances of miscalculation or clumsy handling—prove the rule, the over-all success of the OPA program. At the last minute we decided to borrow from my prewar experience in business by preparing a series of 104 placards that provided a forceful visual presentation of the whole OPA, anti-inflation story. The placards were crude in lettering and design partly because we had no chart experts on our staff and partly to avoid the impression of professional salesmanship. Replicas of the charts, each a little larger than letter size, were bound and placed before every committee member so that they could refer back to previous charts and to provide them with a record of the presentation. As far as I know, this was the first occasion when a chart presentation was used before a Congressional committee. Since then, of course, they have become routine.

We had previously worked out procedures and agenda with each of the two committee staffs. This called first for my over-all presentation, which we knew would take the better part of the first day; the questions by the committee members would then follow.

At ten o'clock on the morning of the presentation I appeared rather nervously before the members of the Senate Banking and Currency Committee, who were in a most friendly mood. With the help of our charts, I reviewed the disastrous consequence of the failure to control prices during World War I, the even more critical importance of avoiding another failure, and the constructive role which Congress had played at an early stage by passing legislation to prevent inflation.

Following our strategy, I described some of the most bizarre and humorous of our blunders. "We have had the unique opportunity," I admitted, "to make more mistakes than any other agency or body in the history of the United States." I explained that many errors were due to the incredible complexity of our job. In reference to gasoline, for instance, I commented, "OPA was given the responsibility for an utterly new program and inevitably there were many mistakes, much fumbling and a great many delays. If we had it to do over again we could obviously do a lot better.

"But," I added, "this brand-new challenge had to be met and somehow we met it. Gasoline consumption is now less than half what it was before the war . . . but somehow everyone gets to his job and the primary needs are met."

When I had finished, Chairman Wagner thanked me for a "masterful job in getting up these charts"; Senator Albert W. Hawkes of New Jersey beamed and said, "As the only Republican member present, I liked that you admitted your mistakes."

One Washington reporter later described the impact of the charts in the following way:

> This new chart is known as the attack-upon-consciousness-chart. You can't escape it. Shut your eyes and there's the professor reading aloud. Avert your gaze and you find yourself staring at the same words in your hands. . . . The only possible way to combat a chart like this is to stand up and yell.

A striking testimony to the effectiveness of our chart presentation was the fact that the next year the National Association of Manufacturers appeared before the committee with 112 charts of its own.

By far the most important consequence of this first presentation was that it persuaded a clear majority of the committee of the importance of continuing government price control and rationing. The new authorization bill as agreed to by the committee contained a few inconvenient but no disabling amendments. On balance, it was agreed that our Congressional debut was a success.

While I can't honestly say that I looked forward to these appearances, they were stimulating, and, as various members began to pursue their own personal gripes, they were even entertaining. On one occasion Senator Tobey went after Jim Brownlee on apple prices. To quote from the record:

TOBEY: . . . in regard to the price ceilings on apples . . . if little apples are put in with big apples, then the seller gets top prices for a basket of apples that may not be top grade. What is the common sense in that? Where is the justice in it? . . . I remember talking to you on the telephone and you said to me, "I am head of the apple division." I said to you, "All right, did you ever raise apples?"

BROWNLEE: I have no objection to being called a theorist . . . any man in my position who deals with eight million different prices has to be a theorist.

TOBEY: But the thing I asked you, why instead of some impractical theoretical bureaucrat, I asked you, why you did not bring in the horny-handed son of New Hampshire or another apple growing state who knows something about apples?

In the course of these long hearings we developed some effective tactics. For instance, the opposition leadership in the House and Senate often supplied younger committee members with cards on which were typed questions designed to throw us into confusion.

When we saw a Congressman referring to a card, it was a good bet that he was asking a question prepared by someone else. After he had read his question, I would politely say that I had not fully understood the question and would he elaborate at greater length. On many occasions this led to the acute embarrassment of the questioner, who had no knowledge of the situation or price regulation to which his question referred.

Among the opposition to OPA, Senators Taft and Wherry were the most persistent. Wherry, who was described in the records as the "lawyer, furniture dealer, and undertaker of Pawnee City, Nebraska," and by his less respectful associates as the "merry mortician," had a better sense of humor than Taft, but he shared Taft's view that OPA had no business regulating profits. I maintained that we had no interest in profits, but in prices, and that the cases were rare in which industry had suffered because of OPA.

It is true that any ceiling on prices places, in greater or lesser degree, a limit on profits. But under wartime price ceilings profits in almost all industries were excellent and in many industries had soared beyond all reason. If our purpose had actually been *profit* control, it could be said that we did a mighty poor job of it.

One of my exchanges with Wherry on this subject was reported by columnist Frederick Othman, who wrote:

> The Senator is a furniture merchant back home in Nebraska and what he wanted to know was where did Bowles get that chart saying profits of small furniture dealers were up 185%. Bowles said he got the figures from the furniture dealers. "Not from furniture dealer Wherry, he didn't," Senator Wherry said. "How can you increase your profits on furniture when you have no furniture?"
>
> Bowles went on. Hardware store profits up 460%. "That's impossible," cried the Senator.
>
> But Bowles kept going. Department stores profits 1324 percent higher than before the war.
>
> "What?" Wherry demanded.
>
> "One thousand three hundred and twenty-four percent," Professor Bowles replied, pointing to his chart.
>
> "That's an awful big figure," interjected Senator Allen J. Ellender of Houma, La. "Are we to understand department stores have been allowed to do that? If it's true, then OPA has been a failure."
>
> "Yep," said Senator Wherry.
>
> "Nope," said Professor Bowles, trying to explain that prices didn't go up but volume did.
>
> "Dumb," muttered Wherry. . . . "That's just plain dumb."

Senator Taft genuinely feared inflation and at the outset had favored limited and selective controls. But his commitment to the interests of business caused him to view with alarm the influx of "theorists" into OPA.

When I, a Yale man like himself and a businessman to boot, was appointed OPA Administrator, I am sure that he expected the Office of Price Administration to get back on what he considered the right track. It must have been an unhappy moment when he learned that on the critical issue of administering price controls, as on many other issues, he and I were poles apart. When after many long discussions I refused to modify my position, his frustrations were intensified.

Taft had always felt that the best OPA could do was to limit price increases during the course of the war to around 10 percent a year. Although such an increase compounded over a period of several years would create major and needless hardship for millions of people and add many billions more to our national debt, I agreed that, in theory at least, we could assume that the Republic would somehow survive. However, I could not see how once price increases began to feed on each other the annual increase could be limited to 10 percent; what we would eventually get would be a runaway inflation.

Taft's legal training led him to take one question at a time, to analyze it, and then to make his decision, and this was the procedure he persistently urged me to adopt in setting price ceilings. Over and over again I replied htat in raising one firm's prices we might be raising costs for ten thousand firms and that it would require a staff many times greater than that of OPA to handle the avalanche of appeals. But he remained adamant to the end.

A typical exchange between us on the subject took place in the hearings of the Banking and Currency Committee a year or so after I became OPA Administrator.

"Senator," I said, "you have always felt that a gradually rising level of prices throughout the war was not only right but desirable."

"It is necessary," asserted Taft.

"I maintain," I said, "that you cannot permit inflation to begin to creep because pretty soon it will stop creeping and start to run."

"I don't agree," Taft declared.

"We have never agreed," I replied.

Taft's opposition also grew out of his philosophical conviction, shared by many conservatives who remained committed to the economic dogma of Adam Smith, that any limitation on profits, direct or indirect, even in wartime was wrong. He interrupted the testimony of Jim Brownlee, the Deputy Director for Price Control in 1944, for example, to say, "The only basic difference in philosophies that I see . . . is the question of the apparent tendency of your Administration to say, 'The one important thing is stabilization, and to stabilization we will sacrifice justice to the individual producer or the individual processor.' "

It made no difference to Taft that earnings in the textile or any other industry had always been uneven, that they were now, in the midst of a world war, far higher than ever before, that fewer firms were going out of business than ever before, let alone that a wartime policy had to concern itself with the larger picture of national welfare. This was another Taft-Brownlee exchange:

BROWNLEE: If during wartime you are going to say, "Make OPA a price escalation agency, one that will increase prices every time your costs go up," you would have inflation and no price control left. I think we will all agree to that.

TAFT: No. I don't agree with that.

Taft was particularly opposed to volunteer price panels which we established in all war price and ration boards to check compliance in the local stores and to investigate all consumer complaints about above-ceiling sales. At one stormy hearing of the Banking and Currency Committee he asserted, "You assume that these people [businessmen] are crooks. . . . You go outside the government to spy on other people."

Chairman Robert Wagner mildly observed that the majority of those present regarded these volunteer price checkers as courteous and dedicated citizens fulfilling an important role. Taft replied, "It is absolutely un-American, contrary to law and contrary to the Constitution. They are against the businessmen."

"Most of them *are* businessmen," I said.

"It would seem," observed another member of the committee, "that the Senator from Ohio [Taft] has the impression that anybody serving the government gratis is violating the law."

Even after all our disagreements over the renewal of the Emergency Price Control Act in 1944, in an effort to establish some basis of understanding, I wrote Taft late in June of that year:

> I want to thank you for your courteous, friendly and intelligent efforts to work out the Stabilization Extension Act. I know how hard it was and the amount of patience it required.
>
> There are, of course, some parts of it that worry us a bit, but it also means a lot to us to be working under a Congressional charter. . . .

In deference to Taft's sensibilities, I had failed to stress in my letter that most parts of the new act that "worried us a bit" were directly attributable to his zeal. Later, to my acute embarrassment, Taft included my polite letter in a full-page advertisement for his re-election to the Senate to demonstrate that he was not as opposed to OPA as his Democratic adversary had charged.

Following his re-election in 1944 Senator Taft redoubled his efforts to remold the Price Control Act to conform to what I believe were sincere but mistaken ideas on the subject of stabilization. In an understatement of his general philosophy, he asserted in the 1944 hearings, "There is no one, at least that I know of, in the Senate who has any intention to scrap the Price Control Act or to substantially modify it. . . . The only question we have before us is the number of amendments which may in some way affect prices which may result in some increase in prices, but which are designed to correct serious injustices."

I later wrote Senator Wagner the following in rebuttal to Taft's views:

> From the start of the war [Senator Taft] has been opposed, as a matter of principle, to the government's stabilization policy. He was for "controlled

inflation" when the Congress passed the Emergency Price Control Act in January, 1942. He was for it when the Stabilization Act was passed in September, 1942, and again when the Stabilization Extension Act was passed in June, 1944.

The Senator's philosophy that it is futile and not particularly desirable to try to keep the value of the dollar stable has been often and fully expressed.

I then quoted Taft's statement to the Senate on July 30, 1942, in which he said:

> On the other hand, a reasonable price increase, say at the rate of 10 percent a year, is not necessarily dangerous if it is under proper control. In fact, my own view is that the price structure should be more or less flexible, and that it may be actually desirable to increase some prices instead of decreasing them or holding them stable.

In 1945 Senator Taft raised the profit issue again in his proposed "cost-plus" amendment, which would have sharply raised most prices. On this issue he very nearly succeeded in winning a majority. I again outlined my opposition in a letter on May 23, 1945, to Senator Wagner:

> No better formula for chaos in the transition period from war to peace could be devised. . . . What is needed in changing our structure of controls as the transition proceeds is flexible, balanced action with due discrimination to avoid nullifying the gains of relaxation by destroying the bases for business planning.
>
> The present staff of this office could not begin to carry the administrative workload which Senator Taft's amendment would place upon it. Moreover, I do not believe that a staff could be held together, or recruited, which thought that the control of unit percentage profit margins instead of prices was an objective worthy of effort and sacrifice.

To Senator Taft's credit, it must be said that his sense of logic and integrity on many questions led him to end up favoring things he had once been flatly against or vice versa. But this virtue was never apparent in his dealings with OPA. In fact, five years after I left Washington, Taft was to lead a group of Republican Senators in the unsuccessful opposition to my confirmation as Ambassador to India.

Although Taft lost the primary debate on price controls, which he continued to call "profit control," he won a number of important battles along the way. One such victory was on food subsidies. In early 1944 I conceded in my testimony before the Senate Banking and Currency Committee that "Congress has expressed its disapproval of the subsidy program."

This was an understatement. Although totally essential to the stabilization program, food subsidies survived only because we persuaded President Roosevelt to veto two Congressional bills which would have barred them, one in June, 1943, and again in February, 1944. After each veto the power of the Commodity Credit Corporation to pay subsidies was extended by a simple Congressional resolution which enabled the program to continue.

The Washington *Post* noted in its editorial of November 18, 1943, "Unfortunately the subsidy fight now raging on the Hill is not being conducted along rational lines." The paper later condemned the Congress for allowing itself to be a "football of special interests." Congressman Henry Steagall of the House Banking and Currency Committee responded to this accusation with the bland assertion that the proposed Congressional ban did not involve a "particle of politics." "I think," he said, "that it is possible for Republicans to be right once in a while."

Budget appropriations hearings were not as long and tedious as those for our annual authorization, and with support from the Bureau of the Budget we avoided serious cuts. We were fortunate that Elmer Staats, who later became Comptroller General of the United States, was at that time the Bureau of the Budget staff member assigned to the Office of Price Administration. Statts made an important contribution to our efforts to improve the efficiency of our operation and to secure the funds that were required to carry on our work.

Throughout the Congressional debates on OPA, we were staunchly defended by the Congressional Committee for the Protection of the Consumer, two of whose leading figures were Representative Thomas E. Scanlon of Pennsylvania and Representative Howard J. McMurray of Wisconsin. The House Select Committee to Investigate Executive Agencies, whose chairman was Congressman Howard W. Smith of Virginia, was among our most bitter critics.

In its first report on OPA, issued on July 27, 1943, the investigation committee criticized our rent regulations; its second report, issued November 15, 1943, dealt similarly with price control and rationing. The report began by saying that OPA had issued 3,196 regulations, amendments and orders, many of them "illegal, absurd, useless and conflicting." It also charged that OPA had set up for itself an extrajudicial procedure which "jeopardized the nation's system of civil liberties." In view of the well-known racist views of its chairman, this particular conclusion was ironic.

When I asked for evidence, Chairman Smith explained to me that "The practical difficulty is a lot of folks did not want to let their names be known for fear of retaliation of some kind." He added as a kindly afterthought, "I am not saying that that fear is justified."

Smith wrote me in November, 1943, to invite me to his own private showing of examples of OPA's alleged unfairness in setting prices for apparel, which he said had been furnished by "various interested citizens," and were available "in physical form" for my perusal, adding that "they could have been readily augmented by many thousands more, time and space permitting."

The items had been furnished by members of the National Retail Dry Goods Association, and with few exceptions they were impossible to identify. Among the items whose manufacturers we could trace, on investigation we found that most of these were outright frauds.

An example of these frauds was reported in an article I wrote on January 19, 1946, in *Collier's* magazine in which I said, "A pair of good 39-cent shorts was labelled as 'out of production because of OPA policies.' The truth is that the manufacturer is making almost 500,000 pairs of these shorts a week, and is selling them below the legal ceiling."

One particular problem which brought me frequently to Capitol Hill throughout the entire war was inflation in the cost of new home building and in the prices of houses put up for sale. In the early years of the war these costs were kept under reasonable control by a simple regulation requiring that no house could be built that cost more than $8,000.

As we drew closer to the end of the war, the market in real estate began to pick up steam and the price of existing housing moved rapidly upward. Tens of thousands of newly married men from the armed forces would soon be returning to set up families, and unless steps were taken, the real estate market would go out of control.

Several of my associates felt that in the crisis atmosphere after Pearl Harbor the OPA's authority might somehow have been stretched to put ceilings on the sale prices of existing homes under the Price Control Act. However, because of the more immediate pressures this opportunity (if, in fact, it existed) was overlooked, and I felt that it was necessary to seek a Congressional authorization rather than to proceed on the assumption that I had this authority.

At first we were so appalled by the complexity of the problem that we almost gave up in despair. However, a simple approach occurred to us: the ceiling price of each house could be set at the last price at which it had been sold prior to the regulation. For instance, a man would have the right to sell his house to a buyer at whatever price he could persuade him to pay for it. However, if the new buyer should later decide to sell the house, the price he had paid for it would automatically become the ceiling for the next sale. This regulation could have saved the returning members of our armed forces hundreds of millions of dollars. But it was stalled and eventually blocked in Congress under pressure from the real estate lobbies.

One quality in Congressional dealings, which at first I found difficult to understand, was the veneer of gentility and courtesy that overlay even the most violent disputes. The older members, in particular, had learned how to say the most outrageous things to each other in the nicest sort of way. This tradition had developed for a variety of reasons. First was the general recognition that two, four or six years of consistent enmity toward a fellow member was a long time, and that life was short. Second was the knowledge that the vicissitudes of politics often made for strange bedfellows. Today's opponent on one issue might be tomorrow's ally on another. Third was the simple fact that people of opposite persuasions often find themselves personally liking their adversaries in spite of their ideological differences.

Regardless of their views toward OPA, our opponents on the Hill with few exceptions were honest and sincere men. But as a newcomer to Washington I was alarmed by the lack of general concern for ethics, and my concern has grown over the years. While members of the executive and judicial branches were expected to be above blame, Congress seemed ready to excuse actions of its own members that it would not tolerate in others.

In "normal times" this is deplorable, but in wartime it was even more so. I recall one particularly lurid example. Just before our appearance before the Senate Appropriations Committee, our Enforcement Division unearthed a serious violation of our pricing regulations by a close relative of a senior member of the Senate Appropriations Committee.

It was a blatant case. The relative had been systematically mispricing his product and keeping two sets of books to avoid detection. The OPA investigator had conclusive evidence, leaving no doubt of the man's intent, and an indictment against him was returned in Federal Court. The Attorney General's office promptly proceeded with the case.

The Senator then told me that he would strongly oppose the OPA appropriations until the charges against his relative had been dropped.

I was weary with the irresponsible attacks on OPA and the general disregard of the public interest by presumably respected political and business leaders. Since the worst thing they could do to me was to send me back to Essex, Connecticut, I decided to fight back. I wrote two speeches for my next scheduled radio broadcast—one a run-of-the-mill account of current problems, and the other a detailed item-by-item description of my conflict with the Senator and his relative.

I privately showed the Senator both speeches, stressing that he alone could decide which of them I would give over the radio the following Wednesday night. If our budget were held up by his action, I would explain why. "It is your decision," I said. The appropriation went through without a hitch.

Although the Congressional pressures to do away with or to cripple the OPA program seemed to me at the time utterly irresponsible, I believe the blame in the vast majority of cases rested less on the individual than on the system. As I came to understand even more clearly when I served as a member of the House in 1959–60, a Congressman or Senator, no matter how conscientious, has an almost impossible task. The magnitude of the problems with which he is required to deal is appalling, and it is impossible for him fully to understand more than a small fraction of the issues on which he must pass judgment.

One of the most impressive and well-balanced Congressional performances of the war period was that of Senator Harry S. Truman of Missouri, who, as chairman of the Senate "Watchdog" Committee, was responsible for investigating all phases of the war effort. Like every other committee chairman whose mandate was related to the war, Truman was deluged with mail, telegrams and visiting constituents protesting one OPA action or another.

But Truman from the beginning understood the magnitude and complexity of our task and the pressures under which we often worked. Because of this understanding and his personal confidence in the integrity of OPA, on no occasion did he succumb to the temptation to call a public hearing in which to rake us over the coals. On perhaps a dozen occasions in three years he asked me to drop by his office informally the next time I was on "the Hill." On each visit I saw him alone with no committee or even a staff member present.

He would simply show me the most recent flurry of critical letters and ask me for an explanation so that he could "reply to these letters intelligently." Since in every case I was always able to answer his questions satisfactorily, that was the end of it. It was a uniquely restrained use of Congressional authority.

CHAPTER 9

MY RELATIONS WITH FDR

THE FIRST TIME I MET PRESIDENT ROOSEVELT was in early 1943 shortly after Leon Henderson left the Office of Price Administration. Henderson had recommended that I be asked to take responsibility for the Rationing Division of the Office of Price Administration, and presumably the purpose of the meeting with Roosevelt was to persuade me to accept.

We were off to a slow start. The President had apparently mislaid his notes and wasn't sure who I was or what he was supposed to ask me to do. However, I admired a ship model on a table near his desk and we discovered our mutual interest in sailing. The conversation then continued for a half-hour, most of it devoted not to the subject of rationing but to foggy summers on the Maine coast.

My next meeting with Roosevelt was in August, 1943, a week or so after I arrived in Washington to become General Manager of the Office of Price Administration. Roosevelt had agreed to my appointment on the assumption that because of my business background I must be a Republican and he preferred Republicans for high positions in the politically vulnerable wartime agencies, since presumably their presence in the Administration would help to keep politics out of the war effort and vice versa. When he discovered that I was a Democrat who had voted for him as a delegate at the 1940 Convention in Chicago and a supporter of his prewar New Deal in the bargain, his reaction, I am sure, was mixed.

After Prentiss Brown's resignation a few weeks later and my appointment as Price Administrator, I saw Roosevelt regularly until his death in April, 1945. Although I had heard and read much about his personal charm, I never ceased to marvel at it. In even the most trying of situations he maintained a serenity and sense of confidence that were contagious.

While he was looked upon as a "radical" by most business leaders, he was quite traditional in his economic thinking. The thought of our unbalanced federal budget so concerned him in the mid-1930's that he took the advice of his more conservative advisers and sharply reduced federal spending while there were still eight million unemployed, thus producing the recession of 1937.

Roosevelt was conscious of the blind opposition of most businessmen, and since he felt, with considerable justification, that he had saved the capitalistic system from collapse in 1933, this irritated him profoundly. But when war became imminent, he understood the importance of uniting the country and winning the confidence of his old opponents, and he was willing to go more than halfway to achieve this. This prompted him in 1943 to remark to a press conference, "Dr. New Deal is dead; Dr. Win-The-War has taken over."

In the fall of 1943 a number of us began to worry about our government's readiness to apply the economic lessons learned in the war to our postwar domestic economy. Even with ten million of our ablest young men in the armed forces, we were producing more than double our output in the best prewar year. If we could do this in time of war, why could we not at least equal this performance in time of peace?

I shared these thoughts with Judge Samuel I. Rosenman, Roosevelt's top adviser, with whom I had established a warm and understanding relationship, and Rosenman asked me to put my ideas on paper. The result was a memorandum to the President suggesting that he propose to Congress a "Second Bill of Rights" which would include the right of every American in the postwar world to a decent home, the right to an education in line with his abilities, the right to modern medical care, the right to a job with good wages, with a guarantee of full production for businessmen and farmers.

I recommended that the President schedule a speech presenting this comprehensive postwar program to the American people immediately after his return from the Cairo-Teheran conferences with Churchill which were scheduled late in November. He planned to leave for home on a Navy cruiser on December 2, and I suggested that he might prepare his final draft of the speech during his return voyage across the Atlantic.

In this speech, as I saw it, he would describe his meetings with American soldiers, sailors, Marines and airmen in the Mediterranean area, express his admiration for their spirit and courage and then voice his personal interest in their concern about the kind of America they would return to after the war.

I suggested that the President might say that he had been bombarded with questions from young GI's which were disturbingly uniform in theme. "When the war is over, will I be able to get a good job? . . . Will I be able to get a good education? . . . Will I be able to own a farm? . . . a small business?"

In the speech as I outlined it, the President would then spell out his concept of a "Second Bill of Rights" on which he would base his requests to Congress for his postwar legislation, and which in more general language might ultimately become part of the Constitution of the United States, similar to Thomas Jefferson's Bill of Rights. I proposed that following his speech he present to Congress each month in the coming session, legislation designed to deal with one element of his "Second Bill of Rights." In February, for instance, he might propose legislation to provide adequate housing for every American family; in March, education; in April, public health; and so on.

I added that if the President should decide to proceed with this plan, he and his Administration would be identified in the public mind with a dramatic effort to create a new postwar America of opportunity and individual dignity with a greater measure of economic, political and social justice.

I admitted that Congress, in the negative mood which prevailed at the time, would probably fail to take significant action on such proposals. But this would set the stage for him to take his case to the American people and express his determination that we should never turn back to the hunger, fear and insecurity of the 1930's. If Congress refused adamantly to take the necessary steps, he would have no alternative but to run again for President on the solid postwar domestic platform provided by the "Second Bill of Rights."

Rosenman was keenly interested and said he would do his best to persuade the President to consider the proposal before he left Washington for Cairo on November 11. A few days later my memorandum was returned to Rosenman with a handwritten note from the President asking, "Sam, what do I do about this?" Rosenman urged me not to be discouraged and added that, as the President thought about it, he believed the idea would appeal to him.

Roosevelt returned to Washington on December 17, but there were no indications that he planned to deliver the speech. I was about to give up when Sam Rosenman told me in confidence that the President was planning to use my material as the basis for his forthcoming State of the Union message on January 11, 1944.

The President had a bad cold on January 11 and did not deliver his message to Congress in person. It was read for him. But that night he went on all national networks for one of his famous "fireside chats," in which he presented the message to the radio audience. It followed my proposed text closely, even to the title, a "Second Bill of Rights." In the same speech he also used the phrase "economic bill of rights," which later became the preferred title.

The message contained the following:

This Republic had its beginning and grew to its present strength under the protection of certain inalienable political rights—among them the right of free speech, free press, free worship, trial by jury, freedom from unreasonable searches and seizures. They were our rights to life and liberty.

We have come to a clear realization of the fact that true individual freedom cannot exist without economic security and independence. Men in need are not free men. People who are hungry and out of a job are the stuff of which dictatorships are made.

In our day these economic truths have become accepted as self-evident. We have accepted, so to speak, a second Bill of Rights under which a new basis of security and prosperity can be established for all—regardless of station, race, or creed.

Among these are:

The right to useful and remunerative jobs in the industries, or shops or farms or mines of the nation;

The right to earn enough to provide adequate food and clothing and recreation;

The right of every farmer to raise and sell his products at a return which will give him and his family a decent living;

The right of every businessman, large and small, to trade in an atmosphere of freedom from unfair competition and domination by monopolies at home and abroad;

The right of every family to a decent house;

The right to adequate medical care and the opportunity to achieve and enjoy good health;

The right to adequate protection from the economic fears of old age, sickness, accident, and unemployment;

The right to a good education.

All of these rights spell security. And after this war is won we must be prepared to move forward in the implementation of these rights, to new goals of human happiness and well-being.

I ask the Congress to explore the means for implementing this Economic Bill of Rights—for it is definitely the responsibility of the Congress so to do.

The President did not, however, follow through on the part of my plan that called for the introduction of legislation in Congress every month designed to implement, one by one, each point on the "Economic

Bill of Rights." Although Rosenman, others and myself continued to press for this postwar domestic legislation, the President's attention was focused on the problem of winning the war and we made little progress.

Another reason, I believe, why he failed to introduce this legislation in the 1944 session of Congress was that he was reluctant to run for a fourth term and determined that he would not actively campaign for one. Although it sounds remarkably naïve for such a sophisticated political leader, I believe it was his original hope that he could somehow remain aloof from politics, concentrate on his Presidential responsibilities, and still be re-elected for one more term in November, 1944. The American people knew him; if they really wanted him to serve for a fourth term, he would do so. But he would not lift his little finger to get it—unless, he added characteristically, the opposition should distort the record.

Mrs. Roosevelt, Sam Rosenman and other intimates did their best to persuade the President that his position was unrealistic. Mrs. Roosevelt, I was told, persuaded him to put on the leg brace that he had not worn for several years and learn to walk again in the upper hall of the White House. It was not until the campaign began and Dewey made a series of misstatements of fact that FDR was persuaded to come out swinging in the familiar Roosevelt tradition.

But many of us remained concerned. Although military victory was gradually coming into sight, his campaign for re-election centered almost entirely on the war; the problems of our postwar economy were receiving slight attention. We were confident that Roosevelt would win, but once the war was over his opponents could argue plausibly that he had no public mandate for the liberal, full-employment program which we believed to be essential in the postwar era.

Then, in mid-October Sam Rosenman called on me to draft a speech outlining our proposals for the postwar period. I went to work at once. In my draft the President would establish as our national postwar goal the total commitment of all our human and material resources to the building of a new and more democratic American society.

According to our economists, "full employment" in the postwar period would mean 57 million jobs, and my version called for whatever government and private investment might be required to create that number.

After a year of disappointment, I had little hope that anything would come of my efforts. But on the night of October 28, when I was working late in my office, the telephone buzzed and my secretary, Marcella Eastman, said, "Turn on your radio—quick—Roosevelt is on with our speech." In classic Roosevelt fashion, the President had rounded off the figure of 57 million jobs which I had given him for full employment, and as a result the speech has gone down in history as the "sixty million jobs" speech. The following excerpts will illustrate the general thrust:

> Last January, in my message to the Congress on the State of the Union, I outlined an Economic Bill of Rights on which "a new basis of security and prosperity can be established for all."
>
> Now, this Economic Bill of Rights is the recognition of the simple fact that, in America, the future of the worker, the future of the farmer lies in the well-being of private enterprise; and that the future of private enterprise lies in the well-being of the worker and the farmer.
>
> To assure the full realization of the right to a useful and remunerative employment, an adequate program must, and if I have anything to do about it will, provide America with close to sixty million productive jobs.
>
> I foresee an expansion of our peacetime productive capacity that will require new facilities, new plants, new equipment—capable of hiring millions of men.
>
> I propose that the government do its part in helping private enterprise to finance expansion of our private industrial plant through normal investment channels.
>
> Business, large and small, must be encouraged by the government to expand its plants, to replace its obsolete or worn-out equipment with new equipment.
>
> The foreign trade of the United States can be trebled after the war.

On the Wednesday morning after the election, Mrs. Roosevelt telephoned Steb to ask us to come to dinner at the White House on the following Saturday night on a "very informal basis." To our surprise, there were only the President, Mrs. Roosevelt, Steb and I. We then realized this was Roosevelt's way of expressing his appreciation for my having pulled out of the Connecticut Senate campaign in 1944 and remaining OPA Administrator, to which I referred in Chapter 5.

Shortly after we arrived, Roosevelt entered the room in his wheelchair, started mixing martinis and launched into a discussion of the election. The President was in good spirits and particularly amused by a story in the evening newspaper describing Dewey's "exhaustion" after the election and his trip south to recuperate. The President described his last long day of campaigning on the day before election through the streets of Brooklyn in an open car during freezing rain; the contrast between his physical stamina and his younger opponent's apparent lack of it greatly pleased him.

After dinner I had an opportunity to discuss with Mrs. Roosevelt my concern over our lack of planning for economic and social development in the postwar period. She had been not only a supporter of our proposals but an active promoter of the Economic Bill of Rights.

Mrs. Roosevelt suggested that I outline for the President the specific actions which would be required to carry out our proposed objectives, with particular reference to the President's "sixty million jobs" speech in Chicago.

The following day I started work on another memorandum to the President. After listing the actions required to carry out the program he had agreed to in principle, I proposed that I be authorized to put together a small staff and work out the details. This would enable the President to spell out a dramatic new domestic postwar program in his inaugural message and then present it item by item to Congress.

I sent copies of this memorandum to Judge Rosenman and Jim Byrnes, asking for their support. Rosenman reacted positively. However, Byrnes was noncommittal; his attention was devoted to more immediate questions.

On a Sunday afternoon in early December I called on Mrs. Roosevelt at the White House to tell her of my lack of progress, and she spoke quite frankly of her own frustrations. Her husband, she said with her extraordinary objectivity, continued largely to be focused on the problems of the war and consequently almost all of his visitors were diplomats, generals or admirals.

Under these conditions she felt that her primary responsibility was "to bring the American people to the President." Although she was, as always, hopeful, she had nothing encouraging to report. The President was then in Warm Springs, Georgia, and she said that she spoke with him on the telephone every morning, often stressing the need for an immediate beginning to our postwar planning.

"I have learned by experience," she said, "to recognize the point at which the President's patience is about to give out and he will begin to scold me. At that moment I hurriedly say, 'Franklin, my car is waiting, I must be on my way. I shall call you again tomorrow.'"

However, in his State of the Union message of 1945, the President indicated that he planned to offer specific proposals at an early date in the future. Just before he left on his February trip to Yalta to meet Churchill and Stalin, shortly before his death, he asked Sam Rosenman to "begin to get the material together for three special messages to Congress" on social security, education and health.[1] The first time I felt really assured of the President's readiness to tackle the challenge of postwar America was in my last talk with him just before he left for Warm Springs in late March.

Although the President looked tired, he did not seem as worn out as

1. Samuel I. Rosenman, *Working with Roosevelt*, New York, Harper & Brothers, 1952, p. 469.

many people later described him. When I commented on his bad cold, he said, "Warm Springs will cure that in a week!"

The President asked me what I planned to do after the war, and I replied that I did not intend to go back to business and I hoped to find some role in government, dealing perhaps with the new housing, welfare and educational programs that were urgently needed.

Suddenly the President said, "I have just the job for you. How would you like to be the first Secretary of the new government department I plan to set up after the war—the Department of Public Welfare, which will also include health and education?" I replied that there was no job that I would rather tackle.

The President's death on April 12, 1945, shocked the nation and the world; not only those of us who had believed in his leadership and ability, but many who had bitterly opposed him.

When the news came in on the news ticker, I was called out of a meeting with OPA's steel advisory committee, which included most of the leaders of the steel industry. For the preceding thirteen years, they had considered Roosevelt an advocate of "creeping socialism" and a threat to everything they had been brought up to believe in. But when I reported the news, there was the look verging on fear on many of their faces.

They and many others like them found it difficult to visualize the United States Government without Roosevelt at the helm. A whole generation had grown into adulthood since that dramatic March day in 1933, when, in the depths of the Depression, our newly inaugurated President told us that America had nothing to fear but fear itself. It was difficult right then for most Americans to visualize our national government except as a projection of his policies and character.

Much has been written about Roosevelt, and it is difficult to add any fresh insights. But on one subject I am in a position to speak with authority and with conviction. Many of Roosevelt's critics have charged him with being a bad administrator. With this judgment I cannot concur. Although Roosevelt's techniques were unorthodox, he was, I believe, a remarkably effective administrator. In large measure this was because he was aware of the inflexibility of the old-line federal agencies and the stifling weight of the federal bureaucracy which had accumulated over the years.

When he became President in 1933, Roosevelt knew that the Department of Labor, the Department of Agriculture, the Department of Commerce and other established governmental organizations were not capable of moving quickly enough and decisively enough to administer the radical new "crash" programs which were required to get our economy moving again. Consequently, he bypassed most of the established government machinery to set up temporary administrative agencies designed to deal pragmatically with emergency situations. Among these "alphabet" organizations were the Works Progress Administration (WPA), the National Recovery Administration (NRA), the National Youth Administration (NYA), the Farm Security Administration (FSA) and many others.

As we moved toward World War II, and it became apparent that massive new demands would soon be placed upon our economy, FDR adopted the same approach. Instead of assigning administrative responsibility for agriculture programs to the Department of Agriculture, labor programs to the Department of Labor, programs concerning business to the Department of Commerce and so on, he established a set of brand-new temporary war agencies: OPA, WPB, WFA, OWI and the rest. At least in their initial stages these new agencies were relatively free of the overstaffing, cumbersome procedures and negative habits of mind that ultimately come to plague all large organizations whether governmental or private. The administrators considered themselves politically expendable and were so considered by the President.

Instead of fighting this encroachment on their bureaucratic preserves, the established federal departments seemed to welcome it. It relieved them of new responsibilities in uncharted areas of government which would inevitably bring them into conflict with Congress and subject them to criticism from the press. Moreover, they knew that eventually these emergency organizations would outlive their usefulness. The battered wartime administrators would then depart from the scene, whatever functions remained would be assigned to the established departments, and the relative calm of "normal times" would once again be resumed.

Roosevelt also had an unorthodox way of getting rid of important officials who he felt were not competent to handle their jobs. Instead of publicly firing them, he would gradually reduce their responsibilities and authority. The official in question would begin to discover that his administrative responsibilities were eroding and that he was being consulted less and less. More often than not he took the path of least resistance and sent his resignation for "personal reasons" to the President, who "reluctantly" accepted it with appropriate praise for the departee's "untiring contribution to the war effort."

This approach does not meet the usual textbook standards of government administration. It was untidy and confusing to the public as well as to the participants. But it often allowed Roosevelt to avoid politically costly front-page collisions with strong-minded individuals who did not measure up, while enabling them to slip quietly out of Washington with a minimum of damage to their reputations.

Although, as I have noted, endless books, articles and analyses have been written about Roosevelt, what I believe may be the most important book of all has not yet appeared. This book, which might appropriately be entitled "Mr. and Mrs. Franklin D. Roosevelt," would deal with the partnership that existed between the President and his remarkable wife. For all that he succeeded in doing she deserved a major share of credit. She helped bring to the surface his compassion, his concern for people and for human dignity. And it was she, in a sense, who brought the American people to him and encouraged him to give himself to the people. Their relationship is a challenge to the ablest of our biographers, and I earnestly hope that someday this book will be written.

CHAPTER 10

THE LINE BEGINS TO BEND

ON APRIL 13, 1945, the day after Roosevelt's death, I sent my resignation to President Truman. Although this is a traditional action by all Presidential appointees when a new President takes over, I was sufficiently battered to feel that it really was someone else's turn.

Ten days later when I was called to the White House, Truman was still in a state of shock. The impossible had occurred and suddenly he had inherited all the burdens of the American Presidency. Truman described with deep feeling his hopes and his fears, and when he said that I must stay in what he described as "the toughest domestic job in Washington" until the war was finally won, there was nothing for me to say but yes.

I assumed I was making a long commitment. The impending collapse of the Germans would assure ultimate victory in the Pacific, but the Japanese forces still remained formidable and the war could be expected to drag on for many more months.

Before the defeat of Germany military requirements had been absorbing more than half our entire production. Yet even though the danger of a runaway inflation under these conditions was obvious, we had barely managed to maintain the Congressional and business support necessary to keep the lid on. Now with more than half of the war won, the pressures for decontrol and a return to "normal conditions" would be even more difficult to resist.

A story which was going the rounds in Washington at that time illustrated the current mood. The Southern members of the Senate and the House had always felt a somewhat proprietary interest in the city of Washington, and this greatly increased during the 1930's. Throughout the Depression most of the Southern states had suffered even more heavily than the rest of the country from low agricultural prices and lack of investment capital, which explains why Southern Democratic leaders brought up in the Populist tradition played a major role in putting through Roosevelt's New Deal. With Germany's defeat signaling the beginning of the end, their nostalgic desire for the good old days when Washington was a Southern city began to grow.

The story concerned two Southern Senators discussing the likely length of the war. One asserted that the war would go on for at least five more years. When his friend asked what made him so pessimistic, he replied, "Even though the Germans have quit, it will take us at least two more years to beat the Japanese and then another three years after that to drive the damn-Yankees out of Washington." To which his friend responded, "You shouldn't talk that way about the Yankees. They are our allies, like the Russians."

The time had now come to take the initiative in removing controls wherever possible. On June 13, in a letter to William H. Davis, who had recently left the chairmanship of the War Labor Board to become Director of the Office of Economic Stabilization, I wrote:

> We are all aware that the end of hostilities in Europe requires a thorough re-examination of the scope of price controls as well as other wartime controls generally. Price controls must be lifted as rapidly as the need for them disappears.
>
> The time has now come, in my opinion, when decontrol can and must be intensified. . . . Between now and the defeat of Japan the supply of many materials will greatly increase and price pressures will begin to ease in a number of areas.

I recommended that decontrol begin immediately for products or services where there was no reason to anticipate an increase in prices above the present ceilings; or where they were insignificant in the budget of the bulk of American families and would not compete for the raw materials used in war production.

But we knew that we were entering a particularly dangerous period. Following the armistice in 1918 the Administration had promptly removed all price and production controls; indeed, Bernard M. Baruch, who had been in charge of the program, had resigned the next day, informing President Wilson that his work was accomplished. In Chapter 2 I wrote of the ensuing collapse of the economy in the winter of 1919. We were determined that this time the cycle of boom and bust must be prevented.

What worried us now was the enormous accumulation of savings.

While we had built a price, wage and rent control dam with surprisingly few leaks, the amount of savings behind that dam had been steadily growing. If the public should become convinced that the dam was about to be removed or to collapse, those savings would inundate the market to bid up prices, and the inflation would quickly get out of hand.

The only long-range solution was increased production. But it would be months before there were enough peacetime commodities, such as washing machines, automobiles, radios, and the like, to absorb the bulk of this pent-up purchasing power.

During the war, Leon Henderson, myself and others repeatedly had warned the Treasury Department and the Congress of precisely this danger. To reduce the pressure to manageable proportions, we had advocated either much higher wartime taxes or a compulsory savings plan or a combination of the two until the production of consumer goods and services could begin to match the demand.

Even at the war's peak we had been unable to persuade the Treasury Department or the White House to seek the necessary Congressional action. Now with the war half won it would be impossible. Under these circumstances, the only hope of avoiding a very sharp rise in prices was to keep our stabilization program reasonably intact. Whenever these controls were dismantled, we must expect a rise in prices, but if they could be maintained for a year or two, the rise might be limited.

Suddenly, in early August came the nuclear attacks on Hiroshima and Nagasaki, and a year sooner than we had anticipated the war was brought to a close with a suddenness which rivaled its beginning.

Having fulfilled my April commitment to stay "until the end of the war," I once again sent my resignation to the White House. And once again the President asked me to stay. The first time, just after Roosevelt's death, I felt I had no choice; but now I was sorely torn. On the one hand, I told the President, I felt a deep commitment both to the objectives of the program and also to the men and women with whom I had worked so closely for these difficult years.

On the other hand, I had been OPA Administrator for three exhausting years, and in my efforts to "hold the line" I had been under heavy fire from a group of Senators and Congressmen who, even though they had been and probably still were a minority, were both dogged and articulate. If I stayed any longer, they would assert that I secretly enjoyed controlling things and that I wanted a permanent job.

If a fresh individual took over at this point, I said, all but the most irresponsible of our critics would in all decency give him time to settle down, and he might look forward for at least a few months to a bureaucratic honeymoon. Since the acute period of inflationary danger would probably be over in eighteen months, this respite might be all that was needed to see us through.

Then there was my obligation to my family. Since the day after Pearl Harbor I had been working an average of eighty hours a week. I badly needed a rest and I was eager to renew my acquaintance with my wife and children. Finally, I told the President I thought we could persuade most of our key people to stick to their jobs for the last crucial year regardless of my own decision. With the exception of Jim Brownlee, my deputy in charge of the Price Department who had recently resigned after a mild heart attack, our organization was still largely intact.

The President brushed all this aside. If I left now, he asked, how could I convince others that they should remain? He had been President for only four months and needed experienced people in key positions and that included me.

Finally, we adopted a compromise. I would stay until January 1, 1946, and with the President's support firmly hold the price line regardless of the ripe fruit and dead cats that would be thrown in my direction. By that time I would be established as a kind of ogre and no one, including the President, would ever want to see me again. The brief period of respite my successor might expect could be prolonged by easing some of the old price ceilings. This might enable the Administration to maintain a reasonably acceptable price level for a year or two more, when the controls could be dismantled without serious danger. I returned to my office, called a meeting of my principal associates and after considerable discussion persuaded all but one or two to stay as long as I did.

We had no illusions about the difficulties in working out a balance between wages and prices during the reconversion period. Since the "hold the line" order, labor with few exceptions had cooperated with business and government to increase production and to maintain price stability. But their "no strike" pledge had ended on V-J Day. Although labor had come to trust OPA's ability to stand up under pressure, they were doubtful, now that the war was over, that the Administration as a whole was prepared to continue to cope with the inevitable demands from business.

A crucial labor-management conference on the reconversion period originally scheduled for immediately after V-J Day had to be postponed because of disagreements over an agenda. Administrative confusion in the wage stabilization program, following the unexpected termination of the war and some of Truman's new appointments, added to the uncertainties.

The situation in regard to wages was, in fact, extremely complex.

On one hand were the vast reserves of savings with their enormous inflationary potential to which I have referred; on the other was the fact that several million workers would now have a sharp cut in take-home pay as reconversion from war production to peace production took place. A cutback to a forty-hour week from the wartime forty-eight-hour week, with the eight extra hours paid on a time-and-a-half basis, would be equivalent to the loss of twelve hours or fully one-fourth of the former weekly wage.

Since it was clear that this fragile situation could not be expected to remain on dead center indefinitely, and no one seemed prepared to take the lead, I decided on my own initiative discreetly and informally to explore with a few key labor and business leaders the posibility of establishing a new wage-price balance to carry us through until a reasonably adequate supply of goods and services was assured.

After some exploratory talks (which I emphasized were wholly off-the-record) with Philip Murray, president of the CIO and of the Steelworkers; William Green, president of the American Federation of Labor; and Walter P. Reuther, president of the Automobile Workers, I posed the following question: Was it possible to develop a new wage-price formula that would enable us to avoid the strikes which would only serve to cut back production and further increase the dangers of inflation?

Their response was cautiously affirmative, and the following formula emerged: all hourly wage rates would immediately be raised 10 percent by the Wage Stabilization Board, and OPA would do all it could to minimize the impact of this wage increase on prices. On this basis labor would agree to forgo all strikes for one year. The labor leaders all thought they could sell this to their rank and file.

I then met confidentially with Eric Johnston, president of the U.S. Chamber of Commerce, and two or three other respected business leaders, told them of my discussion with the labor leaders and asked if they thought business in general would cooperate in such a program.

Their response was equally encouraging, and I thought we might be on the verge of an important breakthrough. One year of uninterrupted production would go far toward restoring the production levels required to meet the shortages that had accumulated during the war years and thereby hasten the elimination of both price and wage controls.

But the story had an unhappy ending. Lewis B. Schwellenbach, a Senatorial friend of President Truman, who had become Secretary of Labor on May 23, was determined to play a more active policy-making role than had Roosevelt's Labor Secretary, Miss Frances Perkins. Wage stabilization, he felt, was one of his key responsibilities, and even though he knew very little about it, he was not prepared to leave the decisions to others. During the summer he had been in conflict with the War Labor Board over wage policies. In mid-September at his request the Board was incorporated into the Department of Labor, and the National Wage Stabilization Board was created to assume some of WLB's old duties.

I pointed out to Schwellenbach, with whom I had excellent personal relations, that we were moving through an explosive domestic period and that whoever got caught in the middle between labor and industry was likely to get hurt. Will Davis of the Office of Economic Stabilization and Willard W. Wirtz, formerly of WLB and now the head of the new Wage Stabilization Board, were, like myself, already battered and expendable. Would it not be wiser, I suggested, for him to remain aloof as Miss Perkins had done and then a year or so later, when the pressures were dying down, emerge unblemished as a fresh face with new ideas?

Schwellenbach, who was ill and not regularly available for discussion, refused to recommend that Truman go ahead with my 10 percent plan. He was persuaded that the danger of inflation was exaggerated and that we could safely remove most controls immediately. Since the President was unwilling to overrule his newly appointed Labor Secretary, I knew my proposal was doomed.

As the weeks wore on, the pressures from the labor rank and file on Murray, Green and Reuther and other leaders became, as we had feared, more than they could withstand. On September 14, Walter Reuther demanded a 30 percent wage increase for his one million United Automobile Workers, which turned out to be the opening gun of a nationwide drive for higher wages. After several weeks of unsuccessful negotiations the workers at General Motors went out on strike on November 21. In December, Philip Murray of the Steelworkers followed with a request for a similar increase, announcing that if his negotiations with U.S. Steel failed he would close the steel industry in January.

In the meantime, OPA was being swamped with letters from consumers who had supported us throughout the war and who were now concerned about the future. Although they were weary of rationing, they feared higher prices and hoped that somehow we could continue to hold them in check.

The first ration programs to go were gasoline and fuel rationing, followed by tires. After the surrender of the Germans in May, 1945, the military demand for fuel had sharply decreased, and with the sudden collapse of Japan these programs were no longer needed.

In the broadcast from the White House on the evening of August 15, V-J Day, I had the pleasure of telling the American people, the vast

majority of whom had given us their support and cooperation throughout the wartime years, that we had lifted gasoline rationing. "Now," I
said, "you can take your gasoline and fuel oil coupons and paste them
in your memory book. . . . Rationing has been lifted, too, on all canned
fruits and vegetables . . . also stoves. . . . It's a pleasure for us at last to
be able to bring you good news."

While we were eager further to relieve our administrative burden by
getting rid of meat rationing, this raised certain difficulties. Stories of
famine conditions in the war-torn areas of Europe and Asia were beginning to appear in the press, and extensive plans were under way for
relief shipments of American grain.

As long as we held down the prices of meat we could limit the amount
of grain that could profitably be fed to cattle and hogs. Although this
meant somewhat less meat and fewer fancy cuts of beef for American
families, it released large quantities of grain to famine-threatened areas
overseas.

Since continued rationing was required to reduce the pressure on
meat prices, this led to another divisive controversy within our government. One highly respected citizen, brought in by the President as a
special adviser, was so exasperated by my efforts to assure larger amounts
of grain to ease hunger overseas that he exploded in a White House
meeting with the comment, "The Chinese have been starving for centuries. Why should we get so excited about them now?"

We had the strong support of Fiorello La Guardia, Herbert Lehman
and others in the United Nations Relief and Rehabilitation Agency, who
were responsible for the famine relief shipments and who felt as I
did that people should be given priority over pigs. However, it was
inevitable, I suppose, that the psychological pressures to eliminate controls in the new post-emergency atmosphere would make this a battle
we could not win.

The War Food Administration insisted that rationing of meat was no
longer necessary, and the President after some hesitation supported this
position in a meeting in his office. He then turned to me and said that
since I had carried the burden of these rationing programs for three
years, I should at least have the privilege and the pleasure of going on
the radio and telling the housewives that they could also throw away
their meat rationing coupon books. I felt strongly enough about this issue
to say, "Thank you, Mr. President, but this is a privilege that under the
circumstances I shall leave to others." Consequently, the War Food Administration announced that meat was no longer rationed and the lid
was off the amounts of grain that could be fed to hogs and cattle. OPA
made no public comment.

Throughout October, November and December, we faced the anticipated flood of pressures for price increases. The pressure was particularly intense in regard to consumer durables and automobiles, which had not been produced since before Pearl Harbor.

Senator Taft, as we anticipated, launched a formidable movement on Capitol Hill for the immediate liquidation of all economic controls. Although he and I agreed that rapidly increased production of consumer products, particularly durable goods, was the only way to control inflation, we parted company as usual on how to achieve the increased production. The Senator believed that the answer was higher prices (and profits). We maintained that the answer lay in pouring the recently returned soldiers into the labor pool as rapidly as we could muster them out of the Army while retaining a reasonably stable level of prices and wages.

The most effective way to give returning veterans and others confidence in the effectiveness of the inflation control program, we thought, was to bring consumer products on the market at approximately the prices of October, 1941, just before Pearl Harbor, when a series of price increases had occurred. Thanks to our court- and Congressional-approved pricing standards, which required first the wholesaler and then, if necessary, the retailer to absorb whatever increases we might be forced to give the manufacturer (as long as profits at their level remained "generally" above the 1936–39 level of the industry), we came through reasonably well.

The pressure for higher prices was a heavy burden on OPA, but I felt that it was understandable. The war had been long and difficult, and businessmen were weary of all government controls, with trips to Washington, and with prolonged talks with bureaucrats who somehow never seemed quite to understand their problems. However, I began to feel somewhat less tolerant when in an effort to force wholly unnecessary increases in prices a number of professional lobbyists began to blame us for shortages of consumer goods. I was particularly disturbed to read full-page advertisements demanding that I change our OPA policies prepared by my old firm, Benton & Bowles, for the National Association of Manufacturers.

The reason for these shortages, of course, was the war. For four years such "consumer durables" as refrigerators, washing machines, most kitchenware and a host of other products were not produced at all because the first priority was to meet the military requirements. This had created a huge backlog of demand which would take some time to fill.

The refusal of the War Production Board to continue most production controls, which were an essential element in the price control operation, made matters worse. For instance, when the War Production Board, over my protests, removed most production controls on textiles, the industry promptly shifted its looms to such items as curtains and bedspreads from which price controls had been removed. As a result returning veterans had difficulty finding pajamas and shirts. A flood of publicity releases and advertisements poured into newspaper offices and into Congress blaming these shortages on OPA.

By early November, 1945, most key staff members of the War Production Board had already left Washington to resume their peacetime occupations, many of them, as they left, gaily canceling the production regulations they had been administering. As controls over production were removed, manufacturers were free to concentrate on whatever items were most profitable. This created additional shortages of essential consumer goods.

There was much less pressure for relaxation of rent controls, which had been extraordinarily effective during the war. The pressures of millions of tenants to maintain effective rent controls, reinforced by returning veterans, were stronger than most members of Congress were prepared to challenge.

Since most products under price control are shipped across state lines, price controls required national legislation. But rent controls in many areas continued for several years under city or state jurisdiction after price controls had been discontinued. Mayors, governors and state legislators could not ignore skyrocketing rents in their constituencies and still remain in office.

During this difficult period, the morale throughout the OPA's national, regional and district offices stood up remarkably well. Most OPA employees felt they had been carrying out a crucially important wartime responsibility and they were anxious to see it through. This same spirit was evident in the war price and ration boards.

On V-J Day the OPA organization consisted of 5,428 local boards, with 275,000 volunteers and 63,217 paid employees. Within two months after the surrender of Japan we had cut our paid staff by 2,500 and a month later by an additional 15,000. By January, 1946, the ration department had been completely abolished.

Ultimately, I believe, the efforts of our local price and ration boards will be recognized as one of the most important developments in World War II. Their effectiveness cannot wholly be judged in terms of efficiency, which, nevertheless, was high. Even more important was the willingness and even eagerness of countless everyday Americans to serve their communities and their country when they were given a chance to do so. Most OPA volunteers signed up for "the duration," and with relatively few exceptions they stuck to their difficult, unglamorous jobs as long as their services were needed.

In the last months of 1945 as I watched this vast organization shrink in size and responsibility, I confess that I had mixed feelings. I felt a sense of pride that this complex federal program had successfully been administered by the people themselves in direct day-to-day dealings with their own neighbors and fellow citizens, coupled with relief that this program was no longer needed.

At the same time I wondered how many of the departing volunteers would find equally satisfying roles in peacetime development of their neighborhoods and communities. I did not express these emotions to anyone but my closest friends. But the nagging question remains: How can we find in peacetime the "moral equivalent of war"?

While we had anticipated the clamor to do away with controls that came from business, organized labor and many members of Congress and the Administration, we had not foreseen the backing that the public as a whole would continue to give us. Instead of being bruised and bloodied as we expected to be, we became increasingly identified as guardians of the public interest and heroes of the consumers. Cartoons depicting me in the role of Horatius at the bridge and as the Little Dutch Boy with his finger in the dike were commonplace. Occasionally, we even had some applause from Capitol Hill.

Our public support was widely reflected in the press.

The Milwaukee *Journal* stated on November 14, 1945:

> Few people today will argue that price controls should be immediately and indiscriminately dropped, yet hundreds will appeal for freedom to make their own prices for the products they sell. Chester Bowles says that that doesn't make sense. It doesn't.

The St. Louis *Post-Dispatch*, on November 16:

> In Chester Bowles rests the will and hope of the quiet millions who do not send delegations and dispatch telegrams. The premature end of what he stands for, they know, would commence an insane orgy of prices, hurting the quiet millions hardly more in the collapse at the end than in the dizzy rise.
>
> One can only wonder what keeps Bowles in the OPA front line against all the vicious assaults, while the resolution of his own superior grows steadily weaker.

The New York *Post*, on December 7:

> Bowles, as head of the Office of Price Administration, is fighting with magnificent courage—and, unfortunately, fighting almost single-handedly, so far as government officials are concerned—to save the country from a glorious ruinous spree of rising prices. Such a spree would be an unmitigated disaster for every one of us.

This support was also evident in the public opinion polls that we had conducted regularly throughout the war. In mid-November, 1945, I received the following from our information department:

> According to the countrywide survey which we have just completed, the public support we have had for the last three years is undiminished. The way in which OPA has handled not only price controls but rationing is still overwhelmingly approved by the women who do the shopping. Ninety-one percent say that OPA has done a "good" or "fairly good" job in handling price controls and only 9% say it has done a "poor job." The support of what remains of rationing is almost equally great.

Despite continued attacks by special interest groups, OPA held prices down through 1945 thanks to substantial public support and the backing of President Truman, as shown in this G. K. Berryman cartoon. *Courtesy The Washington (D.C.) Star.*

This was support which neither the President nor I had anticipated in August when he had agreed to release whatever might be left of me on January 1, 1946. I had become a symbol of "holding the line" to the American public, and my presence in Washington seemed to be a psychological reassurance that inflation could and would be controlled.

Consequently, the President, who was under great political pressure himself to give in here and give in there, asked me to stay for six months longer, as he said, "until the Price Control Act is assured one more year's extension from Congress," and to see that price and rent controls were eliminated in a careful and orderly way as production grew to meet consumer demands. We assumed that all wartime controls would be eliminated by July 1, 1947.

I told the President frankly that I thought he was asking me to stay in an impossible job. The OPA, I said, could not continue to function with almost no support from other agencies within the government. I described my continuing difficulties with the War Production Board and the reason why without production controls price controls were nearly impossible.

The President listened attentively and seemed to understand the almost hopeless conditions under which we were working. The discussion went on for more than an hour and I finally gave in. If the President would firmly direct the WPB and other relevant government agencies to carry out their responsibilities, if I could plan on a two weeks' rest before February 1, and if I could again get my family's agreement, I would stay until July 1.

Why I agreed, I do not honestly know. Probably there was a variety of reasons: a knowledge that if I left most of my associates would go too, a desire not to let the President down, a faint hope that somehow we could still carry out our objectives, influenced by the extraordinary support we were still getting from most of the people.

But this time I met stiff opposition on my own home front. Our decision to leave Washington in January had been firm, and Steb and the children were at least as pleased as I was at the prospect. But, finally, it was agreed once again that instead of our long-postponed return to Connecticut we would vacation for two weeks at Yeoman's Hall just outside of Charleston, South Carolina, and then carry on until July 1.

But within a few days OPA confronted yet another crisis—this time in regard to steel prices—that shook us up considerably. As I have mentioned earlier, the steelworkers had announced that they would strike in January if the industry did not meet their wage demands. Industry, in turn, had told the government it needed a price increase to enable it to do so. Since a strike in the steel industry would slow production in many other industries and thereby further add to the inflationary pressures, the government, committed to both increasing production and reducing inflationary pressures, was caught in the middle.

The situation was familiar. The leaders of the steel industry, most of whom had been cooperative during the war, were, I believe, genuinely convinced that following the war our economy would slip back to prewar levels of production and that their plants, which had been expanded during the war, would soon be operating at no better than 50-to-60 percent capacity.

If this assumption were in fact correct, a price increase would have been necessary. However, as OPA saw it, demand for steel for the next few years would significantly exceed the present production capacity. Consequently, we were convinced that the steel industry could grant a moderate increase in wages and continue to earn very generous profits at the current price of $55 a ton.

We therefore rejected the U.S. Steel request for a $7-a-ton increase, but to avoid any possibility of hardship agreed to a price rise of $2.50 a ton. The industry promptly announced that this was inadequate. In this atmosphere negotiations broke down, and the steelworkers went on strike on January 21. According to Washington gossip, the industry's position was based on the conviction, following private talks with John Snyder, whom the President had recently brought in as Director of War Mobilization and Reconversion, and staff members of the Office of Reconversion, that the Administration could eventually be persuaded to grant additional price concessions. Consequently, they were in no hurry to bargain.

These rumors (which later turned out to be correct), in view of the recent assurances which I had been given by the President, were profoundly disturbing. But since there was nothing more that I could do for the moment, Steb and I decided to take the brief vacation we had promised ourselves. But before leaving for Charleston I wrote the President on January 24, again underscoring my concern over the government's apparent inability to stand up under pressures in regard to the domestic economy and my fear of the consequences.

DEAR MR. PRESIDENT:

As I write this letter, I am fearful that we are on the brink of failure—not because this agency is unequal to its task, not because we lack public support, not because the policies you have declared are weak or unwise, but simply because repeated statements and actions of responsible officials are leading business, labor, and the public to believe that the Administration does not really intend to hold to the position it has officially taken.

I have reviewed for you a number of the issues on which a weak course, rather than a firm course, has been taken over the objections of the Office of Price Administration. They exemplify a trend that has been growing since V-J Day. In its day-to-day operations, OPA encounters chronic reluctance and frequent refusal by other agencies to exercise the powers they possess to aid the stabilization program. Instead of vigorous, constructive cooperation and support, they have one solution to suggest to OPA for almost every problem: increase the ceilings or remove the controls.

The cumulative effects of such a state of mind and the actions which accompany it are soon felt. For the industry seeking the relaxation of some control or in quest of a price increase, it does not take long to learn where to go to get results. As a consequence, in addition to resisting the usual pressures from industry groups and from members of Congress, we in OPA have had to fight off the still more effective pressures from the very agencies of the government on whose cooperation we should have the greatest reason to rely.

The steel situation is a case in point. . . . That a major industry can obtain a concession by pressure tactics is bad enough, but the common knowledge that an industry's blunt rejection of the first concession will extract a better one totally undermines the position of OPA.

This poses a practical question: How can I effectively go before Congress seeking extension of price and subsidy legislation as I have for the last two years when the declared policies of the Administration which I am charged with executing are constant targets for attack in public statements, in conferences with industry, and even before Congressional committees by high officials of other government agencies and departments?

It is not yet too late to re-establish the integrity of our efforts, but it is rapidly becoming too late. If you make it clear to the responsible officials of the government that a firm anti-inflation program must promptly be substituted for the present policy of "retreat," I believe that the government can ride successfully through this crisis and emerge with its prestige enormously enhanced. Otherwise, the stabilization policy will, I believe, progressively disintegrate.

After a week of golf and sun at Yeoman's Hall, Steb and I were just beginning to unwind when one night on the way into dinner we happened to hear a news broadcast from Washington reporting that John Snyder had agreed to the steel company's demand for an increase of $7 a ton—nearly three times the amount we had decided upon.

The only other occasion when OPA had been overruled on a price ceiling involved rubber pricing in 1944. But this case, coming at a critical moment, was much more serious. Not only would such an increase in steel prices raise the costs of the consumer durables and automobiles on which we had just set price ceilings, but it was totally uncalled for.

I immediately called my office to say that we were returning on the night train and asked that meetings be set up with Snyder and with the President for the next day.

My talk with Snyder convinced me that he failed to understand the problem or its implications, nor apparently did key members of his new staff. My visit with the President, who seemed harassed and tired, was equally unsatisfactory. His position was that he had no alternative but to back up the man who was in effect his deputy.

I had been asked to appear before the House Banking and Currency Committee on the following Monday in my role as OPA Administrator, presumably to answer questions on what, thanks to our enterprising press, was now publicly known to be a serious conflict within the Administration on steel prices. Inevitably, the first question addressed to me would be: "Did you or did you not approve of the recent increase in steel prices?" There were only two ways I could answer this question: first, I might falsely maintain that I knew about the additional increase and in general had approved it; or second, I could tell the truth, that I had vigorously opposed the additional price increase and that it had been ordered by John Snyder without my knowledge while I was out of town.

Obviously I could not lie to the committee, and I had no desire to continue to take public responsibility for a program over which I had to admit to Congress and the public I had no control. This left me with no alternative but to resign. That night I met with several close friends in my home in McLean to write my letter of resignation. I was angry through and through and as a consequence my resignation letter was blunt; it included the following paragraphs:

DEAR MR. PRESIDENT:

The Administration is facing a serious crisis in the fight against inflation. . . . We find ourselves in this situation for reasons which I have mentioned to you on other occasions, i.e., because members of your official family who are working on this program have lacked team work and unity of purpose; because government has failed to maintain a consistent policy; because too often it has succumbed to pressures rather than facts; and because for these very reasons business in general has become convinced that on any really important issue the government will bargain and trade in spite of the clear limitations of law and the established standards.

The House Banking and Currency Committee has expressed its willingness to postpone until Monday its hearings at which I am scheduled to appear. I cannot go before that committee which will inevitably probe deeply into the steel price conflict and honestly express my belief that the present program or any counterinflationary program under John Snyder's leadership and authority can hope to succeed.

I welcomed the strong leadership which both Jimmy Byrnes and Fred Vinson in the Office of War Mobilization and Reconversion gave to the stabilization program. If a man with their convictions were today in a position of top authority, I would be more than willing to go along, confident that in spite of past mistakes we could somehow win through to a successful conclusion.

But this is not the case, and under the circumstances the only possible decision for me is to resign. This I hereby do.

Believe me, I have arrived at this decision with extreme reluctance. I would not have stayed with this thankless and difficult task for four long years if I had not felt a deep sense of personal responsibility for the integrity of the operation and for the results which both you and the Congress have directed OPA to achieve.

I have also been conscious of the tremendous burdens that you carry and I had hoped that I could help lighten those burdens and contribute to the success of the programs and policies for which you stand. This, I fear, is no longer possible.

I am sorrier than I can say that circumstances have led me to this decision.

On Wednesday morning, shortly after my letter was delivered at the White House, I received a call from Bernard Baruch, who since his World War I inflation control assignment had been a kind of "father confessor" to our Presidents. This was closely followed by a call from James Byrnes, who was now Secretary of State.

I first met with Baruch, who strongly urged me to stay at my post. As he often had, he referred to the disastrous results of his own premature removal of price, production and wage controls after World War I and expressed the fear that, once OPA began to fall apart, the whole inflation control program would go with it at a most critical moment.

An hour later Byrnes went over the same ground with me and then proposed a plan, which he emphasized was his own idea and in no sense official. "Would you," he asked, "if the President should ask you to, agree to become Director of Economic Stabilization? This would give you control not only of prices, rents and rationing, but also of wages and production." In this position, Byrnes explained, there would be no danger of my being caught again in the situation I now found myself.

My first reaction was totally negative. But after we had talked about the President's difficulties and Byrnes had presented persuasive arguments that somehow I, and I alone, could still get the stabilization program back on the track, I agreed to discuss the situation with President Truman.

Byrnes then left the room, presumably to call the President, and a few minutes later he returned and asked me to accompany him to the White House. Truman had agreed to Byrnes' proposal, and he now strongly urged me to accept it. With deep reluctance and, I might add, with a clear awareness that the difficulties ahead could well prove insurmountable, I accepted.

CHAPTER 11

THE LINE FINALLY BREAKS

THE OFFICE OF ECONOMIC STABILIZATION had changed little since its beginning in 1942 under James F. Byrnes. OES had no operational responsibilities (these were in the hands of OPA, WPB and the Wage Stabilization Board); it had only a small staff, less than fifty people. But it had the power to set policies on all programs relating to the control of rents, prices, production and wages.[1]

I knew that much of my own time would be spent in meetings with officials within our government and with businessmen, labor and farm representatives and members of Congress; this meant that my most immediate need was for an experienced and tough-minded deputy. Jim Brownlee was the ideal choice. He had left Washington following a heart attack in August, and I doubted that he would be available. But I decided to call him anyway.

I finally located him in the locker room of a golf club in Florida just after he had completed his first round of golf in nearly a year. When I told him what I had agreed to do and why I needed his help, there was a prolonged silence, which he broke by suggesting several alternative possibilities. When I explained why each of these men was out of the question, he asked, "When do you want me to be there?" "Monday morning," I answered, to which he replied, "That's a date."

When I put the receiver down, I felt shaken. Jim was as aware as I of the headaches and brickbats that lay ahead, and his health was still in question. But he knew I needed help and he was prepared to provide

---

1. Unfortunately, as we have seen in Chapter 2 and Chapter 10, OES responsibility in regard to taxes was not clearly defined in the stabilization legislation passed by Congress. This omission proved to be costly.

it regardless of the personal sacrifice. Rarely have I felt so grateful to any individual.

Henry Hart, one of the most creative lawyers in OPA, became my general counsel. John T. Dunlop, professor of labor relations at Harvard, assumed responsibility for OES relations with the Wage Stabilization Board. Bice Clemow from OPA came along as my executive assistant, and Doug Bennet assumed responsibility for our press relations, which I knew would be of crucial importance.

I was particularly encouraged when President Truman agreed to my suggestion that Paul A. Porter, who had demonstrated great administrative ability as Deputy OPA Administrator for Rent, take over my post as OPA Administrator; he was sworn in on February 25, 1946. After several cliff-hanging discussions, the other key members of the OPA staff, with only one or two exceptions, agreed to stick with the program.

On February 23, 1946, the first day in our new offices in the stately Federal Reserve Building, I was confronted with a situation that had nothing to do with inflation, and one that shocked me. Three of the dozen or so lawyers and economists I had brought with me from OPA were black, and the secretary to Bice Clemow was a Japanese-American girl who had been with us throughout the war. Just before lunch I was told that our black employees and the Japanese secretary would not be allowed to use the regular lavatories or to eat in the cafeteria.

OPA's policy of equal rights and opportunities regardless of race, creed or color had been criticized by the many exponents of racial discrimination both in the executive branch of our government and in Congress; some of these racists referred to OPA as "nigger heaven." With the war over, they were now determined that the old racial bars would be restored.

Two weeks before, I had written to Arthur S. Flemming, head of the United States Civil Service Commission, protesting the discrimination against black employees of the Office of Price Administration who were seeking transfers to peacetime jobs within the government. My letter follows:

We in OPA owe our Negro employees, who constitute 14% of our Washington staff, a debt of gratitude for their loyalty and good performance. However, I am concerned with their future opportunities in government. My assistant on personnel matters, whom I had asked to assist them in finding suitable positions, tells me that he is running into difficulties.

Although the State Department needs several messengers, they insist that they must be young, white, male and Gentile.

In the Weather Bureau and the Department of Commerce he was

asked whether the applicants were of "light complexion" and he was told
that they would not be interested in interviewing any "colored applicants."

The Naval Research Laboratory indicated they had no Negro employees
and did not have facilities for them.

The Civil Aeronautics Administration, when reviewing the application
of one Negro employee, asked what university she attended. When she
replied Howard University (which as you know is largely Negro), she was
informed that they did not anticipate any vacancies for which she might
qualify.

I strongly urge that you and the Civil Service Commission take whatever steps may be necessary to assure Negro employees who are no
longer needed by the Office of Price Administration employment opportunities in line with their attributes and experience.

To my dismay, we had now encountered the same problem in the
stabilization program itself. I called Marriner S. Eccles, Chairman of the
Federal Reserve Board, whose administrative office ran the building,
and told him the story. Eccles replied that while he deplored the situation
there was nothing he could do about it. Several of his associates on the
Federal Reserve Board, he said, had "quite prejudiced views on the
subject" and he hoped we would be patient. I replied that, while I
recognized his difficulties, we would have no alternative but to request
the White House to move our offices out of the Federal Reserve Building
and provide us with space elsewhere.

Eccles, who, I believe, personally welcomed my ultimatum, said he
would do his best. Two days later we received word that all discriminatory rules had been withdrawn.

The following month we were plunged into one of the most difficult
crises in the crisis-ridden history of the stabilization program. This time
the onslaught came not from those who wished to raise prices, but
from those who had been among our most ardent supporters—organized
labor.

The steel strike had been settled on February 15 by an 18½-cents-
per-hour wage increase following Snyder's action over our protests in
granting the industry a $7-per-ton price increase. When the Wage
Stabilization Board reluctantly agreed, labor, and indeed almost everybody else, assumed that this increase would automatically apply to all
labor agreements and that OPA would then authorize price increases to
cover the extra costs.

However, I was convinced that the impact of a general wage increase of that magnitude would be more than the program could stand.
It was precisely to avoid such a situation that immediately after the

Japanese surrender I had tried privately and unofficially to negotiate an agreement for a general 10 percent wage increase (about half that obtained by the steelworkers after a costly strike) in return for a pledge by labor that there would be no strikes for at least one year.[2]

Consequently, with a sober understanding that we were opening up a hornet's nest, OES issued a ruling that the 18.5 percent wage increase[3] obtained by the steel industry would be accepted as the highest wage increase to which any manufacturer might agree in negotiating with his union. However, under no circumstances would any wage increase be accepted as the basis for a price increase unless it was called for under our normal "generally fair and equitable" pricing standards. In other words, as long as the existing prices provided an industry with an adequate profit, any wage increase to which it might agree must come out of profits. This was a tough ruling, and we knew that its impact on labor would be explosive.

The next day the leaders of organized labor descended on me as a group to demand that the 18.5 percent wage increase should promptly and automatically be extended to all labor contracts. I replied that our ruling would not be modified, and suggested that it was time for business and labor, instead of expecting government to provide all the answers, to get back into the habit of collective bargaining—a habit which had been broken during the war period.

The next few weeks were among the most dismal I can remember. A steady parade of labor leaders, including the most powerful and up to then the most friendly, passed through my office, each of them in his own way angry, sad, critical and, in several cases, abusive. On one occasion when I was in bed for a few days with the flu, Phil Murray, president of the CIO Steelworkers Union, for whom I had the warmest regard, appeared without warning at my home in McLean and subjected me to a going over I shall never forget. Although his steelworkers had won their 18½ cents per hour, he was speaking, as president of the CIO, for labor in general.

Then suddenly the sun came out. As I entered my office one morning after a particularly stormy session with a labor delegation the previous afternoon, I was told that Phil Murray wanted me on the telephone. "Tell him," I said to my secretary, "that I have gone to the dentist." Then I had second thoughts; this was no way to treat a friend, even one who now disagreed with me so militantly. Reluctantly, I took the call. To my

2. During the winter of 1946 the number of strikes reached an all-time high.
3. The steelworkers obtained an 18½-cents-per-hour increase. Since the basic wage in steel was then about 61 an hour, this also worked out to about 18.5 percent.

amazement, Phil's manner had changed completely. "An old acquaintance," he said, "has just loaned me his forty-foot motor cruiser in
Florida and I am about to leave for a week's fishing. You looked dead-
tired when I saw you yesterday, Chet. How about coming along? I
solemnly promise not to mention strikes, price ceilings or wage rates."

This was no time for me to go fishing, but I felt an immense sense
of relief; it was his way of saying that while he disagreed with my
decision, he accepted it as final and wished to restore our old relationship.
Ten days later the CIO, which for three unforgettable weeks had been
accusing me of every crime a wartime bureaucrat could commit, gave
a small dinner in my honor at the Carlton Hotel and all fourteen of their
vice presidents were present. This was followed by a similar dinner by
the AFL a week or so later. I took these gestures to mean that they
accepted my decision, however reluctantly, and that labor would continue to support me.

OES's crucial ruling forced the labor unions and business back to the
negotiating tables. Two months later, when the negotiations had largely
been completed, reports indicated the average raise in wages had not
been 18.5 percent, but 11 percent, only one percent over the figure labor
itself had informally agreed to accept six months earlier before the
General Motors and U.S. Steel strikes which had cost both labor and
business heavily and slowed down the process of reconversion.

OPA meanwhile was working long hours to establish price ceilings on
the flood of products coming on the market for the first time since
Pearl Harbor, and also to make whatever price adjustments were legally
required to maintain "generally fair and equitable" profits.

To add to our problems, in February the price of cotton emerged as a
major issue. Some of the strongest support for OPA during the war had
come from Senators and Congressmen from cotton-producing states in
the South. We had their backing not only because millions of their low-
income constituents benefited from price control, but also because we
had managed to avoid placing a ceiling price on cotton. This exception
occurred because of the Commodity Credit Corporation's huge reserves
of surplus cotton. In order to keep the price of raw cotton from going
above twenty cents a pound, we would increase the flow of surplus cotton
into the market whenever prices threatened to rise above that price.
This enabled us to keep cotton prices down, while leaving members of
Congress from cotton-producing states free to boast to their constituents
that cotton was the one product of any importance on which there was
no price ceiling.

Now the government's cotton reserves were nearly exhausted, and we
had a choice between two unappealing alternatives: (1) we could leave

cotton prices free to seek their own level,[4] which would assure us continued Southern support in Congress but would result in higher textile and apparel prices; or (2) we could impose a price ceiling on raw cotton, which would enable textile and apparel manufacturers to continue to sell at their current prices.

This was one of the few occasions when my staff was deeply divided on an issue of importance, and the discussions in my office were long and emotional. Even some of the most staunch supporters of our "hold the line" policy argued for a compromise. The inflation control program, they said, was in its last year or so of usefulness, and it was essential that we keep the political support of the Southerners.

Others argued that the most important element thus far in our ability to "hold the price line" had been our consistent refusal regardless of political pressures to compromise on our pricing standards. I shared this view. We had made no exceptions before, and somehow I could not bring myself to make one now. A ceiling on cotton was put into effect, and, as predicted, much of our Southern political support went out the window. In the forthcoming debates over the renewal of the Price Control Act this loss was keenly felt. In retrospect, I think those who advocated a compromise on this issue were right and that I was wrong.

Another crisis occurred the next month that grew out of a blatant case of political blackmail. A few irresponsible individuals, some within the government, had assured the wheat farmers that if they refused to ship their wheat and rice to market at the existing price levels, the government would be forced to increase the price of wheat to secure the grain required to continue our shipments to the war-ravaged areas of Europe and Asia.

This tactic of creating an artificial shortage in order to force an increase in prices and profits was one the cattle owners and meat packers had attempted to use against us during the war. Now the farmers, whose earnings were already at record levels, had decided to take advantage of the mass hunger abroad to raise their incomes.

At first President Truman, who was under constant pressure from all directions, did not fully understand the problem. As a result, one lovely spring night on his yacht, *Williamsburg*, on the Potomac, he was persuaded by a group of farm bloc Senators to agree to a 25-cents-a-bushel increase in the price of wheat.

The next morning when I heard of his decision, I was thunderstruck and telephoned the President to express my concern. This campaign, I said, was unconscionable; the increase in wheat would inevitably spread

4. The increase would probably have been around 35 percent.

to all grain prices including corn, which would force us to raise meat prices and in turn would destroy the fragile balance with wage controls. With his usual frankness Truman expressed his regret at having agreed so quickly and told me he would call a meeting for the next morning to review the question.

The dozen or so people present at the meeting in the President's office included Secretary of State Dean Acheson; Henry A. Wallace, former Secretary of Agriculture, who was then Secretary of Commerce; John Snyder and several others. As I looked around the table, the only potential source of support I could see for my position was Henry Wallace.

The President began by announcing what he called his "tentative" decision to support the Department of Agriculture's request for a wheat price increase. He then asked for my comment. I repeated what I had said the previous day over the telephone, adding that during the war American wheat farmers had made far more money than in any other period in our history and that while their prices were fixed so were their costs. A price increase, I said, would have a disastrous impact on the entire economic stabilization framework, already under heavy strain. After some inconclusive discussion, the meeting was adjourned.

I had no doubt about the outcome. The President, having previously committed himself to the Senators and given me the courtesy of a hearing, would, I thought, now officially overrule me. I returned to my office deeply depressed and told the bad news to Jim Brownlee and my other associates.

A few minutes later the telephone rang, and it was the President. "I have thought this all over carefully," he said, "and I guess that you and I are in the minority. I have decided not to grant the price increase." Later I learned that all the others present at the meeting, including Henry Wallace, had supported the price increase.

While the President had come out on our side, much pressure had already been generated by rumors of an impending price rise. Many wheat growers, egged on by a few irresponsible leaders, continued to hold their wheat off the market while the empty grain ships waited at the docks. Three months later we were forced to grant an increase.

Yet most farm bloc leaders remained generally in favor of price controls. During the war price controls held down their costs of fertilizers, machinery, gasoline and construction materials. Now the farmers were concerned that as price controls weakened, their costs would go up and the prices they received for their products would ultimately go down. What they wanted in peacetime was a ceiling on farm costs and a floor under farm prices. Indeed, just as we began to lose the support of organized labor, the farm bloc emerged as one of the most powerful voices for continued stabilization, a development that greatly disturbed our two principal Senate opponents—Senators Taft and Wherry.

In the meantime, a new threat developed to the wage-price formula. While this formula had been reluctantly accepted by Murray, Green, Reuther and other labor leaders, John L. Lewis, president of the United Mine Workers of America, had ignored it. I admired what Lewis had done for the miners in raising wages, shortening hours and improving working conditions. I also admired his rejection of featherbedding and his readiness to encourage more efficient methods as long as his miners got their proper share.

Yet Lewis had been irresponsible in regard to inflation throughout the war. He asserted that he was fighting for the rights of working people. Although soldiers, as well as citizens, might suffer in the meantime, they would thank him when the war ended because he would have raised wage rates and the economy would be in a healthy state. This judgment, however well intentioned, was unrealistic.

Now with the war at an end, Lewis announced that he was going not only for a higher wage increase than those secured by the leaders of the CIO and the AFL, but also for a major welfare fund and other fringe benefits to take care of hospitalization, retirement, pensions and the like.

Obviously, this was not the time for a major adjustment of this kind. The primary need right now was to keep inflationary pressures in check until production of consumer goods was more in line with demands. Any additional leaks in the dike would lead to a flood. What Lewis was proposing was more than a leak.

The first step in our efforts to counter Lewis' demands was to put together a program that we could live with and one he would find difficult to reject. We did not question Lewis' readiness to shut down the coal mines. But we thought he was shrewd enough to recognize the need for public and Congressional support.

Our package program contained a welfare plan more moderate than his extreme demands, paid for partly by the manufacturers and partly by the workers. Then we quietly encouraged a small electrical company to request in cooperation with its workers the precise welfare program to which we were prepared to agree. When they did so, we studied it, discussed it and then approved it in a widely publicized document in which we defined what a welfare fund could collect and what a welfare fund could not collect under our Wage Stabilization Standards. This gave us a clear precedent with which to deal with Lewis.

Precisely according to his schedule, Lewis presented his demand for a package of wage increases plus a welfare program. And we promptly responded by referring him politely to the precedent we had already set, reiterating that it was the limit that we would accept. Lewis rejected this as inadequate, and on April 1 his coal miners went on strike.

Lewis maintained his pressure through the press and resisted all efforts to come to a settlement, despite the pleas of President Truman. But we did not budge either. Finally, after the government had taken over the mines to assure continued production and a series of negotiations had taken place, an agreement was arrived at. When Lewis came out of the last meeting, scores of reporters and radio people were waiting for the word. Someone shouted, "John, how did you come out?" Lewis roared with laughter, slapped his thigh and said, "How do you *think* John Lewis came out? John Lewis won."

With only a cursory glance at the highly complex contract agreement, most of the newspapermen ran off to their typewriters to write stories which generally reflected Lewis' claim. After they had an opportunity to read the agreement carefully, it began to be clear to everyone that John Lewis had failed to get what he was after. The contract generally fell within our standards. But I shall never forget the skill with which the old warrior handled that press conference. However, soon Lewis joined the voices calling for an end to the stabilization program, and late in 1946 another coal strike broke out.

In mid-April, 1946, we once again went before the Congress with a request for the renewal of the Price Control Act. The familiar lobbies, with some new postwar additions, were there to greet us, and we knew the decision of Congress would be close.

Most consumers were aware of the increasing pressure for higher prices, and, as in the past years, hundreds of thousands of them wrote to their Congressmen and Senators in support of continued controls. The flood of letters was the largest of my three years in Washington, but it came too soon. Opposition leaders skillfully dragged out the debate while the lobbyists increased their activities. The consumers, having written their letters of support, turned to other things.

In May, 1946, in a final effort to save the program for what we believed to be the final year, I worked out a plan with Henry Hart and John Dunlop. We knew that we could not persuade Congress to appropriate the $3 billion necessary to maintain the existing food subsidy program beyond October 1, but if we could persuade Congress to reduce the subsidies gradually, the impact would be materially lessened.

A gradual reduction in turn might enable us to keep the consumer price level from rising more than 5 percent in the next twelve months, and if we could persuade the unions of our ability to restrict the price rise to that figure, they might agree to the one-year "no strike" pledge which I had unofficially proposed immediately after V-J Day.

On a confidential basis I discussed the possibility with the two top staff economists of the CIO and AFL, who had consistently supported us. "Labor," I said, "has received an average increase of 11 percent in wages. In order to save the stabilization program, can your leaders and the rank and file be persuaded to forgo any work stoppages for one full year, or until the Consumer Price Index rises by five percent—whichever comes first?"

They responded positively and agreed to do all they could to persuade the key labor leaders, Phil Murray, Walter Reuther and Bill Green, to go along. A few days later I received word that the labor leadership, with the single exception of John L. Lewis, would agree to our proposal provided they were publicly requested to do so by the President.

Together we worked out the language of a proposed press statement which I agreed to ask the President to issue following a well-publicized meeting with the labor leadership in his office. The proposed statement began as follows:

> The Presidents of the American Federation of Labor and the Congress of Industrial Organizations have accepted my request for a year of uninterrupted production and the peaceful settlement of all industrial disputes.

It went on to say labor had agreed that if Congress would enact legislation which permitted effective price control to continue for the "no strike" period, it would cooperate with both industry and government and agree to government arbitration of any disputes.

The proposed Presidential statement continued:

> I could not in conscience ask Mr. Green or Mr. Murray to take the statesmen-like step which they are prepared to take except upon the assumption that the stabilization laws are extended in the form in which I have requested. Obviously labor could not be asked to tie its own hands if it were left unprotected with respect to the prices which make up its living costs and determine the value of its earnings.
>
> On the one hand, we can make good the opportunity, which general economic conditions now afford, of a period of full and uninterrupted production, at stable prices and wages, of the goods we need so much— a period which would finally and definitely put an end to the terrible threat of inflation.
>
> On the other hand, we can throw away this opportunity and embark instead on a period of unstable prices and costs, labor unrest, continued shortages, inflation and final collapse.
>
> I think that Congress and the country are entitled to the assurance

that, if we take the first course, labor will do its part. That assurance has now been given. With this assurance there should be no doubt of the choice which Congress and the country will make.

The proposal ended by specifically asking Congress to enact stabilization legislation until June 30, 1947, without crippling amendments. It called upon industry and the general public to offer their support because, as I put it:

> The next year will substantially determine the destiny of our national economy for years to come. These months will establish whether we shall have orderly stabilization and industrial peace and a safe return to a free market and free collective bargaining, or whether we shall have a disorderly race between prices and wages, production stoppages and eventual collapse and depression. These months present a golden opportunity for a vast outpouring of goods to meet our huge domestic demand and the tremendous needs of the rest of the world.

With the suggested press statements in hand, I confidently went with Henry Hart to the White House to present our proposal to Truman. But we had failed to take into account an important personal factor. At that moment the President was extremely angry with John L. Lewis and with the Railway Brotherhoods and in no mood for agreement of any kind with any labor organization.

For an hour or more I argued that this proposal was our last hope of securing Congressional approval for an effective Price Control Act and saving the stabilization program. Any member of Congress who in the face of this agreement voted for an amendment designed to raise prices or rents would be casting a vote for inflation, and his constituents would know it. "This," I said, "is a battle we can still win." Finally, Truman gave way. "If you can get Schwellenbach to agree to this," he said, "then I will go along."

However, Schwellenbach's illness by that time had been diagnosed as terminal cancer; he was on the West Coast and impossible to reach. But even if we could have talked to him, it may be argued that it would have been too late to change the course of events.

On Capitol Hill the debates on the Price Control Act had deteriorated into legislative chaos. One memorable afternoon the members of the House of Representatives passed literally any special-interest amendment anyone proposed. In the midst of the confusion, my good friend, Herman Kopplemann of Hartford, Congressman from the First Congressional District of Connecticut, soberly proposed an amendment which stated, "The Congress of the United States hereby expresses its deep sympathy to the American consumer." It went roaring through on a voice vote with no one even bothering to consider what it said. The next morning, with some embarrassment, it was eliminated.

In the closing hours of the debates, Senator Taft and Senator Homer E. Capehart of Indiana, in particular, made me personally the issue, claiming I sought to perpetuate my power and to maintain "socialistic controls" over the economy indefinitely.

The mangled remains of our anti-inflation legislation would soon be on the President's desk. We had come to the end of the road. On June 28 I sent the following letter of resignation to President Truman:

DEAR MR. PRESIDENT:

Effective control of prices and rents under the Price Control Bill, which seems likely to pass the Senate today, would be flatly impossible. The bill would simply serve to legalize inflation.

Thousands of substantial price increases would be inevitable. The cost of living would climb rapidly. Black markets would multiply. There would be serious delays in production.

I have recommended to you after a sober and objective study of the alternatives that face us that this bill be vetoed as soon as it reaches your desk.

The Price Control Act runs out at midnight, June 30th; this fact places you in a particularly difficult position.

Nevertheless, following the receipt of a veto message from you there is still reason to hope that the responsible members of Congress will squarely meet the issue which confronts us, and provide the legislation which is essential if we are to maintain a stable economy.

I have participated in the fight to keep down the cost of living for four and one-half years. The great majority of our people, who understand clearly the gigantic issues which are involved, have given me their wholehearted support.

But in carrying out my responsibilities, it has been necessary for me to say "no" one hundred times for every occasion on which it was possible to say "yes." I have been forced to step on many important toes. Inevitably my efforts in behalf of all the people have antagonized those minority groups which seek special concessions.

As you know, I had hoped to leave Washington following V-E Day, again after V-J Day, and again last February. On each occasion I agreed to stay on only at your insistence. However, a few bitter opponents of price and rent control have claimed that I am personally anxious to extend these essential controls indefinitely and unnecessarily.

The announcement of my resignation at this time, effective July 10th, will eliminate any vestige of doubt as to my own position and further sharpen the grave issue which Congress must face in the next 72 hours, in the event of your veto.

I recognize the tremendously heavy burden which rests on your shoulders, and appreciate, as do tens of millions of other Americans, the courageous efforts that you are making in the interest of the country as a whole.

In the future if there is anything that I can do to be helpful to you personally or to the Administration, I hope that you will call upon me.

With my very best wishes.

Very sincerely,
CHESTER BOWLES

The President's reply, which arrived a few hours later, follows:

DEAR CHET:

Now that the Senate has taken the legislative action which you forecast in your letter of this date, I have no alternative but to accept your resignation as Director of Economic Stabilization, effective at the close of business on July tenth next.

Deeply as I regret to see you leave the Administration I can sympathize heartily with the reasons which impel you to this step. I accede to your request most reluctantly. I am mindful of your desire to leave Washington, often expressed since V-E Day, and appreciate your self-sacrifice in remaining at your difficult post as long as you did.

Your action in submitting your resignation before the Senate had acted is an emphatic answer to the fantastic charge of spokesmen for selfish interests that you sought extension of the Price Control Bill in order to perpetuate yourself in office.

In expressing my deep regret at your leaving the Government, I know that I am merely adding my voice to one much greater—the voice of the American people. The people of this country know how conscientiously and faithfully you have worked to protect their interests both during war and during the transition from war to peace.

They know that under your leadership the Office of Price Administration and the Office of Economic Stabilization have been a powerful bulwark against the forces in our economy which might long since have destroyed the security and the hopes of millions of workers and their families. They know your personal fearlessness and integrity, which time and again you demonstrated in speaking out vigorously for the basic principles of this Administration.

The hope that you may remain in public life as a champion of the principles of this Administration, and the assurance that I may continue to call upon you from time to time for counsel, will be some consolation for the loss of so tireless and effective a public servant as you have been over a period of more than four difficult years.

With every good wish.

Very sincerely yours,
HARRY S. TRUMAN

The President, as I had recommended, vetoed the bill. In July the cost of living index rose 6 percent over June, which was nearly double the rise in the last three years. The Congress managed to put together another bill, and although it was almost as weak as its predecessor, President Truman was persuaded to sign it. Predictably, prices continued their sharp increase, and on November 9, 1946, the President decided to put the last remaining remnants of the inflation control program out of its misery. By this time prices had risen by a total of 13 percent since July. The next year or so was to bring a further upward movement of prices and wages and the costly inflation against which we had warned.

In late July of 1946, as the debate over the stabilization program was in its final stages, Steb and I and two of our children, with my governmental responsibilities behind us, were, as we had been three long years ago, when FDR had asked me to come to Washington, once again sailing the New England coast. In the little town of Cutler near

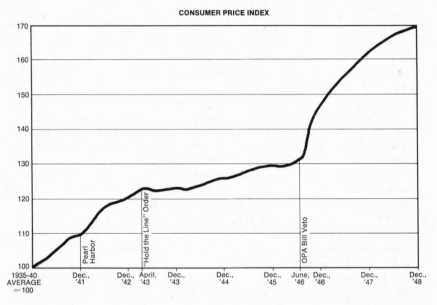

CONSUMER PRICE INDEX

The above graph illustrates how, after President Roosevelt's "hold the line" order of April, 1943, prices and rents were held in check for more than three years, until the line was finally breached by the failure of Congress in June, 1946, to renew the OPA legislation. During this time industrial production doubled, even with more than ten million of our ablest men in the armed forces. After the collapse of OPA, prices rose rapidly, as we had predicted, before leveling off in January, 1949.

the Canadian border we stopped to get some ice and groceries, and I took the occasion to buy a new battery for our radio.

At seven o'clock I was idly turning the dial and suddenly there was the familiar voice of Fulton Lewis, Jr., our most vociferous radio critic with "the latest news from Washington." As on so many of his broadcasts in the last three years, the first item involved me: "Today," soberly announced Lewis, "the stock market dropped four points on the rumor that Chester Bowles would soon be returning to Washington to restore the price control program."

POSTSCRIPT

Following the break-up of the price control program in 1946, prices had risen steadily until January, 1949, when they finally reached their peak.

The next year, on June 25, 1950, when the Korean War broke out, the possibility of a new rise in the price levels was still very much on President Truman's mind. Two days later, the same day that the President ordered U.S. troops to intervene in Korea, he asked me to come to the White House to discuss the problem of inflation.

I reminded President Truman that OPA had been an enormously complicated operation. One of the primary lessons that we learned was that an effective control system required regulations affecting almost all economic activity, including rationing, and controls over production and employment, as well as over wages and prices. Unless the emergency lasted longer than seemed likely, I thought the inflation could be kept within acceptable limits by a sharp increase in taxes plus minimum production controls, with no direct general wage and price controls or rationing.

If, however, he should decide to establish general controls, I suggested that the first step should be immediately to freeze both wages and prices at some previous date, say, May 1. I took strong issue with those who suggested that we "wait and see." A general appeal by the President to the public, business and labor for restraint in price and wage demands would result in some people holding their prices in line while the others, disregarding the government's plea, increased their prices without conscience.

This would mean that the most irresponsible would be in a position to profit from the war, while those who cooperated with the government would lose out. Moreover, if at some later time it was decided to freeze all prices and wages, we would be freezing in all the inequities which had accumulated during this period. The government would face widespread bitterness and, as a result, lack of cooperation.

Unhappily, the government first postponed action, urged everyone to cooperate, and then in September, 1950, established across-the-board price and wage controls. This produced all of the inequities and bitterness which I had feared, and which had been largely avoided during World War II.

PART II

Connecticut Politics

◆

"The country needs and, unless I mistake its temper, the country demands bold persistent experimentation. It is common sense to take a method and try it; if it fails, admit it frankly and try another. But above all, try something."

FRANKLIN D. ROOSEVELT

CHAPTER 12

INTRODUCTION TO POLITICS

IN THE FALL OF 1945 and on into 1946, working Sundays and often in the evenings, I wrote my first book, *Tomorrow Without Fear*, which Simon and Schuster published in the summer of 1946. In it I made three points: (1) why we had stumbled into the Great Depression in the 1930's; (2) how during the war years we had demonstrated the fantastic production capacity of our economy; and (3) how we could now put this capacity to work in the postwar years to abolish poverty and to assure every citizen the right to economic, social and political justice.

The Great Depression had made a profound impression on me. As I watched our economy (which in the 1920's had been hailed as one of the greatest works of man) steadily disintegrate, with the growth of unemployment, slums, ill health and misery, I had come to believe that radical changes in our philosophy of economics and government were essential.

Roosevelt's New Deal had lifted the spirits of our demoralized people and, with a succession of imaginative economic measures, had demonstrated the positive role government could and must play. Nevertheless, when Hitler's armies invaded Norway in 1940, there were still eight million Americans out of work. The New Deal was only half a success, and many frustrated economists told us that there was little more that we could do about it. Ours, they said, was a "mature economy," and we must learn to live with a certain amount of scarcity in the midst of plenty. Our period of rapid economic growth was behind us. Our population would increase more slowly; our country was largely developed; the frontiers were gone. There would be less need, they said, for the energy and investment that had been necessary to open up the West and the South and to build mushrooming new cities to house the flood of immigrants.

If it were, in fact, true that our national economic pie could not be expected to grow significantly, we faced an explosive political dilemma; the only way labor could raise its wages would be at the expense of the stockholders; farmers could expand their slice of the economic pie only at the expense of consumers; and industrialists could earn more profits only by keeping down wages and raising prices to the consumer. This would set labor against management and the farmers, the farmers and labor against the industrialists, with the interest of the consumers lost in the shuffle. It was a recipe for class warfare and for a dog-eat-dog society in which no group could prosper except at the expense of some other group.

The enormous production levels which we had achieved during the war should, of course, have laid to rest the myth of a "mature economy." But mythology is resistant to reason. The war had provided a guaranteed market for all that we could produce, but now this guarantee was gone. Would not a new postwar government, which after the long years of Democratic Party dominance would probably be controlled by Republican conservatives, attempt to return to the old economic dogma which had led us into the Great Depression?

In *Tomorrow Without Fear* I tried to answer these questions by spelling out all that we could do if only we had the will to do it. There was no valid reason, I wrote, why we could not maintain and then steadily increase the $200 billion Gross National Product created during the war, with no significant unemployment. Although several million members of our armed forces were now rejoining the work force, this would be balanced by the return to a forty-hour work week and by the fact that many women and high school students who had taken temporary jobs during the war were returning to their peacetime pursuits. By the late 1960's, I predicted, our Gross National Product could be raised to at least $400 billion, at the then current price levels.[1]

In the early stages we would no doubt be faced with many deep-seated inhibitions and prejudices about the role of government. However, as increased production began to free most families from economic want, and as our federal, state and local governments assumed a new, dynamic role, even those most fearful of change would begin to see that

1. Although this caused me to be labeled as a "visionary," the performance of our economy has, in fact, significantly surpassed the targets I suggested in 1946. In 1969 the GNP was well above $900 billion, which even at 1945 price levels was higher than my prediction. What is wrong now is the maldistribution of our national income and our failure to establish rational priorities.

problems of racism, poverty, housing and ill-health could now be solved on a scale never before imagined.

The same feelings which led me to write *Tomorrow Without Fear* also interested me in running for elective office, an idea which had first occurred to me in 1938 when Eleanor Roosevelt, to whom I had gone for personal advice on what I might do after leaving business, had suggested it. It was also through her that I had met Senator Francis T. Maloney, the senior Senator from Connecticut, who became a close friend.

In November, 1946, both the Connecticut governorship and the Senate seat then held by Republican John A. Danaher were at stake. As soon as the war had ended, many of Connecticut's Democratic leaders had begun offering to support me for either office. As I considered the possibilities, the governorship began to emerge as the most challenging.

The pressure on our postwar government to take on increasing responsibilities would lead to a growing concentration of political and economic power in Washington. This increase would, I felt, be compounded by the inability of our tradition-bound state and local governments to carry their fair share of the burden. In most states the rural areas, with a decreasing minority of population, largely dominated the state government.[2] When the cities, facing severe shortages in housing, schools, transportation and the like, found these conservative, rural-based state assemblies indifferent to their needs, they would simply bypass their state governments and appeal directly to the federal government.

The question whether stronger state governments able and willing to tackle the problems could correct this imbalance was not new. Already there was some evidence that a better balance could be developed.

In the early 1900's Governor Robert M. La Follette of Wisconsin had looked on state and local governments as small-scale laboratories for testing and perfecting national policies. During his tenure as Governor from 1901 to 1907, he persuaded the legislature of Wisconsin to adopt legislation far ahead of the times. Alfred E. Smith, elected Governor of New York in 1922, had also fought with considerable success for efficient and responsible state and local government. Later Governor Theodore F. Green of Rhode Island and Governor Alfred E. Driscoll of New Jersey had accomplished similar reforms.

However, friends with long experience in politics warned me that Connecticut was totally unprepared for any such political experiment.

2. Connecticut was among the most dramatic examples of this situation. Under the Connecticut State Constitution adopted in 1816, each of the smallest towns, many of them with a population of less than 2,000, had the same number of votes in the State House of Representatives as the largest cities.

Connecticut, they said, was "different." It had become known as the "land of steady habits" precisely because the dominant political and business forces were so firmly committed to the status quo.

While I was impressed by these warnings, I was not convinced. My work as OPA Administrator had given me confidence in the good sense of the people and their willingness to support innovative political leaders with a program. In addition, I had come to enjoy grappling with the problems involved in putting together realistic policies and in making those policies work. If the opportunity presented itself, I would, I decided, seek the Democratic nomination for Governor of Connecticut.

Before leaving Washington in early July, 1946, I discussed the Connecticut political situation with Senator Brien McMahon, whom I then knew only casually. McMahon had been elected in 1944 to the Senate seat for which I had originally intended to run, and following the tragic death of Senator Maloney on January 16, 1945, he had become recognized as the leader of the Democratic Party in Connecticut.

He was a complicated individual with many of the characteristics of a traditional conservative politician but with a sense of liberalism which often somewhat unexpectedly shone through on critical questions. For instance, he had been among the first to recognize the political and military implications of nuclear power and had become one of the strongest advocates in Congress of international controls. However, keenly conscious of the conservative atmosphere in Connecticut, Brien was in no hurry to develop close political relations with advocates of change.

In mid-August I called on McMahon to find out where he stood in regard to the Democratic nominee for Governor. By that time Wilbert Snow, former Lieutenant Governor who had briefly become Governor when Republican Governor Raymond Baldwin had resigned to take Francis Maloney's Senate seat, had announced his candidacy and with his charm, wit and liberal views was already receiving attention.

In regard to our candidacies, McMahon was no doubt torn. I believe he recognized the need for a more effective state government, but since Democratic prospects in the 1946 election were not exactly bright, he might have also reasoned that this was a good year in which to eliminate potential political rivals. After some polite fencing, McMahon said he would support the man, Snow or myself, who seemed more likely to win.

A public opinion poll conducted at McMahon's suggestion in late August indicated that it was most unlikely that any Democrat could be elected Governor, but that I would be beaten less badly than Snow. Therefore McMahon agreed to support my candidacy and to urge other state leaders to do likewise. From my work in OPA and my regular weekly broadcasts I was well known to most Connecticut residents. I felt that this would be helpful in the election itself. But my first task was to win a majority of the delegates at the State Nominating Convention in September, and to accomplish this I had to convince the party leaders.

By and large, my whirlwind schedule of visits around the state went well. John Golden, the major Democratic political figure in New Haven; John A. McGuire, Democratic State Chairman; and Cornelius J. Mulvihill, Democratic leader in Bridgeport, had all known me as a friend of Senator Maloney, and they promptly assured me of their support. McGuire agreed to become my campaign manager. The only real opposition seemed to be from a few political leaders whose toes I had stepped on when as State OPA Administrator I had refused to clear any of my appointments through the Democratic state organization and from a few die-hard businessmen, such as Francis Smith of Waterbury, a former State Chairman, who were upset because I had refused to approve the price increases they demanded during the war.

However, I made one mistake. The biggest delegation to the State Convention would be from Hartford, and I knew that my meetings with the leadership there would be of critical importance. I was told that the key leaders were Mayor Thomas J. Spellacy and John P. Kelly, Democratic leader of the South End of the city, and hence the meeting was built around them. John Bailey of Hartford, then State Statute Revision Commissioner, was not invited to the meeting for the simple reason that I had never heard of him.

When Bailey, who was young, able and ambitious, discovered that the "regular" Democratic leaders of Hartford had agreed to support me after a meeting from which he had been excluded, he decided to seize on this issue to make a bid for the city leadership. Since the leadership of the local Democratic organization had come out for me, this automatically placed him in opposition.

On September 10, when I announced my candidacy for the Democratic nomination at a meeting in New Haven, I was still unaware of Bailey's opposition or, for that matter, of his existence.

My support came not only from several influential political leaders but also from members of the trade union movement, from schoolteachers and from older people living on fixed incomes. Relatively few of these people had been closely identified with the Democratic political organization in the past, but because they associated me with FDR, and above all with the struggle to hold down rents and prices, they were eager to help.

The one labor group that held back initially was the Railway Brother-hoods, which had several thousand members. At a meeting one night in New Haven I was asked by their leaders if I would agree to support legislation requiring extra brakemen on freight trains operating in Con-necticut if they would agree to support me. I swallowed hard and replied, "Only if you can demonstrate to me that such legislation will contribute significantly either to efficiency or to safety." I assumed that we would part company at that point, but they decided to back me anyway.[3]

The night before the Nominating Convention I was assured by Mc-Guire and his co-workers that I had the nomination wrapped up. At midnight, when their checks indicated that 850 of the 1,245 delegates were with us, Steb and I went confidently off to bed and slept soundly. Unhappily for us, John Bailey did not sleep at all. Instead, John threw his formidable energies and talents behind Bill Snow.

By breakfast the following morning even an amateur politician like myself could see that the situation had changed. I was deluged with local leaders who the night before had seemed firmly in our camp but who now wanted to see me "urgently and alone."

These visits followed much the same pattern: while they were still inclined to support me, pressure from the Bailey-Snow forces had raised certain questions about my willingness if elected to work with the Democratic state organization. They wanted direct access to the new Governor's office on matters of patronage; could I assure them that access if they helped nominate me and if I were elected? One organiza-tion leader, who I was told controlled thirty delegates, made his point with particular bluntness. "I have two speeches in my pocket," he said. "In one speech I second you and in the other I second Bill Snow. I'll deliver whichever one seems likely to assure me the most patronage jobs in my district."

Another asked if I would agree then and there to make his brother a judge. All I could say to such individuals was that I would carefully consider their recommendations but I could not agree in advance to appoint people whom I had never seen.

And so the switch to Snow, which Bailey had organized so skillfully, gathered momentum.[4] Senator McMahon, as my more knowledgeable friends had predicted, did nothing.

3. This one of many incidents convinced me that you rarely lose politically by sticking to your convictions, even before groups or individuals who see things dif-ferently.
4. This does not imply that Bill Snow won the nomination by making deals that I refused to make. However, my refusal helped feed the suspicion that I would build my own organization, and this loosened many delegate commitments on which we had depended.

The *coup de grâce* was administered by John R. Everett, a young assistant professor of philosophy at Wesleyan, who placed Snow's name in nomination. Everett, who as this is written is president of the New School in New York City, was eager not only to help his fellow faculty member but also to launch his own political career. His eloquent nominating speech brought down the house. Even before the balloting had been completed, I decided that the best I could do was to help unite the party; so I moved that Snow's nomination be made unanimous and pledged my full support.

It was an impressive victory for John Bailey, who delivered all but 52 of Hartford County's more than 200 delegates to Snow, thereby emerging as the most powerful political figure in Hartford, while establishing his skill as a political manipulator and negotiator on a statewide basis.[5] Following the convention, Bailey was elected Democratic State Chairman, a post he has held ever since, including seven years as Democratic National Chairman.

It was ironic that I who had been tagged by many politicians during OPA days as a "do-gooder," had had the support of such big-city machine leaders as Mulvihill and Golden. Even more ironic was the fact that I had been defeated by relative newcomers who, like myself, had almost no political base.

After the nominee for Governor had been chosen, the convention recessed for an hour while the party leaders—both those who supported me and those who had opposed me—met to discuss the choice of a Senatorial nominee to run against the popular Ray Baldwin, who had first been elected Governor of Connecticut in 1938.

The nomination was first offered to me as a consolation prize. However, by this time we were even more determined to sink our roots in Connecticut, and so I declined.

At that moment, Joseph R. Tone, a respected former labor leader then with the Department of Labor in Washington, happened to walk by the open door of the smoke-filled room; someone spotted him and called out, "Come on in, Joe, how about running for the Senate?" Rather stunned, Tone replied, "I have a government job which I can't afford to give up."

To this the organization leaders had an easy answer; if he lost the election, they would get him another government post as good as the one he now had. A few minutes later Tone was nominated and ap-

5. Bailey's breakthrough occurred when he persuaded a majority of the Hartford delegation to vote against the unit rule which Mayor Spellacy had assumed would enable him to deliver the entire 200 votes to me. When instead of the 200 which it was assumed would be for me, I received only 52 Hartford votes, the "bandwagon" shift to Snow grew rapidly.

proved unanimously by the convention, and thus the Democratic Party
found itself a Senatorial candidate.

The next day, the *New York Times* described my downfall:

> Chester Bowles retired today to his Essex estate, his contemplated
> political career temporarily interrupted by a combination of forces which
> yesterday defeated his bid for the Democratic nomination as Governor of
> Connecticut.
>
> Despite predictions of a Bowles victory, the former OPA Chief's po-
> litical inexperience proved no match for an organization drive against
> him. With John Bailey of Hartford carrying the ball, Bowles' strength
> was decimated on the first ballot.

After the convention, Steb and I sent a contribution to Bill Snow's
campaign fund and then worked hard for his election and for the whole
Democratic ticket, making speeches all over the state.

However, the result was preordained. After fourteen years of almost
solid Roosevelt-inspired Democratic victories and continual crises, a
majority of Americans were eager to see what the Republicans could
do. In Connecticut, Ray Baldwin's Senatorial race gave additional
strength to the Republican candidate for Governor, Dr. James L. Mc-
Conaughy, former president of Wesleyan. In fact, it was to strengthen
their state ticket that the Republican organization persuaded Baldwin
to run for a full Senate term instead of retiring as he had planned to
do. McConaughy was elected Governor by a massive plurality, and Baldwin won an equally impressive victory for the Senate.

A few days after the Republican landslide, an old political acquaintance said that he would like to tell me a story which he thought had
a bearing on my political career. It concerned an Arab trader who one
day wandered into the market place looking very sad. When asked what
had upset him, he said that he had lost his donkey. He remained down-
cast for several days, but then one morning suddenly broke into a smile.
When asked if he had found the donkey, he replied, "No, but it just
occurred to me how lucky I was not to be riding on the donkey when
it got lost."

Although we had expected the Democrats to lose in many states, the
magnitude of the nationwide Republican sweep was a surprise to almost
everyone. Roosevelt had transformed the Democratic Party into a dynamic instrument of political, economic and social change. Now with
Roosevelt gone the Democratic Party seemed to have lost much of its
vigor and sense of direction. Millions of voters who considered themselves Roosevelt Democrats felt frustrated and without a secure political
base. This mood played into the hands of the extreme left.

During the war years the U.S.S.R. and the United States had worked as allies with a common objective—the defeat of Nazi Germany. In this wartime atmosphere of cooperation and common purpose many prominent citizens, who before the war were terrified at the very thought of Communism, had worked with other members of their countries to form Soviet-American Friendship societies.

I remember one conservative Connecticut family which several years after the war discovered to its horror a huge Soviet flag tucked away in the attic. The wife had made it for a Soviet-American Friendship dinner in 1944, and it had long since been forgotten. The husband sternly directed that it should be burned at once; there would be no way to explain it to the neighbors at this stage. The wife, in the interest of economy, suggested that she turn it into curtains for the living room and insisted that no one would know the difference. However, her husband pointed out that even with the hammer and sickle removed you could still see the design where the stitches had been, and the flag was burned.

One of the by-products of the wartime good feeling between the U.S. and the U.S.S.R. was that Communist-oriented labor leaders in many key unions achieved a respectability they had not previously enjoyed. This was further increased by their diligent efforts to boost our production of military equipment, which was as important to the U.S.S.R. as it was to the U.S.A. After the war these labor unions inevitably moved toward an extreme left-wing position. They were joined by many democratic liberals, such as Henry A. Wallace, who were opposed to Communism as an ideology, but who assumed that they could cooperate with individual Communists on issues of common interest.

Although I had known Henry Wallace during my years in Washington, he remained in my mind an enigma. Like Wendell Willkie, he thought in broad world terms. He was passionately committed to full production, to the development of a more balanced economy with increased opportunity for all, and to the cause of world peace.

Since the Communists played a rough political game, it was inevitable that he and many others who naïvely tried to cooperate with them would be badly burned in the process. In some cases the scars stayed with them for the remainder of their political careers; some were so shattered that they swung to the other extreme and condoned, if not actually supported, the McCarthy witch hunts of the early 1950's.

If a fragmentation of the Rooseveltian consensus was to be prevented, fresh thinking, fresh faces and a fresh sense of commitment were urgently needed. Without these changes I felt that many of the younger generation, most of whom had fought in the war, would either drift into political apathy or identify themselves with the extreme left.

Out of this situation grew the proposal for a new political organization independent of both political parties which would be committed to the liberal principles of Franklin Roosevelt. Many liberal Democrats, including myself, felt that such an organization would provide a refuge for those Democrats who were disturbed about what appeared to be a political drift to the right within their own party, who were even less inclined to accept the current Republican doctrine, and who recognized the folly of working with the extreme left. James I. Loeb, editor of the *Adirondack Daily Enterprise,* a small newspaper in Saranac Lake, New York, was a particularly persuasive exponent of this concept.

A meeting was held in Washington in early January, 1947, at which I was present and which was attended by a large number of prominent labor leaders, ex-New Dealers and Roosevelt liberals, with a sprinkling of liberal Republicans. After two days of discussion the new organization —Americans for Democratic Action—was launched. Its task would be to spell out and support democratic liberal principles but, as an organization, to remain aloof from either political party, throwing its weight behind candidates it felt might be most effective in carrying out its objectives; anti-Communist but left of center.

Although there was and is much disagreement on the subject, I believe that ADA performed an important function during this confused period. It was generally successful in providing many thousands of people who were frustrated by the lack of direction in both major parties with a political base.

However, I regret that ADA was unable to communicate more effectively with the voters. Gradually it emerged as a group of elite liberals, who seemed more interested in analyzing political problems on a lofty abstract level than in working at the grass roots to develop the fresh political concepts which were required to move our domestic and foreign policies into more realistic and imaginative channels. Although I agreed with ADA's position on most issues (and still do) and indeed was asked to become its first chairman, I felt I could be more effective working within the Democratic Party in Connecticut.

Steb and I devoted most of the winter and spring of 1947 to traveling throughout Connecticut, meeting people, learning more about the problems of its various areas and expressing our views on public affairs. Our tours took us at least once into each of its 169 towns and cities and involved tens of thousands of miles of driving in all kinds of weather over nearly every road in the state.

I spoke to innumerable Rotary Clubs, Parent Teacher Associations,

Leagues of Women Voters, etc., and Steb spoke to many more. We joined the Grange. Much of our time and energy was focused on meetings arranged for us by the local Democratic organizations, varying in attendance from 25 to 250. It was an exhausting schedule, but because it once again brought us close to the people of Connecticut and gave us new insights to their concerns and objectives, we enjoyed it.

I took every opportunity to go on radio programs in the state and also nationally. I also wrote many articles for the Sunday *New York Times Magazine* and other publications. My speeches and broadcasts covered a wide range of postwar economic problems, including prices, housing, schools, unemployment and occasionally foreign affairs. The fact that prices, as we had predicted, were still going merrily upward helped to strengthen my position.

I studied the state budget and state and federal programs and responsibilities. I stressed the need to expand Social Security, to adopt government-sponsored medical insurance, to raise the minimum wage, and to improve the welfare system.

Our emphasis on Connecticut's crowded schools and lack of housing for low- and middle-income families was particularly effective. Some 300,000 people had been attracted to Connecticut during the war by the high wages in our defense plants, and most of them had decided to remain here. This, plus the fact that there had been almost no public construction in Connecticut since Pearl Harbor, had placed an almost unbearable strain on our already inadequate schools and housing facilities.

I stressed the low pay of teachers, the need for a state program of rent controls as the federal government program was eliminated, and the inadequacy of our mental hospitals (with which I was personally familiar as a former trustee of the Norwich Hospital).

I seized upon the annual Jefferson-Jackson Day Dinner in New Haven in the winter of 1948 as a major opportunity to express my political beliefs and objectives. I told the audience of some eight hundred Democrats, including all the party leaders in the state, that if the election were held the next day, at least 100,000 Connecticut voters who considered themselves lifelong Democrats would turn their backs on the party of Jackson, Jefferson and Roosevelt to vote for Henry Wallace.

By splitting the liberal vote this would assure the election of a Republican President and a government even more committed to the status quo. The hope for the Democratic Party in Connecticut and elsewhere was not simply to press for the programs outlined by Franklin D. Roosevelt, but to bring those programs up to date. A warmed-over New Deal, I said, was not enough. We would deserve to win in 1948 only if we committed ourselves to a far-reaching and imaginative effort to eliminate economic, social and political injustice. If we hedged at this critical moment, we would suffer a devastating defeat and we would deserve that defeat. While the response from the audience was encouraging, the bluntness with which I spoke no doubt shocked some of the old-timers.

My conviction that major changes were needed in American society and that we were running out of time presented me with a dilemma about whom to support for the Presidency in the national election of 1948. In the fourteen months I had worked under President Truman I had developed not only a warm feeling toward him personally but respect for his integrity and courage. However, I was concerned about his ability under present circumstances to provide a fresh sense of national purpose and commitment.

Although most of his difficulties were unavoidable, they were nevertheless real; as President, he was a primary target for every disgruntled group or individual in America. His lack of able advisers added to the impression of confusion and lack of national leadership.

When Truman assumed the Presidency after FDR's death, he was surrounded by a Cabinet and staff selected by his predecessor. The new President assumed (no doubt correctly) that they would compare every move he made with what FDR might have done. This, plus his conflicts with labor, which had strongly supported Roosevelt, left him uncomfortable and insecure.

When the Roosevelt appointees, most of whom were exhausted by years of work under high pressure, gradually dropped out in the first year of Truman's Presidency, he replaced them with men he knew would be loyal directly to him and not to the memory of Roosevelt. With very few exceptions, these were men he had known personally for many years; many of them were from Missouri. Several of these new advisers (John Snyder was one example) not only disagreed with Roosevelt's New Deal, but they were even ill at ease with Truman's own liberal instincts. Since Truman, in my opinion, depended too heavily on the advice of his associates and not enough on his own good judgment, they often succeeded in pushing him in the wrong direction.

My own experience during the last year of the economic stabilization program was a case in point. On three occasions Truman had rejected my resignation and prevailed on me to remain in the government. Yet, because he looked on John Snyder as his principal deputy on domestic questions, he overruled my decision in regard to steel prices and approved an unnecessary increase which very nearly wrecked the program.

It can also be argued that he delegated too much power on foreign policy questions to Dean Acheson, who with all of his brilliance was wrong on several key questions, notably his agreement to commit our government to the support of the French effort to maintain their colonial position in Indochina.

The Democratic Party setback in the elections of 1946 helped convince President Truman that the country had moved to the right, and he became even more inclined to listen to the conservative voices in his government. Moreover, even under the best of conditions the election of 1948 would be a difficult one to win. Most of the electorate, sick of being governed by Democrats, were so bent on a change that only a miracle could reverse the situation.

A conviction spread within the Democratic Party that in spite of his courage and personal strength Truman could not win in 1948 and that the only hope was to nominate some relatively fresh individual who could start with a clean slate. Because I shared this conviction, I made a mistake I have regretted ever since.

On April 2, 1948, at Groton, Connecticut, I made a plea on nation-wide radio for Mr. Truman to step aside. After paying tribute to Truman's record as a Senator and his decency and courage, I pointed out that many liberal Democrats were drifting out of the party to join the Wallace movement, and that unless some way could be found to change this situation we were headed for a bad defeat. While this situation had been created more by circumstances than by Truman himself, I said, the only hope was to nominate someone else. Many influential members of the Democratic Party throughout the country, including Brien McMahon and John Bailey, agreed, and the movement grew.

Among the alternatives proposed was General Dwight D. Eisenhower, who had recently resigned as Commander in Chief of the Allied Armies in Europe to become president of Columbia University. No one knew Eisenhower's political views, and I felt it was quite possible that he did not have any. I decided to find out. I called his office at Columbia University and an appointment was arranged for the following day. After a two-hour discussion I was convinced: (1) that he wanted to become President; (2) that this desire was qualified by his reluctance to participate in the turmoil of political life; (3) that his ideas on domestic policy were almost wholly unformed; and (4) that he was incredibly naïve politically. As evidence of this latter point General Eisenhower seriously asked me at the end of our discussion if it might be possible for him to be nominated by both parties. I came away badly shaken.

However, my dilemma was soon resolved. At the Democratic National Convention in Philadelphia, which I attended as a delegate from

Connecticut, any doubts about Truman's willingness to lay down a liberal program and to fight for it were abruptly terminated.

The keynote speech by Alben W. Barkley of Kentucky, majority leader of the Senate, was one of the greatest political presentations I had ever heard. Truman followed with an equally forceful acceptance speech in which he charged the "do-nothing" Eightieth Congress (which had just adjourned) with failure to pass urgently needed legislation and dramatically announced that he was calling them back into a special session to complete their work. These two speeches transformed the atmosphere within the Democratic Party from one of hopelessness to one of dedication and even to a certain cautious confidence.

Our misjudgment of Truman's strength was due in large measure to a failure to take into account not only his own incredible fighting spirit but also the recent changes in his Cabinet and in his staff. Fortunately for Truman, the Democratic Party and the country, most of Truman's old cronies had quickly become weary of Washington life and responsibilities and had drifted back home, leaving the field open for a team of strong, dedicated young liberals. Clark Clifford, who was brought into Truman's official family as a naval attaché, emerged as a dynamic leader-organizer. He recruited many able people for top positions and helped persuade Truman to return to the liberal positions where he had always been most comfortable and boldly to speak out on the issues.

This transformation was reflected at the convention, not only by the Barkley and Truman speeches, but by the successful effort to commit the Democratic Party to a liberal position on civil rights, which for nearly a century it had been sweeping under the political rug.

The national strength of the Democratic Party had for a century and a half been based on a coalition between Northern liberals and city organization leaders on the one hand and Southern Populists on the other. First put together by Thomas Jefferson to win the key election of 1800, it was reaffirmed in the early 1930's. The Depression had hit the South particularly hard, and Southern politicians once again found common cause with liberals and city machine politicians from the North. It was leaders such as James Byrnes of South Carolina and Sam Rayburn of Texas who had guided through Congress Roosevelt's proposals for Social Security, subsidized agriculture, TVA and work relief for the unemployed.

The political price that Roosevelt and the Northern liberals had been forced to pay for Southern support for the New Deal was a heavy one: a political moratorium on the issue of civil rights.

At the 1948 Convention this compromise was openly challenged.

At the outset, supporters of a strong civil rights plank had only three votes on the Resolutions Committee of 106. But a brilliant speech by Hubert Humphrey, Mayor of Minneapolis since 1945 and a candidate for the Senate, called for a stiff antisegregation plank in the Democratic platform. If the Southern delegations did not agree, Humphrey said, they should go home. The Alabama delegation, which was seated directly in front of our delegation, promptly proceeded to do so.

The threat of the Minnesota and Connecticut delegations to take the issue to the floor regardless of the support of other states provided powerful leverage. After a bitter debate, the Democratic Party, for the first time in its long history, faced up to the issue of racial discrimination. The civil rights amendment was adopted and the Southern wing was in effect told, "These are the views for which the Democratic Party stands. . . . Accept them or go elsewhere."

During the convention there was much discussion of Democratic candidates for the governorships, the Senate and the House, and I was frequently asked about my own plans, which were now rapidly taking shape.

CHAPTER 13

THE CAMPAIGN OF 1948

MY DECISION TO RUN FOR THE GOVERNORSHIP of Connecticut, regardless of the adverse outlook, was influenced in large measure by an old friend, Emil Rieve, with whom I discussed the question during the convention. Rieve, who had been one of the most effective supporters of the anti-inflation program during the war, was then national president of the Textile Workers Union of America, which had several strong locals in Connecticut.

When I casually suggested to him that the prospects were far from bright and the very thought of the long months of campaigning made me shudder, his reply was sharp. "I agree," he said, "that you and Truman are likely to lose. But it is your responsibility, and mine, to put up the best battle we can. You're going to run for Governor, and I'm going to raise $20,000 to help finance your campaign."

I suspected that the sudden interest some key Connecticut politicians were also showing in my candidacy for Governor reflected their belief that the Democratic Party was headed for another disastrous defeat and that 1948, like 1946,[1] was a good year to get rid of the remaining Rooseveltian liberals. This feeling no doubt in part explains why the organization professionals also supported the nomination of Adlai Stevenson and Paul Douglas in Illinois, G. Mennen Williams in Michigan, and others.

When Steb and I returned to Connecticut from the convention, I told John Bailey I was eager to run and that I was counting on his support. Bailey agreed and assured me that he would immediately go to

1. Until 1950 the Connecticut governorship was a two-year term. Thereafter it has been a four-year term.

work. A few days later he called to say that the party leaders with few exceptions would back my candidacy. Attorney Thomas J. Dodd, who had been a well-known figure in Connecticut politics for several years, and who I had assumed would oppose me, had surprisingly agreed to accept the nomination for the lieutenant governorship.

A few days later, Dodd, urged by his supporters, abruptly reversed his position. At a press conference in Hartford he announced that he was not interested in being Lieutenant Governor after all and would oppose me for the gubernatorial nomination. However, on the day before the Democratic State Convention, Dodd once again switched gears and, for reasons unknown, agreed not only to withdraw but to second my nomination.

Traditionally, the candidate for Governor has the right to choose the slate which runs with him or at least veto anyone he feels not qualified. After the keynote speech by Franklin Roosevelt, Jr. at the opening of the convention on Friday evening, with Dodd out of the running and my nomination assured, I called the political leadership together to discuss other members of the ticket. This was my first experience in a political "smoke-filled room"; it began, appropriately, at midnight.

Since I was a Protestant, and a Unitarian at that, I was told it was essential that a Catholic be nominated for Lieutenant Governor. I had no objection to this and agreed to support William T. Carroll of Torrington, an attractive personality, well known throughout the state. I also agreed to the nomination of our dear friend, Winifred McDonald, an ex-school-teacher from Waterbury, for the nomination as Secretary of State, and Raymond S. Thatcher as Comptroller. This left two positions—Congress-man-at-Large and the State Treasurer.

The nominee of each political party for Congressman-at-Large, I was told, had always been of Polish descent, while the nominee for Treasurer had always been Italian. This struck me as nonsense, and I said so. The time had come to abandon such political mythology and select the ablest people, regardless of their religion, race or national origin.

The question was debated for more than an hour, and finally we agreed to a compromise; we would break loose from the tradition to the extent of switching the two positions. Consequently, we nominated Henry J. Gwiazda, a lawyer of Polish descent from New Britain, for Treasurer and Fred Trotta of New Haven, who was of Italian descent, for Congressman-at-Large.[2]

2. As it turned out, Gwiazda and Trotta were the only members of our state ticket who lost. This was generally accepted by the traditionalists as proof that it is dangerous to depart from political tradition.

At 4 A.M. I emerged from the meeting in something of a daze, returned to our room in the hotel, woke up Steb to tell her what had happened and then caught a few hours of sleep.

The convention reconvened at 10 A.M. the following morning, and the first order of business was the nomination for Governor. My name was placed in nomination before the convention by Wilbert Snow. Bridgeport leader Connie Mulvihill made a seconding speech, followed by Dodd, who called for my nomination by acclamation.

In my acceptance speech I reviewed the urgent needs of our state and the program I would undertake if elected. Although Connecticut was one of the two or three wealthiest states in America, it was shockingly ill-prepared legally, financially and administratively to tackle even its most urgent problems. As Governor, I said, I would undertake to change this. The reaction was enthusiastic. Indeed, something of the excitement that was so impressive at the National Convention in Philadelphia was evident here in Hartford. As someone remarked, "If the Democrats are beaten, as everyone says they will be, they obviously don't know it."

After a big send-off Steb and I, with Doug Bennet and a few close friends, left for Essex; whatever our prospects might be, we had at least accomplished one thing: the Connecticut Democratic Party was for the first time in many years unified behind a program that recognized the needs of its people.

Three days later I began my campaign with a radio broadcast over most Connecticut stations. This was six weeks before any previous candidate for Governor in Connecticut had gone into action; for the next eleven weeks we knew our days would be chaotic and exhausting.

I had genuine respect and liking for my opponent, Governor James C. Shannon, who as Lieutenant Governor had suceeded Governor Mc-Conaughy upon his death on March 7, 1948. Shannon belonged to the more liberal wing of the Republican Party, he was a member of a trade union, a Catholic in a predominantly Catholic state, and a decent human being, who I knew would be a formidable opponent.

Immediately after launching my campaign I asked a New York polling organization to analyze the political outlook in Connecticut. Although I was curious to know how much support I had in comparison to Governor Shannon, my primary purpose was to find out what most concerned the people and what they expected their government to do about it.

The results of the poll were given to me in early September, accompanied by a letter with the following comment from the pollster:

As OPA Administrator I made weekly radio broadcasts over 400 stations in an effort to win and hold public support, without which OPA would have been smothered by lobbyists for higher prices and their Congressional backers.

Marie Hansen—*Life Magazine* © *Time Inc.*

Steb and I with Sam, Cynthia, Sarah, Chester, Jr., and a newly acquired St. Bernard, in Essex just after I was defeated for the gubernatorial nomination in 1946.

Our house on the Connecticut River in Essex, which we built two years before Pearl Harbor. During the years covered by this book we lived in Washington, Hartford and New Delhi, but Essex was and will always be our home.

Steb on our 72-foot schooner *Nordlys*—which we had built in 1935 and on which we spent most of our free time before the war—taking a noon latitude sight of the sun en route to Bermuda, April, 1937.

My oldest daughter, Barbara, at the helm of *Nordlys*.

With President Truman on his 1948 campaign train. When he drew the biggest crowds in Connecticut's political history, we had a preview of his unexpected victory. *Hartford Times*

With Jan Masaryk, Prime Minister of Czechoslovakia, just two weeks before the Soviet-managed *coup d'état* which drove him to commit suicide. Early in 1948 Steb and I were traveling on behalf of the United Nations Appeal for Children, of which I was International Chairman.

With John Bailey shortly after I was elected Governor. After blocking my nomination in 1946, John became a strong supporter and close associate in my 1948 campaign and during my incumbency.

Steb acting as chauffeur during my 1958 campaign for Congress. Though at first I protested that plastering my name over our car was "too conspicuous," my campaign manager convinced me with "How can you win an election without being conspicuous?"

Adlai Stevenson at Saybrook station in 1954, following a weekend visit to Essex. A fellow student at Choate School, he was elected Governor of Illinois the same year I became Governor of Connecticut. From then on we often met to discuss many questions of common interest.

Eleanor Roosevelt, whom we had come to know and respect in Washington during the war, was the keynote speaker at the State Democratic Convention which renominated me for Governor in July, 1950. *Hartford Courant*

With President Kennedy in December, 1961, after I was sworn in as the President's Special Representative and Adviser on Asian, African and Latin American Affairs.

During a visit to Colombia, South America, in August, 1962. While studying rural development we met this Peace Corps Volunteer in a village some distance from the capital, Bogotá.

Chief Justice Earl Warren, a close friend since the days we were both governors, swears me in as Under Secretary of State, with Steb and Secretary Dean Rusk looking on.

Steb and Emperor Haile Selassie of Ethiopia during our visit to Addis Ababa in 1962 when I attended the Conference on African Economic Development as head of the U.S. delegation.

With President Tito of Yugoslavia in 1961, when I visited Belgrade on a special mission. Tito was a profound admirer of President Kennedy.

Addressing an Indian Army battalion in Ladakh in December, 1963, on my visit to various Indian troop units on the Chinese border. When the Chinese attacked India along the Himalayan border in October, 1962, the U.S. shipped in large supplies of military equipment to strengthen the Indian Army.

Reviewing the honor guard of Indian troops before the President's palace, formerly the residence of the British Viceroys, as part of the ceremony of presenting my credentials to the President.

Steb and I with Jog Falls in the background during our visit to the Sharavati Dam in the state of Mysore, 1965. *USIS Photo*

Steb sponsors an exhibit of American graphics at Roosevelt House. Although we did not actually live there—it was much too big and formal—we used it extensively for receptions, meetings and often to display art by young American and Indian painters.

NBC televises a half-hour discussion I had with Jawaharlal Nehru during our visit to India in 1955.

A visit with Ambassador Edwin Reischauer (center) in Tokyo. One of our most effective ambassadors, now Director of Japanese Studies at Harvard, he shared with me the belief that the future stability of Asia—and our own ability to disengage from Asian conflicts—depended on the willingness of the Asian people, particularly those of India and Japan, gradually to develop an effective working relationship.

A hand pump insecticide sprayer, being used near an irrigation canal fed by a tube well. India's "Green Revolution" has been brought about by the increased use of hybrid seeds, fertilizer, pesticides and irrigation.

Courtesy Ford Foundation

This dam at Sharavati, one of many constructed to provide electric power and supply irrigation, was built almost entirely by the hand labor of some 200,000 workers. Others, such as Bhakra Nangal, which is equal in size, have been built with the most modern equipment.

With Mrs. Indira Gandhi on the day of her election as Prime Minister of India, following the tragic death of Lal Bahadur Shastri in January, 1966.

Greeting Prince Norodom Sihanouk while heading a U.S. mission to Cambodia in January, 1968, to discuss the problem of border infiltration. Although not easy to deal with, Sihanouk was deeply committed to Cambodian independence.

Miss Maniben Kara, an organizer and leader of the textile
workers and Bombay dockers in
the 1930's, was later elected
president of the Indian International Trade Union Confederation. An impressive manifesta-
tion of Indian democracy has
been its acceptance of equal
status for women in all phases
of public life.

A social worker explains a contraceptive device. The current population control
program is by far the largest of any developing nation and has been given top
priority. However, the task is formidable and the best India can hope for is to
balance out its population at around 800 million by 1990.

Courtesy International Planned Parenthood

V. V. Giri, a major political force in India for forty years, became the
fourth President of India upon the death of Husain. Like most Indian
leaders, he had served several prison terms under the British.

The widow of former P
Minister Lal Bahadur Sh
bids Steb good-bye at the ai
as we leave for home.
known outside of India, S
was, in my opinion, one c
great men of our time.
USIS

"This is going to be very discouraging to you because you clearly can't win." The poll showed I would lose by 220,000 votes, more than double the majority by which anyone had ever been defeated for public office in Connecticut. Whatever I did or said in the campaign, the letter added, would affect the outcome by "probably no more than ten or fifteen thousand votes; that is assuming that you run a good campaign and your opponent runs a bad one."

Fifty-four percent of the people sampled said they intended to vote for Governor Shannon, and only 23 percent for me; the remaining 23 percent were undecided. My opponent's two-to-one advantage was discouraging and unexpected. Even more perplexing was the fact that of those who planned to vote against me a large percentage supported the programs I intended to advocate. According to the poll, Connecticut citizens wanted the state government to provide a publicly financed housing program; a large public school building program; greatly increased Old Age Assistance benefits; modernized mental hospitals; an enlarged and more responsive welfare system; and better organized and more efficient administration of the state government. In effect, the people were saying, we don't want a Democratic Administration, but we want the things the Democrats stand for.

I did not question the results of the poll. I had been dealing with polls for many years and, like most people in public life at that time, had come to accept them as accurate within a few percentage points. The polling organization which I had selected was run by experienced people. I was convinced I would not win. In retrospect, I believe the most difficult thing I have ever done in my life was, with this "knowledge" in the back of my mind, to throw my heart and energies into the 1948 campaign.

To avoid discouraging my supporters we decided that the poll should be treated as "top secret." Until after the election no one besides Steb and me knew it existed except Doug Bennet and Marcella Eastman, both of whom had worked with me since the early OPA days in Hartford.

On Sunday afternoon, the day after receiving the poll, I was scheduled to speak to several hundred textile workers in Manchester, near Hartford. Since this was my first appearance after learning I had no chance of victory, I knew it would be trying, but inadvertently I made it even more difficult. At lunch before leaving for Manchester we had lamb with gravy, followed by vanilla ice cream with butterscotch sauce. Somehow I got the butterscotch sauce confused with the gravy, and poured the gravy liberally over my ice cream. Since I particularly like vanilla ice cream with butterscotch sauce, I approached it with considerable vigor. I can still remember the result. For many months I was unable to eat either lamb or ice cream. After lunch, Steb and I left for Manchester, where I presented my views with all the energy I could muster. Despite a receptive audience, it was not a particularly auspicious beginning.

Steb and I were concerned about the effect of our impending political defeat on the three youngest children. Barbara and Chester, Jr. would be disappointed, but they were old enough and sophisticated enough to take it in their stride. However, Cynthia, Sally and Sam (who were then twelve, ten and nine years old respectively) had been already overexposed to the rough and tumble of political life. As OPA Administrator I had been denounced, condemned and on one occasion even hung in effigy. When Steb took the children to the House of Representatives during the final debate on the renewal of the Price Control Act, they had heard a series of speakers, each striving to outdo the others, denounce not only the program for which I was responsible but me personally.

Our children seemed to have weathered that particular storm, but on top of the OPA experience the extravagant statements and personal attacks which are, unfortunately, a factor in almost every political campaign might seriously upset them. We decided to call them together for a family discussion. I pointed out that while I had no chance of winning this election, we felt that I had a responsibility to present my views to the Connecticut voters. Although I would be attacked again as I had been in the past, it would be over in two or three months.

Then we unfolded a plan for the winter months which we knew they would find exciting. Immediately after the election, we would take our new fifty-six-foot yawl, *Mara*, to Charleston, South Carolina, leave her there until after Christmas and then in early January sail to the West Indies for a six months' cruise. Barbara and Chester, Jr., who both loved the water, could, I was sure, be persuaded to join us for two weeks or so. Although this would mean the loss of some time in school for Cynthia, Sally and Sam, their records were good and they could quickly catch up, particularly since we would work with each of them two or three hours a day.

When the children had recovered from the shock, we spread out some charts on the living room floor and began to plan where we could go and how long we would stay at each island, and their enthusiasm began to rise.

With Doug Bennet as my campaign manager, we set up a headquarters in Hartford and recruited a staff. Jean Joyce, who worked with me in the OPA, came up from Washington to help. Penn Kimball resigned from *Time* magazine to head up my publicity staff, and Joseph P. Lyford, who worked for the *Herald Tribune,* also joined us.

Although I tried to put the poll results out of my mind, I found it impossible. For one thing, there was the problem of raising campaign funds. Even when you appear to be a winner, this is not an easy task. But if my prospects had been reasonably good, I could have at least said to a prospective donor, "If we had another ten or fifteen thousand dollars to pay for a few more radio programs, I believe we could come through in November." I could not honestly say this. To be frank, I would have to say, "Although I will be beaten, more campaign funds will enable me to make a stronger case for the public policies which you and I believe in."

This was a disturbing personal dilemma, and despite the secrecy of the poll I found it difficult to seek campaign funds or to urge others to raise funds for me. My total campaign expenditures amounted to only $68,000, three-fourths of which came from labor organizations such as Emil Rieve's.

With the effective support of John Bailey and various local and regional political leaders, we set out to build an organization to cover every neighborhood, community, village, city and town in Connecticut. I was on the radio every night and made an average of eight or ten speeches a day.

Drawing heavily on our wide acquaintanceship built up during OPA days and strengthened by Steb's and my travels around the state following my loss of the 1946 nomination, we involved several thousand people in our campaign. They worked long hours ringing doorbells, telephoning prospective voters and, without complaint, doing the drudgery that goes with political campaigning. A number of young faculty members at Yale and Wesleyan Universities volunteered to help in developing programs and speeches.

Many of these volunteers had never participated in politics; I was particularly pleased that they included many college students and young veterans. Robert Sussler, then at the Yale Law School and now a New London lawyer, headed our student program. The members of our local "Bowles for Governor Clubs" included many former OPA ration board volunteers, a large number of whom were registered Republicans.

Through Steb's efforts, we also developed some campaign music. The tune of "MacNamara's Band" became "Chester Bowles' Band" to provide a special appeal to our Irish supporters. Another of Steb's productions, to the tune of "Buttons and Bows," was recorded and used over and over again on sound trucks and on the radio:

Come and join the Democrats,
We'll meet you at the polls.
All the people know what they want:
It's prices down, houses up;
Everyone vote for Truman and Bowles.

Tired of living with your mother-in-law
In a house that's much too small?
Vote for a man with a housing plan
And watch the Republicans take it on the lam;
Everyone vote for Truman and Bowles.

Time for a guy who really cares what we all seek;
So we'll work much longer, harder for that guy to win next week.
Tired of prices gone sky-high?
Let's put out the do-nothing guys;
Vote for a guy who really tries;
Prices down, houses up;
Everyone vote for Truman and Bowles.

We had a total of six sound trucks operating twelve hours a day. Our arrangement called for a nominal payment if we lost and a very generous one if we won. Since we assumed that victory was out of the question, this seemed a sound business-like approach.

The sound truck operators worked overtime with great enthusiasm. A favorite location was in front of a supermarket; from this vantage point the announcer would say, "When Bowles was in Washington, hamburger cost you only 32 cents a pound and you could buy a cup of coffee for a nickel. Look what they cost now."

In a speech on September 18, I said:

> No prominent Republican has done anything to stop this unbelievable pressure on the pocketbook of America, but prices have gone higher and higher. President Truman gave the Congress a workable plan of control, but it was thrown into the waste paper basket, and prices continued to go up. These prices will eat us out of house and home. If it keeps up, it will come down with a crash.

Since no Governor could do much about them, I felt mildly apologetic for introducing the question of high prices and inflation. However, not unreasonably we believed that as Governor I could encourage massive statewide picketing and consumer strikes against high prices, a device housewives successfully used in combating the sharp inflation that followed World War I. As former OPA Administrator I could also use the governorship as a platform from which to arouse national opposition to inflation.

As Steb and I spoke and spoke all across the state, the crowds grew both in numbers and in enthusiasm. Like my OPA broadcasts, my speeches treated issues simply in terms I felt the people would react to. I proposed a plan for building betwen 12,000 and 15,000 homes in the next two years, as the first step in a seven-year program to build 56,000. I presented a specific plan to finance new school construction on a major scale. I asserted that the overgrown, politics-ridden state government must be reorganized from top to bottom. While carefully avoiding personal debates, I pulled no punches on important issues on which the Republicans had been deficient.

When Governor Shannon made the claim that the Republicans deserved the major credit for the state's labor legislation, I responded forcefully. On October 7 the Governor said:

> It is a fact that not a single bit of progressive liberal labor legislation would be on the statute books of Connecticut today without the assistance of the Republican Party.

I responded:

> It is only on those occasions when public opinion and a vigorous Democratic bloc in the State Assembly have overcome the opposition of Republican die-hards that a Governor has been able to get things done at all.

My views were supported by the CIO, which issued a statement that "In General Assembly sessions since 1945, all the labor legislative agents know the frustration experienced in drawing labor legislation weak enough to pass the Republican House." Joe Tone, who had been Labor Commissioner for eight years during Wilbur Cross' Democratic governorship, added that he could not recall Shannon ever appearing before the labor committee on behalf of any bill.

After Shannon had reportedly refused to debate with me I pointed this out to the voters. On October 19 I said in a New Haven speech:

> It has long been apparent he has no taste to consider or discuss my proposals. My opponent has been extremely reluctant to say anything at all that might be construed as a specific commitment to the voters of Connecticut.
>
> I call it hypocrisy. I call it political cynicism. I call it bankruptcy of the spirit and surrender to the tactics of expediency. Such utter contempt for the intelligence of the voters of Connecticut can only be the product of tired and frightened minds. Democratic government is not established or maintained by evasion.[3]

3. Shannon's campaign tactics, however, were by and large as clean as his less enlightened associates would allow them to be.

The climax was reached in late October when Harry Turman came to speak in Connecticut. Steb and I, John Bailey and other political leaders met the President in Springfield, Massachusetts, and returned with him to Connecticut on his special train. He gave me a warm and enthusiastic welcome, with no sign of resentment over my earlier opposition to his candidacy.[4]

When I asked how his campaign was going, he said, "Marvelously." When I asked if he felt we had a fair chance to win, he produced a typically Trumanesque answer. "What do you mean a 'chance'?" he demanded. "We can't possibly lose."

As the train slowed down at the textile town of Thompsonville, I went with the President to the rear of the car where the microphones were set up. When we opened the door, I could hardly believe my eyes. Although the population of Thompsonville was no more than fifteen thousand, at least thirty thousand cheering people were there to greet us. They were massed in the streets, on the railroad tracks, on top of buildings and cars. Most of them must have come miles to hear Truman speak.

As the train continued toward Hartford, I asked, "How in the world do you produce crowds like that?" Truman replied, "Just wait until we get to Hartford!" He was right. The crowd was estimated at more than 100,000 people, the biggest in Connecticut history and even larger than those Roosevelt had drawn. We both spoke in the Hartford Times Plaza and then proceeded to New London and New Haven, where the crowds were equally impressive. We left the President in Stamford with the conviction that the outcome was likely to be somewhat less one-sided than the pollsters had predicted.

Nevertheless, the poll still hung over us. I began to wonder if my situation might not be similar to that of Wendell Willkie in 1940: there were not enough supporters to elect him, but those who were for him were deeply committed. The result was impressive crowds and great enthusiasm, followed by a decisive defeat. By running an energetic, hard-hitting campaign I had generated intense enthusiasm among a significant number of the voters, and this explained the crowds. But it would be foolish to assume that they represented a majority of the people who would vote in November.

As the campaign moved toward the Election Day climax, our confident competition stuck to a strictly negative approach. According to their speeches, they too believed in more housing, more schools, modern

4. The fact that on no occasion did Truman ever chide me about my suggestion six months earlier that he step aside reflects his generous nature.

hospitals, etc. But to cope with these problems immediately would cost more money than the people of Connecticut, the "land of steady habits," were willing to spend.

Governor Shannon in late August had set the tone when he said of my housing proposal:

> One of these plans proposes a magical solution which would result in creating 56,000 additional dwelling units.
>
> It is enlightening to note that the proponents of these plans blindly disregard the heavy burden of expense which would immediately be imposed on taxpayers.
>
> While there is no desire on my part to moralize, I do feel that the most important responsibility of public officials is to devise plans which are possible of fulfillment.
>
> There can be no claims of integrity in the broad exploitation of ideas which clearly and definitely go beyond the possibility of accomplishment. Unfortunately, many people believe that this latter technique so widely used in commerical advertising is good public practice.

There is a pattern to the political campaigns of many conservative candidates which I have seen repeated on many different occasions. As Roosevelt once remarked, one reason why liberals often appear to be disorganized and disunited while conservatives appear much more united is that there are many ways of going forward but only one way of standing still. Perhaps for this reason conservative candidates often find themselves around the middle of October short of speech material while their opponents continue to pour out proposals for schools, urban planning, new priorities and the like.

Inevitably, this leads to uneasiness among a conservative candidate's advisers and there is increasing agreement that "something must be done." The "something" may take several forms. In its most virulent form it may be hastily contrived charges that the liberal opponent is a "pink," "woolly-minded," an advocate of "creeping socialism," or "knowingly or unknowingly committed to a foreign ideology."

In a milder form it may express itself in political gimmickry which, although harmless enough in itself, contributes nothing to the political dialogue.[5]

In 1948 a Republican tactic was to describe me as "a rich yachtsman with a phony concern for the common man" or "the visiting yachtsman from New York." We responded to this particular gambit by persuading several hundred owners of sailboats and motorboats to write angry letters to the Republican candidates and to the press, stating that if the Re-

5. In the election of 1950 we shall encounter this phenomenon in its more virulent form.

publican Party was opposed to people owning boats, they could count them out on Election Day.

As part of my campaign I made a series of eight statewide radio broadcasts[6] in which I examined various aspects of the Republican record. In one, for example, as reported by the Hartford *Times* on September 1, I "criticized the handling of the State's $15 million construction program, asserting that the State is supervising the work 'without a single architect and with only seven inspectors,' and suggested that the job be placed under an efficient 'Department of Public Works and taken from the politically-ridden comptroller's office.'"

In another statewide radio broadcast on September 28, I charged that the State Welfare Department was going out of its way to pauperize thousands of our elderly citizens. "Old people," I said, "are separated from their savings, insurance policies and even their telephone before becoming eligible to receive grossly inadequate assistance. Our state government has an adding machine where its heart ought to be."

The news report of this broadcast noted that "Bowles had three elderly guests with him on his program who demonstrated hardship under present state aid and eviction laws."

The night before the election, I finished up our campaign at Polish Hall in New Britain. Once again, there was an overflow crowd and great enthusiasm. On my way back to Essex accompanied by John Bailey and other Democratic leaders, someone said, "Let's each put our estimate of how the vote will come out in a sealed envelope and compare them when the returns are in."

I was sure of one thing: the pollsters would turn out to be wrong in predicting that we could not change more than ten or fifteen thousand voters; we knew we had done better than that. But the thought of actually winning never seriously entered my mind. I wrote down, "Shannon by 60,000 votes."[7]

On Election Day any candidate for public office is a lonely individual. After tumultuous weeks of speaking, traveling and campaigning, there is sudden quiet; he is no longer the center of things.

Steb was busy all day at the polls in Essex, checking voter registrations and sending out cars to bring Democrats to the polls. After we voted together around noon I thought of stopping at the boat yard to look over our yawl on which we expected soon to be off for the Caribbean. However, it occurred to me that the workmen there might think I had given up before the returns were in. So I returned to the house and

6. In recent years I have been asked, "Why didn't you use television?" Older readers will recall that in 1948 it was in its very early stages.

7. Bailey, unaware of the poll, proved his political acumen by hitting it on the nose. "Bowles," he wrote, "by a few thousand."

with Cynthia, who was at home with a cold, once again spread out our West Indies navigational charts on the living room floor and discussed the islands we were most eager to visit.

When the polls closed at six o'clock, there were only a dozen or so of our family and closest friends in the house. The radio people had set up their equipment in my library, and at twenty minutes past six the first returns reported on the voting machines began to trickle in from Hartford, a city carried by Roosevelt in 1936 by a 21,000 plurality. The first precincts which reported indicated that I was running substantially ahead of FDR's vote in his biggest year. We couldn't believe it.

By seven o'clock the final returns were in for the three largest cities. We had carried Hartford by 23,000 votes, New Haven by 16,000 and Bridgeport by 6,000. Other cities were showing the same favorable trend.

However, as the small-town vote came in, our lead gradually began to shrink, and as midnight approached, we were leading by only a thousand votes. Then came the dramatic announcement from Windham County that I had carried two more textile towns by good majorities—Putnam by 600 votes and Plainfield by 850—and it was all over.

At midnight Governor Shannon graciously conceded. By that time cars from all over Connecticut were heading for our house. By 1 A.M. there were more than a thousand people there to celebrate.

There was, however, one note of sadness: Cynthia, Sally and Sam's dream of a Caribbean cruise had been demolished. They would be going to school and in a strange new city—Hartford.

Truman lost Connecticut by 15,000 votes. But in addition to my victory we elected the Lieutenant Governor, the Secretary of State and the Comptroller, picked up 48 seats in the State House of Representatives and gained control of the State Senate 22 to 14. The final tally read Bowles 431,268, Shannon 428,983.

At ten o'clock the following morning I called Harry Truman at his home in Independence, Missouri, to congratulate him on his victory. "It must have been a nerve-racking night for you," I said. To which he replied, "I never doubted the outcome. I was sound asleep by midnight."

The Hartford *Times*, which had been neutral during the campaign (the only daily newspaper to support me was the *Yale Daily News*[8]), made the following editorial comment:

> Chester Bowles of Essex is the seventy-second Governor of Connecticut, by a breathtakingly narrow margin. Fighting against what appeared to be an irresistible tide, Mr. Bowles nevertheless ran well ahead of the

8. I did, however, have the support of a few weekly papers, one of which, the Bridgeport *Herald*, had a sizable circulation.

national ticket in a victory that confounded all but those most closely associated with him.[9]

It would be difficult to think of anything Mr. Bowles could have done to strengthen his candidacy that he did not do. Not only was he off to a flying start but he set out to make his already familiar name a household word.

Mr. Bowles is regarded in liberal circles as a potential national leader in rebuilding the national Democratic Party. This may explain the unusual vigor with which his campaign was conducted.

During his campaign Mr. Bowles concentrated most of his fire on the bread and butter issues that were closest to the hearts of the majority of voters. But what this vote means most of all is that Connecticut rejected the theory of status quo, and voted for change.

The defeat of Governor Shannon, while far from devastating, demonstrates that Mr. Bowles succeeded in capturing the imagination of Connecticut voters. He became the most controversial figure in the state campaign. Indeed, toward the end, Mr. Bowles was the principal issue.

The next two years on Capitol Hill will be interesting. Mr. Bowles will not take blind opposition lying down. He has demonstrated that he is no political babe in the woods, but an astute and resourceful man.

9. It confounded my close associates and myself as well.

CHAPTER 14

THE LEGISLATIVE CONFRONTATION

AFTER TWO DAYS OF WADING THROUGH congratulatory mail, we sailed out of Essex harbor on *Mara,* bound not for the Caribbean but for a brief vacation in the Chesapeake Bay. The breeze was fresh out of the west, and it was a long beat to windward in chilly mid-November weather.

Although I had promised Steb that for the next ten days I would concentrate on wind, weather and family affairs, I found myself spending part of each day going over state records, recent legislation and the like.

The closer I got to it, the clearer it became that the governorship of Connecticut had been made to order for doing nothing. Until the 1930's it had been considered a part-time job and had been normally filled by Republican Governors who felt that the less government did, the better it was for everyone, including the Governor.

In 1930, a Democrat, Wilbur L. Cross, the sixty-eight-year-old Dean of the Yale Graduate School, had been elected to the first of four two-year terms. These were the Depression years, with a strong liberal government in Washington from 1933 on, big Democratic majorities in almost all the state legislatures, and a public ready and eager for the constructive changes in our society that were clearly overdue.

As a Democratic Governor with a Republican-controlled legislature, Cross was admittedly limited to some extent in what he could do. However, Governor Cross' compromises went well beyond necessity. He proved to be a Grover Cleveland Democrat who had no desire to disturb the traditional political calm of Connecticut by introducing controversial proposals. As a result a major opportunity to adapt the government of Connecticut to the requirements of our changing society was lost.

This failure is in striking contrast to the neighboring state of Rhode Island, where Governor Theodore Green confronted similar problems and opportunities. Green, using the leverage provided by his own popularity and the funds generated by the New Deal in Washington, set out to modernize the political structure of Rhode Island. After a bitter struggle, he reorganized the Rhode Island legislature, modernized the court system, and transformed an antiquated state bureaucracy into an effective instrument of orderly economic and social change.

Although I knew that our state government was complicated, I was appalled to discover that there were 202 separate institutions, commissions and departments. Moreover, to deal with this bureaucratic maze the Governor had no office staff except an executive secretary, who by the statute was paid only $6,000 a year, plus two or three stenographers, and a public relations officer.

In a Republican Administration this presented no problems; the Governor could call on any or all of his 202 commissioners, department heads and bureau chiefs for assistance with the knowledge that since they were almost all members of his own party he could count on their cooperation and loyalty. When I became Governor, I doubt that there were five Democrats among the top two or three hundred state officials. Thus I found myself in much the same position as a General Motors president would be with a board of directors appointed by Ford.

Doug Bennet agreed to become my executive secretary—at a major financial sacrifice. The state budgetary people, who although appointed under a Republican Governor were, I think, secretly pleased to see the new Governor take his responsibilities so seriously, helped by establishing several new staff jobs in the Governor's office.

To head our staff I hired Philip H. Coombs, a young economist with whom I had worked in Washington. Phil passed up a chance to become head of the department of economics at Amherst College to take this job. Edward J. Logue, who had just graduated from the Yale Law School, also joined my staff as legal secretary—at the princely salary of only $3,612 a year. In recent years Ed has become one of America's most distinguished experts on urban development and as this is written is president of the New York State Urban Development Corporation. Another young lawyer who joined my staff was Abram Chayes, a recent graduate of the Harvard Law School, whom I later brought into the State Department in 1961 as General Counsel, a post in which he performed brilliantly; later he was appointed professor of law at Harvard.

Most of my campaign staff stayed with me, including Jean Joyce, Joe Lyford, who became my press secretary, and Penn Kimball, who concentrated on our new budget.

While most state employees were grossly underpaid, I discovered that the Governor came off rather well. His salary was only $12,000 a year, but he was also furnished a house (known to my predecessors as the "Governor's Mansion," a title which we changed to the "Governor's House") and a domestic staff of four servants. In addition, he was provided with a State Police officer as his chauffeur, a Cadillac limousine, a station wagon, an airplane flown by the National Guard, all the food his family and guests could eat, plus laundry and all utilities. In order to live in equal "comfort," a private individual would have required an income of at least $150,000 a year before taxes.

My predecessors had worked out these prerogatives in a way that made it virtually impossible for anyone to determine where the money came from. One state hospital, for instance, would provide all the meat for the "Mansion," another would provide the vegetables and fruit. One servant would be on the payroll of one department, another on the payroll of another, and so on.

The inauguration program on January 5 was heavy with tradition. It began with a luncheon given at noon by outgoing Governor Shannon at the Hartford Club, followed by a parade to the State Capitol led by the "Governor's Foot Guard" and the "Governor's Horse Guard."

The Foot Guard, of which there were two companies, was established in 1773 by the colonial government just before the Revolutionary War. Since then they have traditionally worn the scarlet uniforms and huge bearskin hats of His Majesty's Cold Stream Guards. The Horse Guard, mounted on beautiful but somewhat temperamental horses, were equally impressive in their colonial uniforms.

However, on this state occasion a soggy wet snow had been falling and consequently our honor guard was not at its resplendent best; the soaking-wet bearskin hats must have weighed twenty-five pounds each. When a battery of artillery fired a nineteen-gun salute, the horses added to the sense of disarray by scurrying in all directions. Finally, everything was restored to its proper order, Governor Shannon escorted me to his former office and bade us a friendly good-bye and good luck.

There with our family, staff and friends, we settled down to wait for the summons to the House Chamber, where I was scheduled to deliver my Inaugural Address to a joint session of the House and the Senate at two o'clock. However, the schedule-makers had failed to take into account the mood of the Republican majority in the House.

By one parliamentary device after another, they held up my affirmation from two o'clock in the afternoon until nearly eight o'clock that night. Eventually they ran out of gimmicks and the traditional bipartisan delegation appeared to escort me to the joint House and Senate reception in the House Hall. As I entered, the Republicans applauded politely and the Democrats cheered vociferously.

The Democrats controlled the Senate by 22 to 14. However, in the House of Representatives the Republicans had 179 members and the Democrats only 93; yet this was the first occasion since the Civil War that the Democrats in the House had the one-third quorum required to demand a roll call. Most legislation, regardless of its importance, had normally been passed or defeated by a voice vote, with no record of how any individual member voted. This enabled a member of the House to claim to one constituent that he had voted for a certain piece of legislation and to another that he had voted against it.

Although I had many Republican supporters, most of the Republican political leaders looked on me as a dangerous New Dealer whose sole redeeming factor was that I had once run my own business.[1] My Inaugural Address was largely directed at my conservative opposition and was designed to ease this concern and to establish a basis for cooperation. I said:

> In a philosophical sense we Americans divide broadly into four political patterns. At one extreme are the reactionaries who make no bones about their preference for the past over the present—much less the future. At the opposite end of the political spectrum are the radicals who dislike our economic, political and social structure so intensely that they would destroy it if they could. Between these extremes of right and left are the conservatives and liberals.
>
> The fact that liberals and conservatives have traditionally agreed on the principles of democracy but disagreed on how to apply these principles to best serve the public interest creates the political dynamics of our democratic society. . . .
>
> You conservatives are right when you say that too much government is dangerous, but sometimes you overlook the fact that if we refuse to employ enough government in the face of problems which only government can solve, then we may eventually end up with much more government than otherwise might have been needed.
>
> I believe the challenge which you conservatives must face is how to make conservatism in Connecticut relevant to our ever-changing social needs. You rigidly regard too much centralized power with suspicion. Re-

---

1. I have heard businessmen say, "Never trust the judgment of a man who has never met a payroll," while politicians say, "Never trust the judgment of a man who has never carried a precinct." I was now qualified on both counts.

member then that strong and effective local institutions are the best assurance that we can have against the arbitrary use of centralized authority.

Political pressures, many of them contrary to the interests of our people, will be brought to bear against all of us during the weeks ahead. I urge you, in all earnestness, to reject them and to listen instead to the voice of our Connecticut people. These are trying times; and for those who believe as we do in the dynamic future of our American democracy, there is urgency in the air.

The Inaugural Ball was scheduled for 10 P.M. that evening in the State Armory. As soon as my speech had been completed, we climbed into our newly acquired Cadillac driven by State Police officer Charles Heckler, who soon became a warm friend, and set out for the Governor's House on Prospect Street. Since none of us had been there, including Heckler, we had to stop on several occasions to ask bystanders for directions to our new home.

The Inaugural Ball was an impressive but overcrowded affair. The Governor's Foot Guard and Horse Guard were there, with the water squeezed out of their bearskin hats and their horses safely back in the stables. The next day the newspapers reported that while it was a colorful function as always, the many students, labor leaders, schoolteachers and welfare workers in attendance gave the affair a "somewhat different" flair. Although it was not as "different" as the Andrew Jackson inaugural, it was clear to friend and foe alike that changes were in the wind.

In spite of the olive branch I had held out to the Republicans in my inaugural speech, I had no illusions about the difficulties that lay ahead. Through their control over the House, the Republican leadership held the power to veto any legislation that we might propose, and it would have been naïve to assume they would not use it. These leaders, John R. Thim, Speaker of the House, George C. Conway, majority leader of the House, and Charles S. House, minority leader of the Senate, were all personally agreeable (I even suspected on several occasions that Charlie House secretly agreed with our proposals). But their primary objective was to prevent my re-election in 1950.

My relationship with the Democratic leadership of the two houses was close. Alfred F. Wechsler, majority leader in the Senate, and John P. Cotter, minority leader in the House, were young, liberal and personally committed to the program we had presented during the campaign. From the outset they worked in close cooperation with me and my staff.

To demonstrate my desire to cooperate with the leaders of both parties, I suggested that whenever the General Assembly was in session I would welcome them to my office for an informal off-the-record discussion of pending legislation. Predictably, the Republicans turned the proposal down, but meetings with the Democratic leadership were held regularly.

To give the rank-and-file Democratic members of the House and Senate a sense of personal involvement, we also invited them to informal seminar-like discussions on all new legislation. Before introducing a housing bill, for instance, Phil Coombs and other staff members would present to the Democratic legislators an analysis of the shortage of housing in Connecticut, what other states had done under similar circumstances (most states had done nothing), and why our proposals seemed to be the most practical approach. Everyone was encouraged to speak out, to criticize and to offer suggestions. (We also invited the Republicans to these sessions, but none ever showed up.)

As we had done in OPA, we succeeded in creating a spirit of cooperation and commitment which generated an extraordinary degree of unity and vigor within our own party. During both the regular legislative session and the special sessions which it was later necessary to call, close to one hundred Administration-supported bills were introduced. On each of them *all* Democratic members of the two houses voted affirmatively. I know of no other political party operating through a democratically elected legislative body which has matched that record.

As the incoming Governor, I was legally responsible for presenting a complete budget to the General Assembly by February 1, 1949—less than a month after my inauguration. Because the State Assembly met in regular session only every two years, the budget appropriations were also for two years. The budget I recommended to the legislature would, therefore, set policy for my entire term. As far as anybody could remember, a complete budget had never been delivered on the prescribed date. This, I thought, was a good place to break another tradition, by presenting the budget to the General Assembly on time.

We were committed to a large construction program for schools, housing, mental hospitals and our state universities and teachers colleges, and I was determined to meet this commitment. We were also committed to an efficient, cost-conscious Administration. This was a good place to demonstrate to the public and members of the General Assembly our determination to see that the state funds would not be wasted. Under existing practices construction costs would be needlessly increased by local building codes and "featherbedding" agreements not to use labor-saving devices, devices which had been designed during the Depression to create more jobs and increase the sale of building materials.

I discussed the situation with the building trade labor leaders, pointing out that the substantial building program I planned to present to the legislature would create thousands of new jobs. Under the circumstances there was no conceivable justification for make-work practices which limited the number of bricks a man could lay in a day or required that all paint should be applied with a brush and not by spraying. I would not, I said, recommend a construction program of this magnitude to the General Assembly unless they first agreed to forgo all featherbedding practices on construction financed by the state.

If they agreed, I would then see that any worker employed on a state-financed construction project was paid the regular union rate whether he belonged to a union or not. This would prevent contractors from using lower-paid nonunion workers as a means of lowering their bids.

This proposal hit at some deeply ingrained practices which were not easy for even the best-intentioned labor leaders to change. However, they finally gave me the pledge I was seeking and lived up to it fully.

Similarly, we set out to break local building codes which required excessive thicknesses of walls, unnecessary plumbing or electrical work and the like. These building codes went far beyond legitimate safety needs. I insisted that no state loans would go to construction projects in any city that clung to outdated building codes.

Our goal of presenting a complete and detailed budget to the legislature was one of the most difficult exercises that I have ever asked a staff to undertake. Someone estimated that more than two thousand man-hours went into it, and I can easily believe it. Penn Kimball, who had been a great source of strength during the campaign, was in charge, assisted by Ralph Sollot, a budget expert from New York City who later served in the Department of Defense, and Lyle Fitch, a young professor from Wesleyan who later became City Administrator of New York City.

On one occasion I remember leaving my office shortly after midnight, with Kimball, Sollot and a few others still hard at work. When I returned the next morning, they were still there in the identical positions I had left them the night before.

Through this exhausting effort we managed for the first time in recent years to produce a tight, easily understood assessment of the Connecticut fiscal situation—on the date prescribed by law. It was a balanced budget which maintained all present services and added several new ones with no increase in taxes. Revenues matched projected expenditures, and, as in our OPA presentation, charts, diagrams and graphs helped make each recommendation clear. On the morning of February 1 every member of the state legislature found a copy on his desk, and at noon I delivered my budget message to a joint meeting of the House and Senate. It was nine thousand words long, with more than 150 pages of facts and figures, and it took me over an hour to deliver.

Our most important proposed departure from current practice involved the financing of state construction projects. Instead of following the traditional practice of including the entire cost of new building in the current budget, we recommended bond issues that would be paid off over a period of years as business expansion is financed. The "pay as you use" approach, which spread the capital cost over the expected life of each building,[2] would enable us greatly to expand the present amount of building with no increase in taxes. This change in budgetary policy was the primary issue between my Administration and the opposition.

The Republican Old Guard members in the House of Representatives quickly grasped the implications of our proposals, and they dug in. Two days after my budget presentation the opposition attacked the budget as too big, too complicated and, worst of all, as a departure from past practice. The Republican chairman of the House Appropriations Committee, Nelson L. Carpenter, demanded that we return to a traditional, line-item budget (which obscured as much as it revealed) and proceeded to draw one up. Consequently, the Appropriations Committee found itself with two budgets.

Such was the beginning of the five-month regular legislative session, during which we were to achieve certain of our objectives, fail in others and postpone two of the most important for special sessions. In general, our batting average was higher than I had expected.

Probably the most important breakthrough was in housing. As I have mentioned, the war had caused more than 300,000 people to move to Connecticut, many permanently, creating a serious housing shortage among low- and lower-middle-income families. Privately financed housing could not conceivably meet the demand at rentals that those in the greatest need could afford to pay. In my travels throughout the state I had been shocked at the housing conditions in many areas. A clean home in good surroundings was the very basis of a united, secure family. During the campaign, at the top of my list of objectives I had proposed that to meet this need the state finance the building of 56,000 homes over a period of years and that at least 12,000 new housing units should be built by the state in the next two years.

Such a program could provide housing at substantially lower rents, first, because the state could borrow money at far cheaper rates than the private developer and, second, because the state and local housing author-

2. In the case of schools this would be forty to fifty years.

ities were not expected to make a profit.[3] The rental covered the interest and principal on the state loans for the actual construction of the house, and also all related administrative costs, making it self-financing.

At that time interest rates were extremely low, and in financing these homes we planned to use the cheapest money of all—one-year state-guaranteed notes, which then carried an interest rate of less than one percent. It was a simple matter to refinance those notes every year, adjusting the rents up or down to cover the interest cost. It was innovative, but no one could find anything wrong with it, and eventually the legislature went along.

We also proposed a second program, offering local housing authorities direct subsidies to build and operate housing for those low-income tenants who could not afford to pay even the rents of the break-even rent program. Whereas the break-even program called for rents of around $50 a month, rentals for the subsidized program would be around $35 a month. This would require a direct contribution by the state government of $900,000 annually.

The public pressure behind our housing program was strong. As the legislative debate began, the halls filled with lobbyists of all kinds, veterans who could not find adequate housing, contractors, architects, merchants who saw a new market for washing machines, rugs and new furniture, plus the leaders of the building trade unions who saw an opportunity for increased employment. Through my weekly radio programs I encouraged these supporters to speak out.

The subsidy program for low-income families met strong opposition in the legislature, and we were forced to drop it. But after long negotiations the rental program, which involved no cost to the state, was agreed upon.

We also secured agreement on a new program for state-financed construction of single homes for sale at about $7,500 each, using the same financing technique as the rental program, which would enable many more low-income families to own their own homes. In the end the legislature agreed to a total program which would provide fifteen thousand state-financed units to be built in two years, half rental and half for purchase.

The original intention for financing the housing for sale was with long-term mortgages granted by tax-free state bonds at 2.5 percent. However, with the Republicans in full agreement, we decided (mistakenly) to finance them with the same one-year notes used in the rental program. Unlike the rental program, however, in which rents could be adjusted to reflect changes in the interest rate, the state's sale price was final and

3. The construction and equipment were, of course, provided by private architects, contractors and business firms.

was based on the interest rate over the twenty-five-year length of the mortgage. Everyone mistakenly assumed that the interest rates would be stable. But later interest rates rose substantially, and the state, of course, was called upon to make up the difference. At this point the home ownership program, for which the Republicans had claimed credit, suddenly became the "Bowles program."

To administer this extensive rental-purchase program, we hired an experienced housing administrator, Bernard E. Loshbough, whom I had known as Director of the Housing Authority in Washington, D.C.

After five weeks of legislative debate, in the face of heavy pressure from the landlords, we also persuaded the House to accept an antieviction program preventing landlords from using the threat of eviction to persuade tenants to agree to pay rents well above the legal ceilings.

At our initiative, the General Assembly passed some significant civil rights legislation well in advance of other states. This legislation established the legal right of every citizen regardless of race or religion to buy or rent a house in any locality, to have equal access to restaurants, barbershops, etc., and not to be denied employment on discriminatory grounds. The moribund Civil Rights Commission was given the power to enforce the law, and I appointed a group of tough-minded members with Elmo Roper as chairman.

As in all other states, the Connecticut National Guard still refused to allow blacks to enlist. I asked for a unanimous vote in changing this, and Connecticut became the first state to desegregate its National Guard.

The day after this bill passed the State Assembly I received a telephone call from a Major General in the Defense Department in Washington who stated that the integration of the Connecticut National Guard would jeopardize the Defense budget with the Southern bloc in Congress and that consequently the Department of Defense could no longer provide the Connecticut National Guard with equipment. I asked the General to put this decision in writing and then called Clark Clifford at the White House. Two days later I received an official apology from the Defense Department for this "misunderstanding."

Later the Civil Rights Commission made a study to determine what racial barriers still existed to admission in Connecticut universities. The results showed that any black or Jew who was highly qualified in terms of high school grades was accepted without question. But applicants from these minority groups who were average college material or slightly below average often faced a different situation: a white, Anglo-Saxon Protestant had a far better chance of being accepted than a member of a minority group. This report was made available to the heads of all universities and forced a re-examination of admission policies.

The 1949 General Assembly also accepted most of my proposals in regard to welfare. In the rich state of Connecticut there was a ceiling of only $50 a month on payments to recipients of Old Age Assistance, with the federal government paying half. Under the existing law, state social workers were also required to force many recipients of Old Age Assistance to leave their homes, sell their cars and even to give up their telephones. The General Assembly agreed not only to remove the ceiling but to revamp the criteria and improve training for social workers. Interestingly enough, the strong support that we received on this legislation came not only from the older recipients but also from their children. In many cases the state had previously forced sons and daughters to take their older relatives into already badly crowded homes regardless of the often adverse effects on family relationships.

During the regular session the legislature was also persuaded to enact an emergency teacher-training program to ease Connecticut's critical teacher shortage. While there were four state teachers colleges in Connecticut, which we were anxious to improve and expand, it was clear that they would be incapable for some time of producing the vast number of new teachers we needed. We recommended, and it was agreed, that qualified liberal arts students would be offered an opportunity to teach in Connecticut public schools after passing a special abbreviated course of training, thereby qualifying for an emergency teaching certificate. Although many members of the educational bureaucracy bitterly opposed the plan, there was no better alternative, and eventually we won our point.

We also secured funds for several new buildings at the University of Connecticut and at our teachers colleges.

Another initiative of ours, which I believe still holds considerable promise, involved the financing and management of hospitals or other institutions. As we visited the state hospitals, Steb and I were often disturbed by the mediocre management in some institutions, largely due to the relatively low salaries the state was able to pay.

It occurred to me that the situation might be solved by bringing the state's ability to finance the building of hospitals together with the ability of private individuals to provide better management. After many discussions we worked out the following formula, using the New Britain Memorial Hospital as our first proposed project: (1) The state would provide $3 million for the construction of the hospital with a bed capacity of 165 patients. (2) The hospital would be operated by a board of directors of eighteen, twelve of whom would be appointed by the original trustees, with the other six appointed by the Governor. (3) The beds would be occupied by patients nominated by the state welfare organizations, with the cost per patient based on the accounting rules established by the American Hospital Association to enable the hospital to operate on a break-even basis. (4) The only state control would be through an audit which would be made annually and by an agreement that the state could take over the management of the hospital on one-year notice whenever it wished to do so.

Since then the New Britain Memorial Hospital, with its bed capacity increased to two hundred beds, has become recognized as one of the best-managed hospitals in the United States. The success of this experiment, involving state-financed construction combined with private management under an agreed set of ground rules, should, I believe, be given serious consideration by the urban, state and federal governments.

I had placed major emphasis during the campaign on efficient and more effective state government. A first step was taken when the General Assembly, in the face of strong opposition from the House leadership, authorized funds for a commission to study the state government and to recommend changes.

In the hope that I could thereby win major support from members of the business community, I appointed a commission made up entirely of businessmen, all but one of whom were Republicans. To head the commission I selected Carter W. Atkins, the competent director of Connecticut's Council of Public Expenditures, an organization established and financed by a large number of Connecticut businesses to serve as a watchdog on state expenditures. I also appointed G. Keith Funston, president of Trinity College and later president of the New York Stock Exchange; James Lee Loomis, president of Connecticut General Insurance Company; Oliver B. Ellsworth, a Hartford banker; and my old associate James G. Rogers. Jim, after leaving Washington, where he had established a reputation as a brilliant administrator, had set up an investment banking office in Stamford. This five-man commission was to report to me on or before January 1, 1950; the story of its report appears in the next chapter.

In view of the opposition's deeply rooted antipathy to change, and the narrowness of my victory at the polls, this record of legislative successes at the regular session of the General Assembly was better than might have been expected; in large measure this was due to our success in promoting public support. Yet several other proposals for urgently needed legislation were blocked in the House.

Among the most important of those defeats was the refusal of the House to pass legislation which would allow the local communities to build schools on a "pay as you use" basis. The House also balked at my proposal to set up a commission to study the quality of education in

Connecticut—an idea in which Steb took a great interest. We were concerned that we might devote all of our money and energies on brick and
mortar to solve the shortage of classrooms and fail to give enough attention to what happened within the classroom. The new commission, I proposed, should consider in depth the curriculum, teaching techniques,
teacher training, and the relationships between students and teachers
and also parents.

The Republican leaders did not take kindly to this proposal. They
insisted on a commission composed entirely of professional educators
and businessmen, while I wanted a broad cross section including, in
addition to businessmen and members of the educational establishment,
laborers, social workers, young people and members of racial minorities.
Although my education study bill was killed in the House, I later used
my contingency fund to convene on March 27, 1949, a study group of
outstanding people headed by Norman Cousins, which considered and
carried out the work anyway.

I also failed to persuade the Republican House to change the manner
in which judges were picked for the lower courts. The judges, who
handled minor civil and criminal matters for the most part, were the
lowest rungs of the judiciary. In the past the legislature itself had selected these judges with no participation by the Governor and, I might
add, with no political holds barred. Each legislative session set the stage
for wild and often unprincipled wheeling and dealing in the selections.
This was in contrast to the higher judiciary in Connecticut, which then,
as now, enjoyed a reputation for high integrity and nonpartisanship.

Moreover, since lower court judges were part-time appointees, a judge
might appear one day as a lawyer before a judge who the next day would
appear as a lawyer pleading a case before him. This resulted in a system
of legal give-and-take which made a mockery of the judicial process;
eventually the public demanded a change. A referendum had been placed
on the ballot in the election the previous November providing that henceforth these judges would be appointed by the Governor for terms determined by the General Assembly. It had received a large majority.

Shortly after my inauguration I sent a message to the legislature
suggesting for its consideration a system which would eventually provide
for a six-year term, with one-third of the judges coming up for reappointment every six years. To establish this cycle, one-third of the new judges
would be nominated for a six-year term, one-third for a two-year term,
and one-third for a four-year term. Thereafter each would serve a full
six-year term provided he was reconfirmed by the Governor and legislature.

Although my proposal was accepted by the Senate, there was no response from the House. In an effort at least to open up a dialogue, we

came up with several variations. However, it soon became clear that the Republican leaders in the House had no thought of passing the legislation until they had a Republican Governor.

A similar case involved appointments to the three-man State Public Utilities Commission. For many years the Republican Party in Connecticut had been dominated by J. Henry Roraback, the Republican National Committeeman who also happened to serve as president of the Connecticut Light & Power Company.

Under his "guidance," legislation was adopted which he correctly assumed would assure Republican control over the members of the Utilities Commission for many years to come. This legislation called for each incumbent to remain in office until his successor had been approved by both houses of the General Assembly. Since the Republicans had controlled the Connecticut House of Representatives for more than a hundred years, this assured them of veto power over any Democratic appointee. On the few occasions when the Democrats controlled the Senate, as they did in 1949, the usual practice was to arrange a deal— the Republicans would get one appointee and the Democrats the next.

Since the terms of two of the three incumbents were about to expire, there were about to be two potential vacancies. Although the current members of the Commission were, as far as I knew, honorable men, none of them had any experience whatsoever in the highly complicated field of public utilities. (One of them, I recall, was in the poultry business, another was the owner of a small store.)

The Republican leaders assumed that in line with political tradition I would select a Democrat and they would select a Republican. However, in the larger interests of the consumers of gas, electricity and other public utilities, I selected two highly professional individuals, each with long experience in setting public utility rates. One happened to be a Republican, and the other an Independent. I did not see how they could be turned down.

The Senate promptly approved these men, but the Republican-dominated House took one quick look and, with no evidence of embarrassment, did not even bother to hold hearings; this meant that the unqualified "tame" incumbents remained in office.

As for my proposal that a sales tax, which falls most heavily on those least able to pay, be replaced by an income tax—it never had a chance.

It was the general assumption, not only among the Republicans but among many members of the press, that Democratic administrations such as ours were no more than temporary interruptions and if the Republican opposition simply sat tight until my two-year term blew over, a Republican would be back in the Governor's chair and they could then return to the good old ways. As a result we ended the regular session with considerable unfinished business.

One piece of business that I felt deserved our attention but which was clearly not ready for legislative action was the high cost of medicine and medical care, and the resulting tragic impact of "catastrophic illnesses" on tens of thousands of Connecticut families.

I knew that any proposal we might make to ease this burden would be politically explosive and must be approached cautiously. My first step, therefore, was an off-the-record discussion with three outstanding physicians who I thought might share my concern, one from the Yale University Medical School and the other two from Hartford Hospital.

After briefly sketching the problems, I said I was prepared to support a state-financed medical insurance program to cover "catastrophic illness," with another state-financed arrangement to provide for a complete annual health check-up for every citizen who requested it. I asked: (1) Could a practical program be put together at reasonable cost? (2) How could the state medical people be brought into the plan in a way that would avoid arousing the old battle cry of "socialized medicine"? Their reaction was enthusiastic.

With their help we then put together a list of doctors and hospital administrators representing a cross section of the Connecticut medical profession. This list included the president of the State Medical Association, a vice president of the National AMA who lived in Connecticut, and several respected doctors and hospital managers; it totaled some twenty people.

On a confidential basis they were invited to an off-the-record meeting in my office. In opening the discussion I stressed that I was speaking in confidence and hoped that any reference to this meeting could be kept out of the press. My sole desire, I said, was to explore with them the possibility of creating an effective state medical insurance system which, with the cooperative support of most doctors, would bring more adequate medical service to our people, and perhaps encourage other states to come up with similar efforts. As a gesture to their own selfish interests, I suggested that this would also assure all doctors, hospitals and druggists full payment for their services.

I realized that the American Medical Association, in spite of the rapid expansion of medical care for veterans, had traditionally been opposed to government-financed health programs for nonveterans. However, I wondered if a primary reason for their opposition had not been the failure of those who sponsored these proposals to ask the medical profession itself to play a major role. Would it be possible, I asked, for the state to work with responsible members of the Connecticut Medical Association and with hospital administrators to devise a fresh nonbureaucratic approach to an old problem?

They listened politely, looked at each other rather nervously and said nothing. When I saw they were unprepared to discuss such a radical proposal on short notice, I said I realized that I was confronting them with a brand-new idea and that they might want first to consult with each other over possible ways of working toward what I assumed was a common goal. We could then meet again and hopefully make some progress. They seemed relieved, and agreed to another meeting in two weeks.

The second meeting was equally unproductive. After considerable skirmishing, one of my original three confidants volunteered that the group was divided on what could and should be done and suggested that I outline any specific ideas that I had in mind and they could then offer their frank views.

I suggested that the question might be divided into three sections: (1) how to ease the financial burden of catastrophic illness; (2) how to assure earlier diagnoses before an illness becomes unmanageable; and (3) how to train more doctors in Connecticut.

In regard to "catastrophic illness," I suggested a plan under which any Connecticut family faced with the costs of a major illness might itself pay up to 10 percent of its annual income. If the costs exceeded that amount, the remainder would be paid by the State Department of Health from regularly appropriated funds.

In regard to the second question, I suggested that an annual health examination should be provided free to every person in the state; mobile clinics might be used in the rural areas. As to the third point, I said that there was only one medical school in the entire state—the Yale Medical School—and it was graduating no more doctors annually than in the 1920's. Connecticut was a rich state, which could and should have a second medical school with equally high standards. The Hartford Hospital might combine with the University of Connecticut to meet this need.

A general nodding of heads encouraged me to suggest a third meeting, which was held about a week later. But rigid concepts are difficult to change. About half of the group said that they were prepared to support my program and the other half were opposed or uncertain.

In view of this division and with all the other legislative problems, it would be unwise to press for legislation this term. Thanking them for their cooperation, I told them that, despite our failure to agree, the meetings had at least been conducted amicably and without unwanted publicity.

Throughout the regular 1949 session, while other legislation passed or failed, and other debates raged, the major questions of how—and whether, which was the real issue—we were to finance programs of school and other state building construction went unanswered. The legislature was required by law to adjourn at midnight, June 8, 1949. But the big day came, and there was still no sign of compromise on the budget.

I had lunch in my office and waited. I had dinner in my office and waited some more. At eleven o'clock that night the Republican leaders unexpectedly appeared in my office on the assumption that by that time I would be willing and eager for a political deal.

At ten minutes to twelve someone pointed out that the law restricting the length of the regular session could be interpreted as referring to standard time, not daylight saving time. So the clock was turned back by one hour and the discussions continued. At midnight standard time we still had failed to agree on a budget, or on essential legislation to expand and modernize state mental hospitals and schools. Indeed, I had no authority to spend any funds after July 1, 1949, except for highway construction, which came from a special fund. It was a travesty of the democratic process.

There was nothing to do but call the two houses to a joint session, politely express my regret at our inability to reach agreement and adjourn the Assembly as the law required. I announced that I would call a special session to begin the following Monday morning. With the Secretary of State shouting, appropriately for once, "God save the State of Connecticut," the regular session of the 1949 General Assembly staggered to a close.

That afternoon the Hartford *Times* ran the following editorial:

After adopting the slogan, "Whittle it down," the Republicans began a blind attack on the Bowles budget. On the evening of adjournment they came out with a document that caused deep consternation to those who thought they understood it and plain confusion to the rest.

Lunging wildly for an issue that might meet with some measure of popular support, the Republicans again turned to the sales tax.

Meanwhile, the obstructionists had halted everything and the final hours of the session were ticking away. It became apparent that the entire business of the state had become a pawn in a squeeze play against the Governor. The question was whether the Republicans could put him in a hold and force him to abandon his platform and that of his party, in order to get anything done at all. Their gamble was that the Governor's sense of responsibility to the state would prove stronger than his pride in his own program or loyalty to his own party.

Three of the most important items have been left for the special session. These are the state budget, the question of how much money the state shall devote to its educational program, and what it intends to do to remedy the past neglect of state institutions. Not one of these problems is new. All of them have confronted the legislators at least since the first of February. But the spirit of take-it-or-leave-it barred the way to their solution.

CHAPTER 15

THE SPECIAL SESSIONS

IN THE FIRST SPECIAL SESSION, after some predictable wrangling, the General Assembly approved a budget for the next two years in which expenditures were balanced with revenues. But once again the House leaders rejected my proposal for a major bond issue to help local communities finance the school-building program on a "pay as you use" basis. As a "substitute" they appropriated $7 million for school construction to be paid for out of current tax revenues; this would finance the building of only four or five schools throughout the state.

After vetoing the $7 million construction item, I adjourned this emergency session with the following statement: "We shall meet again in the fall. At that time I shall again present to the General Assembly the needs for a state school-building program on a scale large enough to meet the needs of our educational system."

The Hartford *Times* commented as follows:

> Governor Bowles' veto of the Republican $7,200,000 appropriation for school building to be paid for out of current revenues was a sound decision. The question now is whether the Republican majority in the House intends to let a sensible long-range proposal for school building aid to be paid for over a period of years go through, or whether it still thinks it can "beat Bowles" by denying adequate school buildings to the children of Connecticut.

The special session devoted to school building was scheduled for November 9, 1949. Since there was no reason to expect the House leadership independently to reverse its position, we knew that our only hope for success was through public support.

I made several broadcasts designed to focus public attention on the crisis in our schools and the need for legislative action. In one broadcast that created considerable stir I said, tongue in cheek, that two "respected but mistaken men," Republican Majority Leader George Conway and Speaker of the House John R. Thim, were the key to the situation. "So far," I said, "they seem not fully to grasp the needs. But I am confident they would welcome an opportunity to discuss the problem with parents of children throughout the state. Why not go to their homes next Sunday or telephone them and give them your views?"[1]

I also conferred with educational leaders throughout the state, Republicans as well as Democrats, and asked for their cooperation. The response from thoughtful citizens, including scores of school board members and teachers, was impressive. In the early fall, shortly after the schools reopened, we launched a "Visit Your School Week."

Thousands of parents visited the schools, and the majority came home shocked by the conditions. In most towns the schools were on two shifts, some with as many as fifty children to a class, with different grades often taught simultaneously in the same room.

In my statement to the two houses which opened the special session on the school crisis, I spelled out the issue and then outlined my proposals:

> This special session will test the sincerity of each individual legislator and each political party. Do we or do we not want to strengthen our educational system? If we do, then are we or are we not willing to take necessary steps to carry out this objective?
>
> The question is sharp and clear and impossible of honest misunderstanding. For nearly a year we have been talking about building schools. We have now reached what in colloquial terms might be called the "put up or shut up" phase of the discussion.
>
> As we enter this session we each carry a heavy responsibility. It is my responsibility to outline the need and to offer a specific realistic program to meet these needs that can be financed within our agreed-to budget.
>
> This I have done; what happens now is in your hands.

The next day the Hartford *Times* commented editorially: "At length and in detail, Governor Bowles has set forth the problem of State aid for the building of schools and offered a program for its solution. There is no evidence that it will be accepted by the Republican majority in the House."

This proved to be too dismal a prognosis. Although the debate continued week after week with every indication that the opposition was determined to stand firm, our statewide program to spell out the issues

1. Hundreds of disturbed parents followed this suggestion.

and to win public support began to show results. As the opposition leaders began to sense the extent of our support, genuine negotiations began.

The bill on which the leaders of both parties finally agreed was almost precisely what we had recommended, including a retroactive provision to cover schools built since 1945. Cities and towns would receive regular payments from the state to help them pay off the bonds which they had issued, and there were no limitations on the number of new or expanded schools that the localities could build; the legislation was to remain in effect indefinitely.

Building proceeded rapidly, and within two years 94,000 schoolchildren were studying in modern schools built under the program. By the early 1960's, more than three-fourths of all schoolchildren in Connecticut were enrolled in modern schools constructed under this program.

With this major accomplishment behind us, we looked forward to the recommendations of the Commission on State Government Reorganization, authorized by the General Assembly during the regular 1949 session. The report of the Commission was delivered to me on February 1, 1950. It was an impressive document which went far beyond my own expectations and, I believe, those of any leader in either party. It was the clearest and most comprehensive blueprint for the organization and operation of a modern state government that I had ever seen.

The report stated unequivocally that "The citizens are not getting one hundred cents' worth of government service for their dollar. Not only has the cost of state government gone up, but the government is costly for what it does." It also asserted that "The best interests of the public are not being served by this system of government. Too often the agencies under this decentralized system respond to interests which are special and local rather than to the larger interests of the people of the state as a whole."

The report called for the consolidation of our 202 commissions, boards and departments into 14 operating departments, 3 central service agencies and the Governor's office.

All special funds would be abolished, including the Highway Fund, and all tax receipts would go into the General Fund. County government, which constituted a needless bureaucratic layer in a small state such as Connecticut, would be abolished, while home rule for the cities and towns would be greatly expanded.

The proposed new State Constitution would provide for initiative and referendum and the recall of elected officials. The State Senate would be redistricted on the basis of population after every federal census, and there would be a 40 percent reduction in the size of the House of Representatives. Annual sessions, an annual budget and an increase in the legislative salaries to enable more high-caliber men and women to serve the General Assembly were also provided for. A direct primary system would abolish the convention method of selecting all candidates.

All local courts with their part-time judges would be abolished and replaced by a new Court of Common Pleas. Also abolished would be the 120 probate courts, which were traditionally ridden with politics, and a new Probate Division of the court system would be established.

These far-reaching proposals recommended by a distinguished Commission of five members—four of them members of the opposite party— made a deep impression on a state which had been insulated from change by the inadequacies of a state government designed for a different era.

The only recommendation the Commission did not make which I had hoped for was the creation of a unicameral Assembly. The tradition of two legislative houses was an historical accident. The British Parliament established two houses (the House of Commons and the House of Lords) as a device gradually to transfer power from the aristocracy to the people as a whole. The two houses of our Federal Congress had been established, not because they would be more democratic or efficient, or because of the British model, but as a compromise required to win the support of both the larger and smaller states at the Constitutional Convention of 1789.

Our State Constitution, as in all other states with the exception of Nebraska, had for no good reason followed the pattern of two houses set by the Federal Congress and by the British.

I believed that the "people as a whole" in Connecticut could be best served by one house, the members of which would be elected from districts of roughly equal population. This, I thought, was the simplest means of preventing the rural majority in the House from vetoing legislation of special importance to the urban areas, which led desperate local officials to take their problems to Washington, thereby increasing the trend toward centralized government.

If the proposal for a unicameral General Assembly were regarded as too radical, we should, I felt, at least establish the principle of equal representation for all members of the House, rural or urban. Under the current system 4 percent of the population of Connecticut could in theory elect a majority in the House of Representatives. Since all towns incorporated before 1850, regardless of population, sent two members to the House, the six smallest towns, with a total population of only 2,200 people, could (and often did) outvote the five largest cities, with a total population of 700,000.

In 1964 when it became apparent that the states themselves were unlikely to come to grips with this situation, the Supreme Court of the United States decided that all state constitutions must be rewritten to assure those citizens who live in cities a political voice equal to those who live in rural areas. This ruling may turn out to be one of the most important judicial decisions in American history.

The Commission report presented a radical organization plan to bring policy-making and administration much closer to the people. For this very reason I knew it would be bitterly opposed by every vested interest in the state.

My instinct was to move cautiously, to praise the report and then call for a public discussion of its recommendations, requesting respected citizens of both parties to establish a statewide organization with a speakers bureau to stimulate discussion meetings in every town and neighborhood. The election was less than eight months away. Once the report had been fully explained and discussed throughout the state, I could make it the primary issue in my campaign for re-election in November, 1950, with the certainty of strong bipartisan support.

The five members of the Commission argued strongly against such delay. They pointed out that at a regular session of the Assembly the legislation required to put these proposals into effect could be lost in the maze of "normal business" and either amended to death or quietly slipped into committee pigeonholes.

They also pointed out that several proposals required constitutional amendments which could legally be placed before the voters for decision in a referendum only when the Governor was up for election. If the proposals were to appear on the ballot next November, I would have to secure the approval of the legislature before that time. Otherwise, these amendments would have to wait until 1954, since the governorship would change to a four-year term in 1950.

Since the public and press reaction to the report had been excellent, the Commission members were confident of statewide, bipartisan support for the reorganization proposals; the business community in particular, they felt, would be solidly behind them.

After lengthy discussions I made the following proposal: if I could persuade the Democratic majority in the Senate to support the recommendations in the report and if the members of the Commission and their supporters among the business community could secure a similar agreement from the Republican majority in the House, I would call a special session. The Commission members agreed, and we proceeded to take soundings among the leaders of the two parties.

I invited the twenty-two Democratic Senators to dinner at the Governor's House to discuss the report and determine how best to proceed. I made it clear that I favored the recommendations and with one or two minor exceptions was prepared to support them all.

As I anticipated, there were many dissenters. The changes, they said, were sound, but the Democrats had far more to lose from such a radical government reorganization than did the Republicans. Our party had been out of office for most of the last century, and we were at long last entitled to our fair share of the patronage available in the present system.

I was supported in my rebuttal by all of the key leaders, including John Bailey, Lieutenant Governor Carroll and the Democratic leaders in the Senate and House. We argued that we were moving into a new and more sophisticated political era. Good government had become good politics. The Democratic Party had an opportunity to lead the fight for a more effective state government and that opportunity should not be thrown away.

It was well after midnight before we convinced the last of the doubters, and the twenty-two Democratic members of the Senate agreed unanimously to support the Commission's recommendations without qualification.

The next morning I reported to the members of the Commission that the Democrats in the State Assembly at least would solidly support their recommendations. A few days later representatives of the Commission told me that the Republican leadership had also agreed to cooperate, but that they could not actually say so in advance because the reorganization would then become established publicly as the "Bowles Program."

Nevertheless, the Commission members assured me that we had nothing to worry about; the Republicans, under continuing pressure from the press and from the business community, would have no alternative but to go along. With this assurance we proceeded, with a certain degree of uneasiness, to call another special session of the General Assembly.

My address to the opening of this joint session in March, 1950, vigorously supported the recommendations of the State Reorganization Commission, noting that it would save at least $20 million annually and would assure much greater efficiency in our governmental operation.

Our present Constitution, I said, had been created for a far simpler era when there were no railroads, airplanes, radios or automobiles; no industrial plants, no crowded cities, no pollution and no fear of mass unemployment or atomic wars. It was a Constitution geared to a predominantly rural society. Since our society had changed drastically, it was time to modernize its government. In closing my presentation I said:

> During the next few weeks, we will demonstrate, each of us—Democrats and Republicans alike—whether our easily enunciated slogans calling for better government are something more than political clichés.
>
> Let me make my own position clear. I accept the report of the Commission on Reorganization with enthusiasm. I endorse it wholeheartedly. I urge you, the members of the Connecticut General Assembly, to take the action necessary to put it into law.
>
> The report offers both parties an opportunity to join together in a nonpartisan effort to modernize our state government and to strengthen our Connecticut democracy.

The legislative hearings began a few days later. The first witness was Charles L. Campbell, president of the Connecticut Light & Power Company and president of the Public Expenditures Council, of which the chairman of the Reorganization Commission, Carter Atkins, was director. Instead of the strong support we all had assumed would be forthcoming, Campbell said in sum that the Commission's proposals were theoretical, wrong and, worst of all, tampered with a system of government which had served us well since 1818.

With few exceptions, each governmental department head then opposed that part of the program affecting his operation. After first congratulating the Commission for its "great contribution," for example, the chairman of the Aeronautics Board opposed incorporation into the Motor Vehicles Department. Likewise, the State Highway Commission opposed its inclusion in the Highway Department; the Board of Education its inclusion in the Education Department; and so on.

Within two or three days it had become clear that we had made a serious political mistake. I should not have called a special session until I was certain that the Republicans were genuinely committed to the program. Instead of trusting the assurances of the Commission members, who had little political experience, I should have personally called the Republican leaders and laid it on the line.

If they had agreed generally to support the recommendations of the predominantly Republican Commission, we could have removed the issue from politics and all shared in the credit. But if they had opposed these recommendations, I would have carried the issue into every town in Connecticut during my campaign for re-election and asked the voters to provide me with so strong a mandate that at the next regular session the program could not have been ignored. But, unfortunately, it was too late to go back.

The many lobbies which felt that they might fare less well in dealing with a more efficient state government then began to bring up their artillery. Conscious of the strong press support for the Commission's recommendations, they were careful in their initial statements not to attack the report directly. It was, they said, a praiseworthy effort, but in this respect or that certain changes were required.

Several of them zeroed in on the proposal that all tax revenues should go into a general fund instead of the present earmarked special funds. Previously, for example, the contributions of the teachers and others toward their pension funds had been placed in special funds, each earmarked for payment of pensions to a particular group. Under the new proposal the full resources of the state would be behind every pension fund, which provided additional protection against any loss due to corruption or mismanagement. If there had been time carefully to explain the reason for this change to the teachers and others in advance, there is no doubt that they would have seen that it was in their interest. As it was, a series of lobbies charged that this was a nefarious plot to divert to other uses the savings of the schoolteachers and other public servants.

The State Grange and Rural Roads Association lobbied against the abolition of the Highway Fund, and contractors and others who had a stake in the loosely administered state highway construction program were told that money previously earmarked for road building would henceforth be controlled by "New Deal crackpots" and diverted to other uses.

The proposed consolidation into one department of the regulating agencies to protect the consumer, businessman and others against malpractices by the banks, insurance companies and public utilities was another target for special attack. Officials of insurance companies, banks and public utilities feared that consolidation would mean new teeth for regulations which were not normally well enforced.

Traditionally, commissions earned from the sale of insurance to cover losses to state institutions and property had been distributed by the party in power among those party leaders who happened to be in the insurance business. Since each party benefited from this when it was in office, and since the amount of the insurance was substantial and of major importance to the insurance companies, it was rarely, if ever, publicly challenged.

The report recommended that this arrangement should be replaced by a self-insurance system (used by the federal government and many state governments), which would save the state money by bypassing the insurance companies, thereby eliminating the premiums altogether. The insurance lobby, of course, raised an uproar over this proposal, even though one member of the Commission who had endorsed the reform was the president of a large Hartford insurance company.

As we watched this parade of special interests, I remembered Steb's wise comment. "You have always," she said, "grossly under-estimated the number of influential people who have a vested interest in bad government." Although many organizations, such as the labor unions and League of Women Voters, strongly supported the Commis-sion's recommendations, it was clear that if the program was to be salvaged, a compromise was essential.

On April 18 I presented such a compromise to a joint session of the Assembly which attracted a good deal of support. Several groups which had originally opposed the reorganization proposals, including Campbell's Public Expenditures Council, came out for the revised plan.

Our opponents in the House responded by adopting a less negative tactic. The reorganization proposal, they said, in general was a good thing and eventually should be put into effect. But as a practical matter at least four hundred pieces of legislation would be required and this would take many months.

When this rationalization began to appear in the press, I asked Abe Chayes and Ed Logue to recruit a legal team to produce the necessary legislation as quickly and quietly as possible. On the ground that we all needed more time to think, I suggested to the leadership of the two houses that the legislature recess for a couple of weeks. With obvious relief, they agreed.

Chayes, Logue and a dozen or so faculty members from the Yale Law School then proceeded to produce a miracle. Instead of four hundred pieces of legislation, they packed all the necessary legislation into forty-three bills; instead of taking "many months," they took two weeks.

They delivered the bills to me on a Saturday. I went over them care-fully with my associates that afternoon and evening, and on Sunday, after reading an encouragingly moderate press statement on the report by House Majority Leader George Conway, I called him and invited him to dinner at our home in Essex the following evening for a private, off-the-record discussion. He hesitated for a few seconds and then agreed to come.

After dinner I laid out the forty-three pieces of legislation on a table and said with a smile, "Here are the four hundred bills that you said would take a year to put together." Conway picked up the first bill, glanced through it, then picked up another and another and finally said: "This is a remarkable job of drafting."

I told him we were prepared to accept all of these bills with whatever changes it was agreed were indicated. He and his Republican associates could first introduce them into the House, pass them and send them to the Democratic Senate, where they would be accepted as Republican-sponsored legislation. Since four out of the five Commission members were Republican, it would be impossible for me or any other Democrat to exploit these reforms politically. I added that if it would make things easier for him, I would even criticize the bills and otherwise indicate whatever reluctance he felt might be politically helpful.

Conway avoided a specific commitment. He said, however, that he was genuinely impressed and that he would immediately discuss my proposal with his associates.

Within a few days six of our bills passed both houses, with the initiative in each case coming from the Republican House leaders. I was amused to see that among the six was a bill that transferred the Mosquito Control Board, which had been an independent operation, to the Health Department. The high priority given this bill was obviously due to the desire of the Republican state organization to get rid of a maverick, antiorganization Republican who had supported me in 1948 and who for some years had been in charge of our mosquitoes.

But the story had a dismal ending. On May 25 the tough, highly partisan Republican National Committeeman, Harold E. Mitchell, returned from an extended out-of-state business trip. When he heard of my private dealings with Conway, he called a meeting of the opposition leadership. They were naïve, he said, to embark on a cooperative effort of this kind. Regardless of how sincere they appeared, Democrats could never be trusted; somehow, he said, we would arrange to get the credit.

The next day, May 26, without further discussion the House abruptly adjourned, and there was nothing for the Senate to do but follow suit. We were, of course, bitterly disappointed. In spite of my original blunder in regard to timing, we had almost succeeded in getting our legislation through.

At the heart of the matter, as Alan Olmstead in the Manchester *Herald* pointed out, was a basic philosophical difference about what government should or should not be. His comments include the following:

> There is a deep, fundamental ideological controversy involved in the report of the State Reorganization Commission. The basis for this controversy is to be found in the word "democracy" and the word "republic" as our dictionary defines them.

"Democracy," says the dictionary, is "a theory of government which, in its purest form, holds that the state should be controlled by all the people, each sharing equally in privileges, duties and responsibilities."

"A republic," says our dictionary, is "a state in which the sovereignty resides in *a certain portion of the people* [italics added], and the legislative and administrative powers are lodged in the officers elected by and representing the people."

The real fear of those who oppose the Report is that it would establish too much "democracy" in Connecticut. It is their view that only a "certain portion of the people" are fit to hold authority, fit to do the governing, that a Republic means government by an elite, or by the "best fitted." This concept has considerable ideological charm for those who conversely are afraid of "mob rule," which is their definition of extreme democracy.

Now the old fashioned town meeting was democracy in its purest form, and it has, nostalgically at least, the approval of even those who claim we are a republic. . . . The fact is that some consider the people of the small towns fit to govern themselves, but do not consider the population of cities equally fit. They fear and distrust plain, direct majority rule in the state as a whole. For such people, a weak Governor, a slow and obstructionist legislature, and cumbersome procedures for all changes are actually Connecticut's strengths, and protections against the potentially unwise and uninformed whims of the people as a whole.

This issue of whether Connecticut is a republic or a democracy will be largely determined by the ultimate fate of the Report.

Democracy often moves slowly, but it does move, and in recent years long-overdue changes have helped to modernize Connecticut's government. Most of the proposals I presented in 1950 have now been enacted into law, largely through the efforts of Governor Abraham Ribicoff. The major changes are as follows:

1. The executive branch has been reorganized into eighteen departments.
2. The legislature, starting in 1972, will meet annually rather than every other year.
3. The local courts, with their part-time judges, have been abolished and replaced by a system of lower state courts and a circuit system.
4. Local city and town governments have been given more voice in their own affairs.
5. County government has been abolished.
6. Following the Supreme Court's ruling of "one man, one vote," the State House of Representatives has been reorganized to give the cities equal voice with the rural areas.

CHAPTER 16

POLITICIANS AND POLITICS

BEFORE MY INAUGURATION IN JANUARY, 1949, I had only a vague under-standing of the complex political forces with which a Governor must deal. While I had worked with political leaders of both parties in Washington, I was distrustful of the so-called "professional politicians" who control and operate the state and local political machines.

However, my worries about my ability to work with the state Demo-cratic organization proved largely groundless. Because I took its leaders into my confidence and because John Bailey acted as an effective com-munications link between the party and my office, I was able to convince most of them that what I was striving to do was not only good govern-ment but also good politics.

Bailey had organized my campaign for the nomination with skill, and I had come to rely on his advice on tactics and timing. He was interested not only in politics as such but also in the art of government. He had an unsurpassed knowledge of the legislative process, worked hard at his trade, and personally read every bill that came out of committee. I not only strongly supported his election to the chairman-ship of the State Democratic Committee; I consulted with him on almost all matters relating to my operation.

At first I worried about John's ability to adapt to the positive role that I expected to play as Governor or to my legislative priorities. But he quickly saw that I held strong views on what I wanted to do, and he not only respected them but worked loyally to develop legislative and public support.

Our personal relationship was further strengthened by the fact that

John was blessed with a keen sense of humor. He found politics stimulating and exciting. He and his wife, Barbara, and their four children were at our house a good deal, and we grew to know each other well. Steb and Barbara became close friends.

I had, of course, become acquainted with all the Democratic leaders in the course of my fight for the nomination in 1946 and the election in 1948. Now I set out to understand what they really wanted and to establish a working relationship. Did they simply want to gain power and influence, as was generally assumed, or was it something more complex? Would it be possible to develop a continuing relationship with them which would not require me to compromise my principles but would still provide a basis for communication and cooperation?

In my travels throughout the state I seized every opportunity to talk to these leaders, to seek their advice, to explain as best I could why I, too, was a politician and what I wanted to accomplish. Steb's contribution was enormous. She rarely forgot names or faces, and her natural liking for people came through quickly and easily in her political contacts.

Although these politicians were not accustomed to working with individuals like me with a totally different background, they gradually began to realize that while I saw politics not as an end in itself (as did many of them) but as a means to an end, the "end" was no more nor less than an effective state government.

With such Democratic regulars as John Golden of New Haven, Connie Mulvihill of Bridgeport, John Tynan of Middletown[1] and Jack Kelly of Hartford, I managed with reasonable success to develop a relationship based on mutual understanding and respect. They and many others were not only loyal but in their different ways offered their friendship. Contrary to the established image of the "machine politician," most of the organization leaders not only were as honest as their counterparts in business or the professions, but in some cases they possessed a genuine idealism and liberalism. With few exceptions, they were second- or third-generation Americans whose parents and grandparents had endured poverty and privation and had worked hard to educate their children and to establish a degree of personal security.

In retrospect, I believe they regarded my Administration as an exciting experience which introduced them to a new kind of political operation they had not known before. At last the political game they played with such gusto could give them rewards of self-respect they had

1. Over his political career Tynan also gave a political helping hand to such outstanding men as Wilbert Snow and Stephen Bailey, Mayor of Middletown.

rarely experienced, even on occasion at the sacrifice of certain conventional rewards such as patronage.

I learned that the word of a professional politician is often more reliable than that of a relative newcomer to politics. Once a professional politician made an agreement, you could generally count on him to stick to it. This quality, it may be said, was largely a testimony to his pragmatic common sense. Once a politician earns a reputation as a potential double-crosser, his effectiveness rapidly disappears.

Generally speaking, the old-line professionals are also less vicious in their electioneering oratory than are many amateurs. It is one of the paradoxes of politics that many of those who set out to run for office presumably for idealistic reasons emerge among the least principled campaigners.

Their rationalization seems to be as follows: in giving up private life to enter political life they are making a great personal sacrifice; politics is necessarily a "dirty business," and consequently if they are to be elected and in a position to bring "clean government" to the people, they must not be squeamish about bringing irresponsible and even libelous charges against their opponents. What irritates me most about such people is their bland assumption that after the campaign furor is over those whom they have so recklessly libeled should be prepared to let bygones be bygones on the grounds that it is all part of the "game" of politics.

Most professional politicians know from experience that the man you oppose today may be your potential ally tomorrow. If you hit him below the belt in a political campaign, future cooperation becomes impossible.

I also learned that political machines are far more complicated than I had previously imagined. Their role can perhaps be summarized as follows:

1. Political "machines" are essential, and they only exist and survive if manned by a sufficient number of people whose aspirations are modest and who, for whatever reason, stick to their objectives through fair and foul weather.

2. The question of whether a particular machine is good or bad depends essentially on whether there happen to be enough decently motivated people available who will apply themselves to the unglamorous activities necessary to keep them afloat.

3. The power of these machines and their internal discipline can easily be overestimated; often the balance of power within the organization is far more fragile than it appears to be, which means that it can be readily upset by a good man who is prepared to make the effort.

4. In many cases the "pros" who man the machines are capable of rising to the challenge of unusual leadership, even if it constrains them from customary practices of dubious morality.

5. Political loyalty and effective support are at their peak when a man is in office with his hand effectively on the throttle of power, but they can be very fickle as soon as he leaves office and is once more in open competition for power.[2]

To avoid misunderstandings and conflicts in regard to patronage, we set up strict ground rules. For instance, it was the usual practice in Connecticut, as elsewhere, for a local political leader to leak to the press the fact that he would soon be meeting with the Governor to recommend the appointment of Mr. So-and-so to such-and-such a position, knowing that to prevent an open conflict the Governor usually would feel forced to go along—and that the local leader's prestige would increase accordingly.

I made it clear at the outset that if I should read in the newspapers that a Democratic leader was coming to Hartford to tell me who to appoint to a certain post, that nominee, regardless of his competence, would be automatically disqualified. I would be glad to receive party leaders' recommendations, but only if they were presented to me in confidence. If we disagreed, we would discuss other possibilities, including outstanding Independents who might strengthen the image of the local Democratic organization. Once we agreed on an appointee, they would be given whatever credit might result. While I could not give them veto power over my appointments, I would never embarrass them by appointing someone who would create difficulties for them.

This formula, firmly stated and rigidly adhered to, as had been our practice in OPA, worked out well. Political leaders were primarily anxious to appear influential, and they had no great difficulties in accepting our ground rules.

The one occasion when a break occurred involved the Democratic National Committeeman from Connecticut, Paul Connery of Norwalk, a powerful member of the state organization. When I refused to appoint an obviously unqualified individual whom he had recommended, he became so abusive that I asked him to leave my office and not to come back. Later he was voted out of his post as National Committeeman by the State Central Committee. Such firm action made it clear that our insistence on qualified people was not subject to compromise.

2. For example, in 1958 John Bailey did not hesitate to employ the skills which he had used to further my programs as Governor to block my nomination for the Senate and to nominate Thomas J. Dodd.

One of my responsibilities as Governor was to appoint some 130 individuals each year to part-time, unpaid positions on state commissions and boards. These included the trustees of mental hospitals, child care centers, education boards, penal institutions and a wide range of state supervisors. In view of Connecticut's diffuse administration, these appointments were particularly important. For instance, the three state mental hospital boards each ran its hospital with no direct control by the Governor except through his power to appoint the trustees.

Traditionally, most of these "prestige" appointments had been passed out by the party in power to major financial contributors or to those with close personal ties to the party. Thus the board members were chosen largely from the upper-income groups, regardless of their qualifications or lack of them. Although many served faithfully and well, we were determined to involve more men and women with special expertise who had a better understanding of our less privileged citizens.

Steb, who had been a social worker and chairman of the school board in Essex, was invaluable in helping to select qualified people to fill these posts. She had campaigned all over the state, spoken in dozens of towns, and had come to know many hundreds of dedicated men and women in all walks of life with special interests and high qualifications. With her help, we put together a list of some four thousand potential candidates.

At my request, Katherine T. Quinn, Secretary of the Democratic Party and right hand of John Bailey, attended all meetings at which our selections were made, to help avoid political blunders. While she was less than enthusiastic about some elements of our legislative program and suspicious of political mavericks such as I, she accepted our standards and, I believe, genuinely tried to help us meet them. Even our opponents would probably agree that our appointees for these positions were significantly better qualifed than in the past.

I was also concerned (needlessly, it turned out) about my relations with the labor unions. Since my opponent, Jim Shannon, was himself a member of an AFL local in Bridgeport, most of the AFL groups had been neutral during the campaign. However, the CIO unions had contributed $51,000 of the $68,000 that we spent in the campaign, which meant the CIO could truthfully say they had enabled me to be elected. What did they expect from me in return?

Shortly after the election I posed this question to Mitchell Sviridoff, the extraordinarily able thirty-two-year-old president of the state CIO. Mike, a New Haven native, was self-educated, resourceful and committed not simply to the interests of labor but to the needs of all citizens. Because of his unique qualities, his influence went well beyond labor circles. Mike's answer to my question was firm and clear. All that he and his people asked of me was that I serve the state as a liberal Governor. And he meant it. On no occasion did he ask me for any favor or special treatment.

The legislative standoff on the appointment of lower court judges caused perhaps my most difficult political problem. As I have mentioned, when the General Assembly adjourned June 1, 1949, the Republicans had assumed that by simply taking no action on the judgeship referendum they had successfully frozen the 126 Republican and 2 Democratic incumbents into their posts. Presumably, these men would remain there until a Republican Administration was elected which could shape the future selection procedures to their advantage.

However, my legal advisers, William S. Gordon, Jr. (Deputy Secretary of State), Ed Logue and Abe Chayes, were convinced that even in the absence of legislation I had the legal right to appoint the 128 judges. Although it was difficult for me to believe that the State Supreme Court would support me in this action, we decided to give it a try.

As evidence of our good faith, we decided to appoint one-half Democrats and one-half Republicans. There were several able Republicans among the incumbents, whom I asked to stay. However, each refused on the ground that he could not accept reappointment from a Democratic Governor under these circumstances without destroying his political credentials within the Republican Party.

The next few weeks were a political nightmare. Literally thousands of Democratic lawyers descended on the State Capitol, each clamoring to be appointed and most of them claiming personal credit for having elected me. Our task was to sort out the qualified people from among the many political hacks. When the smoke and dust finally cleared away, not only had I made my 128 selections but I had developed an ulcer as well.

I was still convinced that this was a futile exercise and I was beginning to begrudge the time and energy we had expended on it, when, to our astonishment, the Supreme Court decided unanimously in favor of our position, and my appointees were duly confirmed. In its decision, the Court highlighted the fact that, while the constitutional amendment specified that the appointees were to be made mutually by the legislature and the Governor, the legislature had refused to act. Therefore the Governor was entitled to act on his own.

As for my selections, I felt we had made the best choices possible under the circumstances. But it had been a hasty operation under great pressure and, given the blatant political nature of these judgeships in the past, I feared that many if not most of my new appointees would drift back into the traditional shoddy pattern of behavior.

I called in several of my appointees in whose integrity I had particular confidence, told them of my fears, and suggested that they propose to their colleagues the establishment of a set of self-imposed ethical standards. Bill Gordon pointed to California's Council of Judges, which had developed a code to guide the behavior of its local court judges as a possible model. Under this code any judge charged with or suspected of improper behavior was asked to appear before a committee on ethics elected by the judges themselves. We quietly urged—I might say insisted —that a similar code be adopted in Connecticut. This was done, and partly, at least, as a consequence these highly vulnerable appointees performed without scandal and in many cases with genuine distinction.

Governors of states are inevitably targets for lobbies, and because of the many controversial proposals with which I was associated it was inevitable that many of them would zero in on me. Surprisingly enough, two of the most powerful lobbies during the 1949 session of the General Assembly were organized by the dentists and by the sports fishermen.

A lobby for dentists pressed for the enactment of legislation to protect themselves from what they considered unfair competition from "dental technicians." A fishermen's lobby also brought heavy pressure to increase state appropriations sharply to increase the number of trout stocked each year in lakes and streams without increasing license fees.[3] The day this particular item came up for debate some three or four hundred burly men in high boots and red-and-black-checked outdoorsman shirts assembled in the State Capitol.

One of the most painful episodes in my political experience opened in October, 1948, a few weeks before the election, when a reporter from a large daily paper, which had persistently failed over a period of years to find any redeeming features in my public career, suddenly asked me for a private appointment on an "urgent matter."

The reporter told me that his paper was aware of certain illegal activities in the State Liquor Commission, whose duties were to enforce all laws and regulations affecting the sale of liquor in Connecticut. If I would expose this corruption, he said, his paper would maintain a benevolent neutrality during the campaign. When I pressed for evidence, he said that he could do no more than assure me that the charges were accurate. I replied that without solid evidence it would be irresponsible to make the matter a political issue.

3. This would require the state to subsidize trout fishing; if we took this step, there was no valid reason then why the state should refuse to subsidize other sports, by providing free basketballs, footballs and the like to citizens requesting them.

As the campaign progressed, I received several anonymous letters also charging corruption in the Liquor Commission. When, following my election, the flow of letters increased, it became clear that an investigation was in order.

I was uncertain how to proceed. The chairman of the Commission, John T. Dunn, Jr., was a prominent Republican political leader. The two men whom I would normally ask to conduct an investigation were also strongly partisan Republicans. The Commissioner of Police, Edward J. Hickey, had publicly contributed to my recent opponent's campaign fund, and the Attorney General, William L. Hadden, was one of the three or four most powerful leaders in the Republican organization.

Nevertheless, because I respected Hickey's record as a police officer, I decided to open up the subject to see how he would react. I told him that, while I had no desire to embarrass him by asking him to investigate a prominent fellow Republican, I would appreciate his professional advice on how best to handle the situation. Hickey replied that his primary obligation was to the state and that he was prepared to launch a thorough investigation, which he agreed was indicated.

On June 1, 1949, Hickey made his report, which included the following charges:

> I have found substantial evidence of questionable conduct and neglect of duty in office by one of the Commissioners of the Liquor Control Commission, namely, Chairman John T. Dunn, Jr. This questionable conduct and neglect of duty pertains to probable violations of the Liquor Control Act and probable violations of the criminal laws. . . .
>
> From May 1, 1945, the date of his appointment, and continuing to the present time, Commissioner Dunn has had personal dealings with permittees of the Liquor Control Commission and with persons applying to that Commission for liquor permits. With more than 134 permittees he had negotiated and effected in the past year and a half over 555 policies of insurance on stocks of liquor, on property, and on the business of permittees of the Liquor Control Commission. The annual premiums total far in excess of $52,527.72. All of these business dealings have been with persons coming before Commissioner Dunn in his official capacity, and upon whose cases he sat in judgment. . . .
>
> Conclusion: Effective enforcement of the liquor laws and the gambling laws as they relate to permittee premises is seriously impaired because of existing conditions and practices.

Despite Dunn's denial of the allegations, the evidence was so damaging that I suspended him pending a hearing.

Because of his own close party ties I suggested to Attorney General Hadden, who normally would be responsible for prosecuting the case, that he might want to stand aside and appoint a special prosecutor. His answer, like Hickey's, was forthright; regardless of any personal embarrassment, he said, it was his responsibility to uphold the law.

In order to avoid the charge that I was vindictively attacking a high-ranking Republican appointee, I withdrew from the usual role of Governor as the hearing officer and asked Justice Newell Jennings of the State Supreme Court, a lifelong Republican, to act in my place.

According to the testimony, the system for some years had worked as follows: if a tavern served liquor to minors or allowed its bar to remain open after the legal closing hour, the owner could buy himself out of the usual penalties—a fine and temporary suspension of his license to sell liquor—by taking out an insurance policy with Dunn. Dunn, who was represented legally by Thomas Dodd, was found guilty, and I dismissed him from office.

Instead of being credited with having cleaned up this corruption, my Administration promptly became the target for bitter attacks by many tavern keepers, often supported by national liquor companies. The reasoning of the tavern keepers was remarkably distorted. They had carefully instructed their bartenders and waiters strictly to obey the laws. In the past if one of their employees had disregarded these orders and violated the law, it was possible to avoid a suspension by buying an insurance policy from the Commissioner. Now they faced suspension of their licenses because their employees had failed to follow instructions. It was, they insisted, unfair.

Another political incident, with broader implications for Connecticut, involved ex-Governor Ray Baldwin, who had been elected to the U.S. Senate in 1946. Shortly after I became Governor, Baldwin called on me in my office. We had known each other, not intimately, but favorably and well. After a brief personal exchange he reminded me that because of impending resignations due to age I would be called upon in the next two years to appoint three new Justices to the State Supreme Court. He said he had some ideas on the subject and asked that I talk with him before I made the appointments.

However, since the first appointment was not due for several months and I was busy with the General Assembly, I neglected to follow up. A month or so later, one of Baldwin's close friends came to see me. "Ray Baldwin," he said, "is anxious to talk with you about the Supreme Court appointments you will soon be making."

In early April, 1949, after two or three more visitors had made the same point, I called Baldwin's Senate office to say that I would be in Washington the following week to testify before a Congressional committee on housing and slum clearance and would like to call on him at that time.

Baldwin opened our conversation by saying that he had decided to resign his Senate seat and would like to be appointed Chief Justice of the Supreme Court in Connecticut. After catching my breath, I pointed out that he still had four years left in his term. While as a Democrat I would welcome one less Republican in the Senate, I felt that he had an obligation to the people of the state to serve out his term.

Baldwin replied that he and Mrs. Baldwin had carefully considered the question and had agreed that he should not continue in the Senate. The more conservative Republican leaders, he said, had tagged him a "liberal" and had set out to limit his opportunities for constructive action. He had been denied good appointments, kept off important committees, and generally hemmed in and frustrated. He also implied that the situation within the Republican Party in Connecticut had increased his frustrations. Most of the party leaders owed their present positions to Baldwin, who had singlehandedly rescued their party from the doldrums in 1938. Yet recently he had been able to muster only one vote for his nominee for National Committeeman in the Republican State Central Committee. Politics can be a heartbreaking business and Ray was a sensitive man.

The situation was too politically explosive to discuss any further on an off-the-cuff basis. I told Ray that he had given me a lot to think about and that we would talk again.

As I considered this political blockbuster on my return trip to Hartford, I became increasingly aware of its far-reaching implications. At that time the number of Republicans and Democrats in the Senate was equal. If Baldwin resigned from the Senate and I appointed a Democrat, the Democrats would have a majority of two.

In Hartford, I shared this development only with Steb, Doug Bennet, Phil Coombs, John Bailey and a few others on my staff. But the first vacancy in the Court would not open up for nearly six months and we were busy with many immediate issues. Consequently, we did not immediately come to grips with Baldwin's proposal, and this delay apparently convinced Baldwin that I was not taking it seriously.

A few weeks later he visited Connecticut, and soon I began to hear rumors that he was thinking of running against me for the governorship in 1950. This gambit may not have been his own doing, but it was traced to mutual friends and was clearly calculated to make me uneasy and to force a decision.

When the story of his gubernatorial ambitions began to appear in the political gossip columns, I called Ray and told him that the rumors would make it difficult for me to appoint him to the Supreme Court since it would be interpreted as a move to bribe him into giving up his candidacy. This would be damaging to his reputation as well as to mine.

Ray replied that he had no intention of running against me. I told him that, while I was gratified to hear this, the story was out and only he could kill it. If he said nothing and told his talkative friends to do likewise, the rumor would be deflated, and then at an appropriate time he could quietly deny that it had ever entered his mind. Then and only then could we discuss his desire to leave the Senate for the Connecticut Supreme Court. Within two or three weeks the story was dead.

This incident persuaded me that I could no longer let the matter slide. I was prepared to accept Baldwin's resignation and appoint him Chief Justice, a post for which he was highly qualified—but whom could I put in the Senate? I wanted to make sure that my choice was one we could be proud of and who would add strength to the liberals.

My first thought was to select someone associated with the party in Connecticut or at least someone who was well known. Abraham A. Ribicoff, who was at that time serving as Congressman from our First Congressional District in and around Hartford, was an obvious possibility. Abe had already established a reputation as an excellent vote-getter, and his appointment would help to strengthen my position. But I was not sure at that time that he could fully be counted upon as a liberal force.

Further to complicate the situation, I knew John Bailey himself was eager for the post. Although John had loyally supported me and could be counted on for a good voting record, he was firmly established in the public mind as a political boss. However unfair it might be to him, I was convinced that he would not help the ticket and would be unlikely to be elected in his own right in 1950.

I also thought seriously about Mitchell Sviridoff, but decided that his appointment might be interpreted as a pay-off for the support labor had given me in the previous election.

I then considered possibilities outside politics. Two men particularly stood out in my mind: Philip C. Jessup, professor of law at Columbia University, a member of the United States delegation to the United Nations, an expert in world affairs, and later a member of the International Court of Justice, who lived in Litchfield County; and George N. Shuster of Stamford, an educator experienced in foreign and domestic affairs who was then president of Hunter College. I knew these men personally and had the highest respect for their integrity and ability.

When I called on Jessup at the UN, he somehow sensed what I was about to propose and attempted to head me off. "Please," he said, "do not suggest the possibility of my going to the Senate. I cannot consider it and I do not want whoever you do appoint to think of himself as your second choice." Jessup stuck to his point, adding that he had no experience in politics and did not think he would be good at it. Shuster was pleased to be asked but felt that his roots in Connecticut were not strong enough.

Another possibility was my former business partner, William Benton. After leaving Benton & Bowles in 1935, he had become vice president of Chicago University and headed the Encyclopaedia Britannica. For the last few years he had lived in Southport in Fairfield County. In addition, Bill had served with great competence as Assistant Secretary of State for Public Affairs. This had given him a taste of public life, and I knew he liked it.

However, there were serious obstacles. Benton had no political connections in Connecticut or elsewhere. He was not a registered Democrat but an Independent. Moreover, he had given generously to the campaign of Republican Clare Boothe Luce for Congress in 1944 when she defeated Margaret Driscoll, then counsel and lobbyist for the state CIO, in a particularly bitter campaign.

Finally, whatever I might say, his appointment would be interpreted as a political plum to an old personal friend.

I tried to put Benton out of my mind. But I could not escape the conviction that he was the most able man available.

I decided to discuss the question with our mutual friend, Anna Rosenberg, who had been closely associated with Franklin Roosevelt, in New York. Anna agreed that I would be sharply criticized for an appointment which would be interpreted as a pay-off to an old friend, but that Bill would make an outstanding Senator. I also discussed the problem with my friend and OPA associate, David Ginsburg, a distinguished Washington lawyer with a keen sense of politics. Dave also recognized Benton's abilities but expressed the view that the political price I would be required to pay might be too high.

Finally, I sought the advice of President Truman. He was delighted at the prospect of having a Democratic majority in the Senate, knew Benton and liked him, but said it was a decision that only I could make.

As the inevitable leaks occurred, the political pressure rose, resulting in many strange proposals. The most extraordinary was from a generally respected Connecticut citizen who in many ways was qualified for the appointment. He made the following bald proposition: (1) he wanted the Senate appointment for only two years; (2) while he was there I could write his speeches for him, and he would take whatever positions I suggested; (3) at the end of the two years he would nominate at the State Convention anyone I might select for the full six-year term; and (4) he would raise $100,000 to help finance my campaign for re-election. When I turned him down, he was flabbergasted and insisted on coming to Hartford to make the proposition all over again on the assumption that I must have misunderstood him.

Brien McMahon, who had been as amazed by the Baldwin proposal as I, was favorably inclined toward Benton. Some cynics suggested that this was because he knew Benton's appointment would create difficulties for me with the public and key members of the Democratic state organization. But I believe McMahon honestly felt, as I did, that Benton would make a good Senator who, once the political dust had died down, would be a credit to the party.

Meanwhile, I thought of something that had not occurred to either Baldwin or me earlier. If I appointed him Chief Justice, we would be bypassing two of the present Justices of the court who were about to retire and who assumed that on the basis of seniority they would have an opportunity to serve, for a matter of a few months, as Chief Justice. I told Baldwin that I had agreed to make him Chief Justice and was prepared to go through with it. However, in his own interest he should consider the difficulties that he might have in dealing with his colleagues.

As an alternative I could simply appoint him as one of five Justices. Then within a year or so following the coming resignations he would automatically be in line for Chief Justice. If I were re-elected, I would, of course, appoint him Chief Justice when his turn came; if the Republicans won, I assumed they would do the same thing. I urged him to think this question over and assured him that I would abide by his decision.

A few days later Ray called to say that I was right and that he would accept the lesser appointment to avoid any possibility of resentment from his new colleagues. A few days later I called a press conference at which I announced his appointment to the Court[4] and that of Bill Benton to the Senate. I did so with my eyes wide-open to the adverse effect it was likely to have on my own political position, but with the conviction that he would make an outstanding Senator (which he did) and that I could survive whatever political damage it did to me (which, as future developments indicated, I couldn't).

Although I knew that John Bailey was personally disappointed, he did all he could to help me through what was at best a difficult situation. In retrospect, I believe that it was even more important to him than I realized.

4. Governor Lodge, who succeeded me in 1950, managed to manipulate the seniority situation in a way that kept Baldwin from becoming Chief Justice during his term. It was a Democrat, Governor Abe Ribicoff, who finally appointed him Chief Justice in 1959.

Benton came to be recognized as one of the three most steadfast and courageous liberal Senators of this period. With Hubert Humphrey and Herbert Lehman, he was one of the "irreducible liberal three." Before leaving for Washington Bill volunteered that he would never vote on any controversial issue without first getting my views. I replied that this was nonsense; I had not put him there as my mouthpiece, but to think, speak and vote as his conscience dictated. A few months later he called to say that he had taken me at my word and had just finished denouncing Joseph McCarthy on the floor of the Senate—to which I said, "Good for you."

CHAPTER 17

THE CAMPAIGN OF 1950

THE REPUBLICAN STATE CONVENTION OPENED in New Haven on June 15, 1950. The nominee for Governor was John D. Lodge, a first-term Congressman and brother of Senator Henry Cabot Lodge of Massachusetts. For the Senate seats Prescott Bush was nominated to run against Bill Benton (for a two-year term) and Joseph E. Talbot to run against Brien McMahon. Attorney General Bill Hadden, who had placed his oath of office above his political affiliation by prosecuting the case against his fellow Republican, Liquor Commissioner Dunn, was as a consequence denied the nomination for another term.

The Republican platform called for many of our proposals to the 1949 General Assembly, which had been blocked by the House Republican leaders. Clearly, our opponents were convinced (rightly, I am afraid) that most voters are inadequately informed or at best have short memories.

The Democratic State Convention was held at the Bushnell Memorial in Hartford on July 28 and 29. I was nominated without opposition by Richard C. Lee, Mayor of New Haven. Lieutenant Governor William T. Carroll, Secretary of State Winifred McDonald and State Comptroller Raymond Thatcher were also renominated, and Alfred F. Wechsler, who served effectively as majority leader of the State Senate, was the choice for Attorney General.

Mrs. Eleanor Roosevelt interrupted a visit to California to give the keynote address. She was at her best—warmhearted, dynamic and wise —and received a tremendous ovation.

The Resolutions Committee, under the chairmanship of Professor Stephen K. Bailey of Wesleyan (later Dean of the Maxwell School of

Public Administration at Syracuse University), produced a challenging and responsible document. The platform covered a wide range of issues: expanding job and business opportunities; education; care of the aged; civil rights and racial tensions; welfare; medical care; and taxes.

Specifically, the platform called for prompt action by the General Assembly on the report of the Reorganization Commission, the delegation of greater authority to the cities and towns, the elimination of the out-dated county system of government, the establishment of a direct primary and other similar measures. It favored the immediate calling of a state constitutional convention to update our 1818 Constitution.

We also recommended that the new General Assembly further expand our housing and education programs and take action on the catastrophic-illness program which I had unsuccessfully pursued earlier in the year. Other programs we supported were a child study and treatment home for emotionally and mentally disturbed children, better treatment of alcoholism as a disease and improved attention to the problems of mental illness.

It was quite a package, and any citizen might reasonably ask how we expected to pay for it. The answer was by economies in government, by spreading capital costs over the life of buildings (instead of charging them all to the current budget), plus the fact that as production increased the state income would grow with it. The platform stressed that our first term's program had been accomplished within a balanced budget without any new taxes or increases in present taxes.

Immediately following the convention I presided over more than thirty political seminars throughout Connecticut for party leaders and other interested individuals to determine the questions most concerning people and what they felt we should do about them. These meetings, which often lasted past midnight, were a heavy physical burden, but they helped to achieve the objective which I believe is essential above all others to effective government: a greater measure of participation among the people.

While we knew that of every ten working people who voted, eight would support me, past experience indicated that normally less than one-half of them actually voted. Organized labor sought to remedy this situation by a massive program of registration and voter education. We also set out to register and learn the concerns of black voters, who in the past had been largely neglected.[1]

Early in the campaign an incident occurred which confirmed my suspicion that in politics anything could happen—and probably would.

1. The number of blacks living in Connecticut was relatively small, probably no more than 3 percent of the population, but it was beginning to grow.

Vivien Kellems, an articulate, attractive but unpredictable Connecticut lady, had decided to run for Governor as an Independent to focus attention on what she believed to be the inequities in the federal income tax. In order to have a place on the ballot she needed ten thousand signatures on a special petition, and with no political organization to collect them she needed help.

We were asked for assistance. If the Democrats would help Miss Kellems to get the necessary signatures, we were told that she could be persuaded to aim all her shots, which were always newsworthy and often very effective, at my Republican opponent. We were sorely tempted. The Democratic organization in Hartford could easily get these signatures in a few days by house-to-house canvassing, and most of the ten to twenty thousand votes she would receive would be normally Republican votes.

Several of my associates thought that we should accept this offer. They argued that there was nothing illegal about it, and as to its ethics, why should Miss Kellems be denied an opportunity to present her views as a candidate for Governor? But the whole exercise made me feel uncomfortable, and I vetoed the idea.

The campaign began in earnest in early September when Lodge launched the first of a long series of personal attacks on me, largely based on the assertion that I had broken my campaign promises.[2] Lodge told the voters I had promised to build 56,000 homes. He also said I failed to live up to a "promise" to reduce prices.

I replied that, as Lodge well knew, the figure of 56,000 homes was our estimate of the *need* for new homes in Connecticut, which my program proposed to meet over a seven-year period. In less than two years we had already built 9,000, with 5,000 more under construction.[3]

As for prices, they had started to drop for the first time in four years the very month I had taken office. While I could take no credit for this, I thought the voters should know that, as a member of what Truman had described as the "do-nothing" Eightieth Congress, Lodge had voted consistently against every proposal to hold prices down.

Lodge could not deny that a huge construction program was now under way in all parts of the state; the evidence was there for everyone to see. Thousands of houses and scores of new schools and new hospitals were being built. In addition, there were new dormitories at the Univer-

2. Lodge was an example of an amateur politician who thinks that professional politics involves foul play as a matter of course. He was also a good example of a conservative without a program. This combination often, as in the case of Lodge, causes the candidate to depend on mud-slinging and character assassination.

3. By the end of my two-year term approximately 14,000 had been completed.

sity of Connecticut and at the four teachers colleges. But a team of professional public relations advisers worked out a clever way of turning our accomplishments into a Lodge asset. The theme was as follows: The Democrats have indeed started many new projects, but who is going to pay for them? Bowles is pushing the "land of steady habits" into bankruptcy.

All government financing is complicated and confusing even for well-informed citizens, and the fact that the construction costs were being spread over a period of from thirty to fifty years was easily lost in the shuffle. Consequently, Lodge's simple accusations, repeated night after night over the radio and in speeches, were effective. By early October the question was being widely asked: While Bowles' construction program was well and good, where, in fact, was the money coming from?

To give further credence to this campaign oratory, the Republicans came up with an effective political gambit. The flow of tax income in Connecticut, as in all states, was uneven from month to month. In the summer and fall of the year it reached its low ebb; in winter and early spring the flow sharply increased. According to the normal practice of both Republican and Democratic governors, the state had borrowed money from special funds such as the Highway Fund in the period of low tax income and then repaid the loan when the flow of tax income increased. This practice avoided temporary bank loans on which interest would be required. To my knowledge, it had never been questioned by either party.

One day in early July the State Treasurer, Joseph A. Adorno, a Republican, appeared in my office to tell me that tax revenues were so low that "the state cannot pay its bills." There was not enough money, he said, to meet the next payroll. The only way out was to borrow money from the banks.

I replied that he knew as well as I that this was a routine situation and that he should proceed to borrow temporarily from the special funds according to the usual procedure.

Adorno refused, saying that he planned to borrow from the banks and was asking my authorization to do so. If I should withhold this authorization, he said he would be "forced" to announce that the state could not meet its next week's payroll. I expressed my disgust and told Adorno he was setting a dangerous precedent which might someday boomerang on the Republicans. Adorno simply repeated the lines he had been asked to deliver; borrowing from the banks, he said, was the way we were going to do it this year.

That night John Bailey, Doug Bennet, Phil Coombs and other associates met with me at the Governor's House to decide on counterstrategy.

Two different views were expressed. Some felt we should meet Adorno head on, denounce his political trick, demand publicly that he follow the traditional practice of borrowing from the special funds instead of the banks, and then begin an educational program to explain the real situation to the voters. Others felt that the issue was not that important and that if we said nothing it would be a one-day wonder, which everyone would soon forget.

We finally agreed to do nothing, which turned out to be a costly error in judgment that in all likelihood was the decisive factor in determining the outcome of the election. Moreover, having decided not to make a public issue of it, we should at least have limited the authorization to a single $18 million loan covering the estimated gap until the seasonal rise in the winter. This would have meant only a single news story, which would be hard to keep alive.

However, I failed to impose such a restriction, and Adorno seized on this second error to borrow a million dollars from the bank each week until election day. Each time, he explained to the press that the money he had been "forced to borrow" had come just in time to meet the state payroll. This gave Adorno nearly twenty opportunities between July and November to announce publicly that the state was bankrupt.

Adorno and Lodge were fully aware that the budget was in balance. But since the exact figures would not become available to the public until the auditor's report was published in June, 1951, eight months after the election, they were safe to produce a steady stream of spot announcements, advertisements and news stories on the same theme: No doubt we have more housing, schools and hospitals, but Governor Bowles has bankrupted the state in the process.[4]

Belatedly we did our best to explain the facts. Ray Thatcher, the State Comptroller, issued a hard-hitting statement, and to my great satisfaction, I received the courageous public support of State Finance Commissioner James B. Lowell, a lifelong Republican, who, with no prompting from me, stated unequivocally, "A balanced budget has been achieved." Nevertheless, the Adorno maneuver tended to reinforce the impression created by the reorganization report that the Bowles Administration was trying to do too much too fast. Even many of our strongest supporters began to worry.

At the same time, the opposition had been quietly organizing pressure groups which felt, rightly or wrongly, that their interests might adversely

4. On July 1, 1951, seven months after the election, the Connecticut State Auditor's Report stated that the budget during my incumbency was, in fact, balanced, with a small surplus. Connecticut during this period was one of only three states which managed to balance its budget with no increase in taxes.

be affected by the changes we had proposed. These included the lobby for the dentists, still upset over my veto of a bill that was in their interest but not in the interest of their patients; trout fishermen, who still wanted better-stocked streams but no increase in license fees; and a small but articulate group of schoolteachers who had been wrongly convinced by Republican leaders that the central fund which was proposed by the Reorganization Commission to guarantee their pension funds would enable the state to use the funds for other purposes. The liquor lobby with substantial funds, much of it contributed by large out-of-state liquor corporations, organized a campaign that included a call on every bar and tavern in the state to charge that I was about to close all liquor stores and establish a state liquor monopoly with a large increase in prices—an idea that had never entered my head.

My effort to introduce a statewide public medical program to meet the costs of long illness had aroused grave fears in the American Medical Association national headquarters in Washington. Soon AMA teams from outside Connecticut began to tour the state as the opening gun in a lavishly subsidized campaign. From then until Election Day in November these teams not only called on doctors to warn them of this particular aspect of the Bowles version of "creeping socialism," but also pressed druggists to give them their charge account lists so that anti-Bowles literature could be sent to Connecticut families.

We fought back. I asked the president of the State Medical Association, who had participated in the meetings I had held earlier on my proposal, to come to my office. He had impressed me as a decent individual, and I could not believe that he was personally sympathetic to the tactics of the national AMA. I reminded him that I had kept my promise to avoid publicity about our meetings and my proposals. However, the AMA attacks on me were so grossly distorted that I had no alternative but to set the record straight. I showed him a draft of a radio talk in which I proposed to tell the full story. He read it with obvious embarrassment, agreed that it was accurate in all respects and, as he left my office, he somewhat furtively wished me good luck. I suspect that he voted for me.

In my speeches I stressed that while the cost of medical care was currently an explosive subject, the American people would sooner or later demand and get action. Why could we in Connecticut not produce a constructive program tailored to our own needs without waiting for the federal government to develop a program to which many might be opposed?

I told the public I was not suggesting that state government interfere with the relationship of doctor and patient, and that the program I proposed would be under the direction of professional people themselves. But, I said, the need was too great to ignore and "we cannot use our traditional fear of government as an excuse to sit back and do nothing."

Despite my efforts to set the record straight on a proposal in which most Connecticut citizens had a major personal stake, the efforts of the AMA lobby were damaging. Indeed, I did not fully understand its effectiveness until a few days after the election when I went to my doctor for a routine physical examination. As soon as I entered his office, he said: "In behalf of the many public-spirited and decent doctors in the state, I offer you an abject apology. Practically every doctor in the state was personally covered by AMA representatives during the campaign and urged to work and vote against you."

When I expressed my doubts that this made much difference, he replied, "That is where you are wrong. Many patients respect the judgment of their doctor as they do that of their clergyman. In the week before the election I had seventeen calls from patients asking me how I would advise them to vote for Governor."

The campaign called for the familiar grinding round of rallies, dinners and Sunday picnics at which I and other speakers reviewed the record of the last two years and made commitments for the future. We were encouraged that everywhere the crowds were large and enthusiastic. Also, our campaign funds were substantially greater than in 1948, and several major newspapers, including the Hartford *Times* and usually the Bridgeport *Post*, now supported us. Even the papers which supported Lodge were in most cases far more objective than in 1948.

In mid-October Brien McMahon arranged for a private statewide poll. Whereas in 1948 I had been led to believe I could not win, now we were to be misled in the opposite direction. The director of the 1950 poll even assured me that I would carry Fairfield County, largely populated with "refugees" from the New York State income tax, which no Democrat had carried since Governor Cross in 1930. "You are a shoo-in," McMahon assured me. Since this was the first time I had heard this phrase, I remember the conversation well.

Undoubtedly this bit of good cheer had a debilitating effect on our campaign.[5] Since I seemed to be comfortably ahead, in all probability once the frenzy and the fury of the election were over, I would be the Governor for the next four years, no matter what I did during the campaign. The reorganization program, which I felt was the principal

5. It may seem strange that on two occasions I was so seriously misled by polls. But, having won in 1948, it was easy to forgive the inaccuracy, and I was told that new techniques had been introduced to correct the earlier errors. Moreover, during my business career I had been deeply involved in market research in which polling techniques were used with success, and consequently I was even more inclined to trust them than most of my contemporaries.

issue, could be passed only if I could muster some conservative support. My relationship with the House leaders (which because of our rotten-borough system would surely be Republican) was likely to be less contentious if I acted and spoke in a restrained and relatively nonpartisan manner during the campaign, and they might therefore be more inclined to allow the reorganization legislation to go through.

For these reasons I did not even chide the Republican leaders about the liquor scandal or their refusal to renominate Attorney General Hadden. However, I did hit hard at the blatantly false material that was being distributed through the mails by various lobbies. I was also sorely tempted to make at least one strong speech on the unbalanced rural-dominated membership of the House of Representatives.

There was an interesting basis for such a speech. In the first decade of the century, a determined attempt had been made to modernize the even then outdated State Constitution. A Constitutional Convention had been called, and there seemed to be majority support for the democratic principle of equal weight for each vote whether it was cast in a village or a city, even though the movement from the rural areas to the cities had not yet fully developed.

But just as the Constitutional Convention was reaching its climax an elderly Republican from a small town rose and made a speech which stopped the proposed reform in its tracks. He had just been to New York and there, he said, he had seen the "dregs of Europe" landing by the thousands on Ellis Island. These Polish, Jewish, Italian and Greek immigrants, he continued, smelled of garlic; they wore shawls over their heads and almost none could speak English. Many of them would soon be on their way to New Britain, Hartford, Bridgeport, New Haven and other Connecticut cities. Within a generation or two, he said, these people would become a political majority, and unless the rural minority which was predominantly white, Anglo-Saxon Protestant maintained its veto power in the state government, heaven only knew what evils would befall Connecticut.

My inclination was to bring this issue into the open, and I wrote a speech designed to do so. "The grandchildren of these immigrants who came to Connecticut half a century ago," I wrote, "smelling of garlic, bearing strange names, speaking strange languages and living largely in our cities, are a half-century later still denied equal political rights under our State Constitution. This we can no longer tolerate. Every Connecticut citizen, regardless of his or her national origin, his religion or the color of his skin, and regardless of whether he lives in a city or a small town, is entitled to equal rights and an equal vote. Let us bury this bigotry once and for all and let us bury it deep."

I knew that this speech would have a dramatic impact in Hartford,

New Britain, Waterbury, New Haven and other industrial cities where second- and third-generation immigrants now constituted a sizable majority. But I also knew that it would be considered a declaration of political war by the Republican House leaders. While it would win many thousands of votes, it would hinder my ability to deal effectively with the rural Republican-dominated House of Representatives after I was elected. Since we were confident that the election was won in any event, the speech was never given.

While television had progressed since 1948, it still had only a limited audience and we used it sparingly. But on the Friday night before the election both Lodge and I bought time. Lodge spoke first and I spoke immediately afterward. As I waited in the next room watching Lodge on the screen, my amazement grew. Line by line, paragraph by paragraph, he was in effect charging me with being a Communist. His indictment appeared largely based on my membership in the Americans for Democratic Action, which had been organized primarily to provide a democratic *alternative* to Communism. As Lodge spoke, pictures of Marx, Lenin and Stalin flashed on the screen alternating with pictures of me.

When he had finished, I went before the same cameras, threw away my prepared speech and denounced Lodge's McCarthy-like performance. I still like to think that Lodge's speech lost more votes for him than it gained, but this may be wishful thinking.

At the time none of us took into account the effect on the election of events far removed from Connecticut, which proved important and some observers felt decisive. In early October, 1950, several Connecticut National Guard elements were ordered to Korea, and before they left I spoke to them of the historic importance of the United Nations' efforts of which they were a part. A few weeks later the Chinese suddenly attacked from across the Yalu, badly defeating General MacArthur, who was caught unaware. This defeat was a shock to the whole country, but particularly to voters in Connecticut who had just seen their sons go marching off to war. Inevitably, the party in power bore the brunt of the reaction even though we had nothing to do with the cause. According to many pollsters, the debacle on the Yalu caused a shift of 10 percentage points in Lodge's favor in the last ten days of the campaign.

On Election Day, 1950, as in 1948, Steb and I voted just before noon; I then returned home, while Steb continued to work at the polls. Cynthia, Sally and Sam, who had a holiday from school, were also helping at the polls and in our headquarters in Essex. As in 1948, the radio technicians moved in at six o'clock and set up their equipment in my library.

There was a dramatic contrast with election night in 1948. In addition to the twenty or so close friends who were with us when the first reports came in two years before, some two or three hundred confident supporters were now crowded into our home. The fact that this was the first birthday of my first grandchild, Timothy Bowles, made it a doubly important occasion. When the children asked, "Do we have to go to school tomorrow?" I answered, "Only if we lose."

A half-hour after the polls closed at 6 P.M. the first reports began to come in from Hartford. Our margin there was about the same as in 1948, 24,000 votes. Then came New Haven, which we won by a comfortable 12,000 votes, New Britain by 6,000 votes, and Bridgeport by 6,000 votes. In the cities we were running at least as well as in 1948.

The first sign of trouble came from the small city of Torrington, which we should have won by at least 1,000; instead, my margin was just over 100. As the evening progressed, we watched our impressive lead in the cities gradually being whittled away by the votes in the small towns.

A report by Alma Lockwood of the Bridgeport *Post* on election night at our home in Essex included the following:

> Usually crowds appear when the political bandwagon is gaining steam, when the fires are lighted and victory seems assured. In Essex the procedure was different.
>
> The first shadows of the approaching reversal appeared to be a signal for the crowds to pour in from all directions: college students, party leaders and workers, neighbors, labor leaders, and men in sweatshirts; all came to share either the bitter or the sweet.
>
> When the results from the election in Coventry came in showing an increase in the Bowles plurality over 1949, the room cheered as one man; when the losses were reported in Norwalk, it groaned as one.

By 1 A.M. it was clear that we had lost the State by 16,000, a margin of less than one percent. In the Senate race, Brien McMahon won by a comfortable plurality over Talbot, and Bill Benton squeezed by Bush by 1,400 votes. But the Republicans made substantial gains in the State Assembly, adding twelve seats in the House and cutting the Democratic majority in the Senate to two votes. I conceded and congratulated my opponent over the radio microphones in my library. By that time our house was jammed with people. When I walked into the living room to join them, I was met with an uproar of emotion.

How can the outcome be explained? Of one thing I am sure: the Republicans, with all their tricks and gambits, did not win the election; I lost it. I lost it for two reasons: first, because we tried to do too much too quickly and because, knowing what we had accomplished, we assumed that the public must know this too, and that consequently the

Republican campaign, deplorable as it was from an ethical standpoint, was bound to fail; second, because we were overconfident and failed to campaign hard. Our daughter Sally, who was politically wise even at the age of twelve, came close to the truth when she said just before Election Day, "This campaign has been nowhere near as much fun as it was in 1948." I knew what she meant. In 1948 everybody was singing, cheering and having a great time. This time it was too dignified and a bit stodgy.

In regard to the first point I must admit the following political weakness: whenever I have been confronted with a state of affairs which is contrary to the public interest, I have felt compelled not only to change it but to change it right away. This sense of urgency, of immediacy, made me challenge deeply rooted special interests and habits of mind with a force which produced a bitter and often irrational reaction among those who had a stake in the status quo.

I have written of my conviction that our Connecticut State government was antiquated, shoddy and ineffective, and, most important of all, undemocratic. As in most state governments, a pattern of inefficiency and conservatism had developed which left the growing cities no alternative but to bypass the state capitals and take their cases directly to Washington. Unless a new sharing of responsibilities could be developed, our overburdened federal government would sooner or later lapse into near-total ineffectiveness.

If I had decided at the outset to pace my efforts over two terms, a total of six years (the first term of two years and the second term of four years), all the devious maneuvers and all the money in the world could not have defeated us.

If we had chosen to pursue the reorganization plan more slowly, I believe that it would have almost certainly gone through. But, as I have written, there were some persuasive legal arguments in favor of acting more quickly, and my compulsive, deep-seated desire "to get things done" made me susceptible to these arguments, particularly when I was assured that the business communities throughout the state would be solidly behind me.

My all-out support of this reorganization plan allowed every conservative group to unite in opposition when nothing else would have brought them together. My failure to challenge the devious Adorno "bankruptcy" gambit allowed the Republicans to cultivate the apathetic "silent majority" through a campaign based on the fear, however misleading, that our program, appealing though it might be, was something we could not afford.

As for my personal reaction to the distortions and shoddy maneuvers of the 1950 election, anyone who enters public life must face the probability that his opponents, particularly if they sense impending defeat, will use every device—moral or immoral, legal or illegal—to defeat him and thereby to protect themselves from the worst of all political fates, oblivion. Although deplorable, it is a fact of life that every public-spirited individual—Republican, Democrat or Independent—must take into account.

Occasionally we have the pleasure of watching a demagogue destroy himself by his own dishonesty and extremism. Joe McCarthy, for instance, made the politically fatal mistake of taking on the Protestant churches, the Army, the Navy and Air Force all in the same week. But, unhappily, in many cases, as in 1970, the political tactic of character assassination still works, and it will continue to work until more people take greater interest in the operation of their government.

CHAPTER 18

INTERLUDE

I WOULD BE LESS THAN HONEST if I did not admit that we dreaded the inaugural luncheon which the retiring Governor traditionally gives for the newly elected Governor. However, Steb and I mustered the best smiles we could for the occasion and ultimately we were on our way back to Essex, driving our own car, once again ordinary citizens between jobs.

Shortly after the election, President Truman and Clark Clifford, among others, suggested that I return to Washington. But after our intensive domestic experiences in OPA and in the Connecticut governorship, Steb and I found our thoughts turning more and more to foreign affairs.

My experience abroad dated back to 1946 when I had been a delegate to the first session of UNESCO in Paris. On that occasion, in addition to my work at UNESCO, I had an opportunity to explore the war-battered French economy, to discuss the economic future of Europe with that remarkable man, Jean Monnet, and to visit Berlin, a city of crushed people and appalling war devastation.

At the invitation of General Bedell Smith, then our Ambassador to the Soviet Union, Bill Benton and I, during a lull in the sessions, had planned to visit Moscow; Smith's plane had been sent to pick us up in Berlin. However, despite our official status and visas the Soviet officials were in no hurry to give us the necessary clearance. First, we were told the weather was bad; second, the weather was better but the Soviet navigator who always flew on the Ambassador's plane was sick; third, the navigator was better but the weather was bad once again; and so on. After a five-day wait, which had given us both our first glimpse of the "Iron Curtain," we had returned to Paris.

After my return to the United States shortly before Christmas, 1946, at his request, I had called upon Trygve Lie, Secretary General of the United Nations. Lie was concerned about the administrative confusion in the United Nations and after several visits had asked me to become Assistant Secretary General for Administration. Before making a decision, I had spent two or three weeks studying the UN administration, becoming increasingly appalled by the built-in confusion. Under the procedures of the General Assembly, I felt it would be nearly impossible to transform the UN into a smooth-running organization. Reluctantly, I had turned the job down.

Trygve Lie had then asked me if I would act as his special assistant on administrative affairs, which was more or less a part-time job; for the next year or so I had met with him once or twice a week to deal with specific questions of administration and management; this had been a stimulating experience and I had developed great personal regard for Lie.

This experience had brought me into close contact with Aache Ording, a remarkable Norwegian official of the UN. Ording had sought my assistance in organizing a world-wide United Nations Appeal for Children with a proposed annual target for $200 million. The funds, which were to be raised by volunteer committees all over the world, would go to the United Nations Children's Fund to provide children in war-torn areas with food, clothes and health care. He hoped the United Nations Appeal for Children would not only benefit children, but that it would also help create international understanding and encourage greater cooperation among all people regardless of ideology. Steb and I had been so impressed with the possibilities that I agreed to become international chairman.

In January and February, 1948, Steb and I had traveled through Europe on behalf of this program. Although the war had been over for nearly three years, the suffering of the children, many of whom had lost their parents, had been unforgettable. In France, Italy and the countries of Eastern Europe we had found ourselves underestimating their ages by three or four years because their growth had been stunted by chronic malnutrition.

The UN appeal fell short of its financial objective, but it successfully focused attention on the problem and increased world respect for the United Nations. Eventually it led to the creation of UNICEF.

During this period my interest in American aid to the underdeveloped countries, then gaining their political independence, had increased. On January 17, 1947, in a speech in behalf of foreign assistance at Freedom House in New York City, I had said: "If the American people will support the investment of only 2 percent of our total income each year for the next twenty years in the development of less fortunate countries, we may change the tide of history."

A few months later, on May 25, in an address in Chicago I had elaborated on these remarks, highlighting the important role of agriculture. I said:

> We will need nothing less than a revolution in world agriculture. We will need broad planning for the valley development of the great rivers of Asia, South America and Africa. We will need greatly to increase the production of modern farm machinery. We will need vast irrigation projects and tremendous new fertilizer plants.
>
> Above all, in many countries we will need to encourage land reform programs so that the land can be owned by those who work it, rather than by absentee landlords.

The first time I felt that some positive action along these lines might be possible had been in late October, 1948, at a luncheon in Washington with Brien McMahon and Clark Clifford. Three months later, presumably through the efforts of Clifford, the concept we had discussed appeared as "Point Four" of President Truman's Inaugural Address.

The State Department, I later heard, had not been consulted about this proposal in advance, which may explain why it took several months for specific recommendations to take shape. When they appeared, they were largely focused on technical assistance, which had been correctly assumed to be the easiest program to sell to a skeptical Congress. The picture of confident, vigorous Americans, ready and willing to get their hands dirty, skilled in agriculture and engineering, showing "backward natives" how to get things done, was not only appealing to our national ego but had the added advantage of requiring only a small budget.

The program had actually been launched in 1950 when, at the request of the Indian Government, a number of technical experts from the United States arrived in India to undertake several engineering and educational projects.

In early spring of 1951, while Steb and I were considering various alternatives in international service, I had several talks with William Foster, who then headed the Economic Cooperative Administration, which had grown out of the Marshall Plan. Foster asked me to become Regional Director of our new aid programs in Southeast Asia, with headquarters in Bangkok. I was intrigued with the proposal, but the possibility quickly faded when Senator Robert Taft made it clear to the Truman Administration that he was in no mood to forget our conflicts during OPA days and would strongly oppose my appointment. Since bipartisan support was essential to our foreign economic assistance programs, there was no sense in pursuing the idea.

President Truman then suggested two or three ambassadorships. When I said that I doubted any of these would interest me, Truman asked me if there wasn't some country I would like to go to. To my own surprise, I found myself answering, "India." "Why in the world," asked the President, "would you want to go to India?"

I had never been in India, although Steb had spent three months there following her graduation from college. But I had read a great deal about its problems and prospects and had come to see India as the political and economic key to a free and stable Asia. It was not only a matter of India's size and geographical position; the struggle by Gandhi and Nehru for freedom from British rule through nonviolent means had established India as a testing ground for democratic government in a period of rapidly receding colonial dominance.

Even while explaining my interest to Truman, it did not occur to me that this was a practical possibility since we already had an Ambassador to India. But a few days later the President telephoned to ask, "Did you really mean it when you said you would go to India as Ambassador?" I replied that I would discuss it with my family and let him know within a week.

Each member of the Bowles family recognized that this decision was of critical importance to all of us. Nevertheless, a few days later I called the President to report that our family decision was unanimously affirmative.

I was told later that Secretary of State Dean Acheson had been less than enthusiastic about my appointment because of my "inexperience." But our many friends in the Administration and in Congress, particularly Hubert Humphrey, Mike Monroney and Bill Benton, who was by then greatly respected, had strongly supported the idea, and Acheson had concurred.

The next order of business was my confirmation by the Senate, where Senator Taft was lying in wait. In addition to his old score against me during the OPA debates, Taft wrongly assumed that I had persuaded Ray Baldwin to leave the Senate in 1949, thereby establishing a Democratic majority. He announced that he regarded my confirmation as a personal issue and that he would oppose it, adding that I was "not fitted either by temperament or experience for any diplomatic role." The proceedings dragged along. Later I heard that Senator Taft had personally called each Republican member of the Senate to request him to vote against my confirmation.

The vote was close; indeed, I achieved the dubious honor of having

more Senators vote against my confirmation as Ambassador than had opposed any other candidate in recent memory: 37 Republicans went along
with Taft. But the Democrats, for once, were unanimously in favor, and I
was pleased to see them joined by six or seven Republicans, including
John Lodge's older brother, Henry Cabot Lodge. Thus the decks were
cleared and I became a card-carrying Ambassador.

The account of my first tour as Ambassador to India, which lasted
from October, 1951, to March, 1953, appears in the final part of this
book, with a report of my second tour from July, 1963, to April, 1969.
However, I shall touch on several significant points at this time.

It was during these seventeen months in India that I became aware of
the contribution that a well-planned, well-administered American assistance program could make in a developing country which was prepared to use such help wisely. I also became convinced that if the rich
countries failed to help the poor countries in Asia, Africa and Latin
America, bitterness, political turbulence and conflict would be the inevitable result.

The first significant capital grant or loan made by the United States
anywhere under Point Four was a grant of $54 million to India during
my first weeks as Ambassador.

In January, 1952, I urged Congress and the Administration to increase this program. I had the strong support of Averell Harriman and
others, but the State Department, under Dean Acheson, was less inclined
to go along. However, I eventually persuaded President Truman to include in his 1953–54 budget, which he presented to Congress just before
leaving office, a $200-million-a-year, five-year-term development fund for
India; an item which was eliminated when the Eisenhower Administration took over.

Steb and I would have been willing to stay in India for another year,
as Paul Hoffman (former head of the Marshall Plan) and other Republican friends reported that the newly elected President wanted me to do.
But my vindictive old adversary Senator Taft, in cooperation with John
Lodge, succeeded in eliminating this possibility.

When I returned to Connecticut, I felt that the most important contribution I could make in regard to public policy was to help create a bridge
of understanding between the Western and Asian worlds. Six months
later, Harper & Brothers published *Ambassador's Report*, a personal
account of our life in India and our impressions of India and Asia. A
second book, *The New Dimensions of Peace*, which appeared a year later,
described what I believe to be the four most decisive revolutions of modern times: the American Revolution, the Soviet Revolution, the Chinese
Revolution and the Indian Revolution—and suggested that twentieth-

century Americans might learn from each. Both books had a substantial sale not only in the United States but in various parts of the world, particularly Asia.

Between 1953 and 1958, in addition to my writing, we traveled widely abroad and throughout the United States. To prepare for a trip to Africa in the winter of 1955, we spent several days in Washington, where to our amazement we found only three people in the entire State Department working full time on African affairs. A visit to the Congressional Library was equally revealing. Only three nations were listed under "Africa"— Ethiopia, Liberia and South Africa. When we asked for material about the Congo, we were told to "see Belgium." When we sought information on Kenya, we were referred to the United Kingdom.

Yet it was becoming clear to any knowledgeable observer that the African drive for independence was gathering momentum and that the colonial nations would soon be left with only two choices: to withdraw gracefully, as the British had done in India, Burma and Ceylon, or to be precipitously pushed out, as the Dutch had been in Indonesia.

On our African tour I kept a journal, and excerpts illustrate the mood of Africa as I saw it five years before the wave of independence actually began:

> Fifty miles outside of the Gold Coast[1] capital city of Accra we attended a meeting of village headmen with a young man from the Anglo-Egyptian Sudan, who had come all the way to the Gold Coast to see the village work and progress toward independence. He and I were both asked to speak of our "mission" to the Gold Coast and to this village. I did my best and my audience was attentive and polite.
>
> Then the young man from the Sudan spoke eloquently of Sudanese independence and hopes for the future. The elders sat in rapt attention and interrupted frequently with applause. My reception was polite; his was deeply moving. I was a white man from America. He was a black man of Africa—the new drowsy Africa that is just coming awake.

* * *

> I asked a British district officer who came to the Gold Coast in 1938 to describe his responsibilities at that time. "First, law and order," he said. "Then communications and communicable diseases." (Communicable diseases are those to which Europeans are prone.)
>
> I asked him what his job is today. He answered without appearing to catch the significance of the change: "First, village roads and water. Then schools, malaria control, village dispensaries, improving agricultural production."

* * *

> An Englishman in Uganda said to me, "Freedom can come too fast. But that is far less dangerous than to have it come too slowly. Africa will

1. Now Ghana.

never be really 'ready' for freedom. But we are driving a heavy wagon down a steep hill. Unless we keep the horses moving fast, the wagon will run right over them."

*   *   *

The faith of the African in education must be seen to be believed. Much of this interest is based on an understandable appreciation of what education can do, but some of it has a psychological and political quality to it as well. Because the white man can read, write and solve mathematical problems, he came to Africa as master. When the black man can do these things, he automatically takes his place beside the white man.

Our public efforts in this part of the world generally appear clumsy. Our information programs in Africa, as elsewhere, are overly preoccupied with satisfying Congress. This is sometimes as frustrating as the dilemma of an advertising agency trying at the same time to sell goods over the radio and to develop programs that please the client's wife.

The American Negro could be an important bridge between America and modern Africa, and we should encourage cultural interchanges in dozens of different ways. The mere presence in Africa of American Negroes as visiting lecturers, teachers, government employees, would do everyone concerned a world of good.

From Ethiopia we flew to Pakistan and then spent three weeks in New Delhi visiting old friends, including Jawaharlal Nehru. Because there was no U.S. Ambassador there at the time (indeed, for half the time between 1954 and 1959 there was no American Ambassador present in New Delhi), Steb and I presented our Chargé d'Affaires with a tactical problem.

In this unpredictable age of John Foster Dulles with its lingering overtones of Senator Joe McCarthy, few Foreign Service officers were prepared to stick their necks out by being openly friendly to a former Ambassador who was a liberal Democrat. It was not until I made a speech at the New Delhi Council for World Affairs on the realities of the U.S.-India relationship, which was enthusiastically received and widely publicized, that the Embassy indicated it knew we were in town.

Later in London the reception from U.S. officials was so chilly that we spent most of our time with our dear friend, Mrs. Vijaya Lakshmi Pandit, Nehru's sister, who was then serving as Indian High Commissioner. When the U.S. Embassy failed to respond to my request that they schedule a series of meetings with key British officials, the Indian Embassy made the appointments.

Soon after our return to Connecticut in March, 1955, I received an invitation to give the Berkeley Lectures at the University of California on the "New Emerging Africa." I declined on the ground that I had been in

Africa less than two months; but when I was told that they could find no one experienced in foreign affairs who had been there even that long, I agreed to speak.

I gave my lectures in April of the following year, and the University of California Press published them in a little book entitled *Africa's Challenge to America*. The lectures emphasized the pace of African nationalism, which I believed would increase far more rapidly than most Western leaders then anticipated. My views were generally considered farfetched, but the pace of change was in fact far faster than I predicted.

Following the Presidential election of 1956, Steb and I embarked on another overseas trip. We went first to India, accompanied by my assistant, Harris Wofford, and Dean Rusk, then president of the Rockefeller Foundation. From India, Steb, Harris and I revisited Pakistan and Afghanistan and then in early February flew over the breathtaking Hindu Kush Mountains and across the Oxus River to Tashkent in Soviet Uzbekistan, where we spent a week, later visiting Moscow and Leningrad.

It was six months after the Hungarian Revolution, and the Russian people still did not quite know what had happened, but they were conscious that something had gone wrong. Relations between the United States and the Soviet Union were then particularly chilly. It had taken us almost three months to get visas, and my book, *The New Dimensions of Peace*, in which I concluded that the American Revolution had had far more impact on world events than had the Soviet Revolution, was under violent attack in the Soviet press.

Nevertheless, we felt a warmth and friendship which amazed us. On our first night in the U.S.S.R. in a restaurant in Tashkent, when it became known that we were Americans, the whole room stood up and offered us a toast. This happened again in Samarkand. Although this warmth was less evident in such large and sophisticated cities as Moscow and Leningrad, we felt it still there under the surface.

When we asked the Intourist representative for an opportunity to talk to students at Moscow University, we were told that it would "not be practical at this particular time." But one evening Steb insisted that we go anyway. Somehow we managed to talk our way into the main university building, ending up with a dozen or more students in a dormitory room talking until past midnight. We were surprised to hear that one student was about to receive his Ph.D. in American Studies with a dissertation on Thomas Jefferson, while another student had just completed his doctoral thesis on Abraham Lincoln.

On the day of our arrival in Moscow we asked for an appointment with Premier Khrushchev without the slightest expectation that anything would come of it. However, two days before we were to leave for Poland, while visiting a collective farm outside of Moscow, we received word that Khrushchev wanted to see me.

Our meeting lasted four hours (with no lunch). Khrushchev was articulate and frank on most points and I thought genuinely wanted to understand Americans. With regard to China[2] he was circumspect. When I suggested that both the Soviet Union and the United States might ultimately face a common problem with China which could bring us closer together, he merely nodded his head.

Following our Soviet visit we spent a week in Poland, where we felt the same sense of personal warmth and desire to communicate. We then left for Belgrade to meet our friends, Joza Vilfan and his wife, Maria, whom we had come to know well in India where he served as Yugoslav Ambassador. He had since become executive assistant to Marshal Tito, and through his offices we had an opportunity for two long talks with Tito. These helped bring our impressions of the Soviet Union into clearer perspective, particularly since even at that early stage it was clear that Yugoslavia had embarked on an approach to government that was far different from either the Soviet Union's or our own.

On our return to Essex in late March we found waiting many speaking invitations from all parts of the country, and I had plans for more books. The currents of American foreign policy under Eisenhower and Dulles were taking us in a direction which I believed dangerous and increasingly irrelevant to the forces which were likely to shape the future.

I resumed the extensive and exhausting series of speaking tours which I had started in 1953 at the rate (according to my secretary's count) of ten a month, often with a schedule almost as harried as that of a Presidential campaign. One day I would be in Michigan, the next in California, the next back in Essex to write. I spoke at every major university in the country and at many smaller ones as well. In addition, I spoke to business groups, workers, teachers and farmers. The audiences varied from five hundred to as many as eight thousand at the University of Michigan, University of Chicago and other universities. Much of my emphasis was on economic development in the developing countries.

In its early years foreign economic assistance received substantial support, not only from benevolent organizations such as church groups and from liberal organizations in general, but also from a large segment of the American people. Public opinion polls in the fifties consistently indicated that a majority of the American people favored such assistance.

But for a variety of reasons Congressional support dwindled. For one

2. This was three years before the Soviet-Chinese break began to be evident.

thing, because the program was brand-new with little experience to go on, it faced frequent difficulties. Whereas the Marshall Plan relied upon an abundance of skilled European labor, scientific expertise and managerial capacity, conditions were totally different in Asia, Africa and Latin America, and American technicians and managers who were accustomed to American or European surroundings found it difficult to adjust.

For another thing the Administration failed to explain what foreign assistance could and could not do. The economic assistance agency's annual presentation to Congress was largely supported by expedient arguments designed to keep the program alive for twelve more months. It was clear from what I had seen, read and heard that U.S. economic assistance to developing nations should have only one purpose: to help a nation which is prepared to help itself speed the rate of its development and build a solid basis for its expanding society. Unhappily, this primary function was lost in a maze of specious claims that suggested the primary objectives of foreign aid were to win allies, to buy votes in the UN General Assembly, to win the global popularity contest and the like.

When the program predictably failed to achieve the inflated goals that Administration representatives claimed for it, many Congressmen and Senators quite reasonably felt let down and misled. The confusion of objectives also resulted in a number of mistakes, which increased the skepticism about the program's value.

Moreover, these were the years when the Cold War was at its height, and the pattern of foreign economic assistance inevitably was shaped by this conflict. The power to allocate economic aid drifted into the hands of the geographic bureaus in the State Department, where the emphasis was usually on what political effect our aid might have on the recipient government rather than on its effectiveness in increasing agricultural output, building schools, damming rivers and modernizing transportation.

Another result of the Cold War atmosphere was the insistence by the Administration that economic aid should be coupled with military assistance in order to present to Congress a more appealing political package, despite the fact that the two rarely belonged together. I was sure that economic development assistance should be separated from our military assistance programs (which were highly inflated and badly administered at best).

Particularly in the early years, the Administration had been hesitant to create a close working relationship with such international development agencies as the World Bank and with the various agencies of the United Nations such as the World Health Organization and UNESCO.

Under these conditions it was not surprising that the Administration could not find and hold able and courageous administrators. Those few who might have been capable of doing justice to the opportunities never stayed long enough to master the complexities of a program which was new in concept and in objectives.

My speeches and lecturing gave me an opportunity not only to develop and express my views on foreign policy but also to learn a great deal about how Americans in all walks of life and in all parts of the country thought and felt. I became convinced that Washington leaders, from the President down, gravely underestimated the intelligence and capacity of the average American to understand complex problems and to come up with sensible answers. Although the tens of thousands of miles of travel involved made it a rugged and exhausting experience, in thinking back over those years I believe the effort was well worthwhile.

In 1956 I gave the Godkin Lectures at Harvard. My theme was the cyclical nature of American politics. On three or four critical occasions our country had been confronted with a situation which divided our people and called for drastic changes in political direction. I noted that each time even the wisest of our predecessors had failed fully to understand the dangers into which we were drifting, with the result that, instead of marching into what proved to be a new era with flags flying and bands playing, we had stumbled into it.

However, on each occasion we had successfully emerged from our confusion and produced the leadership, backed by a strong new political consensus, needed to develop an effective approach to our new problems. I wondered if a similar breakthrough might not lie ahead.

At about this time I also wrote a book on foreign affairs with the rather poor title of *Ideas, People and Peace,* in which I developed much the same theme as in my speeches, with particular emphasis on the need for involving the people themselves in the process of economic growth as a basis for political stability.

In spite of my many other interests, I remained close to Connecticut politics. During my tour in India Ed Logue had been my executive assistant. I had asked Ed and his wife, Margaret, to come because I knew they would not only contribute to my work as Ambassador but would also help keep me in touch with the political forces at home. With Ed's help I kept up a voluminous correspondence with many of my former Connecticut political associates, such as John Bailey.

At that time I intended to run for re-election as Governor in 1954, and Bailey was, of course, a key factor. As I wrote to Doug Bennet on December 31, 1952 from New Delhi:

John has written me many long letters. They are good letters, warm, friendly, which reflect John's instinctive understanding of political forces. Some of his points are made directly, some indirectly, but as I read them they add up to the following:

1. The Connecticut political pot is boiling, but he is trying to quiet it down. This is far too early to make any decision on 1954. He will try to keep sentiment in the party from jelling in any direction.

2. He will always remember our good relationship and close friendship and I can probably count on him personally.

3. The "boys" are desperate for victory as they are getting older. 1954 is the last gasp of the Connecticut political Old Guard (John doesn't call them that).

4. Liberalism was the basis for Democratic Party success, but now nearly everyone has a job, a house and many of them a camp on a lake; consequently a liberal program in the New Deal tradition may no longer be the way to political victory for the Democrats.

In another letter to Doug I remarked that, while the old crude McCarthyism seemed to have had its day, I sensed a new political technique beginning to take shape which, although less dramatic, could be as debilitating to our political morality as McCarthyism. The new technique, as I saw it, was as follows:

1. The prospective candidate tells the political bosses that if elected he will turn over all questions of political patronage to them with no questions asked.

2. Once elected, he votes rather liberally, although being careful to absent himself on the really hot issues.

3. He avoids supporting liberal candidates of his own party, and privately condemns them in conversations and off-the-record speeches.

4. He praises the opposing party on specific issues and condemns his own from time to time, prefacing his remarks by: "What I am about to say no doubt will earn me the opposition of many machine politicians in my own party (they have already been bought with patronage promises) and it may cost me this election. But there is something more priceless than political victory. Win or lose, I must live with myself. So I say with all the sincerity in my soul . . . etc."

After our return to Essex in early May, 1954, I received a flood of requests from political groups in Connecticut and throughout the country to speak, and I accepted many of them. Although this writing and my speaking in California, Kansas, Texas, Iowa and other parts of the country, like my service in India itself, had diverted me somewhat from my quest for the governorship, a series of visits with Bailey and the state leaders convinced me that I could win.

In the early spring of 1954 I discussed my plans with Adlai

Stevenson, with whom I had stayed in touch while overseas. While Adlai had lost his bid for the Presidency in 1952, his unique personal qualities and enthusiastic following convinced me that he was assured the Democratic nomination in 1956. I told Adlai that as Governor of Connecticut I could help him at the nominating convention. If he won, I would, if he wished, resign the governorship to work in his new Administration, preferably in foreign affairs.

Adlai said he was confident I could win the governorship and make a major contribution not only to Connecticut but to the cause of better government in general. However, he felt that it would be a mistake for me to plan to resign in 1956 in the middle of a four-year term. Consequently, he urged me to make my choice now: either run for the governorship and if elected stick with it, or work with him in his campaign with the intention of taking a key position in his Administration.

This view was persuasively reinforced a few weeks later in talks with two of Adlai's closest associates, Willard Wirtz, a law partner, and William Blair, Adlai's executive secretary and alter ego.

Adlai's advice, which I knew in my heart was sound, placed me in a dilemma. Friends throughout the state felt strongly that I should run against Lodge, and I was personally eager to do so. However, working with Stevenson in foreign affairs was also enormously appealing. Moreover, both Steb and Doug Bennet took a dim view of my again entering the Connecticut political arena. Much of what I had set out to do, they said, had been accomplished. My future contributions should be in foreign affairs.

Consequently, after considerable internal turmoil, I decided to remove myself as a candidate for Governor and place my bets on Adlai Stevenson's winning the election of 1956. If Adlai was beaten again, I would still have some options: I could run for the Senate in 1958 or (assuming Lodge and not a Democrat won in 1954) for the governorship.

During the next few weeks Steb and I went through some trying sessions with close friends who continued to press me to run against Lodge. The record of our Administration, which had been subjected to such distortion in the 1950 campaign, was now clear to everyone. The school and home building programs were now recognized as being spectacularly successful, and the budget had, as we had said, been balanced. Under the circumstances my friends were convinced that I could easily be nominated and win; and in view of our defeat in 1950 what sweeter experience could be imagined? Only with great difficulty was I able to stick with my decision to withdraw; and my uncertainties remained with me right down to the wire.

I was chairman of the State Democratic Convention, and the night before the balloting, dozens of leaders and delegates from all over the state pleaded with me to allow my name to be presented to the convention the following morning. They were confident that I could still be nominated, some enthusiasts even said by acclamation. Although I was sorely tempted, I decided that it was now too late to reverse myself. With the benefits of hindsight, I now believe this was a wrong decision.

The election was a close affair, with the Democratic nominee, Abe Ribicoff, beating Lodge by 3,115 votes. I campaigned in Abe's behalf and later had the satisfaction of seeing him persuade the General Assembly to pass most of the remaining legislation that I had advocated a few years earlier.

During the next two years Adlai Stevenson and I met and talked on many occasions in his home in Libertyville, Illinois, our home in Essex, in New York, Washington and elsewhere. In July, 1956, he was easily renominated for the Presidency. Immediately after the convention, he asked me to set up a headquarters in Chicago and to take responsibility for planning his campaign and organizing and writing his speeches.[3]

I was eager to assume this responsibility, but I was unable to do so. During the first eight or ten months of 1955 Steb had not been well, and in early December, 1955, she had been operated on at the Lahey Clinic in Boston for a brain tumor, which turned out to be benign. However, an infection set in following the operation, requiring a second operation in October, 1956, just before the election. Under the circumstances it was impossible for me to devote my full time to Stevenson.

I did all I could between visits to the hospital and spent several days with him on campaign trains and on speaking tours. I was one of the very few people close to him who argued that his primary issue was the conduct of foreign affairs and the means by which we might achieve a communications breakthrough with the Soviets. However, his staff urged him to concentrate on domestic issues, and this he did. But by all odds the most effective speech he made was in Cincinnati late in the campaign when he eloquently argued for a new approach to world peace.

Adlai's defeat left me no alternative except to continue my activities of the past few years. But as 1956 turned to 1957, I found that I had had my fill of an interlude which, however valuable in affording me time to shape my views and test them out in public, lacked the appeal and challenge of public office. Ribicoff, who had been a popular Governor in his first term, had the support of the Democratic Party to run for reelection. But the Connecticut Senate seat held by William A. Purtell would be open in 1958, and I decided to seek it.

3. As everyone knows, he generally wrote his own.

CHAPTER 19

THE SENATE CAMPAIGN OF 1958

FOR PERSONAL REASONS, I would prefer to leave the 1958 campaign for the Senate nomination in Connecticut to those historians who might consider it worth studying. But I do not see how in good conscience I can omit it from this record of my public career.

The campaign involved many complex and unpredictable factors which even many years later are difficult to diagnose or even to describe. At the beginning, I do not think Bill Benton intended to run against me. He was conscious of the political risks I had taken in appointing him to fill the Senate vacancy left by Ray Baldwin and the heavy price that I had paid in my relationship to Abe Ribicoff, John Bailey and other Democratic leaders who wanted the nomination themselves.

Bill had been profoundly distressed at my defeat in 1950. In 1952 he offered to refuse the renomination for the full six-year term to the Senate and to nominate me in his place.[1]

Precisely why he ended up opposing my candidacy for the Senate in 1958 has never been wholly clear. But the two major factors were, no doubt, Bill's liking for the Senate, where he had made an outstanding record as a liberal legislator, and the insistence of some of his followers that somehow he could win.

Moreover, Bill quite sincerely read into our voluminous correspondence a degree of uncertainty in regard to my intentions that I never felt. At least eight of my letters to Benton between April and August, 1957, are directly on the subject of my possible candidacy. As I reread the letters now, with the knowledge of what was in my mind, I honestly cannot see how he could have assumed, as he did, that I would not be-

1. In 1952 Benton lost his Senate seat to William Purtell by 90,000 votes.

come a candidate. Yet Benton is quite accurate in saying that I never actually said so. He made it clear from the beginning that he was eager for the nomination himself, and in his letters and in several conversations he urged me to consider other fields such as newspaper publishing. Nevertheless, he repeatedly stated that if I had a better chance than he to win the nomination, he would support me.

His argument in behalf of his own candidacy rested on the premise that he could ultimately win the support of Abe Ribicoff and John Bailey, who he assumed would either openly or covertly oppose my candidacy.[2]

When I left for a cruise off the coast of Maine in September, 1957, I thought it was agreed that neither of us would announce his candidacy without further discussion. However, in mid-September when Tom Dodd called Bill to say he was about to announce his candidacy and urged Bill to follow suit, Bill announced his the following day. The announcements came to me without warning. Obviously, Dodd had every reason to encourage Bill to enter the race since when I came in, as I am sure he knew I would, this would split the liberal vote. But Benton may have reasoned that once he announced his own candidacy I would withhold mine even though I might not be particularly happy about his action.

When we returned to Essex, Steb and I talked with our friends about how to proceed. Neither of us ever doubted I would make the race; the question was one of timing. The convention was still a year away, and it was our impression that the tempo of the campaign was much too fast.[3]

Moreover, substantial funds would be required to finance my staff, mailings, radio, TV and office expenses, and the close friends on whom I had depended to raise funds for my two previous campaigns reported that several former contributors were so baffled by the impending Benton-Bowles clash that they were unwilling to contribute to either of us. For these reasons we decided to withhold a formal announcement of my candidacy until March.

In the meantime, I knew I was likely to receive (and did receive) many invitations to speak throughout the state from nonpolitical organizations which would not have invited me had I been an announced candidate for the Senate.

In early November I asked Lou Harris, one of the best pollsters in the business,[4] to find out how Dodd and I stood among registered Democrats.

2. On this point Benton turned out to be right, although one reason they opposed me was my failure in 1949 to appoint one of them to the Senate instead of Benton.

3. Very rarely in Connecticut does a candidate who is not an incumbent announce his candidacy before midwinter or early spring.

4. Needless to say, I was now skeptical about polls. But Harris was able to convince me that he had succeeded in correcting the weaknesses of the old polling techniques which had on two occasions misled me in the past.

Probably because no one thought Benton would remain in the race once I had entered it, his name was not included in the study. According to the poll, Dodd was ahead by 58 to 42 percent.

Even without this poll I felt that I could run well ahead of Dodd in an open election in which Republicans and Independents as well as Democrats could vote. But Dodd would not be easy for a Protestant such as me to beat in a Democratic primary. For thirty-five years there had been an Irish Catholic Senator from Connecticut. The incumbent, William Purtell, was a Catholic, as was Dodd. Knowing Connecticut politics and particularly the Democratic Party, 75 percent of whose rank and file at that time were Catholic, I sensed that this might be the biggest hurdle I had to overcome.

In January, however, I had a reassuring discussion with Mayor Dick Lee, John Golden and other New Haven leaders. Two or three weeks later, Dick announced that he had no intention of running for the Senate himself. While I suspected that Dick as a liberal Catholic might be harboring the hope that he would emerge from the wings as a last-minute compromise, it looked as though the New Haven delegation, one of the two largest in the state, would be in my corner.

I formally announced my candidacy on March 5, the day before the annual Jefferson-Jackson Day Dinner. Immediately I began a series of intensive speech-making tours, emphasizing my concern that the United States make fresh efforts to negotiate with the Soviet Union, to reduce the arms burden, to attain full employment, to extend Social Security to cover medical expenses and to make further progress toward racial equality. The response of the Democratic rank and file to my candidacy had been good from the start. By late April it was clear that we had been winning supporters more rapidly than we had anticipated; in city after city we found a reservoir of strength deeper than we had realized.

One favorable factor was my strong support outside Connecticut. Connecticut was already behind John F. Kennedy for the Presidency in 1960, with Abe Ribicoff taking a leading role, and Kennedy and I had a cordial although not close relationship. Since Kennedy had himself been a target for religious bigotry (there were many who openly opposed him on the grounds that "the United States was not yet ready" for a Catholic President), I was sure the last thing he wanted was a political Donnybrook in neighboring Connecticut in which the Catholic-versus-Protestant question played a major role. One of the charges already brought against me not so quietly was that Steb and I were Unitarians and Unitarians, it was alleged, do not believe in God. In retrospect I doubt this situation ever actually caught Kennedy's attention.

As the campaign developed, I became increasingly convinced (wrongly, as it turned out) that when the chips were down neither Governor Ribicoff nor John Bailey would support Dodd, who had vehemently opposed Bailey, Ribicoff and the organization on many occasions. Dodd's principal strength in the party had always been rooted in dissident groups whose major objective was to throw Bailey out.

By early May I was convinced that with Bailey's and Ribicoff's blessing I could win the nomination easily. If they would remain genuinely neutral, I thought I would have an odds-on chance of winning on my own. Several newsmen who had talked directly with Ribicoff had come away with the impression that he would ultimately have no alternative but to oppose Dodd and support me. In respect to Bailey, a major question was Katherine Quinn, his right hand with considerable influence over the distribution of patronage. She was a strong supporter of Tom Dodd.

In the meantime, Benton seemed to be making little progress. He had delegates in Stamford and in Waterbury, but neither we nor anyone else considered him a serious competitor in an open convention. However, I was puzzled with John Bailey set out to convince me that Benton's delegate strength was a lot stronger than either of us knew it to be. Later, it occurred to me that Bailey, who had been heavily wooed by Benton, might actually attempt to nominate him as a last-minute compromise to "avoid a split in the party," regardless of his lack of delegate strength. Since I had sent Bill to the Senate in the first place, Bailey might have assumed I could not object too strongly. Dodd, Bailey must have felt, might be persuaded to accept some other post. The fact that Bailey and Ribicoff continued to insist they were neutral gave this possibility added plausibility.

In mid-May, 1958, I asked Lou Harris to conduct another poll solely to determine the likely outcome of a Benton-Bowles primary. If, as I suspected, I was far ahead, this would be helpful if Bailey actually tried to push Benton through. Harris strongly urged me to include Dodd in the poll. Recent informal probings he had made in Connecticut had convinced him that I had gained considerable strength among the party rank and file since his November poll, and that I could surely beat Benton, and probably Dodd as well. I agreed to a three-way check.

The results of the poll and Lou Harris' interpretation of them, which were delivered to me one week before the convention in June, are as follows:

> This will sum up the final results of the survey we have conducted for you. . . . We used a sample which is a miniature of the rank and file of the Party in Hartford City, Hartford County, New Britain, New Haven County and Bridgeport City.

We asked these Democrats how they would vote if primaries were held. The results clearly show that if conditions were similar to what they are now, you would decisively defeat Dodd in a primary. The final figures, weighted to give each sub-segment of the sample its proper proportion of registered Democrats, comes out to 64 percent for you and 36 percent for Dodd.

The results of the other pairing, between you and Benton, show that you would literally swamp him in a primary by a margin of 88 to 12 percent. Here are the area breakdowns on these results:

	Overall State Weighted	Hartford County	Hartford City	New Britain	New Haven	Bridgeport
Bowles	88%	88%	89%	87%	88%	64%
Benton	12%	12%	11%	13%	12%	36%
Bowles	64%	50%	45%	58%	77%	81%
Dodd	36%	50%	55%	42%	23%	19%

Against Benton you would effectively carry every area surveyed. Against Dodd, you run least well in Hartford City. But you would take every other area by substantial margins. Put another way, Dodd is able to carry only his home city of Hartford, but could do no better than break even in the county as a whole. The further Dodd gets away from his base, the weaker he becomes.

Overall, we would reach two conclusions on these pairings:

1. That as far as Dodd and Benton go, they have marked signs of being sectional candidates, while you show state-wide strength.

2. That while the organization support for Dodd might make the primary race closer, our experience has been that even with full backing of the Governor and the State Democratic organization it would still be doubtful that Dodd could defeat you.

On the other hand, with the Governor's support and the organization support, you should be able to defeat Dodd in a primary very handily. It is our professional conclusion that at this point you are in a very strong and leading position for the nomination with the rank and file Democrats in Connecticut.

May I add the personal hope that a primary can be avoided since this would divide the party next November.

A few days before the results of the poll were delivered to us we made a careful check of our delegate strength throughout the state. A team of volunteers working twelve hours a day talked personally with each delegate either in person or by telephone. The check indicated that we had 448 delegates, Dodd 332 and Benton about 100 in a convention of 880 delegates.

Shortly after I announced my candidacy I had suggested that my close associate, Phil Coombs, whom Benton knew and respected, might hold regular meetings with John Howe, who was equally close to Benton, to avoid misunderstandings between us. When this survey of our delegate strength and the Harris Poll showing our surprising support among the rank-and-file Democrats became available, Phil suggested to John Howe that they discuss the circumstances under which Bill might withdraw in my favor. But to our surprise Howe reported that Benton was unwilling to talk about it. He claimed that his commitment to certain delegates precluded even discussing such a possibility. Although this was disappointing, the Harris Poll convinced us that our main problems were behind us.[5] We had sent a copy of the poll to Governor Ribicoff and to John Bailey immediately after receiving it, and they also undoubtedly knew from their own survey our delegate strength at that time.

At this point I made the third major mistake in my political career.[6] In April and early May, before our present strength was clearly established, the leaders of several large delegations to the convention had expressed the fear that a hard-fought primary between Dodd and me would split the party and lead not only to the election of a Republican Senator but to the defeat of Ribicoff. Consequently, they had offered me their support on the strict condition that I would agree to accept the decision of the convention and would not resort to a primary.[7]

I had agreed to accept this condition because: (1) I thought that, with the support of the large delegations assured and with Bailey and Ribicoff neutral, I would win a clear majority at the convention; and (2) the November Harris Poll had indicated that Dodd would be likely to win a majority of the registered Democrats in a primary against me, an assumption the subsequent June Harris Poll indicated was no longer valid.

The June poll totally changed the situation, and we should have abruptly changed our strategy to fit it. I should have released the results to the press, declared that in view of this clear evidence of my strength among the rank and file of the Democratic Party I was hereby releasing those delegates who had promised to vote for me on the condition that I would not hold a primary, and announced that if I failed to win a majority of the delegates I would enter a primary which I was likely to win by a large margin. Had I taken this position, the situation would no

5. Harris pointed out that since the poll was largely concentrated in the cities, and I was probably even stronger in the small towns, he believed the poll understated rather than overstated my advantage.

6. The first being my failure, due to overconfidence, to run a tougher campaign against Lodge in 1950; the second being my failure to run for the governorship in 1954.

7. In Connecticut any candidate who receives the support of 20 percent of the delegates can call for a primary.

doubt have turned out differently.[8] The last thing Ribicoff and Bailey wanted was a hard-fought statewide primary in which I would swamp Dodd and establish a strong independent political position.

But because they had assured me personally that there would be no pressure, direct or indirect, from the organization in behalf of Dodd or anyone else, because our delegate strength was steadily growing, and because our rallies had drawn from two to five times as many people as Dodd's, this dramatic gesture did not seem necessary.

A few days before the convention we began to hear that Katherine Quinn was quietly working for Dodd. Then came the announcement that Francis Smith of Waterbury, a former state chairman and lumber dealer whom I had alienated as OPA Administrator and who had opposed me ever since, had become Dodd's campaign manager and had begun to tell the press "off the record" that he had Bailey's unspoken support.

Still another straw in the wind was the news that Ray Thatcher, who was again the likely candidate for Comptroller on the ticket with Ribicoff and in a position to control much patronage, unexpectedly came out for Dodd. Two days before, Ray had told one of our checkers that he was solidly with us.

However, for reasons which now seem difficult to understand we continued to assume that Bailey would keep his pledge of neutrality. Several key party leaders had come out for me with the private "consent" of John Bailey. In addition to John Golden, Dick Lee and the New Haven delegation, these included John Tynan of Middletown, Connie Mulvihill of Bridgeport and Thomas Keating of Danbury.

The night before the balloting started we gave a traditional pre-convention cocktail party at the Statler Hotel in Hartford. We had a good band and, thanks to Steb, some excellent songs, with all the usual convention signs, balloons, whistles and political paraphernalia. The warmth of our reception helped restore our confidence that Bailey and Ribicoff would keep their pledge of neutrality.

But Katherine Quinn and Ray Thatcher shrewdly set up the Dodd headquarters, not in an upstairs suite as we had, but on the ground floor of the Statler, and from this vantage point launched an old-fashioned wheeling-and-dealing operation. Since the elevators—as at most political conventions—were so jammed that it was almost impossible to go up or down, the lobby was much the best place for delegate brokers to be.

During the evening Phil Coombs, Doug Bennet and others did their utmost to persuade the Benton group to face up to the facts. They

8. Even with no poll to back him up, Dodd took a similar position, and it proved effective.

reported that while a great majority of the Benton delegates were ready to switch, they had pledged themselves not to do so unless released, and Bill with a few die-hard advisers still remained convinced that there would be a deadlock between Dodd and me and he would somehow emerge out of the confusion as the compromise candidate.

In view of the strength we knew we had not only with the voters as a whole but with registered Democrats, it is hard to explain why we did not release our poll to the press Friday night, when it would have been a first-page story next morning before the voting started, and announce that if the organization deprived me of a majority on the convention floor by pressure on the delegates, I would run and win a primary.

Even today I cannot provide convincing answers. There were probably many reasons. For one thing, while we knew that considerable skulduggery was going on, we thought the bulk of the delegates were still holding firm.

More important, we were convinced that Benton would not permit Dodd to use him to split the liberal vote and send Dodd to the Senate. We believed once Benton saw what was happening he would agree to place my name in nomination and urge his delegates to support me.

Finally, there was no doubt the psychological difficulty of switching a firmly held position on a critical question when you are dead-tired. I may add that Steb alone recognized there was only one thing to do and that was to challenge Bailey and the organization, and she has never forgiven me for failing to see it myself.[9]

The next morning before the voting began there was new evidence that we had misjudged the situation and that not only John Bailey's lieutenants but Bailey himself was working to assure Dodd's nomination. At breakfast our staunch New Haven supporters came up with the news that the Meriden delegation with which they were usually allied refused to make a firm commitment to support me.

Under the convention rules the roll call was called by Congressional Districts, starting with the First District—Hartford County—where Katherine Quinn, John Bailey and Tom Dodd had their greatest strength. To head off a possible stampede to Dodd, we distributed a memorandum to every delegate explaining how the balloting was likely to develop. We would run behind in the beginning, with every prospect of a strong pick-up at the end when the polling reached the Third, Fourth and Fifth Districts (southern and western Connecticut), where our delegate strength was greatest.

9. Not until 1970 was the Connecticut Democratic organization's authority challenged with a statewide primary.

By the time the convention opened at 10 A.M. it was clear that the Quinn operation had been successful and that unless Benton agreed to pull out and nominate me Dodd would be nominated.

Phil Coombs in a last effort told Alphonsus Donahue, Bill's primary supporter in Stamford, that if Bill wanted to prevent this there was still time to join forces. According to our count, Benton had 106 delegates pledged to support him, 90 of whom, if they were released, would support me. This, Phil pointed out, would create a new favorable psychological atmosphere.

But Donahue returned to report that Benton was convinced that I had misgauged my own strength and his. Phil then talked to Elmo Roper, an adviser to Benton, but with the same discouraging result. By now the issue was clearly not Bowles against Benton, but the liberals against Dodd and the conservatives. But the Benton people still refused to see it that way.

My nomination by James Egan, a Hartford attorney, set off a floor demonstration with a parade up and down the aisle, led by Steb's band. Jack Zaiman, the veteran political reporter of the Hartford *Courant*, described the situation in the following terms:

> On the Senate fight there was no reliable advance count. . . . As a result, Saturday morning at the Statler Hilton before the delegates left for the convention, rumors were a dime a dozen. First it was said that Bowles was ahead, then Dodd was ahead, then Benton was pulling out, Bowles was angry at Benton and vice versa. Benton was throwing his votes to Dodd, Benton was throwing his votes to Bowles. And a hundred others.
>
> The drama began to pile up when the delegates got to Bushnell Hall where the convention was held. Great pressure began to build up on Benton to withdraw in favor of Bowles. One conference after another was held between Bowles' supporters and Benton's. But the two men did not meet . . . and Benton refused to budge.
>
> Following the nominating speeches there was a big demonstration for Dodd, a small one for Benton, and a very large one for Bowles. Some veteran observers believe that the Bowles demonstration was the biggest in any State political convention in modern times. . . . In any event it was by far the best organized, noisiest and longest. As the Bowles band played and tickertapes wafted from the balcony, the Bowles supporters set up a chant of "We want Bowles," and Bowles posters and slogans sprang up throughout the hall of delegates as delegates got into the swing of the demonstration.

However, what we needed at this point was not cheerleaders, rousing songs and placards but delegates we could count on.

The roll call started with Hartford County. After Ribicoff and Bailey had each passed (in order to establish their "neutrality"), Quinn and her West Hartford delegation, with one exception, voted for Dodd.[10] The delegates, as we feared, assumed (correctly) that this must be what Bailey and Ribicoff wanted, and as the roll call proceeded, many delegates who had intended to vote for me, seeing that Benton still refused to budge and that we were headed for defeat, switched to Dodd to avoid needlessly weakening their own position with Bailey and the state organization. Litchfield County, for instance, the last county called and where two out of every three delegates were pledged to me before the balloting started, ended up two to one in favor of Dodd.

Even with the advantage of hindsight, I am not really certain of what occurred. There are three relevant questions. First, why did Governor Ribicoff, who had never been listed among Dodd's admirers, and who had the final word, in the last analysis accept Dodd?

Second, how could John Bailey, whose political power was directly challenged by the growing Dodd organization, quietly support Dodd?

Third, why did Benton, at Dodd's urging, enter the race and split the liberal vote, and why did he fail to switch his support to me when he saw that without his support I would lose and that Dodd, whose political philosophy was directly opposed to his, would win?

The general consensus among the most knowledgeable political observers, which I believe is probably reasonably accurate, is as follows: Ribicoff, who had served ably and skillfully as Governor, wanted above all a massive majority in his own campaign for re-election.[11] With me running against Senator Purtell, the national and foreign policy issues would be strenuously debated and the focus would be on the Senatorial, not the gubernatorial, race. On one occasion Bailey frankly made this point, although I didn't take note of it at the time. "A contest between you and Purtell for the Senate," he said, "would produce some spectacular political fireworks. This is a tribute to you personally, but it is not helpful to your candidacy as far as Abe is concerned."

Bailey, whose loyalty was to the Governor, who in Connecticut, as in most states, has the primary political power, was given the formidable task of nominating Dodd without splitting the party and performed with his usual skill.

For instance, two days before the convention he told Tom Keating of Danbury, who controlled fifteen delegates, and Connie Mulvihill of

10. The only member of the West Hartford delegation who refused to follow Katherine Quinn's lead in supporting Dodd was Bailey's independent-minded young son-in-law, James Kennelly.

11. He won by a majority of 246,368, by far the biggest majority in Connecticut political history.

Bridgeport, who controlled forty delegates, that, in line with their past political association when I was Governor, they were free to vote for me. He had the delegates so accurately counted that he could afford to do this.

In retrospect I believe Benton was genuinely convinced by his well-wishers that a deadlock would occur and that he would emerge as the compromise choice. While he no doubt felt uncomfortable in opposing me, and thereby splitting the liberal vote, once started he could not stop.

Although Ribicoff's and Bailey's decision was primarily based on the political factors to which I have referred, my decision not to appoint either one to the Senate to fill Ray Baldwin's place in 1949 undoubtedly rankled, particularly with Ribicoff as his stature grew and his perspective broadened.

In retrospect, I could have saved myself a lot of trouble if I had sent Abe to the Senate instead of Bill. But Bill was an outstanding Senator, and when all is said and done, I could and should have been able to win the nomination regardless of Ribicoff, Bailey or Benton. If I had been more political-minded, I would not have made the mistakes I did. But I have always been primarily issue-oriented, program-oriented and cause-oriented, and I do not regret it.

CHAPTER 20

CONGRESSMAN FROM CONNECTICUT

THE SENATE NOMINATION had been a bruising battle, and many were bitter over the outcome. In an effort to counteract the impression that the liberal wing of the party had been ignored, Bailey through various emissaries urged me during the final moments of the convention to accept the nomination of Congressman-at-large.[1] I flatly refused.

When Governor Ribicoff called the day after the convention to ask me to run for Congress from the Second District in eastern Connecticut, where we live, my inclination was again to refuse. However, the alternative was to return to the semiprivate life of writing and lecturing, of which I had had my fill. Not only would a seat in Congress enable me to serve the people of my state, but it would also provide an excellent platform from which to speak out on national issues, and to press for important domestic legislation.

Moreover, if I were elected, I would have a good chance of becoming a member of the House Foreign Affairs Committee, which would give me far more influence on foreign policy than I would have as an ex-Ambassador and ex-Governor living in Connecticut. I would also be in a better position to involve myself in the 1960 Presidential campaign, which at the time looked like a three-way race between Hubert Humphrey, Adlai Stevenson and John Kennedy for the Democratic nomination.

The Second District constitutes the eastern half of Connecticut. It was largely rural, the three biggest towns being Middletown, Norwich and New London, each with a population of around 25,000. Traditionally it was Republican; only three Democratic Congressmen had been elected

1. At that time no district had been established for Connecticut's sixth Congressman. Instead, he was elected from the state as a whole.

269

there since the turn of the century. However, my campaign for the Senate nomination had convinced me that my views on both domestic and foreign policy had strong grass-roots support, and I was confident I could win. Consequently, I agreed to run if the Congressional nominating convention wanted me to do so. But after my experience at the state convention, I would not lift a finger to get the nomination. With this decision behind us, Steb and I left for two weeks in Maine, leaving our future up to the convention.

This time the situation was reversed. As the organization-backed candidate it was I who was the beneficiary of a controlled convention, and I won easily over Leo B. Flaherty, a young, liberal lawyer from Rockville. A severe storm in Penobscot Bay made it impossible for us to return to accept the nomination in time, and our daughter, Sally, then nineteen years old and a sophomore at Smith College, accepted the nomination on my behalf.

My Republican opponent was Horace Seely-Brown, the incumbent, who had already served five terms. Seely-Brown was a decent person who generally voted with the more liberal wing of his party.

The Congressional District was divided into eight State Senatorial Districts. Instead of the usual helter-skelter schedule of speeches, we decided to concentrate one full week in each of the eight smaller districts. This drastically reduced the amount of driving we had to do and increased the impact of our campaigning in each area.

Our mornings and afternoons were largely devoted to a series of six to eight coffee parties a day and our nights to rallies and meetings. Each coffee party was attended by from thirty to sixty people, most of them women. The volunteers who organized these parties made special efforts to persuade Republicans and Independents to attend. The Democratic leaders were kept busy serving coffee and brownies.

I was impressed with the genuine concern most of these women felt about public questions, and I soon discovered that the most effective approach was to spend a minimum of time on mere pleasantries and to answer their questions frankly and even bluntly.

One of their major concerns, for instance, was unemployment. The textile towns in eastern Connecticut were at that time hard-hit. The mills and machinery were old, wages were low, there was very little new capital and many mills were closing down. It was folly, I said, at this stage, to attempt to compete with the modern, highly efficient textile plants opening in the South. The men who had originally built the textile industry in Connecticut were vigorous entrepreneurs; now the old vigor was gone and most of the grandsons and great-grandsons were content to live off the savings accumulated by previous generations.

What we needed was a greatly increased flow of capital into new metalworking industries, which would pay good wages, assure management a reasonable profit on its investment, and provide the necessary tax base to finance new schools and improved public services.

At that time the general economic outlook in eastern Connecticut was further clouded by fears of both recession and inflation, which were then affecting the country as a whole. Despite sagging business conditions and increased unemployment, prices were continuing to rise, and the people I spoke with wanted their Congressman to do something about it.

Although the Electric Boat Company in Groton, which then, as now, produced many of our nuclear submarines and employed nearly ten thousand men at high wages, was located in my district, I campaigned for meaningful arms control. In Washington, I said, there were many faint-hearted people who lacked faith in our productive capacity and our ability to adapt to new situations. Privately and even publicly, by inference they maintained that heavy expenditures for defense were essential if we were fully to employ our people. In saying this they appeared inadvertently to be accepting the doctrine of Karl Marx, who asserted that a capitalist economy needed war or the threat of war to keep its people employed.

I for one was not ready to accept this "solution." The needs of America for new schools, for housing, urban development, hospitals and modern transportation were, I said, limitless, and as military spending was reduced, spending to meet human needs could rapidly be expanded and new job opportunities greatly increased. With all that needed to be done to make America what we wanted it to be, idle men, idle machines and idle capital were indefensible.

Our campaign tactics included the encouragement of various committees, including the Educators for Bowles Committee, the Farmers for Bowles Committee, and the Republicans for Bowles Committee. These organizations distributed fliers explaining why I had their support for the Congressional seat. The educators supported me with particular enthusiasm because of my long-established concern for schools. My record as Governor gave them confidence that as a member of Congress I would fight for school aid from the national government to help relieve the mounting tax burden on real estate in the cities and rural areas.

Family farmers, who were still numerous in eastern Connecticut, were, I said, the traditional basis of a democratic America. When I was OPA Administrator, the farmer had received 54 cents of every dollar that consumers spent on food. In 1958 he was getting only 35 cents. Obviously, the present government in Washington was uninterested in the small farmers.

A particularly effective element of our campaign was a series of newspaper columns I wrote, set in the style of a Walter Lippmann or Marquis Childs column, which appeared in all the weekly papers, and three or four times a week in the dailies. Through these columns and the use of radio I spelled out my views on the subjects which the discussions at our coffee parties indicated were uppermost in people's minds.

My opponent made no effort to debate the issues, and when it became apparent he might lose, his frustrated campaign managers followed the usual pattern of personal attacks. However, the people of eastern Connecticut, as elsewhere, were becoming much more politically sophisticated than in the Joe McCarthy era, and I won by a large majority.

The first order of business was to put together a staff. I called my old friend and former assistant, Tom Hughes, who was then working for Hubert Humphrey, and asked him to help me find a good administrative assistant. Tom promptly replied, "What's the matter with me?" Although I was reluctant to hire one of his key people, Hubert knew of our close relationship and generously urged Tom to come with me.

I also hired James C. Thomson, Jr., who had been working with me in Connecticut for the last two years; Robert Donaher of Willimantic, who was already in Washington; and an extraordinarily wise and talented young secretary, Pat Durand, who had been active in my campaign.

Nineteen fifty-eight was a good year for the Democrats, and there was a big influx of new Democratic Congressmen into Washington. I still remember the first meeting of us "freshman Congressmen" with Speaker Sam Rayburn in the Democratic Party caucus at which he spelled out the traditional basis for a successful career in Congress.

We newcomers, he said, should at the outset keep quiet, learn the rules and study the methods of the old-timers, who through long experience had learned how to maneuver in committee hearings and in debates on the floor. Back the leadership, he said, in effect, and the leadership would back us. This was the way to secure good committee assignments and favorable action by the Appropriations Committee on requests for federal funds for public works projects, including military installations, in our districts. By "loyally" supporting the House majority leadership and by close personal attention to our constituents we would, he said, be elected over and over again and assure our steady progress up the seniority ladder.

I had been in government and around politicians long enough to be familiar with this theme (although I had no intention of respecting it), but many of my younger colleagues were shocked. In speeches on the floor a few brave individuals emphasized their determination to think, speak and act for themselves, regardless of what the "leadership" thought or did or said. The result was predictable: they failed to get on the committees that they most wanted, and later as the appropriation bills were introduced, that flood-control dam, that new airport or that Veterans' Hospital which they wanted for their districts somehow failed to be included.

With some notable exceptions, the result of this system of self-serving conformity was that most committee chairmen were elderly men whose only real qualification was the fact that they had been there longer than anyone else. Seniority took precedence over merit, hard work or debating skill. Nevertheless, there they were, in positions to block legislation they didn't like or, as seniority lapsed into senility, didn't even understand. And there they will remain until more Americans become aware of the heavy price they pay for a national legislative body whose procedures are anachronistic.

Another obstacle to more effective government in Washington or elsewhere is the premium placed on demagoguery and political conflict. Anyone in public life soon learns that he will gain far more newspaper space and television time by picking fights with prominent individuals than through thoughtful discussion and positive proposals.

My first major speech in the House of Representatives was a carefully prepared presentation which took an hour to deliver and on which I had worked hard for two or three weeks. There were a large number of members on the floor, and the speech was warmly received not only by Democrats but by several Republicans; yet not a single sentence was reported in the press.

This taught me a lesson. After completing my next speech, which dealt with the domestic economy, I put it away in my desk drawer and waited for some well-publicized happening to which it could be tied. The opportunity came three weeks later when Vice President Nixon, in a careless moment, suggested that increased unemployment might be a good thing because it would help keep down prices.

I promptly got out my speech, inserted two or three strong opening paragraphs attacking his "irresponsibility" and "lack of concern for ordinary people" and asked the Speaker for time to deliver it the following day. Two days later my speech was on the front page of every newspaper in the country and on all the network TV news broadcasts.

Genuine disagreement and debate are healthy and productive, and people holding different views have not only a right but an obligation to speak their minds. But when newspapers and TV commentators give more space to extreme and contentious charges and countercharges than to responsible discussion which, as they say in the vernacular, "lacks a news peg," they put a premium on name-calling and extremism and prevent the development of constructive dialogue on public questions. The key to economic or social progress is a continuing effort by all responsible people to communicate more effectively with those who hold different views and, whenever possible in good conscience, to establish common ground.

When we first arrived in Washington in late 1958, Steb and I rented a lovely house with a small garden on Q Street in Georgetown and lived there for more than a year. Rather unexpectedly, we received notice that the owners were returning, and our lease would soon terminate. After carefully surveying the Georgetown area, we purchased a house in February of 1960 at 2808 N Street. After some necessary reconstruction we moved in around April 1.

One of our first decisions was to build a swimming pool, which was one of the wisest things we ever did. We had many good friends among members of Congress, the press, the embassies and within the government, and the pool became a gathering place for many of them on hot weekends and after long days. However, we limited our formal social life to the bare minimum. Anyone who works hard at being a Congressman or a Senator finds too few hours in the week to do what he really wants and needs to do.

Generally, I would arrive at the office around 8:30, spend the morning in conferences, in keeping up with my correspondence, hearings and discussions with my staff, and most of the afternoon on the House floor listening to speeches and in discussions in the outside lobbies. Rarely would I return home before 7:30 or 8:00.

Immediately after the war we had sold our seventy-two-foot schooner, *Nordlys*, which after three years in the Navy was in bad shape, and bought a fifty-six-foot yawl. Cynthia, Sally and Sam, who were with us in Washington, had, like their older brother and sister, Ches, Jr. and Barbara, become expert sailors, and all we needed was our family to make up a crew. But during the mid-fifties they had begun to ask, "Do we *have* to go sailing this weekend?" Steb and I had then decided that the time had come for us to become nautically self-sufficient. In 1957 we bought a thirty-nine-foot yawl which we could sail ourselves, brought it to Chesapeake Bay and kept it in Galesville Harbor, less than an hour out of Washington. On weekends in the spring and fall we often drove out on Friday nights and spent two days sailing and exploring the inlets and rivers of that lovely body of water.

In addition to my legislative duties in Washington, I continued to do a great deal of public speaking throughout the country. The difference in time zones between the East and West Coast made it possible to leave Washington at 5 P.M. and arrive in San Francisco or Los Angeles at seven or so, make an after-dinner speech, leave for Washington at midnight and appear at the office—often more dead than alive—by breakfast time. I did this on many occasions.

In my speeches and my work in Congress I dealt with both foreign and domestic policy in roughly equal proportions. In regard to our economy, my emphasis was on the need for a fresh look at our national priorities, which were becoming increasingly out of line with the real needs of our society. Largely because of the early influence of my Aunt Ruth Baldwin, I was particularly concerned with the impact of racial discrimination, and I spoke to many groups whose primary interest was civil rights.

The economic difficulties in my own Congressional District made me particularly conscious of the process of urban decay that often grew out of a vicious cycle of forces which are difficult for any community adequately to cope with through its own tax resources. When taxes are raised to provide better schools and facilities, old industries are often driven out. However, a run-down city or town without modern schools finds it difficult to attract the new industries needed to employ its people and stimulate trade.

This cycle, I said, could and must be broken. I introduced legislation in the House (John F. Kennedy introduced the same bill in the Senate) to provide grants to those towns where the unemployment level was running above the national levels. These additional funds would enable them to modernize without raising local taxes, and in addition provide loans for job retraining, and help improve rail, electric power and other facilities.

In my testimony on this bill before the House Committee on Banking and Currency on March 19, 1959, I said:

> The reasons for extending federal aid to communities stricken by floods or tornadoes are equally valid for communities which have been devastated by the less dramatic but just as devastating impact of technological change. The exhaustion of a coal mine that had previously been the primary source of employment, the abandoning of a railroad line or the closing of a large factory can bring suffering and hardship to millions of men, women and children through no fault of their own.
>
> Consider the problem of a middle-aged worker in eastern Connecticut who has just lost his job because a textile mill closed down. He has worked for years to develop certain skills. He and his family have sunk

deep roots in the community, with his children settled in school, his home paid for, and his social activities centered in various local organizations. Yet this man is thrown out of work through no fault of his own.

It seems to me that he has a right to expect better alternatives than financial liquidation or being forced to move out of a community which he and his family consider home. These are brutal, nineteenth-century alternatives which by now we should have outgrown in terms of national policy.

This bill, which passed both houses, became law as the "Area Redevelopment Act," whose purpose was "to establish an effective program to alleviate conditions of substantial and persistent unemployment and underemployment in certain economically depressed areas."

I also introduced the "Housing Act of 1959," designed to extend present legislation to cope with urban renewal and the improvement and expansion of public housing. Other domestic legislation I introduced included a proposal to amend the Social Security Act to remove the limitation on the amount of outside income a person could earn while receiving full benefits; and a proposal to assist communities which had been economically disadvantaged by our foreign trade policies, such as the removal of certain restrictive tariffs.

One of the key issues then was inflation. On February 26, 1959, I made a speech before the House, from which excerpts follow:

> Last summer when our unemployment was hovering around the 5 million mark, Administration spokesmen and business leaders announced that the biggest problem facing our country was not unemployment but inflation. Indeed, it was argued, unemployment was *necessary* to curb inflation.
>
> When the election results came in last November, fiscal fears in many prominent quarters increased to a new tempo. Newly elected "radical spenders," it was said, would descend on Washington like a hoard of locusts and send us all into skyrocketing inflation.
>
> Mr. Speaker, what our economy needs are incentives to expand production, lift it out of our paralyzing, self-induced fears. It needs incentives to encourage growth and to make competition palatable, just as consumers need the encouragement of fair prices and better values. The way to stop inflation and bring down prices is to provide good jobs for all who are able to work.
>
> We are being blocked, as on previous occasions in our economic history, by a massive negativism which finds it much easier to stand still than to search for feasible ways of moving ahead.

I was appointed to the House Foreign Affairs Committee and devoted a great deal of time to foreign policy. My experience overseas had led me to believe that our economic development assistance was often spent for the wrong reasons in the wrong places. Our military aid program, I felt, was largely wasted. In country after country I had seen it used clumsily as a political instrument with no relation to military security; much of it was frankly designed to strengthen the hand of right-wing leaders with little or no popular support who were thought to be anti-Communist and pro-U.S.

Portions of an exchange I had during the 1959 committee hearings on the Mutual Security Act with the Assistant Secretary of State for Near Eastern and South Asian Affairs, William M. Rountree, provide an example of my views. The following is excerpted from the *Congressional Record*:

MR. BOWLES: Mr. Secretary, as you know, I am a staunch friend and supporter of the mutual aid program. What concerns me is our overemphasis on the military in some areas.

I know that you agree, for instance, that the security of South Asia is dependent upon the political stability of the area. I wonder if you feel in retrospect that the Pakistan arms agreement of 1954 has added to the political stability of that area, or has it invited the Soviet Union into Afghanistan and seriously and fundamentally disturbed relationships between Afghanistan, Pakistan and India, relationships upon which the future of the whole area obviously depends?

MR. ROUNTREE: Mr. Bowles, I would be less than frank if I said that the implementation of our military assistance program in Pakistan during the years that you mentioned has not created problems for us in our relations with other countries. . . .

MR. BOWLES: A British general said to me in 1957: "I don't know how many thousand Britishers and Indians died to keep the Russians out of Afghanistan. But I do know that since the signing of the U.S.-Pakistan arms agreement Russia has made more progress in this area than it had in the previous hundred years."

I don't think that this is an overstatement.

If half of the cost of this arms agreement had been spent in developing the waters of the Indus for the common use of Pakistan and India, we might have done much to bring these two great nations together; instead, our action has helped to increase their differences.

In the course of my two years in Congress I worked to bring about those changes in the foreign aid program which I had advocated as a private citizen. I was pleased to see the program begin to jell after C. Douglas Dillon took over as Under Secretary of State and Christian A. Herter became Secretary in April, 1959, following the death of John Foster Dulles.

As a member of the House of Representatives, Herter had headed the committee which prepared the legislation for the Marshall Plan. He was interested in a broader concept of assistance to the developing nations. Dillon, too, was quick to grasp its significance. During the last two years of the Eisenhower Administration, largely through the efforts of those two men, a significant portion of the appropriated funds was spent effectively. American foreign aid in the late 1950's, for instance, was a major factor in keeping the Indian economy afloat and Indian democracy alive.

In the early fifties the Eisenhower Administration, encouraged by many former isolationist Congressmen and Senators from farm states, had begun a program of food shipments overseas to supplement our economic development aid. However, the amount of grain in storage in the United States amounted to hundreds of millions of tons—enough to feed the American people for nearly two years. Annual storage costs exceeded a billion dollars.

In 1956, during the Democratic Convention in Chicago, I had discussed this paradox with Senator Hubert Humphrey, who was also disturbed by the spectacle of vast supplies of American "surplus wheat" lying idle when so many people were hungry. Thanks largely to Humphrey's efforts, legislation empowering the Administration to ship massive amounts of our surplus products, including wheat, was later accepted by Congress. This program became the Food For Peace program.

Further to strengthen our economic assistance program, I proposed an amendment to the Mutual Security Act which established a set of standards to guide the allocation of American developmental assistance. Under this amendment, which was accepted by both House and Senate, the Administration was required carefully to examine the effort each recipient country was making to solve its own problems. Only if its government appeared to be making a genuine effort to do so would American aid be forthcoming.

A second amendment, which passed the House but failed in the Senate under pressure from the Department of Defense, would have required that our military aid be used only to maintain a nation's independence and where it would not create regional instability or lead to an arms race. The purpose was to halt the flow of American arms to countries, often governed by right-wing dictators, which were endangered not by direct aggression, subversion or infiltration, but by basic economic needs, injustices and the frustrations of the people.

I also succeeded in changing the preamble of the Mutual Security Act. Previously, the Act had begun:

(a) Through programs of assistance authorized by this Act and its predecessors, the United States has helped thwart Communist intimidation in many countries of the world, has helped Europe recover from the wounds of World War II, has supported defensive military preparations of nations alerted by Communist aggression, and has soundly begun to help peoples of economically underdeveloped areas to develop their resources and improve their living standards.

I proposed new, more positive language to begin the Act, moving the old section (a) down a paragraph to become section (b). The language accepted by the House and Senate read:

(a) It is the sense of Congress that peace in the world increasingly depends on wider recognition, both in principle and practice, of the dignity and interdependence of man; and that the survival of free institutions in the United States can best be assured in a world-wide atmosphere of expanded freedom.

The Act also contained the following language:

(2) The Congress recognizes that the peace of the world and the security of the United States are endangered so long as international communism and the nations it controls continue . . . to bring under their domination peoples now free and independent. . . . The Congress declares it to be the policy of the United States to continue so long as such danger to the peace of the world and to the security of the United States persists, to make available to other free nations and peoples upon request assistance of such nature and in such amounts as the United States deems advisable . . . to help them maintain their freedom.

In trying (unsuccessfully) to change this, I made a speech to Congress, on April 20, 1959, saying:

By the use of this language we have in effect turned Communism into a natural resource like oil or uranium. In this market place of the Cold War, a noisy Communist minority has become worth its weight in gold.

The apocryphal account of a Monacan Foreign Minister's visit to Washington to secure ten million dollars in aid is well known in every world capital.

The arrangement was ready to be signed and sealed, so the story goes, when the American negotiator turned to the Monacan official and casually remarked: "I understand you have been having fearful trouble recently with your Communist agitators."

The Foreign Minister proudly replied that Monaco was almost free of Communists. The startled American official shook his head sadly. "Congress," he said, "will never stand for a grant of ten million dollars to a country with no Communists."

The disheartened Monacan official returned home by way of Paris and, as a last resort, called on the French Foreign Minister. After explaining his predicament, he asked if it might not be possible to borrow a few angry, window-breaking French Communists to help bolster Monaco's application for American aid.

His French counterpart looked at him soberly. "My friend," he finally said, "I am afraid we must refuse. Although France is anxious to be a good neighbor, we need every single Communist that we have."

As long as the preamble of the Mutual Security Act reads as it now reads, Communist agitators may logically say to their Asian, African and Latin-American audiences: "The Soviet Union offers you loans and technicians to speed your economic development. For this you are grateful.

"But should you not be equally grateful to Moscow for the aid you get from Washington?

"In their own official statement of purpose at the beginning of their mutual security legislation, the Americans frankly state that if they were not so frightened of us Communists, they would give you nothing."

I also sponsored a bill in the House to establish an international commission headed by the World Bank, to consult with the governments of South Asia on their economic plans and assist them in carrying them out. This consortium had been proposed by Under Secretary of State Dillon, and was sponsored in the Senate by Jack Kennedy. I also introduced a bill, despite the strong military lobby in Connecticut, to establish an Arms Control Research Institute.

A particularly constructive development during my term in Congress was an organization of liberal Democratic members who met regularly to hear outside experts or to discuss questions of particular importance in the legislative area. There were some sixty to eighty of us in the House who held generally similar views on most issues, and through the study group our power to work together was increased and we were able to become more effective on such crucial problems as foreign aid, education and housing. This "Democratic Study Group" is still in operation.

As the election year of 1960 approached, invitations for speaking engagements became more frequent. Within the course of two months, for instance, I spoke to six different Jefferson-Jackson Day Dinners, with a series of lectures at Grinnell College in Iowa thrown in for good measure. The states I visited most frequently were Wisconsin, Minnesota, California, Michigan and Illinois. Minnesota, for which I developed a special affection, was the home state of some old friends who were also unusually articulate and effective but talkative political figures.

On one occasion when I was the featured speaker, I listened to a speech first by Governor Orville Freeman, who outlined the impressive achievements of his administration as Governor, then an even longer speech by my friend Hubert Humphrey, followed by two or three others of equal length by lesser-known lights. It was ten minutes after twelve when I was finally introduced—presumably as the climax of the evening. As I got up to speak, I noticed the great number of yawns throughout the audience. I scrapped my prepared speech, made a few casual and brief remarks and sat down. It was my most effective speech in many weeks.

In Washington, in Connecticut, and in the course of my increasing number of speaking tours I was beginning to be asked about my personal position in regard to the national elections of 1960. Would I go along with the Connecticut State organization, which supported Kennedy, or would I support Stevenson as in 1956? What about Hubert Humphrey? These were not easy questions. But I was soon called on to find answers.

PART III

Working with Kennedy

◆

"No one can doubt that the wave of the future is not the conquest of the world by a single dogmatic creed but the liberation of the diverse energies of free nations and free men."

JOHN F. KENNEDY

CHAPTER 21

A NEW ADMINISTRATION

In February, 1960, in the Senate Office Building, Senator John F. Kennedy announced at a press conference, to the astonishment of many of my friends, that I had agreed to become his chief adviser on foreign policy and that we would be working closely during the campaign.

The events leading to this announcement had been in the making for four months. In October, Kennedy's chief aide, Theodore C. Sorensen, had called at my home on Q Street. We talked at some length about the political situation in general and the likely issues in the campaign, particularly foreign policy. A few days later Ted called again to say that Kennedy was anxious to have me as his foreign policy adviser. He suggested that not only would Kennedy appreciate my accepting this role, but that it would also put me in a good personal position if Kennedy won the nomination and were elected.

The next week I met with Senator Kennedy. After some discussion on the political outlook and his candidacy, he asked me what I thought of the proposal relayed by Sorensen. I told Kennedy I was pleased and interested, but that because of my long, close association with Adlai Stevenson I could not agree until I knew Adlai's plans. He said he understood and suggested I discuss the matter with Stevenson and that we then have another talk.

On the following day at luncheon in New York, I told Stevenson of the offer, stressing that my first commitment was to him, and asked him to tell me as frankly as he could about his own political plans. He replied that he had no intention of seeking the nomination. In fact, he was planning to leave in midwinter for a long visit to Latin America.

I asked whether he would agree to support Kennedy when he returned in April if he was satisfied with the Senator's positions on domestic and foreign policies, and if he was not, whether he would oppose him, perhaps by announcing his own candidacy. I offered to make no commitment myself until he had decided definitely. Adlai said that while he appreciated my desire to support him, he had no answers to my questions and that I should not feel obligated to him in any way.

My second personal choice as a candidate was Hubert H. Humphrey, with whom I had been working closely in Congress and who was an old friend. But much as I admired and liked Humphrey, I did not believe he could win the nomination in a contest with either Kennedy or Stevenson.

I was convinced that the Presidential election of 1960 represented a potential political breakthrough in both domestic and foreign affairs. During the Eisenhower years the country had been marking time. His conservative Administration had tolerated a high level of domestic unemployment. Its foreign policy had largely been shaped by Cold War considerations and by the classic assumption that peace and a stable order could be maintained only by a balance of military power.

Only the most naïve among liberals assumed that world peace and brotherhood could be achieved by a few treaties and some good intentions. The ghastly record of warfare and violence stretching back to the beginnings of history reflected the fragile nature of civilization and the potential savagery that lay just below the surface. An effective balance of power could do little more than extend the interval between wars (the Pax Britannica lasted for ninety-nine years, from Waterloo to the Marne). Sooner or later the balance would be shattered by weak leadership, inept diplomacy, the presumed superiority of some new weapons system, or an accidental spark such as the Archduke's assassination at Sarajevo which touched off World War I. If all that stood between the human race and oblivion in the next fifty to one hundred years was a balance of power, I would not bet much on the future of the human race.

The only realistic approach, I believed, was to buy whatever time we could by maintaining a military power balance, but with no illusions about its fragile nature. We could only hope that within this period the necessary peace-keeping apparatus could somehow be created within a strengthened United Nations which ultimately would become the basis for a system of world order.

In a book written in the summer of 1959, entitled *The Coming Political Breakthrough,* I focused on the critically decisive importance of the 1960 election. I referred in particular to the cyclical nature of American politics as I had done earlier in the 1956 Godkin Lectures— the petering out of once great political movements which had largely served their purposes and the birth of new movements which at critical moments had carried us forward under new leadership in a fresh burst of energy and commitment.

Although we had avoided a depression since the war, our economy had been operating well below capacity. Abroad, the continents of Asia, Africa and Latin America were seething with revolutionary ferment and demands for a better life, their leaders adopting rhetoric borrowed from our own Revolution, while we ourselves appeared to have lost sight of its principles.

As Toynbee once remarked, more powerful than the atomic bomb was the fact that in the most remote villages of the world people would come to realize that poverty, disease, malnutrition and ill health were not inevitable acts of God, but conditions which could be changed. But we continued to back the Chiang Kai-sheks, the Diems, the Portuguese colonialists and Latin-American dictators.

As the leader of the kind of world-wide liberal movement which I envisioned, a new American President would be faced with the opposition of many powerful vested interests committed to the status quo. But on his side would be all the human forces for freedom, proclaimed in our own Revolution, which had been gradually evolving and were now inspiring young leaders in every corner of the world.

While Jack Kennedy was largely an unknown quantity, there was no one else likely to be elected who could be expected to provide the leadership necessary to give liberalism a new life and sense of purpose. Kennedy was young, attractive, an able speaker, with courage and character. While it was clear that he was not yet thinking in terms of the revolutionary changes which I believed the times required of us, a comparable charge could have been brought against his greatest predecessors at a similar stage in their political careers. On the eve of the Civil War Lincoln in his First Inaugural had asserted that he had no right to free the slaves, and in 1932, with sixteen million people out of work, FDR had promised that if elected he would balance the national budget. Yet once faced with the responsibilities of the Presidency at a critical moment in history, these men had achieved greatness. Was it not possible that Kennedy would rise to the present challenge?

Kennedy had publicly commented on *The Coming Political Breakthrough* with words that strengthened my belief that we saw the world from much the same perspective:

> Chester Bowles has performed another important service. In this book he sets forth for all Americans an agenda of creative action which would restore the balance of our policy at home and abroad. This book is not an

exercise in nostalgia or a mere recital of idle hopes. Rather, he shows concretely the nature of our national tasks during the next decade. Our nation has an accumulation of problems—foreign, domestic, and military —that we must now face. The rug must soon be lifted and the issues which have been swept under it must be grasped. Chester Bowles has given all Americans a clear vision of the future promise of American politics.

In late October I told Kennedy I would become his foreign policy adviser. My one condition was that under no circumstances would I be asked to participate in a political confrontation for delegates with either Stevenson or Humphrey. I could be far more helpful to him and the party if I were free to help bridge whatever differences might develop among these three men, differences that might deepen the worrisome divisions within the party. With this Kennedy expressed agreement.

As he walked with me to the elevator from his suite in New York's Carlyle Hotel, Kennedy remarked that he was delighted we would be working together. He added that I should not be unaware of my own potential as a candidate. If, he said, it became clear that he himself could not get the nomination, "I want you to know that my support will go to those who were the first to support me." I recognized this as a bit of political seduction, not as a serious statement of intent.

It was agreed that I would announce my support for him immediately, with my role as foreign policy adviser to be announced early in 1960. Kennedy emphasized that while he appreciated my political support, it was my experience in foreign affairs he needed most. But I knew my primary importance to Kennedy was that I would associate him in the public mind with the foreign policy concepts now identified with Steven-skeptical liberals. The fact that no well-known member of the liberal son, Humphrey and myself, among others, thereby reassuring many wing of the Democratic Party, such as Eleanor Roosevelt, Walter P. Reuther, Adlai Stevenson or G. Mennen Williams, had yet come out in support of Kennedy strengthened this opinion.

This point was recognized in the press on November 5, when Alan Olmstead reported in the Waterbury *Republican*:

> Bowles becomes the first nationally prominent member of the party's more liberal grouping to make a definite public choice of Kennedy. His is the first public blessing Kennedy has received from the wing of the Democratic Party which otherwise specializes in clinging to potential candidates of its own against him.
>
> It is said that if Kennedy should be standing near the nomination, with the party's liberal wing watching its own possibilities fading, but uncertain and uneasy about its alternative course, Bowles could become the

one to certify to his fellow liberals that Kennedy was close enough to being their kind of candidate, and thus, perhaps, lead a national break-up of the party liberals toward Kennedy which would clinch the nomination for him.

In early February Kennedy's letter requesting me to take on this post and my letter of acceptance were given to the press. Kennedy's letter included the following:

> The search for a just and durable peace is the basic issue of the 1960 campaign. I have long been impressed with your own insights and your ability to articulate the fundamental foreign policy issues facing the American people. I am asking, therefore, if you would be willing to serve as my chief foreign policy adviser, effective immediately. . . .

The gist of my reply was:

> I am delighted to accept as your chief foreign policy adviser.
> As you have stated, the search for a just and durable peace is the basic issue of the 1960 Presidential campaign. Everything we hope for here at home will depend on our ability to achieve a more peaceful world.
> The need is for a fresh, affirmative, American leadership that will give direction, shape and tone to our policies. I shall help you in every way I can in promoting our common foreign policy views.

In the months following the public announcement of my new role, Kennedy and I usually had lunch together once a week, and I continued to feel that our views on foreign policy were generally similar. We agreed that the State Department was in urgent need of fresh minds, more flexibility and tighter organization. Kennedy also seemed to share my concern over the inadequacy of our economic assistance program, the gross misuse of military aid and our inflexible position in regard to China, Taiwan and Southeast Asia. I was asked to go over most of Kennedy's speeches and make suggestions, but they were largely written by Ted Sorensen and Kennedy himself. Kennedy also went over the speeches that I made on controversial subjects, often making suggestions.

In February, 1960, during a weekend visit to Essex I received an unexpected call from Paul M. Butler, Chairman of the Democratic National Committee. Butler said that he had just met with the key party leaders, who were unanimous in wanting me to become chairman of the Democratic Platform Committee. I told him my association with Jack Kennedy made it doubtful whether I should accept. I was sure, I said, that it might invite criticism from many people, including Kennedy's opponents, particularly Lyndon B. Johnson and Stuart Symington. Paul replied that the party leaders had discussed this question fully and decided that it was in no sense a liability.

I tried to reach Kennedy, but he was in the Caribbean on a brief vacation. I then called his brother Robert F. Kennedy, who urged me to accept the platform chairmanship and assured me that Jack would agree. With this encouragement, I consented.

In the next week or so I spent most of my time reading the past platforms of the two parties and comparing them with the records of the parties once they had reached office. It was not a reassuring exercise. I was particularly struck with the fuzzy language, obviously designed to obscure objectives rather than to clarify them. I felt one way to change this pattern would be to increase the number of people actually involved in the preparation of the platform. If more individuals had some personal responsibility for what the party claimed that it stood for, the platform might once again become the serious statement of principles and objectives that it had originally been intended to be.

Consequently, I proposed that we hold preliminary local, state and regional hearings in all parts of the country to give every interested citizen an opportunity to speak his mind. These preliminary hearings were in addition to a full week of nationally televised hearings prior to the National Convention, at which national leaders in a wide variety of fields, from schoolteachers to poultry raisers, would testify and make their recommendations.

By the first week in April the regional hearings were under way, and, because they were unique in American politics, they attracted a good deal of press and TV attention. Local individuals and groups representing a wide variety of viewpoints made their presentations to the teams of well-known political leaders drafted for this service. The proceedings of each meeting were recorded and sent to me.

Traditionally, delegates to both Democratic and Republican conventions, and, more important in recent years, TV audiences as well, had been subjected to monotonous recitals of past achievements and future hopes, most of which went in one ear and out the other, and probably lost more support than they gained.

I persuaded the National Committee that the core of our platform should be relatively brief so that it could be read in no more than a half-hour. In addition, they agreed that a documentary film outlining the accomplishments of the Democratic Party since Roosevelt's election in 1932 should be prepared and shown to the convention delegates and the TV audience just before the presentation of the platform itself.

In April and May, 1960, with the help of my associates, Thomas L. Hughes, Abram J. Chayes, James C. Thomson, Jr. and David Ginsburg,

I prepared a rough draft of a platform which reflected not only our own views, but also those of hundreds of citizens who had attended our local and regional hearings.

When I showed Kennedy the draft in mid-May, he gave it only a cursory glance.[1] I also showed it to R. Sargent Shriver, Kennedy's brother-in-law, whom I had come to know well in recent months and who happened to be on the same plane with us en route to the convention. Bob Kennedy, at my insistence, read the final draft somewhat more thoroughly at breakfast the day before its presentation, but he made no suggestions. Since my own position and views were accepted within the party and throughout the country, and since I was platform chairman, that seemed to be enough for them.

The Platform Committee hearings went smoothly. In fact, testimony in favor of a strong civil rights plank was so overwhelming that the Southern spokesmen who favored continued segregation were reluctant to speak out. To avoid being charged with a one-sided presentation, I telephoned several Southern Senators and governors and urged them to present their recommendations before our committee so that all points of view could be heard and considered—even those with which most of us disagreed.

After the hearings were completed my rough platform draft was presented to the Executive Committee and agreement was easily reached. It then went before the Platform Committee itself, made up of two delegates from each state. We made a special effort to keep the discussions within the committee confidential and off the record, something that had never been done before. We knew that if leaks occurred, the pressures on us would become overwhelming to add new but irrelevant amendments to placate small but vociferous special groups. We wanted the platform to remain simple, clear and forthright.

In a further effort to lessen the inevitable conflicts with the Southern members of the committee, I invited them to a private, off-the-record conference at breakfast on the first day of our discussions. In this meeting I stressed our determination to present a strong civil rights plank to the convention, and added that we had the votes to do so. However, I was anxious to avoid as far as possible language that would arouse a passionately negative response in their states and force them into making bitter speeches.

After careful negotiation, coupled with a firm approach on the key issues on which I had majority support, the first draft of a platform, which many observers described as the most specific and forthright in

1. I doubt that he read it carefully until after the nomination.

many years, was accepted by the committee with very little dissent. Although the Southern members of the committee placed a minority report before the convention objecting to the strong civil rights plank, there was no meaningful opposition, and the platform was adopted by the convention delegates without change and, even more surprising, without costly oratorical fireworks.

My personal feelings about the efforts of the Platform Committee were expressed in my introduction, in which I said, in part:

> Much will be said about our disagreements on civil rights—although these were expressed without bitterness or rancor. Decidedly more important than our disagreements, however, was the unity among us in the field of world affairs and economic policy.
>
> I believe that never before have we achieved a broader, more democratic consensus in the Democratic Party than we discovered in this year's platform deliberations. It is a consensus which shows that we know what is required of us, and that as Americans and as Democrats we are eager and ready to meet the challenge ahead.

The solemn commitments we had built into the platform represented policies which not only Jack Kennedy but also Adlai Stevenson, Hubert Humphrey and other liberal leaders had been advocating throughout the country. If taken seriously by the party rank and file, I hoped they would provide the solid foundation for a political breakthrough and encourage the new President to exert the kind of leadership that would be required to achieve it.

During the fall of 1959 I had begun to receive some scattered and unsolicited publicity about my possible role as a dark-horse candidate for President. Buttons proclaiming "Draft Bowles," "The grass roots are rooting for Chester Bowles," and the like began to make their appearance. The January 11, 1960, issue of the *New Republic* carried an article proposing my candidacy, which concluded:

> This journal believes that the candidacies of Jack Kennedy and Hubert Humphrey—and Adlai Stevenson—are still very much alive, but it also foresees the real possibility of a deadlock. It is not too soon, therefore, to consider attractive, new liberal alternatives. And it is for this reason that discussion of Chester Bowles has practical significance.

Soon Bowles-for-President committees were formed in Wyoming, California, Massachusetts, Missouri, Connecticut, New York, Pennsylvania and Washington, D.C.

While I appreciated the compliment, this movement was embarrassing and I discouraged it. A "Draft Bowles" effort could create misunderstanding, not so much with Kennedy personally, who I am sure did not question my personal commitment to him, but with some of his professional political campaign operators, who were more interested in power than in ideas and who looked on the more liberal elements in the Democratic Party as competitors rather than working partners. I outlined my position in letters to my well-wishers as follows:

> The situation is simply this: the likelihood of Presidential lightning passing the front runners and striking me is extraordinarily remote. It would take a deadlock to bring this about, and in a convention which no longer adheres to two-thirds' rule, a deadlock is virtually impossible.
>
> I am personally committed to the candidacy of Jack Kennedy and I do so with great enthusiasm. I have developed a substantial admiration for him, and I believe that he can lead us to victory and a new era of exciting political action. . . . In these circumstances my effectiveness within the party is best served by vigorously discouraging your attempts to organize in my behalf.

Despite my efforts to dampen down this movement, it caught fire in Los Angeles just before the start of the Democratic National Convention. On Friday, July 8, an impressive Bowles-for-President booth was set up in the Biltmore Hotel near the room in which the Platform Committee was holding its hearings, and volunteers began to distribute Bowles campaign buttons and literature. At the same time Bowles-for-President representatives issued a press release announcing that a press conference would be held Saturday morning. The last thing we needed was more publicity of this kind.

The Los Angeles Bowles-for-President Club had organized a large dinner meeting that night. At my request, my aide, Jim Thomson, interrupted the proceedings to ask that the news conference be canceled. Robert A. Rutland, a UCLA professor and leader of the Los Angeles group, a staunch and devoted supporter whom I had long been trying to dissuade from pressing my candidacy, finally agreed to put the Bowles-for-President movement to rest. He told the group that he and his associates had been impressed with my repeated requests to cease and desist from further organized activity on my behalf, and the press conference was canceled.

In the meantime a series of meetings were held to discuss the Vice Presidency. Although I strongly supported Humphrey, the bitter primary campaign in West Virginia had left too many scars. When Kennedy told me that he thought Johnson was the wisest choice, I expressed my surprise and pointed out the disadvantages of nominating a running mate whose actual views were so little known and whose major talent was legislative manipulation. Kennedy smiled and said, "But he'll never accept." The implication was that by offering the second spot to Johnson he could gain credit with the South and that Johnson could be counted on to refuse.

Kennedy's nomination opened up the near-certainty that if he were elected he would ask me to work with him in some capacity on foreign policy. However, before the National Convention had convened, I had been unanimously renominated at the Connecticut Convention in New London for re-election as Connecticut's Second Congressional District Representative. I accepted the nomination because I wanted to continue in public life regardless of what happened at the National Convention.

A few days after the Los Angeles Convention I went to Hyannis Port to discuss my problem with Kennedy. I told him I was confident I could easily win the Congressional election and was reluctant to give up my seat without a clearer idea of what lay ahead. At the same time I recognized that it would be unwise for him to make commitments until after the election. Kennedy said he was counting on me to devote a major share of my time to his national campaign, and he was confident that two or three weeks of hard campaigning in Connecticut would be sufficient to assure my re-election there.

During this conversation Kennedy for the first time specifically raised the possibility of my appointment as Secretary of State. Mutual friends who knew Kennedy better than I did had assured me that there was an even chance I would be selected, but I had remained skeptical. While many people assumed otherwise, I was not really close to Kennedy. On the basis of his experience and world prestige, Adlai Stevenson had seemed to me the logical choice for Secretary of State. Adlai was even less close to Kennedy than I, and following the last-minute drive for Stevenson at the convention Kennedy still looked upon him as a political rival. But he was among the most distinguished of Democrats, and foreign affairs had always been his primary interest. If Adlai was selected, as I then thought he would be, I saw myself as his Under Secretary, where my long administrative experience and my long and close personal relationship with him would be helpful.

As far as my running for Congress was concerned, there were two ways in which I could proceed. One was to take my chances on Kennedy's election in November and pull out of the Congressional race. This, of course, involved a large measure of risk: if Kennedy was defeated, I would prematurely come to the end of the political road. The other alternative was to campaign for re-election to Congress, but to devote all the time I could to Kennedy's national campaign. If Kennedy won and asked me to join him in Washington, I would then resign my Congressional seat. But this would require a special election, which would involve the risk of losing the seat to a Republican, whereas if I pulled out now, William St. Onge, my former campaign manager, who shared my views, could undoubtedly be nominated and probably elected.[2]

The situation was complicated by the fact that two other Connecticut party leaders, Abe Ribicoff and John Bailey, appeared to be headed for major posts in the Kennedy government.[3] If Kennedy won, I knew that they would privately press him to leave me in Congress on the grounds that two Connecticut leaders in Washington would be company but three a crowd, while publicly taking the position that I should remain in Congress to continue to build a liberal political structure in traditionally Republican eastern Connecticut.

There was also the matter of obligation to my supporters. A great many people had worked hard to put me in Congress and were prepared to work just as hard to keep me there. The young people who had been excited by what I stood for were full of enthusiasm and commitment. It would be pleasant to see the result of their efforts recorded in the ballot box.

The situation was further complicated by Kennedy's fear that if I dropped out of the Congressional campaign, some Stevenson supporters might assume he had already asked me to become Secretary of State, which might dampen their enthusiasm for his campaign. Knowing Stevenson as I did, this seemed to me unlikely; he was not the kind of person who would sulk in his tent or allow his supporters to do so.

After some tortuous discussions, I decided that the wisest and most responsible course was to put my faith in Kennedy's election, to pull out of the Congressional race immediately and to devote all my energies to his election to the Presidency.

With Bob Kennedy's help, I put together a letter of resignation from the Connecticut race, and of commitment to the Kennedy national campaign, which eased the fears of many Stevenson supporters. I was relieved that my constituents in the Second Congressional District by and large understood and respected the reasons for my decision. As I look back on it, in spite of the unhappy experiences that lay ahead I still believe that my choice was the correct one.

By the time I reached Washington in early September, the Speakers Bureau of the Kennedy organization under Sargent Shriver, Archibald

2. As it turned out, Bill St. Onge was defeated by a narrow margin in 1960, but won in 1962 and served as Congressman from Connecticut's Second District until his death in 1970.

3. Ribicoff became Secretary of the Department of Health, Education and Welfare, and Bailey became Democratic National Chairman.

Cox and Kay Folger had prepared a full schedule of speaking engagements. These were largely concentrated in states outside New England where I was particularly well known—California, Illinois, New York, Michigan, Minnesota, Wisconsin, Iowa, Kansas and Pennsylvania.

It was agreed that Connecticut and the other New England states were not a problem. Connecticut party Democrats had been committed to Kennedy from the beginning. And since the speeches he made in his nearby home state of Massachusetts were picked up in Connecticut as well, his photogenic face was familiar to every Connecticut resident who owned a TV set.

In the two months before the election I made a series of speaking tours which kept me going every day from midmorning until late at night. These tours were interspersed with two- or three-day visits to Washington to dig up material for future speeches, to go over drafts of speeches being prepared for Kennedy, and to discuss with Kennedy, often by long-distance telephone, the foreign policy questions which might come up in his daily press conferences. Either Tom Hughes or Jim Thomson, and usually Steb, went with me on these speaking tours. Steb was often called on to make speeches of her own.

Following my return from one of these tours, I issued the following statement through my Congressional office:

> This trip has convinced me that one issue stands paramount in the minds of voters throughout our country, and that is the issue of peace. Wherever I travel, I find a deep conviction that somehow we must move toward creating the conditions for a peace that is more than peace through nuclear terror.
>
> How do we create such conditions? How do we achieve a peace based on order, justice and compassion—a peace which will allow our society and those of other peoples everywhere to develop freely, unfettered by fear and the armaments race? Which candidate and which party can best lead us toward such goals?
>
> These are the questions which most deeply concern the men and women I met during my trip—the farmers of South Dakota, the businessmen of San Francisco and Portland, the students of our great state universities, the working people and housewives everywhere I traveled.

Another of my roles in the campaign was to act as Kennedy's representative with foreign policy officials in the Eisenhower Administration, particularly Secretary of State Christian A. Herter. In the election of 1948 Truman had asked the intelligence people to keep his opponent, Thomas E. Dewey, fully informed on critical situations. Although Truman agreed that Dewey had the right to say what he wished, he believed that if Dewey and his associates had access to the factual

information on which the Administration based its foreign policy decisions and statements, they would be more likely to act responsibly.
President Eisenhower had continued this practice in the election of
1956, but the Nixon campaign managers made it clear that they did
not intend to continue to do so in 1960.

At luncheon in Washington I discussed the situation frankly with
Secretary of State Herter, whom I had come to know and admire when
he was Governor of Massachusetts and I was Governor of Connecticut.
Herter thought for a minute and then observed that as a member of the
House Foreign Affairs Committee I was already cleared for top-secret
information and had a right to background briefings. He suggested I call
on him each week, not in my role as Kennedy's foreign policy adviser,
but as a Congressman. On that basis he would keep me fully informed,
and, of course, I would inform Kennedy.

During the last five or six weeks of the campaign, Herter and I met
regularly once a week at his home on N Street. These briefings enabled
Kennedy, myself and other Democrats to conduct our side of the debate
in a way that would not jeopardize national interests. The Bay of Pigs
invasion of Cuba, which I later learned was then well along in the
planning stage, was the one important subject which Herter never
mentioned.

The story of Kennedy's narrow victory is familiar. As I spoke
throughout the country, I developed the mistaken view that Kennedy
would win by a large majority. Election night at our house in Essex,
which was the same crowded affair it had been on previous election
nights, began in a jovial atmosphere. As we watched the Kennedy vote
roll up in Connecticut, the first state to report, my judgment seemed
to be confirmed. His plurality reached nearly 100,000. But then came a
series of setbacks; the atmosphere became tense, and it was nearly dawn
before we could begin to relax.

Two days later Kennedy asked me to act as his representative in
Washington with foreign diplomats who might want to see him in the
preinaugural period, and Steb and I returned to our home on Q Street.
The official explanation was that the President-elect's time was filled to
overflowing by the recruitment of Cabinet and staff officers, the development of a legislative program and budget, and the drafting of his
Inaugural Address. But even if Kennedy had had time to burn, discussions with foreign representatives before taking office would have
been a mistake. The Eisenhower Administration, in its waning weeks,
confronted a series of touchy international problems. Rumors about
what Kennedy had said about this or thought about that would only
have added to the confusion.

During the month of November I had a long series of off-the-record discussions with foreign envoys—including Ambassador Wilhelm Grewe from West Germany, Chiang Kai-shek's Ambassador, George K. Yeh, Mikhail A. Menshikov of the U.S.S.R. and many others.

None of these talks had any great significance, but they served the useful purpose of informing me—and, through my reports, Kennedy —of the questions that soon were likely to be placed on our doorstep and providing some valuable insights as to what various foreign nations expected of the new Administration.

I was particularly impressed by the genuine sense of relief that the Soviet emissary seemed to feel about Kennedy's election. He emphasized that his government hoped for a long period of reduced tension, and that it was eager to begin informal discussions about the means of creating a more constructive relationship.

CHAPTER 22

THE TEAM OF RUSK AND BOWLES

On December 4, 1960, the Rockefeller Foundation Board of Trustees, of which I was a member, convened at Williamsburg, Virginia, for its annual meeting. Among the other board members present were John J. McCloy, chairman of the Chase Manhattan Bank, former Assistant Secretary of War and U.S. High Commissioner for Germany; Dr. Ralph Bunche, Under Secretary General of the United Nations and winner of the Nobel Peace Prize; Robert A. Lovett, partner in the banking firm of Brown Brothers, Harriman, Inc., and former Secretary of Defense and Under Secretary of State; and Dean Rusk, former Assistant Secretary of State and the Foundation's president.

With the exception of Rusk, each of us had been publicly mentioned as a possible choice for Secretary of State. During our two-day discussions of Foundation business we were one by one called to the telephone. Each call, however routine, created its own air of speculation. In the last afternoon session I was sitting next to Rusk when he, too, received an urgent long-distance call. As he left the room, I sensed intuitively that it might be Kennedy calling. A few minutes later Rusk returned, sat down and passed me a note: "That was Kennedy. He wants to see me tomorrow morning in Washington. What do you think he wants to talk to me about?" On another piece of paper I wrote: "He's going to ask you to become Secretary of State."

One week earlier, at breakfast at his home in Georgetown, Kennedy had said to me: "I want to ask you a hypothetical question: if you were Secretary of State, what kind of an organization would you set up?" I thought about it for a moment and answered, "I think I'd start by asking Dean Rusk to become Under Secretary." Kennedy then asked if

Rusk was not the president of the Rockefeller Foundation. I don't think Kennedy had ever met Rusk, and I may have been the first to bring up his name. I was quite sure at the time and I am sure now that Kennedy's question had had no personal significance for me. He often asked hypothetical questions, and I believed this was no more than that.

After the Rockefeller Foundation meeting ended Rusk returned with Steb and me to Washington and stopped at our house on Q Street for dinner. He asked many questions about Kennedy, his personal characteristics and his ideas on foreign affairs.

Although Rusk had never been active in politics, he was a Democrat, and, indeed, in 1960 had headed the Stevenson-for-President Committee in Scarsdale, New York. I first met him in 1951 when he was Assistant Secretary for Far Eastern Affairs. When John Foster Dulles resigned from the chairmanship of the Board of Trustees of the Rockefeller Foundation in 1952 to become Secretary of State, Rusk, who had worked closely with Dulles in the State Department, came in as the Foundation's president. In 1953 shortly after my return from my first term as Ambassador to India, when I had been invited to become a trustee of the Foundation and a member of the Executive Committee, we had renewed our acquaintance.

During my six or seven years on the Rockefeller Foundation Board, I had developed both affection and respect for Rusk. I never felt that I knew him well (I doubt that anyone outside his family did), but I was impressed with his orderly mind, his thoughtfulness and his remarkable capacity to express himself. When Steb and I traveled with Rusk for nearly a month through northern India in 1957, we observed his apparent ability to communicate with Asians, which encouraged us to think that he understood their problems and aspirations. Certainly nothing in our earlier acquaintance or our conversation that evening at our Georgetown house foreshadowed the differences which later developed.

When Rusk left our house around midnight, he volunteered to telephone after his breakfast meeting with Kennedy to give me a report. He called at about 10:30, just before returning to New York and said, "Well, that's one possibility that we can cross off our list. Kennedy and I could not communicate. If the idea of making me Secretary ever actually entered his mind, I am sure it is now dead."

Although Kennedy had hoped to make his State Department appointments quickly, thereby avoiding the usual build-up of political and personal pressures, there were many complex considerations and inevitably the process dragged.

At first, speculation as to the new Secretary of State focused largely on Adlai Stevenson, with me as the first alternative. Gradually, however, Stevenson's name began to drop out of the speculative news stories and Georgetown cocktail gossip, as pressure from some of Kennedy's close political associates began to build against him.

I was then joined in the rumor mill with such company as David K. E. Bruce, Robert Lovett, John J. McCloy, Eugene R. Black and Senator J. William Fulbright. The Southern Senators, led by Vice President-elect Lyndon Johnson, pressed hard for their Arkansas colleague. But Fulbright's prospects were soon smothered under pressure from black organization leaders who could not forgive him for signing the Southern Manifesto, from organized labor, and from some Jewish groups whom he had offended by his position on the Middle East.

The deflation of the Fulbright balloon had an indirect negative impact on my own chances. Several Southern Senators argued that if Fulbright was disqualified because he had backed racial segregation by signing the Manifesto, I should be eliminated because of my militant advocacy of racial integration and my sponsorship of the strong civil rights plank in the Democratic Convention platform.

My advocacy of fundamental changes in American foreign policy and my support for expansion of federal urban development, housing, educational programs and government-sponsored medical insurance further established me as a target for the hard-line Republican conservatives who led the G.O.P.'s Congressional wing.

The current cliché that Kennedy wanted to be "his own Secretary of State" and to control the formation of foreign policy himself was an oversimplification of the facts. But, understandably, Kennedy was reluctant to appoint a Secretary of State who might become unduly controversial and create difficulties with Congress and the public.[1] This inevitably lessened the chances of contenders with their own public following and with pronounced public views on foreign affairs, such as Stevenson or myself.

Dean Rusk had sufficient credentials to be named Secretary, and, being relatively unknown, he was not an easy target for public criticism. About all that was known of his views was that he had recently published an article in *Foreign Affairs* in which he had argued persuasively that the President should take the lead in foreign policy.[2] Consequently, in

---

1. Once, when Kennedy sought his views on possible candidates for Secretary of State, Robert Lovett was said to have inquired, "Tell me honestly, are you looking for a Secretary of State or are you looking for an Under Secretary?" Kennedy reportedly remarked wryly, "I guess I am looking for an Under Secretary."

2. In *To Move a Nation*, Roger Hilsman cites a "particularly critical newsman" as saying of Rusk, "There are two facts about Dean Rusk that are revealing . . . the first is that he was Assistant Secretary of State for Far Eastern Affairs during the Korean War. The second is that no one remembers it."

spite of Rusk's negative report on his visit with Kennedy, I was not surprised when the rumors soon began to circulate that Rusk would be asked to become Secretary of State.

On Sunday, December 11, I received a call from Bob Kennedy, who said that the President-elect would like to talk to me on the telephone from Palm Beach later that night. The call came at 9:30. Kennedy told me that he had decided to make Rusk Secretary of State and wanted me to become the senior Under Secretary.[3]

At that moment two considerations were uppermost in my mind: first, after fifteen years of deep concern over our foreign relations and nearly a decade of personal involvement, I was delighted to have an opportunity to implement my ideas; and second (Steb insists that this is to some degree a rationalization), I was less disappointed than I had expected not to be offered the top job.

I readily understood why Kennedy felt that Rusk, obviously competent, but less well known and less partisan, filled his requirements better than I. Despite the lesser rank, the Under Secretary was just as close to actual policy-making and even more occupied with the work I enjoyed most—the day-to-day business of involving more people in the development of policy, of building a smooth-running organization and of mustering public support.

In mid-December as Rusk and I moved into our temporary offices in the State Department for the remainder of the transition period, I thought a great deal about the opportunities and limitations of my new post and how I could operate most effectively in it. My first obligation, as I saw it, was to remove any suspicion in Rusk's mind that I still wanted his job and to make it clear that we were not in any sense competing for Kennedy's support and trust. I was determined to build Rusk's confidence in me as his deputy and in his own capacity to deal with Congress, the public, the press and representatives of foreign governments without any second-guessing by his chief subordinate.

During the war years in Washington I had seen at firsthand the bitter relationship between Secretary Cordell Hull and his Under Secretary, Sumner Welles. On many occasions Welles went directly to Roosevelt about questions of policy of which Hull had almost no knowledge. Consequently, in many foreign embassies and within our own government it was assumed that the best way to present a problem or secure a decision was to see Welles, not Hull.

3. The senior Under Secretary is the Deputy Secretary of State, who acts as Secretary in the Secretary's absence. He may be designated as Under Secretary for either Political or Economic Affairs. Kennedy gave me my choice and I chose Political Affairs.

Rusk was not well known to the press, public or Congress, and even less to the Democratic Party leaders, most of whom I had known for years. He was equally unknown to the political operators who had managed Kennedy's 1960 campaign and who were now moving into important positions in the White House and elsewhere in the new Administration. In addition to myself, at least three other Presidential appointees named to the State Deparment—Adlai Stevenson at the UN, Mennen Williams in the African Bureau and Averell Harriman as a roving Ambassador—were well known nationally not only as former governors, but also as advocates of foreign policy innovations in matters on which Rusk had taken no public position. Another potential obstacle to Rusk's influence with the White House was the appointment of the brilliant and articulate McGeorge Bundy as Kennedy's Special Assistant for National Security Affairs, who was now in a position to see the President several times a day.

If Rusk and I were to work together on a relaxed and effective basis, I felt that Bowles the public advocate and political figure must now become Bowles the loyal and self-effacing chief of staff. I decided to reduce my personal contacts with the President to the bare minimum and to limit my discussions with members of the White House staff to matters which I was clearly in a better position to handle than Rusk. I would also reduce my public visibility by refusing, at least for several months, invitations to appear on network TV shows, by keeping my press conferences on a background basis and, most difficult of all, by sharply restricting my contacts with members of Congress, both in the Senate and in the House, where I had made many close friends over a period of twenty years.

In our first discussion Rusk described my role as that of his "alter ego." He likened the relationship he wanted to develop with me to that which existed between Secretary George Marshall and Under Secretary Robert Lovett during the Truman Administration. He made this comment several times, and I think he sincerely wanted it that way. But the successful Marshall-Lovett relationship was based on the fact that Marshall delegated total responsibility for the day-to-day operation of the Department to his Under Secretary. Rusk made it clear that he wanted the administrative strings in his own hands.

In order to clarify our relationship, I suggested, and Rusk agreed, that I prepare two memoranda expressing my views, one on the formulation of our foreign policy and the other on its administration. I thought these memoranda would also be useful in getting Kennedy to focus his attention on the organization of the Department.

During the previous few weeks Kennedy had shown little interest

304 PROMISES TO KEEP

in this subject. Although he wanted the Department to be an effective instrument both in the preparation of policies and in their implementation, the President-elect had neither the time nor the inclination to grapple with the questions involved in achieving this objective. Indeed, in a sense, I felt that Kennedy took administration for granted.[4]

Having been involved in administration for my entire adult life, I knew something of its difficulties and requirements. Indeed, in August, 1946, Secretary of State James F. Byrnes, who had been impressed with our success in transforming the once chaotic Office of Price Administration into a smooth-running organization, had asked me to become his Under Secretary with full responsibility for reorganizing the Department. I had reluctantly refused because of my commitment to stay on as OPA Administrator through the reconversion period. Later as Ambassador to India from 1951 to 1953, I had also seen at firsthand how the administrative rigidity of the State Department often stifled the abilities of talented members of the Foreign Service.

The first of my two memoranda on the formulation of foreign policy summarized my objections to Eisenhower Administration policies and called for a departmental review of our relations with other nations, including those we did not recognize, such as China. In it I said:

> Most of the policy assumptions under which we now operate are hand-me-downs from a period in which the balance of power was vastly more favorable to us than it is now. Although we cannot disregard the commitments that grew out of these assumptions, it is essential that we give more thought to the assumptions themselves. Some of them were questionable in their original setting. Others have been overtaken by events.

I pointed out that the Eisenhower Administration's preoccupation with anti-Communism and military alliances had convinced many thoughtful observers both in the United States and abroad that American foreign policy officials were largely insensitive to the political forces shaping the world.

I suggested that this impression, highlighted by the criticism which had been leveled at the Eisenhower Administration for nearly ten years by Democrats such as Kennedy, Fulbright, Stevenson, Harriman, Humphrey and myself, had been an important and possibly the decisive factor in Kennedy's narrow victory in November. As I put it in my memorandum to Rusk, "There is not only an urgent need but a clear public commitment for a fresh approach to foreign policy."

4. A Georgetown wit once remarked that Kennedy's concept of administration was to call his brother on the telephone and say, "Bob, I want these three things done by Tuesday."

I pointed out in my second memorandum to Rusk that:

> Regardless of the abilities of the present top State Department leaders,
> they have been associated in the public mind and in the minds of the
> leaders of the world with a long series of American setbacks.
>
> Moreover, it is inevitable that many of these individuals should have
> a commitment to the present program under which we have been operat-
> ing for the last eight years, and consequently, it will not be easy for them
> wholeheartedly to support and administer the fresh approaches which the
> world situation requires and to which we are committed by the election
> of President Kennedy.

I suggested that only after the most careful consideration should
we retain in a high policy-making position any senior Foreign Service
officer who was closely associated with the present policies. Instead,
I recommended we recruit down through the level of Assistant Secretary
"people who are unhampered by past loyalties and associations, and
who are in a position to inspire a new spirit and willingness among those
who are working under them."

I believed the choice of Assistant Secretaries would be vital to a
successful effort to foster more affirmative, creative thinking throughout the Department and in our overseas missions. Many career men
had become skilled in the use of ambiguous or evasive language in
dealing with controversial subjects, so that their views could be interpreted in any number of ways. In many cases this occurred because
the opinions (or prejudices) of an Assistant Secretary or Ambassador,
pro or con, could make or break an FSO's career. We could not successfully encourage subordinates to challenge accepted ideas unless their
superiors were themselves open-minded and receptive to innovation.

I urged in my memorandum to Rusk that:

> We should encourage Foreign Service officers to speak more frankly
> through departmental channels even though this brings them into con-
> flict with accepted policies, attitudes, and interpretations of the Depart-
> ment. Those officers who take unpopular or unorthodox positions on com-
> plex issues which are rejected by the White House or the State Department
> should not be penalized. On the contrary, ways should be found to show
> them that we appreciate their courage in expressing their convictions.

The established flow of decision-making in the Department contributed to the difficulties in bringing new ideas to the fore. In the State
Department policies originated at the lower levels, and were passed up to
the top for decision. It was only human for those who had helped
create the old policies to drag their feet in regard to new ones. For
example, whenever the Secretary and Under Secretary desired a new

approach in a certain area, the appropriate "country desk"[5] was asked to produce various alternatives. The desk often first ignored the request in the hope that it would be forgotten and then, if it was insisted upon, would come up with the same old approaches in a new dress. The "revised" policy then gradually worked its way up through the bureaucracy, gathering initials at each level, often at the expense of further compromises.

Finally, having been fought over for some time at the various levels, the paper belatedly arrived at the offices of the Secretary and Under Secretary, who had little or no knowledge of the compromises built into the final version or, except in a general way, of the alternatives. The next step was a high-level meeting at which a discussion of the recommendations took place. At this point, little could be done except to either knock the paper down and start over or accept it as it was, possibly with some moderate amendments.

This weakness in the process of policy-making and revision, I believed, could be solved only by reversing the procedures from the bottom up to the top down. On important policy questions requiring revision, a half-dozen or so top people, including the Secretary himself, should first meet to discuss the validity of the present policy and the various broad alternatives. As options were presented, the appropriate bureaus and "country desks" could be brought in to develop them further. The advantages and disadvantages of each of several approaches could then be carefully considered.

I delivered my two memoranda to Rusk in late December with the intention of discussing them carefully with him and other officials after he had studied them. But Rusk did not respond directly to either of them. A few days after receiving them he casually remarked that while he might have some small differences in implementation, he understood my views. Instead of insisting on a frank discussion of the memoranda and a further review with the President, I mistakenly chose to interpret Rusk's vague verbal response as agreement.

As the weeks passed, I began to sense the consequences of this failure to talk out matters of procedure, priorities and objectives. Rusk and I had little opportunity to meet regularly. We both faced increasingly tight schedules, crammed with interviews and briefing sessions (most of which were devoted to proving that what we were now doing was justified and should not be tampered with, much less changed in any fundamental way). But even when time was not a factor, Rusk seemed to avoid open discussion of differences.

A series of full-blown discussions at the outset would have brought

5. State Department jargon for the group responsible for our relations with individual countries.

to light certain fundamental differences between my views and Rusk's. Rusk was far more comfortable with the traditional State Department approach than I was, or I believed the President to be. His service in the State Department under Truman had left him with an almost mystic commitment to what he reverently referred to as "The Department." This feeling was reflected, to his great credit, in his indignation over the shabby treatment accorded the many capable Foreign Service officers who came under fire from Senator Joseph McCarthy and his fellow Communist-baiters.

But it was also evident in his article for *Foreign Affairs,* in April, 1960, in which he wrote that the primary task of the State Department was not to think up "new ideas." In 1960 I felt (as I feel today) that in the conduct of its foreign policy the United States Government was urgently in need of "new ideas": new ideas concerning our relations with Russia and China, with Europe, Africa, Asia and Latin America; new ideas about economic development, about our national priorities and objectives, about the size, shape and purposes of our military establishment and so on.

In the absence of any formal delegation of authority it seemed to be agreed that my first responsibility was to help recruit the men who would act as our principal associates. Among the most important of these appointments were the Assistant Secretaries for the five geographic bureaus, the Under Secretary for Economic Affairs, my two Deputy Under Secretaries, one for Administration and one for Political Affairs, the Director of the United States Information Agency (USIA), and the Director of the Agency for International Development (AID).[6] In these and a number of other posts, such as Director of Intelligence and Research, the Director of Educational and Cultural Affairs and the Legal Adviser, I was determined to bring in men who shared my sense of urgency.

Because the Cold War mentality had dominated much of the work of the U.S. Information Service in the 1950's, I was particularly anxious to find a new Director who would instill a fresh sense of integrity into our informational work as well as to develop more effective policies and guidelines. My first choice was Edward R. Murrow of the Columbia Broadcasting System. After a brilliant record as a war correspondent Murrow had earned a reputation as an objective and thoughtful news analyst and commentator. He had led the mass media's belated effort to expose Joe McCarthy.

When I suggested Murrow, both Rusk and Kennedy were skeptical,

6. Recruitment for the Agency for International Development is discussed in Chapter 30 in the context of foreign economic assistance.

acknowledging his unique qualifications, but questioning whether he could be persuaded to leave his lucrative position as CBS's top commentator for a relatively low-paying government job with little public visibility. Nevertheless, they authorized me to offer him the post, and it took him no more than thirty seconds to accept. His only question was: "When do I start?"

For the post of Under Secretary for Economic Affairs, Rusk and I agreed on William A. Foster, an internationally-minded Republican who had followed Paul Hoffman as Director of Overseas Aid in the Truman Administration. Kennedy approved, and Foster promptly accepted my offer.

However, influential Democrats on Capitol Hill, disturbed over Foster's Republican background, pressed the White House for the appointment of George Ball, a distinguished law partner of Stevenson's and a Democrat. Ball had specialized in international economic negotiations, was a close friend of Jean Monnet, the father of the European Common Market, and was thought to be one of the relatively few Americans who could communicate with Charles de Gaulle.

When the President decided to reverse the earlier decision and substitute Ball for Foster, it was my unpleasant task to rescind our offer to Foster. With his long background in the unpredictable ways of Washington, Foster took this bit of confusion in his stride and later became head of the newly created Arms Control and Disarmament Agency, where he served with distinction for eight years. Ball, of course, was to become a major element in the reshuffling of the State Department leadership which occurred some months later.

A new Director was also needed to bring more drive, competence and judgment to the Bureau of Intelligence and Research. My choice for this post was Roger Hilsman, a West Point graduate turned political scientist, who headed the research staff at the Library of Congress. I had come to know Hilsman during my two years in Congress, and since my affection and respect for him were matched by President Kennedy's, his appointment was quickly agreed to. Tom Hughes, who had been my associate in Connecticut and later my administrative assistant in Congress, became Hilsman's deputy.[7]

I proposed that we upgrade the Director of the Bureau of Educational and Cultural Affairs to an Assistant Secretary. The new Director's first task, as I saw it, was to establish the domestic policy-making role of the State Department in all matters of international cultural and

7. In 1963 Hilsman became Assistant Secretary for the Far Eastern Bureau and Hughes became Director of Intelligence and Research, remaining in that post until 1969.

educational exchange which were under the jurisdiction of the government. Some sixty thousand full-time foreign students were in the United States, but we had no precise idea where they were, what they thought or what they were getting out of their studies here.

In addition, thousands of other young foreigners were brought here by various agencies for special training who had no contact with the State Department whatsoever; some forty thousand were brought in by the Defense Department alone. It would be useful, I thought, to arrange for as many of them as possible to spend at least a week or two on a university campus, where they would come to know more about how American students thought and felt.

My nominee for the post of Director was Philip H. Coombs, who had worked with me during my term as Governor of Connecticut and who in 1960 was a senior member of the educational department of the Ford Foundation. Rusk agreed and Coombs accepted with enthusiasm.

For the post of Legal Adviser I nominated Abram Chayes, a Harvard Law School professor. Rusk at first questioned the proposal on the ground that at thirty-eight Chayes was "too young and inexperienced." Although Rusk would have preferred a "distinguished international" lawyer, none appeared to be available, and he finally agreed on Chayes. Chayes, who was a competent operator with a positive approach to foreign policy and a brilliant mind, seemed to me the ideal type for this position. I had known him intimately when he worked on my gubernatorial staff. He had clerked for Justice Felix Frankfurter and practiced law in Washington. In 1960 he was one of the youngest and most promising members of the Harvard faculty. During the Kennedy campaign he had worked as a key member of Solicitor General Archibald Cox's research staff. In the next three years Chayes established himself as a constructive and articulate force on a wide range of political issues which had traditionally been ignored by the Legal Adviser's office.

Another post for which we were able to recruit an outstanding man was my Deputy Under Secretary for Administration. Roger W. Jones, head of the U.S. Civil Service Commission under Eisenhower and a Republican, impressed me as liberal, imaginative and determined to pursue the more modern policies of placement and promotion needed both to improve the performance and morale of the Foreign Service and to attract and to hold outstanding young men and women. Rusk agreed, and Jones proceeded to bring in an able supporting staff, including William J. Crockett and Herman Pollack. Together they brought a heretofore unequaled distinction to the Department's Bureau of Administration.

The Deputy Under Secretary for Political Affairs became our major recruiting problem. I recognized that our choice for this post would have a profound effect on our operations. He would work directly with me, outranking the five geographic Assistant Secretaries and acting as my liaison with the various bureau chiefs. He would also be the Department's chief liaison officer with the Pentagon and CIA.

For these reasons I felt it was important that the appointee should be someone I knew well, in whom I had personal confidence, who agreed with the Kennedy approach to foreign affairs and who could be counted on to see that the bureaus faithfully and imaginatively carried out the President's policy decisions.

For several weeks, Rusk and I discussed various possibilities. I strongly favored David Ginsburg, the Washington lawyer with a brilliant record in the New Deal period and as a wartime administrator, who possessed a solid understanding of foreign relations. But Rusk vetoed Ginsburg and expressed a strong preference for a Foreign Service officer.[8] In turn I argued against several of Rusk's nominees, who I felt lacked the commitment and innovative spirit needed for the Deputy Under Secretary post.

Finally, in late January, in view of Rusk's strong feelings I saw no alternative but to agree to the appointment of U. Alexis Johnson, an experienced Foreign Service officer with whom Rusk had worked in the Truman days. I understood that the Deputy Under Secretary was by tradition a Foreign Service officer, and I sympathized with the reasons, since it assured that career men would have an important voice in the Department. But my concern stemmed from Johnson's close association with Walter S. Robertson, who as Assistant Secretary for Far Eastern Affairs was in my view responsible for many of our mistakes in Asia during the 1950's.[9] I ended up with a Deputy who, however likable and skilled, had an approach to foreign policy totally different than mine.

Except for the post of Deputy Under Secretary our most important appointments were the Assistant Secretaries to head the five geographic bureaus—for Europe, Latin America, Africa, the Near East and South Asia, and the Far East.[10] It was essential, as I saw it, to fill these positions with competent officials who were personally loyal to the new

8. Ginsburg later was asked by President Johnson to become Under Secretary of State for Economic Affairs.
9. Later developments proved that my concern was fully justified.
10. The terms "Near East" and "Far East" are British colonial legacies. "Near East" is nearer London, and "Far East" is farther from London. Happily, in the Johnson Administration the term "Far Eastern" was finally changed to "East Asian and Pacific."

President, who genuinely shared his views on international questions and who could be counted upon skillfully and persistently to promote those views. Although things could have been worse, my initial high hopes and expectations did not materialize.

The Latin-American operation was chaotic from the start. Shortly after the election, Kennedy had appointed Adolf A. Berle, the distinguished New Dealer and former Assistant Secretary under Roosevelt's Good Neighbor Policy, as a Special Assistant to the President with the duties of Assistant Secretary of State for Latin American Affairs.

While Berle's special status reflected Kennedy's wish for a new relationship with our southern neighbors, his hazy position in the Administration hierarchy made it almost impossible to get a grip on the Latin American Bureau, which badly needed a house cleaning. A number of Foreign Service officers had comfortably adjusted themselves over the years to close relationships with such right-wing dictators as Batista, Trujillo and Stroessner, and Berle's undefined responsibilities did not permit him, me or anyone else to solve this problem.

In mid-January I finally received a go-ahead from Kennedy and Rusk to hire a regular Assistant Secretary, with Berle presumably, though it was not explicitly stated, limiting his own role. I approached Clark Kerr, president of the University of California, about the job. Kerr expressed keen interest on the condition that I could straighten out the jurisdictional and policy confusion involving Berle. When it became apparent that this was not immediately possible and that some duplication would remain, Kerr very sensibly rejected my offer.

A few months later, after the Bay of Pigs fiasco had illuminated the nearly total confusion in this bureau, I was authorized to renew the offer to Kerr and he agreed to come. But by that time his board of regents was unwilling to give him a leave of absence, and the post remained in limbo. Finally, after several weeks during which I continued without success to press for the appointment of someone who understood the political realities of Latin America, I had no alternative but to go along with the selection of Robert Woodward, a career Foreign Service officer who was then our Ambassador to Chile.

Woodward was capable and thoughtful, but lacked the required stature, imagination and insight into the steadily developing revolutionary trends in Latin-American politics and their implications for the United States. Much of the initiative for Latin-American policy-making drifted from the Department into the White House and eventually into the office of a young Kennedy speech writer, Richard N. Goodwin.

Despite what many considered a rather abrasive personality, Goodwin was one of the few sources of imaginative thinking during this period. Although he had little previous experience in Latin-American affairs, he was able to generate new ideas while the Department stuck doggedly to its old judgments. This helped to confirm Kennedy's increasingly lower assessment of the Department.[11]

For the Near Eastern–South Asian Bureau we recruited from outside the Department a knowledgeable and competent man whom I had known for years. Phillips Talbot, later head of the Asia Society, had considerable academic expertise in South Asian affairs coupled with many visits to that area. Unhappily, after I became Ambassador to India in 1963, Talbot and I found ourselves in serious conflict over the question of military assistance in the subcontinent.

In our choice of Assistant Secretaries for the two bureaus of perhaps greatest importance—Europe and the Far East—as in the Latin-American post, we ended up with agreeable, experienced but tradition-minded career Foreign Service officers. Although I recommended that we would be best served by asking Averell Harriman to fill either of these posts and Harriman told me that he would accept, the Secretary's reaction was firmly negative.[12]

As head of our European Affairs Bureau we retained Foy D. Kohler from the Eisenhower Administration. Kohler was professional and intelligent, but at that time still committed to the Acheson-Dulles-Eisenhower policies, which since the economic recovery of Europe, the emergence of West Germany and the development of Soviet nuclear power were, in my view, in urgent need of revision.

In regard to the Far Eastern Bureau Rusk accepted my recommendation that we transfer the incumbent Assistant Secretary, J. Graham Parsons, who had replaced Robertson and shared many of his views. Parsons was a competent individual of the old school, and I recommended his appointment as Ambassador to Sweden, where he served with distinction.

As Parsons' replacement, Rusk selected Walter McConaughy, a veteran Foreign Service officer and another associate of Rusk's from his days as Assistant Secretary for the Far East. McConaughy, who was likable and mildly liberal, had also labored for many years in Robertson's Asian vineyard. Nevertheless, he did support my effort to persuade

11. In November, 1961, Kennedy appointed Goodwin as Deputy Assistant Secretary in the Latin American Bureau at the same time Woodward was replaced. As Deputy Assistant Secretary from 1961 to 1963, Goodwin was sabotaged by the Department and, in spite of his earnest efforts, accomplished little. While some may see this as proof that men like Goodwin have no place among the "professionals" of the Department, I believe it is a persuasive argument for more of the kind of administrative changes I advocated.

12. While Rusk offered no reason, it was evident that he would feel challenged by Harriman's national stature.

the Secretary and the White House to recognize Mongolia, and proved to be more conscious than many others that our approach to Asia was urgently in need of change.

In contrast to the other geographic bureaus, the situation in the Bureau of African Affairs was encouraging from the outset; indeed, it was exactly what I had hoped the tone of each bureau would be. Even before Kennedy appointed Rusk and myself, he had asked G. Mennen Williams, the buoyant Governor of Michigan, to become Assistant Secretary for African Affairs. Williams, who had been a strong supporter of the civil rights movement, was committed to a policy of anticolonialism and support for African nationalism. His deputy, J. Wayne Fredericks, long experienced in African affairs, whom I helped to recruit from the Ford Foundation, brilliantly complemented him. The African Bureau proved to be a model in regard to the development and implementation of fresh plans, serving to highlight our mediocre success in staffing the other bureaus.

POSTSCRIPT

Nine years later, in 1970, William B. Macomber, Deputy Under Secretary of State for Administration, proposed a series of radical reforms in the organization and management of the State Department, many of which were parallel to my recommendations in 1961. However, unlike past efforts, including my own, his had the full support of the Secretary and were prompted in part by the accumulation of frustrations on the part of many younger, talented FSO's and the increasing difficulty of attracting able men to the Foreign Service.

In an address on January 14, 1970, Macomber made the following points:

> Many of the ideas I will present today are distilled from earlier efforts. Their newness no longer jars. The groundwork for what we seek has been laid. We are asking not for revolution but for the acceleration of an evolution which has already begun.
>
> In the intervening years it has become clear that we can no longer take refuge in a tidy division of talent. For now it represents an abdication of responsibility. We still must take the lead in policy formulation, but if we are really going to lead we must also be prepared to manage and orchestrate the overall spectrum of our nation's activities abroad.
>
> We are going to keep the promotion channels unclogged. We are going to correct the top-heavy character of our system. We shall be even on the lookout for older officers who have lost their drive.

Older and more experienced officers do not seem to have natural advantages in the critical areas of creativity and innovation. Here, clearly, our younger officers should feel neither humility nor inhibition. In fact, it can be argued that creativity can better come from those who do not already know too many reasons why too many things won't work.

While I was pleased to see these long-overdue changes being seriously considered, I found it ironic that their urgency was in large part created by the mismanagement and questionable policies that should have long since been corrected. It is a telling comment on the slow, painful and costly way by which changes are achieved in a bureaucracy.

CHAPTER 23

EMBASSIES AND AMBASSADORS

TRADITIONALLY, ambassadorships in many U.S. missions abroad had been viewed by the party in power as political plums with which to reward its most generous campaign contributors. This practice was hard to defend even in the relatively quiet past when our involvement in world affairs was marginal. In a world buffeted by unpredictable new political forces, the choice of ambassadors on this basis would be totally irresponsible. I had discussed with Kennedy the need to strengthen our overseas missions and found that he shared my views. Although Kennedy naturally left the door open to make a few appointments on personal grounds, he and to some extent even Rusk agreed that recruiting a new breed of envoy should be at the top of our agenda; I was given primary responsibility for recruitment.

The career officers who had risen most quickly in the State Department hierarchy during the 1950's and who now headed many important missions abroad had, with several notable exceptions, largely accepted the Dulles perspective of a world in which the good guys (the Americans) and the bad guys (the Soviets) would remain locked in combat for the foreseeable future. Normally, these men would expect to continue as ambassadors, no matter what the changes in Administration. However, I believed it essential that we distinguish between those who could be expected conscientiously to carry out the policies of the Kennedy Administration and those who were so committed to the old policies they could not be expected to change direction.

I decided that the abilities of all Foreign Service officers qualified for ambassadorial posts should be carefully reviewed. This review should include outstanding employees of the United States Information

Agency and the Agency for International Development, which, while closely associated with the State Department, had previously been by-passed in regard to ambassadorial appointments. We needed to place particular emphasis, I thought, on the younger officers. At that time no one under fifty held the rank of career minister or career ambassador. (I once startled President Kennedy by remarking that under the existing Foreign Service promotional system the highest grade he could expect to achieve at his age, forty-three, was an FSO 3, a little more than halfway up the promotional ladder.)

To reward outstanding service, we should assign a number of Foreign Service officers to prestigious embassies in Europe. Most of these posts had previously gone to wealthy campaign contributors on the spurious grounds that a Foreign Service officer with a relatively modest salary and a limited expense account could not afford to carry on the necessary entertaining. Based on my own ambassadorial experience, I felt this argument had been grossly overdone.[1] In the very few situations where it was valid the President should be prepared to ask Congress for additional entertainment funds, so that we could appoint the best man for the post—not the best rich man.

In our review we should isolate those senior Foreign Service officers in their fifties and early sixties who were simply marking time in unimportant tasks until retirement. It was my view that, in their own interest as well as the government's, men in this category should be encouraged to retire from the service with a generous pension. With several years of active life remaining, most of them could develop stimulating and rewarding second careers in university teaching, international trade or the like. This would help clear the way for the more rapid promotion of talented young officers.

At the same time I felt we should also consider retired Foreign Service officers, still in the active age group, who had resigned for reasons that did not reflect on them personally, and who might now be persuaded to return to service. A prime example in this category was George F. Kennan, then at Princeton's Institute for Advanced Study, who was clearly capable of making an important contribution in a challenging new post.

In addition, those Foreign Service officers who had been unjustly forced to resign or passed over for promotion under the depredations of Joe McCarthy should now have their clouded records cleared.

There were also sources of ambassadorial talent outside the Foreign

---

1. In addition to his salary and entertainment allowance, an ambassador was provided with a fully furnished house, servants, a car and travel expenses. Steb and I had no difficulty living within my salary and allowances.

Service which were relatively untapped. In the universities, the foundations, business and labor unions there were many able men with both a broad understanding of world affairs and a desire to serve their country. They should be considered together with men already in the Foreign Service.

The actual selection of ambassadors turned out to be a huge task which required checking hundreds of individuals, making thousands of telephone calls and conducting many long interviews. Between January and April of 1961 it absorbed at least one-third of my time. Although some of my associates felt that in view of all our other problems the time that I spent in this effort was out of proportion, I do not agree. The result was a significant strengthening of American representation abroad and eventually a far better-coordinated and efficient administrative performance.

The first step was a decision that any ambassador who had performed effectively and who had served less than three years at his present post would be asked to remain. With one or two exceptions, these were all Foreign Service officers. However, this left more than half of the ambassadorial posts to be filled. Most of the appointments we made to fill these vacancies were also Foreign Service officers, many under forty-five years of age. The remainder were men with academic or professional experience particularly relevant to the nation in which they were posted.

One of my most difficult tasks was to reverse a decision of our predecessors, made just before we took over, to assign seven senior, tradition-minded Foreign Service officers to serve in seven newly independent African states headed by radical young leaders. Instead, we chose young, energetic men, eager to live and work in the new Africa, who understood and respected the political changes taking place there.

As Ambassador to Guinea we nominated William Attwood, foreign affairs editor of *Look* magazine, who worked with Stevenson and me during the 1950's on speeches and Democratic programs. I first asked Bill to head my personal staff, but his wife was determined not to live in Washington. When I asked what job would interest him, he replied, "There is only one thing I'd really like to do and that is to become Ambassador to Guinea. I know President Sékou Touré and I believe I can work with him."

Our relations with Guinea at the moment were at the lowest possible ebb, and no one in the State Department, as far as I knew, was on speaking terms with Sékou Touré. But Attwood was able to accomplish far more in Guinea than anyone, including himself, anticipated. On

his visit to Washington in late 1961, Touré was so impressed with
Kennedy that, to the surprise of most Washington observers, he supported him during the Cuban missile crisis in October, 1962, rejecting a
request by the U.S.S.R. for air traffic rights for Soviet planes flying to
Cuba. Later, Attwood served as Ambassador to Kenya before returning
to *Look* as editor in chief.

Edmund A. Gullion, a Foreign Service officer whom I had met in
Saigon in August, 1952, and whom Kennedy also knew and respected,
was posted to the Congo, a major trouble spot. He played a key role
in support of the United Nations' effort to prevent the secession of
Katanga. Gullion later became Dean of the Fletcher School of Law and
Diplomacy at Tufts University.

For newly independent Senegal, we nominated Philip M. Kaiser,
whom I had known when he was Assistant Secretary in the Labor Department in the Truman Administration. He was experienced in economic affairs and particularly sensitive to the attitudes of the newly
independent nations.

As Ambassador to Togo I selected Leon B. Poullada, a relatively
junior Foreign Service officer whom I had met in Afghanistan a few
years before. When I asked him on the telephone if he would accept
the appointment, he could not believe I was serious. William J. Handley, a career Foreign Service officer who had served outstandingly with
USIA in the fifties became Ambassador to Mali.

Robinson McIlvaine, who had been with the State Department since
1954, went to Dahomey, but only after a hassle. Previously, Bob had
published a small Pennsylvania newspaper, the Downingtown *Archive*,
which strongly supported Eisenhower, and his original appointment in
the Department had been a reward for his support. Nevertheless, he had
demonstrated great competence and wanted to pursue a Foreign Service
career. When Democratic leaders in Pennsylvania heard he was about
to be promoted by a Democratic Administration, they raised an uproar.
Some members of Kennedy's staff suggested that it was not worth
a battle, but I felt that a question of principle was involved and insisted
on going ahead. After a long telephone talk with Pennsylvania's Democratic Governor David L. Lawrence, we finally managed to clear the
way.

Our appointments to other countries reflected a similar pattern of
expertise combined with a capacity for fresh thinking. For our mission
in Tokyo, Jim Thomson, my assistant, who had just secured his Ph.D.
in Chinese history, suggested Edwin O. Reischauer, professor of Japanese
history and far Eastern languages at Harvard. I had some difficulty in
persuading Reischauer to accept the post, and when I finally succeeded,

I ran into strong opposition, much of it covert, from senior Foreign Service officers who felt that by tradition this embassy should be assigned to one of the old career China Hands. Ironically, among the arguments used against Reischauer was the fact that he had a Japanese wife. Although Kennedy wavered at one point, Senator William Fulbright gave me strong support and this appointment was finally confirmed.

I was particularly pleased to persuade George Kennan to take a leave of absence from Princeton to become Ambassador to Yugoslavia. His internationally known writings and his knowledge of the U.S.S.R. enabled him to establish a close relationship with President Tito which did much to improve U.S.-Yugoslav relations.

For my old post in New Delhi, Kennedy had already settled on John Kenneth Galbraith, whom I had first met in OPA days. Ken's competence in economic development and his eagerness to challenge official myths made him an ideal choice for New Delhi. If any ambassador could focus White House attention on the long-neglected South Asian area, I knew it would be Galbraith.

David Bruce, former Under Secretary of State under Truman, went to London at the President's special behest, and Kennedy appointed General James M. Gavin to France. Other examples of successful ambassadorial appointments include John Badeau, for ten years president of the American University in Beirut, to the United Arab Republic; William Stevenson, former president of Oberlin College, to the Philippines; Kenneth Young, an ex-businessman with experience in Asia, to Thailand; and William B. Macomber, a Republican who had served under Eisenhower as Assistant Secretary for Congressional Affairs, to Jordan.

In Latin America, American representation was seriously ingrown. Once a Foreign Service officer became proficient in Spanish and was recognized as a "Latin America expert," he was likely to spend his entire career shuttling around the continent from capital to capital. As a result many had become committed to the status quo and were out of touch with the new political forces which were challenging the established power structures, particularly in the rural areas.[2]

I shared my concern over this situation with Puerto Rico's Governor, Muñoz Marín, during a weekend visit Steb and I paid him in early January, 1961. A personal friend of long standing, Muñoz was known and respected throughout most of Latin America. He told us he was encouraged by the liberal approach the Kennedy Administration was

2. As we considered the parochialism of many of our Latin America specialists and the equally parochial qualities of our Middle East specialists, one of my associates remarked wryly that we might be better off simply to reverse their assignments, with the Arab experts going to Latin America and the Latin America experts to the Middle East.

striving to introduce into U.S.–Latin-American relations. At my request he agreed to make available two of his ablest associates, Teodoro Moscoso, to become U.S. Ambassador to Venezuela, and Arturo Morales-Carrión, to fill an important staff position in the Latin American Bureau. These appointments created an uproar in various echelons of the State Department. The appointment of a Puerto Rican as U.S. Ambassador to a major Latin-American nation in particular was looked on as a dangerous break with tradition.

The most outstanding of new Latin-American ambassadors was a Foreign Service officer who had been one of McCarthy's targets a few years earlier. Fulton J. Freeman, whom we sent to Colombia, succeeded in Latin America largely because he was not a member of the State Department's "Latin American Club," having previously served in Europe. An experienced liberal diplomat, Freeman saw Latin America from a fresh and realistic perspective, with its growing revolutionary ferment as well as its vested interests.

Other Latin America appointments which I look back on with some pride include James I. Loeb, a founder of Americans for Democratic Action, who became Ambassador to Peru; John O. Bell, former Deputy Director of the economic assistance program, who almost single-handedly had kept this agency going in spite of the opposition of Congress and public indifference, as Ambassador to Guatemala; Ben S. Stephansky, who had served as U.S. Labor Attaché in Mexico for ten years and had a profound understanding of Latin-American revolutionary forces, as Ambassador to Bolivia; Lincoln Gordon, a Harvard economist, as Ambassador to Brazil; Charles W. Cole, former president of Amherst College, as Ambassador to Chile; and John Bartlow Martin, a former journalist, as Ambassador to the Dominican Republic.

Traditionally, Ireland was looked upon as a political plum, and I was unable to persuade Kennedy to break the tradition. His choice was Matthew McCloskey, a Philadelphia contractor and long-time Democratic Party contributor.[3]

Israel as well was normally a purely political appointment, but in view of the importance of the post, I felt that the safest appointment would be a Foreign Service officer with no political ambitions or connections. This time Kennedy agreed, and I nominated Walworth Barbour, the Deputy Chief of Mission in London, who at the end of 1970 was still in Tel Aviv.

In all of our appointments there was only one major blunder. Apparently in a weak moment, Kennedy promised his personal friend, Earl

---

3. To my relief, McCloskey served in Dublin with distinction.

E. T. Smith, who had served briefly and ineptly in Cuba in the last stages of the Batista era, that he would be named as Ambassador to Switzerland. Since Switzerland had just agreed to handle U.S. interests in Cuba and since Smith was bitterly opposed to the Castro regime and it was bitterly opposed to him, this was not a happy choice.

When the Swiss Government discreetly passed the word that Smith would be difficult to swallow, Kennedy blew up. Soon the word was passed that members of the Administration should demonstrate their distaste for the Swiss Government reaction by blackballing all functions of the Swiss Embassy. It was a childish performance, which reflected no credit on Kennedy and was not in character.

It is hard to think of a more qualified group of ambassadors than those we selected. Although I was charged with bypassing the Foreign Service, the record shows that by May 1, 1961, four months after the Kennedy Administration took office, the number of embassies headed by Foreign Service officers was at an all-time high—a little more than three out of four. The opposite impression was no doubt created by the fact that during this period some thirty ambassadors or former ambassadors were persuaded to retire. Another factor that was often overlooked was that the ambassadors chosen from outside the Foreign Service were not the usual influential businessmen or campaign contributors, but men experienced in foreign affairs and with unusual qualifications.

Closely associated with the selection of ambassadors was the redefinition of the function and responsibilities of the ambassador. As the personal representative of the President of the United States in a foreign country, an ambassador was expected to know not only the country and its leaders but also its people and to win their confidence and respect.

In many national capitals even our ablest chiefs of mission were also hampered by a tradition of social exclusiveness and artificiality which contributed to an aloof and autocratic impression. This tradition placed too much emphasis on entertaining the capital elite and too little on the ambassador's less glamorous responsibilities, including the primary need for getting to know the country, its institutions and its people.

In my mind Benjamin Franklin, perhaps the most effective American ambassador of all time, was a model of what a modern ambassador should be. Although Franklin had represented the American people at Europe's most aristocratic and glittering court, Versailles, he rejected the pomp and artificiality of diplomatic living and brought a fresh approach to his dealings with diplomatic colleagues and government officials. His manner was direct and genuine, and its effect was dramatic.

According to one biographer, Bernard Fay, "Franklin couldn't step

on to the street without being surrounded by an enthusiastic crowd. They
were overjoyed to find the Ambassador from America simple and dignified. They were delighted that he should wear a plain brown suit without ribbons and that he should go without a wig."

While the temptation to wear a wig no longer existed, in many
other respects diplomatic life still resembled the court of Louis XV. I
believed that American representatives abroad in the 1960's who conducted themselves with Franklin's warmth and simplicity—who got to
know the people as well as their leaders—would receive an equally warm
response and would be in a position to act with equal effectiveness.

Before I became Ambassador to India in 1951 I had made two requests of President Truman. First, I would want not only to deal officially with India's central government but also to meet and know the
regional and local government leadership and, indeed, the Indian people
themselves; this meant that I should be free to travel extensively
throughout India.

Second, since I would be responsible for the effectiveness of all U.S.
Government programs there—the United States Information Service, our
economic development program and other activities—I should be
authorized to select all key personnel and generally to direct their
operations.

Truman had agreed on both of these points, and, as a result, my role
had been considerably broader than that of most other American ambassadors. Now, ten years later, the proliferation of American Government programs in many parts of the world in the late 1940's and 1950's
had further increased administrative confusion and duplication. Since
World War II, agencies such as the Central Intelligence Agency, Food for
Peace, the United States Information Agency, the Peace Corps and the
Agency for International Development had been created, all with sizable
overseas missions, while the old-time departments, Labor, Commerce,
Agriculture, Treasury and, particularly, the Defense Department, had
gradually expanded their overseas operations. For example, on the eve
of World War II the U.S. Embassy in Paris employed only seventy-eight
people, includng the staffs of four non-State Department agencies. But
early in the Kennedy Administration the Embassy had over seven hundred employees, including the staffs of twenty-three agencies.

This meant that an effective ambassador could no longer limit his
role to the traditional reporting, negotiating and entertaining; he must
become involved in the entire range of American operations in the
country to which he was assigned. If the U.S. Information Service was
being poorly handled or if the Foreign Aid program was ineptly and
insensitively administered, for example, I believed the ambassador

should have the primary responsibility to take whatever administrative measures, including changes in personnel, might be required to change the situation.

One factor that I had not foreseen was the reluctance of some professional diplomats to assume responsibilities beyond their traditional duties. The broader role we prescribed for the ambassadors gave them responsibility for activities involving the risk of error which they might have preferred to leave to someone else. Under the old system they had been allowed more or less to ignore such activities as economic development programs, United States information activities, cultural exchange and the like, where they felt their competence and experience were limited.

Another reason many of our ambassadors were reluctant to settle conflicts between American agencies operating in the countries to which they were assigned was the fear, often justified, that the State Department could not be counted upon to support them in Washington.

A first essential step, I thought, would be an edict directly from the President to each ambassador clearly establishing his authority and his responsibilities. The President agreed, and I set out to secure agreement from the various agencies affected on a memorandum establishing the new lines of authority.

I discussed the problem with representatives of the Departments of Defense, Agriculture and Labor, the Peace Corps, United States Information Agency, Central Intelligence Agency and other agencies whose overseas personnel were to be subject to greater ambassadorial direction. It became clear that complete agreement on a change of the dimensions I had proposed would be almost impossible to achieve, since nearly every agency insisted that it should be considered a special case. If we were to wait to negotiate an agreement with each of them before taking action, it was evident that the action might never be taken. Kennedy again agreed that we should go ahead and then settle on an *ad hoc* basis any conflicts which might develop.

On May 29, 1961, President Kennedy sent a letter to each ambassador directing him to expand his traditional duties and to secure a firm grip on all the activities of his mission. Several paragraphs follow:

> The practice of modern diplomacy requires a close understanding not only of governments but also of people, their cultures and institutions. Therefore, I hope that you will plan your work so that you may have the time to travel extensively outside the nation's capital. Only in this way can you develop the close, personal associations that go beyond official diplomatic circles and maintain a sympathetic and accurate understanding of all segments of the country.

In regard to your personal authority and responsibility, I shall count on you to oversee and coordinate all the activities of the United States Government. I shall give you full support and backing in carrying out your assignment.

If in your judgment individual members of the Mission are not functioning effectively, you should take whatever action you feel may be required, reporting the circumstances, of course, to the Department of State.

I have informed all heads of the departments and agencies of the Government of the responsibilities of the Chiefs of American Diplomatic Missions for our combined operations abroad, and I have asked them to instruct their representatives in the field accordingly.

The next step was to hold a series of regional meetings of ambassadors to discuss the implications of the President's directive. These meetings were critically important. Although the ambassadors by and large were pleased to be armed with a Presidential directive strengthening their authority and responsibility, most of them were doubtful that the new directive really meant what it said. Already the various agencies and departments were, as might be expected, beginning to interpret the directive each in its own way.

I was accompanied to each regional meeting by high-ranking representatives of each of the agencies involved, the heads of which I had finally been able to convince that this was a serious effort to modernize our overseas operations, that it had the full backing of the President and that I was determined to see it through. We invited not only the ambassadors, but also their wives, administrative officers and principal foreign aid, information and military advisers.

The attendance of the ambassadors' wives was an important innovation. As every Foreign Service officer knows, a wife sensitive to local problems, aware of our government's interests and objectives and eager and able to help can be a tower of strength in any overseas mission, large or small. For better or for worse, it is the ambassador's wife who sits beside the highest officials of foreign governments at dinners and formal functions. Thus, to broaden their knowledge and understanding of our objectives and operations, the wives attended all but the most highly classified discussions.

Each meeting, at which I acted as chairman, began with a comprehensive discussion of the policies of the new Administration, with special reference to the way these policies affected the particular region. I then fully described the new mandate which the ambassadors had been given and outlined the resources and programs which were available to them in meeting their responsibilities. Finally, the ambassadors tried to give the Washington representatives of the various U.S. organizations who were accompanying me a clear picture of the practical problems they confronted.

The six regional meetings held covered all U.S. missions in Latin America, Africa, the Near East and South Asia and the Far East. Although our missions in Europe were perhaps in the greatest need of this administrative therapy, the European Bureau managed by various devices to postpone the meeting from one date to another, so that it was never held.

Nearly two years later, in the winter of 1963, with the President's encouragement I made an extensive survey of the operation of each embassy. Each agency under the ambassador's authority was asked to provide me on a confidential basis with its analysis of the effectiveness of the ambassador in working with its representatives in the mission.

Although there were a number of inadequate performances, most of our envoys had been reasonably successful in integrating the operations of the various agencies and eliminating confusion and interagency conflict. Their success was usually in direct proportion to the amount of time, energy and resourcefulness they had devoted to the task. As might be expected, the younger ambassadors, by and large, functioned most effectively under the new system. Several of the senior ambassadors, particularly in Europe, continued to be reluctant to assume personal responsibility for "controversial" programs such as the USIS, Peace Corps and AID.

The fact that in the last ten or fifteen years the influence of the United States has continued to diminish in most parts of the world is, by and large, the fault not of our ambassadors but of events beyond their control. Even the most able and experienced chief of mission is rarely able significantly to influence the views of those in Washington who make the policies under which he operates.

CHAPTER 24

THE BAY OF PIGS

To THIS DAY, the sequence of events that led to our unsuccessful attempt to overthrow the Castro regime with a brigade of Cuban exiles in April, 1961, is unclear to me. The State Department as an organization had been virtually excluded from the planning and decision-making process, and I knew only in general terms of plans inherited from the previous Administration for a covert paramilitary operation designed to overthrow Fidel Castro.

If Rusk knew more than I about the proposed operation (and I assumed he did), he did not discuss it with me in any detail, nor had anyone within the State Department been asked to work on it.[1] Although it was clear that grave problems of international law and treaty interpretation would be involved, the Department's Legal Adviser, Abram Chayes, knew nothing of the project. The director of the Department's Bureau of Intelligence and Research, Roger Hilsman, was similarly in the dark, despite the necessity for a balanced intelligence estimate of Castro's domestic support in the event of a landing or major infiltration.

Even Adlai Stevenson, who would be called upon to defend any such United States action on the floor of the United Nations, was not informed. The participants in the actual planning had been limited to special groups in the Central Intelligence Agency, the Defense Department and the White House.

During the last few weeks of March, Rusk was attending a series of meetings abroad, including the SEATO Conference at Bangkok. As Act-

---

1. I have always assumed the Secretary of State would have been informed in detail, but I cannot support this with facts. Rusk has never told me how much he knew in advance about the Bay of Pigs.

ing Secretary in his absence, I bore the responsibility of representing the State Department at White House meetings. At that time I knew that the military force of Cuban exiles was completing preparations in a training camp in the mountains of Guatemala. But that was about all I did know.

On several occasions I discussed the plan in general terms with the four or five people in the second echelon who knew of its existence. At these meetings I vigorously opposed it and was joined by Ed Murrow. McGeorge Bundy and Deputy Secretary of Defense Roswell Gilpatric spoke of the plan only in the most general terms; if they were in fact opposed to it (as I believe they may have been), they obviously felt that it was too late to stop it.

By the time Rusk returned to Washington at the end of March I had learned enough to cause me deep concern. On Friday, March 31, shortly after he reached his office, I personally gave him a memorandum stating why I opposed the plan. I wrote:

> On Tuesday, April 4th, a meeting will be held at the White House at which a decision will be reached on the Cuban adventure.
>
> During your absence I have had an opportunity to become better acquainted with the proposal, and I find it profoundly disturbing.
>
> Let me frankly say, however, that I am not a wholly objective judge of the practical aspects. In considerable degree, my concern stems from a deep personal conviction that our national interests are poorly served by a covert operation of this kind at a time when our new President is effectively appealing to world opinion on the basis of high principle.
>
> In sponsoring the Cuban operation, for instance, we would be deliberately violating the fundamental obligations we assumed in the Act of Bogotá establishing the Organization of American States. The Act provides:
>
> —"No state may use or encourage the use of coercive measures of an economic or political character in order to force the sovereign will of another State and obtain from it advantages of any kind.
>
> —"The territory of a State is inviolable; it may not be the object, even temporarily, of military occupation or of other measures of force taken by another State, directly or indirectly, on any grounds whatever. . . ."
>
> I think it is fair to say that these articles, signaling an end of U.S. unilateralism, comprise the central features of the OAS from the point of view of the Latin-American countries.
>
> To act deliberately in defiance of these obligations would deal a blow to the Inter-American System from which I doubt it would soon recover. The suggestion that Cuba has somehow "removed itself" from the System is a transparent rationalization for the exercise of our own will.
>
> We cannot expect the benefits of treaties if we are unwilling to accept the limitations they impose on our freedom to act.
>
> Those most familiar with the Cuban operation seem to agree that, as

the venture is now planned, the chances of success are not greater than one out of three. This makes it a highly risky operation. If it fails, Castro's prestige and strength will be greatly enhanced. The one way we can reduce the risk is by commitment of direct American military support.

A pertinent question, of course, is what will happen in Cuba if this operation is canceled and we limit ourselves to small and scattered operations?

There is the possibility that the Castro effort will be a failure without any further intervention from us. It is not easy to create a viable Communist state on an island, totally dependent on open sea lanes, with a large population and inadequate resources.

It appears likely, however, that Castro will succeed in solidifying his political position. If this occurs and the Soviet Union should attempt to provide an aggressive Castro with substantially larger amounts of arms, including naval vessels, we would have the power to throw a blockade around Cuba and to extend it, if necessary, to petroleum supplies.

Technically, this, too, would be an act of war. However, I believe we would find it vastly easier to live with direct action of this kind in the face of what we would fairly describe as an open Soviet move to establish Cuba as a military base than with the covert operation now under consideration.

Under the very best circumstances, I believe this operation will have a much more adverse effect on world opinion that most people contemplate. It is admitted that there will be riots and a new wave of anti-Americanism throughout Latin America. It is also assumed that there will be many who quietly wish us well and, if the operation succeeds, will heave a sigh of relief.

Since President Kennedy took office on January 20th our position has been dramatically improved in the eyes of the world.

I believe it would be a grave mistake for us to jeopardize the favorable position we have steadily developed in most of the non-Communist world by the responsible and restrained policies which are now associated with the President by embarking on a major covert adventure with such very heavy built-in risks.

I realize that this operation has been put together over a period of months. A great deal of time and money has been spent and many individuals have become emotionally involved in its success. We should not, however, proceed with this adventure simply because we are wound up and cannot stop.

If you agree that this operation would be a mistake, I suggest that you personally and privately communicate your views to the President. It is my guess that your voice will be decisive.

I told Rusk that if the White House seemed determined nevertheless to proceed with the plan, I would want to be immediately informed so that I could take my personal objections directly to the President.

Late Tuesday afternoon, April 4, after the White House meeting, Rusk told me the plan had been greatly modified and that he did not feel it was necessary for me to see Kennedy.[2] Rusk volunteered to let me know if the original plan was reinstated so that I could personally present my objections to the President. Since the Secretary was now back in Washington, my role as the State Department representative in the National Security Council White House meetings ended.

I do not believe that Rusk deliberately misinformed me. Indeed, in talks with key Defense Department officials on Thursday, two days after my talks with Rusk, I also received the impression that the size of the operation had been drastically reduced and that its objectives were much more limited. Nevertheless, stories asserting that a U.S.-sponsored invasion was imminent continued to appear in the press. While I told James Reston of the *New York Times* on Thursday, April 6, that these stories were in error, he and other journalists remained convinced that the invasion was still forthcoming.[3] Later, of course, it became evident that there had, in fact, been more solid information about this project in the National Press Club than in the State Department.

By Friday, April 14, I had become sufficiently alarmed by these continuing press rumors to write a longhand letter to the President strongly opposing any invasion and asking for an immediate opportunity to express my views directly to him. When I brought the letter to my State Department office on Saturday morning to have it typed and delivered, the news was already on the wire service that B-26's flown by Cuban pilots had hit the Havana airfield; I realized it was too late. The amphibious invasion at the Bay of Pigs came on Monday, and by Tuesday morning it was obvious that it was a total failure.

On Thursday, April 20, at the President's request I attended a meeting of the National Security Council in the White House to review the situation. Thirty or forty of the highest officials in the government were present at what turned out to be the grimmest gathering in my experience in government, and that includes some grim meetings.

Kennedy was shattered. His public career had been a long series of successes, with no serious setbacks. Here, for the first time, he faced a major situation where his judgment had led him seriously astray. The

2. The essential modification Rusk mentioned was a reduction in the size of the operation, putting it on a par with a number of other recent similar guerrilla operations which had attracted no great attention. I recall that I asked Rusk whether he thought the "modified" operation would make the front page of the *New York Times*. He replied that he doubted it.

3. As a matter of fact, the full story was set up in type by the *New York Times* for their Friday morning edition. When the White House heard of this, the President called the *Times* and persuaded them to kill the story. If the story had been run, I believe the plan would have been canceled.

reactions around the table in the Cabinet Room were emotional, almost savage. The President and the U.S. Government had been humiliated; something must be done. The discussion rambled in circles, with little coherent thought. After listening for some forty-five minutes, President Kennedy got up and walked toward his office.

Concerned by the militant mood of most of those at the meeting, I walked out after him and asked for an opportunity to discuss the situation. I proposed both of us forget for a moment that he was President of the United States and I was Under Secretary of State. We had known each other for many years; I would like for a moment to speak as a friend.

It was clear, I said, that we faced a disastrous setback. But setbacks for any American President in this unpredictable world were to be expected. What history would primarily be concerned with would be how the President reacted to such setbacks. Although the emotional pressure to retaliate in some way against Castro was powerful, this pressure must be resisted. Above all, the situation must not be allowed to deteriorate into a head-to-head personal contest between the President of the United States and Fidel Castro. Now was the time for sober second thoughts, for deliberation and for a minimum of public comment.

At that point Vice President Johnson, Bob Kennedy and Robert McNamara, the Secretary of Defense, joined us, and Kennedy simply said to me, "Thank you." The conversation continued another ten minutes.

That night I wrote down the following observations about the meeting:[4]

> What worries me most is that two of the most powerful people in this Administration—Lyndon Johnson and Bob Kennedy[5]—have no experience in foreign affairs, and yet they realize this is the central question of this period and are determined to be experts at it.
>
> The problems of foreign affairs are complex, involving politics, economics and social questions that require an understanding both of history and of various world cultures.
>
> When a newcomer enters the field and finds himself confronted by the nuances of international questions, he becomes an easy target for the military-CIA-paramilitary-type answers which can be added, subtracted, multiplied or divided.
>
> This kind of thinking was almost dominant in today's conference, and

4. I did not keep a journal or diary, but periodically I wrote my impressions of various situations down while they were fresh in my mind.

5. I should add that while this was true of Robert Kennedy in the early months of the Administration, his judgments of world policy rapidly matured in the next year.

I found it alarming. The President appeared by all odds to be the most calm, yet it was clear that he had been suffering from an acute shock and it was an open question in my mind as to what his ultimate reaction would be.

On Saturday President Kennedy again convened the National Security Council. Emotions were still high, and specific proposals were made that the United States should move directly against Castro. I stressed that if the United States with its 180 million people attacked a neighboring nation of six million, we would simply compound the disaster. An invasion of Cuba would almost certainly fail unless it were supported by major American forces. Even if it succeeded, Castro would emerge as the hero in what would surely be viewed throughout the world as a struggle between David and Goliath. By and large, these comments were brushed aside, although there was significantly more evidence of support than at the earlier meeting.

The President made no commitment and limited himself largely to asking questions, but I returned to the State Department with renewed forebodings. While the verbal fireworks were admittedly the emotional reaction of people unaccustomed to defeat whose pride and confidence had been deeply wounded, this hardly gave me confidence that we were not on the verge of making a rash decision we would surely regret.

The situation was a classic example of the unpredictable, precarious nature of high-level decision-making on critical questions in this or any modern government. Normally thoughtful individuals, who were tired, frustrated, personally under attack, and dealing with tense and difficult questions, were being pressed to take steps which could only compound the mistakes that had already been made. The Bay of Pigs debacle, I thought, would put the minds of the White House group to the supreme test.

The next NSC meeting on Monday, April 24, was somewhat more dispassionate. Yet anyone who attended only this meeting and none of the earlier ones would have been concerned by what remained of the fire and fury. For instance, there were proposals for all kinds of barely clandestine harassment to punish Castro for defeating our abortive invasion attempt. There was even vague talk of imposing economic sanctions against nations, such as Mexico and Brazil, which had voted to condemn our action in the UN.

Gradually the emotional pressure diminished and reason returned. As the meeting came to a close, the President, who seemed to have regained his confidence, said that we had no alternative but to live with the humiliation our error had created and respect the attitudes of other nations who had disagreed with our actions.

Following this meeting, the draft of a cable outlining U.S. policy in regard to future actions, statements and attitude was prepared by Latin American Bureau officials to be sent to all United States embassies. When the cable reached my desk for approval early in the evening, I saw that it completely misrepresented the decisions reached that afternoon. It seemed actually to instruct our envoys to those nations which had relations with Cuba to bring pressure to bear on their host governments to cut those relations and to sever trade connections.

I called Secretary Rusk at his home and told him of my objections. He agreed, and the cable was rewritten accurately to convey the President's more moderate views. The new version directed our ambassadors to avoid giving the impression that we wanted to force their host governments into positions they would not take independently. They were also asked to avoid reckless statements which would support the impression that the U.S. was a wobbly, insecure, vindictive power.

Largely because the President had kept his head in the face of the emotional backlash, the Bay of Pigs was not as calamitous as it could have been. Nevertheless, for all the President's gallantry in publicly assuming full personal responsibility, the humiliating failure of the invasion shattered the myth of a New Frontier run by a new breed of incisive, fault-free supermen. However costly, it may have been a necessary lesson.

Inevitably, the conflict within the government following the Bay of Pigs disaster was reflected in a variety of unpleasant ways. One which involved me was a story in *Time* magazine that I had "leaked" to the press my opposition to the proposed invasion in order to embarrass the President and that Bob Kennedy and I had nearly ended up in a fist fight. Both assertions were ridiculous. It was no secret, then or now, that not only I, but also Bill Fulbright, Ed Murrow, Jerome B. Wiesner, Science Adviser to the President, and several others had opposed the plan. (How could such a "secret" possibly be kept in our government?) As for Bob Kennedy, it was true that his initial reaction to the news of the Bay of Pigs fiasco was emotional and militant, but he and I never discussed the question. Although he and I often saw situations from quite different perspectives in this early period, if he had lived to be nominated for the Presidency in 1968, I would have done all I could to help him be elected.

Blame for the Bay of Pigs fiasco has been placed primarily on the Central Intelligence Agency, and, as everyone knows, it played the major role. Inevitably, this well-publicized responsibility has compounded the public, press and Congressional criticism of the CIA as a whole. Much of the criticism is valid, but I believe that the responsibility should be more broadly shared.

The difficulties the CIA has encountered in the last few years are largely due to the fact that under pressure from the White House, State Department and Bureau of the Budget, as well as from its own empire builders, its operational responsibilities were expanded far beyond the intentions of its creators.

Activities which should have been administered by the State Department, the United States Information Agency and other agencies dealing with foreign affairs were assigned to the CIA simply because Congress could not be persuaded to provide the appropriate agencies with the necessary funds. The CIA, with its more flexible budget, could always "find the money."

Practically all of the CIA's economic studies of Russia, China and other countries and many of its political studies could have been more appropriately handled by the Bureau of Intelligence and Research of the State Department. Similarly, all cultural exchange activities should have been delegated to the Cultural Affairs Bureau of the State Department, with an adequate budget to carry them out.

The political vulnerability created by this vast, expedient overextension of the CIA was recognized by many of us, and possible alternatives were discussed. Shortly after Kennedy took office I made a series of recommendations for a reorganization of CIA activities. After the Bay of Pigs I recommended to Rusk that the CIA should be abolished and its functions absorbed by offices more directly responsible to the State Department. But even when the stories of CIA involvement in many nonintelligence activities broke in the newspapers, no significant effort was made to correct the situation.

CHAPTER 25

THE LAOS CRISIS

ON THE DAY BEFORE Kennedy's inauguration, President Eisenhower stressed ominously that the incoming Administration might immediately have to make a series of fateful decisions to "save" the embattled nation of Laos from being overrun by the Pathet Lao forces, which North Vietnam's President, Ho Chi Minh, had supported since 1949.

Previously, Secretary of State John Foster Dulles had described Laos as a "bulwark against Communism" and a "bastion of freedom," and American policy had reflected this assessment. The Royal Laotian Army had been provided with American military training advisers. With a population of only two million people, Laos had already been the beneficiary of more than $300 million in American aid—the equivalent of $150 per person.

Between Kennedy's election and his inauguration the State Department's Far Eastern Bureau, headed by Assistant Secretary Parsons, formerly Dulles' Ambassador to Laos, had intervened in Laos and, with the cooperation of the CIA, engineered a rightist coup which it was assumed would assure an anti-Communist government. In December, 1960, the moderate, prodemocratic Prince Souvanna Phouma had been driven out of office by the "pro-American" forces of Phoumi Nosavan.

On several occasions before his election, I had discussed with Kennedy the potential dangers of the situation in Laos in relation to the whole Southeast Asia region. "The program on which the Eisenhower Administration embarked in Laos," I wrote in a memorandum to him, "strikes me as one of the most appalling, naïve, misguided and badly administered efforts that has come to my attention in the last few years, and we have seen some bad ones." I believed that some form of neutralization was the only practical answer, and Kennedy agreed. After he became President, he continued to follow the Laotian situation closely.

In our early discussions in the State Department in January, 1961, I proposed that our first step toward neutralization should be to resurrect the 1957 Vientiane agreements. These had established a neutralist ruling coalition, including Souvanna Phouma and his half-brother, Prince Souphanouvong, the Pathet Lao leader who was supported by the Hanoi Government. While Souvanna Phouma was critical of the United States, he was a genuine neutralist, firmly opposed to a Communist government.

After being forced out of his own country with the heavy involvement of the United States, it was not surprising that Souvanna Phouma strongly denounced the United States' actions in general and Assistant Secretary Parsons in particular. We could not expect to recapture his confidence overnight—particularly since several of his adversaries in the U.S. Government (including Parsons) had not yet been replaced by Kennedy appointees.

However, it was argued that a viable neutralist government could not be put together unless the Pathet Lao were first prevented from taking over the country by force, a theory which led to a broad consensus (which I did not share) that American military intervention should take place "if necessary."

This line of reasoning ignored the obvious fact that U.S. military action in Laos against the Pathet Lao would destroy any possibility of ever establishing a coalition government. If we were serious about the neutralization of Laos, I argued, it was imperative that we develop a strategy that would preclude any direct American military commitment.[1]

Another factor was the position of the Soviet Union. On January 6, two weeks before Kennedy's inauguration, Soviet Premier Khrushchev had made a major speech pledging Russian help for "wars of national liberation." The guerrilla war in Southeast Asia was clearly within the purview of Khrushchev's definition, so much so that Russian planes were already making frequent air drops of equipment and supplies to the Pathet Lao forces.

Khrushchev's speech and the military air drops were generally accepted as evidence that the Soviets had set out to eliminate American influence from Southeast Asia and to expand their own. I agreed that this assessment might be accurate. But it seemed equally plausible that Khrushchev's objective might be to prevent the Chinese from gaining control over the Pathet Lao. Moscow might logically feel that influence over Southeast Asia should not go to either the Chinese or the Americans by default.

On February 9 I told Rusk in a memorandum that in my view the

1. A team of American advisers was already involved.

military approach to Laos which we inherited from our predecessors was "foredoomed to failure." Not only would the continuation of this policy by the Kennedy Administration jeopardize our political goal in Laos, but it would also place us in a colonialist position similar to the French. As usual, his response was equivocal.

However, the increasing Soviet air drops and the continuing Pathet Lao victories over the Royal Laotian Army held the headlines.[2] By mid-March, with few exceptions (one of them being Ambassador at Large Averell Harriman), State and Defense Department officials felt that the situation had become much too serious for us to pursue a nonmilitary political strategy. Kennedy had not yet taken a public position.

Purely diplomatic considerations aside, I felt it would be a mistake to commit ground forces to Laos unless the U.S. were seriously prepared to embark on a major land war with China, which I regarded as pure folly. The Chinese, I suspected, were no more likely to allow us to establish a solid American beachhead in Laos on their southern border than they had been to permit us to advance through North Korea to the Yalu River in 1950.

On several occasions I suggested to the Joint Chiefs of Staff, individually and collectively, that the possibility of a massive Chinese advance into Southeast Asia, arising out of China's serious land and petroleum shortages, was a potential military danger even if we did not seem to threaten China by establishing U.S. forces close to China's southern border. They replied that whether the first move came from us or from the Chinese, their contingency plans for Laos called for the introduction of American troops into South Vietnam. Advancing westward, these troops would seek to block any Chinese intrusions through the mountains into Laos. When I pointed out that the force which they contemplated was grossly inadequate and that we could hardly count on the Chinese to limit their pressures to what we could contain, they admitted that if our troops were in danger of being overrun, nuclear weapons might be used.

At a meeting at the White House in mid-March, I again expressed the opinion that the Chinese would not accept an American military presence in Laos. This was brushed aside on the grounds that it would probably not occur, and that if it did, the military measures were available to cope with them (meaning again, I assumed, the use of nuclear weapons). A second White House meeting which I attended that month

2. The "Laos Crisis" in February, 1961, was precipitated by the actions of Kong Le, an anti-Communist Laotian paratroop colonel whose reaction to the U.S.-sponsored coup was to join forces with the Pathet Lao in capturing the strategic Plain of Jars.

also failed adequately to consider the full implications of an American military response to counter the Pathet Lao.

Secretary Rusk was scheduled to attend a SEATO meeting in Bangkok the last week in March. With various qualifications, the President authorized him to offer the American military forces that might be required to hold the entire region against the Pathet Lao and the increasingly restive Vietcong in neighboring Vietnam.

Such a commitment, I feared, would foreclose any hope for a political settlement. An offer of American troops, however carefully hedged, would lead the Thai Government and the Diem Government in South Vietnam, as well as the Phoumi Nosavan Government, promptly to step up their pressures for direct American military aid on the premise that the United States itself now agreed that the only solution was military. Inevitably, they would then oppose even more stubbornly any effort to secure a political accommodation with their opponents, and stiffen their opposition to essential internal economic and social reforms.

On March 21 I sent Rusk a memorandum proposing an alternative policy which might enable us to avoid a direct military commitment. I suggested that the United States, joined by India, co-chairman of the International Control Commission for Laos, present a four-point program for settlement, to include reaffirmation of the principle of a neutral, unaligned Laos; an immediate cease-fire based on a withdrawal from current battle lines by both sides; an international conference for Laos along the lines proposed by Prince Norodom Sihanouk of Cambodia; and an interim government to be composed of the three Laotian Prime Ministers, including Souvanna Phouma, who had held office since 1957 —regardless of their political views.

Two days later, as Rusk was leaving for the Far East, I wrote him a more detailed memorandum,[3] of which excerpts follow:

> Here are several factors which in the meetings I have attended have not adequately been taken into account.
>
> 1. In Korea, we operated, after the first few hours, under the full authority of the United Nations. Here we will be operating under the authority of SEATO, an organization which is mistrusted by most Asians, particularly by the Indians, Burmese and other neutrals whose views have a profound effect on world opinion.

3. The reader may wonder why I communicated so frequently with the Secretary by means of memoranda. There are two reasons: First, in dealing with a complex situation in government, or indeed any large organization, it is important to spell out on paper the problem and recommendations for solution, since the spoken word is easily forgotten or twisted. Second, partly because of the extreme pressures of Rusk's job and partly because of his natural reticence, it was almost impossible to persuade him to set aside the necessary time for a full discussion of the longer-range factors which might be involved.

2. Although Korea was far from home, we had a long seacoast on which to operate, and a solid military base in Japan, only a few hundred miles away. In Laos we would be operating under the worst conceivable conditions from a logistical point of view.

3. If we commit American troops to Laos, there is a strong possibility that we will be hit by Pathet Lao, Vietcong and North Vietnamese troops who will vastly outnumber us. If the Soviets should restrain these forces through their influence in Hanoi, the response may come from the Chinese.

4. If powerful ground troops are thrown at us and our own forces are overwhelmed, we face an impossible choice: either we retreat under fire, with the most humiliating implications to our prestige and influence, or we resort to nuclear weapons, which would be catastrophic in its effects on Asian and world opinion.

It is bad enough for us to get ourselves into a vastly overcommitted position. It will be even worse if we fail fully to take account of the dynamics of the situation and become caught up in an escalating dilemma which can easily get out of control.

Nor do I think we can ignore the possibility that if the Soviet Union is planning a continuation of the Cold War, they may see some advantages in embroiling the United States with the Chinese in a relatively untenable military position nine thousand miles from our shores.

The first need is to avoid provocative statements that will push either the Communist Chinese or the Soviets into a corner and make it difficult for them to reach a compromise with us.

More than that, in the very weak position in which we now find ourselves, I believe we should be prepared to make political concessions, if this is the only way that our direct American military participation can be avoided in Laos.

The decision to stake America's power and influence on a wobbly situation nearly as close to the Chinese border as Cuba is to the United States, by spending $300 million in an attempt to turn two million gentle, unwarlike, Laotian men, women and children into nation of battle-hungry Turks, will appear strange indeed in the history of our time.

The same day I wrote my memorandum, March 23, Kennedy told a press conference that if the Pathet Lao attacks did not cease, even "those who support a truly neutral Laos will have to consider their response." Ground forces in Japan and on Okinawa were readied for combat, and ships from the Seventh Fleet moved into the South China Sea. At the SEATO meeting four days later, Rusk secured troop pledges from Thailand, Pakistan and the Philippines, although France declined to commit itself. Through Ken Galbraith in New Delhi, the President persuaded Nehru publicly to support a cease-fire in the hope of forestalling the actual use of troops.

Despite this diplomatic initiative, I remained concerned to see the

Department of Defense still grinding out military plans. On March 25, as Acting Secretary with Rusk away, I sent a memorandum to the White House arguing that our political and diplomatic position would be materially strengthened if we openly and wholeheartedly backed Souvanna Phouma.

I warned once again of a major clash with the Chinese if we sent troops in. "If the situation were reversed," I wrote, "and either the Soviets or the Chinese moved military forces into Cuba, we would be under heavy political pressures for immediate and strenuous action to throw them out. Why should we expect the Chinese to act less directly on their own doorstep?"

I once again asked the Pentagon for a review of their actual plans for the contingency of an American military operation in Laos. Military planners tried to avoid the issue by telling me that my fears of Chinese intervention in the event of an American landing were exaggerated. When I insisted that they tell me what they proposed we should do if they turned out to be wrong, it became clear that their only "contingency plan" remained a nuclear response. The thought that we should attempt to "save Laos" by a nuclear attack struck me as preposterous.

Meanwhile, the Chinese Foreign Minister, Chen Yi, in the course of a visit to Indonesia, stated that the introduction of American troops into Southeast Asia would be matched by Chinese forces. Intelligence analysts quickly pointed out that the language was identical to that used in 1950 by Chou En-lai when the Chinese warned the United Nations that an advance by MacArthur to the Yalu would provoke a direct Chinese military response.

On April 1, to our intense relief, Khrushchev indicated that he would consider a British proposal to revive the International Control Commission for Laos and to set in motion steps that would lead to a peace conference. This development suggested that a way could be found out of the imbroglio short of war. At the same time, in the Far Eastern Bureau of the State Department, in the Pentagon and elsewhere in the government, officials finally began to see that U.S. military intervention in Laos might have consequences that would dwarf our immediate concern with the Pathet Lao and their limited Soviet logistical support.

These hopeful signs underscored the need for us to persuade Souvanna Phouma that we were genuinely seeking a political settlement. At an unscheduled meeting in New Delhi with Averell Harriman, Souvanna said he was convinced that the Laotian people did not want a Communist government and that the most promising way to create a workable alternative was to return to a coalition government according to the 1957 Vientiane agreements. Such a solution, he emphasized, would be feasible only if the United States agreed to forgo its support of Phoumi Nosavan.

But throughout April and May the pendulum continued to swing back and forth. For days the Bay of Pigs occupied the headlines, and when Kennedy decided not to attempt to rescue the Cuban exile brigade with American forces, he felt it was important to let Khrushchev know this did not mean that we were also prepared to abandon Laos. To reinforce the point, the President, mistakenly I thought, ordered our military advisers in Laos, who had previously worn civilian clothes, to wear their uniforms and make no effort to hide their support of the troops of the pro-Western Phoumi.[4]

This saber-rattling encouraged the proponents of a military "solution" once again to come up with new proposals for the introduction of a full contingent of American troops. One study that I found particularly alarming concluded that the Chinese could be kept out of Southeast Asia by 300,000 U.S. troops plus assistance from our allies, with the admission that at some stage nuclear weapons would probably be required. If this occurred, the report admitted, the Russians could be expected to introduce their volunteers supported by nuclear weapons. This frightening scenario had a certain comic opera quality. But if the Pentagon itself took this analysis at all seriously, the need for an alternative was all the more urgent.

By that time those of us who had been pressing for a more flexible position and for a negotiated settlement had become convinced that some sort of military operation was likely to be agreed to, and that the best we could do, under the circumstances, was to limit its dimensions.

Then suddenly the pendulum once again swung toward a more rational and less military approach. On May 1 the quiet negotiations between the British and the Soviets produced an agreement on a cease-fire, and the re-establishment of the International Control Commission. Ten days later the Commission announced the "general and obvious discontinuance of hostilities." This was followed by the convening in Geneva of a fourteen-nation conference to negotiate a political settlement, with Averell Harriman heading our delegation.[5]

4. On the other hand, the Bay of Pigs probably threw some cold water on the heated debates over our "response" to Laos. For a question raised by the Bay of Pigs episode was how we could expect to stop Communism in Laos with U.S. troops if we couldn't do so in Cuba. President Kennedy was said to have wryly asked this question. In an April 29 memo to Dean Rusk, I made the point that a decision to send American troops ten thousand miles to Laos, a country most Americans could not find on the map, to fight the Pathet Lao would appear incongruous to Congress and to most Americans in view of our recent decision not to send troops to aid the Bay of Pigs invaders only ninety miles off Florida's shores.

5. Kennedy reportedly told Harriman most emphatically not to come back without a settlement.

Although it has been claimed that it was the threat of U.S. armed intervention that had saved the day, the reasons for the breakthrough were, in my opinion, far more complex. For one thing, as much as the Hanoi Government opposed the United States' position, it had no desire to be "saved" by its giant neighbor, China. Likewise, the Soviet leaders had every reason to avoid a major confrontation which the Peking Government could so readily turn to its advantage. Although the Soviets were no doubt pleased by our dilemma in Laos, they must have realized that once the situation got out of hand they, too, would be faced with some hard decisions. Finally, officials in the Defense Department began to have second thoughts about the wisdom of advocating plans that would risk a distant land war with a probable nuclear climax.

Unhappily, the Geneva Agreements which Averell Harriman skillfully negotiated during 1961 and 1962 did not assure peace. While they bought some time, as they were intended to do, the war in Vietnam eventually spilled over into Laos. As the pressure on the Vietcong increased, the North Vietnamese increased the flow of military supplies and troops into South Vietnam. The safest supply route in South Vietnam was the so-called Ho Chi Minh Trail, located largely in Laos. Beginning in 1963, the flow of men and supplies over the Ho Chi Minh Trail increased steadily, at its peak reaching an annual figure estimated at between 60,000 and 100,000 troops and hundreds of thousands of tons of supplies.

This traffic was, of course, in direct violation of the 1962 Geneva Accords. Hanoi's effort to maintain the flow inevitably led to a Laotian-approved U.S.–South Vietnam effort at bombing the trail. The Pathet Lao, of course, remained a danger to the central government.

In August, 1967, when I visited the drowsy Laotian capital city of Vientiane, the so-called "secret war" along the Ho Chi Minh Trail was in full swing. In a long talk, Prime Minister Souvanna Phouma expressed grave concern about the movement of North Vietnamese through his country and about the support Hanoi was giving to the Pathet Lao insurgents and the implications for the future of his country.

While there had been what amounted to an unspoken agreement to limit military action in Laos to this area, their thrust in early 1970 indicated that the Pathet Lao have the capacity to push to the Mekong River, which forms the border between Laos, Thailand and Cambodia, if they decide to do so.

How the Laotian struggle in which we and the North Vietnamese have been active but illegal participants develops depends, of course, on the final outcome in Vietnam.

CHAPTER 26

SPELLING OUT OUR DIFFERENCES

In early June, 1961, Khrushchev and Kennedy met in Vienna. In judging Kennedy at that time Khrushchev was no doubt impressed by two factors. First, Kennedy had demonstrated immature judgment in approving the Bay of Pigs adventure, and, second, after it had failed, he hesitated to take direct military action as he, Khrushchev, had done in Hungary.

This led Khrushchev to assume that he was dealing with a weak and vacillating new American President, and he set out to intimidate him by taking a harsh position, particularly in regard to Berlin. Although he succeeded in sending Kennedy back to Washington in a high state of alarm, the consequences were scarcely what Khrushchev had intended. Soon, several of my colleagues were seriously proposing that to underline American firmness and test Soviet intentions the President should send heavily armored convoys up the Autobahn to Berlin, an action perilously close to challenging the Soviets to a game of "Russian roulette."

This reaction added to my growing concern over the first six months of the Kennedy Administration's efforts in foreign policy. To be sure, we had recruited many able people and, after two exercises in cliff-hanging, had managed to avoid a military invasion of Cuba and the commitment of American military forces in Laos. In addition, we had successfully resisted pressures for a U.S. military takeover in the Dominican Republic, which had developed out of the fear, following Trujillo's assassination on May 30, that Castro might decide to beat us to it. But these were narrow escapes, and they underscored the disturbing ease with which the new Administration moved toward military "solutions" to foreign policy questions.

Shortly before the abortive meeting in Vienna, after a particularly disturbing session at the White House I wrote down the following personal observations in a notebook:

> The question which concerns me most about the new Administration is whether it lacks a genuine sense of conviction about what is right and what is wrong. I realize in posing this question I am raising an extremely serious point. Nevertheless, I feel it must be faced.
>
> Anyone in public life who has strong convictions about the rights and wrongs of public morality, both domestic and international, has a very great advantage in times of strain, since his instincts on what to do are clear and immediate. Lacking such a framework of moral conviction or sense of what is right and what is wrong, he is forced to lean almost entirely on his mental processes; he adds up the plusses and minuses of any question and comes up with a conclusion. Under normal conditions, when he is not tired or frustrated, this pragmatic approach should successfully bring him out on the right side of a question.
>
> What worries me are the conclusions that such an individual may reach when he is tired, angry, frustrated or emotionally affected. The Cuban fiasco demonstrates how far astray a man as brilliant and well intentioned as President Kennedy can go who lacks a basic moral reference point.

During these first difficult six months of 1961 I had had my first significant experience with the "military mind." I was concerned by the narrow military perspective that even some of our ablest military leaders brought to bear on what were primarily political questions. I was even more alarmed by their ability to influence what our government said and, in some cases, actually did.

It was understandable that high military officers dealing with urgent questions of national defense would give a high priority to such tangible elements of power as aircraft carriers, communications, logistics, artillery, tanks and the like—elements that anyone, including members of Congress, could see, weigh and enumerate—and that many of them would come to believe that if enough force were brought to bear on a problem, this problem could be solved.

But I had assumed that among the new crop of military leaders who rose to positions of authority during the 1960's there would be many more with a keener awareness of political and economic forces. Each year at our National War College and the three service war colleges, several hundred of our most promising military officers were given an opportunity to put aside for one year their military duties and study in depth the nonmilitary elements that helped shape international relations.[1]

1. Since the 1950's I had lectured regularly at these war colleges. I underscored the particular stake the American military had in the development of balanced, realistic foreign policies. When blunders occur, I pointed out, it is members of our armed forces, not the diplomats, who are called upon to do the dying.

Nevertheless, when the Army and Air Force colonels and Navy captains who in the 1950's had seemed so keenly aware of the political and economic forces affecting our foreign policy moved into their present positions of seniority and authority, they often appeared as bellicose and parochial as had many of their predecessors. (I might add that the first time I saw evidence that our top military leaders were beginning to lose confidence in the military numbers game that was largely responsible for the Vietnam debacle was in a meeting in the Pentagon following my return from India in May, 1969.)

The tendency of the new Administration to reach for military answers to political problems could not fully be explained in terms of Pentagon pressure, or the fears generated by crises, or Khrushchev's irresponsible onslaught on Kennedy at Vienna. Another factor was that in dealing with foreign policy many Democratic liberals in and around the Administration found themselves on unfamiliar ground.

The issues on which they had built their careers were related largely to the domestic conflicts of the New Deal and post–New Deal periods. In relatively few instances, such as in the case of Adlai Stevenson and myself, had they previously taken a major interest in foreign affairs. Consequently, when foreign policy questions moved to the top of our national agenda in the late 1950's, they were ill-prepared for their new roles. And yet, accustomed as they were to speaking and writing authoritatively on domestic questions, they often tackled the complex and unfamiliar issues of foreign policy-making with the same exuberant assurance.

In addition, the judgment on foreign policy issues of many liberals, even those with experience in foreign affairs, was distorted by their determination to establish themselves as "realists." Having been charged with "woolly-headedness," "softness on Communism" and similar crimes during the Republican Administration, they felt it necessary to demonstrate they were, in fact, tough characters.[2]

It was they who were largely responsible for the "counterinsurgency" flurry which led to the development of the "Green Berets."[3] It was assumed that by borrowing the guerrilla techniques of Mao Tse-tung and Che Guevara, with some of our own cowboys-and-Indians tradition

2. However, as I noted in the spring of 1961: "Any thought that this Administration is tough-minded in the administration of our military assistance program is a serious mistake. I do not know of any national leader who has come to Washington and asked for arms who has not gone home with more than he expected to get, regardless of the legitimacy of his claim. We are almost as big pushovers for the Salazars, the Chiangs, the Diems, the Ayub Khans as the previous Administration."

3. This particularly appealed to Robert Kennedy, at that early stage of his political development.

thrown in for good measure, we could beat our adversaries at their own game. Walt Rostow, who in the 1950's was an able economist in the field of overseas development and the author of the well-known book, *The Stages of Economic Growth*, is a classic example of the militarized liberal.

It was ironic that not only President Kennedy but many nonmilitarized Democratic liberals such as Stevenson, Humphrey, Fulbright and myself had inadvertently helped to strengthen the United States military potential for overseas adventurism. The way this developed is a revealing commentary on the complex process of policy-making.

In 1954, under heavy budgetary pressures, John Foster Dulles set out to develop a less expensive but effective way to "contain Communism." The result was his proposal for "massive retaliation at a time and place of our own choosing," as a deterrent to Communist intrusion in various strategic parts of the world. His views were outlined in an article in *Foreign Affairs* in January, 1954. Six weeks later I strongly challenged these in an article I wrote for the *New York Times Magazine*.

The Eisenhower Administration, I pointed out, seemed to be saying that in dealing with future armed Soviet or Chinese aggression into non-Communist territory anywhere in the world, it would rely chiefly upon nuclear attacks by the Strategic Air Command against major cities in the U.S.S.R. or China.

This, I wrote, posed a series of critical questions: (1) Should we place our principal reliance in Asia upon a method of retaliation which carried what were unacceptable risks? (2) Even if we were prepared to risk nuclear war over a limited aggression, would not the new policy tempt the Soviet leaders to underestimate our readiness? (3) If they calculated that we would not risk general war in response to a limited aggression and succeeded once in calling our bluff, would not much of the deterrent value of the policy disappear overnight? (4) Would the proposed new policy make our European friends more or less eager to be associated with us?

Our diplomacy, I concluded, must avoid becoming hypnotized into negation by the actions of the Soviet Union and China. But equally important, it must maintain an attitude which our forefathers in the Declaration of Independence described as "a decent respect for the opinions of mankind."

My opposition to Dulles' thesis was endorsed by many Republican and Democratic leaders, including former Secretary of State Dean Acheson and key members of Congress; the opposition soon became so strong that the concept was abandoned. What we failed to foresee was the overreaction of the Defense Department. The military reasoned that if our government was unwilling to blow up Moscow or Peking to deter the Soviets or Chinese from subverting strategically located governments, our *only* alternative was to build up American ground, air and naval capacity to enable us directly to oppose insurgent movements supported by the U.S.S.R. or China.

Thus our justified opposition to Dulles' proposal of nuclear retaliation may have helped lay the basis for an expansion of our Army, Air Force and Navy which we did not foresee and would not have supported.

During the years of the Cold War the word "power" had become probably the most important word in the vocabularies of diplomats and military leaders. It was my feeling that the loose use of this word both reflected and contributed to many of our policy problems. One evening in the home of a Washington friend, the word "power" was bandied around to such an extent that I finally asked the half-dozen people present to tell me what they meant by "power." Each came up with much the same definition: nuclear power, air power, sea power, steel production, communications, alliances, transport, technology, military training and equipment, overseas bases and the like.

Nevertheless, as I saw it, this definition of power was inadequate. In the last twenty years half of the people of the world had changed their form of government even though "power," as so narrowly defined by these friends, had been heavily on the side of the status quo. The record clearly indicated that material "power" in the traditional sense was likely to come out second best in a contest with ideas which move men to great efforts and sacrifice.

There were many examples: In China Mao Tse-tung with ten thousand ragged men, a thousand rifles and a revolutionary idea which appealed to the impoverished masses of his country ultimately destroyed the Nationalist armies, armed, trained and supported by the United States, which was then said to be at the peak of its "power." The fact that Mao's objectives were distasteful to most of us is not relevant; his ideas generated a massive public response which enabled him to dominate all of China—and in today's world that is very relevant indeed.

In India the British with all their tanks, planes and aircraft carriers were unable to cope with the power of ideas, freedom and human dignity generated by Gandhi. And so it was in Indonesia, Burma, the Middle East and much of Africa. One by one the colonial nations which possessed traditional material "power" in abundance were forced to give up their overseas possessions by able indigenous leaders whose millions of followers were determined to be free. The inadequacy of our own version of "power" in Vietnam is the most recent example.

This point is illustrated by the scathing question which Stalin once posed to a visitor who spoke of the "power" of the Vatican. "But how many divisions," Stalin is said to have inquired, "has the Pope?" The Soviet-dominated governments of Eastern Europe could have told Stalin that the power of the Pope was substantial, even in their own regimented countries.

By June, 1961, I was convinced that unless the makers of American policy in the State Department and White House could be persuaded to support a radical but essential shift in foreign policy, we would sooner or later be confronted with a full-blown disaster. The time had come to challenge not simply our military reaction on specific questions such as Cuba, Laos or Berlin, but the whole approach of the new Administration to world affairs. Where was the United States Government headed in its dealings with the world? What were our objectives? Were we, in fact, doomed to an endless struggle with the U.S.S.R. or China, with only a precarious balance of power between us and disaster, or was there a feasible way to genuine peace?

I decided to prepare a memorandum which would present frankly and comprehensively my convictions on the direction which the Kennedy Administration should take in respect to foreign policy. I would review our first six months in office, assess our mistakes and lost opportunities, and suggest some paths for the future which might serve to strengthen our position. The memorandum was sent to the Secretary in late June.

The impression many foreign friends had of us today, I wrote, was of bellicose rhetoric, backed by deadlier and more costly weapons than ever before. (A recent survey in India indicated that two-thirds of those interviewed believed that the United States was most likely to start World War III.) The Pentagon's public relations budget was twenty-five times that of the State Department. Was it strange that under the circumstances the general impression of our image overseas was predominantly a military one?

This militaristic impression had an historical base. John Foster Dulles had mistakenly assumed that if NATO worked well in Europe, there was no reason why it should not work well elsewhere. This miscalculation had led us in the 1950's into a costly crash effort to set up alliances and bases wherever we could find anyone to play host. The result was that we appeared to accept Chiang Kai-shek's interpretation of events in East Asia, the views of Syngman Rhee on Korea and Japan, the Shah of Iran's views on the Middle East and Batista's views on the Caribbean, while simultaneously describing ourselves as "leaders of the free world."

The Kennedy Adminstration had, to be sure, taken some positive

steps in its first six months. Adlai Stevenson's presence in the United
Nations had given our role there a new sense of importance and dignity.
Studies under John J. McCloy were developing some promising ideas on
disarmament and arms control. The State Department had been
strengthened, and the President had announced his new "Alliance for
Progress" for Latin America, which had caught the imagination of our
Spanish-speaking neighbors to the south.

While all these gains were important, I wrote, they were in no sense
adequate. In Europe, for instance, where the situation had changed
drastically in the last ten years, our policies had not begun to reflect the
change. No longer did America have the almost unlimited foreign exchange reserves and virtual monopoly over nuclear power which had
previously assured us a decisive voice in West European affairs. It was
inevitable that sooner or later leaders in France, Germany or the United
Kingdom would rise to challenge our "leadership." The wise course
would be to forge a new, more realistic relationship before we were
forced to do so.

I gave particular emphasis to the question of Germany, perhaps the
key to a stable Europe. We had taken a strong position against a united
Germany unless it were to have closer ties with the Western nations.
But was this a realistic position? Would we accept a united Germany
associated with the Soviet Union? Could we not live with *both* Germanys
until they united of their own free will?

The half-billion people of North America and Western Europe together, I pointed out, commanded the world's greatest concentration of
economic, political and industrial resources. What could and should we
be doing to create a greater sense of unity and common purpose and
to move toward political and economic integration? In other words,
was there any way we could begin to institutionalize our common
economic and political interests?

What more could we do about disarmament? Admittedly, Soviet
suspicions, fears and ambitions presented at the moment a formal
barrier to any major agreement. But had we really thought through our
own position? Did we know what we were really prepared to give if the
Soviets should suddenly show signs of talking seriously?

In regard to the developing nations we faced a challenge which we
had scarcely begun to cope with. In Asia, Africa and Latin America new
forces of nationalism and anticolonialism were on the march, a fact
which presented us with difficult choices. In Africa, for example, could
we afford to support Salazar and Portuguese colonialism and to continue
normal relationships with the Union of South Africa? It was fantastic, I
suggested, that we should remain silent while Portugal, the weakest,
most backward nation in Europe, continued to stress its "rights" to gov-

ern twelve million Africans who had been exploited for more than a hundred years.

In regard to Latin America I suggested that we were now running the danger of becoming so obsessed with Castro that it was increasingly difficult for us to think rationally of the area as a whole. Sooner or later revolution—violent and bloody or nonviolent and relatively peaceful— was certain to erupt throughout Latin America. The masses of poverty-stricken peasants and workers would not forever remain silent while the benefits of American aid and private investment went largely to the rich and privileged. Where, I asked, did the United States Government stand on this question?

I also pointed out the grave danger of maintaining a position in Southeast Asia which most of the world found indefensible. Why did we assume that China would accept a powerful American military presence near her southern border when we would not tolerate a similar Soviet position in Mexico or Canada?

Our present course in Asia was doomed to failure, and should be replaced as rapidly as possible by one which would encourage an Asian response to Asian problems. Our objective, I wrote, should be the gradual development of a consensus involving such non-Communist Asian nations as India and Japan, with the support and cooperation of Australia and other Asian nations.

I closed my memorandum with an expression of confidence in our capacity to deal with these problems and forces, provided we organized ourselves effectively and established policy guidelines which would lend consistency to our day-to-day operation. It was inevitable, I wrote, that most of my time and that of the Secretary and our top associates would be devoted to specific and immediate questions. The flood of cables arriving every day from our embassies demanded our attention and required prompt decisions. But missing was a clear sense of objectives supported by the President and articulated by Rusk, myself and other chief officials to guide our day-to-day actions.

Recently I had held a series of policy review meetings with the top staff of each of the State Department bureaus at which I brought up many of the ideas contained in my memorandum. I knew that several participants had pointed out to Rusk that the views I expressed varied significantly from "established policies." They had sought Rusk's assurance that I was not speaking for the Administration as a whole. I, too, had often heard officials justify an action on the grounds that the policy in question had been in effect throughout much of the Eisenhower era and, they assumed (accurately, I am afraid), was still in effect.

Many policy-makers were persuaded that the American people would not permit them to replace long-standing policies with new ones of untested merit, sure to be controversial. I felt, however, that we should not limit our efforts to what we knew the American people would readily accept or Congress would support. If a democratic government could not devise ways to do what was required of it, then it would almost certainly fail.

I believed that many leaders greatly underestimated the public's capacity to understand and its willingness to support realistic new foreign policies, once the way had been pointed with clarity by strong executive leadership. Our most notable foreign policy actions since the war had originally been controversial—Lend-Lease, the Truman Doctrine, the Marshall Plan, Point Four, etc.—and in each case the decision had been made under adverse political conditions. Yet because the Administration had explained the need for the proposed action logically and forthrightly, the necessary public support on those occasions had been forthcoming. A responsibility of the State Department in its dealings with the American public now, I believed, was to strive to dispel with the facts the dangerous clichés on which much of what passes for "public opinion" is based. "What a grim joke it would be," I wrote to Rusk, "if the history books record that the people of a great nation dedicated to free speech and communication failed to appreciate or understand the quite obvious forces which destroyed it."

As a result of this effort, a large group of influential press and radio people were invited to Washington for a two-day conference, at which I acted as chairman, to consider foreign policy questions in depth. These meetings were so successful that we scheduled a series of similar regional meetings in such cities as Denver, Chicago, Cleveland and Louisville, to which we invited newspapermen (including the editors of weeklies), radio commentators, heads of Leagues of Women Voters and other opinion-makers.

Although these meetings were well attended, lively and, I think, successful, they may have added to the growing (and quite correct) impression that I was advocating a broader, less doctrinaire approach to foreign policy than was actually in effect.

In addition to my detailed memorandum proposing a review in depth of our foreign policy, I continued to press Rusk to establish my authority as Under Secretary to make the administrative decisions required to transform the Department into an effective instrument of foreign policy. I also continued my efforts to persuade the Secretary to define our own working relationship.

I had hoped that my memorandum and my other efforts would lead to a frank and free discussion of where we were heading among the

President, Rusk, Bob McNamara, McGeorge Bundy, myself and others. But it did not.

At the very least, I hoped that it would lead to a frank and open discussion between Rusk and me on the wide range of subjects I had opened up. One evening when Steb and Rusk's wife, Virginia, were both away, Rusk and I had a long talk at my house which continued for two or three hours. I reminded Rusk that when I became Under Secretary I had reduced my contacts with the White House to a minimum in order to eliminate any possible basis for misunderstanding between us. But, I said, the only result had been that many of my old friends in the White House and in Congress were now taking me to task for administrative conflicts and confusion in the State Department that I had no authority to correct. Rusk was cordial, but talked around the issue. While it was a pleasant enough evening with a man for whom I retained personal affection and even respect, it could not be described as an exchange of views.

The discussion that materialized a few days later was not what I had anticipated.

CHAPTER 27

THE CONFLICT COMES TO THE SURFACE

ON THURSDAY, July 6, Rusk asked me to lunch in his office. He appeared nervous, and within a few moments I knew why.

"Last night," he said, "I was thinking of the frustrating job you have and how unhappy it must make you. Why don't you free yourself from the Department and take on the job of roving ambassador? You already have excellent contacts in Asia, Africa and Europe, and you could easily make them in Latin America." He observed that Harriman was unable to handle all that needed to be done, particularly since he was now in Geneva spending full time on the Laotian situation.

My first impulse was to ask what he meant. But it seemed all too clear. I replied in as dead-pan a manner as I could muster that, while I would like to do more traveling and perhaps could in the future, my present job was important, and I felt that I could contribute most to the Administration in Washington. That was the end of the conversation.

Returning to my office, I telephoned Abe Chayes and told him what had happened. Abe was incredulous and said I must have misunderstood. I replied that it sounded to me like a not particularly subtle hint that I resign as Under Secretary. Abe insisted that the Administration wouldn't dare handle me in such a crude way and that I had probably read too much into Rusk's words. He nearly managed to convince me.

But soon there was further evidence that something was in the wind. In that week's issue of *U.S. News & World Report* a story appeared alleging that I was a serious personal problem for Rusk because of my "end runs" around him to see the President directly on policy questions. Another story in *Newsweek* reported that "within the State Department there is a good deal of shooting at Chester Bowles." When contacted, the

Newsweek reporter attributed his information to "a White House aide at a dinner party." Rusk heatedly denied the report, and in fact I deliberately had not talked to the President alone since early December, six months ago. Yet no retraction was ever printed.

On Sunday, July 9, Charles Bartlett, a close journalist friend of the President, produced a widely read article in *News Focus* and the Chattanooga *Times* asserting that numerous Foreign Service officers were angry at me because so many senior men had been asked to retire. The State Department regulars, Bartlett wrote, "maintain that Bowles has created a sense of disorder and insecurity which will persist as long as he remains Under Secretary. They are, in short, after his scalp."

On Tuesday, July 11, Rusk asked me to come to his office after the early morning staff meeting. He brought up the Bartlett piece and said he knew it was absurd but added, uncomfortably, "Really, wouldn't you like to switch to this roving ambassador job, or perhaps to a key embassy such as Chile or Brazil?"

I asked him to tell me frankly whether this idea was his or the President's, and Rusk, looking still more uncomfortable, replied that it was Kennedy's. I called the President, and he invited me to lunch the following day.

At the White House, I first had a swim with Kennedy, followed by lunch upstairs in the family section. Kennedy opened the conversation by saying that he might have made a mistake in not making me Secretary of State in the first place, and that if he had done so, things might have been different. However, Rusk was Secretary, and the Department had not come through with the new policy approaches the President had wanted. This concerned him very much and called for some changes. While he knew the shortcomings of the State Department could not reasonably be blamed on me, I was a logical target. Again, I was asked how I would like to go to Chile.

I expressed surprise that he and Rusk had not talked with me earlier about the situation. I was as unhappy as he about the inadequacies of the State Department, but I doubted whether he fully understood the problems involved. I added that I had no desire to move to an embassy under any circumstances. My obligation, I said, was to help him to shape the State Department into a more effective instrument for carrying out his policies. I noted that this development had caught me by surprise and I wanted time to think about it. I asked if we could meet again the following Monday, July 17, and the President agreed.

In the next few days many newspapers began to carry front-page rumors of my impending resignation. These included articles by Joseph Alsop and Murrey Marder in the Washington *Post*, Walter Redder in the

Minneapolis *Tribune* and Rowland Evans, Jr. in the New York *Herald Tribune*. According to these reports, "highly placed White House spokesmen" charged that I was at home only with "big thoughts," while "members of Kennedy's political staff" were said to carry a grudge against me because of my refusal in 1960 to campaign against Hubert Humphrey in the Wisconsin and West Virginia primaries. In addition, I was charged with having openly expressed my opposition to the Bay of Pigs operation and, most extraordinary of all, with having no experience or interest in administration.

A few days earlier, Abe Chayes had casually told me of a dinner party in Georgetown at which McGeorge Bundy had stated that no one in the White House knew precisely who was responsible for the lack of direction and initiative in the State Department, but that it was clear that changes would have to be made. And, Bundy added, "You can't change Rusk." Abe said that he had not taken this comment seriously at the time, but in light of my conversation with Kennedy and Rusk this judgment had been wrong.

By Friday, July 14, with Kennedy out of town, the situation was moving toward a crisis. Scores of friends within and outside of the government, Democratic leaders in various parts of the country and members of Congress telephoned, wrote and called at our Georgetown home to express their concern and offer their help. Walter Reuther called from Detroit and Adlai Stevenson from Florence, Italy, both advising me to stay put. Orville Freeman and Soapy (G. Mennen) Williams, with whom I had dinner that night, were both indignant and offered similar advice. I had no intention of quitting and so assured my friends. If the President wanted me to leave, he would have to say so and publicly explain why. If this should occur, I was prepared to meet the issue squarely and set the record straight in detail.

The attacks on me necessarily involved what I believed to be our outdated foreign policy, and hence the conflict increasingly took on ideological connotations. Thus the question of whether Kennedy would support me in the face of these attacks, for which some of his friends and associates were responsible, began to be viewed, somewhat unfairly, as a measure of his commitment to "liberalism."

At breakfast on Monday just before my scheduled appointment with President Kennedy, I read on the front page of the *New York Times* under the by-line of James Reston that Kennedy was expected to ask for my resignation that day.

I decided to take the initiative as soon as I entered Kennedy's office. First, I reiterated my previous recommendations for a reorganization of State Department personnel, for a new structure to clarify the lines of authority and for a review in depth of the assumptions on which our present policies were based. I then showed Kennedy two memoranda I had written on the Department's operational problems as well as my warning to Rusk against the Cuban adventure, which I discovered Kennedy had never seen or heard of.

Kennedy read the three memoranda with obvious interest. I then said that I had carefully considered the suggestion he had made to me a few days before and had decided that under the present circumstances I would not accept appointment to an embassy nor would I leave my post as Under Secretary of State unless I was publicly removed. For eight months, with no support from either the White House or the Secretary, I had worked hard to reorganize the Department. Many problems remained, and if he or Rusk would give me the necessary authority, I would deal with them.

President Kennedy did not directly comment on my refusal to step aside. He simply pointed out that a difficult situation had developed for both of us and added once again that he regretted the news stories. I pointed out that the current uproar in the press had raised an immediate problem for me since I was scheduled to depart within a week for a series of ambassadorial coordination meetings in Africa, the Middle East and Asia which had been set up some time ago.

Kennedy said I should go ahead with the trip and that he would make a public statement to the effect that I was staying on and that the situation remained unchanged. He added that when I returned from abroad, we could resume our discussions and decide where to go from there. He told me he wanted to keep the decision confined to himself, Rusk and me so that no more leaks would occur.

Although on the latter point I knew he was sincere, there was soon fresh evidence that some members of the President's staff were unprepared to take the President's statement about press leaks seriously. Shortly after I left Kennedy's office a reporter on the Washington *Post* called me to tell me that Kennedy's press secretary, Pierre Salinger, had just completed a background press conference in which he had said that my resignation was "not *currently* expected," and then had added off the record that I might not be around for very long.

Under these circumstances it was not surprising that the newspapers next morning continued to leave my status uncertain. As soon as I reached my office, I called Rusk to say that unless Kennedy was prepared to clarify the situation, my pending trip abroad must be abandoned. Rusk agreed, and the following day at his press conference Kennedy made a statement flatly denying rumors about my pending resignation, but adding that he would not hesitate to ask any official to change jobs if it meant his efforts would be better spent.

Most of the press articles continued to reflect this uncertain state of events: i.e., while I was staying on, this did not mean that things were settled. The following editorials appeared on July 18:

Columnist Peter Edson's article in the Washington *Daily News*, entitled "Bowles Has Staying Power," asserted:

> The big blowup over the possible firing or resignation of Chester Bowles as Under Secretary of State is one of the occupational hazards of politics. The attempt to get Mr. Bowles was an inside job which didn't quite come off.
>
> The mixup came at a bad time. . . . Relations with Russia are ready to explode on half a dozen fronts. Secretary of State Dean Rusk must confer with allied Foreign Ministers in Europe. Under Secretary Bowles himself is off on a three-week fact-finding trip to Africa and South Asia.
>
> If ever the Kennedy Administration needs steadiness and no palace politics, this is the time.
>
> The mention of McGeorge Bundy—top special assistant to the President—as an eventual successor to Under Secretary Bowles is now officially denied. But it is not without interest.
>
> Mr. Bundy came to Washington with a good reputation in administration at Harvard College. But the Bowles record as an administrator looks superior from every point of view. He was successful in business before he got into politics. In his public careers he has been wartime price administrator and economic stabilization director, congressman, governor of Connecticut and ambassador to India. These are apparently the characteristics that have made the President decide to keep him on the job.

The Washington *Post* summed up the situation in an editorial entitled "The Bowles Affair":

> The first full scale internal political hurricane of the Kennedy Administration has broken about Chester Bowles, Under Secretary of State, with a display of thunder, lightning, wind and rain reminiscent of New Deal days.
>
> Mr. Bowles brought to his job the experience of an administrator gained as a governor and in earlier Federal posts. He has worked hard at making his own personality complementary to that of his chief; and this has not been easy for one who has been the top man in most of the places he has hitherto served.
>
> On the detailed kind of work involved in straightening out the administrative jungle of the State Department he seems to have done well. The Department will be better off for his handling of personnel, his recruitment of new people, his influence on ambassadorial appointments, his impact on the foreign service, his contributions to the cultural affairs office, and his management of protocol responsibilities to new nations. He has supervised the establishment of the new operations center. He helped

put through needed amendments to the Foreign Service Act. The International Labor office has been given a better setup. He has lent his sympathetic help to subordinates who have cut out needless reports, eliminated departmental committees and otherwise simplified procedures. He has skillfully handled the program to give ambassadors more control over all United States operations in their countries of assignment.

Most of the criticism of Mr. Bowles is that his most grievous offense is that he is still Chester Bowles. It is pretty hard for him not to be that.

My personal feelings were mixed and my interpretation of these events uncertain. I could only guess about their origin. As I wrote to Adlai Stevenson on July 23:

> On no occasion in the last six months has there been the slightest suggestion of warning from the President, Dean Rusk or anyone else. Nor, incidentally, did anyone have the courage to attach his name to any of the personal attacks, which were authorized by "high Administration authorities," "White House sources," etc.[1]

The logic of recent events seemed hard to grasp. Kennedy had taken office with a frequently expressed determination to make substantial changes in American foreign policy which were similar to my own views. Indeed, this is why I had supported him and worked for him in 1960. However, ever since he had entered the White House he had bounced from one international crisis to another, and the President had become understandably frustrated and uncertain. In a sense I carried some share of responsibility since out of a determination not to undermine Dean Rusk I had made no direct appeal to the President for support for the changes in policy direction and administration for which I had been fighting and which I still believed the President wanted.

As I wrote Stevenson:

> . . . this was a fundamental error. Anyone who has been in public life as long as you and I cannot wish himself out of it. For this reason it is a mistake for him ever to be more than ten feet from a microphone through which he can reply to whatever public criticism may be made of his actions.

Of one thing I was certain: the Department's problems were not going to be solved merely by replacing me.

With the question of my status suspended—if not solved—I left on July 25 for three regional administrative conferences. Since the rumors still continued, the situation was uncomfortable at the outset, but I received a warm response at the first ambassadors' meeting at Lagos, and

---

1. The letter appears in its entirety in an appendix, since it stands, years later, as an accurate summary of my feelings at that time.

as the trip progressed, I began to feel better. Ted Sorensen's brother, Tom, of the United States Information Agency, I was later told, sent back glowing reports of the content of the meetings and of the welcome that I received at each of them.

On my return to Washington in late August I called on the President to report on the trip. He showed an unexpected interest in my account of our progress in reorganizing our overseas missions and seemed warm, friendly, genuinely glad to see me and at ease.

For the first time since I became Under Secretary, he asked for my views on what was wrong with the Department's operations. I told him, also for the first time, of the specific changes I had proposed, the differences I had with Rusk in regard to the kind of people we needed and why I felt that these differences were at the heart of our difficulties. I added that because I felt this was primarily my problem to work out with Rusk, I had not discussed it with him until he raised the question with me.

After some discussion the President asked that I send him a private memorandum outlining my views. I wrote the memorandum as the President requested, but after considering whether the President's reference to "private memorandum" meant for his eyes only I decided that I would feel more comfortable if I sent a copy to Rusk.

A few days later the barrage began all over again with a vicious column by Joseph Alsop which appeared in a large number of syndicated newspapers. The story ridiculed Kennedy and Rusk for supposedly allowing themselves to be manipulated by me and a lot of "wild liberals," with whom, it said, the President was not anxious to tangle. Alsop concluded: "The President would have made no audible protest if Bowles had suddenly decided to join a community of Indian swamis on his recent visit to his favorite subcontinent." At the same time, several of Kennedy's associates were widely quoted as being surprised that I had not long since fallen apart under the pressure.

Shortly after Labor Day I went to the White House to see Ted Sorensen in the hope that he could explain precisely what had happened and what the President really wanted. Sorensen said that as far as he knew the question of my status was now settled. However, after a half-hour's exchange I began to suspect that he knew no more about the situation than I did. He did remark that I had amassed a powerful coalition of determined opponents in Washington. These included senior Foreign Service officers whom I had forced to retire to enable us to promote more younger men, the Acheson-oriented Cold War elements in the State Department and in the White House, and the ultraconservatives on Capitol Hill in both parties who looked on individuals such as Stevenson and me as "radicals."

Another factor, Sorensen thought, was increasing impatience among many people close to the President with the nonaligned position of many underdeveloped nations. While the United States was embroiled with Russia over Laos, Berlin and nuclear testing, they were irritated that many underdeveloped countries refused to take sides. Since for many years I had given public encouragement to the new nationalistic forces in Asia, Africa and Latin America, this, too, had played into the hands of my opponents.

The following morning Rusk and I were scheduled to have breakfast together. At first he was nervous and uneasy, but gradually he relaxed and our conversation became almost as easy and natural as in the days when I first knew him. However, when I brought up the upcoming conference of the nonaligned nations at Belgrade, Yugoslavia, his mood suddenly changed. "It is high time," he said, "that they decided what side of the Cold War they are on." Although I knew he was worried and frustrated over Berlin and the Russians, I was startled by this reflexive reversal to a doctrinaire position.

I then tried a different subject—the need to strengthen the five geographic bureaus. At first he did not respond directly. But as I continued to press the point, he said sharply, "I don't agree that we should grab the first fresh face we see and bring him into the State Department."

Clearly we were miles apart. I think this was the first time that I admitted to myself that there was nothing more I could ever do or say to bridge the gap.

CHAPTER 28

THE CONFLICT BOILS OVER

IN EARLY SEPTEMBER, 1961, a few days after our return from a brief
vacation in Maine, there seemed to be significant progress toward a
tighter organization in the Department. At a meeting with George Ball,
Alex Johnson, myself and one or two others, Rusk assigned to me for the
first time a clear set of responsibilities which included authority for administration and personnel, policy planning and long-term operations
in general. Ball would spend more time backstopping the Secretary on
crisis situations.

After several days had passed and no announcement was forthcoming, I suggested to Rusk that he send a memorandum to the State
Department staff outlining the new delegation of authority. He de-
murred on the ground that the timing wasn't right. The press, he
said, was still harping on our difficulties in July. Since this might more
logically have been interpreted as a reason publicly to clear up the
confusion, I concluded that "his decision" may have been made in response to a suggestion from the President. Since it was understandable
that Kennedy might not wish to involve himself further in the differences
between Rusk and me, it remained to be seen how seriously Rusk would
take his suggestion.

My skepticism was compounded a few days later when the annual
review of our budget was scheduled to get under way and I suggested
that I take charge of the "cutting and healing" operation with the head
of each bureau. Rusk replied that he would take charge of the operation
himself.

As the weeks went by, the confusion deepened. The Department
was almost without direction, and inevitably the White House staff

under McGeorge Bundy assumed more and more responsibility for questions which should have been handled by the State Department. When President Kennedy announced on October 11, 1961, that he was sending a high-level mission to explore the situation in South Vietnam, it was headed not by Harriman, myself or some other State Department official, but by General Maxwell Taylor and Walt Rostow, both of the White House staff, with only a small, low-level State Department contingent. This indicated that the State Department had either abdicated its responsibility or that the President, with no confidence in the State Department, had decided to take it away. In either event, it was, I thought, a grave mistake, and I emphatically said so.

A few days later I left for several weeks of conferences in Asia and Latin America. Upon my return in mid-November I was not surprised to find that the recommendations of the Taylor-Rostow mission were heavily oriented toward military action.[1]

My spirits were lifted somewhat by the report of the Senate Government Operations Subcommittee on National Security issued in mid-November, which strongly criticized current State Department operations and offered many of the same recommendations that I had been advocating for nearly a year. This report was of particular significance because it was chaired by Senator Henry M. Jackson of Washington, a friend of Kennedy's and his choice for Democratic National Chairman during the 1960 campaign.

Although I had, of course, known of the committee's investigations and had been asked to appear as a witness, I had decided to take no part, since I did not want the Secretary to think I was seeking personal support for my own views and undermining his own on Capitol Hill.

A year before, the committee had issued a somewhat similar report, which criticized the overbureaucratization of policy formation under President Eisenhower. This had prompted Kennedy to reduce the National Security staff in the White House. I was delighted to see that the second report was equally pungent and perceptive in pointing out weak points in the State Department operation. Its main criticisms were that the State Department was not asserting its leadership across the whole front of foreign policy, that it had not adequately staffed itself for such leadership, and that instead of foreseeing problems and dealing with them before they developed, the Department was inclined to wait until they were full-blown crises.

The State Department, the report stressed, needed more executive

1. These recommendations are discussed futher in Chapter 32.

managers—men broadly experienced in dealing with the full range of national security problems. The administration of foreign policy, the report observed, had become "big business." This placed a high premium on the ability to manage large-scale enterprises—to make decisions promptly and decisively, to delegate and to monitor. The need for able "take-charge" men was particularly urgent down through the Assistant Secretary level and at our large missions abroad.

The Jackson report encouraged me to make another try to secure the Secretary's agreement to review our administrative setup. Immediately after the daily staff meeting Monday morning, November 27, I met with Rusk once again to urge the changes I had been proposing in the European and Asian bureaus.

My recent visit to the Far East and Southeast Asia, I said as tactfully as I could, had confirmed my fear that American policies in that area were increasingly detached from the realities. One year after Kennedy's election we were operating on much the same mistaken assumptions that had been laid down by John Foster Dulles and Assistant Secretary Walter Robertson.

Although Harriman was still involved in the Laos negotiations in Geneva, I suggested to Rusk that he should be asked to assume the directorship of the Asian Bureau on his return. This appointment would be important, I said, not only for its ultimate effect on our operations in that area but for its morale-building effect throughout the Department. It would also help us to persuade George McGhee, who had been reluctant to give up his chairmanship of the Policy Planning staff, to become Assistant Secretary of the European Bureau.

Rusk replied, as on previous occasions, that for a variety of reasons, which he did not specify, he was not prepared to make either move at this time. His only specific comment was that a change in the Assistant Secretary for the Far Eastern Bureau would be unfair to McConaughy because he had "just bought a new house here in Washington."

Five days later, on the morning of the Harvard-Yale football game in New Haven, Rusk called me at my home in Essex, where we had gone for the weekend, to say he would like to see me as soon as possible. I explained that I was involved that day and evening in a family reunion which had been planned before my recent trip abroad and that unless it was an emergency I would rather wait until after the weekend.

When I asked him what the subject was, he replied obliquely that it concerned "administrative changes." I reminded him that we already had a luncheon appointment for Monday, but he said that that would be a busy day and we should meet on Sunday.

I was sure that the changes which Rusk wanted to discuss did not involve my two Assistant Secretary proposals, since he had dismissed them so abruptly a few days earlier. Still, I did not suspect that the meeting had anything but a routine purpose, principally because there had been no hints in the press of major developments in the offing. I ran into Arthur Schlesinger at the game and told him of Rusk's call, but he could cast no light on what lay behind it.

On Sunday afternoon when I walked into Rusk's office, he handed me a press statement announcing a series of major changes. I was to leave my post as Under Secretary to replace Averell Harriman as roving ambassador. Harriman was to take over the Far Eastern Bureau (which I had been advocating for some time); George Ball was to replace me as Under Secretary; and George McGhee would replace Ball as junior Under Secretary, the third-ranking officer. Dick Goodwin and Walt Rostow were moving from the White House to the State Department, Goodwin to become Deputy Assistant Secretary for Latin American Affairs and Rostow to head the Policy Planning staff. McConaughy, who Rusk had insisted in his conversation with me a few days earlier must remain as Assistant Secretary for East Asia, was to be moved to an overseas assignment.

Evidently, Kennedy had accepted some of the proposals I had made in response to his request for my recommendations several weeks before, and in the last two or three days had directed Rusk to put them into effect. The elevation of the liberal Harriman, which was an excellent move in itself, would help draw the teeth of liberal Democrats who would be opposed to my being sidetracked. This wholesale reorganization ultimately became known in Washington circles as the "Thanksgiving Day Massacre."

Kennedy's press secretary, Pierre Salinger, Rusk said, was scheduled to announce these changes to the press in Hyannis Port within a few hours. This meant that I had a choice either to leave the Administration then and there or to try to work out a new role within it.

The advantages of leaving the Administration were obvious. A complete break would set me free to spell out publicly the weaknesses in our foreign policy and in our State Department organization, the dangers of our increasingly military-oriented approach, and what I had been striving fruitlessly to do for the last twelve months to change the situation and the obstacles which I had encountered. A decision to return to private life would also be easier for Steb and me to live with personally, since any new government assignment, regardless of how it was described by Kennedy, would involve difficult adjustments.

However, I resented being confronted without warning with an ultimatum. So I told Rusk that regardless of Salinger's impending press conference I was unwilling to decide until I had an opportunity to consider the alternatives and talk with Steb and some of my friends.

Rusk then called Ted Sorensen, who apparently had been asked to stand by in the White House with his political fire extinguisher, and suggested that he talk to me. A few minutes later Ted arrived in my office. He insisted that in spite of all the fireworks the President still genuinely wanted me to stay in the Administration.

I told Sorensen that if I must decide one way or the other immediately, my decision was to resign and that under no condition would I accept a vaguely defined "roving ambassadorship." Sorensen then asked if I had in mind an alternative role. After a few moments' thought I replied that the only post that would appeal to me was one that involved specific responsibilities working on the formulation and administration of foreign policy directly with the President. Sorensen telephoned Kennedy at Hyannis Port and a few minutes later reported that the President would be delighted to explore such a possibility; within twenty-four hours he would make a specific proposal that he was confident I would accept.

At about six o'clock, I left my office for Abe Chayes' home in Georgetown where we were joined by Harris Wofford, his wife Claire, and David Ginsburg, each of whom was almost as shattered as I. When I returned to our house on N Street around ten, the telephone was ringing. It was Steb, who was still in Essex; she had heard the news over the radio, chartered a private plane and would be in Washington in two or three hours. She arrived shortly after midnight, and her cool judgment helped me to sort out my own turbulent reactions.

I don't entirely recall what I said that night to either Steb or my friends at the Chayes' house. I do remember I was angry over the devious manner in which the situation had been handled, shocked at its suddenness and saddened as I reviewed the events of the preceding year.

My friends have often charged me with failing to see my efforts in this difficult year in balanced perspective. I accomplished, they say, far more than I realized. To whatever extent this is true, the explanation may lie in the fact that I expected too much. In my previous two major experiences in government—as Administrator of OPA and as Governor of Connecticut—I had been propelled into positions of great responsibility which I had not really anticipated, but which had worked out far better than I or anyone else expected, while on this occasion I had come well prepared, with high expectations and after a year of hard work had relatively little to show for it.

As Under Secretary of State I felt secure in my background, clear in my objectives and confident of my abilities. In regard to administration, which I saw as a primary responsibility of the Under Secretary, the Department, although in dire need of reorganization and reinvigoration, was by no means in as bad shape as OPA had been when I took over in 1943. In regard to the formation of foreign policy I was no amateur dealing with unfamiliar problems, but a former Ambassador who had successfully run one of our largest overseas missions, a long-time student of foreign affairs and a former member of the House Foreign Affairs Committee, with a wide circle of friends and acquaintances throughout the world, many of them in high places.

My close association with Kennedy even before his nomination as his chief foreign policy adviser and my long and cordial personal relationship with Rusk had given me every reason for confidence. It never occurred to me that my judgment on all phases of foreign policy-making and administration would not be listened to and in most cases supported by the President and Secretary. Because I had expected so much, my disappointment over the outcome was all the keener.

Although the State Department was the only organization in which I had worked since my late twenties where I was not fully in charge, I do not think this was a factor. I was psychologically adjusted to my role as Number Two and, as a matter of fact, rather welcomed the freedom this gave me to avoid the official functions and airport-greeting ceremonies, which I had always disliked.

I realized, of course, that in the complex area of foreign policy there were bound to be disagreements, but I was prepared to work them out as they arose, in a rational and open manner. I was no stranger to controversy and to the infighting of Washington bureaucracy; during World War II I had survived many bitter confrontations with such battle-scarred professionals as Harold Ickes and Fred Vinson.

But the differences between my wartime OPA experience and this one were fundamental. As OPA Administrator I could always count on strong intellectual, political and emotional support first from President Roosevelt and later from President Truman. They were both committed to the control of inflation, and I managed to put together and administer an organization that was equal to the task.

My desire to do all I could to strengthen Rusk's own position placed a premium on his support of my efforts and on the similarity of our views. But Rusk and I proved to be poles apart.

I often wonder why I did not sense this possibility earlier. I can only say that at the Rockefeller Foundation Rusk had impressed me as concise and articulate, and an able and decisive administrator. As Secretary of State, however, he seemed to accept the vast and often rigid State

Department bureaucracy as a fact of life beyond his and my capacity to change. His energies and efforts were invariably directed at the problems that were presently on his desk, with little evidence of concern about how and why they arose in the first place.

On domestic questions Rusk was genuinely concerned about social problems. Although a Southern Democrat, he was liberal in regard to race relations. His foreign policy thinking, however, had been shaped during the early, bitter, disillusioning years of the Cold War. Although I think he tried to take a less rigid view, he never succeeded in seeing any international conflict in terms other than those of the Cold War. Every nation, he felt, had an obligation to make a choice: was it for or against the United States? Furthermore, once Rusk had explored a situation carefully and reached a conclusion, it was difficult to budge him, even though the conditions under which his original decision had been reached might have changed significantly.

Most of the top staff in the State Department were, of course, aware of the gap that existed between Rusk and me on matters of administration and policy-making. Lucius D. Battle, head of the State Department Secretariat, in particular, was in close touch with both Rusk and myself and made a persistent effort to bridge our differences whenever possible. I think he thoroughly understood what I was trying to do, and there is no doubt but that he knew more about Rusk's temperament and general motivation than anyone else in the Department.

Luke had worked with Rusk when he was Assistant Secretary of State, and they were old friends. Although I had not known him previously, we quickly developed a close personal relationship and understanding, and I often turned to him for advice on how best to handle a particularly complex question with Rusk. Almost all of the memoranda I wrote to Rusk went through Luke's hands. Indeed, he often agreed to read them in an early draft version and, with his keen knowledge of and respect for Rusk, he made many helpful suggestions. But even his persistent efforts could not bridge the gap.[1]

The only one of Kennedy's advisers who understood the difficulties between Rusk and me was Arthur Schlesinger, Jr. In his book, *A Thousand Days*, he made the kindly comment that "Bowles was the hapless victim of conditions which he had diagnosed better than anybody else."

Despite my deep differences with Rusk, it is only fair to say that I know of no man in public life who worked harder to meet his responsi-

1. In 1963 a career Foreign Service officer, Samuel W. Lewis, who in 1961 served as a member of my staff, wrote an independent analysis of my relationship with Rusk. This appears with Lewis' permission in an appendix.

bilities as he saw them. He was totally loyal to the two Presidents whom he served. If he was wrong on Vietnam and other issues, as I believe he was, his conclusions were reached in good faith.

On several occasions after 1961 I sensed that Rusk was on the point of opening up a discussion in depth of our past relationship, and I earnestly wished that he had done so. However, his sense of reserve invariably triumphed, and the frank talk for which I was so eager never materialized.

At a State Department ceremony in July, 1969, after my return from India, I was given the Award for Distinguished Service by the Department. After a few brief remarks by the new Secretary, William Rogers, Rusk was asked to comment.

"Chet Bowles," he said graciously, "has contributed many ideas which are now an integral part of American foreign policy. In regard to the many more ideas of his which were not accepted—only the historians can determine who was right and who was wrong."

That, I agree, is a good place to leave it.

CHAPTER 29

LAUNCHED IN A NEW ROLE

ON MONDAY MORNING, December 4, the day after the State Department reorganization, Ted Sorensen came to my house to outline the new position to which the President had referred. The title was impressive: the President's Special Representative and Adviser on Asian, African and Latin American Affairs—and with it went a raise in salary, ambassadorial status, a White House car and other status symbols of officialdom.

When I met the President at the White House later in the day, I expressed my frank skepticism about what it all meant; my ability to make a useful contribution, I said, would largely depend on the closeness of my personal relationship with him. Although he had often spoken on foreign policy matters precisely as I hoped he would, I was concerned by the lack of personal rapport between us. How otherwise could recent developments be explained? I was not, I said, the tough, terse, yes-or-no type he apparently found it easiest to work with, and there was nothing I could do to become one.

Kennedy denied that communication was a problem. The primary point, he said, was that I was the strongest asset the Administration had in Asia, Africa and Latin America, and therefore I was indispensable to his programs and plans. We talked for an hour and my doubts persisted. But the President spoke with such earnestness and conviction that I agreed to give his proposal a genuine try. As a starting point he suggested that I accompany him to Latin America two weeks later.

The trip, which included Venezuela and Colombia, was a success, and I returned with the feeling that I had contributed significantly. Kennedy handled himself with skill, saying all the proper things and saying them eloquently, while playing down what I had begun to fear was an obsession with Castro.

But, as the following entry in my notebook in early December indicates, I still seriously questioned my ability to affect our foreign policies from within the Administration.

> I do not believe that this type of gadfly operation is something I will want to continue for very long. If the President honestly wants this sort of thing from me, it should be clear by the end of the summer, in which case I will continue to work with him indefinitely. However, it would be a mistake for me to remain here if I do not feel a genuine confidence in our relationship and in my ability to get things done.

In early February I left on an extensive trip to explore trouble spots in the Middle East, North Africa, South Asia and East Asia, accompanied by three members of my staff—Samuel Lewis, William Polk and Annabelle Mitchell.

Although I discussed the likely issues at length with the President, the itinerary and the trip itself did not originate in the White House; it reflected my desire to gain a clearer perspective on recent developments in Africa and Asia and on our overseas operations in general and to break loose for a few weeks from the tense and contentious atmosphere of our national capital.

I will not attempt to describe the trip in detail, but the following highlights will suggest the wide variety of subjects which were covered.

I was eager to visit Iran for two reasons: first, because I had never met the Shah and I was anxious to know more about his general approach to economic development, defense and other questions; second, because for several years I had been intrigued with the possibility of opening up an assured trade route from landlocked Afghanistan through Iran to the outside world.[1]

In the last few years Pakistan had on several occasions closed its border to all goods exported from Afghanistan and transported across Pakistan to foreign countries; the objective of these embargoes was to force Afghanistan to modify its views on various issues dividing the two nations. During these intervals, which on one occasion had lasted several months, Afghan exports had to be shipped to the outside world either through the U.S.S.R. or by rail across northern Iran—both of which added greatly to the transportation costs and hampered Afghanistan's ability to achieve economic self-sufficiency.

I had in mind the possibility of using some of our economic assist-

1. Other landlocked nations which face somewhat similar problems include Bolivia, Nepal, Laos and several new African nations.

ance funds to construct a new seaport at Bandar Abbas in southern Iran at the entrance to the Persian Gulf, with a modern road from the port to the town of Zahidan near the Iran-Pakistan border and then across Afghanistan to the capital city of Kabul. This would provide a much more direct route, and the Afghans with whom I had discussed the possibility were, of course, enthusiastic. I was eager to secure the Shah's general approval for this project and, if it was forthcoming, to visit the proposed site.

I was favorably impressed with most of the government officials with whom I talked in Teheran, particularly the Minister of Agriculture, who described his commitment to a large-scale land reform program. It was also reassuring to talk with some of the able young graduates of European and American universities who, despite their criticism of their government, had returned to Iran to become involved in various aspects of its administration. The response from the relatively few peasants who had thus far benefited from land reform and cooperatives was enthusiastic. On the negative side of the ledger were the still appalling poverty and social injustice, and the lack of trained people working in the rural areas to carry out new programs.

I spent a long, and I thought fruitful, evening with the Shah. The dinner, at which we were joined by Ambassador Julius Holmes and the Iranian Foreign Minister, started at 8 P.M. and involved quantities of excellent French food served on a succession of gold plates. The Shah impressed me as genuinely concerned about the needs of his people, but at least equally concerned about his need for sophisticated military equipment, which in my view had but little relevance to Iran's security or prosperity.

When I asked him what defense problems particularly concerned him, he came up with some surprising answers in the following order: first, Nasser and Egypt (which is a thousand miles away); second, the Afghans, who, he said, might be backed by Russian Uzbeks dressed in Afghan uniforms; and third, the Iraqi. The Soviets, he said, were primarily *our* problem.

I strongly argued the case for more intensive economic development against what I thought (but didn't say) amounted to a playboy military approach. To my distress, Ambassador Holmes came down more often than not on the side of the Shah. Nevertheless, when we finally rose from the dining table around midnight, I felt that I had largely convinced the Shah (a) that he was unlikely to get the increased military assistance which he wanted from the United States and (b) that the developmental aid which I offered as a substitute might indeed be a better long-range investment for him and for the people of Iran.

I was also successful in arousing his interest in and securing his informal approval of my proposal for a new port at Bandar Abbas linked by a new road to Kabul. But predictably, he was less than enthusiastic about my suggestion that it be an internationalized project that would enable the Afghans to ship their exports across Iran under bond.

My visit in an Air Force plane to the Bandar Abbas area was encouraging; the American Army engineers who met me there agreed that the project was practical and that a modern port could be completed in four or five years. As we explored the possibilities in greater detail, it was clear that not only would the port be of immense potential value to Afghanistan in providing a secure outlet to world markets, but that it would open up a potentially rich area of Iran for increased development and trade.[2]

From Teheran I flew to Cairo for a series of talks with Nasser. My purpose there was threefold: (1) to persuade Nasser to abandon his disruptive efforts in Africa, in particular in the Congo; (2) to persuade him to cease his threatening attacks, verbal and otherwise, on Jordan and Saudi Arabia; and (3) to explore the possibility of an arms-ceiling agreement between Israel and the U.A.R. If Nasser's reactions on those questions were reasonably positive, President Kennedy had assured me that we would agree to help ease the U.A.R.'s economic difficulties.

In my two three-hour talks with Nasser I found him restrained, soft-spoken, with an excellent command of English, an appearance of frankness and a probing mind, but handicapped by a lack of a sense of history or knowledge of economics.

He also seemed frustrated with the sterility of his own Pan-Arab movement, his inability to persuade the oil-producing Middle Eastern countries to turn over a significant share of their foreign exchange income to him and, on top of it all, the disastrous failure of his cotton crop, the principal source of his foreign exchange.

On several occasions he referred to his disenchantment with Marxist philosophy and his concern over Soviet objectives in the Middle East in general and in the U.A.R. in particular.

The differences between the U.A.R. and the United States were deep, and I had no illusions about the obstacles to bridging them. But, in view of Nasser's current difficulties, I thought it might be possible to persuade him to divert his formidable energies from subversion and conflict to the economic development of his own country.

2. The Port of Bandar Abbas was completed in 1970, and most of the facilities are now in full operation. Although substantial amounts of trade to and from Afghanistan now go through there, my proposal that Iran internationalize the port was rejected by the Shah.

In regard to Africa I made more progress than I anticipated. Partly, no doubt, because Nasser's efforts at subversion in the Congo and elsewhere had not been productive, he accepted my assurance that we had no desire to turn the Congo or any other part of Africa back to the former colonial masters and were interested only in helping to build independent African nations with rising living standards for their people.[3]

My effort to persuade Nasser to take a less belligerent stance in regard to Jordan and Saudi Arabia was less successful. Nasser said these were reactionary regimes which were doomed to collapse and that he would continue to "reply" to their attacks on him. He was interested but not convinced by my suggestion that the place to prove that he was a genuine revolutionary was in the U.A.R. itself; only if he could bring a greater measure of economic and social justice to his own people, I said, could he firmly establish his own credentials.

When I pressed the case for an understanding with Israel at least in regard to the size of their respective military forces (public if possible, but private if for political reasons that was impossible), Nasser was again polite but adamant. His own military, he said, would never accept such an agreement; if he should even suggest the possibility, he would be thrown out.

Thus I succeeded in my most immediate task and, not surprisingly, failed in the other two. A small economic mission headed by the distinguished economist, Edward Mason of Harvard, visited the U.A.R. a few weeks later and worked out a limited economic agreement largely involving wheat shipments. This, I thought, was essential as evidence of our good faith in respect to Nasser's assurance that he would relax his pressure on the Congo.

The night I left Cairo I wrote some brief comments about Nasser in my notebook: "The Middle East impresses me as a madhouse, with Nasser one of the few Arab leaders with whom it is possible to talk and reason. In spite of his irresponsible position in regard to Israel, he may be the only Arab leader with enough mass support to make the concessions which will ultimately be required if there is ever to be a settlement."

In Addis Ababa, the capital of Ethiopia, I met Steb, who had flown earlier from Washington to Nigeria, where our youngest son, Sam, and his wife, Nancy, were teaching school. Steb had divided her ten-day stay between Ibadan, where Nancy was awaiting the arrival of what

3. The U.A.R.'s disruptive activities in the Congo were, in fact, curtailed.

turned out to be Eve, our third granddaughter, and Ilorin, where Sam was teaching. On the way to Nigeria she had visited three of our other West African embassies; Ambassadors Phil Kaiser in Senegal, Bill Attwood in Guinea and Leon Poullada in Togo were old friends and eager for a firsthand account of my recent adventures in Washington.

Steb's luggage had been lost somewhere along the way, and for the remainder of our trip she lived in borrowed clothing. This, she discovered, had certain advantages; when we left one place, she simply returned what she had borrowed and proceeded on her way with no luggage to pack.

In Addis Ababa I acted as chairman of the U.S. delegation to the United Nations Conference on African economic affairs. The increased degree of sophistication among the African delegates was most impressive in view of the short time African leaders had had to adjust to their awesome political, economic and social problems. When we first visited Africa in 1955, African planners were primarily concerned with such status symbols as nuclear power plants, steel mills and airports. Now their emphasis was largely on education, followed by agricultural development, with industrial growth where it should be, as an outgrowth of the other two.

We emerged from the Conference with spectacularly increased goodwill from the Africans, more because of Soviet mistakes than anything else. In the usual alphabetical order, I was scheduled to speak just before the chairman of the Soviet delegation and, knowing that he undoubtedly had a prefabricated speech written and cleared by the Soviet Foreign Office, I addressed my remarks directly to him.

Let both nations, I suggested—Soviet and American—pledge to keep the Cold War out of Africa. We Americans were prepared to work as partners with the U.S.S.R. to improve the lot of the African people who had just emerged from colonial control; as we saw it, it was our common responsibility and privilege as developed industrial nations to hold out a helping hand.

This produced an extremely warm response from the otherwise all-African audience, and the Soviet chairman then rose rather hesitantly, pulled a speech from his pocket and, in bitter, classic Cold War language, launched into a tirade against the "American imperialists," "Wall Street warmongers" and the like. The contrast between the two presentations, one following directly after the other, was dramatic, and my Soviet colleague was embarrassed; so much so that later in the evening he quietly took me aside to assure me that none of his remarks had been directed at me personally.

I had two long talks with the Emperor of Ethiopia, the "Lion of

Judah," whom I had come to know quite well during several previous visits. Like the Shah, I found the Emperor concerned with economic and social reform, but even more concerned with military power, in spite of the fact that he faced no significant military threat within fifteen hundred miles. Unhappily, here as in many other countries, U.S. policies had encouraged such thinking.

Haile Selassie and I discussed the question of Ethiopia's national priorities, and I felt that I made a considerable impression. Although his people were particularly deprived and backward, I pointed out that he was investing far larger sums on military defense than on education and public health. Within a few years, I said, Ethiopia would be lagging further and further behind those African nations which were putting first things first.

Instead of seeking costly planes and tanks as a thinly disguised "payment" for the use of our communications center on the Ethiopian coast of the Red Sea, would it not be wiser to ask us for a fair rental for the use of this area in the form of annual cash payments that he could invest in education for his people? To this approach the Emperor, after some initial misgivings, gradually worked up a considerable enthusiasm.

The most impressive element in the Ethiopian situation, we thought, was the emergence of sizable groups of Western-educated, patriotic, committed and impatient young people who were beginning to come forward in the government services and the professions. When we first visited Ethiopia in 1955, there had been scarcely a dozen college graduates in the entire country; now there were several hundred. They were eager for progress and likely to become an increasingly important political factor.

From Addis Ababa we flew directly to India. We found Nehru disillusioned by the Chinese and cautiously optimistic about India's economic prospects. He was greatly attracted to Kennedy and asserted on several occasions and in different contexts that he hoped our government would avoid becoming involved in Southeast Asia, where "America's ability to influence events is and always will be strictly limited." He had high praise for Ambassador Kenneth Galbraith.

Before going on to Thailand we stopped for a few days in Pakistan. I knew President Ayub Khan as a charming, Western-oriented Sandhurst military man with, unhappily, little understanding of Asia or its people. During our discussion he was almost as contemptuous of his own East Bengalis (to whom he referred as "they") as he was of the Indians and the Afghans. His insensitivity and even arrogance in discussing the United States and President Kennedy were breathtaking.

As we talked I began to wonder if Ayub Khan had not become a greater obstacle to the development of an enlightened U.S. policy in Asia than Chiang Kai-shek. The political inadequacies of the Generalissimo were becoming increasingly understood in Washington, while Ayub Khan with his British charm was still managing to confuse a great many influential American policy-makers.

When Secretary Dulles signed the U.S.-Pakistan arms agreement in 1954, he placed a massive supply of American weapons in the hands of an irresponsible "ally" whose political views were more often than not in conflict with our own.

One encouraging factor in Pakistan was a significant improvement in the economic situation to which a group of Harvard University economists headed by my former OPA associate, Dick Gilbert, were making a major contribution. But it was difficult to see how a politically astute *nonmilitary* successor could develop the power and influence ever to oust Ayub Khan and establish a democratic government.

We next visited Thailand for a few days, where I received much the same impression I had had on previous visits. My report to the White House and State Department included the following comment: "A relatively prosperous, happy people, who sooner or later will come to see that the American presence in their country is more likely to act as a lightning rod to Communism rather than as a shield."

We then spent a few days in Cambodia, which I described in my report as

> quite prosperous, with broad-scale land ownership, good soil, plenty of water, an attractive people, and above all the determination to remain free.
>
> The Cambodian Army is built more or less along the lines of our own army engineers.[4] It devotes much of its energies to building roads, schools, clinics, with antiguerrilla measures thrown in for good measure. As a consequence Communist guerrillas have been almost eliminated in Cambodia, and I am confident it could not be brought into the Communist orbit except by overt aggression by North Vietnam or China.
>
> Sihanouk, although difficult to deal with, is politically astute, with a sense of showmanship and patriotism which endears him to most of his people. If only there were a Sihanouk in each of the four Southeast Asian countries that used to be known as French Indo-China,[5] I believe this area would be far more stable than it is today.

Sihanouk gave us the red-carpet treatment, with American flags

4. It was largely trained by General Edward C. D. Sherrer of the U.S. Army.
5. Laos, Cambodia, North and South Vietnam.

along the boulevards and an official dinner followed by a performance by the magnificent Royal Cambodian Ballet.

In Phnom Penh I spent many hours studying the plans for the development of the Mekong River which flows through or borders on Laos, Thailand, Cambodia and South Vietnam. This project not only had enormous promise for the generation of electrical power, irrigation and improved navigation, but could someday be a decisive factor in bringing these countries together. We flew up the Mekong from Phnom Penh as far as the Laotian border in a small plane at a height of only two or three hundred feet to see some of the proposed dam and power sites. We also spent a day at the vast Hindu temples at Angkor Wat in northern Cambodia, which I had never seen but which Steb had visited thirty years before. They were overwhelming.

From Phnom Penh, Steb and I flew in an Air Force plane to Manila, where I had extended talks with President Macapagal and Vice President Palaez. Both of these men were cordial but, even more important, frank. While the foreign policy of the Philippines, they said, would continue to be friendly to the United States, they were determined to present themselves in Asia as genuine Asians and not as "Asian Uncle Toms."

I agreed that their capacity to contribute to a peaceful and stable Asia would depend not so much on what we Americans thought or said about them but on their own ability to communicate effectively with the Indonesians, Malays, Burmese and other Asians—as fellow Asians. Macapagal gave us a very pleasant dinner at the President's palace.

We left early the following morning for the Philippine city of Baguio, where the Regional Conference of U.S. Ambassadors to East Asian Countries was held. Steb and I had forgotten how beautiful Baguio was. When we were last there, it was in the rainy season and most of the mountains were obscured. This time it was beautifully clear and cool. It was the general impression of those of us who had attended all of the regional Ambassadorial Conferences that the one at Baguio was the best organized.

Averell Harriman and I chaired the Conference together, and since as usual we were in agreement on all essential points, it worked out effectively. Harriman's bluntness in discussing our mistakes in East Asia in general and China in particular and on the need to assume control of our own policies in the future was refreshing, although one or two members of the Old China Hands Club who were still stationed in the area (I believe wrongly) looked a bit startled.

After five days in Baguio we flew to Tokyo via Okinawa, where we stopped for a few hours. I found our vast military base there depressing, located as it was in the middle of an alien society in which the adjustment problems appeared intense and very poorly handled.

During our four days in Tokyo I had an opportunity for long fruitful discussions with Ambassador Ed Reischauer about a subject which I felt then, and do now, to be of crucial importance to the future of Asia: the need for an all-Asian consensus or association free of U.S., Soviet or Chinese control, with Australia, Japan and India as its eventual base. With Ambassador Reischauer I also visited the Foreign Minister and other officials. I met informally with the American press and on the last day held a conference with the Japanese press in the course of which I indiscreetly asserted that "in my personal opinion" it was unrealistic to assume that China belonged to Taiwan or that Taiwan belonged to China; each, I said, should be considered separate from the other. The next day the Generalissimo not unexpectedly expressed his strong dissent.

Our return to Washington from this extensive and generally successful trip was in many ways difficult. Because Steb and I had accumulated over the years an extraordinary amount of goodwill in Asia and in much of Africa, we felt a sense of security and confidence there in our ability actually to do something about the problems which confronted us.

In contrast, Washington was like a cold bath on a January morning; we were quickly made aware of the dead-handed grasp of the bureaucracy, the unwillingness of all but a few top leaders to consider old problems in fresh terms, or even soberly to discuss impending problems, which, it was assumed, could be expected to go away if only they were left alone.

There were, however, two encouraging notes: first, the unusually warm response I received following my speech at the Press Club in which I reported on my trip; and second, the fact that I received a prompt call from the President, who asked me to come to give him my impressions and recommendations on the following day.

Our discussion was long and relaxed, and once again I was impressed by his extraordinary mind and how quickly he grasped complex facts and figures. He was particularly pleased at what I believed to be my success in convincing both the Shah of Iran and Emperor Haile Selassie of Ethiopia that it was most unlikely that further requests for U.S. military assistance would be acted upon favorably, and that the interests of their two countries would be better served in any event by an equivalent amount of money for building dams, fertilizer plants and the like.

But my "success" turned out to be illusory. When first the Shah and then a mission from Ethiopia arrived in Washington a few months later, they were clearly resigned to this switch in the nature of U.S. assistance and ready to accept it. However, the Shah, reasoning that there was no harm in making one more try, asked the Pentagon for new supersonic planes and, instead of getting the turndown that he expected after his talk with me, was told that his request would be granted. The Ethiopians, to their surprise, also received a favorable answer.

This goes to show that within the vast expanse of the United States Government the most misguided policies generate a momentum of their own which even senior officials, presumably speaking for the President himself, find it difficult, if not impossible, to stop.

CHAPTER 30

FOREIGN ECONOMIC ASSISTANCE

UPON MY RETURN from Asia I discussed with my personal staff, almost all of whom had decided to stay with me, how we could contribute most effectively in my new role. We concluded that we should select situations of particular importance in which our current foreign policies were failing to meet our objectives and develop precise recommendations for improvement. It would then be my task to persuade our busy and harried President, and the preoccupied State Department, to consider them carefully and to put them into effect.

For a number of reasons we decided to start with the foreign aid program, and particularly economic assistance. For ten years this program had suffered from lack of competent leadership and realistic operating standards. In the 1950's Kennedy and I had often discussed the need for a totally different set of objectives and operating procedures. He was particularly interested in my ideas on the process of economic growth and its political implications which I had developed during my service in India and later in my travels and studies in Africa and Latin America. I believe that this common interest was one of the reasons why he asked me to become his chief adviser on foreign policy before his nomination.

In the late 1940's discussions with a remarkable Chinese development expert, James Y. C. Yen, a protégé of Dr. Sun Yat-sen, father of the Chinese Democratic Revolution, gave me my first insights into the importance of a rural political base for economic growth in a developing nation. Dr. Sun's objective was to assure every Chinese cultivator the right to work his own land and to receive the benefits of his efforts. Although Dr. Sun was blocked by the entrenched feudal land-

379

owners who in the 1920's dominated most of rural China, James Y. C. Yen was able in the 1930's to establish a somewhat similar integrated rural development involving some twenty million people in South China.[1]

Here, I began to see, was the key to economic growth and ultimately to political stability in the developing countries. After gaining firsthand experience in rural development in India in 1951–53 I supplemented this experience by a special study of the Japanese rural development which had preceded the postwar development of the modern Japanese industrial society.

At the end of World War II Japan's cities were devastated, communications disrupted, the people demoralized, and industrial capacity was cut to a fraction of prewar levels. An outmoded land tenure system, under which more than one-third of all the rural families owned no land at all, had added to the sense of hopelessness.

In 1946, at the urging of General MacArthur and some astute members of his staff, the Japanese Government launched a land reform program designed, in the words of the legislation, "to insure that those who till the land of Japan shall henceforth have an equal opportunity to enjoy the fruits of their labor." Between 1946 and 1949 the Japanese Government established a ceiling of seven and a half acres as the limit that could be owned and cultivated by a single family. All holdings above that level were purchased by the government. Absentee landlords were required to sell all their land.

The government then resold this land on easy terms to four million tenant farmers and landless laborers. As a result, 94 percent of all rural families in Japan became for the first time landowners in their own right. This gave them a new sense of hope, dignity and, above all, a clear incentive and opportunity to improve their lot.

Given the importance of a solid rural base in any developing country, it is interesting to note that among the slowest to grasp its dynamics have been the Marxist Russians and the capitalistic Americans. Marx was largely concerned with the urban areas; he devoted only one sentence of his 1848 *Manifesto* to problems of agriculture.

Both Lenin and Mao Tse-tung used land ownership as a political instrument to gain power. But because of the political difficulties in imposing an authoritarian regime in a land of peasants who have tasted the

1. Following the defeat of the Japanese in 1945, Dr. Yen unsuccessfully urged Chiang Kai-shek to launch a nationwide rural development program. According to Dr. Yen, the Generalissimo told him, "As soon as we have defeated the Red Armies, we shall move forward rapidly with your program." To which Dr. Yen responded, "You will never win the war on the battlefield until you first win the struggle in the rice fields. If you do not now bring new hope and opportunities to the peasants, you will never defeat the Red Army." Within four short years Dr. Yen's warning had been fulfilled.

benefits of owning their own farms, both the U.S.S.R. and China soon reverted to large farms, dependent on expensive machinery, manned by thousands of workers with little personal incentive to increase production and in no position to question the system itself.

American farmers in this century have depended largely on machinery and large land holdings, for quite different reasons. The competition for labor with urban factories has given American farmers no alternative but to introduce large amounts of machinery to cut their labor costs per acre. This in turn has placed a premium on large land holdings, where the machinery can be used most effectively. In the U.S.S.R. the effort to free more workers for industry has led logically to more mechanization.

The first thing that an American farm expert in Asia has to learn is that the function of farm machinery, by and large, is not to raise output per acre but to allow more work to be done by fewer people. When there is an oversupply of labor, as in most Asian nations, agricultural machinery has its limits. And I suspect that Soviet agricultural experts are in a similar position. In any event, I can vouch for the fact that most Russian and American experts in Asia find it hard to believe that in Japan, where the average farm is less that three acres, and in Taiwan, with the average farm around four acres, the output per acre is larger than in most of heavily mechanized rural America or in the U.S.S.R.

From my experience in economic development over the years, I have summarized the process by which I believe sound progress can take place in a developing country:

1. Recognition by the government of the primary importance of agriculture. In a crowded country such as Japan this means small, efficient farms owned by the cultivators themselves, which serve to increase their personal sense of involvement and security.

2. Guaranteed price levels for all important agricultural crops to assure continuing incentives for high agricultural production.

3. Development of marketing cooperatives to assure more efficient distribution and to help hold down prices to the consumers.

4. Easily available credit at low interest rates to enable all cultivators to purchase hybrid seeds, fertilizer, pesticides, improved tools, to dig wells or otherwise provide an assured flow of irrigation water, and for increased electrification in the rural areas.

5. As farm production and farm incomes rise and the demand for consumer goods increases, generous tax incentives to encourage the building of small factories in nearby towns. These factories provide jobs for unemployed landless laborers and part-time employment for cultivators when their work on the farms is completed. At this stage the

introduction of *small* tractors enables the cultivators to reduce their time in the fields and thereby to earn more wages in nearby factories.

6. Incentives to expand heavy urban industry, whether through the public or private sector, as the demand for steel, electric power, machinery, improved transport and the like grows.

Closely related to the question of output—either agricultural or industrial—is the relationship between increasing production and economic justice created by that production. Most economists agree that the rate of economic growth is dependent on the accumulation of capital and the reinvestment of these capital savings to expand production further. Expanding economic justice is obviously impossible without expanding production. But some conservative economists argue that a really determined effort to bring a wider distribution of the newly produced wealth will bring the process of growth to a dead stop. Nevertheless, if a society is to develop an acceptable degree of political cohesion, a reasonable balance must be developed between the two objectives.

The politics of economic growth is further complicated by the fact that as living standards rise and people become more secure, the pressure for even more rapid progress grows in geometric proportions. The following words of Alexis de Tocqueville, written in 1835, are still relevant:

> Only great ingenuity can save a prince who undertakes to give relief to his subjects after long oppression. The sufferings that are endured patiently as being inevitable, become intolerable the moment it appears that there might be an escape. Reform then only serves to reveal more clearly what still remains oppressive and now all the more unbearable; the suffering, it is true, has been reduced, but one's sensitivity has become more acute.

This simple but often neglected fact is, in my opinion, rapidly becoming one of the most important political challenges of our times. The thought that economic growth, instead of creating political stability, may actually lead to more political turbulence is a new and, to many privileged people, a disturbing one. There is, I believe, only one valid answer. Not only must production rise, but more and more people must become personally involved in the process of growth and benefit directly from this growth.

The response of national and local leaders confronted with the inevitable hope-inspired protests should not be to retreat in fear, but to redouble their efforts to encourage and help the people to become active participants in the struggle to conquer poverty and to lessen injustice.

It was Kennedy's intention, following his election, to launch a new approach to foreign economic assistance based on these concepts. The first step was the selection of an outstanding administrator, and he asked for my recommendations.

I first suggested Harlan Cleveland, Dean of Syracuse University's Maxwell School of Public Administration, who had the necessary administrative ability and a keen understanding of the principles of economic growth which I have just described. But this did not work out. Adlai Stevenson, our Ambassador to the United Nations, argued that Cleveland was even more urgently needed to fill the slot of Assistant Secretary for International Organizational Affairs. After some delay because of differences that Cleveland had with Kennedy's political staff during the campaign, it was agreed that Cleveland should be offered the Assistant Secretary post, which he promptly accepted.

We finally settled on Henry R. Labouisse, an administrator with broad international experience in economic development who had formerly served with distinction as head of the United Nations Relief and Works Agency for Palestine Refugees.

A few months later, in March, 1961, President Kennedy sent a foreign aid proposal to Congress, which called for both a reorganization of AID, integration with other aid-giving agencies, and also the establishment of a higher standard of performance by the recipient countries. I was more directly responsible for shaping the content and drafting the language for this message than for any other Kennedy speech.

Kennedy stressed that our objective "should be not to buy friends, but to help create independent nations capable of standing on their own feet and of making their own free choices." He also rejected the practice of using our assistance funds to prop up repressive, totalitarian regimes, and urged Congress to "look beyond economic growth to the creation of societies offering a broadening measure of individual opportunity and justice."

The President's message emphasized that in all devoloping nations rural programs were of primary importance, not only because of the need for increased agricultural production, but because most people lived on the land. Of particular importance was his recommendation that "those nations which have the talent and determination to achieve rapid integrated economic and political growth should be given highest priority."

In October, 1961, when Congress approved the President's proposed reorganization and endorsed his plea that our objective henceforth should be to foster planned national development—not to bolster the political power of right-wing generals—we felt that at long last genuine progress was being made.

The authorization of new "performance" criteria as the basis for the distribution of economic assistance reflected this growing understanding by Congress that factors other than Cold War competition with the Soviet Union or China would henceforth govern the work of the new Agency. The 1961 Act provided that:

> Assistance will be based upon sound plans and programs, be directed toward the social as well as economic aspects of economic development; be responsive to the efforts of the recipient countries to mobilize their own resources and help themselves; be cognizant of the external and internal pressures which hamper their growth and emphasize long range development assistance as the primary instrument of such growth.

In regard to rural development as an integral part of the national growth process, it stated:

> When the President determines that the economy of any country is in major part an agrarian economy, emphasis shall be placed on programs which reach the people who are engaged in agrarian pursuits or who live in the villages or rural areas.

To establish the status of these principles as official American doctrine, both to Washington and to the developing nations, I made several major speeches in my role as Under Secretary. Two of these were in Latin America, where in many areas the barriers to economic progress and social justice were most firmly fixed.

In October, 1961, in Mexico City I compared the American political, economic and social revolution with the revolution that had transformed Mexico in the 1920's and 1930's. I expressed the hope that similar efforts to bring new opportunities, high living standards and a greater sense of dignity would spread throughout Latin America to benefit the exploited and the forgotten.

Pointing to the fact that only 1.5 percent of the people in Latin America (those who owned fifteen thousand acres or more each) actually possessed half of all the agricultural land in the entire continent, I stressed the need for sweeping land reform, tax reforms, rural public health measures and the like.

"Poverty," I said, "must be recognized as a form of tyranny in itself; economic development as the liberating force. Yet economic development will fail in its purposes if its benefits go primarily to a wealthy elite."

I expected a negative response, at least from officials of the government and those with a stake in the status quo, but the reaction was quite different. The following excerpts from a USIS official report of Mexico's reactions to my speech and to private talks with high Mexican officials reflect this reaction:

> Embassy officers have been impressed (and a little bit mystified) by the across the board favorable reaction to the Under Secretary's speech.

Not even the "fat cats" have dared to attack it publicly, even by insinuation.

The speech pleased the church, the progressives, the nationalists and the super patriots. What is particularly mystifying to some is the whole-hearted approval of the speech by those press organs directly controlled by the Mexican Government.

We rather incline toward the explanation that Mexico reacted favorably to a frank, blunt, liberal speech that said things that no American official, to our knowledge, has ever said publicly in this country.

It is interesting that even the influential Marxist-oriented magazine *Siempre* had a favorable editorial entitled "At Last They Have Understood Us."

A few months later I followed this up with a somewhat similar speech to a large audience of businessmen in Bogotá, Colombia. I stressed that their natural political allies were not the wealthy feudal landlords, among whom I knew many in my audience had close friends, but rather the masses of peasants in the rural areas. Indeed, I said, all that they as businessmen had in common with the rural landlords was their ability to send their sons to Princeton, Cornell or the University of Chicago and to buy their suits from Brooks Brothers.

The rural landlords, I said, with some notable exceptions, felt that it was in their interest to hold back education, to delay improvement in transportation systems and otherwise to keep the peasants who tilled their land ignorant, unprotesting and politically apathetic. This I pointed out, was dramatically contrary to the interests of the businessmen, since it was more prosperous, awakened peasants who alone could provide the mass markets to purchase in quantity the goods which the businessmen produced. I concluded that the businessman and the peasant had much to gain by working together as political allies for improved education, increased farm income, modern health facilities and increased per capita income.

"Social and political reforms," I asserted, "must go hand in hand with economic growth. Otherwise increased output may simply widen the gap between the rich and the poor, increase social tensions and create the ingredients for a political explosion."

In closing I added the following warning:

Let me say with deep conviction that the United States Government does not intend to subsidize the status quo in Latin America or anywhere else. My country cannot properly be expected to support governments which are unable, unwilling or unprepared to take hard decisions which are essential if our common economic, social and political objectives are to be secured.

In saying these things I hoped I was, in fact, speaking for President

Kennedy and the new Administration. At least I had proved that an American official could still speak his mind in forthright, liberal terms without turning himself into a target for criticism and cries of "Gringo go home."[2] But I was concerned by the apathetic Congressional reaction to the 1962 foreign aid appropriation bill. As I studied the debates and talked to my former colleagues in Congress, I became convinced that a major reason for this lack of support was the continued reluctance of many decision-makers in AID genuinely to accept and to carry out the new concepts contained in the President's message, the 1961 foreign assistance act and my own speeches.

Labouisse had been asked to undertake too much, in operating the existing program while trying to develop a complete plan of reorganization, and a few months after his appointment he asked to be relieved.[3] This added to the difficulties in changing the nature of our foreign assistance.

Soon after the 1961 Act had passed Congress I had urged the President to proceed at once to establish specific criteria reflecting his interpretation of the legislation and then to direct the program's administrators consistently to apply these criteria in the future to all foreign economic assistance projects. These criteria, I felt, would serve much the same purpose as the wage and price ceiling criteria which we had developed in the Office of Price Administration during the war. They would relieve pressures on AID officials (often generated within Congress itself) to use our economic assistance funds to buy off anti-American politicians in the recipient country or to put "our men" in key posts, and enable the AID staff to concentrate their energies where they belonged: on the dynamics of economic and social development.

In spite of the urgings of myself and others, many AID officials seemed still unable or unwilling to distinguish between political pressures for economic assistance generated by the Cold War conflict and the genuine economic and social needs of nation-building which were their primary responsibility.

One solution to this problem, I thought, might be to switch all AID policy decisions which involved political questions from the regional or country desks, which were staffed with technical people with little or no political experience, to the AID administrator or the Secretary of State.

2. Unhappily, American policy in Latin America has continued to fall far short of the objectives which I outlined with such confidence. We still seem to be more comfortable in the political company of the generals and the landowners. Unless there is a miraculous change in U.S. policy in the early 1970's, revolution, probably most of it violent, or a further estrangement from the "Colossus of the North" seems inevitable.

3. He is now administering UNICEF.

This would underscore the political nature of these decisions and avoid confusing them with the economic development criteria which AID should alone be concerned with. It would be better yet, I felt, if all economic assistance funds which Congress appropriated for purely political reasons could be financed from a special contingency budget and thereby shut off entirely from the decision-making process of AID.

To emphasize the Administration's genuine commitment to the principles the President had proposed and Congress had accepted, I prepared a memorandum recommending a set of specific criteria for the allocation of AID funds, and distributed it widely throughout the Administration. In this memorandum I proposed that AID should, first, publicly reiterate the economic and social nature of its objectives and, second, spell out precisely the working standards which would henceforth guide its decisions. The series of questions I posed closely followed those I had spelled out in a speech on the floor of the House of Representatives in 1959. The answers to these questions, I felt, would help provide a solid, nonpolitical basis for granting economic assistance:

1. Does the prospective recipient government have the ability to maintain internal stability and to carry out a comprehensive economic and social program?

2. Has it prepared a long-range national economic development plan to allocate effectively both its own internal resources and its foreign aid?

3. Is it taking steps to distribute its tax burden more equitably?

4. Does it have a reasonably efficient, honest corps of public administrators?

5. Is it generally committed to an effective land reform program and to an integrated effort to bolster the rural sector of its economy?

6. Is it committed to an integrated approach to rural development involving agricultural extension services, a price support program, cooperative marketing arrangements and readily available credit?

7. Has it set forth realistic objectives in national housing, health, education and population control, with pragmatic plans for putting them into effect?

8. Is it generally favorable to private investment (outside of utilities, transport, national resources, heavy industry and other investments more suited to government investment)?

9. Has it set up firm foreign exchange controls to halt excessive luxury imports and flights of capital abroad?

10. Does it recognize the crucial importance of population control?

11. Does it have substantial public support?

I recognized that there would be a number of nations that we would want to assist which could not meet all these criteria. But the answers about the applicant countries would, I believed, suggest distinct categories of nations and clarify the kinds of assistance we should make available to each.

These suggested standards for allocating assistance were stern. But such measures were now required, I felt, if our reorganized assistance program was to secure and hold the support of Congress and fulfill its critically important function of nation-building.

"The more clearly these standards are understood by the recipient countries," I wrote, "the more closely they are coordinated with the policies of international lending agencies and other capital exporting nations, and the more consistent we are in applying them, the less will be the pressures on us to violate them and the more effective the results."

I pointed out that such criteria would have to be handled with great sensitivity and that even so they would be resented by proud new nations on the ground that they represented interference in their domestic affairs. Nevertheless, I felt that the United States Government should clearly draw a line between economic standards, which are justified, and political conditions, which are not. Economic criteria, tactfully and discreetly handled, are the best insurance that our funds are not spent on useless monuments or unfinished stadiums, but actually reach the people who should benefit. Multilateral aid through the UN and its related agencies should, I felt, be increased steadily and eventually carry most if not all of the load. But neither our government nor most others were as yet prepared to appropriate fully adequate funds for these international agencies.

My sole purpose in proposing these criteria was to assure that whatever funds our government provided as economic assistance were put to better use, an approach I had been persistently advocating for the last ten years. However, a number of people, including both friends and foes, interpreted my recommendations as a proposal for a reduction in foreign economic assistance. This misinterpretation, ironically, produced the first favorable coverage I had ever received in my entire public career from certain conservative newspapers.

The Chicago *Tribune*, which for twenty years had failed to find any good in me or my proposals, said it was now willing to overlook "Mr. Bowles' past if his conversion is genuine, and if he can persuade other stubborn backers of foreign aid that much of it has been a total loss."

The New York *Journal American*, which had been equally critical, asserted editorially: "What Chester hath done is to write a memo completely reversing his give-give-give-give-away position on foreign aid."

However, most commentators understood that my proposals, far from suggesting a cutback in the quantity of aid we distributed, actually sought more aid to those nations which could most effectively use it.

Perhaps the most understanding comment came from the Washington *Post*, which said: "Mr. Bowles' proposals indicate the direction in which the program must move in the future if the Administration is to avoid the kind of debacle it has just experienced in Congress."

The reaction abroad was not altogether happy. In an early confidential version of my memorandum I listed certain nations as examples of those which I felt, because of their own economic ineptness, failed to qualify. Inevitably, this unedited version reached the press, and soon I was being chastised by various right-wing governments because of my comments on their performance and the low classification I gave them as recipients of assistance. But like most such flaps it soon blew over as "high-classification" countries began to make their voices heard.

The President repeatedly made it clear to me that in all this effort I had his full personal support, and I believe he meant what he said. Judging from the strong public approval that my proposals received in the press and in Congress, Kennedy's public support of them would, I believe, have been not only helpful in making the program more effective but politically helpful as well. Nevertheless, whatever the reasons, the clear ringing endorsement from the White House of my interpretation of the President's economic assistance objectives which I had hoped for never materialized.

In April, 1963, when David Bell, a Harvard economist, with four years of practical administrative experience in Pakistan, moved in as Director, the foreign assistance program was, for the first time in its existence, under truly professional management. In 1967 he was replaced by his equally able deputy, William S. Gaud, with another outstanding individual, Maurice J. Williams, as his second-in-command.

POSTSCRIPT

Ten years later the questions are often asked: How successful have our foreign economic assistance programs been? Have they been worth the cost? Where have they succeeded and where have they failed?

The answers are complex; indeed, almost anything you say about the AID program, good or bad, is true. However, I believe a few principles can be stated with confidence.

1. In several countries the program has been successful largely because of the massive amounts of money which have been invested in it. In South Korea and Taiwan, for instance, a high rate of economic growth has been achieved which would not have been possible otherwise.

2. In a second group of countries, notably India and Pakistan, there has also been significant progress with a far lower investment per capita (aid to India, for instance, at its peak level was less than $2 per capita compared to annual inputs of more than $100 per capita in some countries which, for good reason or bad, were given high priorities).

American economic assistance even at this relatively low per capita level played a major and likely decisive role in enabling India and Pakistan to achieve their present rather encouraging rate of economic growth.

3. In a number of other countries U.S. economic assistance has been neither massive enough nor sufficiently well planned and directed to achieve its objectives.

On balance I believe that well-planned economic assistance in adequate amounts from the United States and other developed nations in close cooperation with the World Bank can make a major and in many cases decisive contribution to the stability and progress of those developing nations which are able and willing to use such assistance effectively.

CHAPTER 31

A FRESH LOOK AT CHINA

DURING THE 1950's Jack Kennedy often expressed to me the view that American policy in regard to China was unrealistic, and must ultimately be changed. In February, 1960, shortly after he asked me to become his foreign policy adviser, we had a long discussion on the subject in my Congressional office. I had just completed the final draft of an article for the April issue of *Foreign Affairs* entitled "The China Problem Reconsidered," in which I challenged the folklore that still accepted Chiang Kai-shek as President of China and urged a reappraisal of our relations with both the Peking and the Taiwanese governments. Since this was a complex and controversial subject and as Kennedy's foreign policy adviser anything I wrote would now be interpreted as reflecting Kennedy's view, I wanted to be sure that we were in general agreement.

Kennedy read the draft and endorsed it without reservation. What I wrote, he said, needed saying; adding that this article by me at this particular moment "might open at least a few minds to the possibilities."

In 1960 most Americans still saw China through the eyes of the thousands of missionaries who had gone there in the nineteenth and early twentieth centuries to build universities and establish hospitals. When China's revolutionary consciousness erupted under Sun Yat-sen and forced the collapse of the Manchu Dynasty in 1911, it was the ideas of Western democracy, as interpreted by these missionaries, which largely inspired Dr. Sun's program of economic and social reform and modernization. "I am a coolie and the son of a coolie," he declared proudly. "I was born with the poor and I am still poor. My sympathy has always been with the struggling masses."

As President of the new China Republic, Dr. Sun had turned first to America for capital assistance and technical advice in building a modern nation. It was only in 1923 after he had been repeatedly rebuffed in Washington and London by bankers and government officials to whom China was as remote as the moon that he had turned reluctantly to Moscow.

Chiang Kai-shek, who assumed power after Dr. Sun died in 1925, gave democracy in China a second chance. Many of Chiang's achievements were impressive, but for the majority of the Chinese the grinding hardship of peasant life continued. The relatively meager gains which were evident in some areas only raised their expectations and increased their restlessness. In 1938, under pressure from the invading Japanese, Chiang had been forced to abandon the coastal areas and take refuge in Chungking, far into the interior. Cut off from the more liberal views of the Western-oriented Chinese in the large cities, he came under the influence of the feudal landlords, who were out of step with the awakening Chinese people.

This opened the door wide for Communist political leaders to recruit millions of young men for the Red Armies with their version of Lenin's revolutionary slogan "land to the tillers": the simple promise that every peasant soldier would be given his own piece of land when the war against the "imperialists" had finally been won.

American policy remained tied to the destiny of Chiang Kai-shek for several reasons. First, we deplored the Japanese invasion and sympathized with China's efforts to defend itself. Second, the missionaries, who had great influence on our China policy, remained convinced that with all his defects there was no alternative to Chiang (his wife was a Christian and later he became one). And third, the Generalissimo and his government on Taiwan created one of the most effective political lobbies of all time to influence the American people, press and Congress.

As the Communists continued to make gains throughout the 1940's, the United States became increasingly associated in the minds of most Chinese with the reactionary political elements under whom they had suffered for so long. As a result, in December, 1949, when Mao Tse-tung and his Red Armies marched into Peking and became masters of China, several incidents occurred, notably the attack on our Consulate General in Mukden, which served to increase bitterness on both sides. When the Chinese forces in October, 1952, crossed the Yalu River to attack the UN Army in Korea, American policy became increasingly militant, and serious proposals to "unleash" the Generalissimo against the mainland became part of our official posture. The fact that no Nationalist attack on the mainland could hope to succeed without major American support, probably including use of nuclear weapons, was lost in the torrent of Cold War oratory.

In 1952 the Republican charge that the Democrats had "lost China" struck a responsive chord with the frustrated voters and contributed significantly to the G.O.P.'s resurgence and to the noxious political development which became known as "McCarthyism"; most opposition leaders were effectively silenced. Under the prodding of Joe McCarthy and other ardent supporters of the Generalissimo, most Americans became convinced that the Nationalist Government on Formosa was the mainland's legal government, that the Chinese seat in the UN General Assembly and Security Council belonged to the Nationalist regime, and that we must relentlessly oppose the admission of Communist China to the community of nations, even though almost one-quarter of all mankind lived there.

Throughout the 1950's an almost mythical political power was attributed to the "China lobby" with its claim to be a "Committee of One Million." Its effective lobbying made any reappraisal of our relationships with Chiang Kai-shek and the mainland a matter so controversial that only a few foolhardy souls within the government, like myself, dared even to discuss it.

Moreover, many State Department officials still idealized the political relations with China which had developed during the last century. Secretary Hay's Open Door policy in 1900 was remembered with pride as a benevolent effort by the United States to keep the Great Powers from dividing China as they were then dividing Africa, while the humiliating treaties which the British, French and Americans forced the Manchu emperors to sign in the mid-nineteenth century had conveniently been forgotten. These treaties, which among other privileges gave the three powers the right to collect taxes and establish special courts in China, had not been repudiated by the United States Government until two years after Pearl Harbor.

One result of these attitudes was the almost submissive spirit with which our government addressed Chiang's claim to the mainland. Fed by his supporters in Congress, the Administration and the press, Chiang's expectations had become so bloated that it was impossible to deal with him on a rational basis.

Another factor which contributed to the inflexibility of America's approach to Asia through the 1950's was the assumption that "the Communist world" was a monolithic body of some 900 million bellicose likeminded Communists directed by Moscow and stretching from central Germany to the Gulf of Japan.

In October, 1951, when I first discussed world politics with Jawaharlal Nehru in New Delhi, he had expressed the conviction that China and the Soviet Union by the logic of history and the realities of geography were destined sooner or later to come into conflict. Nehru felt that a major mistake of American policy in Asia at the time was our assumption of continuing Chinese-Soviet cooperation into the indefinite future.

This insight opened my mind to the possibility of a fundamental shift in Asian relationships sometime in the future. On many occasions in writings and speeches in the 1950's, I had pointed out these possibilities, and for this "heresy" I had been promptly taken to task. Monolithic Communism, according to the conventional wisdom, was here to stay, and this "wisdom" was deep-rooted. For instance, in 1957 at a symposium on Chinese-Soviet affairs several eminent Sino-Soviet specialists discussed Chinese-Russian relationships for two days without a single reference to the possibility that the Soviet Union and China might someday fail to see eye to eye. However, by June, 1959, a new major political development began to emerge: China and the U.S.S.R., as Nehru had predicted, were developing serious political differences; the so-called "monolithic" Soviet-Chinese bloc was not as monolithic as many had assumed.

Under these circumstances I felt it might now be possible to begin to develop an Asian policy based on the realities. To assume that Chiang Kai-shek was still the ruler of 650 million mainland Chinese was clearly absurd. The Peking Government, although beset with difficulties, had been in firm control of China for more than ten years. Although it would be the ultimate in naïveté to expect our differences with China suddenly to disappear, I felt we should seek quietly and persistently to establish a more normal relationship with the Peking Government if and when the opportunity presented itself.

A first step might be discreetly to explore the possibility of easing restrictions on journalists, scientists, educators and businessmen who might want to travel in China. In its current antagonistic mood, the Peking Government would almost certainly refuse visas to Americans. But at least the onus of barring contact between citizens of the two nations would be lifted from our backs. Within a few years, moreover, it was conceivable that changing conditions might persuade the mainland Chinese to begin gradually to lower their barriers.

On many occasions since 1954, when Secretary of State Dulles decided to sign the SEATO[1] pact, I had argued that the United States could make a far more valuable and historically durable contribution to the security of non-Communist Asia by avoiding promises of American troops and infusions of American military assistance, advisers, planes and bomber pilots.

---

1. The Southeast Asia Treaty Organization consisted of the United Kingdom, France, Australia, New Zealand, Pakistan, Thailand, the Philippines and the United States.

Over the long haul Chinese pressure on their neighbors, and particularly the independent nations of South Asia, could effectively be met only if the large Asian powers—Japan, Australia, India and Indonesia—recognized their common stake in a stable Asia and organized their resources to achieve it.

Although this would take time and indeed might be impossible, the assumption that the United States from a distance of ten thousand miles could organize, control and lead a coalition of lesser Asian powers which could act as an effective military and political "balance" to China was unrealistic. As I saw it, only in the event of a massive aggression by the Chinese Armies should we consider military involvement and then only through the United Nations.

Although I recognized that even a loose informal association of the non-Communist Asian nations to assure their own security and development would take time, I was convinced that as they gained more confidence their growing sense of nationalism would provide a far more effective barrier to Chinese expansion than direct American intervention in their behalf.

Taiwan, I felt, should be regarded as a bona fide independent nation rather than as a temporary refuge for anti-Communist exiles. This would save the Chiang Kai-shek Government the hundreds of thousands of dollars it was spending every year to persuade the American press, Congress and people that it was now capable of re-establishing its position on the mainland if we would only provide the necessary support.

Genuine nationhood would also encourage the democratization of Taiwan's totalitarian political process, which gave most of the power to two million Chinese exiles from the mainland, while virtually ignoring the rights of the more than eight million native Taiwanese. An independent Sino-Formosan nation, I thought, could present to Asia and the world a dramatic contrast between a modernized non-Communist Chinese society, free from mass regimentation, and with an increasing measure of political liberty and economic opportunities for its citizens, on the one hand, and the authoritarian Chinese regime on the mainland, on the other. In building a society the younger generation of Taiwanese and Chinese émigrés from the mainland could, I felt, find a common sense of purpose.

What I was proposing in effect was not a "two China" policy but a "two nation" policy. By making it clear that we had no intention of supporting a Nationalist invasion of the mainland and concentrating on the effective orderly growth of a new, independent Taiwanese nation we would deprive Peking of an excuse for counterhostilities.

I was under no illusion about the difficulties that stood in the way. Not only were there the inflexible positions of Chiang Kai-shek and Mao

Tse-tung, but such complex procedural problems as China's Security Council seat. But it could, I believed, be made the starting point for a comprehensive review of the present means of selecting Security Council members which had been established in 1944. Since France with a population of some fifty million people was entitled to be a permanent member, what about Japan, India and Brazil?

During the Presidential campaign of 1960 Kennedy, who in general agreed with this approach to China which I have described, cautiously challenged some of the sterile political mythology on which our China policies were then based. Nixon quickly accepted the challenge, and unlimited American guarantees to the Nationalist Government on Taiwan promptly became a hot issue. In answer to a newsman's questions during one of the televised debates with Nixon in October, Kennedy outlined a position toward the coastal islands of Quemoy and Matsu, which were still in Chiang Kai-shek's hands, identical to the one in my April *Foreign Affairs* article. While continuing to support our commitment to the independence of the Nationalist regime on Taiwan, he said that the extension of the pledge to include Quemoy and Matsu was an open invitation for Mao Tse-tung to draw us into a military conflict ten thousand miles from our shores.

Vice President Nixon, anxious to counter Kennedy's campaign charges about America's faltering prestige overseas under the Eisenhower Administration, promptly conjured up visions of another Munich. If we should pull back from Quemoy and Matsu, he warned, the Communist Chinese would sooner or later end up in California. For several days, to the undoubted delight of both Chiang Kai-shek and Mao Tse-tung, Nixon and Kennedy exchanged charges of gross irresponsibility, warmongering and appeasement. But gradually their positions became closer, other issues came to the fore, and Quemoy and Matsu faded into the background.

Since Kennedy was elected by an exceedingly narrow margin, he was in no mood once in office to take unnecessary risks. His more cautious advisers, with the support of the State Department's Far Eastern Bureau, persuaded him that any relaxation of the hostile posture of his predecessors toward the Peking regime would be courting political disaster. Although I was still convinced by our earlier discussion that the President was anxious to breathe new life into our China policy, it was apparent that any significant relaxation in our policy would have to await a resounding Kennedy re-election victory in 1964.

Consequently, I was distressed but not surprised when the President asked me, during my confirmation hearings before the Senate Foreign

"Now, Mr. Bowles, Tell Us Just What You Think Is Out Here Beyond The Edge Of The World"

The above cartoon, which appeared at the time of the Senate hearings on my confirmation as Under Secretary of State, reflects the anticipated confrontation between my views on China and those still held by many Senators and Congressmen. © *1961 by Herblock in The Washington Post.*

Relations Committee in late January, 1961, to play down the differences between my ideas about China and the generally accepted wisdom generated by the partisans of Chiang Kai-shek.

Although the China lobby had made an effort to muster Senatorial opposition to my confirmation, the hearings were relaxed and amicable. In response to the inevitable question about the possibility of China's being voted into the UN, I swallowed hard and said, quite accurately, that I saw no imminent likelihood of change in our policy of nonrecognition and nonadmission. During the subsequent questioning I managed to avoid creating any headlines that might underscore the fact that the new Under Secretary and Chiang Kai-shek held widely differing views about the future of the Chinese mainland and of Taiwan.

Nevertheless, I was determined to continue to promote, whenever an opportunity presented itself, the more flexible Asian policy which I had been advocating for many years and which I knew Kennedy in his heart agreed with.

One such initiative involved Mongolia, a strategically important new buffer state on the Manchurian-Siberian frontier which in the spring of 1961 applied for admission to the United Nations. Mongolia, which had a common border with both the U.S.S.R. and China, was a bone of contention between these two nations, each of which sought pre-eminence there. Mongolia's application for membership in the United Nations was approved by the General Assembly and passed on to the Security Council, where I feared it would be vetoed by Nationalist China. However, at the last minute an impasse was averted by persuading the reluctant Generalissimo to abstain on the question, and on October 25, 1961, Mongolia became a member of the UN.

During this period of UN negotiation and maneuver I also pressed for the establishment of a U.S. diplomatic mission in Mongolia and a Mongolian mission in Washington, both of which the Mongolian Government made clear it would welcome. This exchange, I felt, would illustrate that our policies in Asia were no longer dictated by Chiang Kai-shek and at the same time provide us with new insights into an area about which we knew little.

The Far Eastern Bureau vigorously opposed an exchange of ambassadors with Mongolia on the ground that it might be interpreted as a "softening" in our position toward China.[2] Nevertheless, my counter-arguments were at first favorably received, and indeed had the support not only of President Kennedy but also of Secretary Rusk.

But when rumors of the effort to recognize Mongolia as an independent nation reached the China lobby, spearheaded by the "Com-

2. This, of course, was my intention.

mittee of One Million against the Admission of Red China to the UN,"
my support began to disintegrate. Then a few Congressmen applied
the *coup de grâce* by threatening to destroy our foreign economic assistance program. Although, as I pointed out, these individuals had always
opposed foreign assistance anyway, this caused the Administration to
drop the subject entirely.

On two occasions as Under Secretary I also made attempts to soften
the rhetoric used by the United States toward China. In July, 1961,
during a visit to West Africa I asserted at a press conference that among
its evils a Chinese invasion of Formosa "would violate the right of 'self-
determination' of eleven million people living there." However, predictably, the Taipei Government was outraged over my use of the phrase
"self-determination," even in this context, and promptly protested. President Kennedy felt compelled to issue a statement reaffirming American
support of Chiang's sovereignty over the mainland.

A month later in Tokyo I again broached the subject in a press
conference:

> We Americans have felt close and friendly to the Chinese people for
> over a hundred years, and we are unhappy about the block which stands
> between us now. But since the Communist Chinese Government threatens
> the independence of eleven million people in Formosa, I think we took
> the right course, much as we deplore having to take it.
>
> We hope that the day will come when the Chinese Government may
> take a different attitude. The Taiwanese have the second highest living
> standard in Asia. They entertain no desire to live under Communism.
> They seek self-determination. Consequently, we are prepared to defend
> their independence just as we would that of Berlin.

This statement explicitly denied both Chiang's pretentions on the
mainland and Mao's to Formosa. Even though it sought to shift the
burden of the diplomatic impasse from Taipei to Peking, the Nationalist
Chinese were again outraged. A Taiwan newspaper commented:

> This would mean that the U.S. assistance for Taiwan's security is not
> directed to the Chinese Government struggling to recover the lost land,
> but to an independent administration on Taiwan so that it can be free
> from Communist aggression. In supporting the so-called independence on
> Taiwan isn't Bowles advocating two Chinas?
>
> Does this not mean that the U.S. fails to recognize the Free Chinese
> Government as the only lawful government to represent China? Mr.
> Bowles as Under Secretary of the State Department should know this is
> the U.S. policy. His erroneous statement . . . gravely injures American
> prestige and honor. . . .
>
> Although we know that the U.S. foreign policy is decided by President

Kennedy and not by Under Secretary Bowles, we do not think it is good
for the United States when one of her important diplomatic administrators
makes such irresponsible utterances, destroying the mutual confidence
and unity among the allies. . . .

My case for a change in U.S. policy in regard to China and Asia was,
however, given fresh impetus by growing evidence of the split between
China and the U.S.S.R. For many years a flood of Soviet industrial assistance, military equipment and skilled technicians had been steadily
bolstering China's growth rate and, simultaneously, it was assumed, had
been forging unbreakable ideological bonds between the two countries.
But gradually it became evident that China's Great Leap Forward had
failed to materialize, that Soviet technicians were leaving in droves and
that some Soviet loans were being canceled.[3]

In the late 1950's China's economic plans had begun rapidly to out-
run available resources, and the slowdown in Soviet aid compounded its
problems. In 1961 and 1962 China's growing internal economic strains
were intensified by droughts, and the harvests ran far short of their
targets.

In late January, 1962, shortly after I left my post as Under Secretary,
I again discussed with the President our relations with China and found
his interest keen as ever. I reminded him of Lord Castlereagh's plea at
the Vienna Peace Conference in 1815 ("We have," he said, "come here
not to win diplomatic trophies but to return the world to peaceful habits")
and urged that he reject the pressures developing in Congress and the
Administration to take advantage of the weakening Sino-Soviet ties by
playing one nation against the other.

A war between China and the U.S.S.R. would, I felt, be a disaster
which could easily spread. As for the current U.S.-China conflict, it had
been building up for years and it could not be expected to disappear overnight; nor would the Sino-Soviet rift easily be repaired. We must, I said,
cultivate infinite patience. However, if China's dwindling food supply
made it necessary for the Peking Government to import food (which
could only come from the U.S., Australia or Canada), and we were
to make significant amounts available, China might be expected to relax to some degree its bitter antagonism toward the United States.

This conversation led to a promising proposal. Some weeks earlier,
at the President's suggestion, I had embarked upon a study of China's

3. Confirmation of a split between the two countries came from both Soviet and
Chinese sources. In late 1961 even the Peking *People's Daily* described the Soviet retrenchment as "perfidious" and charged that the U.S.S.R. "tore up 343
contracts and supplementary provisions and in addition heavily slashed its shipments of several categories of equipment."

food problems, their implications for the future and the steps the United States might, under favorable conditions, take to help solve them.

In my report, which went to the President in mid-January, I wrote: "China's food crisis simply cannot be solved through 'internal' actions by the Peking Government in the foreseeable future. Although the vagaries of weather will make some years better than others, the recurring shortages will not only create grave hardship among the Chinese people but also present a continuing threat to China's economic growth and political stability."

My analysis suggested that the Chinese leadership might sooner or later be faced with three fateful choices: (1) to do nothing, on the assumption that one more famine would not change the course of history; (2) to purchase wheat from the non-Communist food-exporting nations, such as Australia, Canada and the United States, through normal trade channels; or (3) "by overt or covert means to seek control of the food surplus areas of Southeast Asia, an operation which would risk a major war."

The conclusion of my report suggested that:

> If my analysis is correct, it points to a need for study of ways in which our own abundant agricultural resources may be used not only to save tens of millions of our fellow human beings from hunger but also to encourage the Chinese Government to adopt a more constructive role in Southeast and East Asia. Such a study is particularly needed in the context of the Sino-Soviet rift, since the Soviets are in no position to help fill China's grain shortage.
>
> In my view, our study should focus on the possibilities of bilateral commercial transactions, third party sales, or some form of a World Food Bank whereby U.S. resources can constructively be brought to bear on China's development.

Both the President and Secretary of State were receptive to my proposal that on both humanitarian and political grounds we probe the possibility of working with China on the food question. Therefore, in my second discussion with President Kennedy in late January, 1962, just before leaving for a series of visits to the Middle East and Asia,[4] I posed two questions:

First, would we be prepared to sell a limited amount of wheat to the Chinese on an emergency basis for hard currency and without political conditions? Second, if China would agree not to attempt to change its existing borders by force (without necessarily forfeiting its claims to territories outside its present borders), would we be willing to offer much

4. This visit was to be part of the trip I took in February, 1962, which is described in part in Chapter 29.

larger quantities of wheat on a continuing, low-interest, long-term basis?

The President readily agreed to the first proposal and suggested informally three to five million tons. In regard to my second proposal, he said that if some reliable means of communication could be opened up, he would consider an agreement for ten or twelve million tons of American wheat annually (about 30 percent of our entire wheat crop) on a long-term, easy-credit basis, provided China agreed to abandon its present military-political pressures on its neighbors.

I then suggested that we might further encourage the Chinese Government to take a more responsible role in Asia by offering to invest a substantial capital sum in the building up of a neutralized Southeast Asia. In that case China might eventually find it more profitable to trade there than to fight. To this, too, the President's response was affirmative.

Kennedy asked if I had considered how we could discreetly explore these possibilities with the Peking Government. I replied that U Nu, the Prime Minister of Burma (who had managed to maintain friendly relations with his northern neighbors), might be a good intermediary. On my trip throughout Southeast Asia I could stop in Rangoon for a confidential discussion with U Nu, whom I had known for many years and with whom I could talk frankly.

The President agreed, and we next discussed the basis on which I should advance these proposals. Were they to be my own ideas, for which the President took no responsibility? Were they official United States policy? Or were they proposals which I had discussed in general terms with the President, but which had not yet been formally approved? Kennedy opted for the third of these choices.

When I reached New Delhi in mid-February, I discussed my mission in confidence with Nehru, who, as I anticipated, was most responsive. However, since by that time he was barely on speaking terms with the Chinese because of differences over their common border, all he could do was wish me good luck and to offer some astute advice on how best to approach U Nu.

To avoid the possibility of newspaper leaks, my appointment with U Nu was quietly set up as a routine courtesy call through the Burmese Embassy in New Delhi. Then came a twist of fate that may have had historic implications. The day before I was scheduled to leave New Delhi for Rangoon, U Nu's government was overthrown by a *coup d'état,* and he was placed under custody by the new government.

With this avenue abruptly closed, I suggested to the President on my return to Washington that we approach the Chinese through our sporadic ambassadorial conferences in Warsaw. However, at this moment the Peking Government launched fresh attacks against the "American imperialists," and the opponents of my proposal within our government suggested that we postpone any direct approach to the Chinese until the "dust had settled." Since the dust is unlikely to settle in Asia during our lifetime, the opportunity never came.

In retrospect, I believe that the wheat sales plan floundered not because of U Nu's unavailability as a mediator (some other indirect means could have been substituted), or because of China's propaganda attacks on the United States, which were routine, but largely because many Administration officials persisted in their belief that any change whatsoever in our China policy was dangerous. Old habits of mind die slowly, particularly in the making of foreign policy.

As I wrote in my 1960 article in *Foreign Affairs*: "For too long now we have remained at the mercy of events set in motion by leaders in Taipei and Peking. . . . We have failed to take into account adequately the long-range forces which seem certain to shape future developments. . . . Until we do, we shall continue to be severely hampered in our relations with all of Asia."

In Southeast Asia in the years that followed we were destined to pay an appalling price for this failure in human lives, wasted resources and national disunity. Ironically, it was the Vietnam disaster which, in 1969, produced the first indication that we might at some stage welcome a relaxation in our relations with China.

CHAPTER 32

VIETNAM: THE MAKINGS OF A DEBACLE

As HISTORIANS REVIEW our experience in Vietnam, a major question will be: why did presumably able, thoughtful American officials allow themselves to become committed to such unrealistic goals with so little understanding of the forces with which they would be called upon to contend? It is a tragic story:

When World War II ended, the French, who had been humiliated militarily and politically, were determined to maintain as much as possible of their former imperial glory and were convinced that colonial retreat in Asia would weaken their hold in Morocco, Tunisia and elsewhere in French Africa.

In August, 1945, when the Japanese surrendered, the French promptly set out to restore their former colonial position in "French Indochina." When the early negotiations failed with Ho Chi Minh, the leader of the independence movement of the nationalist forces,[1] they abruptly turned to military force. In November, 1946, the French Navy shelled the seaport city of Haiphong, killing some four thousand Vietnamese, most of them civilians. A full-fledged conflict then became inevitable.

If Franklin D. Roosevelt had lived, I am confident that he would not have permitted the French to return to Indochina or the Dutch to Indonesia; about this subject he felt strongly. On one occasion when I asked him if he was similarly opposed to the British retaining control over India, he remarked casually, "Oh, the British will not be a problem, they are wise enough eventually to leave of their own accord."

---

1. Ho had fought side by side with U.S. forces against the Japanese and was thought to be genuinely eager at that time for a settlement acceptable to both the French and the Vietnamese.

After Roosevelt's death a series of events combined to push us into supporting the French effort. At that time our primary strategic objective with the French Government was to persuade it to contribute twelve divisions to the recently organized NATO defense forces in Western Europe. As a *quid pro quo* for those divisions (which failed to appear) Secretary of State Dean Acheson in May, 1950, called for American military aid to France to "assist in restoring stability and in permitting the Associated States of [French] Indochina to pursue their peaceful and democratic development." The ultimate result was the shipment of some $2 billion worth of modern military equipment. While the French insisted that their objective was not to re-establish their former colonial position, but rather to "block Communism" and to "protect French property" (phrases calculated to salve American consciences and to win American support), no knowledgeable observer took these rationalizations seriously. Nevertheless, at the time these events in distant Asia were looked upon as relatively minor in comparison with those in Europe, and Truman, with profound faith in his Secretary of State, went along with Acheson's views—with disastrous consequences which did not become evident until years after Acheson left office.

Those who write the history of our times will, I believe, regard this political "bargain" as one of the most ill-considered acts in American history.

By 1951 the French forces in Vietnam totaled 140,000 professional soldiers, supported by 150,000 French-trained, French-equipped and French-led Vietnamese troops. But even this massive force was barely able to hold its own against a far smaller number of ill-trained, ill-equipped and ill-nourished but deeply committed Vietminh guerrillas fighting for their independence.

When Steb and I first visited Saigon in the summer of 1952, French casualties already totaled 38,000 dead, including 11,000 officers. U.S. military aid to France in Indochina was already two and a half times as great as our entire world-wide Point Four program, and equal to our Marshall Plan contribution to France itself.

Before leaving New Delhi for Saigon, I had discussed Southeast Asia at length with Prime Minister Nehru, who had known Ho Chi Minh casually for several years. When Ho Chi Minh stopped briefly in Ceylon in 1946 on his return to Vietnam from Paris, Nehru had sent an envoy to explore his objectives and his political orientation. The emissary reported that while Ho regarded himself as a Communist, he felt that it would be his intense nationalism and not his ideology that would largely shape his policies. As evidence of this he reported that Ho Chi Minh saw himself primarily as a patriotic leader of Vietnamese nationalism and had asserted that he was determined to withstand Chinese encroachments as vigorously as he would those of the French.

As an ardent young student in Paris in 1919 during the negotiations over the Treaty of Versailles, Ho had been profoundly stirred by Woodrow Wilson's views of self-determination and had repeatedly asked for an opportunity to explore with the American President how Wilson's concepts of political freedom, which were arousing such high hopes in Europe, could be extended to free the people of Asia and Africa. Unhappily, the appointment was never arranged.

The failure of the French, with all their military power, to maintain their position in Indochina was due to the same reasons that Chiang Kai-shek had failed in China, and that we ourselves were later to fail in Vietnam. There was a disastrous gap between the political realities and the French Government's approach to them. This was illustrated for me by a series of confidential exchanges I had in Vietnam with Prime Minister Nguyen Van Tam, a man of considerable courage and distinction whom the French had somehow persuaded to assume this figurehead position. In August, 1952, when I called on Van Tam in his office, he frankly and indiscreetly expressed his personal view "that the French effort was doomed."

When I asked him why, he replied, "Let me tell you a simple story. When the Communists capture a village, they announce that all debts of the peasants to the moneylenders are canceled and that henceforth all land belongs to the peasants who actually work the land.

"When the French forces recapture the village," he continued, "their first step is to restore the landlords and moneylenders to their former positions of power, and, as might be expected, the embittered villagers promptly join the Vietminh guerrillas en masse. How," Van Tam asked wearily, "can we win a civil war on that basis?"

In May, 1953, when I made a second visit to Vietnam, I was again warmly greeted by Prime Minister Van Tam, who said with an air of mock satisfaction: "The French have learned a lesson. You will remember our conversation last summer? Well, I have great news for you. Now when the French recapture a village, they allow the peasants to keep the land which the Communists have given them. Thus, if a peasant is to become free, the Communists must still first occupy his village and give him his land; then the French must 'liberate' the village so that he can keep the land."

With few exceptions, most notably Edmund Gullion, later Ambassador to the Congo, who headed the political section of our Saigon Embassy in 1952, the American officials totally misjudged the situation. On February 4, 1954, two months before the collapse of the French military stronghold at Dienbienphu which spelled defeat for their entire effort, Admiral Arthur W. Radford, Chairman of the Joint Chiefs of Staff, was quoted in the *New York Times* as testifying before the House Foreign Affairs Committee that "The development of a broad strategic concept by the French and Vietnamese commanders in Indochina, supported by the United States financial and military assistance, should insure within a very few months a favorable turn in the course of the war. . . . Communist prospects of achieving any decisive immediate successes are nonexistent."

In July, 1954, when the Geneva Agreements were signed, there was some basis for hope that a stable peace might be assured by the free elections which the agreements called for to determine the future governments of North and South Vietnam. But South Vietnam's President Ngo Dinh Diem, on one pretext or another, refused to cooperate, and, with our connivance (the United States never actually signed the accords), the elections were never held.

The Ho Chi Minh Government in Hanoi, bitter over what it considered to be a deliberate violation of the Geneva election agreement, launched a new campaign of terrorism against the Diem Government. Diem promptly turned to us for assistance, which we agreed to provide. This led step by step to our massive involvement.

At first Diem demonstrated a heartening degree of courage and understanding, but gradually, like most of our allies in the underdeveloped world, slipped under control of the great landlords and other right-wing elements who were determined at any cost of blood, suffering and deterioration to maintain the status quo. Rejecting what he believed to be halfhearted advice from the United States, he refused to place a ceiling on land holdings (as he had promised), to clean up corruption in the villages and cities and to grant even minimal local powers in a society long accustomed to strong political institutions at the village level.

In spite of this mounting evidence that Diem was incapable or unwilling to create a political base for an independent South Vietnam, much of the discussion in the Departments of Defense and State and, increasingly, the White House continued to center around Diem's military capacity to counter the Vietcong.

In February, 1961, I first urged Dean Rusk to consider the expansion of the neutrality concept established for Laos in the Geneva Accords in 1954, to embrace the rest of Southeast Asia, excluding North Vietnam and East Pakistan, but including Thailand, Burma, Cambodia, Malaysia, South Vietnam and Singapore.

Neutral status, I said, might be guaranteed by the United States, Britain, France, the Soviet Union, India and Japan. It was even conceivable that such a plan might appeal to the Soviet Union's interest in keeping Communist China from moving to absorb Southeast Asia into its sphere of influence. At least it would enable us to move out of the stifling confines of the SEATO pact as a legal justification for our presence in Southeast Asia and give our future actions an air of broad international cooperation rather than one of narrow anti-Communism.

Further, I pointed out if in the face of such an arrangement Ho Chi Minh insisted on invading the South, it would be clear that his action constituted aggression against an independent state whose neutrality had been established by international agreement. My proposal was greeted in the State Department with a resounding silence, some raised eyebrows and even, I am told, some discreet questions as to whether I realized that I was inadvertently playing the Communist game. Rusk did not respond.

When I had discussed American policy in regard to South Vietnam with Kennedy shortly after his election, he expressed only a marginal interest. But following the Bay of Pigs, his confrontation with Khrushchev in Vienna and the resumption of nuclear testing by the Soviets, I sensed that, subconsciously at least, he was searching for some issue on which he could prove at a relatively low cost that he was, in fact, a tough President who could not be pushed around by the Soviets, the Chinese or anyone else.

In October, 1961, General Maxwell Taylor and Walt Rostow, both White House advisers, were sent on a mission to Vietnam. Rostow had by that time emerged as a supporter of the hard-line approach. Taylor, on the other hand, consistently opposed any further direct U.S. involvement in an Asian land war. When I had first met him in Seoul in May, 1953, when he was Commander in Chief of the UN armies in Korea, he had described to me in graphic terms the difficulties of such involvement. Although it was generally assumed that he had been included in the mission as a balance for Rostow's more extreme views, their report, I understand, turned out to be a joint document.

Several of its recommendations had been under consideration for some time—helicopters, B-26's, military advisers and training experts. But the report also called for the introduction of regular American troops, with the possibility that massive numbers might be required.[2]

It was my view and that of several others, particularly Abe Chayes, that the acceptance by the President of these recommendations or

2. In his book *To Move a Nation*, Roger Hilsman writes: "The Taylor report also proposed the introduction into Vietnam of over ten thousand regular American ground troops, initially, and accepting the possibility that as many as six full divisions might eventually be required." This number, in fact, turned out to be approximately the size of the American forces later introduced.

anything close to them would constitute a long step toward a full-blown war of unpredictable dimensions. In an effort to transfer the debate from the military to the political arena I again introduced my proposal for a neutralized Southeast Asia in a somewhat new form: i.e., that we expand the negotiations in regard to the neutralization of Laos which were still under way in Geneva to the neutralization of the entire area, including not only Laos but both Vietnams, Cambodia, Burma, Thailand, Malaysia and Singapore.

Averell Harriman reacted favorably to this proposal. As head of our negotiating team he had developed working relationships with representatives of the other side and, while recognizing the difficulties, felt that some such plan might be feasible. The Soviet Union, he thought, might be persuaded to share responsibility for insuring the provisions of the agreement.

My recommendations, with those of the Taylor-Rostow mission, were vigorously debated in the Department and the White House. Although Kennedy did not comment directly to me on my proposal, it was my impression that he looked upon it as a praiseworthy goal, but one for which the "time was not yet ripe." Other accounts of this period support this view: "Chester Bowles' idea . . . was an imaginative proposal, but it seemed either too early or too late."[3] "There was one imaginative proposal—a notion put forward by Chester Bowles. . . . So far as I know, President Kennedy did not make any specific comment on this suggestion. . . ."[4] "Robert F. Kennedy in February, 1967, was finally prepared to admit to himself that prophets like Chester Bowles had been right all along and that he, his brother and their friends had been tragically wrong."[5]

President Kennedy's decision was to go part way: he would increase the number of U.S. military advisers in Vietnam but forgo, for the present at least, the introduction of American troops. This represented a defeat for my proposal and a partial victory for the military view. Inevitably, it further upset the precarious balance on foreign policy questions between the Defense Department and State Department, and, as it turned out, set the stage for the nearly total militarization of our Southeast Asia policy and the ultimate debacle in Vietnam.

By the winter of 1962 the general view among policy-makers seemed to be that the "Communists must be taught a lesson." Rusk was said to view Vietnam as the place to stop Communism in Asia. This catchall use of the word "Communism" served only to confuse the issues in Asia and to encourage the search for a military "solution."

3. Arthur Schlesinger, Jr., *A Thousand Days*, p. 503.
4. Roger Hilsman, *To Move a Nation*, p. 423.
5. Jack Newfield, *Robert F. Kennedy: A Memoir*, p. 133.

Many thoughtful people felt Communism continued to represent a vast monolithic force committed to the total destruction of the United States and the Western world. Yet Communist China and Communist Russia were teetering on the brink of open hostilities. The government of Yugoslavia, which also called itself Communist, was far removed from either the Soviets or the Chinese in its economic and political philosophy. Similarly, the North Vietnamese brand of Communism was different from that of the Chinese, Russian or Yugoslav, and there were various other versions in India, Burma and elsewhere.

By all odds the primary political force in Asia, Africa and Latin America was not Communism, or democracy, but nationalism. Ho Chi Minh and his followers looked on the war in Southeast Asia primarily as a struggle for national independence and identity, not as a crusade to force their own or any other version of "Communism" down the throats of their unwilling neighbors.

The traditional antagonism of the North Vietnamese for the Chinese has, in my opinion, been a more important force than their common commitment to the theories of Marx. Chinese-Soviet competition for influence in Southeast Asia may prove to have been an equally crucial factor. The fact that Hanoi has been able to secure weapons and support from both the Soviet Union and the Chinese has made it unnecessary for the Hanoi Government to face the question: "Is it better for us to be 'saved' by the expansionist Chinese Communists than to be overrun by the imperialistic American capitalists?"

Because so many officials were operating under mistaken assumptions, I believed it necessary for the President to state publicly what our position was in Southeast Asia. Following my return from another visit there in late May, 1962, I wrote, borrowing a phrase from John Foster Dulles:

> If there ever was a need for an "agonizing reappraisal," it is here and now. This reappraisal must look far beyond counterguerrilla tactics and fortified townships to the political factors which in the long run alone will prove decisive.
>
> American history is replete with tragedies born of our failure to relate our military efforts to political objectives.

By early June, 1962, I had worked up a formal proposal for such a reappraisal for the President. I proposed that the President make a major speech in which he would precisely define our objectives in Southeast Asia. I envisioned the effect of this speech as similar to that of Woodrow Wilson's speech in 1918, setting forth his Fourteen Points, which put our participation in World War I into a framework of objectives that anyone could understand. Kennedy would spell out what we were prepared to do to arrive at a peaceful solution to the Vietnamese conflict. The speech would declare that our objectives in Southeast Asia were no more and no less than what the people wanted for themselves: guaranteed national independence, more rapid economic development and maximum freedom of choice within their own cultures and religions. It would firmly identify the United States Government and people with peace, development, anticolonialism and increasing regional unity.

Such a clarification of our objectives by the President would be immediately reassuring to the politically sophisticated people in both neutral and aligned states of the region, and it would give the American presence in Southeast Asia—whether military, political or economic— the affirmative, understandable, appealing purpose which had been largely lacking since the days of Roosevelt. It would also encourage the U.S.S.R. to press for stabilization and neutralization of the region, and would remove any valid excuse for Chinese Communist aggression based on a misunderstanding of our objectives.

I suggested that the President proclaim our complete disinterest in any military base or presence in Southeast Asia. Since most Asians suspected that we had permanent strategic ambitions in this area, this assurance, I said, would help us to escape being tagged as colonial successors to the French. "Our future policy," I wrote, "should be based on five simple points:

1. We welcome the recent agreement in regard to a neutral and independent Laos. We congratulate Prime Minister Souvanna Phouma and pledge our full support to his new government in its efforts to eliminate civil strife and political subversion from whatever source.
2. We continue to hope that a peaceful settlement may also be possible in South Vietnam, still torn by bloody and unnecessary fighting.
3. Once the fighting is ended and a peaceful settlement achieved, we will contribute generously to rebuilding those areas destroyed by war and to the establishment of prosperous economic conditions.
4. Under conditions of peace, we will join with all interested nations in the speeding up of plans for the rapid development of the lower Mekong basin with a U.S. pledge of substantial sums for the development of the river's potential.
5. Under conditions of peace, we will also join with other nations in guaranteeing the independence and security of all Southeast Asia against either overt aggression or covert subversion by any foreign power.

Somewhat to my surprise, the response to this comprehensive proposal was encouraging. Kennedy not only agreed that the time had come to clarify our objectives and plans for Vietnam and the adjoining areas; he was enthusiastic.

Rusk also agreed, and we met to consider the procedures. I suggested that I visit on an official basis the capitals of the nations of the area (except North Vietnam) and meet with the heads of state on a confidential basis to express our concern about the present escalating military trend and the President's desire to offer a bold and appealing peace initiative and to seek their advice on how this could best be accomplished.

The day following this meeting, I sent Rusk a memorandum suggesting that the basis of my discussions should be a regional charter for all Southeast Asia. Rusk agreed, and plans went rapidly ahead. The Far Eastern Bureau, at Rusk's request, prepared cables to our embassies, confidentially setting up my visits and meetings with the heads of government. Throughout the preparatory meetings in the State Department I had stressed, and it was understood, that my mission would receive a minimum of publicity, since the discussions we contemplated would deal not only with Vietnam but with a host of long-range political and economic problems throughout the region.

By July 18 I had prepared the following draft for study by the Department and the White House:

PRINCIPLES FOR A PRESIDENTIAL "PEACE CHARTER FOR SOUTHEAST ASIA"

I. OUR OBJECTIVES

   A. Achievement of peace throughout Southeast Asia so that the peoples of each nation may realize their full potential within the framework of their own traditions, cultures and religions.

   B. Renunciation of force, in accordance with the United Nations Charter, as an instrument for solving disputes among the nations of Southeast Asia.

   C. Under conditions of peace, withdrawal of all foreign troops from Southeast Asian territories, except those provided at the request of governments in order to train forces for purposes of national defense.

   D. Respect for the neutrality of any nation that seeks to remain unaligned with any of the great powers.

   E. Increased international cooperation for the more rapid development of Southeast Asia's natural and human resources.

II. POLITICAL STEPS TO ACHIEVE THESE OBJECTIVES

   A. Prompt termination of the guerrilla warfare which is now threatening the independence of South Vietnam, with the withdrawal north of the 17th parallel of all Vietminh cadres.

   B. Broad guarantees by the Great Powers of the sovereignty, independence, and territorial integrity of the Southeast Asian nations.

(Query: What "Great Powers"? U.K., France, U.S., U.S.S.R., mainland China, India, Pakistan and Japan?)

C. Similar guarantees against all forms of internal subversion, endorsed by both great and small powers with major interests in the Southeast Asian area, to the end that Southeast Asia may cease to be a battlefield in the Cold War.
D. Establishment of an agreed system of inspection of possible violations to undergird these guarantees, under the aegis of the United Nations.

III. ECONOMIC INSTRUMENTS TO ACHIEVE THESE OBJECTIVES

A. Strengthening of such regional associations as ECAFE [Economic Commission for Asia and the Far East], the Asian Productivity Organization, the Colombo Plan Organization and the Association of Southeast Asia.
B. Development of the Lower Mekong Basin under an International Authority to increase the industrial capacity of the four riparian states (Thailand, Vietnam, Laos and Cambodia) and to provide a greatly expanded food supply for world distribution through peaceful international trade. (Note: Including mainland China as long as her government keeps the peace.)
C. Creation by the Southeast Asian states of regional production and marketing authorities for the principal staple exports of the region: rice, teak, tin, rubber and jute.
D. A comprehensive study of the practicability of creating a Southeast Asian Common Market.
E. Creation, under the aegis of the existing regional associations, of regional communications systems, educational institutions, shipping lines, air lines and coordinated industrial development plans to assist in meshing the economies of the nations of the area.

IV. OUR AMERICAN COMMITMENT

On the basis of these principles the United States Government will lend its wholehearted efforts to the achievement of a lasting peace in Southeast Asia with an increasing measure of opportunity, freedom and justice for the 200 million people of this area.

Once the political steps to establish such a peace have been taken, the United States will devote a major proportion of the funds which it is now forced to spend on military operations in Vietnam, Laos and Thailand, to the peaceful, economic and social development of the entire region.

Although I knew that many officials in the Far Eastern Bureau were strongly opposed to this effort, I assumed that with the approval of the President and Secretary there would be no turning back at this point. However, I underestimated their capacity for resistance. The opening gun of the effort to reverse the President's and Secretary's decision was a detailed rebuttal to my draft Southeast Asian Charter. Like other memoranda supporting the deeply rooted "Let's do nothing for the time being" state of mind, it described my proposals as "unrealistic, impractical and premature." It closed with the comment which in the next few years was soon to become basic American dogma: "The primary problem we must recognize is that the Hanoi Government has not yet been given adequate reason to call off its aggression in South Vietnam. This remains the hard obstacle to the realization of our good intentions towards Southeast Asia."

In another memorandum on August 16, 1962, rebutting the arguments of the bureau, I replied:

> On the basis of such reasoning, Wilson's Fourteen Points could be condemned as an empty gesture, Secretary Marshall's 1947 speech at Harvard viewed as a visionary bit of do-goodism, Truman's Point Four proposals as unrealistic, and the Alliance for Progress as a blatant case of international daydreaming. . . .
>
> At present we are faced with a most difficult security situation in South Vietnam. Although our military authorities appear hopeful about the outcome, qualified *outside* observers place the odds for a clear-cut victory for the Saigon Government at less than fifty-fifty. . . .
>
> If, as many fear, the situation deteriorates, we may be forced within the next year or so to choose between committing more and more American troops and material to what the President's political opponents will describe as "another Democratic war," or withdrawing in embarrassed frustration.
>
> For the U.S. Government to adopt the classic "Let's wait and see" posture under such circumstances strikes me as sterile and foolhardy. . . .

However, in the face of opposition from members of the bureau, Secretary Rusk, presumably with the President's agreement, reversed the decision. I was told that the mission, which was scheduled to leave in the middle of September, 1962, had simply been postponed, on the grounds that the "timing," as usual, was "inopportune." October, it was said, might be a good time to discuss it again.

By the time October came, we were involved in the Cuban missile crisis, and the timing continued to be wrong. No more was said about my trip or my proposal.

In November, 1962, General Earle G. Wheeler, later Chairman of the Joint Chiefs of Staff, in a speech at Fordham University, said, "It is fashionable in some quarters to say that the problems in Southeast Asia are primarily political and economic rather than military. I do not agree. The essence of the problem in Vietnam is military."

In the early spring of 1963, after I had accepted Kennedy's offer to return to India, I made one more effort. On March 7, 1963, I wrote a memorandum to President Kennedy which said:

I hesitate to play the role of Cassandra again in regard to Vietnam and Southeast Asia. However, I remain deeply concerned about the outlook there, and having talked to Mike Mansfield about his report and the fragile nature of our present position, I feel that I should frankly express my misgivings to you.

I see nothing in the present course of events to dispel my conviction, expressed to you and the Secretary on several occasions, that if this course is pursued, the Southeast Asia situation will ultimately have a serious impact on the Administration's position at home and abroad.

Although the general outlook here in Washington and in Saigon now seems to be cautiously optimistic, it may be worthwhile to remind ourselves of the confident assumptions of the Eisenhower Administration in a somewhat similar situation during the winter of 1954. . . .

Nine years have passed and now it is we who appear to be striving, in defiance of powerful indigenous political and military forces, to insure the survival of an unpopular Vietnamese regime with inadequate roots among the people. And now, as in 1954, many able U.S. military authorities are convinced that the situation is moving in our favor and that victory can be foreseen within two to three years.

I wonder if these assurances are not based on a dangerously false premise, i.e., that the Communists will not embarrass us by upping the military ante . . . ?

I once again suggested an immediate review in depth of our present Vietnam policy within the framework of South Asia as a whole and that the speech which I had prepared for the President a year before be updated for early delivery on TV or elsewhere by Kennedy or Rusk, Averell Harriman or some other major Administration spokesman. But there was no response.

In mid-July, 1963, on our way to New Delhi to assume my new post as Ambassador, Steb and I stopped in Saigon for several days. My worst fears about the deterioration of the situation there were confirmed. Ambassador Frederick E. Nolting, Jr. had recently left and Ambassador Henry Cabot Lodge had not yet been appointed; a chargé d'affaires was the senior officer. This had encouraged the various factions in the official American community to do even more freewheeling than they might otherwise have indulged in. The American Embassy was at odds with the American military, and both were at odds with the American press. It was not a reassuring spectacle.

Neither was what I found in the Vietnamese Government. The Embassy set up a meeting for me with President Diem at nine o'clock on the morning after our arrival. When I noticed that nothing further had been planned for that morning, I suggested that we fill in the time between eleven o'clock and luncheon with other appointments. My control officer (a young Foreign Service officer) shook his head. "Don't be concerned about that," he said. "I will be very surprised if your Diem appointment breaks up before 1 P.M."

How right he was. My talk with Diem, or rather his talk with me, lasted until ten minutes after one o'clock, which made us late for a one o'clock luncheon. In the course of this four-hour-plus meeting I asked something like four or five questions, each of which took no more than a minute. President Diem carried on from there. I left the meeting deeply concerned; President Diem seemed to be living in an unreal world of his own. Again and again, he described military and political situations within his country which were distorted, and offered sanguine analyses of Chinese and Soviet objectives and interests. His predictions of the likely course of action were, if anything, even more unrealistic.

One other event bothered me during our five-day visit. I managed to spend a day or two in the countryside accompanied by American and South Vietnamese officers and military escorts armed to the teeth. In so short a time and under such circumstances it was impossible to get a clear view, but I remember vividly the reactions of the Vietnamese children. On previous visits to rural areas in a dozen or so Asian countries, including Vietnam, I found it had always been possible, with a few hastily learned phrases, to communicate with the children. But on this trip, through fear of war or resentment at the American military presence, the children were silent.

By the time we were scheduled to leave Saigon I was deeply disturbed. In a private cable to the White House I described the rapidly deteriorating situation and expressed my particular concern about Diem. "President Diem," I wrote, "is living in a world of his own and seems to be completely out of touch with the real situation. Any attractive South Vietnamese brigadier general with a little courage and organization could, I believe, take this place over in twenty-four hours."

I recommended that President Kennedy send an individual in whom he had personal confidence unobtrusively but immediately to Vietnam to make an independent analysis. I specifically recommended Thomas Hughes, who was then serving as Director of Intelligence and Research in the State Department. Although I was later told that my emergency cable was the occasion for a series of high-level meetings, nothing came of it.

My visit confirmed all my fears about the role we were trying to play in Vietnam, and I made an entry in my notebook which was to prove prophetic:

> Our present course of action within a rigid political and military framework dominated by Diem is very likely to fail, *and for this failure we may eventually be called upon to pay a heavy price, both in Asia and here at home.*

Our intervention in Southeast Asia is a disturbing demonstration of the extent to which a great and powerful nation, with the very best of intentions, once it loses touch with political realities, can delude itself and its people and be forced to pay a price out of all proportion to its objectives.

CHAPTER 33

CHALLENGE IN AFRICA:
THE CONGO CRISIS

IN MID-OCTOBER, 1962, I left Washington with Steb and two members of
my staff for a four weeks' visit to Africa which was to take me to seven
countries, with brief stops in another five, checking on operational problems in the various missions, examining proposals for economic assistance and generally renewing our acquaintance with a continent and a
people which had always had a special appeal to us both.

On October 13, the day before our departure, we received photo-
graphic evidence of large-scale Russian shipments into Cuba of heavy
Il-28 bombers.

By coincidence, I had a long-planned luncheon appointment that
day with Soviet Ambassador Anatoly Dobrynin, with whom I met
frequently and informally to exchange views. I expressed to Dobrynin
my concern about the shipments and warned him that a stiff reaction
from our government was inevitable. He seemed genuinely surprised
and insisted that the report must be untrue. I replied that I hoped he
was right but that if he was wrong, he would not be the first nor the
last ambassador in modern history to be deceived or ignored by his
government in such a situation.

When I returned to the office, I wrote a memorandum describing my
conversation with Ambassador Dobrynin, including his categorical
denial, sent it to the Secretary of State and the President and went
home to pack for our trip, on which we were leaving early the following
day. A week later when the Cuban missile crisis took shape I was in
Africa.

My trip was to involve me in another quite different kind of crisis which brought the United Nations itself to the brink of disaster. Although I did not know it when we left Washington, events in the Congo were reaching a head.

Since 1960, when the Congo became independent, it had been beset with dissension and violence. The basic issue was whether the copper-rich province of Katanga, which was controlled politically by Moise Tshombé, would be permitted to become a separate state or whether the Congo would exist as a united country. Belgium had substantial financial interests in Katanga, which it was assumed Tshombé could be trusted to protect. Because of the Congo's immense size, its strategic location in the explosive southern third of Africa and the efforts of the U.S.S.R. to establish a foothold there, the confrontation affected the whole of Africa.

When Steb and I first visited the "Belgian Congo" in January, 1955, not even the most optimistic Congolese patriot dreamed that in five years his country would be an independent nation. What we then saw was a vast country almost the size of India with a population of only thirty million Africans dominated by a tiny white Belgian minority. While there was some economic progress, it was heavily weighted in favor of industrialization and the urban areas, with the predominantly rural areas, where most of the Congolese lived, receiving only meager benefits. This pattern I felt was dangerous. "Progress in the Congo," I had written in 1955, "is moving ahead at best in arithmetical progression. The *demand* for progress, however, is moving ahead in geometric progression."

What I found most alarming was the attitude of the Belgian Government and the insensitivity of even the most able of its colonial administrators to the political forces developing throughout the entire continent. While the Belgians were embarked on a well-organized development plan that seemed logical from their narrow perspective, it was, I felt, based on a false assumption: that by providing the urban Congolese with reasonably good jobs, clean houses, medical care and elementary education for their children, political stability and continued subservience to Belgian colonial rule could be assured. What was missing was the sense of dignity and personal involvement without which stability is impossible—in Detroit or Los Angeles, the Congo or anywhere else.

The Belgians refused to allow more than a few Congolese to secure an advanced education—even a technical education—for fear that they would then demand a growing share of responsibility in the shaping of their own future. As for the absence of the right to vote, the Belgians asserted that this did not represent discrimination against the Africans; *no one* had the right to vote, neither Belgian nor Congolese.

The contrast between the British and Belgian colonial attitudes toward education in Africa was both dramatic and instructive. The British colonies appeared on the surface to be less politically stable, but that was precisely because, except in Southern Rhodesia, they were committed to giving Africans the experience in government which was necessary for the future. In 1955, Sir Andrew Cohen, the Governor of Uganda, explained the British perspective to me in the following terms. "We are headed," he told us, "for many turbulent and difficult years here in Africa. It will be easier for all of us if the Africans speak good English and have a sound knowledge of English law."

Whereas the British believed quite genuinely that the more university graduates the better, most Belgians recoiled in horror at the thought of education for Africans. At the time of our 1955 visit three thousand Africans from Ghana were studying in English-language institutions abroad, with an impressive Oxford-model university for a thousand additional students under construction outside Accra. In contrast, only eleven Congolese college students were studying in Belgium, none elsewhere. The barely begun university outside Léopoldville was expected to graduate no more than six or seven students each year for the foreseeable future.

Until the British and French decided in 1959, 1960 and 1961 to grant independence to their colonies most Belgians assumed that their own rule would continue for decades. But when the British and French began to cut their African colonies loose, the Belgian Government abruptly revised its policy and announced its own intention to withdraw.

On June 30, 1960, six months before Kennedy took office and less than six months after the dramatic shift in Belgian policy had been announced, the Congo was granted independence. It was irresponsible for the Belgians suddenly to assume that in six months an orderly switch could be made from Belgian to Congolese administration and that democratic institutions for which no basis had been laid could successfully replace the despotic methods under which the Congo had been governed for generations. It was not surprising that within two weeks the Congo had fallen into administrative chaos. As I had written following our visit there in 1955, "The danger lies not so much in the possibility that the Belgians will not compromise eventually with the force of nationalism, but that when they are finally forced to do so they will find 'their' Africans almost totally inexperienced in handling the responsibilities which they are certain to demand and eventually to get."

Less than a month after independence, Moise Tshombé announced that the province of Katanga had seceded from the Congo under his presidency and would henceforth function as a separate government with close ties to Belgium, underwritten by military and economic assistance. At the same time Congolese troops in other parts of the Congo mutinied against their Belgian officers, some Belgian citizens were killed, and the Belgian Government dispatched troops to protect Belgian lives.

In an atmosphere of mistrust, hatred, panic and extraordinarily fast-moving events, the new Congolese President, Joseph Kasavubu, and his Prime Minister, Patrice Lumumba, requested the assistance of the United Nations to help end the Katanga secession and restore national unity.

The UN, under the firm leadership of Secretary Dag Hammarskjöld, responded with a peace-keeping mission of some fifteen thousand troops, a large part of whom were Indians, with the understanding that it would remain neutral on the political issue dividing the Congo. But Lumumba, anxious for the immediate overthrow of Tshombé, turned to the Soviet Union for assistance, an act which led to his imprisonment and eventual assassination in early 1961.

Tshombé's suspected complicity in the assassination aroused the fury of most of newly independent Africa, and his continued alliance with Belgium made his overthrow and the re-establishment of a unified Congo a matter of urgency to the millions of Africans for whom the issue was now one of nationalism vs. colonialism.

The speed and strength of the African independence movement had caught almost everyone in Washington as in other national capitals by surprise, and our government was ill-prepared for the hard new decisions required. The disarray was compounded by the fact that top officials in the Defense Department and the European Bureau of the State Department, with a very few exceptions, were opposed to any U.S. move in the United Nations or elsewhere that would upset either the European colonial powers which were allied with us in NATO or even racist South Africa, which the Navy considered to be of great strategic importance.

Before his nomination and election in 1960, Kennedy and I had discussed the developing situation in Africa on many occasions. He had read a series of lectures on Africa which I gave in 1956 at the University of California at Berkeley, which appeared in book form under the title *Africa's Challenge to America,* and expressed full agreement with my analysis and conclusions. In his Inaugural Address he had offered a pledge of assistance to underdeveloped countries, including those of Africa, "not because the Communists may be doing it, not because we seek their vote in the United Nations, but because it is right."

The fact that Mennen Williams, who had a strong labor and civil rights record and shared my antipathy for colonialism, had been appointed Assistant Secretary for African Affairs even before Rusk's appointment had been announced underscored Kennedy's interest in Africa. The appointment of Wayne Fredericks as his deputy and the ambassadorial appointments of such men as Bill Attwood to Guinea, Phil Kaiser to Senegal and Edmund Gullion to the Congo had also helped make it clear to the African states that the United States' indifference to the new Africa, which had characterized the Eisenhower years, was being fundamentally changed.

With the eloquent Adlai Stevenson as its spokesman in the United Nations, the Administration had adopted an attitude of friendly cooperation with the new African states. This was particularly impressive to them because on several issues it brought us into direct conflict with our European allies, which were striving to retain their special colonial privileges. Another positive factor was Kennedy's youth and vitality, which appealed to the young African leaders, and quickly won for him the personal respect and admiration not only of African leaders but of the people of Africa in a way that no other American President had ever done—or has done since.

With regard to the Congo, Kennedy had opposed Tshombé's secession and had supported the action of the United Nations from the beginning, despite the difficulties this created for him in Europe and among Katanga advocates in the United States. Nevertheless, I was concerned that if the situation reached crisis proportions, other priorities might be given precedence and the pressures to write off the Congo, despite the negative impact this would have on our relations with Africa, would prove too great. Although our current advantages in Africa were substantial, their foundations were in many respects fragile and for this reason, I felt, provided no solid assurance for the future. The only way to convince proud African leaders that the United States understood their problems and encouraged their independence was through forthright action.

A test of our new policies was soon provided by the U.S.S.R., which seized upon the situation in the Congo to castigate the UN for refusing to support more stringent military action against Tshombé and to imply that it might find it necessary to intervene unilaterally (it had already provided weapons to Lumumba). These moves, which were strongly supported by the U.A.R.,[1] were calculated to impress African radicals and discredit whatever favorable ground the United States had developed among these new leaders.

In response, Kennedy was easily persuaded to underscore publicly

1. My discussion with Nasser on this subject is described in Chapter 29.

and strongly U.S. support for the UN and to warn Russia against intervention. A few months later, we pledged our support to the coalition, anti-Tshombé Government which had emerged from the earlier chaos following Lumumba's death, headed by Cyrille Adoula.

Nevertheless, the Congo problem smoldered through 1961 into 1962, with Katanga still a separate entity and the Léopoldville Government barely in control of the rest of the country, while the impatience and cynicism of other newly independent African states in regard to the ability of the UN to handle the situation continued to grow.

In mid-December, 1961, Tshombé had indicated to Kennedy that he would meet with Adoula, and from March to June, 1962, intermittent negotiations took place in Léopoldville. However, in spite of heavy pressure from the UN, Tshombé refused to surrender the independence of Katanga. The talks ended and the situation further deteriorated.

During our October, 1962, trip to Africa, Steb and I, while impressed by the sense of movement in most of the countries we visited, were concerned about the growing bitterness and sense of hopelessness that we encountered in the southern third of the continent.

The white minority which constituted Southern Rhodesia's Government, for example, seemed to be living in much the same political dreamland as when we first visited there in 1955. Both Nyasaland and Northern Rhodesia[2] were scheduled for independence by 1964, and it seemed likely that this prospect would lead to a further move to the right in Southern Rhodesia as the nervous whites there clamped down on all potential "troublemakers." The ultimate birth of a free Southern Rhodesia under democratic majority rule was bound to be a long and painful affair.

My talks with African leaders throughout this explosive area made it clear that the Congo was the key: the failure of the United Nations there would quickly lead to the polarization of forces and counterforces throughout much of the continent. Tshombé had already made a mockery out of the plan proposed by U Thant in August, 1962, for economic sanctions if steps were not taken toward reunification with the central Congolese Government. Meanwhile, he had ordered his forces, consisting largely of a few hundred white mercenaries recruited in South Africa, to resume their harassment of outlying UN units.

We flew directly from Salisbury in Southern Rhodesia to Brazzaville, the capital of what was formerly known as the "French Congo," just across the Congo River from the former Belgian capital of Léopoldville. Since a mission led by Under Secretary George McGhee had just left Léopoldville and I was anxious to avoid adding to an already highly

2. Now the independent countries of Malawi and Zambia.

confused situation in the Congo itself, I met our Ambassador, Edmund Gullion, in Brazzaville. Gullion, who had Kennedy's confidence as well as my own, reported that Tshombé had handled McGhee skillfully, which was not surprising since Tshombé was far more accustomed to dealing with Americans and Europeans than with the Africans whom he claimed to represent.

According to Gullion, Tshombé flatly denied the charge that he was not negotiating in good faith with the UN and the central Congolese Government. Yet, since Tshombé obviously had no intention of compromising his differences with the Congolese nationalists, this was a blatant falsehood. Nevertheless, McGhee, who was an experienced diplomat in regard to Europe and the Middle East, but who had had little experience in the infinite complexities of Africa, accepted these assurances at their face value. A contributing reason for McGhee's desire to maintain a connection with Tshombé was, no doubt, the strong arguments of the European Bureau, which was itself influenced by the British, French and Belgian financiers who owned the copper mines in Katanga and who believed that their interests could most readily be protected in a separate state dominated by Tshombé.

Gullion further reported that when McGhee left he was genuinely convinced that for the United States to support a UN crackdown on Tshombé, supported if necessary by a UN agreement to impose more rigorous economic sanctions on Katanga, would make a difficult situation worse.

With this analysis I strongly disagreed. Any relaxation of our pressures on Tshombé, as I saw it, would be a grievous error. Tshombé would continue to move closer to the white-supremacist powers in Angola, Mozambique, Rhodesia and South Africa. This, in turn, could lead to the grimmest of all possibilities—a bloody confrontation between the bulk of black Africa supported by the U.S.S.R., on the one hand, and the white supremacists in South Africa, Rhodesia and the Portuguese colonies, plus Tshombé and a reluctant Belgium, on the other—with the United Nations and the United States on the sidelines and rapidly losing whatever influence they had once had.

Since our government was still reeling from the impact of the Cuba crisis, I knew it would be difficult to persuade any top official to concern himself with a brand-new crisis of this magnitude. However, difficult or not, I was convinced that we could no longer afford to vacillate in the Congo. If the Kennedy Administration attempted to do so, it would jeopardize and very probably destroy the favorable position it had laboriously been developing in Africa for the last two years and further weaken the United Nations.

On my way back to Washington via West Africa, I sent the Department a cable from Guinea strongly urging forthright U.S. support for the UN unification effort, a blockade of Katangan copper exports, and additional UN forces to guarantee the collection of internal taxes by the central Adoula Government, which had been deprived by Tshombé of the substantial revenues from Katanga and was facing severe financial problems.

The members of the McGhee mission, who had just returned to Washington and were backed by the European Bureau in the Department, had urged delay. G. Mennen Williams, his deputy, Wayne Fredericks, and the African Bureau specialists, however, supported the recommendations in my cable. Williams had effectively stressed for some time the perils of trusting Tshombé, who, he pointed out, for more than two years had sabotaged all attempts to unite the Congo.

Immediately upon my arrival in Washington on November 9, I wrote a report to the President pointing to three basic factors which were converging to sabotage the UN efforts:

First, Tshombé's remarkable political skill in dealing with Americans and Europeans.

Second, Chinese military pressure on the Indian border, which had developed in October and would almost certainly force the withdrawal within a few weeks of the competent, well-led Indian forces which were the mainstay of the UN military effort.

Third, and in some ways most important, the strong suspicions of many young African leaders, with a vague knowledge of Marxism and an unhappy personal experience with colonial rule, that capitalist countries like America, Britain and France could never be expected to oppose the corporate views of the Belgium-controlled mining and manufacturing interests, which favored a separate Katanga. My recent talks with African leaders had left me with no doubt of their concern over this likelihood.

Almost everywhere in Africa, I reported, Tshombé was considered an African "Quisling," with the potential capacity to throw not only the Congo but all of black Africa into chaos.

Kennedy was interested in my report, and when we met two days after my return, he asked me to spell out precisely what course of action I favored. That night I prepared a memorandum of recommendations which I delivered to him the next morning. This memorandum, dated December 12, made the following recommendations:

> 1. A politically united, economically viable Congo is essential to the stability of the central and southern third of Africa and to U.S. world interests generally.

2. The Adoula Government, which, with all its weaknesses, offers the best and very possibly the *only* remaining hope for Congolese stability and unity, is now on the verge of collapse.

3. Since Tshombé could not hope to head a *united* Congo, he will continue to maneuver for an independent Katanga. Therefore we can expect him to continue his present delaying tactics, which are based on the assumption that we have already run out of determination and that the UN will soon run out of troops and money.

4. Although the Belgian Foreign Minister's, Paul-Henri Spaak's, recent moderate stand is welcome, the Belgian, British and French governments prodded by the copper interests, particularly the Union Minière, will continue to oppose effective economic sanctions to force Tshombé to cooperate.

5. Because of the imminent withdrawals of Indian and other troops and Tshombé's stubborn opposition, the UN's capability to unify the Congo will be exhausted within 30 to 45 days.

6. If the United Nations fails, we will be faced in all probability with a chaotic, unmanageable situation in central Africa, out of which any one of several developments may occur, all of them unfavorable to us, ranging from a Soviet takeover to a major U.S. commitment of money and manpower to prevent it.

We will also see the end of the UN as an effective administrative instrument of diplomacy, for which we will carry a heavy burden of responsibility.

I then proposed a series of steps through the UN, to be agreed to in advance, with each step followed by a brief interval during which Tshombé would be given a chance to sign a unification agreement with guarantees for his legitimate interests.

First, if a Tshombé-organized Léopoldville coup against Adoula seemed imminent, we should tell Adoula we would back him and his allies in a move to disband Parliament and to govern directly for the duration of the national emergency. In return, Adoula would pledge himself to oppose Soviet intervention in the unification fight and to protect Tshombé's legitimate interests as a province leader during the unification process.

Next, our officials through speeches and background press conferences should try publicly to unravel the complexities of the Congo conflict in order to mobilize public support for an anti-Tshombé policy. The heavily financed Katangan public relations operations in America, directed since 1960 by Michael Struelens, had for several months been effectively confusing the situation and had created considerable public and Congressional support for Tshombé's position. Now Struelens' visa was about to expire, and by simply refusing to renew it we could end his operation.

Should Tshombé refuse to sign an acceptable agreement within one week, I proposed a series of immediate military operations by the United Nations command. These would include UN bombing of Katangan white mercenary ground forces and airplanes, a ground blockade of Elisabethville, the Katangan capital, aimed at cutting off the outlet for copper exports through Northern Rhodesia, and a parallel UN paratroop movement to cut off the export of Katangan copper to the Portuguese colony of Angola.

These recommendations became the center of an all-out conflict within the Administration. On one side was a large majority, including the Joint Chiefs of Staff and the Defense Department supported by the European Bureau of the State Department, where most of the senior officers still clung to the belief that ex-colonial areas in Africa were not our concern and should eventually end up as spheres of influence of their former colonial rulers.

On the other side was a small group, including Adlai Stevenson, Williams, Fredericks and myself, who were convinced that only through the development of an international conscience with an effective United Nations to back it up could we ever hope to dampen down conflicts that could eventually blossom into major wars. If we failed to support strong UN action in this clear-cut situation, whatever hope there might still be of building a strong and effective international peace-keeping organization would be shattered

There was, as I saw it, no middle ground. The effort to negotiate a settlement had reached an impasse, and the date of departure of the UN Indian troops was getting nearer. Thus the President had to choose between supporting increased UN use of force to prevent Katanga's secession or pulling out entirely. These opposing views were bitterly debated in a series of White House meetings, all of which were attended by the President.

I was interested to see the Pentagon strongly favoring withdrawal of the UN forces on the grounds that Tshombé's mercenaries were a formidable force with which the UN could not deal. To contemplate UN forces being chased out of the Congo by a disorganized group of South African racist mercenaries was more than I could swallow. I wryly remarked at one meeting that it was a reasonable guess that each contract signed by a mercenary included a clause stating that under no circumstances would he be required to fight any farther than one thousand feet from a bar. Moreover, if the South African mercenaries had one good look at a battalion of Indian Gurkha troops, which were the backbone of the UN force, they would not stop running until they got back to Johannesburg. There were some at the table who laughed and others who scowled. The President was among those who laughed.

Two days later the President made a firm decision to continue full support for the UN, and the pieces quickly began to fall into place. A State Department study group concluded that support of the UN action was the only way to insure stability in the Congo. The respected Belgian Foreign Minister, Paul-Henri Spaak, had stated on December 11 that, despite his government's own self-interests in the Congo and its initial opposition to the UN, Belgium would support the UN. This statement may be credited in large part to the efforts of Under Secretary George McGhee, who now also supported the President's decision even though it was contrary to his earlier recommendation. Except for a few European powers such as Portugal, we now had strong support for a far more comprehensive and effective UN-based effort.

In late December the UN forces moved in and by mid-January, 1963, Tshombé's forces had been so badly mauled by the Indian units that he announced his willingness to end the divisive two-and-a-half-year-old secession.

It was a reassuring experience. The United States Government had made the necessary moves to reverse a situation that I believe would have spelled disaster for the UN, and to underscore our conviction that the integrity of the new African nations now took precedence over the nineteenth-century interests of the European powers.

After this crisis had passed I took advantage of the new focus on the problems of Africa strongly to urge the President and Secretary to re-examine our relations with Portugal, which, although the least industrialized of all the NATO powers, still remained by all odds the major colonial force in Africa. As everyone knew, our uneasy political support of Portugal in the UN on questions involving colonialism was part of the price we paid for the use of the Azores as a naval and air base where most of our shorter-range planes refueled on their way to and from Europe.

I renewed a proposal that I had previously outlined in a memorandum to the President on June 4, 1962, and which had received little attention then. My proposal was for a major loan to the Portuguese Government by the U.S. and its NATO allies with which to modernize its economy, in return for which Portugal would agree to the independence of Angola, Mozambique and its other African possessions and give the United States and the West European nations a long lease on the Azores. Although Salazar would reject it out of hand, I believe many younger Portuguese would have welcomed it as an opportunity to modernize their economy and to emancipate their sixteenth-century colonial holdings in the bargain. But since no immediate decision was involved, my proposal was never seriously discussed.

The relatively favorable relations between the United States and Africa that were established in the Kennedy years were subsequently weakened by our involvement in Vietnam, our intervention in the Dominican Republic in 1965 and our refusal to take meaningful steps against South Africa's racist government (or, for that matter, to make faster progress in solving our own racial conflicts). Yet, by and large, our record in Africa was probably more consistently liberal and enlightened than in any other continent.

POSTSCRIPT

While the Congo experienced continued difficulties during the 1960's, it celebrated the tenth anniversary of its independence in 1970 in an atmosphere of stability and hope. The reasons, I believe, are the role of the United Nations, large inputs of United States economic assistance and the emergence of able leadership from among the inexperienced Congolese leaders.

One of the most important turned out to be Joseph D. Mobutu, a former soldier. Until 1965 Mobutu concentrated his efforts largely on the organization of a loyal and competent Congolese Army which unexpectedly developed into a solid foundation of the central government.

Once established as President, Mobutu, who in 1970 was thirty-nine years old, demonstrated considerable skill as a politician and administrator. By subduing the remnants of the white mercenaries he established a high degree of local stability and order. He then demonstrated political courage by imposing a strict currency devaluation, which, while hitting many people heavily, placed the Congo economy on a solid base. Relations with Belgium improved and many foreign experts returned. Thanks to rapidly rising world copper prices, the Congo's foreign exchange reserves rose to nearly $250 million in three years. The Congo had come a long way from the crisis that erupted in 1962, with excellent prospects for continued stability and growth.

CHAPTER 34

FROM WASHINGTON TO NEW DELHI

FOLLOWING OUR RETURN from Africa in November, 1962, I had planned
to send my letter of resignation to Kennedy immediately after Thanksgiving. Although the proposals I had put forward in the previous eleven
months, including those dealing with Vietnam, had been politely considered in both the State Department and White House, they had produced very little in the way of action.[1]

I had been in public life long enough to expect a certain amount of
buffeting and frustration as an occupational risk. But in a year of effort
all I felt I had managed to do was to make a few of my colleagues feel
momentarily uncomfortable about their fixed positions without really
changing their minds, much less their policies.

I had completed a final draft of my resignation letter when an unpleasant event occurred. In an article in the *Saturday Evening Post*,
Charles Bartlett and Stewart Alsop attacked Adlai Stevenson for the
advice he was alleged to have given the President during the Cuban
missile crisis. Unnamed officials were quoted as saying that "Adlai
wanted another Munich."

Because of Bartlett's presumably close relationship with the President it was assumed by unfriendly critics that Kennedy himself was
seeking to embarrass Stevenson and thus to edge him out of office.
The Washington *Post* printed a Herblock cartoon depicting Stevenson with a knife in his back with the caption, "It must have come
from above."

I felt that the affair was less complicated than was generally as-

1. The Congo was an exception.

430

sumed. The State Department and Pentagon were still filled with people whose views on foreign policy had largely been shaped by the Cold War and who were willing and eager to believe the Bartlett-Alsop charge. I knew that they were every bit as scathing in the personal denunciation of Stevenson's views as they had been of my own. The article, I thought, reflected the division among Kennedy's advisers and the rigid, anti-liberal atmosphere among many of the senior Foreign Service officers in the State Department.

I assumed, as did most others, that Kennedy would promptly condemn the leak and the sentiment behind it. But all he criticized was the leak itself and the trouble it caused. His failure fully to support a distinguished American who had twice been the Democratic nominee for President strengthened my determination to leave the Administration.

Based on the events of the last two years, I assumed that the Bartlett-Alsop piece was only the first salvo in a new campaign to purge Washington of foreign policy "liberals," in whose company I was obviously included. Nor could I forget that the chain of events that led to my removal as Under Secretary of State also began with a Bartlett column, interpreted much the same way as the anti-Stevenson piece.

I waited a few days for the stories to peter out, and then on December 2, 1962, I took my letter of resignation to Sorensen; I asked him to read it and then personally to give it to the President. Sorensen said I was "much too sensitive" and urged me to change my mind and withdraw the lettter. I replied that my decision was firm and that there could be only three explanations of this year's developments:

First, that the President's personal assurance that the Special Representative's post was an important post which would bring me close to the President on foreign policy questions had never been intended to be taken seriously. I did not believe this.

Second, that somehow I had provided the President and the Secretary of State with inadequate, mistaken or irrelevant advice on the Asian, African and South American continents. I felt this was hardly the case. Third, that the situation was as my letter stated.

Sorensen again said that he wished I would reconsider my decision, but that if I insisted, he would personally deliver my letter to the President.

My letter made these main points:

> In the last seventeen months I have traveled some 80,000 miles to confer on the spot with the leaders of twenty-nine Asian, African and Latin American countries and to appraise our operations and policies in each of these nations. As a result of this effort I have made a number of specific policy recommendations to you and the Secretary of State.

I do not know how many of these recommendations ever reached your desk. However, there is no evidence that any of them received anything but the most cursory attention from your immediate advisers, who have been largely absorbed by problems of Europe, the U.S.S.R. and Cuba.

In view of our personal conversations of a year ago, and the assurances given me at that time by the Secretary, Ted Sorensen and McGeorge Bundy, I find this situation puzzling.

When you asked me to become your "adviser on foreign policy" in October, 1959, you emphasized that your request was based on the similarity of our views and objectives in regard not only to Asia, Africa and Latin America, but also to the Soviets.

Whatever our differences in style—and some tell me that is our real trouble—I remain convinced that your approach and mine to foreign policy matters are in fact very close. I am all the more concerned, therefore, about the impasse which has developed.

It has been suggested by some of our mutual friends, in a way of explanation, that since none of your present close advisers on foreign affairs were themselves involved in the public dialogue on U.S. foreign policy which led up to your election in 1960, they have viewed as "expendable" the positions many of us had taken and were taking in regard to Asia, Africa and Latin America.

Since they were less politically committed and exposed, it is said that they look on those of us who fought the fight against narrow Cold War concepts during the Dulles era as "controversial targets" for the Goldwaters and the John Birchers, and therefore a political liability to you and your Administration.

Their focus on Europe and the sense of exasperation with which they often approach the problem of the developing nations may derive from the fact that they have had almost no firsthand experience with these continents; for instance, not one of them, as far as I know, has ever visited Africa south of the Sahara.

If the special tasks in these continents, for which I am equipped by interest and experience, were now being adequately performed by others, the difficult circumstances in which I have had to work would have long since induced me to leave the Administration. However, these tasks— particularly in Asia, Africa and the Middle East—are given only the most cursory attention by our top policy-making associates until the underlying forces erupt to create a crisis.

I accept the need for the high priority given the Western Alliance, the Atlantic Community and assorted crisis points. Much of our energies must necessarily be absorbed in dealing with such vital matters.

But I fail to understand—and deeply deplore—the fact that no one in your Administration at a high level who is closely associated with you and has your full confidence has been giving priority attention to what is frequently referred to as the "outlying areas"—in other words, to that part of the world where most of the human race lives.

As a result of their heavy European orientation and a dearth of relevant experience among the upper echelons in the White House, Defense and State Departments, the response of your chief advisers to the problems of Africa and Asia has been one of peevish reluctance. When forced to act in response to specific crises, we have often ended up at the last minute doing the right thing—thanks largely to your own personal insights. But we have appeared to do so grudgingly, irritated that demands for action from these particular nations should be made upon us at all. Over and over again we have passed up opportunities to take the initiative and to help shape the course of events—rather than be controlled by them.

In such a context, it is baffling to me that my own readiness to play a role in connection with these vital and neglected matters has not only been ignored but obstructed. There is clearly enough to be done in these critically important areas to require all the energies of a high-level "adviser and representative," as I was described.

In other words, there is still plenty for *someone* to do in Asia, Africa and Latin America; and I would much rather work toward these objectives, which I continue to believe you and I still share, as a member of your Administration than as an outsider.

But, since there seems to be no way in which I can more effectively bring my experience to bear in this context, there is no alternative but for me to work outside the Administration for the policies which I have been advocating for years.

An hour or so after delivering this letter of resignation Sorensen called to report that the President had read my letter, most emphatically did not want me to leave the Administration, and that he looked forward to a visit with me on Tuesday of the following week, December 11.

I met with the President in his office for about forty-five minutes. He stressed that he did not want me to leave under any circumstances, and as we reviewed the various issues with which the Administration had had to deal, he asserted that the record would show that he had come down on my side of the intra-Administration debates more often than not.

I agreed that this might be statistically correct, but that these decisions had come just as we were about to go over the cliff. The issues themselves should have been foreseen and handled at a much earlier point. On many occasions, I said, it was like watching a movie in which the "bad guys" seemed to be winning, until the last minute when the tables suddenly turned and the President saved the day.

In closing our discussion Kennedy asked me to postpone any action until we had another chance to talk. He would be leaving for Florida soon and would like to think the whole situation through and talk with me after Christmas. Although my instinct was to press for a decision, the President was at that moment faced with raging public speculation over the recent article attacking Adlai Stevenson, and I did not want to add to his difficulties.

The President returned from his Florida vacation on January 9, and I saw him in the late afternoon of January 11. During the Christmas holidays I had become sufficiently impatient to write yet another letter to Kennedy, discussing some political elements of the present situation which I felt were important not only to his political career but to our national interests. I stressed in particular the importance of developing a foreign and domestic policy that would place him in a strong position for the 1964 campaign and that would provide a strong mandate for his second term.

My letter emphasized that if the Administration did not act decisively on a wide range of foreign policy issues within the next twelve months, it might lose its last opportunity to do so. The most immediate of these was undoubtedly Southeast Asia. But in addition to these were policies in South Asia, the Congo, Latin America and the Middle East and our ability to reach a realistic agreement with the Soviet Union to lessen the arms burden, which was reducing our capacity to deal with many domestic issues. By January of the next year Kennedy would be under heavy pressure from his political advisers to avoid controversy both at home and abroad because of the impending elections. Consequently the time to make the critically important reviews of our foreign policy that I had been persistently advocating in the past few months was now, when he still had some political elbow room.

I also pointed to the emergence of what I believed to be a new kind of political animal in America, an individual who is liberal in domestic affairs and reactionary in foreign affairs, to the point where his philosophy is almost a mirror image of the Maoist theory about inevitable conflict. Such people, I argued, could be a far greater threat to America's national interests abroad than readily identifiable extremists like Goldwater, because the latter's conservative views on domestic issues, such as Social Security, civil rights and housing made it unlikely that they could muster any significant support from the public as a whole.

In the end I decided not to send the letter, but to discuss these matters personally with the President.

When I walked into his office following his return from Florida, I was impressed with the fact that Kennedy looked stronger and healthier than I had ever seen him. After an interruption to discuss some Congressional business he came to his point. "Galbraith is getting out of India in May or early June," he said. "How would you like to take his place?"

The offer hadn't been entirely unexpected. Galbraith, it was widely known, wanted to return to Harvard after two years. However, I had suspected that the more likely request would have been for me to take over the Alliance for Progress.

Kennedy had urged me to accept the latter position a year before. Having learned the dangers in accepting fuzzy assignments of authority, I had replied that I would be delighted to do so provided I were publicly given full authority, subject only to him and Rusk, for all phases of our Latin-American relations—diplomatic, economic assistance, military, USIS and intelligence. The President assured me that I would in fact be responsible for all these activities. But as we talked I became concerned that his proposal was more of an expedient move than a carefully thought-through decision actually to change our policy framework in Latin America. Hence, I had declined.

That evening Steb and I discussed at length the President's proposal that we return to India. While we were both happy at the thought of going back to New Delhi, there were several factors that argued against my accepting Kennedy's proposal. First, I was reluctant to run away from the political struggle in the United States. The Kennedy Administration had fallen far short of my hopes. I had looked upon it as an historic turning point both at home and abroad; as the climax of our efforts to promote a better distribution of wealth, to ease racial tensions, to rebuild our cities, to strengthen our educational system and to improve not only material life but the quality of our society; and in world affairs to promote national independence, to help raise living standards and to do everything possible to end the Cold War and encourage peaceful, constructive cooperation with the U.S.S.R. and hopefully someday even China.

Thus far our performance had fallen far short of our expectations. The liberal views which people like Humphrey, Stevenson, Mennen Williams, Averell Harriman and, to a certain extent, Kennedy had presented so vigorously in the late 1950's were now rarely heard anywhere in Washington.

In a "round robin" letter to my family I summarized my feelings:

> The country's need is not for a liberal movement in a traditional sense but for a genuinely radical evaluation of American society, of our economic institutions, racial tensions, maladjustment of income and of the full use of our resources as well as of our relations to the world as a whole.
>
> There is little hard thinking being done here in Washington on any of these questions. The political breakthrough which I anticipated following the election of 1960 has not made its appearance. This is because

there is almost no intellectual leadership that has seriously challenged the conventional wisdom or ventured beyond the limited and now inadequate concepts of the New Deal.

Following the election of President Kennedy, the leadership of the American liberal movement naturally gravitated to the White House, but unhappily the Administration itself has seemed more concerned about husbanding the President's wide popularity, getting him re-elected, and generally muddling from crisis to crisis as elegantly as possible than in pressing overdue economic and social reforms.

A second reason for not returning to India was a concern over my ability significantly to affect our relations with India. Steb and I both knew that it might be difficult for us to recapture the unusual position we had in India in 1953; India had changed, and until the recent Chinese attack on India the U.S.-India relationship had deteriorated following our misguided agreement in 1954 to equip the Pakistan military.

We also knew that the new forces which were shaping India's hopes, fears and objectives would not be easy to communicate to our government. Moreover, once I was safely established in the U.S. Embassy in New Delhi, ten thousand miles away, how could we be sure that Kennedy and Rusk, particularly in view of the past, would actually give me the support that they had promised? Because of these factors a return to India might prove to be one more frustrating experience, of which I had had my full share.

However, on the positive side of the ledger, Jawaharlal Nehru, whom we had both known as a personal friend since 1951, was still the primary political force in India. The Congress Party was still dominant in the central government, and in most of the states; and Steb and I had warm memories of President Radhakrishnan, whom we had come to know when he was serving as Vice President. Moreover, the fact that India is ten thousand miles from Washington would assure me considerably more opportunity for personal judgments and tactics than I had in the State Department. Cables from overseas, as Ken Galbraith and a few others had demonstrated, often had a far greater impact on the White House and State Department than even the most carefully prepared high-level interdepartmental memoranda.

However, by far the most persuasive argument was the coincidence of two major events involving the Soviet Union, China and India which created an unparalleled opportunity for a fundamental change in our Asian policies. My experience in public affairs had taught me long ago it is timely reaction to events such as these which largely shapes history; skillfully marshaled arguments can often establish doubts about the wisdom of an existing policy, but that policy is unlikely to be changed unless an event occurs that shatters old relationships and opens up opportunities for new ones.

The first of the events to which I refer was the break between the Soviet Union and China, which had gradually been drifting apart for the last three or four years. The implications for the future of a continuing split in what many observers had wrongly assumed to be the "monolithic Communist bloc" were both great and unpredictable. The second event was the recent China-India conflict. Nehru's patient efforts to create a degree of harmony with China had begun to deteriorate in the late 1950's because of the dispute over the Indo-Chinese border in the Himalayas. At first this dispute had been discreetly kept under cover, but eventually it had erupted in the Chinese attack on India in October, 1962. and the disastrous defeat of the Indian forces on many sections of the long front.

These two historic events had combined to create a brand-new situation in Asia. With old relationships coming unstuck, we could expect a period of flux during which the United States might have an opportunity to develop a fresh and more realistic approach.

The extent of this opportunity had been underscored by the quickness with which the Indians had turned to us for military support following the Chinese attack in the fall. Our response had created almost overnight a new, highly favorable attitude in India toward the United States.

For fifteen years I had strongly and consistently opposed U.S. policy in Asia, which had been based primarily on military alliances with several rightist Asian governments with an open-ended commitment to support them under any and all circumstances. Now with the door wide-open for the development of an alternative policy which would necessarily include a closer relationship with India, I could not turn my back on the challenge. However, in view of my experience in the last two years I decided, in accepting an appointment as Ambassador to India, to include some reservations. In my letter of acceptance, on February 18, I told President Kennedy of my concerns.

My own views on the importance of a viable India to a free and politically stable Asia, I pointed out, were strongly held and widely known. Because of this, my assignment there would be interpreted as a reaffirmation of policies which I had long advocated. If the Administration's actions in the months following my appointment should fail to reflect these policies, my effectiveness would be gravely jeopardized, and I would be placed in an intolerable position.

While, I wrote, I did not suggest that we could foresee all the conditions that might affect our future relations with India or predetermine what actions Congress might take, I wanted to be sure not only that the Administration shared my views on the opportunity which now existed for us in India and in Asia, but that the Administration would be prepared to go to bat for them with Congress and the general public to secure the necessary budgets and authority.

"In other words," I wrote, "unless there is a deeply rooted and clearly understood consensus on U.S. objectives and priorities in India and South Asia, I am not the right man to represent the United States in India."

I also expressed the hope that the President would continue to welcome my views on foreign policy and domestic political questions not directly involving India, that I might feel free to communicate directly with him, and that this relationship would be understood and accepted in the top echelons of the State Department.

Although the President's response was forthright and reassuring, I still had grave doubts about the support I could expect from Dean Rusk and the State Department. When I raised these doubts with Dean directly, he suggested that I write him and Kennedy a memorandum specifically outlining the policies toward India and its relations with the rest of Asia which I would advocate. This, he said, would clarify any differences which might exist among us.

On March 12 I submittted an outline of these policies, emphasizing India's economic needs, the importance of accepting India as a primary force in Southeast Asia (which meant an end to the special status that Pakistan had been granted since the Dulles days), the need for sensitivity in dealing with Indian politics and, finally, the recognition of India's potential role in cooperation with Japan, Indonesia and other independent Asian nations in working toward a stable Asian balance, which, with U.S. support but not leadership, would eliminate the possibility of more Vietnams.

A few days later Kennedy told me he had read the memorandum which I had written at Rusk's suggestion, that he had always agreed with me in regard to India's importance to a stable Asia, that he agreed with my assessment of the new opportunities that existed there following the disruption in Soviet-China and India-China relationships, and that I could count on his full support. Rusk was less forthcoming. Although he did not specifically disagree with anything I had written, his strong bias came through clearly in the two or three talks we had on the subject. Indeed, in my last visit with him a week before my departure, he was so negative that I said, "Dean, if I felt that you really meant all you have been saying, I would be foolish indeed to accept the President's proposal. But I assume that your criticisms reflect the frustrations that all of us who deal with India feel on certain occasions and that you often feel even more strongly than others. So I am going anyway."

Inevitably, I began to be drawn into the day-to-day policy process in regard to India. When the Chinese invaded northern India in the fall of 1962, the United States and Great Britain had supported India vigorously. But we had also—rather ineptly, I thought—seized upon India's acute need for U.S. assistance as a lever to force the Indians to make concessions to the Pakistani in regard to Kashmir, which no democratic Indian Government could make and survive. Since the Pakistani had been outspoken in their support of China when India was under attack, it was my opinion that this effort was a nonstarter. Had Pakistan taken a neutral position, or, better yet, one favorable to India, I believe a rapprochement between the two countries, including a Kashmir settlement, could have been achieved. Regrettably, Pakistan's harsh pro-Chinese position killed whatever chances there might have been for such an accord.

The situation was further complicated by the fact that the Chinese war had revealed the inadequacy of India's military defenses. When the Chinese attacked, we and the British had immediately shipped in some $70 million worth of military equipment to meet their most urgent needs. Now the Indians had turned instinctively to the United States and Britain to help them finance the long-overdue modernization of their military forces. Indian plans were relatively moderate, in the neighborhood of $100 million a year for five years (we had previously given Pakistan over $800 million of equipment).

However, our government dragged its feet, partly in the mistaken hope that it might persuade India to make greater concessions to settle the Kashmir dispute, and even more out of fear that by sending military equipment to India we would upset the Pakistani and thereby jeopardize the U.S. military base at Peshawar in Pakistan on which our intelligence people placed great importance.

Meetings on India's request for U.S. support in modernizing the Indian Army dragged on throughout the winter of 1963 with no appreciable progress. In late April the President called a meeting in his office attended by Secretary of Defense McNamara, Rusk, Phil Talbot, the Assistant Secretary for South Asia and the Middle East, McGeorge Bundy, Robert Komer, Bundy's assistant, and me. The consensus of the meeting, including both Rusk and McNamara, was strongly opposed to a five-year program to help modernize the Indian armed forces, largely on the grounds that it would disrupt our relations with Pakistan.

I took the opposite view. The Chinese attack on India, I

said, was likely to open up new relationships in Asia which, although unpredictable in their direction or dimensions at this point, might create favorable opportunities for an entirely new approach to Asian stability. It might involve the gradual development of a new working relationship between the two largest non-Communist Asian nations, Japan and India. Although I had opposed most military aid programs, this situation was exceptional; India was seriously threatened by China, not only along the 2,500-mile Himalayan front but also from Burma, which China could use as a passageway into India. Pakistan's recent support of the Chinese had increased India's worries. Consequently, I recommended a military program for India in the neighborhood of $100 million a year, for five years. I had no doubt that if we were not prepared to help India to this extent, India would have no alternative but to go to the Soviet Union for the military equipment. If so, almost certainly the Soviets would grasp the opportunity to establish a closer relationship with this major, strategically placed nation.

The possibility of this chain of events was rejected by almost everyone at the meeting except, I discovered later, the President himself. The idea of the Soviet Union's giving military equipment to India on any basis was dismissed as unrealistic. India, it was said, had no place to go but to the United States. If we proceeded to help them, we would get ourselves into hot water with our "allies," the Pakistani (who for the last several years, with a strong lobby in Washington, had been manipulating American policies in Asia with a skill matched only by the Nationalist Chinese).

Following the meeting the President asked me to come into his office. While the consensus of the meeting was against me, he said that he was inclined to think that I was right. Therefore, he said, this subject should be the first for me to explore on my arrival in India. As soon as I had a firsthand impression of India's attitudes and needs, I should return to Washington for further discussions.

In April and May I was busy with the recruiting of new staff members. As I looked over the personnel roster for the New Delhi mission and the the three consulate generals in Madras, Bombay and Calcutta, I was concerned by the number of vacancies in key positions. Although I would have preferred to have had experienced men already on the scene, the vacancies gave me an opportunity to pick a staff in whom I already had personal confidence.

The most important post was the Deputy Chief of Mission, who acts as the deputy to the Ambassador, assuming his responsibilities when he is out of the country and acting as general manager and coordinator in the operation of the mission itself. I felt it was important that this post be filled by an outstanding Foreign Service officer. After considering a dozen or more possibilities, I settled on Joseph N. Greene, Jr., who was at that time serving as DCM in Nigeria and whom Steb and I had met on our various visits there. We had stayed at his home and had come to know Jerry as an extremely able administrator and his wife, Kitty, as an attractive and competent associate.

The Peace Corps and USIS were both in charge of experienced directors whom I was eager to keep and who agreed to continue. However, the post of Director of Economic Assistance, which next to the DCM I considered the most important post in the mission, was about to become vacant. Although Tyler Wood had been in this post for five years and was anxious to renew his acquaintance with the United States, I persuaded him to stay on temporarily.

Another position which was open was the Cultural Affairs Attaché, who plays a key role in dealing with universities, libraries and particularly with India's young people. The person who immediately occurred to me as best fitted for the task was Robert R. R. Brooks, Dean of Williams College, who had been my close associate since OPA days and in whom I had the utmost confidence. To my delight, I found that Bob and his wife, Mary, were in the mood for a change.

As head of the economics section I selected Leonard Weiss, a Foreign Service officer with a brilliant mind, imaginative, deeply committed and anxious to serve in India. He also proved to be a fortunate choice and soon became not only a key member of my staff but one of my closest personal advisers. I persuaded Charles E. Lindblom, a professor of economics at Yale, with whom I had worked as Governor of Connecticut on housing and school programs, to become my special adviser on economic affairs, and Colonel Amos Jordan, who was teaching political science at West Point, to assume a similar role on military questions.

Finally, as staff assistants, I hired Richard Celeste, a Rhodes Scholar who had done graduate work in education at Yale; Brandon Grove, a young Foreign Service officer with whom I had worked in Washington; and Douglas Bennet, Jr., whose father had worked closely with me in almost everything I had done over the past twenty years. These three young associates were crucially important in helping Jerry Greene and me develop an integrated, smooth-running organization.

After an exchange of cables with Ken Galbraith, we set the date for our arrival in Delhi in mid-July, about two or three weeks after his departure. We decided to go by way of the Pacific, taking a steamer from San Francisco to Japan and from there by plane to several East and Southeast Asian countries to help bring us up to date on developments in that area.

We had rented our Washington house on N Street, but decided to keep our Essex house open in charge of a caretaker and his wife. This would enable our children, who were deeply attached to Essex, to go there for weekends, Christmas holidays and other occasions. Although this was somewhat extravagant, we felt that it was an important element in maintaining the unusually close personal ties within our family. In mid-June we took off for San Francisco on the first leg of our journey. At that time we expected to stay in India for no more than two or three years. As it turned out, we remained there six years, which were among the most pleasant and stimulating of our lives.

CHAPTER 35

JOHN F. KENNEDY

IN MY FAREWELL VISITS with friends and associates before leaving for New Delhi the discussion naturally turned to President Kennedy, in terms not only of my own frustrating and disappointing experience, but of his effectiveness, conviction and likely place in history. Since then additional impressions, memories of half-forgotten events and the views expressed by others who knew him in different contexts have been constantly adding new dimension and perspective to my evaluation of this remarkable man.

Although I doubt that historians will rank Kennedy as one of our greatest Presidents, I believe that had he lived he would have almost certainly become one. Kennedy's charm, wit, intellectual capacity and eloquence would have assured him an important position in any era. But because he also represented the coming of age of the new postwar generation, no newly elected American President aroused greater expectations not only in his own country but throughout the world.

Yet on January 20, 1961, when Kennedy took his oath of office, I believe his political philosophy was still largely unformed. As a Congressman and Senator he had consistently voted "right" on labor and welfare legislation, housing, civil rights and the like, which were the issues by which liberals were distinguished from conservatives in Massachusetts and elsewhere. But the driving energy with which Kennedy sought the Presidency was generated not by a clear idea of what he wished to achieve, but primarily by his passion for accomplishment for its own sake—the Presidency represented the next and ultimate rung up the political ladder.

Even as his real convictions began gradually to take shape, the tra-

443

ditional criteria of "liberalism" or "conservatism" seemed less important to Kennedy than the ability of intelligent, sensitive and rational men, whatever their politics, to weigh alternatives and make the right choices. Instinctively, he distrusted any view which smacked of a firmly held philosophical belief. This in large measure was why he was attracted to analytically brilliant men such as Robert S. McNamara and McGeorge Bundy.

From mid-1959 until his election in 1960 I often accompanied Kennedy to meetings with labor and civil rights groups. On almost every occasion he was uneasy and occasionally contentious, as though uncomfortable with the demands put upon him to demonstrate his liberal credentials by a show of emotional commitment to liberalism, a commitment he did not possess.

This adherence to "pragmatism," on which Kennedy and many of his associates set such store, often accounted for what seemed to me a needlessly long process of deliberation on clear moral issues, to which I thought his response should have been quick and unequivocal.

Every man in a high public position is constantly pressed for decisions on a variety of subjects, a significant number of which involve matters of principle on which presumably he has long since reached his conclusions. Indeed, his reactions on such questions may be so predictable that there is no need for the decisions even to reach his desk. This enables him to focus his attention on the more complex or less familiar issues where the guidelines are less well established or nonexistent.

I do not, of course, suggest that what I have referred to as "principles" should be accepted indefinitely as the basis for final policy judgments. As circumstances change, old forces weaken and new ones take shape, and the principles that guide one's thinking must be constantly subjected to review and modification. It is here that young men often have major advantages over the ablest of older men in public life. As long as the assumptions and principles which have shaped their careers remain valid, men such as Konrad Adenauer and Charles de Gaulle can serve effectively to a ripe old age. Their downfall occurs when conditions change and they no longer have the ability to take these changes into account.

Nevertheless, when CIA chief Allen Dulles proposed to the President of the United States that our government finance and sponsor an invasion of Cuba by one thousand Cuban expatriates in clear violation of previous treaty commitments, there was no need, in my opinion, for a series of endless White House meetings to examine the proposal from a hundred different angles. The answer to Mr. Dulles' proposal should have been promptly and finally negative. The proposals to send American ground troops to Vietnam, to invade the Dominican Republic or to continue to arm Taiwan while seeking more normal relations with China belong, as I see it, in the same category.

In previous chapters I have described some of the crises that developed within the Administration, often because a consistent framework of firm moral principle was missing. In Chapter 26, assessing the performance of the Administration's officials, I observed that while under normal conditions the pragmatic approach was successful, it had real dangers. My words applied to Kennedy himself. "What worries me," I noted, "are the conclusions he may reach when he is tired, angry, frustrated or emotionally affected."

In the area of domestic affairs I recall an incident in respect to race relations which seems minor in retrospect but which was disturbing at the time. I had been asked to deliver a convocation speech on February 15, 1963, at Lincoln University in Pennsylvania, at that time composed almost wholly of black students. Like many others, I was disheartened by the slow pace of integration following the Supreme Court's 1954 decision on public schools. After a full decade of effort the accomplishments, it seemed to me, were minimal and it was time to say so.

The speech I had prepared challenged the record not just of the Administration but of our whole society, including many who regarded themselves rather contentedly as "liberals." My prepared text observed that black Americans "have a right to feel let down and bitter. The American people and their government have not lived up to the promise of this great judicial decision. Too many of us have been content to sit back and to say by implication, 'The Supreme Court has spoken and victory has been won.'"

As I was about to go on the auditorium stage to deliver my speech, I was told that there was an urgent call for me from the White House; the President was on the line.

Kennedy said he had just read my speech and was disturbed by it. In effect, he said, it was a "call to rebellion." I replied that it was a simple and frank reiteration of a position which I, and, I assumed, the Administration had taken long ago. Moreover, I explained, the speech had gone through the prescribed procedures; it had been approved by the White House, mimeographed and distributed to the press on the previous day, and I was scheduled to deliver it in approximately two minutes.

"If I call it off now," I told him, "or if I water it down, difficult questions will be asked both of you and of me, and a relatively minor issue could be blown into a major news story which would embarrass us both." After some discussion, Kennedy agreed that I should go ahead. He did not mention the incident again.

I am sure that the President's reaction to this speech did not reflect any personal opposition to desegregation. But having won by only a narrow margin in 1960, he was hesitant to open up any controversial questions unless it became necessary. What disturbed me was that on such a clear-cut issue he should have allowed even the slightest doubt about the propriety of my words to enter his mind.

It is a fact that until 1963, when Bob Kennedy became convinced that more determined action was necessary, those who were closest to Kennedy in the day-to-day process of administration were either not particularly committed to civil rights or did not give it a very high priority—or, most of all, feared the political effects of a white backlash.

Sargent Shriver, the "family man" on civil rights in the campaign, and Harris Wofford, my friend and former associate who headed the civil rights section in the 1960 campaign, and others, such as Soapy Williams and I, were not listened to when the President decided to go slow on the promised Executive Order on housing and on new legislation.

Every President attracts not only a coterie of devoted and loyal friends and admirers but also various political camp followers who are more interested in promoting their own interests than in furthering those of the President to whom they attach themselves. In Kennedy's case his lack of a consistent world view or a committed political philosophy affected his choice of key colleagues and advisers, and their failures in the same regard in turn affected him.

Kennedy's style put a heavy premium on the analysis, advice and persuasiveness of those closest to the President and resulted in an "inner circle" of unusual composition. It is particularly revealing that many of those who had the greatest influence on Kennedy's policies after he became President had failed publicly to support his nomination, and in some cases even his election.

Traditionally, it is assumed that those who come out first for a winning candidate or those who come out last are the most likely recipients of Presidential favors, the former being in the position of having taken a major risk in behalf of the candidate when others were waiting for more convincing evidence of his impending success, the latter being able to say that it was because of their courageous last-minute endorsements that his victory had been achieved.

In the Kennedy Administration many members of both of these traditionally favored groups found themselves, ironically, at a disadvantage. The assumption seemed to be that however helpful their efforts may have been in the past these individuals had been tarnished by the recent political hurly-burly and consequently had become subject to particularly bitter criticism from opposition members of Congress, the press and the public. Those who had played no role in the election might therefore be less likely to stir up criticism.

As a consequence, by the spring of 1961 many Democratic leaders who had privately, and even not so privately, opposed Kennedy's nomination, and in some cases even his election, suddenly awoke to find themselves among his key political advisers. Dean Acheson, who had publicly ridiculed Kennedy's first major foreign policy speech on Algeria and had bitterly opposed the approach to world affairs that most of us around Kennedy favored, is one example. Following the crisis over Berlin created by the Kennedy-Khrushchev encounter in Vienna, he emerged for a time as a central figure in the White House discussions.

Although I believe Kennedy was by and large disturbed by the specific advice Acheson offered, he nevertheless allowed him to dominate the debate within the government for some weeks. As a consequence, instead of the bold new initiatives which had been promised and which might have included more forthright proposals for negotiation, the options placed before the President were cast in the familiar Cold War alternatives of when and where "to stand up militarily to the Russians."

Finally, with pressure from Senators such as Hubert Humphrey and William Fulbright and support from Administration officials such as Arthur Schlesinger, Abe Chayes and Carl Kaysen, a Kennedy adviser, Kennedy was persuaded to recast the problem in broader terms than Acheson's original arguments.

Due to the complexity of Kennedy's personal style and his varied interests, it is impossible to characterize with any degree of precision the men and women with whom President Kennedy chose to work closely and who as a result influenced him most (and who in turn took on many of his characteristics). However, at the grave risk involved in all such generalizations, it seems to me that they could be roughly divided into several groups.

Some, of course, were purely political operators, the majority from Massachusetts, who had successfully nursed his ambitions and brilliantly managed his campaigns. Since most of these men were not hampered by ideological considerations, they felt much less commitment to the programs which so many of us, including the President, had expounded in the 1950's. I doubt that many of them even bothered to read the 1960 Democratic platform, which many of us saw as our declaration of faith.

Their own political faith was simple: their man was brighter, smarter and consequently better equipped to govern than any of his opponents. Their objectives were equally simple: to do what was necessary to elect Kennedy President and then to stay as close as possible to the new center of power and its status symbols—White House stationery, a limousine and a white telephone connected directly to the President's desk.

Although these professionals were as a matter of habit opposed to anyone who described himself as a Republican, I often wondered if in their hearts they were not almost as opposed to those Democrats who had worked with Roosevelt and Truman to create the New Deal and who had tried to carry it forward in the postwar years. Almost instinctively, they looked with suspicion on anyone with a committed liberal philosophy, and felt more comfortable with their fellow pros, who were less concerned with such matters.

Another faction among the Kennedy supporters, who were distinguished by their wealth, wit and charm, were the glamorous, glittering members of the "political jet set," who attached themselves socially to Jackie and Jack. It is doubtful that many of these jet-setters had much interest in economic, social or political ideas or programs; what concerned them was the prestige that came with being "close to the White House."

As they saw it, Kennedy's association with the liberals was a matter of political expediency, for which, in view of the closeness of the election, they forgave him. As "traitors to our class" Adlai Stevenson and I particularly drew their disdain.

Whatever their convictions, most of the people around Kennedy felt it necessary to take on at least some jet-set characteristics to assure their position in the New Frontier. (I shall always remember the photograph of Treasury Under Secretary Henry Fowler doing the "frug.")

Even when all of these negative elements are taken into account, the fact remains that many of Kennedy's advisers were able, committed, aware of the accumulation of problems which America faced at home and abroad and eager to do something about them. They shared my view that a warmed-over New Deal was not adequate and that what was required was a dynamic program which truly reflected our national priorities. But on critical issues we were usually outnumbered.

Beyond all these were his father and mother, whom I knew only casually, and most of all his brother Bob, who may have had as much influence on the President as all the rest put together.

The sum of Kennedy's political ambitions, personal inclinations, Presidential style and often conflicting advice from the inner circle and other associates combined with the course of events to produce a paradoxical mix of approaches, alternately reassuring and alarming. A good example is provided by two of Kennedy's innovative commitments, the Peace Corps and his determination to put a man on the moon.

The Peace Corps idea promised to add a new dimension to our foreign policy by creating a bridge between dedicated young Americans and the millions of Asians, Africans and Latin Americans who knew America only through the movies. It quickly caught on among the college generation, and many thousands of young people volunteered their services. Under the energetic direction of Kennedy's brother-in-law, Sargent Shriver (whom Kennedy said, only half facetiously, he had appointed so that when the Peace Corps failed it would be easier to fire its Director), the idea was quickly transformed into a program which Kennedy pushed through Congress and firmly supported through its shaky beginning in 1961. Within a year it had become one of our best-known, most effective and least controversial of our overseas programs.

In 1957, when the Soviets startled the world by placing the first satellite in orbit, the American Government and people responded with a panicky rush into scientific activity of all shapes and sizes in an effort to prove that we would not be left behind. With his deep competitive instincts and self-image as a man of action who was determined to "get America moving again," Kennedy saw this as a challenge.

James R. Killian, who was Science Adviser to President Eisenhower, strongly opposed adventures into space simply to outdo the Russians, and Jerome Wiesner, Science Adviser to President Kennedy, shared many of Killian's doubts. But on April 12, 1961, when the Soviet Cosmonaut Yuri Gagarin orbited the earth and became the first man to fly in space, Kennedy's competitive spirit boiled in frustration. Two days later, to sharpen his sense of defeat, came the Bay of Pigs fiasco, his first serious setback.

The President's mood was reflected in a memorandum he fired off almost immediately to Vice President Johnson, to whom he had assigned responsibility for the coordination of the space effort. "Do we have a chance of beating the Soviets," he demanded, "by putting a laboratory in space, or by a trip around the moon, or by a rocket to go to the moon and back with a man? Is there any other space program which promises dramatic results in which we could win? How much additional would it cost? Are we working 24 hours a day on existing programs? If not, why not?"[1]

My personal relationship with Kennedy in many ways also reflected the paradoxes of the Kennedy era. Although some of my associates still disagree, I remain convinced that on foreign policy questions my position and that of Kennedy (after he had fully thought through the alarming implications of some of the alternatives he was invariably urged to accept) were, in fact, extremely close.

Although it may be no more than my own wishful thinking, I believe that Kennedy himself felt more comfortable in taking a creative,

1. Referred to by Hugo Young, Bryan Silcock and Peter Dunn in an article, "Why We Went to the Moon," published in the *Washington Monthly*, April, 1970.

people-oriented position and that this helps explain why on so many occasions he supported the more moderate minority position against a majority of his advisers. I refer in particular to the proposed invasion of Cuba following the Bay of Pigs, the proposed intervention in the Dominican Republic following the assassination of Trujillo, the proposed introduction of ground forces into Laos, the proposed escalation from advisers to combat troops in Vietnam of the Taylor-Rostow mission report, the proposed withdrawal of the UN from the Congo and the proposed shipment of additional arms to Pakistan in 1963.

When I mentioned these examples to my colleagues as evidence of the more confident, more liberal Kennedy I hoped would ultimately emerge, I was invariably charged with giving Kennedy credit for not doing things which he should never have considered doing in the first place.

One factor that I am sure kept him from moving further in a liberal direction was the inherent need he shared with many liberals to prove that he was not really "woolly-headed" or sentimental, as his hard-line critics claimed, but rather "tough-minded and realistic," as all good foreign policy-makers are expected to be. As a result he often allowed what in the early stages might have been quite manageable situations to slide or to be so studied and restudied that eventually they blossomed into full-blown crises.

Gradually, I came to realize that Kennedy's personal style would prevent him from boldly advocating the liberal program that I and other Democrats had outlined in the party platform for 1960. Nor could he be expected to apply firm and consistent pressure on the State and Defense Departments to accomplish a unified set of foreign policy objectives such as I had urged as Under Secretary.

As a consequence, subconsciously I think, I tried to get the President, publicly at least, to *express* his liberal convictions, with the hope that once he did so this would serve to strengthen his liberal cast not only in his own mind but among the public, press and Congress. As he gained experience and confidence in his Presidency, I also believed he would lose some of his political caution and emerge as a bold and innovative leader. This development was, in fact, becoming more and more evident in the last few months of his career.

For instance, on several occasions he told friends that if he were re-elected by a sizable majority in 1964, he would be less vulnerable to day-to-day political pressures and consequently in a position to straighten out our China policy. In fact, I believe Kennedy's timidity in regard to foreign affairs may have been due in large measure to the closeness of the 1960 election. He had expected to win by a comfortable majority, and the fact that he barely scraped through made him cautious. I suspect that his strategy was to build up maximum political strength in his first term and then, following what he hoped and expected would be a decisive victory in 1964, to take the bold steps which some of us were advocating. If this judgment is correct, it further underscores the tragedy of his untimely death.

Another example of the evolution of Kennedy's position on world affairs was his speech on June 10, 1963, at the American University, in which he announced his willingness to negotiate with the U.S.S.R. on the cessation of nuclear testing in the atmosphere. Although he spoke in his usual pragmatic terms, a new moral dimension had been added, that I had not seen or heard before:

> First, let us re-examine our attitude toward peace itself. Too many of us think it is impossible. Too many think it unreal. But that is a dangerous, defeatist belief. . . . Our problems are man-made; therefore they can be solved by man. And man can be as big as he wants. No problem of human destiny is beyond the reach of human beings. Man's reason and spirit have often solved the seemingly unsolvable, and we believe they can do it again.
>
> I am not referring to the absolute, infinite concept of universal peace and goodwill of which some fantasts and fanatics dream. I do not deny the values of hopes and dreams, but we merely invite discouragement and incredulity by making them our only and immediate goal.
>
> Let us focus instead on a more practical, more attainable peace, based not on a sudden revolution in human nature but on a gradual evolution in human institutions, on a series of concrete actions and effective agreements which are in the interest of all concerned. There is no single, simple key to this peace, no grand or magic formula to be adopted by one or two powers. Genuine peace must be the product of many nations, the sum of many acts. . . . For peace is a process, a way of solving problems. . . .
>
> World peace . . . does not require that each man love his neighbor; it requires only that they live together in mutual tolerance, submitting their disputes to a just and peaceful settlement. And history teaches us that enmities between nations, as between individuals, do not last forever. However fixed our likes and dislikes may seem, the tide of time and events will often bring surprising changes in the relations between nations and neighbors.
>
> So let us persevere. Peace need not be impracticable, and war need not be inevitable. By defining our goal more clearly, by making it seem more manageable and less remote, we can help all peoples to see it, to draw hope from it, and to move irresistibly toward it.

Ted Sorensen had told me about this speech in early May and had asked for my suggestions. I responded as I had on previous occasions, but with little confidence that the President, in view of his current conflicts with Congress on several legislative issues, would say what I thought desperately needed saying. I was particularly pessimistic because he had told me in a recent conversation that the Senate was dead set against any halt to nuclear testing and he could see little hope for agreement.

However, in late May, following a private lunch with Soviet Ambassador Dobrynin at my home on N Street, my hopes had begun to rise. After several minutes of sterile wrangling, Dobrynin had expressed what seemed to be a genuine willingness to consider a new approach to the problem of nuclear testing in the atmosphere.

Before returning to my office, I stopped at the White House to tell Kennedy of this conversation. To my relief, Kennedy's reaction was wholly positive. While he remained doubtful that he could get the necessary two-thirds majority in the Senate, he said that he would go ahead anyway if the Soviets would only give him something worth presenting. "It may sound corny," he said, "but I am thinking not so much of our world but the world that Caroline will live in." He went on to say that even if he could "muster only ten votes in the Senate," he was determined to present the treaty with his recommendation for approval.

By the end of July, after his eloquent plea at the American University for a measure of nuclear sanity, we had negotiated our first major agreement in the defense field with the Soviets. On September 24 Kennedy's appeal to the Senate to implement the treaty agreement easily secured the necessary two-thirds majority with a vote of 80 to 19.

The question of what course Kennedy would have taken on Vietnam if he had lived will occupy historians for generations to come. It is my personal opinion that he would have eventually pulled back and that the introduction of U.S. general troops and the bombing of North Vietnam, which followed the Tonkin Gulf incident, would not have taken place. This opinion is largely based on my confidence in Kennedy's courage on other occasions in admitting that a policy was wrong and reversing it. I am also encouraged in this view by his words on a CBS television news program with Walter Cronkite on September 2, 1963:

> Unless a greater effort is made by the Vietnamese Government to win popular support the war cannot be won. In the final analysis, it's their war. They're the ones who have to win it or lose it. We can help them, give them equipment, we can send our men out there as advisers, but they have to win it, the people of Vietnam. We're prepared to continue to assist them, but I don't think that the war can be won unless the Vietnamese people support the effort. In the last two months the Saigon Government

has gotten out of touch with the people. The repressions against the Buddhists were very unwise. But all we can do is to make it clear we don't think this is the way to win. It's my hope that this will become increasingly obvious to the government, that they will take steps to try to bring back popular support for this very essential struggle.

Had Kennedy lived, I believe he would have become identified as a world leader whose thinking was not only pragmatic but increasingly guided by liberal principles which distinguished between what is right and what is wrong—and who was no longer embarrassed to say so.

I am confident that he would have also come to see that as often as not policies which make sense when considered one step at a time do not necessarily combine to make any sense at all. I have a deep conviction that if he had lived, he would have recognized the folly of our Southeast Asia policy, reversed our course of action and thereby altered the course of history.

Despite our personal difficulties I think Kennedy sincerely wanted to keep me in the Administration, not only because of my experience in foreign affairs but because he felt that I could balance to some extent the more military-oriented influences around him.

As for my own position, I stuck with Kennedy in spite of the difficulties because I felt convinced that he not only respected what I believed in but that he was becoming increasingly willing to stand behind policies based on these beliefs.

To some extent, I believe my failure to achieve many of my objectives during my years with Kennedy can be explained by political ineptness mixed with some wishful thinking. My most serious personal blunder was to cut myself off from my own sources of influence: my past association with the President, my former colleagues on Capitol Hill, Democratic Party leaders and the press.

In judging Kennedy's impact on perhaps the least tangible but most important issue, that of dignity for all men, we should never underrate his unique personal contributions. Even in his brief three years as President, he came to symbolize, not only to Americans but to tens of millions of people throughout the world, a new postwar generation moving into world affairs with a freshness and commitment that promised great things. In remote villages of India, Steb and I often saw pictures of Kennedy side by side with those of Gandhi and Nehru. Prime Minister Shastri's youngest grandson was named "Kennedy."

When Kennedy died, heartfelt tributes came from every corner of the world that were almost unprecedented. In India at the memorial service in front of the American Embassy, President Radhakrishnan and Prime Minister Nehru were joined by all the members of the Cabinet and Parliament and by thousands of simple Indian citizens who had come to love President Kennedy and to look at him with hope for the future.

As for my personal summation of Kennedy, I can do no more than quote from a brief comment I wrote in the midst of the State Department upheaval in July, 1961, at one of the darkest moments of my public career, when I was in no mood to be charitable:

> Whatever may be said for the President's methods of operations (and they leave a good deal to be desired as far as I am concerned), there is no question that he is moving toward a deeper understanding of foreign affairs. Indeed, he is the most solid force that can be counted on in Washington, or, indeed, anywhere else, to act rationally and responsibly.

PART IV

Ambassador to India:
A Search for Alternatives
in Asia

◆

"A change of supreme importance has now come over the world scene, and that is the renascence of Asia. Perhaps when the history of our time comes to be written, this re-entry of this old continent of Asia into world politics will be the most outstanding fact of this and the next generation,"

JAWAHARLAL NEHRU

CHAPTER 36

THE AMERICAN MISSION IN INDIA

WHATEVER DOUBTS we may have had about the wisdom of our return
to India began to disappear on the day of our arrival in New Delhi,
July 17, 1963. The warmth of our welcome was reassuring, and we
were excited by the prospect of visiting familiar places and seeing old
friends. Most important, for the first time in two years I felt free to
speak my own mind and to act. Ten thousand miles from Washington's
stifling bureaucracy and with a clear mandate from the President, I was
now in a position to explore the possibilities of a new relationship with
India and a fresh approach to Asia as a whole.

The critical element in our decision to return to India had been two
historic events: the break between the Soviet Union and China and the
equally dramatic break between India and China. Since then a third
development had occurred that was likely further to loosen old relationships and set the stage for further change: the growing involvement
of the United States in Southeast Asia. From the start I had been
convinced that the assumptions behind our military commitment there
were unrealistic. Now the limitations of U.S. military power in Asia
and the political weakness of an American-led coalition of lesser Asian
powers were becoming increasingly evident.

These events in combination, I thought, would ultimately shatter
the assumption accepted directly or indirectly by the Truman, Eisenhower and Kennedy Administrations[1] that a coalition of smaller Asian
nations could somehow "contain China" if only America firmly guided
the coalition and backed it with adequate will and resources.

The foundations for a politically stable Asia, capable of balancing

1. Later, also, by the Johnson and Nixon Administrations.

the power and weight of China (until the day when China was prepared to work constructively with its neighbors), could, I believed, be
provided only when the non-Communist nations of Asia, in their own
interests, began to work together. This would depend largely on the
willingness and ability of Japan, India and Indonesia, where most non-
Communist Asians live and which had thus far refused to become
directly involved, to assume far broader political and economic responsibilities for the peace and increasing prosperity of the region.

Many observers dismissed this development as most unlikely, and admittedly the obstacles were formidable. For instance, would India recognize her potential role in Asia? And if so, could India achieve the
political stability and economic growth rate necessary to enable her to
play this role? How would Japan with its burgeoning economic capacity
choose to use its new power? Could India and Japan, which had never
been close, come to understand each other and work together on matters
affecting their common interests? Could the Southeast Asian nations set
aside their historic differences and find some basis for cooperation?
Would they accept Japan and India as partners? Could the United
States be persuaded to assist India and other Asian nations adequately
with development loans without offending their political sensibilities?

Before beginning the story of my effort to help move American policy
in this more realistic direction, it might be useful to provide some background on the American mission in New Delhi for which I was now
responsible, and my efforts to strengthen it. As Under Secretary of
State I had encouraged ambassadors to assume greater responsibility,
and I had persuaded President Kennedy to give them the necessary
authority. Now I had the opportunity to practice what I had been so
persistently preaching since I first served in India in the early 1950's.

I saw four parts to this task: the organization of the Embassy
itself; the morale of its employees and their involvement in Indian life;
the fostering of a better understanding of the United States on the part
of India; and the reverse—a better understanding of India by Americans. By and large, I achieved some success in all four of these areas,
although I am sure that some of the changes that I made in our operations did not survive long after our departure.[2]

To strengthen the mission, a first priority was to provide a clearer
sense of policy direction and to assure greater coordination in and among

---

2. After we left India in 1953 following our first assignment there, a friend wrote
me that the wheels of our departing plane had scarcely left the ground when
Embassy officials began to rewrite my administrative orders, many of which had
upset traditional Foreign Service procedures.

the various departments—State Department, United States Information Service, Peace Corps, Agency for International Development and our military mission.[3] As in most large overseas American missions, there was considerable confusion over who was responsible for what and even over what we were supposed to accomplish.

Regular staff meetings on an informal basis proved invaluable in developing a sense of involvement in the work of the mission as a whole, in avoiding conflicts, in keeping everyone informed and in encouraging creative thinking. Each morning, for example, a brief meeting was held in my office, attended by my deputy, my two staff assistants and the heads of the various departments—a dozen or so in all—to consider the latest cables and to assign responsibilities for following through on the various items on the agenda.

Once a week a much larger meeting was held to which members of all sections of the mission were invited, including junior officers. At this larger meeting we considered issues which affected our operations. One week, for example, a political specialist would present an analysis of the Indian political situation in South India; followed the next week by a member of the AID staff describing the progress of the family planning program; then an up-to-date report on the Peace Corps or the progress of Indian agriculture and the like.

Another critical operational need was for closer coordination among those responsible for our political and economic reporting. Among the weekly reports that came to my desk might be a *political* analysis of the current situation in the Punjab side by side with an *economic* analysis by a different specialist covering the same state. Although these might both be excellent reports written by professionals, the interplay of economic and political forces was inevitably by-passed because each section wished to avoid encroachment on the other's territory. Probably the most important single *political* development in India each year was an economic event—the success or failure of the monsoon rains.

After much discussion we decided to combine political and economic analyses and reporting into a Department of Political and Economic Affairs headed by a Minister-Counselor. Under this new arrangement each officer dealt with all aspects of a problem. Since he was now in a position to go beyond the traditional role of simply describing the situation from the restricted perspective of his own specialty, we expected each officer to make recommendations to deal with the situations he had described.

Another area where coordination was lacking was between the

3. The military group had been set up to administer the flow of emergency military assistance, following the Chinese attack in October-November, 1962.

Peace Corps and the economic assistance program. The problem was dramatized by an incident that occurred during a visit to the Punjab shortly after our arrival. A group of Peace Corps Volunteers working on poultry farms told us of their concern about a strange new disease that was killing many baby chicks. On my return to New Delhi I sent an urgent message to the Department of Agriculture asking them to send a poultry expert to help with this problem.

Much to our embarrassment, they replied that one of the ablest poultry experts in the United States, a member of the faculty of the University of Michigan, was already located at the Agricultural University at Ludhiana, less than ten miles from where these Peace Corps Volunteers were operating. Within a week we had worked out a system that assured closer coordination and which both groups came to welcome.

Another need was for improved and more coordinated administration. The State Department, AID, Peace Corps, USIS and the military each had its own personnel, travel and housing staffs. By combining all administration services under a single director we saved considerable funds and greatly improved our operations.[4]

Another problem of organization was the lack of a close relationship between the Embassy and the three U.S. consulates in Madras, Calcutta and Bombay. For example, the consulates had not been receiving copies of many important cables between New Delhi and the State Department. As a result, the consuls general often lacked an adequate understanding of our operations.

It was a simple matter to clear up this particular omission. But to assure closer coordination of programs, I made regular visits to each of the consulates. Twice a year we also held two-day conferences in New Delhi attended by the consuls general and members of their staffs, which enabled us to explore all phases of our work throughout India, to share experiences and to discuss ways to improve our operations.

The improvement of morale throughout the mission was as important to an effective operation as the improvement of administration; indeed, the two were closely associated. Americans serving overseas not only have different jobs and family responsibilities than at home, but they are surrounded by a different culture. Often the tendency is to withdraw into an "American community" and to limit all other personal contacts. Health also becomes a major source of concern among many

4. This break with bureaucratic routine was abandoned within a year after we left New Delhi.

overseas mission employees. Foreign germs seem more dangerous than our own, and harrowing tales of wrong diagnoses and wrong treatment add to the sense of uncertainty.[5]

Morale was also adversely affected, I thought, by traditions of formality and rank. In a large mission such as New Delhi, many members of the staff rarely see either the Ambassador or his wife except under formal, official circumstances. To help correct this, Steb and I had a luncheon every Tuesday with a dozen or so lower- or middle-level employees and their wives, whom we would not normally meet. Steb also gave a "newcomers' tea" once a month for all newly arrived Americans in India.

We also encouraged wives of senior officials to call on the usually rather nervous wives of newly arrived officers, which seemed to us to be a more neighborly custom than expecting a new arrival to call on the wife of her husband's superior, which has long been the custom in the Foreign Service. We also encouraged informal dress throughout the year. I wore a dinner coat not more than three or four times a year. When the hot weather started in early April, most of the men switched to "bush shirts," with short sleeves and open at the neck.

There was also the question of our relations with the representatives of other countries. Like other national capitals, New Delhi is addicted to diplomatic dinners at which ambassadors and their wives exchange gossip and try to soak up more information than they give out. During our first week in New Delhi we received invitations to six of these dinners and accepted three. Although our hosts were cordial and the food excellent, it was clear that as a regular routine these affairs would add little to our knowledge of India, but a great deal to our physical burdens.

My daily schedule included between ten and twelve hours in the office, with frequent evening meetings or speaking engagements. Moreover, the early evening hours were especially important since the ten-hour difference in time between Washington and New Delhi meant that cables sent from my office as late as 7:30 P.M. would be on the Secretary's desk that same morning. Something had to give, and the choice was not difficult. Relations between America and Australia, Brazil or the Philippines are not likely to be settled in New Delhi.

However, we were concerned that our diplomatic colleagues might interpret our refusal to become too involved in the diplomatic social life

5. Actually, records show that there was less illness on a per capita basis in the American mission in New Delhi and in many others than in the State Department in Washington. In eight years in India, for example, Steb's illnesses consisted of two light cases of pneumonia. On three occasions I developed amoebic dysentery. However, there is now an effective treatment for it, and in eight years I lost only two days from my official duties because of illness.

of New Delhi as evidence that we were stuffy and unsocial. To meet this problem, we worked out various schemes which enabled us to develop and maintain the necessary relationships while avoiding long, dreary diplomatic dinners. For instance, whenever we turned down an invitation for dinner at the home of one of our ambassadorial colleagues, we made it a point to invite him and his wife to lunch alone at our house the following week. In this way we got to know each other much more effectively than we would have as participants at the same large dinner parties and avoided the impression of being aloof.

We were meticulous, however, in attending the "National Day" receptions which are given by each embassy each year, usually from 6 to 8 P.M.[6] Steb and I attended the most important ones together and alternated on the others. We also gave a series of music and dance recitals and dinners at one- or two-month intervals, usually with about 150 guests. They began promptly at seven o'clock, and after a half-hour of cocktails and soft drinks we presented an Indian music or dance recital. This lasted about an hour, and then came dinner. By 11 P.M. most of the guests had left. Steb, with the help of her social secretary, Bimla Bissell, a young Indian woman married to an American, planned and managed these affairs with great skill, and they enabled us to keep in touch with foreign diplomats, members of Parliament, ministers and civil servants, businessmen, educators and welfare workers whom we might not otherwise see.

We also spent a portion of our "free time" with young people— Indian and American, including many Peace Corps Volunteers—who came through our house in large numbers. In addition, there was of course a steady flow of visitors.

In the first two years of our second assignment, we invited our Indian employees, their wives and children to our Christmas functions. But since few of them were Christians, Steb organized an Indian mela specifically for them. We held it each year on Diwali, in late October or early November, the gayest of Indian holidays, with its "festival of lights." Although a purely Indian occasion, it was reminiscent of an American country fair, with trained bears, trapeze artists, fireworks and the like.

Two days before Christmas the Embassy had an open-house carol sing, which was usually attended by several hundred people. On Christmas Day itself Steb and I held open house. Through the churches and

6. Since July 4 falls during the hot monsoon season, we scheduled United States National Day during the lovely winter months on the birthday of a great American President. One year it would be Lincoln, another Jefferson, and so on. But instead of limiting our government list to the diplomatic elite, we also invited some eight thousand people, including schoolteachers, welfare workers and lesser government officials.

newspapers we invited Indian citizens from all walks of life. The first year we scheduled it from 10 A.M. to 6 P.M., and some ten thousand Indians—villagers, students, workers, businessmen and officials— showed up; it was an exhausting experience. In following years we cut this down to three hours, but still the crowds were huge.

I seriously doubt that these less formal social patterns, for which Steb was largely responsible, will long survive the pressure of Foreign Service tradition, but I believe we were successful for six years in presenting to India a fresher, warmer, more human impression of the United States while saving Americans on our staff from the strain of trying to be more formal than they would normally be at home.

Our morale-building efforts received an important boost from our decision to change the status of Roosevelt House from that of the Ambassador's official residence to that of a mission center. Although Roosevelt House was a magnificent piece of architecture, its formal grandeur and vast spaces made us feel uncomfortable. A few weeks after our arrival we mustered the courage to move into a more homelike, one-story, three-bedroom cottage with a lovely garden at 17 Ratendon Road. We had lived there ten years before and had come to like it second only to our home in Essex.

As a mission center, Roosevelt House was a success. Official meetings, press conferences, teas, receptions and formal dinners were held there. It was also available for groups within the mission, club meetings, school dances, film showings, art exhibits and the like. Its swimming pool was open to American and Indian employees, including visiting Peace Corps Volunteers who were constantly coming through New Delhi. We established a mission Cooperative Association responsible for maintaining recreational facilities, including a highly popular eight-team softball league which included British, Indian and Japanese teams as well as American.

The American Women's Club was also effective in encouraging wives to find useful activities in art, music, welfare work and teaching outside the American community. It was particularly rewarding to see the Marine Security Guards, under the leadership of Master Sergeant Johnson Lykins, take an intensive interest in India and make a personal contribution to better understanding between India and America. One of the projects they worked on, for example, was a home for lepers near New Delhi.

Perhaps the most effective instrument in encouraging our staff to become more personally involved in Indian life was the two-week intensive orientation course which all newly assigned employees and their wives were required to attend, with older children welcome. We had set this up during my first tour as Ambassador, and somehow it had survived the interval. The course was largely planned and taught by Indians with special expertise in the various aspects of the curriculum. It included an analysis of India's economy, social and political structure, foreign policy, religions and attitudes. There was also a taste of Indian history, art, music and dance, with visits to villages, hospitals, family planning clinics and schools.

The worst vantage place from which to form a balanced opinion of any country is its national capital. Most of those people who come there—whether it be New Delhi, Washington, Warsaw or Buenos Aires—arrive with a problem to be solved, a special advantage to pursue or an ax to grind. During my wartime service, for example, almost everyone I met in Washington agreed that the OPA was a first-class mess, and at times, after a long stint without traveling, I began to wonder if this were not true. However, as soon as I ventured into the rest of the country, I invariably found strong support for what we were trying to do and appreciation of what we were able to accomplish.

In India, therefore, I encouraged all our employees to travel. Steb and I visited not only every state but also every city of any size, almost every university, every major industrial enterprise or dam, together with hundreds of villages. I can think of no occasion when we returned to Delhi without our confidence being renewed and our perspective broadened.

In the course of our travels I spoke to every conceivable audience— students, businessmen, farmers, laborers, villagers and soldiers. Steb was almost equally active, often speaking in Hindi, which I never really learned. I found that my audiences welcomed my willingness to speak bluntly not only on Indo-American relations but also on controversial questions of economic development, where I thought India had gone wrong. I knew that in so doing I was likely to be charged with interference, and this is precisely what Communist Party representatives in Parliament and in various state assemblies often did. But with rare exceptions, I was encouraged to speak my mind as an accepted friend of India.

In our dealings with India and other Asian or African nations after World War II, the United States started with many advantages, the most important of which was our revolutionary tradition. More than 150 years ago, Foreign Minister Metternich of Austria, referring to the role of young American volunteers in the Greek rebellion against the Turks, remarked bitterly, "Wherever there is a revolution, you will find the Americans promoting those which fail and cheering those which succeed."

Most leaders in India, as elsewhere in Asia and Africa, had been profoundly affected by the liberal, anticolonial tradition of Jefferson, Jackson, Lincoln and Roosevelt. In drafting its Constitution, India borrowed many ideas and even phrases from the revolutionary pronouncements of the United States. It begins with the phrase, "We, the people of India . . ."

I often reminded Indian audiences of the sensitivity that our long years under British rule had created in the United States and our understanding of their difficulty in realizing that they, too, were now an independent country. In this regard they liked my story of Big Bill Thompson's campaign for Mayor of Chicago in 1928. As the campaign drew to a close and his speech writers ran out of relevant material, he promised one night, if elected, to keep the British Navy out of Lake Michigan. This created such enthusiasm that the night before the election he carried his commitment still further. "If King George ever comes to Chicago," he said, "I will personally throw him out." When a voice from the crowd asked if he were referring to King George III or King George V, Thompson is said to have exclaimed, "My God, don't tell me that there are two of them." (P.S. He was elected.)

Although India and America have much in common, including their commitment to democratic institutions, we had been subject to quite different forces, and our experiences on many questions had led us to different conclusions. Moreover, the people of both countries had developed seriously distorted views of the other. Partly as a consequence of the steady flow of American movies, many Indians visualized America as a land of cowboys, gangsters, CIA agents, millionaires and movie stars, while many Americans visualized India as a land of too many babies, cows and monkeys, famines, maharajas, polo players and cobras, with economic and political problems so appallingly great that neither we, the Indians nor anyone else could solve them. It was part of our task to bridge this communication gap.

The record of the United States Information Service in the post–World War II period was uneven. In some countries, such as India, under a succession of imaginative directors and interested ambassadors it had been highly successful. But in others, often in an effort to please the Congressional Appropriations committees, it attempted to depict America as a paragon of virtue, affluent, powerful, fat and prosperous, with, as far as the eye or ear could tell, no problems or conflicts.

For instance, in 1954 when the Supreme Court made its momentous decision in regard to school desegregation, tens of millions of people throughout the world who listened to the Voice of America were given the impression that racial problems in America were now largely solved. When the Little Rock school integration confrontation followed shortly thereafter, our credibility suffered correspondingly.

By the time of our arrival in 1963, Indo-American relationships had improved, partly because most Indians liked most of the Americans they had met, from the GI's in wartime to those Americans now living and working in India; partly because of the assistance we had contributed to the Indian economy; and partly as a result of the prompt American and British response to India's request for assistance after the Chinese attack on India in October, 1962.[7]

My feeling was that we should not expect India to abandon its nonalignment policies, nor should we even attempt to press Nehru in this direction. What was far more important was for our two nations to understand each other's fears, hopes, attitudes and objectives.

In New Delhi and throughout India I spoke with great frankness about America and its many problems, but always with my primary emphasis on our efforts to cope democratically with these problems. For instance, I did not deny that racial tensions in America were very real, nor did I claim that we had dealt adequately with them. Perhaps because of their concern about their own caste system, Indians generally accepted this. Indeed, there has been a remarkable lack of criticism in India over our failure fully to integrate American society—less, I believe, than in almost any other Asian or African country.

On such foreign policy questions as U.S. objectives in Europe, or our differences with China or the Soviet Union, I also felt that frankness was the best approach. My views on Vietnam were already well known in India, so I suggested that we leave the question of our original involvement to the historians and concentrate on the best way to end the fighting and insure a better future for Vietnam's long-suffering people.

Much of the burden for correcting the distorted views of America held by many Indians was on the United States Information Service,[8] under the able leadership of William Weathersby, who in 1967 became my deputy. During my first assignment in India, the USIS had published the *American Reporter,* a twelve-page fortnightly newspaper in eight Indian languages with a circulation of about 450,000. When I returned to India in 1963, I was delighted to see that this paper was still in opera-

7. An indication of this paradoxical new relationship was Nehru's agreement that the United States be permitted to set up a Voice of America radio station on Indian soil which would carry both Indian and American broadcasts to Southeast Asia. At the breakfast table on our first day in New Delhi, I read in the newspaper that India had withdrawn from this agreement. Although some pressure had been brought to bear by the Communists, the most effective opposition came from individuals and newspaper editors who were normally friendly to America, but who questioned the wisdom of such a close tie to the United States.

8. The entire USIS program in India is paid for in rupees from the vast holdings which we accumulated as payments for our shipments of PL-480 "Food for Peace" wheat.

tion, still well edited and still dealing honestly with the common problems of America and India. It also reported world-wide developments in the fields of science, education and politics; interviews with recent prominent visitors and excerpts from speeches by prominent American officials. In 1964 I began to contribute to the *American Reporter* a regular column, which was also published regularly in papers throughout India with a total daily circulation of two and a half million. In these columns I outlined my personal views on such questions as economic development, economic justice and world politics.[9]

At least half of our information program in India was designed to reach young people. A particularly effective USIS program was its series of "American Cultural Weeks" at various Indian universities. These comprehensive presentations of American problems, accomplishments, music, art and political views often lasted four or five days. To help conduct the various seminars, we recruited wives of Foreign Service officers, Peace Corps Volunteers, Fulbright Scholars and specialists from a variety of fields, as well as our own USIS staff.

When we first went to India in 1951, Nehru was so much the center of things that it was almost unnecessary for me as the U.S. Ambassador to call on anyone else. He had practically the sole power to make decisions, and he used it without hesitation. On our second tour, the situation had dramatically changed; the various ministries now had the power to make all but the most crucial decisions involving their special areas of responsibility. This meant many more people for me and my associates to see and to know.

The Indian senior civil servants with few exceptions were bright, sophisticated and usually badly overworked; our relations with them by and large were excellent. Here again we learned that the most effective way was to speak frankly, to admit our own mistakes (as we tactfully called attention to theirs) and to seek their views on how to accomplish our common goals.[10]

One particularly useful means of bringing key officials of the Indian and American governments closer together were formal annual conferences, whose sites alternated between the two countries. The first of these took place in August, 1968, in New Delhi. After considerable negotiation an American team came to India under the chairmanship of Under Secretary Nicholas deB. Katzenbach that included some of

9. On no occasion did either the White House or the State Department ever tell me what or what not to say.

10. I once tried this approach on the Soviet Ambassador. I had no sooner given my introductory line, "We are dealing with a new world and both your government and mine are bound to make mistakes," than he interrupted to say: "The Soviet Union makes no mistakes."

our ablest experts in economics, politics, Chinese and Soviet affairs and the like. For three days we talked frankly and in depth about common problems with our counterparts in the Indian Government, behind closed doors and with no press to report the exchanges. Rather to the surprise of the team from Washington, the differences between our two governments turned out to be almost negligible. A second meeting, held in Washington after my departure in 1969, was, I understand, equally successful.

Steb and I took a particular personal interest in the Peace Corps, which did a great deal to counteract unrealistic impressions of the United States. India's population equals that of Africa and Latin America combined, and our Peace Corps contingent was the largest in the world. When I arrived, there were some six hundred Volunteers; by the time of our departure in 1969 the number was around a thousand. They were engaged in a wide variety of work, including irrigation, birth control, agriculture, social work and nutrition.

One of the primary reasons why the Peace Corps was effective in India was, I believe, our insistence on "in-country training." Instead of training in the United States under simulated conditions, the Volunteers, after initial screening, would come directly to India, where they were assigned to villages similar to those in which they would be working. Here their training was largely supervised by Indian civil servants and by Indian members of our own staff. At the end of two months' training those who had not qualified returned home. The remainder were told that, although they were now accepted, they were still free to change their minds, and their passage would be paid to the United States. Usually at this point three or four more out of a group of eighty or so would decide to drop out. But the remainder, who had come to know India at firsthand and had made their own decision to stay, almost invariably stayed for the two full years.

I made it a point personally to talk to each group of Peace Corps Volunteers within two or three days after their arrival in India and also to talk with them shortly before they left. In addition, Volunteers were always welcomed at our house and at various Embassy functions, and we met scores of them working in villages during our travels around the country.

The exposure of various CIA activities by the *New York Times* in the spring of 1967 hurt us throughout the world, particularly in India, where we had developed especially close and extensive relationships with Indian universities and with individual scholars, none of which were in any way connected with intelligence operations. Naturally, the U.S.S.R. moved in to make the most of it.

One Russian propaganda gimmick was the repeated charge by the Soviet radio that Indians and other foreign students in the United States had been turned into CIA agents and were returning to subvert their own countries. As I once wrote to my family, "What greater evil could there be than to smear these thousands of young Indians who had been educated in America, so that every favorable comment they make on the U.S. is a basis for suspicion and they are finally driven to criticize America to prove their patriotism?"

Part of the covert operations against our mission involved the use of forged letters allegedly written by me or by well-known Indians. These letters usually went through a step-by-step sequence: (1) A document would be forged picturing the United States in some evil role. (2) The story would then be printed in a small Communist newspaper in East Germany or Bulgaria or in a Communist paper in Western Europe. (3) It would then be reprinted in India in the Communist-financed pages of *Blitz, Patriot* or *Link*. (4) The story would then be given first-page coverage in *Pravda*. (5) The final exposure would be a broadcast on Radio Moscow. During our eight years in India such propaganda gambits were routine affairs.

On several occasions I tried to discuss these tactics with the Soviet Ambassador. Why, I asked, does your radio seek constantly to undermine our efforts to create a stable India? In view of your conflict with China, an independent India is equally important to you. But I didn't get far. He would agree that our objectives were similar, but then claim that he could not understand why I should come to him with this problem since Radio Peace and Progress in Moscow was a private organization over which his government had no control.

On one occasion I wrote an open letter to the director of Radio Peace and Progress stating that I was informed by the Soviet Ambassador that his government had no control over the broadcasts of his station. Consequently, I was asking him directly to tone down these broadcasts in the interests of Soviet-American understanding and a more peaceful world. We then gave the letter to the newspapers, where it created considerable amusement.[11]

The various Communist elements in Parliament,[12] plus Communist-subsidized newspapers, plus generous Soviet financing, operating in a free society, with a free press and free speech, was a tough combination

11. Actually, I do not believe the Soviet Embassy in New Delhi fully controlled Soviet propaganda broadcasts, which often backfired on the Soviets because they reflected so little understanding of India.

12. As we shall see in a later chapter, the Communists in India were badly split. But one subject on which they could usually find common ground was the alleged misdeeds of the "American imperialists."

to buck. It succeeded in persuading millions of Indians that their own democratic political parties were all corrupt (although they were probably no more so than the Democrats and Republicans back home). It also spent considerable time, energy and money following the CIA "revelations" in the *New York Times,* creating suspicion about relationships in Indian-American projects which were perfectly proper, in an effort to establish that all Americans in India were spies.

By all odds our most effective response was to point out that the CIA "revelations" had been brought to light not by Soviet KGB agents but by hard-working American newspaper reporters. But even more important in neutralizing these attacks was the fact that there were tens of thousands of Indians who knew Steb, myself and other members of the mission and what we were trying to do. As a result in most situations we could count on the support of a very large number of Indians, many of them in important positions.

Tourism had increased significantly since my first assignment, and every year some forty thousand Americans were now visiting India. Although most of them came to see the musty "old" India described in the guidebooks, we made an effort to give them at least some understanding of the "new" India. An effective element in this program was a Visitors Center in our Embassy, which among other activities provided information about United States Government activities near such ancient tourist attractions as the Ajanta Caves or the Taj Mahal—a nearby Peace Corps operation or a new dam being built with American assistance.

Any group of American visitors, however small, could arrange through the Visitors Center for a briefing by a Foreign Service officer on the political and economic situation in India. With larger groups I often took an hour or so personally to answer questions about this important, diverse and fascinating country.

American businessmen, like most foreign businessmen in India, or other nations, including the United States, often run into maddening problems of bureaucracy, red tape and delays. To help them keep their perspective on the opportunities as well as the problems in India, we invited them and their Indian partners and associates to New Delhi two or three times a year for a day's conference on various phases of economic development and Indian economic policy.

We also encouraged the development of three Indo-American chambers of commerce—one in Delhi, one in Bombay and one in Calcutta— each of which brought together several hundred American businessmen and their Indian colleagues for regular discussions of common problems.

The American press representatives in India were, on the whole, an able, conscientious group.[13] I made myself available to them at any time, at their request, on a "background" basis. Whenever indicated, we invited them to a press conference in my office to fill them in on current problems. Many of the Indian press came individually to see me, and in addition, every two or three weeks, I held a regular background press conference at Roosevelt House with representatives of thirty or forty Indian newspapers, with whom I talked with great frankness. It was a great tribute to their integrity that on no occasion did any of my off-the-record comments appear in print.

It should be added that India's contribution to better understanding between our two countries has not always been characterized by tact, consistency or diplomatic handling of touchy issues. This stems in part from India's own acute sensitivity, nurtured during the colonial period, to any act which can be interpreted as outside pressure. In some cases it is a consequence of internal Indian political pressures not fully visible to the American eye and therefore not understood by Americans.

During the Dulles "everyone-stand-up-and-be-counted" period, India aggressively took a nonalignment position in respect to the Cold War. Although the United States ultimately accepted India's right to have views of its own, overburdened American officials, with little understanding of Asia and Asians, were often irritated by the self-righteous approach of many Indian leaders.

But this does not excuse our own ineptness. A great nation cannot afford to base its foreign policy on frustrations and irritation. It is critically important to the long-term interests of the American people that our Congress, our press and our government understand what is happening in India and what is likely to happen in the future. With one-sixth of the world's population, India is bound to be an important, if not decisive, factor in the future of Asia. The chapters that follow will, I hope, contribute to that understanding.

13. One of their greatest difficulties was that many of their editors, who knew little or nothing about India, would print any bizarre story of strange Indian ways that reflected the existing stereotype, but would reject news stories which dealt with the many positive changes that were taking place.

CHAPTER 37

A LOST OPPORTUNITY

THE FIRST OFFICIAL ACT of a newly arrived ambassador in a foreign capital is to present his credentials to the head of state. On the second day after our arrival the chief of protocol picked up Steb and me at Roosevelt House to escort us to the President's palace[1] for my ceremonial call on President Radhakrishnan. We were met by an honor guard composed of one hundred cavalrymen in brilliant red uniforms on magnificent horses and a company of infantry.

After we had been escorted through the palace gates, we left our car in the courtyard and were introduced to the President's handsome young military aides. An Army band played our two national anthems, and after briefly reviewing the honor guard, we entered the palace, where we were greeted by the President.

Radhakrishnan was a rare human being, former Oxford professor, head of UNESCO, Gandhian patriot and, at seventy-three years of age, as keen and charming as ever. When we had known him as Vice President, we considered him among our best Indian friends. I had been grateful for the candor with which he discussed the problems facing our two governments and his astute comments on the Indian political scene. When I asked to what extent our earlier relationship would be changed because of his Presidential status, he assured me that we could pick up precisely where we had left off ten years ago.

By tradition my next call was on the Prime Minister. During our first assignment in India, in the early 1950's, Steb and I had come to know Jawaharlal Nehru well. During the ten-year intervening period, I had seen Nehru in New York, Washington and New Delhi on a dozen

1. In British days it had been the home of the Viceroy.

or so occasions, and through these visits plus an occasional exchange of letters we had kept in touch with each other's views.

Nehru gave me a warm welcome. Although he had aged in his physical appearance, his mind seemed as alert as ever. I was particularly anxious to discuss the five-year military assistance program which India had requested. President Kennedy, who I knew was favorably inclined, had asked me to explore the question as rapidly as possible and report my findings back to him. Although I knew this question was as much on Nehru's mind as it was on my own, it was introduced in a manner which I had not anticipated.

India, Nehru said, deeply appreciated the action of the American and British governments in promptly providing shipments of military equipment after the 1962 Chinese attack.[2] We had moved swiftly and expertly, and the Indian people would be forever grateful. But why, Nehru asked, did the United States attempt to use India's difficulties with China as a lever to force him to make concessions to Pakistan on Kashmir?[3] Pakistan, Nehru reminded me, had publicly supported the Chinese attacks on India. Yet at the very moment when Indian emotions against Pakistan were high, we had attempted to force him to make compromises which the Indian people and the Indian Parliament would not possibly accept, and which no Indian Prime Minister could make without being voted out of office.

If the Pakistani had sided with India or at least remained neutral on the Indo-Chinese conflict, Nehru said, an atmosphere would have been created in which he could have made very significant concessions in regard to Kashmir. Therefore it would have been far more logical for us to have pressed Pakistan to forgo its support for the Chinese than to have pressed for Indian concessions that India could not possibly make in the heavily charged atmosphere of that time.

Nehru raised this matter not contentiously, but as a puzzled friend. After considerable discussion I believe I made some progress in persuading him that, however mistakenly directed our approach may have been, the intent was sincere. President Kennedy, a good friend of India, was eager to improve relations between Pakistan and India and to free both nations for the task of modernization and development. That was one reason why I had agreed to return to New Delhi.

Ultimately this discussion led us to the question of India's request for U.S. military assistance. Following India's establishment as an independent nation in 1947, the Indian Government had decided to keep its

2. This emergency equipment was covered by a grant of $65 million.
3. Nehru was referring to the Indo-Pakistani negotiations on Kashmir which had been launched as a result of U.S. prodding in the winter of 1962–63.

military expenditures at the maximum level of one percent of its Gross National Product,[4] thereby freeing resources for economic development. It had been India's hope that Pakistani antagonism would gradually moderate and that China's energies would be focused primarily on its own internal development. When the Chinese unexpectedly attacked, the Indian Army was armed with obsolescent weapons, and had had inadequate training; as a result India had experienced a military disaster.

I then told Nehru of an incident which had occurred just prior to China's attack. When I stopped in India in March, 1962, for a brief visit, the Commander in Chief of the Indian Army, General Brij Kaul, whom I did not know, requested to see me. He told me that he expected an attack by Communist China between July and October of that year and asked what the United States could be expected to do to assist. When I expressed my skepticism about such an attack, General Kaul insisted that Chinese troop movements into Tibet and the carefully calculated build-up of tensions indicated that the Chinese were preparing to move from the negotiating table to the battlefield.

When I asked Kaul if the Prime Minister knew he was discussing these possibilities with me, he replied in the negative. Nor did he follow through on my suggestion that he discuss it with Ambassador Galbraith, who would then put the question to Washington. Nehru's only comment was: "I wish he had told me, too."

I might add that another reason for India's defeat was its decision not to use its Air Force against the long Chinese communications lines for fear that if it did so the Chinese would bomb Calcutta and New Delhi. In late November, 1962, with the Indian Army near collapse, Nehru had written to President Kennedy asking for the immediate delivery of fourteen squadrons of U.S. fighter planes to protect the northern Indian cities, and three squadrons of bombers, which would enable the Indian Air Force to attack the Chinese communications lines. Three days after the receipt of this letter the Chinese began to withdraw, and the decision was never made.

In view of India's defeat and the continuing belligerence of the Pakistani (who were armed with modern American weapons), Nehru said that India now had no alternative but to develop the military strength appropriate to a nation of its size and exposed geographical position with two unfriendly neighbors.

Nehru stressed that the military strategy he had in mind was a relatively moderate one but that Indian forces must be large enough and adequately armed and trained to discourage either Pakistan or China in-

4. In 1963, U.S. expenditures were approximately 8 percent; Turkey, Greece, France and many other countries were spending from 5 to 7 percent.

dividually from attacking India. If China and Pakistan *together* attacked India, he hoped that support from the United States and other countries would again be forthcoming. Time, he said, was of the essence. Therefore he would be grateful if I would talk directly to Defense Minister Yeshwantrao Chavan and other Indian officials who were familiar with India's military needs and then persuade President Kennedy to make an early decision.

In the following weeks I met regularly with Defense Minister Chavan, the former Chief Minister of Maharashtra, who had been drafted by Nehru to replace Krishna Menon soon after the Chinese attack, and his staff. The budget figure for U.S. military aid with which we were working was $75 million a year for five years, in addition to our previous 1962 emergency assistance of $65 million, with the hope that the British could be persuaded to provide another $15 or $20 million annually.

The Indian request was for a $500 million program, to be spent over a period of five years.[5] The Indians were particularly anxious to fully equip their frontier mountain divisions, some of which already had American machine guns, rifles, radios, trucks and jeeps. Their second most important priority was modern airplanes to bolster their obsolescent Air Force, and third a radar warning screen to help protect North Indian cities from a Chinese air attack.

The United States military mission in New Delhi, headed by General John E. Kelly, consisted of roughly one hundred officers and men. In addition, Colonel Amos (Joe) Jordan, on a special leave of absence from West Point, where he headed the political science department, was a member of my personal staff.

The initial task of the military mission was to handle the flow of military equipment under the original agreement immediately following the Chinese attack. In cooperation with their opposite numbers in the Indian military establishment, General Kelly and his team worked out a plan which it was agreed would provide the best possible use of the additional funds which we hoped and believed our government would now make available. By the end of October we reached a tentative agreement which included modern aircraft, further equipment for twelve mountain divisions and the radar network, at a cost of $75 million a year for five years.

Once the proposed military program had tentatively been put together, I asked the Prime Minister two related political questions. First, if the program was agreed to by my government, were the Indians prepared to negotiate with the Pakistani for the establishment of a ceiling

5. The Pakistani had already received on a grant basis some $850 million worth of American military equipment.

on their respective military establishments? Every dollar spent on military equipment meant so much less for the domestic economies of both countries, and the last thing South Asia needed, I suggested to Nehru, was an arms race.

Second, I expressed our concern in regard to China, which seemed to be in a somewhat more belligerent mood than either the Indians or we had anticipated. While I realized that the Indian military was for a variety of reasons unable to become directly involved in Southeast Asia at this time, our government would welcome India's *political* cooperation in developing a peaceful solution that would assure the independence of South Vietnam, Laos and the other nations in this area. If the Chinese should actually invade the nations of Southeast Asia (which I did not anticipate), we hoped that India would do all it could to support our efforts to defend them. In respect to all of these questions the Prime Minister responded promptly and affirmatively.

Since the French withdrew in 1954, India had taken a moderate position in regard to Southeast Asia. On his visit to Washington in November, 1961, Nehru had indicated that a substantial consensus existed between the United States and India on the problems of Southeast Asia. Kennedy had assured Nehru that in Vietnam he would press Diem to liberalize his regime and in Laos he would support a coalition headed by Souvanna Phouma. In turn, Nehru had assured Kennedy that if necessary India would use its political capital accumulated during its years of support for Souvanna Phouma to encourage a non-Communist political evolution in Laos.

Kennedy had inferred from this early talk with Nehru that India would not object openly to some U.S. military advisers or military equipment in Vietnam, but would oppose intervention by U.S. combat troops. This assessment was correct; it was in 1965, when we introduced combat troops, that India began to move away from us.

My personal views on providing a military assistance program to India were mixed. In the last fifteen years much of our military assistance outside Europe had been given to persuade other governments to support United States foreign policy. In some instances it was a thinly disguised price that we paid for the use of military bases, which we built at great cost on land provided by our "allies." But once we had begun to provide military aid, it often became almost impossible to stop, and we found ourselves captives of our own policy. Whenever one of the recipients sensed that we might be considering a reduction in our military assistance, we were likely to be informed in one way or another that unless we maintained the present flow of weapons our bases would be in jeopardy and our so-called ally would "be forced to reconsider" its support of our foreign policy.

But I believed that India's security problem was a special case, and that the objectives of our assistance there were totally different from those in such countries as Iran or Ethiopia, and certainly Pakistan. India had a 2,500-mile-long border with China, plus an additional 600 miles of border with Burma. Chinese troops had already demonstrated their belligerence by crossing the India-China border, and unless India succeeded in modernizing its armed forces, it was quite possible that China would choose to do so again on a larger scale.

Since Pakistan, whose Army had been largely equipped and trained by the United States, had supported the Chinese effort of 1962, it certainly could not be depended upon to remain neutral if the Chinese launched another attack. Our failure to assist India while we continued heavily to support Pakistan would seem strange indeed. Moreover, India in its present nervous mood was determined to modernize its Army by one means or another. While Nehru hoped that it would be the United States which provided the necessary support, it was clear that if turned down, he would with genuine reluctance approach the Soviet Union, which was now as anxious as the United States to hold China in check. It was on this basis that I justified in my own mind a military program for India in 1963.

I left for the United States in mid-November with a tentative agreement with the Indian Government in my briefcase for President Kennedy's consideration. With Nehru's somewhat surprising readiness to take a sympathetic political position in Southeast Asia, with his willingness to negotiate a ceiling on military expenditures with Pakistan, and with the President's backing, I was confident that I had a much better than even chance of success. However, I knew that the influence which Pakistan had developed over a period of years at high levels in the State and Defense Departments would be formidable. The origins of our relationship with Pakistan are an interesting commentary on how U.S. foreign policy was often shaped during these years. This relationship deserves a closer look.

The rationale of the United States' interests in Pakistan's military strength may be traced to a book, *Wells of Power*, written by a British civil servant, Sir Olaf Caroe, which came to the attention of the U.S. State Department in the early 1950's. As Caroe pointed out, in British colonial days the stability of the Middle East and Southeast Asia largely depended on three elements: British diplomacy, the British Navy and the Indian Army. Following the British withdrawal from India and the establishment of Nehru's policy of noninvolvement in 1948, the Indian Army had been neutralized; hence, Caroe argued, a substitute must be found, and Pakistan was the most likely possibility.

When this strained bit of geopolitical reasoning was first unveiled in the winter of 1952 during my first assignment to India, I strongly questioned it. My arguments were supported by Sir Archibald Nye, former dupty to Field Marshal Montgomery, and then British High Commissioner in India. After many long discussions and countless cables, I convinced President Truman that large-scale military assistance to Pakistan would be a serious mistake. If Soviet Army forces moved overtly into the Middle East (a most improbable turn of events), Pakistan, separated from the U.S.S.R. itself only by a relatively weak Afghanistan, would almost surely remain aloof no matter how many arms we gave them.

In the fall of 1953, Ayub Khan, who at that time was Commander in Chief of the Pakistan Army,[6] arrived in the United States, presumably for a medical check-up. However, it soon became apparent that his visit had other purposes. In discussions with the State Department and Pentagon he persuasively advocated the Caroe thesis. The State Department, which under my prodding had explored the pros and cons of the idea when it was first proposed and had reached a negative decision, continued to disagree.

At that point members of Ayub Khan's staff leaked the story to the newspapers. Soon articles began to appear, citing "informed sources," which alleged that the State Department was actually rejecting an opportunity for a military alliance with a nation of 100 million "hard-fighting Muslims" who were willing, even eager, to take on whatever Communists we might designate. At this time, Senator Joseph McCarthy's influence was at its height, and a vision of a State Department "infiltrated" with Communist spies scheming to deprive the U.S. Government of a new source of military support was easily conjured up.

Soon stories began to appear of behind-the-scenes maneuvering within the State Department and Pentagon for a review of the earlier negative decision. Of particular concern was the report that Secretary of State Dulles, exasperated by Nehru's refusal to sign the Japanese Peace Treaty which he (Dulles) had negotiated or to "modify" India's non-aligned foreign policies, was in favor of the proposed build-up of the Pakistan military.

On December 21, 1953, I wrote to Dulles cautioning him against a military pact with Pakistan. Prime Minister Nehru, I wrote, would react strongly against any program to supply modern U.S. equipment to the Pakistan Army. In fact, rumors of the impending military pact had already set off anti-American sentiment in India and elsewhere in the

6. Later President of Pakistan.

Middle East and South Asia, and I thought it entirely possible that Nehru might feel it politically expedient to go along with the anti-American sentiment for a time in the hope that he could thereby control it and gradually modify it. However, I knew this would only serve to make a bad situation worse. The United States would be likely to react angrily to whatever Nehru might say, and our reactions in turn would call for further criticism of U.S. policy by Indians, who were, in fact, eager for American friendship and understanding.

The Soviet Union, I wrote to Dulles, would be presented with a tempting choice of alternatives. The Soviets would surely offer India military assistance to match our assistance to Pakistan. This offer might be supported by substantial Soviet economic aid to bolster the Indian Five-Year Plan. I concluded:

> The proposed arms agreement with Pakistan, far from furthering our national objectives in the Middle East and South Asia, will add danger-ously to the grave instability that already exists there. I am convinced that the proposed United States–Pakistan military agreement may indeed set in motion a chain of events which in the next ten years can lead to political developments in India and South Asia which will have grave implications for our future relations in this area and indeed in all of Asia.

As rumors of an impending U.S.-Pakistan arms agreement continued to grow, the Communist Party of India seized the opportunity to launch mass agitation for the immediate purchase of "defensive" arms from the Soviet Union. In late December, 1953, in an effort to keep the Communist Party of India from appropriating this political issue, Nehru made a speech strongly opposing U.S. military assistance to Pakistan on the grounds that it would bring the Cold War to India's own borders. Two weeks later, he characterized the proposed military aid as an "anti-Asian step, a step toward war, not peace, a step which will bring war or the threat of war to our frontiers."

On February 25, 1954, President Eisenhower approved the arms agreement with Pakistan. In a public lettter of explanation to Prime Minister Nehru he said:

> What we are proposing to do and what Pakistan is agreeing to is not directed in any way against India, and I am confirming publicly that if our aid to any country, including Pakistan, is misused and directed against any other, I shall undertake immediate and, in accordance with my Constitutional authority, appropriate action both within and without the United Nations to thwart such aggressions.

On March 1, in a formal reply to President Eisenhower's letter, Nehru wrote, "Although I appreciate the assurance you gave me, you are, however, aware of the views of my government and our people in regard to this matter." He added that he was convinced that President Eisenhower bore no ill will toward India and that his decision to give arms to Pakistan was well intentioned, but that the effects were "bound to be unfortunate." The first result he pointed out was "a sense of upsetting things" and the creation of insecurity between India and Pakistan. Nehru expressed doubt that President Eisenhower could, as a practical matter, prevent "aggression" by Pakistan with United States arms.[7]

The Congress and public were told that the purpose of our military assistance was to enable the Pakistani to join in the common defense of South Asia and the Middle East against a Soviet-Chinese attack, while the State Department and the U.S. Embassy in New Delhi continued to offer India similar assurances.

India's Army, Navy and Air Force, like those of Pakistan, were at that time totally dependent on U.S. and British equipment left over from World War II, and the Indians still hoped that the equipment we sent Pakistan would not be enough to upset the balance. Consequently, in the summer of 1954, when large amounts of modern U.S. military equipment to Pakistan, including tanks, began to be unloaded on the Karachi docks, the Indian press and public, supported by the leaders of all parties from extreme left to extreme right, reacted bitterly.

The Indian Government pointed out that the military equipment that we were giving to Pakistan had no relevance to our alleged military objectives. If the Pakistan Army were actually designed to become part of a U.S.-sponsored defense system to discourage a Soviet or Chinese military movement through the Himalayas or the Hindu Kush Mountains, it would be seeking equipment appropriate for fighting in the mountain areas. However, the equipment we supplied Pakistan—tanks, motorized artillery and the like—was suitable for use only on a relatively flat terrain, in other words, on the plains of North India. Moreover, from the outset the Pakistan Government had itself made clear that it had no quarrel with either the U.S.S.R. or China and privately admitted that its military build-up was, in fact, directed against India.

To balance the increasing strength of the Pakistan Army and Air Force, which we were equipping with F-86 and F-104 fighter planes and Patton tanks, the Indians dipped into their limited foreign exchange reserves to buy Centurion tanks and Hunter fighter planes from the British and Mystère fighter planes from the French. The fact that India's purchases were limited reflected its continued trust in the

7. The Pakistan-India war of August and September of 1965 unhappily proved Nehru's judgment to have been correct.

United States' pledge that under no circumstances would we "permit" the equipment given to Pakistan to be used against India.[8]

In the late 1950's a new element appeared which further strengthened our commitment to Pakistan. This was the development of a large U.S. military base at Peshawar in Pakistan. Alert American reporters soon discovered and publicized the fact that, in addition to its strategic value in case of war with the U.S.S.R., the base had been established to gather information on scientific developments in the U.S.S.R. through the the use of sophisticated electronic equipment. The U-2 in which Francis Gary Powers embarked on his flight across the U.S.S.R. on May 9, 1960, took off from the Peshawar airfield.

As the Pentagon and State Department placed greater and greater emphasis on the importance of our air base in Peshawar, the capacity of the Pakistan Government to influence U.S. policy in South Asia increased correspondingly, until it gained what amounted to a political hammer lock on that policy.

President Kennedy had from the beginning shared my concern about our lopsided policy toward Pakistan and India. Nonetheless, in early July, 1961, when President Ayub Khan came to Washington to press the new President to carry out what he quite inaccurately described as the "promise" of the Eisenhower Administration to supply a squadron of F-104's, he had no great difficulty in winning the approval of the new Administration. Kennedy, obviously, had succumbed to the familiar pressures of his top advisers.

Nevertheless, in mid-November, 1963, when I reported to the President my talks with Nehru in regard to India's request for U.S. military assistance, he was greatly pleased. He indicated he would fully support my proposals regardless of the Pakistan situation. But before calling a meeting of the National Security Council he wanted me to develop the broadest possible support in the Pentagon and State Department. He left no doubt in my mind but that he would go through with the agreement in any event, but that if I could win the active support of Dean Rusk and Robert McNamara it would be that much easier for him.

The President told me he would schedule the National Security Council meeting on Tuesday, November 26, the day before I planned to return to India. Four days before the meeting was to have taken place, the President was assassinated.

8. Dulles sought to rationalize our assistance to Pakistan on the ground that India would also be given U.S. equipment if it asked for it. But this would have required India to abandon its policies of nonalignment and to associate itself militarily with the United States in Asia, which India was not prepared to do; nor, I might add, as events have since demonstrated, was Pakistan.

President Johnson, not unreasonably, was anxious to consider the many problems for which he had assumed responsibility from his own perspective, and for that reason the decision was postponed. However, I suggested to the new President that he ask General Maxwell Taylor, in whose judgment I understood he had great faith, to visit India, talk to the heads of the government and to make his own assessment, and the President agreed. General Taylor arrived in New Delhi in early December and stayed with us for about ten days. He traveled extensively through North India, visiting many Indian Army and Air Force units along the Chinese border. His report fully supported my recommendation.

But the new Administration soon found itself under heavy pressure from the Pakistan lobby in the State and Defense Departments and in Congress, and continued to postpone its decision. This delay was particularly worrisome since by that time it was clear that if we rejected India's request, the Indian Government, greatly fearful about its long and exposed mountain border, would feel that it had no alternative but to ask the Soviets to supply the equipment which it had sought from us, and that the Soviet answer would be affirmative. The fact, which by now was well known, that the delay since President Kennedy's death was largely the result of Pakistan pressure on the new Johnson Administration was by this time beginning to introduce a new set of tensions into the situation.

I continued by cables and letters to share my concern with the President, Dean Rusk and Robert McNamara, and in mid-March, 1964, what appeared to be a favorable decision was finally reached. The size of the program would be $100 million annually for five years (half in grants and half in sales), with the understanding that the amounts and types of equipment would be decided later.

However, it soon became apparent that, while McGeorge Bundy and other members of the White House staff had secured an agreement in principle, the State Department and Pentagon were not yet prepared to risk our base at Peshawar by providing the kind of military assistance that India needed.

But the flow of cables and memoranda from New Delhi continued, and by May of 1964 we had persuaded Washington to reach a tentative agreement on a proposal that largely met India's requirements. I returned at once to Washington for the final negotiations, followed shortly thereafter by Defense Minister Chavan and other Indian defense officials. After two weeks of negotiation we succeeded in producing a program satisfactory to India and agreed to by the Secretaries of State and Defense. President Johnson was also prepared to accept it, and the final meeting to nail everything down was scheduled for noon on May 28 in the White House.

But once again fate intervened. On Wednesday, May 27, I was awakened at 6 A.M. by a telephone call and was told that Nehru had suddenly died.

Three hours later I left for India on the President's plane to attend the funeral with Dean Rusk, several American officials and most of the Indian team who had come to Washington to negotiate the agreement.

Before leaving Washington I talked to McGeorge Bundy and Robert Komer of the White House staff, who had strongly supported my recommendations and stressed the need for a quick approval. An uncertain new Indian Government, I said, would be in office within a few days, and it would be greatly reassured if we were promptly to demonstrate that it had our full confidence. They agreed and added that if either the Secretary of State or Secretary of Defense would recommend this action to the President, the authorization for me to tell the Indian Government that the military aid program had been agreed to and would be on my desk within two or three days. They expressed the hope that I could secure Rusk's agreement on the flight to New Delhi while they talked to McNamara.

But the authorization never came. Dean Rusk successfully avoided the subject during our eighteen-hour flight to New Delhi, and although the White House staff continued to support the agreed proposal, the officials in the South Asian Bureaus of the Pentagon and State Department seized upon Nehru's death to persuade the President and the two Secretaries that the wisest course was to delay until, in their words, "the dust has a chance to settle."

By that time normally sober-minded officials in the White House and the State Department had convinced each other that the Peshawar base was, in fact, "vitally important" to the future security of the United States. Although this wildly exaggerated assertion was repeatedly challenged by more knowledgeable but lower-level intelligence experts in Washington, proposals for shifting these facilities from Peshawar to a less politically sensitive area were brushed aside.

Under these circumstances it was inevitable that the Indian Government, which had been waiting impatiently for eighteen months, would turn to the U.S.S.R. for the military assistance which it felt was so essential to its own survival.

The Soviets had belatedly awakened to the fact that the disruption of their relations with China gave India much greater importance in their world strategy. The Soviet Union had previously supplied a few planes and some SAM's (Surface to Air Missiles) and had discreetly suggested the possibility of building plants in India in which to manufacture MIG-21 planes. Although India made it clear that it would prefer to base the modernization of its armed forces on American equipment, the Soviets were now ready and waiting to move in if and when we rejected the Indian request. In mid-August, 1964, the same Indian military negotiating team, headed by Defense Minister Chavan, with whom we had so nearly reached agreement in Washington departed for Moscow, and two weeks later they returned with all they had asked for, and more.

POSTSCRIPT

The fears and confusion at high levels in Washington created by the possibility that Pakistan would cancel our agreement on the Peshawar air base were no doubt the most immediate cause for the delay and the final negative decision.[9] But there was a deeper and, in my opinion, even more worrisome element: the men primarily responsible for making American foreign policy, including not only the new President, but Rusk, McNamara and Rostow, had very little understanding of the economic and political problems of Asia—either South Asia or Southeast Asia, where the effects of American involvement have been so tragic.[10]

This lack of understanding was due to a number of reasons. One was the strong European orientation of most of the men who had dominated American foreign policy since World War II. Until recent years most writing and research on Africa, India and South Asia were done by Europeans, largely British, and most of them reflected the frustrations, prejudices and colonial attitudes which had accumulated during their long dominance over these continents. World history taught in most American and West European schools still begins in what is now Egypt, Iraq and Iran and then proceeds first to Greece, then to Rome and then to northern Europe, and finally spills across the Atlantic to the United States and Canada. The history and culture of the ancient lands of China and India receive only cursory attention, and then usually from a European point of view. Moreover, most Americans originally came from Europe, as did our languages and much of our culture. Every American over forty-five years of age grew up in an era in which most of the world was made up of colonies dominated by Europe.

During the Truman Adminstration I doubt that more than one or two members of the Cabinet ever visited South Asia except as a member

9. In spite of the heavy political as well as military price we paid for the Peshawar base, Pakistan in 1968, in an effort to please the U.S.S.R., refused to renew the agreement and we were forced to move out the following year.

10. To Robert McNamara's credit, he later changed his views and, as President of the World Bank, he is now one of the most effective advocates of an enlightened and realistic Asian policy.

of a military unit during the war. Under President Kennedy the number was not much greater.

Following World War II with the collapse of colonialism, the situation was totally changed. Although Europe was still of primary importance to us and to world peace, it no longer dominated Asia and Africa, and, as a result, what happened in those great continents became of crucial importance in itself. Unhappily, many influential Americans not only in the government but in business, in the press and in our universities failed to adapt themselves to this fundamental change, and there are many in key posts who have still not adapted to it.

I could see little hope of revamping American policy in Asia unless the views of our policy-makers could be brought into balance with the realities that would certainly shape the new postcolonial world. Consequently, for six years in my daily cables and memoranda to the White House, State Department and Pentagon, I stressed and restressed this theme: Asia is a different world; the people's hopes and fears are rooted in two hundred years of colonialism; the forces shaping Asia, and Africa too, are not capitalism or Communism, but nationalism. We can never create the necessary understanding of India, its people and its potential role in the future of Southeast Asia unless we grasp these realities and base our plans upon them.

As part of this effort I tried to persuade top American newsmen to visit India long enough to see what was actually happening and to write about it, not just the dramatic "newsworthy" developments, but the problems the people faced and how they saw themselves and us. Several came, were impressed and wrote extensively and persuasively about these problems. But most continued to focus on the "good stories," with little regard for the less newsworthy but perhaps more important aspects of India.

I also wrote, and on my various visits to Washington talked with, friends and other members of the Senate and House of Representatives on both sides of the aisle whom I had come to know during my long years in public service. Each year I personally invited a number of them to come to India and see the situation as it actually existed. But India is a long way away and a vast country, and most Congressional trips abroad are hasty affairs. The average number of Congressmen and Senators who came to India each year was no more than eight, and most of them stayed only three or four days, including the inevitable day off to see the Taj Mahal and watch the snake charmers. In 1965 by a prodigious amount of letter writing I managed to bring the figure up to thirty-eight, but it then dropped back to "normal."

For the great majority who I knew would never come, I prepared every two or three months a comprehensive "off-the-record" Congressional memorandum dealing with India's political developments, economic growth, relations with the United States and with neighboring countries and the like. Accompanying each memorandum was a personal letter in which I urged the Congressman or Senator, if he could not actually come, at least to take an hour or so carefully to study my memoranda. Three or four hours' reading a year about a country of great strategic importance, with one-sixth of the world's population, the recipient of our largest economic assistance program, and which still managed to govern itself democratically, did not seem to me excessive. A similar memorandum went at regular intervals to some fifty or sixty members of the American press whom I knew personally.[11]

In my regular letters to the President and Secretaries Rusk and McNamara, I dealt not only with India but with our dilemma in Vietnam. I had several discussions about Vietnam with Vice President Johnson before the death of President Kennedy and he had heard me express my opposition to our military involvement there at meetings in the White House and elsewhere. I did not raise this question during the first few months of his Presidency, first because it was not directly my business, and second because my primary concern was to secure his approval of the Indian defense program.

However, in the spring of 1964 I wrote the first of a series of a dozen or more letters to President Johnson expressing my views on American policy in Southeast Asia, with special emphasis on the need for political, economic and social reform. Following is an excerpt from this first letter, dated May 19, 1964:

> What worries me most about the situation in Vietnam is the continuing lack of an effective political appeal which will undercut the Communist position in the rural areas and rally the Vietnamese peasants in support of their government.
>
> There is enough good land in Vietnam to enable every rural family to have fifteen acres or so that will belong to him in perpetuity and which will give him a degree of prosperity and a sense of permanent security and dignity. Unless we press the government in Saigon to undertake a program of this kind and unless we do so quickly no amount of American military assistance, no amount of training or exhortation, will keep Vietnam and perhaps much of Southeast Asia from falling into Communist hands.

As I look back on my long and intensive effort to share my own experiences in Asia with those who were in a position actually to set our policies, I must sadly admit that I can claim very few converts.

---

11. To avoid any possible charge of misuse of government funds, I paid for the cost of the Congressional and press letters myself.

CHAPTER 38

IMPRESSIONS OF JAWAHARLAL NEHRU

NEHRU'S DEATH marked the end of an era. Gandhi and Nehru had led the successful nonviolent struggle for Indian independence. Nehru and Sardar Patel had transformed India into a republic, and Nehru almost alone had held India together and set it on its present course. Now Nehru was gone, and it was difficult to imagine India without him.

No one who knew Jawaharlal Nehru would attempt to describe him in a phrase. He was many-sided, full of conflicting enthusiasms, doubts and sorrows. Yet there has seldom been a public figure more open with his problems and his thoughts.

Nehru went to Harrow, one of the most exclusive schools in England, and then continued on to Cambridge. Like many other educated Indians, he often felt the conflicting pull of East and West. "I have become a mixture of the East and the West," he once wrote, "out of place everywhere, at home nowhere. Perhaps my thoughts and approach to life are more akin to what is called Western than to the Eastern, but India clings to me as she does to all her children in innumerable ways. I am a stranger and alien in the West, I cannot be of it. But in my own country also, sometimes I have an exile's feeling."

He also once remarked, "Some feel the world might be better off if it had fewer moral crusaders, but everyone wants not only to carry out a moral crusade in his own environment, but to impose his moral crusade on others." Although his avowed skepticism left little room for religious dogma, he never allowed that skepticism to cloud his belief in the dignity of the individual.

Although he was born into one of the wealthiest families of the top Kashmiri-Brahman caste, Nehru chose to devote his life to struggle for his country's freedom. He spent more than thirteen years as a prisoner of the British. His father, Motilal Nehru, one of the most distinguished lawyers in India, was at first concerned about Jawaharlal's rebellious spirit but eventually, like so many others, he came to share his son's commitment to India's freedom and eventually served a prison term himself.

With independence in 1947, Nehru's life took on a new aspect. Gandhi had looked on the Congress Party solely as an instrument to secure independence. Once the objective of a free India had been achieved, he proposed to convert the party into a nonpartisan organization to serve the Indian people. However, by 1948 Congress had been built into one of the most powerful political organizations in the world, reaching into even the most remote villages of India as well as every town and urban neighborhood.

Nehru and his associates, differing from Gandhi's view, saw Congress as an essential instrument of orderly, democratic government. The very fact that it was not tied tightly to any particular dogma or doctrine enabled it to absorb a wide range of political viewpoints, much as the Democratic Party has done since 1932, and Nehru, backed by Congress, soon became the most powerful man in India.

The sources of Nehru's strength among the educated people of India were obvious. I find it more difficult to explain his hold upon the illiterate people of the villages and city slums. To some extent this was due to his association with Gandhi, who on many occasions declared, "Jawaharlal is my political heir." Partly, I believe, it reflects the tradition of renunciation which characterizes the great leaders of Indian history, and Nehru's understanding that India's future would largely be determined in the villages, where most of the people live. His pragmatic approach to economic development led him to recognize this simple fact that has been neglected by many professional economists.

In a personal conversation Nehru was the most articulate man I have ever met. He always seemed to talk fully and freely, to say just what he thought, to make every effort to see that his listener understood his viewpoint, regardless of what he might think of its merits. Nehru never painted the world in harshly contrasting blacks and whites, but in subtle intermediate shades. He seemed sometimes to reach a conclusion almost reluctantly, as though hesitant to give up the good that lay along other paths. His conversation often consisted of literally thinking aloud, and he explored all sides of a problem until its full complexity was felt.

However, my first meeting with him in October, 1951, was a dismal failure. At that time his sister, Mrs. Vijaya Lakshmi Pandit, whom

Steb and I knew well, was India's Ambassador to the United States. Mrs. Pandit had been gratified at my appointment and may have written her brother somewhat over enthusiastically of the close association that she hoped would grow up between us. Whatever the reason, our first meeting lasted no more than fifteen minutes, during which Nehru, to my dismay, appeared to have gone to sleep.

My first real discussion with Nehru came two weeks later, and it was one I shall never forget. He invited Steb and me to dinner with him and his daughter, Indira, and after dinner he asked me into his study, where we talked until nearly one o'clock in the morning. Never have I listened to a more articulate survey of world affairs.

Since the late 1940's, Nehru said, American foreign policy had been based on a series of assumptions which were, in his view, at best questionable and at worst dangerously wrong. Of these the most worrisome was the conviction of many informed Americans that the primary threat to their security was a world-wide Communist conspiracy, in which the Soviet Union and China were closely cooperating. The primary world-wide political force, in his view, was not Communism but an intense nationalism.

The Chinese-Soviet association, he said, was unlikely to last for more than a few years. Not only did the Chinese traditionally look down on the Russians as semibarbarians, but the Russians were the only imperial power that had retained control over what for centuries had been Chinese territory. In dealing with China, he said, the Soviets feel a sense of cultural inferiority; in addition, they are concerned about the vast and rapidly expanding population of China pressing against their eastern or southern borders. It was only a matter of time, he said, before a confrontation of some kind would occur.

Nehru also suggested that Stalin faced an impossible dilemma in regard to his domestic policies. If Russia was to become an advanced nation with the benefits of modern technology, education, Nehru said, must be pressed at all levels and on an intensive scale. But an educational effort of that magnitude would inevitably, over a period of years, affect the attitudes of the Soviet people and lead to a liberalization which Stalin did not anticipate. A well-educated man, Nehru pointed out, is bound to think his own thoughts and to develop his own judgments. Scientists, physicists and engineers cannot be expected to concentrate solely on scientific matters without regard for the implications for their country and the world.

Nehru was already convinced in 1951 that the Soviets had made their choice. Stalin would move ahead, he thought, with a massive educational program, and take his chances on containing the political pressures which would almost certainly be generated in the process.

Soon, he said, we might see the beginnings of a somewhat more liberal trend in the Soviet Union.

Nehru also expressed the view that the Soviet Union would soon launch economic assistance programs similar to our own in many developing nations. This, he suggested, would introduce a new and unpredictable factor in the relations between highly developed Europe, America and the U.S.S.R., on the one hand, and the developing nations such as India, on the other.

Nehru expressed concern over the long-term problem Communist China posed for India. But he was convinced that the nonaligned bridge-building role he was playing in Asia was not only in India's interest but in the interest of Asian stability, and indeed in the interest of the United States and the cause of world peace.

He staked his hopes for a peaceful relationship, not on Chinese goodwill, but on the assumption that the Chinese leaders needed a period of peace in which to solidify their revolution and to build a solid economic base. Nehru often compared what he believed to be Mao Tse-tung's long-range strategy with that which Stalin followed in the late thirties when he even made a deal with Hitler in the hope of preventing a Nazi attack and gaining more time to strengthen the Soviet economy.

When I first met Nehru in 1951, he was sharply critical of the United States. I believe that one of the most important reasons for this critical view was our failure seriously to discuss with him and his government the peace treaty with Japan. The Truman Administration, in an effort to assure support from the leaders of both political parties, had asked John Foster Dulles to negotiate the peace treaty and to muster worldwide support for it, particularly in Asia. Dulles, who was never known for his sensitivity in such matters, personally conferred with leaders in every Asian nation with the sole exception of India.

As one of the few Asian nations which had not been overrun by the Japanese, India was potentially the most willing in the bitter aftermath of the war to support a moderate and constructive approach to postwar Japan, and there is no doubt that our failure to consult Nehru hurt Nehru's pride. Moreover, Nehru felt that if given the opportunity he could have helped us to avoid a serious mistake in regard to the Japanese treaty.

If he had been consulted, Nehru said, he would have warned us against the danger of combining in a single document direct U.S.-Japanese security agreements in regard to American military bases with provisions ending the military occupation and re-establishing Japan's sovereignty.

In the future, he said prophetically, the clauses which gave the United States military the right to maintain bases in Japan would be interpreted by many Japanese as the price their government had been forced to pay to end the U.S. military occupation. To avoid this interpretation not only by the Japanese but by others, Nehru favored a two-step approach.

First, he suggested, a peace treaty should be signed re-establishing the full sovereign rights of Japan, including those islands whose inhabitants had an historical affinity to the Japanese people and which had not been acquired by aggression from any other country. Once this agreement had been signed, the United States and the new sovereign government of Japan could negotiate mutually acceptable treaties in regard to security relationships, military bases and the like, with much less danger of future misunderstandings.

The United States Government had abruptly brushed these suggestions aside and insisted on combining both objectives. Nehru had then refused to go to San Francisco to sign the treaty, and the United States Government reacted strongly. On June 9, 1952, India and Japan signed a separate treaty of "peace and amnesty."

Another cause for U.S.-Indian tensions during my first tour as Ambassador to India was our insensitive handling of India's request in the winter of 1951 for a loan with which to purchase two million tons of American wheat after the monsoon rains had failed in many parts of India. During the Congressional debates a series of amendments were considered which would have required India to make certain adjustments in its foreign policy as a *quid pro quo* for the wheat. Although the amendments were defeated by narrow margins, Nehru felt we were taking advantage of India's food shortage to drive a hard bargain.

Later, in the fall of 1950, Nehru aroused our official ire by criticizing General MacArthur's UN Army invasion of North Korea. Although India did not send troops to Korea, it had sent several hospital units and voted with the United States–led majority on June 25 for a resolution describing the North Korean action as a breach of the peace and asking North Korea to "withdraw forthwith their armed forces to the 38th parallel." From then on India's primary role was that of mediator. Soon after MacArthur's brilliant victory following the Inchon landings in September, 1950, the Chinese Foreign Minister in Peking summoned the Indian Ambassador to his office in the middle of the night and asked him to warn the United States that if the UN forces crossed the 38th parallel and approached the Yalu River borderline between China and North Korea, China would enter the war in force.

Nehru promptly passed this warning on to the United States Government. When questioned by the White House, MacArthur asserted that he "knew Asia and the mind of Asia better than anyone else." In the unlikely event that the Chinese did attack, he asserted that he would "destroy them quickly with my Air Force." The United Nations armies then proceeded north to the Yalu, where they were badly defeated by the Chinese.

Nehru later pointed out that the peace treaty between North Korea and South Korea, to which we agreed in July, 1953, established the cease-fire line approximately at the 38th parallel, which we could have settled for in September, 1950. He reminded me that since then more than 25,000 additional Americans and many more Chinese and North and South Koreans had been killed, all for no purpose. And yet, he said, presumably responsible American leaders had called him a Communist or "fellow traveler" because he had warned them accurately of the consequences of their efforts to move to the Yalu.

In the late summer of 1952 during my first assignment in India I had sought out Nehru on an unofficial personal basis to persuade him to make another effort to bring the war to a close. In the forthcoming United States election campaign, I said, the Korean War would be the primary political issue. By Election Day in early November the Democrats and Republicans would be equally committed to end the war by a strong offensive. Since no word of approval or disagreement came from Washington in response to my report of my first conversation, I urged Nehru a few days later to propose a new basis for a peaceful settlement among the UN, North Koreans and Chinese when the United Nations met in October. This he did.

The response of the Soviets was belligerently negative, and at first the Chinese and North Koreans showed little enthusiasm. However, soon after Stalin's death in March, 1953, the North Koreans and Chinese indicated their willingness to negotiate on the basis of the proposals that Nehru had made in the General Assembly the previous October.

In the following months highly efficient Indian military units were entrusted with policing the truce, which involved repatriation of prisoners. This was a delicate task, and even Nehru's many American critics admitted that it was skillfully handled.

Unfortunately for U.S.-Indian relations, the vocally anti-American Krishna Menon, who had played a central role in the Korean negotiations, soon became a familiar spectacle on American television sets. Since it was assumed that Menon was personally close to Nehru, much of the irritation which he generated transferred itself to the Prime Minister.

When in the 1950's I told friends that I did not believe Menon had a decisive influence on Nehru's actions, their natural question was,

"Why then does Nehru keep him in his Cabinet?" The answer was probably rather simple; with a few exceptions, the Congress Party leadership which dominated the Indian Cabinet was made up of plodding and rather dull political leaders. Whether or not he agreed with Menon's views, Nehru with his keen sense of humor and imagination found Krishna Menon good company. But, following Menon's miserable performance as Defense Minister at the time of the Chinese attack in 1962, Nehru found it necessary to remove him from the Cabinet, and he has long since ceased to have an important political influence.

Nehru also clearly foresaw the outcome of the French struggle to maintain their colonial hold on Indochina. In January, 1954, he stated in a press conference that the French were doomed to lose the war and that it was to their advantage to try to make peace on the best basis possible before it was too late. This statement was challenged not only by the French, but by many Americans. In March, 1954, an official American military spokesman stated that this warning reflected Nehru's "sympathy with Communism." Two weeks later Dienbienphu fell to the Vietcong and the French were forced to withdraw from all of Indochina.

Following the debacle I seriously doubted that the "live and let live" relationship which Nehru had tried so hard to establish between China and India in the early 1950's would last. In October, 1954, in an article in *Foreign Affairs*, I wrote:

> It would be a mistake to consider the Indo-Chinese agreements which were made this summer in New Delhi as a Chinese diplomatic victory. The Chou En-lai–Nehru statement proposed that the Indo-Chinese treaty on Tibet serve as a model for all of Asia. The preamble of this treaty lays down five principles for friendly relations.
>
> The Indians cannot be unaware that China violated all five of these principles in taking over Tibet in 1951, nor has anyone suggested that India has failed to live up to them in her relations with China.
>
> If the restatement of these principles now by Chou En-lai and Nehru means anything it is that the Chinese have agreed to start living up to a set of principles which have been blatantly and recently violated by the Chinese themselves. The Indians on their part are obviously hoping, as we of the West have so futilely hoped in the years following the war, that China with its many internal problems will settle down to peace and harmony.
>
> Arguments from western sources no matter how persuasive will have little effect in persuading the skeptical Asians that they are hoping for the impossible. For this reason agreement between Nehru and Chou En-lai, instead of promoting closer Chinese-Indian relationships, may prove to do the opposite. In any case, it provides a clear test of Chinese intentions.
>
> If the Chinese follow the example of the Soviet Union in the 1920's

and 1930's and decide temporarily to relax their pressure and consolidate their revolution, India and other free Asian nations will be given a badly needed breathing spell in which to put their own economic and political houses in order.

If, as it seems more likely, China disregards her new promises and embarks either directly or indirectly on further expansion, the real nature of Chinese Communism will become obvious to many Asians for the first time. Such a development following Chou En-lai's recent commitments in New Delhi and Rangoon may provide the non-Communist people of free Asia with the kind of psychological shock that was felt throughout the West following the Soviet-managed coup d'état in Czechoslovakia and the death of Jan Masaryk in 1948. India is the key to the situation. How far would India go in opposing a Chinese advance in Asia? Right now, no one knows.

I later learned that Nehru had this article reproduced and distributed to all his embassies. Clearly, he was less certain of Chinese restraint than he admitted publicly.

Nehru was often accused of anti-Americanism. But this, I think, was untrue. Although he carried some of the upper-class British prejudices against the boisterous and self-assured approach to life of many Americans, with some notable exceptions, he liked them.

Nehru had a particularly high regard for America's revolutionary past. In preparing for the Bandung Conference on Afro-Asian unity in 1955, for which Nehru was in large measure responsible, the organizers deliberately selected the nineteenth of April, 1955, as the opening day. This was the 180th anniversary of the Battle of Lexington-Concord, where American farmers broke into armed rebellion against British colonial rule. The opening ceremony that night began with the reading of Longfellow's "The Midnight Ride of Paul Revere." The resolutions which were finally adopted by the Conference were phrased in the language of Jefferson and Lincoln.

Interestingly enough, the Chinese delegation, in order to establish some degree of rapport with the Asian-African nations, felt it expedient to vote for these resolutions. Nehru believed that another concession he had been able to wring from the Chinese as a result of the Conference was the abandonment of their first series of attacks on the islands of Quemoy and Matsu.

Nehru's chief criticism of the United States, which he often reiterated, was our lack of understanding of the burning aspirations of the Asian people. Very few Americans, he said, have "any understanding of the mind and heart of Asia." Such comments should not lightly be brushed aside; Nehru expressed over the years not only his own beliefs and convictions but the yearnings of the masses in Asia and Africa. It is fair to say that in general what Nehru said is what most Asians think. There was an Asian way of looking at the world, which Nehru expressed most eloquently. If we Americans are to live in peace with the one-third of all humanity who live there, we must indeed develop a better understanding of "the mind and heart of Asia."

For the first fourteen years of India's freedom, Nehru almost completely dominated the scene. Although his colleagues, the public and the press had the constitutional right to debate, criticize and challenge, their respect for Nehru was so deep that he was in the unprecedented position of holding almost totalitarian powers within the framework of a democratic government. Nevertheless, with each passing year new forces and new problems tended more and more to divide the leadership which had won the struggle for independence and weaken the bonds that held it together. By the early 1960's divisive pressures and conflicting personal ambitions among his colleagues, which Nehru had successfully contained in the earlier years, began to break into the open.

The language problem was one example. Nehru and his associates were convinced that a free and united India required a common language. Although Nehru and many other Indian leaders spoke English as eloquently as any American, Canadian, Australian or Britisher, in their new nationalistic mood most Indian leaders were determined that the choice be made from among the fourteen indigenous languages of India. Hindi, which was more or less understood by 40 percent or so of the people, was favored in the northern and central states. But southern leaders rejected Hindi and favored the continuation of English. Agreement was finally reached that Hindi would eventually become the national language but that English would be retained indefinitely in government and the universities. In an effort to encourage an orderly evolution and to discourage pressure for various regional languages, the first state borders were established on the basis of geography and economics rather than language.

During our 1955 visit to India we could see that Nehru's concept of state borders based on geography rather than language was beginning to break down. Pressure for linguistic states in East and Central India was becoming explosive. The fact that these deeply rooted differences did not lead to the fragmentation of India, as so many foreign observers expected, testifies to the extraordinary political skill of Nehru and his associates and also to the generally underestimated feeling throughout India that regardless of caste or religion they are Indians first.

By the time of our next visit in 1957 the political conflicts over language had shifted to the Bombay area in western India, where serious riots occurred between the Marathi-speaking people and the Gujarati. However, once again with remarkable political skill, Nehru combined compromise with force, and after some worrisome weeks an agreement was reached to establish two states, with Bombay the capital of Maharashtra and Ahmedabad the capital of the new state of Gujarat. Although still occasionally plagued with political turbulence, these have become two of the most prosperous states in India.

In January, 1964, Nehru suffered a stroke which left him badly shaken. In the following months it was tragic to watch him gradually go downhill until his death on May 27, 1964. We had luncheon alone with Nehru and his daughter a week before he died. The memory I carry with me is of a tired but great and gentle man who had come to feel at peace with himself and with mankind. On a table by his bedside when he died, in his own handwriting, were the lines of Robert Frost:

> The woods are lovely, dark and deep,
> But I have promises to keep,
> And miles to go before I sleep,
> And miles to go before I sleep.

In the last five months of Nehru's life President Radhakrishnan had become increasingly concerned about Nehru's ability to manage the affairs of government. On several occasions he expressed to me in a half-joking manner the wish that somehow after Nehru's death or retirement the whole country could operate under "President's rule" for a few months. This, he said, would enable him in his role as President to ease some of the accumulating political conflicts and make some of the difficult but necessary decisions before turning the government over to a new Prime Minister and Cabinet.

Following Nehru's death, if President Radhakrishnan had, in fact, proposed that the political leaders of all parties should be given a chance to catch their breath and refocus their plans and policies, his judgment, I believe, would have been almost unanimously accepted by the Indian people and their political leaders.

However, Radhakrishnan was a man of great personal integrity. He realized that he was in the historic position of being the first President of India to interpret the Constitution on the occasion of the first change of government and hence in a position to establish the model and traditions for future Presidents to follow. So instead of suspending parliamentary government for even the brief interval provided by the Constitution, he called in the senior member of the Cabinet, Gulzari Lal Nanda, and asked him to present his recommendations for a new government within the next six days.

CHAPTER 39

LAL BAHADUR SHASTRI

ON June 2, 1964, six days after Nehru's death, Lal Bahadur Shastri was elected the second Prime Minister of India. For several weeks, Shastri was ill,[1] but by early August he had picked up the reins of government. He was an appealing man. Although he was scarcely five feet tall, his warm smile, his sharp questions and his simple, direct, pragmatic approach gave an impression of unusual strength.

It has often occurred to me that Indian politicians may be divided generally into two groups, one of which might be referred to as the "Adamses" and the second, the "Jacksonians." The "Adamses," of which Nehru is the prime example, had grown deep roots in the Western world and particularly in the United Kingdom, where a large number of Indian leaders received their education. Here they learned not only to speak eloquent English but to acquire many European attitudes. As a consequence, many of the "Adamses" were torn between two worlds— East and West.[2] The "Jacksonians" on the other hand, of which Shastri was an example, had rarely if ever traveled outside of India, and had no such inhibitions or confusion about their identity or their roots. They were, by and large, more earthy and pragmatic and closer to the masses of the people to whom they felt they belonged.

Steb and I had known Shastri and his wife in his various ministerial roles for fifteen years, and in his new role a warm relationship quickly grew up between us. As Prime Minister, Shastri seemed to grow from day to day. Although for thirty or more years he had labored in the

1. Later we learned that it had been a mild heart attack.
2. This often led many of them paradoxically to assume what appeared to be "anti-Western" positions in a subconscious effort to demonstrate that they were, in fact, genuinely Indian.

shadow of Nehru, now his confidence steadily increased. In his handling of several delicate political situations his skill seemed comparable to that of Nehru in his prime. His influence in the Congress Party grew rapidly, and soon the regional and state leaders who had put him in office were congratulating themselves, with good reason, for having made a wise choice under great pressures.

In October I began to talk to Shastri about the possibility of a visit to the United States; neither the Prime Minister nor his wife had ever been out of India and he was obviously eager to go. However, he suggested that the meeting should not be scheduled until the fall of 1965, which would give him time to settle down in his new role as Prime Minister. The State Department and White House quickly agreed to the visit but suggested, for a variety of reasons, that it be scheduled for the spring of 1965, to which Shastri with considerable reluctance agreed. Steb pressed Mrs. Shastri to accompany her husband, and she, too, accepted.

In an article, "Train to Allahabad," Steb later wrote:

> On Christmas Eve Chet had a conference with the Prime Minister, and I had gone along to talk with Mrs. Shastri about her coming trip to the United States. She was eagerly looking forward to it and we spoke about the various things she might like to see and do there. . . . We must have talked longer than we realized for there stood Chet and the Prime Minister, finished with their business.
>
> "I don't know that my wife should accompany me to Washington," Shastri said. "It will be just a brief trip." But Mrs. Shastri just chuckled and wagged her head. And as our eyes met, I knew that she would surely get the last word on that.

I was distressed, although not surprised, a few weeks after the date had been agreed upon to learn that because of the State Department assumption that Pakistan and India should always be bracketed together, regardless of their differences in size, importance, and the nature of their problems, President Ayub Khan of Pakistan had been invited to visit the United States a few weeks after the visit of Prime Minister Shastri. This was as illogical as the President of France's refusing to invite the President of the United States to France unless a similar invitation were sent to the President of Mexico.

But the worst was yet to come. In mid-April my assistant, Dick Celeste, interrupted a meeting to hand me a news broadcast from Karachi stating that President Johnson had decided to "disinvite" both Prime Minister Shastri and President Ayub Khan. There had been no previous intimation of this in any cable or correspondence. Plans for the program had been progressing smoothly.

I knew that the impact of such a development on Shastri and other Indians would be shatttering, and I tried to convince myself that it must be a mistake. I sent an urgent cable to the State Department asking that the decision, if it had in fact been made, be reviewed and reversed. A few hours later Rusk replied that, to his regret, the news was accurate and that the President's decision could not be changed. We would have to do our best in what he knew was a difficult situation.

I shall never forget the meeting I had with the Prime Minister at his home that evening. He and Mrs. Shastri had come to look forward eagerly to their visit to the United States. Now he had been rudely and publicly embarrassed. He was a sensitive man, particularly in matters affecting foreign policy, where he felt less secure than in dealing with domestic affairs, and, worst of all, there was nothing I could say or do to ease his reaction.

The anger of the Indian Government was reflected in a chilly press statement:

> The United States Ambassador on several occasions has urged the Prime Minister to visit the United States. On January 18th, Ambassador Bowles forwarded a message from President Johnson specifically suggesting that the visit be scheduled for the middle of March. This was later changed to early June at the President's request. The invitation has been withdrawn. Our Ambassador in Washington has informed the Secretary of State that the unusual manner in which this step has been taken will cause misunderstanding in India.

In a few days I learned from friends in the Department that three weeks earlier the President had suddenly decided that he could not handle all the commitments he had made for the coming weeks. He had asked the State Department to cancel both the Shastri and Ayub Khan visits. Dean Rusk, who was aware of the adverse consequences but was out of the country, had sent a message asking that any announcement be held until he had an opportunity to urge the President to change his mind. The announcement was delayed until his return, and when Rusk's effort failed, no time was left to cushion the blow. If I had received even a three-day warning, I am confident that I could easily have persuaded Shastri to agree to a later date, particularly since he had favored this in the beginning. The morale of the entire American mission was deeply affected.

One unhappy incident followed another. In the spring of 1965 it became evident that because of the failure of the monsoon India would need greatly increased shipments of wheat for the coming year.[3] We in

3. The U.S. had been providing India with an average of two million tons of wheat per year since 1951. The Indians paid for these shipments in rupees.

the New Delhi mission assumed that Washington would approve a new food agreement without delay, but our cables on the subject were answered evasively or not at all. When I sought to find the reasoning, I received a private message from friends in the State Department that it was a direct result of President Johnson's annoyance at Shastri's criticism of our increasing military involvement in Vietnam and his resentment toward Indian press criticism of his abrupt canceling of the Shastri visit.

Not unnaturally, the Indian press had reported that Shastri had been critical of the sudden withdrawal of his invitation to the United States, and he had also made a mild suggestion that the bombing of North Vietnam was unlikely to bring peace (a view shared by most of our friends). Indeed, stories were even appearing in the Washington press that "highly placed officials," etc., were boasting on a "background basis" that a food squeeze would bring the Indians to heel.

At this critical moment, a disgruntled American reporter who was personally unhappy in India for a variety of reasons, including the bad telephone service, poured gasoline on the flames. Over a period of six months he had collected all of the adverse comments on President Johnson that he could cull from India's freewheeling press, which he now consolidated into a "news story" and wired it to his paper as evidence of a "well-planned plot" by the Indian Government to blacken the American President.

When the story appeared in the American press, all hell broke loose. The State Department spokesmen called in the reporters and on a "background basis" offered an incredible analysis of Indian knavery. A cable to me from a normally responsible member of the President's staff proclaimed that "the President will not allow himself to become a target for blackmail and slander."

Then, when we were about to convince ourselves that the U.S.-Indian relations could sink no lower, Pakistan sent five thousand guerrillas into the Kashmir Valley in August, 1965. The Pakistan Government had expected the Kashmiri people to welcome the infiltrators with open arms. But they were poorly trained, poorly disciplined, poorly organized and poorly informed, and many Kashmiri cheerfully cooperated with the Indian Army in rounding them up. It was as irresponsible and inept a performance as our own abortive effort at the Bay of Pigs.

At this point a brief outline of the origins of the dispute over Kashmir may be in order. After the agreement to partition the Indian subcontinent in 1947, the Indian Government had the problem of dealing with the 550 princely states which constituted about one-third of India.

Through the brilliant negotiating abilities of V. P. Menon and Sardar Patel, the Indian princes were persuaded to forefeit the traditional but hazy political power which they enjoyed under the British and to accept the jurisdiction of either India or Pakistan. According to the agreement, each princely state could choose to attach itself either to Pakistan or to India *provided* it had a common border with the country which it had chosen.[4]

Kashmir, which bordered on both India and Pakistan, had a Hindu ruler, with a predominantly Muslim population in the Kashmir Valley.[5] Moreover, for many generations Kashmir had been yearning for independence, or at least semiautonomy under Indian rule similar to that of the Himalayan kingdoms of Sikkim and Bhutan.

Consequently, the Maharaja delayed his decision in the hope that Kashmir could somehow work out a special relationship with India and Pakistan. In October, 1947, to force his hand, Pakistan sent guerrilla fighters from the northwest frontier provinces to compel a merger with Pakistan. As the invading force neared the capital city of Srinagar, the Maharaja, in a state of panic, opted for India, and his decision was officially approved by the Viceroy, Lord Mountbatten, who by common agreement was presiding over the liquidation of British India.

Indian troops were hurriedly flown in to meet the tribal invaders (who were by then openly supported by the Pakistan Army). They had cleared the airport and were pushing the invaders back when Nehru agreed to a cease-fire on January 1, 1948, and called upon the United Nations Security Council to brand Pakistan as an aggressor and direct it to withdraw all its forces. But the Security Council was reluctant to make a finding on the ground that it might drive the Pakistani into an even more militant stand.

After much discussion the Secretary General was directed by the Security Council to send a team of negotiators to the subcontinent to reach an agreement. Although a variety of proposals were offered, the impasse continued, with the Pakistani occupying roughly 40 percent of Kashmir and the Indians the rest. This was the status of the "Kashmir Problem" when we arrived in India on our first assignment in October, 1951, and there it still rested when we returned in 1963.

From my earliest contact with the issue I had been convinced that this was not a problem that the United States or any outside nation

4. Although East Bengal was separated by nearly a thousand miles of Indian territory, it became part of Pakistan, but Bengal was not a princely state and thus had a different origin.

5. Of the other two sections of Kashmir, Jammu is largely Hindu and Ladakh is Buddhist. But the bulk of the people live in the valley.

could solve. The best hope was that eventually some event might occur which would break the ice and lead India and Pakistan to a solution. As I pointed out in an earlier chapter, such an opportunity arose when the Chinese attacked India in October, 1962. If Pakistan had supported India or had even agreed to maintain a benevolent neutrality at that time, a wave of goodwill toward Pakistan would have swept India that might have made a Kashmir settlement possible. Instead, Pakistan strongly backed the Chinese, and the tragic conflict between Pakistan and India was intensified.

In the last month of Nehru's life, I believe, his primary objective was to find a way out of this impasse. When we lunched with Nehru a week before his death, the question was uppermost in his mind, and, indeed, he could talk of little else. I am convinced that he felt then that he was close to a solution built around Sheik Abdullah, a Kashmir Muslim political leader who was an admirer of Nehru and Gandhi and who was strongly supported by the people of the Kashmir Valley. When Nehru died, this effort ground to a stop.

After Shastri had recovered from his first heart attack and settled in as Prime Minister, he began gradually to move toward the Nehru-Abdullah formula for settling the dispute. However, the Pakistani had long been convinced that one Muslim soldier could outfight ten Hindus, and, unhappily for them and for India, Pakistan's military leaders, who had taken this myth seriously, decided that the time had come to bring military pressure directly to bear on India and to settle by force the differences which had defied negotiation.

The Pakistani guerrilla infiltration into Kashmir was only the first act of the drama. When United Nations observers on the cease-fire line reported to the Secretary General that Pakistan had, in fact, embarked on an aggression against India, it was assumed in India that this UN report would promptly be published and the Pakistani action condemned.

But high officials at the United Nations were convinced that if the report were publicized, Pakistan would be driven into a corner, and a negotiated peace would become impossible. The refusal to publish the report reminded the Indians of the United Nations' failure for a similar reason to declare Pakistan an aggressor when it invaded Kashmir in 1948 and persuaded India that it could not expect fair treatment from the United Nations.

With this history of what it felt was ill treatment at the hands of the UN, India decided to take direct action against Pakistan's infiltration of Kashmir in August, 1965. In late August Indian Army units attacked the Pakistani forces at the Hagi Pir Pass, which was the major infiltration route for Pakistani guerrilla forces then entering Kashmir. Since this pass was several miles on the Pakistan side of the cease-fire line established in 1950, we were at once fearful that the Pakistani would react by expanding the war.

In early September a Pakistani armored brigade, equipped with American tanks, artillery and machine guns and supported by American planes, crossed the Indo-Pakistani frontier in the Jammu area and moved to cut off communications between northern India and the Kashmir Valley. Since the roads and rivers were flooded by the monsoon rains, the Indians were unable to bring up the forces needed to meet this thrust and the Pakistan forces quickly moved some ten or fifteen miles into Indian territory. In an attempt to draw off the Pakistani, the Indians launched a diversionary thrust farther west; two Indian divisions moved across the Punjab border and headed for Lahore.

During the next two or three weeks the course of the war caught almost everyone, including the Indians, by surprise. The Pakistani, although armed with American equipment and with many units trained by American officers, were driven back. Almost half of the U.S.-provided Patton tanks in the Pakistan Army were destroyed or badly damaged by Indian fire. More than one hundred were captured intact.

During September the Chinese, eager to keep the situation stirred up and alarmed over the progress being made in the negotiations for a cease-fire, sent India an ultimatum. India, the Chinese alleged, was guilty of stealing several hundred Tibetan yaks; unless these were returned with suitable apologies within seventy-two hours, the Chinese would take "suitable" military action. Fortunately, this gambit failed. After intensive negotiations involving our embassies in Delhi and Rawalpindi, the State Department, the British and the United Nations, an Indo-Pakistan cease-fire was arranged, and the Chinese ultimatum was not renewed. Although the war had lasted less than four weeks, an estimated three thousand were killed on each side.

The Indian Government, press and public were predictably critical of the use of American equipment by the Pakistani. Over and over again it was pointed out to me that every Indian casualty had been caused by an American bullet, an American shell or an American hand grenade.

Eleven years had elapsed since President Eisenhower's 1954 assurance to Nehru that he would "take appropriate action" if any U.S. arms were ever used against India, and Nehru in reply had expressed doubt that as a "practical matter" the President would be able to prevent aggression by Pakistan troops equipped with U.S. arms. Nehru's doubts had been vindicated.

The American Congress and public had been told the purpose of our military assistance was solely to commit Pakistani to the common defense of South Asia and the Middle East against a Soviet-Chinese attack. But the possibility of losing our Peshawar base still dominated American policy in South Asia. Our government was clearly determined to duck the implications of our pledge to keep the Pakistani from using U.S. weapons in aggression against India. While we did suspend all military aid to Pakistan, it was suspended to India as well.[6] Our Ambassador in Pakistan, Eugene M. Locke, "protested" the Pakistani aggression, but privately and in only the mildest terms. Even in the face of a Pakistan statement that we had made no protest whatsoever Washington remained officially silent.

I had strongly urged the State Department to issue some kind of public rebuke to Pakistan so that I could more effectively face the irate Indians. Back had come a cable recognizing my "predicament"; but no statement was forthcoming. I could, the State Department said, say whatever I felt would be helpful off the record or as background.

That afternoon in a background press conference I did my best with this meager ammunition. I told of our "protest" to the Pakistan Government; the Pakistani insistence that the arms were used in self-defense; our "stern warning" to the Pakistani not to use them again. Now, I said, we were in a dilemma: should we chastise the Pakistani in public to satisfy Indian public opinion—and risk the failure of the current negotiations—or should we remain silent? Difficult as this made it for me, I felt we should say nothing further. The Indian correspondents reacted with understanding; they realized that my statement was an effort to put the best face possible on a situation which three American Presidents[7] and five American ambassadors[8] had repeatedly assured them could never happen.

I then expressed my grave fears of the war hysteria being whipped up in India by frustrated political leaders, proclaiming their government had been humiliated by China, attacked by Pakistan and double-crossed by the United States. A government beset by such problems is often eager for almost any device that will restore national unity. I appealed to the press for greater responsibility and sanity. I did my best, but under the circumstances it was less than adequate.

Many Americans still tend to accept Pakistan's defense of its invasion of Kashmir on the specious grounds that it was acting in the

6. It was alleged that India, too, had used U.S. equipment. However, after carefully investigating the situation we reached the conclusion that the only Indian units in the area armed with U.S. weapons were two reserve mountain divisions which were not involved in combat.

7. Eisenhower, Kennedy and Johnson.

8. Allen, Cooper, Bunker, Galbraith and myself.

name of "self-determination" for the Kashmiri. This is a dangerously simplistic approach. If the principle of self-determination were applied to every religious or tribal group in Africa, there would be fighting in every country on the continent. The United States fought a Civil War in which nearly a million people died to *prevent* the Southern states from exercising "self-determination."

In November of 1965 when the atmosphere had eased a bit, I again brought up the importance of inviting Shastri to Washington. At that time India was beginning to feel the full impact of the crop failure due to a failure of monsoon rains throughout most of India. I suggested that an easing of the Indian food situation by the announcement of increased shipments of American wheat would make it unnecessary for Shastri to appear in President Johnson's eyes as quite so much of a supplicant. But my assumption in regard to the easing of the atmosphere in Washington turned out to be premature. A few days later I received a personal cable from Secretary Rusk saying that if Shastri expected us to make concessions to persuade him to come to the United States, "India was in for a long, hard winter." The cable then proceeded to outline the U.S. position, which as a matter of fact was quite reasonable.

In my private reply to Rusk I described his message as "paradoxical." The things the Secretary wanted Shastri to agree to were not unreasonable, but if "the harsh tone of your message to me accurately reflects the atmosphere in Washington, a meeting between Shastri and Johnson at this time would be a disaster and, regardless of how historians would assess responsibility, both countries would be genuinely hurt." A few days later a message arrived saying that the Shastri visit would be worked out.

In January, 1966, a peace conference arranged by Prime Minister Kosygin began in Tashkent, Uzbekistan. Shastri showed extraordinary negotiating capacity, coupled with a willingness to go more than half way in dealing with the Pakistani. At Tashkent Shastri had achieved a considerable rapport with President Ayub Khan. There were very few Indian leaders, or, indeed, leaders from any country, who could have mustered the courage Shastri showed. The Indian Army, at great cost, had won several positions from Pakistan which were of strategic importance to India in its defense against future Pakistani or Chinese attacks. But Shastri knew that total withdrawal was essential to assure a solid base for the kind of over-all peace agreement with Pakistan that he was seeking.

When he somewhat nervously described the situation to his military leaders, their reply was direct and simple: "Mr. Prime Minister, this is strictly a political decision. We shall do what you tell us to do." Shastri told me of this exchange the following day with understandable pride in the Indian military's commitment to democratic government implied by their response.

On January 11, only a few hours after the peace document had been signed at Tashkent, Shastri suffered a heart attack and in a few minutes was dead. The news reached us in New Delhi at 4 A.M., an hour or so after it occurred.

The sense of shock we all felt is reflected in these paragraphs from Steb's article, "Train to Allahabad":

> As the peace talks started in Tashkent, everyone in Delhi, in the whole world, we felt, was holding his breath. . . . As news gave increasingly little hope that any agreement would be reached, our spirits sank. We thought of Shastri, frail yet determined, and of the terrible pressures and burdens upon him. Then Chet called me Monday afternoon and said, "He's done it! They're signing an agreement, it's coming over the ticker." The news seemed miraculous. I hung up the phone in excitement—and then had to call back to find out what the communiqué was. We all rejoiced that night.
>
> It was four in the morning when the call came from Chet's deputy, Jerry Greene. "Steb, let me speak to Chet," and his tone instantly reminded me of that other early morning when he called to give us the news of Kennedy's assassination. And now again I heard Chet saying, "Oh no, no."
>
> That morning we drove over together to sign the book at the Prime Minister's residence. "Won't you come and see Mrs. Shastri?" they asked. As we were taken to the private rooms, which were starkly bare and simple, I thought of the words of an Indian policeman who helped us through the crowds outside. He said, "Our Shastri was just like one of us. He was the leader of our country, but lived like us. His house was larger, but inside it was no different from my family's home in our village in U.P."

The next day Vice President Hubert Humphrey, representing President Johnson, with Dean Rusk arrived in New Delhi on the President's plane to attend the funeral. The funeral procession crowds were equal to the multitudes following Nehru's death eighteen months before. In a sense Shastri's death was the more tragic, coming at the beginning of a career as Prime Minister which, I believe, would have been impressive. If he had lived, I believe that closer relations would have almost certainly developed between India and Pakistan. Even on the explosive Kashmir issue some kind of agreement might have been negotiated.

Mrs. Shastri invited Steb to go with her on the funeral train which carried Shastri's ashes to be immersed in the Ganges at the Sangam, where the Ganges and Jumna rivers join with the mythical underground river, the Saraswati.

Steb, who was the only non-Indian on the train, described the extraordinary outpouring of grief by Indians of all castes, religions and states in these words:

> As we waited near the gleaming white coach that was to carry the ashes, we heard the approaching beat of the death march.
>
> To muffled drums there came [her son] Hari, slowly, slowly carrying the urn, the family following. . . . And there came all the Ministers of State; Indira Gandhi was weeping openly. . . . Many of us there were reminded of that other occasion, just nineteen months before, when this train received the ashes of Jawaharlal Nehru. It was then a Mr. Shastri, hardly known to the outside world, who had, quietly, in tears, been in charge of the arrangements. . . .
>
> Then the train started and the crowds along the platform and along the tracks were weeping and reaching out. The last of Shastri was leaving them. . . . Out through the train yards filled with faces, the coach rolled. . . .
>
> As I looked out the window it seemed as though all the people of India were standing out there waiting and watching the train. . . . At the many station stops, Shahdara, Ghaziabad, Khurja, Aligarh, Kanpur, and the rest, they waited by the hundreds of thousands, milling and crowding up to the train . . . to catch sight of the urn, then bowed over praying hands. . . .
>
> The further we went into the countryside the more intense seemed this pageant of grief and love. On the whole route I don't believe there was a soul unaware of what that coach bore. At crossings, sometimes, the train would slow down and receive the namastes of the peasants gathered there, pulled up with their carts, tongas, bicycles and camels.
>
> As we sped by, we saw the villagers come out of their homes, standing in doorways and on mud walls and rooftops to greet the train. . . . Most poignant of all were the lone figures in the fields, a man standing by a Persian well, a farmer holding the reins of his bullock team: they would stop and face the speeding train and bow their heads in simple, solitary homage.[9]

Steb and Mrs. Shastri continued their close friendship for as long as we were in India. She was one of the last to say good-bye to us at the airport when we left for home three years later.

9. The complete article appears in an appendix.

CHAPTER 40

NEHRU'S DAUGHTER TAKES THE HELM

FOLLOWING THE DEATH of Shastri, Mrs. Indira Gandhi became Prime Minister in as smooth a transition as when Shastri had succeeded Nehru. Some differences within the Congress Party were evident. But whatever scars developed were, on the surface at least, quickly healed, and the organization retained its traditional unity.

When Nehru died, many observers believed his daughter was determined to take his place. I doubt this; she had always seemed relaxed and happy in her role as her father's hostess and confidante, and I do not think that at that time she harbored ambitions to succeed him. When I saw Indira two days after the funeral, she was badly shaken. What she would most like to do, she told me, was to drop everything and go to London for a few months to live with her sons.

Steb and I had known Indira for many years, and in the first year or so after our return to India we had seen her often. Under the weight of her new responsibilities she inevitably became somewhat more distant and harder to reach. Except on one or two memorable occasions, I had found it easy to talk both to Nehru and to Shastri. But in spite of our long friendship, my visits with Prime Minister Indira Gandhi were often unproductive. In the course of an exchange of views she allowed long silences to develop. On one or two occasions I made up my mind that I would say nothing more until Mrs. Gandhi broke the ice. But after two or three minutes of silence it was always I who capitulated and opened up a new subject.

During the next few months Mrs. Gandhi began to emerge as an astute politician.[1] On several occasions her skill in handling sensitive

1. During the struggle against the British for independence, Mrs. Gandhi had served some time in prison, but the only political office which she had held under her father was as President of the Congress Party in the late 1950's. At that time she had handled the Communist agitations in Kerala decisively and successfully.

situations and in developing compromises with her opponents when none seemed possible reminded me of Franklin D. Roosevelt in his prime. She combined a keen sense of timing with great physical and moral courage. She never hesitated to move into an unfriendly crowd, and almost invariably she managed to put hecklers in their place and to win a majority of her audience.[2]

While Mrs. Gandhi lacked an understanding of the process of economic development, she had three extraordinarily able men who did understand it working closely with her in her first two years as Prime Minister: Chidambara Subramanian, the Minister of Agriculture, L. K. Jha,[3] her Executive Assistant, and Asoka Mehta, an economist and former leader of the Socialist Party who had joined the Congress Party two or three years before. Chavan, the Defense Minister, who had developed into an effective political figure, also joined the inner circle after a brief flirtation with a group of Congress MP's who urged him to seek the prime ministership for himself. These men, working together, formed an articulate, pragmatic and competent team which during a critical period won and held her confidence.

Mrs. Gandhi had consistently taken a moderate position in regard to Pakistan and Kashmir and was eager to take advantage of the new spirit generated at Tashkent to explore the possibility of further agreements. Unhappily, the Pakistan Government was not so forthcoming. To protect their own political positions, President Ayub Khan, Foreign Minister Bhutto and other Pakistan leaders had created the impression in Pakistan that the Indian Army had been defeated. How, then, could they explain the compromises which would necessarily accompany an India-Pakistan settlement? Indeed, if Pakistan had actually "won" the war, how could they explain the fact that the bulk of Kashmir still remained as it had before the fighting started?

Nevertheless, Mrs. Gandhi had many long talks with Sheik Abdullah, the Kashmir leader who it was generally agreed was the most likely key to the situation. I knew the Sheik well from my first assignment to India, and on several occasions after my return he had suggested a meeting. However, I was fearful that I would be accused of interfering in Indian internal affairs, and so reluctantly I put him off. When I reported this to the Indian Foreign Office, they urged me to put aside my diplomatic inhibitions and do what I could to help him see the opportunity for a settlement and the extent to which it depended on him.

Our discussion was long, friendly and frank and, I thought, en-

2. In the 1967 election campaign in the state of Orissa, some rowdy threw a stone which hit her in the face and broke her nose; in spite of the bleeding she simply covered it up with her handkerchief and went on to complete her speech.
3. Later India's Ambassador to the United States.

couraging. I said that since he was the only person who could conceivably bring about a settlement of Kashmir he carried a heavy responsibility. I then suggested a formula similar to the one proposed by Nehru just before his death in 1964: (a) Abdullah would publicly assert that Kashmir was part of India and that he intended to run for the office of its Chief Minister. (b) In his campaign for election (the success of which was very nearly assured) he would stress that the Kashmir Valley, which was the most important area, should be granted a special semiautonomous status within the Indian nation. As the newly elected Chief Minister he would negotiate the terms of the special status with the central government of India in New Delhi. (c) India would agree that the Pakistani be given permanent possession of the area (which amounted to about 40 percent of the total) which they had occupied in the brief struggle in 1947, while India would be given permanent possession of Jammu and Ladakh.

Although Abdullah was resentful over the action of the Indian Government in keeping him in prison or under house arrest for several years, because of his alleged secret discussions with Pakistan,[4] and was himself a devout Muslim, he believed in a secular state and would have much preferred a permanent special relationship with India to the absorption of Kashmir into Pakistan. This came through clearly in our discussion. But when counterpressures were brought to bear on him by Kashmir extremists, he wavered. As a result the differences between Pakistan and India remained on dead center. The Pakistan Government insisted on a Kashmir settlement as the prior condition for agreements in regard to trade, communications and the general normalization of relationships. India expressed its willingness to discuss Kashmir, but argued that the more realistic approach was first to solve the more easily manageable problems, and then, in what should be a more favorable atmosphere, the Kashmir issue could be considered.

There are three reasons why this impasse is likely to continue until some positive new factor develops:

1. The Indian and Pakistan Governments view the partition of 1947 from totally different perspectives. Pakistan interprets it as a break between "Muslim Pakistan" and "Hindu India." India argues that it is not a Hindu state, but a *secular* state in which people of all religions are guaranteed equal rights and opportunities under a democratic constitution.

Therefore, as long as Pakistan claims the Kashmir Valley on the grounds that its population is predominantly *Muslim*, India has no alternative but to reject the claim. If the Pakistan claim were accepted,

4. I question the validity of these charges, although members of his family may have been so involved.

they say, what would happen to the sixty million Muslims who live elsewhere in India—more than those who live in West Pakistan itself—do these Muslims belong to Pakistan too, and if so where will they live? And what about the eleven million Christians living in India and the twelve million Sikhs?

2. Any democratically elected Indian Government that negotiated away a large strategic area that the Army had twice defended at great cost on the battlefield would be promptly voted out of office. (President Johnson once asked me why India would not agree to a plebiscite in the Kashmir Valley. In reply, I asked him what would have happened if the Mexican Government in the 1870's and 1880's had suggested to the President of the United States that a plebiscite be held in Texas to determine whether it should belong to America or to Mexico. As a good Texan, President Johnson's reply was brief and to the point: "If the President of the United States even considered such a proposal, he would be impeached.")

3. The Kashmir Valley is strategic to the defense of North India. A substantial part of the Indian Army in Ladakh is now facing the Chinese on the Tibetan side of the Himalayan Mountains. If the Pakistani should occupy the Kashmir Valley, it would be impossible for India to supply these troops the year round since the only all-weather road from India runs straight through the Kashmir Valley to Srinagar and from there to Kargil and Leh.[5]

Consequently, if India should withdraw from the Kashmir Valley, it would be forced to abandon a vast area in Ladakh which would promptly be occupied by the Chinese, bringing them four or five hundred miles closer to New Delhi.

Despite these obstacles to a settlement, the situation is not hopeless. It is my hope that a Kashmir relationship with India similar to that of Puerto Rico and the United States may someday evolve.[6] This would give the people of Kashmir some sense of independence and identity, and as emotions settled down, the relationship might come to be accepted by Pakistan as well.

Since Washington had previously agreed to reschedule Shastri's visit to the United States, I was pleased when Mrs. Gandhi agreed to carry through with the visit in the spring of 1966. There were many subjects for discussion. The most immediate was wheat.

5. India is building a new road over the 13,500-foot Rhotang Pass through Kulu, Manali, Lahul and Spiti to Leh. Construction was started in 1963 with earth-moving machinery and trucks provided by the American economic assistance program. However, since it will be snowbound at least five months of the year, it offers no real alternative to the present road through the Kashmir Valley.

6. At their request I provided copies of the documents establishing the U.S.-Puerto Rico relationship to Abdullah and the Indian Government.

The nearly total failure of the Indian monsoon in the crop year of 1965 had been followed by what began to appear to be a poor crop for 1966. Two nationwide droughts in succession had not occurred in India for nearly a hundred years. If the situation continued to deteriorate, the only way India could be saved from a famine, which at that point would have placed unbearable strains on the Indian political system and economy, was by drawing on our huge stockpiles of wheat.[7] There was also the matter of the resumption of U.S. economic assistance and the consideration of additional funds for the so-called "Big Push,"[8] which had very nearly been agreed to just before the Pakistan-India war, and which we believed could go far toward making India self-sufficient by the late 1970's.

I was also encouraged by a cable from Secretary Rusk in early March saying that the President was interested in a plan I had proposed in 1963 for an Indo-American Foundation, financed by the huge reserves of rupees that we had accumulated from the sale of wheat over a period of years. The Foundation would have an Indian President, an American deputy, a board of trustees half American and half Indian, a staff largely Indian, and it would be located in India.

Organized along the lines of the Rockefeller and Ford Foundations, the Foundation would be endowed, under my proposal, with $300 million worth of rupees. This would provide the Foundation with an income the equivalent of $10 to $14 million a year to be used to finance university projects, scientific research and the usual wide range of foundation activities. The Foundation would have the special advantage of providing a source of funds to finance the kind of fresh experimental concepts that the Indian Government, like most democratic governments, hesitates to undertake for fear of political criticism if they fail to work out. At the same time it would reduce the vast accumulation of rupees controlled by the United States Government, which Indian political leaders, with good reason, looked upon as a potential source of inflation should they be misused.

My proposal had been received with enthusiasm by Shastri and those few others in the Indian Government who knew about it. In the winter of 1964 we had drawn up an agreement, but it had been blocked in Washington for a variety of bureaucratic reasons. Now the President, searching for some dramatic gesture to please Mrs. Gandhi during her visit, had apparently run across this proposal and decided it was time to launch it.

Steb and I preceded Mrs. Gandhi to the United States by a few days

7. The story of our efforts to meet India's emergency needs and the conflicts which this created appears in the next chapter.
8. Discussed in detail in Chapter 43.

so that I could work out an agenda with the White House and State Department and be there to greet her.

Her arrival on March 28 was a gala affair. We met her plane at Andrews Air Force Base outside Washington and were transported by helicopter to the White House lawn. While I was uncertain how she and President Johnson would hit it off, I was reassured from the moment the President greeted her. He went out of his way to be cordial. In his remarks the President said:

> Madam Prime Minister, we are very glad that you are here. I feel very privileged to welcome you as the leader of our sister democracy. I have even greater pleasure in welcoming you as a good and gracious friend.
>
> Someone has said that all pleasure is edged with sadness. Only two months ago we looked forward to receiving your gallant predecessor here in our capital in Washington. We share your grief in his sudden and untimely death.
>
> Our thoughts also go back to the visits of another great Indian leader, those in 1949, 1956 and 1961 of your late father. Few have ever held a larger place in the hearts of the American people, and few ever will. We like to think, Mrs. Gandhi, that he belonged to us, too.
>
> We want to learn how we can best help you and how our help can be used to the very best effect. Your people and ours share the conviction that however difficult the problems there are none that a strong and vigorous democracy cannot solve. Mrs. Johnson and our daughters and I look forward to renewing an old friendship; to matching, if possible, in warmth and spirit your own hospitality in the years past. Let me say once more how much we appreciate your making this long journey at this busy time to visit us here in the United States.

Mrs. Gandhi responded in an equally warm and confident manner. Later the President told me that he was particularly impressed by the political astuteness she displayed in a long private conversation he had with her in his office. In addition, there were, of course, discussions between her and members of her staff and their American counterparts on a wide variety of subjects, ranging from India's need for more soybean oil to the likely intentions of the Chinese in Southeast Asia.

The official dinner at the White House was a glittering affair with the usual exchange of toasts by the President and Mrs. Gandhi. During the President's toast, he announced the United States was prepared to go ahead with the Indo-American Foundation.[9] The President pulled an additional rabbit out of the hat by offering Mrs. Gandhi the ship

9. I had consulted with the Indian Government before leaving New Delhi to make sure that their decision to go ahead with the proposal on the basis of the agreement we had negotiated in 1963–64 still held good and received an affirmative reply.

Anton Brun (Harry Truman's old yacht, *Williamsburg*), which had been rebuilt and equipped for deep-sea research. The Indians wanted a ship of this kind for offshore exploration in the Arabian Sea and the Bay of Bengal.

The final event was a cocktail party at the Indian Embassy, followed by dinner for a smaller number. Although the President, according to protocol, had not been invited to dinner, he came to the cocktail party and enjoyed himself so much that he asked if he could stay on for dinner. His toast, delivered in his Texas drawl, was once again a glowing tribute to Mrs. Gandhi and her government and an assurance of everlasting friendship and understanding; indeed, the clouds seemed at long last to be drifting away.

Mrs. Gandhi then proceeded to wow the Press Club and the Council on Foreign Relations and left behind an extraordinary glow of goodwill and bright expectations. Of even greater importance, I thought, was the sense of confidence the visit gave her not only in the support of the United States but in her own abilities.

However, on my return to India most of the old difficulties, and one or two new ones, were there to greet us. The President's announcement of the Indo-American Foundation had come as a complete surprise to the Indian press, Parliament and public. I had expected there would be attacks from left-wing sources, but I was most concerned by the attacks by economists and political scientists at Delhi University, many of whom had been educated in the United States, and who, we assumed, would have the clearest understanding of the many advantages that would stem from our proposal. However, in India, as in other new countries, intense nationalism was an important and growing force, and the left-wing assertion that this Foundation represented an attempt by the United States to subvert the Indian educational system made a deep impression on even normally sensible people who were good friends of the United States.[10]

It was particularly disturbing that the problem could easily have been avoided if only we had been able to explain publicly in advance what the Foundation was being set up to do and how it would operate. We had been fearful that if the press were to learn that the proposed new American Foundation was an idea which we had originally presented to President Kennedy, President Johnson might have refused to go through with it. Therefore discussions about it within the Embassy and with the Indian Government had been treated on almost a top-secret basis. The Indian

10. There was no validity whatsoever to the charge of American control. As I have indicated, the board would have been half Indian, and the President would have been an Indian, as would most of the staff.

public, press and universities were totally unprepared for the proposal.

If I had only had a week or two for press conferences and meetings and perhaps one or two speeches before the announcement, I am confident that I could have created an atmosphere which would have removed all barriers. However, Mrs. Gandhi was jittery about the opposition to the idea, and there was nothing to do but set it aside until a more auspicious moment.

On the other hand, we were encouraged to hear that the Indian Government had decided to devaluate the rupee, a step which the World Bank, many key officials in the Indian Government and our own economists felt was essential to spur Indian exports and to stimulate faster economic growth. But once again the political resistance in India was immediate and stormy and for much the same reasons. The leftist opposition attacked the decision as an American imperialistic plot and pointed to the "U.S.-controlled World Bank" as its primary source. The devaluation was also strongly opposed by several important members of the Congress Party who did not understand its economic implications or the conditions which made it necessary.

The situation was worsened by its effect upon the Indian people. Devaluation would of course raise the price of imported goods, but it should have had no effect on goods produced in India, such as food. Nevertheless, many Indian shopkeepers raised their prices anyway, which caused the public to blame devaluation for all higher prices.

But still greater difficulties lay ahead. In July, 1966, two months after her visit to Washington, Mrs. Gandhi left for a state visit to Moscow, obviously calculated to balance her visit to the United States. But the balance somehow got out of hand, and the joint press statement issued by Mrs. Gandhi and Premier Kosygin at the end of her visit called for an end to our bombing of North Vietnam and also contained vague references to the nefarious "imperialistic powers." These could be—and were—generally interpreted as attacks on the United States because of our rapidly growing involvement in Southeast Asia. This set off new fireworks in Washington.

On their return from Moscow, some of my friends in the Indian Foreign Ministry who had accompanied Mrs. Gandhi described to me the skill with which the Soviets managed this propaganda coup. The drafting of the joint statement was handled by the Soviets in cooperation with a relatively low-level member of the Indian mission. It was then shown to Mrs. Gandhi at a particularly hectic moment of her schedule and in the absence of her more responsible advisers. Whatever its origin, it demolished much of the goodwill in Washington which had been created during her visit there.

Even the President's last-minute present of the good ship *Anton Brun* ultimately backfired. According to the schedule, the vessel was to be delivered in Bombay in September, 1966. When September came and no *Anton Brun* was in sight, I cabled the State Department asking about the delay. I was told that Senator Wayne Morse was holding up the transfer. When I wrote to Senator Morse, however, he replied that he had no objection to the gift.

When three more months had passed and still no *Anton Brun*, I cabled again, only to be told that it had been discovered that new engines would be required and there was no way to pay for them. After a cable exchange with Paul Nitze, Secretary of the Navy, this hurdle was cleared.

Four months later I cabled once again, urgently asking when we might expect the *Anton Brun*, only to receive word that "Unfortunately the *Anton Brun* sank last week in New York Harbor while being launched from dry dock."

Against a background of concern and uncertainty, the fourth Indian general elections were held in February, 1967. In each of the first three national elections—1952, 1957 and 1962[11]—the Congress Party had established substantial majorities in the central Parliament and in the state assemblies. For two full decades Nehru's leadership had provided a unifying force. With his prestige, political skill, the devotion of the people and his deep commitment to a free and democratic India, Nehru knew—and the world knew as well—that his decisions would be respected.

The 1967 election marked a watershed in Indian politics. The Congress Party for the first time was confronted with an entirely new political situation. Although it had never received more than 44 percent of the total vote cast, the fragmented opposition had made it possible for Congress to maintain large majorities in both the national Parliament and state assemblies. With Nehru gone, opposition leaders from extreme left to extreme right in most parts of India came together with a single objective: to break the long domination by the Congress Party. The result was a series of Rube Goldberg political coalitions or "united fronts" which were committed to work together regardless of their differences in regard to programs and ideology.

This was a shrewd and effective political tactic, and it achieved its objectives. Although the total Congress vote in 1967 was reduced by only 3 percent, to 41 percent, the usually large Congress Party majority in the

11. It so happened that Steb and I were in India either in an official role or as visitors during each of these four elections.

national Parliament with 521 members was cut to 22 seats, and in 8 of the 17 state assemblies the Congress for the first time found itself in the minority.

We viewed the results with mixed feelings. There was no doubt that the Congress Party had lost much of its effectiveness, and there was little evidence of its being rejuvenated from within. But the wide spectrum of political views represented in the "united fronts" made it difficult, and in some states literally impossible, for the newly elected coalition government to govern.

Nevertheless, the election itself impressed me as a new fresh wind blowing through India. One hundred and seventy million people had voted, and it was clear that a majority were looking for new, young faces and fresh thinking. There was very little disorder. It was a quiet, business-like and enormously impressive undertaking.

But the orderly conduct of the election proved in many parts of India to be the calm before the storm. The most explosive situation developed in West Bengal, with its brooding, turbulent, impoverished Calcutta. Here the left-wing (Maoist) Communist Party as part of the United Front had secured enough votes to enable it to select the Deputy Prime Minister, the Home Minister (who controls the police) and the Minister of Education. And there was no reason to doubt that their objective was violent revolution. One young non-Communist leader in Calcutta announced, "We are prepared to wade through rivers of blood to reach our goals."

In the national Parliament, after some maneuvering by the growing opposition within her own party, Mrs. Gandhi was again elected Prime Minister. Gradually the country settled down.

In March an incident occurred which for a time at least took our minds off the elections, political unrest, wheat and the problems of economic assistance. On the evening of March 6, Stalin's daughter, Svetlana Alliluyeva, passport in hand, suddenly arrived at our Embassy doorstep and asked for a visa to go to the United States.

Svetlana had come to India in December to immerse the ashes of her late Indian husband in the Ganges. She had had a difficult time persuading Soviet officials in Moscow to allow her to leave Russia, and her stay had been officially limited to two weeks. However, she had been so impressed and excited by the free, democratic atmosphere of Indian society that she had decided not to return to the U.S.S.R., but to live in India for the rest of her life.

On several occasions the Soviet Embassy sent members of its staff to the small village of Uttar Pradesh, where her husband had lived and where she was now staying with his relatives. But she had refused to accompany them to New Delhi.

When Svetlana mentioned her wish to remain in India to an Indian official who was related to her late husband, he told her that India's relations with the Soviet Union were so sensitive and so important that it would be impossible to allow her to remain in defiance of her own government. It was at this point that she decided to defect to the U.S.A.

When Svetlana appeared at the American Embassy and produced her Soviet passport, the Marine guard recognized that something unusual was in the air and promptly notified me and key members of my staff.

At first I was skeptical. I did not even know that Stalin had a daughter, and I felt that it might well be some new ploy by the Soviets to create difficulties. While we were considering what to do, we asked Svetlana to write down who she was, why she wanted to leave Russia and why she wanted to go to the United States. The result was an eloquent, articulate and convincing ten-page letter written at my desk in the Chancery with a ballpoint pen on a yellow pad.[12]

The situation was loaded with politically explosive possibilities. Although the Soviets in India and elsewhere were continuing to play a hard game, I believed that sooner or later fruitful discussions between the U.S. and the U.S.S.R. might become possible and ultimately lead to a détente. At that time we were, in fact, seeking Soviet assistance in settling the conflict in Vietnam. The last thing I wanted to do was to place unnecessary strains on an already tense and uncertain relationship. But clearly we could not ignore or reject Svetlana's appeal. This would be a gross violation of our traditional commitment to political asylum.

This left only two courses of action. The first would be to provide temporary asylum in our Embassy or my official residence, Roosevelt House, which according to international law could not be violated even by the host government, India. This would give her time to retain a lawyer and appeal to the Indian courts for the right to leave India.

But there were some serious disadvantages. The announcement that Stalin's daughter had repudiated Soviet citizenship and had taken refuge in the home of the American Ambassador to India would create a sensation throughout the world. Within forty-eight hours Roosevelt House would be surrounded not only by Indian police but by scores of reporters, television teams and curiosity seekers. The Soviet Union, em-

12. This letter is reprinted in Svetlana's book, *Only One Year*, pp. 200–204.

barrassed by this situation, would bring heavy pressure to bear on the Indian Government to force the Indian courts to decide the case in their favor.

Since the Indian high courts are independent of the government and, by and large, are as deeply committed to constitutional law as our own, they were likely to decide in Svetlana's favor. The frustrated Indian Government would then be caught in the middle. In such a highly charged situation no one could give ground and everyone concerned would be hurt. The adverse effect on relationships among the United States, India and the Soviet Union would be serious.

The second possibility was to say nothing and to get her out of India as quickly as possible. Her passport, which the Soviet Embassy had fortunately returned to her that day on the assumption that she would soon be returning to Moscow, was in good order and required only an American visa—which I had authority to provide. A quick check of the airline schedules revealed that a Qantas Airlines plane bound for Rome would come through at one o'clock in the morning, four hours away. There were still two vacant seats, and these we immediately reserved.

Before finally committing ourselves to this course of action, however, I felt obligated to make sure that Svetlana had carefully considered the implications of leaving her own country. We asked her once again to consider the drastic step she was taking. She would be leaving her home and her family, probably forever. A reception was being given that night for a visiting official at the Soviet Embassy, and it was still not too late for her to slip back into the room in the Soviet Embassy hostel where she had spent the previous night, and then take the Soviet plane to Moscow two days later—according to her original plan.

Svetlana promptly rejected this suggestion. "If neither democratic India nor democratic America will accept me," she said, "I shall tell my story to the newspapers." It was clear from the set of her jaw that she meant precisely what she had said, and I could see no reason to pursue the suggestion.

At nine o'clock that evening I sent an urgent cable to the State Department stating that Svetlana Alliluyeva was now in our Embassy, that the Indian Government would be reluctant to allow her to stay in India, and that she was determined not to return to the Soviet Union. We had considered all the possibilities, and, on balance, I had decided to give her a visa and put her on a plane to Rome that night with a member of my staff as escort. She could be met in Rome by State Department officials, and we could then think through the various possibilities and implications before making a final decision. I added that I would proceed with this plan unless I received word to the contrary before the plane left in four hours.

Later I was told that my urgent cable arrived in the State Department and was decoded only eighteen minutes after it had been sent, which was about noon in Washington. It was, however, never answered. I assume that the harried State Department and White House were only too glad to have me take responsibility. At 1 A.M. on March 7, accompanied by Bob Rayles, a young Russian-speaking Foreign Service officer, Svetlana left New Delhi's Palam Airport on the first stage of a journey which eventually took her to a new life in the United States.

As far as we could tell, the Soviet Embassy did not miss her until late the next day. In any event, it was not until then that the Indian Government heard what had occurred. As we had anticipated, the Soviets immediately charged that the whole affair was a CIA kidnaping plot in which the Indian Government must have cooperated. The Indian Minister of External Affairs, caught in the middle, turned on me with the charge that I had "smuggled her out of the country in the dead of night." Presumably to ease angry charges from the Soviet Embassy, I was handed an *aide-mémoire* charging me with illegal procedure. Since the *aide-mémoire* was filled with inaccuracies, I refused to accept it. Within a few days the issue was officially dropped.

When I met the Soviet Ambassador at a reception a few days later, he was at first predictably chilly. I pointed out that our long tradition of political asylum made it impossible for me to reject her appeal, and that the direct-action procedure that we had followed was not only legal, but in the best interests of Svetlana, the Soviet Union, the Indians and ourselves. No one, I said, could have gained from a confrontation.

I added that I believed that sooner or later he and his government would see the issue from a more balanced perspective and agree that our admittedly unorthodox handling of the situation had saved him, his government and India considerable embarrassment and bitterness. Although I could hardly expect him to agree with me, he dropped the subject and thereafter resumed our normally cordial relationship.

In July, three months later, we met Svetlana at our home in Connecticut shortly after she arrived in the United States. Since then we have developed a warm regard for her as an individual and respect for her thoughtful and generally hopeful view of our turbulent world. She is now married to a distinguished American architect, and intends to become an American citizen. In a recent letter she wrote that she looked forward to her role as a "happy housewife."

This interlude was soon behind us when in early April, 1967, we received a cable informing us that the decision we had dreaded most had now been made: the U.S. had decided to resume limited military aid to Pakistan. The action came all wrapped up in rationalizations about promoting arms reductions. Probably because so few members of Congress understand the fine print in operations of this kind, the State Department and White House had actually secured Congressional approval of the transaction on the grounds that it would help "avoid an arms race." Consciously or not, it was a masterpiece of deviousness.

Under existing circumstances Pakistan and India had three possible sources of arms: (1) they could purchase spare parts to activate existing equipment; (2) they could purchase equipment from sources over which we had no control, i.e., Russia or France; (3) they could purchase American equipment from "third countries" over which we had licensing controls (i.e., the equipment could not be sold by the third country without U.S. approval).

The Pakistani assumed that the new U.S. decision meant not only supplying spare parts for their F-86 planes and Patton tanks, damaged in the recent war with India, but also slackening restrictions on the purchase of U.S.-manufactured arms, particularly tanks, from third countries.

To meet Pakistan's request for tanks, the U.S. Government asked first the West Germans, then the Belgians, then the Italians, and finally the Turks to "sell" one hundred semiobsolescent U.S. tanks to Pakistan for a nominal price with the assurance that we would approve the sale, and then replace the third country's tanks which had gone to Pakistan with an equivalent number of our most modern tanks "to strengthen our NATO forces."

Predictably, these "third countries," which were reluctant to antagonize India by becoming a party to this gambit, each in turn leaked the story to the press, and after a period of uncertainty the Johnson Administration, already caught in a "credibility gap" in Southeast Asia and elsewhere, decided not to widen the gap any further. Consequently, the agreement with Pakistan was limited to spare parts; and the request for U.S. tanks to be provided by a third country was set aside for "further study."

In March, 1970, a year after I left India, the Pakistani request for the tanks was renewed, and, according to press reports, this time the U.S. response was favorable. It was a senseless performance. Why should the Nixon Administration, with a relatively clean slate, seriously consider a proposal that would simply repeat the blunders and shabby diplomatic gambits of its predecessors?

There was considerable opposition in Congress, and I added my protest in a "guest editorial" in the *New York Times*. Again the decision was delayed; but six months later, in October, 1970, an agreement was reached which, according to press reports, permitted Pakistan to purchase one squadron of F-104 fighter planes, a squadron of B-57 bombers (the only conceivable purpose of which could be to bomb Indian cities) and a sizable number of armored personnel carriers.

Whose interests are served by such a decision? Certainly not the interests of the American people in South Asia, or the cause of world peace, or the welfare of the people of Pakistan, who are more in need of tractors than of tanks. A few military leaders in Pakistan, perhaps, and the American firms that manufacture the equipment, but that is all.

In the 1930's, Sir Basil Zaharoff, chief arms salesman for the British firm of Vickers, was described as "the merchant of death." Now the "merchants of death" are governments, and death has become nationalized. The United States alone sells on the average of $2 billion worth of arms to foreign governments each year. Pentagon-sponsored arms salesmen moving from country to country, peddling military equipment in these critical times, present, in my opinion, a sorry spectacle.

CHAPTER 41

LBJ AND AMERICAN WHEAT

DURING MRS. GANDHI'S VISIT to the United States in March, 1966, President Johnson assured her that the United States would do everything possible to meet India's emergency needs for food. He told Mrs. Gandhi that he intended to send a special message to Congress shortly to seek its endorsement of U.S. assistance.

In the President's special message to Congress on March 30, he faithfully carried out the promise. He said, in part:

> During this past week I have discussed the Indian food problem with the Prime Minister of India, who has been our welcome and distinguished guest here in Washington. I am persuaded that we may stand, at this moment, on the threshold of a great tragedy. The facts are simple; their implications are grave. India faces an unprecedented drought. Unless the world responds, India faces famine.
>
> Strong efforts by the Indian Government, and our help, have so far averted famine. But in the absence of cooperative and energetic action by the United States, by other nations and by India herself, some millions of people will suffer needlessly before the next crop is harvested. This, in our day and age, must not happen. Can we let it be said that man, who can travel into space and explore the stars, cannot feed his own?
>
> Indian leaders have rightfully turned to the world for help. Pope Paul VI has endorsed their plea. So has the World Council of Churches. So has the Secretary General of the United Nations. So has the Director General of the Food and Agricultural Organization. And, so, in this message, does the President of the United States. . . .
>
> It is not our nature to drive a hard mathematical bargain where hunger is involved. Children will not know that they suffered hunger because American assistance was not matched. We will expect and press

for the most energetic and compassionate action by all countries of all political faiths. But if their response is insufficient, and if we must provide more, before we stand by and watch children starve, we will do so. I, therefore, ask your endorsement for this emergency action.

India is a good and deserving friend. Let it never be said that "bread should be so dear, and flesh and blood so cheap" that we turned in indifference from her bitter need.

Despite these eloquent words, it was evident that there was little understanding at the higher levels in the White House or State Department of India's predicament. Not only did we fail to secure a specific commitment and schedule of grain shipments; we had to fend off well-intentioned but inappropriate "solutions" to India's agricultural problems which would only have added to our difficulties. For instance, during a special visit to Washington in July to discuss the Indian food situation, I heard that the Department of Agriculture, without talking to me, had recommended to the President that one thousand U.S. Department of Agriculture extension workers be sent immediately to India to introduce "American know-how" to the Indian cultivators. Worse still, I heard the President was excited about the idea and was likely to approve it.

The very thought of this mass migration of one thousand American "experts," most of whom would start with little or no understanding of the special problems of agriculture in Asia, suddenly hitting the Indian countryside with 950 wives, 2,500 children, 3,000 air conditioners, 1,000 jeeps, 1,000 electric refrigerators (many of which wouldn't work), 800 or 900 dogs and 2,000 or 3,000 cats was appalling.

That night I sent a special private cable to my staff in India alerting them to this development and asking them to meet immediately with Indian officials and persuade them to make a formal request for five hundred Peace Corps Volunteers to work especially on agricultural problems. The cablegram with the official Indian request arrived within twenty-four hours, and by some fast work and a good deal of persuasion I managed to substitute the Peace Corps operation, which I knew we could handle effectively, for the more expensive, complicated and disruptive Department of Agriculture proposal.

In a long and encouraging talk with the President a few days later I pointed out that the Food for Peace Bill had passed Congress, the Indian Government's program for rapidly increasing its own production had met our highest hopes, and I felt the time had come to go beyond vague assurances of assistance. We now needed commitments on the specific amounts and dates when the grain would be shipped, so that India could establish its enormous national rationing program on a more solid basis.

To my relief, President Johnson promptly called a White House meeting of some thirty Senators of both parties, which I attended, and delivered one of the most eloquent appeals on behalf of human justice I had ever heard. The issue, as he put it, was clear: The United States is a fortunate country with vast food reserves. We are decent people who believe in carrying our share of the burdens of the world. Would the Senate support a massive program of food shipments to help India weather her present difficulties? There was no Cold War appeal to fears of Communism, to the possibility of winning Indian support for our political positions or other political gimmicks which, unhappily, we often tie, openly or covertly, to such appeals. It was straightforward, clear and in our best American tradition.

The President then went around the room asking each Senator for his personal opinion. There was unanimous agreement that the effort must be made.

On the second day the President called a similar meeting of about sixty members of the House of Representatives. Again he made an extraordinarily effective presentation in the very best tradition of American decency and democracy. His appeal was so persuasive that even those individuals who might be expected to take a negative position began nodding their heads.

With a favorable Congressional response to his appeal, we assumed the President would instruct the State Department, AID and Department of Agriculture to proceed with the grain shipments. Instead, he embarked on a foot-dragging performance that I still fail to understand. Assuming personal charge of the program, he adopted what was referred to in Washington as a "short tether" approach, holding up authorization for new shipments until the very last moment. Even the senior officials in our government dealing with India's food problem became so intimidated that they refused to make even those decisions which they could have made for themselves.

India's harried officials and our own harried mission were kept on tenterhooks until the last possible moment before we received word that a new series of shipments, which were all that stood between tens of thousands of people and starvation, had been authorized by the President and were on their way. This placed the Indian rationing system under an almost impossible strain. India's needs could be met only by an uninterrupted stream of grain ships, an average of three arriving at Indian ports every day. The time schedule was so tight that it was often referred to as a "ship-to-mouth" operation. Even the delay of a few days in ship departures from American ports was reflected in the most tragic terms in the drought-ridden areas.

The situation was made even more difficult by the fact that sensitive Indian officials seemed almost to be searching for ways to prove that India's integrity as a sovereign nation could never be bought with American wheat. The Indian Government swamped President Johnson with pleas to stop the bombing of North Vietnam. On one memorable occasion Mrs. Gandhi, following charges by Communist members of Parliament that by accepting U.S. wheat she had "sold out" to the American imperialists, sent warm birthday greetings to Ho Chi Minh. Her purpose, I believe, was largely to prove that these charges were false.

Predictably, the U.S. Government's reaction, and particularly that of the President, was violent. Cables from Washington burned with comments about "those ungrateful Indians," and the shipments of wheat were further delayed. Our official logic in regard to India seemed to run as follows: India is poor, we are rich, and India must have our assistance. Therefore it follows that if India cannot support U.S. policy, it should at least refrain from criticizing it, or accept the consequences.

This spirit at its worst was reflected in the remark a high White House official once made to me as we discussed one of Mrs. Gandhi's requests for America to "stop the bombing." Mrs. Gandhi, I asserted, was only saying what U Thant and the Pope had said over and over again. "But," replied the official, "the Pope and U Thant don't need our wheat."[1]

By the fall of 1966 it was clear that the monsoon had failed for a second consecutive year, and the food outlook again began to look desperate. We began daily to report to Washington the rapidly worsening food situation, particularly in Bihar and eastern Uttar Pradesh, where some millions of people were now threatened with starvation. We also carefully assessed and reported on the successes and shortcomings of India's efforts to modernize its agriculture and move toward self-sufficiency. We pointed out the likely need for substantial increases in the wheat shipments which had previously been requested.

These reports were based on visits to rural areas throughout India by members of our staff who had long experience in Indian agriculture and food distribution. Our estimates in the past had been remarkably accurate and we were confident that they were equally so on this occasion. They had the unqualified endorsement of the World Bank team which had been in India for several weeks studying the food situation and of the highly competent agricultural staffs of the Ford and Rockefeller Foundations in India.

1. Dean Rusk often showed this kind of petty irritation. Once when I was pressing the wheat issue, he asked impatiently, "Tell me one thing that India has ever done for us?" My reply was that India, with one-sixth of the human race, had survived as a working democracy and the world's biggest common market for almost twenty years, and that this itself was quite a contribution.

However, on November 11, 1966, out of the blue arrived a cable from Agriculture Secretary Orville Freeman in which he abruptly announced a plan for a general check-up on the Indian food situation. The cable included a patronizing and unreasonable message which I was asked to deliver at once to Minister of Agriculture Subramanian. The next morning I sent a cable to Secretary Rusk in which I stated:

> Secretary Freeman's cable in which he states that he is sending a special mission here next week more accurately to assess India's food situation and tells me to transmit an extraordinarily insensitive message to Subramanian has just arrived. The tone and context of these messages constitute an indictment of the competence and judgment of the United States Mission in Delhi which is both unjustified and unacceptable.
>
> If I should deliver Freeman's letter to Subramanian, Mrs. Gandhi and the Indian Government could only conclude that (1) the President has no confidence in the judgment of his Ambassador in Delhi and his staff; (2) the American Government is taking advantage of India's acute food crisis to bring political pressure to bear on the Indian Government. The press is bound to draw one or both of these conclusions in any event.
>
> Therefore, I shall not deliver Freeman's message to Subramanian unless I am ordered to do so by the President.

Within a few hours I received by cable a contrite reply asserting that, of course, the State Department and the White House had complete confidence in the New Delhi Embassy. The delay in wheat shipments and the proposal for a team from Washington to review the situation, it was said, were part of an effort to convince Congress that the Administration was "hardheaded" in dealing with aid problems; this would be helpful in maintaining a steady flow of shipments to India. As for the insensitive letter which Freeman had asked me to deliver to Subramanian, it was suggested that I forget it.

I was puzzled as to how this situation had developed. Orville Freeman and I had been good friends since the late 1940's when he was Governor of Minnesota and I was Governor of Connecticut; we had worked together closely in the political arena. Moreover, it had been I who had stimulated his interest in Indian agriculture, which began with a very useful visit he made at my invitation in April, 1964. I concluded that this incident reflected the confused, jittery, dog-eat-dog atmosphere in Washington which had become particularly evident in regard to questions involving India since the President had begun personally to oversee the wheat shipments;[2] there was a good chance, I

2. On one occasion during a discussion of India's food problems before a group of Senators President Johnson unmercifully chastised Secretary Freeman because he did not have on the tip of his tongue certain figures on soybean production.

thought, that the cable had been written by a staff member and that Freeman had not even seen it.

By this time the U.S. press had become aware of our difficulties, and a number of editorials appeared strongly supporting our position. The *New York Times* commented editorially on November 29, 1966:

> President Johnson's decision to interrupt American grain shipments to India in mid-December, just as famine threatens and critical elections approach, is a serious error. A continuous "bridge of boats" is vital because India's port facilities can barely meet the country's annual import needs now.
>
> The White House statement that the new drought required a new survey is unconvincing. It does not explain why shipments are being held up while the study is made. The new drought may increase the need for American grain. It certainly cannot reduce it. This situation leads Indians to suspect that the hold-up may be partially due to President Johnson's displeasure with Prime Minister Gandhi's recent call for a halt in the bombing of North Vietnam.

On December 11 the Washington *Post* commented:

> A major interruption in January grain arrivals in India has been averted by the timely gift of 100,000 tons of wheat from Canada and an emergency $10 million Indian purchase of 150,000 tons from Australia.
>
> The Administration is continuing to delay action on new food aid commitments including a short-term, 2-million-ton agreement envisaged in Indo–United States discussions since July. This means that a break in grain arrivals during the first week of February is now almost inescapable.
>
> A variety of explanations have been suggested to justify the delayed decision. One interpretation is that the President wants to dramatize his desire for Soviet and other international participation in helping food-deficit countries. Another is that he wants to shock India into more meaningful agricultural reforms and more equitable sharing of its own food resources.
>
> There are good reasons for a firm American policy that, in the long run, will assist India in resolving its recurrent food difficulties. But people sometimes starve to death in the short run and India is on the brink of famine. It also is on the eve of an election and starvation does not ordinarily induce an electorate to behave rationally.
>
> We have good reason to hope that India will continue to be an enclave of relative stability in Asia and we desire a continuation of its essentially democratic system. Whatever else our policies do, they must not be permitted to prejudice these long-run ends.

Whatever President Johnson's motives, his tactics were causing hardship and humiliation in India. The Indians, desperate for help, were never quite sure what would be forthcoming. But knowing the explosive side of President Johnson's makeup, they never dared say so out loud. John Lewis and I, and our mission in general, were as worried as the Indians and embarrassed as well.

Two weeks after my exchange with Washington over Freeman's proposal I received a cable from the State Department saying that while the President did not question the accuracy of our reports, he felt that it would be usfeul if two teams—one consisting of U.S. agriculture experts and the other of members of Congress—came out in the next two weeks. Having made my point in the earlier exchange, I promptly agreed.

The Congressional committee consisted of Congressman Robert Poage, a Texas Democrat and chairman of the House Agriculture Committee; Congressman Robert Dole, Kansas Republican, also a member of the House Agriculture Committee; Senator Gale McGee, Democrat from Wyoming; and Senator Jack Miller, Republican from Iowa, a member of the Senate Agriculture Committee. In a country the size of India, it is not easy in a limited period to secure a balanced view of any situation, and agriculture is particularly complex. But this committee, maintaining a heavy schedule, reached deep into rural areas all over India and their report was comprehensive, balanced and constructive. They reported to the President unanimously and without reservation that the flow of wheat to India should be continued.

The committee from the Department of Agriculture made an equally conscientious survey, including not only the rural areas but the rationing setup and the "ship-to-mouth" distribution system. They, too, reported to the President that far from overstating India's food needs we were probably understating them.

On February 6, 1967, Congressmen Poage and Dole introduced legislation in the House to assure the flow of wheat to India. They said:

> The food crisis that India faces is very real and serious. India needs help. We feel that the resolution which we introduced today will serve as a bipartisan expression of the sense of Congress supporting the efforts of our government to come to the aid of the Indian people in this time of critical food shortage.

In addition, each of the four members of Congress made a separate statement expressing his own views which appeared in the *Congressional Record*. Congressman Dole's statement was typical:

> Last December, at the request of the President, the gentleman from Texas [Mr. Poage] and I visited India and found the dimensions of the food crisis alarming. The self-help efforts now being carried out in the disaster-plagued nation, in my opinion, offer real hope and encouragment.

The Government of India is placing increasing emphasis on agricultural development. Now in the fourth 5-year plan agriculture's priority has been established as second only to national defense, and public investment scheduled for agriculture during the fourth 5-year plan will more than double that for the third 5-year plan.

There are signs of encouragement in fertilizer production, increased supply of credit through cooperatives, development of water and soil resources, increased yields through the new high-yielding seed varieties, and a number of other programs designed to increase food production.

Progress is being made, and, in my opinion, the Government of India, and the Indians themselves, are earnest and sincere in their self-help efforts.

The *New York Times* again commented:

If India were seriously delinquent in self-help measures, there might be an argument for a squeeze at a more propitious time. But an inter-agency memorandum in October, a special task force in November and a Congressional visit in December have all indicated that India's program is generally satisfactory.

Even Secretary of Agriculture Freeman, the chief doubter last summer, now believes that the Indians are making "an earnest effort." The President's main objective, Mr. Freeman indicated, is not so much to pressure India as to force the Soviet Union and other countries into sharing the American aid burden.

The objective is laudable. But the method chosen to achieve it, at a time when the subcontinent is living from ship to mouth, involves a dangerous gamble. It amounts to playing Russian roulette with the life of Prime Minister Indira Gandhi's moderate democratic Government. And a misfire, as Moscow undoubtedly has noted, is likely to see the United States, not the Soviet Union, blamed for thousands of famine deaths.

Throughout 1967, in large measure because of these reports, a reasonably steady flow of wheat was maintained. Were it not for our wheat shipments, India could not possibly have met the desperate grain shortages of 1965, 1966 and 1967, and the result would have been a famine of either large or moderate proportions.[3]

Much of the credit for this huge outpouring of 26 million tons of American wheat belongs to the able middle and lower levels of the White House, the State Department and the Department of Agriculture, who

---

3. The story of how India *avoided* a devastating famine has never been told. Disasters make better news than success. As they walked down the gangways from the incoming planes, foreign newsmen arriving in Delhi to cover the "famine story" often asked, "Where can we see the nearest bodies?" When they were told that so far there were no bodies and we were earnestly hoping there would be none, they felt a certain letdown. Although there were a few hundred deaths in which hunger was a factor, I doubt that many of these could be attributed solely to "starvation."

understood the situation from the beginning and patiently and persistently struggled to persuade their superiors. However, it is fair to say that if I and my associates in the Embassy had not pushed and pulled, argued, cabled and written, the necessary wheat would not have been forthcoming.

Much credit was also due to the Indians themselves. They organized a remarkably efficient rationing system and transportation system. Working around the clock, many thousands of workers unloaded the wheat from the ships, and then by trucks and by rail it was distributed to the villages and towns where the need was most urgent. Although we had many inspectors constantly watching this effort, it is extraordinary that no black market scandal of any substance ever came to light.

By January, 1968, thanks to the dramatically improved harvest following the excellent 1967 monsoon, it was evident that the Indian Government would require considerably less wheat than in the previous crisis years. According to early estimates the amount would be no more than three million tons, which was a third or fourth what it had been in each of the previous two years.

Then suddenly the situation was turned upside down. In the spring of 1968 I had a communication from the State Department and the Department of Agriculture saying that the United States Government had excessively large supplies of wheat and could I not persuade the Indian Government to *increase* its request to six million tons? This, it was said, would build up India's own reserve stocks (and incidentally stiffen American grain prices in an election year).

Since our mission and the Indian Government were greatly pleased that the shipments could be reduced and the Indians were taking justified pride in their own greatly increased production, we were at first reluctant. But it was true that the extra two or three million tons of imports would enable the Indians to build a much bigger reserve and allow a great deal more flexibility in distribution. Consequently, we recommended to the Indian Government that it request the larger amount. After much discussion it agreed to make the request and to reorganize its ration plans to fit the increased supply.

These plans called for the additional wheat to begin to arrive in September. But the weeks slipped by and the White House authorization that would start the additional grain ships on their long journey to India was not forthcoming. Cable followed cable, but there was no action. By mid-October the Indian Government, which by this time had adjusted its rationing plans to include the anticipated extra wheat, was facing another crisis. Unless the additional wheat (which it had not originally asked for) was immediately forthcoming, the ration, which had been adjusted upward following our assurance of larger supplies, would have to be sharply reduced at a time when the government faced a major political crisis in Bengal and elsewhere.

We continued to cable, to write and to send staff people to Washington, but with no visible result. President Johnson, for reasons that no one could fathom, was continuing to withhold the authorization which would send the grain ships on their way. Dean Rusk, Orville Freeman and other members of the government, I felt, understood the irony of the situation and were doing their best, but clearly with no success.

Three days before the U.S. elections in early November I received a confidential message from a friend in the State Department reporting that a meeting had just been held in the White House at which the State Department and Department of Agriculture had pressed hard for the authorization but that the President was adamant; he would wait until the new Congress under a new President had been installed and leave the decision to him. In the meantime, India could go without.

On Monday morning, the day before election, following a worrisome weekend a personal cable for me arrived from the President that left us dumfounded. The President had approved the immediate shipments of the grain and at the same time released funds for the economic aid program, which had also been held in abeyance and for which we had very nearly given up hope.

Election Day for the American mission in India, as in the United States and throughout the world, was one of intense interest. The United States Information Service set up a political information center not only in New Delhi but in Madras, Calcutta and Bombay, where thousands of Indians and foreigners[4] as well as Americans gathered to watch the results as they were posted state by state on a gigantic bulletin board. When the day was over, we knew that Richard Nixon, who had visited India twice while I was Ambassador,[5] would be our next President.

As I watched the results being posted, I found my mind constantly drifting back to the enigma of Lyndon Baines Johnson. He has been analyzed ad infinitum, but no one has yet been able to explain him, and I wonder if anyone ever will. My own experiences with him are evidence of his complexity.

    4. Several members of the Soviet Embassy spent most of the day at the center in New Delhi.
    5. After his visit in early 1967, Nixon had sent me a letter of thanks in which he said in part: "What pleased me most was the opportunity to get your very candid and informative appraisal of Indian-American relations as well as your views on what changes in our foreign policy could be made in the years ahead. This is certainly a period in which there is a great necessity for stating new ideas."

I first met Johnson in 1944 when as a young Texas Congressman he had had the courage to vote in opposition to an unnecessary increase in oil prices then being maneuvered through Congress by Harold Ickes and the Petroleum Administration for War with strong support from Senators and Congressmen from the oil-producing states. He and Mike Monroney of Oklahoma, both from states where oil revenues are often tied tightly to political contributions, were major factors which turned the Congressional tide in our favor. It was an act of great courage.

My reactions to his possible candidacy for the Presidency in 1960 were, however, unfavorable, in large part based on his record as a Senator and a political operator. I did not believe that he could be counted on to take a clear stand on civil rights and similar domestic issues, while on foreign affairs he was without experience. For these reasons I ducked an opportunity to second Johnson's nomination to the Vice Presidency at the 1960 Los Angeles Convention.

Nevertheless, once in office Johnson produced a program that went beyond FDR's New Deal or Kennedy's New Frontier. He succeeded in securing Congressional approval for almost two hundred measures to assist farmers and rural areas in addition to the creation of a Cabinet-rank Department of Housing and Urban Development and the fostering of such imaginative new programs as Model Cities; the creation of a Cabinet-rank Department of Transportation; the first federal safety standards for motor vehicles; new measures to protect consumers; the largest manpower program in our history; the declaration of a "war on poverty," with many new and radical "poverty programs"; increased aid to education; the National Teacher Corps; Medicare for the benefit of millions of older people; plus the 1964 Civil Rights Act, the most far-reaching civil rights legislation in one hundred years. It was a magnificent performance and all the more impressive because it was unexpected.

But in foreign affairs it was a different story. President Johnson had little feeling for the people of the developing new nations, although his antecedents could have given him the basis for learning. On one occasion when discussing with him the problems of overseas development, I remarked that while I was not sure that he fully understood what I was saying, I was confident that his Populist father and grandfather would have understood me. This comment intrigued the President, and he asked what I meant. I replied that the problems of the people of India, Nigeria, Brazil and other developing countries were very similar now to those of Texas and other Western states around the turn of the century. At that time the Populists were fighting for new schools, new roads to allow the farmer to reach the market towns, lower interest and freight rates, rural medical care and the like. This, I said, was what Texas wanted then, and it was all that the people of India wanted today. He asked me to write a speech for him on the subject and I did, but he never gave it.

My chief dealings with President Johnson, of course, largely concerned India. To this day his actions and his state of mind remain a puzzle. As we have seen, on at least five occasions in the critical years of 1965, 1966 and 1967 the President put the Indian Government and people through a needless ordeal in regard to food supplies with no valid explanation even to me and my associates, who had to work every day with exhausted and desperate Indian officials.

In the six years of our second assignment to New Delhi we shipped to India a total of 26 million tons of wheat, nearly three-fourths of our entire average annual crop; and nearly one thousand ten-thousand-ton shiploads of wheat a year at the peak. Twelve percent of the Indian people lived on American wheat, and there was no doubt that it saved millions of them from starvation. But our public posture through most of the critical period was one of confusion, irresponsibility and, as one Indian friend bitterly asserted one evening, "something approaching sadism."

The extent of my exasperation is indicated by a journal entry for February 6, 1966:

> LBJ's performance remains beyond comprehension or belief. After all the big talk about "fighting hunger in India" as we would "fight a war," we have provided in the last two months between 300,000 and 500,000 tons less than the Indians could have shipped, unloaded and transported. Yesterday with the remark that even the Secretaries of State and Agriculture, whom he has just seen, did not know what he was going to do, he belatedly made available three million tons.
>
> It is a cruel performance. The Indians must conform; they must be made to fawn; their pride must be cracked. Pressure to improve India's performance was sensible, but that had been assured in 1965. Once the Indian commitment to modernize their own agriculture had been made was the moment for bold, effective, confidence-creating gestures. Instead came more pressure, more mystery, with the poor State Department trying to explain each move or refusal to move as a logical result of India's failure to do all kinds of things that no sensible person ever expected them to do. It is in this way that distrust and hatred are born among people who want to be our friends.

Despite our best efforts in India to maintain India's trust in our intentions the impression developed that the United States was more interested in gaining a political advantage or forcing a change in India's foreign policy than in helping fellow beings who were in desperate need of help. The tragic thing about all these impressions and suspicions is that they were in fact totally untrue. Most Americans, including the President himself, felt a responsibility to save India from a disaster, and we saved it.

Although President Johnson had briefly visited India once or twice, he knew little about it, and was in no mood to learn. He mistrusted anyone who pleaded India's case, on the grounds that he must be prejudiced in India's favor.

Loyal staff assistants such as Bill Moyers, Joseph Califano, Jack Valenti, Douglass Cater and George Reedy worked hard to keep the President's policies on the track and often, because of his rapidly shifting moods, took a great deal of abuse in the process. On one occasion I was testifying before the Senate Foreign Relations Committee when the word came that the President wished to see me immediately. The chairman, Bill Fulbright, promptly excused me and courteously postponed the hearings. I rushed to the White House, only to wait more than an hour before the President could see me. It turned out that the matter was of small importance. I don't even recall what it was. I am sure that the President did not intend to wreck my day. Probably he said thoughtlessly, "Get Bowles over here right away," and a nervous staff member dutifully proceeded to do so.

Johnson's political Waterloo was Vietnam. As our military involvement grew, the political repercussions at home and abroad intensified. Although many others carried a large share of responsibility, the public resentment focused on him. There were relatively few Americans, regardless of their political affiliations, who had not honestly wanted to help Eisenhower and Truman when they blundered; but not Johnson. As his problems increased, there were few helping hands.

Once he became personally committed to a victory he could not win, he seemed obsessed with those who did not fully share his views. At one meeting in the summer of 1966, literally half our time together was taken up by almost paranoiac references to Bobby Kennedy, Wayne Morse, Bill Fulbright and others. He would allude to an obscure news reference and then with his aide, Jack Valenti, embark on a frantic search through the pages of various newspapers to find it. He made particularly scathing references to the *New York Times*, whose current offense had been to have put his most recent speech on NATO back on page 18.

After this meeting, I wrote in my notebook:

> In Johnson I see a man headed for deep trouble, with the probability of an increasing obsession with his "enemies"; and steadily growing public disenchantment—depending largely on events for timing, but with a near-

certainty in regard to the ultimate result. A break on Vietnam might still provide a breathing spell; a disaster in Vietnam could speed the day of political reckoning. The continuation of the war will make Johnson more irascible and even more inclined to shoot from the hip. His many accomplishments will be forgotten, and his personal qualties will earn him an increasing measure of dislike and distrust.

To strike a balance between his foreign policy failures and his domestic accomplishments is a task for the historians. But it would be grossly unfair if his extraordinary legislative record, which rivaled Roosevelt's and surpassed Kennedy's, were lost sight of. He dealt boldly and, by and large, successfully with every public issue that had concerned liberals since World War II.

Nor should it be forgotten that Johnson was genuinely eager to create a new and constructive relationship with the Soviets; indeed, deep inside of him this may have been his greatest ambition. He was excited at the possibilities opened up by his visit with Kosygin at Glassboro and thrilled by the favorable public response. If an opportunity for meaningful negotiations in Moscow or elsewhere had developed, I believe Johnson would have welcomed it with enthusiasm and pursued it with skill. But because of Vietnam and the Soviet takeover in Prague, the opportunity never came.

I have expressed the belief that Kennedy would have seen the danger in time and avoided a full commitment to Vietnam. With Johnson, Vietnam became an obsession, and it destroyed him.

CHAPTER 42

CHINA, RUSSIA AND INDIA

INDIA'S ABILITY to play a constructive role in Asia will depend in large measure on its success or failure in dealing with its own internal problems. But another major factor will be the relations which develop among China, Russia and India.

Lenin recognized this when he wrote that the ultimate victory of world Communism would come through the revolutionary alliance between the Soviet Union and the "exploited people of Asia, Africa and Latin America." "In the last analysis," he said, "the future of the world will be determined by the cold fact that Russia, China and India represent a crushing majority of the people of the world." A working relationship among these three nations, with their vast resources and with nearly half of the world's population, Lenin felt, could bring overwhelming political and economic pressure to bear on such neighboring nations as Japan, Germany, the United Kingdom and France. This is what Lenin meant when he remarked that the "road to Paris lies through Calcutta and Peking."

But a half-century later Lenin's prophecy is a long way from fulfillment. The Chinese attack on India in 1962, for one thing, put an end to India's hope that under existing conditions China could be expected to play the role of the good neighbor. Although the Indians were humiliated, the Chinese assumption that this attack would create political divisions throughout India proved to be incorrect; on the contrary, the Indian people, even in the southern states far removed from the conflict, rallied strongly to the defense of the government, and Indian unity and morale reached a new high.

537

The Indo-Chinese conflict is an important element in the international scene not only because of the vast size of these two nations (together they represent more than a third of all mankind), but because China is a totalitarian nation attempting to build a new society in a new way, while India in its drive for development is still deeply committed to democratic procedures. If India succeeds in its efforts to achieve an adequate rate of growth with reasonable political stability, the case for democracy in Asia will be greatly strengthened.

Since the brief Indo-Pakistan war in 1965, India's primary security concern has been the possibility that the Pakistani, who openly supported the Chinese territorial claims against India, might join the Chinese in a major attack along India's 2,500-mile northern frontier. If such an attack should occur, Indian tacticians assume that Pakistan's role would be a thrust into Ladakh to open a second front, with the promise that if India were defeated Kashmir would be transferred to Pakistan.

There were occasions when I wondered if this grim analysis might not eventually prove valid. The extraordinary network of hard-surfaced roads which the Chinese had built for thousands of miles along the Indo-Tibetan border provided the Chinese with the capacity rapidly to move large military units along their entire southern border, thereby providing several options for attack on India.

But the Indian military, as we have seen, has now been modernized, expanded and reorganized. Both the Indian Army, with its more than one million men, well led, well equipped and with high morale, and the Indian Air Force, with some seven hundred planes, are entirely composed of volunteers; the first term of enlistment is six years, with the option to re-enlist for six more years. Each soldier and officer is required to return to his village once a year for two months to help work the farms and to renew his contact with the civilian population. I have visited Indian Army posts and regularly delivered lectures on foreign policy to Indian officers in the defense colleges; on each occasion I have been impressed with the caliber, quality and intelligence of both officers and men.

Because India's military strength has grown, it now seems to me that an attack by China, directly or in cooperation with Pakistan, is most unlikely. Even if the Indian military capacity were less impressive, I find it difficult to visualize the conservative, land-holding leaders who largely dominate West Pakistan, regardless of their bitter antagonism toward India, throwing in their lot with a Chinese regime which would almost certainly gobble them up before the exercise was finally completed.

We may, however, see increased Chinese *covert* activities in North Burma, Assam, in the turbulent Communist-oriented city of Calcutta and in uneasy East Pakistan. If such a low-key softening-up effort were successful, it is conceivable, but still unlikely, that China might attempt to outflank India's Army and Air Force in the well-defended passes in the Himalayas, by a thrust through Burma.

Indian Government leaders, and particularly the military, are conscious of these possibilities, but quite confident of their ability to handle them. In 1967 some three thousand Naga tribesmen from eastern India did cross northern Burma to the Chinese state of Yünnan for a year's training in guerrilla warfare. However, the following year when a sizable number armed with Chinese weapons returned covertly to Nagaland, the Indian military, backed by an effective political-economic development effort, succeeded first in containing this force and then in largely destroying it.

No one can speak with assurance about the future policies of the Chinese Government. Some assert that the Chinese are committed to a world-wide ideological crusade based on their own version of the Marxist-Leninist doctrine; others argue that China is simply a resurgent power, seeking to avenge the humiliations which have been thrust upon it by the West, and confident that sooner or later it can restore the Middle Kingdom with China as the center of the world; still others see China's foreign policy as a reflection of its fierce drive for modernization.

The Chinese are a competent, tough, determined people, with the largest population in the world on a vast land area and with very considerable natural resources, backed by a long history and a deeply rooted cultural tradition. It is my impression that the Chinese past is probably more important in determining the present Chinese mood than its ideological ties to Communism. China draws its inspiration and its dynamism largely from its historical concept of its place in the world, adapted to our present era. Chinese leaders, it seems to me, are inclined to be Chinese first and Marxist-Leninist second, with the ideological concepts which they have superimposed on Chinese society adjusted to China's own requirements and history.

The Soviets clearly misjudged their own ability to dominate China. It is doubtful that China had ever entertained the idea of playing a secondary role in the relationship. As long as the Soviet Union and China were moving in the same general direction, China was content to go along. When the Soviets began to modify their policies to fit what they believed to be changed conditions, a break with China became inevitable.

In regard to China's future relations with the Soviet Union, China resents not only the fact that the U.S.S.R. maintains its grip on more than a million square miles of former Chinese territory but that the

Soviet Union has not hesitated on occasion to work with the United
States in the interest of moderating world tensions. In July, 1963,
Gromyko said, "The two greatest modern powers have left far behind
any other country in the world. If they unite for peace, there can be no
war. If any madman wants to go to war, we have but to shake our
fingers to warn them off." This remark no doubt intensified China's
disdain for the U.S.S.R.

China's ambitions seem to remain unlimited. Chinese leaders assert
that they will "not only overtake the capitalist countries and surpass
them," but will also "overtake and surpass the Socialist countries as
well." They seek ultimately to emerge as the revolutionary superpower,
operating at the storm center of the world, with an irresistible appeal
to the have-not nations with their hundreds of millions of bitter, dis-
possessed and underprivileged people.

Part of China's strength in today's world lies in the fact that Mao
has placed major confidence in the strength of the peasantry as opposed
to the Marxist-Leninist assumption that the decisive power rests with the
industrial proletariat. As the Chinese see the world, it is in the villages
of the world, surrounding the cities, where lies the future.

China has placed its bets on world revolution, and they are likely to
remain there until some internal political eruption occurs, or a new
Chinese leadership at some point comes to the conclusion that its goals
are simply not attainable. But right now China is convinced that "the
four seas are raging, the five continents are rocking," and they may be
expected to maintain their militarily cautious but politically aggressive
course.

There is very little the U.S., the U.S.S.R. or any other nation can do
right now to affect what goes on inside China. But there is a great deal
we can do, when and if circumstances change, to ease legitimate Chinese
fears and to encourage China in a more rational relationship with its
neighbors and with the world. In the meantime, we should avoid above
all any attempt to set China and the Soviet Union against each other.
A Chinese-Soviet war would be a catastrophe, not only for those two
great nations, but for all of us.

As the Soviet-Chinese conflict has taken shape, Soviet policy toward
India has gradually become more favorable. When the break between
China and the U.S.S.R. became evident in the early 1960's, India's leaders promptly moved to improve their relations with the Russians. But
the Soviet reaction was at first slow and uncertain. When the Chinese
attacked India in 1962, the Soviets first assumed a neutral position. But
the U.S. refusal to meet India's request for equipment to modernize its

military forces in 1963–64 gave the Soviets an opportunity to redress their mistakes and opened the door to a wholly new Soviet-Indian relationship.

Until the Second World War Indian leaders, deeply engrossed in their struggle for independence, viewed the Soviet Union as a nation opposed to colonialism and dedicated to peace. Few influential Indians approved of the Soviet political structure, but neither did most of them understand its brutality and contempt for individual rights.

When the Nazis invaded the U.S.S.R. in 1941, promotion of Communist revolutionary doctrine overseas was muted as the Soviet people were organized and focused on a single-minded effort to beat back the Nazi invaders. All over the world Communist parties were instructed to put aside any activity that might weaken the Allied effort to destroy the German-Japanese-Italian alliance.

As a consequence, Communist-dominated unions by and large became orderly, hard-working and committed to the war effort. Even in the colonies of the Allies the Communist leaders, their fellow travelers and political allies were instructed for the time being to abandon anti-government activities and create no difficulties for the British or French. Indian Communists and other extremists of the left largely dissociated themselves from the struggle for independence from British rule.

The reaction of the Indian people and their leaders was bitter. Their distress was compounded by Soviet attacks on Gandhi as a reactionary Hindu leader, while Nehru was described as the "Chiang Kai-shek of India." His policies, it was charged, were bound to "lead to subservience to the American imperialist camp." Indeed, it has only been in the last few years that Gandhi's biographical sketch in official Soviet papers has given even lip service to his accomplishments in behalf of an independent India.

As the war period faded from the public consciousness and particularly after Stalin's death in March, 1953, there was a cautious but marked improvement in Indo-Soviet relations. In August of that year Malenkov spoke warmly of India's contribution to ending the Korean War and expressed the view that Indo-Soviet relations would "continue to develop and grow in strength."

At the same time a certain amount of empathy for the Soviet Union began to develop among younger Indians, particularly those who had been caught up in the rhetoric of Marxism with little knowledge of the actual workings of Soviet society.

But Nehru himself had few illusions about Stalin. A few days after Stalin's death, the Prime Minister and his daughter, Indira, had a quiet family dinner with Steb and me at 17 Ratendon Road. Stalin was the center of much of the conversation. When I casually remarked that, despite his sins, Stalin had a rather kindly face, Nehru snorted. "You have never seen him," he said, "and I have. Stalin has the coldest, cruelest face I have seen on any man."

Although a five-year Indo-Soviet trade agreement had been agreed to in 1953, the first Soviet loan for Indian economic development was signed in the late winter of 1955. When Steb and I visited India in January, 1955, several friends in the Indian Government, who were as opposed to Communist ideology as we were, told us that the U.S. 1954 decision to provide military equipment to Pakistan had convinced them that to maintain a balance India must accept some assistance from the U.S.S.R. I was also told that limited agreements had been reached under which Russia would provide a dozen or so Soviet technical advisers. An agreement with the Soviets to finance and build a steel mill, they said, was under discussion.

The latter situation was moving faster than India had anticipated, and several Indian officials expressed their concern. "Why," they asked, "don't you Americans agree to build the mill? There is still time." When I returned to the United States, I asked to see President Eisenhower to discuss the possibility. My letter was routinely referred to the "working levels" of the State Department, where a minor official brushed aside my report in disbelief. "I cannot conceive," he said, "of the Soviet Union giving any meaningful economic assistance to India, and most certainly they will not build a steel mill. Even if I should be wrong on that one point," he added, "any mill that they set up in India would be obsolete and no longer of use to the Russians."

One year later, on February 21, 1955, the Soviet Union agreed to spend $140 million to build one of the most modern steel mills in Asia. The Bhilai steel complex was completed in 1960 and is now turning out nearly two million tons of steel annually. Another, larger Soviet steel mill will be completed by 1973.

India and other Asian nations face a serious dilemma, which we must seek to understand. While we all share the hope that China ultimately will become a good neighbor with which the independent Asian nations can live with a reasonable degree of security and normal exchange of goods, there is nothing in the Chinese situation today which makes this appear likely in the near future.

Following the defeat of the Chiang Kai-shek forces in China in the late 1940's, most Asians assumed that a close Chinese-Soviet relationship would develop and endure;[1] consequently, a close relationship with the

1. Nehru, as we have seen, was an exception.

United States seemed essential to their security and continued independence, even though "neutral" nations such as India continued to stress their nonalignment. When the Chinese-Soviet axis broke up and Chinese troops moved across India's northern borders, India instinctively turned to the United States for assistance. However, our decision not to assist India in modernizing its armed forces, coupled with the quick favorable response from the Soviets to their request, and the strong public reaction in the United States to our military involvement in Southeast Asia convinced the Indians that they could no longer count on us in case of a Chinese attack, but that they probably *could* count on the Soviets.

In our concentration on Vietnam we have largely lost sight of steadily developing Soviet interest and influence in Asia. The evidence of this interest which has received most attention in the American press is the increased Soviet naval force in the Mediterranean, their intense desire to reopen the Suez Canal and the presence of various Soviet naval units in the Indian Ocean. But the new Soviet involvement in Asia goes far beyond these tactical military maneuvers.

In Moscow in June, 1969, the Secretary General of the Soviet Communist Party, Leonid Brezhnev, noted in a speech at the World Communist Party Conference, "We are of the opinion that the course of events is putting on the agenda the task of creating a system of collective security in Asia." This Dullesian assertion has not publicly been amplified, and every government in Asia has been interpreting it in different ways. India's reaction to Brezhnev's statement was cautious. Mrs. Gandhi discreetly let it be known that India would prefer a non-alliance security setup composed of Asian states guaranteed by both Russia and America.

A key to Brezhnev's meaning appeared in advance of his speech in an article in *Izvestia* in May, 1969, in which it was asserted that the same countries which have won their freedom from colonialism "will strengthen the peace by their own joint opposition to expansion and imperialism." The forces of "expansion" in this case were clearly the Chinese, who were charged with harboring designs against a number of Asian countries. Peking promptly responded by accusing Brezhnev of "fishing in the dung heap of imperialism."

Moscow is obviously reaching for a way to contain China by associating the Asian nations in some loose formation under Soviet domination and leadership, and we should not underestimate the strength of the Soviet appeal even to those nations, such as Thailand and the Philippines, which have clung to us in the past. Like all Asian nations they fear China in varying degrees, and the United States appears increasingly confused, uncertain and even irrelevant. Unless an alternative Asian security system evolves, it seems likely that in the coming years they will turn increasingly to the Soviets, who are ready and willing. Recently, a Soviet official, when asked "What is the basis of Soviet foreign policy in Asia?" replied, "We simply occupy the empty seats."

Even Japan, our second-largest trading partner, is not exempt from Soviet blandishments. From the standpoint of geography and industrial capacity the Japanese are in a position to be extremely helpful to the Soviets in building up eastern Siberia. The Soviets are offering the Japanese major concessions of natural gas, timber and power, in return for Japanese industrial equipment.

There are formidable obstacles to a close association; for instance, the Japanese resent the refusal of the Soviets to return the islands taken from them after the war. Since the Kuriles and the small islands off the shore of Hokkaido screen the Soviet Pacific naval bases on the Siberian coast and assure the U.S.S.R. control of the strategic Sea of Okhotsk, these issues will not easily be settled. Nevertheless, a gradually growing Soviet-Japanese rapprochement has a certain political-economic logic, and we should not be surprised if it continues to develop in the future.

The Soviets have even provided military equipment and assistance to Pakistan in an effort to lure it away from China, and have already succeeded in persuading Pakistan to push the United States out of the Peshawar air base, which the Pentagon wrongly assumed it had secured in perpetuity by grants to Pakistan of nearly $1 billion in military equipment.

The Soviets look on India much as did John F. Kennedy: as a critically important factor in shaping the future of Asia and as a counterweight to an unpredictable China. A united, well-armed India on China's southern flank, they believe, will discourage Chinese pressure on the central and eastern areas of the U.S.S.R. And so, on the heels of our own adverse reply to the Indian Government for military assistance, they seized the opportunity to equip the Indian Army and Air Force with Soviet weapons, to expand trade programs and economic assistance, and massively to increase their programs of cultural exchange.

Soviet tactics and strategy in India, however, are often inept and at cross-purposes. The Soviet wing of the badly divided Communist Party usually assumes a generally moderate position in support of Mrs. Gandhi's coalition, while the left wing is oriented toward Peking. But the Soviet-controlled moderates take every advantage of India's commitment to free speech to weaken Indian democracy, and shamelessly admit their allegiance to the U.S.S.R. At election time Communist flags identical to those of the U.S.S.R. are prominently displayed throughout India. When high Soviet officials come to India, they often have long, closed-door sessions with Indian Communist leaders. This arouses deep resentment and suspicion among many Indians.

The Soviet Union has also brought heavy pressure to bear on India on economic issues. Their objective is clearly to push, prod and persuade the Indians toward a more tightly controlled economy. But here again they make their share of mistakes. On many occasions the Soviets—like the United States—have given India to understand that it was about to receive assistance or other economic concessions from Moscow which never materialized. Inevitably, this has produced a certain disenchantment among Indian leaders. Most Indians, regardless of politics, are eager for the day when neither Soviet nor American assistance will be needed. Only then, they feel, can India achieve genuine independence.

As a totalitarian state, the Soviets have certain advantages in dealing with India. But they are handicapped by a number of other factors. First, there is the language gap. While practically all educated Indians speak English, relatively few learn Russian. Second, among many Soviet officials and specialists there is a certain disdain for India and Indians, which they do not even bother to hide. Moreover, most Indian political leaders and top civil servants are aware that the Soviets play a rough political game and that as long as Moscow controls the flow of spare parts and ammunition for most of the basic equipment of the Indian military forces, India will remain in a precarious position.

In spite of the lack of natural rapport between most Indians and most Russians, the Soviets understand better than have American policy-makers the deep sense of insecurity which the Indians feel as a consequence of their long domination by foreign invaders, most recently the British. In a calculated effort to build up India's sense of national importance, a steady flow of Soviet high officials, cultural groups, dance teams and circuses arrive at Indian airports throughout the year. The Soviets are now spending more than five times as much as the United States spends on similar cultural exchanges.

While Soviet inroads into Asia may cause some legitimate concern, we should not lose our heads over it, particularly since at this stage our mistakes have left us with little or no alternative. Most Asians have no more desire to be "saved" by the Soviets than by the Americans. Just as an American-dominated Asian alliance to contain China has been rejected by the bulk of the Asian people, so it seems likely that the Soviet version suggested by Brezhnev will in the long run similarly fail. In Asia, as in other parts of the world, nationalism is a far stronger force than ideology.

In regard to China, I believe every effort should be made to ease our present tense relationships and to bring this potentially great nation into the world community of nations. But it is foolish to expect much progress in the immediate future. As always, events will undoubtedly play a major part, and as much as possible, China will set its own timetable. In the meantime, it would be unwise for us to give way to anger, irritation or premature hopes.

As for India, its interest in Asia and particularly Southeast Asia goes back many centuries. "Greater India" was the title of a chapter in an Indian history book which Cynthia, Sally and Sam studied in New Delhi during our first assignment there in 1951–53. Its map shows Indian settlements in Ceylon, Burma, Malaya, Java, Sumatra, Borneo, Bali and Cambodia.

Nehru often commented to me on the uneasy Indian-Chinese confrontation that existed in Southeast Asia between 400 and 1200. Indian influence was moving gradually east and north and Chinese influence west and south. The line between the two cultures is still evident in Indonesia, Cambodia, Vietnam and Thailand.

For the next several centuries under the impact of Muslim invasions and later British rule, India's focus was toward the West. Now in response to its concern about Chinese expansion the pendulum of Indian foreign policy may be expected to swing, once again, to the East.

CHAPTER 43

PROSPECTS FOR INDIA

INDIA'S ABILITY to contribute to a more stable and prosperous Asia depends in large measure on the extent to which it can put its own economic and political house in order. What are the prospects?

When India became free in 1947, its government faced economic chaos. The railroads, which had been operating under heavy strain with few repairs during the war, were sadly run-down. Although a considerable amount of unsophisticated irrigation had been developed, many of the canals and tanks were in poor repair and the available irrigation water was totally inadequate.

Most industries were equipped with outdated and worn-out machinery which could operate at a profit only as long as wages were low. Although some progress had been made in building schools and health centers, there had been no significant national programs, and improvement depended largely on the interest and initiative, or lack of it, of the local officials.

Yet there were several positive factors. Although badly run-down during the war period, India's railroads were extensive. A good road system had been built. Perhaps most important, solid foundations had been laid for an effective nationwide Civil Service.

Before independence, to be sure, the Indian Civil Service had been largely concentrated on tax collections, local security and communications. Now it found itself with an overwhelming set of new problems such as mass education, public health, industrial development and agriculture. But there was determination to broaden the administrative apparatus to meet the new challenge.

The concept of national planning in India was adopted by the Congress Party in the mid-thirties, and the first chairman of the National Planning Committee, established in 1938, was Jawaharlal Nehru. Many Indian political leaders and economists had studied the Soviet system of five-year plans under which priorities are established and production goals set. These leaders were also intrigued with the teachings of Harold Laski of the London School of Economics, who believed that only through democratic socialism could mass production be assured side by side with an increasing measure of economic justice.

They recognized that planning in the Soviet Union was conducted through totalitarian directives and that economic planning in a democratic India would call for radically different techniques. National planning in India, it was agreed, should start with democratic discussions in the villages, with the programs gradually taking shape as they moved up through the districts to the states and finally to the center. To some extent India has managed to do this.

One of my first visits outside New Delhi following our arrival in India in October, 1951, was to the Etawah district in the Punjab, where I had been told an experimental new rural development program was getting under way in some eighty villages with a total of perhaps forty thousand people.

Steb and I spent three days there, and we were greatly impressed. What struck me in particular was the fact that this program, like that of James Y. C. Yen in China before the Communist takeover in the late 1940's, was based on an integrated approach; it dealt simultaneously with agriculture, education and public health, with a heavy emphasis on local initiative and the involvement of the villagers. In Etawah each "village development worker" after several months of generalized training was assigned to five or six villages. When he ran into difficulties on some aspect of the program in a particular village, he could call in the appropriate specialist in school building, public health, agriculture or well-digging to help him. This program caught my imagination, and on the way back to New Delhi we began to calculate how all of rural India might someday be covered by a vast extension service program organized along these lines.

The next morning I asked for an appointment with the Prime Minister. Having long since learned the value in calling on a major political figure of presenting him with a memorandum outlining precisely what I wanted him to do, I put together a proposal for a nationwide campaign for village development. Since I had just been informed that a $54 million U.S. grant for development would soon be made available to India and that it was our responsibility in cooperation with the

Indian Government to develop the most effective way to use it, the visit was well timed.

Nehru listened with interest to my outline of the work of Dr. Yen in China and the remarkable progress of the Japanese, who had embarked on a similar effort to develop their rural areas. But he remarked with a sigh that while this concept was appealing, it was impractical in India on a large scale since the educated young people were unlikely to respond. Etawah, he thought, was a special case. I was surprised that a man with Nehru's commitment both to democratic economic progress and to young people should react so negatively, and I said so. As our discussion continued, Nehru's doubts seemed to ease, and when I left two hours later, he was talking in enthusiastic terms about the possibilities.

In March, 1952, at his request I presented to Nehru a comprehensive memorandum stating the case for a mass program which, adequately funded and assigned a high priority, could, I believed, be extended to cover all of rural India, however lightly, in ten years. Although more dramatic results could be achieved by concentrating the available funds in a few limited regions, I stressed the political need to give every Indian villager some evidence that the Indian Government was interested in his welfare. I also urged Nehru to take a leaf from President Roosevelt's book and establish a separate administrative department to handle this new program.

Nehru agreed with both of these recommendations, so in early April, 1952, with generous Ford Foundation assistance, the first training course was set up for some fifty carefully chosen Indian civil servants, each of whom had been nominated to act as a community development director responsible for about a hundred villages. The program was to be independently administered under a Director of Community Development answering directly to the Prime Minister and independent of the established ministries.

On Gandhi's birthday, October 2, 1952, the ground was broken for the first development block in a village ten miles from New Delhi. Since then the rural programs had moved forward, some excellent, some promising and some grossly inadequate, as I am sure Nehru anticipated. And just as Roosevelt's decision to set up special "expendable" new organizations met resistance from the established agencies which were being bypassed, so the Indian Ministries of Agriculture, Health, Education and Irrigation set out to undercut the concept of an independent Community Development organization.

It was also inevitable that the village-oriented approach which I advocated should face vigorous competition for scarce resources from advocates of more rapid industrialization. In the mid-1950's the latter were encouraged by the beginnings of economic aid largely for industrial purposes from both Western and Soviet bloc nations.

As the need for more rapid growth in the developing nations became evident, the West European nations and Japanese, having largely recovered from the war, began to be in a position to help. To speed this help, Under Secretary of State Douglas Dillon proposed the pooling of our economic assistance to India through a "consortium" of Western nations, plus Japan, headed by the World Bank, and the flow of foreign aid sharply increased.[1]

By 1963 this increase in foreign economic assistance, coupled with a determined and, by and large, effective effort by the Indian Government, had begun to produce encouraging results. Since we left India in 1953 the number of bicycles in the cities and even in the villages had multiplied tenfold, and there was a growing number of small cars called "Ambassadors," scooters and motorcycles. Wristwatches, transistor radios, flashlights, one-burner kerosene stoves and other evidences of a gradually rising standard of living were also evident.

The production of electrical power had been increased seven times. At least half of this increase was made possible by U.S. economic assistance which enabled the Indian Government to purchase the necessary equipment—almost all from American companies. The Indian railroad system had been rebuilt, modernized and expanded. India was even building its own railroad cars and locomotives—diesel, steam and electric.

Several new, heavy-industrial plants largely financed by loans from the U.S.S.R. were turning out complex, sophisticated machinery, including huge generators. The machine tool industry had also grown rapidly. The president of Hindustan Machine Tool Company once told me, with understandable pride, that they would soon be exporting some units to Europe and the United States.

There were three times as many children attending school at all levels, with a million and a half students in the universities. The number of graduate schools for medical students had grown from sixteen following independence to over a hundred. Several modern scientific institutes had been set up. One at Kanpur, sponsored by a consortium of American universities including M.I.T., Princeton, Caltech and others, was most impressive. Eight new American-financed agricultural universities were operating, each modeled after our land-grant colleges; indeed, each with direct ties to an American land-grant university.

1. In 1959 a resolution endorsing this concept was introduced in the Senate by Jack Kennedy and by me in the House.

However, in regard to population control, progress had been painfully slow. This delay reflected several factors. First, the Ministry of Health for a period of ten or fifteen years had been headed by ministers who were not interested in the subject and, indeed, had serious reservations about it. Second, contraceptives which were safe, sure, simple and cheap had not yet been developed. Third, the Indian Government had not known how to get at the problem, nor, indeed, had anybody else. In India, as elsewhere, there was a kind of blind hope that some magical scientific development would suddenly come out of the blue and solve the problem. The development of the "pill" aroused particular interest.

Those with a pessimistic turn of mind could still find ample evidence to bolster their view that India, because of the vast magnitude of its administration problems, could never hold its population in check. But others of us who had watched India's development over the years were cautiously hopeful. The administration of the antimalaria program was an example. When we arrived in India in 1951, it was estimated that there were 100 million cases of malaria in India each year. Since malaria usually struck around harvest time, the effect on Indian food production was considerable. In 1953, with the support and encouragement of the Rockefeller Foundation, the World Health Organization and the United States, the Indian Government started a program to eliminate the mosquitoes that spread malaria. This program covered all the villages in India in which malaria was a problem—250,000 in all. Each received two or three sprayings of DDT each year. By 1963 malaria had dropped from 100 million cases a year to something less than 100 thousand.

As we began travels around India in August and September of 1963, our impressions about the general economic situation were, on balance, rather positive. Although slums and poverty were still evident everywhere, the people generally were better fed, better clothed and looked healthier. The average daily caloric intake was about one-fourth higher than when we had left in 1953. In the winter months most Indians now wore shoes. Even in the villages many of the children had warm sweaters.

Yet in September, 1963, when I visited several *rural* areas with my economic adviser, Ed Lindblom, on leave from his position as professor of economics at Yale, we returned to Delhi in a much less confident mood. As I told Nehru in a long conversation the following day, what worried us most was the lack of interest among most cultivators in the new hybrid rice seeds developed in the Philippines or the wheat seeds developed through Rockefeller Foundation research in Mexico.

There was also alarmingly little interest in the use of fertilizer, improved use of water, increased availability of rural credit or improved marketing programs. But the primary obstacle to greater food grain production, we felt, was the low prices paid to the farmers. The Indian Government wanted low food prices in the cities to dampen down urban unrest, and an important factor in carrying out this policy was the shipment of American wheat, which was largely distributed in the cities.[2] By holding down food prices in the cities, however, this program had inadvertently held down the cultivators' income and left them no incentive to adopt modern techniques. Thus most of them were producing only enough food to feed their own families.

In my talk with Nehru I also expressed my concern over the slow pace of land reform. The Indian Government had initiated a sweeping redistribution of land in the early 1950's, breaking up the vast "zamindari" estates which were established under British rule, some of which totaled as much as 10,000 acres. But they did not go nearly as far as in Japan or Taiwan. Although a 30-acre ceiling had been established in most Indian states, there were still many holdings of 50 to 150 acres, and the existing legislation in regard to tenancy rights and the division of the crops between landowners and tenant cultivators was often not enforced. Over one-fifth of all Indian rural people still owned no land at all, and others only a tiny plot. This, we felt, could eventually develop into the major source of political unrest.

The most immediate needs, as we saw them, were to increase the use of fertilizer, to develop more modern techniques of irrigation, to adapt the extraordinary new hybrid seeds to India's climate and soil conditions, and to press for expanded rural credit at low interest rates. If the Indian Government could be persuaded to assure the cultivators year after year a price high enough to encourage them to take the risks involved in new methods and expanded production, we felt that there was reason to hope for a new dynamism in the largely agricultural villages.

In the spring of 1964 this was spelled out in a memorandum, "Long-Range Assistance Strategy for India," in which we made the following proposals:

1. Shipments of U.S. wheat should be more carefully related to India's own national food prices and marketing program. A tactful but determined effort should be made to persuade the Indian Government to adopt a version of our agricultural price support program to assure the cultivators a reasonable profit.

2. The number of U.S. technical assistance advisers at the eight Indian agricultural universities which we had helped build in the 1950's

2. With their Marxist orientation gained from Harold Laski and others, Indian planners in the 1950's were more concerned about political unrest among the urban proletariat than among the rural peasantry, which Mao Tse-tung later demonstrated was a far greater potential revolutionary force.

should be increased and greater care should be taken in their selection. This was essential to the adaptation of the hybrid seeds to India's soil and climatic conditions and their acceptance by the cultivators.

3. Our joint efforts should be accelerated in the so-called "Intensive Agriculture Districts" which had been set up, with the help of the Ford Foundation, as large demonstration areas where cultivators could see the results of a program combining hybrid seeds, fertilizer, water, etc.

4. New Peace Corps programs should be established to communicate the new agricultural techniques as effectively and widely as possible.

5. A substantial increase in fertilizer resources should be assured through hard-currency loans with which to finance fertilizer imports during the next few years, and through joint ventures with major U.S. and other foreign companies to increase Indian fertilizer production capacity over the longer term.

Next in importance to agriculture in our proposed new economic assistance program was aid to Indian industry, both the public and private sectors, to reduce India's dependence on imports and to expand its own exports wherever possible, thereby reducing its dependence on foreign economic assistance.

Traditionally, India's foreign exchange had largely been earned by sales of jute and tea. In recent years the sales of these two commodities had been gradually heading downward as other developing nations began to compete as suppliers. The only answer was greatly to increase the export of other products, particularly manufactured goods. This we felt would require increased incentives to private enterprise, much of which was enmeshed in a tangle of red tape and harassed by outdated political slogans.

As in other developing countries, industry in India often suffered from a doctrinaire, semi-Marxist approach. Most Indian political leaders and economists, because of long and bitter experience under British colonialism, looked on capitalism with somewhat the same jaundiced eye that Teddy Roosevelt viewed the great monopolies in America sixty years ago.[3] As a result of this built-in fear of "capitalistic exploitation," vast bureaucratic organizations were developed for the purpose of licensing, price control, control of imports and exports, and use of raw materials and scarce items.

The effect had been to stifle or discourage private investment in new fields of industrial development, such as fertilizer production. For example, in the early weeks after our return in July, 1963, I had talked to a steady stream of American businessmen, most of whom were

3. Many of the British-Indian corporations in India in the early years of this century were in the worst tradition of this exploitative capitalism, which Karl Marx had attacked so effectively.

interested in investing in India but who felt frustrated by the bureaucratic barriers.

Our recommendations also stressed the need to improve the efficiency
of public sector plants. One result of India's deeply rooted suspicion of
large private sector plants—particularly those supported by foreign
capital—was that heavy industrial production became increasingly delegated to the public sector.

I had no quarrel with public sector plants so long as they were
efficient. But this, I believed, could be accomplished only if the
government-owned plants were set up on an independent basis with
their own boards of directors and managers, as had been done in
Germany, France, Italy and in our own TVA. When the bureaucracies
in the various ministries tried to run them directly, political pressure
to promote unqualified people and the fear of making mistakes almost
invariably led to inefficiency, delays and financial loss to the government.

The third priority established in our Long-Range Assistance Strategy
was a greatly expanded population control program. An analysis of
India's potential economic growth made it clear that while India probably
had the capacity to feed and support its rapidly growing population in
a reasonably adequate fashion for some time to come, it did not have
the resources to provide the increased consumer goods and the improved
services—schools, transportation, housing—which should result from
significant economic growth. Thus a population control program sufficiently effective to stabilize the population within a realistic time span
was essential if the individual Indian citizen was to realize a significant
improvement in his own living standards as a result of national economic
growth.

These three priorities—increasing agricultural production, developing and improving domestic industrial capacity (with particular emphasis on exports) and controlling the rate of population growth—were,
we felt, the prerequisites of an economically self-sufficient India. Much
of my time during the next six years was spent in pressing either my
own government or the Indian Government to support policies and programs which were related to these goals.

I was particularly concerned by the small number of Indian leaders
who were articulating the major requirements for a developing India. I
soon began to wonder if I could find some way of saying some of the
things that needed saying without affecting Indian sensitivities. In
October I decided that the need justified the political risk, and consequently I delivered a series of four lectures on economic development
at Delhi University.

The first lecture stressed "five essentials of nation building":

1. Adequate capital from both domestic and foreign sources.
2. Enough goods and services to persuade people to contribute the personal effort that development requires.
3. Adequate skills for management, administration, production and citizenship.
4. A willingness and ability in overcrowded nations such as India and Pakistan to curb a rapid population increase.
5. A unifying sense of national purpose, with effective communications between the people and their leaders.

In the second and third lectures I focused on the dynamics of rural development and on the problem of reconciling industrial growth with social justice. Wherever possible, in speeches such as these I tried to encourage Indians to study the dramatically successful Japanese experience. For example, in my lecture on rural development I observed:

> The American rural experience is challenging and instructive, but in my opinion the developing nations of Asia, Africa and Latin America have most to learn from a study of Japan, which was the first Asian country to transform a tradition-bound agricultural economy based on subsistence farming and hierarchical social relationships into a dynamic contributing element of a modern economic system.

The fourth lecture was devoted to a discussion of the economic problems and prospects of India and China and emphasized India's many advantages in the inevitable competition.

These lectures were published in a short book entitled *The Makings of a Just Society*[4] and sent with a personal note to more than ten thousand economists, civil servants, publishers and elected officials throughout India. They were published in full by several large newspapers, and to my relief there were no references to my "interference" in India's internal affairs.

In addition, I continued to prepare informal memoranda for the Prime Minister—usually at his specific request—setting forth my own thinking regarding priority economic questions ranging from rural development to fertilizer production.[5]

During the first year I spent at least one-third of my time working on economic development problems. After five years of outstanding

4. I chose a "just society" as the objective rather than "a more productive society" to emphasize the importance of assuring the individual citizen a better, fuller life, not simply more "things."
5. One of these memoranda is reprinted in an appendix.

service, Ty Wood had agreed to stay on as AID Director, but only until I found a successor. In the spring of 1964 I had the good fortune to meet John Lewis,[6] an able economist on leave from Indiana University who was then serving as a member of the President's Council of Economic Advisers. After several long talks I persuaded him to join us in India. Under John's leadership we developed what I believe to have been the most effective AID mission in the world, staffed with men and women who were not only professional and highly competent in their own field, but also attentive to the special attitudes, interests and sensitivities of the Indian people and their government, and the limitations under which foreigners, however well intentioned, consequently must function.

Because of its vast size and its far better than average administrative competence, India was the largest recipient of economic assistance outside of Vietnam.[7] Although the needs were urgent, the Indian leaders were particularly sensitive to pressures from Western nations.

With free speech, a free press and a democratic parliament, the Indian Government has been heavily pressed by the well-organized and well-financed Communist minority to take public positions on foreign policy questions which were bound to cause an adverse reaction in Washington and thereby increase the difficulties in persuading Congress to authorize an adequate level of assistance.

Consequently, time and time again we had to restate the basic premise of our effort in order to help keep both governments on the track. For example, I took the occasion at one point in a column in the *American Reporter* entitled "Why Does America Help India to Grow?" to state:

> For the past fifteen years American assistance to India has had a direct and clear purpose: it is designed to help India become an economically self-sufficient and politically viable nation.
>
> Such an India will make its own massive contribution to world peace by demonstrating to the people of Asia, Africa and Latin America that democracy can achieve what totalitarianism, either Communist or Fascist, can never achieve: a society that is both prosperous and free.

The government of India was committed to developing a self-reliant economy as quickly as possible, and it generally shared our view of the priority tasks to be accomplished. A favorable factor was the Indian Government's stress on austerity and individual sacrifice, which has been far closer to the hard realities of economic development than in most Asian, African and Latin-American countries.

6. Lewis left India in 1969 to become Director of the Woodrow Wilson School of Public and International Affairs at Princeton University.

7. On a per capita basis our assistance to India was approximately $1.50, which placed it close to the bottom of the list of developing nations which were receiving U.S. assistance.

The foreign exchange which India received in the form of economic assistance or from exports went largely to build the Indian economy and not—as in so much of Latin America—to provide luxury items for the relatively few privileged people at the top. Through extremely heavy import duties, the importation of foreign cars, refrigerators and other luxury items which would eat into the Indian foreign exchange reserves was reduced to a dribble.

The Indian Government was determined to raise the maximum amount of capital savings for development purposes from within India itself. Eighty percent of the industrial capital which has thus far been available to modernize and expand the Indian industrial base has come not from foreign lenders or donors but from the savings of the Indian people.

In the spring of 1965 we went a step further and submitted to Washington a much more detailed proposal, prepared under John Lewis' direction, for bolstering the Indian economy. The proposal was based on the premise that with adequate foreign economic assistance for the next five years India might be expected to achieve the major economic breakthrough necessary to make it self-sufficient and thus enable it to do without foreign economic assistance.

If the United States, the World Bank and other members of the Consortium could be persuaded to provide enough additional foreign exchange to support for a five- or ten-year period a new growth-oriented economic policy, India, we believed, under favorable conditions could achieve a self-sustained rate of growth by the late 1970's. Our proposal—which came to be called "The Big Push"—aimed at self-sufficiency in food production in five years and in foreign exchange earning power in a decade.

Without U.S. economic assistance, our studies indicated India could increase its annual output by barely enough to keep pace with its population growth. With the current economic assistance provided by the World Bank, the United States and its associates (about $2 billion annually), we could expect an annual growth rate of about 5 percent, which after taking into account the population increase would amount to a little less than 3 percent per capita. But with a 40 percent increase in these assistance levels, India's rate of growth could be increased to an impressive 7 percent annually by the late 1970's, which would be about 5 percent per capita.

A "Big Push," we suggested, would enable us gradually to reduce and eventually to terminate economic assistance to India, leaving this potentially great country self-reliant and in a position to assume greater responsibility for the political stability of Asia. The annual cost to the

United States would be no more than the cost of ten days of warfare in Vietnam.

During a visit to Washington for consultation in 1965 I stressed to the President the importance of a favorable decision on our proposed aid program by comparing the present circumstances with those concerning our so-called "loss" of China to Communism in the late 1940's. Our inability to affect the final result then, I said, was not due to any failure of President Truman or Secretary Marshall, but rather to our lack of awareness in the late 1930's and early 1940's of the forces which were relentlessly pushing China toward disaster. Because our attention at that time was focused on domestic economic problems and the growing crises in Europe, we did not bring our influence to bear on the situation in China, although an effective and sensitive U.S. policy might have led to a very different outcome. Let us not, I urged, repeat this mistake in India.

When I returned to New Delhi in late July, I was convinced that we were winning not only the support of our government but also the full backing of the World Bank. However, I overestimated my powers of persuasion; the authorization for our proposed increase in economic assistance on which we were counting did not materialize.

By this time a delay in granting economic assistance to India, or any other country whose leaders had criticized our increasing involvement in Vietnam, was interpreted (often correctly) as an attempt by the Administration to force the recipient nation to change its position. A series of newspaper leaks about the status of the new India aid program during the month of August strongly hinted that this was the explanation. These rumors were picked up by the Indian press and provoked a number of sharply critical editorials and political cartoons in many normally pro-American Indian newspapers.

Alarmed at the political implications, I wrote President Johnson's chief assistant, Bill Moyers, on August 26, to enlist his support in persuading the President that these pressure tactics would boomerang:

> We are deluged with editorials and cartoons lamenting more in sorrow than in anger that the United States has lost its sense of values. To give you some flavor of the current Indian mood I am attaching some recent press comment, all taken from pro–United States newspapers in the last two days.
> As I consider the present situation I am sure of at least three things:
> 1. The use of our economic assistance or Peace Corps programs to pressure the Indians to adopt a foreign policy which they believe to be contrary to their national interests will fail.
> 2. These tactics will make us sitting ducks in India for the Soviet

propaganda machine, the Indian Communists and the Krishna Menons.

3. The tactics will seriously injure the United States and the good name of Lyndon B. Johnson not only in Asia but elsewhere.

However, the President's attempt to force a change in India's public attitude toward our involvement in Vietnam and my efforts to persuade him that such pressures would backfire soon became academic. On August 5 Pakistan had launched its abortive effort by some five thousand guerrillas to take over Kashmir. By early September a full-scale war had developed between India and Pakistan, and in the eyes of Washington officialdom a whole new situation now came into being. Instead of giving a green light to the "Big Push," our government promptly stopped all economic assistance not only to Pakistan but to India as well.

But the seeds had been sown and many key members of the Indian Government had begun to sense the possibilities.

In December, 1965, India's Agricultural Minister, Subramanian, one of India's ablest administrators, announced a comprehensive program designed rapidly to increase food grain production which had been unanimously approved by the Cabinet. It pledged the Indian Government to a series of actions which we, together with many brilliant Indian economists and experts from the World Bank, Rockefeller and Ford Foundations, had been strongly advocating. These included a massive increase in the hybrid seed program, more readily available credit for the cultivators, expansion and improved use of irrigation water, and a fertilizer industry with twenty or thirty times the existing capacity.

The failure of the monsoon rains in 1965 and 1966 brought India to the brink of disaster. But it also showed farmers and government officials alike the urgent necessity for modernizing agricultural methods along the lines of the Subramanian proposals.

It was agreed that the single most important requisite was to increase the market price paid to the cultivators, thereby providing a greater incentive for them to work longer hours, to take certain risks and to try new techniques.

Greatly increased use of fertilizer was a second requirement. Fertilizer on the international market is an expensive commodity, and, as we have seen, Indian fertilizer production in 1963 was grossly inadequate. By 1965 plans were introduced to build a large number of fertilizer plants in India. In the meantime we would do our best to provide enough foreign exchange to import the necessary fertilizer until the Indian production reached an adequate level. It was agreed that the minimum level of fertilizer required by 1975 would be four or five million tons (in terms of nitrogen). The new fertilizer plants would require considerable foreign capital and technology, and this provided its own set of problems.

Experiments at the eight new agricultural universities which we had helped build in the late 1950's had already demonstrated that the new hybrid wheat and maize seeds developed by the Ford and Rockefeller Foundations in the Philippines could assure impressive increases in production. However, ample irrigation water and fertilizer were essential elements in the new procedures, and there were serious risks from rust and other plant diseases, which required constant research by the newly trained Indian experts, to assure the frequent adaptations required to meet changing conditions.

There was also the problem of rural credit. In India most cultivators had traditionally depended upon the moneylenders, who often charged interest as high as 50 percent annually, to carry them from one season to another. Rural banks which could provide money at lower interest rates were essential.

Another element of major importance was irrigation. The great river valley developments, to be sure, had provided many millions of acres of irrigated land. But these enterprises were necessarily controlled by the government, which decided when and in what quantity water would be moved through the canals into different areas. The Indian cultivators naturally preferred to have direct control over their own water supply. This led to the digging of tens of thousands of tube wells, financed by government loans directly to the cultivators, each equipped with an electric or diesel pump. A single well could provide irrigation for between five and fifty acres depending on the location and size of the pipe, and assure at least two crops annually. This vast well-building program created additional pressure for rural electrification, for well-digging machinery and local rural industries.

In one important aspect of development planning I am somewhat of an economic heretic. In a democratic country such as India I believe it is important to economic growth to emphasize the production of more consumer goods—better housing, bicycles, wristwatches, etc.—as well as capital goods. This runs counter to much of the dogma of economic planning, which holds that only capital goods produce growth.

The savings which produce capital goods come out of increased productivity as well as from self-denial. In a totalitarian country fear of the "authorities" is a major factor in enforcing self-denial and producing savings. But in a democratic country the techniques of terror are ruled out. Since exhortation to forgo improvements in living standards in order to create more capital savings to build faraway industrial plants gets scanty response from a depressed people, the solution must be to make economic progress visible to the people. Unless there is a prospect that their wants can be met, there is no reason to expect weary, insecure, ill-nourished people to work harder, to adopt new methods and to take the risks of change. This, I believe, is one of the key elements in a development program.

With the support and help of John Lewis and other members of our U.S. mission, I continued to preach this doctrine for economic growth all over India. This educational effort helped encourage India's gradual shift away from long-term, slow-pay-off, capital-intensive projects toward more modest industrial enterprises, often located in the rural areas, which produced immediate and visible results.

One of the most important elements in our economic assistance was the use of the rupees which under Public Law 480 (the Food for Peace program) the United States received from the sale of wheat to India over a period years.[8]

Until 1968 this wheat was paid for in Indian local currency, which could be spent only in India.[9] According to our agreement with the Indian Government, 20 percent of these rupees was made available to pay the cost of operating the U.S. mission in India—salaries, travel, furniture, housing, the building of our Chancery and the like. Another 11 percent was set aside for loans to U.S. business firms in India under the so-called Cooley Amendment. The remaining 69 percent was lent at 5 percent interest to the Indian Goverment for development projects.

We were eager to spend more of our rupee reserves to expand the circulation of USIS-printed magazines in India, to increase our program of textbooks for Indian schools and for other programs. Since these rupees could be spent only in India, the Bureau of the Budget had no objection as long as they did not appear as dollar expenditures in our national budget. However, the Appropriations Committees of the Senate and the House, particularly that of the House under Congressman John Rooney of New York, strongly opposed this. If we wanted rupee appropriations, Rooney insisted, we must present our requests in terms of dollars.[10]

8. I have already referred in Chapter 40 to the foundation I unsuccessfully attempted to establish with our rupee holdings.

9. As India's food problem eased, an increasing percentage of our wheat shipments have been paid for by long-term dollar loans at low interest rates. Nevertheless, the rupees from past transactions have continued to accumulate.

10. The Bureau of the Budget opposed the Rooney view on the ground that the rupees were in no sense equivalent to dollars. If these rupees were included in our budget as "dollars," they would unnecessarily press against our dollar debt ceiling and create a highly inflated and distorted impression of our actual budget.

Congress had its way. When we asked it to approve increased sums of rupees to expand our cultural or informational programs or for other purposes, we were required to request them in terms of dollars. Since in the eyes of Congress there was no longer a distinction between the two kinds of programs, rupee programs were slashed along with dollar programs, regardless of the fact that the cost of the rupee programs to the U.S. taxpayer was nil.

Whatever dollars were appropriated for these particular programs by Congress went to the Treasury, where they were exchanged for rupees for our use in India. The dollars were then balanced off against the accounts of the Commodity Credit Corporation to "pay" for the wheat which the farmers originally sold our government.

Although these transactions gave the impression that the Commodity Credit Corporation was being repaid for its original loans, it was a meaningless bit of bookkeeping. The American taxpayer did not benefit, and our programs in India were needlessly restricted. In spite of my repeated efforts to free more of these U.S.-owned rupees to strengthen our operation in India (personal letters to every member of Congress and to the press, and direct pleas to Presidents Kennedy and Johnson), it was a complicated subject, and since the position of the Appropriations Committees was strongly held, no one wanted to take on the battle.

The situation was eased somewhat by the passage of the Mondale Amendment in 1966. This enabled us to provide India with the rupees needed to finance several ambitious new programs. These included a loan of slightly more than a billion rupees ($140 million equivalent) as "seed" money to expand rural electricity for irrigation, village lighting and rural industry. Two billion rupees ($267 million equivalent) went to help finance low-cost housing and 350 million rupees ($50 million equivalent) went to expand the sizable population control program. A great deal more could be done at no cost to the United States.

Although the failure of the monsoon rains in both 1965 and 1966 was a devastating setback even in those areas which received normal rains, we could begin to see rural India coming alive. Within three years the number of acres sown with hybrid seeds had moved from two million to nearly 35 million acres. Domestic fertilizer production rose from a 1963 level of less than 100,000 tons (nitrogen) to one million tons. This was supplemented by over a million additional tons of imports. By 1968 food grain production rose from a 1966 figure of 76 million tons to 105 million tons even though the rains in 1968 were barely normal.

The Green Revolution demonstrated that a small-sized holding of five to ten acres, properly cultivated, can provide an impressive income for an Indian family. In addition, as the cultivators' purchasing power grew, the need for small industrial plants to produce consumer goods began to develop in the rural towns. By 1968 these were already beginning to provide part-time jobs for many cultivators between harvest time and planting time.

Boosting food production helped ease the critical problem of increasing population. It was in no sense an answer; it simply postponed the day of reckoning. But again there was reason for cautious optimism. Instead of diminishing on the assumption that the need was less urgent, Indian interest in population control increased steadily. This was partly because the Indian people and government had increasing confidence in their abilities to handle difficult nationwide programs.[11]

However, India cannot afford any illusions about the magnitude of the challenge of population growth. It is a problem far more difficult to cope with than increasing food production. If the Indian Government can persuade even one out of four cultivators to plant new seeds, use new fertilizers and new techniques in irrigation control, a breakthrough in agriculture is assured.

But not so in population control. The arithmetic of the population explosion is overwhelming. In 1963, for example, roughly 21 million babies were born in India. With a death rate of some 9 million people per year, no less than 12 million births would have had to be prevented in 1963 to assure a stable population. Each year the figure increases. This means that something like 80 percent of all married couples of child-bearing age must be persuaded to use contraceptives.

The danger lies not in the possibility that India will ultimately starve to death, but in the probability that if the increase in population is not halted within the next fifteen or twenty years, the improvement of living standards will be painfully slow, with explosive political implications. There will not be enough schools or teachers, clinics or doctors, and consumer goods will be available only to the most affluent. Psychological problems caused by too many people living in too small a space will increase. Already in Calcutta and Kerala one feels suffocated by the masses of people.

In the spring of 1965 the government set out to lower the birth rate, which was then 41 per thousand, to 25 per thousand by 1975.[12] Although I am doubtful that this ambitious target can be met, there are several

---

11. The massive malaria-control program to which I referred earlier and the Green Revolution are examples.

12. This would mean a drop from an increase of 2.4 percent annually to an increase of 1.5 percent.

encouraging factors: For one thing, there is almost no religious block to l irth control like that which severely handicaps the efforts of many countries of Latin America. I know of no political leader, left, center or right, who has openly opposed birth control. The program is backed by an extensive public education effort. Thirty percent of the Population Center's budget goes to public education, and the budget itself is limited only by what can effectively be used. By 1966 everywhere we went we saw billboards depicting a mother and father and three children with the slogan, "One, two, three—stop." There was also advertising in the newspapers. Thousands of public clinics have been established in the cities. In the villages are many more thousands of "family health centers," each staffed by a doctor, two or three midwives and a few assistants.

When the program began in 1965, the primary emphasis was placed on the "loop," and several million were inserted in the first two or three years. When it began to become evident that the "loop" had serious limitations,[13] the Indian Government switched to a wide range of techniques, some of which would appeal in some areas and some in others. One of the most important is the vasectomy, a male operation that takes no more than five to ten minutes. It has been performed on several million men who had their wives' consent and who already had three children.

In several states cash incentives have been established. The patient receives, for example, one hundred rupees, with ten extra rupees to the doctor, and ten to the man who refers the patient to the clinic. All birth control devices are free of charge.

There are also plans for raising the minimum legal age for marriage, and abortions have already been liberalized. These were the major factors in the success of the population control program in Japan, which brought the birth rate increase down from 3 percent to less than 1 percent in fifteen years.

In India, as in America, there are wide differences in administrative effectiveness and commitment among the states. In many Indian states the record on population control is encouraging; in others it is much less so. This is one reason why Americans who visit India come back with such widely varying reactions. But one thing is sure: if India can balance out its population by 1985 at around 750 million (the present population of China), it will have achieved a modern miracle.

Aside from population control, future prosperity depends largely on three factors: the degree to which a substantial increase in exports can

13. Many women complained of pain and occasional bleeding.

be achieved; the availability of investment capital and foreign economic assistance; and the matter of land ownership.

By 1968 we were encouraged that Indian exports had begun to increase rapidly, in spite of the fact that the old export stand-bys—tea and jute—were running into more competition from the production of other developing areas. Most of the increases are in industrial products, including heavy industrial equipment and earth-moving machinery.

Moreover, India's imports of wheat and other agricultural commodities, which cost around $250 million in foreign exchange each year, are being reduced; and there is reason to hope that by 1975 these imports may no longer be necessary.[14] Fertilizer imports, which amount to another $250 million annually, are being reduced as expansion of the Indian fertilizer industry takes place.

Another $100 million is being spent annually to import petroleum, and about $120 million for copper, zinc, lead, tin and other metals. Here, too, there are encouraging factors. A major effort is being made to locate indigenous sources of these metals, and India's own production of them may gradually begin to come closer to fulfilling its needs. Large petroleum deposits have also been coming to light, although the Indian Government has been slow to exploit them.

There are three ways in which the United States, the World Bank and Consortium nations can in the years ahead help India achieve a self-sustaining economy: (1) by agreeing to a debt moratorium for a period of five to ten years; this would eliminate or reduce the $500 million India now has to pay the West each year in hard currency for principal and interest on past loans; (2) by reducing our own tariffs on goods imported from India and other developing nations; and (3) by continuing and, if possible, enlarging the flow of nonproject loans through our economic assistance program.

If one or more of these sources of foreign exchange is not made available during the next five or ten years, I doubt whether the Indian growth rate can rise much beyond 3 percent annually. On a per capita basis this would mean close to economic stagnation. If the World Bank Consortium assistance program were at the same levels as in 1964 and 1965 before the war with Pakistan, the prospect might be for a 5 percent growth rate. If the program were restored to the level of the late 1950's, India's increase in gross national income each year might reach 6 to 7 percent. Compounded from year to year, this could produce a startling

14. On February 10, 1967, India announced: "1971 is the cut-off date after which no further imports of wheat on a concessional basis will be sought. The target of achieving self-sufficiency in the production of food grains by 1970–71 is to be pursued vigorously." This does not mean that India may not, from time to time, purchase food grain for hard currency in the world market.

change in the Indian economy and, I believe, in the political balance in Asia in the next ten years.

The difficulties are great, and unhappily a bold effort of this kind seems unlikely. America and most other nations of the West are increasingly focusing on other problems, cynical about the "profitability" of "helping others" and in a general mood of irritation and frustration. The sensitive Indians, on the other hand, are becoming less eager to receive foreign assistance, on the ground that it places them in the role of beggars and subjects them to political pressures. So the odds are that this opportunity for rapid growth will be missed.

However, with the new approach of the World Bank and a continuing rise in Indian exports, the foreign exchange required for a 5 percent increase in the GNP may be available. This would increase India's per capita income by about 3 percent annually, which if wisely distributed might be enough to maintain reasonable stability and a sense of progress.

The crucial question, "who owns the land," particularly in the rural areas, may turn out to be the single most important element in determining India's success or failure in the next twenty years.

As I have pointed out elsewhere in this book, rapid increases in agricultural production are bound greatly to widen the gap between those who own the land and those who work it as landless laborers. Most Indian political leaders have somewhat belatedly come to recognize the importance of a broader-based rural prosperity, and many of them see the need for a greater measure of economic justice for the landless peasant. The many who have visited Japan and the few who have visited Taiwan have seen the importance of low ceilings on land holdings, which guarantee every family at least some land, as a means of assuring political stability. But when it comes to lowering the present ceiling of thirty acres per family (which is generally poorly enforced) to the ten-acre ceiling which is in effect in Taiwan, the Indian leaders run into formidable obstacles since large landowners are a major and often decisive political factor in the national and state assemblies.[15]

An alternative approach, which I have advocated and which has been seriously considered by liberal Indian leaders, would be to eliminate taxes on small land holdings, say, up to five acres, and then impose a gradually increasing land tax on all holdings between five and ten acres, with a very sharp progressive rise in taxes on farms of more than ten acres. At the same time, if taxes on small rural industrial plants (brickyards and canning factories, for example) were largely eliminated for a period of, say, ten years, many are confident that a new agro-

15. As in Kansas, Nebraska, Iowa, etc., in the first half of the century.

industrial dynamism would sweep rural India. The cultivator with more than ten acres would have a strong incentive to sell that part of his heavily taxed land holdings over ten acres and to invest the proceeds in a factory which would be relatively free from taxes for an appropriate period.

At present the demand for laborers to till the large farms is very great, and farm wages in many parts of India have risen spectacularly. But this, too, is creating a new and disruptive movement toward rapid but in many cases premature mechanization. To cut their labor costs, many of the large cultivators are buying tractors. This cuts their labor costs, but unless new factory jobs can be made available, it will lead to massive unemployment and rapidly increasing political turbulence. This is already occurring and spreading rapidly. In West Bengal, for example, the Maoist wing of the Communist Party is very effectively exploiting this issue as its counterpart did in China in the 1940's. As long as there are not enough jobs for all who are willing and able to work, the only alternative I can see is for the government to provide direct employment in building dams, roads, parks and other improvements.

A related question is the debt burden on millions of Indian families who in many cases have been paying interest rates of from 20 to 40 percent for many years. The long-range solution is of course a modern credit system. But, in the meantime, I believe debts the interest on which has already been paid three or four times over should be reduced or eliminated. This is a drastic move, but India is facing a potentially revolutionary situation, and our experience in China and Vietnam should have taught us by now that radical political and economic moves are the only way that bloody revolutions can be avoided. If the burden of rural debt could in this way be eased, the prospects for a viable Indian rural society would be greatly increased. Some of the younger non-Communist leaders are beginning to come to grips with such problems, but, in my opinion, not sufficiently.

Among the most encouraging omens for the future of the Indian rural economy are the findings of Professor McKim Marriott, an outstanding social anthropologist from the University of Chicago. In 1950 Dr. Marriott made a six-month study of a village in the Aligarh district of western Uttar Pradesh about one hundred miles away from New Delhi. Dr. Marriott spent six months in this village, studying in depth each family, each piece of land and the hopes, fears, traditions and daily life of the villagers, including caste differences, religious attachments and the like.

At that time there was almost no irrigated land. The diet of the villagers was meager; few ate more than twice a day. Every last calorie, according to Dr. Marriott, was extracted from the environment. Although the farmers knew the value of manure as fertilizer, there was none available since dried dung cakes were the only fuel for cooking. There were twenty-four different castes, and religious rites were developed by blind superstition. There was no school or industry. There was widespread fear and distrust of government officials. The whole atmosphere was one of utter hopelessness—some eight hundred people simply striving to stay alive.

Eighteen years later Dr. Marriott returned to the Aligarh village for a six-month follow-up study. He found a dramatically changed situation. The first tube well had been dug a few years before. Since then ten or twelve more had been completed, each of which produced ample irrigation water for two crops. The yield of the crops was about double what it had been, and as new hybrid seeds become more and more available, it may be expected to grow steadily.

In Dr. Marriott's words:

> There are no empty fields these days. As one crop comes out of the ground they start sowing a new one. You see standing crops on every side. Labor is being imported into the village from the cities, therefore reversing the usual process. Some families are even beginning to dream of tractors and mechanical tools to grind the grain and to ease the manual labor. The wells are now all electrified, drawing their power from a nearby power line.

The sharp rise in income and living standards had had a most constructive effect on the social organization. Caste differences were eased significantly, and everyone in the village had begun to vote in elections. More than half the village's children were in school, with quite a few going to a high school nearly six miles away.

"There is an awareness," Dr. Marriott concluded, "that something important is happening in the village . . . the most exciting thing about it is that most of the changes seem to happen through the power of the people. There is new initiative, new leadership and new hopes for the future."

Although much of India still clings to the old ways, anyone who travels through the rural areas is bound to be impressed with the evidence of economic progress in many areas similar to that described by Dr. Marriott, and with it a sense of increasing confidence among the people. The familiar stereotype of the apathetic, hopeless Indian peasant bogged down in the traditions of his forefathers is steadily giving way under the impact of new opportunities and objectives.

Although India's central government is wobbly and subject to heavy pressures, many able young people are beginning to come forward to assert that the present promising but inadequate economic progress can be intensified if the government will simply keep out of the way. Government red tape must be more ruthlessly slashed, and the stifling influence of the Soviet Union's outworn concepts of development must be discarded. Right now India urgently needs to encourage foreign private investment on a partnership basis, not only for the foreign exchange but to introduce more modern industrial technology. This requires far more incentives, which the left-wing parties strongly oppose. But a strong central government is also essential to economic growth and to an increasing measure of economic and social justice. Somehow a balance must be struck.

India's political prospects are closely associated with its economic growth. Greater production seems to open men's minds to the possibility of new opportunities. Unless the people can become directly involved in their own progress and the rapid increase of their country's output, this increase, as I have repeatedly pointed out, will lead to greater political turbulence.

Ever since India gained her independence in 1947 observers have been saying that India, with its fourteen major languages, its half-billion people, its many different and often conflicting religions and its divisive caste system, is sooner or later bound to disintegrate. But I doubt it. Western Europe has approximately the same population as India, and the same number of languages. The physical differences between Greek and Swede or Belgian and Portuguese are at least as great as the differences between Punjabis and Madrasis, Bengalis and Marathis. And the separate political histories of England and Italy are about as different as those of Madras and Bengal.

If by a miracle Europe were suddenly united under one constitution, with one prime minister, one legal system, a common market and with federal and state legislatures, it would mean the fulfillment of a vision that generations of Europeans have pursued since the days of the Romans.

For the first difficult twenty-three years of its existence India has succeeded in doing what Europe has thus far failed to do. In the face of severe economic and political pressures, India has somehow maintained freedom of speech, freedom of the press, due process, parliamentary procedures and national unity. In the Western sense, India *is* a functioning democracy.

Democracies are never tidy. They stumble and fumble and often take longer to make decisions than is good for them. But one of democracy's advantages is that it allows people to blow off steam, to voice their disagreements and to vent their dissatisfaction before the breaking point is reached.

Much as most of the Indian people have come to distrust the Congress Party and to question the abilities of other moderate parties, they are not yet in a genuinely revolutionary mood. Under present circumstances a Communist takeover in India seems unlikely. But there is a real possibility that the Communists may develop enough political leverage to block the more flexible, incentive-oriented economic measures which are so urgently needed. This could provoke a situation similar to that in France before the Second World War, when the Communists, while unable to seize power, were able to keep a long succession of non-Communist governments from governing. The result was stagnation, a grave weakening of French society and the final collapse of France itself under the impact of Hitler's panzer divisions.

Although caste divisions in India remain a divisive factor, considerable progress has been made. Laws have been passed which forbid caste discrimination and outlaw "untouchability," and as economic conditions gradually improve, the caste conflicts will ease. But an abrupt collapse of the caste system is not in the cards, and, in my opinion, might create more problems than it solved.

What is more likely to occur is a gradual erosion of caste injustices, inhibitions and loyalties similar to the erosion of racial barriers in the United States. However, the Indian caste barriers should be easier to deal with than our racial barriers since there is usually no way to tell a person's caste by his appearance.

Religious differences in India present a more serious problem. Until about A.D. 1200 India was able to absorb a long series of invaders, who, with minor exceptions, accepted the Hindu culture, philosophy and religion which they found there. But the Muslim invaders who later overran North India were as determined as the Hindus to preserve their own cultural identity. Thus India developed two rival religious communities, each with strength sufficient to make it impossible for one to dominate or absorb the other.

At present the Muslim minority in India totals some sixty million, with an additional twelve million Christians, ten million Sikhs and smaller numbers of Buddhists, Jains, Parsis and Jews. These minorities have chosen to live in a secular state, and Indian leaders take justified pride in the extent to which most of them have been integrated in Indian society. However, the fact remains that from time to time in many parts of India religious antagonism still erupts in senseless violence.

Thus the outlook for India must be described as uncertain. But there are several positive factors. With some notable exceptions, Indian leaders are united in their efforts to deal positively with the religious conflicts. Here many younger people are beginning to play a constructive role. A young Hindu student recently wrote me: "The youth of India is no longer enamored by either Muslim or Hindu institutions and is anxious to pull down the walls of tradition which separate the two communities."

Half the population of India is under twenty-five years of age. These young people are not enthusiastic about re-enacting the horrors of partition or carrying on the animosity between the two major religious communities which has punctuated the past seven hundred years. The large majority, instead, are determined to break the deadlock of the decades, and, while conscious of the problems which are involved, they are ready to welcome the laws, science and technology which may help them to bind themselves more closely together. In another letter a Muslim graduate student wrote:

> Both religions preach tolerance. Whatever may be said about Islam being propagated by the sword, it is basically a tolerant religion; there is evidence to show that the prophet Mohammed himself protected and helped Christian missionaries, and Hinduism by its very philosophy brooks abundant tolerance.

Despite the encouraging signs that most young Indians, like young people in the United States, are striving to find new answers to old problems, religious conflicts, since the beginning of time, have not easily succumbed to reason, and progress no doubt will be slow. It took the United States 185 years to elect a Catholic President, and in every major city in the United States tensions among nationality groups, races and religions continue to cause anxiety.

Another political problem is that of language, to which I have previously referred. A riot may start in a North Indian city in which the demonstrators denounce English, tear down English signs and insist that Hindi be immediately established as the national language. In response, similar demonstrations break out in South India in which the demonstrators denounce Hindi and call for English as the national language in order to prevent their own regional languages (Tamil, Bengali, etc.) from being replaced by Hindi.

But India's talent for adjustment and compromise usually makes itself felt. Respected and relatively noncontroversial leaders may be expected to come forward and say, "This situation deserves careful study to bring out the facts and to offer a solution acceptable to everyone." There is a general nodding of heads, and the study begins. When it is completed two or three years later, its authors are commended by the press, and the report, like others before it, begins to gather dust on library shelves while the situation goes on much as it did before.

In the future an educated Indian will no doubt need to know three languages—Hindi, English and his own regional language. Although this is a burden, it is not in any sense an impossible one; most educated Europeans speak two, three or four languages.

With all their political contradictions and turbulence, I know of no people with greater capacity than the Indians to hammer out an agreement among differing groups and to sweep under the rug issues on which agreement for the moment is impossible.

But suppose Indian representative democracy does break down, what then? Will the Army take over, as in many other less developed countries? It is possible, but not likely. As I have already indicated, the Army is strongly nonpolitical. Equally important is the fact that the Indian Constitution, probably unwittingly, assigns great power to the President.

There is little doubt that in the drafting of the Indian Constitution it was assumed that the President would play much the same role as the ruling sovereign of the United Kingdom. Although holding the symbolic power of a British sovereign, he would not be expected to exercise it, any more than the British sovereign does. However, there is a fundamental difference. Although unwritten in constitutional form, the actual distribution of power between the British sovereign and Parliament is rooted in hundreds of years of tradition. The Indian Constitution, on the other hand, is supported by no such tradition. While the drafters of the Indian Constitution intended them to be symbolic, in clear language it assigns to the President real powers.

A literal reading of these provisions clearly indicates that the executive power resides in the President, who "appoints" the Prime Minister and "approves" his Cabinet. The Supreme Court of India and other qualified students of constitutional law maintain that the President is bound to adhere to the advice of the Cabinet and the Parliament. However, as we all know, court decisions are always subject to reconsideration as constitutions are reinterpreted under changing conditions.

As long as the Congress Party had control over the Indian central Government and the states, the specific constitutional powers of the President presented no problem. The Congress Party, in effect, had the power to nominate the President and to assure his victory. In the next few years, however, a majority can be assured only by a coalition. In a crisis produced by the inability of a party or coalition to govern, a strong President, with the support of some of the key political leaders, the military, a significant proportion of the press and a fresh interpretation of the Constitution by the courts, could emerge with much the same powers that Charles de Gaulle had in France, with the sole constitutional requirement being that he stand for re-election in five years.

Precisely what political system will finally emerge from this interplay of political, academic and social forces, only a very brave or very foolish man would attempt to prophesy. As I repeatedly emphasized to all who would listen—and to many who would rather not—the forces that hold India together are usually underestimated by observers who do not know the country well and who have not read its history. Through all the maze of languages, religions, castes, parties and economic positions, there runs a common denominator of Indianness: north, south, east and west, people think of themselves as Indian. A visitor to any part of India knows he is in India. And a united India, with one-sixth of the world's population, will play a key role in the future of Asia.

CHAPTER 44

FAREWELL TO INDIA AND ASIA

SHORTLY BEFORE Richard Nixon's inauguration as President of the United States I submitted my resignation, in accordance with customary procedure. Six years had gone by since I had accepted Jack Kennedy's offer that I serve as his Ambassador to India; six years since I had written: "Unless there is a deeply rooted and clearly understood consensus on U.S. objectives and priorities in India and South Asia, I am not the right man to represent the United States in India." In those six years the consequences of our failure in 1963 and 1964 to persuade Washington to respond affirmatively to India's request for military assistance had become clear. Although I opposed military assistance in general, and have never thought that a military alliance between India and the United States would be desirable or possible, I believe that a moderate five-year program of military aid to help modernize India's Army and Air Force following the 1962 Chinese attack might have made a decisive difference in the course of events in Asia.

When I last talked to Kennedy three days before his death he saw the opportunity clearly, and I am convinced he would have provided this assistance. But when the new Administration, following Nehru's death in May, 1964, not only "postponed" India's requests, forcing India to go to the U.S.S.R., but a few months later introduced American ground forces and airpower into Vietnam on a massive scale, the opportunity was lost, and our relations with India became increasingly uneasy.

The Indian Government's consistent policy of pressing for negotiations while denouncing the bombing of North Vietnam by the U.S. Air Force had infuriated President Johnson. But both Shastri and, later, Mrs.

Gandhi shared the conviction of the British, the Canadians, the Pope and the Secretary General of the United Nations that only when the bombing was stopped would serious negotiations become possible, and, wheat or no wheat, they never attempted to suppress their views.

My letter to President Johnson in the spring of 1964 expressing my concern about Vietnam had been followed by a score of letters to him with specific suggestions, particularly in regard to land reform, on how the United States might find a way out of the military impasse into which we had stumbled. The following excerpts from these letters are illustrative:

March 15, 1967:

I recognize the problem of persuading the South Vietnamese Government to take revolutionary action in regard to land reform which I have been advocating. However, I wonder if Chang Kai-shek and President Park of South Korea, both of whom have had extraordinary success with this kind of land reform program, might not be persuaded to lend their support? Chiang Kai-shek in particular is in a position to express his regrets to General Ky that he did not move along these lines on the Chinese mainland as he did later with such effectiveness on Taiwan.

New schools, clinics and roads for the rural people of Vietnam are important. However, unless the South Vietnamese Government is prepared to change the basic power structure in the villages, relieving the peasants of the burden of high land rentals and assuring them their rights to own the land they till, the struggle simply cannot be won.

Please forgive me for persisting on this subject. However, I am deeply persuaded that we still have an opportunity dramatically to switch the whole economic-political focus of our South Vietnamese effort toward a position that will capture the imagination of the Vietnamese peasants. At the same time we can convince the people of the United States and the rest of the world that our objective is not to restore the status quo in South Vietnam but to create a vigorous new democratic society which is responsive to the people's needs.

May 18, 1967:

Although Vietnam is not directly my business, I would like again to take the liberty of expressing my private views directly to you on what I believe to be the critical situation which is developing there.

I do so, first, because many years of experience in Asia have given me some feeling for the forces which are shaping events there, and, second, because I feel that whether my views prove to be right or wrong they are different from those which are normally presented to you by your advisers.

On several occasions I have proposed that we bring to bear on the Saigon Government whatever pressures are required to persuade it to launch a program which would assure each rural family in South

Vietnam twelve or fifteen acres of land. This could include those members of the Vietcong who lay down their arms before a certain date.

Several respected TV and newspaper reporters on their way home from Saigon have recently told me that right now the Saigon Government is moving in the opposite direction. When American and South Vietnamese troops take over a rural area from the Vietcong, they assert, the rights of the landlords are promptly restored, and in some cases there has even been an effort to collect a percentage of the crops as back rent.

If these stories are correct, we can never succeed in "pacifying" the South Vietnam rural areas regardless of the size of our commitment, money and men, or the dedication and ability of those who are carrying it out. The peasants of Asia want doctors, schools and roads; but even more they want pride, dignity and economic and social justice.

In each case the President and Secretary had responded by agreeing that my idea was "excellent," but that I should realize that the first order of business was to defeat the enemy; after that, they said, reform such as I suggested would be needed. Their words reminded me of the views that had led Chiang Kai-shek to disaster on the Chinese mainland in the 1940's.

A variant of their standard reply was that even if the Saigon Government could be persuaded by U.S. pressure to announce that land would be made available to every rural family, the promise could not be implemented until the defeat of the Vietcong, since the Vietcong controlled much of the countryside. My response to this rationalization is typified by the following excerpt from a letter to the President, written February 27, 1967:

> You face a problem somewhat similar to that of Lincoln in regard to the freeing of the slaves. The arguments against the Emancipation Proclamation were similarly focused on the claims that (1) it would upset many property (slave) owners in the border states; (2) that it could not be enforced in areas not occupied by the Union Army; and (3) that even after the war it would involve enormous administrative difficulties and expense.
>
> Nonetheless only after Lincoln made the hard decision did the war become meaningful for most Americans (including many in the Southern states) and to the millions of onlookers overseas.
>
> For these reasons I hope you will reject the old arguments about administrative difficulties, bad timing, loss to our property-owning friends, etc., and come out boldly for a sweeping irrevocable land reform proposal. Only in this way can we make our present efforts convincing and meaningful to the honest doubters in the United States and in other countries.

I visited Southeast Asia three times during my last six years in India. The last occasion was in January, 1968, when President Johnson sent me to Cambodia to discuss with Prince Norodom Sihanouk North Vietnam military violations of the Cambodian border areas. The Pentagon had been pressing for the right of "hot pursuit" across the Cambodian border, and my visit was obviously part of an effort to relieve this pressure.

Very few Americans had ever been to Cambodia, and many misconceptions had developed about the country and Sihanouk. I had met Sihanouk on several occasions and liked him. Although he was unpredictable, ruthless and shrewd, all his talents, good and bad, were focused on keeping Cambodia independent and free of war. But he also had a sense of humor.

In a radio speech to the Cambodian people in 1962, for instance, Sihanouk stated that he was greatly distressed about the behavior of his son, who could not be trusted in matters of the heart, and who had already led several young ladies astray. Sihanouk reported that he had married him to a girl of outstanding character who he assumed would put an end to his indiscretions. Unhappily, Sihanouk had to report that his son had recently returned to his former habits and he, Sihanouk, felt obligated to warn the young ladies of his country that he could no longer be held responsible for his son's behavior.

In another radio broadcast to the people in January, 1968, after Sihanouk had officially agreed to my forthcoming mission to his country, he said, "The Americans are trying to woo me for reasons that are obvious. First, they sent Jackie Kennedy, who stayed here a full week. When she was unable to seduce me, they decided to send Chester Bowles, who is obviously much less seductive than Jackie Kennedy. I suggest that Chester Bowles save his time, visit Angkor Wat and then stop by at Phnom Penh on his way back to Delhi, when I shall be delighted to have tea with him."

My instructions made it clear that my mission was calculated to head off a major intrusion of the United States into Cambodia to root out the Vietcong and North Vietnamese forces established there. Such an invasion appeared to me and to many people in the Department, including, I am told, Dean Rusk, as one more dangerous mistake.

We left New Delhi for Phnomh Penh on January 8, 1968, accompanied by Philip Habib, Deputy Assistant Secretary of State for East Asian Affairs; Herbert Spivack, Minister-Counselor for Political and Economic Affairs in New Delhi; and several other members of my staff. We were met at the airport by Madame Chin Renn, Secretary of State for Information, a charming lady who greeted us warmly.

The formal meetings began the following morning. Prime Minister Son Sann proposed a full exchange of views that would enable him to re-

port to the Prince in preparation for our first serious meeting with Sihanouk the following day. I emphasized that the United States recognized the
neutrality, sovereignty and territorial integrity of Cambodia, and wished
to support the Royal Cambodian Government's efforts to preserve its
independence. We were, however, concerned that the war in Vietnam
might intensify in future months. If this should result in more and more
Vietcong and North Vietnamese forces seeking refuge in Cambodia, it
could lead to an expansion of the fighting.

The Prime Minister replied that when Vietcong contingents crossed
the Cambodian border, they were immediately disarmed or asked to leave.
The Commander in Chief of the Cambodian armed forces, General Nhiek
Tioulong, also forcefully defended Cambodia's ability to detect and prevent Vietcong incursions and criticized the United States and South Vietnamese attacks on Cambodian outposts.[1] Whatever differences there
might be in our estimates of the border problem, he added, the two
governments must both find a way to help the International Control
Commission guarantee Cambodia's neutrality.

The next day, accompanied by the American delegation, I had a
long discussion with Sihanouk, at the Prince's official residence. The
Prince said that he could not understand why the United States was attacking North Vietnam and "other small countries," while avoiding a
confrontation with the Soviet Union and Communist China, which were
actually promoting the conflict. Ho Chi Minh, Sihanouk said, was no
minion of Peking; he was a true nationalist. It would be in our interest to
help him maintain his position. If we failed to do so, we would push
Hanoi into the arms of the Chinese, which was precisely what Ho Chi
Minh wanted to avoid.

I emphasized that we had no desire to carry out military operations
anywhere in Cambodia. Prince Sihanouk replied that he accepted this
assurance and added that he personally had no use for any Vietnamese,
"red, blue, north or south."

Later, in a quiet private visit, Sihanouk volunteered that he would
not object to the United States' engaging in "hot pursuit" in unpopulated
areas of Cambodia. He pointed out that while he could not say this publicly or officially, if the United States followed this course, it might even
help him to solve his problem. But I doubted that he meant it.

In the discussions next day Prime Minister Son Sann expressed his
government's satisfaction with the course of the conversations and
brought up the question of restoring normal diplomatic relations with
the United States. The only problem, he said, was the wording of the
announcement. He suggested the following formula: "The United States

---

1. Neither one really believed this.

unconditionally respects the territorial integrity of Cambodia with its present borders, and recognizes the inviolability of these borders." I replied that this seemed reasonable and I only wished that I had the authority to negotiate an agreement. However, I would strongly recommend that my government should respond positively to his proposal.

"Would the United States," Sann then inquired, "be willing to offer assurances against any movement across the border by the South Vietnamese or American troops?" I replied that Cambodia was on the edge of a savage war which had become difficult for us or anyone else to control. We would do our best to see that no further border incidents occurred, but I could not provide an absolute guarantee in a situation as volatile as this. The Prime Minister accepted my assurance that the United States would do everything possible to avoid border incidents, and did not press any further for a "guarantee" which I knew, and he suspected, the U.S. Government would not agree to.

The next step was to put together a communiqué, which was signed by Prime Minister Son Sann and myself, representing our two countries.[2] Further toasts were exchanged in a cordial atmosphere. There seemed little doubt that on the Cambodian side fears of "hot pursuit" by U.S. and South Vietnamese troops, which had been strongly rumored in the American press, had now been allayed; it never occurred to any of us that less than two years later we would actually invade Cambodia.

Upon our return to New Delhi we were met by a large delegation of American, Indian and foreign newspapermen who were eager to hear the details of the trip. A few hours later a cable flash came from Washington stating that at a State Department press briefing an official had said that my agreement with Sihanouk did not change the situation in any respect. I sent an urgent message to the White House saying that the President should either publicly support or publicly disavow the agreement. A few hours later the White House spokesman came through with a clear statement that the President fully endorsed the agreement between Ambassador Bowles and Prince Sihanouk.

Later events in Cambodia, the overthrow of Sihanouk and the subsequent introduction of U.S. troops there with the result of widening the scope of the war in Vietnam, have served to emphasize for all to see what became evident to me during my visit. Sihanouk's policies, though often irritating to the United States, were an effective means of guarding the neutrality of Cambodia.

If there were ever doubts about Sihanouk's interest and objectives, they were dispelled in a revealing article in the April, 1970, issue of

2. I took the responsibility of not sending it to Washington for approval because I felt the delay at this stage might lead to a breakdown in our agreement.

the *Pacific Community,* which must have been written in January or February, before his overthrow in late March:

> The United States, for its part, would be only too happy to see "punished" this "insolent" country of Cambodia, resolutely non-aligned, which always withstood that power. But the Communization of Cambodia would be the prelude to a Communization of all Southeast Asia and, finally (although in a longer run), of Asia. Thus it is permitted to hope that, to defend its world interests (and indeed not for our sake), the United States will not disentangle itself too quickly from our area—in any case not before having established a more coherent policy which will enable our populations to face the Communist drive with some chance of success.

By now it should be clear that I believe America has much to learn about Asia and that the learning process is dangerously slow. We were drawn into Vietnam by a combination of idealism, ignorance and belief in our own "power"; but events have demonstrated, at great cost, that American military power has strict limitations. We cannot "save" any nation which is unwilling to save itself. The power that will continue largely to shape history will stem far more from ideas and dedicated leadership than from military might. Gandhi, "armed" only with ideas and dedication, pushed the British out of India. Mao Tse-tung with ten thousand men and a thousands rifles generated the power to destroy Chiang Kai-shek. But we with all of our wealth and might failed in Vietnam.

I have emphasized in previous chapters that a politically stable Asia can be assured only by the Asians themselves. Not only must they make an all-out effort to provide better living standards for their people; they must also learn to work with other Asian people for common objectives. A nation that cannot keep peace within its own borders is unlikely to maintain its sovereignty for very long. This, in the long run, is a sufficient reason alone why the United States should not become involved in the internal civil wars of Asia or anywhere else.

What is required now is a fresh approach to the problems of Asia, with no link of any kind with the United States, the Soviets or China, initiated by Asians, directed by Asians and supported by the great majority of Asians. The following scenario which I suggested informally to the State Department in April, 1970, meets these standards and might conceivably have created a basis for a breakthrough at that time:

1. A respected neutral Asian leader whose nation has not been aligned with the U.S., the U.S.S.R. or China would propose a conference of Asian nations (North Vietnam and South Vietnam, Burma, Laos, Cambodia, Thailand, Malaysia, the Philippines, India, Japan and probably Australia, but not China, Russia or the United States).

2. He would state that the objectives of this conference were three-fold: (a) to organize a genuinely Asian effort to achieve a cease-fire where the Great Powers have failed; (b) to negotiate a political settlement to the war perhaps with coalition governments in both North and South Vietnam which the combatants could be persuaded to accept; and (c) to develop a program for the economic rehabilitation of the Southeast Asian area, including Burma, which the U.S.S.R., the U.S. and China would be asked genuinely to support with *no political strings*.

3. He would suggest that the ultimate step would be the establishment of a permanent independent Asian organization which would meet regularly to consider common problems and to coordinate economic development efforts—in effect, an Asian League of Nations.

The call for the conference would state that Southeast Asia has been suffering under war conditions for thirty years, with vast physical and material damage, much of it produced by outsiders, and that as a consequence the progress of the 200 million people who live there has been set back for generations.

In such a setting the Asian nations, regardless of ideology, would independently discuss their mutual problems and possible solutions, free of the influence, real or imagined, of the United States, Russia or China.

A gesture in this direction was actually made, and for a time it seemed promising. But it was Indonesia that sponsored the proposal, and it was obvious that Indonesia, which had been in the process of negotiating a large loan from the United States, would not be acceptable to the U.S.S.R., China or North Vietnam as a negotiator. Prime Minister Lee Kuan Yew of Singapore conceivably might have made more progress.

The primary task in any case for America should be humbly to seek to understand how Asians think and feel and what they are struggling to accomplish. Once we develop a greater sensitivity, our relations with the Asians will significantly improve. Our role should then be limited to economic assistance to those nations which are prepared to help themselves. The role of the American military should be limited to assisting Asian nations in resisting any massive aggression by the Chinese Army across international borders, which is a most unlikely development under present conditions.

Particularly if we are to encourage a gradually evolving association of India with other independent Asian nations, we also need to develop far more sensitive understanding of India's objectives, fears and psychological reactions. Also required will be continued, generous, well-planned economic assistance in cooperation with the World Bank and Consortium nations to provide India with the necessary push toward self-sufficiency.

With the $160 billion that we have poured into Vietnam since the early 1950's we could have underwritten the legitimate needs of every independent nation in Asia, Africa and Latin America that was prepared to put its own economic house in order. In regard to India alone, expenditure there of less than 2 percent of our average annual military and economic budget for Vietnam would have gone far toward assuring the success of this critically important democratic experiment.

The United States will no doubt find it easier to develop common political ground with Asian nations when they no longer are in the humiliating position of having to accept our financial assistance. In the meantime, we may expect that India's leaders, as well as other recipients of American assistance, will consider it politically necessary from time to time to prove to their own citizens and to the world that they have not sold their sovereignty to a foreign government. This is no different than the way the early leaders of our own country reacted.

As for our efforts to persuade the President, Secretary and Congress to recognize the importance of India to a stable Asia and to appreciate the major economic gains that were being made there, we accomplished very little. Sixteen years after the abysmal blunder of arming Pakistan against India there still seems to be no recognition at high levels in Washington of the irrational nature of this move and its heavy cost in our relations with India. Even the Soviet success in persuading the Pakistan Government to push us out of the Peshawar air base for which we paid such a heavy political and economic price seems to have been written off as a bit of hard luck.

At the "working levels" of the State Department there were many well-informed, dedicated and cooperative people who backed our efforts to the hilt, but they made almost no impression on the harried individuals who "make policy" on the Department's seventh floor or in the White House.

The one exception was Kashmir. When we left India, the State Department and the White House were, I believe, finally convinced that the United States Government could not solve the Kashmir dispute through some magic formula or by a new exercise in political arm-twisting.

We can also take some credit, I think, for keeping certain conflicts between America and India from getting worse. As I think back over the diplomatic aspects of my work in India I wonder whether my greatest accomplishment may not have been in keeping potentially explosive situations from actually exploding. On many occasions a timely meeting or discussion or persuasive argument avoided a costly blow-up. India's bitterness over President Johnson's "disinvitation" of Shastri, our crude handling of the wheat shipments, and India's reaction to the casualties inflicted on their troops by American military equipment during the Indo-Pakistan war are cases in point.

Finally, we managed to put together what I believe to be the most efficient U.S. overseas mission that I knew of. For six years I had the advantage of a brilliant staff with high morale and a deep sense of commitment to our common objectives.

The many years we had been in India were underscored by my elevation in September, 1968, to Dean of the Diplomatic Corps. Diplomatic deans are selected in order of seniority, and the only one of the eighty ambassadors who had been in India longer than we, was our good friend Octavio Paz, Ambassador from Mexico, who also is known as one of the world's great modern poets. As I began to creep up the line of diplomatic seniority, I had for some months become increasingly concerned by the possibility that the responsibilities of the deanship might be added to our already heavy schedule. However, Octavio was quick to reassure me, "You can relax. We love India and I expect we shall be here for many years."

A few weeks after he had given me this assurance, student riots broke out in Mexico City, which the police handled with considerable ruthlessness. Paz, who had been a strong liberal force in Mexico for many years, was so shocked by the news that he publicly protested the action of his government. This resulted in his resignation, and, ready or not, I found myself in the position of Dean.

The Dean's primary responsibility is to give a diplomatic reception for each outgoing ambassador and, according to custom, the Dean as host is expected to offer on these occasions a brief, witty, eloquent toast and tribute (an exercise for which I have no talent whatsoever). As it turned out, my service as Dean of the Diplomatic Corps was not particularly onerous, but it supported my feeling that we had been in India long enough.

In March, 1969, when we still had had no word from Washington on my replacement, I cabled that we would like, if possible, to leave India in late April and hoped that this might be convenient for President Nixon. A week or two later the date was confirmed.

As the time grew closer, we came to realize that our roots in India were even deeper than we had assumed them to be. Not only had we come to know a great many Indians in all parts of the country very well, but the sights and sounds of the Indian cities and villages had become a part of our lives. We knew that the last weeks in India would involve a good many good-byes, farewell receptions, dinners and the like. To reduce this ordeal to the minimum, Steb and I made a tour of India, spending two days each in Calcutta, Madras and Bombay. After a day in New Delhi, we then took off for what we both considered one of the most beautiful spots in India—the Kulu Valley in the foothills of the Himalayas, two or three hundred miles north of Delhi. It is a narrow valley created by the Beas River which eventually flows into the Indus. It is thirty miles in length, with a maximum width of a mile or so. On three sides it is closed in by snow-clad mountains, some of which are twenty thousand feet high. We spent five days there in a "forest rest home" where Nehru used to stay, with the roar of the nearby Beas River fed by melting snows from the Himalayas, and spring with its apple blossoms and flowers all around us.

On our return to Delhi, we found that our departure strategy had been less successful than we assumed. The functions and difficult good-byes which might have been spread over two or three weeks were now all crowded into eight days.

The Indian employees at the mission gave us a memorable farewell reception, and there were other good-bye meetings with the Peace Corps, USIS, AID, the Diplomatic Corps and our many Indian friends.

On April 29, 1969, we took off on an Air India plane. Although we had dreaded the farewells at Palam Airport, we shall never forget their warmth and magnitude.

EPILOGUE

IT WOULD BE beyond the scope of both this volume and my own capacity for me to deal in anything but the most general terms with tomorrow's world. Yet the experience gained in my twenty-nine years of public life may justify a few observations.

The challenge in the years ahead is unprecedented. New technology is opening up limitless opportunity for mankind; but it is also creating economic, political and social pressures which, if uncontrolled or misdirected, could ultimately destroy us. Because the United States is most advanced technologically, the impact of this revolution has hit our country first. The problems which confront us today will eventually confront every nation regardless of its ideology.

Consider the question of war and peace. Whatever hope there may be for peace still rests, as it has for hundreds of years, on a balance of power between the major nations or groups of nations. Yet at best such a balance has only served to lengthen the time between wars. Sooner or later an event has occurred—the assassination of an archduke, the emergence of a Hitler, a breakthrough in weaponry by one nation or another—which has upset the balance and once again plunged the world into war. There is no reason to assume that the present uneasy balance is any more likely to survive; and in this nuclear age this could mean the destruction of much of mankind.

To "protect" themselves, the United States and the Soviet Union have accumulated nuclear weapons with an explosive force equal to fifteen tons of TNT for every man, woman and child on earth, according to a recent report by the Stockholm International Peace Research Institute. The Arms Control and Disarmament Agency estimates that world expenditures on armaments were $200 billion in 1969. According to a 1970 estimate by UNESCO, this is more than the entire world spent on public education and public health.

America's own military budget now accounts for roughly one-third of all our government expenditures. This vast expenditure distorts our economy, undermines our democracy and frightens our friends and ourselves as well as our enemies. Recently General David M. Shoup, former Commandant of the U.S. Marine Corps and a member of the Joint Chiefs of Staff, went so far as to assert that "militarism in America is in full bloom."[1]

At the same time our fragile international peace-keeping machinery has become less and less effective. With 127 nations now in the United Nations, with two of the five "great powers" no longer great, and with the largest power, China, in fact not represented at all, the original UN Charter is largely irrelevant to the current needs.

With a rapidly decreasing death rate, population growth throughout much of the world is threatening to outstrip available resources. The only way that food supplies and food requirements can be brought into balance in the next twenty years will be sharply to reduce the global birth rate. Otherwise, the increases in food production made possible by the "Green Revolution," in India and elsewhere, will only postpone the disaster.

America's domestic economy is also in dangerous imbalance. Our trillion-dollar Gross National Product, instead of being allocated on a priority basis to meet the problems of urban decay, slums and inadequate schools, hospitals and medical services, and to improve the quality of our lives, has largely been expended on more and more consumer goods, most of which have a calculated high rate of obsolescence, on super-luxuries for our more affluent citizens, and on gadgetry unlimited.

By 1985 the average family income, which was $8,600 in 1970, will grow to $15,000 at present levels of purchasing power. This additional income could provide ample funds to improve the quality of our environment and our lives, lessen the gap between the rich nations and the poor nations and still enable us Americans to continue to have by far the highest standard of material living the world has ever known. But there is no evidence that the more affluent members of our society are prepared to support the legislation necessary to achieve this.

The economic imbalance is increased by inflation, which continues to eat into our savings as prices and wages chase each other upward, while our government proceeds on the assumption that the only acceptable cure for higher prices is less employment. The right to strike, which was fully established only in the 1930's as a means of assuring workers the right to bargain for a fair share of the income they helped to create, is now often being misused to bring political and economic pressure against the community as a whole.

Motor vehicles, factories and power plants are poisoning the air we breathe, while industries and archaic sewer systems pollute our rivers.

1. April, 1969, edition of the *Atlantic Monthly*.

At the same time, the family, religious and community ties which provided previous generations with a sense of personal security and direction have become weaker, and tens of millions of people are morally adrift. This has intensified racial conflicts, added to the rise in crime and drug addiction and widened the gap in understanding between the generations.

Congress, which was intended by the authors of our Constitution to be the primary vehicle for adapting our society to new forces and changing circumstances, rolls on much as it has for the last one hundred years. The system of seniority, buttressed by skillfully conceived rules of procedure, often enables small minorities controlled by politically powerful individuals and special-interest groups to prevent critically important action on domestic and foreign policy legislation.

The executive branch, as George Reedy has pointed out in his book, *The Twilight of the Presidency,* has taken on a resemblance to a monarchy, which it was never intended to have. Like the Congress, the Administration, whether Republican or Democratic, appears incapable of coping effectively with the steadily growing forces for change.

Faced with this awesome array of unsolved problems, it is not surprising that millions of younger people, and thousands of older ones as well, have become cynical and defeatist. The only realistic way out, many of them assert, is not only to do away with the so-called "Establishment" that dominates our economic, social and political system, but to do away with the system itself and make a fresh start.

I share their concern, but reject their conclusion. Two hundred years of American history have demonstrated the incredible ability of human beings in a free society somehow to make their way through seemingly impossible dilemmas and to improvise effective responses to new forces. It is, I believe, within our capacity to do so again.

The Constitutional Convention of the 1780's set out to create a new kind of society designed to assure certain "inalienable" rights and responsibilities to the people as a whole, rather than to foster and safeguard the interests of elite and privileged groups, which had traditionally been government's role. In 1800 Thomas Jefferson, the leading advocate and spokesman for the revolutionary new concept that government should belong to the people, was elected President and the world's first democratically conceived government (however imperfect) was established.

By mid-century changing economic, social and political conditions had brought us to a new moment of truth. Our country was sorely divided by the slavery issue and whatever domestic dialogue was left was hopelessly bogged down in secondary issues.

In an editorial written in 1856, my grandfather, Samuel Bowles, editor of the Springfield *Republican* and one of the period's most outspoken liberal voices, expressed the urgent need for a new majority consensus capable of dealing with the crisis in the following words:

> Old Party names must be forgotten, old Party ties surrendered, organizations based on secondary issues abandoned, momentary self-interest sacrificed to the country and its welfare, and all must stand together and fight and labor side by side until the great question which overshadows all others has found issue in triumph of justice.

Eventually a new political consensus did emerge which enabled Americans to re-establish their political unity, abolish slavery, develop the continent and shape the economic and political forces generated by the Industrial Revolution to more democratic ends.

In 1932 we reached a third political watershed when our economic system very nearly collapsed under the strain of a new set of pressures, and again there were many who predicted national disintegration. But again out of turbulence and conflict a new majority political consensus emerged in support of Roosevelt's proposals for new government institutions to deal with new conditions and to "promote the general welfare."

We are now faced with a similar watershed as new political, social and economic forces create new problems for which we are unprepared. The conflicts of hawks vs. doves, of blacks with their grievances vs. whites with their fears, of farmers, businessmen and workers, of "hard hats" and students, of a vast array of special pleaders for this cause or that, are pulling our society apart, while the primary question of national decline or national resurrection, whether there is to be a world, and, if so, what kind of world it will be, are in danger of being lost in the confusion of parades, epithets, confrontation and violence.

What kinds of changes are required in our institutions, procedures and priorities to enable us to adjust our society to a new era? The most important question before us is the preservation of peace.

Only a greatly strengthened UN, armed with effective, adequately financed peace-keeping machinery and, ultimately, world law with enforceable disarmament, can enable us to break the cycle of war and peace which has plagued mankind for centuries and which in this nuclear age can destroy us all. And only through a strengthened UN can we effectively cope with such problems as air and oceanic pollution which require world-wide action.

As Secretary General U Thant observed in a speech in August, 1970,

"If the United Nations is to be effective in procuring peace, we must make the transition from power politics to a policy of collective responsibility toward mankind." A Charter Review Conference is provided for in the original UN Charter for this very purpose, and a separate world constitutional convention is a possibility. Whatever the forum, however, the best-qualified men from all over the world should be meeting right now as Madison, Hamilton and the early Federalists started meeting in the 1780's.[2]

Although it is generally (and perhaps correctly) argued that the world is "not ready" for even small steps toward world government, it would be a mistake to underestimate the ability of the masses to grasp big concepts and to follow enlightened leadership that spells out what is required of us all. Public opinion polls in October, 1970, indicated that nearly 90 percent of all qualified American voters believe that the United Nations must be made more effective, and their view is shared by equally large majorities in many other countries.

Our most important domestic question is whether we can establish some system of priorities that will assure that our wealth, skills and energies go where they are most needed by our people as a whole. America can no longer afford in the name of the "free market" to turn loose our enormous productive capacity without clearly defined objectives. There are many means of making such planning effective, including tax incentives, tax penalties and subsidies. But while good planning is regarded as essential by the managers of any private corporation, many reject planning by *government* as "creeping socialism."

Another critical question is education. For more than a century we Americans have placed great faith in universal public education as the ultimate means of meeting human problems. Yet today many of our best students charge the academic curricula with irrelevance; the present aim of education, they say, is no more than the pursuit of degrees which promise greater earning power.

I believe that a broader educational focus is essential to the survival of our free democratic society. In addition to providing a "marketable" skill (which may prove obsolete in a few years), a modern education system should help growing numbers of students to understand and deal with the effects of the technological revolution and the complexities of modern society, and to distinguish the charlatans in public life from responsible and enlightened leaders.

Many readers will assert that only a minority of our people would

2. Various sources for the financing of a greatly strengthened United Nations have been suggested. One of the most appealing is to allocate to the UN a share of the world's oceanic and polar resources.

agree to the major structural adjustments which I believe will be required. They will remind us that it took a revolution in the eighteenth century, a Civil War in the nineteenth and a disastrous depression in the twentieth to prod our predecessors in much less complex periods into making the changes in institutions and procedures necessary to meet changing conditions. Only a catastrophe or series of catastrophes, they will say, could create the more flexible political atmosphere in which such changes might be politically acceptable to a majority of our people. If they are right—and they may be right—the prospects for mankind are indeed bleak.

Yet there are many positive elements which in all the confusion I believe are being overlooked. The United States is divided, confused and frustrated. But, ironically, there is an extraordinary degree of soul-searching taking place. Never in my memory have so many Americans seemed so ready to analyze our conflicts, to explore our weaknesses and to search, however hesitantly, for workable solutions. This spirit is reflected in the increasing willingness of millions of individuals who are at odds on other questions to join together to combat overriding common dangers. The widespread support for ending the war in Vietnam is one example. Another is the growing public concern over the pollution and destruction of our environment.

It may be said that even though these are relatively simple issues, we have not yet succeeded in dealing with either one. On such critical questions as the establishment of workable peace-keeping machinery and national priorities there is little sign thus far of the majority consensus that would be required to deal with them effectively.

Yet this is no time to throw up our hands in despair. It is a time for fresh ideas and new perspectives, for enlightened policies and politically wise new leaders who understand not only the dangers but also the opportunities of the new world into which we are moving.

But solutions to the problems which confront us will not suddenly emerge full-blown from the minds of political leaders. Rather, they will develop gradually and painfully out of the interplay of economic, social and political forces in the cities, towns and neighborhoods of America. The necessary adjustments in our institutions, our values, our objectives and our priorities will be possible only if the great majority of people are directly and personally involved in the process.

I do not assume that the struggle for a better tomorrow *will* be won. But I do maintain that it *can* be won. Civilization, which has evolved so painfully through the centuries, need not be allowed at this stage to destroy itself, while our goals of freedom, justice, democracy and peace slip beyond our reach.

I am hopeful that this account of my years in public life may provide some encouragement to those who are now beginning their careers, and who are concerned about the task of social innovation and political reform. They have my good wishes, and, as long as I have breath and strength, they will have my collaboration.

Their task is no less than the fulfillment of the democratic political objectives of the generations that preceded them: life of quality and of high value, the rights of men successfully defended, the rule of reason, and eventually the confederation of the world.

Essex, Connecticut,
January 4, 1971

APPENDIX I

Inaugural Address of Chester Bowles, Governor of the State of Connecticut, to the General Assembly, January 5, 1949[*]

Mr. President, Mr. Speaker and Members of the Connecticut General Assembly:

By law and by tradition, we are gathered here today to consider how we may best carry out the responsibilities which the people of Connecticut placed in our hands on November 2. During the next few months, we shall be working closely together in the development of our legislative program. What we do, or what we fail to do, will affect, for good or ill, the life of every Connecticut citizen.

In this Inaugural Message, I shall touch but briefly on my specific recommendations for legislative action. This is not because my recommendations are lacking in urgency, but because I believe that our success will be determined by our ability to develop a common ground of understanding and respect; and that the first step in the development of such understanding is a full and frank discussion of principles.

Let me say at the outset that I do not believe we can afford the luxury of narrow-minded partisanship. Political parties are instruments by which we make our democracy responsible and effective, not weapons to harass and stultify the orderly development of government. They cannot be allowed to become ends in themselves.

In times past, we in Connecticut have been accustomed to lead the search for new methods to refine and improve the democratic process. An early Connecticut citizen, Thomas Hooker, gave the world its first written constitution. Connecticut abolished slavery eighty years before the Civil War. In the 1800's, Connecticut took a prominent part in Jefferson's fight for political democracy and Jackson's fight for increased economic democracy.

Connecticut was one of the first states to establish public schools and hospitals for the mentally ill, the deaf and other handicapped persons. In the present century, Connecticut, by its support of the reforms of Republican

* In this speech, to which I referred in Chapter 14, I try not only to express my general philosophy of government, and to outline the programs which I felt were necessary, but also to ease the inevitable conflicts between my office and the Republican-dominated State House of Representatives.

593

Theodore Roosevelt and Democrats Woodrow Wilson and Franklin D. Roosevelt, has continued in the forefront of enlightened governments.

Contrary to the dire prophecies of the conservatives, the legislative reforms of the past have not ruined industry and trade, corrupted the poor or led to socialism. Instead, industry and trade have developed hand in hand with social progress, and Connecticut has become one of the wealthiest states in the Union.

It is our responsibility at this session of the legislature to reaffirm the liberal tradition of our state; to push forward the frontiers of security, freedom and opportunity for every Connecticut citizen.

Our task will not be an easy one. We are living in a period which breeds sharp controversy and in which unhealthy and dangerous signs of extremism are all too apparent. As public problems become more complicated, many of us are tempted to reduce issues to political clichés and to wrap our own ideas and those with which we disagree into separate vacuum-packed containers, labeled respectively "Good" and "Evil."

In our complex and often frustrating world, this kind of reaction is understandably human. But if we expect our efforts during the next few months to be effective, we must strive constantly to minimize our conflicts, and to broaden, wherever possible, our areas of agreement.

In a philosophical sense, we Americans divide broadly into four political patterns. At one extreme are the reactionaries who make no bones about their preference for the past over the present—much less the future. At the opposite end of the political spectrum are the radicals who dislike our economic, political and social structure so intensely that they would destroy it if they could. Between the extremes of right and left are the conservatives and liberals.

At least 90 percent of us fit more or less generally into these two middle groups. So let us disregard the extremists and examine the difference between those of us who consider ourselves liberals and those who consider themselves conservatives.

The fact that liberals and conservatives have traditionally agreed on the principles of democracy but disagreed on how to apply these principles to best serve the public interest creates the political dynamics of our democratic society.

Since Colonial times, conservatives have continued to be conservative; but the reforms which their fathers opposed have become the established institutions which the sons upheld as sound and desirable.

Liberals have continued to be liberal, but they are learning that idealistic dreams and brilliant schemes are not enough; that public programs must be worked out the hard and careful way and made to fit, not just the views of a handful of theorists, but the complicated needs of all of our people.

The pulling and hauling of the liberals and conservatives, while healthy and desirable, is often an uncomfortable process. In the heat of controversy, liberals are sometimes inclined to class all conservatives as "reactionaries" or even "fascists," plotting to set up a Wall Street dictatorship. Conservatives, similarly, are sometimes inclined to class all liberals as "radicals" or even "Communists" determined to destroy our Constitution, enslave our people and wreck our private enterprise system. Against this kind of political hysteria, let me repeat, we must all be everlastingly on guard. In this explosive world it is more than just unhealthy. It is dangerous.

Now let us examine the liberals and conservatives a little more closely. Those of us who consider ourselves liberals feel a justified sense of pride in the accomplishments of the American liberal tradition. Since the days of Jefferson and Jackson, we have been in the forefront of the struggle to achieve an increasing measure of economic, social and political democracy for all of our people.

We who consider ourselves liberals, however, have no right to be smug. Although Franklin Roosevelt's New Deal achieved many great things for the American people, it never did solve the problem of unemployment. In 1939, six years after Herbert Hoover left the White House, there were still seventy thousand men and women walking Connecticut streets in search of jobs.

At the risk of establishing myself as a heretic, let me add that I am not too certain that we liberals have the final answer to unemployment today. Full production and full employment have been established in the postwar years—not because we have finally developed the basis for a permanent balance between wages, prices and profits, but largely because of our vast military expenditures and the program of Marshall Plan aid to Europe. In a sense, our employment problem has been solved, not through our own economic and political wisdom, but by the intransigence of Marshal Joseph Stalin.

We who consider ourselves liberals have a bad habit, too, of skipping lightly over some of the more boring details of governmental operations. We are great hands at writing eloquent declarations. But we sometimes fail to consider the administrative problems involved in putting our policies into effect. Frequently, in our impatience for a better life for all of our people, we have underestimated the hard realities of budget and finance.

The goal we liberals must set for ourselves is to to make Connecticut a proving ground of *competent* liberalism. Good government must display a healthy respect for other people's money. Sound government requires the fullest application of our energy toward practical ends. Intelligent government should be as economical and diligent an operation as we are accustomed to associate with Yankee enterprise.

I have been frank in analyzing the shortcomings of those of us who call ourselves liberals. Perhaps those of you who consider yourselves conservatives may feel that I am entitled now to suggest a few of your own handicaps.

If I may say so, I believe that your fundamental problem lies not in any lack of humanity and good will; but in your failure to recognize the urgency of many of the needs of our people; in your tendency to feel that public problems, if left alone, will eventually solve themselves; in your reluctance to use governmental powers to solve problems which clearly cannot be handled by any other means.

You conservatives are right when you say that too much government is dangerous. But sometimes you overlook the fact that if we refuse to employ enough government in the face of problems which only government can solve, then we may eventually end up with much more government than otherwise might have been needed.

I believe the challenge which you conservatives face is how to make conservatism in Connecticut relevant to our ever-changing social needs. You rigidly regard centralized power with suspicion. Remember that whatever success we may have in solving our problems here in Connecticut will ease the pressure to pass those problems on to federal jurisdiction. Strong and effective local institutions are the best assurance that we can have against the arbitrary use of centralized authority.

We liberals and conservatives will continue to disagree. Undoubtedly, we will disagree at some points in the Connecticut legislative session of 1949. But let us strive to see that our disagreement, if it comes, is an honest disagreement of principles and procedure, and not a disagreement born of the political clichés and the blind prejudices which make constructive thinking impossible.

I have a feeling that the extent of our real differences is often exaggerated. As an example, consider the development of our educational system.

A little more than one hundred years ago, there did exist a tremendous controversy throughout Connecticut and much of America on the subject of education. The liberals proposed that free public schools should be established and that every child, regardless of the income of his parents, should be taught at least to read and write. The conservatives of that day felt that education for the so-called masses was fraught with revolutionary dangers, and the fight raged hot and heavy for more than a generation.

Since then, liberals and conservatives have worked side by side in all of our 169 towns and cities to develop our Connecticut schools. Today—thanks to these joint efforts—we are providing most of our children with a reasonably good education.

I wonder, however, if our present educational standards are really as good as they should be? The average Connecticut boy and girl drops out of school at the end of the second year of high school. This is no better than the national average. Only one out of seven Connecticut boys and girls goes on to college. Again, this is no better than the national average, which includes low income states, such as Mississippi, Louisiana, and Tennessee. This means that we are lagging behind many other states.

Is there any real disagreement between us when I say that our Connecticut school system should be improved and strengthened in every practical way?

The future of our civilization depends on the ability of liberals and conservatives together to solve through democratic action the complicated problems which surround us. These problems are certain to grow in complexity as the years go on. They represent an ever-growing challenge to our educational institutions. We cannot build a future which will safeguard the children. But we *can* build children which will safeguard the future.

We need *better* schools. We also need *more* schools, and quickly. If we don't take action soon—bold, forthright action—our school system, instead of growing stronger, will begin to come apart at the seams.

The problem is clear. The number of births in Connecticut in 1948 was more than double the number in 1939. Unless we build new schools in a hurry, instead of twenty-five children in a classroom we will soon have forty to fifty; and, as a result, substantially lower educational standards. Our cities and towns cannot finance the building of the necessary schools without state aid. Surely most of us, conservatives as well as liberals, will agree that such aid on a generous basis must be forthcoming at this legislative session.

We will need many new teachers, too—50 percent more at least—if we expect even to maintain our prewar standards of education. I am sure that both conservatives and liberals in this Assembly will vote together again to expand our facilities so that the necessary teachers can be trained in the next few years.

We must remember, too, that the crisis in education extends beyond our primary and secondary schools. There is a growing agreement among us that every qualified boy or girl is entitled to an opportunity to go to college, regardless of the income of his parents. We must work toward that ideal as rapidly as possible. Connecticut University is badly overcrowded. A continuation of the building program there is essential.

Our labor laws, no less than our ideas on education, offer us an opportunity for nailing down the fiction that conservatives and liberals are doomed to perpetual disagreement. When unemployment compensation, workmen's compensation and Social Security were first proposed, many conservatives disagreed. But in the last few years, in their speeches and political platforms, they have accepted these programs as essential factors in our increasing economic democracy.

Can't we agree now to bring these programs up to date? If unemployment insurance and workmen's compensation are right in principle, why should we continue to limit their coverage to employees of firms employing more than four or five workers? Why don't we give *every* Connecticut worker the right to this basic protection? Other states have already taken this step. Why should we in Connecticut lag behind?

Here's another point. In theory at least, we have accepted the principle that workers should be protected against loss of employment for reasons beyond their control. Thus a worker receives compensation if he receives an injury on the job. He gets compensation if the plant shuts down for lack of orders and throws him out of work.

But what happens if he is unable to work because of illness; or because he breaks an ankle playing baseball with his youngsters? Should he be denied reasonable compensation? I don't think so, and I hope that a majority of you—conservatives as well as liberals—will agree.

Here's still another point on labor legislation. In some Connecticut factories, men and women, working side by side with equal skill at identical work, receive different rates of pay. Why not stop this obvious discrimination?

Let's take Old Age Assistance. Today, there is a $50 limitation on the aid, exclusive of medical care, which the state can give to a needy old person. In many cases, this is insufficient to provide a decent minimum of food, clothing and shelter. The only limitation on Old Age Assistance should be the actual need in each individual case; need established by expert social workers, and based on the current cost of living. I am sure that we can agree on that.

Some of the eligibility requirements—the so-called "pauper clauses"— in our Old Age Assistance Act are clearly wrong. They destroy the purposes of the Act and take away something of the dignity to which our old people are entitled. Let us act together in the next few months—conservatives and liberals—to put our Old Age Assistance program on a decent human basis.

Let's move on to the question of housing. Our lack of modern housing at fair prices is undermining our society at its very foundation. When adequate housing is lacking, families are broken and torn, children are brought up in squalor and bitterness, and the sense of security which can develop only in decent homes becomes impossible.

Our tragic lack of housing is a problem which concerns every individual in our state—conservatives, liberals, all of us—regardless of our incomes. Democracy can easily lose its meaning to those who are forced to double up in slum tenements.

The housing crisis did not develop overnight. Even before the war, one-third of our people were inadequately housed. Since then, tens of thousands of Connecticut homes and tenements which were scarcely fit for minimum living in 1939 have deteriorated still further. Our population has increased substantially. Home building has been held down, first by the war and then by scarcities and high prices. As a result the shortage has grown steadily more critical.

Today, as everyone knows, even the most efficient of private builders cannot build homes to rent for less than $85 a month. That's exactly three times the *average* rental that Connecticut families are paying today. It's more than twice as much as most families can afford. The gap between the kind of rentals which our people need and the new rentals which private industry can now build at a profit is staggering.

If we expect to build homes at rentals that the majority of people can afford to pay, we must provide some kind of government help. This fact must be clear to all of us—conservatives as well as liberals. So let us move boldly ahead together to meet our crucial housing problem. Let us authorize an all-out building program for the coming biennium—with rentals in reach of the average Connecticut family.

Here is another point on the housing crisis. The critical shortage of housing and the gradual emasculation of our federal rent control program has led to an epidemic of evictions, which I am sure must disturb all of you —regardless of your political viewpoint.

The Eviction Act passed by the special session last August has certain basic defects which make it almost ineffective. I hope that an eviction law with some real teeth in it will be passed by this session of the Assembly.

We also need a stand-by rent control act to take the place of the monstrosity which passed the last Assembly. I defy anyone—conservative or liberal—to explain how this Act could possibly be made to work without turning rent control into the most sordid kind of political football. Read it sometime and see if you don't agree with me.

Another problem on which action is urgently needed has been referred to as the "Shame of the States"—not just the conservative states or the liberal states, but all the states. I am referring to mental hospitals. If any of you doubt the urgency of the situation in Connecticut, I suggest that you visit any one of our state hospitals during the next few weeks.

The legislatures of several states are now taking vigorous action to correct this long-neglected problem. Will we in Connecticut refuse to accept the challenge? I do not believe so.

Here's another question—minimum wages. When a federal 40-cent minimum wage was established in 1938, many of you conservatives viewed this step with sincere alarm. Since then, most of you have accepted it as reasonable and fair.

The 40-cent-an-hour minimum wage of 1938 has now lost half its purchasing power. I propose that we establish an over-all minimum wage here in Connecticut that will take into account the increase in the cost of living— in other words, 75 cents an hour. I hope that there is no disagreement on this.

Our limit on savings bank insurance policies should also be brought in line with living cost increases. I suggest an increase from $3,000 to $5,000.

One last question. Conservatives and liberals alike believe in equal rights for every citizen, regardless of race, creed or color. And yet today—January 5, 1949, nearly a hundred years after the Civil War—it is still impossible for a Negro citizen to volunteer for our National Guard. The reason for this lies in the traditional Army regulations. You alone can correct this shameful discrimination in the State of Connecticut.

These, then, are the main features of the economic and social program on which I hope you will take action in the coming session. As men of good will, I am confident that we can reach agreement on them. I shall offer you more detailed recommendations on each in the next few days. In the meantime, let us add them all up.

Could this program, by any stretch of the imagination, be considered extreme? Not unless you are prepared to repudiate a basic tradition of New England—the tradition of social responsibility.

In our smaller towns, rural areas and city neighborhoods the principle of the friendly neighbor has been accepted and firmly established since Colonial days. When your neighbor's barn burns down or a falling tree crushes in a section of his roof, you pitch in with hammer and saw. If he becomes sick, you call a doctor and see that his children are taken care of after school. In the traditional New England community the slogan, in other words, has rarely been "Live and *let* live," but rather "Live and *help* live."

The legislative economic and social program which I have outlined adds up, it seems to me, to a Connecticut good neighbor program on a statewide scale. If we agree on it, we will have taken a bold step together toward our democratic goal of a high minimum level of security plus maximum opportunity and freedom for every Connecticut citizen.

But effective modern government calls for more than a willingness to apply the principle of the friendly neighbor to the problems of our state. In addition to warmth and human understanding, our government should possess a high degree of administrative efficiency.

Our Yankee forefathers gave us the principle of social responsibility in human relations. They also taught us to despise waste, inefficiency and lost motion in any form. Government today, faced with complicated new problems in a complicated new world, is necessarily big government. But the fact that government is big does not mean that it must be clumsy.

Since election day, I have been almost continually occupied in a detailed study of the finances, budget and operation of our state government. With the aid of an able group of assistants, I have probed deeply into the workings of our governmental machinery. I have personally interviewed most of our 108 state departments and commissions.

The task has been a big one and the time has been short. I do not pretend to know all the answers. But I do know this: If we are going to make our Connecticut State government really efficient, we have a big job ahead of us.

Our long overdue effort to modernize our state government can easily bog down in political bickering. To avoid this, I propose the appointment of a temporary nonpartisan commission with a mandate to study our state government with the utmost care and to report as soon as practicable its full recommendations. This commission should be set up at once so that there can be no delay in tackling this essential job.

Part of the responsibility of this temporary Commission on Organization should be a reclassification study of our state wage scales. In the meantime, I urge you immediately to establish the $180-$240 increase of 1946 and the 10 percent increase of last winter as a permanent part of our basic salary structure. This represents simple justice to the sixteen thousand men and women who work for our state government.

There are several other emergency actions which we must take promptly in the interest of increased efficiency in our state administration.

All of us—conservatives as well as liberals—agree that we must do everything within our power to bring labor and management together and to reduce the differences which lead to strikes. This will require a completely new kind of Department of Mediation and Arbitration. We need legislation on this.

We must also establish a new department to handle housing. Our present housing administration was developed before the nature of the housing crisis became clear. When I say that it is wholly inadequate to our present urgent needs, I do not mean to cast any reflection on the caliber and integrity of the men now in charge. But if we expect to get homes in a hurry, we must have the tools to handle the job.

Another urgent administrative problem involves our public works program. As I have already pointed out, most of our schools, buildings, hospitals and institutions, were well below standard in 1939. For many reasons—some good and some not so good—very little has been done since then to expand, improve or even to repair them. The situation today has passed the point where we can temporize, delay or postpone.

Our long-deferred building needs are so vast that we cannot possibly meet them all in the next two, four or even six years. Obviously, we must tackle first things first. For this reason, I have requested all departments, including the Highway Department, to prepare their building recommendations on a ten-year basis, with a clear statement of priorities. This will enable us to move ahead with the greatest possible efficiency and economy.

On a ten-year basis, our building program will clearly become more manageable. More than that, a long-range program of this kind will provide a bulwark against unemployment and recession here in Connecticut. By planning our public works in advance, we will be in a position to speed up our building program if hard times threaten, and thus take up any slack which occurs in private employment. Such foresight here would also enable us to get our full share of federal funds as quickly as such funds are made available.

The size and importance of our building program calls for the establishment of an independent Department of Public Works headed by the most competent staff we can find.

There are several other administrative problems on which I hope you will also take action. We should revise the system of payment for our probate judges, many of whom are now paid more than the members of our State Supreme Court of Errors. We should require State Attorneys to give full time to their work. We should rewrite our election laws. We should provide recourse to state primaries so that our political parties will be more directly responsible to the rank-and-file membership. Liberals and conservatives who are sincerely interested in better government should find no difficulty in agreeing on these questions.

Let me now discuss briefly some of the more important questions on the development of our budget for the next biennium.

There is nothing to be gained by refusing to face up to the fact that

Connecticut is confronted with a difficult economic problem. The figures presented to me by the various state agencies in making their budget requests for the next biennium totaled $400 million, which is $160 million more than these same agencies will spend for the current biennium. These estimates, delivered to me on November 15, in accordance with the law, were drawn up before Election Day—in other words, before anyone knew whether the next budget would be presented to you by a Republican or Democratic Governor.

Some of the requests for additional funds were the direct result of price increases in the last two years. Food and clothing for our institutions and welfare services are up nearly 40 percent. Building repairs and upkeep are substantially more expensive. Most of these price increases will necessarily be reflected in our budget for the next biennium.

Some of the requests for additional funds were based on recommendations for expanded services, many of them highly desirable. The most urgent of these will appear in my budget recommendations. The others must be canceled or postponed.

Fortunately, the new housing program and the increase in Old Age Assistance will require only $4 million for the coming biennium, which is less than 2 percent of our present total expenditures.

The total addition to our 1949–51 budget due to increased costs of essential services, increases in present services, and for new programs will be manageable without undue increases in our total tax income. The difficulty lies not so much in the cost of current programs, but in the cost of the badly needed new buildings and long-postponed major repairs, which make up the bulk of the $160 million increase which has been requested.

Some of these requests are, I believe, unnecessary. But a major part of them are not only justified but long overdue, and must be included in our ten-year building program. The most urgent needs should be scheduled for the coming biennium.

The question of financing this long-postponed building program is crucial. In any well-run business such a program would be paid for out of capital reserves accumulated in the period when building was impossible. That is the way American corporations have financed the tremendous capital expansion which has been in progress since 1946, an expansion running into billions of dollars.

Every well-run state government has followed the same procedure. California, Michigan and New York and many other states have been able to handle most of their postwar building through reserves which were prudently built up during the war years. New York State alone put aside a postwar building fund of $540 million. California's fund totals $476 million.

Our postwar needs here in Connecticut, as in other states, have been obvious for many years. It is unfortunate that we lacked the simple foresight to put aside the necessary funds to handle them. Our inadequate $16 million "postwar building fund" has long since vanished—most of it into the General Fund—to pay for current operating expenses.

As a result, we must now start from scratch in tackling the problem of financing this long-term building program—a program which was, from the start, an obvious postwar necessity. A bond issue of some kind seems inevitable.

One final word about the budget which I shall present to you on February

1. In past years the budget has been presented on a piecemeal basis. The separation of expenditures and income into special funds and budgets has made an over-all understanding of the state's financial situation difficult.

The new budget for the coming biennium will be a complete, comprehensive statement of Connecticut's needs, resources, income and commitments. It will give you not only my best judgment of the total minimum program required, but also a statement of our total income needs and the sources through which I recommend these needs should be met.

I sincerely hope that the consolidated budget which I shall present to you on February 1 will help you in the General Assembly to a clearer understanding of the over-all financial problems of our state, and encourage you to tackle my budget recommendations, not piecemeal but as integrated parts of an over-all program.

There is one final subject on which I shall comment briefly. Rising prices have threatened the stability of our economy and the security of our people for the last two and one-half years. They have added substantially to the cost of our state and local governments. These inflated prices have been unnecessary as well as dangerous.

There is at least some indication that the price problem may begin to ease in the next few months. The November and December Cost of Living statements of the Department of Labor clearly show a downward trend.

I am confident that the newly elected government in Washington will, if necessary, use all the power of the federal authorities to see that the upward rush of prices is not resumed. We here in Connecticut should continue to watch developments carefully. Needless to say, I shall use whatever practical means I can to ease the cost of living problem in our own state.

I have outlined the tremendous task that lies before us. I have stressed, not the differences which may divide some of us, but the areas in which all of us —conservatives as well as liberals—can surely work constructively and effectively together.

The legislatures which have met here before you have frequently touched greatness. Others have bogged down in mediocrity under the pressure of petty politics and of selfish interests.

Political pressures, many of them contrary to the interests of our people, will be brought to bear against all of us during the weeks ahead. I urge you, in all earnestness, to reject them, and to listen instead to the voice of our Connecticut people. These are trying times; and for those who believe as we do in the dynamic future of our American democracy, there is urgency in the air.

Let us pray then that God may give to all of us the vision to see the possibilities that lie before us; the tolerance to work with one another on the basis of understanding and respect; the humanity never to turn our faces from the needs of our people; the courage to move forward toward a tomorrow without fear.

APPENDIX II

Considerations Regarding the Selection of Top Policy-makers
Memorandum to Dean Rusk from Chester Bowles
December 18, 1960*

My purpose in writing this memorandum is to outline some of my views for your own consideration. In this area, as in others, I believe we are very close on basic principles, and where differences do exist this approach may help us to isolate and eliminate them by further discussion. Once we have established a broad common approach, we can operate with a minimum of discussion and delay.

1. Let us consider briefly the general background against which our principal choices will be made.

The world situation with which we must deal is acutely dangerous, most Americans regardless of party are keenly aware of this fact, and there is a general belief that these dangers are largely due to the inadequacies of U.S. policy during the last few years.

Furthermore, the impression is widespread that our officials dealing with foreign policy, both in Washington and throughout the world, have in many cases been insensitive to changing conditions and forces. This impression has been deepened by such books as *The Ugly American,* which, although grossly unfair, has been widely accepted.

Senator Kennedy, his rivals for the Democratic nomination, the party spokesmen (such as Bill Fulbright) and Democratic candidates for the House and Senate have concentrated much of their fire on our foreign policy inadequacies for the last several years, and particularly during the recent campaign.

Having made some four hundred speeches on foreign policy during the past year (more than two hundred during the campaign itself), I am convinced that our foreign policy difficulties were the single most important question in the minds of the voters on November 8. Indeed, if Nixon and other

---

* This memorandum, to which I referred in Chapter 22, is one of two I prepared as Dean Rusk and I began to work together during the Presidential transition period. My purpose was to help clarify our working relationship and also to focus President Kennedy's attention on the organization of the State Department.

Republicans had not stated their own concern and pledged themselves to modify our present policies, I believe the Democrats' margin of victory would have been considerably greater.

2. In my opinion, the Democratic attacks on the conduct of American foreign affairs, although often narrowly partisan, were largely founded in fact. In Europe we have seen confusion and lack of leadership; in Asia we have been equally inconsistent, and often dangerously doctrinaire. Until recently Latin America and Africa, in the face of clear evidence of the mounting dangers, have been largely ignored.

Therefore it seems to me that there is not only an urgent need but a clear public commitment for a fresh approach to foreign policy in most areas of the world and the refocusing of American energies and influence in dealing with other nations.

Regardless of the abilities of the present top State Department leaders, they have been associated in the public mind and in the minds of the leaders of the world with a long series of American setbacks.

Moreover, it is inevitable that such individuals should have a commitment to our present programs which will make it difficult for them wholeheartedly to support and administer the fresh approaches which the world situation requires and to which we are committed by the election of President Kennedy.

3. This brings me to a consideration of the Foreign Service itself. Although I have not had as much day-to-day contact with the Service as you have, my association has been considerable, not only during my own period as Ambassador but also during extensive travel in the last few years.

I am sure you will agree that the critical clichés about the Foreign Service which are widely accepted, and which are particularly deeply rooted on Capitol Hill, are grossly unfair to most Foreign Service officers. Many of them have been deeply opposed to many of our policies and tactics in the last few years, restless because of the lack of sensitivity and direction, resentful because of the lack of Administration support during the McCarthy period, and profoundly hopeful of Senator Kennedy's election. Many others, while less conscious of the political considerations, are ready to cheerfully accept the new Administration in the conviction that the situation will now be improved and greater opportunities available to them. The number of Foreign Service officers who are opposed to the new Administration is, in my opinion, strictly limited. If we provide the necessary leadership, sense of direction and sensitivity to individual attitudes and problems, I am confident that we can count on a high degree of loyalty, intelligence and competent service from the Foreign Service generally.

At the same time, I believe we should frankly face the fact that there is urgent room for improvement, involving not only methods of operation and selection but also of personal attitudes. Anyone with an intimate knowledge of our foreign policies and of the forces with which we must contend will agree that a sizable percentage of our representatives abroad have been slow to understand the full dimensions of the challenge we face and the requirements that this challenge imposes on their own efforts and attitudes.

4. This suggests the need for certain standards which I believe we should apply in selecting our top Department policy-makers:

a. They should have a broad understanding of the historical forces which are shaping the world and the practical problems of foreign policy-making and administration.

b. They should be dedicated to the public service, willing to commit themselves for the "duration," able to work as members of the team, lacking in personal ambition, willing to be personally expendable, intensely and personally loyal to you, the President and the Service generally.

c. They should have the capacity for fresh affirmative thinking, and for dealing with the new powerful forces which are shaping events throughout the world.

If these general standards appear reasonable, it would suggest the need for the appointment of fresh, competent individuals at all top foreign policy posts, down through the rank of Assistant Secretary. It would also suggest that in selecting these people, with a minimum of exceptions, we bring in people from the outside who are unhampered by past loyalties and associations, and who are in a position to inspire a new spirit and willingness among those who are working under them.

5. At the same time we should consider immediate steps to improve the morale of Foreign Service officers and others in the Department. There are several means by which we can accomplish this.

a. The appointment of outstanding officers to head two or three top embassies in Europe. If this requires larger allowances, I suggest we ask for them at once. In one or two cases, however, this might not be necessary.

b. We can launch a survey of the entire Service under competent Foreign Service officers, with particular emphasis on the need to speed the promotion of particularly outstanding officers. Because of the present seniority and retirement system many mediocre officers end up in charge of embassies while they wait for retirement age, thereby slowing down promotion for outstanding younger men. We might consider the procedure of the armed forces, which weeds out mediocre older individuals by enabling them to leave the service with high honors and an adequate pension if their further promotion is not indicated. This would give a new sense of lift and encouragement to the more able people in the younger age brackets.

c. We can search out those employees who unjustly suffered in the McCarthy period and see that the record is cleared. Although this might create some difficulties, I believe we would receive widespread public support, and the impact on the Service would be profound.

d. We can make it clear to the members of the Foreign Service that individuals will not be penalized for affirmative and creative thinking. We should encourage Foreign Service officers to speak more frankly through departmental channels even though this brings them into conflict with the accepted policies, attitudes and interpretations of the Department.

Those officers who take unpopular or unorthodox positions on complex issues which are rejected by the White House or the State Department should not be penalized. On the contrary, ways should be found to show them that we appreciate their courage in expressing their convictions.

e. Finally, by the public statements we make, by our tact in handling individuals, by our fairness in dealing with individual problems, by the sense of policy direction and leadership which we provide, we can create a new, confident atmosphere throughout the Department.

6. This brings me to what I believe to be the most important consideration of all, the responsibilities of our ambassadors. What is their job, and by what standards should we judge their performance?

Historically, the ambassador has been a direct appointee of the Head of

State, with the task of representing the President in a foreign capital and reporting through him to the State Department on the developments affecting the interests and the security of the United States. At the beginning of the war period it became obvious that this concept of his role was too narrow, and efforts were made to broaden it. It was agreed that the ambassador must also feel responsible for the improvement of the position of the United States by whatever means were available to him.

This requires that the ambassador should be an administrator, responsible not only for the proper handling of his traditional responsibilities but also in a general way for the entire U.S. Government operations in his area.

If the U.S. Information Service is being poorly handled, if the Mutual Security program is ineptly and insensitively administered, if the operations of the U.S. military programs are creating difficulties with the government, the ambassador has the responsibility not only for reporting the situation to Washington but for taking all administrative measures within his capacity to change it.

As you well know, many of our professional diplomats have been slow to accept this broader concept of the ambassador's role, which expands their own opportunities for error by drawing them into areas of operation in which they have limited competence and experience.

Nevertheless, I believe it is important that we clearly lay down the role of an ambassador as an operator and administrator, and that this concept be uppermost in our minds in making our selections. It also appears essential that we set up operating procedures which will enable us to apply a tactful but firm pressure to see that each ambassador is in fact acting in the broad operational role to which we have assigned him.

Let me conclude by suggesting a series of judgments by which we can expedite the task of choosing ambassadors.

a. First of all we should recognize the existence of some exceptional situations which may require us in some degree to modify the standards which I have suggested. I am thinking particularly of a limited number of countries in which a single individual or small clique more or less totally dominates the political scene.

Where such situations exist, I believe we should make a determined effort to find an indivdual who may possess the capacity to break through the existing communications wall and win the confidence of the individual who dominates the country in question.

For instance, if we can find individuals capable of winning the confidence of Nkrumah, Nasser, Salazar, Franco, Tito, Sukarno, etc., we should be ready to sacrifice some other considerations.

b. Having isolated these nations for special consideration, we could then postpone detailed consideration for those embassies which are now in the charge of Foreign Service officers who are carrying out their responsibilities in a competent way and who have expressed no desire to be transferred. These ambassadors could be immediately notified that for the time being at least we are satisfied with their performance and expect them to stay on, and that as soon as the pressure of immediate decisions are behind us we will talk with them in detail about the future.

c. We can set aside those posts where a noncareer ambassador is performing in an outstanding fashion. Regardless of his politics and the means by which he entered the service, I am strongly in favor of retaining anyone whose performance has been outstanding and on whose future loyalty we can count.

d. This would leave only three groups of ambassadors for whom replacement would be immediately necessary:

(1) Those occupying posts where individual capacity to deal with the Head of State is of special significance, and where that capacity, regardless of other qualifications, is not now evident.

(2) Foreign Service officers who have been posted in some capital for a long period of time or who either should be relieved or who are anxious to be relieved.

(3) Noncareer officers whose abilities are not outstanding enough to warrant their retention.

By some such system of clarification we should be able to eliminate the need for any action for substantially more than half of our embassies. This will make our immediate task much more manageable.

Whenever we go outside the career service, I suggest we give special consideration to retired Foreign Service officers who are still in the active age group, who resigned for reasons that do not reflect on them personally and who might now be persuaded to return to the service. We might also consider scholars from our universities who can bring a high degree of competence and understanding to areas which have been their specialties.

I hope we can avoid to a maximum degree any compromises on the necessary qualifications for political or other reasons. We have every reason to be encouraged on this point.

7. In conclusion, I would like to suggest the need for handling all these personnel decisions with the speed that is consistent with a sober, responsible and thorough consideration. So far we have been extraordinarily free from outside pressures. This has been due primarily to the high standards which Senator Kennedy has set on all recruitment; nonetheless, the fact that Congress is not yet in session is also a contributing factor.

When the Congress does return, we will begin to receive many personnel suggestions from Capitol Hill. In many cases theirs will be serious, sober recommendations which we will want to consider carefully. In other cases they will represent the Congressman's or Senator's desire to carry out a commitment by at least presenting the name.

In any event, the more expeditiously we can handle this work of selection, the less the pressures, the better the decisions and the quicker we can move on to the major task of refocusing and revitalizing American foreign policy.

APPENDIX III

Some Requirements of American Foreign Policy
Memorandum to the Secretary of State and Other
Administration Foreign Policy Officials
July 1, 1961*

Here are some questions about various elements of United States foreign policy which I believe to be in immediate need of overhauling. Although the list is in no sense complete and thoughtful men may disagree on some of the questions which I raise, I hope it may stimulate further long-range discussion.

May I take this opportunity to express my admiration for and appreciation of George McGhee and his able and dedicated Policy Planning Council. Many of the suggestions on the pages which follow are now under consideration in the Council. The purpose of this memorandum is to encourage their further efforts and to support their goals.

1. Policy in Regard to Europe

Beyond the limited recommendations of the Acheson Report on NATO, we have produced almost no new ideas on Europe's development since the proposal for a European Defense Community. The Soviets have consistently held the initiative in pressing their own conceptions of Europe's future.

The major recurrent question in regard to Europe has been: "Does the Kremlin really mean what it says in regard to Berlin?" Disturbingly little thought has been given to answering the question: "What can we Americans propose that will offer new hope for a more secure Europe if the Soviets should accept—or deprive the Soviets of the initiative if they should refuse?"

In retrospect it seems clear that we should have provided the President with some affirmative proposals for his discussion in Vienna, and that the intensified review now taking place should have started in February.

* By June, 1961, I was convinced that unless the makers of American foreign policy could be persuaded to support a radical but essential shift in foreign policy, we would sooner or later be confronted with a disaster. This memorandum, to which I referred in Chapter 26, reviews our first six months in office and suggests my personal views on how our foreign policy might be strengthened.

In this instance we may properly be indicted for the very sins for which we criticized the previous Administration—failure to grasp and hold the initiative.

In my view we need to approach our relations with Europe from a much broader perspective. We have talked a great deal about the common purposes of the Atlantic Community, but have we fully faced up to the practical demands and opportunities that these purposes imply?

In the past few years the concept of European unity has taken great strides toward fulfillment. Our ultimate interests are profoundly in harmony with this development.

Together, the 500 million people of North America and Western Europe command the world's greatest economic, political and industrial resources. How can we begin to build the basis for close integration? What can we propose now to institutionalize our common political and economic interests?

Britain now appears on the verge of moving into the Common Market. What are the possibilities for the development of associate memberships in a Common Market which might eventually include North America? Could a trading partnership of this kind gradually be transformed into a loose political confederation?

It is generally agreed that until a permanent settlement is agreed to we can give no ground in regard to Berlin. But do we or the Soviets really want to see Germany united? And if not, is there some room here for maneuver?

Disarmament appears as far away as the moon. But would a proposal for the reduction of force levels with full inspection in Western and Eastern Europe necessarily fall on barren ground? What are the possibilities for regional arms limitations within a band of territory extending from the Atlantic to the Urals?

Although the practical difficulties in such an arrangement (once suggested by both de Gaulle and Adenauer) are obvious, may it not form the basis for a proposal to the Soviet Union that might conceivably break the arms control deadlock? Would it not at least put the Kremlin on the defensive before the world?

In the absence of an arms control agreement with a realistic inspection system, can we do no more to assure the defense of Europe?

Is it really true that 500 million Americans and West Europeans cannot provide sufficient ground forces to stop the Red Army, drawn from 200 million Russians? Is there no way to utilize the tough fighting qualities of the Yugoslavs in the defense of Europe?

If war should come, have we taken adequate account of the impact on our communication lines of the deep political divisions within France and Italy, divisions born largely of the appalling and continuing gap between rich and poor, and dramatized by Communist minorities in each country that make up more than 20 percent of the electorate? And if the Communists can muster one out of four votes under conditions of nearly full employment, what will happen when these countries face a full-blown depression?

I have the utmost respect for Foy Kohler and his able colleagues in the Bureau of European Affairs. However, it seems to me it is essential that we find some way to bring fresh minds and energies to bear on our policies in regard to Europe.

II. *Policy in Regard to Africa*

In Africa one prophecy, at least, can be made with confidence: In the years ahead, the continent will continue to seethe with internal conflicts and revolutionary changes.

Our primary objective should be to keep Africa outside the Sino-Soviet bloc. This may best be assured by the neutralization of much of the continent.

Although a great deal of flexibility and restraint will be required, the currently changing attitudes in Ghana, Guinea and Mali show what can be achieved through such a strategy.

The region south of the Congo presents a particularly explosive problem. Here serious outbreaks of violence are virtually inevitable in the next few years.

The Portuguese attempt to maintain their rule is almost certain to fail. The course of events in Mozambique is liable to repeat the situation in Angola.

It is fantastic that the weakest and most backward nation in Europe should continue to stress its "rights" to govern ten million Africans whom it has exploited, abused, whipped and enslaved for more than four hundred years. Even more fantastic are its demands for American support in this impossible enterprise.

Salazar may be expected to apply increasing pressure on us. We will be told that the Azores are essential to the defense of Berlin, that we cannot turn our back on our NATO ally in a critical period, that the Portuguese in Europe are more important than the Africans in Africa, and that the upheaval there is due to the Communists in any event. Will we stand up to this pressure?

Southern Rhodesia may soon be moving toward a racial crisis. There are few who doubt but that the Republic of South Africa will blow up in due course. When this occurs, will we be able to say that we took every practical measure to prevent or temper the holocaust?

Can the UN be effective as a direct operating trustee in further African crises? What has been learned from the Congo experience? Is some other political instrument available?

These clearly predictable problems deserve a greater measure of our own attention.

III. *Policy in Regard to Latin America*

In Latin America, prior to the setback in Cuba, President Kennedy had taken a bold and promising initiative. It is now essential that we follow through on this beginning, that we prevent the Castro irritant from throwing us off balance, and that we avoid an impression of obsession with the Cuban situation.

Political agreements with the nations of Latin America on hemispheric security will involve some compromise on our part. The best likelihood for such agreements lies not in a rehashing of the Cuban situation, or in pressure on our OAS associates to accept our interpretation of what has occurred there in the last two years, but in the development of political machinery that can effectively combat further hemispheric intrusions or aggression by Cuba or any other nation.

The danger in Cuba, as I see it, lies not in the newly acquired MIG's but in the possibility that this small island with its ready-made system of docks, power plants, railroads and other basic infrastructure will be used by the Soviets to perpetrate a gigantic economic and political fraud.

On the existing economic base a substantial but manageable economic investment could result in rapidly expanding living standards and a Communist showcase that could deeply impress other Latin-American peoples. The fact that this miracle was made possible by Cuba's small population and existing capitalist-built infrastructure, which could not easily be duplicated in less favored nations, would not be understood.

The creation of vigorous Latin-American nation-states impervious to Communism will require much more governmental assistance than is now contemplated, plus increased private investment by American businessmen.

We should consider techniques by which the U.S. Government may help to guarantee such investment. We must also consider commodity agreements on a really adequate scale for stabilizing the prices of raw materials.

Yet an increase in industrial production and the easing of the fluctuation in the raw material markets will not in themselves create viable economies. An equally pressing need is for a sweeping redistribution of wealth, with special emphasis on the two-thirds of the people who live on the land.

This requires that assistance go directly to the rural as well as the urban people. It calls for tax systems based on an ability to pay, taxes that are really collected. It calls for land reforms, for control of luxury imports, less graft and special influence, for a greater sense of dignity and justice.

The development of a special division within the AID to deal with rural problems in Latin America and elsewhere on an *integrated* basis should be seriously considered.

This should enable us to bring together a staff of specialists in total rural development—land reform, low interest credit, better seeds, school and road building, public health, improved local government, and internal security based on a local militia with the will to defend the new economic and social gains of the community.

The challenge to American policy-makers in Latin America can be simply stated: Can we muster the administrative tools and personnel competent to help create a democratic rural revolution in depth? Above all, can we persuade the Latin-American governments of their own urgent responsibility for more competent planning and a greater willingness to struggle against their own vested interests?

IV. *Policy in Regard to Asia*

The central problem we face in Asia is the existence of Communist China. China is the one nation that can endure an all-out nuclear war without sacrificing its existence. To assume that our present relationship with China can be stabilized along existing lines is folly.

The threat of Communist China is threefold:

First, it embodies the evangelistic zeal of Marxism-Leninism; a zeal that, in its bellicose Chinese expression, professes no fear of nuclear war.

Second, Communist China embodies the recurrent force of Chinese imperialist expansionism, a force that has often probed the extremities of Asia throughout history, and which is now refueled by a vigorous Chinese nationalism.

Third, modern China represents a classic "have-not" situation of the prewar Japanese and German variety. The arable land of China is grossly inadequate to meet the agricultural needs of her growing population, while bordering on China are weak nations, relatively uncrowded, that possess the very resources which China needs so urgently.

Together, these three aspects of Chinese expansionism make China a paramount threat to all the nations on its periphery. The most vulnerable and inviting objective for Chinese conquest, however, is Southeast Asia with its great Mekong and Irrawaddy river systems, its rich abundance of rice and oil, of land, water and sun, and its relatively low ratio of people to land.

In the years immediately ahead, our two chief aims must be to find effective methods, first, to contain China's military potential, and second, ultimately to relieve China's food requirements and thereby to release her pent-up energy and hostility through channels other than conquest.

On the periphery of China, we have heretofore based our military position on nations almost wholly lacking in the essential elements of power—not only in resources and industrial potential but, in several cases, in the willingness of their people to fight for the U.S.-supported reactionary societies that currently exist there.

The problem of Laos is not an isolated phenomenon. Under the best of circumstances South Korea, Taiwan and the nations of Southeast Asia provide an unreliable barrier to Chinese expansionism.

Our current defense structure—SEATO and the bilateral pacts—is adequate in this region only if Mao Tse-tung and his associates are considerate enough to limit their military pressure to our sharply restricted capacity, at the end of a ten-thousand-mile supply line, to contain that pressure with orthodox weapons.

Should China choose to move vigorously into Southeast Asia under present circumstances, we would face two alternatives: either an all-out response with the full use of nuclear weapons; or a humiliating retreat from our sweeping commitments to the defense of Asia.

The ugliness of these alternatives underscores the urgent need for a more creative effort to build a new power balance in Asia. Such a balance, capable of discouraging Chinese expansion, must be anchored in the two major non-Communist Asian power centers—India and Japan.

I do not suggest that this balance can easily be brought about. On the contrary, it may prove to be politically impossible.

If this should be the case, I can see no way to avoid a nuclear war or a precipitous and humiliating withdrawal from Asia in the next five to ten years.

This helps frame the crucial questions: Will India come to see that a Chinese move into Southeast Asia will mean the fall of Burma and direct, overwhelming pressures on India's frontiers? Can Japan be persuaded that Chinese occupation of Southeast Asia will further imperil Japan's vital markets and trade routes, and eventually turn her into a Chinese satellite?

I do not know the answers. But I do know that no more urgent task faces

American diplomacy than the creation of a new Asian power balance solidly based on these hard realities.

In pursuit of this objective our approach should be restrained and tactful. Neither India nor Japan can be expected to move into a formal alliance with us. Yet each must be encouraged to recognize its own stake in the containment of China, the limitations of American power in dealing with this danger, and the consequent necessity for the major non-Communist African powers to take the initiative in "guaranteeing" the security of Asia against China's aggressions (as did the United States in regard to the Holy Alliance and Latin America through the Monroe Doctrine) with the tacit support of American air and naval power remaining in the background (in the role of the British fleet).

In South Asia, India's relations with Pakistan must undergo fundamental constructive change. An Indo-Pakistani-sponsored Monroe Doctrine for South and Southeast Asia with the tacit support of Japan and with increasing acceptance from the nations of the area may ultimately substitute for the present wobbly SEATO arrangement.

While pursuing the immediate objective of containing Chinese military expansionism in Asia, I believe that American policy must simultaneously seek some means gradually to relieve the pressures that are created by China's food shortages.

Is it not folly to assume that a chronically food-deficient China can be anything but expansionist and dangerous?

This suggests a key question: Within the next decade can the agricultural capacity of the United States, Canada and Australia be brought to bear on this situation in a way politically acceptable to the Chinese Communists? As a *quid pro quo,* could the Peking Government be persuaded to accept Red China's present boundaries?

At present the answer appears impossibly negative. But time, patience and hard logic may combine to change this situation. Where can we begin to make a start?

In the meantime we will continue to face some serious dangers in regard to the Nationalist Government on Formosa—dangers which I do not believe we have adequately taken into account.

If we seriously intend to release ourselves from the straitjacket which has characterized our Far Eastern policies in the last several years, we must assume that explosive pressures will be generated in Taipei which may take any one of several forms.

For instance, it would be a mistake to dismiss the recent CIA reports of a Nationalist Chinese effort to invade the mainland sometime during the next six months.

The Nationalists are capable, of course, of a substantial initial move, with their present petroleum supplies adequate for several days.

This would confront us with an immediate decision of the utmost complexity. If we provided support, we would face a major war; if we held back, the Nationalist effort would almost certainly fail for lack of supplies.

In that case we would be charged with letting down an ally who was said to be on the edge of a massive victory. It would be hard to imagine a more critical political predicament.

There is also the possibility of a *coup d'état* on Formosa which would depose the Generalissimo and attempt to turn Taiwan over to the government in Peking. Although this is not likely, it cannot wholly be dismissed.

It is essential that we start now to plan our response to such possible developments.

v. *Policy in Regard to the Middle East*

Although the Kuwait crisis has rippled the surface, the Middle East in general has been reasonably calm in recent months. Indeed there have been some positive gains, among them the development of sharp differences between the U.A.R. and the Soviet Union. Although it would be a mistake to overstate these differences, Nasser appears to have drifted into a more neutral position.

However, the basic problems which threaten the stability of the Middle East remain. The demands of the great bulk of the people, who are wretchedly poor, are largely unmet and their frustrations increase correspondingly.

Serious mistakes were made by the previous Administration in dealing with this critical area.

For instance, in the spring of 1955 when the Soviets were pressing for a summit meeting at Geneva, rumors developed that the Czechs were about to supply Egypt with major shipments of arms. If we had conditioned our attendance at Geneva on an assurance that these arms shipments would not be made, some kind of arms embargo might have been negotiated.

This opportunity was neglected, and the Czech equipment began to arrive on the docks of Cairo, less than six weeks after the Geneva conference had closed.

Another opportunity presented itself after the Suez crisis in 1956. A call for an arms embargo at that time would have frozen the situation in a shape favorable to both us and the Israelis.

It is also possible that strong pressures behind a Middle East Development Corporation in that fluid period might have been effective. Although this idea was proposed at that time by Bill Fulbright, Hubert Humphrey, myself and several others, and was considered by the Administration, nothing came of it.

This is now water over the dam. But has the time not come to examine our relations with the Middle East in much greater depth?

Is there no way to bring the oil resources of the Middle East to bear on the incredible poverty that exists there on a more integrated basis? Is it really impossible to work out an agreement on arms ceilings which would not immobilize our efforts in regard to Turkey?

Although the answers to these questions may be negative, I do not think we have yet made an adequate effort.

vi. *The Question of Allies, Client Nations and Independents*

When a nation which the Soviet Union has wooed expresses a preference for "neutrality," the U.S.S.R. suffers a defeat, and a victory may be chalked up for freedom. Slowly, we have come to recognize this fact; at least, we no longer press all nations to choose sides.

However, we still regard neutralism as less than our highest aim for other nations. If Burma and Cambodia should come out strongly "on our side," we would be enormously pleased.

Yet can it not be argued that the American presence in such nations acts as a lightning rod that adds fire and effectiveness to Chinese propaganda? In some ways may it not weaken the strength of the local government in its battle against Chinese without and Communists within?

In this regard, we should particularly consider the example of Burma. Here is an apparently weak and unstable nation, with a long common frontier with Communist China, that has nonetheless been able to put down seven separate internal rebellions in ten years.

This was possible in large measure because none of these rebellions were aided and abetted by the Communist Chinese.

Had we been heavily and directly involved with the Burmese Government, the Chinese would have been handed a convenient "imperialistic" target, and it is fair to assume that Burma would have been faced with formidable and very likely overwhelming pressure from the north.

In the current global conflict, nations large and small can be most appropriately divided into three groups:

1. *Allies*. In a realistic sense these are limited to those with a similar stake in democratic societies (Canada, Britain, etc.); those who for reasons of their own are fearful of or antagonistic to the Soviet Union (for example, the Turks); and those whose geographical position makes them of special importance to us if war should come.

2. *Client Nations*. These we might define as states whose independence is important to us but who are unable to stand on their own feet (Jordan, South Korea, etc.).

3. *The Independents*. These would vary greatly in their attitudes and views. Many of them, but not necessarily all, would pursue policies of neutralism—a situation which, in most cases, operates in our interest and contrary to the interest of the Soviet Union.

Our primary objective in every part of the world should be the emergence of vigorous, independent nation-states. The public commitment of such states to a direct Cold War association with the U.S. is much less important than their commitment to their own development and freedom. Vigorous national independence may serve our objectives as well; rarely does it serve those of the Russians.

Considerable work has already been done by Policy Planning on this and related subjects.

VII. *The Need to Strengthen Our Standards of Foreign Aid*

In Asia, Africa, the Middle East and Latin America, we now have an unparalleled opportunity to make a fresh start on the basis of thirteen years' experience in foreign aid programs.

We have no better instrument, potentially, for associating ourselves with the constructive, progressive forces of the world and for thwarting, blunting and deflecting the forces both of feudalism and of Communism.

Yet we have not yet put that instrument to its fullest use.

What is required now is a powerful new determination that our aid must go to those countries that are best able to use it with effectiveness. In establishing this standard we must gradually but firmly disassociate ourselves from the perpetuators of social injustice.

We generally agree that this is our intention. The new legislation will require it. But are we really prepared to meet the heavy forces that will continue to press us toward expedient decisions in support of the status quo?

In much of the world today the choice facing the people involves three possibilities: the old feudal status quo, varieties of fascist dictatorship, or Communism.

It is imperative that in each case we provide and publicize our own democratic alternative; that we spell out our proposals to the nations' leaders, and make known where we stand to the people in the market place, the universities and in rural areas where most of them live.

In spelling out such choices on a country-by-country basis, we will be taking the first step toward the creation of a new non-Communist world community and not simply a formal alliance of nations of varying stages of antagonism to the Soviet Union and of willingness to do our bidding.

This will require us to blueprint a course of proposed action in each underdeveloped country that embodies programs for land reform, rural credit, agricultural extension, public health, roads, austerity taxation, resource development and literacy; all contributing toward the creation of a more just society that encourages individual participation in the process of national development.

It also requires us tactfully to inform the people of that country of the reforms which we advocate, so that they may associate us with liberal democratic change, not simply with negative anti-Communism.

One objective should be a free-world community, with a growing stake in independence, to which we can offer some dramatic economic advantages: commodity agreements, economic aid, loans, technicians and favorable trade relations on a scale that meets their needs.

VIII. *The Need, in the Meantime, for a Firm, Patient and Sophisticated Approach to the Soviet Union*

We are now moving steadily toward a crisis in regard to Berlin and Germany. The next few months will profoundly test our wisdom, our patience and our nerve.

I believe we should accept this challenge as an opportunity, not simply to reassert our position in Berlin, but to open up the whole question of Germany, Central Europe, the reduction of military force levels in a broad area, covering both Western Europe and Western Russia, and indeed all questions that threaten the peace.

There is a possibility that the situation in the months ahead will develop to a point where the social, cultural and economic contacts which have been gradually established with the U.S.S.R. may be jeopardized.

However, if the atmosphere permits it, I believe we should continue to do all we can to cultivate increased cultural, social and political contacts with the Soviet leaders and people.

We should also explore ways to involve the Russians in the long-term containment of Communist China. Clumsy overt efforts to create a Sino-Soviet split will be inevitably self-defeating. But we should seek a rational basis for conversations with the Russians on the common problem we share in preventing a Chinese explosion that would involve us both in war.

Finally, if circumstances permit, we should seek every opportunity to stress to the Soviets the inherent dangers of their obsession with secrecy. Because we have so little real knowledge of Soviet capabilities, we are forced to prepare for the worst. This escalates the arms race and increases the danger of war by miscalculation.

IX. *The Need Better to Inform the American Public and the Congress on Foreign Affairs*

The key to an effective U.S. foreign policy is not only abroad but here at home. Many of us accept the need for drastic changes in the thrust and emphasis of our foreign relations. Yet many of us have been persuaded that the American people will not permit us to do what is required to create a more rational world.

Faced with this conflict, we rationalize away the requisites and tell ourselves that we can somehow make do with policies that largely ignore the thrust and potential of China and that make us appear ready to settle for the status quo in most areas, with a few mild concessions to human aspirations elsewhere.

This, I believe, is the central challenge. What a grim joke it will be if the history books record that the people of a great nation dedicated to free speech and communication failed to appreciate or understand the quite obvious forces which destroyed it.

In dealing with the American public we must strive to demolish some lingering dangerous clichés that persist among a small but influential minority of our people. The most dangerous of these is the theory that our nation must ultimately choose between going to war to "solve the Soviet problem" or withdrawing from world affairs to let nature take its course.

It is difficult for impatient Americans to realize that for some questions in world affairs there are no immediate answers. We cannot control the forces that are moving mankind; but within limits we can learn to shape them, to cushion them and often to guide them into safer channels.

This calls for a mature awareness of our irrevocable commitment to rational dealing with other nations and to the relentless pursuit of peace. We can afford neither to strike out recklessly nor to run away.

In the months immediately ahead, this will require of us a sharply improved public information effort. At present, the amount of military information and propaganda from the Pentagon and the foreign policy information from the State Department are in the ratio of twenty to one.

It is my opinion that most Administrations traditionally have tended to underestimate the public's capacity for understanding and its willingness to support realistic foreign policies once the way has been pointed with clarity by strong executive leadership.

In closing, may I add that there are two ways for the State Department to deal with the President. One is to find out where we think he is going and to help him get there.

The other is to determine what we think is right for him to do, and then vigorously and thoughtfully to present our case, even though he may disagree with it and even though our views may on occasion bring us into conflict with the Pentagon and other agencies.

This latter approach is, I believe, the only responsible course.

In the next few years the chips are down. We move towards a series of historic decisions which may decide the course of events for generations to come. One of the most critical lies just ahead in regard to Berlin.

It is possible although unlikely that the outcome may be war—in which case there will be little left with which to concern ourselves.

It is also possible that we will successfully surmount the challenge and emerge from the clash of national wills with our status in Europe unweakened but having sacrificed in large measure our relations with the emerging peoples of the southern hemispheres under pressure from our more reactionary allies and supporters.

Finally, we may emerge stronger in our relations with Europe, tested in the face of the gravest of Soviet challenges, having successfully reaffirmed our belief not only in the dignity but also in the *capacity* of free men to create a more rational world.

APPENDIX IV

Letter to Adlai Stevenson in Paris, July 23, 1961 *

The Honorable Adlai Stevenson
American Embassy
Paris, France

DEAR ADLAI:

I was grateful for your telephone call; also for your letter with its warm reassurance. I would have given a great deal if you had been in Washington when this nasty business developed. I badly needed someone with your background and experience whom I could trust and with whom I could talk frankly. I am leaving on Monday, the 24th, for Lagos, and shall not be back until the 12th of August. This means that we will again miss connections. For this reason I thought it might be useful for me to outline in detail what has occurred, with my own rather uncertain interpretations of its implications and its origins.

As to the latter, I can only guess. On no occasion in the last six months has there been the slightest suggestion of warning from the President, Dean Rusk or anyone else. Nor, incidentally, did anyone have the courage to attach his name to any of the personal attacks, which were authorized by "high Administration authorities," "White House sources," etc.

Most of our mutual friends believe it originated with and was masterminded by the same factions against whom we fought in the Democratic Advisory Council.

In early December when I accepted the post of Under Secretary, I did so, as you know, with some reservations since the functions of this office had never been clearly defined.

However, recent news stories which suggested that I am not interested in administration missed the point entirely. Indeed, it was my belief that the State Department organization was inadequate and clumsy and that my years

---

* This letter to an old and warm friend, to which I referred in Chapter 27, accurately reflects my feelings over the attacks which began in July, 1961, on my position as Under Secretary, and about what I felt were the underlying causes.

619

of administrative experience would enable me to help greatly to improve it that led me to take a job which otherwise had little appeal.

From the outset I was anxious *not* to appear to be in competition with the Secretary for public recognition. As Ambassador to the United Nations it was necessary and inevitable that you would be prominently in the public eye. As Secretary, Dean also had a major role to play in publicizing and explaining foreign policy. I felt that it was essential that I help build up his primary role and presence, and this I have earnestly tried to do.

For this reason I held no press conferences (except a few backgrounders), made only two television appearances and only three relatively unpublicized speeches in six months.

May I add that this was a fundamental error. Anyone who has been in public life as long as you and I cannot wish himself out of it. For this reason it is a mistake for him ever to be more than ten feet from a microphone through which he can reply to whatever public criticism may be made of his actions.

In any event, I managed to stay out of the newspapers from the time I went through my Senatorial hearings with the usual questions about "two Chinas" until early May, when a single sentence in *Time* accused me of leaking the story of a difference of opinion on the Cuba fiasco (which was totally false), and an equally brief note in *Newsweek* reported that Dean and I were having "personal differences" because I allegedly insisted on discussing policy questions directly and privately with the President. (The first time I have talked with him alone since breakfast at his N Street home in late November was last week at the White House.)

No one paid much attention to these stories until Charles Bartlett of *News Focus* and the Chattanooga *Times* picked up the latter as the basis for a Sunday column and embellished it with a lot of petty hearsay to the effect that I was being criticized by members of the Foreign Service for my policy views.

The night his story ran, a member of the White House staff at a party in Georgetown asserted, "completely off the record," that "someone in the State Department has to go. It cannot be Rusk. So it will have to be Bowles." Joe Alsop's wife was there, along with several others, and from then on the rumors from "highly placed sources" started flying fast.

I immediately asked to see the President, who, while expressing his disappointment about the news stories, asked if I would consider taking an embassy abroad.

This is a luncheon which I shall never forget, and not because of its implications in regard to my future. In the first place, I have never heard the President talk as thoughtfully and passionately on foreign affairs. He said precisely the things you and I have been advocating for years, and he said them well.

He then expressed his deep disappointment at the failure of the State Department effectively to translate his views into action. He went on to say that changes must be made, and since it was generally assumed that the Under Secretary was in charge of administration, I was the logical one to change.

Since I have spent most of my waking hours for six months trying to create an administrative apparatus that would do precisely what the President wants done, I was in a somewhat baffling dilemma.

It seemed to me that the first thing to do was to help him to see what was missing and why, leaving my own future role for later consideration. So I suggested that I come back on Monday to talk in greater detail. I added that I was not interested in an embassy.

This was on Wednesday, July 12. During the next three days all hell broke loose and the most incredible stories came flying through the air, all based on the utterances of nameless authorities and all adding up to the prophecy that I was about to be eased out of the State Department.

Inevitably, these tactics aroused strong reactions from our mutual friends here in Washington and elsewhere. At dinner on Saturday at our home, Soapy Williams and Orville Freeman agreed that I should not allow myself to be pushed quietly aside since the real conflict had nothing to do with my role in administration but rather the positions I had taken in regard to Cuba, Laos, Angola, Berlin and other policy questions.

Some of the stories from "highly placed sources" clearly came from conservative Democratic political circles, i.e., although I had supported Kennedy, it was alleged that I had refused to help him defeat Hubert Humphrey in the Wisconsin primary (one of the conditions on which I agreed to work for Kennedy was that at no time would I take any action which was in open conflict with your interests or Hubert's, and Jack thoroughly understood this); that I had failed to discuss the Democratic platform with Jack or his staff people and that this had forced him to accept liberal planks to which he was deeply opposed (not only did Jack see the platform, but so did Sarge Shriver and Bob Kennedy, and all of them made good suggestions).

Other news stories during and after the weekend came from friendlier newsmen who were alarmed by the widespread press gossip of my impending "ouster."

Most of the flak, however, reflected the same old battles that you and I have been dealing with for years involving differing views on Europe and the southern continents.

In my talk with the President on Monday, July 17th, he again made excellent sense on foreign policy. And again he showed the same lack of understanding of *why* he was not getting the kind of performance he should get out of the State Department, and the same unawareness of the primary role of the Achesonians in the effort to push me out.

It was agreed, however, that the situation should remain exactly as it had been, that I would leave on my trip, and that he would make a clear statement to the press that would restore the basis for a constructive, working relationship.

However, the statement issued late that afternoon by the White House press people said that my resignation was not "currently expected," and naturally, the stories began all over again to the effect that this was a papered-over agreement, good only until the situation blew over. When the newspapers the next morning continued this refrain, I told Dean Rusk that it was impossible for me to continue unless the President cleared up the confusion. This the President did to my satisfaction at his Wednesday press conference. I came back to the office that morning.

So much for the developments themselves. Now a few comments on the basic problem—the Department.

Any thoughtful observer knows that a great many good things have been done in the last six months, many of them associated with your excellent operation in and around the United Nations. However, the President is wholly right in saying that we have missed the boat badly in other areas.

Our Latin-American operation, for instance, is extraordinarily weak. In the Far East very little has actually come through in the way of improved policy. (And we may soon pull back from that.) In Europe we have been guilty of failing to create a fresh position on Berlin and Central Europe which would have allowed *us* to take the initiative before Khrushchev made his demands at Geneva, and therefore there has been continued fumbling in trying to come up with an adequate response to *his* challenge.

As I see it, there are two fundamental reasons for our difficulty.

1. In my opinion, the whole process of policy-making in the Department is wrong and must be fundamentally changed. Instead of being formed by the people at the top, it is formed in large measure in the lower levels.

Thus if we want a new policy in regard to a critical situation in a certain area, the appropriate desk puts together a set of recommendations, which gradually rise up through the bureaucracy, gathering initials at each stage of their progress, usually at the expense of various compromises.

Finally, having been fought over for some time, the paper arrives at the office of the Secretary and Under Secretary, who have little or no knowledge of the compromises which have been made, much less of the alternatives. The next step is a meeting preparatory to a National Security Council meeting at which there is a discussion of the recommendations around the table, dominated by people who are already totally committed to the paper at question.

At this point, there is very little to be done except to knock the paper down and start over or to accept the paper as it is, with moderate amendments. This is the heart of our difficulties, as I have learned from hard experience in recent months.

Last February, for instance, I was determined to see us get a head start on Berlin so that the President would have a solid position before the inevitable spring showdown. I first tried to work through the Policy Planning staff with George McGhee and his assistants. However, Policy Planning ran into a barrage of objections and foot-dragging from the European Bureau, and after three or four attempts, their efforts were smothered.

I then tried to open up the subject directly through my staff assistant, Charlie Rogers, but at the end of three or four weeks he came back bloody and baffled, and at about that time Laos and Cuba hit us and the effort died out.

Another example is Haiti, for which I have been trying to shape a new policy since last February. I am going away now with the job not yet completed, having run into a solid wall of people who insist that the situation is impossible, that nothing can be done about it and that it is foolish to try.

The fresh, new policies which are so desperately needed should be made from the top down, and not from the bottom up. If the subject is Germany, Dean Rusk, you, perhaps Foy Kohler, Abe Chayes and I should spend a leisurely evening together early in the game and talk over in general terms the implications of the German problem and the various policy possibilities. The more promising ones should then be assigned to task forces, using not only the Bureau of European Affairs, but also Policy Planning, and possibly one or more outside groups. Able staff assistants should then be given the responsibility of following through, for keeping the top executives informed of the progress and for warning us when the progress is bogging down or moving up dead-end streets.

Through this system the ideas and direction would start where they should start—at the top of the Department with the President's chosen top executives, and then move down to the specialists and technicians, who have their own essential roles to play. Until we start to operate on some such basis, the State Department will continue to fail to satisfy the President's very proper demands on it.

2. The second source of failure in the State Department involves people. On December 18th I wrote a letter to Dean Rusk in which I strongly urged that we bring in able outside people to head all the bureaus of the State Department. In those few instances when this appeared unwise or impractical, I suggested that outsiders with a fresh view and perspective be introduced as deputies.

The purpose, of course, was to make sure that our policies are controlled by able individuals who understand and believe in the policies which the President, you, Hubert Humphrey, Bill Fulbright, I and others have been strongly advocating for so many years.

I felt then and I feel increasingly certain now that you cannot take individuals, no matter how able or honest, who have been working on the narrow, sterile policies which have been in effect throughout much of the Eisenhower era and expect them to understand, support and administer the new emphasis and the changes which we all agree are required.

In every bureau where new people have been introduced—people who see foreign policy in the same terms as the President, you, I and others—we have a greatly improved operation. Where fresh blood has *not* been introduced, we have varying degrees of sterility and a stubborn opposition to change.

Harlan Cleveland and Dick Gardner, for instance, have brought a new freshness and vigor to the Bureau of International Organizations. Phil Coombs has brought a new perspective into the Bureau of Educational and Cultural Affairs. Abe Chayes has invigorated the Legal Adviser's office. Roger Hilsman and Tom Hughes have performed an equally important function in Intelligence and Research.

The same effect has been achieved in the Administration Bureau, through a single individual—Roger Jones—who spotted two extremely competent career people who for years have been fighting losing battles for fresh policies and to whom we gave new authority.

In the geographic bureaus, Soapy Williams has brought a new vigor and new direction to African Affairs. He has been greatly helped by his able deputy, Wayne Fredericks, with experience in Africa and a clear understanding of the forces which are being generated there.

Phil Talbot has also performed ably in Near East and South Asian Affairs, although he urgently needs a strong new deputy on the Middle East, where we have simply been reiterating old thoughts and policy.

However, in the bureaus of Europe, the Far East and Inter-American Affairs, we have introduced almost no new blood. Indeed, the only exceptions are Tom Finletter, who, in NATO, has little influence on over-all European policy, and Morales-Carrión in ARA, who has largely been shunted aside.

In these key bureaus, where unhappily, all our crises have occurred, we have skilled professionals, men of great honesty and integrity, who, however, find it virtually impossible to understand, much less to effectuate, the new policies which Kennedy is trying to put into effect, and which we have supported for so many years.

Another crucially important post, of course, is that of Deputy Under Secretary for Political Affairs.

could be remedied. By changing only three or four top people (promoting them to embassies, on which they would look with great relief), by the addition of six or seven able young deputies from the outside who have experi-

The real tragedy of our present situation lies in the ease with which it ence in the area and who would bring to it a fresh point of view, plus a process of policy-making which moves ideas from the top down rather than from the bottom up, and finally with four or five staff assistants for the Secretary and myself to see that the policy direction set by the President, the Secretary, you and myself is actually carried through, we could vastly improve the performance of the State Department and give the President what he is seeking.

In spite of this experience, I continue to have a high regard for Dean Rusk. Although no one man can be expected to have *all* the attributes needed in that job, he has a high percentage of them. As I see it, there are two principal weaknesses, both of which could largely be overcome with our help.

First of all, as we both know so well, Dean is not easy to communicate with, and since it is hard to know what he is thinking, barriers are set up against the kind of free discussion and coordinated action which is sorely needed.

Second, I believe he does not fully accept the limitations of "The Department" itself. The Foreign Service is full of able men. However, it is folly to expect many FSO's to administer policies which differ sharply in emphasis, and in some cases in substance, from those of the last Administration, to understand what the new President is trying to do, and to help him to switch the focus of our foreign operations.

I should add one pertinent fact: namely, as you undoubtedly know, that the large-scale staffing of assistant secretaryships by FSO's is a phenomenon of the post-Wriston era—and by no means an unmixed blessing.

My own position remains unclear, and I will appreciate all you can do to help me think it through. I would prefer to stick in my present post, but only if the President and Dean are prepared to move the people who should be moved and to change the process of policy formation. If this were done, I believe I could quadruple my effectiveness, and that the results would quickly make themselves felt in the White House.

If they are unwilling to make these changes, then I will be glad to do some reshuffling with George Ball, leaving us both in our Under Secretary positions. In that case, I would devote my major time to the development of policy on special situations, such as the Middle East, Southeast Asia, northeast Brazil and other areas, to work more closely with the Policy Planning group, and to apply a generous amount of my time to the badly needed task of interpreting foreign policy in this country and abroad.

Of one thing I am sure: In view of the attacks to which I have been subjected, I cannot accept any change that will be interpreted as a demotion.

This is not simply a matter of personal pride. Unless I carried the title of Under Secretary, I would be substantially less effective in what I do or say both overseas and in Washington. Unless Dean and the President understand this point, I may be able to make a bigger contribution outside the Department.

Adlai, forgive me for this long letter, but I did want you to have the full story, particularly because the group who have misled the President in such an extraordinary way about me have no greater regard for you.

With my warmest regards,

Sincerely,
CHET BOWLES

APPENDIX V

Random Musings about Chester Bowles
and the Department of State
by Samuel W. Lewis, May 26, 1963 *

At bedrock was a fundamental difference between Bowles and Rusk on the philosophy of executive management. Rusk is by background and bent a "staff man" who believes in using the organization, in trusting the experts who make it up, and in getting the organization to function smoothly by cleaning up lines of authority and responsibility. He also is a basically modest person, very conscious of the limited power of men to alter broad courses of events.

Bowles from his earliest experience with government (OPA) has been dissatisfied with organizations as they were when he found them, impatient with the career staff's endemic caution, and convinced that organization charts mean little in and of themselves. Rather, to him the key to executive management is the recruiting of a group of top-level people wholly sympathetic to the broad policy goals and concepts of the top man. Given the right key men, Bowles believes the organization and its charts will follow. He then is ready to rely heavily on delegation of authority, but only after this basic congruity between the top man and his chief aides has been assured. He also has faith in the power of talented men to make a real imprint on the tides of history if they boldly strike out to do so.

These two philosophies were never resolved. Bowles' view prevailed in recruiting most of our ambassadors, and in the Department for some of the "functional" bureaus, such as Cultural Affairs, but for only *Africa* and the *Near East–South Asia* among the five regional bureaus. Europe, the Far East and Latin America remained in the hands of men who had been key figures in the previous Administration's foreign policy decisions, and the strategic post of Deputy Under Secretary for Political Affairs went to a careerist, U. Alexis Johnson, after Bowles had unsuccessfully pressed for an outsider. Rusk's confidence in the careerists, especially in men from the career ranks

* These "Random Musings," to which I referred in Chapter 28, were first shown to me as I began this book in 1969. They present an independent analysis of the problems which developed between Dean Dusk and me in 1961, and were written two years later by a young Foreign Service officer who was a member of my staff.

626

with whom he had worked earlier in the Department (like Johnson), protected these areas from Bowles' broom. Latin America was a special case, however, which falls really in neither category; there the shadow of Adolph Berle's special status as head of the "Latin American task force"—though soon recognized as a bad choice for the permanent head of ARA—muddied the situation until long after the Bay of Pigs invasion, and no top man would consider the job so long as Berle was still around. By the time the Berle problem had been resolved, the Cuba fiasco had befallen, and no one in his right mind from outside could be prevailed upon to accept. So the job fell to the careerists to fill, and to ward off the importunings of Dick Goodwin at the height of his White House prestige.

The result was a top staff to a certain extent divided in its orientation, perhaps even in its initial loyalties. The frustrations must have been great on all sides. Rusk instinctively drew back from the proposals for sweeping policy change emanating from the African Bureau, while Bowles applauded. Bowles fumed at the continuation of previous policy lines in Europe and the Far East. Dean Acheson was not far from the mark in a caustic off-the-record speech he made to the Foreign Service Association in mid-1961, when he likened the Department to a medieval court, in which the King reigned but did not rule, and where powerful feudal barons exercised almost unlimited power for often contradictory ends in the various regions under their sway (e.g., the "Duke of New York," the "Viscount of Africa," etc.).

Since this situation has not changed materially over the one and a half years since Bowles moved out of the under secretaryship, it seems clear that *he* was not the basic problem. Despite the musical chairs game which has continued, there is still a lack of strong policy guidance from the *top* of the Department which might harmonize the frequently conflicting policy lines taken by the various bureaus. Rusk has chosen to be a "Special Assistant to the President for Foreign Affairs" rather than the Secretary of a large Department. He serves as an able counselor for JFK (among many), a splendid negotiator abroad and at home, and a thoughtful policy-maker on specific issues. But he has left the running of the Department's policy-making machinery and its administrative structure to others.

This is not uncommon. What is more uncommon and more debilitating, however, is his reluctance to commit himself in advance to give strong policy guidance to his subordinates. There has been, and is now, little sense of unified command in the Department. The feudal barons continue to rule their domains, striking independent treaties of alliance with one or more of the President's immediate staff to ensure favorable support from the White House, leaving the Secretary as merely one more voice in the room at the final policy debates, instead of his serving as the President's responsible deputy for foreign affairs.

Whatever were the defects of the Dulles foreign policy—and they were many—Dulles did have a strong point of view on all major issues and left little doubt down the line in the Department after the first few months of his administration as to what sort of policies he favored. This strong sense of policy direction often infuriated those below him who felt he refused to be guided by their expert knowledge. But it did have the virtue of consistency. And since Dulles' views were known and largely predictable, it made lower-level policy-making and policy implementation much easier.

Under this Administration such a coherent policy viewpoint has been hard to perceive; issues are not resolved at lower levels but are kicked up to the White House for eventual resolution. Since the eventual range of decisions there reflects the shifting balance of Washington power, not a single-minded and single-directed point of view, future decisions again must be brought back to this level for resolution. It has been rightly said that under Eisenhower you may not have thought much of the decisions, but at least once they were made they tended to stay made. Under JFK you have to get a crucial decision made not once but a dozen times. They just don't "stick." And this quality of decision-making reflects, to some degree, the "laissez-faire" philosophy of executive management espoused by DR, as well as the powerful policy direction afforded other departments such as Defense and CIA, each of whom daily challenges State for the pre-eminent voice in the making of policy on one issue or another.

One recurring dirge since January, 1961, has been that State is an administrative mess and that it needs someone to clean it up. Bowles was accused, among other things, of not having put his mind to "managing the store," as an Under Secretary supposedly should have done, but rather spending his time and energies dreaming up grandiose policies, which Rusk would not approve. There is a grain of truth here, but only a grain. Few Under Secretaries since World War II have been "store managers," and, moreover, there is a great deal of confusion as to what sort of "administration" we are talking about.

First, there is the key problem of "administering policy" in the Department, that is to say, making the day-to-day operating decisions on telegrams of instructions to our posts abroad, resolving concrete disputes between geographic bureaus and steering the world-wide diplomatic machinery. This function has almost always been in the hands of the third or fourth man in the Department—rarely in those of Number Two. The Number Two man must inevitably function largely as an alter ego for the Secretary in those innumerable meetings, discussions with foreign ambassadors and ceremonial functions which fill so much of a Secretary's time. From 1953 to 1959 the role was filled by Robert Murphy, then until 1961 by Livingston Merchant. These senior career diplomats carried out Dulles' policies and saw to it that the bureaucratic machinery implemented his wishes, and those of Eisenhower and Herter after Dulles' death. During the Eisenhower years there were four Under Secretaries: Smith, Hoover, Jr., Herter and Dillon. Of the four only Smith played anything like the "Chief of Staff" role, and that because of his wartime experience in just such a capacity.

It would have been highly unusual, therefore, had Bowles taken over this type of function. But, undeniably, the policy-management function was badly neglected during the first six months of JFK's Administration. Why? Because from the time of Merchant's departure in late January, 1961, until Alex Johnson entered on duty about May 1 as Deputy Under Secretary for Political Affairs, the key job was vacant! Raymond Hare, who had been Merchant's deputy, was lacking in the necessary bureaucratic talents. He silently slipped back overseas without leaving a ripple (to perform, however, very ably as an Ambassador in a role for which he is well fitted). Rusk and Bowles jousted cautiously about a replacement for Merchant, CB wanting an energetic outsider wholly sympathetic with the tenets of Kennedy-

Stevenson-Bowles ideas about foreign policy. Rusk wanted a career man, Alex Johnson, whom he had worked with in the Department in the late 1940's. Rusk won, but meanwhile time had gone by. Bowles had been working night and day to recruit a new breed of ambassadors, to try to bring in new and sympathetic leadership for the key regional bureaus (only partly successful), to impart a new spirit and new way of looking at many old problems to the bewildered and resentful career staffs of some of the bureaus, to serve as alter ego to a man he admired but could seldom comprehend, to persuade a cautious Rusk to undertake bold innovation while the iron was hot, and at the same time to tend to the daily policy-management chores which are a more than full-time job for anyone, even for so able a man as Livingston Merchant. Little wonder that the White House complained about State's performance from time to time.

After Johnson came on board in early May, order began to be regained, and paper again flowed more smoothly through its accustomed channels. But the harm had been done to Bowles' image at the White House.

The second type of "administration" for which Bowles allegedly was responsible is the normal housekeeping chores—budget, personnel, etc. *No* Under Secretary has ever paid very much attention to these subjects, nor has any Secretary. The housekeepers of the Department have been (since 1953) Lourie, Saltzman, Loy Henderson, Roger Jones, Bill Orrick and now Bill Crockett. Bowles took more interest in this side of management than had any of his predecessors, working closely with Roger Jones on a good many planned improvements in State's admittedly archaic administrative system. But although he often asked Rusk for full authority over this area, especially over top personnel selection, it was never explicitly granted. Neither Jones nor Bowles ever felt they had Rusk's full confidence or support in their efforts at reform—nor in fact did they. The result was halfhearted beginnings, little more. It suffices to say that Under Secretary George Ball has been far *less* of an "administrator" in the housekeeping sense, showing no interest whatsoever in this side of the job.

To Bowles "administrative management" meant getting the best top people he could find, then giving them their heads. To Rusk it meant holding down budgets, cutting off positions, paring the Department to its necessary hard core in order to reduce organizational "layering" and speed up movement of papers and decisions. Neither had, obviously, a completely satisfactory philosophy of administrative management. And Bowles' philosophy could work only if he were in the top job with a complete free hand—which he was not.

Being a second-in-command is hard for anyone; doubly so for Bowles, who had never worked for anyone else in his entire career. But he worked very hard at being a loyal deputy, trying to mesh his ebullience and activism with Rusk's contemplative, cautious pragmatism. But they really could not communicate. Bowles could never elicit Rusk's real thinking about the best approach to problems and could not stimulate with him the kind of oral "brainstorming" about broad issues which is Bowles' intellectual bread and butter. Failing to spark an oral dialogue, he fell to trying to say in memos to Rusk the things that he felt needed saying, and to ask for the policy guidance he realized was needed. Still silence. The memos, because of the frustrations, became longer; the rhetorical questions became repetitive, because no response was stimulated. There was no real meeting of minds, because Rusk kept his in some secret place. Their styles were worlds apart, and the gaps in style prevented effective communication from ever taking place. Yet I am convinced that basically they see the world in much the same light.

After Cuba there was a rapid hunt for scapegoats. The State Department was ready-made, and Bowles was ready-made. He had friends in the press who knew he had opposed the fiasco; he had something of a following in one wing of the party and was not wholly dependent on the White House for everything, an intolerable annoyance for the bright young satraps; he was "softheaded" and idealistic, a believer in the power of ideas—not a hard-headed pragmatist like the man in the White House; he was too decent and kind a person to be a good political infighter, and they knew it. So they went after him, with lots of specious arguments, and a few valid ones. They first discredited him by blaming him for all the ills of the State Department, they lulled him to sleep, they suddenly administered the *coup de grâce* while he was away for Thanksgiving.

But removing Bowles did little to improve the Department's functioning in their eyes; so then Roger Jones had to go, and McGhee and Orrick, and several others. Yet still the lack of central policy direction continues, even though the papers do flow more smoothly now thanks to an Executive Secretariat which knows well its tasks, to Alex Johnson and, now most importantly, to Averell Harriman, who begins to bring vigorous central direction to policy operations long lacking. But still the lines of authority and direction run from the White House staff to the various Assistant Secretaries. And it would be hard to contend that the Department belongs to Dean Rusk.

APPENDIX VI

*Letter to Lal Bahadur Shastri, Prime Minister of India,
from Ambassador Chester Bowles
New Delhi, India, October 17, 1964**

DEAR MR. PRIME MINISTER:

In several recent speeches you have expressed your deep interest in the welfare of the common man—his food, housing, medical facilities and employment opportunities.

It was this special emphasis on increased human rights which encouraged me to speak so frankly in our talk a few days ago on the need for a greatly increased effort in the Fourth Plan on measures to improve the living standards of the Indian masses. This letter is in response to your request for a detailed outline of my views.

Rapid economic development under any economic system requires sacrifices from the general public. No nation, unless it plows part of each year's production back into productive facilities, can achieve the kind of continuing economic growth India wants and needs for the long-term benefit of her people.

In a democracy such as India, however, where the consumers are also voters, there is a limit to how long the common man's needs can be postponed. If I read the signs correctly, these limits are now being reached, and unless economic development is more oriented toward the people's immediate needs, political protests and dissension seem likely to grow.

Under the first three plans, in addition to a fourfold increase in electric power and a major expansion in steel production and railroad modernization, many thousands of schools have been built; medical facilities have been improved; malaria has been largely eliminated; and there has been a significant expansion in the production of consumer goods.

Nevertheless, in the last decade the actual numbers of the unemployed, the illiterate and the ill-housed have also increased, and the gap has grown

---

* This letter, prepared at Prime Minister Shastri's request three months after he took office, presents my views on the need for greater individual incentives to speed economic development in India. It illustrates the unusually close relationship which quickly grew up between the new Prime Minister and me, as it had previously with Nehru.

between the living standards for which the masses of people have hoped and the direct benefits they have actually received.

In my opinion this situation can be reversed with no adverse effect on the growth of heavy industry. In other words, you do not have to choose between industrial growth and the improvement of living conditions. India is in the happy position of being able to offer its lower-income families many tangible benefits that will gratify their craving for personal improvement, stir their incentives and enlist their participation in economic development in a manner that will actually *increase* the tempo of industrialization.

Let us discuss this opportunity in terms of six major requirements: more food, more jobs, wider distribution of land, better use of capital already at hand, increased investment in human resources and population control.

I

More and Better Food. We believe that the most important single benefit that the government can offer the Indian public is more food and better-balanced diets. Since everyone agrees that more food-grain production is an urgent necessity, I shall not dwell on the need itself. However, I would like to underscore the extent to which India's food deficiency has placed a significant drag on national progress generally, including industrial development.

As long as food production lags, every increase in national income pushes up the prices of food and increases public resentment. Since rising prices necessitate added restrictions on purchasing power, investment in all sectors must be curtailed and fiscal and monetary policy, instead of being used as a major stimulant to economic growth, must be employed as a depressant.

Fortunately your government has now embarked on a positive program to reverse this situation. With additional fertilizers and pesticides, stronger and more reliable price incentives, and better extension and other agricultural services, I believe we can count on impressive early gains in agricultural production.

Our people have been working closely with your Ministry of Agriculture on many phases of your agricultural problems. If there are any additional ways in which we can help in your intensified push for increased food-grain production, please let us know.

II

More Jobs. The failure of the expanded cottage industries program to ease the problem of idle manpower has been disappointing. But the problem itself remains and must be dealt with. It seems to me essential that the Fourth Plan come boldly to grips with India's vast and growing problem of unemployment and underemployment.

In my own country during the Great Depression of the 1930's we experienced mass unemployment, idle machinery and idle capital side by side with limitless unfulfilled human needs. It was not until the early 1940's that we realized we had the power and competence to put all our able-bodied citizens to work productively and at good wages. Similarly, I believe it is now within the power of your government to achieve a massive increase in employment opportunities, both urban and rural, without inflation, and I can imagine no greater benefit that you could confer on India's millions.

In the context of India's pressing need for basic capital infrastructure the energies of jobless people represent an enormous potential asset which can be applied to the work of economic development with very little diversion of investment.

India urgently needs irrigation channels, highways, bridges, drainage ditches and canals, wells and sewage systems, schools, homes and health centers to support the growth of commerce, industry and agriculture.

While construction of this sort requires only the simplest tools and a minimum of materials, it offers employment to large numbers of workers. Thus a well-conceived public works program will allow India to capitalize on her abundant supply of labor and at the same time provide millions of under-privileged men and women with the increasing incomes and the sense of personal participation and dignity which are now denied to them.

Some observers will counter these proposals with the warning that the purchasing power generated by increased employment would lead to a run-away inflation. This concern is seriously expressed, and it deserves a serious answer. In several Latin-American countries the impact of inflation on na-tional development has in fact been crippling.

However, inflation should not be permitted to become a political bogeyman that blocks the process of economic growth. If Japan, Germany and other war-torn countries had allowed fear of inflation to dominate their postwar planning, they would still be in economic doldrums.

Inflation occurs when increasing incomes after taxes are not matched by comparable supplies of consumer goods. One way to deal with the problem is to remove the excess income by massive increases in taxes. The other is to provide a flood of consumer goods on which the excess income can be spent.

Too much emphasis on the first of these techniques condemns large sec-tions of the people to squalor, unemployment and despair, while major em-phasis on the second increases employment, raises living standards and creates an atmosphere of hope and national dedication. Moreover, the pro-duction of more consumer goods means that a normal tax rate will produce substantially increased tax income.

If the common man were urgently pressing for a flood of complex and costly consumer durables, his demands could be met only at the expense of heavy industry. However, his needs are simple and easily met from readily available resources.

Every villager would like an extra sari for his wife. There is a great need for shoes. Most rural families want tiled roofs, two or three new charpoys, a smokeless chula, better cooking equipment and a decent house.

Most of these contributions to better living can be produced with materials and production skills which are now readily at hand. Little or nothing would be required in the way of foreign exchange, and the diversion of indigenous resources from heavy industry would be insignificant. At the same time, the process of meeting these demands calls for more and more labor, which further eases the tensions and waste that characterize the present mass un-employment.

Additional goods and even more jobs can also be provided by the fuller use of existing plants and equipment and by policies that not only permit but encourage small businesses to grow into medium-size businesses. In our opinion present constraints on the growth of small labor-intensive firms make the least rather than the most of the employment and production potential of these industries. One such constraint is the bias in favor of larger firms in the allocation of raw materials.

We also believe that there are major opportunities for expanding employment in agriculture. As cultivators use more pesticides and fertilizer and make better use of increasing supplies of irrigation water to raise output, the need is for more labor, not less. In addition, the expansion of agricultural output means more jobs in the production of tools, materials and simple machinery, as well as more jobs in the marketing of agricultural output.

For all these reasons, I suggest India should radically raise its sights with respect to employment. More specifically, I suggest that the first thrust of a more adequate employment policy should be a greatly intensified program of rural public works.

Such a program conceived on an adequate national scale calls for bold experimentation and possibly some unorthodox patterns of administration. My own experience in the United States during the Great Depression and the emergency conditions of World War II suggests that sweeping new programs can often best be carried out by totally new agencies, often of a temporary nature, organized for special purposes and independent of established governmental bodies and procedures.

A staff group in our AID mission has been set to work analyzing the whole vital but diffuse subject of public works programs in India. As findings emerge from this study, we shall, of course, pass them along to your government. We are anxious to assist in the development of a dynamic rural works effort in any way we feasibly can.

III

Wider Distribution and Better Use of Land. The third great benefit that India can confer on her underprivileged majority in the rural areas is to assure every cultivator some land of his own. I believe that a major goal of the Fourth Five-Year Plan should be to provide every adult male villager either with his own land or with a job at a decent living wage. Although India has eliminated the zamindars and enacted considerable legislation to widen the ownership of the land, it is generally agreed that the implementation has not matched the breadth of the original vision.

I realize that political opposition to genuinely effective land reform is as powerful in India as elsewhere. However, it is unlikely ever to become *less* powerful and, since further land reform can contribute in a major way to a long-term political stability, we believe that the unfinished business in this area should be tackled as quickly and effectively as possible.

I would also like to stress that the demand for land is in no sense at war with the need for rapid economic development. On the contrary, the small farmer's pressing motivation is to extract the maximum from his land. Once he is assured fertilizer, adequate supplies of water, credit and rewarding prices, experience demonstrates that he will push his production to significantly higher levels. This in turn allows him to earn more income and to help provide an expanding market for manufactured goods.

There is no politically painless way to deal with this complex and controversial problem. However, the most constructive and least embittering way to meet it may be through the establishment of a progressive land tax system based on the size of the holdings. If this is coupled with generous tax incentives for new small businesses and the offer of technical assistance, many thousands of large landholders may be encouraged to shift their investments from farmland to job-producing local enterprises.

Incidentally, in my own country the technique of using the tax system to discourage those forms of capital investment which run counter to our national interest and at the same time to offer tax rewards to those that benefit large numbers of our people has proved to be a far more effective instrument in shaping our economy along constructive lines than administrative restrictions and directives.

IV

Better Use of Capital at Hand. A major reason why the energies of the common man have not been fully enlisted for economic development in India is that materials and tools, as well as machinery, have been made available to relatively few people. Meanwhile, hundreds of thousands of small businessmen who have the intelligence, skill and energy to make a major contribution to their country in terms of goods and employment have been confronted with an allocation system for scarce materials and machinery that favors the larger units. This, in turn, dulls the energies of small firms and discourages their expansion.

Although much is being done to encourage and assist small businesses, I believe that much more can be done. A whole range of promotional devices— technical assistance, managerial consulting services, improved credit and very possibly major tax incentives—can be made available to help small businesses to get established and rooted, particularly in the rural areas.

Such a development can be a major factor in creating the consumer goods necessary to soak up increased purchasing power generated by higher food prices and public construction work, while at the same time providing full-time employment for rural unemployed and part-time employment for the cultivators of modest holdings.

V

Increased Investment in Human Resources. Although increased capital investment is essential, experience indicates that a satisfactory rate of economic growth is impossible unless the people individually and in groups are caught up in the development process. It is also clear that India cannot become a modern industrialized nation with her present level of literacy and organizational and vocational skills.

This means that the common man must be aroused and equipped; he must be given new aspirations and the competence to pursue them.

I am persuaded that man himself is India's most underdeveloped resource, and that an increased investment in human resource development could pay off handsomely in more rapid economic development, including industrialization, as well as in increasing satisfaction for individual citizens.

Some of this investment will take the form of education for children, which millions of Indians prize more than they do any consumer goods; some will take the form of universally available medical services, perhaps no less prized; some the form of vocational training to open up new employment opportunities; some the form of water supply and improved sanitation, which reduce the toll of sickness and absenteeism as well as adding to the amenities of life; and some the form of improved housing facilities.

Because the latter point has so often been involved in controversy, I would like to offer my personal views in somewhat greater detail.

With the single exception of adequate food, the home in which people sleep at night is the most important influence in their lives. Better housing for the rural and urban poor alike will substantially improve their health and stamina. It will also help bring them out of their misery, open their eyes to the potentialities of life in twentieth-century India, stimulate their energies and improve their abilities.

Yet many observers still tell us that housing for the underprivileged majority is too vast a burden for the Indian Government to undertake, and in any event shortages of cement and other scarce materials make an extensive housing program a practical impossibility. In view of the miserable conditions under which tens of millions of families now live this negative reasoning seems to me wholly unacceptable.

There is no shortage of labor in India, and shortage of building materials can be dealt with effectively in two steps: first by making sure that the present supply is used to build new homes for those who need them most, and second by increasing the amount of materials that are available.

When my own country was faced with similar shortages during the war, our government postponed, through a system of priorities, any construction that did not directly serve our national objectives. At the same time, we clamped a tight limitation on the size and value of dwelling units that could be newly constructed.

If the vast quantities of building materials that are now going into high- and middle-income housing in India were devoted to really low-cost housing, five or six times as many housing units could be built from the existing supply of building materials.

Moreover, there is no reason why the present production of building materials should not be sharply increased. Cement is short today largely because the prices have been set so low that there is no incentive to raise production. We believe that a modest price adjustment would substantially increase production with only an insignificant diversion of scarce resources. At the same time, new construction techniques can sharply reduce the amount of cement that is required.

There is also a vast potential in cheap building materials such as cinder blocks which could be rapidly developed into major enterprises. Rural housing can be constructed almost entirely with locally available materials plus small amounts of coal shipped in to fire the brick kilns. A new technique enables relatively simple and inexpensive hand-powered machines to create highly acceptable building blocks out of some kinds of ordinary earth.

At present, India is thought to be building roughly 300,000 homes annually, most of them for the middle- and high-income families. If the Fourth Plan provides a high priority for the welfare of the average Indian citizen, I believe that the annual production of homes could be increased tenfold and several million more people offered employment at good wages in the process.

VI

Family Planning. What India is able to give her people in the way of expanded opportunities and greater personal dignity will be determined not only by the amount and distribution of industrial output but also by the number of people among whom it must be shared.

Progress has been made in developing effective and acceptable family planning techniques. The need now is for mass education and for the introduction of these techniques throughout India.

This is a formidable administrative challenge which, in my opinion, can be successfully met only if a special agency is established with a fully adequate budget, able leadership, outstanding personnel and the authority to move with vigor and speed.

Through a coordinated, dedicated effort of this kind, malaria in India was virtually eliminated in a decade. A similar effort in population control might well enable you to reduce your population growth to the Japanese level of one percent annually within a similar time span.

The effect on India's per capita income growth would be dramatic. For example, if your population growth rate had been held to that level during the 1950's, the advance in per capita incomes would have been nearly doubled.

VII

A New Deal for India: Food, Jobs, Land and Capital in Hand. Taking all these possibilities together, I believe that your expressed concern for the common man can be made the heart of a great new liberal, progressive, socialist —call it what you will—forward thrust in Indian developmental policy.

As a foreigner deeply committed to India's rapid economic development, I hope it may be made clear to every citizen, as well as to every interested observer abroad, that the Government of India:

I. Recognizes that every generation can directly share and deserves to share in the benefits of economic development.
II. Intends to find for every willing Indian a productive role to play in India's economic development—through jobs for each adult able and willing to work, a reasonable access to tools and materials, and land for the cultivator.
III. Recognizes that man himself is India's greatest resource and invests generously and confidently in his development.

In closing may I emphasize again that there is no need for India to choose between rapid economic growth and social justice in a free society. On the contrary, economic expansion is most rapid in those nations which provide the greatest freedom and incentive for the individual citizen.

My government and my countrymen are deeply committed to India's success as a democracy. But we believe that this success can be assured only if the welfare of the everyday Indian citizen is given a higher priority in your national planning.

I am leaving for the United States in early November for consultations with President Johnson. After you have had a chance to consider these personal thoughts I will look forward to discussing them further.

With warmest regards,

Sincerely,
CHESTER BOWLES

APPENDIX VII

"Train to Allahabad" by Steb Bowles
As told to Joanna Macy
from News Circle *Magazine, New Delhi, March, 1966**

On Christmas Eve Chet had a conference with the Prime Minister, and I had gone along to talk with Mrs. Shastri about her trip to the United States. She was eagerly looking forward to it and we spoke about the various things she might like to see and do there. She has difficulty understanding my brand of Hindi and I hers, so we talked mostly through an interpreter. But there was close feeling between us.

She would nod and smile and press my arm. You know, Indian women have very strong hands and their grip conveys an inner strength, too. We must have talked longer than we realized for there stood Chet and the Prime Minister, finished with their business.

"I don't know that my wife should accompany me to Washington," Shastri said. "It will be just a brief trip." But Mrs. Shastri just chuckled and wagged her head. And as our eyes met, I knew that she would surely get the last word on that.

As the peace talks started in Tashkent, everyone in Delhi, in the whole world, we felt, was holding his breath. On that Saturday, just before the close of the Tashkent conference, I went alone and called on Mrs. Shastri. She was looking lovely with the pallu of her khadi sari draped up, as always, over her head, just revealing the vermilion mark in the parting of her hair, and on her forehead a large red tika mark.

As usual, she received me in one of the formal official rooms of the Prime Minister's residence-office at Number 10 Janpath. Next to it, connected by a covered walkway, are their private quarters, the house that has been for years the Shastri home. As I left that day Lalita Shastri said, smiling, "Next time you come I will take you into my own home." I did not know then that it would be so soon—and so tragic.

---

* This article, to which I referred in Chapter 39, describes the journey of the funeral train which carried Prime Minister Shastri's ashes to be immersed in the Ganges. It indicates the deep emotional feeling which Indians held for this remarkable man who was hardly known outside his own country.

As news from Tashkent gave increasingly little hope that any agreement would be reached, our spirits sank. We thought of Shastri, frail yet determined, and of the terrible pressures and burdens upon him. Then Chet called me Monday afternoon and said, "He's done it! They're signing an agreement, it's coming over the ticker." The news seemed miraculous. I hung up the phone in excitement—and then had to call back to find out what the communiqué was. We all rejoiced that night.

It was four in the morning when the call came from Chet's deputy, Jerry Greene. "Steb, let me speak to Chet," and his tone instantly reminded me of that other early morning when he called to give us the news of Kennedy's assassination. And now again I heard Chet saying, "Oh no, no."

That morning we drove over together to sign the book at the Prime Minister's residence. "Won't you come and see Mrs. Shastri?" they asked. As we were taken to the private rooms, which were starkly bare and simple, I thought of the words of an Indian policeman who helped us through the crowds outside. He said: "Our Shastri was just like one of us. He was the leader of our country, but he lived like us. His house was larger, but inside it was no different from my family's home in our village in U.P."

There amidst the coming and going of family and friends and officials was Lalita Shastri, huddled in a quilt on a charpoy. She cowered there like a struck animal, dazed and hurt. Her pink sari was rumpled, her hair undone and streaming about her face; and so I would see her in her grief again and again over the next twenty-four hours.

In early afternoon we met the plane from Tashkent and the body of Shastri was taken to his residence. Crowds had been gathering there since dawn in front of Number 10 Janpath. I felt I wanted to go there again and, just like the simple Indians to whom he belonged, pay my respects to him. The thought of sweeping up in a diplomatic limousine distressed me, so I had the car drop me a block away and started walking.

The police were now trying to turn away the massive streams of people, though they still waved the automobiles through. One stopped me curtly. "No one allowed on foot here!" And a man standing nearby said, "You cannot get through to the house, you know." "I'm going to try, anyway," said I. But a few steps later another constable barred the way, ordering me off. I did not say who I was, perhaps because it seemed not right at all, and not what Shastri would have wanted, to hold off everyone but those with cars.

The fellow who had spoken up before, and who was amused by my persistence, came up to me. "See, I was right. . . . But if you really want to get to the house," he said, "we can go down that side alley. I think we can sneak through there." So off we went, a gentleman from the Congress Party joining us. They were kind and helpful. I hope I will see them again.

On the way we negotiated a four-foot wall, admittedly a bit awkward in a sari. "Why, you're even spryer than my old mother," said my guide. "How old's your mother?" "Seventy-two." "Well, I should be spryer, I'm not that old yet."

When we reached the house, I was recognized and taken to the Shastri family quarters, where the pitch of emotion was higher even than in the morning. The body of the Prime Minister was carried in. His face looked quiet, serene. I realized I had seldom seen him without his Gandhi cap. Then, to the chanting of the bhajans, he was taken out and placed on the covered walkway, to lie in state.

Now all his people of Delhi could pass and see him and the street and gates were opened and the surging, silent masses swept in. Later on in the evening I came again with friends, for it was an unforgettable scene, and I felt caught to the hearts of these people in this shared moment.

The lights and the incense burning, the growing heaps of flowers, the shuffling, shawled humanity passing with palms pressed in namaskar, and interwoven through it all the haunting bhajans being sung. Wailing, sorrowing, grieving, they reminded me, except for their stronger rhythm, of some of our Negro music, like Serena's lament in *Porgy and Bess*.

All through the long hours Lalita Shastri was beside the body of her husband and squeezing his legs as if she could give him strength, moaning and sobbing, to the point of exhaustion. One wondered she had any tears left. Supporting her were her daughters and beside her her sons and grandchildren.

The old uncle who had paid for Shastri's education was there too, dressed like a pilgrim, with a staff in his hand and wearing little round Gandhi spectacles. And the family pundit from Benares, who always wore a piece of red cloth over his head; it was he who gave all the instructions for the cremation and other rituals.

The next morning, with Hubert Humphrey in our car, we followed in the long procession through a sea of humanity down to the simple ghat by the Jumna. There we watched Hari Shastri, the eldest son, ignite the funeral pyre. Mrs. Shastri, as is customary for the widow, did not come. The next day she participated in the ceremony at the ghat where the family collected the ashes.

Then for the following ten days until the ashes were taken to Allahabad for immersion, the garland-draped urn was displayed at 10 Janpath for the streams of people who came daily and all through the nights to take "darshan" and to pay their respects. Flower sellers sat out on the street, and the garlands looked gay on the arms of people coming in. At the other gate where the visitors filed out, vendors of sweets and channa (spiced gram) had set up stalls.

Twice again I went to sit beside Mrs. Shastri, once bringing a basket of fruit for the family. I got to know them all—Hari, who is a sales manager in an automobile firm here, and his brothers, students at St. Stephen's and St. Columba's, and his sisters and their husbands and the children. And there were the old family servants, too—Ram Nath, Shastri's bearer, who had always been with him, even to Tashkent, and Bharat Singh, the peon. Again and again they told me, lovingly, untiringly, of how they had known him and how they had served him and what kind of man he was—they said it so simply, a good man. *"Bohot achcha admi tha."* We did not talk much, Mrs. Shastri and I; a chair would be brought and I'd sit beside her and she'd hold and squeeze my arm. It seemed to mean something to her to have me there, I felt that strongly.

And so I found myself asking Mr. Venkataraman, Shastri's secretary, "Is it appropriate for anyone not of the family to go with them to Allahabad?" He said immediately yes. But I went on, "I want Mrs. Shastri to think it over if she really wants me to come." Then came the message to my home: Mrs. Shastri says please to come. Thoughtfully she also invited Bimla Bissell, who works so closely with Chet and me and who had on two or three occasions visited Mrs. Shastri with me.

On Monday morning, the twenty-fourth of January, the Asthi Special stood waiting and ready at the Delhi Railway Station. By a different route from the public procession Bimla and I made our way down to the platform and found the compartment, a two-person "coupe," assigned to us. Then, as we waited near the gleaming white coach that was to carry the ashes, we heard the approaching beat of the death march.

To muffled drums there came Hari, slowly, slowly carrying the urn, the family following. Until I saw it come, I had not known one could feel so much about just a thing, an urn. And there came all the Ministers of State; Indira Gandhi was weeping openly.

On the platform stood the diplomats, too, and members of the press, and many of us there were reminded of that other occasion, just nineteen months before, when this train received the ashes of Jawaharlal Nehru. It was then a Mr. Shastri, hardly known to the outside world, who had, quietly, in tears, been in charge of the arrangements.

The white coach was bare inside except for simple sheeting on the floor, bolsters around the edges and the teakwood platform in the center where the urn stood up between two picture windows. I was asked in, and here I sat cross-legged beside a daughter of Shastri, amidst the family, while leaders of the country filed through to give their last namastes and floral tributes.

I'll never again smell marigolds without that moment coming back. Each was carrying his own grief, and I did not want to stare, but sat with head bowed like the others of the family. I watched a procession of feet go by me —President Radhakrishnan, Indira Gandhi and the others. Some barefoot and some in socks; one sock I watched had a large hole in it and all around the air was heavy with flowers and the chanting of bhajans.

Then the train started and the crowds along the platform and along the track were weeping and reaching out. The last of Shastri was leaving them, and with them I felt the beginning of a terrible finality, more even than when he was burned, and I cried. Out through the train yards filled with faces, the coach rolled and Mrs. Shastri and Hari were at their posts, beside the windows at each side of the urn, with palms pressed, acknowledging the crowds.

Never, during that whole long journey, did Mrs. Shastri turn from the waiting faces of her people. Whenever there was even the smallest group outside, she would be at the window, never sparing herself in what we sensed she felt as her last great duty to her husband. Although a compartment next to ours was available for her to go and lie down, she never left the car. We wondered how she could carry on.

During the trip bhajans were sung without a break, and in stark contrast to the chanting stood the stiff, immobile figures of the honor guard. Men of the four services stood at the corners of the platform, heads bowed, hands folded on the butts of their upright rifles.

Back in our compartment, Bim and I had a cup of coffee to brace up. Soon, some of the family and office staff stopped by; the children came, too, and we passed out cookies. They were wonderful to me; I was the only foreigner among them, yet they knew I felt part of it all.

Drinking our coffee we relaxed and chattted together and we reminisced about the man he was. Everyone near him felt Shastri was saintly, and they told how in his quiet way he could get anyone to work their hardest, do their utmost to please him. As I looked out the window, it seemed as though all the people of India were standing out there waiting and watching the train. I thought how I should be using the movie camera I had brought, but I did not want anything to come between me and these wonderful people.

At the many station stops, Shahdara, Ghaziabad, Khurja, Aligarh, Kanpur, and the rest, they waited by the hundreds of thousands, milling and crowding up to the train to see. Up they pressed, some bringing flowers, some joining in the singing of the Ramdhun broadcast from the coach, as they craned to catch sight of the urn, then bowed over praying hands. Many wept when they saw Mrs. Shastri. At each stop the offerings of blossoms and garlands were taken aboard, and some of the flowers from previous offerings, that were heaped about the urn, were given out in blessing.

Crowds of that multitude were hard to manage and the police had to shove to keep them in order and slowly moving past the coach. Messages went out from Mrs. Shastri to them, "Please be gentle." In all the crush, perilous to the point of injury, I remember most the patience of the crowds. Even when they were pressed and squeezed and almost mashed against the barriers, I saw no gesture, no expression, of irritation or complaint.

At Kanpur, where we stopped for two hours, they estimated that 200,000 poured through the station. Down a stairway they pressed, squeezing through a gate on the platform near the coach; there the incredible crush seemed even greater. On the table by the coach where the offerings of wreaths were piled, stood an officer in smart uniform with a microphone in one hand and a walking stick in the other. He would wave his stick in the direction they should move, and, exhorting, encouraging, he would shout over and over, "Bohot achcha, bohot achcha. Tik he, tik he!"

The further we went into the countryside the more intense seemed this pageant of grief and love. On the whole route I don't believe there was a soul unaware of what that coach bore. At crossings, sometimes, the train would slow down and receive the namastes of the peasants gathered there, pulled up with their carts, tongas, bicycles and camels.

Then across the countryside the train would pick up speed. We could see into courtyards and into village streets; the land was so green it was hard to believe there would be a drought. The fields of mustard were a beautiful yellow. "It is the color of spring," said a woman by my side, and we remembered that this very day in India spring begins, the day of Basant, when women traditionally put on yellow saris. But this Basant we all wore white for mourning.

As we sped by, we saw the villagers come out of their homes, standing in doorways and on mud walls and rooftops to greet the train. Each time the pattern of recognition would repeat itself; first, the excitement of suddenly identifying the car, then the reverent bowing of the head with hands held palms together, then the immediate turning to the next person to share the moment and point, as if saying, "Did you see it? Did you see her?"

Most poignant of all were the lone figures in the fields, a man standing by a Persian well, a farmer holding the reins of his bullock team: they would stop and face the speeding train and bow their heads in simple, solitary homage.

At sundown I was sitting again in the white coach, having come here several times during the day. Now, in the evening, it came more alive—more people coming in and joining in the singing of the bhajans. Many they sang were poems written by Mrs. Shastri herself over the years, and many were songs sung to her. I kept hearing the name Lalita in the chanting. And

Lalita Shastri, sitting beside me to the left of the urn and having now a respite of two hours betwen stops, closed her eyes to the music. Exhausted, she began to nod and soon her head was on my shoulder and I was holding it so she could sleep. The world went dark outside and Bim fetched my shawl and arranged it over us as we sat there in the swaying car.

By eight in the morning we pulled into Allahabad, and there I was in our tiny compartment, half into a fresh sari of Bim's; she maintained that mine was too rumpled to wear that day. "Hurry, hurry, let me help you," said a cousin of the family, coming in with a troop of children. "No woman in India ties a sari the way I do," I said impatiently. "I'll just manage by myself," and I did, in spite of the many helpful, tugging hands.

Crowds of thousands were waiting outside and lining the streets to the Sangam. A grandson ran up to me with the message that Mrs. Shastri asked me to sit with her on the truck carrying the ashes. I could hardly believe it and thought that he'd mistaken me. "Do you know who I am?" I asked the boy. "Why, yes, you're Mrs. Bowles." But I declined. I believe she genuinely wanted me, but all the onlookers would not know that and would wonder why I was there.

The Sangam, the confluence of the three sacred rivers, the Jumna, the Ganges and the invisible, mythical Saraswati, is a place of vast, sandy flats, shifting and changing. At the Kumbha Mela, just a week before, pilgrims had converged to bathe there, and some of their numbers swelled to over a million the crowds who gathered there now for the immersion of Shastri's ashes.

A short pier was built out over the water for the ceremony, the Asthi Visarjan, and joining the family there was the Prime Minister, who had flown down with Cabinet members from Delhi early that morning. Gondola-like boats were waiting for us, scores of them, all hung with flowers and their decks strewn with garlands and blossoms. It all had a holiday air as we pushed off from the banks in the morning sunshine, bumping into each other as we maneuvered about to view the immersion. Overhead helicopters were circling and small planes flew low to scatter rose petals on the water in the two traditional acts of homage. Hari Shastri stepped to the edge, tipped the urn and poured the ashes. A cannon boomed. And everyone in their boats threw garlands and scattered flowers on the water until the river was like a carpet, everywhere except for the exact spot where the ashes had fallen.

There, a strong current took the ashes and the wreaths cast by the Shastri family, right out in a straight line. One had so strongly the feeling of Shastri's ashes joining with those of Nehru and of Gandhi and of countless Indians—all merging together in Mother Ganga. Hari dipped up Ganges water, sprinkling it on those standing near him on the pier and everyone in the boats sprinkled each other, too, and then that was all, the ceremony was over.

When I was hurriedly awakened in my berth the next morning, I found that our train had pulled into the Delhi station an hour ahead of time, as if, eager and efficient, it were hastening to draw us back to the present and the future. Puddles of water gleamed on the platform and the air was still wet with the long-hoped-for rain that, although far too brief, had finally come. I breathed in the beautiful, precious, moist air and felt my first lift since those days of shared grief had begun so long ago.

The day that greeted us was January 26, Republic Day. After breakfast together, Chet and I joined the throngs along the vast, straight sweep of Rajpath to view the traditional, but ever new Republic Day Parade. Down from the President's Palace marched the regiments and the cadets, the schoolchildren and the folk dancers, colors flying and bands of drum and bagpipe; down they marched, one felt the stern, invigorating young pride of it all, toward the great arch of India Gate rising in the morning mist over a mile away.

I looked at the faces about me in the stands. There were the newly sworn members of the Cabinet. And there was Indira Gandhi, looking serious, but confident and young. Thinking of the dignified and smooth way in which the change of leadership had taken place, I sensed keenly the vitality and continuing thread of Indian democracy.

Near us sat the Pakistan High Commissioner and his family. I remembered that he had flown down to Delhi from Tashkent in the same plane with Shastri's body. And not far away I saw General Chaudhuri, the Chief of Staff, sitting relaxed, and I thought of the negotiations for the withdrawal of the armies that were under way. Already the Tashkent agreement, Shastri's last act and gift to us all, was taking effect, creating a new spirit, a new atmosphere. After all the sorrowing of the past days I felt again, but perhaps with a greater confidence than ever, the bright promise of India's future.

INDEX

The abbreviation CB is used for Chester Bowles.

Abdullah, Sheik, 502, 509–510
Acheson, Dean, 149, 173, 247, 248, 345, 405, 447
Addis Ababa, 372–373
Adenauer, Konrad, 444
Adorno, Joseph A., 235–236, 242
Adoula, Cyrille, 423, 426
Afghanistan, trade routes from, 369–371
Africa: CB in, 249–250, 372–374, 418–420, 423–425; independence of new nations, 249–250; ambassadors to, 317–318, 422; U.S. policy on, 348–349; Nasser's influence in, 371–372; United Nations Conference on, 373; Congo crisis, 418–429; British colonies, 420
African Affairs, Bureau of, 313
Africa's Challenge to America, by CB, 251, 421
Agency for International Development (AID), 307, 316, 322, 325; reorganized, program of, 383–384, 386–390; in India, 459, 460, 556
Agriculture Department, 67; extension workers for India proposed, 524; committee sent to India, 529
Alliance for Progress, 348, 435
Alliluyeva, Svetlana, 517–520
Alsop, Joseph, 353, 358; article on Stevenson, 430–431
Ambassadors: choice of, 315–325; functions of, 321–325; regional meetings of, 324–325, 376–377
Ambassador's Report, by CB, 248
American Hospital Association, 200
American Medical Association, 203, 237–238
American Reporter, 466–467, 556
Americans for Democratic Action, 170, 240
Anti-Inflation Committee, Seven Point Program, 37–38
Anton Brun, ship, 513–514, 516
Appropriations Committee, Senate, 114–115

Appropriations Committees, House and Senate, 102
Area Redevelopment Act, 275–276
Arms Control and Disarmament Agency, 585
Arms Control Research Institute, 280
Asia: Soviet influence in, 543–545; conference of nations proposed, 580–581; problems of, 580–582; *see also* Southeast Asia
Assam, Chinese activities in, 538
Atkins, Carter W., 200, 213
Attwood, William, 317–318, 373, 422
Ayub Khan, Mohammed, 374–375, 478, 481; visit to U.S. planned and canceled, 498–499; and Kashmir dispute, 505, 509
Azores, U.S. base in, 428

Backman, Kenneth B., 26
Badeau, John, 319
Baguio, Regional Conference of U.S. Ambassadors, 376–377
Bailey, Barbara, 219
Bailey, John, 173, 184, 186, 212, 221n., 227, 235, 254–255, 258–259, 269, 295; opposes CB in campaign for governorship, 1946, 165–167; supports CB as candidate for Governor, 1948, 176–177, 181; working with CB, 218–219; as possible Senator, 228, 230; in CB's campaign for Senate nomination, 261, 263–268
Bailey, Stephen, Mayor of Middletown, 219n.
Bailey, Prof. Stephen K., 232–233
Baldwin, Raymond, 164, 167, 247, 258, 268; Senator from Connecticut, 168; Connecticut Supreme Court appointment, 226–230; Senator needed to replace him, 228–230
Baldwin, Ruth Standish, 3–4, 6, 275
Ball, George, 360; Under Secretary for Economic Affairs, 308; replaces CB as Under Secretary of State, 363
Bandar Abbas, 370–371

Bandung Conference on Afro-Asian
    unity, 494
Bankhead Bill, 30
Banking and Currency Committee,
    House, 102, 140, 275–276
Banking and Currency Committee, Sen-
    ate, 70, 102, 106–111
Banking and Currency Committees,
    House and Senate, 52, 55–56, 102,
    104–105
Barbour, Walworth, 320
Barkley, Alben W., 104, 174
Bartlett, Charles, 353; article on Steven-
    son, 430–431
Baruch, Bernard M., 127, 141
Batista, Fulgencio, 347
Batten, George, Company, 6
Batten, Barton, Durstine & Osborn, 6
Battle, Lucius D., 366
Bay of Pigs invasion, 297, 311, 326–333,
    340, 444, 449, 450
Belgium: Congo ruled by, 419–421, 425;
    in Congo crisis, 428
Bell, David, 389
Bell, John O., 320
Bennet, Douglas J., 22, 144, 227, 235,
    256, 264; in CB's gubernatorial cam-
    paign, 1948, 178–180; executive sec-
    retary to CB, 190; letters from CB,
    254–255
Bennet, Douglas, Jr., 441
Bennet, Phoebe, 22
Benton, William, 244; in advertising,
    6–7, 9; as Senator, 229–231, 247; in
    campaign of 1950, 232, 241; candi-
    date for Senate nomination against
    CB, 258–268
Benton & Bowles, 6–7, 9, 21, 47, 48,
    133
Berle, Adolf A., 311
Berlin: CB in, 244; armored convoys to,
    proposed, 342
Berryman, G. K., cartoon, 136
Bhutto, Foreign Minister of Pakistan,
    509
Bissell, Bimla, 462
Black, Eugene R., 301
Blacks: in OPA, 64, 144–145; discrim-
    ination against, in government offices,
    144–145; in National Guard, 198; in
    Connecticut as voters, 233; CB's speech
    on, 445–446
Blair, William, 256
Bogotá, CB's speech in, 385
Bolivia, 369n.
Bombay, 496; U.S. consulate, 460
Bowles, Allen, brother of CB, 3
Bowles, Barbara, daughter of CB, 8, 45,
    180, 274
Bowles, Chester: family, 2–4; education,
    4–5; early career, 5–10; reading
    schedule, 7; children, 8; Connecticut
    State Tire Ration Administrator, 14–
    20; Connecticut District Director of
    OPA, 20–26; offered OPA position in
    Washington, 26–28; General Manager
    and Administrator of OPA, 43–115,
    126–141, 364–365, see also Office of
    Price Administration; broadcasts to
    consumers, 69–70; relations with Con-
    gress, 102–115; relations with Roose-
    velt, 116–125; offers to leave OPA,
126, 128–129, 137; resigns from OPA,
    140–141; Director of OES, 141–158;
    resigns from OES, 154–157; Tomor-
    row Without Fear, 161–162; candi-
    date for Governor of Connecticut,
    1946, 164–168; campaign for Demo-
    cratic Party, 170–172; Jefferson-Jack-
    son Day Dinner speech, 171–172; can-
    didate for Governor of Connecticut,
    1948, 176–187; elected, 187–188;
    as Governor, 189–243, see also Con-
    necticut; inauguration, 191–193; In-
    augural Address, text, 593–602; gub-
    ernatorial campaign, 1950, 232–243;
    speeches, 239–240; loses election, 241–
    242; in Europe, 244–245; with United
    Nations, 244–245; speeches on foreign
    aid, 245–246, 252–254, 384–385; Am-
    bassador to India, first time, 247–
    248, 250, 322; Ambassador's Report,
    248; The New Dimensions of Peace,
    248–249, 251; in Africa, 249–250,
    372–374, 418–420, 423–425; Berkeley
    Lectures, University of California,
    250–251; Africa's Challenge to Amer-
    ica, 251, 421; in Soviet Union, 251–
    252; Godkin Lectures, Harvard, 254,
    286; Ideas, People and Peace, 254;
    plans to run for re-election as Gov-
    ernor, 254–256; campaign for U.S.
    Senate nomination, 258–268; cam-
    paign for election to Congress, 269–
    272; in Congress, 272–281; speeches
    in House, 273–274, 276; bills intro-
    duced by, 275–276, 280; before House
    Foreign Affairs Committee, 276–277;
    Mutual Security Act amendments
    proposed, 278–279; as Kennedy's ad-
    viser, 285, 288–289, 296–298; foreign
    policy, views on, 286–287, 304–305,
    343–351; The Coming Political Break-
    through, 286–288; chairman of Demo-
    cratic Platform Committee, 289–292;
    possible candidate for Presidency,
    292–293; renominated as Congress-
    man, resigns, 294–295; possible Sec-
    retary of State, 294–295, 301; Under
    Secretary of State, 302–314; see also
    State Department; memoranda to
    Rusk, 304–305, December 18, 1960,
    text, 603–607; and Bay of Pigs in-
    vasion, 326–333; in Laos crisis, 334–
    341; memorandum on foreign policy,
    July 1, 1961, 347–349, text, 608–618;
    resignation suggested, 352–359; let-
    ter to Stevenson on resignation, 357,
    text, 619–625; resigns as Under Sec-
    retary of State, 363–365; State De-
    partment Award for Distinguished
    Service, 367; President's Special Rep-
    resentative and Adviser on Asian,
    African and Latin American Affairs,
    368–378; tour of Middle East, Africa
    and Asia, 369–378; foreign aid pro-
    grams, 379–390; China, recommended
    policy on, 391, 394–403; Vietnam
    policy, statement on, 411–415; Congo
    crisis, recommendations on, 425–429;
    resigns as Special Representative,
    430–434; Ambassador to India, second
    time, 434–442, 457–486, see also

India; letter to his children on ambassadorship, 435–436; Kennedy's relationship with, 444–446, 449, 454; speech on civil rights, 445–446; memoranda and reports on India, 485–486, 555, text, 631–637; lectures on Indian economic development, 554–555; *The Makings of a Just Society*, 555; resigns as Ambassador, 574; in Cambodia, political mission, 577–579; Dean of Diplomatic Corps, 583; leaves India, 583–584

Bowles, Chester, Jr., son of CB, 8, 13, 45, 180, 274

Bowles, Cynthia, daughter of CB, 8, 27, 180, 187, 240, 274, 546

Bowles, Dorothy, sister of CB, 3, 13

Bowles, Dorothy Stebbins (Steb), wife of CB, 8, 21, 23, 27–28, 45, 137–139, 156, 166, 168, 176, 189, 199, 200, 215, 227, 240, 244, 246, 248, 256, 259, 260, 270, 302, 319; in Connecticut State Defense Council, 13; dinner with Roosevelts, 121; in campaign for Democratic Party, 170–171; in gubernatorial campaign, 1948, 178, 180, 181, 183, 184, 186; helps CB as Governor, 219, 222; travels, 245, 249–252, 372–373, 376–377, 405, 415, 418, 419, 423, 441; in CB's campaign for Senate nomination, 264–266; in Washington, 274, 297, 300; in campaign for Kennedy, 296; and CB's resignation as Under Secretary of State, 363, 364; and CB's appointment as Ambassador to India, 435, 436; in Embassy at New Delhi, 461–463; in India, 464, 468, 470, 472, 489, 497, 508, 541, 542, 548, 584; "Train to Allahabad," quoted, 498, 506–507, text, 638–644

Bowles, Julia Fisk, first wife of CB, 6, 8

Bowles, Nancy (Mrs Samuel Bowles), 372

Bowles, Samuel, grandfather of CB, 3, 588

Bowles, Samuel, son of CB, 8, 180, 187, 240, 274, 372–373, 546

Bowles, Sarah, daughter of CB, 8, 180, 187, 240, 242, 270, 274, 546

Bowles, Sherman, cousin of CB, 5

Bowles, Timothy, grandson of CB, 241

Brazzaville, 423–424

Brezhnev, Leonid, 543, 545

Bridgeport *Herald*, 187n.

Bridgeport *Post*, 238, 241

Broadcast Magazine, 16

Brooks, Mary, 441

Brooks, Robert R. R., 66, 441

Brown, Prentiss M., 26, 28, 29, 59, 116; letter from CB, 26–27; as OPA Director, 41

Brownlee, James F.: in OPA, 47–48, 129; discussion with Tobey, 107; discussion with Taft, 109; in OES, 143–144, 149

Bruce, David K. E., 301, 319

Bunche, Ralph, 299

Bundy, McGeorge, 303, 327, 351, 439, 444, 482, 483; and CB's resignation, 354, 356, 361

Bureau of the Budget, 112, 333, 561

Burma, 402; Chinese activities in, 538–539

Bush, Prescott, 232, 241

Butler, Paul M., 289–290

Butler, Ralph Starr, 6–7

Byrnes, James F., 81, 93, 122, 141, 174, 304; Economic Stabilization Director, 39, 143; CB's relationship with, 58–60; letter to CB, 59

Calcutta, 517, 538; U.S. consulate, 460

Califano, Joseph, 535

Cambodia, 546; CB in, 374–375, 577–579; Vietcong and North Vietnamese in, 577–578; U.S. relations with, 578–580

Campbell, Charles L., 213, 215

Capehart, Homer E., 154

Caroe, Sir Olaf, *Wells of Power*, 477–478

Carpenter, Nelson L., 196

Carroll, William T., 177, 212, 232

Castlereagh, Lord, 400

Castro, Fidel, 342, 349, 369; and Bay of Pigs invasion, 326, 330, 331

Cater, Douglass, 535

Cavers, David F., 45, 48

Celeste, Richard, 441, 498

Central Intelligence Agency (CIA), 322, 323; and Bay of Pigs invasion, 326, 332–333; faults of, 333; in Laos, 334; Soviet propaganda on, 468–470

Chamber of Commerce, U.S., 66

Chattanooga *Times*, 353

Chavan, Yeshwantrao, 475, 482, 484, 509

Chayes, Abram, 190, 215, 223, 290, 352, 354, 364, 408, 447; Legal Adviser in State Department, 309, 326

Chen Yi, 339

Chiang Kai-shek, 347, 375, 377, 380n., 575, 576, 580; CB's recommendations on policy with, 391, 394–395; China controlled by, 392

Chicago *Tribune*, 388

Childs, Marquis, 100

China: intervention in Laos possible, 335–336, 339–340; U.S. policy on, 345–346, 391–403, 457–458; Mao Tse-tung's power in, 346; land reform in, 379–381; CB's recommendations on policy, 391, 394–403; under Sun Yat-sen, 391–392; under Chiang Kai-shek, 392; Communist control of, 392; in United Nations, 393, 396, 398; U.S. relationship with, 393, 396, 398–403; Soviet Union in conflict with, 393–394, 400, 410; North Vietnam supported by, 410, 578; India threatened by, 425; break with Soviet Union, 437, 457; India attacked by, 437, 439–440, 457, 473–474, 537–538; Pakistan supports, 439, 440, 473, 477, 502; Nehru on, 489–490; India's peaceful relationship with, 490, 493–494; and Korean peace negotiations, 492; in Bandung Conference, 494; in Kashmir crisis, 503; India and Soviet Union, future relations with, 537–546; in India, covert activities, 538–539; Marxist-Leninist doctrine in, 539–540

China, Nationalist, *see* Taiwan

Chin Ren, Madame, 577
Choate School, 4
Chou En-lai, 339
CIA, see Central Intelligence Agency
CIO, CB's campaign supported by, 183, 222
Civil rights: as issue in 1948 Democratic Convention, 174–175; Connecticut legislation on, 198; in Democratic platform, 1960, 291–292; Kennedy's position on, 445–446
Civil Rights Act (1964), 533
Clay, Lucius, 58
Clemow, Bice, 144
Cleveland, Harlan, 383
Clifford, Clark, 174, 198, 244, 246
Coal miners' strikes, 151
Cohen, Sir Andrew, 420
Cole, Charles W., 320
Collier's, article by CB, 113
Collyer, John L., 17
The Coming Political Breakthrough, by CB, 286–288
Committee for Economic Development, 66
Commodity Credit Corporation, 112, 147, 562
Common Sense magazine, 10
Communism: influence in U.S., 169; as campaign issue against CB, 240; foreign aid and, 279–280; Dulles' policy of containment, 345–347; in China, 392, 539–540; monolithic, concept of, 394, 410; in Southeast Asia, 410; in India, 468–470, 479, 541, 544–545, 556, 567, 570; in World War II, 541; in France, 570
Congo: Nasser's influence in, 371, 372; crisis in, 418–429, 450; Belgian rule of, 419–421, 425; CB's recommendations on, 425–429; tenth anniversary of independence, 429
Congress: OPA relations with, 102–115; Rayburn's rules for success in, 272–273; CB in, 272–281; delegation sent to India, 529; and economic aid to India, 561–562
Congressional Committee for the Protection of the Consumer, 112
Connecticut: State Defense Council, 13; State Tire Ration Administration, 14–20; OPA regional district, 20–26; state government, 163–164, 190, 209–215, 242; CB as candidate for Governor, 1946, 164–168; Democratic Party, CB's work for, 170–172; CB as candidate for Governor, 1948, 176–187; CB elected, 187–188; CB as governor, 189–243; budget, 194–196, 236n.; building program, 194–198, 234–235; housing, 196–198, 234; Civil Rights Commission, 198; civil rights legislation, 198; teacher-training program, 199; welfare program, 199; hospitals and institutions, management of, 199–200; Commission on State Government Reorganization, report, 200, 209–215; school-building program, 200, 207–209; education study plan, 200–201; judicial reform, 201–202, 223–224; Public Utilities Commission, 202; medical care program proposed, 203–204, 237–238;

Constitution, new, proposed, 209–210, 213, 239; state government reorganization, proposals for, 209–215; legislation on reorganization, 215–217; state commissions and boards, 222; judges, appointment of, 223–224; lobbies of dentists and fishermen, 224, 237; State Liquor Commission, 224–226; Supreme Court appointments, 226–230; Senator to replace Baldwin, 228–230; CB's gubernatorial campaign, 1950, 232–243; finance as campaign issue, 235–236; medical care as campaign issue, 237–238; Congressional Districts, 269–270; economic conditions, 270–271
Connecticut Medical Association, 203–204, 237
Connery, Paul, 221
Conway, George C., 193, 208, 215–216
Cooley Amendment, 561
Coombs, Philip H., 190, 194, 227, 235, 263, 264, 266, 309
Cotter, John P., 193
Cotton price ceiling, 147–148
Cousins, Norman, 201
Cox, Archibald, 295–296, 309
Crockett, William J., 309
Cronkite, Walter, 452
Cross, Wilbur L., 183, 189–190, 238
Crute, Stanley, 16
Cuba: Bay of Pigs invasion, 297, 311, 326–333, 444, 449, 450; missile crisis, 318, 418, 430; Switzerland handles U.S. interests in, 321

Danaher, John A., 29, 163
Davis, Elmer H., 58, 92–93
Davis, William H., 58, 131; letter from CB, 127
de Gaulle, Charles, 308, 444, 573
Democratic National Convention, 1948, 173–175
Democratic Party: after Roosevelt's leadership, 168–170; CB's work for, 170–172; in 1948 campaign, 173–175; Platform Committee, 1960, CB as chairman, 289–292
Democratic Study Group, 280
Depression, effects of, 7–8, 161
Dewey, Thomas E., 296; campaign for Presidency, 1944, 74, 120, 121
Diem, see Ngo Dinh Diem
Dienbienphu, 406, 493
Dillon, C. Douglas, 277–278, 280, 550
Dobrynin, Anatoly, 418, 452
Dodd, Thomas J., 22, 177, 178, 221n., 226; in Senate nomination campaign, 259–267
Dole, Robert, 529
Dominican Republic, U.S. military intervention in, 342, 450
Donaher, Robert, 272
Donahue, Alphonsus, 266
Douglas, Paul, 176
Driscoll, Alfred E., 163
Driscoll, Margaret, 229
Dulles, Allen, 444
Dulles, John Foster, 250, 252, 277, 300, 315, 334, 362, 375, 394, 410, 471; foreign policy, 345–347; and military

aid to Pakistan, 478–479, 481n.; and Japanese peace treaty, 491
Dunlop, John T., 144, 151
Dunn, John T., Jr., 225–226, 232
Dunn, Peter, 449n.
Durand, Pat, 272

Eastman, Marcella, 16, 120, 179
Eccles, Marriner S., 145
Economic Cooperation Administration, 246
Economic planning: in World War II, 32–42, 46; need for, 161–163; rural development in, 379–382
Edson, Peter, 356
Egan, James, 266
Eisenhower, Dwight D., 252, 297, 334, 361, 542; proposed as Democratic candidate for President, 173; and military aid to Pakistan, 479–480, 503; Nehru's correspondence with, 479–480, 503
Eisenhower Administration: foreign aid in, 252–254, 278; foreign policy in, 286, 304, 345–347; intervention in Laos, 334–335; and military aid to Pakistan, 478–481
Electric Boat Company, 271
Ellender, Allen J., 96
Elliott, Harriet, 32
Ellsworth, Oliver B., 200
Emergency Court of Appeals on OPA, 52–54
Emergency Price Control Act, 32, 34–36, 51–52, 69–70, 75–76, 95, 100; amendments proposed, 88, 91; annual authorization, 102, 103, 107, 110, 151; Taft's attitude toward, 110–111; last debate on, 153–154; Truman's veto of, 156
Emerson, Thomas I., 75
Essex, Conn., 9, 22–23, 442
Etawah, rural development program, 548–549
Ethiopia, 372–374, 378
Evans, Rowland, 354
Everett, John R., 167

Farmers: OPA relations with, 67–68; in Connecticut, 271; economic development and, 380–382; mechanization and farm output, 381–382; see also Land reform; Rural development
Farm organizations, 67–68
Farm products: price control, 30, 37, 40; subsidies on, 41–42, 55–56, 67; price increases, postwar, 148–149
Fay, Bernard, 321–322
Federal Bureau of Investigation, 84
Federal Reserve Board, 145
Field, Richard H., 48
Fitch, Lyle, 195
Flaherty, Leo B., 270
Folger, Kay, 296
Food for Peace program, 278, 322, 524, 561
Ford Foundation, 549, 553, 559, 560
Foreign Affairs: Rusk's article, 301, 307; Dulles' article, 345; CB's articles, 391, 396, 403, 493–494

Foreign Affairs Committee, House, 276–277
Foreign aid: CB's speeches on, 245–246, 252–254, 384–385; Point Four program, 246, 248; in Eisenhower Administration, 252–254, 278; military programs, 277; CB's programs, 379–390; Kennedy's proposal, 382–383, 389; see also under names of countries
Foreign policy: of Eisenhower Administration, 286, 304, 345–347; CB's views on, 286–287, 304–305, 343–351; of Kennedy Administration, 342–345, 347–351; military leaders in, 343–345, 347; CB's memorandum on, July 1, 1961, 347–349, text, 608–618; see also under names of countries and regions
Foreign Service officers, 305; as ambassadors, 315–317, 321
Formosa, see Taiwan
Forrestal, James V., 29
Foster, William A., 246, 308
Fowler, Henry, 448
France: in Indochina (Vietnam), 404–407, 493; U.S. aid to, 405; African colonies, 420; Communism in, 570
Frankfurter, Felix, 309
Franklin, Benjamin, 321–322
Fredericks, J. Wayne, 313, 422, 425, 427
Freeman, Fulton J., 320
Freeman, Orville, 281, 354; and Indian food situation, 527, 532
Frost, Robert, poem, 496
Fuel oil: shortage, 24–25; rationing, 80, 131
Fulbright, J. William, 301, 319, 332, 345, 447, 535
Funston, G. Keith, 200

Gagarin, Yuri, 449
Galbraith, John Kenneth, 436, 441; in OPA, 34, 41, 44, 47; Ambassador to India, 319, 338, 374, 434–435, 474
Gandhi, Indira, 489, 508–517, 541, 543, 544; character of, 508–509; in Kashmir dispute, 509; visit to U.S., 511–514, 523; visit to Moscow, 515; birthday greetings to Ho Chi Minh, 526
Gandhi, Mohandas K., 346, 487, 580; Nehru and, 488; Soviet attitude toward, 541
Gasoline: shortage, 24–25, 77–78; rationing, 77–80, 131; black market in, 78–80
Gaud, William S., 389
Gavin, Gen. James M., 319
General Foods Corporation, 6–7, 47
General Maximum Price Regulation, 38
General Motors Corporation, strike, 131
Geneva Agreements: on Laos, 340–341, 407, 409, 411; on Vietnam, 407
Germany, U.S. policy on, 348
Ghana, education in, 420
Gilbert, Ethel, 65
Gilbert, Richard V., 39n., 48, 375
Gillette, Frederick B., 6
Gilpatric, Roswell, 327
Ginsburg, David, 32, 34, 41, 52, 229, 290, 310, 364
Golden, John, 165, 167, 219, 260, 264
Goldwater, Barry, 434

Goodwin, Richard N., 311–312, 363
Gordon, Lincoln, 320
Gordon, William S., Jr., 223, 224
Gore, Albert, 33
Government Operations Subcommittee on National Security, Senate, 361
Great Britain: mediation in Laos, 339–340; control of India, 404; African colonies, 420; supports India against China, 439, 473; Constitution, 572
Green, Theodore F., 163, 190
Green, William, 130–131, 152
Green Berets, 344
Greene, Joseph N., Jr., 441
Greene, Kitty, 441
Grewe, Wilhelm, 298
Grinnell College, 280
Gromyko, Andrei, 540
Gross National Product: 1940, 33; increase of, predicted, 162; misuse of, 586
Grove, Brandon, 441
Guevara, Che, 344
Gullion, Edmund A., 318, 406, 422, 424
Gwiazda, Henry J., 177

Habib, Philip, 577
Hadden, William L., 225–226, 232, 239
Haile Selassie, 373–374, 378
Hall, Leonard W., 99
Hamm, John E., 32
Hammarskjöld, Dag, 421
Handley, William J., 318
Hanoi Government, see Vietnam, North
Harriman, Averell, 248, 303, 312, 352, 362, 409, 435; in Laos crisis, 336, 339–341; in Far Eastern Bureau, 363; at Baguio Conference, 376
Harris, Lou, 259–263
Hart, Henry, 48, 144, 151, 153
Hartford Courant, 14, 24, 44–45, 266
Hartford Times, 25, 186–188, 207, 208, 238
Harvard, Godkin Lectures, 254, 286
Hawkes, Albert W., 106
Hay, John, 393
Heckler, Charles, 193
Henderson, Leon, 26, 31–32, 39, 116, 128; as OPA Director, 34–35, 37, 41; on Emergency Price Control Act, 35
Herblock, cartoons, 97, 430
Herter, Christian A., 277–278, 296–297
Hickey, Edward J., 225–226
Hillman, Sidney, 32
Hilsman, Roger, 301n., 408; Director of Bureau of Intelligence and Research, 308, 326
Hitler, Adolf, 490
Ho Chi Minh, 407, 408, 410, 578; in Laos crisis, 334; and French in Indochina, 404; ideas and objectives of, 405–406; Mrs. Gandhi's birthday greetings to, 526
Hoffman, Paul G., 66
Holmes, Julius, 370
Hoover, Herbert, 6, 34
Hospitals in Connecticut, management of, 199–200
House, Charles S., 193
Housing: price inflation, 113–114; Connecticut program, 196–198, 234
Housing Act (1959), 276

Housing and Urban Development, Department of, 533
Howe, John, 263
Howell, G. Evan, 99
Hughes, Thomas L., 272, 290, 296, 308n., 416
Hull, Cordell, 302
Humphrey, Hubert, 231, 247, 272, 278, 281, 292, 345, 354, 435, 447; in Presidential campaign of 1960, 269, 286, 288, 293; at Shastri's funeral, 506
Hurley, Robert A., 13–14, 16, 19
Hutchins, Robert, 9

Ickes, Harold L., 58, 78, 365, 533; opposes oil price control, 89; on fur price control, controversy with CB, 89–91
Ideas, People and Peace, by CB, 254
India: Point Four Program in, 246, 248: CB as Ambassador to, first time, 247–248, 250, 322; U.S. wheat for, 278, 389–390, 491, 499–500, 512, 523–532; Galbraith as Ambassador to, 319, 338, 374, 474; in International Control Commission for Laos, 337; Gandhi's power in, 346; survey on opinion of U.S., 347; CB visits, 374; British in, 404; China threatens, 425; CB as Ambassador to, second time, 434–442, 457–486; U.S. policy on, 436–440, 458, 473–477, 481, 484–486, 490–493, 574, 582; Chinese attack on, 437, 439–440, 457, 473–474, 537–538; and Pakistan in Kashmir dispute, 439, 473, 500–506, 509–511, 559; Pakistan's relations with, 439, 473–475, 538; U.S. military aid to, 439–440, 473–477, 504; Soviet military aid to, 440, 477, 479, 482, 483–484; Kennedy honored in, 453–454; U.S. military mission to, 459, 460, 473–476; U.S. relationship with, 464–466, 470–471, 484–486, 500; Constitution, 465, 572; Communist propaganda in, 468–470, 515; policy on Southeast Asia, 476; U.S. military aid to Pakistan opposed, 478–480; Communist Party, 469n., 479, 517, 544–545, 556, 567; Johnson's policy on, 484, 500, 512, 523–532, 534–535, 558–559; visitors from U.S. encouraged, 485; CB's reports and memoranda on, 485–486, 555, text, 631–637; Nehru's government of, 487–488, 495–496; Congress Party, 488, 508, 509, 515–517, 570, 572; and Japanese peace treaty, 490–491; Japanese treaty with, 491; in Korean War, 491–492; China and, peaceful relationship, 490, 493–494; languages of, 495–496, 571–572; Shastri as Prime Minister, 497–500, 505–506; partition of, in 1947, 500–501; Mrs Gandhi as Prime Minister, 508–517; Indo-American Foundation proposed, 512–514; devaluation of rupee, 515; protests against bombing of North Vietnam, 515, 526, 574–575; elections of 1967, 516–517; U.S. food shipments in 1966, 523–532, 534–535; U.S. agricultural experts proposed for,

524; China and Soviet Union, future relations with, 537–546; Chinese activities in, 538–539; military strength, 538; Communism in, 541, 556, 570; Soviet economic aid to, 542, 550; Soviet strategy in, 544–545; rural development, 548–549, 567–568; national planning, 548–550; economic aid through Consortium of nations, 550, 557, 565, 581; education, 550; industrial progress, 550, 554; population control and health, 551, 554, 563–564; agriculture, 551–553, 559–560, 562–563, 566–567; land reform, 552, 566–567; U.S. economic aid to, 550–562, 565–566; "Long-Range Assistance Strategy for India," memorandum, 552–553; capitalist exploitation feared, 553–554; CB's lectures on economic development, 554–555; Green Revolution, 562–563; exports and imports, 564–565; political prospects, 569–573; caste system, 570; religious differences, 570–571; association with other Asian nations, 581–582

Indo-American Foundation, 512–514
Indochina, French in, 404–407, 493
Indonesia, 546, 581
Inflation, 586; after World War I, 30–31; World War II effects on, 33; controls under OPA, 36–37; Seven Point Program against, 37–38; in housing prices, 113–114; postwar control program, 133–135; after end of price control, 156–157; as campaign issue in 1948, 182; CB's speech on, before House, 276
International Peace Research Institute, Stockholm, 585
Iran: CB in, 369–371; trade routes from Afghanistan through, 369–371; U.S. aid to, 378
Iran, Shah of, see Mohammed Reza Pahlavi
Izvestia, 543

Jackson, Henry M., 361–362
Japan: CB in, 377; rural development, 380–381; India and, in U.S. policy, 458; peace treaty with, 478, 490–491; Nehru on U.S. relations with, 490–491; Indian treaty with, 491; Soviet influence in, 544; aid to India, 550
Jefferson, Thomas, 174, 587
Jennings, Newell, 226
Jessup, Philip C., 228–229
Jha, L. K., 509
Johnson, Alexis, 310, 360
Johnson, Lyndon B., 289, 301, 449, 562, 576; Vice Presidential candidate, 293–294; and Bay of Pigs invasion, 330; and military aid to Pakistan, 482, 521; policy on India, 484, 500, 512, 523–532, 534–535, 558–559; letter from CB on Vietnam, 486; relations with Shastri, 498–500, 505; on Kashmir plebiscite, 511; and Indo-American Foundation, 512–514; Mrs. Gandhi entertained by, 513–514; and wheat for India, 523–532, 534–535; CB's impressions of, 532–536; program as

President, 533; policy on Vietnam, 535–536
Johnston, Eric, 66, 130
Jones, Marvin, 58
Jones, Roger W., 309
Jordan, Amos (Joe), 441, 475
Jordan, Nasser's relations with, 370, 371
Joyce, Jean, 180, 191

Kabul, 370, 371
Kaiser, Philip M., 318, 373, 422
Kasavubu, Joseph, 421
Kashmir: India and Pakistan in dispute over, 439, 473, 500–506, 509–511, 559; Mrs. Gandhi's policy on, 509; problems summarized, 510–511; U.S. policy on, 582
Kashmir, Maharaja of, 501
Katanga in Congo crisis, 419–421, 423–427
Katzenbach, Nicholas deB., 467
Kaul, Gen. Brij, 474
Kaysen, Carl, 447
Keating, Thomas, 264, 267
Kellems, Vivien, 234
Kelly, Gen. John E., 475
Kelly, John P., 165, 219
Kennan, George F., 316, 318
Kennedy, Jacqueline, 577
Kennedy, John F., 275, 280, 287, 371, 374, 375, 443–454, 458, 514, 536, 544, 550n., 562, 574; candidate for Presidency, 260, 269, 281, 288, 293–297; CB as adviser to, 285, 288–289, 296–298, on CB's The Coming Political Breakthrough, 287–288; letter to CB, 289; letters from CB, 289, 430–434; Secretary of State, choice of, 294–295, 299–302; election, 297; and State Department, 303–304, 308, 311–313; ambassadors appointed, 315, 318–321, 323–325; letter on functions of ambassadors, 323–324; and Bay of Pigs invasion, 326–333, 340, 444, 449, 450; and Laos crisis, 334–336, 338, 340; meets Khrushchev, 342; foreign policy of, 342–345, 347–351; and CB's resignation as Under Secretary of State, 353–361, 363–365; appoints CB as Special Representative and Adviser, 368, 377–379; in Latin America, 368–369; character and ideas of, 377, 443–448, 450–454; foreign aid proposal, 382–383, 389; policy on China, 391, 396, 398–403; debates with Nixon, 396; policy on Vietnam, 408–411, 414–415, 450, 452–453, 476; policy in Africa, 421, 422, 429; in Congo crisis, 425–428, 450; and article against Stevenson, 430–431; CB's letter of resignation as Special Representative, 430–434; appoints CB Ambassador to India, 434–435, 437–438; policy on India, 439–440, 473–475, 481; CB's relationship with, 444–446, 449–454; associates and advisers, 446–448; moon landing planned by, 448–449; death of, 451, 453–454, 481; speeches, 451–453
Kennedy, Robert F., 290, 291, 295, 302, 344n., 409, 446, 448, 535; and Bay of Pigs invasion, 330, 332

Kennelly, James, 267n.
Kerr, Clark, 311
Khrushchev, Nikita: CB meets, 251–252; in Laos crisis, 335, 339–340; Kennedy meets, 342
Killian, James R., 449
Kimball, Penn, 180–181, 191, 195
Kleberg, Richard M., 88
Knudsen, William S., 32
Kohler, Foy D., 312
Komer, Robert, 439, 483
Kong Le, Colonel, 336n.
Kopplemann, Herman, 153–154
Korea, economic aid to, 389
Korean War, 240, 337, 339, 392; prices in, 157–158; India and, 491–492; peace negotiations, 492
Kosygin, Aleksei N., 505; and Mrs. Gandhi, 515; Johnson meets, 536
Krishna Menon, Vengalil K., 492–493
Krug, Julius A., 94
Kulu Valley, 584

Labor: manpower control proposed, 38; in wage and price control, 41; OPA relations with, 66–67, 129–131; OES relations with, 145–147, 150–153; "no strike" pledge proposed, 152–153; Communist influence on, 169; CB's relations with, as Governor, 222–223; see also Wages
Labouisse, Henry R., 383, 386
La Follette, Robert M., 5, 163
La Guardia, Fiorello, 132; attacks OPA, 72–74; advice on investigations, 84
Land reform: in Asia, 379–381; in India, 552, 566–567; in Taiwan, 566
Laos, 334–341, 369n.; U.S. intervention in, 334–337, 450; International Control Commission for, 337, 339, 340; CB proposes settlement of problem, 337–339; Geneva Agreements on, 340–341, 407, 409, 411; Ho Chi Minh supply route to Vietnam, 341; Souvanna Phouma's regime encouraged, 476
Laski, Harold, 548, 552n.
Latin America: U.S. relations with, 311, 349; ambassadors to, 319–320; Alliance for Progress, 348; Kennedy and CB visit, 368–369; U.S. economic aid in, 384–386
Lawrence, David L., 318
League of Nations, 9
Lee, Richard C., 232, 260, 264
Lee Kuan Yew, 581
Lehman, Herbert, 132, 231
Lenin, Nikolai, 380, 537
Lewis, Fulton, Jr., 157
Lewis, John, 529, 556, 557, 561
Lewis, John L., 152, 153; demands for mine workers, 150–151
Lewis, R. A., cartoon, 101
Lewis, Samuel W., 369; "Random Musings about Chester Bowles and the Department of State," 366n., text, 626–630
Liberalism: in politics, 170; political technique against, 255; in foreign policy, 344–345
Lie, Trygve, 245
Lincoln, Abraham, 287

Lincoln University, CB speaks at, 445
Lindblom, Charles E., 441, 551
Little Rock, school integration disorder, 465
Little Steel Formula, 38
Lobbyists, 86–101; in Connecticut, 224, 237
Locke, Eugene M., 504
Lockwood, Alma, 241
Lodge, Henry Cabot, II, 232, 248, 415
Lodge, John D., 230n., 248, 256; candidate for Governor of Connecticut, 232, 234–236, 240
Loeb, James I., 170, 320
Logue, Edward J., 190, 215, 223, 254
Logue, Margaret, 254
Looby, Archie, 23
Loomis, James Lee, 200
Loshbough, Bernard E., 198
Lovett, Robert A., 299, 301, 303
Lowell, James B., 236
Luce, Clare Boothe, 229
Lumumba, Patrice, 421, 422
Lyford, Joseph P., 181, 191
Lykins, Johnson, 463

Macapagal, Diosdado, 376
MacArthur, Gen. Douglas, 240, 339, 380, 491–492
McCarthy, John T., 18–19
McCarthy, Joseph, and McCarthyism, 6, 169, 231, 243, 307, 316, 320, 393, 478
McCloskey, Matthew, 320
McCloy, John J., 299, 301, 348
McConaughy, James L., 168, 178
McConaughy, Walter, 312–313, 362, 363
McDonald, Winifred, 177, 232
McGee, Gale, 529
McGhee, George, 362, 363; in Congo crisis, 423–425
McGuire, John A., 165, 166
McIlvaine, Robinson, 318
McMahon, Brien, 166, 173, 230, 238, 246; supports CB as candidate for Governor of Connecticut, 164–165; candidate for U.S. Senate, 232, 241
McMurray, Howard J., 112
McNamara, Robert, 330, 351, 439, 444, 481–484, 486
McNutt, Paul V., 58, 103
Macomber, William B., 313–314, 319
Makings of a Just Society, The, by CB, 555
Malenkov, Georgi M., 541
Mallon, W. L., 99
Maloney, Francis T., 29, 163, 164
Manchester Herald, 216–217
Mao Tse-tung, 344, 346, 380, 395–396, 540, 552n., 580
Marder, Murrey, 353
Marriott, McKim, 567–568
Marshall, George C., 303
Marshall Plan, 253
Martin, John Bartlow, 320
Martin, Joseph, 34
Marx, Karl, 271, 380
Mason, Edward, 372
Matsu (island), 396, 494
Maxon, Lou R., 27, 43–44, 55
Medical care, Connecticut program proposed, 203–204, 237–238
Medicare, 533

Mehta, Asoka, 509
Mekong River, 341, 376, 411
Menon, V. P., 501
Menshikov, Mikhail A., 298
Metternich, Klemens von, 464
Mexico, economic aid in, 384–385
Mexico City: CB's speech in, 384–385; student riots in, 583
Middle East, CB's tour of, 369–372
Military expenditures, 585–586
Military leaders in foreign policy, 343–345, 347
Miller, Jack, 529
Milwaukee *Journal*, 135
Minneapolis *Tribune*, 354
Mitchell, Annabelle, 369
Mitchell, Harold E., 216
Mobutu, Joseph D., 429
Mohammed Reza Pahlavi, Shah of Iran, 347, 370–371, 378
Mondale Amendment, 562
Mongolia, 398–399
Monnet, Jean, 244, 308
Monroney, A. S. Mike, 102–103, 247, 533
Montague, Joseph C., 95
Montgomery, Donald E., 66
Morales-Carrión, Arturo, 320
Morgenthau, Henry, 84
Morrison, James H., 88
Morse, Wayne, 516, 535
Mortimer, Charles, 6–7
Moscoso, Teodoro, 320
Mountbatten, Lord, 501
Moyers, Bill D., 535; letter from CB, 558–559
Mulvihill, Cornelius J., 165, 167, 178, 219, 264, 267
Muñoz Marín, Luis, 319–320
Murray, Philip, 130–131, 146–147, 152
Murrow, Edward R., 327, 332; Director of USIA, 307–308
Mutual Security Act, 277; amendments proposed by CB, 278–279

Nanda, Gulzari Lal, 496
Nasser, Gamal Abdel, 370–372
National Association of Manufacturers, 96–98, 106, 133
National Automobile Dealers Association, 98-99
National Defense Advisory Commission, 31–32
National Guard, Connecticut, desegregation of, 198
National Retail Dry Goods Association, 91–92, 113
National Security Council, 329, 331
National Teacher Corps, 533
National Wage Stabilization Board, *see* Wage Stabilization Board
NATO (North Atlantic Treaty Organization), 347, 405, 421
Nehru, Jawaharlal, 250, 338, 374, 402, 405, 436, 437, 453, 466, 467, 497, 516, 546, 584; on Chinese-Soviet relations, 393–394, 489–490; CB's interviews with, 472–475, 488–491, 551–552; and U.S. military aid to Pakistan, 478–481; Eisenhower's correspondence with, 479–480, 503; death of, 483, 487, 496; CB's impressions of, 487–496; Gandhi and, 488; on Stalin, 489–490, 541–

542; on U.S. policies, 489–492; and Korean War, 491–492; Americans, opinion of, 494–495; in Kashmir crisis, 501, 502; Soviet attitude toward, 541; and national planning, 548–549
Nehru, Motilal, 488
Nelson, Donald M., 57, 58, 88, 94
Nepal, 369n.
New Britain Memorial Hospital, 199–200
New Deal: agencies, 123–124; effects of, 161
New Delhi: U.S. Embassy, 458–463; National Day receptions, 462; American Women's Club, 463; Marine Security Guards, 463; Roosevelt House, 463, 518; Indian and American officials, conference of, 467–468; Visitors Center, 470
New Dimensions of Peace, The, by CB, 248–249, 251
New Haven *Register*, 45
New Republic, 86–87, 94, 292
News Circle, article by Mrs. Bowles, text, 638–644
News Focus, 353
Newsweek, 352–353
New York *Herald Tribune*, 354
New York *Journal-American*, 388
New York *Post*, 135
New York Times, 6, 14, 28, 34, 168, 329, 354, 407, 468, 470, 521, 528, 530, 535
New York Times Magazine, 171, 345
Ngo Dinh Diem, 407, 416–417, 476
Nguyen Van Tam, 406
Nhiek Tioulong, Gen., 578
Nitze, Paul, 516
Nixon, Richard M., 273, 297, 574, 583; debates with Kennedy, 396; elected President, 532; letter to CB, 532n.
Nixon Administration, military aid to Pakistan, 521
Nolting, Frederick E., Jr., 415
Norodom Sihanouk, Prince, 337, 375–376, 577–580
Nye, Sir Archibald, 478
Nye, Gerald P., 31, 32

Office of Economic Stabilization (OES), 92–93; CB as Director, 141–158; and steel industry wage increase, 146–147; CB resigns from, 154–157
Office of Price Administration (OPA), 26–27, 147, 304; Connecticut district, CB as director, 20–26; CB offered position in national organization, 26–28; CB as General Manager and Administrator, 29, 43–115, 126–141, 364–365; established, 32, 35; Henderson as Director, 34–35, 37, 41; statement on wage increases, 39; Brown as Director, 41; criticism of, 43–50; economists in, 44–46, 49; lawyers in, 44–47, 49; reorganization, 47–48, 61–65; businessmen protest against, 48–49; price regulations, CB's interpretation of, 51–54; Supreme Court decisions on, 53; local ration boards, 62–63, 134; personnel standards, 64; Office of Advisory Committees, 65; labor support of, 66–67; farmers and, 67–68; consumers and, 68–71; Consumer Information Service, 69; Home

Front Pledge, 71; public opinion of, 71, 135–136; politics avoided in, 72; enforcement program, 75–83; investigations to prevent corruption, 83–85; lobbyists and, 86–101; relations with Congress, 102–115; program after war, 127–139; organization reduced, 134; overruled in steel price increase, 138–140; CB resigns from, 140–141; Porter as Director, 144
Office of War Mobilization, 58
Ohio State Grange, 68
Okinawa, 376–377
O'Leary, Paul M., 34
Olmstead, Alan, 216–217, 288–289
O'Mahoney, Joseph C., 31
O'Neal, Edward A., 68
Ording, Aache, 245
Othman, Frederick, 108

Pacific Community magazine, 580
Pakistan: U.S. military aid to, 277, 375, 436, 450, 475*n.*, 477–481, 484, 503–504, 521–522; troops pledged for Laos, 338; relations with Afghanistan, 369; CB in, 374–375; U.S. economic aid to, 389–390; U.S. relations with, 438–440, 473, 477–482; relations with India, 439, 473–475, 538; Chinese attack on India supported by, 439, 440, 473, 477, 502; and India in Kashmir dispute, 439, 473, 500–506, 509–511, 559; in partition of India, 1947, 501; Soviet aid to, 544
Palaez, Vice President of Philippines, 376
Pandit, Vijaya Lakshmi, 250, 488–489
Parsons, J. Graham, 312, 334, 335
Patel, Sardar, 487, 501
Pathet Lao, 334–341
Patman, Wright, 32, 34, 99, 100
Paz, Octavio, 583
Peace Corps, 322, 323, 325, 441, 448–449; in India, 459, 460, 462, 463, 468, 524, 553
Pearl Harbor, attack on, 10, 13
Perkins, Frances, 130, 131
Peshawar, U.S. military base, 481–484, 544, 582
Petroleum: prices, subsidy on, 57, 89; rationing, 78; price control opposed, 89
Philippines, 543; troops pledged for Laos, 338; CB in, 376–377
Phoumi Nosavan, 334, 337, 340
Poage, Robert, 529
Point Four program, 246, 248
Political machines, 220–221
Politicians, professional, 218–221
Polk, William, 369
Pollack, Herman, 309
Porter, Paul A., 34, 144
Portugal: colonialism of, 348–349, 428; U.S. relations with, 428
Potter, Russell, 26
Potter, Zenas L., 104; letter to CB, 105
Poullada, Leon B., 318; 373
Powers, Francis Gary, 481
Price, Garrett, cartoon, 15
Price control, 30–42; Roosevelt's "hold the line" order, 30, 41, 55; wages and, 30, 37–38; price schedules, 32;

opposition to, 33, 36, 38–39; selectivists in, 33; prices frozen, 37–38; Roosevelt's Labor Day message, 1942, 40; OPA regulations, interpretation of, 51–54; lobbyists against, 86–101; of furs, 89–90, 96; in textile industry, 91–94; in meat industry, 94–96; of automobiles after war, 98–101; removal of, planned, 127–137; postwar, 147–158; graph, 156; in Korean War, 157–158
Price Control Act, *see* Emergency Price Control Act
Puerto Rico, U.S. relationship with, 511
Purtell, William A., 257, 258*n.*, 260, 267

Quemoy (island), 396, 494
Quinlan, Francis, 16
Quinn, Katherine T., 222, 261, 264–267

Radford, Adm. Arthur W., 407
Radhakrishnan, Sarvepalli, 436, 453, 472, 496
Radio Peace and Progress, Moscow, 469
Railway Brotherhoods, 166
Rationing: tires, 14–20, 23, 131; public reaction to, 23–25; products rationed, 24; sugar, 24, 77; canned food, 46; gasoline, 77–80, 131; counterfeit coupons, 79–80; excess coupons invalidated, 80–83; end of, 131–132
Rayburn, Samuel, 174, 272
Rayles, Robert, 520
Redder, Walter, 353
Reedy, George, 535, 587
Reischauer, Edwin O., 318–319, 377
Rent control, 35–36; rents frozen, 37; postwar problems, 134
Reston, James, 329, 354
Reuther, Walter P., 34, 130–131, 152, 288, 354
Rhee, Syngman, 347
Rhodesia, Northern, 423
Rhodesia, Southern, 420, 423
Ribicoff, Abraham, 217, 228, 230*n.*, 257, 258, 295; elected Governor of Connecticut, 257, 267*n.*; in Senate nomination campaign, 259–261, 263–264, 266–268; asks CB to run for Congress, 269
Rieve, Emil, 176, 181
Robertson, Walter S., 310, 312, 362
Rockefeller Foundation, 551, 559, 560; Board of Trustees, 299–300
Rogers, James G., Jr., 48, 64, 200
Rogers, William, 367
Rooney, John, 561
Roosevelt, Eleanor, 29, 120–122, 163, 288; relationship with her husband, 125; keynote speech at Connecticut Democratic Convention, 232
Roosevelt, Franklin D., 14, 16, 28, 31, 59, 95, 174, 185, 287, 365, 549; "hold the line" order, 30, 41, 55; and OPA, 32, 34, 56–57, 83–84, 112; opposition to, 33; calls for war production, 33; messages on price control, 37–38, 40–41; asks CB not to run for Senate, 71–72; CB's relations with, 116–125; "Economic Bill of Rights" speech suggested by CB, 117–120; "sixty million jobs" speech suggested by

CB, 120–121; death, 123; as administrator, 123–125; Democratic Party influence by, 168, 170; Truman as his successor, 172; on British rule of India, 404
Roosevelt, Franklin D., Jr., 177
Roosevelt, Theodore, 553
Roper, Elmo, 198, 266
Roraback, J. Henry, 202
Rosenberg, Anna, 229
Rosenman, Samuel I., 37, 39, 117, 118, 120, 122
Rostow, Walter, 345, 363, 484; mission to Vietnam, 361, 408, 409, 450
Rountree, William M., 277
Rural development: in China, 379–381; in Japan, 380–381; in foreign aid program, 384–385; in India, 548–549, 567–568
Rusk, Dean, 251, 333, 398, 401, 435, 436, 439, 481–484, 486, 512, 532, 577; Kennedy's choice of, 299–302; Secretary of State, 302–313, see also State Department; CB's memoranda to, 304–305, Dec. 18, 1960, text, 603–607; ambassadors chosen by, 315; and Bay of Pigs invasion, 326–329, 332; in Laos crisis, 337–338, 340n.; and foreign policy, 349–351; CB's conflict with, 352–353, 355, 358–360, 362–366; character of, 365–367; CB urges him to expand neutrality in Asia, 407–408; policy on Vietnam, 409, 411–412, 414; and CB as Ambassador to India, 438, 439; and Shastri's visit to U.S., 499, 505; at Shastri's funeral, 506; attitude toward India, 526n.; CB's message to, on Indian food situation, 527
Russia, see Soviet Union
Rutland, Robert A., 293

Saigon, 405, 415
Saigon Government, see Vietnam, South
St. Louis Post-Dispatch, 135
St. Onge, William, 295
Salazar, António de Oliveira, 348, 428
Salinger, Pierre, 355, 363
San Francisco Chronicle, 83, 88
Saturday Evening Post, 430
Saudi Arabia, Nasser's relations with, 370, 371
Scanlon, Thomas E., 112
Schlesinger, Arthur, Jr., 363, 366, 447
Schwellenbach, Lewis B., 130–131, 153
Scranton, Asa, 16
SEATO (Southeast Asia Treaty Organization), 337–338, 394, 408
Seeley-Brown, Horace, 270
Select Committee to Investigate Executive Agencies, House, 112–113
Seymour, Charles, 10; Diplomatic Background of the War, 1870–1914, 4
Shannon, James C., 191, 222; in Connecticut gubernatorial campaign, 178, 179, 183, 185, 187
Shastri, Lal Bahadur, 453, 497–507, 512; visit to U.S. planned and canceled, 498–499, 505; Johnson's relations with, 498–500, 505; in peace conference on Kashmir, 505–506; death and funeral, 506–507; letter from CB, text, 631–637; Mrs. Bowles' article on his funeral, text, 638–644
Shastri, Lalita, 497–499, 507
Sherrer, Gen. Edward C. D., 375n.
Shoup, Gen. David M., 586
Shriver, R. Sargent, 291, 295, 446, 449
Shuster, George N., 228–229
Sihanouk, see Norodom Sihanouk
Silcock, Bryan, 449n.
Small Business Committee, House, 99
Small Business Committee, Senate, 53
Smallwood, Robert, 48
Smith, Alfred E., 163
Smith, Gen. Bedell, 244
Smith, Earl E. T., 320–321
Smith, Francis, 165, 264
Smith, Harold D., 37, 39
Smith, Howard W., 112–113
Snow, Wilbert, 178, 219n.; candidate for Governor of Connecticut, 164, 166–168
Snyder, John, 149, 172; and steel price increase, 138–140, 145
Social Security Act, amendment proposed, 276
Sollot, Ralph, 195
Son Sann, 577–579
Sorensen, Theodore C., 285, 289, 358–359, 364, 368, 431, 433, 451
Sorensen, Thomas, 358
Souphanouvong, Prince, 335
South Africa, 421, 424, 427, 429
Southeast Asia: neutrality in, advised, 407–409; Communism and nationalism in, 410; CB's statement of policy, 411–415; Peace Charter, draft of, 412–413; U.S. involvement in, 457–458, 476; Indian policy on, 476
Souvanna Phouma, Prince, 334–335, 337, 339–341, 411, 476
Soviet-American Friendship societies, 169
Soviet Union: as ally of U.S., 169; CB plans to visit, 244; CB in, 251–252; in Cuban missile crisis, 318, 418; in Laos crisis, 335–336, 339–341; U.S. foreign policy on, 345–346, 348; in Middle East, 370, 371; in Africa, 373, 419, 424; farming in, 380–381; China in conflict with, 393–394, 400, 410; North Vietnam supported by, 410; in Congo crisis, 421–423; break with China, 437, 457; military aid to India, possible, 440, 477, 479, 482, accepted, 483–484; space exploration, 449; nuclear testing agreement, 451–452; propaganda on CIA, 468–470; Nehru on, 489–490; and Korean peace negotiations, 492; Mrs. Gandhi visits, 515; and Svetlana Alliluyeva's defection, 517–520; India and China, future relations with, 537–546; Gandhi and Nehru criticized in, 541; economic aid to India, 542, 550; influence in Asia, 543–545; strategy in India, 544–545
Spaak, Paul-Henri, 426, 428
Spellacy, Thomas J., 165, 167n.
Spence, Brent, 102, 104
Spivack, Herbert, 577
Springfield Daily News, 5

Springfield *Republican,* 3, 5–6, 588
Stalin, Joseph, 346–347; Nehru on, 489–490, 541–542; daughter of, *see* Alliluyeva, Svetlana
State Department: Kennedy and, 303–304, 308; appointments in, 305, 307–313; policy-making in, 305–306; McCarthy's investigation of, 307; reforms proposed in 1970, 313–314; ambassadors, choice of, 315–325; and Bay of Pigs invasion, 326–329, 333; and Central Intelligence Agency, 333; Senate Subcommittee report on, 361–362; changes proposed by CB, 362–363; staff changes, 363; CB's resignation from, 363–365; CB receives Award for Distinguished Service, 367; in Indian affairs, 459, 460
State governments, 163; Connecticut, reorganization, 209–217; constitutions, 210–211
Statts, Elmer, 112
Steagall, Henry, 32, 112
Steel industry: strike threatened, 131, 137–138; price increase, 138–140, 145; wage increase, 145–146
Stephansky, Ben S., 320
Stevenson, Adlai, 4, 176, 292, 344, 345, 354, 359, 383, 435, 448; advises CB on governorship, 255–256; candidate for Presidency in 1956, 257; in Presidential campaign of 1960, 269, 281, 285–286, 288; possible Secretary of State, 294, 295, 301; Ambassador to United Nations, 303, 348, 422; and Bay of Pigs invasion, 326; letter from CB, 357, text, 619–625; in Congo crisis, 427; attacked in article by Bartlett and Alsop, 430–431
Stevenson, William, 319
Struelens, Michael, 426
Subramanian, Chidambara, 509, 527, 559
Sun Yat-sen, 379–380, 391–392
Supply Priorities and Allocations Boards, 32
Supreme Court: *Gillespie Rogers–Pyatt Co.* v. *Bowles,* 53; decision on state constitutions, 211; decision on school integration, 445, 465
Sussler, Robert, 181
Sviridoff, Mitchell, 222–223, 228
Switzerland, controversy on Ambassador to, 321
Symington, Stuart, 289–290

Taber, John, 47–48
Taft, Robert A., 35, 52, 68, 88, 102, 150, 154; attacks "OPA propaganda," 70–71; CB's disagreements with, 108–111; Brownlee's discussion with, 109; wants all controls removed, 133; opposes foreign appointment for CB, 246–248
Taiwan, 377, 389; agricultural output, 381; U.S. policy on Nationalist government, 392, 393, 396, 398–403; CB's recommendations on, 394–395; land reform in, 566
Talbot, Joseph E., 232, 241
Talbot, Phillips, 312, 439

Tashkent, peace conference on Kashmir, 505–506
Taylor, Gen. Maxwell: mission to Vietnam, 361, 408, 409, 450; in India, 482
Thailand, 543, 546; troops pledged for Laos, 338; CB in, 375
Thatcher, Raymond S., 177, 232, 236, 264
Thim, John R., 193, 208
Thomas, Norman, 4, 5
Thompson, William (Big Bill), 465
Thomson, James C., Jr., 272, 290, 293, 296, 318
Time, 45, 332
Tito, Marshal, 252, 319
Tobey, Charles W., 102, 107
Tocqueville, Alexis de, 382
Tomorrow Without Fear, by CB, 161–162
Tone, Joseph R., 167–168, 183
Touré, Sékou, 317–318
Toynbee, Arnold J., 287
Transportation, Department of, 533
Treasury Department, 128; Secret Service branch, 84
Trotta, Fred, 177
Truman, Harry S., 132, 142, 144, 151, 244, 365, 405, 478; chairman of Senate "Watchdog" Committee, 115; as President, asks CB to continue in OPA, 126, 128–129, 137; letters from CB, 138–141, 154–155; CB's letter of resignation from OPA, 140–141; and wheat price increase, 148–149; and "no strike" proposal, 153; CB's letter of resignation from OES, 154–155; letter to CB, 155; asks CB for advice on inflation in Korean War, 157; CB's opinion of, as candidate, 172–173; nominated at 1948 Democratic Convention, 174; in campaign of 1948, 184, 296–297; elected, 187; CB asks his advice on Benton as Senator, 229; Point Four program, 246, 248; appoints CB as Ambassador to India, 247–248, 322
Tshombé, Moise, in Congo crisis, 419–428
Tynan, John, 219, 264

U-2 plane, 481
UNESCO, 244, 585
United Arab Republic, 371–372, 422
United Automobile Workers, 131
United Nations, 586; CB's work for, 244–245; Eisenhower Administration and, 253; strengthening of, 286, 588–589; Conference on African Economic Affairs, 373; China in, 393, 395, 396, 398; Mongolia in, 398; in Congo crisis, 421–428; in Kashmir crisis, 501, 502
United Nations Children's Fund (UNICEF), 245
United Nations Relief and Rehabilitation Agency, 132
United States Information Agency (Service) (USIA, USIS), 307, 315–316, 322, 323, 325, 333, 441; in India, 459, 460, 465–467, 532
U.S. News & World Report, 352

University of California, Berkeley Lectures, 250–251
U Nu, 402
U Thant, 423, 588–589

Valenti, Jack, 535
Vientiane agreements, 335, 340
Vietcong, 337, 341; in Cambodia, 577–578
Vietminh, 405
Vietnam, North, 407; Laos and, 341; Chinese and Russian support of, 410, 578; Communism and nationalism in, 410; bombing of, 500; Indian protests on bombing, 515, 526, 574–575; forces in Cambodia, 577–578
Vietnam, South: sending of U.S. troops planned, 336–337; Laos as supply route to, 341; Taylor-Rostow mission to, 361, 408, 409, 450; French in, 404–407, 493; Geneva Agreements on, 407; beginning of U.S. involvement in, 407; Kennedy's policy on, 408–411, 414–415, 450, 452–453, 476; CB's statement of policy, 411–415; Indian policy on, 476; CB advises Johnson on, 486, 575–576; Shastri criticizes U.S. action in, 500; Johnson's policy on, 535–536, 574–576; Indian culture in, 546; Cambodian view of U.S. action in, 578, 579; U.S. failure in, 580; forces in Cambodia, 578–579; Asian conference on, proposed, 580–581
Vilfan, Joza, 252
Vilfan, Maria, 252
Vinson, Frederick M., 58, 81, 89, 365; and textile price control, 92–94
Voice of America, 465, 466n.
Vose, Prescott, 26

Wages: price control and, 30, 37; frozen, 37–38; Little Steel Formula, 38; aircraft workers' demands, 39; OPA statement on, 39; Roosevelt's Labor Day message, 1942, 40; postwar formula proposed, 129–130; increases, 131, 145–147; in steel industry, 145–146; Lewis' demands, 150–151; in Korean War, 157–158
Wage Stabilization Board, 130, 131, 145
Wagner, Robert: chairman of Senate Banking and Currency Committee, 102, 104, 106, 110; letters from CB, 110–111
Wallace, Donald H., 48
Wallace, Henry A., 149, 169, 171, 173
War Food Administration, 132

War Labor Board, 131
War Manpower Commission, 30
War Policies Commission, 31
War Production Board, 57, 88, 133–134; and textile price control, 92–94
Washington Daily News, 356
Washington Monthly, 449n.
Washington Post, 82, 94, 112, 353, 355–357, 389, 431, 528
Waterbury Republican, 288
Weathersby, William, 466
Wechsler, Alfred F., 193, 232
Weiss, Leonard, 441
Welles, Sumner, 302
Wheat: price increase, 148–149; surplus, and foreign aid, 278; for India, see under India
Wheeler, Gen. Earle G., 414
Wherry, Kenneth S., 53, 67–68, 102, 150; CB's exchange of opinions with, 107–108
Wiesner, Jerome B., 332, 449
Williams, Frances, 64
Williams, G. Mennen, 176, 288, 303, 354, 435, 446; Assistant Secretary for African Affairs, 313, 422, 425, 427
Williams, Maurice J., 389
Willkie, Wendell, 169, 184
Wilson, Woodrow, 4, 6, 9, 127, 406, 410
Wirtz, Willard W., 131, 256
Wofford, Claire, 364
Wofford, Harris, 251, 364, 446
Wood, Tyler, 441, 586
Woodward, Robert, 311
World Bank, 280, 390; and India, 550, 557–559, 565–566, 581
World Health Organization, 551
World War I: inflation after, 30–31, 127; profiteering in, 31
World War II: CB's attitude toward, 9–10; Pearl Harbor attack, 10, 13; production of war materials, 33–34; agencies established, 124; end of, 128; Soviet Union as ally of U.S., 169; Communism in, 541; see also Price control; Rationing

Yale Daily News, 187
Yale Medical Schol, 204
Yale University, Sheffield Scientific School, 4–5
Yeh, George K., 298
Yen, James Y. C., 379–380, 548–549
Young, Hugo, 449n.
Young, Kenneth, 319

Zaharoff, Sir Basil, 522
Zaiman, Jack, 266

ARMS AND ARMOR OF THE
SAMURAI
The History of Weaponry in Ancient Japan

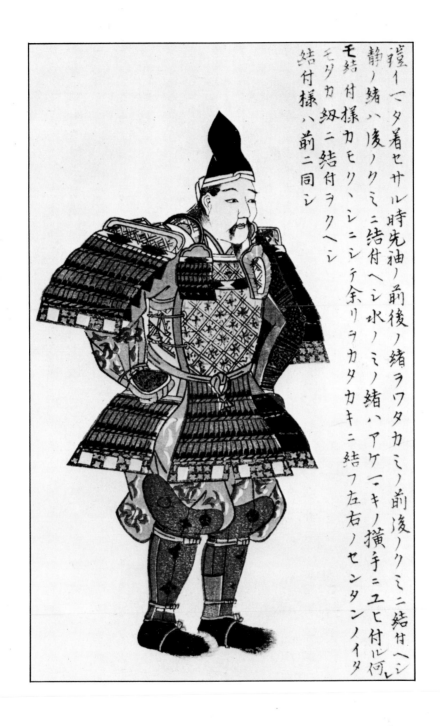

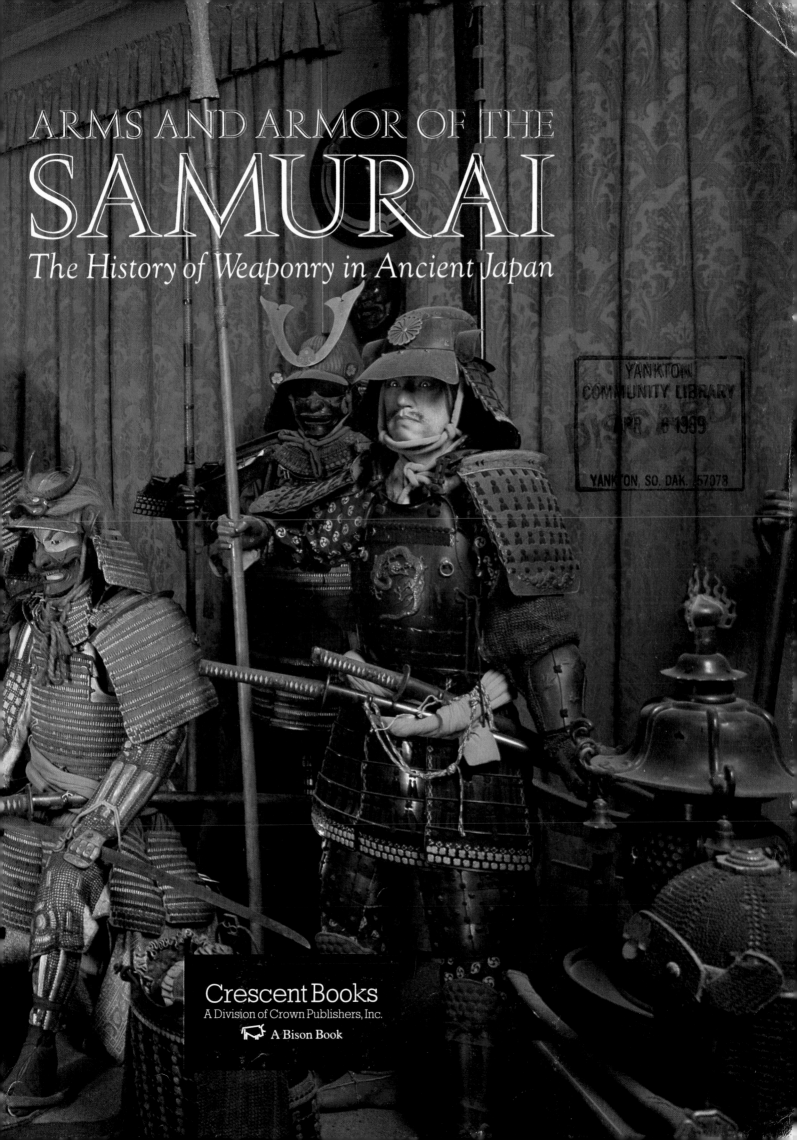

ARMS AND ARMOR OF THE
SAMURAI
The History of Weaponry in Ancient Japan

Crescent Books
A Division of Crown Publishers, Inc.
A Bison Book

The 1988 edition published by
Crescent Books, distributed by
Crown Publishers, Inc.
225 Park Avenue South
New York, NY 10003

Produced by
Bison Books Corp.
15 Sherwood Avenue
Greenwich, CT 06830
USA

Printed in Hong Kong

Lettor, se truovi cosa che t'offenda in
questo modestissimo librino non te
maravigliar. Perche DIVINO, et non
humano, e quel ch'e senza Menda.

(Reader, if you find something that offends
you in this modest little book, do not be
surprised. For divine, not human, is that
which is without fault.)

From an Italian book of the 17th C.

**Library of Congress Cataloging-in-Publication
Data**

Bottomley, Ian & Hopson, Anthony
    Arms & Armor of the samurai by Ian Bottomley &
Anthony Hopson
        p.   cm.
    ISBN 0-517-64467-3 $12.98
    1. Arms and armor—Japan—History. 2.
Samurai.   I. Title.
 II. Title: Arms and armor of the samurai.
U821.J3T87   1988
355.8'241'0952—oc 19

*Page 1: Samurai of the
Nambokucho period wearing an o
yoroi.*

*Pages 2-3: Two hundred years
and half a world away: a
collection of Japanese armour
assembled in the 1930s and 1940s
displayed in an English country
house.*

*Pages 4-5: Samurai in action as
depicted in the thirteenth century
scroll, the Heiji Monogatari
Emaki.*

Contents

Foreword 7

ONE *The Origins of the Warrior Class* 8

TWO *The Samurai during the Gempei Wars* 22

THREE *The Kamakura and Nambokucho Periods* 46

FOUR *Civil Unrest: the Ashikaga Shogunate* 70

FIVE *The Evolution of Modern Armour* 94

SIX *The Arrival of the Southern Barbarians* 124

SEVEN *Japan in Isolation: the Edo Period* 154

Glossary 184

Bibliography 189

Index 190

Foreword

by Dr Y Sasama President of the Japan Armour and Militaria
Research Association

Although not formulated until some time during the seventeenth century, the code of Bushido is as old as the samurai class itself. The philosophies of Buddha, Chu-Tsu, Confucius and the ancient Gods of the Shinto faith were tempered by the spirit and thought of the Japanese people to produce an ethical system which the samurai strove to follow. The true spirit of Bushido requires a sincere observance of the following eight points:

Jin – to develop a sympathetic understanding of people
Gi – to preserve the correct ethics
Chu – to show loyalty to one's master
Ko – to respect and to care for one's parents
Rei – to show respect for others
Chi – to enhance wisdom by broadening one's knowledge
Shin – to be truthful at all times
Tei – to care for the aged and those of a humble station.

At the very heart of this discipline, formed by generations of samurai, was the realization that there was a need for such an ethical base as well as the need to learn the techniques of survival on the battlefield.

The study of Bushido is a difficult path, and one which the authors have striven to follow. Indeed, through long years of studying Kendo and Iai do, they have come to understand the fundamentals of Bushido. In the true spirit of the sixth tenet, they have broadened their knowledge by making an extensive study of the weapons, equipment, armour and defences of the samurai.

The current upsurge of interest in the West has led to the authors, regarded as experts in the field, being asked to fill the need for an introductory volume on the subject. As a Japanese, I am extremely happy if the results of their lengthy studies lead to a better understanding of Japan, its history and its people. For this reason I can recommend this work.

Periods of Japanese History and Art

The dates used in this book are those published by Suwa Tokutaro in his *Nihonshi no Yoryo*, Obunsha, Tokyo, 1957.

Jomon	– 8
Yayoi	8 – 300
Yamato	300 – 710
Nara	710 – 794
Early Heian	794 – 898
Late Heian	898 – 1185
Kamakura	1185 – 1333
Nambokucho	1336 – 1392
Muromachi	1333 – 1573
Sengoku	1482 – 1558
Momoyama	1573 – 1603
Edo	1603 – 1868

Notes on the Japanese used in the text

Many of the characters used in the study of arms and armour are of some antiquity they will not be found in a modern character dictionary and substitutes are used for others. Furthermore, even characters that are in general use are on occasions read in a way that is peculiar to the subject. To avoid errors, the authors have made every effort to check all of the terms used in this book against readings, often written phonetically, by modern Japanese authorities. The Hepburn system of Romanization has been used throughout with the exception of the indication of long vowel sounds. In many cases, compound terms have been split, without hyphenation, to ease pronounciation.

The reader should be aware of the frequent modification that is made to the initial sound of the second component in compound words. Typical changes are:

hoshi + hachi = hoshi bachi
uchi + katana = uchi gatana
hineno + shikoro = hineno jikoro

Names used in the text are those by which the person is most widely known and are written in the traditional way with the family name first. Equally, the traditional names of provinces have been used.

Left: A superb ni mai do gusoku of the Edo period complete with all its accessories.

CHAPTER ONE
The Origins of the Warrior Class

Right: Haniwa of fired clay from a tomb of the Yamato period representing the style of armour now called tanko (lit short armour).

Japan is unique among the world's major powers in being a country which, until recent times and with but two minor exceptions, fought all its battles on its own soil. No other nation has seen such long civil strife in which group after group struggled to gain power, only to be toppled in turn. These groups sought not the throne, which continued in an unbroken line, but the power to manipulate through it, while maintaining all the while the semblance of royal control.

In such a climate it is hardly surprising that the study of military matters was held in high esteem. This, and the fierce family pride of the Japanese, has resulted in the preservation of ancestral and votive arms and armours from the eighth century down to the middle of the last century, when they were finally laid aside in favour of the uniforms and weapons styled on those worn in the West.

Mythology has it that the sun goddess Amaterasu sent her grandson from heaven to Japan to bring the sacred symbols of power –

Right: Yamato period tanko having the plates laced together with leather thongs.

the sword, the comma-shaped jewel and the mirror – and to bring order to the people. Archaeology suggests that the people we now know as the Japanese are the descendants of successive waves of invaders from the Chinese and Korean mainlands and from the islands of Southeast Asia. Establishing themselves at first on the southern island of Kyushu, they set about consolidating their position and driving northwards the original inhabitants of Caucasian type, who are now represented by the few Ainu who survive on Hokkaido.

The invading peoples brought with them a knowledge of working bronze, and produced spear and arrow heads that differ little from those found from the Bronze Age cultures of Europe. During the period from the second century BC to the second century AD, further groups brought with them two important innovations: the working of iron and the practice of dolmen burial. It is from these sometimes enormous burial mounds that the remains of armours, swords and spear heads have been excavated which allow us to reconstruct in almost every detail the military equipment in use at the time.

Iron plates of considerable size and intricate shape demonstrate the skill with which these early armourers could handle their intractable raw material, and show that a long tradition of iron working must have existed in their homelands. There remains, however, one curious anomaly. In the earliest finds, the plates of the armours were fastened together with leather thongs, a feature which suggests that they were copies in iron of earlier versions made entirely from leather or perhaps bark. Evidence that this was probably the case is given by the use until recent times of remarkably similar hide armours in the Szechuan region of China. It was not long, however, before both rivets and rudimentary hinges were incorporated in these constructions, showing that even at this remote period the Japanese were quick to adapt new technologies to their needs. These early armours, now called *tanko*, were designed for fighting on foot with sword, spear and bow, and closely resemble the tonlet armours developed at the beginning of the sixteenth century in Europe for foot combat tournaments – a remarkable example of parallel development, albeit centuries apart.

Tanko were provided with a *kabuto* (helmet), which was characterized by a prominent beaked front which jutted out over the brow to protect the wearer's face; a feature that gives rise to their modern Japanese name of *shokaku tsuki kabuto* (battering-ram helmet). Their main constructional element was an oval plate, the *shokaku bo*, slightly domed for the head with a narrow prolongation in front that curved forwards and downwards where it developed a pronounced central fold. Two horizontal strips encircling the head were riveted to this frontal strip: the lower one, the *koshimaki* (hip wrap), formed the lower edge of the helmet bowl; the other, the *do maki* (body wrap), was set at about the level of the temples. Filling the gaps between these strips and the shokaku bo were small plates, sometimes triangular but more commonly rectangular in shape. Because the

front projected so far from the head, the triangular gap beneath was filled by a small plate, the *shoshaku tei ita*, whose rear edge bent downwards into a flange that rested against the forehead.

Fastened through holes in the koshimaki at the sides and back, were a series of broad leather thongs onto which were laced about five horizontal U-shaped strips of iron forming a defence for the neck, called the *shikoro* on all later helmets. Each strip was hung in such a way that it overlapped the one above to leave no gaps, and yet allowed either side or the back to move independently upwards with the wearer's movements.

Worn with these rather curious but no doubt effective helmets was a body armour, *do*, similarly constructed from plates riveted to a framework of strips. Almost all the surviving examples fitted closely to the body, and had a pronounced waist so that they sat firmly on the hips.

The do excavated from the earliest tombs are provided with an opening down the front which was fastened by ties of cloth. This style must have involved considerable gymnastics and needed several assistants to put on the do, since the strips of iron from which it was made are continuous around the body and the whole affair had to be sprung open to admit the wearer. This defect was recognized and rectified in later models which, from the heavily corroded remains, appear to have been fitted with a hinged section on the right

Below: Shokaku tsuki bachi from the Yamato period.

Opposite page left: Saddle of lacquered wood. Momoyama period.

Opposite page right: Umabari, a type of lancet carried in a pocket in the face of a sword scabbard for bleeding horses.

Right: Yamato period tanko of riveted plates.

Below: Horse muzzles of russet iron.

front or, occasionally, on both sides. The deep cut-outs for the arms left a standing extension at the front, reaching to the upper chest, and a similar, rather higher, section at the back. To these extensions were fastened a pair of cloth shoulder straps called *watagami* (over the shoulders), which transferred some of the not inconsiderable weight from the hips to the shoulders.

Protecting the lower body and tying over the flanged lower edge of the do was a flared skirt, called rather appropriately the *kusazuri*

(grass rubbing), since it reached to just above the knee. Like the shikoro, it was made of 10 or more horizontal lames, laced to internal leather thongs, and split down either side to allow some movement when walking. No protection was provided for the lower legs at this date, but rock carvings show that long baggy trousers were worn, tied with a drawstring just below the knee.

The shoulders and upper arms were covered by an arrangement of curved plates, the *kata yoroi* (shoulder armour), running from front to back and extending as far as the elbow, which were permanently fastened to a plate defence for the neck and upper chest called *akabe yoroi* (neck armour); the combination is almost identical to the 'Almain collar' worn in Europe during the sixteenth century with munition armours. Unlike the European version, which was worn under the shoulder straps of the cuirass to help distribute the weight, the Japanese wore it above the watagami, overlapping the top edges of the do at the front and back. Completing the outfit were long, tubular, tapering cuffs of plate fitted with a small panel of leather-laced scales which formed a defensive cover for the back of the hand.

As was normal on all later armours, the metal surface was given a coating of natural lacquer as a protection against the humidity of the Japanese climate. Some slight decoration to what must have been very sombre-looking armours was afforded by a border of leather thonging, sewn through holes along the sharp edges of all the major elements, and by a bunch of pheasant-tail feathers tied to iron prongs provided for that purpose on top of the helmet.

Found with these armours were the remains of simple self bows (made from a single piece of wood), arrowheads, socketed spear heads and long swords with straight single-edged iron blades. The swords were carried in scabbards covered in sheet copper and decorated with punched designs. Some had a hilt ending in a bulbous, slanting pommel of copper, *kazuchi no tsurugi* (mallet-headed sword), while others, *koma no tsurugi* (Korean sword) had ring-shaped pommels, occasionally enclosing silhouettes of animalistic design. The lengths of these weapons vary between just under two feet (0.6m) to four feet (1.2m) with three feet (0.9m) being the average. Two of these swords were excavated in Higo and Musashi provinces; they have inlays of silver representing horses and flowers on their blades and were probably imported from China. In most cases, some form of *tsuba* (flat hand guard) was fitted and this was pierced, generally with a trapezoidal opening. However, some have been found with comma-shaped holes representing the sacred jewels, which must surely point to native manufacture.

Thus equipped, the Yamato people, as they called themselves, lived a frontier life that was already beginning to show something of the social structure of historic Japan. A contemporary Chinese document, the *We-jen Chuan* notes that the peoples of the outlying islands of Tsushima and Iki sailed to the markets of both the Northern and Southern Dynasties of China. Of the southern region of Japan it records that 'in the various kingdoms there are markets where necessary items are traded. The Yamato Court oversees them.' This is a clear indication that the colonized territory was already divided into provinces responsible to a central court.

Naturally, this young, vigorous nation was awed by the sophisticated culture of its powerful neighbour, China. Religion, technology, government and the arts of China were assiduously studied and slavishly copied whenever possible. The system of Chinese writing was adopted and adapted to the spoken language of the Japanese, to become the bane of Japanese and non-Japanese students ever since. Artists and craftsmen were persuaded to come to Japan to train Japanese pupils in their styles and methods. In short, what occurred was almost a wholesale importation of one culture and its superimposition on another. However, Buddhism, the imported religion, did not entirely supplant the indigenous Shinto religion; the two co-existed peacefully and still do today.

Among the imports were a considerable number of horses or, to be more accurate, ponies, of the type used by the Mongols on their periodic expansions from the steppes of Central Asia. They were sturdy, shaggy-

Right: Stirrups of russet iron decorated with chrysanthemums and clover in silver overlay. Edo period.

Below: Tsuki mabisashi bachi, a type of helmet introduced from the Asiatic mainland together with armour of scale construction and horses.

coated beasts which later commentators describe as having wild dispositions and, particularly true of stallions, a tendency to bite the knees of their riders. Uncouth animals they may have been, but they were invaluable to the Japanese because they could cover considerable distances over rough terrain. Initially the Japanese used the same harness as their Chinese counterparts, a wooden saddle reinforced and decorated with metal, and plain, open stirrups suspended by chains. By the early Heian period, the stirrup had acquired an enclosed toecap and a rearward extension of the tread; this was quickly modified, by the loss of the sides of the toecap, into the characteristic open-platform stirrup, which the Japanese continued to use until the nineteenth century. Not only horses were imported, lamellar armour was also adopted from the Asiatic mainland, and modified to suit Japanese taste.

Armour of lamellar construction is of great antiquity, having originated somewhere in the Middle East. It was used by the Egyptians and, later, the Romans, spreading eastwards into Central Asia and northwards into Eastern Europe, reaching as far as Scandinavia. Although differing in minor details, lamellar armour was always constructed from more-or-less rectangular, overlapping scales of metal or leather, laced together into rows which were then laced vertically, each row overlapping the one above so that the tops of the scale heads were visible. The result was a flexible defence whose efficiency lay in its ability to absorb the energy of a blow in the lacing sandwiched between the rows of scales before penetration could begin. It was in fact an early version of the laminated armour that modern military technology has only recently rediscovered.

Although the tanko continued to be made, the new style of construction was developed into a complementary armour for mounted use. Called *keiko* or *kake yoroi* (hanging armour) and made entirely from iron scales laced together with leather thongs, these armours were similar in form to the armour made and worn in Tibet as late as the nineteenth century and to the few surviving armours made by the Ainu peoples in northern Japan. The do of a keiko resembled a sleeveless coat, opening down the front and provided with a flared skirt extending to mid-thigh. At the waist was a row of elongated incurved scales, which rested on the hips, with sometimes a similar row along the lower edge of the skirt, whose purpose is obscure. Over this was worn a collar and upper-arm guards combination comparable with that worn with the tanko, but made entirely of scales. The tubular defence for the forearms was no longer of plates, but of narrow vertical splints, this time without any protection for the hand. The legs are always a vulnerable target of a horseman, so leg armour was provided in the form of sections of scales; a tapered section tied above and below the knee, another wrapped around the lower leg with ties at the back.

With the keiko came a new style of helmet, called *mabisashi tsuki kabuto* because of the prominent pierced horizontal peak riveted to the front lower edge. More or less circular in plan, and fitting close to the head, it was constructed in a similar way to the earlier helmets; the koshimaki and do maki were still used, but now took the form of complete rings held together by the infilling of rectangular plates. Closing the top was a circular iron plate, the *fuse ita*, onto which was riveted an ornamental arrangement of two iron cups connected by an iron rod through their bases. It has been suggested that the lower of these cups was to accommodate the wearer's hair, but the fuse ita was solid at this point, making it more likely that the whole arrangement was to carry a plume, which would have been tied to the holes in the rim of the upper cup. The shikoro fitted to these helmets was made of metal strips arranged exactly like those on the shokaku tsuki kabuto.

The distinctive feature of these helmets was the peak. It was lobed in outline and fretted with either a geometric design or one of stylized tendrils. One of these helmets, made of gilded copper and hence unsuited to real use, is decorated with a punched design of fishes and birds which extends onto the plates of the bowl. Since shoes, also of gilded copper, have been found in a tomb, they, like the helmet, were probably made as grave goods for a person of considerable rank.

Left: A haniwa representing a warrior wearing a scale armour called keiko. The neck guard is divided so that the front portions can be fastened under the chin to give greater protection to the face.

Apart from the actual remains of armours and other weapons found as burial deposits, our knowledge of the military equipment is considerably extended by finds of *haniwa*, fired-clay models of figures, animals and inanimate objects, which were placed in the superstructure of the tombs. These do not seem to have been substitutes for people buried with the dead as was common in China, since no evidence of this practice has been found in Japan, but rather served as markers, which were erected upon posts around the mound of the grave. Whatever their real purpose, a large proportion of these charming figures represent warriors, and from them it is possible to see the way in which the two styles of armour evolved and combined as all possible combinations of plate and scales were tried out. This experimentation is hardly surprising since the

armourers themselves were a mixture of native Japanese, Koreans and Chinese. Since few actual armours have been excavated, and most of these are fragmentary, haniwa provide invaluable secondary evidence about styles of armour and helmets. A group of warrior figures show keiko being worn with a simple bowl-shaped helmet of vertical plates, some of which are provided with exaggerated rivets, and surmounted by an inverted iron cup – these helmets are almost identical to those worn in contemporary China. These models differ from surviving helmets in having the shikoro made of scales, split vertically just behind the ears, with the front sections tying under the chin to guard the face. Why no examples have been unearthed of what seems to have been a common type of helmet, while numbers of the rarely depicted mabisashi tsuki kabuto have been found remains a mystery. Possibly peaked helmets were in fact the exception, worn perhaps by nobles as an indication of their rank, while the haniwa represent warriors of lower status, wearing common armour in their role as tomb guardians.

As the Yamato people pushed the frontier and the 'barbarians' further from the court, Emperor Kotoku, backed by the powerful aristocratic Fujiwara clan, gathered together the nobles and announced a new system of government based on that of T'ang China. It was in effect a declaration of absolute monarchy; all lands belonged to the throne and those who worked it would pay for its use in taxes. A series of royal decrees was issued in 646 to this effect, called the Taika Reform. Also included was legislation aimed at establishing internal peace by banning the wearing of swords by all except those guarding the capital and territorial borders. The lack of success of this particular enactment can be judged by the fact that a watered-down version had to be passed again in 696.

By the middle of the eighth century, the court was firmly established in Nara, a city based on those of T'ang China. Prosperity in the country was increasing so rapidly that there was an increasing demand for luxury goods. The famous Sho so in at Nara, established by the widow of the Emperor Shomu in 756 to house his personal belongings as a shrine to his memory, contains among its treasures items from distant parts of the world imported through China. Stored there originally were 90 keiko and 10 tanko; sadly,

Right: Haniwa clearly showing the fabric shoulder straps supporting the tanko.

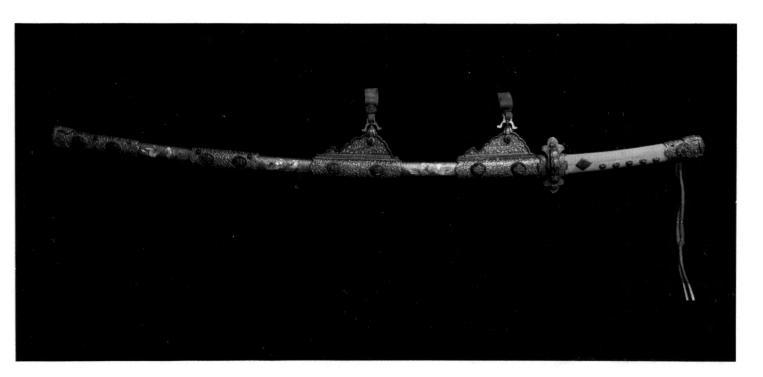

however, these were later borrowed to arm Imperial troops during a rebellion and were never replaced. All that now survive are a few fragments of a keiko laced in purple doeskin; this represents the oldest non-excavated armour in Japan.

Fortunately, the Sho so in collection still contains a considerable number of spears, swords and other weapons. Among the former are socketed spear heads about 10 inches (25cm) long, with elegant diamond-sectioned blades, some of which have a down-curving hook just above the socket. All were referred to in inventories by the generic name of *hoko*, although others with curious crank-shaped sword-like blades mounted on short, cord-bound shafts, are distinguished by being described as *te boko* (hand spears).

Many of the swords preserved at the shrine are undoubtedly of Chinese manufacture but a few at least of the short swords and knives are thought to be indigenous. These, when polished by modern methods, show that the swordsmiths were beginning to experiment with techniques that were to create the most perfect hand-to-hand weapon the world has seen.

Swordsmiths throughout the world have been hindered by the mutually exclusive properties of toughness and hardness of steel. Having only an empirical understanding of the complex metallurgy involved, they adopted a variety of techniques in an attempt to make a blade that was hard enough to take

and keep a cutting edge, yet tough enough not to break easily. The interaction between iron and carbon, and the effect of temperature changes on the combination is enormously complex. Put very simply, iron reacts with an excess of carbon at high temperatures to produce a compound which on slow cooling becomes tough and soft. On the other hand, if the compound is cooled rapidly, the transformation does not have time to occur and the high temperature form is retained, leaving the steel very hard but as brittle as glass. Lowering the level of carbon below a critical limit reduces this capacity to harden until, with almost-pure iron, it ceases altogether. A further factor that has a considerable bearing on sword technology is the fact that all metals are made up from a mass of interlocking crystals whose size influences the mechanical properties of the metal. Deformation causes the crystals to fragment, hardening the metal, but also introduces dislocations that, if taken to excess, cause the structure to collapse. This is exactly the principle we all use to break a piece of wire by bending it back and forth. During this process the metal can be felt to harden as the crystals are progressively broken down, reaching a maximum just before the metal begins to crack. In sword making, therefore, it is important to know just how far the forging process should be taken; too little and the metal is not as hard as it could be, while over-working causes it to become weak and more liable to fracture.

Above: An eighteenth century reproduction of a sword mounting used at court since the Heian period.

*Right: Cross-section of a sword
blade made in variation of the
wari ha kitae technique in which
the steel forming the cutting edge
is sandwiched between pieces of
only partially mixed softer metal.*

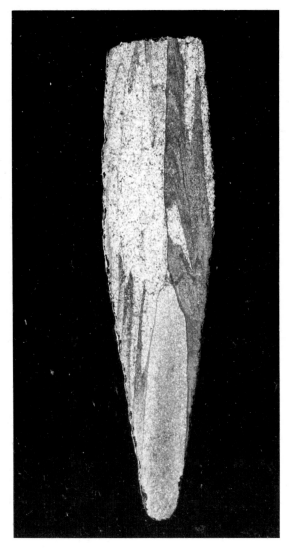

In Europe swordsmiths compromised by making blades that were tempered, that is, they were first made fully hard, but very brittle, then reheated to a lower temperature, allowing some of the hardness to dissipate. This process produced blades that were at once moderately hard and reasonably tough. In India and the Middle East, an alternative compromise was reached; a mixture of high-carbon steel and almost-pure iron, which cannot be hardened, was forged together. This formed a mixture which, when heated and quenched, produced a blade with an edge that had both hard and soft parts, the one sharing its properties with the other and, incidentally, producing the 'watered steel' effect so admired in their blades.

Japan's answer to this problem was sometimes to produce a blade like the Middle Eastern blades, but more often they made a high-carbon-steel cutting edge and welded it to a low-carbon-steel body. This was then heat treated in such a way that only the edge was hardened; although brittle, this was supported and prevented from breaking by the soft, malleable body of the blade. This is exactly the same principle that is now used for tungsten-carbide-tipped machine tools. Over the centuries, many different techniques were evolved that achieved this aim, but all involved the smith in careful preparation of the materials, which he then assembled into a composite billet from which the sword itself was made.

No one now knows when this method of construction was perfected, but by the tenth century blades were being made which had all the characteristics expected of true Japanese swords. Nothing has come down to us of the working methods of smiths from the tenth century, but we know from historic writings and from modern smiths using traditional methods that parts of the process were regarded as religious ceremonies. At these times the forge would be decorated with straw rope and cut-paper, symbols of the Shinto faith, while the smith himself would dress in court robes, after symbolic washing. Some smiths are said to have taken religious observation even further and abstained from alcohol, women and eating certain foods during the forging of a blade. Inevitably there were others who did not carry things quite so far. Noda Hankei, whose work was renowned and much sought-after during the early Edo period, seems to have spent much of his life sleeping off the effects of drink in the more dubious quarters of the capital – his body was found in the gutter one morning cut in two by one of his own blades.

Recent research suggests that in historic times, the manufacture of a blade began with the careful selection of small pieces of steel from the impure mass of slag and metal formed in the blast furnace. These were stacked onto a previously prepared iron plate which was welded to a long iron rod which acted as a handle, and wrapped with paper and string to make a compact block which held the whole precarious pile together. A thin slurry of clay and straw ash in water was poured over everything, both to protect the bundle until it was positioned in the fire, and to act as a flux, easing fusion. The hearth used by the swordsmith took the form of a long, narrow pit lined with clay. Air was supplied by bellows operated by the smith himself and the hearth was fuelled with carefully selected pieces of charcoal. As soon as the correct temperature was reached, the partially fused block was transferred to the anvil and welded solid by the smith's assistants, who struck with sledge hammers at the spot indicated by the smith. By carefully controlling the intensity and position of the blows, the block was drawn out to twice its length and half its thickness while maintaining the width and keeping the edges square. After reheating, the underside of the block was cleaned by pouring water over the anvil then hammering the block on it; this caused an explosive release of steam which carried with it the surface coating of scale and dirt from the fire.

Now followed the part of the forging operation on which so much depended; to cut the block almost in two with a chisel, bending it back on itself and then welding the joint together so that no scale or unwelded gaps were included that would cause weaknesses in the final blade. Great care was taken to ensure that the surface of the anvil, and hence the welding surface it produced, was perfectly smooth and that there were no pockets that would trap scale or slag. That this folding operation was done not once, but sometimes as many as 15 times, to produce metal with fewer inclusions of slag than many modern steel samples, is little short of miraculous and a testimony to the skill and dedication of these master craftsmen. During the long process of folding, heating and welding, impurities in the metal were eliminated and some of the carbon was probably burnt out but, more importantly, the metal was made homogeneous and the grain structure was refined, with a corresponding increase in hardness.

To form steels of intermediate hardness, a compound block would be made by welding soft iron and steel together, and then folding and welding this until the two metals were mixed to the required degree. Repeating the folding process many times produced a virtually homogeneous metal. Fewer foldings however left the two grades of metal in layers which, when the finished blade was polished, were visible as the beautifully patterned surface effects, *hada*, on the finished sword. Sakakibara Kozan, writing in his book *Chukokatchu Seisakuben* on the manufacture of steel for armour, warns that the foldings should not exceed 15 otherwise the 'hardness' would be lost and the steel will become *kuzureru* (decayed). He also warns that if high-carbon steel is used initially, more than

Left: Cross-section of a sword blade made by the kobushi kitae process in which a soft core is wrapped in high carbon steel. In this case the core shows a coarse crystalline structure towards the back and there is a welding defect, visible as a dark line, on the right.

five foldings will ruin it by burning out too much of the carbon. On the other hand, Suishinshi Kawabe Gihachiro Masahide, a swordsmith working in the early nineteenth century who devoted much of his life to rediscovering the secrets of the old swordsmiths, describes in detail how the bed of the hearth could be soaked with water the night before to prevent carbon being lost.

Using these methods, the smith could produce the various grades of steel that he needed for a blade, and by simple tests such as the examination of the colour and texture of a fractured surface, could judge very closely the properties each possessed. His next task was to assemble the different pieces, each carefully shaped, into a billet from which the final blade could be made. It was in the manner by which this was done that most variations occur. Sometimes a block was notched along its length and a strip of high-carbon steel welded in, *wari ha kitae* (split-edge forging). A variant was to wrap the high-carbon metal around a low-carbon core, *kobushi kitae*

(fist forging). A more complex construction using five grades of steel, arranged to form the edge, back, cores and sides, gave what was called rather confusingly *san mai zukuri* (three-plate style), considered to be the best method by an old swordsmith, Horii Taneyoshi, at the end of the last century.

By careful orientation of those pieces of metal that had only received a few folding operations, the smith could regulate the type of surface effects visible on the sides of the finished blade. If the surface was parallel to the folds, small irregularities would reveal a beautiful burl-wood grain when ground flat; if at right angles or beaten on an angle, a striated effect was produced. Some even went as far as corrugating the metal so that when polished it showed regular undulating striations, along the length of the blade.

Once the composite billet had been prepared, it was drawn out into a strip of the approximate size and shape of the blade using a wooden gauge, to determine the proportions and curve. Using a smaller hammer, the smith then carefully shaped the *shinogi* (ridge) and single edge that was characteristic of most blades, leaving the final shaping and cleaning to be carried out with a draw shave and files while the blade was clamped to a wooden block. If after careful examination no defects were revealed and the smith was satisfied with his work, he would then punch a hole called a *mekugi no ana*, through the *nakago* (tang), which was used to hold the blade into its mounts, before passing the blade for hardening.

Giving the blade a hard, tempered edge while leaving the remainder soft was

achieved by coating the blade with a layer of clay which, when dry, was thinned by scraping away all but a thin film from the edge, in a pattern that was characteristic of the smith's working tradition. Masahide maintained that any clay was suitable, if sticky, and that he obtained his from the province of Dewa; he mixed it with powdered whetstone and charcoal before use. He also mentions that his experiments led him to believe that some of the old smiths used borax in addition to the clay, but he was attempting to reproduce by any means that he could find, features of old blades that in the past had arisen from the materials and methods used.

When dry, the clay-coated blade was heated in the specially darkened smithy so that the temperature of the hot metal could be judged by its colour. For a delicate narrow *yakiba* (cutting edge), the blade could only be heated to dull red, to localize the hardening, but for more robust patterns, bright red or orange was permissible. When at precisely the right temperature, the heat-softened blade was plunged edge down into water, which was also at a critical temperature. The layer of clay surrounding the blade delayed the chilling of the body sufficiently to prevent it being hardened while allowing the full rapid cooling to take place along the edge. It was during this stage that the blade assumed most of its graceful curve; the differential quenching caused the back to contract more than the edge. If the smith had misjudged things, this difference in contraction caused undue stressing that could, in extreme cases, cause cracking of the hardened edge with the total loss of the time and labour expended.

Little wonder that this was regarded as the most sacred part of the whole process, and that prayers were offered to a shrine set up in the forge before it was undertaken.

The smith would then chisel his name on the tang, if he had not done so before, perhaps including other details such as the province in which he worked and the date. Traditionally, spring water was considered to be at the correct temperature during the second and eighth months, and most dated swords indicate these months, irrespective of when they were actually made. Any decoration on the blade, such as carvings or grooves, would also be cut into the soft metal body of the blade before it could be finally finished.

In all probability the earlier swordsmiths would then themselves grind the blade into its final shape and keen edge but in later times this was a separate craft. The sword polisher used a dozen or more stones of increasing fineness that not only smoothed and polished the metal, but also revealed the complex structures introduced into the metal by the forging and hardening processes it had undergone. It is from a close study of these details, together with the subtle shape of a blade, that sword appraisers are able to assign a blade to a given maker even when, as is often the case, the swordsmith had chosen not to sign it.

By the middle of the eighth century Nara had become a capital of considerable sophistication, with palaces, mansions and Buddhist temples housing priceless libraries and art treasures from China. The government, however, had grown weak and the Imperial armies were suffering all too many defeats from the Ainu on the northern borders. Ambitious nobles and the clergy were constantly plotting to place their favourites in positions of power at court. By 784 Emperor Kammu could tolerate the situation no longer and, aided by the ever-scheming Fujiwara clan, decided to move the capital to a more auspicious location. After some initial difficulties the site of modern Kyoto was chosen, which although only 25 miles from Nara, was considered sufficiently distant to escape from the influence of the monks. On this gently sloping plain with mountains guarding the northeast (which as everyone knew was the direction chosen by demons to launch their attacks) a new Chinese-style city called Heian-Kyo (the Capital of Peace and Tranquillity) was built. Initially the move was a great success but on Kammu's death in 806, the power struggle to influence affairs of state began once again. Ultimately it was the Fujiwara who gained the ascendance and by using titles such as 'Chancellor' and 'Regent', gained control of the throne by providing a seemingly inexhaustible supply of beautiful daughters as brides for the Emperor.

Entrenched in their magnificent capital and turning inward from the rest of the world, the courtiers and nobles of Heian society developed a refined culture which emphasized poetry, music, art and fashion while much of the remainder of the country, populated mainly by farmers, struggled to exist. Minor members of the Imperial Family and the younger sons of the aristocracy were dispatched to act as stewards of provincial estates and as local representatives of the government. They became in fact a class of landed gentry, *ji zamurai*, the backbone of the armed forces; putting on their armour and rallying with their retainers to suppress rebellion and continue the process of expansion ever northwards. These minor aristocrats formed two major groups; adopting the names of Taira and Minamoto they were based in the western and eastern regions of Japan respectively.

Following the almost wholesale adoption of Buddhism and the resultant cessation of dolmen burials and their associated haniwa, actual examples of arms and armour of the period are reduced to occasional archaeological finds. What evidence there is suggests that armours of plate had finally been abandoned in favour of a version of the keiko, modified into a poncho-like garment with openings under each arm filled by separate pieces fastened to the body. The shape and construction of the helmet was also changing and was now distinctly conical; it was made of vertical tapering plates riveted to a koshimaki at the bottom and surmounted by an inverted iron cup that housed the wearer's hair. Horses were now reasonably plentiful and almost all fighting was between groups of mounted men.

With the Fujiwara firmly in control of the country by manipulation of what were virtually puppet emperors, the Taira and the Minamoto began of gain prestige by acting as the armed forces of the regency in what were mainly policing roles; the Ainu were now an issue only in the extreme north. One particularly troublesome problem was the result of a

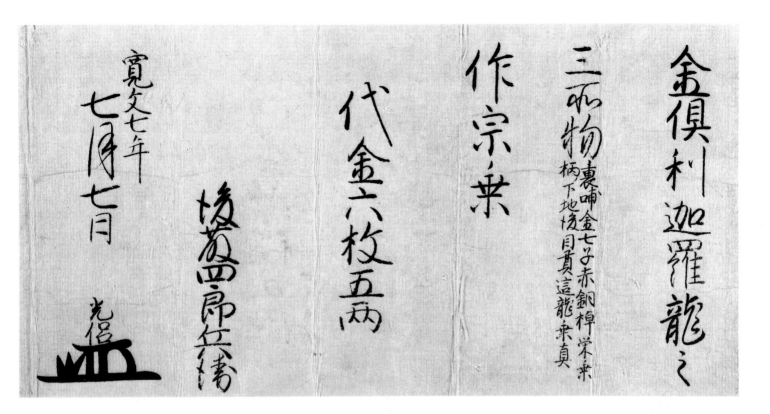

quirk of legislation incorporated in the Taika Reform which exempted some of the nobility and temples from paying taxes on their land holdings. Playing on this, many of the Fujiwara, minor members of the Imperial Family and particularly the monastic orders situated in the mountains to the north of the capital, set up lucrative business schemes whereby they accepted nominal ownership of land in exchange for a small percentage of the annual yield. Looking after these interests, as well as more legitimate affairs of state, became the prerogative of the Taira and Minamoto.

Farther from the capital the situation grew steadily worse throughout the eleventh century as local magnates, virtually ignored by a court totally engrossed in itself, refused to pay taxes, and banded together for self-protection. They formed what amounted to private armies which were fully capable of dealing with such forces as the government could muster. This same blatant disregard for the law was also shown by the monastic orders, which employed their own armies of mercenaries, only slightly legitimized as *sohei* (novices). On several occasions these armies of monks, wearing armour under their clerical robes and wielding their favourite weapon, the *naginata*, marched on the capital, carrying with them sacred palanquins to force the somewhat superstitious courtiers to accede to their demands.

From this time weapons and armour were deposited in temples as votive offerings, indicating the importance and prestige that was beginning to be attached to them – and also perhaps the growing prestige of the military. Some of these deposits have survived almost intact to the present day, but it is impossible to say how many more would have survived had not the temples, in particular, suffered systematic burning because of their involvement in politics during Japan's long civil wars. We must, however, be grateful that at least some of this unique legacy is available for study – unmatched by anything elsewhere in the world.

During this period of growing chaos there were glimmers of light as the occasional Emperor broke free from the grasp of the Fujiwara and either ruled directly or, more commonly, abdicated in favour of a weak son and ruled from retirement. This very Japanese institution of the 'Cloistered Emperors' was insufficient to halt the decline of the brilliant social life that Heian-Kyo had enjoyed for so long. Much of the city was already in ruins and bandits roamed the derelict areas, raiding mansions and palaces alike. In the rest of the country, the 'teeth and claws of the Fujiwara', the Minamoto, together with the Taira, were becoming more self-assertive as they realized the potential power they could wield and the growing weakness of the court.

CHAPTER TWO
The Samurai during the Gempei Wars

As Heian culture gained confidence during the ninth century it looked less often to China for its inspiration, becoming more inward looking and relying more on native sources of talent. The official link was broken in 894 when, exactly 100 years after the capital's founding, the diplomatic mission planned for that year was cancelled. The adoption of Chinese military philosophy declined even earlier and a school for *samurai* (one who serves), the *Butokukan*, had been set up in the capital. Here the martial arts were cultivated by officer cadets of high family.

During the tenth and early eleventh centuries the increased availability of horses led to the evolution of a style of fighting that depended to a large degree on the ability of the combatants to discharge arrows from horseback while charging their opponent at full gallop – wheeling away at the last moment to re-form. This ability to use a bow, *yumi*, was deemed so important, that the term *kyusen no ie* came to mean 'samurai family', although its literal meaning is 'bows and arrow family'. Indeed, all contemporary accounts of battles record the strength of each side solely in terms of the numbers of bows present. As the eleventh century advanced, these tactics acquired some of the ritualistic qualities of the duel. Battles degenerated into a mêlée, with individual warriors shouting challenges, declaring their pedigree and past achievements before launching into an attack on whichever opponent they had singled out. Ceremonies were devised such as that of presenting the heads of the slain to the victorious

Right: Scene from the Heiji Monogatari Emaki *showing samurai and their retainers attacking the imperial palace. Kamakura period.*

commanders after the battle; honour and, more importantly, rewards, were bestowed on those who had killed the highest ranking opponents. With each warrior bent on glory, commanders could do little to control the impetuosity of their forces and any attempt at using them tactically was futile.

Foot soldiers played little part in the military strategy of the day, being relegated to a supporting role. Each noble would be accompanied by a number of lightly armed retainers on foot, who carried their lord's helmet and other equipment to the scene of the battle, but who played no part in the initial stages of the fighting itself; their duty was to rush in between the horses, arrows and flailing swords, to give assistance when their lord or his opponent was unhorsed.

In 1156, the first year of the period of Hogen, a dispute arose over succession to the throne that resulted in calls for support going out from both the current Emperor, Go-Shirakawa, and the 'Cloistered Emperor' Sotoku. Their loyalties divided, both the samurai and the armed monks of Nara took sides. Each group contained a mixture of both Taira and Minamoto, with the result that, as in many civil wars, fathers faced sons

from the opposing lines. This division of the family between the two opposing forces did not always arise from a sense of conviction; the Japanese, being pragmatists, frequently adopted such a strategy to ensure that at least a part of the family would survive, whatever the outcome. The inevitable battle was fought during a July night, with all the formality and style expected of perfect samurai: challenges and counter-challenges were issued, charges were made and arrows shot. The only deviation from good form was the burning of Sotoku's headquarters when it became evident that it would take too long to capture it in any other way, leaving the defenders little choice but to flee.

In itself the whole affair was little more than an incident in which a few were killed and Sotoku was banished, but its legacy was to plunge the country into further civil war. One of the commanders, Taira Kiyomori, was rewarded, much to the chagrin of the Minamoto, by a powerful position at court. Discontent increased when Kiyomori, as skilled in politics as he was in arms, rose rapidly through the ranks, inevitably, perhaps, making enemies among both the Fujiwara and the Minamoto in the process.

Right: Scene from the Heiji Monogatari Emaki. *Armed retainers carry trophy heads on their naginata (pole arms). Kamakura period.*

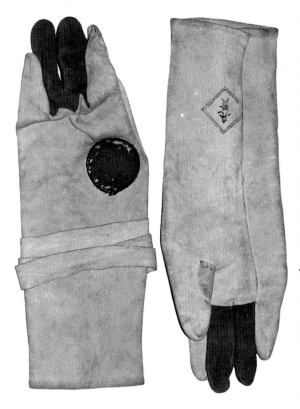

Resentment grew with each promotion until 1160 when a force of 500 Minamoto attacked the palace itself, kidnapping Go-Shirakawa, who was now 'cloistered', and imprisoning Emperor Nijo in an attempt to regain some of their former power. There followed a month of fighting in and around the capital, until the Taira finally regained control of the situation and embarked on a programme of executions and retribution of unparalleled savagery. Every adult Minamoto they could find was put to the sword, with the exception of one old man who had refused to take part in the attack. Only the Minamoto children were spared; they were exiled to various monasteries or adopted into Taira households on the assumption that they no longer posed a threat.

Every written character used by the Japanese has at least two pronunciations – the native Japanese sound for the idea it expresses and the way the Chinese pronounced the character during the Nara period or, more accurately, how the Japanese thought they did. Using the Chinese pronunciation, which was always favoured by scholars of the classics, the names Minamoto and Taira become Gen and Hei which, when compounded, gives the name to the wars between these two great houses – The Gempei Wars.

Historically important as these opening battles of the Gempei Wars were, they illus-trate vividly how parochial Heian society was when a force of just 500 could capture and hold the throne against the Imperial forces for the best part of a month. Even allowing for poor communications, events in the capital meant little to most of the population, to whom the courtiers and their world seemed as remote as the gods themselves.

Although not unknown in Japan, the recurved composite bows of the Asiatic horseman played no part in these battles and were never adopted by the Japanese. The horn and sinew needed for these bows came from cattle, but few were kept because most Japanese were Buddhists, and eating meat or handling anything derived from dead animals was abhorrent to them. In later periods, tasks such as executions or the slaughter of animals and the preparation of leather were carried out by the *eta*, a class of people considered subhuman and totally outside society because of their occupation. That leather figures largely in military equipment supposes that, once prepared, it somehow became transformed and lost its defiling

Left: Glove for archery practice of dark blue leather covering the thumb and first two fingers only. Edo period.

Above: Box of lacquered leather for storing archers' gloves. Momoyama period.

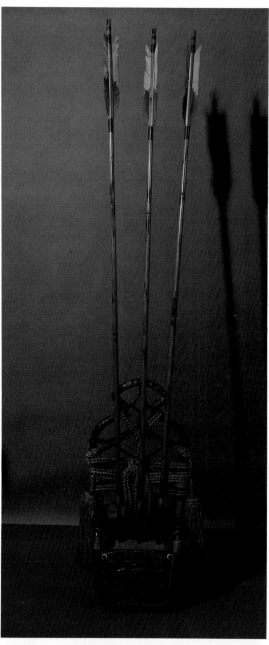

Right: Arrows displayed in an open quiver. Muromachi period.

Below: Various arrow heads, including pierced flat arrow heads with a cherry blossom design.

properties; an attitude of mind similar to that assumed by those who ate venison and assuaged their consciences by calling it 'mountain whale.' The Japanese bowyers, however, turned to the materials they had in abundance: wood and, especially, bamboo.

To obtain the power needed in a war bow while retaining a cross-section of reasonable proportions, it was necessary to adopt a laminated structure. During the early Heian this was achieved by making the bow of deciduous wood and backing it with bamboo; that is the body of the bow was of wood with a thick facing of bamboo fastened onto the side farthest from the archer when drawing the bow. By the middle of the Heian, performance was further improved by adding an additional facing of bamboo on the opposite, or belly side of the bow. Although glued carefully with hide glue, the most powerful adhesive available, joints involving bamboo are notoriously unreliable and they had to be augmented by bindings of rattan which differ considerably in number and position. Additional pieces of wood were spliced in at each end, then glued and bound in position to reinforce the nocks for the string. Bindings of rattan and leather marked the grip. Almost all traditional bows were lacquered to prevent damp weakening the glued joints; the most popular colour scheme was black with the bindings picked out in red. When being carried to and from the battlefield, or when in storage, bows were further protected by tubular bags of cloth which tied at the ends.

Poor glue adhesion imposed a severe limit on the stressing the bow could withstand. To limit the stress, the bow had to be long; an average bow was about 6½ feet (2m) in length, but some were much longer. One bow, said to have been the property of Yuasa Matashichiro, is 8 feet 9 inches (2.7m) long, and is still preserved in the temple at Itsukushima. This temple also houses an 8-foot 6-inch (2.5m) long bow which belonged to Ihara Koshiro. Even bows of less heroic lengths than these would have been hopelessly impractical on horseback had the bowyers not arrived at the simple expedient of moving the grip downwards from the centre and, by careful shaping, making the upper limb do much of the work. This left a short lower limb that could be easily manipulated over the horse's neck.

Tsuru (bowstrings) were of plant fibre, usually hemp or ramie, coated with wax to

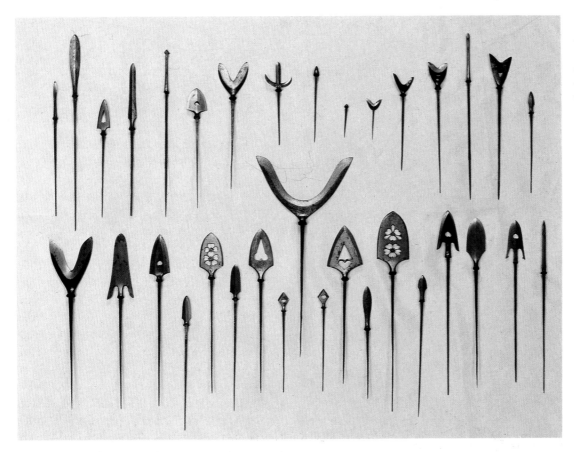

give a hard, smooth surface. The upper end was bound with red silk ribbon, the bottom end with white. Loops were formed by means of a timber hitch rather than being part of the string's construction, or formed by separate cords as in China. The upper loop was also provided with an extra tab of silk so that the string could be held in the teeth, leaving both hands free to brace the bow. In some cases this was too much for one person to manage – one way of gauging the strength of a bow was to count the number of men needed to string it.

Like most Asiatics, the Japanese drew the string with the right thumb hooked under the arrow and locked by the first two fingers resting on the thumbnail. This requires that the arrow be positioned on the right of the bow as viewed by the archer, not on the left as when the string is drawn with the fingers. Unlike the Chinese, the Japanese apparently did not use thumb rings of stones or ivory to protect the ball of the thumb from the pressure of the string, wearing instead a leather glove, *yugake*. Those worn while practicing often only covered the first two fingers and had an enlarged thumb reinforced with horn or leather at the point of contact with the string. In war, where such a glove would have hindered the handling of a sword or

even the arrows, a pair of more ordinary gloves were worn, again reinforced, but only with a small double layer of leather on the inside of the right thumb. Made of coloured or patterned leather, the two centre fingers are for some reason frequently of a different colour from the rest.

To draw the bow the archer held the bow above the head, to clear the horse, and then moved his the hands apart as the bow was brought down, to end with the left arm

27

Right: A quiver that has survived from the Heian period preserved in the storehouse of a temple. These ebira were worn on the right hip, the shafts of the arrows being secured to the upright frame by a cord.

Far right: An Edo period reproduction of an ebira of cane, rawhide and leather. The deer skin suggests that it was made as part of a hunting outfit.

straight and the right hand near the right ear. This style of drawing the bow was formalized by the Ogasawara family. The alternative style, *heiki ryu*, practised by foot soldiers, resembled that used in Europe – the draw was begun with the bow held horizontally, level with the waist. Drawing these asymmetric bows requires a very loose hold by the bow hand since the upper limb moves forward in an arc, ending with the grip at a considerable angle from the vertical. To release, the fingers supporting the thumb were relaxed, allowing the string to slip off the glove and, as it returned to its resting position, allowing the bow to rotate in the hand so that it ended with the string touching the outside of the bow arm. This permitted the Japanese to dispense with a bracer for the protection of the inside of the left wrist, although occasionally a *yugote* (loose sleeve) was worn on the left arm to protect the clothing underneath.

The *ya* (arrows) had bamboo shafts. These were cut in November and December, when they were in the best condition, and prepared by shaving off the nodes and outer skin. The nock for the bowstring was cut immediately above a node, for strength, in the end farthest from the root in the growing plant so that the

taper was towards the nock. Each shaft was softened in hot sand and then carefully straightened, using a notched stick for leverage. On better sets of arrows from the Edo period, shafts were sorted to ensure that the positions of the nodes matched and looked even when carried in a quiver. They were finished by bindings of lacquered fibre below the nock and above the head, to prevent splitting at these vulnerable points, and in many cases the signature of the maker was added on the nock binding in red lacquer.

There were normally three fletchings, although arrows fitted with a particularly large head had four. Because of the problem of adhesion, fletchings were glued in place and then bound to the shaft by the ends of their quills. All manner of feathers were pressed into use, but various eagle, hawk, crane and pheasant tail feathers are by far the most common. On most arrows the fletchings were left either untrimmed or cut parallel to the shaft, using the natural slope of the barbs at each end. For the very best sets, the area of the shaft between and around the fletchings was lacquered gold or decorated in some other way.

Ya no ne (arrowheads) were made by specialist smiths. They sometimes signed their work, either on the blade or in minute characters on the tang. They were produced in a multiplicity of shapes and sizes. Many were highly decorative and enormous; these were never meant to be shot, but were intended for presentation and votive purposes. Fanciful names exist, or have been invented, for the hundreds of varieties, but all can be assigned into one of three major groups.

Narrow four-sided heads These are often almost square in section and are named after the leaf they resemble, for example *yanagi* (willow-leaf shape) or *sasa no ha* (bamboo-leaf shape). Like the bodkin heads of Europe, their purpose was to pierce deep and, if needed, to punch holes through armour. Most war arrows were fitted with heads of this type. Related to these are various acutely pointed heads (*togari ya*), and the less common chisel pointed heads, which both served a similar function.

Barbed broadhead types (hira ne) These are shaped like the base of a flat-iron and are flat in section with a narrow sharpened edge. These exhibit most variation and were often pierced with heraldic or flower designs in negative silhouette, their shape lending themselves to this form of decoration. Less common are specimens with poems or other characters in positive silhouette, in which almost the entire area of the blade is occupied by the decoration, leaving only a narrow band as the cutting edge. Some complete sets have two arrows, one fitted with a decorated hira ne; the other with a forked head. Some historians claim these would have been used against a high-ranking opponent, and others that it would have been shot to signal defeat – both highly improbable reasons.

Forked arrow heads Named *karimata* after their resemblance to a flock of geese in flight, forked arrow heads range in size from a fraction of an inch to as much as several inches across the points. Most were probably for hunting, but several do appear in picture scrolls of battles. In the past it has been suggested that they were used to cut the fastening cords of armour, or to damage the rigging of ships. Despite having four fletchings to prevent the arrow spinning it would have taken a remarkable archer to ensure the arrow struck the cords or rigging with its head at right angles to them, not to mention the difficulty of doing so from a moving

horse in battle. The purpose of forked arrow heads was to increase the chance of hitting something by increasing the width of the head. One type of arrow that was regularly fitted with a forked arrow head had a bulbous whistle of horn or wood immediately below the head and was used for signalling in war, an idea copied from the Chinese.

Whatever the type, all arrowheads were fitted firmly into the shaft of the arrow solely by a long, slender tang forged in one piece with the head; a concave neck separated the tang and head and formed a shoulder to butt against the end of the shaft. They were carried, slung on the right hip, in a quiver called an *ebira*. This had a box-like lower section fitted with a grid of bamboo or hide strips, which gripped the heads, and an openwork frame rising from the back edge to which the shafts were loosely tied by a cord. Drawing an arrow from such a quiver involved grasping it just above the head, lifting it clear of the grid, then pulling it forwards until the shaft was clear of the cords.

The gorgeous panoply these warrior nobles wore was quite different from the crude armours of the earlier periods, and reflects in colours and mountings the refined tastes developed by Heian society. In comparison with later armours they were somewhat angular and had a rather ungainly appearance, but they were admirably suited to the warfare of the time. Made of scales in a similar way to the keiko, these armours incorporated new methods of construction and lacing, and new materials were used in their decoration.

Heian-period scales were large and made either from rawhide or iron. The great weight of armours made entirely of iron prohibited their general use. The two materials were either alternated along each row to give a construction called *ichimai maze*, or the iron scales would be concentrated in those areas needing the greatest protection, giving a con-

 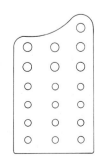 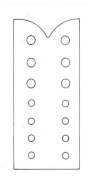

Left: Types of scales (l-r): kozane, the most usual pattern; shikime zane, a rare type of scale assembled with a double overlap resulting in rows of triple thickness; iyozane, a type of scale designed to avoid a large overlap, lightening the armour and reducing the number of scales needed.

Right: Patterns of armour lacing reflected personal taste. There were many styles, just a few of which are illustrated. (Top row from left to right) shikime odoshi, susogoi odoshi, omodaka odoshi, tsumadori odoshi. (Bottom row from left to right) mongara odoshi (the owner's crest forms the basis of this pattern) hadasusogoi odoshi, tatewake odoshi, katatsumadori odoshi.

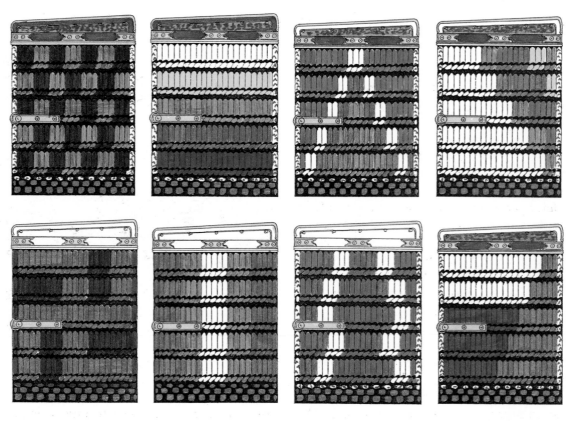

struction called *kane maze*. The hide came from the skins of both cattle and horses and was simply prepared by soaking in water to induce bacterial fermentation which loosened the hair and fatty tissues. After scraping and cleaning, the skins were stretched and dried to give a tough, translucent material whose only real defect was that it absorbed moisture and softened. One famous armour of the Minamoto is said to have been made exclusively from the leather of cows' knees, on the principle that this must be the toughest part of the hide, owing to their habit of kneeling.

Each *sane* (scale), measured about 2 inches (5cm) by 1½ inches (4cm), and was punched with 13 holes in two groups. The lower group of eight holes was called the *shita toji no ana*, and the upper group of five holes the *kedate no ana*. To protect them against damp, they were lacquered before being assembled into rows by leather thongs laced through the lower holes so that each scale overlapped by half the one to its right, giving a double

thickness throughout – a special half scale being added at each end of the row to maintain the thickness. Because the rows constructed in this way had a tendency to sag as the lacing stretched with age, a few armours were made from scales which had three columns of holes, *shikime zane*, which extended the overlap and prevented this, but added considerably to the weight. The leather lacing, called *shita toji*, which fastened

Below right: Individual kozane were fastened together into rows by the shita toji, leather thongs laced through the lower holes in the scales.

Far right: Rows of kozane were assembled into armour by the lacing, odoshi ge (yellow). A thicker braid, the mimi ito, bordered each section while the bottom row of scales had the shita toji laced as decorative cross-knots (red) called hishinui.

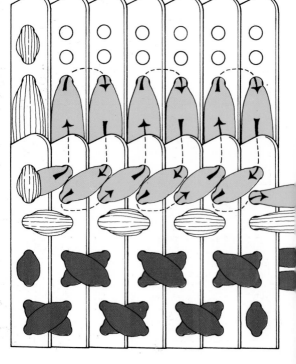

the scales into rows, remained visible on the lowest row of each section and, to make it more decorative, it was laced as a series of cross knots, *hishinui* (lozenge sewing), and picked out in red lacquer. Because of this, the lowest row of scales on a piece of scale armour with this knotting visible is called the *hishinui no ita*.

Once the rows of scales had been prepared, they were fastened to each other vertically by the lacing, called *odoshi ge*. During the early Heian period the odoshi ge was frequently of leather, either plain or dyed with a simple repeat pattern of flowers or geometric ornament. It is the colour, material and pattern of this lacing, together with the style of do, that the Japanese use to describe an armour.

While leather was never totally abandoned as a lacing material, it was only available in a limited range of colours and in relatively short lengths, which made the process of lacing an armour difficult. As a consequence it was soon superseded by a flat silk braid, produced in lengths of about 10 feet (3m). The number of strands of silk dictated the width. These braids were prepared on a special loom or frame in which the worker knelt. The pre-dyed threads, wound on lead-filled bobbins to regulate the tension, were passed over and under pairs of other threads to produce a

characteristically ribbed braid. Occasionally an alternative material, made by wrapping strips of twill silk cloth around a tough fabric core, was used in such a way that the overlap was concealed underneath; the same strategy was occasionally employed later, using cheaper fabrics, for munitions armours.

A wide range of colours were used for lacing. By far the most common colour chosen in later periods was dark blue, because the

Above: The top plate, kanmuri ita, of this Momoyama period shoulder guard is covered with shoehei gawa – printed leather decorated with the date 1352.

O yoroi

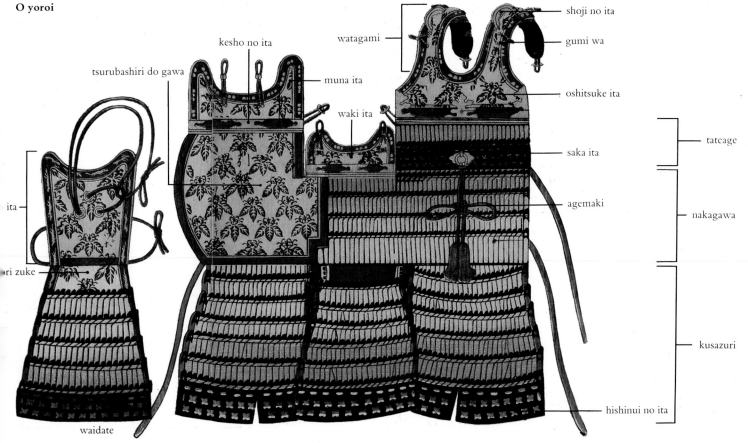

indigo dye used acted as an ultraviolet filter and protected the silk from damage by light. Many of the other colours, particularly the reds (dyed with madder), and the purple (dyed with soya), had just the opposite effect tendering the silk and accelerating its decomposition. For this reason it is uncommon to find armours laced in these colours that have survived with their lacing intact.

Multi-coloured combinations that were not of one of the recognized standard patterns were called *iro iro odoshi* (varied colour lacing); those that used shades of one colour fading to white at the bottom are called *nioi* and if reversed, with white at the top, *susogoi*.

There seems to be no evidence that the colours chosen for an armour represented any family or clan allegiance. An examination of contemporary illustrations of battles shows similar colours being worn by both sides, with apparently a preponderance of red. This might be a product of artistic licence, making for a more striking picture, but it could equally be that red was actually more popular, being considered a martial colour.

The process of lacing began by fixing the completed rows of scales in their correct relative positions by a single lace that supposedly ran continuously down either side of each section and along the lowest of the top group of holes of the hishinui no ita. An examination of surviving armours shows that it was in fact much more common to use

three separate pieces. Because of its importance, this *mimi ito* (border thread) was thicker and stronger than the other lacing and usually of a contrasting colour and pattern. During the Heian period the border thread was white silk decorated with dark-blue chevrons, to which was added later a light blue, forming a pattern known as *takanoha uchi* (hawk's feather). By the Kamakura and Muromachi periods, braids patterned in combinations of white, purple and green, or white, red and green became more popular, the former gaining the addition of dark blue to become the familiar *takuboku uchi* (woodpecker braid) found on most later armours. Some experts maintain that the introduction of the light-green colour did not occur until the Edo period, and that its occurrence on earlier armours is the result of relacing at a later date.

Once the rows of scales were secured in position, the piece was suspended from a stand by a swivel so that it could be turned this way and that, as the remainder of the lacing was put in, always from left to right along each row. Pictures of armourers at work show them using a pair of flat-nosed tongs for the purpose while the ends of the braid were drawn out into a long taper, stiffened by glue, to assist in threading. Some armours from later periods have the braid locked into the holes by small tapering plugs of what appears to be chewed up paper, inserted from the front, but pushed under the lacing so as not to be seen. On the tapered parts of the armour extra lengths of braid were worked in from the widest row, being distributed along it as symmetrically as possible. Sections of the armour which needed to be rigid, such as the do and occasionally the upper rows of the shikoro, had extra leather thongs concealed under the lacing to lock the rows together and prevent them from collapsing into each other.

At the top of the breast, back and shoulder guards, the scales were fastened to metal plates recessed to take them and the joint was covered by a strip of wood, appropriately called *kesho no ita* (cosmetic plate), covered with decorated leather. The whole assembly – plate, scales and strip – was fastened together by gilt rivets, with split copper shanks bent over on the inside. Trapped below this strip and giving a neat finish to its lower edge was a double piping of red and white twill.

Decorative leathers were used extensively, both to cover solid plates of iron, held in

Below: Fabric sock, tabi, dyed in imitation of tsumatagata gawa, one of the many patterned leathers used in the decoration and construction of armour. The big toe is divided to accommodate the thongs of the sandals.

place by *fukurin* (copper gilt edgings), and elsewhere on the armour. All were of a soft, pale suede, either dyed, smoked, or stencilled with patterns. The two former types tended to be used for linings or edgings subject to rubbing; red or blue were the favourite colours if dyed, various yellows and browns if smoked. The smoked leathers could be patterned by pasting paper cut-outs onto the leather before it was smoked to produce a white design on the yellow ground when the paper was removed. For the more pictorial stencilled varieties, the dye was either padded directly onto the leather through a stencil, or a resist was applied to the leather; this left the design in white on a coloured background after dyeing.

During the Heian and early Kamakura periods, the design most often used took the form of Chinese lions arranged into circular medallions, dyed in blue, set in a red diagonal grid of stylized foliage. Later patterns have lions gambolling among rather indifferently drawn foliage in blue or shades of brown with the occasional flower in red, which despite the name 'lion cherry blossom leather' are really meant to represent peonies. Later still, leathers became more pictorial and exhibit a wider range of subjects, including dragons and figures from Buddhist iconography, with the design arranged to fill the space they were to occupy on the armour. Many of these leathers continued in use, becoming progressively more stereotyped into a few basic patterns on the lion-cherry-blossom theme, drawn to a smaller scale more suited to the areas they covered on later armours. One very important pattern deserves mention since it incorporates the date Shohei sixth year (1352), which has led to some confusion. This date was the year in which the pattern was licensed for production, and has nothing to do with when the armour was manufactured; in fact it continued to be made until the end of the Edo period.

The remaining stencilled patterns were more linear, being designed to border the pictorial leathers, and the two were separated by a multicoloured silk piping set into the seam between them. The favourite in the Heian period was red with small groups of white dots at intervals, but on later armours an iris flower growing from the middle of a group of four or six leaves in white on blue became more common. At first these were

naturally depicted but gradually they became more stylized, until eventually the pattern became debased and almost unrecognizable.

Heian samurai wore armour designed specifically for their role as mounted archers and many of its features were dictated by this requirement. Called *o yoroi* (great armour), after the large size of its components, it was to be the only armour considered suitable for the nobility for centuries.

Hachi (helmet bowls) were now almost hemispherical but still retained a slight conical tendency that was to persist for a further hundred years or so. Most were made from overlapping vertical plates, usually eight in number, riveted together along the rear edges by five or six large dome-headed rivets. Because of their often exaggerated size, the heads of these rivets (called *o boshi*, large stars) were made hollow to reduce their weight, giving rise to the alternate name of *kara boshi* (empty stars). One of the terms used for these helmet bowls is *arare boshi bachi*, alluding to the resemblance of the rivets to hail stones. A few helmets which have survived from the Heian period are raised from a single plate, overlaid with strips and fitted with large rivets as reinforcements. Called *ichi mai fuse bachi*, these are the only examples which show that armourers could beat a helmet bowl from a single piece of metal before the middle of the Edo period.

Right: O boshi bachi, a helmet bowl with large standing rivets. Heian period. Note that the rivets are positioned along the edge of the plates where they overlap.

A deep *koshimaki* (plate forming the bottom edge of the helmet bowl) was riveted around the base of the helmet bowl, and at the apex, was a large hole, the *tehen*. The wearer pulled the top of the tall soft hat, worn in lieu of a helmet lining, through the tehen. At first the tehen was rimmed by a shaped iron plate *aoiba za* but later it was also fitted with a *tehen kanamono* (ornate gilt rim). Because the rivets were positioned along the edges of each plate, the large front plate appeared rather bare and was decorated with either a central row of rivets, or by one or more applied iron strips (*shinodare*), emerging from under the aoiba za, and terminating in fleur-de-lis-shaped ends. Positioned on the back plate, which was devoid of rivets, was a gilt ring, *kasa jirushi no kan* (hat-flag ring), from which was hung a silk bow. Originally this ring was added in place of a rivet bordering the back plate, but was soon moved to the central position. As the name suggests, its purpose was to carry a small flag of identification, but it is rarely depicted being worn. Like many details on Japanese armour, the

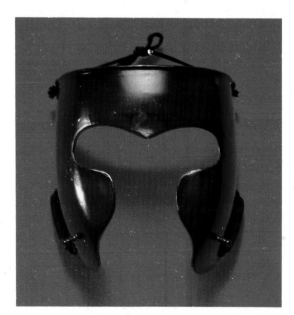

Right: Black lacquered happuri, plate defence for forehead and cheeks, with standing flanges on the cheeks.

Kasa jirushi no kan was retained for its decorative qualities long after the original use had been lost.

A small peak (*mabisashi*) was attached by gilt copper rivets to the front of the koshimaki, hiding the join. It was convex in section and covered with patterned leather held in position by a *fukurin* (decorative rim). To avoid impeding the release of the bowstring, the peak was almost vertical. There were two or, more often, four, holes in the bowl, *hibiki no ana*, through which were knotted leather thongs that provided attachment points for the silk helmet cord which tied under and around the chin. Again, these holes were retained as decoration until the nineteenth century, long after their original function had been lost. Even after protruding rivets were abandoned, four, the *shiten no byo*, were still fitted to prevent a sword from sliding down the bowl and cutting what were, by then, non-existent leather thongs.

The koshimaki also carried a *shikoro* (neck guard) of five rows of tapered scales, giving it a deep conical shape. It reached almost to the shoulders. It was attached by pairs of gilt metal rivets with split shanks, reputedly so that it would tear free if grasped by an opponent; pairs of rivets were used so that in an emergency it could be reattached by a cord. The four upper rows of scales were extended and then bent sharply outwards at right angles, forming the *fukigaeshi*, the distinctive feature found on nearly all Japanese helmets. Its primary purpose was to protect the face from arrows shot at short range after charging the enemy. As soon as the charge was over and the arrow loosed, the samurai wheeled the horse to the right, turning his head in the same direction and bringing the fukigaeshi between his face and the enemy. Because the overlap of the rows was reversed in the fukigaeshi, it also prevented a sword cutting through the lacing between the lames of the shikoro and striking the shoulders. Like the peak, the fukigaeshi were covered with leather, in this case to hide the underside of the scales, and usually had a copper gilt *fukigaeshi no suemon* (chrysanthemum ornament) in the upper outer corner, a decoration that was also applied to the peak and other parts of the armour.

Many samurai are shown in contemporary illustrations wearing an additional defence, the *happuri* (face guard), tied around the brow under the helmet and covering the hel-

Left: Restored and relaced Heian period o yoroi. This type of armour wrapped around the body and had a separate defence for the right side.

met cords. These face guards took the form of a lacquered or leather-covered plate covering the forehead with extensions at either side covering the cheeks. Some had flanges (*yadome*) riveted at right angles to the cheek pieces to act as arrow stops.

Armour for the trunk consisted of four rows of scales called the *nakagawa*, which encircled the whole of the front, left side, and back but leaving a considerable gap under the right arm. Two additional sections made from shorter rows of scales, the *tateage*, covered the upper part of the chest and back. That at the front reached onto the chest and was topped by a solid leather-covered plate, the *muna ita*; the upper edge was shaped at the ends to meet the shoulder straps. The rear tateage terminated in a plate shaped to the back of the neck, the *oshitsuke ita*, from which extended the heavily padded plate shoulder straps (*watagami*). Riveted to the upper surfaces of the watagami were semicircular vertical plates, (*shoji no ita*), which prevented the upper edge of the shoulder guards striking the neck or face during violent action, and protected against circling cuts.

To enable the watagami to be thrown back when putting on the do, the *saka ita* (the middle row of scales in the rear tateage) was laced in reverse and provided with a gilt copper ring from which hung a large heavy silk bow, tied in a special knot. This bow had the double purpose of holding the saka ita down against the pull of the lacing, as well as providing an attachment point for the shoulder guards. Like all do, the o yoroi was fastened to the body by toggles; in this period these kohaze hung on cords attached to the watagami and buttoned into loops anchored to the tateage. These loops were closed by seme

Right: Pictures from a series showing a samurai tightening the draw-strings of the yoroi hitatare and tying on the waidate.

kohaze sliding on them, which locked the loop over the toggles after they had been fastened. This arrangement is the reverse of that found on later armours, where the toggles are always fitted to the muna ita. These fastenings between the watagami and the front of the do were collectively called *takahimo*. Under the left arm, where there was no metal plate, the tops of the scales were wrapped with leather to prevent them snagging on the clothing. The whole front of the do was covered with a large sheet of decorated leather to prevent the bowstring catching on the heads of the scales as it was loosed.

Two small pieces of armour were hung from the ends of the watagami to guard the takahimo and also to some extent the armpits. That on the right, the sword arm, had to be flexible, and consisted of three short rows of scales and a cap plate, and was called the *sendan no ita*. That for the bow arm was a single rigid plate called the *kyubi no ita*. A distinguishing feature of Heian armour is the gentle, lobed shape given to the tops of these plates.

The *waidate* was a secondary defence which filled the gap on the right. It was put on before the do and was tied to the right side of the body by silk cords, one passing over the shoulder the other around the waist. Its upper part was a single leather-covered iron plate which curved with the body and was hollowed at the top for the arm.

Hanging from the lower edge of both the do and the waidate were four *kusazuri*, trapezoidal sections of scales, which covered the lower body and thighs. Those sections at the front and back were attached to the do by lacing, while those at the sides were attached by a band of leather to prevent chafing by the quiver and sword worn at these points. As a slight concession to walking, the lowest row of scales at the front and back were occasionally divided into two sections.

In place of the collar with its attached arm guards that had been worn in the earlier periods, the arms and shoulders were now defended by large, flat rectangular sections of scales called *o sode* (large sleeve). There is some evidence that the warriors during the Yamato period had used shields, but these had to be discarded once mounted archery became the conventional method of fighting. To some extent, sode acted in a similar way to shields; they slid off the arms when they were raised to shoot and hung behind the shoulders, coming into play, like the fuki-gaeshi, as the horse was wheeled round.

The o sode were made of six or seven rows of scales, fastened at the top to a longitudinally curved solid plate, the *kanmuri no ita*. To properly fulfill their role they were fastened by a complex system of cords in such a way that they remained in position yet allowed the arms sufficient freedom of movement for drawing the bow or using the sword. Tied to rings on the ends of the kanmuri no ita were two doubled silk cords with tasseled ends, and a further ring in the middle carried a tie of soft leather. A fourth ring was positioned under the rear edge of the sode, on the third row from the top, to which was tied a single cord. Starting at the top front, the first silk cord and the leather tie were knotted to loops of cord or sewn leather (*gumi wa*) threaded through an elongated metal bead, provided for the purpose on top of the watagami at front and back. The rear cord was tied to the loops of the silk bow on the back of the do. The final cord was tied to the neck of the silk bow, where it hung from its ring. Irrespective of the colour of the armour's lacing, these cords and bows, including that on the helmet, were invariably vermilion; the effect was to create a splendidly coloured detail which matched the lacquered cross knots on the hishinui no ita.

Underneath this polychrome carapace the samurai wore a *yoroi hitatare*, a costume derived from court dress, over a simple kimono and under trousers of white silk. Made of silk brocade, the yoroi hitatare comprised a jacket with voluminous sleeves which had a draw string at the wrist, and a pair of baggy trousers ending just below the knee where another draw string enabled them to be gathered and tucked into the tops of tall, stiff fur boots. The wrist draw strings were tightened, wrapped around the wrists and tied, leaving long loops which were passed over the middle fingers to prevent the sleeves riding up the arms.

No defence was provided for the shins or lower arms until late in the twelfth century, when tubular plate shinguards and an armoured sleeve for the bow arm with an extension over the back of the hand, made their appearance. The inclusion of these new pieces of armour necessitated changes to the way in which the yoroi hitatare was worn. The left sleeve was too voluminous to fit

Left: Trousers from a yoroi hitatare of golden brown brocade. The yoroi hitatare resembles court costume and was worn under armour by nobles of the day.

under the armoured sleeve, so it was left to hang down the back, under the armour. Cloth leggings were tied around the shins to prevent the shinguards rubbing, while the boots were replaced by fur-covered shoes called *kutsu*.

Because of their lowly rank, the noble's retainers wore a simpler form of armour, more suited to their role, called a *haramaki* (belly wrap). It was made from three or four rows of scales forming a nakagawa, in this case extended sufficiently to overlap, always with the back over the front, under the right

Below: Sandals of rice straw, waraji. This type of footwear, initially worn only by retainers, was adopted by all samurai as fighting on foot became more common. Being disposable, distances were measured in the number of pairs worn out by a journey.

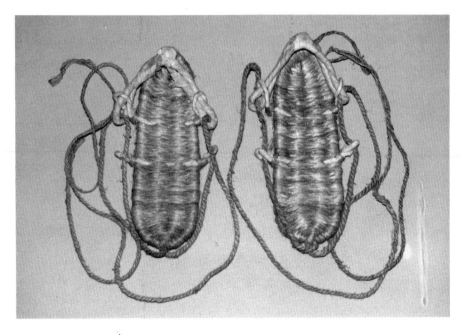

Right: Leather laced haramaki with large shoulder guards. The lacing was originally purple. Heian period.

Far right: Armed samurai wearing an o yoroi. The whole of his equipment was designed with mounted archery in mind.

Below: Brocade kaihan (leggings) were worn under the shin guards.

arm, so obviating the need for a waidate. Tateage were fitted at the front and back with a muna ita, oshitsuke ita and watagami as before, attached by simple braid cross knots to the upper row of scales. Kesho no ita, being too ornamental for retainers, were never fitted. In this instance these knots are properly called *hishi toji* rather than hishi nui, which applies only to those cross knots on the hishi-nui no ita. Unlike the o yoroi, the takahimo fastenings of a haramaki were attached to the muna ita, usually emerging from the outside, but on one surviving example fitted on the inside so that the cords were less vulnerable. Because a retainer spent much of his time

十八、弓

弦ヲ下ヘナシニキリヨリ
上五寸斗ノホドヲトリテ
撮テ持ヘシ軍陣ニ八九ホ
弓本式也雨露
ナドノシメリ
ヲイトウ
更ナシ

Above: Detail from the Heiji Monogatari Emaki.

Below: Heian period blade for a tachi (slung sword), remounted during the Edo period.

Bottom: Chinese style tachi of the Heian period.

walking or running besides his master's horse, the kusazuri were divided into seven or eight sections to give greater freedom of movement to the legs.

No sode were provided, their place being taken by large *gyoyo* (leaf-shaped plates), which were attached to the watagami by cords so that they hung on the points of the shoulders, giving some protection to upper arms. At least one hinged pair has survived; this reduced the tendency for them to become displaced as the arms were raised. Haramaki were undecorated apart from the decorated leather covering these plates, and the occasional chrysanthemum ornament.

Contemporary illustrations often show retainers without helmets. Instead they wore either a happuri or a simple folded cap of lacquered gauze. Judging by these pictures, retainers wore little under their armour other than a shirt-like garment, with the skirts tucked up into the belt. Many were bare footed, although a few are shown wearing

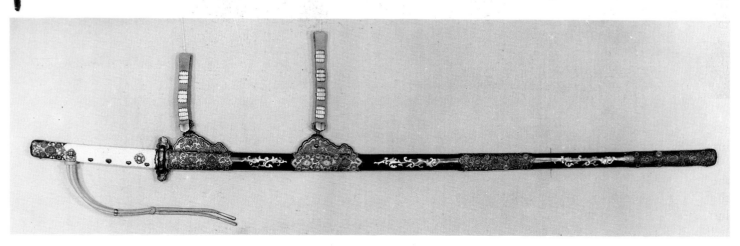

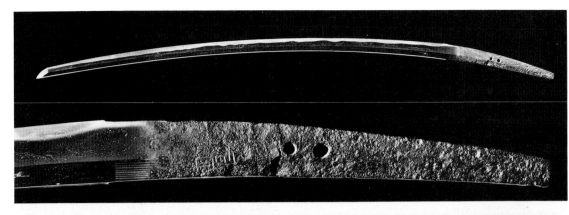

Left: Blade for a long sword in the Yamashiro style by Rai Kuninaga, circa 1330. In this period all long sword blades were made as tachi.

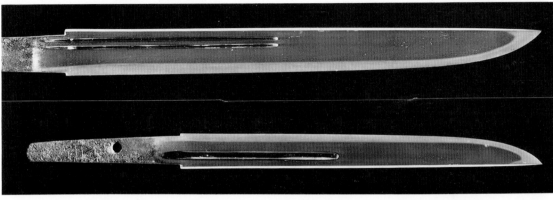

Left: Dirk blade in the Yamashiro style. Signature undecipherable. Most samurai wore a dirk at all times but in war it was only used when unhorsed.

Left: Blade for a long sword in the Yamato style by Kuniyoshi of the Yamato Senjuin group, circa 1300. During the Heian period the long sword was a secondary weapon, used after an initial exchange of arrows.

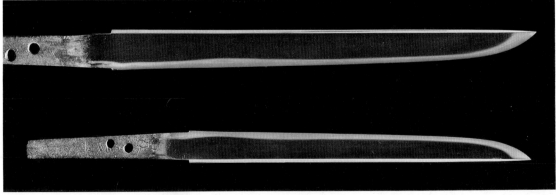

Left: Yamato-style dirk blade signed by Hosho Sadaoki, circa 1360.

straw sandals. Their equipment was improved, like that of the nobles, when the latter adopted the armoured sleeve, *kote*, for the bow arm. It was not long before a similar though more utilitarian pair of sleeves was introduced for use with the haramaki.

Both nobles and their retainers wore long swords, slung at the left hip edge downwards. These were called *bu tachi* (military sword) to differentiate them from the varieties worn at court. Those worn by the nobles were mounted in gold, silver or copper, as befitted their station. Some had the hilt and scabbard coated with plain black lacquer, *kuro zukuri no tachi*; some were bound spirally with a strip of leather under the lacquer which gave them their name of *hiru maki no tachi* (leech-wrapped tachi) while others were decorated by lacquered designs or by mother of pearl inlay. Those carried by the retainers, *no dachi* (field swords), were serviceable but simply mounted, with plain black scabbards. Both types were fitted with hilts that could be held in two hands, but those used by the nobles from horseback had necessarily to be fitted with lighter blades since only one hand was free to wield them. All nobles and many retainers also carried small dirks with short, flat-sided blades, called *katana*, thrust through the *obi* (sash) on the left front of the body. Nobles used these dirks when they were unhorsed and had to grapple with an opponent. Contemporary illustrations also show a ring-shaped object fastened to the sash alongside the tachi. These were reels of basketwork or leather on which

additional bowstrings were carried.

During the Heian period, blade shape and construction reached a state that was so near to perfection that later swordsmiths found it inadvisable to deviate from it. Sword production was mostly concentrated around the home province of Yamato and neighbouring Yamashiro, giving rise to the earliest of the five great traditions of sword making, *go kaden*, in the old sword or koto period. Their blades are characterized by having a very small point section and a gentle, shallow curve, which on early examples became more pronounced near the tang, giving the mounted sword a distinctive upswept hilt. Both areas produced blades that were slim and elegant, as befits the feelings of the age; this is particularly evident in those from Yamashiro.

The following description of the monk Tsutsui no Jomio Meishu in action, from the *Tales of Heike*, gives some idea of the tech-

Below: Screen painting depicting the Taira forces before the Battle of Dan no Ura. This battle saw the Taira totally defeated and virtually annihilated by the Minamoto.

niques for using the long sword at this period:

With his naginata he killed five, but with the sixth it snapped assunder in the midst and, flinging it away, he drew his sword, wielding it in the zigzag style, the interlacing, cross, reversed dragonfly, waterwheel, and eight-sides-at-once styles of fencing and cutting down eight men; but as he brought down the ninth with a mighty blow on the helmet, the blade snapped at the hilt. . .

We have no idea what these styles were but their names seem indicative of sweeping, circular cuts designed to hit with maximum force. Surviving Heian blades are so delicate that it is not surprising that Meishu's broke. An alternative technique practised from horseback was for the sword to be tucked into the crook of the elbow and braced rigid against the body, using the speed and momentum of the charge to deal a slashing cut to the opponent.

A variety of pole arms was carried by both the nobles and their retainers. Paramount among them was the naginata, which by the Heian period had acquired a long blade, widening and curving into a hooked shape at the top. This was fitted into a short shaft some four or five feet (1.2 or 1.5m) long,

bound at the top with metal and fitted with a shoe of iron to protect the lower end. The te boko (spear) of the Nara period survived as a straight, ridged blade, about one foot (0.3m) in length, on a short shaft that could only have been used at close quarters for either stabbing or making short chopping cuts.

Kiyomori's attempts to gain power by wooing the court were doomed from the start because the real power now lay in the hands of the warriors scattered all over the country. As soon as they were old enough, the Minamoto, who had been exiled as children, rallied support, particularly in the Eastern plains of the Kanto. Lead by Minamoto Yoritomo, they struck at the Taira in 1180 and launched the country into a war which raged across the whole country and which even Kiyomori's death in 1181 failed to halt. By 1183, the Taira were demoralized and on the defensive as the Minamoto threatened the capital itself. In an attempt to regroup, the Taira snatched the child-Emperor Antoku, and headed to their homelands in the west. However, they failed to move the ex-Emperor, Go-Shirakawa, who was still exercising power from retirement. Encouraged by Go-Shirakawa, the Minamoto set off in pursuit, gaining even more strength as pre-

Above: Scene from the Yashima Nana *scroll showing Minamoto Yoshitsune (third from left) in a helmet with kuwagata, with retainers and his companion Benkei (fourth from left, mounted) carrying an assortment of improbable weapons.*

Above: Large naginata (pole arm) blades. The Kamakura period blade (right) reputedly belonged to Benkei; the other dates to the Nambokucho period.

Above right: Nineteenth century print by Kunisada shows Minamoto Yoshitsune being taught swordsmanship by tengu, mythical birdlike creatures.

Far right: Camp curtain (jin baku) after which Yoritomo's military council was named. This example bears the mon of the Honda family.

viously uncommitted groups joined what had now become a royal cause.

This terrible episode ended in a battle fought not on horseback, but in ungainly coastal boats opposite the shore of Dan-no-Ura, at the mouth of the Inland Sea. Not only were the Emperor and his retinue drowned, but also the Taira clan was effectively wiped out in the ensuing massacre. Those who did survive committed suicide.

Unlike Kiyomori, Minamoto Yoritomo saw in the courage and loyalty of the samurai an alternative basis for government – what would now be called a military dictatorship. He was still threatened by rival factions,

including one led by his brother Yoshitsune, whom he rigorously and ruthlessly disposed of. Yoritomo extracted permission from Go-Shirakawa to appoint stewards and constables in the provinces and took for himself the title, which had existed for centuries but had become an anachronism, of Seii Taishogun (normally shortened to Shogun and meaning Barbarian suppressing Commander in Chief). Avoiding the capital with its temptations and soft life, he set up residence in the eastern town of Kamakura and established an administrative council, the *bakufu*, to deal with military matters. Since the military held all real authority, he effectively transferred

the seat of power while leaving the bureaucracy of the capital in existence but almost completely impotent.

Despite his efforts at eliminating potential rivals, Yoritomo's death in 1199 saw the title pass in succession to his sons who, by comparison with their father, were weak and unsuited to the task. Masa-ko, Yoritomo's widow, prevented further power struggles erupting by gaining control of the Shogun for her own family, the Hojo. Throughout, this period of strife, this family never took the title Shogun for itself, being content to control the country as regents through another series of puppets.

CHAPTER THREE
The Kamakura and Nambokucho Periods

*Far right: Painting on a door in
Nishi Hongan-ji, Kyoto, of a
samurai wearing a horo. This
cape-like accessory was thought to
have been worn for the awe-
inspiring effect it produced as it
billowed out behind the wearer.*

For the whole of the Kamakura period the country was governed through a tortuous chain of command. In theory, all power came from the Emperor, but in practice he was controlled by at least one retired Emperor, and occasionally two. He in turn delegated control to a Shogun who in his turn was nothing more than a puppet of the Hojo regents. Despite this bureaucratic maze, the country was relatively prosperous. The occasional conspiracy or uprising had little effect other than to transfer, by confiscation, land to the regency, who steadily gained power and influence by giving it to supporters.

Things were not as calm, however, in the remainder of Asia as Genghis Khan and his Golden Hordes moved outwards from their homelands and not only conquered China, but most of Asia and Eastern Europe as well.

There is a theory, as yet unproven and unaccepted by Western scholars, that the Khan was none other than Minamoto Yoshitsune, who had managed to escape his brother's depredations by fleeing to the Chinese mainland; certainly the name Genghis when written in Chinese uses the same character. True or not, by 1268 Genghis's grandson Kublai Khan, turned his attention to Japan, which he felt ought to be a vassal, and dispatched envoys to convey veiled threats to this effect. Confident of their position, the Hojo ignored the warning and sent the ambassadors back unanswered, with the not unexpected result of provoking the Khan, who was unaccustomed to such slights, into taking action.

A great fleet of boats, constructed and manned by Koreans and carrying an invasion force of 15,000 men was launched late in

*Right: Mounted archer of the
Kamakura period wearing an o
yoroi decorated with peonies.*

1274. The small islands of Iki and Tsushima were taken and the force finally landed at Imazu in Hakata bay, Kyushu. Disembarkation began before the main Japanese force had reached the area, and the few local samurai available had little chance. The Mongols were veteran warriors who fought in closely packed and disciplined ranks, manoeuvering to the sound of drum beats. The traditional ritual challenges made by the samurai before battle were wasted on this enemy. Those foolish enough to charge were hacked to pieces as the Mongol ranks opened and swallowed them. Realizing that there was little they could do, the Japanese withdrew behind nearby ancient earthworks to await the arrival of the main army. They had, however, shown the Mongol leaders that the tactic, effective in previous campaigns, of creating total panic in an enemy force was lost on the samurai. The Mongols did, however, introduce two unfamiliar weapons: crossbows, whose bolts easily outranged the arrows of the Japanese; and explosive shells, which were hurled into the enemies' ranks by catapult. These latter seem to have been an idea suggested by Marco Polo, who was staying at the Khan's court. Far from being the terror weapons the Mongols hoped, explosive shells appear to have caused more alarm among the horses than the Japanese, who made careful drawings of them in the pictorial scrolls depicting their exploits for posterity.

Below: Nineteenth century woodblock print showing pole arms in use during the Gempei wars. The artist has included long-bladed spears, which in fact belong to a later age.

Since the day was nearly over, and fearing night attacks as well as being apprehensive about the weather, the Mongols decided to re-embark, burning and looting as they made their way back to their ships. Their fears were well founded, for that night a storm blew up which, despite the shelter of Hakata Bay, wrenched ships from their moorings and swept them onto the coast, effectively destroying the armada and drowning the greater part of the force. Only a few scattered remnants of the huge army remained to be dealt with the following day and only two are said to have survived to report the outcome to Kublai Khan.

A second invasion was launched five years later, this time with 150,000 men in two contingents; one from Korea and one sailing rather later from China. Once again, Tsushima and Iki were attacked first before the Mongols once again landed at Hataka Bay in late June. This time the Japanese were ready and a long defensive wall had been erected, manned from one end to the other by armies from all over Japan. The Mongols' repeated attempts to secure an adequate bridgehead were repulsed, while other samurai in boats fired or boarded the transports by day and night. With the ships rotting under them and disease rife on board, the Korean force withdrew to await the arrival of the Chinese fleet. By August the great armada was assembled and advancing towards Japan while the Emperor and priests of both Buddhist and

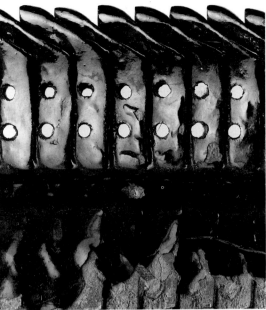

Left: Front (left) and rear of a row of kozane from an Edo period armour. From the Kamakura period the scales were assembled into rows before lacquering, the upper part of each scale being built up with lacquer in front to give a ribbed appearance to the completed row.

Shinto faiths prayed for deliverance. Once again the weather came to their aid; a sudden typhoon of tremendous fury arose and swamped, upturned and smashed the unwieldy transports, causing enormous loss of life. The *kami kaze* (divine wind) subsided as quickly as it had begun, leaving only a fraction of the great armada to limp slowly back to China.

In these brief but telling encounters, the Japanese had their first opportunity to test their equipment and military skills against those of a foreign enemy. It was immediately obvious that the samurai's code of conduct and futile charges were suicidal against an opponent who ignored the rules and shot the horses from under him. His armour, while effective against the arrows and swords of the Mongols provided the wearer was mounted, proved ill-suited to fighting on foot; most of its considerable weight was taken by the shoulders while the kusazuri imposed severe restrictions on walking. Swords, and in particular the points, were said to have broken and chipped against Mongol armour, which contemporary illustrations and descriptions reveal to have been long, skirted coats made from hide and heavy fabric sewn together, worn with iron helmets fitted with leather hoods. Why this should have been a problem when for centuries swordsmen had apparently been cutting through Japanese armour to great effect is a mystery – in all probability they did cut the Mongol armour but became trapped by the layers of thick leather and, being rather delicate, broke as they were wrenched free.

As a consequence of the experience gained during these attempted invasions, dependence on mounted archery went into decline and gradually the horse was relegated to a transport role. Archery became less important, but was never abandoned. The sword and, more especially, the naginata, which had been primarily a retainer's weapon, was taken up by the nobles. A few naginata blades have survived from the Kamakura period. Ranging from some two feet to four feet (0.6 to 2m) in length, they were originally mounted on shafts about four to five feet (1.2 to 1.5m) long. If the *Taiheiki E maki*, a picture scroll of the period, is to be believed, some o naginata had blades six feet (1.8m) long, mounted on proportionately shorter shafts. Like most later blades, these naginata were cut with a complex of short grooves near to the tang, above which the back edge was thinned, but not sharpened, so that the greater part of the blade was a flattened-diamond shape in section. Seen in profile, the curve is slight or non-existent near the tang, becoming more pronounced towards the point. The increase in width near the point gave the blade a rather swollen appearance. As with the majority of Japanese pole arms, the naginata was provided with a tang as long or longer than the blade itself, which fitted into a carefully cut recess in the shaft – a method of attachment that had the advantage of reinforcing the region of greatest stress. Illustrations show that the shaft was oval in section, and retained the metal reinforcement at the top and protective shoe at the bottom as it had in the Heian period. Most appear to

Right: Kamakura period naginata blade.

Above: Detail from Takedori Monogatari *showing fully armed archers and retainers armed with* naginata.

be plainly lacquered, but some are spirally marked, as if they had been wrapped to improve the grip.

Other weapons are occasionally depicted in scrolls, being used by the more flamboyant samurai. One such illustration shows the *kumade* (bear's paw), a species of rake which had a clawed head mounted on a long shaft. A chain is coiled around the shaft, which presumably fastened to the wrist or armour as security against loss in battle. It is shown being used by one horseman in an attempt to drag another samurai from his horse. Very occasionally the *kama*, a species of sickle, was used; it had a straight blade, mounted at right angles to the shaft and sharpened along the under edge. Some were fitted to long shafts,

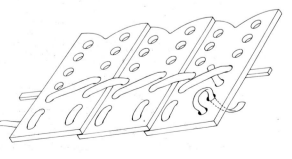

Right: Iyozane laced to a leather thong before lacquering.

to unhorse an opponent before engaging with the sword or dirk, while others were mounted on a short shaft to be used as hand weapons, to hack and cut at the opponent's armour. The te boko (hand spear) of the Heian period had developed into a true spear with a shaft of about 6 feet (1.8m). It was carried by the lower ranks, and was called *kiku-chi yari* after the area in Higo where it was developed. It was still fitted with a short, straight, single-edged blade, prominently ridged to reinforce the point when used for thrusting, but also capable of being used with a cutting action. Contemporary scrolls show some samurai armed with *masakari* (battle axes), fitted with long shafts but, like the kumade and kama, they were rare weapons, carried only by individuals who had developed the special skills needed to use them.

The introduction of new weapons and the changes in strategy were accompanied by a series of small but important changes in the way armours were assembled and lacquered, which quite incidentally did much to improve their appearance. Scales, and consequently the lacing, were narrower and lost much of the clumsiness of their Heian counterparts. The appearance was further enhanced by embossing, or moulding outwards slightly, the visible surface of each scale. This made the scales stiffer and gave the completed row a pronounced ribbed look. Scales treated in this way are described as *kara kozane* (hollow scales), and were used for special purposes until the nineteenth century. In general use, however, they were soon superseded by *moriage kozane* (built up scales), in which the relief effect was produced by a build up of lacquer on flat scales, applied after they had been laced into rows. Since this style of scale became the norm, the descriptive prefix was soon dropped and they were, from this period, referred to simply as kozane.

The manufacture of scales, either from leather or iron, was a lengthy and labour-intensive business. Since kozane overlapped each other by a half, a complete armour used several thousand. During the fourteenth century a new technique of scale construction was devised, based on the type of scales and method of lacing that had been used for keiko in the Yamato and Nara periods, which almost halved the number required. These new scales, called *iyozane*, were slightly wider than kozane and punched with two columns of seven holes, instead of the thirteen of a kozane. When assembled into rows, each scale only slightly overlapped its neighbour and hence covered almost twice the area of the same number of kozane. Having no real overlap meant that lacing alone was insufficient to hold the scales into a row. Consequently they were laced onto a strip of rawhide (*kawashiki*) which showed as a distinct rib under the lacquer when the completed row was viewed from behind.

As they were wider than kozane, and had a smaller overlap, the tops of individual iyozane showed as a distinctive feature above the lacing. Armourers experimented by cutting the top edge into a variety of shapes, only three of which occur with any regularity. Usually the upper edge was cut to form a V-shaped notch. Alternatively, it could be cut into a rounded lobe over each column of holes, or shaped so as to resemble two normal scale heads. In the latter case, the scale would be modelled and lacquered to simulate normal kozane construction.

Lacquered articles have been discovered in Japan that can be dated as early as 500 BC,

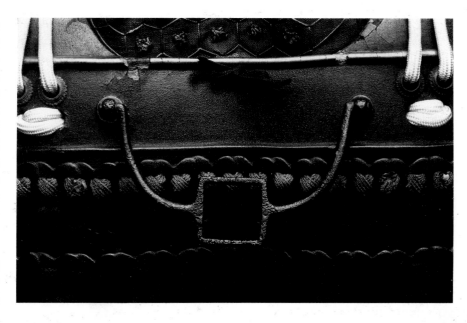

and although lacquer was eventually used in considerable quantities, it was always a valuable commodity, made even more expensive by the labour entailed in its production. To the Japanese its value lay not only in its role as an efficient preservative against the humid climate, but in its long-

Above: Detail of a do made from true iyozane. The hinged bracket is to carry the flag worn on the back of armour.

Below: Purple twill laced o yoroi. The lacing is twill cloth wrapped round tape. Kamakura period.

lasting, lustrous beauty. Unlike Western decorative or protective mediums, whether paints, varnishes or 'japan lacquers', which are complex blends of drying oils, resins and solvents, real lacquer (*urushi*) is simply the processed sap of a small tree, *Rhus vernicifera*, which grows in many parts of Asia. Like rubber, better quality lacquer was obtained by incising the bark of the trunk and collecting the sap in small cups; an inferior grade being obtained from twigs and prunings. After filtering to remove foreign matter, the crude lacquer was gently heated to remove excess water. The finished product was hardened in humid conditions to give a water- and solvent-proof coating that did not scratch or chip easily, and which could be polished to a high gloss.

It was usual to mix pigments with the raw lacquer to enhance its natural dark-brown colour, but the available range was rather limited. Most often it was coloured black, with carbon or, later, iron compounds; a bright-red, with vermilion; or a wide range of brown colours from mixtures of the two. Very occasionally dark-green or blue lacquered objects are found, which involve other mineral pigments since organic colouring matters are destroyed by the lacquer and could not be used. Gold lacquer was frequently used, either produced by coating ordinary black lacquer, while still wet, with gold dust or with leaf, or by grinding the gold dust into raw lacquer to make a kind of gold paint. Silver could be employed in the same way, but its tendency to tarnish to a dull-grey colour made it less popular. This use of precious metals was simulated on cheaper work by substituting tin foil, which when coated with a golden-coloured transparent lacquer looked remarkably effective.

Many elaborate techniques, producing the most varied effects, were invented and used, especially on scabbards, quivers and similar surfaces where the artists strove for novelty while always maintaining their innate good taste. Textured finishes which resisted knocks and felt pleasant to handle were made by incorporating gritty inert materials such as burnt clay or even ground, hardened lacquer into the final coats. Smooth transparent surfaces could overlay the coloured underlayers and enclose within them embedded flakes of metal, mother of pearl or chopped straw, to give finishes of great richness. Realistic imitations of materials like wrinkled leather, bark, bamboo or russet iron were all simulated in this very versatile medium. The russet-iron finish is particularly common on later armours. This fashion resulted partly from the influence of the tea cult with its emphasis on quiet good taste and was partly so that the quality of the metalwork could be seen. A coating of russet lacquer simulated the effect of russet iron without the attendant problem of corrosion.

Lacquering was a long and complex process that began with the careful preparation of the base. Joints in wood had to be filled, and the whole piece smoothed, while metal had to be rubbed with a coarse whetstone to provide a key for the lacquer. A very thin layer of inferior-grade lacquer was applied over the whole surface to act as an adhesive to hold down a layer of cloth or, on cheaper work, paper, which acted as a foundation for the subsequent coats. Further coats of crude lacquer were added to fill the texture of the cloth, each being allowed to harden before being rubbed smooth. Once this base was judged satisfactory, it was levelled and built up with a mixture of lacquer and either flour or burnt clay and sometimes also chopped hemp fibres called *kokuso*. This putty-like mixture was used to produce relief effects or to fill hollows in exactly the same way as a modern finisher would use fillers. When the thickness and surface were judged satisfactory, three or four coats of better quality lacquer were added, each polished to a satin finish with charcoal. Finally, two coats of the best lacquer were added and finished with charcoal dust and ashes of deer's antlers to give the final deep-black lustrous surface.

On most pieces of armour or sword scabbards, the lacquering was now complete but for a more glossy finish a fine coating of special lacquer was applied to give a surface which, while new, was impressive but soon scratched and showed finger marks. If the object was to be coloured or decorated in some other way, further coloured layers or metal dusts, generally being applied over black undercoats to enhance their brilliance, could be applied.

Sakakibara Kozan recommends that decorative lacquering on armours should be carried out by a specialist lacquer artist and not entrusted to the armourer. This suggests that they were accustomed to lacquering their own work, but in view of the complicated nature of the process, it is more probable that each workshop had a lacquer specialist on the staff who could complete the basic processes but who was incapable of fine artistic work.

For a considerable period after the Mongol attacks, there was a general fear of a reprisal throughout the country, as well as considerable discontent among the samurai over the failure of the government to compensate them for their expenses and services. The extensive preparation for the defence of the country had strained the economy, and samurai who had fought petitioned for the traditional rewards for service, which the bakufu just could not provide. The larger landowners away from the centres lost faith in any form of central government, and set up what were almost independent states – foreshadowing later divisions within the country. Sensing this threat, and using yet another squabble over succession as his excuse, the mature Emperor Go-Daigo took the throne and evaded every attempt by the Hojo to unseat him. Outraged, the Hojo resorted to force and in 1333 dispatched an army under Ashikaga Takauji to take the throne by force. Takauji, however, had other plans. Declaring himself initially for the Emperor, he recruited a huge following of samurai who felt cheated by the Hojo, and attacked Kamakura, burning it to the ground. Takauji himself marched on Kyoto (formerly Heian Kyo), killed the bakufu representatives and eventually replaced the self-willed Go-Daigo with a puppet ruler, who granted him the title of Shogun. Go-Daigo took his regalia and fled south to Yoshino in the mountains around Nara, where he continued to reign until 1392 in what became known as the Southern Court, while the Emperors of the Ashikaga continued to rule from the Northern Court of Kyoto.

The whole of this period of turmoil, called the Nambokucho (the period of the Northern and Southern courts), saw almost continual fighting of one form or another as the provincial lords squabbled over land rights. Loyalties lasted only so long as it suited the occasion, being switched from one side to another to take advantage of every opportunity as it presented itself.

However successful the o yoroi had been in the past, it was an impractical armour for use on foot and some nobles abandoned it altogether. Yoroi dating from this period differ in details from those of the Heian

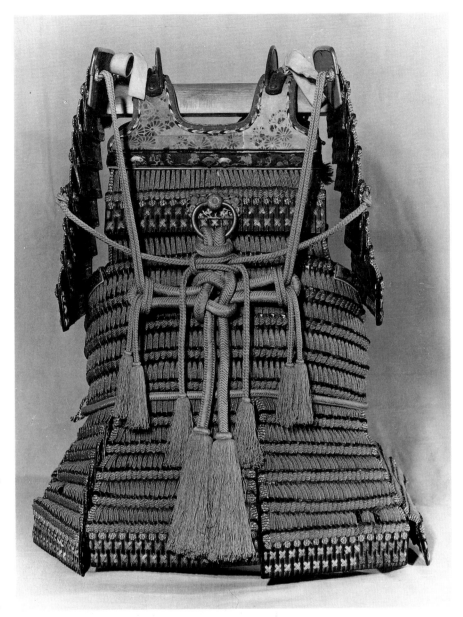

period. All were fitted with front and back kusazuri which had a divided hishinui no ita to assist in walking. The shoji no ita attached to the watagami began to swing forwards and the peak of the helmet moved outwards from the vertical – in both cases to give greater protection to the face. The tops of the sendan no ita and the kyubi no ita lost the characteristic gentle, lobed outline of the Heian period and took on a more zigzagged profile. Some armours had the fastening cords threaded through holes in the muna ita, fastening on the inside, aping the haramaki of the retainers. A new innovation was the introduction of the *waka ita*, an additional plate which was laced to the scales of the nakagawa under the left arm to fill what must have been a rather vulnerable gap. The upper edge of this plate, shaped to fit closely to the arm, was held in position yet given some

Above: Rear view of a red laced maru do yoroi, a hybrid armour incorporating the saka ita, shoulder guards and their fastenings from the o yoroi, with the divided kusazuri and overlap under the right arm of the haramaki.

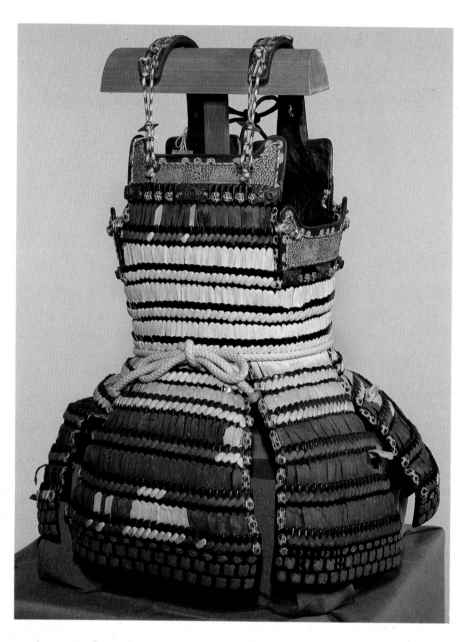

Above: Red and white laced haramaki opening down the back; a very early example of this style of armour. Nambokucho period.

Far right: Green and red laced o yoroi. The colour of the lacing varied to the taste of the wearer. Kamakura period.

degree of movement by small toggles at each upper corner. These toggles were fastened to corresponding loops on the front and rear tateage.

Armours became more of a vehicle for applied ornamentation and decoration. The chrysanthemum ornaments that had been fitted to the leather covering of the fukigaeshi and on the peak of Heian armours were now applied along the hishinui no ita of the kusazuri, the sode and the shikoro. Ornamental plaques of pierced and engraved gilded copper became less stereotyped and were applied to the kesho no ita and the hishinui no ita. They were held in place by gilt rivets; occasionally these represented the *mon* (heraldic device) of the wearer. Further decoration was provided by oversewing the leather crossknotting on the hishinui no ita, with vermilion silk braid. This emphasized the knots

and brought the hishinui no ita into further prominence.

The more practical samurai abandoned the o yoroi and adopted a better quality version of the haramaki worn by foot soldiers. They decorated and embellished it as befitted their rank, and wore it with sode and a helmet. These haramaki were fitted with shoji no ita, an agemaki to which the sode cords could be attached, and the new waki ita under both arms (that under the right arm being of necessity in two parts). Because of their awkwardness, the guards for the fastenings on the do that had been used for the o yoroi were abandoned; they were replaced by a small pair of gyoyo attached to the ends of the watagami to fulfill the same function. A few armours were hybrids between o yoroi and haramaki, having divided kusazuri and the overlap under the right arm like the haramaki, but retaining the leather covering for the front of the do and saka ita of the o yoroi. Like the haramaki, they were provided with sode and a helmet identical to those worn with the o yoroi. These hybrid armours are called *maru do yoroi*.

By the Kamakura period helmets had begun to take on a softer outline. They were almost perfectly hemispherical, with a dozen or more plates with perhaps six smaller rivets in each. Bowls of this shape are called *daienzan bachi* or more simply *maru bachi* (round helmet bowls). This trend towards helmet bowls made with more plates, each fastened by a greater number of smaller rivets, continued throughout the Kamakura and Nambokucho periods. A new and important innovation was the provision of *suji* (small flanges) along the rear edge of each plate, adding considerable strength to the helmet without adding to its weight. Shinodare became almost standard accessories: they were generally of gilded copper rather than of iron as formerly, and built of several layers, each with decorative milled edges. Helmets could be further enhanced by applying the shinodare over plates of silvered or gilded copper, *kata jira*, which occupied the space between the flanges. These relieved the severity of these helmets, acting as a foil to the black lacquer bowl.

Contemporary illustrations show what appear to be the corners of a square of white cloth, or strips of cloth, emerging from between the koshimaki and the shikoro at the sides and back and covering most of the peak

Right: A 32-plate hoshi bachi from the Nambokucho or early Muromachi period fitted with the present neck guard during the Edo period.

at the front – the ends disappearing into the tehen, where they were presumably knotted. This feature appears to be a form of semi-permanent lining, which, if it was tied sufficiently tightly, would lift the bowl off the wearer's head and reduce the concussive effects of a blow. Prior to this development, the inside of all helmets were lacquered but unlined, the wearer's hair and eboshi acting as the only padding. A lining was an improvement in that it made the helmet more comfortable to wear, but it did require that the hair, worn at this period in a queue on top of the head, be undressed before putting on the helmet. Since this change rendered the tehen superfluous, it was reduced in size, with a corresponding increase in the elaboration of the tehen kanamono, which was now made of several chrysanthemum-shaped washers in gilded copper, each of a smaller diameter than the one below.

Towards the end of the Nambokucho period, helmet bowls with standing rivets (*hoshi bachi*) had reached the pinnacle of their development with as many as 36 plates fastened by 15 rivets on each. Of necessity, these rivets had to be thin, appearing long and pointed. Helmets now displayed a profusion of shinodare on the front, back and sides of the helmet bowl in groups of three or five. Where the space between the flanges was too narrow, several plates would be fitted with flush rivets and have the flanges omitted so that larger decorative plates could be fitted. A helmet with four such plates was described as *shiho jiro* (four sides white), or with more, *happo jiro* (eight sides white). The use of the description 'white' in this context refers to the *kata jiro*, now always silvered to act as contrast to the gilded shinodare. The cloth strips had disappeared from illustrations by the Nambokucho period, but some form of

completely internal lining was almost certainly fitted, probably made of leather. In later years these linings were generally of coarse hemp, faced with silk or some other fine cloth, shaped by a close spiral of stitches.

As an alternative to shinodare or, more usually, in addition to them, gilt metal rims were fitted over the flanges. These were almost invariably accompanied by *igaki* (small gilt plates with shaped upper edges) fastened between the flanges and just above the koshimaki to form a decorative band around the base of the bowl. In later years, these plates were formed in one with the gilt metal rims, reducing the number of fastenings and, more importantly, the number of perforations for them made in the bowl itself.

During the late Heian period a few warriors had created a sensation by appearing in battle wearing gilded crests. These quickly became standard, taking the form of a pair of flat gilded metal 'horns' of stereotyped shape called *kuwagata*. They fitted into a special socket (a *kuwagata dai*) which was fastened to the peak of the helmet. Early versions are narrow with their upper ends swelling into two pointed lobes that may represent stylized horns – a conjecture based on the fact that very early examples extend from a plate, decorated with the face of a demon, which fastened to the peak of the helmet. This tradition was occasionally continued into the Kamakura period, and later, by embossing the kuwagata dai into a representation of a demon's head. By the Nambokucho period kuwagata became wider and larger, reaching exaggerated proportions in some votive armours, and exceptionally being embellished by engraved decoration.

Accompanying these changes to the helmet were alterations to the shikoro, which now began to broaden out at the bottom to give greater freedom of movement to the arms. Five rows of scales were still normal although there are references in contemporary literature to *san mai kabuto* (three-plate helmets) that can only refer to the number of lames in the shikoro. Since defence against arrows was less of a consideration, the fuki-gaeshi, while still large, were now no longer bent sharply at a right angle to the shikoro but curved back at a more acute angle to it. In keeping with the trend towards increased decoration, the face of the fukigaeshi might be covered with elaborate gilt-metal ornaments over the decorated leather. A few votive armours were made in which this elaboration was carried to the extreme; almost every available surface, including large areas of lacing on the sode, were covered with the most elaborate pierced and chased metal decorations.

The nobles' custom of wearing the happuri under the helmet became uncommon during the Kamakura period, as the need for protection from arrows fired at close quarters declined. Instead, armour for the lower face, *hoate*, appeared in increasing numbers, becoming even more common during the Nambokucho period. An example of such a mask, covering the chin and cheeks up to the level of the eyes but leaving the nose and mouth exposed, appears in the *Gosannen Gassen Emaki* – a picture scroll dating from the late eleventh century. No other examples are known from this early period. Developed with the hoate and complementary to it, was the *nodawa*, a bib-like protection for the throat and upper chest, which consisted of a U-shaped plate to which was attached, by an intermediary band of leather, two curved rows of scales. Nodawa may occasionally have been attached to the lower edge of the hoate to form a unit, since, as the hoate

increased in popularity, the use of the separate nodawa declined.

Protection for the arms, *kote*, was now universally used and took the form of a fabric sleeve, occasionally of hemp cloth or more usually of gold brocade, to which were sewn lacquered iron plates. The oldest surviving examples consist of large curved plates for the upper and lower arm together with a smaller one for the elbow. These were sewn to the backing by pairs of holes around the edge. A further plate, shaped to cover the back of the hand but having no provision for the thumb, was either sewn to the cuff of the sleeve or hinged to the plate over the forearm, being provided with a loop for the middle finger, and sometimes another for the thumb, to hold it in position on the back of the hand. In keeping with the remainder of the armour, the lacquered surfaces of these plates were embellished by ornaments of gilded copper.

In place of the high fur boots previously worn, *suneate* (shin guards) were now worn with slightly more practical, but still very stiff, fur shoes. During the Kamakura period, suneate were made of three plates hinged together and decorated with applied

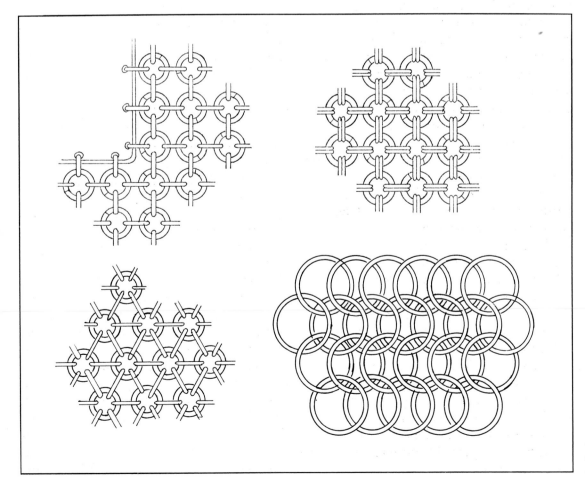

Left: Various types of mail. Top left: So gusari. Top right: Seiro gusari. Bottom left: Asa no ha gusari. Bottom right: Nanban gusari.

Above: *Purple leather laced haramaki with tsubo sode (shoulder guards which curve with the arm and narrow towards the bottom). This simple armour was probably made for a retainer. Nambokucho period. The lacing has faded.*

fastened in place by simple ties of cloth or braid which fitted through metal loops riveted to the plates. By this time, the fur boots were being abandoned by all but the highest ranking officers; straw sandals were adopted as being more suitable for use on foot.

The Nambokucho period saw the introduction of mail, which was extensively used to fill the gaps between plates on minor parts of armour. Unlike the situation in Europe, mail was rarely used as the sole defence. Japanese mail construction is unlike any other with the sole exception of a fragment of Etruscan mail now preserved in Paris. It is based on a system of circular links, which lay in the plane of the mail and oval links at right angles to it. Almost all examples are made from wire of good circular section, showing that it was produced by means of a draw-plate. The links were manufactured by winding wire on a mandrel of the shape required, then cutting down the side of the resulting coil with a chisel to form the individual links. Unlike European mail, which was riveted, the links of Japanese mail were merely butted together, relying on the hardness of the metal and the construction to keep them closed.

In most Japanese mail each circular link was connected to four others by oval links, giving a rectangular arrangement, called *so gusari*, having the advantage of being readily connected to plates. Where greater strength was needed the wire could be of a heavier grade, or the oval links could be made of two or more turns of wire to give a type of double or triple mail, called *seiro gusari*. For areas needing a greater degree of flexibility or only light protection, such as the bend of the arm, *koshi gusari* was made by leaving rectangular spaces in so gusari. An alternative construction, based on a hexagonal arrangement of the same types of links, was also used, but not as widely. In its most dense form, *asa no ha gusari*, each round link of mail was connected to three others by the oval links, but variants of lower density were possible. The fact that none of these are especially common would suggest they had little real advantage over the rectangular forms.

Whatever the type of mail used, it was never used alone, being sewn onto some form of fabric or leather backing or, occasionally, sandwiched between layers of cloth. To prevent rusting, and consequent damage to the underlying fabric, mail was

gilt ornaments like the plates of the kote. Pictures show they were provided with cords along their rear edges, laced in a criss-crossed manner around the back of the leg. Interestingly though, the oldest suneate surviving (at Gifu and Oita Prefectures), which can be dated to this era, are fitted with cords at the top and bottom to tie around the leg. These simple suneate offered no protection to the knees, a considerable disadvantage for mounted use, and a deficiency which was rectified during the Nambokucho period by adding plate knee guards of considerable size to their upper edge. Suneate fitted with these large knee guards are called *o tateage suneate*, always lacquered, generally black even when the remainder of the armour was a more eye-catching colour.

Because the Japanese tended to ride with a high stirrup, the divided kusazuri of the hara-maki tended to slip off the rider's leg, leaving the knee and much of the thigh exposed. Several illustrations of the Nambokucho period depict horsemen wearing what appear to be a pair of short baggy trousers over the yoroi hitatare, marked with vertical lines that have been interpreted as splints or plates sewn onto the cloth – which later became known as *kobakama jitate*. An alternative armour involved laced scales, similarly sewn onto a backing, with the lower rows split into pendant sections for greater flexibility, rather like small kusazuri. This style was later called *hodo haidate* after its supposed resemblance to Buddhist altar cloths, which are similarly cut into sections along one edge. Documentary evidence suggests that something similar had been used in the Heian period but there is no indication of the form it took. No examples have survived from either the Kamakura or Nambokucho periods to show exactly what these early leg armours were like. The book *Taiheiki*, dating from the Nambokucho period, mentions *hiza yoroi* (knee or lap armour) – it would seem therefore that this was the customary term used to describe all types of thigh armour until the Muromachi period, when the more common name of *haidate* began to be used.

A mention must be made of the *horo*, a curious device which had a considerable vogue during the Kamakura period but had appeared somewhat earlier. A type of cloth cape, the top fastened behind the shoulders, and flared out slightly towards the bottom. It gathered in and tied at the waist. Pictures of standing samurai show it hanging loosely in a pouch down the back, but when moving on horseback, it inflated with air and ballooned out behind the wearer. Its purpose remains obscure, but was probably purely to intimidate the enemy, although it may have had some protective value when galloping away after an attack. However, one painting casts some doubt over this hypothesis, since it shows a horo being worn over the face and reaching to the horse's head. It obscures the wearer's vision and presumably limits the freedom of movement of the arms. Whether this is the result of a misunderstanding on the

Above: An Edo period reproduction of a nodawa, a defense for the throat and upper chest. The black lacquered plate is iron, the scales leather.

Left: A mysterious illustration from Gunyoki showing an unorthodox use of the horo (cape-like cloth).

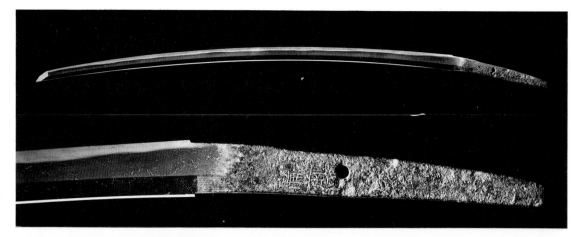

Right: Blade for a long sword in the Bizen tradition; there were more swords made in this tradition than in any other during the Koto period.

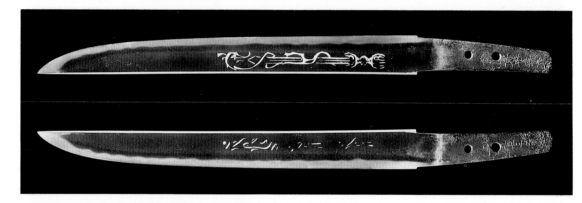

Right: Dirk blade signed Bizen Osafune Kunimitsu and dated 1276.

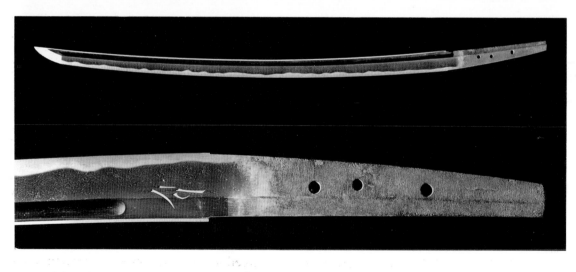

Right: Blade for a long sword in the Soshu tradition decorated with a horimono of a debased sanskrit character.

part of the artist we can only surmise, but the horo was undeniably popular and acquired a considerable mystique in later years, when it was incorrectly revived. Not understanding the principle, these later versions incorporated a framework of bamboo or whalebone to hold the cloth into the shape depicted in old drawings.

While the continuous fighting throughout the Nambokucho period did little to help the prosperity of the country as a whole, it was a period of prosperity for armourers and swordsmiths, and for their suppliers, the producers of iron and steel.

Deposits of iron ore occur widely if some-

what thinly in Japan; mainly in the form of magnetite, a blackish ore and red ferruginous sand. It was the latter that was the first choice of the swordsmiths, but it must always be remembered that a considerable source of metal in ancient times was recycled scrap. In his book on armour making, Sakakibara Kozan states that iron made in Harima and Idzumo was better than that from Bitchu, Hoki, Mimasaki or Iwami and that old saws and agricultural tools were an excellent source of raw material. Masahide boasts in his book that 'there is no iron that cannot be made into good steel.' But he goes on to say that starting with better quality metal can

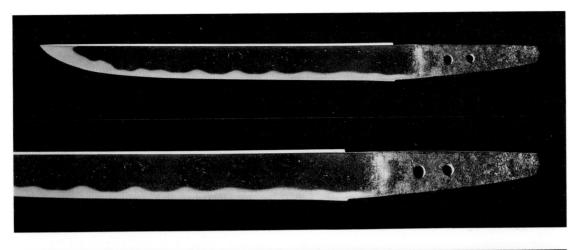

Left: Dirk blade in the Soshu tradition; some of the finest blades belong to this tradition.

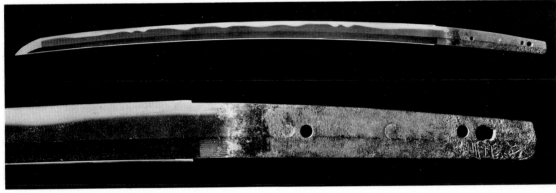

Left: Blade for a long sword in the Mino tradition signed by Kaneuji, circa 1350. This style of sword remained popular into the twentieth century.

Left: Dirk blade in the Mino tradition signed Kanesada, 1270.

save the smith a lot of time and effort.

Iron smelting was always something of a cottage industry, carried out, during the period for which we have written evidence at least, in a rectangular furnace about three feet (1m) by six feet (2m) in area and some six feet (2 m) high. It was often built into a pit dug into the side of a hill to ease the task of charging, and covered with a temporary shed to give some protection from the weather. The walls of the furnace were of clay, which acted as a flux, helping to promote fusion but also limiting the length of time for which the furnace could operate. Charcoal was burnt in the pit to dry out the soil, and later served both as fuel and reducing agent, being added throughout the firing together with further

ore. To maintain a high temperature, air was pumped in through a series of bamboo tubes fitted with cast-iron nozzles embedded in the furnace wall and connected to a second pit alongside in which were housed the bellows, the intervening wall of soil offering some protection from the heat to the men who operated them. At the end of three or four days of successive firings and tappings, from which was obtained cast iron, the furnace was dismantled to obtain the mass of partially fused steel, iron and slag – the raw material of the swordsmith and armourer. In earlier periods, the efficiency of the furnace was such that this bloom was the only product, the temperature being insufficient to effect fusion of the cast iron. This mass could

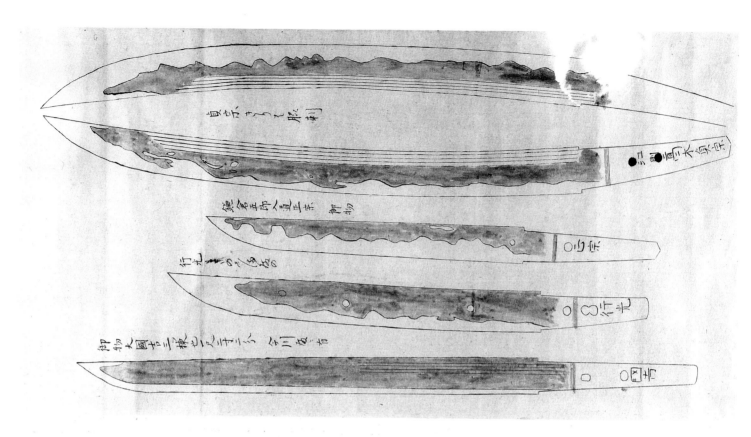

Above: Detail from a scroll of blades by famous smiths. From top to bottom they are by Sadamune, Masamune, Yukimitsu and Kuniyoshi.

be refined by forging to beat out the slag and earthy impurities, but more frequently it was either cut up while still pasty, or thrown into water to fragment and make the selection of the better pieces easier.

To meet the growing need for swords, craftsmen moved to wherever there was a demand, setting up workshops and developing styles to suit local tastes and needs. The provinces of Bizen, Sagami (Soshu) and Mino in particular became important centres of sword making, developing the remaining styles of the five great traditions. Production in Yamashiro began to decline, and in Yamato almost ceased entirely. Many other centres existed of course, but their products show that their techniques were ultimately derived from those of the main traditions.

The Kamakura period witnessed the first golden age of sword making, aided by the recognition given to the craft by no less a person than a retired Emperor. Following the drowning of Emperor Antoku at Dan No Ura, the throne was taken by Go-Toba. After his retirement and, eventually, exile, he devoted himself to the study of swords. Rumour suggested that his hate for the Regent Hojo Yoshitoki, who had forced his exile, was the reason for his interest, but he never exacted revenge. A more likely explanation is that he indulged his passions as a way of staving off the boredom of banish-

ment from the capital. Whatever the truth, he summoned to his palace many of the best swordsmiths of his day, discussing their craft with them, suggesting new ideas and even participating, in a smithy set up in the palace grounds, in the tempering of blades. He is even said to have made blades himself under guidance, several of which still exist.

Lists of the smiths, who attended for one or two months each, show that Bizen was already a leading province in the craft; no fewer than 25 out of the 39 who attended during the years of the second decade of the thirteenth century, came from there. This pre-eminence of Bizen continued throughout the Koto period, which lasted until 1595 – no fewer than 4005 swordsmiths are known to have worked there, compared with 1269 for Mino and 1025 for Yamato. Assuming an average working life for a smith of 20 years, producing, at a conservative estimate, 30 blades of all types annually, Bizen alone would have produced some two and a half million swords during this period, whilst the total for the whole country during the same period would have been nearly 15 million.

It is very difficult to estimate the cost of producing a sword in modern terms, except perhaps in terms of the skilled man hours needed to make it. In the Nara period it took 18 days for the smith to forge a tachi blade, 9 days for the silversmith to make the mounts,

6 days for the lacquerer to make the scabbard, 2 days for the leather worker, with an additional 18 days for labourers. Added to this would be the not inconsiderable cost of the raw materials, making the tachi an expensive production by any standards. A comparable length of time for forging a long blade was noted at the end of the seventeenth century, when the Shogun summoned swordsmiths to make swords at his palace. In each case more than 20 days were required to produce a roughly polished blade. This production time fell rapidly with a shorter blade, a good smith being reckoned to be able to produce a dirk blade in a day and a half.

The enhancement of the status of swordsmiths is reflected by the fact that many of the most famous sported family names, strictly speaking a prerogative of the aristocracy. By the middle of the thirteenth century several smiths were working who have been regarded ever since as supreme masters, and who have never been seriously rivalled. Among them were Toshihiro Yoshimitsu of Awataguchi, Go Yoshihiro of Etchu and, arguably the greatest of them all,

Goro Nyudo Masamune of Sagami. Masamune was the son of Yukimitsu and grandson of Awataguchi Kunitomo, who had been chosen to work with Go-Toba. He made a special point of studying under other great smiths in order to become acquainted with as many aspects of the art as possible. Masamune gained such a reputation that he attracted a number of pupils who themselves became famous, the greatest being his adopted son Sadamune, who attracted pupils in his turn. The surviving blades made by these smiths are regarded as treasures to the present day.

Nambokucho swords differ considerably from those of the Heian, principally in their length and robust appearance. The slim, rather delicate blades of Heian tachi were found wanting during the Mongol invasions and internal fighting which followed and were replaced by heavier and longer swords with longer points, which were sufficiently tempered to allow some reshaping if chipped. To add even more strength to this vulnerable part of the blade, the grooves, which were fairly commonly cut just below

Above: Detail from a scroll of famous blades showing a long sword by Masamune. Its elegant shape has been lost because the blade has been shortened. An owner may have shortened the blade to suit his physique or to comply with one of the many edicts during the Edo period.

Below: An unusual no dachi (field sword) mounted like a conventional tachi and dedicated by Hojo Tokimune. Its total length is 5 feet 9 inches (1.77m). Nambokucho period. Swords of this type were too long to wear, so were normally carried.

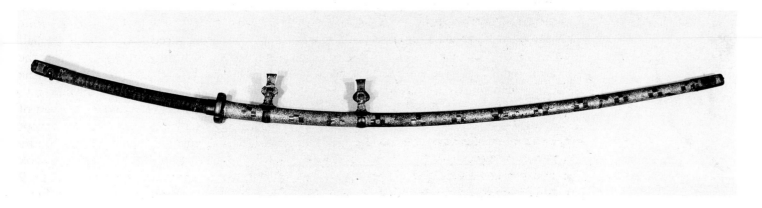

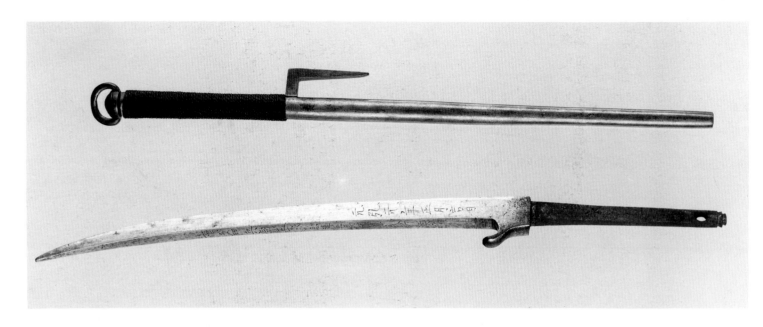

Above: Jitte (top) a club used for parrying swords and a hachiwari (helmet splitter) the latter bearing the signature and date of Masamune as well as that of its maker Shizu Saburo Kaneuji of Mino province. Circa 1730.

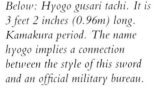

Below: Hyogo gusari tachi. It is 3 feet 2 inches (0.96m) long. Kamakura period. The name hyogo implies a connection between the style of this sword and an official military bureau.

the back to reduce weight, were stopped further back from the point. This tendency to larger, longer blades was taken to extremes during the Nambokucho period with a new type of no dachi with blades of five feet (1.5m) or more in length. Worn slung over the back in plain scabbards, they were carried into action unsheathed and used in much the same way as the two-handed swords of Europe.

The more normal long swords were still worn slung edge downwards from the waist, and the short dirk, with its flat-sided blade, was still carried thrust through the belt on the left front of the body. A few of the surviving dirk blades were designed specifically for armour piercing, as shown by their heavy cross section and acute point. References in contemporary literature confusingly refer to *shito* (stabbing knife), *koshi gatana* (hip sword) and *himo gatana* (braid sword); in all probability they are alternative names for

essentially the same weapon, differing only, if at all, in the style of mounting. One variety of dirk that can be identified in paintings is the *ebizaya maki* (prawn scabbard wrapped), so called because the scabbard and hilt were carved with gadroons like the carapace of the crustacean.

Another strange weapon, reputedly devised by Masamune, and invariably bearing his signature in addition to the smith who actually made it, was the *hachiwari* (helmet splitter). Mounted and worn like the dirk, the hachiwari took the form of a curved, pointed bar of steel, having a small hook-like protrusion at the base. Although it could have been used for piercing, the curvature and hook suggest its main use was as a parrying weapon, being held in the left hand while the tachi was wielded with the right.

The hiru maki no tachi of the Heian was still used, together with new varieties with reinforcing strips applied to the scabbard and

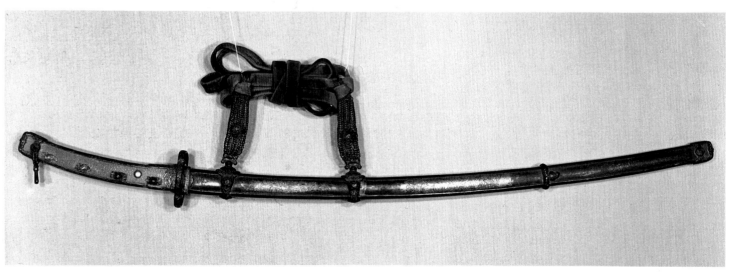

hilt, or with criss-crossed wrappings of leather around the hilt and upper part of the scabbard to improve the grip. This latter type was called *kawa zutsumi maki no tachi* and was provided with a tubular leather cover over the lower part of the scabbard and a leather cover over the tsuba to protect it from the weather and damage in action. It became fashionable to cover the lower end of other types of scabbards with leather or, for the higher ranks, tiger's tail skin.

The components of mounted swords had become fairly standardized and were to continue virtually unchanged as long as swords continued to be worn. Irrespective of the size or style of mounting, all blades were fitted with a soft-metal collar, called the *habaki*, which butted against two shoulders at the junction between the blade and the tang. This relatively insignificant but vital fitting, the only one to belong to the blade itself rather than to the mount, had the dual duty of transmitting the force of a blow from the blade to the hilt, and of providing a seal with the mouth of the scabbard when the sword was sheathed.

Scabbards were generally made of *honoki*, a light straight-grained wood from a species of magnolia whose natural oils acted as a rust preventive. Only occasionally were more decorative woods used – and then mainly for dirks. Some scabbards for field use were fitted with U-shaped metal strips extending the full length at the top and bottom, held in place by gilt rings; the resulting panels at the sides were either lacquered or filled by thin metal plates. One type of sword mounted in this manner can be positively identified as a *hyogo kusari no tachi* (military chain tachi), which was slung from the belt by complex hangers of many fine chains. Whatever the type, all tachi scabbards were fitted with chapes, known as *ishizuke* during the Heian period, but *kojiri* from the Kamakura onwards. Most had at least one *seme gane* (reinforcing band) fitted towards the lower end, which helped to prevent the two halves of the scabbard from separating. The mouth of the scabbard was reinforced by a metal band, below which were two *ashi* (ornate clasps) to which the hangers were attached.

Scabbards for dirks were occasionally fitted with elaborately carved metal mounts matching those of the tachi, but more often they were relatively plain, with perhaps some simple lacquered decoration. They did

Far left: A kogai, an implement which was carried in a pocket on the front of a sword or dirk scabbard.

Left: A kodzuka, a handle of a small utility knife carried in a pocket on the rear of a sword or dirk scabbard.

Below: Kashira (cap of the hilt, top) and a side view and base of the fuchi (reinforcing band at the bottom of the hilt). By the famed Iwamoto Konkwan, these show demons being driven from the house by the throwing of beans.

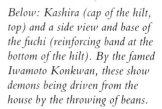

Right: A pair of gilt-leather-covered gyoyo converted into a purse during the Edo period. These leaf-shaped plates, originally used as shoulder guards on retainer's armours, were later used to protect the fastenings of the shoulder straps.

Below: Hilt of a sword bound in variegated silk over metal ornaments which were intended to improve the grip.

Below right: Folding war fan with gilded paper and iron outer ribs overlaid with dragons in silver.

however gain a new feature in the form of implements carried in pockets in the face of the scabbard. One of these, the *kogai*, carried on the outer face of the scabbard when worn, has attracted more supposition and wild theories as to its use than anything else in the field of Japanese arms and armour. In its usual form, the kogai consisted of an ornamented handle, topped by a small spoon-shaped finial, and a narrow, blunt skewer-like blade; some later versions, *wari kogai*, can be split into two parts along the centre line. These mysterious objects are probably nothing more than toilet implements; the finial being for cleaning the ears and the blade for re-dressing the hair after removing the helmet. The split variety appeared at a similar time to the adoption of the very heavily pommaded hair styles worn during the Momoyama and Edo periods. On the rear face of the scabbard was carried a small general-purpose knife, generally called a *kodzuka*, a term which strictly only refers to its decorative hilt. From this time, these accessories became optional for all short swords.

Hilts (*tsuka*) were also of magnolia wood, carefully fitted to the tang and held in place by a *mekugi* (peg), which at this period was of soft metal with ornate end caps. As silk or leather wrappings became more common,

鬼児嶋弥太郎

一壽齋
芳員画

Right: Nineteenth century woodblock print showing a samurai in battle standing on a fallen pavise and carrying a trophy head in his teeth.

Right: Banner of hemp cloth about 11 feet 6 inches (3.5m) long. Muromachi period.

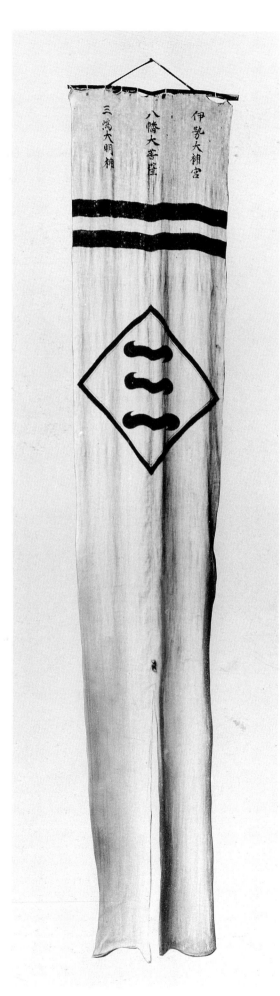

the peg lost its decorative ends, becoming a tapered piece of bamboo or horn. The whole outer surface of the hilt was covered with *same*, the skin from the back of several species of ray found in the China Seas. After cleaning and preparation, the skins reveal creamy-white bony nodules which vary in size with the size of the fish and the position they occupy, being most pronounced in a concentrated patch just behind the head. The size and regularity of these large nodules dictated the price of skins; they were sometimes so valuable that they were ornately wrapped in brocade and given as presents.

Fittings for tachi hilts invariably included a pommel, *kabuto gane* or *kashira*, shaped like the chape, and a reinforcing band at the base called the *kuchi gane* (mouth metal) or, later, the *fuchi*. If the scabbard had metal-re-inforced edges, the edges of the hilt were also fitted with them. Small nails with ornate heads, often in the form of mon or rice bales, were inserted into the hilt both as decoration and to assist the grip, their place being taken by larger ornaments, as the use of bindings over the same became more common. Katana hilts were similarly fitted with pommels and were reinforced at the base; these were sometimes bound but in this period they were more often fitted with a wide metal band, *do gane*, carrying raised ornaments on each face.

Only the tachi was provided with a tsuba (hand guard). A flat disc, it had raised thickened edges, and a lobed outline and was held in place between the habaki and the hilt. It was protected by one or more decorative washers, *seppa*, on each side, which were occasionally expanded to cover most of the face of the tsuba.

Having learned lessons from the methods used by the Mongols, the samurai began to appreciate the advantage of tactics in war and to acknowledge the potential of the common foot soldier. Battles were no longer haphazard scrambles for glory and reward; now the troops were carefully orchestrated in tactical manoeuvres based on Chinese military texts. Lines of infantry armed with pole arms were deployed against cavalry, protected against arrows by *tate* (portable wooden shields). These shields figure prominently in illustrations of battles, and were made almost exactly like their counterparts, the pavises, of Europe – even to having a hinged prop at the back, and being decorated with heraldic

Left: War fan with black lacquered papers decorated with a mon in gold, used for directing troops.

Below left: Sode jirushi, an identification flag worn tied to the shoulder guard. Nambokucko period.

Below: Menuki in the form of male and female dragons. These ornaments were fastened under the binding of sword hilts to improve the grip.

symbols on the front. Heraldic banners, *hata*, in the form of long streamers of cloth some two feet (0.6m) wide attached to a cross bar of bamboo at the top, were used to indicate rallying points. These designated the allegiance of the troops.

Commanders now took a less active role in the actual fighting, being positioned with their guard on vantage points where they could direct the movement of their troops, generally by means of a *gunsen* (war fan). In later periods, these fans were often made with gilded or black papers decorated with a red sun fastened to heavy iron sticks, enabling them to be used as a weapon in an emergency. There was also a non-folding fan, which was a more or less rounded plate of wood, leather or, occasionally, metal, mounted on a handle; the plate was lacquered with the user's mon or with a perpetual calendar showing inauspicious days.

Arrayed in ranks under fluttering pennants of brilliantly dyed cloth and wearing multi-coloured armours, the samurai of the period fought battle after battle in support of one or other of the courts or, more often, for land and the wealth it brought. For the remainder of the population it mattered little who held title to the land they farmed; life was hard.

CHAPTER FOUR
Civil Unrest: the Ashikaga Shogunate

Far right: Reproduction of a Muromachi period o yoroi. It was made by Masuda Miochin Ki no Muneharu in 1860 and presented to Queen Victoria by the last Tokugawa Shogun.

Unlike Yoritomo, who sensibly moved away from Kyoto, the Ashikaga fell into the old trap of setting up the Shogunal Court in the capital. Doubtless they felt it necessary to keep a close eye on the Emperor during the Nambokucho period, but the pleasurable life in the capital appealed far more to Ashikaga tastes than a spartan existence in some provincial backwater. The Ashikaga built magnificent palaces in the Muromachi quarter of the city, giving the name to this period of Japanese history. They spent lavishly, encouraging artists and craftsmen to return to Kyoto to provide the luxury goods they demanded. To pay for this extravagance, unprecedented taxes were levied on farmers; at times over two-thirds of their yearly production was demanded, forcing many to borrow money or pawn belongings to exist.

From the shores of southern Japan and in particular the islands of Iki and Tsushima, pirate-traders had carried out profitable raids on both China and Korea for many years. Answering Chinese requests, the Ashikaga crushed this enterprise and set up official trading operations to import even more luxuries to satisfy their taste for high living. The organization of this and other schemes was delegated to the monks of wealthy monasteries, who acted as advisers and civil servants to the Shogunate. In exchange for brocades, porcelains and other luxuries, the Japanese shipped raw materials and arms, principally appallingly low-quality sword blades, in their thousands.

For the first time, discontent was evident among the lower classes, who up until now had tolerated their lot with surprising good humour. Prior to the fifteenth century, battles and skirmishes had caused some local damage to crops, or had resulted in the burning of a village, but, by and large, the samurai had ignored the peasants and had been ignored by them in return. The burden imposed on the peasant farmers by the be-

Below: Painted screen showing an attack on a fortified mansion. A horseman on the left wears a red dyed horo, which billows out behind him as he charges.

haviour of the Ashikaga, and by those lords who aped their lifestyle, was something that could not be ignored and which touched on everyone's lives. Organized by the *ji zamurai* (local squires), the agricultural community formed themselves into groups called *ikki* for mutual protection and, when forced, retaliated. On several occasions these groups besieged the capital and succeeded in forcing the government to cancel all debts owed to money lenders, and on one occasion even defeated a bakufu army.

To counter these insurrections, the lords built up their armies, even recruiting members of the peasant classes, provided they could equip themselves with arms. These low ranking infantry were aptly named *ashigaru* ('light foot', in the sense of 'light infantry'). Poorly armed and even more poorly led, these unfortunates were motivated almost entirely by the promise of loot rather than by any sense of loyalty, and proved of little value to the commanders of the time.

Even as late as the fifteenth century, o yoroi were still being made and worn by a few high-ranking samurai, but were now anachronistic, and were usually worn only on ceremonial occasions. In battle most samurai wore a development of the simple haramaki-style armour, which wrapped around the body and obviated the need for a waidate.

Since the late Heian period, the necessity for vigil had given rise to the need for a form of protection that could be worn with, or under, everyday wear. The need had been met by a simplification of the haramaki, called a *shita haramaki* (under belly wrap) or more commonly *hara ate* (applied to the belly). These light armours corresponded exactly to the front part of a haramaki, but the nakagawa stopped under the left arm instead of continuing around the body and it had an abbreviated waki ita as on the right. Since there were no watagami, straps were attached to the waki ita and were worn crossed over the back fastened by toggles to loops attached to the muna ita. This fastening was supplemented by cords fastened to the lower rear edges of the nakagawa that tied around the waist. Early versions were normally fitted with three rudimentary sections of kusazuri covering little more than the hips, but a few were made with sections of normal length. In the Kamakura and Nambokucho periods, considerable num-

此ノ圖古画
結城合戦ノ
繪ニ見エメ
リ

矢保呂掛ケタル覩頁タル圖

補

右二ツノ圖一ノ谷合戦ノ繪ニ
見エタリ上ヒ佐光信ノ
古画ナリ

the sides of the hara ate around the body, complete with further sections of kusazuri, to form a do having its opening down the centre of the back, where it fastened by braid ties. These extensions of the nakagawa meant that the rear tateage and the oshitsuke ita had to be split, each half being fitted with a padded watagami in place of the cross straps. Having the opening at the back caused something of a problem with the fastenings of the sode, since there was nowhere to fit the silk bow on the back. One solution was to provide the armour with a narrow centre plate, *sei ita*, suspended from the oshitsuke ita by toggles and tied in at the waist by the waist cord. Most examples of these back plates are fitted with a section of kusazuri that overlapped those attached to the do and a silk bow, enabling the sode to be fastened in the traditional way. More rarely, this plate consisted of only two rows of scales and a top plate; it was just long enough to carry the ring and its bow, but offered no protection from the middle of the back downwards. Other armours seem to have had neither form of back plate, being fitted instead with small rings on each half of the oshitsuke to which the cords from the sode could be tied.

Many haramaki and most do maru continued to be provided with the same o sode that had been designed originally for the o yoroi, together with the wagumi and, in the case of the do maru in particular, shoji ita as well; the latter being particularly necessary when the arms were lifted over the head when using a sword or naginata. O sode were, however, cumbersome and greatly impeded the free movement of the arms, having been devised originally to act as static shields. More satisfactory versions were introduced, fitted closer to the shoulder and moving with the arms when they were lifted rather than slipping off them. This was achieved by forming the kanmuri no ita into a curve and turning its upper edge at right angles to form a standing flange that guarded the neck and, incidentally, obviating the need for the shoji no ita. Like o sode, this top plate was covered with leather held in place by a gilt fukurin and was fitted with a kesho no ita over the scale heads. The remainder of the sode differed depending upon the type. Those designed for haramaki had the rows of scales continue the curve of the kanmuri no ita and tapering towards the bottom, giving rise to their name *tsubo sode* after their sup-

Above: Page from Gun Yo Ki *showing foot soldiers equipped with utsubo. These enclosed quivers are shown covered with cloth dyed in distinctive patterns that may have served as a means of troop identification.*

bers of these very simple do were produced for foot soldiers, who wore them with simple kote and a happuri. Both scale and plate versions for use by troops, and more decorative versions for wear over normal clothes, continued to be made well into the Edo period. They differed from the earlier ones in having the separate kusazuri modified into a single downward-tapering section that covered only the lower abdomen.

For a short while the original name haramaki continued in use to describe an armour opening on the right. However, this type of armour took the name *do maru* (body round) when an entirely new style of do evolved from the hara ate. Taking the old name, haramaki, this style was produced by extending posed resemblance to a jar. The other, which appears to have been worn indiscriminately with either haramaki or do maru, had lames which became progressively flatter and wider towards the bottom and hence were called *hiro sode* (spreading sode). The ring which on Heian period sode had been fitted inside the rear edge to take the rear cord was replaced on all sode by an elaborate kogai kanamono, attached over the lacing on the fourth row of scales. Apart from this minor improvement, the attachment cords, and the method of fastening these sode to the do, remained unchanged.

The traditional style of armour (now called the do maru) and the new haramaki differed in several small ways from those made earlier. The lames of the kusazuri had an inwards curve at each end, making them fit the legs better and giving the region below the waist a bell-shaped outline. This was achieved by lacing a strip of hide to the back of the scales as they were assembled into rows before they were lacquered. Armours also began to develop a slight constriction at the waist, achieved by tapering the scales in

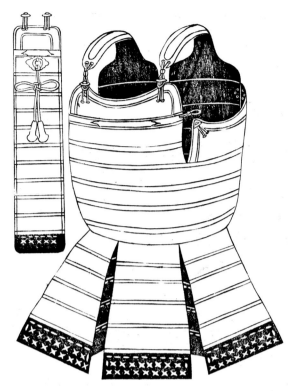

Left: Drawing from Gun Yo Ki *of a Muromachi period haramaki with the opening down the back. The narrow plate is the sei ita (lit back plate) which covered the opening.*

the lower rows of the nakagawa. This transferred little weight from the shoulders to the hips unless, as was sometimes done later, the wearer wore a layer of padding under the

Below: A posed photograph from the late nineteenth century accurately depicts samurai of the Muromachi period. The kneeling page wears a hara ate, covering only the front of the body, and holds a signalling conch.

Right: An Edo period reproduction of a haramaki incorporating a helmet bowl by Saotome Iyetada.

Far right: Sei ita (plate covering the opening of the haramaki) from a Muromachi haramaki. The bottom part covers the trunk and is of leather-laced iyozane, the remainder of kozane, smaller scales, laced with silk.

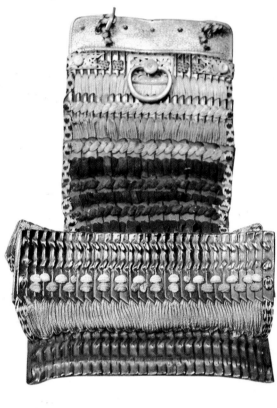

Do maru (Kamakura/Nambokucho period)

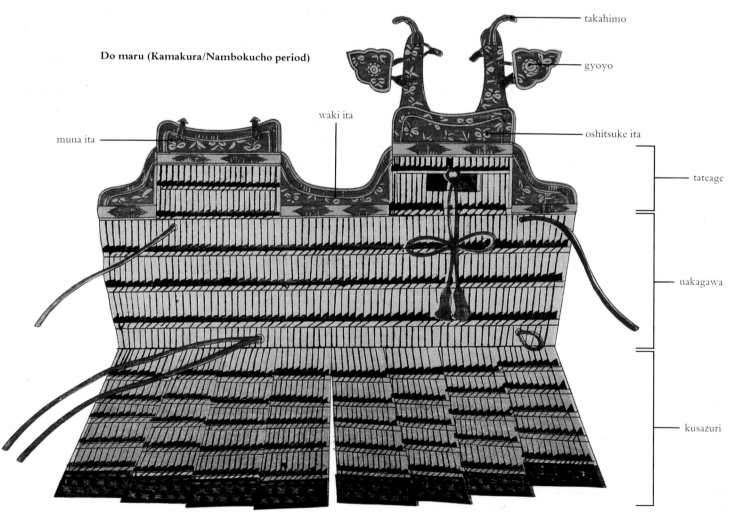

takahimo

gyoyo

oshitsuke ita

waki ita

muna ita

tateage

nakagawa

kusazuri

trousers of the yoroi hitatare. Some armours were made entirely of iyozane, others used a mixture of both iyozane and kozane, employing the former for the nakagawa and the latter elsewhere. One strange form of both do maru and haramaki appeared; it was covered entirely with plain, smoked leather held in place by cross knots on each row of scales. These armours were called *kawa zutzumi do maru* or *kawa zutzumi no haramaki* (leather-wrapped armour), and since few survive, they cannot have been popular – probably because they were rather dull compared with the elaborate colours and patterns of lacing that were now popular for more conventional armours.

As helmets were now invariably fitted with a permanent lining, they were made larger, to keep the sides of the helmet itself away from the head. A further consequence was that either three or four rings were riveted to the koshimaki to provide attachment points for the helmet cord, which could no longer be attached high inside the bowl. Reputedly, the increase in the space between

the lining and the bowl reduced the concussive effects of a blow as well as making the helmet more comfortable to wear.

The extremely elaborate helmets of the Nambokucho period were replaced by more sober helmets. The rivets were countersunk into the surface of the plates and then lacquered over. Decoration was confined to a gilt tehen kanamono, fukurin and igaki, with usually three shinodare applied directly to the

Above: An unusually early kawa zutsumi do maru. In this type of armour the entire outer surface was covered with smoked leather. Nambokucho period.

Above left: Blue laced do maru with o sode, now considerably faded. Kuromachi period.

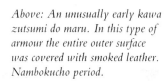

Left: Akoda nari kabuto by Miochin Iyetsugu (1558-1591), who worked in Sagami. The koshimaki has been modified to take the present neck guard at a later date.

75

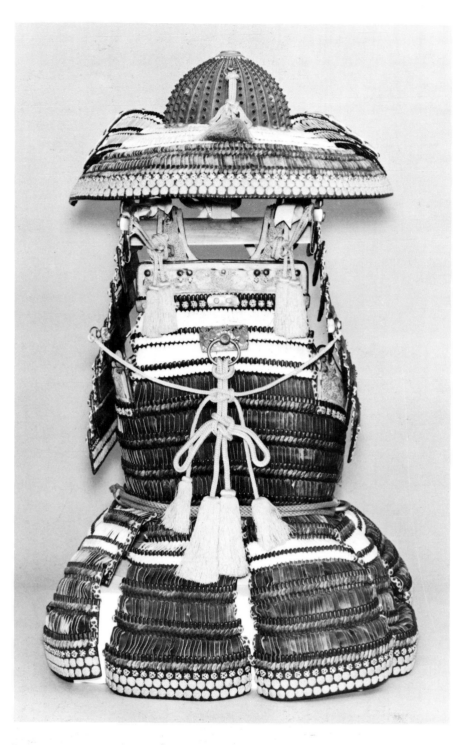

Above: Rear view of a blue and white laced do maru with large sleeves. The wide, spreading neck guard and the fukigaeshi bent backwards to lie along it are typical of the fashion of the time. Muromachi period.

pletely hidden by the enlarged kuwagata dai fastened to it by gilt-headed rivets. An extra socket, the *haraidate* (prayer stand), became a standard addition fitted centrally between the curved sockets for the kuwagata, the combination being called *mitsu kuwagata dai.* In many cases the central crest took the form of a stylized straight sword blade of the type used in Buddhist ritual, and when it did, its socket was elaborately shaped to represent the stylized thunderbolt hilt normally fitted to these swords. For other crests, the haraidate was a simple rectangular tube having its outer face decorated en suite with the other kanamono on the armour.

Continuing the trend that had started during the Kamakura and Nambokucho periods, the shikoro continued to spread, until in its extreme form it was almost horizontal – *kasa jikoro* (named after the umbrella-shaped hat worn by farmers). Although it allowed the arms to move freely, it left the head and neck vulnerable at the sides, so some had an extra protection fitted underneath the shikora. These *shita jikoro* were generally flat rectangular scales laced to a cloth backing, which hung down like a curtain close to the head. At least one helmet survives where the shita jikoro is of more normal construction but is shaped closer to the head, fitted rather incongruously below the regular one. The fukigaeshi continued to be formed from all but the hishinui no ita and was now bent so far backwards that they all but lay flat on the shikoro itself.

Armour for the face became more common in the later Muromachi period, but was by no means universal. When no mask was worn, the upper chest and throat were protected by a nodawa. The hoate continued to be the most popular type of mask, covering the chin and cheeks to just below the eyes, but an abbreviated version, the *hanbo* was also available which covered only the chin and angle of the jaw. Masks were now provided with two or three rows of scales, curved to fit around the throat. Called *yodare kake* (baby's bib), it hung outside the do, filling the gap above the muna ita and obviating the need for a separate nodawa. For those wanting more protection, similar masks, called *me no shita ho* (below the eye mask), were available provided with a nose piece; on most examples this could be removed to convert it into a hoate. Wrinkles, moustaches, imperials, whiskers, beards, and even gilded or silvered teeth were added

lacquer on the front plate and two others on the back plate. Any helmet bowl in which the rivets were no longer visible but the flanges remained prominent are described as *suji bachi.* As the era progressed, the swelling of the bowl increased, particularly at the back, the tehen tilted forwards slightly and the area round it was slightly depressed. The shape resembled the top of the recently introduced pumpkin, and hence these helmets were called *akoda nari kabuto.*

The peak, which now projected forward at a considerable angle, continued to be covered with decorated leather but was almost comto masks to enhance their warlike appearance. Most were lacquered red inside, supposedly to impart a reddish, warlike hue to the features, but since the interior could not be seen when worn, this theory is rather dubious.

Very occasionally a full face mask, *so men*, was worn. One of the few to survive is a black-lacquered example. A combination of a happuri with a hoate, it can be separated at the temples, leaving a T-shaped opening for the eyes, nose and mouth. Another covers the face completely, but is just a skeleton framework fretted from a single piece of iron. The first of these examples still retains its yodare kake, and the holes in the latter show that one was originally fitted.

These *men gu* (face armour) were made either from iron or leather, the important feature being that they fitted the face properly. As an aid to comfort, they were provided with a hole or a tube under the chin to drain away perspiration. The helmet cord was tied to hooks on the cheeks and long projecting studs under the chin. This was found in practice to be a much more secure method of fastening the helmet than when the cord was tied directly to the chin. The lower lip and chin protrude in an exaggerated way on many masks, not only to make them more grotesque but also to form a groove which prevented the helmet cord from becoming dislodged. A great number of different methods were devised for tying helmets;

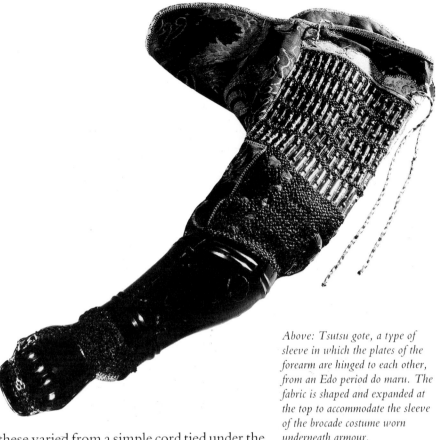

Above: Tsutsu gote, a type of sleeve in which the plates of the forearm are hinged to each other, from an Edo period do maru. The fabric is shaped and expanded at the top to accommodate the sleeve of the brocade costume worn underneath armour.

these varied from a simple cord tied under the chin, to complex arrangements involving up to five rings on the helmet, the cord looping from them and the hooks attached to the mask in all manner of ways – advocates of each method claiming it had special advantages in battle.

A considerable number of complete armours survive from the Muromachi period

Below: Nineteenth century woodblock print showing retainers of the Takeda family dressing for battle.

Above: Men gu (face armour), from various periods. Top row, me no shita ho, which cover the face and nose below the level of the eyes; middle row, hanbo which cover only the chin and lower cheeks; bottom row nodawa, defences for the throat and upper chest.

Right: Masks covering the whole face were never very common. This example is signed Kojima Munenao, a Miochin smith who worked in the late eighteenth century.

which show that armour for the limbs was developing to keep pace with that for the head and body. The kote were now based on fairly tight-fitting sleeves, *iyeji* (foundation), having a core of hemp cloth stiffened with unripe-persimmon juice, lined with thin silk and covered on the outside with linen, hemp or brocade. All three layers of fabric were bound together around the edge with leather or braid edging. The sleeve was laced up the inside of the arm by a cord so that its fit could be adjusted over the under garments. Onto this base was sewn the defensive metal work, which at this period was of two types. One variety generally had three large plates over the forearm, hinged or sewn to each other with braid, and called *tsutsu gote* (tubular kote). The alternative variety was made up from a varying number of narrow splints connected by mail, and was called *shino gote* in reference to the shape of the leaves of bamboo grass. This term occurs in the book *Moko Shurai*, which suggests that this style had been used in the Kamakura period, but no illustrations or examples survive to show what these early versions were like.

Both varieties of kote were provided with a handguard, *tekko*, which was embossed for the knuckles, and which was extended by a strip of mail and a further small plate to cover the first joint of the fingers. Also joined by mail was a shaped plate for the thumb prolonged by another tiny plate. Loops of cord or braid were provided, generally threaded through the mail joints, through which the middle finger and the thumb were passed to hold the tekko in position. A further cord, fastened with a toggle just above the wrist, prevented the weight of the sleeve dragging on the hand.

The upper part of both types of sleeve was covered with mail into which were set plates whose number, size and arrangement varied considerably. One special type that came into use towards the end of the period, particularly for use with the better quality haramaki, had the whole of the upper arm covered by a small plate sode sewn permanently into position. To allow it to fit close to the arm, the plates of this sode were hinged in two places, the lowest lame being cut off at an angle to allow the elbow to bend. Because these kote resembled those shown being worn by the Buddhist divinity, they were called *bishamon gote*. All types of kote were provided with a small domed plate, *hiji gane*, over the point of the elbow and a capping plate, *kanmuri no ita*, divided into three by hinges or mail to fit the shoulder, and flanged for stiffness.

Prior to the late Muromachi period kote had been put on before the do, being held in place by cords or ties of cloth under the opposite armpit or across the chest. While this method continued to be used, towards the end of the period kote appeared which formed part of an abbreviated jacket, *sashinuki gote*. Some had a standing armoured collar, *tominaga sashinuki gote*. Others had the fabric foundation trimmed to the edge of a capping plate with holes for cords, carrying small toggles that fastened to loops on the underside of the watagami; this transferred some of the weight of the kote to the armour rather than directly to the body.

Armour for the upper legs also underwent considerable development during the Muro-machi period, encouraged by the improved techniques developed in the use of pole arms. At the start of the period, an arrangement that had first appeared late in the Nambokucho period was perfected in which rows of kozane were arranged to encircle the knee and lower thigh. This type of haidate took the form of a divided apron of fabric, reinforced with leather to take the weight of the armoured portion. Along the lower edge of

Below: Hodo haidate (defence for the thighs with the lower part divided into sections) from an Edo period reproduction of a do maru.

Bottom: Shino suneate (shinguards) of splints connected by mail. The centre shino is hinged across under the tie to avoid rubbing the instep. Edo period.

Above: Illustration showing the kote (armoured sleeve) being tied around the body under the opposite arm.

form of defence had only a limited vogue. It was superseded by a flatter arrangement of kozane, still attached to an apron-like fabric support, hung in front of the thigh and knee and only loosely fastened behind the leg by a narrow band of fabric. Initially, the scales were in several rows, the lower ones subdivided as they had been during the Nambo-kucho period, but by the mid-Muromachi they were replaced by continuous rows of iyozane (larger scales), laced in reverse so that they overlapped downwards. This arrangement was lighter and easier to make.

On their lower legs, most samurai continued to wear some form of o tateage suneate (shin guard with knee plates), which by the middle of the Muromachi period was sometimes supplemented by an additional plate covering the back of the leg. An alternative, lighter form made of splints, like the corresponding kote, now made its appearance. These *shino suneate* differed from the plate variety in that the shino on the inside of the leg only extended to mid-calf, the lower part being replaced by a patch of leather, *abumi zuri no kawa*, to prevent damage to the stirrup leathers. Some had the defence for the knee omitted, when they were known as *kaihan suneate*, but most are fitted with them, in the form of a standing section of *kikko* or brigandine made from small hexagonal plates quilted between layers of fabric or leather. All samurai now wore straw sandals over soft leather ankle socks which had a separate big toe to accommodate the thongs of the sandals.

The swords and other weapons carried during the Muromachi period consisted of a mixture of the older styles of the Kamakura and Nambokucho periods, and other newly devised varieties. Most still wore the kawa zutzumi no tachi, although an alternative, *ito maki no tachi*, appeared in which the hilt and upper part of the scabbard were wrapped with silk braid in place of leather. One innovation that started early in the period was for the dirk or short sword worn edge upwards through the belt to be increased in length and to be worn as an alternative to the tachi. At first these *uchi gatana* (striking or piercing sword) were relatively short, with light, relatively straight blades averaging about two feet (0.6m) in length. These were more suited to thrusting than the longer, curved blades of tachi. As their utility became recognized, they were made longer and sturdier, being

each section of fabric was sewn three curved rows of scales, the upper row being laced in reverse for flexibility. When worn, the scale sections were tied above and below the knee so as to completely encircle the leg. This restricted movement to such an extent that this

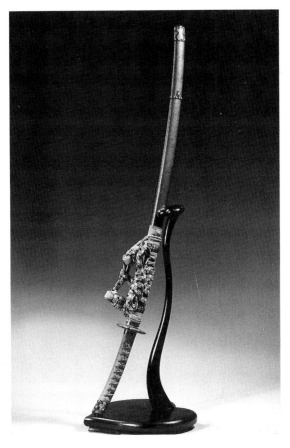

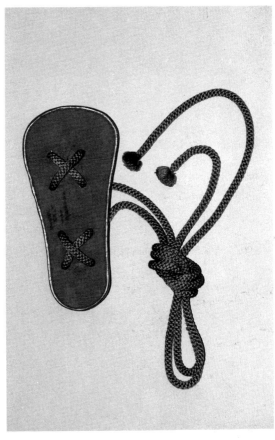

Far left: An ito maki no tachi on a tachi stand. This type of sword has the hilt and upper part of the scabbard bound with silk. Edo period.

Left: A koshi ate or sword carrier. Momoyama period.

mounted in a similar way to the tachi but without ashi and sometimes without tsuba. Like dirks, they were fastened to the belt by a strong braid, threaded through a slotted protrusion on the outer face of the scabbard a few inches below the mouth, called a *kurigata* (chestnut shape). So popular did this style of sword become, that it was eventually adopted as standard wear when in civilian dress, accompanied by a short sword, chiisa katana or wakizashi, mounted in a similar way. Some samurai, whether because of poverty or design, had tachi made with removeable ashi so that they could be worn as uchi gatana. Others wore uchi gatana fastened to a sword carrier, koshi ate, edge downwards in the manner of a tachi.

It is not known why this form of sword mounting became so popular; it may be that it was simply more comfortable to wear, as the sword was held firmly to the body and did not bump against the hip when riding or walking. This was also the case when the sword was carried in a koshi ate, since it was tied closely to the waist. Having the hilt in a fixed position meant that the hand could be guided straight to it when the need arose to draw the sword quickly, rather than having to fumble, as would have been necessary for the hilt of a tachi, which swung on its

hangers. Since the Japanese always removed the long sword when entering a house, leaving it in a rack placed for the purpose by the

Below: Sword guard of russet iron pierced with a design of sickles and a pagoda.

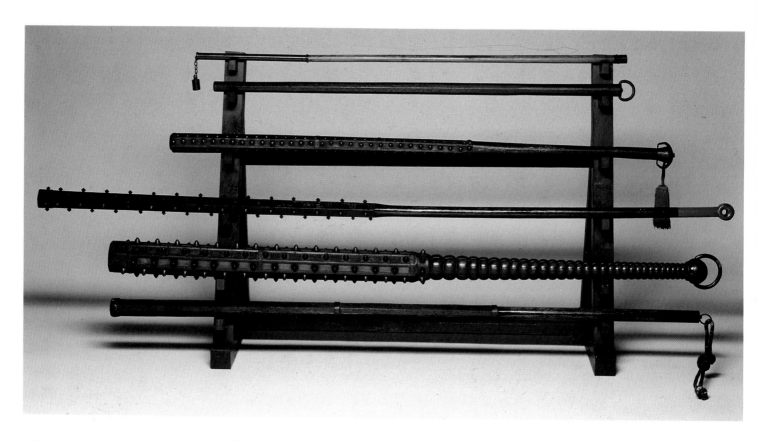

Above: Various types of club. The top example contains a weighted chain which can be flicked out at an enemy.

Below: Pole arms. The bottom two are fitted with parrying bars.

door, the answer may be much more prosaic. The tachi was tied to the belt by its cords, and had to be untied to remove it. An uchi gatana, on the other hand, could be slipped from the belt, or repositioned in it, in just a few seconds.

Those with the strength to do so went into battle carrying the huge no dachi, but most preferred one of the varieties of pole arms. Naginata were still popular, but they had slightly smaller blades than previously, mounted on proportionally longer shafts. In

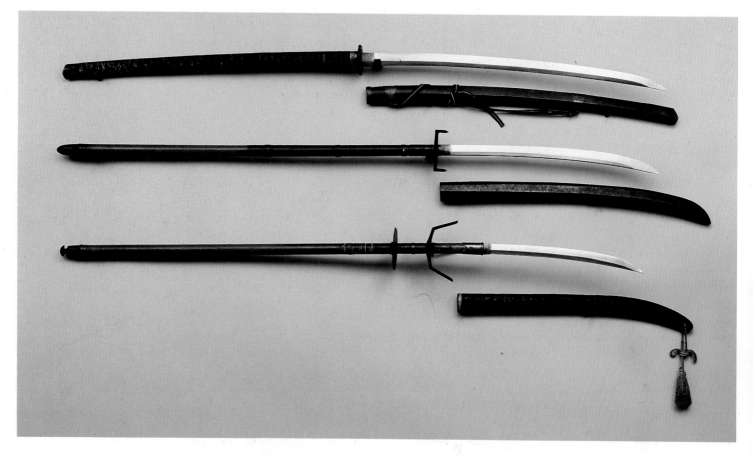

Far left: Utsubo of exaggerated proportions. These quivers offer the arrows complete protection from the weather.

Left: Saika bachi having hinged plates to guard the temples. Helmet bowls of this type, made at Saika on the Kii peninsula, are characterized by the chrysanthemum-shaped plates applied to the top of the bowl.

Below: Two bows. The bow on the left is a han kyu, or half bow, for use in restricted spaces.

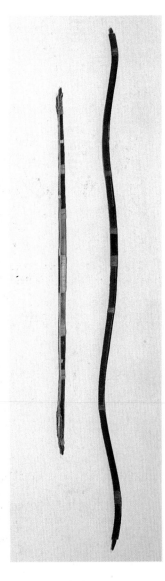

common with all pole arms of the period, naginata shafts now sported several ornamental reinforcing bands around the region enclosing the tang of the blade, below which was a bulbous binding of cord that acted as a hand stop. In use, the hands are continuously slid along the shaft of the naginata, and reversed on it, as different defensive stances are adopted. During these manoeuvres the hand stop acted as a tactile indication to the upper limit of the shaft. It was now usual to lacquer or otherwise decorate only the part of the shaft above the hand stop (the part of the shaft that had to be split to cut the socket for the tang of the blade); the lower part was generally of polished wood.

A few kumade and kama were still being used, but as in all periods they were rare weapons, used only by a small minority. Similarly, a few of herculean stature carried clubs of iron or wood, *kanabo*, of tapering octagonal section, about five feet (1.5m) long, and frequently studded for most of their length. No doubt a blow from such a weapon would have been devastating, but their sheer size and weight would suggest they were meant more for intimidation than for serious use.

A weapon similar in many respects to the naginata appeared around the middle of the Muromachi period. Called the *nagamaki*, some authorities consider it merely a variant of the no dachi. The apparent similarity between the names is illusory; naginata means 'mowing down sword' while nagamaki means 'long wrapping' and refers to the fact that many have their shafts wrapped in a criss-crossed manner, like a sword hilt. In shape, the blades of the nagamaki resembled a large, heavy sword blade, sometimes thinned along the back edge to reduce weight. It was fitted to a short shaft about four feet (1.2m) long and was generally provided with a tsuba or other protection for the hand. Modern enthusiasts who have attempted to use them describe them as clumsy, ill-balanced weapons with little to recommend them. Despite this they enjoyed a considerable vogue extending into the Momoyama period, being favoured by Oda Nobunaga for his front-line troops.

By far the most common pole arm carried was the *yari* (spear). Fitted with a head which was a flattened-diamond shape in section, its length could vary from six inches (15cm) to three feet (0.9m) or more. Unlike the naginata and nagamaki, which had oval shafts to assist in directing the blade, spear shafts were round or multi-faceted, lacquered in the upper part and reinforced with metal rings. Most shafts were of oak, but one formerly in the author's collection was built from wedge-shaped pieces of bamboo, glued together in the manner of a fishing rod. The total length of yari during most of the Muromachi period was a modest six or seven feet (1.8 or 2.1m), but towards the end of the period, foot soldiers were armed with longer spears as a defence against horsemen.

Archery continued to play its role in all Muromachi battles. The power of the bow had been increased by surrounding the wooden core with bamboo on all four sides. A new type of quiver, the *utsubo*, appeared which all but ousted the old ebira. It was enclosed, offering better protection from the weather to the arrows. Most utsubo were more or less cylindrical containers with a rounded upper end and a lidded opening in the side near the bottom. They were worn on the right hip and held in place by straps and cords; the lid was swung aside as the arrows were taken out downwards. When not in use the lid was held shut by a strap. Later utsubo

Right: Oki tenugui kabuto, a type of helmet with almost vertical sides to the bowl and top plates which extend beyond the back of the bowl. The applied flower shaped plates suggest the work of the Saika Haruta armourers.

varied considerably; the upper part swelled outwards like a balloon in some, others were elaborately lacquered or covered with fur. However, during the Muromachi period they were plain utilitarian objects, worn with a cloth cover decorated with stripes of colour or with mon. These covers may have acted as troop identification on the battlefield as well as providing protection.

A curious weapon that survives in considerable numbers made its appearance at the end of the Nambokucho period and became more common during the Muromachi period. The *uchi ne* originally took the form of a very short spear, with a shaft that was only about a foot (0.3m) long and a small but heavy three- or four-sided blade. At close quarters it could be used for stabbing or thrown in the manner of a dart, while for longer ranges it could be held by the point and thrown in a similar way to a knife. Later versions were fitted with exaggerated fletchings to stabilize their flight, and a nock (frequently of ivory) which, because the weapon was a missile was purely decorative. Those that survive from the Edo period generally have a tasselled wrist cord through the shaft near the nock, indicating the tendency to use them more as a stabbing weapon than as a missile.

Unlike the swordsmiths, whose names have survived both on blades and in the literature of the Heian period, reference to armourers is remarkably scarce. Even the name *kanko* (armour person) that was used during the Kamakura and Nambokucho periods has a slightly derogatory implication. By the Muromachi period, however, the situation began to change with the introduction of the more complimentary name, *katchu shi* (armour craftsman) and isolated references to groups of armourers with names like Yuasa, Handa and Gennai appear in contemporary literature. In the book *Sekiso orai* by Ichijo Kaneyoshi, the name 'Wakito' occurs with reference to a group of armour makers, while in *Oninki* an armour is referred to as being a Koizumi yoroi. Koizumi and Wakito are suburbs of Nara, suggesting that there was already a concentration of armourers working there.

Two groups, the Haruta and the Iwai, share the distinction of being the first armourers that can be positively identified in Japanese records. Almost without doubt, the Haruta was the first group to start signing its work and it is probable that it is the same group as the Handa mentioned above. Such signatures, at first chiselled only inside the back plate of helmet bowls, had been preceded by quality control marks in the form of single characters, occasionally applied in red lacquer. Once the practice of signing helmets became common, the *ukebari* (lining) was provided with a vertical slit at the back so that the inscription could be read.

Towards the end of the Muromachi period the Haruta group was known to be based at Nara and it was probably responsible for the Koizumi armour mentioned above. At this time it specialized in making akoda nari kabuto, and continued to make them long after other, more practical, helmets had been adopted by other groups. Because of this adherence to the older style of helmet, the group suffered something of a decline in popularity during the sixteenth century, although it managed to maintain its appointment as armourer to the Shogun. At some period towards the end of the fifteenth century some of the Haruta moved to Kii and flourished by adopting the methods and styles being developed there. Unfortunately little is known about this branch, since it rarely signed its work, much of which can best be described as sturdy if not elegant.

Also working in Nara were the Iwai, about whom even less is known than the Haruta. During the Muromachi period members of this group seem to have been general armourers, but by the Momoyama and early Edo periods they were making armour for the Shogun himself, and for presentation by him, specializing in armour made of hardened leather. The mainline Iwai later became renowned for lacing and tailoring metalwork made by other groups, although a few helmets survive that show it could still make armour itself. Many more members of this group are known to have dispersed to different parts of the country to work as part of the retinue of various *daimyo*.

Towards the end of the fifteenth century a few tentative moves were made that were to transform traditional manufacturing techniques. Apart from minor cosmetic changes to the shape, and the number and size of rivets, helmets were still being made in essentially the same labour-intensive fashion as in the Heian period. An early example of a helmet made and preserved in Tosa province, shows that the armourers there were conscious of the problem and had found a solution; a solution which, although relatively insignificant at the time, was to be extremely important later. Because the shape of this new helmet was, in contrast to the akoda nari, contoured close to the head, it became known, not unnaturally, as the *zunari kabuto* (head-shaped helmet). Of the greatest simplicity, its main constructional element was a long plate running from front to back over the crown of the head, riveted to a rather wide koshimaki at each end, with two further plates filling in the gaps at each side. A simple peak whose lower edge arched over the eyes was riveted directly to the koshimaki in front. In the case of the surviving helmet, a small pair of kuwagata are held in place by these same rivets. An illustration of ashigaru by Tosa Mitsunobu shows the zunari kabuto being worn with a shikoro of cloth, marked as if quilted, but probably meant to represent mail. This is the first example of helmets being made for munition armour, *okashi gusoku* (lent armour), designed for low-cost production.

Below: A saika bachi, a multi-plate helmet made in Saika, decorated with the typical flower shaped plates of the Haruta armourers.

Above: Oki tenugui kabuto of considerable weight devoid of ornament.

Other armourers in the town of Saika on the Kii peninsular were also beginning to experiment. Their inspiration is said to have been a strange helmet washed out of the banking bordering the sea shore, a story which may have an element of truth because their initial productions bear more than a passing resemblance to the tsuki mabizashi kabuto of the Yamato period. What finally emerged were *saika bachi*, differing in detail from each other, yet recognizably related. The helmet bowl was rather higher than a hemisphere and circular in plan. It was made up of about eight vertical plates riveted to a wide koshimaki at the base and had a large, domed, circular plate with a multi-lobed outline at the top. Surmounting this were several more iron plates with a chrysanthemum-shaped outline surrounding the small iron rimmed tehen. All of the rivets involved had small rounded heads fitted with a washer of iron marked with radiating lines, *za boshi*. Many examples had no peak as such; instead the koshimaki continued across the front as a separate piece, cut out over the eyes and embossed with wrinkles and eyebrows. A few examples have small additional plates hinged above each temple, forming a sort of built-in happuri (a feature that also occurred on helmets represented on some haniwa.)

Another form of helmet bowl, whose inspiration can only be guessed at, was also produced by the Saika smiths. It was called *oki tenugui bachi* because it resembled the thin cotton towel worn under the helmet to absorb perspiration. There is some evidence that these helmets may have originated with the Tosa group since the book *Ken Mon Zatsu Roku* describes them as being similar to the *tosa zukin kabuto*. Since *zukin* can be translated as a hood or turban, this reference may be describing a similar but now unknown form of helmet; a view reinforced by the fact that they were called *zukin nari* (hood shaped) during the Edo period. The helmet bowl of the oki tenugui kabuto had the koshimaki extended upwards to form the sides of the helmet, and was capped by two plates, curved downwards at the front and sides only, riveted together along the centre line. These top plates were attached solely along the front and sides of the helmet, leaving the rear edge overhanging the koshimaki and often with a distinct gap beneath, which may have added considerably to the comfort of the wearer in the humid climate of Japan. Once again there was generally no separate peak, the front plate being embossed and fitted with applied eyebrows. Some examples were fitted with a narrow brim riveted around the koshimaki, which turned up at the front to form rudimentary fukigaeshi, while others were repoussed with a groove; in both cases these features were probably added to stiffen the sides and particularly the back since it gained no support from the top plates.

Neither the saika bachi nor the oki tenugui bachi was provided with the usual fittings for crests since generally neither had a peak to which they could be fitted. Instead they had simple iron hooks, *tsunomoto*, riveted to the brow, which in the case of the oki tenugui bachi were frequently double pronged.

So popular did these helmet styles become that the Haruta smiths who moved to Saika took up their production and abandoned their favourite akoda nari. Essentially, their products were very similar to, although perhaps rather more refined than, the rather brutal helmets of the indigenous smiths, and can be distinguished by the applied large diamond or flower-shaped plates, sometimes pierced so as to leave only an outline. These decorative plates became almost a trademark of the Saika Haruta; they used smaller ones under rivet heads in place of the more usual round washers of za boshi.

In the first year of the Onin period (1467), an argument between two families of nobles broke out in the capital. Other nobles joined sides and a prolonged war broke out, fought almost entirely in the city itself. This urban war continued for a total of some 11 years, gradually dying out as the participants lost their sense of purpose and drifted back to their provinces. Some idea of the scale of fighting can be gained from the fact that a single lord turned up with 20,000 men to support one faction; little wonder that a great part of Kyoto failed to survive.

On their return to their homelands, many of the nobles found their domains had been usurped, or divided up among those they had left in charge. Those with the means to do so fought to regain their possessions while others had little alternative but to accept the situation. Fighting flared up throughout the country as the more ambitious saw their chance to gain land and status. This unique situation is summed up by the phrase *gekokujo* (those below overthrowing those above). It was a time of rapid rises to prominence by minor members of the nobility and the equally rapid decline into obscurity of previously important personages. Throughout the remainder of the fifteenth century, and for the whole of the sixteenth, the country experienced almost perpetual warfare, giving rise to the name *sengoku jidai* (The Age of the Country at War).

As the scale of fighting, and the numbers involved in it, increased, the demand for arms and armour rose to unprecedented heights. Scale armours that had served the samurai well over the centuries suffered from defects that became more and more apparent as the magnitude and duration of the conflict increased. Armours had evolved into rich costumes, valued almost as much for their appearance as for their defensive qualities. With their subtle colour schemes and often lace-like metal decorations they were totally unsuited to the rough-and-tumble of the long campaigns that were such a prominent feature of these wars. Sakakibara Kozan's analysis of the situation sums up these disadvantages admirably:

A large quantity of lacing is a disadvantage. When soaked with water it becomes very heavy and cannot be quickly dried; so that in summer it is oppressive and in winter liable to freeze. Moreover, no amount of washing will completely free the lacing from any mud which may have penetrated it, and on long and distant cam-

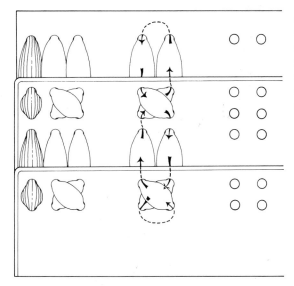

Left: Sugake lacing was adopted as a means of reducing the amount of braid used in the construction of an armour. Large quantities of lacing became heavy when soaked and harboured dirt and vermin on long campaigns.

paigns it becomes evil smelling and overrun by ants and lice, with consequent ill-effects on the health of the wearer. It is also easily damaged because it will retain a spear instead of letting it glide off harmlessly.

Below: Dark green kebiki sugake laced do maru. Sugake lacing (see diagram above) can be seen on the kusazuri.

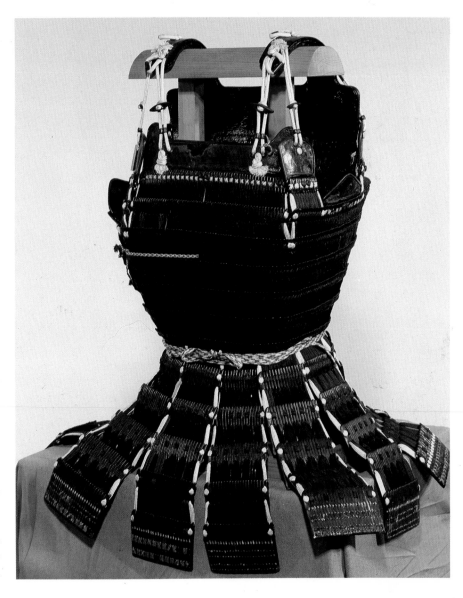

Left: Karuta gane tatami do. These armours of mail and plates sewn onto a fabric backing dispensed with lacing entirely. Since they could be cheaply produced, and folded for storage and transport, they were widely used for arming common soldiers.

Above: Karuta gane tatami kabuto inscribed in red lacquer 'medium size'. This inscriptian suggests it was for issue to low-ranking troops.

Below: Tatami hitai ate, a minimal helmet usually worn by foot soldiers, fitted with a hood of kikko and hair.

What Kozan fails to say, but what is equally important, is that its production involved immense amounts of labour, which could only be afforded by the very wealthy. Armourers, their order books full, struggled to keep pace with the demands placed on them. Not only were the samurai demanding armour, but commanders were also faced with the problem of providing something for the ever-growing numbers of ashigaru being recruited. In the past, when ashigaru had been relatively few in numbers, many had been left to look after their own interests, and a battlefield provided a plentiful supply of spare equipment. This *ad hoc* approach could hardly be countenanced when a whole army needed equipping. Inevitably the answer lay in the abandonment of scale construction altogether and its replacement by plates, but there were many who showed a reluctance to abandon such a well-tried system without first exploring every alternative.

Reducing the amount of lacing was a step in the right direction and could be achieved without changing the method of construction at all. In the traditional *kebiki* (drawn hair) style of lacing, each length of braid connected adjacent rows of scales by alternating from one to another, horizontally from left to right. A new technique was devised called *sugake* (simple hang) lacing in which the length of braid was threaded vertically up the rows of scales from the lowest to the top, then back again, giving the appearance of a pair of laces, cross knotted on each row to lock them in position. These double columns of lacings could be spaced along the rows, keeping the total amount to a minimum. A rare variation of this technique was *mitsu suji gake*, which used groups of three adjacent holes rather than pairs, laced in the same way with an additional length of braid running vertically down the centre holes. In a few cases armours were made of kozane, laced in the sugake style, with all the unused holes filled in with lacquer. While this reduced the lacing problem, it did nothing to reduce the initial labour involved in making the scales. Another method that was tried was to use iyozane, with the completed rows wrapped in lacquered leather and pierced only where needed for the sugake lacing. In this case there was some saving in time since each iyozane covered almost twice the area as a kozane, with the added advantage that there was also a considerable saving in weight.

Above: Chochin kabuto, a helmet which collapses flat for storage, extended, and (below) closed.

While these experiments were being tried, others dispensed with lacing altogether and made armours from small plates sewn onto a fabric backing with the gaps between them filled with mail. Both do maru and haramaki versions of these were successfully created. By hinging the few large plates such as the muna ita and watagami, the whole armour could be folded into a compact package for both storage and transport. They were called *kusari do maru* or *kusari haramaki*, and further differentiated into *karuta gane do* and *kikko gane do* depending whether they were made from rectangular or hexagonal plates respectively. Because they could be folded, all types were known by the generic term *tatami do* (tatamu being the verb to fold). A few were of high quality and obviously made for men of rank, but most were cheaply made munition armours, issued to troops from stores when needed. The fact that many have sections of kusazuri omitted at the back shows they were not all meant for the humble foot soldier; perhaps they were for lightly armoured cavalry which could be deployed rapidly over rough terrain.

All types and qualities of helmets are found accompanying these do, but for munition armours, a simple hood of mail and plates fitted with a nominal shikoro was considered adequate when cost was a consideration. One such helmet in the author's collection has a slit at the back for the wearer's hair and is inscribed inside in red lacquer 'medium-large size'. Even cheaper was the *hitai ate*, a simple plate, shaped to fit the forehead and sewn to a band of cloth which could be tied around the head. This defence obviously derived from the happuri of the Heian period, and was later elaborated and extended further onto the head, by providing it with a peak and making it of two or more plates, riveted loosely at the temples so that it could be collapsed for storage. In this more developed form, called *tatami hitai ate*, it was often sewn to a hood made of mail or of kikko to offer some protection to the remainder of the head and neck.

During the early Edo period, a novel folding helmet was made to accompany tatami do. The most usual type has the bowl divided horizontally into overlapping rings fastened together with sugake lacing, and arranged so that it can be locked in an extended position to a pivoted curved strap by a turn button.

Far left: O yoroi, traditionally from Tamba province. The helmet is decorated with shinodare applied to the front plate, and is fitted with the characteristic spreading neck guard (kasa jikoro) of the Muromachi period. The tsurubashiri gawa, leather cover to the front of the do, is printed with the Buddhist divinity Fudo.

Below: Dark blue laced mogami do. This type of armour was constructed of horizontal strips of steel, individually hinged. Edo period.

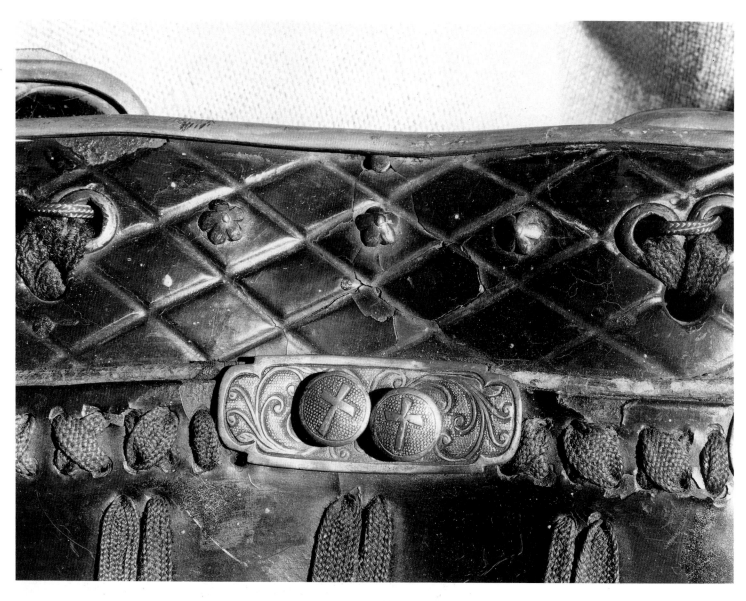

Above: Detail of the sei ita (back plate) of the armour opposite showing the unusual treatment of the lacquer and typical lobed Momoyama style kanamono. The rivets holding these ornamental plaques in position are engraved with the owner's mon; the character 'ju' in a circle symbolizing the Christian cross.

More sophisticated versions have spring-operated studs on each section that snap out and lock over the tops of the plate below as the helmet is extended, the taper of the rings stopping both types from extending too far. Because they resemble the familiar paper lanterns, these helmets are called *chochin bachi*.

While tatami do had solved some of the problems of traditional armours, they suffered from a lack of rigidity which offered almost no protection against the force of a blow. Large rigid sections were needed to dissipate the energy over a wide area. One solution to this problem was to replace the rows of scales with strips of steel, fitted with hinges to enable the wearer to put it on. Called *mogami do*, these armours were of either do maru or haramaki style, with each strip forming the nakagawa divided into five curved pieces joined by hinges in line with the edges of the tateage at front and back. Irrespective of whether they were laced in the

kebiki or sugake style, most had the tops and sides of the plates turned outwards to a small flange, against which a narrow, round beading was modelled with lacquer. Continuing the traditional method of construction, each of these strips was individually lined with leather, which was held in place by the leather ties that fastened the strips of the nakagawa rigidly to each other. These armours were fitted with kusazuri, sode and shikoro which matched the construction of the do; they were made from strips of plate, lacquered and laced either in the kebiki or sugake style.

Even though the mogami style of construction continued to be produced as long as armour was worn, the multiplicity of small hinges, and the rather delicate internal ties which really held the do together were serious weaknesses; further developments were needed before plate armour could be said to be superior to that made from scales.

Right: Mogami haramaki of Naito Yukiyasu, a Christian Daimyo exiled to Manila for his beliefs. This reassembled armour clearly shows the individually hinged plates in the do that characterize this construction. The helmet is an etchu zunari kabuto with the central plate overlapping the brow plate and the lower plate of the neck guard cut with a straight edge at the bottom.

CHAPTER FIVE
The Evolution of Modern Armour

Far right: Detail from a folding screen showing the siege of Osaka Castle.

Right: The main tower of Hamamatsu Castle, which served as an observation platform.

Below: Hamamatsu Castle – a corner tower. Castle building reached a climax in the sixteenth century at the height of the civil wars.

As the fifteenth century drew to a close, fortunes and reputations were gained and lost with a bewildering rapidity. Those with sufficient courage or guile prospered while the weak and indecisive went under. Gekokujo was at its height, with long-established families sinking into obscurity, while newcomers rose to positions of power and prominence.

A typical example of how minor figures achieved fame and fortune is shown by an incident which arose after Ashikaga Masatomo instructed his son to join a monastery. Not having a religious leaning, the son's response was to murder his father and assume control of the family's domain. From indignation or, more likely, using the incident as a pretext for action, an obscure samurai called Ise Shinkuro launched a successful attack on the son, gaining control of the province of Izu in the process. Like so many in his position, Shinkuro changed his name, choosing Hojo, in an attempt to gain respectability,

joining a monastery under the adopted name of Soun. He then set about acquiring the neighbouring province of Sagami, inviting the local lord to a hunt. Needless to say, the lord, not the deer, was the quarry, and Soun emerged with the fortress town of Odawara added to his acquisitions. Using more conventional tactics he completed the conquest of Sagami before passing the task of further expansion to his son and grandson. By the mid-sixteenth century the family were powerful land owners with most of the eastern plains of Honshu under their control. With such treachery and military aggression almost commonplace, it is hardly surprising that the demand for the trappings of war was at an unprecedented level.

Having once acquired land, those who rose to power employed every means they

could to hold onto it, indulging in an unprecedented spate of castle building. Fortresses and strongholds, often little more than temporary stockades or fortified houses, had been built since Yamato times, but by the Muromachi period they had begun to take on a more permanent character, developing into castles, sited to take maximum advantage of the terrain. The golden age of castle building occurred during the sixteenth and early seventeenth centuries, indeed the period is named after a castle. Enormous works at Osaka and Edo were built with multiple towers, moats and outworks extending a mile or more on each side. Natural defensive positions such as hills or mountain crags were the first choice of location, but lakes, rivers and even the sea were exploited for their defensive possibilities. When size and the site permitted, the enclosed area was divided into a series of compartments on different levels and separated by gates and bridges to confuse the enemy should he gain entry. Once inside, his

progress was impeded by one obstacle after another and he was constantly assailed by the arrows of the defenders. In some castles, these 'killing grounds' take on the character of a maze, and abrupt changes of direction are required to reach the heart of the stronghold.

The basis of these structures was a series of platforms of rammed earth, faced with cyclopean masonry that rose in a sweeping curve, often directly out of the moat, and becoming vertical or even overhanging slightly towards the top. On these bases were built the walls of stone or wood that divided the interior. Towers and arrow loops were incorporated where needed to provide defence to the flanks and to cover the areas within. The various gates were sometimes surmounted by towers, usually a single storey high, from which the defenders could pour missiles down onto the attackers. As a precaution against fire, the gates were often plated with iron and the timber structure of the tower, like the other structures of the castle, was heavily plastered. At the heart of

Below: Scene from the film
Kagemusha *showing a*
commander with his pages and
personal guards controlling troops
from a vantage point.

the defence was the main tower, with perhaps subsidiary towers connected to it rising in storeys of decreasing size, with sweeping roofs and overhanging gables. Although it looked impressive, the tower had little military value; it was essentially a command post and watch-tower during a battle. The tower at Osaka stood on a base about 100 feet (30m) square and 50 feet (15m) high; the tower itself was three storeys high, which added another 40 feet (12m) to the total height. The towers were used for storage and similar purposes; the main living quarters were more or less conventional buildings erected in the various courtyards within the walls.

Very few castles were taken by direct attack, but when attempting such an assault, the Japanese used siege equipment similar to that of Europe. The attackers constructed all manner of portable shields and movable towers to enable them to approach the walls. Moats were filled with brushwood fascines, and hooked scaling ladders were employed to scale the walls. Despite these aids, starvation and betrayal were responsible for far more capitulations than any amount of heroic fighting. In one castle the mats covering the floor, normally stuffed with rice straw, were filled instead with dried edible roots which could be taken up and boiled in an emergency.

During the first half of the sixteenth century armourers all over the country continued the break with traditional methods of construction that had begun towards the end of the Muromachi period. Faced with the unprecedented demands being made on them, they were more than ready to adopt the new techniques and novel styles that are now called *tosei gusoku* (modern armour). This important transition did not happen suddenly, nor did the new armours being produced necessarily show all the features that are now associated with the concept. Haramaki and do maru were still being made for the few who wanted them, but these were very much in the minority and most samurai chose the more practical, if sober modern armours.

Below: Scene from the film Kagemusha *showing foot soldiers armed with spears.*

Freed from the constraints of tradition, the armourers conceived a bewildering array of new types of armour that remained in production side-by-side with the older styles until armour was finally abandoned altogether during the nineteenth century. This blossoming of inventiveness coincided with the emergence of new groups of armourers during the late fifteenth and early sixteenth centuries to compete with the long-established Haruta and Iwai groups. Among the first, and by far the most important, were the Miochin, followed later by others, among whom the Saotome group must be singled out because of the extremely high quality of its work.

Much of what has been written about the Miochin is based on writings of the Edo period, and in particular a genealogy of their own creation, designed to enhance their respectability by claiming a long pedigree and association with the famous. In fact, the Miochin were comparative latecomers to the craft; the first independent mention of them as a group is in *Gozuisin Sanjoki*, published in 1506, where they are recorded as being makers of bits for horses. Another reference from the same period, in *Kebukigusa* confirms that they were bit makers and adds that Yamashiro was the centre from which they worked. Even as late as the early Edo period, the *Wakan Sansaizue* lists both the Ichiguchi and Miochin as being makers of horse bits. This association with bits is substantiated to some extent by the large numbers of tsuba signed by Miochins, and especially with the name Nobuiye. These tsuba, which date from the Momoyama and early Edo periods,

are of well-forged iron and are decorated with punching and piercing – both techniques that were used in the making of the cheek plates for bits. These tsuba were probably a subsidiary product made when the demand for horse equipment was low.

Considerable doubt remains as to which of these bit makers first turned to making armour, but several helmet bowls survive from the 1450s that show features suggestive of later Miochin work. They are signed 'Yoshimichi' and 'Takayoshi' but these two never used the name Miochin in their signatures. The first to do so was Miochin Nobuiye who, according to tradition, lived from 1485 to 1564. Judging by the quantity and rather varying quality of work signed with this name, it is more than likely that there were several people who used it – almost certainly unconnected with the group who made the tsuba. Some of these helmets may be the work of pupils, since it was common for them to use their master's name as a mark of respect. This practice (called *okkake mei*) was carried out with the noblest of motives, and with no intention to defraud, but has been responsible for much confusion over attributions ever since. Equally, the master often signed the work of his students if its quality was such that it did not discredit the workshop.

According to Yamagami Hachiro's *Nihon Katchu no Shin Kenkyu* Nobuiye's first signature dates from 1510, when he was 25 years old. The Miochin genealogy states that he was born in Shirai and later moved to Osumi, and was originally named Yasuiye. At some point early in his career he is sup-

Below: A high-sided, flat topped 62-plate suji kabuto by Miochin Nobuiye.

Below right: A 62-plate suji kabuto by Miochin Nobuiye. The neck guard is decorated by a silk frill copied from the ruffs of the Europeans.

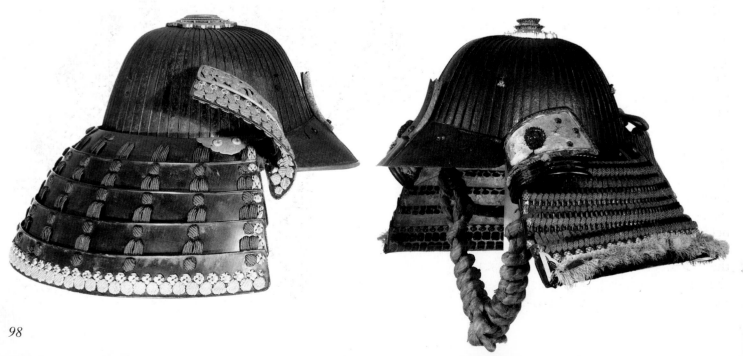

posed to have made a fine helmet for Takeda Harunobu (later Takeda Shingen), a well-known warrior-daimyo, who granted him the right to use the character 'Nobu' in his name in recognition of the quality of his work. Unfortunately there is no evidence for this whatsoever; no Miochin helmets appear in the inventory of the Takeda family's possessions after Shingen's death. There is, however, a Nobuiye helmet inscribed in red lacquer as belonging to Shingen, but this inscription is considered to have been added during the Edo period, probably by the Miochin. The whole episode appears to be little more than an attempt to enhance the reputation of the group by association with the famous.

What cannot be disputed is that the Miochin, and Nobuiye in particular, completed the development of a style of helmet, evolved from the akoda nari, that particularly suited the fashion of the time and the type of warfare then being conducted. These high-sided suji bachi were egg shaped in plan, with steeply sloping sides that flattened rather suddenly towards the top, giving the bowl the appearance of having a distinct 'shoulder'. Many were made from either 32 or 62 vertical plates, but other configurations were not uncommon. Devoid of superfluous ornament that might be damaged in action, they were even left unlacquered, but given a controlled coating of rust, to show the excellent quality of the metalwork. Even decorative leathers were eschewed in favour of a plain steel peak, fitted with a simple iron haraidate held in place by the centre one of *sanko no byo* (three iron rivets), which fastened the peak to the koshimaki. Nobuiye characteristically shaped the haraidate so that it lay close to the front plate of the helmet, and filed its top

edge into a cusped V-shape, below which are two holes arranged vertically. He also shaped and fitted the peak in such a way that its centre was slightly lower than the outer edges when viewed in profile. As on most helmets, the vestigial holes (hibiki no ana) and their protective standing rivets (shiten no byo) were added, slightly higher than halfway up the sides.

Second only to Nobuiye and perhaps even more imitated, was Miochin Yoshimichi, whose products, while very similar, differ in

Above and above left: Eight-plate helmet bowl of heichozan form (high sided, flat topped) by Miochin Yoshimichi.

Below: A 32-plate heichozan kabuto fitted with an ichimanju jikoro (neck guard in which only the top plate is curved in section) by Miochin Ki Yasukiyo. The waved outline of the plates and the rivets hammered over on the outside are unusual. Late Edo period.

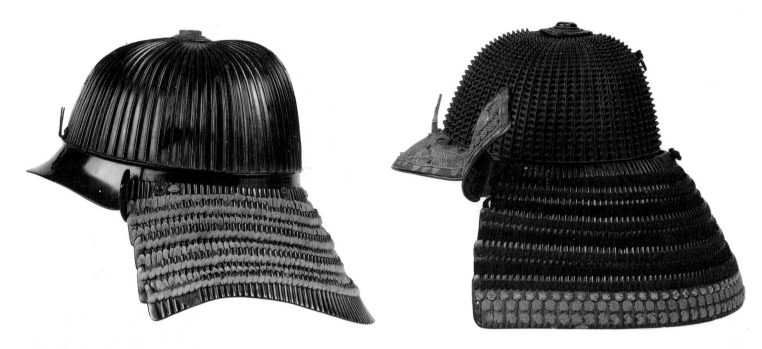

Above: An unsigned goshozan suji bachi of the type produced by the Haruta smiths. Helmets of this type are higher at the back than the front and have the rivets countersunk under the lacquer.

Above right: Ko boshi kabuto signed 'Saotome Iyetada.' The profusion of rivets, while demonstrating the skill of the maker, added considerable weight to the helmet.

Below: A zunari bachi, typified by the longitudinal plate over the centre of the head, fitted with a crest in the form of a fan paper with the character 'yama' (mountain) torn out of it. It is signed by Saotome Iyetada.

having the haraidate standing rather more forward, off the front plate, and pierced with two holes arranged side by side. Yoshimichi's peaks also differ from Nobuiye's in that the centre is higher than the outer edge when viewed from the side. Miochin work was in great demand and inevitably many of the group subsequently moved away to establish their own sub-groups in different parts of the country, sometimes dropping the name Miochin in favour of another. Once the Miochins had shown the way, the Saotome, Haruta and other groups began to produce their own versions of the high-sided helmets, in varying qualities and with slight regional variations.

On some of these helmets, particularly those produced by the Miochins and Saotome, standing rivets were reintroduced; but in an unprecedented profusion that far exceeds the number needed to hold the plates together. Sometimes as many as 22 *muku boshi* (pointed rivets) were fitted to each plate, each carefully graded in size, becoming smaller towards the tehen, and exactly aligned in perfectly straight rows. A typical 62-plate *ko boshi bachi* (small-rivet helmet bowl) might incorporate over 2000 rivets, so closely spaced as to almost hide the surface of the bowl itself. Apart from demonstrating the consummate skill of their makers, it is difficult to see what advantage these helmets possessed; the number of holes needed in each plate and the increase in weight can only have been detrimental. Despite this, they were popular helmets, produced by the very best armourers and incorporated in high-quality armours.

The profiles of these helmets differ depending upon the makers and the taste of their clients. With their love of intricate terminology, Edo period armourers classified them according to the shape of the top and the angle it made with the line of the koshimaki. Those still showing a vestige of the high back of the akoda nari (called by them *reiseizan*, mountain top heaped up) were known as *goshozan* (rear victory mountain); when flat on top they were called *heichozan* (level top mountain), or when higher in front

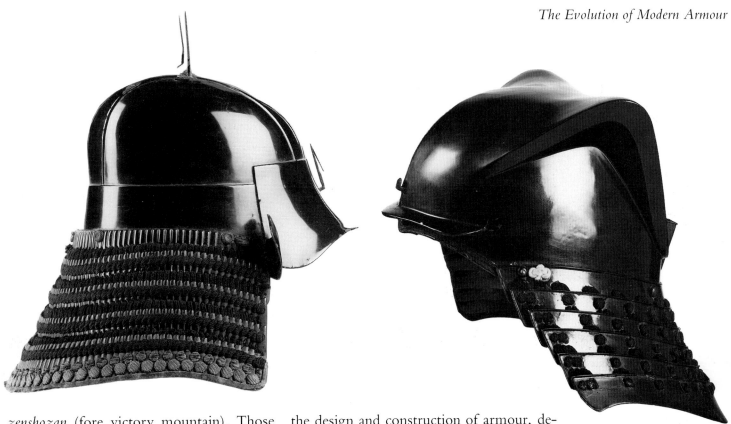

zenshozan (fore victory mountain). Those higher than a hemisphere were called *koseizan* (high built-up mountain), or if the tehen region was depressed, *tenkokuzan* (heavenly valley mountain). Although whimsical flights of fancy designed to impress customers, these names do provide a basis for classification in the absence of anything better.

Hineno Hironari and his brother Yajiuemon, both high-ranking samurai from the province of Mino who took a great interest in the design and construction of armour, developed and popularized the zunari style of construction which had originated in the province of Tosa. The *hineno zunari bachi* that resulted was higher and rather more swollen at the back than the original, with the front overlaid by a brow plate that curved outwards at the base to form a peak. A similar helmet manufactured somewhat later in the province of Etchu was favoured by the Hosokawa family; it differed in construction in

Above left: A typical Hineno zunari kabuto with fittings for crests at the top and front. Zunari helmets of this type have the central longitudinal plate riveted under the brow plate and the lower edge of the neck guard shaped to the shoulders.

Above: Harikaki kabuto, a helmet bowl decorated by a light superstructure of wood, paper, leather and lacquer, in the form of a stylized cap folded back on the head. Momoyama period.

Left: Eboshi nari kabuto, a helmet shaped to resemble a tall cap. Momoyama period.

101

Right: Etchu zunari bachi decorated with dragons and clouds in overlay. This bowl has never been mounted but the armourer has indicated the position for crest holders at the front, sides and top. Late Edo period.

Below: Gold-lacquered zunari kabuto, a style of helmet developed in Tosa, overlaid by mail. Momoyama period.

having the central plate over the crown overlap the browplate rather than being riveted underneath it. Because these helmets were made of a few simply shaped plates, zunari

bachi could be made from heavier-gauge metal and harder steel than more conventional multi-plate helmets. For this reason, better quality versions of this style of helmet became popular with men of high rank and, because they could be made by far less skilled craftsmen, they were the first choice for cheap armours, and were turned out in their thousands from thin metal. Being rather plain in appearance, many zunari kabuto were decorated with coloured lacquer or were covered with hair, bristles, feathers or textured leather. Others relieved the severity by adopting all manner of exaggerated *tate mono* (crests) fitted to the front, sides, top and back of the helmet.

These crests, which were applied to all types of helmets, were often little more than silhouettes of metal, wood or leather, gilded, lacquered, or decorated in some other way. A few, however, are masterpieces of wood carving, embellished with lacquer, hair and other materials. When fitted to the front of the helmet they were called *maedate*, if at the sides, *waki date*, on top *kashira date* or at the back *ushiro date*. The subject matter was sometimes heraldic, but just as often appeared to have been chosen at the whim of the wearer and could depict almost anything.

Hineno Hironari is also credited with what must be the ultimate in helmet decoration, the *harikake bachi*. Using a zunari helmet bowl as a base, fantastic creations in wood, rawhide and paper were built up and subsequently lacquered; these represented anything the imagination could conceive. Since this superstructure was light, size was not a limitation and a few flamboyant samurai appeared on the battlefield wearing helmets that towered several feet above the head or extended several feet from side to side. The subjects represented were legion, ranging from animals and plants to everyday objects and even abstract ideas. Edo period books list hundreds of varieties, ranging from rather conservative copies of hoods and caps, to helmets in the shape of 'peeled winter cherries', 'curled sea slugs' or even the improbable 'helmet in the shape of a snow storm'. However absurd some of these now seem, they were undoubtedly popular in their day and sufficient survive to show the artistry exercised by their makers.

Zunari bachi were not the only simple helmets produced and once the idea had been established that efficient helmets could be made of a few plates, other constructions, the simpler the better, were explored and exploited. Particularly popular were those fashioned in the form of a court cap, *eboshi nari kabuto*, or the closely related helmet shaped like a catfish's tail, *namazu o kabuto*. Both types were made of two plates riveted around the edge at the front, top and back, and opened outwards at the bottom for the head. In common with most simple helmets, they were generally fitted with a brow plate and concave peak combination, in the zunari bachi style, with a small inner plate bridging the gap across the brow to which the helmet lining was sewn. All non-regular helmets, that is those that are neither hoshi bachi nor suji bachi, are generically classified as *kawari bachi* (novel or peculiar helmets).

To accompany the zunari and its fanciful variants, the Hineno devised a new form of shikoro that fitted closely to the neck, falling in a slight concave curve to a bottom plate shaped to the shoulders. The makers of the etchu zunari bachi produced a similar arrangement, but it had a straight edge to the bottom plate. Unlike previous shikoro, only the top plate (*hachi tsuke no ita*) was extended and bent outwards to form rudimentary fukigaeshi, usually decorated with the owner's mon. Some however, abandoned fukigaeshi altogether since they no longer served any useful purpose. Others, called *ite*

Above: A haruta kawari kabuto in the form of a head wearing a court cap. Helmets were made in unusual styles to make the wearer distinctive in battle.

jikoro, had removable or hinged fukigaeshi which could be taken off or swung out of the way when using a bow. These close-fitting shikoro became so popular that other types of helmet were modified to take them; the angled flange of the koshimaki was clipped into tabs, so that it could be bent vertical.

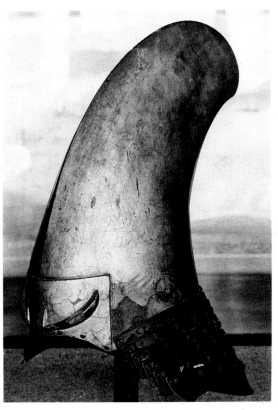

Left: Embossed kawari bachi, an unconventional multi-plate construction, in the shape of a Chinese cap. Momoyama period.

Far left: Naga eboshi kabuto, a helmet in the form of an exaggerated tall court cap.

Right: Six-plate hoshi bachi (helmet with prominent rivets) decorated with dragons in overlay. Kaga work of the Momoyama or early Edo periods.

Far right: Me no shita ho, a mask covering the face and nose below the eyes, of russet iron signed with the words 'Ki Yasukiyo, a pupil of Miochin Muneyasu, made this'. The surface treatment of lines is called sujichigai yasurime.

Below: Harikake kabuto, a helmet with a built up lacquered superstructure in the form of a cap worn by priests of the Nichiren sect.

When not fitted with this close-fitting *hineno jikoro*, helmets were provided with neck guards of more or less rounded outline, the fukigaeshi was formed as a prolongation of the top plate. If all the plates were curved in section it was called a *manju jikoro* (dumpling shikoro), either *o manju* or *ko manju* depending upon its size. If only the top plate was rounded, the remainder being more or less flat, it was called *ichimanju jikoro*; one variant of this form had all the plates except the top one divided into three sections covering the sides and back. Called *gessan shikoro*, this gave great freedom of movement, but was never very popular since the smaller sections offered less protection from a blow. As the hineno jikoro required a vertical koshimaki, it was no longer possible to fit the iron rings for the helmet cord. In their place, cord loops were threaded through holes in the koshimaki and the shikoro, in three, four or five places depending upon the way the owner tied his helmet cords.

Armour for the face, men gu, was now standard and could be either a hoate, hanbo or me no shita ho according to taste. Very few so men were made, except as demonstrations of the armourer's skill, since they restricted the vision far too much to be practical. Whatever the type, they came in all manner of forms; heavily wrinkled or smooth, with or without teeth or facial hair, lacquered or russet iron. Some smiths adopted the standing flange (yadome), which had been used on the Heian period happuri, to guard the helmet cords. All masks were now fitted with a throat defence (yodare kake) as a matter of course, which was either

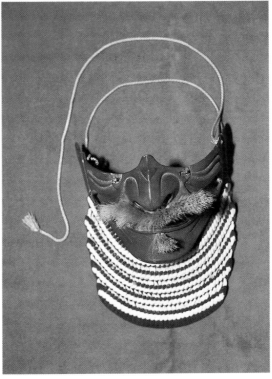

Far left: Me no shita ho with hinged throat defence.

Left: Russet lacquered me no shita ho with a throat defence that extends upwards following the line of the jaw.

laced directly to the mask or to an intermediate band of leather (*komori tsuke*). Nodawa were almost totally abandoned as their function was now superseded by the yodare kake of the mask and the modifications that had been made to the do.

Although practical, plate construction was dull, and many samurai still favoured kebiki lacing, not infrequently for the whole armour, but at least for the *gessan*, as the kusazuri were now called. In order to retain some of the advantages and ease of manufacture of plate construction, armourers devised a way of simulating scales using lacquer.

Kiritsuke kozane (cut-out and applied scales), as they were called, were produced by shaping the upper edge of a plate like a row of scale heads, piercing the plate with holes for lacing, then modelling the surface into a series of vertical ribs with kokuso, before the final lacquering. Properly done, the effect is remarkably realistic, only lacking the deep undercuts between the heads of the scales. A similar method was used to produce *kiritsuke iyozane*, most of which are virtually indistinguishable from a real row of such iyozane scales wrapped in thin leather under the lacquer. In many cases, the makers of kiritsuke

Far left: Kiritsuke kozane, plates covered with lacquer to simulate small scales.

Above: Plate cut out for kiritsuke iyozane and pierced for imitation lacing. The pairs of holes along the lower edge are for internal ties which held the do rigid.

Left: A plate pierced for sugake lacing, where pairs of laces are spaced along a plate or row of scales.

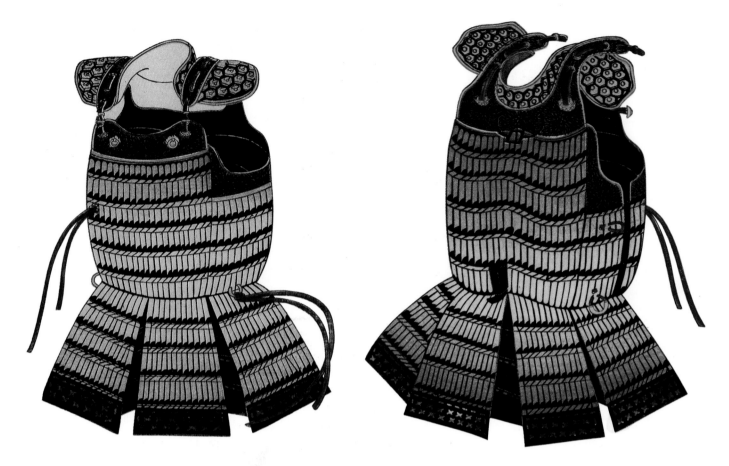

Above and above right: Front and rear views of a tosei do ('modern' armour) from Gun Yo Ki.

iyozane even went as far as fitting a kawashiki, held in place by imitation lacing fastened through two rows of holes drilled along the centre line of the plate. When lacquered, the sewing and the ridge formed by the kawashiki on the inside added considerably to the realism; only the rigidity of the solid plate betrayed the true method of construction.

Complementing the new styles of helmets, armourers devised a whole range of do which most samurai found preferable to the old do maru and haramaki for use in the field. Much of the terminology changed during this period. The muna ita (plate covering the top of the chest) was now called the *oni damari* and the oshitsuke ita (plate covering the top of the back) was called the *boko no ita*. In *tosei do* (modern do) the number of rows of scales, or their plate equivalents, in the nakagawa increased to five. This not only improved the protection for the lower abdomen but also allowed the do to sit more firmly on the hips. For this latter reason, tosei do can also be called *tachi do* (standing do). Similarly, an additional row was sometimes added to the front tateage to improve the protection given to the upper chest. This emphasis on covering a greater part of the body, almost certainly a result of the increased use of straight-bladed spears, is also reflected by changes to

the plates covering the top of the chest and those under the arms. Both plates had their upper profiles modified to fit closer to the throat and arm respectively, and were given a rolled out upper edge, which acted as a stop rib to prevent weapons sliding off into the body. Whereas protection for the neck had previously been provided by the shoji no ita and the shikoro, it was now usual to fit a *tate eri* (armoured collar) usually of kikko, but sometimes of mail. On the inside, these collars were extended in the form of a padded yoke across the upper back and over the shoulders, making the armour considerably more comfortable. The watagami also gained minor defences for the shoulder in the form of *kohire* (little fin), made of either scales, plate or brigandine, fastened along their outer edges. These helped to cover the gap between the watagami and the top of the kote or sode, now exposed to a downwards cut by the introduction of closer fitting shikoro.

Whatever the type, many tosei do were provided with a pouch, *hanagami fukuro* (nose tissue bag), either on the left front, just above the waist, or attached behind one of the front gessan. As its name suggests, it was used to carry paper handkerchiefs and other small necessities when armed. Because the uchi

gatana was more popular than the tachi, those pouches situated on the front of the do had the double function of protecting the lacquer from contact by the tsuba of the swords. Where a pouch was not fitted, it was sometimes replaced by a simple pad of fabric or leather to serve the same purpose.

As tactics improved and the co-ordination of large numbers of troops became important, identification on the battlefield grew in importance. In the Muromachi period, warriors had sometimes worn a streamer attached to a stick in the haraidate. It now became common practice to equip each member of a company with a flag or other identification called a *sashimono*, worn in a holder attached to the backplate of the do. To accommodate this fitting, the back of the tosei do was shaped with a slight vertical groove over the spine. Various arrangements were introduced for attaching the sashimono. Most commonly, a bow-shaped metal bracket (*gattari*), with a square or round holder at its centre was pivoted to the boko no ita. Some gattari are ingeniously hinged in

Left: Byo toji okegawa do, an armour of horizontal plates fastened by prominent rivets. The purpose of the hinged hook attached at the waist on the right is unknown. (Lacing modern.)

Below left: Rear view of a hon iyozane nuinobe do, an armour made in two parts and joined by a hinge under the left arm and laced with sugake lacing.

Left: Nuinobe do fitted with a sashimono of paper plumes. This device was worn for identification on the battlefield.

107

Right: Attachment for the sashimono, the identification emblem attached to armour.

Far right: The war standard of Honda Masashige. The Honda family came to power in the sixteenth century. Momoyama period.

the middle so that they could be removed from the pivots when not required. Alternatively the bracket might take the form of a wooden plate, lacquered or covered with leather and tied by thongs to the boko no ita. Into this upper socket was inserted a lacquered wooden tube (*uke zutsu*). The lower end fitted into a metal cup (*machi uke*) riveted or tied to the lower edge of the do.

The sashimono worn by common troops generally took the form of small flags of silk, hemp or cotton, dyed and printed with mon, stripes or other devices and flown from a bamboo pole some three or four feet (0.9 or 1.2m) long which fitted into the uke zutsu. The upper edge of the flag was supported by a horizontal rod pivoted to the pole in such a way that the flag remained extended and visible, even in windless conditions. Company commanders and other officers frequently wore alternative sashimono, perhaps large fabric or gilded paper feathers, sunbursts or other emblems of gilded wood or leather.

Even larger ensigns and war standards, *uma jirushi* (horse emblem) were positioned at strategic places on the battlefield to act as rallying points during the action and were carried as identification when marching.

Many of these standards incorporate long, coloured ribbons hanging from a finial decorated with a mon mounted on a pole about eight feet (2.4m) high. Other commanders chose large gilded fans, gourds and other objects similarly mounted. Commanders still carried fans with which to direct the movements of their troops; these were even more necessary since the wearing of masks made speech difficult. A new form of insignia, indicating rank, was introduced; it took the form of a tassel of hair or paper, often gilded, which hung from a short baton. These *sai hai* were either tucked into the sash or hung from a ring (*sai hai no kan*) provided for the purpose on the right breast of the do. A second ring, supposedly for a towel but more probably simply to balance the appearance of the do, was added to the left breast on some armours; this became virtually standard during the Edo period.

The new types of do were subdivided and named by the armourers, with their usual passion for terminology, on the basis of what are often quite minor differences in construction. In an attempt at some form of order, laced do will be considered first.

Hon kozane maru do were tosei versions of

the do maru made with the nakagawa extended by an additional row of scales. The equivalent haramaki was unpopular and all but unknown. When made of iyozane with sugake lacing, but in the style of a do maru, they were simply referred to as *iyozane do*. Much more popular and more convenient armours were made by dividing the maru do into two parts under the left arm and fitting a long hinge from the waki ita to the waist. By making the pins of these hinges removable, the do could by split into two separate parts, facilitating storage and transport. A much less common arrangement was to omit the hinge and fasten the two parts of the do by a tie at each side. These *ryo takahimo do* are most commonly, but not exclusively, found as munition armours, since they could be adjusted to accommodate a wide variety of sizes. The use of the term takahimo in this context refers to the ties for the side openings of the do, the term *aibiki* now being used for the fastenings between the watagami and oni damari.

Do made of true scales but divided into two sections by a hinge were given the name *hon kozane ni mai do* (true-scale two-section

do). When the equivalent do was made from imitation scales, they were called *kiritsuke kozane ni mai do*. Iyozane do divided in the same way were called *hon iyozane nuinobe do*, or simply *nuinobe do* if of false scales. (The term nuinobe was used by armourers in several contexts and means literally 'extended sewing'. Why this appellation came to be applied to this style of do is unknown, but it illustrates some of the difficulties encountered in attempting to translate the vague terminology used.) A variant of these laced do had the upper and lower parts laced in different styles; the usual arrangement was to have the nakagawa laced in kebiki and the tateage in sugake. This armour is called *dangae do* (changed rows do) because of their banded appearance.

Similar do to all of the above were produced with four hinges, positioned below the edges of the tateage at the front and back. Since they could be divided into five sections (front, left side, back and two overlapping sections under the right arm) they are called *go mai do*. These were subdivided on the basis of whether they were made from true or false scales in exactly the same way as ni mai do. A

Far left: War standard in the form of two gilded umbrella shapes. These heraldic devices acted as rallying points on the battlefield and were a prominent feature of Momoyama warfare.

Left: Sai hai, a commander's baton, of paper strips on its display stand.

Left: Iyozane do gusoku. In this construction the rows of scales are continuous around the body and had to be sprung open to admit the wearer, imposing a considerable strain on the structure. Momoyama period.

Above right: Blue laced hon kozane ni mai do gusoku, an armour of 'true' scales in two parts which is joined under the left arm by a hinge.

Above far right: Light blue laced yokohagi okegawa do gusoku. In this type of armour the plates forming the do were fastened by countersunk rivets and lacquered over. (Helmet cord modern.)

rare construction had the plate under the left arm divided to form a *roku mai do*. These were generally fastened by ties at each side, becoming *ryo takahimo roku mai do*, but an example formerly in the author's collection was fitted with a hinge as well as ties, enabling the two left sections to be joined.

More popular, and certainly more eco-nomical to make, were do which abandoned lacing and scales, or their imitations, and replaced the scales by plates. Most common were the various forms of do in which the separate strips of plate from which they were made were visible. When these strips were horizontal and fastened with countersunk rivets, that is, without visible fastenings, they were called *yokohagi okegawa do* after their supposed resemblance to a coopered bucket with hoops around it. Most of these are ni mai do, but they were also made in go mai do form. If fastened together in a visible way, different names were used which described the fastenings: *byo toji yokohagi okegawa do* or *byo kakari do* had prominent rivet heads, sometimes in the shape of *mon*; *kasugai do* were made from plates fastened to each other with a type of staple; *hishi toji yokohagi okegawa do* or simply *hishi toji do* were fastened with cross knots of metal, silk or leather; *uname toji yokohagi okegawa do* or *uname toji do* were fastened with simple horizontal sewing.

An alternative construction, usually of go mai do form, was made with the plates arranged vertically, called *tatehagi okegawa do*. In most examples the front and back sections consisted of a large central plate extended by a narrower plate at either side. An important derivative of this type of do was devised in the Yukinoshita area of Kamakura, and called therefore a *Yukinoshita do*. Date Masamune invited Miochin Masaiye and his family to Sendai to make armour in this style for both himself and his troops. During his stay in Sendai, Masaiye introduced changes and brought the style to its fully evolved form. Yukinoshita do were made of five sections which tapered towards the waist. The front and side sections were made of single plates while the back was normally constructed of vertical plates like a tatehagi okegawa do. Each section was provided with hinges riveted to the outside of the plate, unlike other do which had them on the inside, with only the knuckle visible. A distinguishing feature was the oni damari, either in one with the front plate, or riveted solidly to it, pierced with three holes for the aibiki instead of the more usual four. Hinged to the boko no ita were plate watagami with simple flap-like gyoyo hinged to their ends which hung over the aibiki. Plate kohire were provided, hinged to the outer edges of the watagami. Because all parts were hinged, they could be totally dismantled into more or less flat components for easy storage and transport, and quickly repaired or replaced if damaged. During the Edo period, this style, with slight variations, was called *kanto do*, *sendai do* or *oshu do* because of its popularity in these areas.

All types of okegawa do could, and usually did, have the upper plates of the front tateage and the oni damari laced in some way to introduce a certain degree of flexibility. One plain russet iron yokohagi okegawa do formerly in the author's collection had the two upper plates of the front tateage and the lower plate of the nakagawa in front, fitted with rivets sliding in slots in the adjoining plates as an alternative to lacing; exactly the same method of introducing fexibility as was used for European armours. Plate do, but particularly okegawa do, could have the edges of the component plates left plain, decorated with metal rims, or shaped into an undulating outline. Once again Edo period armourers devised extremely fanciful names for these shapes, only a few of which occur with any degree of regularity and are worthy of note.

When the plates of the do were not visible but lacquered smooth, or made from a single plate of iron or leather, the term used is *hotoke do* (alluding to the Buddha, that is, unblemished). Alternatively, the whole front of an okegawa do could be covered with a sheet of leather to give a *kawa zutsumi do* having a similar appearance. These smooth-faced do, as well as the tatehagi okegawa do with their wide front plate, provided a perfect vehicle for decoration in lacquer or damascening in gold or silver, and many were so treated. Others showed cross knots on the smooth surface, purely as decoration since the plates were in fact riveted under the lacquer. This variety is called *hishi toji hotoke do*. Alternatively a hotoke do could be provided with a laced portion to allow some flexibility. When this lacing is at the bottom it is called *koshi tori hotoke do*, or if at the top, *mune tori hotoke do*.

Finally, mention must be made of a range of do embossed in imitation of the human torso. Since these do resemble the guardian statues outside Buddhist temples, they are collectively called *nio do*. Most were made from a single plate, either embossed or modelled with kokuso with breasts, ribs and spinal protrusions that simulate human conditions from extreme emaciation to a comfortable rotundity. Individual varieties are named after divinities whose bodies are depicted in art with the same amount of flesh. A variant of this style, of which at least one example has survived, is called *katahada nugi do* (bared shoulder do) representing a partially emaciated body, lacquered in a flesh colour, which has the lower part and left

shoulder draped in sections of scales laced in different colours to represent clothing.

All types of do were fitted with gessan in seven or more sections. These were almost invariably laced to the do in the kebiki style, irrespective of the other lacing. This lacing was long, which gave great freedom of movement to the legs but left a considerable undefended region that was only partially covered by the thick padded outer belt (*uwa obi*). Some samurai increased the protection of the hips by having a series of mail covered cloth flaps (*koshi gusari*) sewn onto the lower

edge of the do under the lacing, as additional security. The gessan themselves generally matched the construction and lacing of the do, but were often of rawhide rather than steel to save weight. To maintain the curved shape of the leather plates a curved iron rod, (*shikigane*) was laced to the back before being lacquered. Most do had gessan constructed of five plates in each section, but very long versions with up to eight plates in each, which reached almost to the knees, are occasionally encountered.

Worn with these do were all manner of

Above left: Yosekake sugake odoshi ni mai do, a two section do with the lacing arranged in vertical bands.

Above: Hon iyozane nuinobe do. The style of construction and lacquering and colour of the lacing varied according to the owner's taste and pocket.

Left: Dark blue leather laced armour having an okegawa go mai do with both mune tori and koshi tori (five part do of horizontal plates with sections of lacing at the top and bottom). These sections of lacing introduced a degree of flexibility into what would otherwise have been a rigid and uncomfortable do. Armours are traditionally described by the colour of the lacing, but most have now faded.

sode, chosen both to complement the armour and to signify the status of the wearer. Generals and others of high rank continued to wear the impressive o sode or hiro sode of an exaggerated size. Those lower in the social scale wore a more practical size of hiro sode, or a new type called *tosei sode*.

These were only slightly curved, rectangular in shape and of modest size. Tosei sode were designed to be hung from the fastenings of the kote, rather than being hung from the watagami, and had simple cord loops for the purpose fastened through holes in the top plate. In most cases, they were stiffened with

Above: Mid-blue laced go mai do gusoku. An inscription on the do records that this armour was made to the order of Nakagawa Mochinori, a retainer of the Nagato Han by Ki Yasukiyo, in 1848.

internal ties and lined with fabric so that only the lower one or two plates were flexible. To keep them in position, many have a loop of braid or cord fitted to the bottom of the stiffened portion that fastened to a small toggle on the kote, just above the elbow. A few samurai dispensed with sode altogether, considering them to be of doubtful value in

action, but most surviving armours of the period are fitted with them – the wearer could leave them off if he chose to do so.

Only two substantially new forms of kote were added to the shino gote and tsutsu gote of the mid-Muromachi period, although many variations were made which differed in details. The first of these was the *kusari gote*,

made entirely of mail except for the tekko and the kanmuri no ita. It was so sober that it never became popular, and lack of protection against the force of a blow mitigated against its effectiveness. The second variety was initially promoted by the Satake family of Hitachi and rapidly became popular everywhere. The book *Kosei Roku* is the first to refer to *oda gote*; the name is derived from the family of armourers who first made them. Oda gote are characterized by having *hyotan* or *fukube* (gourd-shaped plates) embedded in the mail over the forearm and upper arm. Some are smooth with perhaps an applied flower-shape decoration, but most are pleated (*shiwa fukube*) with rows of tiny lines at each end.

Right: Tsutsu gote, an armoured sleeve with the forearm plates hinged to each other, probably of Kaga manufacture. The plate over the back of the hand is extended by finger plates.

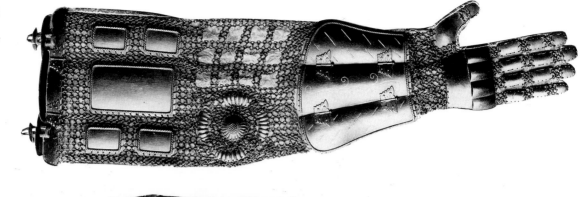

Right: Shino gote, an armoured sleeve with splints defending the forearm.

Right: Oda gote with the characteristic gourd-shaped plates applied over the forearm and upper arm. In this example the plates are closely pleated, with rows of tiny rivets at each end.

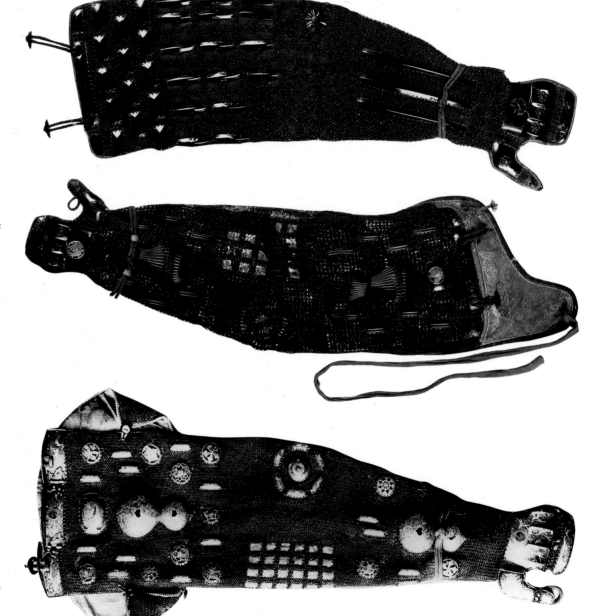

Right: Oda gote of Kaga manufacture. The plates are decorated with silver overlay and set in chirimen nanban Kusari, European-style mail with small, closely packed links.

They were generally supplemented by narrow, fluted plates, *ikada* (rafts), set into the mail at intervals on either side of the fukube. Around the hiji gane (elbow plate) were set four curved strips, similar to ikada but with radial flutes, called *matsuba wa* since they re-sembled conventionally drawn pine needles. Most oda gote are further decorated with a profusion of pierced flower-shaped plates, often of the greatest delicacy, applied to the tekko and kanmuri no ita. Their similarity suggests that the metalwork for these sleeves

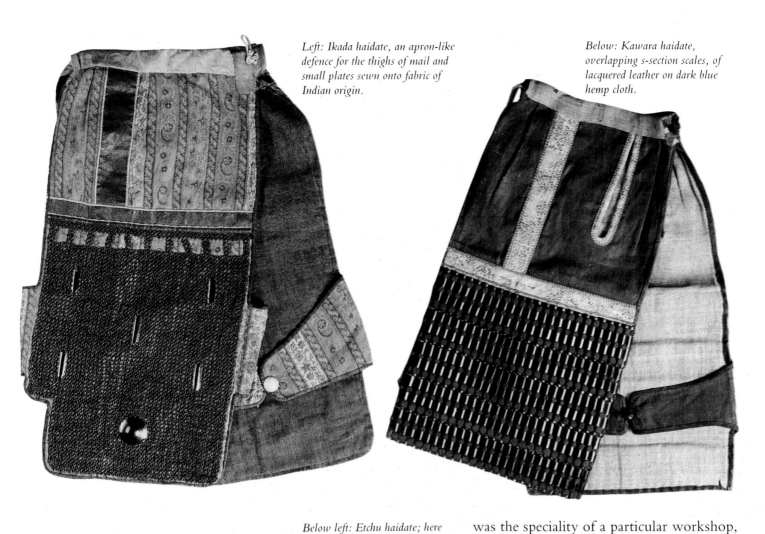

Left: Ikada haidate, an apron-like defence for the thighs of mail and small plates sewn onto fabric of Indian origin.

Below: Kawara haidate, overlapping s-section scales, of lacquered leather on dark blue hemp cloth.

Below left: Etchu haidate; here the armoured section is reduced to a sparse grid of mail and splints.

Below right: Shino haidate has rows of elongated plates connected by mail.

was the speciality of a particular workshop, which supplied them to other armourers for mounting with their own work. Since similarities can also be detected between other components of armours, reputedly by different smiths, it seems probable that by this time raw plate and many standard components were being virtually mass produced and distributed within the trade.

Following the general trend towards sim-

Right: Tsutsu suneate, plate shin guards.

Far right: Kogake of mail and plates. These armoured overshoes were held in place by the ties of the straw sandals.

Below: Wakibiki, an armpit guard, of mail. This was an accessory which could be worn with any armour.

plification, the haidate (knee and thigh armour) was made lighter by modifying the scale construction used in the Muromachi period or by replacing it with mail or plates. *Ita haidate* were made from flat scales arranged into four or five rows containing between seven and fifteen or more scales in each. Those made from the larger scales were lacquered after lacing to stiffen the rows so that they formed almost rigid plates and were frequently decorated with mon or other lacquered designs. An alternative form, called *kawara haidate*, was made from s-sectioned scales which overlapped like roof tiles and then laced together. When mail formed the sole defence, haidate were called *kusari haidate*, but most have some *ikada* (small rectangular plates) fitted into the mail to form *ikada haidate*. A similar type with ikada and plates over the knee, resembling the hiji gane

and matsuba wa of the oda gote was called *oda haidate*. *Shino haidate* consisted of short shino assembled in rows joined by mail, being most abbreviated in the type called *etchu haidate* in which short narrow shino, virtually ikada, were connected in rows by narrow strips of mail to form only a grid of metal over the surface. Whatever the type, haidate could be sewn either onto a divided apron of fabric, matching the fabric of the kote, or to the front of a pair of baggy breeches, which occasionally were armoured with mail at the back. The apron type, except for the very stiff ita haidate, have tabs of fabric on either side that were tied or buttoned behind the leg to prevent the haidate being displaced and bumping against the leg while walking.

Little change was made to the armour for the lower leg, with tsutsu suneate and shino suneate continuing in production. The etchu armourers made one variant of the latter which dispensed with the fabric backing and the knee guard, which was especially favoured when fighting in wet conditions since there was nothing, other than the ties, to become soaked. Some kusari suneate (mail shinguards, sometimes with ikada) were made which suffered from the same defect as kusari gote – they provided no protection from a blow. They do not seem to have been too popular, judging by the dearth of surviving examples when compared to the numbers of surviving plate shinguards.

In addition to the armour itself, and sometimes provided with it, were a number of minor accessories. For the armpits,

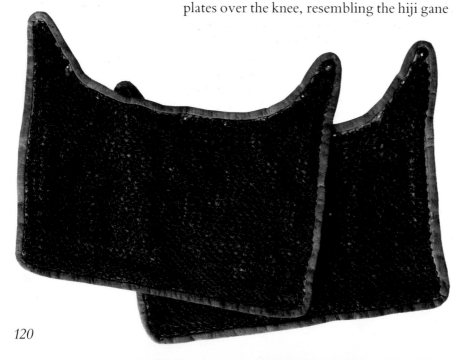

U-shaped pieces of armour made of mail sewn onto a fabric backing (*wakibiki*) were made. They were either laced directly to the underside of the sleeve so that they hung against the sides of the body, or were made as separate pieces which were tied to the body before putting on the do. Other wakibiki were made of plate or scales, which, despite the incorporation of lacing and hinges, were far too stiff to be worn beneath the do. Some Japanese museums mount these hanging under the arm but outside the do, in such a way that they would move into position over the gap above the waki ita with the action of raising the arm, which is almost certainly the way they would have been worn. Neater, and probably far more comfortable, was the *manju wa*, a type of short sleeveless jacket made with flaps that passed under the arms

and over the shoulders to tie on the chest. These were either of mail or kikko and were provided with an armoured collar, obviating the need for a separate armoured collar. Some examples are fitted with fastenings for the sleeves so that they could be put on as a single unit. Armour for the feet (*kogake*) was also available; it was an overshoe without a sole, made of iron or leather plates connected by mail or hinges. Kogake were fastened by ties behind the heel and the ankle and held in place on the foot by the ties of the sandal. Most samurai abandoned the yoroi hitatare for wear with tosei gusoku, preferring instead a narrow-sleeved shirt-like garment, derived from the dress of the lower classes, worn with short breeches and leggings.

Armours had been traditionally stored in lacquered chests which had short flaring legs

Above: A manju wa, a short armoured waistcoat worn beneath armour to protect the armpits and upper chest. It is of silver and blue brocade over brigandine of leather plates. Edo period.

Above: Shitagi, a garment which was worn under armour, of hemp printed with a design of Chinese grass. Edo period.

Above right: Shitagi of hemp cloth having a brocade collar. Edo period.

Right: A box for storing and transporting armour with its leather storage cover. Momoyama period.

Far right: Armour being stored in a traditional chest.

fitted to the sides rather than the corners, and a lid which was fastened by heavy tasselled cords. With the introduction of tosei gusoku and the need for mobility during protracted campaigns, small portable armour boxes were introduced, occasionally made in pairs for more lavish armours. Most are straight sided, about two and a half feet (0.75m) high and rather less than two feet square, but other decorative shapes are common. They were, of necessity, light, and were made from thin wood, wickerwork or even papier mâché, which was lacquered or covered with leather and reinforced at the corners and edges with ironwork. Most have locks or hasps and staples and are fitted with looped hinged handles for carrying on a pole. A few, designed for light armours, had padded shoulder straps and were carried on the back of a single porter.

These improvements to armour, and the necessity for change which the samurai accepted, came at a momentous time. Europeans, exploring the East for trade, brought guns with them. These not only revolutionized the form of warfare the samurai had known, but brought about unity in Japan after centuries of internal strife.

水干與又

布直垂與又

CHAPTER SIX
The Arrival of the Southern Barbarians

Far right: Set of ornate large-bore guns displayed in a rack. This type of gun, kakae zutsu, was designed for attacking fortifications.

Below: Bronze cannon on a sliding mount to absorb the recoil. Cannon, generally rather small, were quickly adopted by the Japanese after the arrival of the Europeans in the 1540s.

During the sixteenth century the sea powers of Europe, in a move to end the monopoly of merchants using the Silk Road across Asia, sent expeditions in search of a sea route to the sources of spice and silk. This long and dangerous voyage was undertaken by a small band of Portuguese adventurers who, in a second attempt to reach the trading centre of Peking, were washed ashore after a violent storm. They landed on the small island of Tanegashima, off the coast of Kyushu, in either 1542 or 1543.

As the first Europeans to set foot in Japan they caused no little sensation, but it was as nothing to the delight and excitement caused by the matchlock guns they carried. The Japanese immediately not only understood their mechanism, but also grasped their

potential and, for an exorbitant sum, these primitive weapons passed into the possession of the local daimyo. It is just possible that the Japanese knew something of guns and gunpowder from the Chinese, but there is no evidence of this in the careful descriptions they have left of demonstration firings. The Lord of Tanegashima was delighted with his purchase and immediately set his swordsmith to work in making copies. Forging a barrel was a simple metalsmithing process, but when faced with cutting the thread of the breech plug the swordsmith was totally defeated; such technology was totally unknown in Japan. The problem was finally resolved, so legend has it, by exchanging his daughter for lessons with another Portuguese who arrived a short time after. To the man's credit, within

six months he had produced a large number of copies (traditionally the figure is said to have been 600), which the Lord of Tanegashima traded, spreading knowledge of this new weapon throughout the country within a short time of its introduction. It is difficult to assess accurately the rate of spread, but by 1555 Takeda Shingen had bought at least 300, and 20 years later, Oda Nobunaga, then a relatively minor daimyo, had 3000 gunners in the army which defeated the forces of Takeda Katsuyori at the battle of Nagashino.

Military planners were quick to reach the same conclusions about the gun as the Europeans before them. It was relatively cheap to produce, effective under the right weather conditions and could, after the minimum of training, turn the rawest recruits into a valuable adjunct to other forces. Here at last was a weapon that could turn the ashigaru from a rabble into the equal of the finest samurai, without the long, arduous training that both archery and fencing demanded. The guns made were smooth-bore snapping

Right: Ashigaru (foot soldier) armed with a musket. The match is coiled around his wrist. Guns of this type made the ashigaru a formidable fighting force, threatening the supremacy of the samurai.

Below: Procession of spearmen and musketeers, their guns covered in striped fabric bags to protect them from the weather.

matchlocks which varied from long muskets for use on foot to short carbines and even pistols that could be handled on horseback, which is curious because such guns were rare in Europe. Guns with similar mechanisms had been in vogue during the 1520s, but in Germany, not in Portugal. In these matchlocks the powder was ignited by the smouldering end of a length of cord impregnated with saltpeter to make it burn evenly. To simplify handling, the cord was held in the jaws of a pivoted lever, the serpentine; when the trigger was pulled a spring propelled the serpentine into the priming powder. Most European guns were far less complex – the serpentine was connected directly to the trigger by a simple mechanical link so that they moved together. It was also the normal European practice to position the serpentine in front of the priming pan. The Japanese guns had it fitted behind, in such a way that it moved away from the user when it was fired.

Gun barrels were made from a U-shaped strip of iron which was welded into a tube around a steel bar or mandrel of slightly smaller diameter than finally needed, to allow for subsequent fine boring and polishing. At the breech end of the barrel, the bore was sealed by a screwed plug and a small pan for the priming powder was welded on the right-hand side. A standing guard of brass was attached where the pan joined the barrel which had the dual function of reducing corrosion from the burning powder and preventing water running down the barrel and seeping under the pivoted brass pan cover which protected the priming from damp and wind. On average, the barrels of existing muskets are about three feet (0.9m) long with a bore that can vary between 0.5 and 0.8 inches (1.27 and 2.03cm) in diameter. A few large-bore (2-3½ inches, 5.08-8.89cm) guns were made with barrels about two feet (0.6m) long that are aptly called *kakae zutsu* (hand cannon). Supported on a rest, these monsters were used to batter down gates or other light fortifications in a similar way to modern hand-held rocket launchers. Most

Right: Interior of gun lock by the Kunitomo group showing the tumbler and springs.

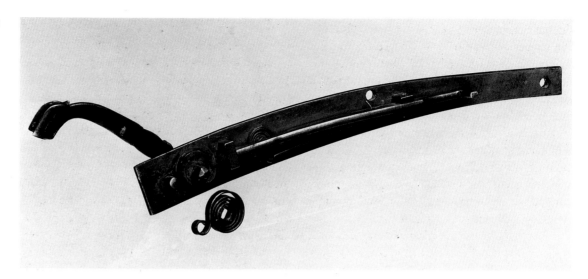

Right: Interior of gun lock by the Kunitomo group showing the tumbler and springs.

are highly decorated. Although called 'wall guns' in the West because of their similarity to the weapons used in European castles and forts, there is no evidence that they were ever used in that role. A further group of guns, called *hiya zutsu*, resemble small cannon. However, they were never used in war; their purpose was, as their name suggests, to shoot fire arrows and launch fireworks at festivals and other public occasions.

During the Edo period a few novelty guns were produced with multiple barrels which either radiated like the fingers of the hand from a common breech block and fired simultaneously, or were arranged with their bores parallel in such a way that they could be rotated to bring each barrel to the firing position in turn. None of these were ever actually used in anger; they were either experimental oddities or symbols of power to be carried in parades – quite a few of the revolving type still exist where it was not even considered necessary to drill touch holes between the pan and the barrels. Contrary to common belief, the gun makers of Japan were not wholly unaware of the developments in firearms that occurred in Europe during the seventeenth and eighteenth centuries. At least one snaphaunce pistol is known and a Japanese wheel lock is reported to exist in the reserve collection of a museum in England. Flintlock tinder lighters were common in the Edo period, and Hokusai depicts a double-barrelled flintlock pistol in his book *Manga*. These guns are rare, not because the gunsmiths could not make them, but because the government of the day actively discouraged any attempt to do so.

Japanese matchlocks often have their barrels decorated with lacquer or, more com-

monly, with overlay (*nunome*) in silver or gold. The more decorative were obviously intended for display rather than for use, being exhibited on racks or carried in front of personages of rank in processions. Themes for this decoration tend to be rather limited, with mon, the ever-popular dragon or the occasional inscription predominating. Some guns are signed by the maker underneath the barrel at the breech, but since many guns were turned out as part of a large contract, they were frequently left unsigned.

Irrespective of size, all guns, including cannon, were fitted with sights in the form of blocks, drilled, grooved and slotted in different ways. The standard arrangement was to fit a foresight just above the muzzle, and a backsight positioned about a third of the length down the barrel from the breech. Most backsights have slots or a combination of vertical and transverse holes, which suggests that they were once fitted with detachable leaf sights to allow for different ranges. To the authors' knowledge, no such additional sight blades have survived. The brass-lined cavities in the stock of some guns may have once held these, but in one specimen known to the authors, this held a supply of bamboo splints, intended for fastening the match into the serpentine. One gun in the author's possession which has every appearance of being of some age is fitted with a silver bead fitted into the rear face of the foresight, enabling it to be seen when sighting against a dark target; a feature having a considerable history that is still used to this day.

The stocks were of red oak, full-stocked to the muzzle, with the barrel held in place by a series of bamboo pins passing through the stock and into lugs dovetailed into the underside of the barrel. An exception to this is the kakae zutsu, some of which were fitted with reinforcing bands around the stock and barrel. All types were equipped with a simple wooden ramrod housed in the stock beneath the barrel. There was no tang attached to the breech plug as was common on European guns; instead the square end of the plug fitted into a recess in the stock, reinforced by a band of brass at this point to prevent splitting. Like the guns on which they were modelled, there is no shoulder stock. Instead they terminate in a form of curved pistol grip designed to be held against the cheek – the recoil being taken by the heavy barrel and by allowing the gun to move backwards and downwards on firing. What little stock furniture there was includes ornamental washers around holes and sometimes a trigger guard, invariably made of brass, both to prevent corrosion and because it could be cast in almost the final form, requiring only the minimum of finishing. A few of the more decorative guns have inlays of pierced and engraved brass let into their stocks.

Locks were of two basic types. The first had an external brass mainspring operating upwards on the tail of a serpentine which pivoted on a brass spindle passing through the lock plate and into the wood of the stock. This pivot was held in place by a bamboo pin fitted vertically just to the rear of the barrel. The serpentine was held in the cocked position by the nose of a long, horizontally operating sear, protruding through the lockplate above the tail, and pivoted against a light internal spring in such a way that it retracted into the plate when the trigger was pulled.

The second, more complicated mechanism, had the serpentine pivoting through the lock plate, and fitted with a tumbler and spiral brass mainspring on the inside. Operating in a notch cut into the tumbler and holding the lock cocked, was a sliding horizontal sear, pulled back by the trigger against the force of a smaller spiral spring. The gun in the author's possession mentioned above is of this type and the bearing surfaces of both the sear and tumbler are fitted with hardened steel inserts as a precaution against wear. In addition the tension of the sear spring can be varied, allowing the user to adjust the trigger pull to his liking.

In both types of lock, no screws were used, all supports were riveted to the lock plate and the various components fastened to them by pins of brass or bamboo. Even the locks themselves were held into the stocks by tapering pins of brass, fitted into tapering holes in the wood of the stock. The positions of these pins is revealed on the opposite side of the stock by inlet brass washers. Most gunsmiths provided an extra hole to allow a punch to be used to push the lock plate out of its recess when dismantling the gun.

The function of the springs operating the

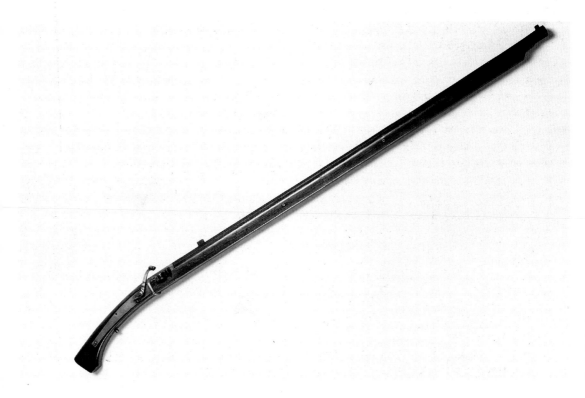

Left: Matchlock musket by the Kunitomo group. Guns of this type were produced in their thousands within a few years of the introduction of firearms.

Far right: The Banrin kabuto (horse rushes helmet) of Toyotomi Hideyoshi with a crest in the form of a spray of leaves.

serpentine of Japanese guns has often been misunderstood, and the apparent inability of the Japanese to make them of steel has been noted. Steel would, in fact, have been inappropriate for the role these springs had to play. All guns of this type relied on the match, with its glowing coal, igniting the priming without itself being snuffed out on the base of the pan. Gunsmiths in Europe were well aware of this danger, even though the speed and pressure exerted by the serpentine was controlled entirely by the trigger pull. To prevent a misfire, the base of the pan of European guns was punched with a pattern of ribs and dots which ensured that at least parts of the glowing coal remained alight. The brass springs of the Japanese, while weak, moved the serpentine with sufficient rapidity, but with insufficient force to damage it when halted by contact with the pan surround, the glowing coal entering the pan to ignite the priming.

Three major groups of gunsmiths are known to have been working in the Momoyama and early Edo periods, but many more individuals worked as retainers for various daimyo. The first of these groups

Right: Ashigaru (foot soldier) putting on armour. Note in all the illustrations of these soldiers, the swords are shown as being put on before the armour.

was based in Kyushu and continued to use the name of Tanegashima even though it had spread into the nearby provinces of Satsuma, Amakusa, Hizen and Higo. All its guns were fitted with distinctive blackened-wood stocks, occasionally further decorated with mon or stylized tendrils in gold lacquer. Most of the guns supplied to the armies during the Momoyama period were the product of the Kunitomo group founded in 1560 in the regions around Kyoto. It was from these makers that Oda Nobunaga obtained the guns which were used with such telling effect at Nagashino. Kunitomo weapons had pale-coloured stocks and generally simple but elegant octagonal barrels. A distinctive feature of the group's work is the practice of filing grooves across the width of the serpentine to resemble the nodes of bamboo. It also used cherry-blossom-shaped inserts around the holes for the lock pins. At best the group made superb guns, but much of its mass-produced work was so bad that it gained the nickname *udon ju* (noodle guns) because the barrels flexed and bent during firing. The third group was centred around the town of Sakai, near Osaka, where production started in 1554. Guns produced by the Sakai workers became renowned for the quality of their locks and ornamental brasswork, so much so that they were frequently commissioned by daimyo to mount barrels by other makers. Their own barrels were generally octagonal, decorated with applied silver designs, and terminating in bulbous fig-shaped muzzles.

Under ideal conditions, these matchlocks had a maximum range of about 300 yards, but were only capable of hitting a man-sized target consistently at 50 yards or so. While this effective range seems limited by modern standards, it was perfectly adequate when the target was a massed group of troops and somebody would be hit, even if it was not the person aimed at. After a few rounds the smoke would have prevented the two armies seeing each other anyway. Modern experimenters have found that reloading took about two minutes, but they were untrained and no doubt were far more careful than a soldier fighting for his life in the middle of a raging battle. During the Momoyama period, the gunners were provided with two flasks, a larger one for the ordinary powder and a smaller one for the finer priming powder. These were made of lacquered wood or paper with tubular nozzles fitted

Above and above right: Okashi gusoku, armour of munition quality comprising an okegawa do with rudimentary protection for the thighs together with a conical jingasa. Armours such as this were made in their thousands for issue to low-ranking soldiers.

with a stopper, which in the case of the larger flasks was itself a tube which acted as a measure for the powder charge. The more advanced commanders equipped their gunners with bandoliers, after the Western fashion, consisting of a series of paper tubes hung from a belt worn over the shoulder, each containing a pre-measured charge of powder. Attached to the belt was a box or pouch to carry the lead balls as well as a priming flask. Using these, the gunner could empty a charge down the barrel, drop in a ball and ram it home in a matter of seconds. What was time consuming was priming the pan and refitting the match without accidentally setting fire to loose powder. To speed up the rate of fire, gunners were arranged in ranks, the front row firing while those at the rear reloaded. By rotating the ranks, a withering and almost constant hail of fire could be maintained while supplies of powder lasted.

As was true of all early guns, the vagaries

of the weather dictated their use. The pan cover was arranged to slide under the vertical flash shield and this did much to keep the priming dry, but only while the pan was kept shut. Many illustrations show short, pistol-like guns *bajo zutsu* being carried in lacquered cases, worn at the waist in a similar way to modern holsters; longer guns had cloth bags which offered some protection while in storage or when being transported. Other paintings depict a stiff-paper shield fitted above and around the lock to keep off the worst of the wind and rain, but this must have made repriming almost impossible. The fact remained that in a good downpour or a high wind guns were at best an unreliable weapon, and at worst were totally useless, other than as a club.

Tanegashima, hinawa ju or *teppo*, as guns were called, enabled the more imaginative commanders with only limited forces to embark on campaigns that would have been suicidal without them. Among the first was

Takeda Shingen, who ordered 300 guns in 1555 for trials. He became such an advocate of their use that in 1571 he issued an order to his generals to reduce the number of spearmen and replace them by gunners. Most of his battles, however, took place in and around his own province of Kai, and so had little impact on the political situation of the country as a whole, but the superb organization he employed to maintain his armies became the model for later commanders.

Following the Shingen's lead, large armies were formed and trained in the use of the new weapon, and drilled in tactics which exploited its potential. Those recruits capable of buying their own armour did so, but the poor samurai and the ashigaru had, as always, to be content with cheap munition armour supplied by their lord. The most rudimentary of these consisted of a simple plate do, sometimes of lacquered rawhide, or more usually an okegawa do of thin metal, painted with the commander's mon or with stripes of colour for identification, and fitted with simple plate gessan fastened to the do by sugake lacing. If they were lucky they were issued with a simple zunari helmet, but most were equipped with a conical iron or leather hat, *jingasa*, lacquered like the do, and worn with a cloth shikoro at the sides and back. In emergencies, these jingasa could, like the steel helmets of more modern wars, serve as a cooking pot or as a wash basin. These simple armours were originally provided with kote consisting of a few plates sparsely linked by mail, sewn onto a stout hemp backing. Only rarely were haidate or suneate provided, since the protection they afforded was not considered worth the extra expense and they also inhibited mobility. All ashigaru were issued with a sword, *okashi katana* (lent sword), and such other weapons or equipment as needed. When on the march, much of the equipment and stores needed by the army was carried on the backs of ashigaru since pack horses were scarce and wheeled transport was almost totally unused.

Born into this world of military aggression and intrigue were three men, two minor nobles and a peasant, who were destined to change the whole direction of Japan's history. None of them was different from or more noble than their contemporaries, except that they were more able than most, but they found themselves in the right places at the right times. Oda Nobunaga was born

in 1534 into a household that had clawed itself to power in the province of Owari by 'geko-kujo' during the 1530s. With a ruthlessness he was to display all his life, when only 17 years old he took control of the family fortunes, against fierce opposition from his relatives. Seven years later, a recruit by the name of Tokichi joined his army as an ashigaru, having stolen money from his previous master with which to buy an armour. He showed such exceptional ability and qualities of leadership that he rapidly rose to become one of Nobunaga's most able generals. This former peasant, later called Toyotomi Hideyoshi, was the second of these men of destiny.

The third member of the trio, Tokugawa Iyeyasu, met with the others in 1558 as an opponent in a tentative border attack on one

Below: Foot soldier armed with a spear. Note how the gessan is draped over the swords and how provisions were carried in a cloth, tied at intervals, and worn around the shoulders.

Right: Renjaku nuinobe do showing the fabric cords passing over the shoulders to emerge at the waist in front.

Far right: Koshi tori hotoke ni mai do gusoku, a smooth-lacquered do with lacing at the bottom. Momoyama period.

Left: Ryo takahimo renjaku do gusoku, a 'modern' armour fastened by ties at each side. Foreign influence is evident in the medial ridge to the do and the use of Indian fabrics for the sleeves and haidate.

of Nobunaga's strongholds. Since Iyeyasu was only 17 at the time, he was a minor commander of Imagawa Yoshimoto, lord of Mikawa, Totomi and Suruga, the last of which adjoined Nobunaga's province of Owari. Yoshimoto had ambition, if little military skill, and in 1560 he had assembled an army of 25,000 to march on Kyoto to tackle the now-feeble Ashikaga. The only real barrier between him and the capital was Nobunaga and his small force of some 2000 or so men. To everyone's surprise, Nobunaga attacked the larger force and, partly by deception, succeeded in killing Yoshimoto. The following year, Iyeyasu, now no longer under obligation, joined Nobunaga as another of his generals.

Nobunaga was not the romantic that Yoshimoto had been, and realized that a direct assault on Kyoto with banners in the van was no longer the way to win wars. He first looked westwards, and gained control of the rich rice-producing province of Omi. He then either took, or stationed agents in, cities such as Otsu, Kusatsu, Kamigyo and, especially, Sakai. As a result of this policy he could provision and supply his ever-growing armies and draw on the services of craftsmen such as Imai Sokyu of Sakai, a supplier of guns. In a brilliant series of campaigns, Nobunaga wiped out the forces of the fifteenth Ashikaga Shogun and continued to conquer province after province, aided by his

generals Hideyoshi and Iyeyasu.

Like the European knight before him, the samurai found the gun a great leveller, showing respect to neither rank nor the quality of one's armour. Even daimyo appeared on the battlefield wearing sturdy tosei armours devoid of superfluous decoration. To alleviate the plainness, many of these armours were lacquered in bright colours, fitted with extravagant crests, or even wigs of hair. Vividly coloured *jinbaori* (surcoats) in expensive fabrics were worn over the armour, even in battle. Tokugawa Iyeyasu, renowned for his frugality, owned two armours of the simplest kind, distinguished only in that they are both lacquered in gold. He also owned another, made after Hideyoshi had jokingly referred to him as the 'Cow of the Kanto', completely covered in hide with the hair left on and with huge buffalo horns on the helmet. Following an engagement against Takeda Shingen, who had selected all those wearing red armour to position themselves in the front rank, Iyeyasu determined to imitate the idea and gave instructions to the Ii family to henceforth wear only red lacquered armour. As a result, any red lacquered armour became known as *hikone gusoku*, after the name of the Ii family's castle town.

A few of the more cautious had bulletproof armours made, and marks of musket balls on some show that they had been subjected to a proof test by their makers. These *tameshi gusoku* were necessarily of great weight and most were provided with some form of solid plate do, and usually a zunari or other simple helmet; the thickness of the plates needed precluded a more complex type of design.

Sakakibara Kozan, although writing over 200 years later, makes reference to armour plate made with a hard-steel face, welded to a soft-steel back. Armourers appreciated that if the steel billet, after folding and welding, was flattened into a plate with the welds parallel to the surface, it was apt to flake when struck. If, on the other hand, it was beaten out with the weld planes at right angles to the plate surface, it split along the lines of the welds. To avoid these defects, a steel billet was formed in the latter way, then cut in two and the halves welded to each other with the direction of the grain crossed: a process called *jumonji kitae* (cross-pattern forging). When this was welded to the backing of softer iron, the face resisted penetration and splitting,

Above: Spears and heraldic banners were carried for identification. All weapons were provided with scabbards to protect them from the humid climate.

and was supported by the malleable back. In an attempt to identify whether this process was actually used, the author carried out Rockwell hardness tests on two pieces of armour by Miochin smiths made about 300 years apart. In both cases there was considerable difference in hardness between the front and back surfaces of the plates that suggests that this method of making plates was, for some armour at least, actually employed.

To enable these and other heavy do to be worn for long periods of time, they were sometimes fitted with an internal system of suspensory cords called *renjaku*; an almost identical solution to the same problem was utilized by the armourers in the Royal

Far left: An armour presented by the governor of Edo to King James I of England.

Far left: Portrait of the Irish noble, Sir Neill O'Neill painted by J M Wright in 1680. The artist has introduced an imported Japanese armour – the style is typical of those produced by the Iwai for presentation and should be compared with those shown on pages 136 and 139. The servant carries the helmet bowl, the neck guard having been fitted around the waist in the manner of a European culet.

Armouries at Greenwich for a very heavy armour for Henry VIII of England. The cords were of braided silk or of cloth sewn into a roll, about an inch in diameter, anchored to the back plate at the level of the shoulder blades then passing over the shoulders to emerge through two holes in the front of the do just above the waist. One rare example that still retains its original renjaku is fitted with a single cord of braided silk, threaded through two holes in the backplate,

at which point its weave changes from round to flat for that portion that sits on the shoulders, becoming round again about the level of the chest. The *renjaku do* was put on in the usual way, then hitched up until the weight was taken off the watagami and transferred to the renjaku, then the ends of the renjaku were tied together in front. A renjaku do in the author's collection has the watagami reduced to flat, unpadded strips of rawhide protected by small steel plates which are

Above left: The second of the two armours presented to King James I of England, recently repaired and relaced. These presentation armours were rather stereotyped and old-fashioned in style but were the normal wear of high-ranking samurai.

Above: Helmet and do inspired by European models. Momoyama period.

Right: A European cabasset modified for Japanese use by the addition of a plate around the lower edge to carry the neck guard. This is one of the very few examples in which the helmet has not been reversed by the Japanese.

inadequate to support the do, except just for the few minutes needed to put it on and adjust the cords. Just how this suspension made a difference is hard to imagine; the actual weight of the do is still taken by the shoulders. Presumably it was the elasticity of the cords that mattered, lessening the jolting of the armour while riding or walking.

Although renjaku were popular, the very heavy tameshi gusoku were never very common and by the mid-Edo period had all but ceased to be made. Most samurai considered the extra weight and the restriction it imposed on movement too high a price to pay for the dubious protection it provided.

Close on the heels of the Portuguese came the Spanish, to be followed in turn by the Dutch and English, all eager for trade and, in the case of the first two nations, keen to gain

converts to the Catholic faith. Because these travellers had to overwinter in Goa or Macao before undertaking the last leg of their two-year journey, their ultimate landfall was usually Kyushu and, in particular, the southern port of Nagasaki. For this reason all Europeans were described by the Japanese as *nanban* (southern barbarians).

The goods they imported were as diverse and varied as the adventurers that brought them, but demand fluctuated as in any market. Will Adams, the English pilot of a Dutch expedition that sailed around Cape Horn before being driven by a storm to Japan, wrote several letters home during his long exile. In one, written to his 'good friend' Augustin Spalding in Bantam in 1613, he offers advice on the kind of goods in demand at the time:

Now the commodities yt ye bring from Holland are these: cloth, leed [lead], still [steel], louking glasses, drinking glasses, dans-klass-glasses [telescopes], amber, dieeper and holland [fabrics], with other things of small importance.

One humorous note was included in a letter from a Dutch merchant to his suppliers requesting the usual imports of cloth, steel, telescopes and the like – his list finished with a plea for several more barrels of cough mixture. In exchange for these imports, the Europeans shipped home products from the exotic East. Adams' letter goes on to describe the current prices and mentions that the ship that came from Pattania carrying luxury fabrics from China, left Japan with exports of porcelain, lacquer wares and munitions among other things.

Among these munitions shipped to Europe were quantities of swords, spears and armours. Several well-known people of the time are known to have owned and prized Japanese swords – among them Sir Francis Drake and Rembrandt van Rijn. Presentation armours and weapons were sent to various European monarchs as diplomatic presents. James I of England received two armours made by Iwai Yozayemon from the Governor of Edo which are still preserved in the Tower of London together with a sword. Others must have been brought by merchants as items for trade since one appears, as an artist's prop, in a portrait of the Irish noble Sir Neill O'Neill. The young arms enthusiast Louis XIII of France collected all manner of weapons in his Cabinet D'Armes. Among the items listed in the inventory of 1729 are

Right: Nanban kabuto, made from a cabasset decorated and mounted in Japan.

armours, swords and polearms that can be identified, despite the rather vague descriptions, as Japanese. Armours sent as diplomatic presents to France are now preserved in the Army Museum in Paris. All these presentation armours were rather old fashioned, being provided with akoda nari kabuto and o sode, but represent the style that nobles were expected to wear as an indication of their status. In the Historisches Museum in Dresden is a wheel-lock pistol whose stock, like its accompanying powder flask, is decorated with black lacquer, inlaid with chips of mother of pearl, in the characteristic style of Momoyama export lacquer. The gun itself, which is Flemish and dated around 1620, must have been shipped to Japan by a Dutch merchant in the unfinished state to be returned for sale after being decorated.

Oda Nobunaga took a very tolerant view of the Europeans, particularly the Jesuits, whom he regarded as a counter to the more militant of the Buddhists. Like many samurai, he admired the military organization and attitude of these 'Soldiers of Christ', while despising the political intrigues of some of the Buddhist sects. On one famous occasion, he surrounded Mount Hiei, to the north of Kyoto, and set fire to Enryakuji Temple, which had lent support to an opponent, killing everyone on the mountain and burning every building in the temple complex to the ground. Oda Nobunaga met his death in 1582, not in glorious battle, but while at his ablutions, betrayed by one of his own generals. Within a year, Nobunaga's death had been avenged by Hideyoshi, who assumed leadership of his forces and continued the process of unification. By the late 1580s the entire country, for the first time in hundreds of years, was virtually under the domination of one man – and that man a commoner.

Among the last to capitulate were the Daimyo of Kyushu, many of whom had been baptized as Christians. Some were undoubtedly true converts, but others regarded Christianity as little more than a new sect of Buddhism, and one that was very much worth encouraging for the trade which followed the priests. Even though wars were sweeping the country, the 'black ships' continued to arrive, bringing with them luxuries and novelties including armour and other weapons, for trade.

At least one sword blade which survives from this period originated in Solingen, Germany; it was reshaped and retempered by a Japanese swordsmith and mounted, as a dirk, in a scabbard covered with imported Dutch leather. In the nineteenth century Masahide wrote that he had examined many Dutch swords and recognized that they were not folded and forged like Japanese swords but were simply beaten out at one heating. Imported steel from Holland and India was especially prized by swordsmiths during the late sixteenth and early seventeenth centuries, no doubt for its sales appeal. Many blades from that time have inscriptions on their tangs attesting that they were made from 'southern barbarian iron'. Masahide, practical as ever, stated that although it looked different in the rough, it worked exactly the same and the swords were indistinguishable from those made of native steel.

Equally popular were sword mounts, particularly tsuba, in the foreign style. A few of the better ones were passable copies, in russet iron and gilding, of the pierced shell guards

Left: Kebiki odoshi go mai do gusoku, a close-laced five-plate do. This armour shows many small features of European influence including a ridge to the front plate, roped rims to the major plates and a pleated ruff around the collar.

of small-swords. As was often the case with fashionable styles, mindless duplication of the unfamiliar motifs resulted in tsuba consisting of little more than a plate pierced with hundreds of holes, amply justifying Western collectors' derogatory description of them as 'coffee strainers'.

Little now remains of the armour entering Japan from the West, and that which does survive consists mainly of breasts and backs, the occasional gorget and various open helmets of the morion or cabasset variety. Armour for the limbs, as well as the various types of close helmets being worn in Europe at the time, seem never to have been used; presumably because they were too different in character to those used by the Japanese.

Genuine nanban gusoku was a rarity that only the rich could afford to acquire and modify to their taste. Rather ordinary quality 'breasts and backs' of Italian or Flemish manufacture seem to have been the usual imports – modified into nanban do by fitting them with gessan and watagami before giving them a russet finish in place of their European polish. When the gorget was worn, it was outside the cuirass, forming what was called a manchira (in an attempt to imitate the Spanish word for cape – mantilla), contrary to the intention of the European armourers who made them.

Rather more common than nanban do are *nanban kabuto*, made from imported Spanish morions or cabassets. These helmets, most of which are raised from one piece of steel, have tall skulls shaped like half an almond that terminate in a small bent stalk at the apex. Some have a narrow brim turned down at the sides and rising to an upturned point at the front

Left: Momonari kabuto, a helmet inspired by the European morion.

and back; others have a narrow flat brim all round. A tubular plume holder of brass or iron was fixed to the back of the skull just above the brim, continuing a row of ornate, brass-headed rivets that fastened the internal leather strap for the lining. Most are of very common quality, being turned out in their thousands for light munition armours in Italy and possibly Spain, although a few were made as alternative light helmets to accompany expensive armours.

In the hands of the Japanese these helmets were adapted to take a shikoro by being fitted with a koshimaki riveted to the inside of the lower edge of the skull, cut out in front over

Far left: A 62-plate ko boshi kabuto, by Miochin Nagamichi. It belongs to the armour opposite. Helmets of this type covered with over 1000 small rivets were supreme examples of the armourer's craft, but of doubtful value in battle.

Left: Me no shita ho (facemask) of russet iron in the Nara style belonging to the armour opposite.

Above: Red, white and blue laced ni mai do, an armour which joins by a hinge under the left arm. One of ten similar armours owned by Toyotomi Hideyoshi and thought to have been used by his guard or by his doubles (kagemusha).

typical watagami have been attached by similar rivets to those at the waist, while the front has been pierced to take shoulder-strap fastenings. Attached to the lining strap are leather iyozane gessan in six sections, lacquered red and laced in dark blue silk. Over the do was worn the gorget, as a manchira, decorated en suite with the cuirass, with the outer edge and the small flange around the neck lacquered red. The helmet has been modified from a typical cabasset by fitting the usual koshimaki and red lacquered shikoro. The small brim has been cut away in front and replaced by a concave peak in the tosei style. All remaining components are of standard Japanese patterns and consist of a hanbo, oda gote, haidate and shino suneate.

For those unable to acquire the real thing, copies of nanban gusoku were made, varying from very accurate reproductions of the originals to strange creations that resemble little else on earth, but which could be passed off to those in the more remote parts of the country who had never actually come into contact with the 'foreign devils'. Attempts to copy nanban do were more or less confined to making them from single front and back plates and shaping the front to form a medial ridge. With helmets, the armourer's imagination ran riot. All sorts of wonderful shapes and styles were produced whose only commonality was that they were not recognizably Japanese. A considerable number had high, almost pointed crowns, overlaid with elaborately shaped iron plates covering the joints. Many are fitted with a horizontal brim that may well have been inspired by Korean or Chinese originals.

One style of helmet modelled on the cabasset that was to prove lasting was the *momonari kabuto* (peach-shaped helmet). The majority of these are similar in shape to the skull of a cabasset but with a flange running from front to back, cut with a step at the apex to represent the stalk. Very few are provided with a brim, being fitted instead with the brow-plate-peak combination of the zunari bachi. These helmets became and remained popular because weapons slid easily off their smoothly curved surfaces, and because they could be made cheaply and easily. This helmet represented one of the few unusual styles which even the poorer samurai could afford.

Those samurai too conservative to wear these obvious copies of foreign styles were nevertheless prepared to accept small but

the eyes. Strangely, the Japanese usually reversed them so that the stalk at the apex pointed forwards, to satisfy the samurai ethic of always advancing. Because the plume holder was then at the front, it was discarded and replaced by a tsunomoto to take a crest. Once again the surface would be russet and perhaps decorated with gold and silver overlay to conform to Japanese taste.

A famous armour of Tokugawa Iyeyasu is one of the few surviving examples that incorporates several pieces of European manufacture. The do was originally an Italian peascod cuirass of about 1580, with a pronounced medial ridge. On the backplate a pair of

Left: Jinbaori, a surcoat worn over armour, of a member of the Honda family.

cloth, which became widely used for military equipment, but never, it seems, for civilian clothing. From the limited colours of the surviving examples, it would seem that it was imported pre-dyed in either bright red, black, brown, yellow or white. For some inexplicable reason, blues and greens are rarely, if at all, encountered. Almost immediately, this fabric became the favourite material for covering kikko work on collars and knee guards, and for making jinbaori and other military clothing. It was so widely used that supply could not keep up with demand, and a trade developed in Kyushu of producing a counterfeit from cotton and rabbit hair.

Since the traders had to stop en route in either India or China, the products of these and neighbouring countries were added to the bill of lading. Ivory, sometimes gathered from the remains of mammoth in the tundra of Siberia, was imported for carvings, the scraps being used for toggles on more expensive armours. From the same region came the

Below: Sheet of embossed, gilded and painted leather made in Holland during the late seventeenth or early eighteenth century as a wall covering. This type of leather was used by the Japanese to cover sword scabbards and so on.

fashionable European influences on their armours. Medial ridges on do were considered beneficial, stiffening the front plate and, on plate do, providing a glancing surface off which weapons would slide. Any do so shaped is described as *omodaka do* (water-plantain leaf) or *hatomune do* (pigeon breasted). Also popular was an imitation of the roping which decorated the rolled edges of most European armours from early in the sixteenth century. Since the edges of Japanese armour were not rolled, this decoration was simulated by shaping the applied soft metal edges of the plates into a rope-like form, to give what was called *nawame fukurin*. Japanese artists of the day loved to depict costumes of the Europeans, especially the long, padded pantaloons and the ruffs worn around the neck and wrists. These ruffs were imitated with small pleated frills of several layers of silk, which were sewn around the collars of better armours, to form what are called *kesho eri*. Occasionally these frills are found elsewhere on the armour, bordering sode or haidate and particularly around the cuffs of kote.

Along with these obvious imitations of European culture were other more subtle influences. New materials were brought into the country which were avidly taken up for their novelty value. Both the Dutch and English imported a closely woven woollen

with rococo scrolls and painted with acanthus leaves in red and white. This leather, called 'gouldleer' by the Dutch, was originally made in sections measuring about three feet (0.9m) by two feet (0.6m), and dates from the beginning of the eighteenth century. In Holland it was generally used for wall hangings, but the Japanese adopted it for covering sword scabbards, saddles and the like.

One of the few imported ideas that proved to be something of a retrograde step, yet which was taken up quite avidly, was mail made in the European manner. In this construction, all links were circular and each was linked through four others. To the mail-maker it was a boon in that he had only one shape of link to make, but when incorporated with plates, as much Japanese mail was, the fact that none of the links lay parallel to the plane of the plates made connecting the two difficult. Despite this, *nanban kusari* became popular, especially for cheaper work, when it was made of thin wire with the joints merely butted together rather than riveted as was the practice in Europe. One variety of nanban kusari that was a distinct improvement, involved the use of very small links in relation to the diameter of the wire. The result, as its name of *chirimen nanban kusari* suggests, was a dense smooth structure whose surface resembled crêpe de chine.

Above: Front plate of a go mai do covered with imported Dutch leather of identical pattern to that shown on the previous page. Note the ties for attaching the gessan which were laced onto a leather belt, a not uncommon feature of tosei armour.

Right: Together with the gun, the yari was the main offensive weapon of the period.

skins of polar bears, which are seen glued to the lower edge of shikoro, sode and gessan, as an alternative to the black fur of the native Japanese bear. A whole range of exotic fabrics appeared, ranging from brocades, velvets and damasks to figured satins, and even the humble cotton and calico. An armour in the author's collection has the sleeves and haidate covered with a block printed Indian chintz, while another has the front of the do covered with a piece of leather that is Dutch in origin, embossed and gilded

Even before the whole of the country was under his domination, Hideyoshi was faced with half a million or so samurai, and an unknown number of the remainder of the population, bearing arms. With little to occupy their time as the fighting drew to a close, they were a potential danger to the unity he was so near to achieving. In 1588 he issued a proclamation that all weapons, other than those belonging to the samurai, were to be seized and used in the construction of a great Buddha. This 'Sword Hunt' more than any other factor, finally divided the population, creating an elite warrior class. The days of the samurai-farmer were now over, and many were faced with the agonizing decision of leaving their land for the service of a lord, or remaining on the land with the consequent loss of status. Those who chose the military life moved to the towns springing

Right: Nagamaki and its scabbard. These pole arms with their long, sword-like blades were popular for arming the front-rank troops of both Muromachi and Momoyama period armies.

Below: Foot soldiers armed with spears carrying a trophy head and looted swords.

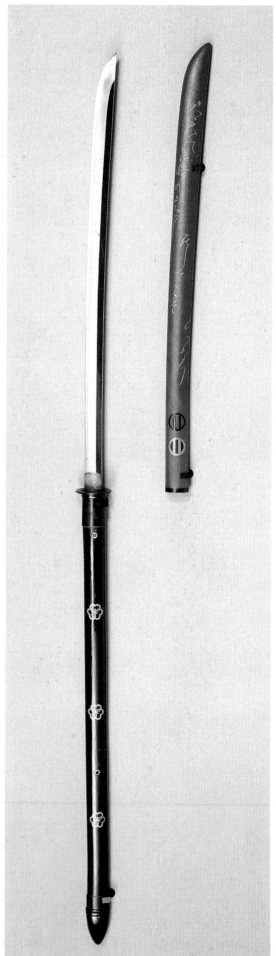

up around the castles of the daimyo, becoming retainers whose lives and actions were controlled by obligation.

Having solved part of the dilemma, Hideyoshi then began to realize a long-cherished ambition that would solve another part – the conquest of China. Because of its vast size and ability to absorb invaders rather than confront them, China's government had grown complacent. Hideyoshi's scheme was to attack and conquer Korea, and use it as a base from which to launch an attack on the Chinese capital. By 1592 he had assembled a force of some 300,000 men, in seven divisions, mainly under the command of Christian daimyo, which was dispatched in a motley collection of boats and ships from Kyushu, Iki and Tsushima.

The muster for the fourth division, commanded by Hideyoshi's former enemy Shimazu Yoshihiro, has survived to give us some indication of the composition of these forces:

15,000 general troops under the command of Yoshihiro's son
300 banners with 5 hand spears
300 spears, of which 200 should be long and 200 (sic) should be hand-spears
Besides these, the men should provide hand spears according to their capacity...
1500 men with guns
1500 men with bows
600 men with sashimono; these should be armoured.

In addition there is the quaint instruction that shows the military mind has always been the same throughout history:

Only distinguished men should be mounted; however, all those who cannot go on foot should be mounted. Therefore, the number of mounted is indefinite. The mounted men might well bear helmet and armour.

The hand spears, *te yari*, referred to in the list were about seven feet (2.1m) in total length, for ease of handling at close quarters. They were fitted with heads about six inches (15cm) long, having a cross section that was either of an elongated-diamond shape, *ryo shinogi yari*, or in the form of a flattened triangle, *sankaku yari*. Both types had cutting edges along both sides. These short spears were carried by both foot soldiers and horsemen, and were handy enough to be swung about to take advantage of their cutting edges, as well as for thrusting. The longer spears were similar except in weight and length and generally had proportionately larger heads. Most were between 10 and 12 feet (3 and 3.7m) long, but Oda Nobunaga is reputed to have used one that was 18 feet in length. Being less easily handled for fighting at close quarters, they were mainly used, like the pikes of Europe, to protect other troops from cavalry. They were gripped near the butt by the right hand and thrust forward with a pumping action through the left hand; metal tubes fitted with a hand guard were sometimes employed to reduce the friction. Many spears were fitted with metal crossbars, *hadome*, a foot or so below the head,

Right: The blade from a yari (top) and a jumonji yari (bottom). The latter is unusual in having its central blade shaped with a sword point.

which could be used to parry a sword or could be hooked behind the opponent's legs to knock him to the ground.

Other types of pole arms in use differed from the yari only in the shape of their heads. *Jumonji yari* consisted of a straight central blade with two others at right angles near the base (their name alludes to their cross shape when mounted). Being sharpened along all the edges, they could be used for striking or cutting in all directions in a similar way to the European halberd. The *katakama yari* (side sickle spear) was similar to the jumonji yari except that it only had one side blade, occasionally curved upwards slightly. Kato Kiyomasa, one of Hideyoshi's ablest generals, was famed for his skill with this weapon, and is supposed to have hunted tigers with it during the Korean campaign. Pole arms with other strangely shaped heads are not uncommon. Some had L- or T-shaped blades sharpened along all the edges and could only have been employed with a cutting action. Like all Japanese weapons, these strange and wonderful pole arms were all provided with scabbards when not in use, some of which must have tasked the ingenuity of their makers to the limit. One curious weapon that could not be fitted with a scabbard had a multi-pronged barbed head mounted on a shaft whose upper end is reinforced with spiked iron strips to prevent it being cut or grasped. These *yagara mogara* were designed to snag in the armour or clothing and were used for pulling down horsemen or trapping and holding men on foot. During the Edo period they became the favourite weapon of the police, being used for taking captives unhurt, as the law at the time required.

Both naginata and nagamaki continued in use, as apparently did the no dachi, the latter more for its psychological impact than for its effect on the outcome of a conflict. These weapons were used with considerable impact at least once during the Korean campaign, as a Korean writer records: 'All the Japanese soldiers carried on their shoulder enormous swords; and when their host was seen from the other side of the river the rays of the sun were reflected upon their blades like flashes of lightning.' However, the books *Cho Hitsu Roku* and *Date Narizane Ki* give the game away by explaining that these 'terror weapons' were nothing more than pieces of wood covered with a paint made from tin.

Almost all except the highest ranks now wore the uchi gatana, (generally abbreviated to *katana*), and the *wakizashi*, both with armour and civilian dress. Those who could afford to do so had pairs of swords, *daisho* (long and short), made with matching mounts and decoration. As it was a period of exuberant luxury despite the wars, daisho from this era tend to be lacquered in bright colours with extravagant gilded or painted decoration – the antithesis of later samurai taste.

The number of archers in the Shimazu muster reflects the importance still being placed on the bow. Its power had been increased yet again; its effective range was by this time almost as long as the gun and its rate of fire was better. The improvement in power and range was achieved by making the bow almost entirely from bamboo. In place of the wooden core used previously, three or four bamboo slats were now glued at right angles between the bamboo back and belly,

Left: A foot soldier with a bow and quiver mounted in a rack for carrying. The gun never entirely replaced the bow and arrow because the gun was useless in wet or windy conditions.

149

*Left: The site of the Battle at
Sekigahara, 1600, at which
Tokugawa Iyeyasu gained control
of the country.*

wood being used only as a filler at the sides.
The bow also had one considerable advantage over the gun – it did not need expensive
powder. Arrows were to some extent re-
usable and in any case a Japanese product;
good powder on the other hand was an

expensive item of trade with the Europeans,
particularly the English, as the homemade
product was inferior.

Despite Hideyoshi's grand schemes, the
Korean invasion, and a second attempt five
years later involving 150,000 men, failed

*Above: Armour and weapons
presented to Mori Kobayakawa
Takakage by Hideyoshi for his
services at the Battle P'yok-je-
yek, during the Korean
campaign.*

Above and above right: Front and back of a jinbaori or surcoat of Kobayakawa Takakage. The mon was granted to Takagake by Hideyoshi and dates this garment to the period just before the owner's death in 1597.

because the lines of supply were inadequate, especially in the face of the efficient Korean navy. Those who survived and returned to Japan were rewarded and honoured in the traditional way, but in reality the whole affair was a disaster, whose only benefit had been

temporarily to remove from the country a number of potentially disruptive commanders and their armies. Among those rewarded was Mori Kobayakawa Takakage, who had led the sixth division in the first invasion. On his return at the end of the first invasion attempt, the Emperor, acting on Hideyoshi's instructions, presented him not only with Hideyoshi's son, whom he adopted, but also with an armour and swords as a reward for his part in defeating the Chinese and Koreans at P'yok-je-yek in 1593. Since Takakage died in 1597, the date of manufacture of this armour, which survives in almost pristine condition, can be narrowed down to the period 1594 to 1597. The importance of this armour, closely examined by the authors, lies in its indisputable provenance, and in that it should represent a model of the type of armour to which a fighting samurai, albeit an elderly one, would have aspired.

The helmet is a 62-plate hoshi bachi, reputedly made by a member of the Saotome family, but more likely Haruta work in view of the concave tosei mabisashi. To enhance its appearance, the peak has been covered with printed leather. The helmet is fitted with a maedate in the form of the imperial chrysanthemum mon flanked by leaves, and waki date bearing the kiri mon used by Hideyoshi; this mon also occurs elsewhere on the armour, having been granted to Takakage for his use. The mask is a typical Nara me no shita ho, lacquered black with the hole under the chin furnished with an ornate gilt eyelet. Unusually, the nuinobe do is provided with renjaku, shoji ita and gyoyo, the latter permanently attached to the watagami. On the front of the do are two rings, the saihai no kan and the tenugui no kan, in copper gilt. This second ring is fitted to the left breast, which is normally regarded as an Edo period innovation. The o sode are also atypical in being lined inside with brocade, like a tosei sode – most o sode only having a narrow vertical strip of leather where they come in contact with the kote. Still accompanying the armour is a lacquered display stand, bags for the individual pieces and its two boxes, which retain their leather storage covers.

Hideyoshi died during the second abortive invasion of Korea, which, incidentally, was commanded by his son Hideaki, whom Kobayakawa Takakage had adopted. Hideyoshi's other son, Hideyori, was left in the protective care of regents, one of whom was Tokugawa Iyeyasu. True to form, the regents manoeuvred to take control, finally polarizing into two groups. One was led by Iyeyasu and the other by one of Hideyoshi's administrators, Ishida Mitsunari. The antagonists finally met at Sekigahara, in the province of Mino, in October 1600. In total, 154,000 troops were in the field, with rather more than 30,000 held in reserve. Guns had no effect on the outcome of the battle since the whole affair took place in pouring rain. It was the bow, sword and spear that won the day for Iyeyasu, but only because Hideaki changed sides at a crucial moment.

As victor, Iyeyasu was in control of a unified country and, being of noble birth, was entitled to become Shogun. Once again the military capital was moved, this time to Edo (now Tokyo), which rapidly grew to become the largest city in the world. For a while he was content to allow Hideyori to live, but by 1614 he felt his position threatened. He found a feeble excuse for an attack in an alternative reading of an inscrip-

Left: Armour display stand for the armour of Kobayakawa Takakage.

tion cast into a bell associated with Hideyoshi's great Buddha, which he interpreted as a slight. Hideyori sent out pleas for help, but only those whose land had been confiscated after the Battle of Sekigahara responded. Altogether some 90,000 packed into Osaka castle, the largest and strongest castle in Japan, and prepared for a siege. Some idea of the scale of the fortifications can be obtained from the fact that Hideyori had moats dug which were 240 feet (73m) wide, and that the perimeter of the outer works was nine miles (14.5km) long. Iyeyasu mustered 18,000 men and eventually, after heavy losses, captured the outworks. There followed a long period of attrition, during which both cannon and miners were used to good effect. The collapse came, however, when the defenders ventured out to fight on the surrounding plains, and were cut off, allowing the attackers to gain entry. Fire completed the task of destruction and Hideyori, trapped in the blazing main tower, committed suicide. Iyeyasu was now in complete control, without serious opposition, but he was now 74 years old. He died the following year, leaving behind a unique legacy to his son – a unified Japan. There was every chance that this situation would continue.

Far left: Stirrups used by Takakage during the Korean campaign.

CHAPTER SEVEN
Japan in Isolation: the Edo Period

Below: Map of Edo and the defensive ring of provinces held by loyal daimyo.

The Edo period officially begins with the establishment of the Tokugawa Shogunate at Edo, but it was not until Iyemitsu, Iyeyasu's grandson, came to power that the period took on its characteristic pace and lifestyle. Iyeyasu, on the whole, had been tolerant of the Christians, but his son and grandson were far less so. Iyemitsu's attitude

hardened after a group of Christian farmers and samurai rebelled against the excesses of the local daimyo at Shimabara in 1637. Intolerant of the political ambitions being shown by the Jesuits and their converts, Iyemitsu inaugurated a programme of expulsions and repression, designed to remove all traces of the religion from Japanese soil. At

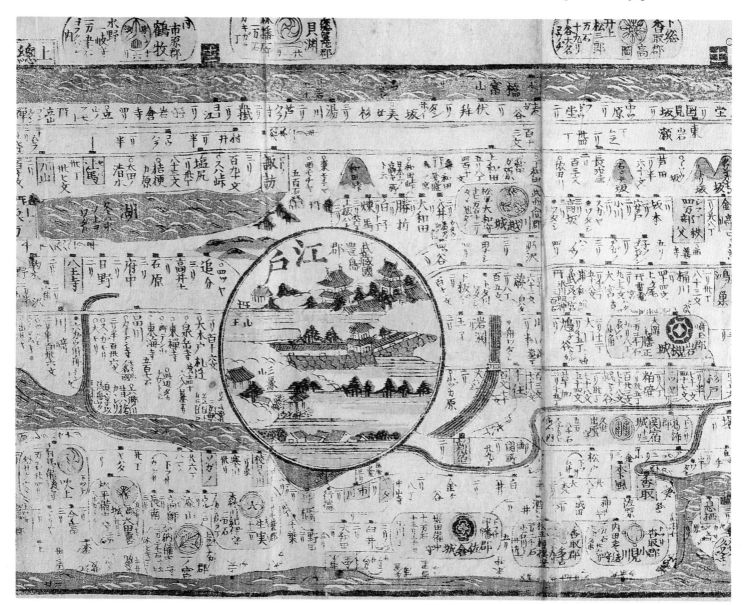

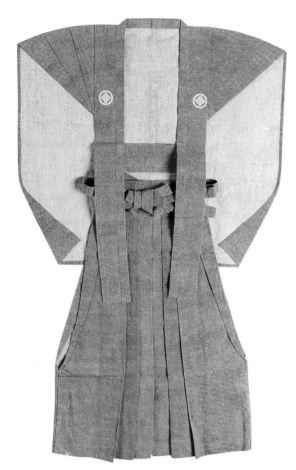

court officials at their head. Below him came the daimyo, previously a loose term applied to any great landowner, but now defined as one whose income was greater than 10,000 *koku* of rice per year (one koku was approximately the amount of rice needed to feed a person for a year). For reasons of security, the daimyo were carefully categorized on the basis of their allegiance to the Tokugawa at Sekigahara. *Han* (territorial holdings) were allotted to daimyo on the basis of their supposed loyalty and Edo was ringed by daimyo whose loyalty could be relied upon. Each daimyo supported and issued stipends to the other grades of samurai who made up his retinue and who in turn might support others of even lesser rank.

Many of the samurai retained by the shogun, and to a lesser extent those of the daimyo, continued in their role as members of

Left: Kami shimo of brown and white hemp cloth decorated with the owner's mon. This costume was worn on formal occasions by the samurai of the Edo period.

Below: Kusari katabira, a mail shirt, with detachable half sleeves (han gote) of European-style mail on brocade. This was an alternative, light defence to plate armour. Edo period.

the same time a policy of seclusion was instigated, preventing all overseas travel and inhibiting contact with the rest of the world; the only exceptions being small isolated trading stations run by the Dutch and Chinese at Nagasaki.

Internally, legislation was enacted which profoundly affected the social structure and life of the country. Of the greatest importance to the arms student was the legislation which confirmed the rigid social structure initiated by Hideyoshi. Under the Tokugawas, society became even more stratified, with almost no opportunity of crossing the divisions between the classes. A constant stream of laws and edicts was issued, but never clearly set down, which attempted to regulate in the minutest detail the lifestyle, behaviour and attitudes of everyone.

At the pinnacle of this social order were, theoretically, the Emperor and the *kuge* (nobles), who made up the imperial court in Kyoto. In practice, the court continued in the almost totally emasculated role it had played for centuries; that of conducting ceremonials, devoid of purpose and designed to keep it occupied. The real apex of the structure was occupied by the samurai – themselves strictly stratified with the Shogun and his various military units and armies, but armies whose roles were becoming increasingly legislative. Even before the end of the seventeenth century, laws had to be passed to ensure that samurai kept their weapons and armour in good order. By 1694, matters had grown worse – the government resorted to passing laws to enforce the practice of the martial arts. Year by year, more and more samurai, who were expected to be equipped and ready for war at all times, found themselves instead struggling with the mountains of paperwork required by the Tokugawa bureaucracy. In this and other ways the government discouraged the formation of power groups while simultaneously recognizing the need for a military class to maintain the social order. Confucian ideals of loyalty were advocated at every opportunity and an idealized version of Bushido, The Way of the Warrior, with its basis in the distant past, was codified. By emphasizing the sword as the 'soul of the samurai' and recounting stories of single-handed bravery and unthinking loyalty shown by the samurai of old to his lord (and by logical extension, through him, to the shogun), skills such as the maintenance of large armies and their tactical use in the field or the use of massed musketry, were gradually eroded.

Thus were the samurai of the period occupied. They bustled about the castle towns wearing their two swords and curious ceremonial dress (*kami shimo*) with its stiffened wings of hemp cloth, carrying out the business of their lord, or keeping the peace in their role as magistrates and police. In Edo, there were two permanent magistrates (*machi bugyo*) controlling 25 assistants (*yoriki*) and below them 120 police officers (*doshin*). These minor officials, the doshin, like their non-samurai attendants, carried as symbols of their office the *jitte* (a steel rod fitted with a side hook), which, together with yagara mogara which were positioned at the barriers and check points dividing the city into areas, were used to disarm and apprehend wrongdoers, without bloodshed. Should a situation arise in which a yoriki needed to be called, he would attend on horseback wearing a mail shirt, *kusari katabira*, fitted with detachable armoured sleeves, under his outer coat, and a lacquered or iron jingasa on his head. His task was to supervise the arrest, using his sword or spear only if all other attempts failed.

Another official duty undertaken by the samurai was the organization of fire fighting, a responsibility of the greatest importance in towns and cities built almost entirely of wood and paper. In 1657, a fire in Edo killed 108,000 people and another in 1772 destroyed half the city. By the end of the seventeenth century, the government had organized squads of trained men, supervised by samurai, who competed to be first to attend the blaze and plant their banner on an adjacent rooftop, thus claiming the right to deal with the outbreak and receive payment. So seriously was this duty taken that in the castle towns the daimyo themselves attended, wearing lacquered paper mâché fire helmets with long, hood-like cloaks attached to them which fastened over the face to give some protection from the heat and sparks.

Positioned in theory just below the samurai, but in practice almost at the bottom of the social scale were the prime producers of food – the farmers. These were organized on a village basis with a headman responsible to the daimyo for tax gathering and production targets. Individuals within the village were responsible to the headman, who in turn was responsible to higher authorities for the villagers. It was in the headman's interest to maintain civil obedience; if anything went wrong, both he and his family would be severely punished. This system of mutual responsibility, for both reward and punishment, was one of the main factors which held

Right: Jingasa of iron decorated with mon in silver overlay. These light open helmets were worn when riding or in camp and were frequently of lacquered leather for lightness. This diminutive example was made for a child during the Edo period.

156

the social structure together. Below the farmers were artists and craftsmen, many of whom in practice enjoyed a status far higher than their supposed station, by reason of their patronage and ability. A few were even granted samurai status because of the excellence of their work, or held positions of authority as advisers and craftsmen in various han. On rare occasions samurai moved socially in the opposite direction, mixing and working with artisans; for example, during the early Edo period Rurisai Genuemon was so obsessed by military strategy and technology that he not only influenced the design of armour but also probably made it himself.

Finally, at the bottom of the social ladder came the merchants and brokers, non-producers who in practice managed to live opulent lives despite the constant edicts from the government to encourage frugality. Many became so rich that they bought respectability, marrying their daughters into samurai families in exchange for the discharge of debts. It was this class of townsmen which was mainly responsible for the cannons of taste so familiar in the art of the Edo period. Outside the social hierarchy, and never satisfactorily categorized, were a few small groups like doctors and priests, as well as the *eta* or *hinin*, people who carried out tasks considered taboo.

Swords could be carried by several of these groups, but only the samurai would wear the pair of swords that were their badge of office. Those who could afford the considerable expense wore daisho, but many more wore whatever they could afford or had inherited. Since the blade of a sword could easily be removed from its mount, it was not uncommon to have different sets of mounts, *koshirae*, made for the same blade for use on different occasions. When a blade was not being used, it was kept in a scabbard and hilt of plain wood, *shirasaya*, and the mounts were assembled on a wooden replica of the blade, *tsunagi*. Swords were always stored in bags of rich brocade, and might then be placed into lacquered boxes, *katana zutsu*, made to house them. Racks, *katana kake*, were positioned by the door of every samurai household to receive the long swords of visitors.

Other classes, if permitted a sword at all, had to be content with a single short sword or one of the many varieties of dirk, generically termed *tanto*, but differentiated on the basis

of the mount. Women of the samurai class carried a small dirk, *kaiken*, in the fold of their kimono, both as a weapon of defence and, in the last resort, as a means of committing suicide. Some townsmen, more brave or more contemptuous of officialdom than others, made the most of things and pushed the length of the blade to the legal limit of approximately 2 feet (0.6m) and wore it in a long scabbard, implying that they were entitled to wear a katana. Members of the merchant class, in particular, had their swords or dirks lavishly mounted, encouraging the production of highly decorative sword mounts, and breaking away from the austere styles that had become fashionable with the samurai.

Below: Fire helmet and cape of a member of the Mori family. The supervision of fire-fighting was one of the samurai's duties during the Edo period.

Above: A cap and cape worn by the women of a daimyo's household in the event of a fire. Fires were a great hazard in the newly built towns and cities springing up around the castles of the daimyo. Edo period.

Above right: Armoured jacket of mail and plates covered with patterned hemp. The absence of mon suggests that this was made for a non-samurai. Edo period.

Right: A highly decorated jingasa.

During the Momoyama period, most samurai had been content with sword fittings that were both functional and showed a restrained taste and a subtlety of design that is still admired today, although their sword scabbards were lacquered in bright colours and designs that appear almost vulgar by comparison with the blacks and sombre colours of the Edo period. Mostly these had been made in iron, patinated to rich shades of brown, and textured to give not only a visual but a tactile quality that cannot be appreciated unless they are handled. The long-established Goto school had produced soft-metal fittings according to their own strict cannons, but these were for wear in court and were never meant for the masses. Townsmen, anxious to display their wealth and intent on living life to the full, signalled the boom in fine metalwork used not only for sword fittings, but also for *netsuke*, pipes and pouch clasps. Their demands stimulated the artists and craftsmen into the production of metalwork that surpasses, both in quality and in design, almost any metalwork made before or since.

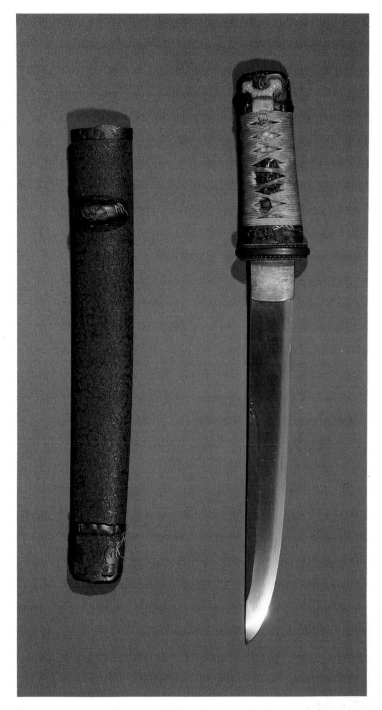

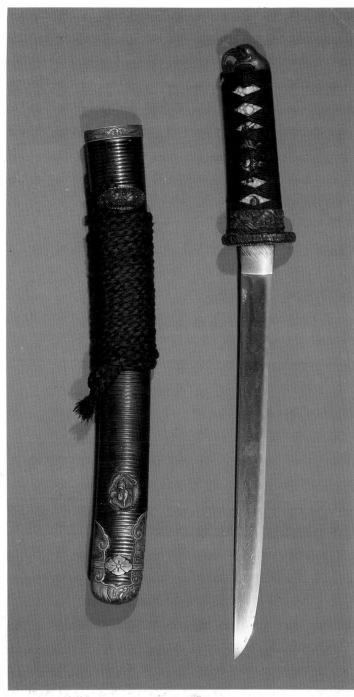

The Japanese have always abhored raw metal, with the exception of gold, silver and the steel of blades, preferring to accelerate corrosion and produce a coloured surface patina. With this in mind, alloys had been devised, centuries before, solely for the colours they developed on their surfaces when chemically treated. Paramount among them was *shakudo*, an alloy of copper containing up to five per cent gold, which acquired a purplish-black patina of great richness. *Shibuichi* was an alloy of copper with about 25 per cent silver, which could exhibit various shades of silvery-grey and had a fine flecked effect if properly mixed.

Added to these two principal alloys were *sentoku*, a type of brass which gave various yellow and brown colours, and various lead bronzes which provided the darker browns and greens. Using these alloys, together with gold, silver, copper and iron, the craftsmen produced coloured pictures of incredible complexity and, in many cases, an artistry that defies their medium.

The techniques these craftsmen employed were similar to those used by jewellers the world over, but developed to levels of technical complexity rarely seen elsewhere. Surfaces were textured using punches which, if rough faced and used in a random pattern,

Above left: Hamidashi, a variety of dirk with a guard only slightly larger than the hilt.

Above right: A tanto (dirk) with a pommel in the form of an elephant's head. Elephants were known only by illustration in Japan.

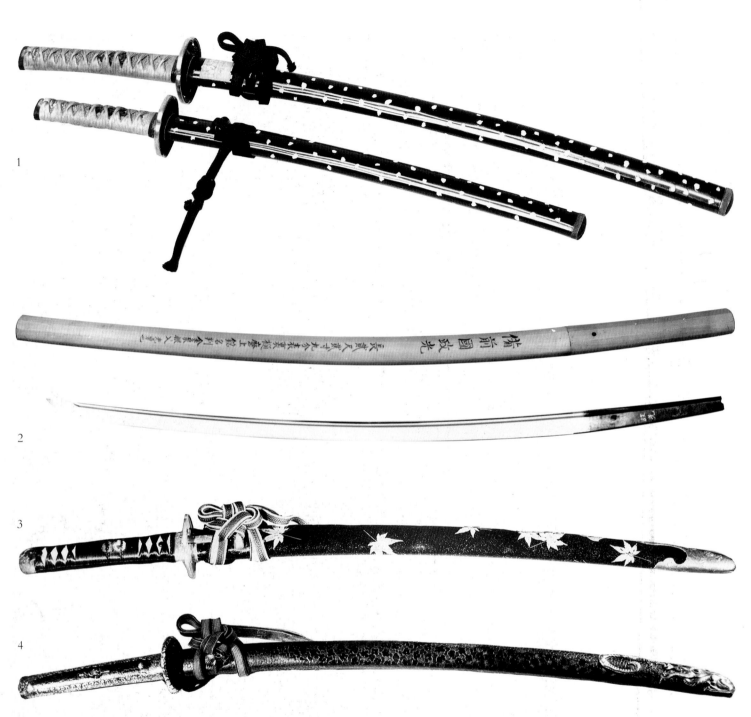

1. Daisho, the pair of swords which only the samurai were permitted to wear. The lacquer of the scabbards is inlaid with fragments of bone.

2. Blade by Bizen Masamitsu and its shirosaya inscribed with the name of the blade's maker. The shirosaya is a plain wooden scabbard used to store an unmounted blade.

3. Short sword in a superb mount typical of the type used by wealthy townsmen.

4. Sword richly mounted in silver as a birthday present.

imitated the surface of stone (*ishime*); while more regularity and a smoother punch gave a texture like wrinkled leather. The most Japanese of these surface treatments was obtained with a minute cup-punch which raised the ground into hemispheres, often so minute as to be all but invisible to the naked eye, but arranged in carefully spaced rows that generally follow the outline of the piece. Early *nanako* (fish-roe ground) was made with a punch having a group of three or more indentations, but later work is so careful and precise, with the hemispheres maintaining straight lines over complex three-dimensional curves, that a single punch must have been used.

Chasing, engraving and carving the metal were also employed to delineate the design. One special engraving technique was *kata-giri*, in which one face of the cut was vertical, while the other formed a shallow angle with the surface – the depth of cut varying the width of the channel. When used on silver or shibuichi, the effect of the shadow cast by the vertical wall of the cut simulated an ink painting on paper. Metals were carved using tiny chisels, and, even more remarkably, finished and polished, apparently as effortlessly as wood or ivory. *Taka bori* involved carving the metal in relief, whereas *shishiai bori* had the design carved in sunk relief, below the level of the surrounding ground.

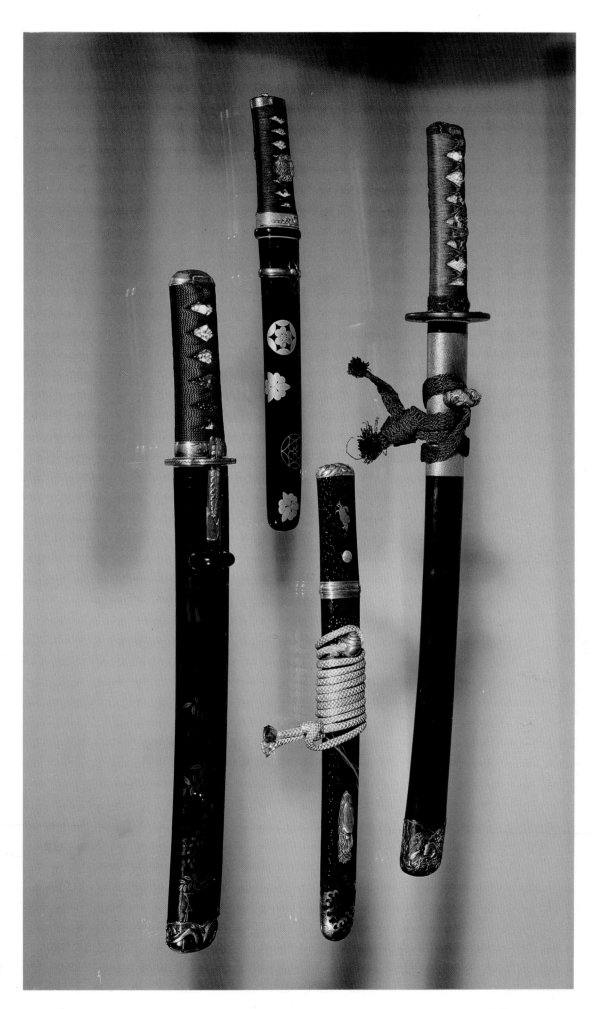

Right: Various dirks and short swords showing the inventive variety of decoration and mountings. During the Edo period swords became more ornamental but were seldom used for their real purpose.

Opposite: A selection of tsuba (sword guards) showing the wide variety of styles, shapes and subjects.

Far left: Tsuba of shakudo, an alloy of copper and gold, with inlay by Goto Mitsutada depicting the rival generals at the Battle of Uji river.

Left: Tsuba by Hitotsuyanagi Tomonaga showing Yuten Shonin exorcising a ghost.

Overlay, *nunome*, was a technique that could only be applied to an iron or steel base, and although not too durable, was capable of great richness and was widely used both for sword mounts and for decorating armour. In this process, the surface of the iron, sometimes already carved, was covered with a series of intersecting cuts made with a chisel or a knife held at an angle to the surface so as to throw up tiny pointed burrs. The overlay itself was limited to different colours of gold, silver or pure copper, other metals being too hard. The design was executed by applying the overlay in the form of wire or foil, tapped and burnished into place so that the teeth-like burrs were forced into the softer metal holding it in position.

Inlay, *hon zogan*, involved cutting a depression into the base, the exact size and shape of the piece to be inlaid, having slightly undercut edges and a raised burr around the outline. Into this was fitted the metal to be inlaid, cut with its sides sloping towards the top, then the burr was forced down onto the edges of the inlay to hold it in place. Sometimes the inlay was polished flush with the surface to give *hira zogan*, but in most cases it was left proud of the surface, *taka zogan*, and subsequently carved. On cheap work soldering was used to fix relief decoration in imitation of taka zogan.

Much fine work which appears to be inlay is in fact fire gilt. This is made by coating the metal where needed with a gold and mercury amalgam, then heating to drive off the mercury and leave the gold fused onto the surface. This same universal technique, often repeated several times to obtain a satisfactory coating, was used to produce the gilt copper so widely used on military equipment.

During the seventeenth and eighteenth centuries the makers of sword fittings gradually moved away from the simple styles in iron, producing more and more complex work. Numerous schools were founded,

Below: Tehen kanamono of a helmet by Saotome Ietada in shakudo decorated with nanako. The artist has lightened the effect of the black shakudo against the dark russet iron of the helmet by interposing a plate of gilded copper.

Above: Detail of a painted screen showing the interior of a workshop for the manufacture of sword fittings.

each developing and perfecting their own techniques but only a few can be mentioned here. Kaneiye and his followers carved away the background of the iron to produce designs in low relief, which might be en-

livened by small touches of gold, inspired by the works of Chinese painters. Workers in the province of Nagato (Choshu) specialized in iron tsuba in which the subject matter was painstakingly depicted in the round by pierc-

figures in battle scenes and other stories from history and legend. Etchizen Kinai and his followers also worked in iron. Their speciality was dragons, with their characteristic long chins, which were carved with the utmost precision in the round. Later groups, among whom the Nara, Yokoya and Yanagawa were important innovators, extended their repertoires by using soft-metal alloys to produce fittings that were works of art, rather than practical, if decorated, utilities. Certain schools developed and perfected particular themes for which they became famous; the Konkan specialized in fish subjects and the Omori in curling waves, dotted with minute flecks of gold spray. As in so many spheres, fashion played its part and was responsible for the production of somewhat banal copies of popular subjects and styles; these were turned out in their thousands by back-street workshops.

Above: Tatehage okegawa go mai do, a five-piece do of vertical plates, decorated with Fudo riding a dragon. Signed by Miochin Muneo and dated 1858.

ing and meticulous carving. The oft-copied school founded by Soten, working in Hikone, used a similar technique, but combined it with overlay in shades of gold and silver to depict minute and skilfully rendered

Right: Blade for a long sword by Inoue Shinkai, circa 1674. Despite the mediocrity of many Shinto swords, craftsmen such as Shinkai produced fine blades.

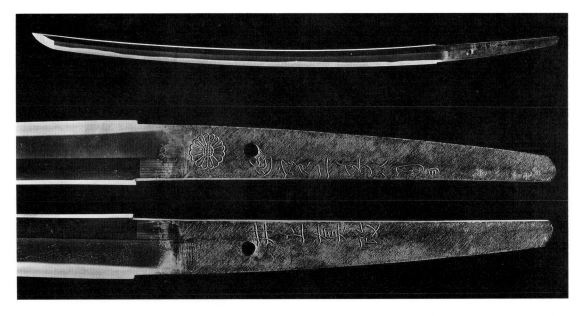

During the Momoyama period sword-smiths had moved all over the country to meet the demands of the armies and as a result cross-fertilization of ideas took place. However, disastrous floods during the sixteenth century wiped out all but a few of the Osafune Bizen smiths, with the result that their influence was largely absent. What emerged during the seventeenth century were new styles that blurred the differences between the original traditions. This chronological boundary, coinciding with the rule of the Tokugawas, heralded the beginning of the shinto (New Sword) period. Initially there was an upsurge of brilliant work, led by craftsmen such as Umetada Myoju and Horikawa Kunihiro at Kyoto, and Noda Hankei in Edo. These in turn trained and encouraged others, such as Tadayoshi of Hizen, whose family turned out consistently good blades

for generations. Rather predictably, many of the swords made during later years of this peaceful period were mediocre, being enlivened only occasionally by smiths such as Nagasone Okisato of Edo and Tsuta Sukehiro and Inouye Shinkai of Osaka. These latter smiths were among the many who catered not only for samurai but for wealthy townsmen, developing flamboyant styles of blades with decorative hamon and extensive horimono, which, while technically superb, were works of art rather than practical swords.

Swordsmanship was practised using wooden blades and, later, padded armour, but few Edo period samurai had experienced the reality of using cold steel against an opponent. Equally, many of the swords being produced were weapons whose real strength was never put to the test. A few samurai

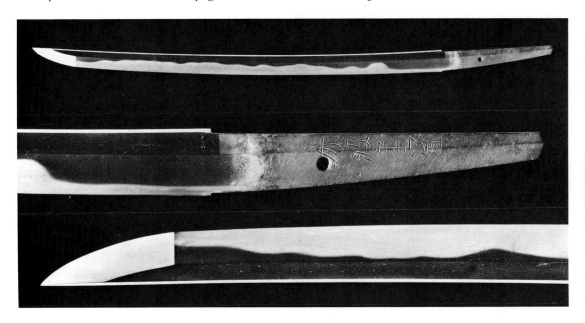

Right: Blade for a long sword by Tamba no kami Yoshimichi (1565 – 1635), a renowned swordsmith of the Shinto period.

Left: Blade for a short sword by Nagasone Okisato Nyudo Kotetsu with the result of a test inlaid in gold recording that two bodies had been cut.

resorted to murdering commoners for some imagined slight as a means of trying out their swords; this was not in itself a crime but it was frowned upon. Others, more humanely, used bundles of wet straw tied around a bamboo pole as a substitute for a human body, or tested their swords on helmets and other pieces of armour.

According to Tokugawa law, the bodies of executed criminals became the property of the state and might be used to test swords, although bodies of murderers, tattooed people, priests and untouchables were taboo. A system of official testing, *tameshi giri*, was established using this raw material supplied by the execution yards. Although requiring official permission, swords could be submitted to one of the hereditary officials drawn from either the Yamada, Chokushi or Nakagawa familes for testing.

For the test itself, the body was arranged on a mound of sand, and tied to bamboo stakes to hold it in position. The tester, wearing kami shimo and carrying a blade fitted into a special iron-bound hilt, then studied the corpse and decided which of his repertoire of cuts was appropriate. Severing the arm at the wrist was considered the easiest, while a cut across the hips, *ryo kuruma*, or a diagonal cut through the shoulder girdle, *o kessa*, the most difficult. After making the cut, first the body was carefully examined, then the blade for damage and for signs of adhering fat. If satisfied, further, more difficult, cuts might be made, and the final result was sometimes inlaid in gold on the tang of the blade. Masahide comments that blades by differing smiths were divided into five categories of sharpness according to the results of such tests, and that experience showed that

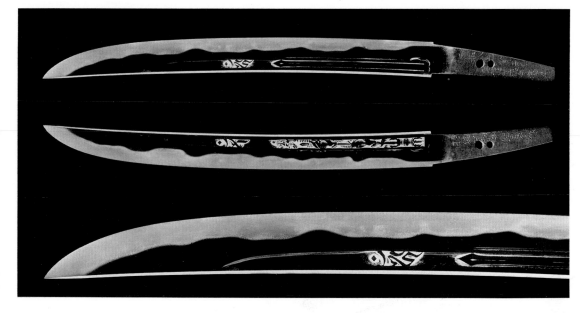

Left: Short sword by Oite Kishu Wakayama Shigekuni dated 1622, an excellent smith of the Yamato Tegai school.

167

Right (both): Page from a heraldic handbook showing the mon and heraldic equipment of Ito Harima no Kami Nagahiro.

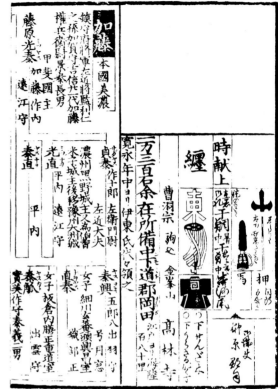

the most efficient length lay between one foot four inches and two feet four inches (40-71cm). Longer swords were too difficult for the average man to use effectively. It was also found that the cross section given to the blade by the polisher had a significant effect on its cutting ability; a slight convexity to the surfaces improved its ability to cut flesh while a flat surface was most suitable for the straw bundles.

One of the ways in which the Tokugawa curbed the powers of the daimyo was to enforce a biannual attendance at court, *sankin kotai*, modified for those whose province was a considerable distance from the capital.

These peregrinations or *daimyo gyoretsu* kept them shuffling between their home provinces and Edo with huge retinues of samurai and servants, whose numbers were specified according to income, stretching their resources to the limit and preventing any idea of insurrection. The roads connecting the capital with the remainder of the country became of great importance, and were provided with inns and waystations to accommodate the members of the processions. There was not, however, free passage; barriers and checkpoints were manned by Tokugawa officials who made reports on traffic to and from the capital and apprehended those

Right: Spears and their heraldic scabbards were carried in processions to identify the travellers.

without proper authorization – particularly the wives and families of the daimyo who were confined in their mansions in Edo as hostages during the absence of the daimyo. As symbols of the daimyo's status, these processions were headed by retainers carrying tall yari with ornamental scabbards whose shape and decoration had heraldic significance. They were followed by others carrying guns, tachi, bows and quivers in special racks and other symbols of rank. The daimyo and his senior staff rode in palanquins, sometimes carrying a small bow for protection, *kago hankyu* (also called *riman kyu* after Riman Hayashi of Kii province who invented the device); these weapons were made as sets comprising a short whalebone bow and diminutive arrows held in a lacquered leather case – the samurai equivalent of the 'derringer'.

The Maeda family of Kaga, considered a potential threat by the Tokugawa, far from being impoverished by this system had the largest income of any – just over one million koku. Like many in their position, they were 'invited' by the shogun to undertake ruinous public works that threatened their financial stability. Determined to avoid the debts that so many in a similar position had been forced into, the Maeda instigated two schemes to bring money into the provinces. They traded with the Dutch and Chinese at Nagasaki, and put the lower ranking soldiers to work making armour. No doubt professional armourers supervised the operation and did the more difficult parts of the work (some Miochin and Haruta smiths are known to have moved to Kaga), but the products they turned out were distinctive. Output began in earnest during the middle of the seventeenth century under the fifth daimyo, and continued until the time of the thirteenth daimyo in 1725. During that time they were responsible for manufacturing a considerable quantity of sturdy and practical armour, as befits that produced by the samurai class. For helmets they had a penchant for kawari bachi or hoshi bachi with zaboshi, to which were applied cut-out iron decorations, sometimes splashed with a silvery alloy, *sawari*, partially fused onto the russet surface to represent dew or rain. One invariable feature of Kaga helmets is that they were never fitted with cords made from the rope-like 'drum cord' as was used elsewhere, preferring instead to use rolled cloth – initially hemp, but later crêpe

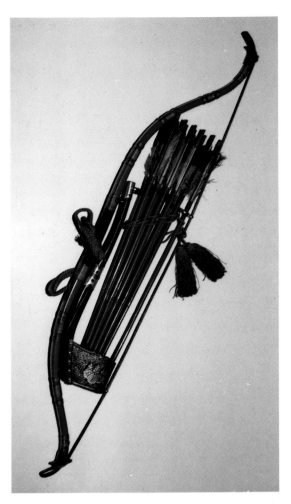

Left: Kago hankyu of whalebone with its quiver of arrows. These diminutive weapons were designed for use from within the cramped confines of the palanquins in which the nobles travelled.

de chine rolled and sewn around a core of soft threads.

Kaga do were of many types, but with the emphasis on those built up from a few relatively large plates, frequently laced in white silk with the edges to the plates finished to one of the standard outlines. When not given a russet finish, many do were covered in

Left: Suji kabuto by the Unkai group of Kaga. The applied iron decoration on the peak, the iron tehen kanamono and the grouped lacing are typical of the work of these armourers. The austerity of the helmet bowl has been relieved by applying boyo (stick-like) shinodare to the plates.

Opposite left: A 120-plate suji bachi decorated with a theme involving a dragon, embossed on the peak, chasing a sacred jewel, mounted in the tehen. A straight-bladed Buddhist sword has been applied as decoration to the front plate while the neck guard has a mon incorporated in the lacing.

Opposite right: Mune tori okegawa do gusoku by Miochin Munesada circa 1653. The helmet and do are engraved with debased Sanskrit characters.

Right: A typical armour made by the Kaga clan in russet iron with white lacing.

wrinkled 'Chinese leather' or were decorated with gold and black lacquer which had a 'hammered' texture. The fronts of many kaga do were decorated with a circular design, generally of a dragon in either applied metalwork or in raised lacquer, a style called *maki e do*.

Particularly characteristic are the watagami, which were hinged to the boko no ita so that they could be removed or swung back when putting on the do. The edges were turned up to form a shallow channel section, which added considerably to their stiffness. On some do, this flange was enlarged around the neck opening at the back, to form a low-standing metal collar. Kohaze were of a distinctive four-lobed shape while the seme kohaze was waisted and grooved around its edge – both parts were frequently made of ivory. Huge numbers of kote were turned out which had the kanmuri ita in three pieces, each with a standing flange on the upper edge, joined by butterfly-shaped hinges. Many were oda gote with the plates damascened in silver and, reputedly, with special types of mail which was sometimes said to be of brass to avoid corrosion. Many of these features were often displayed in the work of the Unkai, a group of Miochin armourers who moved to Kaga, working from the mid-seventeenth to the mid-eighteenth centuries. This group specialized in the highest grade work, producing armours for the wealthy decorated with applied iron work, splashed with sawari, that often draws its themes from Buddhism. Much of their work incorporates exotic materials such as velvet and ivory and often shows foreign influences, no doubt because of the province's connections with the Dutch and Chinese at Nagasaki.

By and large, most samurai during the greater part of the seventeenth century continued to wear the practical armours of the Momoyama period, brightening them somewhat by the addition of more elaborate gilded metal decorations and printed leathers but without detracting from their essential utility. The Neo group of Nara, founded towards the end of the Momoyama period, continued to produce work of outstanding quality – Neo Masanobu, in particular, continued the traditions of Nobuiye and Yoshimichi by producing superb high-sided suji bachi and hoshi bachi, generally of 62 plates. Occasionally they made helmets of 120 or even 140 plates, but these necessitated plates

that were so narrow that the interior edges had to be cut in a waved pattern, to create space for the staggered rows of rivets – this was a wonderful tour de force, but the helmets were weakened by the numerous perforations and were very heavy. As in all periods, leather armour continued to be made, particularly by the Iwai armourers. It was often of considerable thickness and almost as practical as metal and was particularly favoured by elderly men because of its light weight. The basic forms were obtained by shaping the wet rawhide in wooden moulds; these were then modelled with kokuso before lacquering. Both hoshi bachi and suji bachi were produced and, with metal details applied to the basic leather shell, they are virtually indistinguishable from helmets made from steel.

For the first time in their history, the Japanese armourers turned their attention to the protection of the horse. Complete armours, *uma yoroi*, were produced from small embossed scales of leather, generally gilded, sewn onto fabric. Most of these armours consist of a large rectangular section for the crupper, with a small extension along one long edge covering the tail, two triangular sections laced together along the mane forming a crinet for the neck and perhaps an additional panel over the chest resembling a peytral. More elaborate versions incorporated metal plates and mail along the crest of the neck, and had flanchards linking the peytral with the crupper at the sides. The head of the horse was covered by a chanfron, which was often simply of lacquered papier mâché but was occasionally steel, in the form of a dragon's

head or a caricature of a horse. The whole assembly was held in position by ties to the saddle and to other parts of the normal harness, with additional ties or toggles between the adjoining sections of the armour.

As the prospect of war gradually faded, the emphasis on practicability waned in favour of further decoration. The Miochin, in particular, demonstrated their skill by producing embossed or *uchidashi do* which, although often superbly executed, thinned the metal and produced a surface that would trap the point of a weapon. Although not the first to produce such work, Miochin Munesuke (1642-1735) became renowned for it. He specialized in yukinoshita do with superbly embossed front plates. These designs took all manner of forms, but characters, Chinese lions and Buddhist divinities were particularly favoured – the latter were sometimes so deeply embossed that the figure is almost in the round. Munesuke, together with his grandfather Kunimichi, concocted the impressive genealogy of the Miochin family, listing an unbroken lineage from the earliest times and claiming for himself the title Premier Armour Expert of Japan. Adopting the strategy of the Honnami family, who acted as appraisers of swords, Munesuke began to issue certificates of authenticity, giving the provenance and a value to pieces of unsigned and often ancient armour. He invariably attributed authorship to one or other of his fictitious ancestors listed in his genealogy. By the beginning of the eighteenth century the fashion for embossed armour was at its height, with embossed plates forming the main elements of do, sode and haidate. Even complete helmet bowls were hammered from one or more sheets of iron. Miochin Ryoei, whose exact working dates are unknown, excelled in producing

Far left: Red, white and blue laced ni mai do gusoku, having the yurugi ito replaced by mail. Edo period.

Left: Helmet belonging to the armour opposite by Neo Masanobu of Nara.

Top right: Goshozan suji bachi of rawhide lacquered to resemble russet iron.

Right: Interior of the helmet bowl above showing the fastenings of the applied metal suji (flanges).

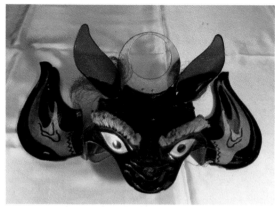

quality, and showed immense mastery of a stubborn medium, as armour it was all but useless – of necessity it was made of soft iron and was sometimes so thin that it could be bent in the hands. Not all embossed work, however, was totally impractical. A few armourers applied the decoration over robust armours, with the joint so carefully fitted as to be imperceptible. Rather strangely, having gone to all this trouble, the solid plate behind the embossing was sometimes cut away.

Above:Horse armour of lacquered leather scales sewn to fabric. Armour for horses was only made in the Edo period and was never proved in battle. Edo period.

helmets modelled to represent sea shells or plant subjects, beaten from a single sheet. Although much of this work was of the finest

Above right: Chanfron for a horse armour in the form of a caricature of a horse. Chanfrons were often of papier mâchè and had little defensive value. Edo period.

Right: Horse harness. The large flanchards were to protect the horse from the heavy iron stirrups.

Below: Uchidashi gusoku by Miochin Ki Munesuke. Embossed armour such as this became popular during the peaceful Edo period as the reality of warfare receded. Mid-Edo period.

Right: Black and blue laced maru do. Edo period.

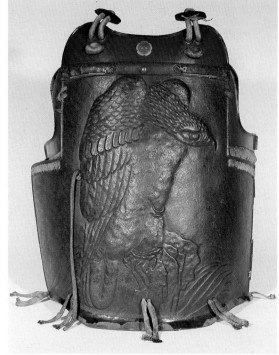

Left: A fantastic armour of loosely tied plates. It resembles a Karasu tengu, a mythical bird-like creature.

Above: Front plate of an uchidashi ni mai do embossed with an eagle. Edo period.

Below: Uchidashi hoate, a face with embossed cheeks by a Miochin armourer. Edo period.

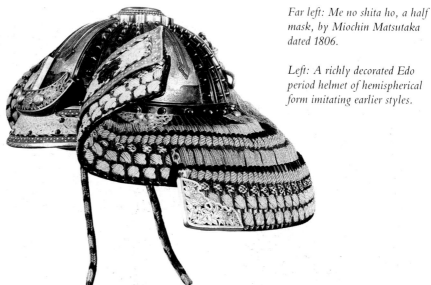

Far left: Me no shita ho, a half mask, by Miochin Matsutaka dated 1806.

Left: A richly decorated Edo period helmet of hemispherical form imitating earlier styles.

During the first decades of the eighteenth century the attitude towards decoration rose to further heights as the emphasis being placed on the legends and heroic epics by the Tokugawa took effect. Samurai yearned for the splendour of the past, encouraged by such books as *Honcho Gunkiko*, a 12-volume work written by Arai Hakuseki, which contained a documentary history of arms and armour illustrated by examples preserved in shrines and temples. In works such as this and *Gun Yo Ki*, published in 1734 by Ise Sadatake, o yoroi, do maru and haramaki were described in detail, together with the swords, costumes and accessories worn with them. The spirit of the antiquarian was in the air and the mood was one of nostalgia.

Catering for this longing, the armourers, and the Miochin in particular, revived the maru bachi, making it either with or without rivets as the customer required. Some were deliberately given a heavy coating of rust to give them an apearance of great antiquity, becoming *sabi mono* (rusty things), designed to evoke an emotion of nostalgic melancholia. Old styles of printed leather were reproduced and o sode were fitted to all types of armours with little thought as to how they should be mounted. Quite correctly, shoji no ita and gumiwa were fitted to the watagami, which incongruously often retained kohire. Being unsure about the various cords and ties, those at the ends of the kanmuri no ita were tied to the front and back gumi, the leather tie being knotted around the watagami – the shoji no ita and the kohire had to be pierced to accommodate it. Fittings for the sashimono were rendered almost unusable because of the bow fitted to the back of the armour, and were further impeded by large, spreading shikoro. Nodawa were provided with these armours, clashing incongruously

Below left: An uchidashi bachi, an embossed helmet bowl in the shape of an egg-plant. Attributed to Ohara Katsunari.

Below: An Edo reproduction of an o boshi maru bachi, a round helmet bowl with large rivets, inaccurate in that the rivets are positioned on the centre line of each plate rather than along the rear edge.

Right: Iro iro odoshi ni mai do gusoku, a multi-coloured two piece armour, showing early features incorporated into a typical Edo armour. The style of this armour is loosely based on a do maru of the Muromachi period.

Far right: Omodaka odoshi do maru, a do maru laced with a pattern resembling a water-plantain leaf, a superb Edo period reproduction of the earlier style.

with the various types of men gu. Being unsure about its position, some tried to wear this neck armour inside the do, no doubt painfully, others just tied it loosely and let it hang on the chest.

Before long copies were being made of the old armours. At first these were ludicrous pastiches incorporating features from different ages, but gradually they became more accurate, culminating in almost perfect copies of o yoroi, haramaki and do maru. Those with money went one better and bought old armours from temples, or searched family store houses, and refurbished them for use. In a plea for sanity, Sakakibara Kozan wrote his book *Chuko-katchu Seisakuben*, urging samurai to abandon these revival armours and return to using the more practical styles of the Momoyama period. A few heeded his plea, and had superb armours in the Momoyama styles made by such smiths as Miochin Muneyasu, but even he continued to make do maru or

haramaki for those who wanted them.

Swordsmiths too, began to look back to the past for their models. Masahide and his followers at the beginning of the nineteenth century initiated a revival of the styles and techniques from the Shinshito period of the Nambokucho period, in particular. Following this lead others, such as Hosokawa Masayoshi, Naotane and his son Naokatsu, reproduced the elegant blades of the Koto period, working in whichever of the five traditions the customer demanded. Much of their work approached the quality of the blades created by the great masters of the swordsmiths' craft but this rebirth was to be shortlived; the outside world was beginning to take an interest in Japan.

During the 1840s the United States of America and the manufacturing powers in Europe were expanding and competing for trade with China. Russian outposts were established bordering the Pacific, and Britain, after an initial probe at Japan's

Far left: Armour in do maru style made for a daimyo of the Doi family. Late Edo period.

Left: Tatewaku odoshi ni mai do gusoku, a two-section armour, laced with vertical bars of colour to represent rising steam. A late Edo armour influenced by earlier do maru.

defences, gained Hong Kong and Shanghai. America, in particular, needed a refuelling post between San Francisco and Shanghai if the newly formed Pacific Mail Steamship Company was to have any chance of success, and Japan was the only suitable site. The United States Government realized that pressure would have to be exerted if successful negotiations were to be concluded. In 1853 four warships sailed into Uraga Bay near Edo carrying Commodore Matthew Calbraith Perry to inform the Japanese of the Americans' intentions. Thousands of samurai assembled, impotent against the guns of the warships, as preliminary negotiations were carried out. In the following year a treaty was signed and within a year, long before the treaty conditions could be met, the first visitors arrived. Within a few years, this trickle of foreigners had become a stream as other countries negotiated for the right to trade and more and more visitors flocked to see the country for themselves.

The attitude of the Japanese towards the arrival of the foreigners was divided. One faction wanted to expel the barbarians and re-

Below: A late Edo period version of a nodawa (defence for throat and neck) known as a guruwa.

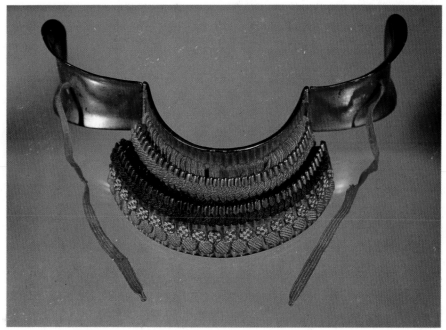

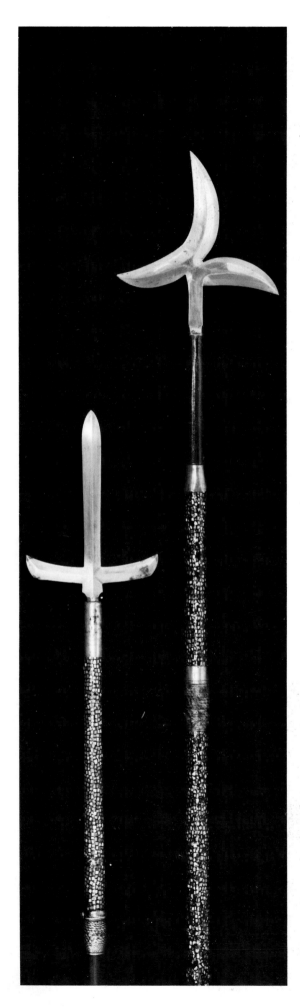

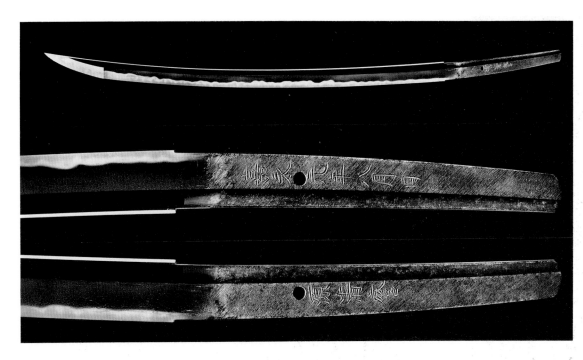

Opposite left: The jumonji yari on the left is a fairly common type, the sickle yari on the right is extremely rare.

Opposite right: A very late 'foreign' armour incorporating a French cuirassier's helmet and cuirass from the Napoleonic period.

establish the Emperor as the true ruler of the country but the remainder sensed the inevitability of a change in the social order. A few took matters into their own hands, reacting with violence not only against foreigners, but also against the more-progressive ministers of state. By 1868 the shogun had abdicated in favour of the Emperor and his last entry into Osaka castle was watched and described by Algernon Mitford, later Lord Redesdale:

... warriors dressed in the old armour of the country, carrying spears, bows and arrows, falchions curiously shaped, with sword and dirk, who looked as if they had stepped out of some old pictures of the Gempei Wars in the Middle Ages. Their jinbaori, not unlike herald's tabards, were as many-coloured as Joseph's coat. Hideous masks of lacquer and iron, fringed with portentous whiskers and mustachios, crested helmets with wigs from which long streamers of horsehair floated to their waists, might strike terror into any enemy. They looked like the hobgoblins of a nightmare.

In November 1868, the Emperor took on the mantle of power his ancestors had lost almost 900 years before, setting up his new palace in Edo Castle and renaming the city Tokyo. For a while the samurai continued to wear their swords, often incongruously matched with

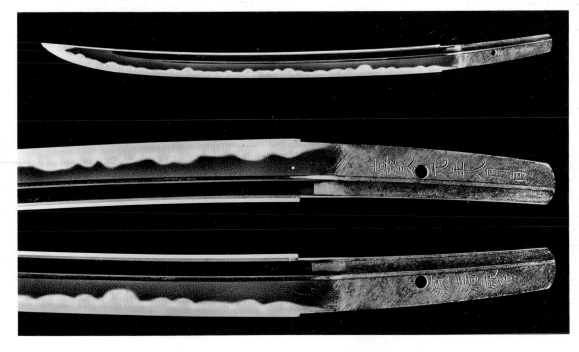

Left: An Edo period armour fitted with a leather cover for the front of the armour in the style of an o yoroi.

Right: A samurai poses before the camera of a 'barbarian'. The era of the samurai drew to a close with the arrival of Westerners during the 1860s.

by the ever-growing numbers of tourists as souvenirs of a vanished society. In his book *Rambles in Japan*, published in 1895, H B Tristam, the Canon of Durham, writes about this phenomenon:

The collections of old armour and swords in these shops were to me as fascinating as a display of the fashions in Regent Street to an English belle, while the prices, as far as I am able to judge, were extremely moderate. I made many purchases at a price really less than the value of the material. . . . In fact, ancient armour was a drug on the market, many of the poorer Samurai being compelled to part with their treasured accoutrements for rice.

In a fervent spirit of modernization and enthusiasm for all things Western, the Japanese discarded without hesitation many of their ancient treasures. A thousand years of accumulated artistry and meticulous craftsmanship in lacquer, silk and metal was abandoned in the space of a few years. Not all craftsmen, however, neglected their traditional skills; a few passed the principles of their trades to their descendants, and their grandchildren are only now beginning to reap the benefits as modern Japanese look back into their history from the technological society they have built. Once again, swordsmiths and armourers are producing heirlooms for future generations so that they might be reminded of their country's past.

European-style frock coats and top hats, but their protected status and the practice of wearing swords was abolished by an edict of 1876. Faced with the problem of making a living, many samurai joined the newly formed armed forces, but others, often too proud to earn a living, were obliged to sell their once-treasured swords and armour to pawnbrokers and curio shops, to be bought

Right: An articulated iron snake produced as a novelty by a redundant armour maker.

Glossary

Abumi A stirrup.

Abumi zuri no kawa Leather patch on the inside of tosei shin guards to prevent chafing of the stirrup leathers.

Ai Indigo colour.

Aibiki Shoulder strap fastenings of a tosei do.

Aizuchi Swordsmith's assistants.

Agemaki Bow of silk cord tied in a special knot hung from rings on armour – an especially large one was hung on the back as part of the shoulder-guard attachments.

Agemaki no kan Ring on back of do from which a large agemaki is hung.

Ago no o benri Protruding studs on chin of mask to prevent the helmet cords from slipping forwards.

Aka Crimson colour.

Akabe yoroi Neck armour – particularly that worn with tanko during the Yamato period.

Akoda nari bachi Style of helmet that developed during the Muromachi period which is distinctly swollen at the back and normally without prominent rivets.

Akome Iron ore.

Aoiba za Decorative iron plate surrounding the tehen of a Heian period helmet bowl.

Arare boshi bachi Term used to describe a helmet bowl made or decorated with large, exaggerated rivets.

Asa no ha gusari Mail in which each round link is connected to each of three others.

Asagi Pale blue colour.

Ase nagashi no ana Hole or tube under the chin of a mask to drain away perspiration.

Ashi Rings around a tachi scabbard to which the hangers are attached.

Ato me ate Backsight of a gun or cannon.

Ayasugi hada Regular wavy grain on surface of a sword.

Bajo zutzu A small pistol-like gun.

Birodo Velvet.

Bishamon gote Armoured sleeves having an integral small sode covering the upper arm.

Boko no ita Top plate at the back of a tosei do to which the watagami are riveted.

Byakudan nuri Transparent lacquer of a golden yellow colour.

Byo kakari do *see* byo toji yokohagi okegawa do

Byo toji yokohagi okegawa do Tosei do of horizontal plates fastened by prominent, often decorated, rivets.

Bu tachi A military sword as opposed to those worn at court or with civilian dress.

Chiisa gatana *see* wakizashi

Chirimen namban kusari European-type mail made with small, densely packed links.

Chochin bachi Helmet bowl that collapses flat for storage.

Daienzan bachi Helmet bowl having a more or less hemispherical shape.

Daimyo Term applied to holders of a considerable area of land – formalized in the Edo period to those with incomes above 10,000 koku per year.

Daisho A pair of swords having matching mounts, normally a katana and wakizashi combination.

Dangaye do Tosei do in which different styles of lacing are used in the upper and lower sections.

Do Armour for the body.

Do dan Mound of sand used to support the corpse in sword testing.

Do gane Ornamental metal band around the central part of a sword or dirk hilt.

Do maki Intermediate strip of iron forming the framework of a shoshaku tsuki kabuto.

Do maru Scale armour wrapping around the body and fastening under the right arm (*see haramaki*).

Donsu Damask.

Ebira Open quiver used in the Heian and Kamakura periods.

Ebizaya maki Dirk mounted in a scabbard and hilt carved with gadroons to resemble a shrimp's carapace.

Eboshi Tall cap of variable shape – often curving rearwards at the top.

Eboshi nari kabuto Helmet shaped to resemble an eboshi.

E gawa Leather decorated with a pictorial design.

Etchu haidate Haidate covered with only a sparse grid of mail and splints.

Etchu jikoro Tosei neck guard falling in a concave curve and terminating in a bottom plate which has a straight lower edge.

Etchu suneate Splint shin guards without a fabric backing.

Etchu zunari bachi Helmet bowl of simple construction having the longitudinal top plate overlapping the brow plate.

Fuchi Reinforcing band around the base of a hilt.

Fukigaeshi The turnback at the front edge of the upper row or rows of a neck guard.

Fukigaeshi no suemon Chrysanthemum-shaped ornaments applied to fukigaeshi of Heian period helmets.

Fujiwara iro A pale lilac colour.

Fukube Gourd-shaped plate applied to armoured sleeves.

Fukurin Applied metal rim.

Fuse ita Plate forming the top of a mabisashi tsuki kabuto.

Fusube gawa Smoked leather having a yellow or brown colour.

Gattari Attachment for a sashimono fastened to back of do at the level of the shoulder blades.

Gessan Pendant armoured sections attached to the lower edge of a tosei do.

Gessan jikoro Tosei shikoro having all but the uppermost plate divided into sections.

Goishi gashira Iyozane scales with heads of rounded shape.

Go kaden The five traditions of sword making during the Koto period.

Gose gawa Red leather decorated with groups of white spots.

Goshozan High-sided helmet having the back higher than the front.

Gumbai uchiwa A non-folding variety of war fan.

Gumi wa Leather loop fitted with an elongated metal bead on the shoulder strap of an armour to which the shoulder guards are tied.

Gunsen Folding war fan.

Gusoku A set of something – a complete armour.

Gusoku bitsu Box for the storage and transport of an armour.

Gyoyo Leaf-shaped plate used as a shoulder protector or to guard the fastenings of the shoulder straps.

Ha Cutting edge of a sword.

Habaki Collar of soft metal around the base of a blade.

Hachi The bowl of a helmet.

Hachiman kuro A very dark blue-black colour used for armour lacing during the Edo period.

Hachi tsuke no ita The uppermost plate or row of scales in a neck guard.

Hachiwara A parrying weapon consisting of a curved tapering square sectioned bar with a hook-like projection at the base.

Hada Forged pattern on the surface of a blade.

Hadome Parrying bar attached to the shaft of a spear.

Haidate Defence for the thighs shaped like a divided apron.

Hakushi Pale purple.

Hamon Outline shape of tempered edge of a blade.

Hanagami bukuro Pouch attached to the front of a do or behind one of the gessan.

Hana gata shobu gawa Blue leather with naturalistically depicted iris flowers and leaves.

Hana ni cho gawa Leather decorated with flowers and butterflies.

Hanbo An abbreviated face mask covering only the chin and lower cheeks.

Haniwa Fired clay figure or model set around the mound of a burial mound.

Happuri Plate defence for the forehead and cheeks.

Hara ate Abbreviated armour covering the front and sides of the body only.

Haraidate Tubular crest holder attached centrally to the peak of a helmet.

Haramaki Armour worn during the Heian and Kamakura periods which wrapped around the body and fastened under the right arm. From the Muromachi period, the term refers to an armour opening down the centre line of the back.

Harikake bachi A helmet bowl decorated and embellished by a light decorative superstructure of wood, paper, leather and lacquer.

Hasso byo A soft-metal rivet with an ornamented head.

Hatomune do Do having a medial ridge.

Hata Long banner hung by a cross bar from a pole.

Hayago Powder flask.

Hei A castle wall.

Heichozan High-sided helmet shape which is flat on top.

Hi A groove in a blade. Alternatively, the term refers to the colour vermilion.

Hibiki no ana Holes in a helmet bowl originally for attaching a helmet cord but later decorative.

Hibuta The pan cover of a matchlock.

Hiji gane Elbow plate of an armoured sleeve.

Hikone gusoku Red lacquered armour.

Hinawa ju Matchlock gun.

Hineno jikoro Close-fitting neck guard having a lower edge which is shaped to the shoulders.

Hineno zunari bachi Helmet bowl of simplified construction having a central longitudinal plate which is overlaid by a brow plate/peak combination.

Hira ne Flat arrowhead of the broadhead type.

Hira zogan Inlay finished flush with the surrounding surface.

Hirumaki no tachi Tachi having the scabbard and hilt spirally bound with a strip of leather under the lacquer.

Hiro sode Shoulder guard which widens and flattens towards the bottom.

Hishinui A cross-knot on the lowest row of scales of a piece of armour.

Hishinui no ita The lowest row of scales of a piece of armour.

Hishi toji A cross-knot other than on the hishinui no ita.

Hishi toji do A variety of yokohagi okegawa do in which the plates are connected by cross-knots.

Hishi toji hotoke do A smooth-faced do decorated by cross-knots.

Hitai ate Late form of happuri worn in place of a helmet.

Hiya zutsu Small cannon for launching fireworks.

Hizara The flashpan of a matchlock gun.

Hiza yoroi Old term for armour covering the thigh and knee.

Hoate A mask covering the chin and cheeks only.

Hodo haidate Haidate having the lower part of the armoured portion divided into pendant sections.

Hon kozane True scales.

Hon zogane Inlay.

Hori A moat.

Horimono Carved decoration on a blade.

Horo Cape-like cloth attached to the back of an armour which inflated with air when riding.

Hoshi A rivet.

Hoshi bachi A helmet bowl with prominent rivets.

Hotoke do A smooth faced do.

Hyo Dark green.

Hyotan Gourd-shaped plate forming part of an armoured sleeve.

Ichi mai fuse bachi Heian period helmet bowl beaten from a single plate.

Ichimai maze Alternation of iron and leather scales along a row.

Ichimanju jikoro Neck guard having only the top plate curved.

Igaki Ornamental plates around the base of a helmet bowl.

Ikada Small rectangular plates set in mail.

Ikada haidate Mail haidate with scattered ikada.

Iro Colour.

Iro gawa Self-coloured leather.

Iro iro odoshi Multi-coloured lacing.

Ishime Irregular rough texture like the surface of stone.

Ishizuke The chape of a tachi scabbard.

Ita haidate Scale haidate.

Ite jikoro Tosei shikoro in which the right fukigaeshi can be removed or folded back for archery.

Ito maki no tachi A tachi in which the hilt and upper part of the scabbard are bound with silk braid in a cross-cross fashion.

Iyozane Type of scale assembled with almost no overlap.

Iyozane do Tosei do of iyozane wrapping around the body and fastening under the right arm.

Ji ita Ornament of a gilt or silvered plate overlaid by shinodare applied to a helmet bowl.

Jinbaori Surcoat worn over armour.

Jingasa Conical open hat of iron or lacquered leather worn as a light defence.

Jitte A parrying bar carried by police during the Edo period.

Ji zamurai Land-owning samurai.

Jumonji kitae Method of forging armour plate with a crossed grain.

Jumonji yari Type of spear head having a central blade with side blades at the base.

Kabuto A helmet.

Kabuto gane The pommel of a tachi.

Kabuto no o The tying cord of a helmet.

Kago hankyu A miniature bow carried in a palanquin.

Kaihan Leggings.

Kaihan suneate Suneate without knee guards.

Kakae zutsu Large-bore gun.

Kake kusari An oval link connecting the circular links of mail.

Kake o The front tying cord of a sode.

Kama A sickle-like weapon.

Kami shimo Ceremonial dress of stiffened hemp worn by samurai during the Edo period.

Kanabo Long club of metal or wood.

Kane maze Technique of concentrating iron scales at vulnerable points of an armour.

Kanmuri no ita Cap plate of a sode or kote.

Kara boshi Large rivet having a hollow head.

Kara bitsu Chest used for storing armour.

Kara kozane Scales embossed from the back.

Karimata Forked arrow head.

Karuta gane do Folding armour of rectangular plates.

Kasa jikoro Wide spreading neck guard, often almost flat.

Kasa jirushi no kan Ring at the back of a helmet designed to carry a small identification flag, but on later helmets usually provided with an agemaki bow.

Kasari suneate Mail shin guards.

Kashira The pommel of a sword.

Kashira date Crest mounted on the top of a helmet.

Katagiri Engraving technique in which one side of the cut is vertical.

Katahada nugi do Type of *Nio do*.

Kata jiro Gilt or silvered plate applied between the suji of a helmet bowl as decoration.

Katakama yari Spear having only one side blade.

Katana Dirk worn in the belt during the Heian period. Alternatively, the characteristic long sword worn in the belt during the Momoyama and Edo periods.

Katana kake Sword stand.

Katana toji Sword polisher.

Katana zutsu Tubular lacquered case for a sword.

Kata yoroi Shoulder armour worn with the tanko during the Yamato period.

Katchu shi Armourer.

Kawari bachi Helmet of other than the conventional multi-plate construction.

Kawara haidate Haidate of S-sectioned scales overlapped like roof tiles.

Kawashiki Leather thong incorporated in the lacing holding scales into a row.

Kazuchi no tsurugi Early straight sword having a bulbous pommel.

Kawa tsutsu maki no tachi Leather wrapped tachi.

Kawa zutsumi do Do covered with a sheet of leather.

Kebiki Close lacing.

Kedate no ana Lacing holding the rows of scales together.

Keiko Early scale armour.

Kesho eri Collar decorated with a silk frill in imitation of a European ruff.

Kesho no ita Leather covered wood strip covering the heads of the scales where they afix to a metal plate.

Kikko A type of brigandine made of small hexagonal plates quilted between layers of fabric.

Kikko gane do A folding do made from hexagonal plates.

Kikuchi yari Early variety of spear with a straight, single-edged blade.

Kikujin Yellowish-green colour.

Kinran Gold brocade.

Kiritsuke iyozane Iyozane simulated by lacquer applied to a solid plate.

Kiritsuke kozane Kozane simulated by lacquer applied to a solid plate.

Kissaki Point section of a sword.

Kiwame fuda Certificate attributing the authorship of armour to a particular maker.

Ko Yellow.

Kobai Dark red.

Kobakama Abbreviated trousers worn under tosei armour.

Kobakama jitate Thigh armour sewn onto a pair of trousers.

Ko boshi bachi Helmet bowl with small standing rivets.

Kobushi kitae Sword construction in which a soft core was wrapped in hard steel.

Kodzuka Handle of a small utility knife carried in a pocket on the rear face of a sword or dirk scabbard.

Kogai Skewer-like implement carried in a pocket on the front face of a sword or dirk scabbard.

Kogai kanamono Decorative plate and ring combination attached to the rear edge of a shoulder guard to which the rearmost tying cord was fastened.

Kogake Armour for the feet.

Kohaze Toggle.

Kojiri Protective metal cap for the end of a scabbard.

Ko manju jikoro Small rounded neck guard.

Koma no tsurugi Early ring pommelled sword originally from Korea.

Komori zuke Intermediate band of leather connecting a row of scales or a plate to some other part of an armour.

Kon Dark blue.

Kosakura gawa Dark blue or green printed leather with an all-over pattern of small flowers.

Koseizan High-sided helmet, usually flat topped, which is taller than a hemisphere.

Koshi ate Sword carrier worn tied around the waist to enable a sword without ashi to be slung edge downwards like a tachi.

Koshi gatana Variety of short sword.

Koshi gusari Variety of mail having rectangular spaces to increase the flexibility.

Koshimaki Strip of metal forming the lower edge of a helmet bowl.

Kote Armoured sleeve.

Kozane A small scale as opposed to those used during the Heian period.

Kozane gashira Top edge of an iyozane cut to resemble two kozane.

Kuchi ba Dull brown colour.

Kuchi gane Metal band around the base of a hilt.

Kumade Rake-like pole arm.

Kura Saddle.

Kuro Black.

Kuro zukuri no tachi Black lacquered tachi.

Kusari Mail.

Kusari do maru Mail and plate version of a do maru.

Kusari gote Armoured sleeve of mail.

Kusari haidate Thigh armour of mail.

Kusari haramaki Mail and plate version of a haramaki.

Kusazuri Pendant sections of scales attached to the lower edge of the do to cover the thighs.

Kusugai do Yokohagi okegawa do in which the plates are joined by a variety of staples.

Kusureru Steel spoiled by over-forging.

Kutsu Stiff boots or shoes of fur.

Kuwagata Flat, stylized horns worn as a crest.

Kyubi no ita Defence for the left armpit, worn with o yoroi.

Mabizashi Peak of a helmet.

Mabizashi tsuki kabuto Ancient style of helmet having a horizontal fretted peak.

Machi uke Socket at the waist on the back of a do into which the sashimono assembly is fitted.

Maedate Crest attached to the front of a helmet.

Maki e do A do decorated with a lacquered design or picture.

Manchira European gorget which was adapted by the Japanese.

Manju wa Short armoured waistcoat worn beneath an armour to protect the armpits and upper chest.

Maru bachi *see daienzan bachi.*

Maro do A tosei version of the do maru, differing from the original versions of the armour in having an extra row of scales in the nakagawa.

Maru do yoroi Hybrid armour between an o yoroi and a do maru.

Masakari An axe.

Masa kogane Iron ore.

Matsuba wa Curved plates arranged in a ring around the elbow plate of an armoured sleeve.

Mei Signature.

Mei no ana A slit in the lining of a helmet through which the signature can be read.

Mekugi Peg holding a blade into its mounts.

Mekugi no ana Hole in the tang of a blade for a mekugi.

Men gu Face armour.

Me no shita ho Face mask covering the face and nose below the level of the eyes.

Menuki Ornaments attached to the hilt of a sword or trapped under its bindings which helped to improve the grip.

Mimi ito Braid around the edges of a piece of armour.

Mitsu kuwagata dai Kuwagata dai with an additional central socket to carry a crest.

Mitsu suji gaki Variant of sugake lacing involving three braids.

Mizu hiki Twin pipings of red and white twill set below the lower edge of a kesho no ita.

Mizu nomi no o Cord attached to the rear edge of a sode.

Moegi Leaf green.

Mogami do Do of horizontal plates, each of which is articulated by separate hinges.

Momen Cotton cloth.

Momonari bachi Pointed helmet inspired by the European morion.

Mon Heraldic symbol.

Moriage kozane Scales having the outer visible surface built up with lacquer.

Muku boshi Rivets with narrow pointed heads.

Muna ita Uppermost plate on the front of a do.

Muna tori hotoke do Smooth-faced do with a top section laced.

Mune machi Shoulder on the back edge of a blade at its junction with the tang.

Murasaki Purple.

Nagamaki Pole arm with a long sword-like blade fitted to a short shaft.

Naginata Pole arm having a curved, single-edged blade.

Nakagawa The part of a do which encircles the trunk.

Nakago Tang of a blade.

Naka kusari The circular links in Japanese mail which lie horizontal to its surface.

Namazu o kabuto Tall, laterally flattened helmet of rounded profile said to resemble the tail of a catfish.

Nanako Surface texture given to ornamental metalwork in which the ground is raised into a series of hemispheres.

Nanban Foreigners, particularly European foreigners.

Nanban gusari International style mail in which each link is meshed with four others.

Nawame fukurin Applied metal edging shaped to resemble a rope.

Neji Breech plug of a gun.

Neri gawa Rawhide.

Nibe Animal glue.

Ni mai do Do in two parts joined by a hinge under the left arm.

Nio do Do modelled to represent the human torso.

Nioi Lacing pattern in shades of one colour fading to white at the bottom.

Nishiki Brocade.

No dachi Simple tachi for retainer's use. Alternatively a very large sword carried rather than worn.

Nodawa Bib-like defence for the throat and upper chest consisting of a U-shaped plate with two or three curved rows of scales attached to it.

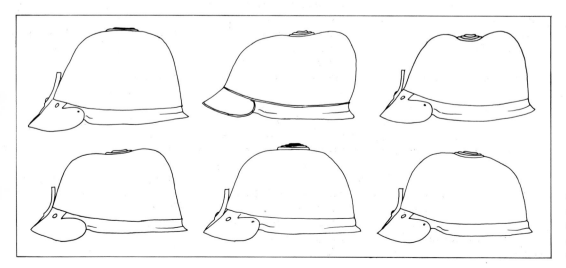

Top row, left to right: Koseizan bachi, reiseizen bachi (akoda nari bachi), tenkokuzan bachi. Bottom row, left to right: goshozan bachi, heichozan bachi, zenshozan bachi.

Nuinobe do *Sugake* laced *ni mai do* made of *iyozane*.

Nunome Overlay of gold, silver or copper on iron.

Obi Belt or sash.

O boshi Rivet having a large head.

Oda gote Kote having gourd-shaped plates applied over the forearm and upper arm.

Oda haidate Haidate of mail with ikada and knee plates resembling those at the elbow of oda gote.

Odoshi ge Lacing material.

Okashi gatana Sword issued to a low-ranking soldier.

Okashi gusoku Armour issued to a low-ranking soldier.

Okke mei A signature applied by another as a mark of respect.

O kessa In *tameshi giri*, a diagonal cut through the shoulder girdle.

Oki tenugui bachi A helmet bowl with almost vertical sides and top plates which are extended rearwards beyond the back of the bowl.

O manju jikoro A neck guard of large, rounded section.

Omodaka do A do having a medial ridge.

Omote kaku kuri Rivets closed on the outside, leaving them only slightly proud of the surface.

Oni damari The uppermost plate of the front of a tosei do.

Ori kugi A hook on the cheek of a mask around which the helmet cord is fastened.

Oshitsuke ita The uppermost plate at the back of a scale armour to which the shoulder straps are attached.

O sode Large rectangular sode.

O tateage suneate Shin guards having large standing plate defences for the knees.

O yoroi Armour having a separate defence for the right side of the body – the classic armour of the Heian period.

Rasha Woollen cloth.

Reiseizan *see akoda nari bachi.*

Renjaku do A tosei do fitted with internal suspensory cords.

Riman kyu *see kago hankyu.*

Rinzu Satin.

Roku mai do A tosei do having five hinges that is divisible into six sections.

Ryo kuruma In tameshi giri, a cut through the pelvic girdle.

Ryo shinogi yari Spear head of diamond section.

Ryo takahimo do A tosei do in either two or six sections with ties at each side of the body.

Sabi nuri A lacquered surface imitating rusty iron.

Sage o A cord or braid attached to the scabbard of a sword for securing it to the belt.

Sai hai A commander's baton hung with a tassel of hair or paper.

Sai hai no kan A ring on the right breast of a tosei do.

Saika bachi A type of multiplate helmet made in Saika.

Saka ita Plate at the back of an o yoroi laced in reverse to allow the shoulder straps to be swung backwards.

Saki me ate Fore sight of a gun or cannon.

Sakura iro Pink.

Same Ray skin used for covering sword hilts.

Samurai Member of the warrior class.

Sane A scale.

Sankaku yari Spear head of triangular section.

Sanko no byo Domed-headed rivets attaching the peak to the bowl of a helmet.

San mai zukuri Sword-blade construction having different grades of steel for the edge, core, back and faces of the blade.

Sarasa Calico.

Sasaheri Leather or braid edging around a fabric portion of an armour.

Sasa no ha Arrow head in the shape of a bamboo-grass leaf.

Sashinuki gote A pair of kote forming part of a short jacket.

Sashimono A flag or other device worn attached to the back of an armour.

Sawari Hard silvery alloy used as decoration on russet iron in the form of partially fused droplets.

Saya Scabbard.

Sei ita Narrow plate worn over the opening of a haramaki.

Seiro gusari A variety of mail in which the oval links are of two or three turns of wire.

Seme gane Decorative reinforcing ring around the scabbard of a tachi.

Seme kohaze A double-holed bead sliding on a loop of cord to close it over a toggle.

Sendai do Alternative name for a yukinoshita do.

Sendan no ita Guard for the right armpit, worn with an o yoroi.

Sentoku A variety of brass.

Seppa Ornamental washers placed on either side of a sword guard.

Shakudo Alloy of copper and gold, patinating to a purple-black colour.

Shi Purple.

Shibuichi An alloy of copper and silver, patinating to a grey colour.

Shiho jiro Helmet decorated with four groups of shinodare.

Shikigane A strip of iron laced behind a leather plate to maintain its shape.

Shikime zane Scale having three columns of holes.

Shikoro Neck guard of a helmet.

Shino A splint.

Shinodare An ornamental strip emerging from the tehen kanamono and extending down the front, sides or back of a helmet bowl.

Shinogi Ridge on a blade.

Shino gote Kote having splints as a defence for the forearm.

Shino haidate Haidate armoured with splints connected by mail.

Shino suneate Shin guards of splints connected by mail.

Shinshinto Swords made in the nineteenth century before the restoration of the Emperor.

Shinto Swords made between 1596 and the end of the eighteenth century.

Shira White.

Shirasaya Scabbard and hilt of plain wood used for storing an unmounted blade.

Shirisaya Leather or fur cover worn over the scabbard of a tachi.

Shishiai bori Sunk relief carving.

Shishi ko sakura gawa Printed leather decorated with Chinese lions and foliage.

Shitagi Shirt-like garment worn under armour.

Shita haramaki *see hara ate.*

Shita jikoro Auxilliary neck guard fitted below the regular one.

Shita toji Leather lacing fastening the scales into a row.

Shita toji no ana Lower group of eight holes in a scale.

Shiten no byo Vestigial rivets applied as decoration to helmet bowls.

Shito A form of dirk.

Shiwa fukube Pleated, gourd-shaped plate used for oda gote.

Shizuka no o Leather tie used to attach an o sode to the rear loop on the watagami.

Shobu gawa Dark blue leather decorated with irises and leaves.

Shohei gawa Variety of shishi ko sakura gawa incorporating the date 1352.

Shoji no ita A standing plate of rounded outline fastened to the upper surface of a watagami.

Shokaku bo Plate forming the top and front of a shoshaku tsuki kabuto.

Shoshaku tei ita Triangular plate under the beaked front of a shoshaku tsuki kabuto.

Shoshaku tsuki kabuto Ancient helmet having a prominent beaked front.

Sode Shoulder guard.

Sode tsuke no o Fastening cord of a shoulder guard.

So gusari Mail in which each circular link is connected to four others – the normal Japanese construction.

So men Mask covering the whole face.

Sori Curvature of a sword.

Sugake Lacing technique in which pairs of laces are threaded vertically up the row of scales to lighten the armour.

Sugi shobu gawa Debased variety of shobu gawa.

Suji Rib or flange.

Suji bachi Multi-plate helmet in which the rivets are countersunk leaving the flanged edges of the plates prominent.

Sumi yagura Subsidiary tower of a castle.

Suneate Shin guard.

Susogoi Shaded colour lacing growing lighter towards the top.

Tabi Sock.

Tachi Slung sword.

Tachi do A do sufficiently long in the body to rest on the hips.

Taka bori Relief carving.

Takahimo The fastenings of the shoulder straps of a scale armour. Alternatively, the fastening of the opening of a tosei do.

Takanoha uchi Braid patterned with chevrons.

Taka zogan Raised inlay.

Takuboku uchi Multi-coloured braid of white, green, purple and dark blue.

Tameshi giri Sword testing.

Tameshi gusoku Armour showing the marks of bullets used to test its defensive quality.

Tanko Early plate armour of the Yamato period.

Tanto Dirk.

Tasuki ni shishi no maru e gawa Printed leather with a design of Chinese lions in a diagonal lattice of foliage.

Tatami do Folding do.

Tatara Furnace.

Mabizashi tsuki kabuto with a fragmentary shikoro. Yamato period.

Tate Free-standing wooden shield.

Tateage The standing parts of a do covering the chest and back.

Tate eri Armoured collar.

Tate hagi okegawa do Tosei do made of vertical plates.

Tate mono Crest.

Te boko Short hand spear.

Tehen The hole in the crown of a helmet bowl.

Tehen kanamono Ornamental metal surround to the tehen.

Tekko A plate forming part of a kote which covers the back of the hand.

Tenkokuzan High-sided helmet whose top dips in the region of the tehen.

Tenshukaku Main tower of a castle.

Tenugui no kan Ring on the left breast of tosei do.

Teppo Gun.

Togari ya An acutely pointed arrow head.

Tominaga sashinuki gote Kote attached to a short jacket having an armoured collar.

Tonbo gawa Printed leather decorated with dragonflies.

Tosei do A 'modern' do, that is those evolved during the sixteenth century.

Tosei gusoku 'Modern' armour.

Tosei sode Small sode hanging from the fastenings of the kote.

Tsuba Sword guard.

Tsubo ita Plate forming the upper part of a waidate.

Tsubo sode A sode curved to the arm and narrowing towards the bottom.

Tsuka Hilt of a sword or dirk.

Tsume gata gawa Dark blue leather decorated with white truncated triangular shapes.

Tsunagi A wooden replica of a blade on which the mounts of a sword are assembled when in storage.

Tsunomoto Hook or spiked form of crest attachment.

Tsuru Bow string.

Tsurubashiri gawa Leather sheet covering the front of an o yoroi which prevented the bow string snagging on the heads of the scales.

Tsurumaki Bow string reel.

Tsutsu Gun barrel.

Tsutsu gote A kote having the plates over the fore arm hinged or sewn to each other.

Tsutsu suneate Shin guards of three or more plates hinged or sewn together.

Uchidashi do Tosei do decorated by embossing.

Uchi gatana Sword worn edge upwards through the belt during the Muromachi period.

Uchi ne Short throwing arrow or dart.

Ukebari Helmet lining.

Uke zutsu Wooden socket into which the sashimono pole was fitted.

Uma jirushi Large heraldic emblem or ensign.

Uma yoroi Horse armour.

Uname toji Lacing in which a length of braid is threaded in and out of a straight row of holes.

Uname toji do Tosei do in which the plates are fastened together by uname toji.

Urushi Lacquer.

Ushiro date Crest fitted to the back of a helmet.

Utsubo Enclosed quiver.

Uwa obi Outer sash or belt.

Uzura gawa Brown leather decorated with white and black spots.

Waidate Piece of armour forming part of an o yoroi which guarded the right side of the body.

Waka ita Plates attached to the upper edge of the nakagawa under the arms.

Wakibiki Arm pit guard.

Waki date Crests fitted to the sides of a helmet.

Wakizashi Short sword having a blade between one and two feet (0.3 and 0.6m) long and mounted with a tsuba – like a katana.

Waraji Straw sandals.

Wari ha kitae Sword construction in which the steel edge is inserted in a slit cut into the body of the blade.

Wari kogai A kogai which divides along the centre line into two parts.

Watagami Shoulder straps of an armour.

Ya Arrow.

Yadome Standing flanges on the cheeks of a mask.

Yagara mogara Pole arm having a multi-pronged barbed head used to entangle an opponent.

Ya hazu gashira Type of iyozane having the upper edge notched.

Yakiba Hardened edge of a blade.

Yamabuki Golden yellow.

Yanagi An arrow head in the shape of a willow leaf.

Ya no ne An arrow head.

Yari Spear.

Yodare kake Throat defence attached to the lower edge of a mask.

Yokohagi okegawa do Tosei do made from horizontal plates.

Yoroi Armour.

Yoroi hitatare Costume of brocade worn under armour.

Yoshino urushi Glossy finishing lacquer.

Yugake Archer's glove.

Yugote Loose sleeve worn on the left arm when practicing archery.

Yukinoshita do A variety of plate go mai do with external hinges.

Yumi Bow.

Yurugi ito Lacing attaching the kusazuri or gessan to the do.

Za boshi Prominent rivet head fitted with a washer cut with radiating lines.

Zenshozan High-sided helmet higher in the front than the back.

Zukin nari kabuto A variety of oki tenugui helmet.

Zunari bachi Helmet construction devised in Tosa which had a longitudinal plate over the centre of the head.

Bibliography

Books dealing entirely or in part with arms and armour.

Katchu no Token *Gen Shoku Nihon no Bijutsu* – Vol XXI, Tokyo

Katchu *Nihon no Bijutsu* – Vol XXIV, Tokyo 1968

Taiho Magazine: Spring 1973, Autumn 1974, Spring 1978, Tokyo

Anderson, L J *Japanese Armour. An illustrated guide to the work of the Myochin and Saotome families from the fifteenth to the twentieth century*, London 1968

Feddersen, M *Japanese Decorative Art*, London 1961

Handa, J and Sasama, Dr Y *Nihin Katchu neihin Shu*, Tokyo 1969

Hawley, W M *Japanese Swordsmiths*, Hollywood 1966

Hickman, B (Editor) *Japanese Crafts: Materials and their Applications. Selected early papers from the Japan Society of London*, London 1978

Honami, K, Sasama, Y Dr and Sone, M *Ko Buki no Shokukin*, Tokyo

Inada, H and Joly, H *The Sword and Same* (Translation of the Sword Books in Honcho Gunkiko together with a treatise on Same), London 1975

Kaneda Chappelear, K *Japanese Armour Makers for The Samurai*, Tokyo 1987

Knutsen, R M *Japanese Polearms*, London 1963

Newman, A R and Ryerson, E *Japanese Art*, London 1964

Robinson, B W *The Arts of the Japanese Sword*, London 1961

Robinson, H R *Japanese Armour (The Concise Encyclopaedia of Antiques: Vol V)*, London 1961

The Manufacture of Armour and Helmets in Sixteenth-Century Japan, (Translation of Chukokatchu Seisakuben by Sakakibara Kozan), London 1962

The Armour Book in Honcho Gunkiko, London 1964

A Short History of Japanese Armour, HMSO London 1965

Oriental Armour, London 1967

Japanese Arms and Armour, London 1969

Sasama, Dr Y *Shumi no Katchu*, Tokyo 1962
Nihon Katchu Zukan (3 vols), Tokyo 1965
Nihon no Meito (3 vols), Tokyo 1973
Zukai Nihon Katchu Jiten, Tokyo 1974
Katchushi Meikan, Tokyo 1976
Nihon Katchu Bugu Jiten, Tokyo 1981

Stone, G C *A Glossary Of The Construction, Decoration And Use Of Arms And Armour In All Countries And In All Times*, New York 1984

Yamagami, H *Japan's Ancient Armour*, Japanese Government Railways 1941

Nihon Katchu Hyaku Sen, Tokyo 1975

Books on related topics

Barr, P *The Coming of the Barbarians*, London 1967

Dunn, C J *Everyday Life in Traditional Japan*, London 1969

Hawley, W M and Kaneda Cheppelar, K *Mon: The Japanese Family Crest*, Hollywood 1976

Kato, H and Yoishimoto, S *Nihon no Kaemon*, Tokyo 1959

Turnbull, S *The Samurai: A Military History*, London 1977

Samurai Armies, London 1979

Warlords of Japan, London 1979

The Books of the Samurai,. London 1982

Samurai Warriors, London 1987

Battles of the Samurai, London 1987

Varley, H P *The Onin War*, Columbia University 1967

Books of value to enthusiasts

Koop, A J and Inada H *Japanese Names And How To Read Them*, London 1960

Rose-Innes, A *Beginner's Dictionary of Chinese – Japanese Characters*, Tokyo 1975

Index

Page numbers in *italics* refer to illustrations

Adams, Will 140
agemaki (silk bow) *53, 54*
Ainu people 8, 13, 20
akabe yoroi (neck armour) 10
Almain collar 10
Amaterasu, sun goddess 8
Antoku, Emperor 43, 62
Arai Hakuseki 177
archers, archery 27-8, 49, 149
  gloves for *25-6*
  in Muromachi period 84
  see also bows, crossbows
arm defences 13, 36, 53, 54
  gyoyo 40, 153
  hiji gane 79, 118, 120
  iyeji 78
  kanmuri no ita 72, 79, 117, 118, 177
  kyubi no ita 36, 53
  sendan no ita 36, 53
  tekko 79, 117, 118
  see also kote, o sode
armour, assembly of 50-51
armour, imported 143-4
  nanban do *137*
  nanban gusoku 143-4
  nanban kabuto *140,* 143-4
  nanban kusari 146
armour boxes 122, *122*
armour lacing 30-31, 53, 75, 87, 89, 91
  Edo period 32
  Heian period 30-32, 51
  Kamakura period 32, 50-51, *54*
  Muromachi period 32
  Nambokucho period *55*
  kebiki style 89, 92, 105, 113
  mitsu suji gake 89
  sugake technique *87,* 89, 91, 92, 105, 107, 13, 133
armourers 14, 52, 84-6, 89, 97-8, 169-72, 174, 177, 183
arrowheads 10, *26-7,* 28-9
arrows *26,* 28, 151
ashigaru 71, 85, 89, 126, *126, 130,* 133
  see also foot soldiers
Ashikaga rule 53, 70-73, 75-87, 89, 91-2, 94, 135
Ashikaya, Masatomo 94
Ashikaya, Takauji 53
Awataguchi, Kunitomi 63

Battle axe 50
body armour *see* do, do maru, haramaki, keiko, kusazuri, maru do yoroi, mogami do, nakagawa, o yoroi, tatami do, tateage, tosei do waidate, watagami
boko no ita 106, 107, 108, 112
bows 10, 22, 25-6, *83,* 84, 149, *149,* 151
  kago hanku 169, *169*
bowstrings 26-7
Buddhism 11, 20, 25, 48, 141, 170
bullet-proof armour 137, 140
Bushido 156
Butokukan, school for samurai 22

Cannon *124-5,* 128
castle building *94,* 96-7
China 46

cultural influence of 11, 14, 20, 22
influence on armour *141,* 170
Japanese ambitions in 148
military tactics copied 68
pronunciation 25
trade with 70, 170
Cho Hitsu Roku 149
Christians 154
Chukokatchu Seisakuben (Kozan) 178
clubs *82, 83*
Confucian ideals 156
crossbows 48

Daimyo 85, 155, 156, 168-9
daisho *see under* swords
Dan no Ura, battle of *42*
Date Narizane Ki 149
Date Masamune 112
decoration 28, 160, 163
  of armour 10, 54, 87, *92,* 145, 163, 172, 174
  of helmets 13, 54, 56-7, 75, 76, *84-5,* 86, 102, *169*
  with special lacquer 41-2, 50, 51-3, 65, 112
  with leather 32-3, 177
  of swords and dirks 52, 64, 66, 68, 163
dirks, 42, 60-61, *64,* 65, 81, *161*
  decoration of 64, 66, 68
  ebizaya maki 64
  hamidashi *159*
  kaiken 157
  tanto 157, *159*
do 9, 13, 32, 35-6, *51,* 108-9, 111-12, 145
  Edo variations of 112
  hatomune do 145
  Kanto do 112
  nanban do *137*
  nio do 112
  nuinobe do *107,* 153
  omodaka do 145
  oshu do 112
  sendai so 112
  uchidashi do 172
  yukinoshita do 112, 172
  see also okegawa do, tatami do
do maru 72-3, 75, *75-7, 87,* 91, 92, 97, 106 109, *175,* 177, *178, 179*
  mogami *91, 92*
  sei ita 72, *73-4*
dolmen burial mounds 9, 14, 20
Drake, Sir Francis 140

eboshi (cap) *33,* 103
Edo 96, 153, map 154, 155, 181
Edo period 85, 98, 154-60, 163-72, 174, 177-9, 181, 183
  armour of *80, 91,* 108, *122,* 140, *155, 176-9*
  armourers 100, 112
  equipment in *12, 28, 32-3, 59, 66*
  helmets in *9, 56,* 86, 91, *99,* 100-101, *102, 104, 173*
  weapons *81,* 84
embossing 112, 172, *176-7*
Europe, Europeans 124, 140, 141, 155, 178
  influence of 141, *142-3,* 143-6, 170
explosive shells 48

Face armour (men gu) 76-7, *78,* 104-5, 177

see hanbo, hoate, me no shita ho, nodawa, so men, yodare kake
firearms 124, *126,* 126-30, 132, 137, 141, 151
  gunsights 128
  gunsmiths 130
  types of lock *128,* 129
    fire fighting 156, *157-8*
    foot soldiers 24, 68, 72, *72,* 84, 97, *133, 147, 149*
  see also ashigaru
Fujiwara clan 14, 20, 21, 24
fukigaeshi (helmet feature) 34, 37, 54, 56, 76, *76,* 86, 103-4
fukube plates 117-18
fukurin, helmet decoration 75, 145

Gempei wars 25
Genghis Kan 46
gessan 105, 113, *133,* 143, 144, 146
gloves, for archery *24-6*
go kaden sword making tradition 42
Go-Daigo, emperor 53
Gosannen Gassen Emaki picture scroll 57
Go-Shairakawa, Emperor 24, 25, 43-4
Go-Toba, Emperor 62, 63
Go-Yoshihiro 63
Goto school of sword fittings 158
Gozuisin Sanjoki 98
great armour *see* o yoroi
gunsmiths 130
Gun Yo Ki 59, 72-3, 106, 177

haidate (thigh armour) 79-80, 120, 133, 144
  etchu haidate *119,* 120
  hodo haidate 59
  ikada haidate, ita haidate 120
  kawara haidate 120
  kusari haidate 120
  shino haidate *119,* 120
Hamamatsu Castle *94*
han, territorial holdings 155
hanagami fukuro (nose tissue bag) 106-7
hanbo mask 76, *78,* 104, 144
hand cannon 127-8
hand spear *see* te boko, te yari
haniwa model figures 8, 14, *14,* 20, 86
happuri (face guard) 34, *34-5,* 40, 57, 72, 77, 104
haraidate (helmet fitting) 76, 99, 100
haramaki (belly wrap) 37-8, *38,* 40, 41, 53, 54, *55, 58,* 59, 72-3, *73-4,* 91, 92, *92,* 97, 106, 109, 177, 178
  adopted by samurai 71, 73, 75
  hara ate (shita haramaki) 71-2, *73*
  mogami haramaki *93*
  see also do maru
Haruta armourer group 84-5, 86, 98, 100, 152, 169
Heian period
  armour 23, 29-32, *31, 35,* 36
  equipment *28, 39-40*
  helmets 33, *34,* 85
  swordmaking 42
Heian-Kyo city (Kyoto) 20, 21, 25, 29
Heiji Monogatari Emaki 4-5, 19, 22, 24, 40
helmets
  bowls 33-4, 54, 56, 76, 98

chochin bachi *89, 92*
crests 56, 76, 102
daienzan bachi 54
decoration 13, 54, 56-7, 75, 76, *84-5,* 86, 102, *169*
  of Edo period *9, 56,* 86, 91, *99,* 100-101, *102, 104, 173*
  European style *140, 142-3*
  harikake bachi 102
  Heian period 33, *34,* 85
  hineno zunari bachi 101-3
  hitai ate *88,* 91
  hoshi bachi *56,* 152, 169, 170-71
  Kamakura period 54, 56
  Kawari bachi 103, *103,* 169
  linings 56, 75
  manufacture of 85-6, 98, 106
  maru bachi 54, 177
  Miochin helmets *98-9,* 98-100
  Momoyama period *101-4*
  for munition armours 91-2
  Nambokucho period 75, 76
  oki tenugui bachi *84,* 86, *86*
  saiki bachi *83, 85,* 86
  Saotome helmets 100
  suji bachi 76, *99,* 169, 170-71, *171, 173*
  zunari bachi 100, 144
  see also Kabuto
Henry VIII armour 139
heraldic devices 54, 69, *109, 168*
hiji gane *see* arm defences
Hineno, Hironari 101, 102, 103
  brother Yajiuemon 101
hishinui no ita *see* o yoroi
hiya zutsu guns 128
hoate (face armour) 57, 76, 77, 104
Hojo family 46, 53
  Masa-ko 45
  Yoshitoki 62
hoko (spears) 15
Honcho Gunkiko (Hakuseki) 177
Horii, Taneyoshi 18
Horikawa, Kunihiro 166
horo (cloth cape) *47, 59,* 59-60, *70*
horses, ponies 11-12, 20, 22, 49
  armour for 171-2, *174*
  harness *10-11,* 12, 98, *174*
Hosokawa family 101
Hosokawa, Masayoshi 178

Ichijo, Kaneyoshi 84
Igaki helmet decoration 75
Imai, Sokyu 135
Imagawa, Yoshimoto 135
Inouye, Shinkai 166
  blade by 166
iron, sources and smelting 60-62
Ise, Sadatake 177
Ise, Shinkuro 94
Ishida, Mitsunari 153
Itsukushima temple 26
Iwai armourer group 84, 85, 98, 171
Iwai, Yozayemon 140
iyozane (scales) *29, 50,* 51, 74, 75, 80, 89, 109
  iyozane do gusoku *111*
  kiriksuke iyozane *105,* 105-6

James I, armour for *136, 139,* 140
Jesuits 141
ji zamurai (gentry) 20, 71
jinbaori (surcoats) 137, 145, *145, 152*
jingasa (hat) 133, 156, *156, 158*
jitte (club) *64,* 156

Kabuto (helmet) 9, 20
  akoda nari kabuto *75*, 76, 85, 86,
    99, 141
  chocin kabuto *89, 92*
  eboshi nari kabuto *103, 103*
  harikake kabuto *101, 104*
  heichozan kabuto *99*
  hoshi kabuto 100, 103
  kawari kabuto *103, 115*
  mabizashi tsuki kabuto *12, 13, 14,*
    86
  momonari kabuto *143,* 144
  nanban kabuto *140,* 143-4
  oki tenugui kabuto *84, 86*
  san mai kabuto 56
  shoshaku tsuki kabuto 9, *9*
  suji kabuto *98, 100*
  tosa zukin kabuto *86*
  zunari kabuto 85, 101, *101,* 102, 133,
    137
  see also helmets
Kaga armourers 169-70
Kagemusha, film *96-7*
kakae zutsu (hand cannon) 127-8, 129
kake yoroi *see* keiko
kama (type of sickle) 50, 83
Kamakura period
  archer of *46*
  armour 32, 33, *46, 51, 54,* 71, 76
  helmets of 54, 56
  pole arms *44, 49*
  scenes of *22, 24*
Kamakura town 44, 53, 112
kami kaze (divine wind) 49
kami shimo ceremonial dress *155, 156*
Kammu, emperor 20
kanabo (wooden club) 83
Kaneiye, metal worker 164
kanmuri no ita *see* arm defences
kasa jirushi no kan (hat-flag ring) 34
kata yoroi (Shoulder armour) 10
katana (dirk) 42, 48
  (long sword) 157
katchu shi (armour craftsman) 84
Kato, Kiyomasa 149
kawa zutsumi no do maru/kawa
    zutsumi no haramaki 75, *75*
Kebukigusa 98
keiko (kake yoroi) (hanging armour)
    12, 13, *13,* 14-15, 20, 29, 51
Ken Mon Zatsu Roku 86
kesho eri, armour decoration 145
kesho no ita *see* o yoroi
kikuchi yari (te boko) 50
Kinai, Etchizen 165
Kiyomaro, Minamoto, swords of *181*
Kobayakawa, Hideaki 153
  armour of 151-153
kodzuka (knife) 65
kogai, kogai kanamono 65, 73
kogake, foot armour *120,* 121
Korea, influence on armour *141*
Korean campaigns 148-9, 151-2, 153
Kosei Roku 117
koshi ate, sword carrier *81*
koshimaki (helmet fitting) 9, 13, 20,
    34, 75, *75,* 85, 86, 103, *140,* 143,
    144
Koshirae (sword mounts) 157
koshiro, Ihara 26
kote (armoured sleeve) 41, 72, 78-9,
    79, 116, 133, 170
  bishamon gote 79
  kusari gote 116-17, 120
  oda gote 117-18, *118,* 120, 144, 170
  shino gote 78-9, 116, *118*
  tsutsu gote 77, 78-9, 116, *118*
Kotoku, Emperor 14
kozane (scales) *29-31, 49,* 51, 74, 75,
    79, 80, 89

kara kozane 51
kiritsuke kozane 105, *105*
moriage kozane 51
Kublai Khan 46, 48
kumade, type of take 50, 83
kusari katabira, mail shirt *155,* 156
kusazuri (hip armour) 10, 36, 40, 49,
    53, 54, 59, 71, 72, 73, 91, 92, 105
kuwagata (crests) 56, 76, 85
Kyoto 20, 53, 70, 87, 135, 155

Lacquer 41-2, 50, 51-3, 59, 112, 141
  to simulate scales 105
  for sword scabbards 42, 65
lamellar armour 12
leather, use of 32, 77, 80, *145,* 171, 177
leg protection 13, 37, *38,* 59
  kobakama jitate 59
  see also haidate, suneate
Louis XIII 140

Maeda family 169
mail 57, 58
  arrangement of *57, 58*
  construction of 58, 146
Manga (Hokusai) 128
manju wa (armoured jacket) 121, *121*
maru do yoroi *23, 53,* 54
Masahide, Suishinshi Kawabe
    Gihachiro 17, 19, 60, 141, 167, 178
masakiri (battle axe) 50
Masamitsu, Bizen, sword of *160*
Masamune, Goro Nyndo 63, 64
masks 76-7, *78*
  see also face armour, me no shita ho
Matashichiro, Yuasa *57*
matchlock guns 124, 126-30, *129,* 132
me no shita ho (mask) 76, *78,* 104,
    104-5, 143
  Nara me no shita ho 153
Meishu, Tsutsui no Jomio, monk 42
men gu *see* face armour, me no shita
    ho
metal alloys 159
metal working 158-60, 163
military tactics 68-9, 107, 132-3
Minamoto samurai group 20-21,
    24-5, 30, 43
Minamoto, Yoritomo 43, 44-5, 70
Minamoto, Yoshitsune 43, 44, *44,* 46
Miochin armourers 98, 137, 169, 170,
    172, 177
Miochin, Iyetsugu, armour by *75*
Miochin, Kunimichi 172
Miochin, Masaiye 112
Miochin, Muneo, do by *165*
Miochin, Munesada, armour by *171*
Miochin, Munesuke, armour by 172,
    175
Miochin, Muneyasu 178
Miochin, Nagamichi, armour by *143*
Miochin, Nobuiye, 98-100, 170
  armour by *98*
Miochin, Ryoei 172
Miochin, Yoshimichi 99-100, 170
  armour by *99*
Mitford, Algernon, quoted 181
mogami do armour *91,* 92
mogami haramaki armour *93*
Moko Shurai 79
Monoyama period 83, 85, 178
  decoration of *92*
  equipment in 11, 25
  helmets of 101-4
  swords of 158, 166
mon (heraldic device) 54, *69,* 102,
    133, 153, 168
monastic orders 21
mongals 68
  invasions by *46,* 48-9, 53

Munenao, Kojima, masks by *78*
munition armour 85, 91-2, 109, 133
Muromachi period *68,* 70, *73,* 83, 107
  armour 32, *56,* 71, *75-6,* 76, 77-8,
    85, *87, 91*
  arms 80, 83-5, 97
  armourers in 84
muskets, musketeers 126-7

Nagamaki (pole arm) 83, *147*
Nagashino, battle of 126, 130
Nagasone, Okisato Kotetsu 166
  sword by 167
naginata (pole arm) 21, *24,* 43, *44,*
    49-50, *49-50,* 83
nakagawa (trunk armour) 35, 37, 53,
    71, 72, 73, 75, 92, 106, 109, 112
  waka ita 53, 54, 71
Nambokucho period 53, 70, 178
  armour of *55, 56, 58,* 71, *75*
  helmets 75, 76
nanban gusoku *see* armour, imported
Naokatsu and Naotane, swordsmiths
    178
Nara city 14, 20, 53
  armourers of 84, 85, 170
Nijo, Emperor 25
Noda, Hankei 16, 166
nodawa (throat and chest protector)
    57, *59,* 76, *78,* 105, 177, *179*

Oda, Nobunaga 83, 126, 130, 133,
    135, 141, 148
O sode (large shoulder guards) 36-7,
    40, 54, 72, 92, 115-16, 141, 146,
    153, 177
  hiro sode 73, 115
  tsubo sode *58,* 72
o yoroi (great armour) *1, 23, 31, 33,*
    35, 35-6, 38, 51, 53, 54, *54,* 71,
    71, 72, 90, 177, 178, *182*
  hishinui no ita 53, 54, 76
  kesho no ita 54, 72
  maru do yoroi *23, 53,* 54
Ogasawara family 28
okashi gusoku *see* munition armour
okegawa do 112, 133
  varieties of *110,* 112, *115,* 165
O'Neill, Sir Neill, armour of *138,* 140
Osafune Bizen smiths 166
Osaka *95,* 96, 97, 153
oshitsuke ita 72, 106

Pavaises *67,* 68
Perry, Commodore Matthew C 179
pistols, wheel-lock 141
plate armour 91-2, 105
pole arms 49, 68, 79, 82, *82,* 148-9
  in Gempei wars *48*
  yagara mogara 149
  see also nagamaki, naginata, yari
Polo, Marco 48

Quivers *26, 28, 29,* 72, 84
  utsubo *83,* 84

Rembrandt van Rijn 140
renjaku, suspensory cords 137,
    139-40, 153
Rurisai, Genuemon 157

Sadamune, son of Masamune 63
saddles *11*
sai hai, commander's baton 108, *109*
Saika town 86, 135
Sakakibara, Kozan 17, 52, 60, 87, 98,
    137, 178
samurai, *1, 4-5, 19,* 22, 44
  armour adjustments by 54, 122
  latterday position 181-2, *183*

as magistrates and police 156
  and Mongol invasion 49, 53
  in Shogunate structure 155-7, 177
sandals *37,* 80
Saotome, Iyetada
  armour by 74, 100
Saotome armourers 100, 152
sashimono, editifaction mark 107-8,
    107-8, 177
sashimuki gote, jacket 79
Satake family 117
scabbards 41-2, 52, 64-6, *81,* 158, *180*
scales *see* iyozane, kozane
Seii Taishogun title 44
Sekigahara, battle of *150,* 153, 155
shields 36, 68
Shikoro (neck defence) 9, 13, 14, 32,
    34, 54, 56, 85, 91, 92, 106, 133,
    143, 144, 146, 177
  hineno 104
  ite jikoro 103
  kasa jikoro 76
  shita jikoro 76
Shimazu, Yoshihiro 148, 149
shinguards *see* suneate
shinodare (helmet fitting) 54, 56, 75
Shinto faith 11, 16, 49
  New Sword period 166
shitagi, undergarment *122*
Sho so in collection, Nara 14-15
Shogun title 44, 46, 53, 181
shoji no ita 54, 72, 106, 153, 177
Shomu, Emperor 14
so men, mask 77, 104
sode jirushi, identification flag 69
Soten metal work school 165
Sotoku, Emperor 24
Spalding, Augustin 140
spears 10, 15, *97, 147, 168*
  hoko 15
  scabbard for *180*
  spearman *126*
  uchi ne 84
  yari 84, *146, 148, 180*
stirrups 12, *12,* 153
suji, on helmet plate 54
suneate (shin guard) 37, 57-8, 80, 120,
    133
  kaihan suneate *38,* 80
  o tateage suneate 58, 80
  shino suneate 80, *80,* 120, 144
  tsutsu suneate 120, *120*
sword guards *81*
sword hilts 41-2, *65,* 66, *66,* 68
sword testing 167, *167*
swords *60-63, 160*
  bu tachi 41, 43
  daisho 149, 157, *160*
  hachiwari 64
  Heian period 63, 64
  hyogo kusari no tachi *64,* 65
  katana 157
  kazuchi no tsurugi 10
  Koma no tsurugi 10
  mounts *15, 81,* 157, *161,* 163-5
  Nambokucho period 63-4
  no dachi 42, *63,* 64, 82, 83
    hiru maki no tachi 64
    ita maki no tachi 80, *81*
    kawa zutsumi maki no tachi 65,
      80
  okashi katana 133
  tsuba 11, 68, *81,* 98, 141, 143, *163,*
    164
  uchi gatana 80-82, 149
  wakizashi 149, *181*
swordsmiths, sword making 15-20,
    16-17, 42, 60, 62-3, 84, *164,* 166,
    178, *183*
  certificate of authenticity *21, 172*

Tachi *see* swords
tachi do (standing do) 106
Tadayoshi of Hizen 166
Taiheiki 59
Taiheiki Amaki, picture scroll 49
Taika Reform, 646 14, 21
Taira, samurai group 20-21, 24-5, *42,* 43-4
Taira, Kiyomori 24, 43, 44
Takeda, Harunobu (Shingen) 99, 126, 133, 137
Takeda, Katsuyori 126
Takedori Monogatari 50
Tales of Heike 42
Tanegashima 124, 126, 130
tanko armour *8, 9, 10, 12, 14, 14*
tatami do, packaged armour *88,* 91-2
tate eri (armoured collar) 106
tate mono (crests) 102
tateage 54, 122
te boko 14, 43, 50, 148
te yari 148, 149
tehen, helmet fitting 34, 56, 76, 86

tehen kanamono 75, *163*
to gasa kabuto *141*
Tokugawa, Iyemitsu 154
Tokugawa, Iyeyasu 133, 135, 137, 144, 153, 154
Tokugawa shogunate 154-5, 166, 168, 177
Tokyo 153, 181
tominaga sachinuki gote, sleeves forming part of a jacket 79
tonlet armour 9
Tosa armourers 85, 86, 101
Tosa, Mitsunobu 85
tosei do, modern do *106,* 106-7, 137
 renjaku do 137, 139-40
 varieties of 108-9, 111-13
tosei gusoku, modern armour 97-8, 115-17, 121-2, *134-5, 142, 171, 173, 178-80*
 hikone gusoku 137
 okashi gusoku *130*
 tameshi gusoku 137, 140
tosei mabisashi 152

tosei sode 115-16, 153
Toshihiro, Yoshimitsu 63
Toyotomi, Hideyoshi 133, 137, 141, 147-8, 151-2, 153, 155
 armour of 131, 144
 sons of 153
Tristam, Rev. H B quoted 183
tsunomoto, crest hook 86
tsuru (bowstrings) 26-7
Tsuta Sukehiro 166

Uma jirushi, identification emblem 108
uma yoroi, horse armour 171-2
Umetada, Myoju 166
United States 178-9
Unkai, ex-Miochin armourers 170
utsubo, quiver *83, 84*

Waidate, body armour 36, 71
Wakan Sansaizue 98
wakibiki, armpit protection *120,* 121
war fans *66, 69*

war standard *108*
watagami (shoulder straps) 10, *14,* 35-6, 53, 71, 72, 91, 106, 112, 139, 143, 144, 153, 170, 177
Wejen Chuan 11

Yamagami, Hachiro 98
Yamashiro 42, 62, 98
 swords, dirks of *41*
Yamato II, 14, 42, 62
 armour of *8-10, 13,* 36
yari, spear 83-4, *146, 148, 180*
Yashima Nana scroll 43
yodare kake (throat guard) 76, 77, 104-5
yoroi hitatare, under-armour dress 37, 59, 75, 121
Yoshimichi, Tamba no kami, sword by 166
yugake, archer's glove *24*
Yukimitsu, son of Masamune 63

ACKNOWLEDGMENTS
The authors would like to express their special gratitude to Dr Yoshihiko Sasama who, over the last twelve years has, in the best traditions of scholarship, freely shared his extensive knowledge and continued to show enthusiasm while patiently answering our many queries. Thanks must also be expressed to Barry Charlesworth, David Drury, Deryk Ingham, Tony O'Neill, Shigeki Oyama, Stephen Turnbull and the late Dr K Yoshida for their assistance and co-operation during the preparation of this work. Finally the authors would like to express their gratitude to Jane Laslett, the editor, who suffered much at our hands and bore it with fortitude, and to Melanie Earnshaw who performed miracles in finding suitable photographs with which to illustrate this book.

The publisher would like to thank Martin Bristow, the designer, Ron

Watson for compiling the index, and the following agencies and individuals for providing the illustrations: B = below, L = left, R = right, T = top, BT = bottom, C = centre, A = above.

BBC Hulton Picture Library: page 73(below). Bodleian Library, Oxford: pp 43[ms JAP d.53(2)(R) first scene], 50[MS JAP d.40 fol. 15R), 62(MS JAP d.55(R)], 63T, [MS JAP d.55 (R)], 126-127 [MS JAP e 2(R) last scene]. Boston, Museum of Fine Arts: pp 4-5, 22, 24, 40T. Collection Ian Bottomley/Photo David Drury: pp 12T, 16, 17, 25R, 28R, 32, 48 both, 51T, 56, 59B, 64T, 72, 74TR, 75B, 80B, 88 both T, 89 both, 99, 100 both T, 101 both T, 102T, 103T, 104T, 105T TL and BR, 107T and BR, 108L, 110, 111R, 113 both, 116L, 118 middle 2, 119T and BL, 120, 121, 128, 129, 134, 143 all 3, 146T, 154, 155 both, 158T2, 163B, 165, 168T, 177BR. Bradford Art Galleries and Museums: pp 40C, 59T, 69T, 77T, 80T, 160T

and 2B, 161, 172 both, 177 T2, 179B. Bramante Editrice/Museo Orientale: pp 84, 85, 91, 103BL, 104B, 118T and BT, 169B, 170, 171L. Trustee of the British Museum: pp 42, 70. Durham Oriental Museum: 66T, 83B, 119BR, 156, 159 both, 173, 176R, 183B. Werner Forman Archive: pp 15T, 26R, 27B, 47, 95, 102, 116R, 131, 140B, 164, 176BR. Geneva, Musée d'Ethnographie: p 180L. Archiv Gerstenberg: p 67. Honda Museum/ Courtesy ISEI, Tokyo: pp 11L, 27T, 45b, 101B, 108R, 109L, 135R, 145T, 168B, 174R. Anthony Hopson: p 132 both. Kyoto Arashiyama Museum: pp 10B, 11R, 34B, 78T, 82 both, 83 both T, 107BL, 114, 115, 124, 125, 139R, 147R, 162, 174L, 175R, 176L, 182. The Metropolitan Museum of Art, New York, pp 9, 88, 90, 175L. Mori Collection: pp 25L. 26L, 33, 37 both, 38B, 66BR, 81T, 109R, 117, 122, 135L, 151 all 3, 153, 157, 158 both B, 169T. National Film Archive: pp 96, 97. The National Trust: pp 2-3.

Peter Newark's Historical Pictures: pp 144, 183T. Tony O'Neill: pp 26B, 31, 66BL, 73T, 74B, 86, 105 TR, 106 both, 111L, 126, 130, 133, 146B, 147L, 149, 179TR. Oyamazumi Jinja: pp 23, 34T, 35, 38A, 44L, 51B, 53, 54, 55, 58, 63B, 64B, 68, 75 both T, 87B. Pitt Rivers Museum, Oxford: p 6. Rijksmuseum, Amsterdam: p 145. Board of Trustees of the Royal Armouries, H M Tower of London: pp 1, 36 both, 39, 79L, 88B, 92, 93, 98 both, 100B, 103BR, 123, 136, 139L, 140T, 141T, 160C, 171R, 174B, 177BL, 180R. The Tate Gallery, London: p 138. Tokyo National Museum/ Courtesy ISEI, Tokyo: pp 8 both, 12B, 13, 14, 18-19. Tokyo Sword Museum/Courtesy ISEI, Tokyo: 41, 60, 61, 65, 69R, 81B, 166, 167, 181. Stephen Turnbull: pp 10T, 94 both, 150. Victoria and Albert Museum, London: pp 44-45, 46, 48, 71, 74TL, 77B, 78B, 81TL, 141B, 163T 2, 179TL.